TEST
Ch 19-21

GRONCHY Ch 1
VEBLEN   P 215-275
          355-431

Basic Business Finance

Text and Cases

Basic Business Finance
Text and Cases

Pearson Hunt, D.C.S.
Professor of Business Administration

Charles M. Williams, D.C.S.
George Gund Professor of Commercial Banking

Gordon Donaldson, D.C.S.
Professor of Business Administration

All of the Graduate School of Business Administration,
Harvard University

Third Edition · 1966

Richard D. Irwin, Inc.

Homewood, Illinois

THIRD EDITION

First Printing, May, 1966
Second Printing, December, 1966

*Case material of the Harvard Graduate School of Business Ad-
ministration is made possible by the cooperation of business
firms who may wish to remain anonymous by having names,
quantities and other identifying details disguised while maintaining basic relationships. Cases are prepared as the basis for
class discussion rather than to illustrate either effective or in-
effective handling of administrative situations.*

Library of Congress Catalog Card No. 66–24587
PRINTED IN THE UNITED STATES OF AMERICA

Preface

This book represents the work of many persons, and complete acknowledgement of all the contributions to a book now in the third edition is impossible. We would like to express here our appreciation of especially significant contributions.

First, we express our gratitude to the many professors who have given us the benefit of their experience with earlier editions of the book and their suggestions for its improvement. Surely this edition will be much enriched by modifications they have recommended.

Further, we want to thank those business leaders whose active cooperation made possible the preparation of case problems from actual situations. Unfortunately, they must remain anonymous.

Along with the authors, who supervised the collection and writing of most of the cases, a number of other present and past members of the faculty of the Harvard Business School played major roles in the preparation of the case materials. The contributions of Professors Leonard C. R. Langer, James T. S. Porterfield, Lawrence E. Thompson, and Robert F. Vandell were particularly important. Professor William W. Sihler prepared the revision of chapters 24 and 25.

Among the research assistants who handled the field work and drafting of cases, James Clauson, Paul Judy, and Lee Bodenhamer wrote two or more cases. Eleven other men wrote cases included in the book.

Miss Carolyn Stubbs, Associate in Research in our school, was extremely helpful as a researcher, editor, indexer, and general organizer of the work of revising the book. We salute her able and devoted work on this book.

Many secretaries assisted in the preparation of the book. Denise Aronson and Carol Middleton have been particularly helpful on this edition.

The cases in this volume are copyrighted by the President and Fellows of Harvard College and are used with their permission.

PEARSON HUNT
CHARLES M. WILLIAMS
GORDON DONALDSON

Graduate School of Business Administration
Harvard University
April, 1966

Table of Contents

vii

List of Cases

Selected List of
Tables, Charts, and Exhibits

xvii

PART I

Introduction

Chapter 1

Introduction

IN THIS introductory chapter of *Basic Business Finance: Text and Cases* we shall begin by describing the finance function in business. Having explained what this book is about, we then describe the design of the book —the point of view from which we approach the subject, the users for whom the book has been prepared, the needs we seek to meet through inclusion of both textual and case problem materials, the objectives of the text and of the cases, and how each should be used. Then we shall briefly outline the substantive plan of the book, that is, the major subject areas covered and the order of their presentation.

After this introduction to the book as a whole, we shall turn to an overall look at the need for funds in business. The importance of using funds effectively and widely used methods of measuring the effectiveness with which funds are being employed are then considered.

The Finance Function in Business

This book is concerned with the finance function of business and how it can be carried out effectively. As the finance function was first defined, it was viewed narrowly as simply the task of providing the funds needed by the enterprise on terms that are most favorable in the light of the objectives of the business. This long-held concept has the merit of highlighting a central core of the finance function—keeping the business supplied with enough funds to accomplish its objectives. Certainly, seeing to it that the business has the funds to pay its current bills and to support programs embarked upon is a basic part of the finance function. Getting the needed funds in the most suitable way and on the best terms possible also is clearly a central part of the finance job.

But the finance function is much broader than one of funds procurement or supply. It can and should contribute to the basic business objective of building values. Speaking broadly, values will be maximized only if the firm's resources are used effectively. Hence, the finance function is vitally concerned with the use of funds within the business, not just the supply of funds to the business.

3

Money seldom is available to the firm in unlimited quantities. In all cases, it has a cost. Evaluation of proposed projects that involve a need for funds should take into account the costs and other problems involved in getting these funds and balance these factors with the amount of added profits or other benefits expected to be achieved through use of the added funds. Moreover, the forecasted profits can seldom be regarded as assured; rather, most profit projections involve a significant degree of uncertainty. Consequently, the degree of uncertainty that should be attached to the achievement of the projected benefits also should be weighed in the decision whether to undertake the project.

To illustrate, let us assume that the production manager of a manufacturing firm is urging the construction of a new plant. This new plant, he predicts, will cut production costs and increase the firm's profits. Yet, to build the new plant will require a large outlay of cash and necessitate heavy borrowing. The financial aspects of the problem do not stop with a decision that the funds can be obtained or even with the decision that they can best be raised in a particular way—say, through an issue to the public of 20-year first-mortgage bonds. Instead, the financial considerations extend toward questions of whether the added profits from the new plant, in the light of the uncertainties involved, adequately compensate for the costs and risks involved in the borrowing. Further, are there alternative methods of getting the same or some of the profits at much less financial burden? Would, for instance, modernization of the existing plant at half the total cost and three quarters of the cost savings achieved by a new plant be a better alternative? Or could the funds required for the new plant be used to better advantage in research devoted to new products that could be produced efficiently with the existing facilities?

The concern of the financial function with the effective use of funds is most vivid in the case of proposed new projects that require funds, like the example above of the new plant. But it may be equally or more important to the firm that the funds tied up in the existing operations of the firm are being employed effectively. For example, action to free up funds by sale or liquidation of low-return divisions or product lines may contribute to the economic progress of the firm as much as careful policies and procedures of evaluating the cost/benefit relationship of new projects.

Altogether, it seems to us clear that the financial function cannot be separated out and divorced from broad consideration of the effective use of funds in the business.

The breadth of the financial function as we see it can be further demonstrated by noting the range of considerations involved in a seemingly narrow financial issue. For example, the board of directors of the company may be considering what dividends to declare on the common stock of the company. Certainly, the board will wish to take into account the financial needs of the business and the opportunities for using the funds that have been made available from profits in the business. But the board will also be concerned with such matters as the objectives and desires of the stockholders, the likely impact of alternative dividend decisions on the short-run and long-term market price of the stock, and the consequent effect of its own dividend action on the ability of the company to sell more common stock at a favorable price in the future.

Further, few firms enjoy financial positions so strong that planning can go forward and decisions can be made on the assumption that any funds required by the plans and decisions will be obtained. Indeed, in a great many less affluent concerns the present or potential supply of funds and the financial aspects of important decisions may well be of dominant importance. The financial situation often is such that the current and future operations of the business must be shaped to fit the funds available, rather than the reverse.

Even the relatively specialized or central-core aspects of the broad financial function—those related to supplying the needed funds—are not to be regarded as narrow or separated from the operations of the business, as we shall see in detail later in this book. The need for funds in a business is affected by every activity of the business and by virtually everything that happens to the business. In order to understand and meet its needs for funds efficiently and astutely, the financial officer must understand the business and keep in touch with all phases of its operations. Probably no other functional area of business is so intimately interrelated with other areas of the business as is the finance function. The successful financial man in business must be not only a "money man"; he must be a businessman.

Organization to Carry Out the Finance Function in Business

The financial function, broadly considered, is much the same in its basic aspects in all businesses. That is to say, financial considerations exist in virtually all concerns, whatever their size or nature. The details of the function may differ widely, but the basic and important features of the job to be done are universal in nature. Many of the important aspects of the financial function are carried on by the top management of the company—the president, executive vice president, the board of directors, or top-management committees. The board of directors, with the advice of the president, treasurer, or other senior officers, may well make the final decision on such issues as building a new plant or liquidating a product line. Though final decisions on matters with strong financial implications may be taken by the board or by officers with overall responsibility in the firm, financial officers generally have an important opportunity and, indeed, responsibility, to contribute to good decision making on issues that cut across functional areas of the business. They should see to it that the financial implications of broad decisions are clearly brought out and are understood by those who must make the final decisions.

The ways in which enterprises organize to carry out the finance function differ widely. In very small concerns the head of the firm often assumes direct and virtually sole responsibility for marketing, production, finance, and still other functions. In medium and large concerns a separate financial department headed by an officer with a title such as treasurer or vice president–finance may be assigned primary responsibility for the narrower funds supply aspects of the finance function. In some concerns responsibilities in the broad financial area are divided between a treasurer and a controller who, in addition to his usual duties as the chief accounting officer of the firm, may be assigned responsibility for such aspects of the finance function as financial forecasting and the appraisal of the effectiveness with which funds are used in various parts of the business. In many large concerns both the treasurer and the controller report to a chief financial officer who often has the title, vice president–finance. To minimize problems of terminology, we shall refer to the officer with primary responsibility for the financial function as the chief financial officer or simply the financial officer, be his literal title president, general manager, treasurer, or controller.

As is suggested by the nature of the finance function, the chief financial officer usually is one of the senior officers of the firm reporting directly to the president or executive vice president and is an important member of the "top-management team."

The Design of This Book

This book is written from the point of view of the chief financial officer in an operating business, a man with responsibilities for getting a job done well. His job involves a need to make or take part in specific decisions and hence is oriented toward responsible recommendations and action rather than abstract theorizing. This viewpoint of the active businessman is in contrast with that of some finance textbooks which seem to be written more from the viewpoint of a detached observer and reporter of the business scene, or with other books written primarily from an investor's viewpoint. It is also in contrast with still other books on finance which are written more or less implicitly from a public or governmental policy point of view, such as that of a congressman heading a committee which has an interest in the financing of business.

The primary emphasis in the book is on financial decision making and administration in a going concern. We do deviate somewhat from our going-concern framework in the chapters dealing with business failure and the financing of new enterprises. Even here, however, the emphasis is on the special problems which management may face at either end of the life cycle of an individual business organization. Our general adherence to the point of view of internal management does not preclude our occasionally looking at business as might an outside analyst—investor, trade creditor, etc.

Since we take a point of view encompassing that of the chief financial officer, we are much concerned with what we term "the funds point of view." While, as we have emphasized, the chief financial officer, along with the president and other top officers, has a real concern for profits and the effective use of assets, typically he has the direct and primary responsibility for seeing to it that the firm does not run short of funds. The term *funds* is often used here and elsewhere synonymously with *cash* or *money*, but a more accurate and complete definition of *funds* would be *the means of payment*. Thus, the purchase of raw materials requires funds; but for a time, at least, credit supplied by the seller can take the place of cash as the medium by which ownership of the materials was accomplished. As the man responsible for seeing to it that the firm has the means of payment it desires, the chief financial officer appropriately is strongly oriented toward a funds point of view.

In this book, textual material and case problems are combined, on the premise that a basic course in finance should serve two major purposes. The text seeks primarily to inform—to provide the student with useful background information about the financing job in business. The case problems are designed to help the student to develop some skills in thinking through financial problems and in reaching sensible decisions for action.

To be more specific, one of the functions of the textual material is to supply a virtual kit of background facts, concepts, and analytical methods in key areas of our subject. For example, before introducing cases dealing with problems in raising funds, we describe the major suppliers of funds to business and the economic and operational conditions which govern the arrangements under which they make funds available to business. Particularly important sources of funds, such as the commercial banks, are treated at some length.

In addition, part of the text material is devoted to introducing techniques of analysis or interpretation of material that can be useful in handling the case problems or in business. For example, a chapter is devoted to discussion of techniques of forecasting future needs for funds and problems in their use.

Still other parts of the text go well beyond the task of painting a factual background or describing financial techniques and attempt to develop basic ideas on some important issues. We hope thereby to stimulate rather than close out student thinking on these issues. In most instances where we have put forward our own ideas on debatable subjects, the student will have a chance to test the usefulness of these ideas in dealing with related issues raised in the cases.

We should make clear, however, that we do not attempt in the text to supply the answers to the case problems that follow. Rather, we hope through the text to bring the student along to a point where he can comprehend the problems posed in the cases and work out sensible answers to these problems. In other words, we hope through the text to equip the student with useful tools for attacking the issues raised in the cases.

Since few students will have had previous training through case problems, some discussion of the case problems is appropriate. Most of the cases are descriptions of actual business problems faced by real firms. The names, and sometimes other nonvital facts, have usually been disguised to conceal the true identity of the firms—indeed, the use of a disguise is usually a condition of permission by the firm for us to use the material. Usually, too, the actual facts of the business situation have been simplified somewhat by omission or alteration of peripheral aspects.

The case problems are intended to be much more than illustrations. Typically, they are problems calling for solution. Seldom is there a single "right" answer to the problem presented, but some actions clearly are better than others that might be suggested. The student should be prepared to defend his particular proposals for action and to give in some detail the reasons for his choice of alternatives.

The Substantive Plan of the Book

It may be helpful to review briefly the major subject areas to be covered and indicate the order in which they are taken up in the book. We first are concerned with helping the student understand the nature of the need for funds in business. The nature and amount of funds needed to operate a business are grounded on the nature of its operations. We seek to help the student to see how operational decisions affect the need for funds and how changes in operations, such as changes in the policy of the firm toward granting credit to customers, affect the finances of business. Attention is directed, in turn, to the investment in inventory, in receivables, in cash and near-cash investments, and in fixed assets. Methods by which the financial officer can play a useful part in controlling the need for funds are also examined.

We then discuss techniques of analyzing the past and current financing of the business as a means of understanding the past needs for funds and the way they have been met.

From a focus on understanding past needs, we then shift to the problems of forecasting future needs for funds. Techniques for organizing information on the future operations of the business into specific forecasts of funds needs are introduced and discussed.

Next, the problem of how the needed funds should best be obtained is taken up. Sources of short-term funds are explored, and the negotiation of suitable terms with these sources is considered. Raising intermediate- and long-term funds is taken up next and at considerable length.

In turning to the sources of long-term funds (Part V), we deal first with the primary source of permanent capital for going businesses—retained earnings—and this, of course, means a discussion of dividend policy. Then, before taking up the analytical issues of corporate capital structure, we present two chapters that give the factual picture of the external capital market and the normal procedures for tapping this market for new funds.

These chapters are followed by a set of chapters (Part VI) which discuss the basic security types in an analytical framework. The underlying considerations of risk, income, and control are presented, and analytical approaches are offered for considering objectively the choices that must be made. At this stage the choices are presented in their simplest form so that the essential features will be more readily apparent.

Part VII, on capital budgeting, deals explicitly and in some detail with one of the major areas of corporate decision making—the selection of long-term investment opportunities. Current analytical concepts are described, including the evaluation of cash flows, the cost of security issues, and the opportunity cost in capital budgeting.

Part VIII, dealing with the bargain for funds, turns attention to a number of the more important variations in long-term capital contracts and observes how modifications in the distribution of risk, income, and control evolve to meet the recognized needs of suppliers and users of capital. This section also includes chapters on leasing as an alternative to ownership, on refinancing, and on the nature and effects of government regulation. The objective of this last chapter is not only to describe the nature of present-day regulation, with special emphasis on the role of the Securities and Exchange Commission, but, more importantly, to bring out the impact of such regulation on the financial practices and policies of individual business corporations.

The final sections of the book group a number of special aspects of business finance under the headings "Financing Growth and Development" and "Business Failure." The financial problems peculiar to the new, small-scale business are presented in some detail. Other chapters deal with valuation and other financial aspects of mergers and with the problems surrounding the firm during a period of serious financial difficulty, contrasting liquidation with the reconstruction of the corporate structure to permit a continuing business.

The Need for Funds: An Overall Look

"You've got to have money to make money!" This business adage is a simple recognition that most enterprises need funds in order to operate profitably. The typical manufacturing firm, for example, needs to maintain some stocks of goods, to extend credit to its customers, to carry a bank account, and to have plant and productive equipment. While the amounts needed in the individual firm are influenced by many factors and developments, and fluctuate over a period of time, the typical going business has and must maintain a substantial continuing investment in inventory, credits to its customers (receivables), cash in banks, and plant and equipment.

Table 1–1 shows the assets and liabilities of all U.S. manufacturing corporations at the end of 1964. Together, these corporations owned assets valued at over $323 billion. Inventories amounted to over $75 billion, or 23.4% of their total assets. Notes and accounts receivable totaled nearly $57 billion, or 17.6% of the total assets. Cash and U.S. government securities, which are a popular medium for investment of

TABLE 1–1

ESTIMATED BALANCE SHEET, ALL U.S. MANUFACTURING CORPORATIONS,
DECEMBER 31, 1964
(Dollar Figures in Millions)

	December 31, 1964	Percentage of Total
ASSETS		
Cash on hand and in bank....................	$ 19,630	6.1%
U.S. government securities.....................	11,427	3.5
Notes and accounts receivable (net)............	56,890	17.6
Inventories................................	75,637	23.4
Other current assets........................	8,568	2.7
Total current assets....................	$172,152	53.3%
Property, plant, and equipment................	251,742	77.9
Deduct: Reserve for depreciation and depletion....	126,622	39.2
Total property, plant, and equipment (net)................................	$125,121	38.7%
Other noncurrent assets.....................	26,002	8.0
Total assets..........................	$323,274	100.0%
LIABILITIES AND STOCKHOLDERS' EQUITY		
Short-term loans from banks (original maturity of one year or less)...........................	$ 8,782	2.7%
Trade accounts and notes payable..............	31,564	9.7
Federal income taxes accrued..................	12,211	3.8
Instalments due in 1 year or less on long-term debt......................................	2,950	0.9
Other current liabilities......................	16,535	5.1
Total current liabilities..................	$ 72,042	22.3%
Long-term debt due in more than 1 year..........	40,695	12.6
Other noncurrent liabilities...................	6,967	2.2
Total liabilities.......................	$119,704	37.0%
Reserves not reflected elsewhere................	2,219	0.7
Capital stock, capital surplus, and minority interest..................................	75,811	23.5
Earned surplus and surplus reserves.............	125,539	38.8
Total stockholders' equity...............	$203,569	63.0%
Total liabilities and stockholders' equity..	$323,274	100.0%

SOURCE: U.S. Federal Trade Commission and Securities and Exchange Commission, *Quarterly Financial Report for Manufacturing Corporations: Fourth Quarter, 1964* (Washington, D.C.: U.S. Government Printing Office, 1965), pp. 12 and 34.

NOTE: In this and other tables in the book the figures have been rounded to the nearest whole number. Hence, totals do not always agree.

cash not needed immediately, together amounted to about $31 billion, or 9.6% of the total. The net investment in property, plant, and equipment was also huge—over $125 billion, or 38.7% of the total. Together, these four major types of assets represented 89.3% of the total assets of U.S. manufacturers.

In building an understanding of the financing of business, it is useful to think of the various assets as representing the investment of funds. Viewed in this light, the outstanding investment in inventory reported on the balance sheet represents funds absorbed or tied up in inventory on that date. If the inventories are built up, more funds are absorbed, or used, in maintaining this type of asset. If the inventories are reduced, funds are released for other uses. In many respects the analogy of a sponge is appropriate. An increase in inventory or other assets soaks up cash or funds; a squeezing-down of the inventory sponge frees cash for other uses.

The typical business commonly has a wide range of alternative or competing uses for its funds. A proposed buildup of raw material inventories may require an implicit choice of use of funds over alternative uses such as purchase of new machines, increased advertising outlays, purchase of another concern, repayment of debt, or higher dividends to shareholders. At a single point of time the asset side of the balance sheet can be regarded as the reflection of a cumulative complex of the investment decisions of management. Similarly, the net changes in asset accounts between balance sheet dates reflect decisions implemented during the intervening period.

Looking at the changes in the aggregate balance sheets for U.S. manufacturers from December 31, 1963, to December 31, 1964, as shown in Table 1–2, we see that the investment in every type of asset except cash and U.S. government securities was expanded during 1964. The increases in receivables, inventory, and net fixed assets represented particularly large uses of funds. Some funds were released for other uses by reduction of the investment in government bonds and in cash.

Under this same concept the items on the liability side of the balance sheet can appropriately be regarded as sources of funds. In Table 1–1, it can be seen that total debts of U.S. manufacturers on December 31, 1964, amounted to nearly $120 billion, or 37.0% of total assets. Stockholders, by buying stock in the companies and leaving profits in the businesses, have been, in effect, the source of almost $204 billion, or 63.0% of the total assets.

The funds required to increase the investment in one asset may be provided by the squeezing-down of the investment in another asset—for example, the added need for funds created by an inventory buildup might be met by drawing down the investment in cash. Alternatively, the needed funds might be secured by increasing a liability—for example, by added borrowing from banks. Or the use could be matched through the sale of

TABLE 1–2

NET CHANGES IN ASSETS AND LIABILITIES OF ALL U.S. MANUFACTURING
CORPORATIONS, 1964
(Dollar Figures in Millions)

	December 31, 1963	December 31, 1964	Net Change
ASSETS			
Cash on hand and in bank	$ 20,351	$ 19,630	−$ 721
U.S. government securities	12,202	11,427	− 775
Notes and accounts receivable (net)	51,523	56,890	+ 5,367
Inventories	70,539	75,637	+ 5,098
Other current assets	8,056	8,568	+ 512
Total current assets	$162,670	$172,152	+$ 9,482
Property, plant, and equipment	232,777	251,742	+ 18,965
Deduct: Reserve for depreciation and depletion	117,676	126,622	+ 8,946
Total property, plant, and equipment (net)	$115,102	$125,121	+$10,019
Other noncurrent assets	24,819	26,002	+ 1,183
Total assets	$302,591	$323,274	+$20,683
LIABILITIES AND STOCKHOLDERS' EQUITY			
Short-term loans from banks (original maturity of 1 year or less)	$ 7,925	$ 8,782	+$ 857
Trade accounts and notes payable	28,539	31,564	+ 3,025
Federal income taxes accrued	11,699	12,211	+ 512
Instalments due in 1 year or less on long-term debt	2,678	2,950	+ 272
Other current liabilities	15,340	16,535	+ 1,195
Total current liabilities	$ 66,181	$ 72,042	+$ 5,861
Long-term debt due in more than 1 year	38,106	40,695	+ 2,589
Other noncurrent liabilities	5,922	6,967	+ 1,045
Total liabilities	$110,209	$119,704	+$ 9,495
Reserves not reflected elsewhere	2,208	2,219	+ 11
Capital stock, capital surplus, minority interest	74,098	75,811	+ 1,713
Earned surplus and surplus reserves	116,077	125,539	+ 9,462
Total stockholders' equity	$192,383	$203,569	+$11,186
Total liabilities and stockholders' equity	$302,591	$323,274	+$20,683

SOURCE: U.S. Federal Trade Commission and Securities and Exchange Commission, *Quarterly Financial Report for Manufacturing Corporations: Fourth Quarter, 1964* (Washington, D.C.: U.S. Government Printing Office, 1965), pp. 12 and 34.

NOTE: Changes in the accounting classification of time certificates of deposit were made in 1964. To make the 1963 data approximately comparable, the cash item was raised by about 14%; and U.S. government securities and other current assets were lowered by over 5% and over 18%, respectively.

more stock—or an increase in the stockholders' investment in the company through the reinvestment of earnings.

Turning again to Table 1–2, we see that the large increase in assets of manufacturing companies during 1964 was financed through increased credit from all the major sources, through important increases in the ownership accounts, and by the drawing-down of the investment in cash and U.S. government bonds.

Organized and careful analysis of sources and uses of funds over a period of time, as reflected in balance sheet changes supplemented with material from income statements, can be a useful aid to understanding the needs of a business and how they have been met. In Chapter 7 we shall explain in some detail the technique of funds flow analysis—which is built around the construction of statements of sources and uses of funds. At this point, it will suffice if the student recognizes clearly that the various assets represent the use or investment of funds, that increases in these assets absorb or use funds, and that decreases in particular assets free or release funds.

Underlying Objectives of Resource Management

The basic reason for being of most business enterprises is to build maximum sustainable values for the owners. True, enlightened owners and managers recognize that the firm also has responsibilities to its customers, its employees, its community, and perhaps to the firm itself as a total organization. But the obligation of management to use the funds contributed to its care by the owners to the maximum advantage of the owners is the paramount one of the financial manager.

Wise choices in the use of funds (resources) and in the ways available sources of funds are drawn upon are central to the building of enterprise values. Generally, the objectives of wise funds allocation and value building are served if profit opportunities and performance are viewed in relation to the scale of resources or funds required to produce them. That is, a given amount of profit return should be evaluated in terms of the percentage profit return on the investment of funds involved. To illustrate, let us suppose that an entrepreneur has an opportunity to buy either of two businesses. Business A promises an annual profit of $24,000 but will require an investment of $240,000. Business B offers only a $20,000 annual return, but the investment needed is $140,000. If all other considerations were the same, surely the 14.4% prospective return on investment in firm B ($20,000/$140,000 = 14.4%) is more attractive than the 10% return ($24,000/$240,000) on investment in firm A.

The usefulness and validity of effort to maximize *return on investment* as an intermediate means to the end objective of building values is gaining increasing acceptance, and return on invested funds is also gaining acceptance as a prime measure of management's performance in handling the funds entrusted to its supervision. Note the choice of words, "a prime measure." We do not argue that other criteria have no relevance or validity or that achievement of a maximum return on investment necessarily will maximize values. Yet the increasing acceptance of return on investment (*ROI*) as a prime objective and measure of performance rests on solid grounds.

First, the return-on-investment objective inherently recognizes the value of capital—the fact that its owners could use their funds to advantage in other ventures—and that capital is seldom available for an enterprise in unlimited amount. Second, it puts a premium on economical use of capital in the firm. Third, use of this performance criterion and objective points to broad avenues for improvement of performance. Fourth, the *ROI* concept has a high degree of what might be termed "administrative feasibility." It is straightforward and can be understood throughout an organization. Moreover, it can be applied to the operations of subsidiaries, divisions, or other subgroupings within the firm.

Alternative Ways to Improved Return on Investment

Return on investment can usefully be calculated both in terms of the return on asset investment and also on that portion of the investment funds of the business that is supplied by the owners. Let us first concern ourselves with the return on total funds or asset investment.

The *return on asset investment* is the product of three key variables: the amount of asset investment, the amount of sales, and the percentage of profit return on sales. The *ROI* can be simply and directly calculated as follows:

$$\frac{\text{Net Profit after Taxes}}{\text{Total Assets}}.$$

A less direct method of calculating *ROI* can be more revealing, however. Under this "turnover" method, *ROI* is calculated as follows:

$$ROI = \frac{\text{Sales}}{\text{Assets}} \times \frac{\text{Net Profit}}{\text{Sales}}.$$

Let us illustrate. Firm X had total assets of $400,000, sales of $1,000,000, and net income after taxes of $40,000 in 1964. Application of the direct formula shows the *ROI* to be 10% ($40,000/$400,000).

Using the turnover formula approach we proceed:

$$ROI = \frac{\$1,000,000}{\$400,000} \times \frac{\$40,000}{\$1,000,000}$$
$$ROI = 2.5 \times 4\%$$
$$ROI = 10\%.$$

Now let us assume that firm X in the following year, 1965, increased sales to $1,200,000 and net income after taxes to $48,000. However, total assets were increased to $600,000. Using the direct formula we note that *ROI* dropped to 8% ($48,000/$600,000). Calculating by the turnover method, we derive the following:

$$ROI = \frac{\$1,200,000}{\$600,000} \times \frac{\$48,000}{\$1,200,000}$$
$$ROI = 2 \times 4\%$$
$$ROI = 8\%.$$

The turnover calculation highlights the fact that the profit return held constant at 4% and that it was the large increase in asset investment relative to sales (reflected in a decline in the turnover of assets in sales to 2 times) that was responsible for the lower *ROI*. If the management of firm X had been able to achieve the sales and profit increases on the old investment base of $400,000, it would have boosted the turnover rate to 3.0 and the return on asset investment to 12% (4% times 3.0).

It should be apparent that success in boosting return on asset investment can be achieved by progress along either of two broad avenues —by increasing the rate of profit on sales or by increasing investment turnover. Investment turnover, in turn, can be raised by increasing sales more than assets or by cutting assets more than sales are reduced. Put differently, increases in sales or profit returns on sales enhance return on investment only if the investment is held to a less than proportionate increase.

So far we have spoken only in terms of return on investment in total assets. The owners of the enterprise—the common stockholders if it is a corporation—may well have an especial concern with the return on the funds they have invested in the business. In calculating *return on owners' investment*, the investment base is the total of the common stock accounts (capital and surplus).

Let us illustrate with firms Y and Z and the following facts:

	Firm Y	Firm Z
Sales.......................................	$1,000,000	$1,000,000
Net income before taxes and interest...........	80,000	80,000
Interest.....................................	–0–	10,000
Net income before taxes......................	$ 80,000	$ 70,000
Taxes @ 50%...............................	40,000	35,000
Income after taxes...........................	$ 40,000	$ 35,000
Total assets.................................	$ 400,000	$ 400,000
Total debts..................................	–0–	$ 200,000
Owners' investment...........................	$ 400,000	$ 200,000
ROI (total assets)...........................	10%	8.75%
ROOI (return on owners' investment)..........	10%	17.50%

Note that we have made the unlikely assumption that firm Y operates with no debts at all, in contrast to firm Z which has financed equally with debt and ownership. Sales and earnings were assumed equal except for the interest costs in firm Z, which were deducted before income taxes were calculated. The extra interest cost cut *ROI* down modestly, from 10% in firm Y to 8.75% in firm Z. But the lesser use of ownership funds in firm Z meant a sharply higher *ROOI* in firm Z (17.5%) over the 10% figure for firm Y. In effect, firm Z borrowed at 5% ($10,000 interest ÷ $200,000) before taxes, and effectively 2½% after taxes, while it was able to earn 20% before interest and taxes on assets ($80,000/$400,000), and 8.75% after interest and taxes. These examples point up the fact that so long as the after-tax interest costs are less than the rate of return on asset investment, the rate of return on owners' investment can be increased by increasing the proportion of borrowed money to ownership funds. This is simply another way of saying that if assets can be made to earn more than the cost of borrowed money, financing through debt is profitable to the owners.

Balanced against the attractions of the opportunity for boosting return on owners' investment through increased use of debt are the added financial risks imposed by borrowing. If interest or agreed loan repayments cannot be met on schedule, creditors can force bankruptcy of the firm. And in liquidation or reorganization of the firm, creditors' claims must be met in full before the owners can recover any of their investment. The decision as to the optimum balance in financing through debt and ownership funds is one of the most important financial decisions in most firms, and one discussed at length later in this book. Suffice it here to recognize the impact of the debt/ownership relationship on the return on owners' investment.

Different Routes to a Satisfactory Return on Investment

Widely varied approaches can lead to a gratifyingly high return on invested capital. Let us examine the results of several successful firms with quite different approaches. These approaches reflect industry characteristics.

First, let us look at Minnesota Mining and Manufacturing Company, which in 1964 showed a return of 13.3% on total year-end asset investment and 18.4% on owners' investment. How were such striking results achieved? The answer lies primarily in a rate of profit on sales unusually high in manufacturing, 11.3%. (The median return on sales of *Fortune's* 500 largest U.S. industrial corporations in 1964 was 5.0%.)[1] Coupled with an asset turnover of 1.18 and an ownership investment turnover of 1.62, the high profit rate produced an unusually high return on total investment and, despite only modest use of debt, on the owners' investment.

Red Owl Stores, a northwestern food chain, in contrast, earned only 1.00% on sales in its fiscal year ended February 27, 1965. Turnover of asset investment was, however, 5.71; and turnover of ownership investment, reflecting substantial debt financing, was 10.59! Consequently, the company earned 5.7% on total assets and 10.6% on owners' investment.

The Dayton Power and Light Company, an Ohio electric and gas

---

[1] *The Fortune Directory: The 500 Largest U.S. Industrial Corporations* (New York: Time, Inc., August, 1965), p. 21.

utility, earned 13.43% on total sales in 1964. Turnover of assets, as in the case of most utilities, was low—only 0.40. Since, again, as with most electric utilities, much debt was used, turnover of owners' investment was much higher—1.02. Though return on total assets was just 5.3%, return on owners' investment was 13.7%.

These numerical examples are simply detailed instances of the statements that we made at the beginning of the chapter, where we said that financial work is the management of assets and the proper provision of funds.

The Need for Pressures toward Effective Use of Assets

As our endorsement of the usefulness of the return-on-investment concept indicates, we believe that vigorous, well-thought-out, and continuing management effort to keep the firm's assets working hard and productively is essential to the success of the business. The financial officer can and should play a leading role in these efforts.

This emphasis may appear misplaced or platitudinous without full recognition of the basic pressures that exist in most enterprises, and particularly in highly profitable ones, toward extravagant or indulgent use of resources. Some of these pressures stem from seemingly innate human qualities—the human animal is not by nature thrifty or wise in his use of resources. For example, all of us like to have the latest and best tools with which to work. And many, if not most, people tend to equate "bigger" with "better." Personal empire-building tendencies also seem almost innate. Further, the sheer convenience of abundant resources at hand is attractive—witness the number of financially pressed families who embrace the luxury and convenience of a second or even third family automobile. Participation in business—especially in a business owned by someone else—does not convert the human animal into a machine that grinds out economically rational decisions.

Even in enterprises whose management generally is imbued with concern for return on investment or similar goals stressing maximum productivity of resources, certain sources of pressure toward indulgent use of assets can be identified. One such is the common preoccupation of management personnel having specialized responsibilities with the gains from increased sales or cost cutting which can be achieved with more capital. Production managers are likely to be keenly aware of possibilities of greater output or of cutting production costs with added laborsaving equipment (larger equipment investment). An expensive shutdown due to exhaustion of raw material stocks provides an obvious push toward the carrying of greater stocks. The sales manager can be expected to be vigorous in exposing the potential for bigger sales through more generous credit extension (larger receivables) or through more complete stocks of goods for sale (larger finished goods inventory). Such added use of resources *may* appear to boost overall return on investment and be desirable. But too often, the partisans of such actions overlook or underemphasize important but less obvious operating costs involved in higher asset accumulation and the costs of the added capital investment required.

The carrying of added raw material stocks, for example, may well mean a need for greater storage facilities, higher property taxes, insurance, and other costs of protecting and caring for the stocks. Further, risks of loss through physical deterioration, obsolescence, or price declines may be significant and yet inadequately recognized. Similar operating costs and risks of loss are likely to be significant in the case of all other types of assets—with the exception perhaps of cash itself, and even cash is subject to the risks of loss of value through inflation.

The _net_ gains, after full allowance for the added operating costs and risks of loss of values involved in added investment, must be compared with the costs or economic burden of the added investment. The objective, of course, should be one of balance—of ensuring that the savings or added revenues from more assets match or exceed the costs of the capital involved. The net return-on-investment concept basically is a device to see that the added assets "pay their way" and to point up the price in lower return on investment of less productive investment.

But even adherence to return-on-investment doctrines does not ensure adequate management recognition of the problems of raising the funds to finance the added investment. In large, prosperous firms the assumption that funds can readily be secured for any investment judged worthy may in fact be justified. But in a great many firms—particularly new, smaller, or less successful concerns—the problems in financing even obviously desirable investment may be formidable, often controlling. Here, management must balance the advantages of moves that call for more capital against the financial problems of getting the needed money. The interest of the financial officer here is immediate and direct. In such cases imaginative effort may reveal ways in which many, if not all, of the gains of proposals for added investment can be garnered with smaller or no added investment. _Often, the easiest and best way to raise funds is to avoid the need for them._

In this introductory chapter, we have spoken repeatedly of the "corporation." These references reflect the great importance in modern business life of the corporation as an organizational, legal, and financial vehicle. Student understanding of the basic features of the corporate form of organization and how the corporate form differs from sole proprietorships and partnerships is important to mastery of materials to come. Chapter 2 seeks to provide the basis for this understanding.

Chapter 2

The Nature of the Corporation in the United States

ANY PERSON visiting even the smallest business district of a town in the United States will observe, if he turns his attention to the matter, that the business which is carried on is owned in a variety of ways. There will surely be shops, dealerships, and services that are owned and operated by one person. Some of these may even have a sign showing the name of an individual and the abbreviation *Prop.*, indicating "Proprietor." Other activities will be found to be owned by a group of persons acting as partners. This will certainly be the case for any law office or medical center, and it will often be the case for other activities where a few persons have decided to join together to form a business. It is not always possible to judge that a firm is a partnership purely from its name, but the use of personal names (Smith & Jones) or the words *and Company* often furnish a clue.

Mixed in with these organizations, which are to be recognized as persons or groups of persons engaged in business, the observer will see, by the use of the abbreviation *Inc.* (*Incorporated*) or *Corp.* (*Corporation*) in the name, that certain firms are designated as having corporate form. Agencies, plants, and offices of larger businesses will be among those which bear the corporate designation. In most communities, for example, our observer is likely to find the business office of the local unit of the American Telephone and Telegraph Company, one of the largest private corporations in the United States. And of course, on the shelves of all the stores the products of corporate business will greatly outnumber the goods that were made by other types of firms.

As he looks for the names which indicate that a business has corporate form, the observer will observe the somewhat puzzling fact that many of the smaller firms are also incorporated. If he should conclude that there must be a variety of reasons why people choose to incorporate their businesses, he would be on the right track.

The differences between the types of ownership are of more than passing importance to all of us. Their significance begins to become apparent whenever one wishes to establish a relation with a firm that requires a commitment of some sort. Who is authorized to speak for the business? Will the business survive those who now speak for it? Where and how much is the ultimate liability of the firm, in case damage is done to me? How can I invest some of my funds in this firm? What participation in control would I have? Any one of these questions has different answers, depending upon the type of business organization that is used. The reader should be able to answer them, among others, after study of this chapter.

Legal Patterns Fall into Two Groups

In order to indicate how some of the questions can be answered, it is necessary to identify the various bodies of rules within which a business must operate. We refer to these rules as *legal patterns*, of which several are available for choice by those who wish to set up a business organization. A complete treatise would describe even those, such as the *business trust* and the *joint-stock company*, which are at present of small importance in the United States. The principal avenues of choice lead to the *corporation* on one side and to the *partnership* or to the *proprietorship* on the other, and our discussion will deal with them. The major concern of this material will therefore be to explain the characteristics of the corporation, on one hand, and the partnership-proprietorship, on the other, so that the reader can understand the factors that enter the decision-making process when the choice is being made for a firm. For the present the business trust can be regarded as very like a corporation, and the joint-stock company as a corporation except for the legal liability that attaches to its owners. A preliminary distinction can then be drawn between the partnership-proprietorship, which is simply a certain person or group of persons in business, and those businesses of corporate type, where there is a legal entity apart from the persons who own and operate the firm.

Present Importance of the Corporation in the United States

Since the corporation has become the predominant form of doing business in the United States, we can well begin our examination of the subject by a review of some important statistics about the varying importance of the corporation in various sectors of the economic activity of the nation. While we shall confine ourselves to the factual situation in the United States, it will be of interest to note that in general the same conditions will be found in any industrialized country where private enterprise plays an important part. Table 2–1 shows not only that one half of the business income is earned by corporations, but also that this form of business organization is dominant in industries such as public utilities and manufacturing, where large-scale units are likely to be needed for efficiency.

To explain more fully the reasons for the use of the corporate form, we now turn to an examination of its characteristics in some detail. They have been organized under the major headings: "Legal Entity," "State Sanction—Corporate Powers," "Financial Contracts," and "Tax Status." In each section primary attention will be given to the corporation. The

TABLE 2–1

COMPARISON OF RELATIVE IMPORTANCE OF INCORPORATED AND UNIN-
CORPORATED ENTERPRISES AS MEASURED BY PERCENTAGE OF TOTAL NET
INCOME BEFORE TAXES, BY INDUSTRY, FOR THE YEAR 1963

| | Before-Tax Corporate Income | |
Industry	Millions of Dollars	Percentage of Industry
All industries............................	$51,267	50.3%
Communications and public utilities........	7,300	99.1
Manufacturing...........................	27,185	94.6
Mining.................................	929	85.9
Finance, insurance, and real estate........	5,687	66.6
Transportation..........................	1,084	54.1
Wholesale and retail trade...............	5,406	30.2
Contract construction....................	521	9.8
Services................................	554	3.7
Agriculture, forestry, and fisheries.........	86	0.6

SOURCE: U.S. Department of Commerce, *Survey of Current Business*, July, 1964
(National Income Number), Tables 44 and 56, pp. 27 and 31.

partnership-proprietorship and other patterns will be referred to only where there are major differences of concern to those selecting the legal pattern of a business.

Legal Entity

The reader should note that the American culture of today provides natural acceptance of the idea that one normally does business with an entity which is separate from the persons dealt with. One thinks of a business as separate from the personal interests of its owner. This division is a complex one, involving characteristics that are not always desirable, but it is important to recognize that it does exist. There is acceptance in our culture of the idea that a business unit is a separable entity, and the law has been specific in making the separation in the case of the corporation, so one can speak of the legal entity that exists in addition to the cultural entity that is generally accepted.

A useful definition of a _corporation_ is: ". . . an association of persons which is in many respects treated as if it were itself a person. It has rights and duties of its own, which are not the rights and duties of the individual members thereof. . . . The rights and duties of the members descend to the successive members of the corporation."[1]

This statement is both the definition of a corporation and an explanation of the meaning of the term *legal entity*. The corporation has status before the law as a person. This means that courts will consider the corporation as a person which may enter into contracts, sue or be sued, and so on, quite independently of the individuals who own its securities. Thus, while the culture confers a sort of entity upon any business unit, the law confines this privilege to the corporation. The other forms of organization are recognized only as groups of individuals.

It should be noted that the conferring of personality upon the corporation does not mean that this kind of person has all the rights and privileges of a natural person. Obviously, there are many types of contract, such as marriage, that a corporation cannot enter into, and there are many types of conduct which corporations cannot undertake. There are, in fact, many laws limiting corporate privileges. The significant thing is that a corporation does have certain important elements of a separate personality in the eyes of the law.

Characteristics of the Corporation Associated with Legal Entity. Certain characteristics of a corporation may be associated with its legal entity. (1) There is the duty to have a corporate name, although as a privilege, other types of firms may select names. (2) There is the privilege of a term of existence which is completely independent of the lives of any natural persons. (3) There is a provision for a board of directors to represent the owners, who may be a great many persons. (4) There is the privilege that the corporation may hold title to property and that its officers may enter into contracts of all sorts without binding the individuals who own the corporation to the obligations it has undertaken. Finally, and often of great importance, (5) the separate entity is subject to different rules of taxation. This last matter will be the subject of a separate section of this chapter.

The foregoing characteristics are available only in limited form, if at all, to the other forms of business organization, and none has all of them. A partnership operates under the rule—exactly contrary to that for the corporation—that any partner may act for the partnership in matters related to the business of the partnership, except where the limitation on the partner is indicated clearly and publicly.[2] The grant of such power to a partner is a necessary convenience if business is to be done efficiently,

---

[1] Cecil T. Carr, "Corporation," *Encyclopaedia Britannica* (11th ed.; New York: Encyclopaedia Britannica Co., 1910–11), Vol. VII, p. 190.

[2] In such case the person is known as a *limited partner* and can take no part in the management of the partnership. He is simply a supplier of capital. A major difficulty faced by limited partners is that states other than that in which the partnership was formed may make the limited partner equally liable with the other partners for debts created in the outside state.

but it has served as the disruptive force that has caused the dissolution of many firms.

The Corporate Name. The duty to select a corporate name includes as a requirement that the name indicate the fact of incorporation.[3] In the United States this is usually done by using the word *Incorporated* as the last word of the corporate title. This is usually abbreviated and read as *Inc.* The word *Corporation* (*Corp.*) is sometimes used. One also finds *Limited* (*Ltd.*), which is the standard British and Canadian practice but appears in the United States only to lend a sort of prestige to the name. Some states have laws which permit the use of *The* _____ *Company* to distinguish a corporation. Other distinguishing words are used in other countries. The French *Société Anonyme* is worth noting because it points out the separate entity characteristic of the corporation.

Most states now permit any form of business unit to adopt a firm name. Often, there is some designation in the title that indicates the type of legal pattern that is used. Business trusts usually have the word *Trust* in their names.[4] Limited partnerships must indicate that some of the partners do not have unlimited liability, but do not do so in their names. In most states the fact of limited partnership is disclosed in a certificate of Limited Partnership, which is filed with the Secretary of State and is thus a matter of public record. The ordinary partnerships and other forms of business use the words *and Company* frequently.

Term of Life. Most corporations avail themselves fully of the privilege of indefinite existence by stating no termination date in their basic documents. Those which do usually find it easy to extend their life by amendment. One author has selected an apt simile by comparing the corporate society to a river. The water in the river, symbolizing the parties to the corporation, is ever changing. The general river, however, does not change; and one thinks of the river as the same entity, even though much water has flowed through it.

The characteristics of a corporation which have just been described can be summarized in the eloquent and frequently quoted words of John Marshall:

A corporation is an artificial being, invisible, intangible, and existing only in contemplation of law. Being the mere creature of law, it possesses only those properties which the charter of its creation confers upon it, either expressly or as incidental to its very existence. . . . Among the most important are immortality, and . . . individuality; properties by which a

---

[3] Insurance *companies*, trust *companies*, and *banks* are usually corporations, though their names may not indicate the fact. These enterprises are incorporated under special laws regulating banking and insurance.

[4] The phrase *the trust problem* to designate the problem created by large-scale enterprise is an historical accident arising from the fact that the first "trusts" used the business trust form. Later, "trusts" used the corporate form much more frequently.

perpetual succession of many persons are considered the same and may act as a single individual.[5]

The historic rule is that a partnership must dissolve upon the death, incapacity, or withdrawal of any partner, except a limited partner. The same is, of course, true of an individual proprietorship. A great many partnership agreements provide in detail the procedure to be followed upon the withdrawal of a partner. A few states permit partnerships to survive without the signing of a new contract. Thus, in many cases a new partnership is formed to take over the affairs of the old one without any disturbance of the business. It must, however, be noted that no such arrangement can avoid the necessity of evaluating the interest of the withdrawing partner, or of paying this value to the partner, or his estate, or other representative. The payment may be made in notes of the new partnership, if this was provided for by the original partnership agreement, but any such notes must be payable in a reasonable time.[6]

Despite the devices that can be created by advance agreement, the process of dissolution of a partnership and creation of a new partnership is usually a period of strain even with goodwill from all parties. It may

---

[5] *Trustees of Dartmouth College* v. *Woodward*, 4 Wheat. (U.S.) 518, 636 (1819). In his first sentence the learned justice was paraphrasing Sir Edward Coke. Case of Sutton's Hospital, 10 Coke's Reports 1, 32 *b* (1613).

[6] The following quotations from a partnership agreement show the extent of complexity sometimes encountered in partnership agreements. Note that the partnership contract foresees problems of valuation as well as liquidation.

Profits and Losses. Salaries of partners shall be treated as expenses. Net profits or losses for each calendar year shall be entered as follows:

  a) Net profits or losses up to and including 10% of the aggregate capital accounts shall be credited or charged to partners in proportion to their capital accounts;

  b) One-half of any remaining net profits or losses up through the next 6% of the aggregate capital accounts shall be credited or charged proportionally to the several capital accounts, and the other half shall be credited or charged against the partners in equal shares; and

  c) All net profits or losses for each year over 16% of the aggregate capital accounts shall be credited or charged in proportion to the several capital accounts.

New Partners. New partners may be elected not less than 60 days after proposal for membership, by the vote of at least two-thirds of the members owning at least two-thirds of the firm's capital.

Withdrawal or Death of a Partner. A partner may withdraw at any time by agreement with the Executive Committee or by giving one year's notice. Withdrawal may be required by a two-thirds vote of members owning two-thirds of capital. Such withdrawal or death shall not work a dissolution of the firm. In case of the withdrawal or death of a partner, the interest of such former partner shall be determined and paid as follows:

  a) The amount credited in his drawing account shall be paid on 30 days' notice.

  b) His credit balance in the capital account, as shown by the last previous balance sheet plus or minus subsequent charges and corrections for the profit or loss of the year, with interest at 6% per annum until payment, shall be paid by the firm in 10 equal annual installments, with such anticipation in the payment of installments as the firm may decide. Such unpaid balances shall be treated as a debt of the firm.

impose severe financial burdens upon the continuing business. Thus, the disadvantages of mortality lead many partnerships to shift to the corporate form. The same is true, of course, of the individual proprietor, if he desires to see his business continue after him.

The Board of Directors. In the proprietorship the ultimate powers of decision are in the hands of the owner. In the partnership, as stated above, any general partner may act for the partnership. In the case of the corporation, most of the powers of ownership are placed in the hands of a board of directors. There are certain questions of such importance that they must be referred to a stockholders' meeting for a vote. These include decisions to merge with another firm, to change the privileges of a class of stockholders, and others of like importance. But in the normal course of affairs the board of directors makes decisions as if the directors were owners, as long as its members act honestly and in good faith. From this situation of representative government comes the possibility—and often the fact—of a separation of ownership from control.[7]

Adolph Berle and Gardiner Means, in their pioneering study,[8] defined location of the control of a corporation as follows: ". . . we may say for practical purposes that control lies in the hands of the individual or group who have the actual power to select the board of directors (or its majority). . . ."[9] In the active sense of day-to-day management, this definition is entirely true, and it is therefore appropriate to study first the location of the voting power which can be used at corporate meetings. Every corporation will have at least one class of shareholders whose members have voting power. In the majority of corporations, all the voting power is found in the common stock, on the basis of one vote per share.

Any shareholder may be elected a director at the annual meeting of the shareholders; but since his holding need be only one or a few shares, his own position as owner may be nominal. In the smaller firms, especially those *closely held* corporations where the ownership of shares is concentrated in a few hands, the membership of the board will be able to know the desires of the stockholder group, and to act accordingly.[10] In the larger, *publicly held* corporations the directors may be unable to sense the

---

[7] Whether a director must be a shareholder is usually prescribed by a corporation's bylaws.

[8] Adolph A. Berle, Jr., and Gardiner C. Means, *The Modern Corporation and Private Property* (New York: Macmillan Co., 1933). Used by permission. The statistical section has become out of date, but the legal analysis is as cogent as ever.

[9] *Ibid.*, p. 69.

[10] In the past, three has usually been the minimum number of directors required by the statutes of most states, although a few states have permitted "a board of one or more directors." Recently, starting in 1961, several states, including Delaware, New York, and Illinois, have enacted laws providing that where all shares are owned by one or two stockholders the number of directors may be less than three but not less than the number of stockholders. See "Further Thoughts on the One or Two Director Statutes," by E. George Rudolph, in *The Business Lawyer*, Vol. XX (April, 1965), pp. 781–88.

desires of a group of shareholders of diversified characteristics. Although there has been a movement to persuade shareholders in the publicly held corporations to attend meetings, the proportion of such owners who do in fact attend has been and will continue to be small. Most persons entitled to vote at such meetings execute a *proxy*, which names someone who is authorized to cast the vote of the absent shareholder. There are, as our readers doubtless know, occasional proxy fights where opposing interests solicit the vote of the shareholder; but the majority of corporations have peaceful annual meetings at which the existing management, having solicited proxies, has a controlling majority of the votes at the meeting. The terms *management controlled* and *minority controlled* are used to describe corporations where the *proxy system* is relied on to provide the incumbent group with the votes needed to elect its nominees to the board of directors.

As far as the large publicly held companies are concerned, the present situation has been aptly described by Mason:

The one-hundred-and-thirty-odd largest manufacturing corporations account for half of manufacturing output in the United States. The five hundred largest business corporations in this country embrace nearly two thirds of all nonagricultural economic activity. These or similar figures are reiterated with such frequency that they tend to bounce off our heads rather than to penetrate. But by now we are all aware that we live not only in a corporate society but a society of large corporations. The management—that is, the control—of these corporations is in the hands of, at most, a few thousand men. Who selected these men, if not to rule over us, at least to exercise vast authority, and to whom are they responsible? The answer to the first question is quite clearly: they selected themselves. The answer to the second is, at best, nebulous. . . .[11]

There are a great many factors to be appraised before one can form a judgment about the desirability of such a situation. Suffice it to say here that corporations are governed by elected boards of directors, which are supposed in legal theory to represent the interests of the owning investors. In many corporations, especially the closely held ones, they do. In other corporations it is not easy for the members of the board to be identified as representatives of any ownership interest. Most directors under such circumstances act in what they believe to be "the best interests of the corporation"; but the exact meaning of that term is not clear—nor can it be, for the corporation is nothing more than an artificial being, with no interests of its own. One much-quoted attempt to provide guidance is the following:

. . . Business firms are man-made instruments of society. They can be made to achieve their greatest social usefulness—and thus their future can be best assured—when management succeeds in finding a harmonious

---

[11] Edward S. Mason (ed.), *The Corporation in Modern Society* (Cambridge, Mass.: Harvard University Press, 1959), p. 5.

balance among the claims of the various interested groups: the stockholders, employees, customers, and the public at large. But management's responsibility, in the broadest sense, extends beyond the search for a balance among respective claims. Management, as a good citizen, and because it cannot properly function in an acrimonious and contentious atmosphere, has the positive duty to work for peaceful relations and understanding among men—for a restoration of faith of men in each other in all walks of life.

. . . .

Those two words, "fair" and "reasonable," mark the asserted claims not only of a corporation's stockholders but of all other groups as well. Very few groups ever believe that they make unfair or unreasonable claims. But often what one group thinks fair is regarded as entirely unreasonable by another. It takes professional judgment, experience, and knowledge of the consequences of specific decisions to resolve all the claims and to keep all the groups in cooperative support of the joint enterprise.

This reconciliation of interest is not always as difficult as it may seem. It is in part a matter of recognizing true long-term interest, as distinguished from interests that may seem real because they are more immediate.[12]

In view of the widespread ineffectiveness of shareholder control, the reader may be disposed to conclude that the common shareholder should be considered as just another source of funds along with the bondholder and preferred stockholder. We disagree with this interpretation for two reasons: (1) The common shareholder alone possesses the legal right to control the management and the business, whether he exercises it or not; and (2) the common shareholder continues to bear the fundamental risks of the business, whether or not he dictates its policies. This leads us to the position that questions of financial policy (which are the matters of principal importance throughout this book) *should* be determined from the point of view of the interests of the common shareholders *existing at the time the policy is being determined*. This interest, when determined, can then enter the balancing process that is implicit in the quotation from Abrams that we gave above.

Limited Liability. As distinguished from other forms of business organization, the corporate form offers *limited liability* to its owners. The following comment has been made on the typical provision of corporation law on stockholders' liabilities:

Stockholders who invest their funds in the capital stock of corporations are protected by law from losses beyond their investment. Thus, a business may fail after accumulating debts to creditors, liability on contracts and judgments against the corporation for its torts. With rare exceptions, stockholders cannot be held liable for any part of this indebtedness.[13]

---

[12] Frank W. Abrams, "Management's Responsibilities in a Complex World," *Harvard Business Review*, May, 1951, pp. 29–30.

[13] Commerce Clearing House, Inc., *Corporation Law Guide* (Chicago, 1965), Par. 133. (For summaries of state laws, see Par. 658 for each state.)

While the legal obligations of a proprietor or of any member of a partnership are described as *unlimited liability*, experience indicates that business creditors are reluctant to levy upon personal assets, if only because of the cost involved. When they do, they often find that most of the assets in the partner's family are in the name of the wife or some other person not a partner. Such insulation from liability is common and expected. It reflects the cultural acceptance of the business as separate from the personal interests of the owners. Nevertheless, where one considers the incorporation of a small firm, the grant of limited liability is often a factor of considerable weight in the decision.[14]

On the side of the publicly held corporation, where limited liability exists as a matter of law, it is now so universally a characteristic of securities that investors take it for granted. The need for this feature is therefore no longer an issue of the investment world. There is, however, one corollary of the grant of limited liability which corporate management needs to bear in mind. The capital contributed by the shareholders is to be kept separate from any earnings that may be received and held by the corporation. Dividends may not be paid out of such capital.

State Sanction—Corporate Powers

All of the material above, which is centered on the legal entity enjoyed by the corporation, has implicit in it the fact that the corporation exists by the grace of legislative power. Artificial persons are created only by legislative action, and the sovereign has always been the agency upon which depends the opportunity to create corporations.

General Incorporation Laws of the States.   For some years past, beginning with New York in 1811, each of the states of the United States has had a "general corporation law," paralleled by a "general banking law" and the like, which permit persons to charter a corporation for any legal purpose, provided they meet certain requirements, which are the same for any applicant.[15] The terms of the laws vary greatly among the states, and some of the differences will be referred to where they are pertinent, but they have the common characteristic of the relative ease with which a corporation can be created. The necessary papers are drafted and filed, moderate fees are paid, et cetera, all within the terms of the statute and without real difficulty.

Incorporation is not difficult in any state, but few states match Delaware, where it is possible for a firm in Wilmington to advertise that

---

[14] The limited liability feature of an incorporated business may be of little use if a banker or other creditor insists on having the debt contract personally endorsed by the principal stockholder(s).

[15] In the case of banks and other financial corporations, the minimum capital requirement may be substantial. Certain types of business, such as utilities, cannot be set up without a finding by a commission that they are "convenient and necessary."

out-of-state persons may employ it to handle all the necessary procedure of incorporation, with the result that:

Corporations are organized, by-laws adopted and records mailed to counsel on the same day. . . . The first meeting is held in Wilmington. Personal attendance of the incorporators is not required. . . . Thus the organization is brought up to the point of holding the first meeting of directors for electing officers and commencing business. This meeting may be held when and where convenient to the directors and forms are furnished as a guide for its procedure.

Federal Corporations Result from Special Enactment. No general corporation statute exists as a part of the federal law, though the Congress has the power to enact one and bills have been submitted for the purpose. There is a general banking law, known as the National Banking Act, under which are chartered banks with the privilege, and duty, of carrying in their title the words *National Bank* (or N.B.A.). Similar laws provide for federal savings and loan associations, national farm loan associations, and other credit agencies; but for the formation of a general business corporation, one looks to the various states.

The federal Congress has chartered numerous corporations by special enactment. These fulfill some governmental purpose, often of a financial nature. The Federal Reserve banks, the Federal Land banks, the Reconstruction Finance Corporation, and the Inland Waterways Corporation are examples of the use of federal statute to create a corporation. On the other hand, the Congress has sometimes provided for the formation of a governmental corporation under state law. This is true, for instance, of the Commodity Credit Corporation of Delaware.

The Definition of Corporate Powers. The saying "The corporation has limited powers" reflects the admitted fact that a corporation can have only the powers that the state permits it to assume. Nevertheless, the statement is misleading. In practice, those who form corporations draft their own definition of powers and provide the powers they desire within the broad limitations of the general law.

At the time a corporation is formed, its powers will be defined by (1) the statutes of the state, which apply to all its corporations; (2) the *certificate of incorporation* (or *charter*, or *articles of association*), which is drafted by those desiring to form the corporation and applies only to the specific firm; and (3) the *bylaws*, further defining the corporation's powers, which are also drafted by the incorporators.

The Corporation Law. Corporations are subject to all law that affects business affairs, but the corporation statute of a state deals with the special characteristics of a corporation, and it is to the provisions of such a statute that one turns when the powers available to a corporation are to be described.

Anyone with imagination who studies carefully any piece of legislation will soon be able to think of situations where the application of the wording of the statute is uncertain. When lawyers speak of "untested" provisions of a statute, they refer to clauses whose meanings have not yet been the subject of a judicial decision. There is no other way to discover the meaning of a difficult clause than by waiting for a lawsuit to develop and observing the court's conclusion. Then it is said that the clause has been "interpreted."

For this reason it must be realized that the corporation law of a state is far more than the text of the legislation. It includes this text and all the judicial decisions relative to it. From this fact flows a reluctance on the part of legislators to change long-standing and fully interpreted clauses of legislation. There is always uncertainty about the exact meaning of proposed provisions which may cause hesitancy in their use and costly litigation before their interpretation. Among the reasons for the popularity of Delaware in the past as a state of incorporation has been the fact that its corporation law has been the subject of much litigation, so that at present the meaning of the statute is well settled.

Although from time to time, judicial decisions tend to confuse rather than clarify the law, the longer the corporation continues to be the principal pattern used by business units, the more nearly perfected its law will be in every detail. Thus, as time has gone by, the greater has become the margin of preference for the corporation over the joint-stock company and the business trust.

Articles of Incorporation and Bylaws. Most general corporation laws make it clear that the state no longer values its privilege to limit the powers of corporations formed for general business purposes. Under such circumstances, it is not surprising that a cautious draftsman may state the proposed powers broadly enough to avoid any necessity of later amendment.

At this point the reader is reminded that this description refers to incorporation under general laws, not under banking, insurance, or other special laws. The draftsman cannot entirely "encompass the world in the English language," as certain activities are in the purview of other laws. Thus, the extremely broad charter of the Chesapeake Corporation, a railroad holding company, conceded the following restrictions:

Nothing herein contained is to be construed as authorizing the Corporation to carry on the business of discounting bills, notes or other evidences of debt, or receiving deposits of money, or foreign coins, or buying and selling bills of exchange, or of issuing bills, notes or other evidences of debt for circulation as money. . . .

Nothing herein contained shall be . . . construed to give the Corporation any rights, powers, or privileges not permitted by the laws of the State of Maryland. . . .

Despite the possibility that narrow definitions of powers may prove embarrassing at a later time, a substantial number of cases exist where the powers that are taken are narrowly stated. This is particularly true of small firms, where the intent of the incorporators is to take advantage of certain of the attributes of the corporation without freeing the future management in every particular. Quite frequently, in such firms one finds that the transfer of stock is limited to certain procedures that give the corporation's directors control over additions to the stockholder group.

Since the bylaws of the corporation are drafted to implement the articles of incorporation, it can be expected that they will not alter the conclusions suggested by the above paragraphs: that the general corporation law of most states does not, in fact, limit the freedom of incorporators to set up a corporation of their own design. While many corporations do operate with closely defined powers, many others do not, and the state is a passive agent. The legal pattern of the corporation need be no more restrictive than that of the noncorporate enterprise.

All state laws permit amendments to the articles of incorporation and bylaws of corporations after they have become going concerns. The usual first step is for the board of directors to pass a resolution that an amendment is needed. The amendment is then presented to the stockholders in a regular or special meeting. An amendment voted on at a regular meeting may require only majority approval by the stockholders. Some types of amendment require a higher percentage or permit dissenting stockholders to ask for the fair value of their shares, and certain amendments reducing the rights of stockholders are forbidden. With regard to bylaws, the directors themselves often have the right to amend routine ones, and the approval of the stockholders is needed only for basic changes.[16]

The state is also a passive agent in the taking of powers by firms that select patterns other than a corporation. A proprietorship is the most free of any special limitation upon its business. Partnerships are, in most states, the subject of a special partnership law; but in the making of the partnership contract, a basic document similar to corporate articles and bylaws, draftsmen are as free when it comes to the particular matter of defining the nature of the business to be undertaken.

Important Distinctions Remain.   The basic differences already referred to in this chapter are (1) that the corporation is a legal entity, and thus that its parties may separate its affairs from their own more completely than is possible under other legal forms; (2) that the corporation has the possibility of an unlimited term of existence; (3) that each member of a partnership, except a publicly announced limited partner, may act in the name of the partnership; (4) that a partnership must go through a dissolution upon the death of a partner, and a new partnership must succeed it; and (5) that the liabilities of a corporation do not attach to its owners or its managers.

---

[16] See Commerce Clearing House, Inc., *Corporation Law Guide, 1965* (Chicago, 1965), Pars. 185–91.

An important basic difference not so far mentioned, and one that cannot be avoided completely by clever draftsmanship, is the limitation put upon a corporation's power to do business in any state. This limitation comes from the general recognition that a corporation is not a person in the sense used in the Constitution of the United States, which guarantees that each state shall confer upon a citizen of any state all those rights which it confers upon its own citizens. In contrast, an out-of-state

TABLE 2–2

STATE OF INCORPORATION AND LOCATION OF GENERAL OFFICE OF 20 LARGEST
U.S. INDUSTRIAL CORPORATIONS
(1964)

Name of Company	Location of General Office	State of Incorporation
General Motors Corporation	Michigan	Delaware
Standard Oil Company (New Jersey)	New York	New Jersey
Ford Motor Company	Michigan	Delaware
General Electric Company	New York	New York
Socony Mobil Oil Company, Inc.	New York	New York
Chrysler Corporation	Michigan	Delaware
United States Steel Corporation*	New York	New Jersey*
Texaco Inc.	New York	Delaware
International Business Machines Corporation	New York	New York
Gulf Oil Corporation	Pennsylvania	Pennsylvania
Western Electric Company, Inc.	New York	New York
DuPont (E.I.) de Nemours & Company	Delaware	Delaware
Swift & Company	Illinois	Illinois
Shell Oil Company	New York	Delaware
Standard Oil Company (Indiana)	Illinois	Indiana
Standard Oil Company of California	California	Delaware
Westinghouse Electric Corporation	Pennsylvania	Pennsylvania
Bethlehem Steel Corporation	Pennsylvania	Delaware
International Harvester Company	Illinois	New Jersey
North American Aviation, Inc.	California	Delaware

*United States Steel Corporation was incorporated in Delaware in January, 1966.
SOURCE OF COMPANY NAMES: *The Fortune Directory: The 500 Largest U.S. Industrial Corporations* (New York: Time, Inc., August, 1965), p. 21. Copyright, 1965, by Time, Inc.
SOURCE OF OTHER DATA: *Moody's Industrial Manual, 1965*, and *Moody's Public Utility Manual, 1965.*

corporation, "foreign" to a state in which it desires to do business, is always required to pay certain fees and to maintain a local office. In some states it may be required to indicate which of its powers it proposes to use in the state; and in a few cases it may be denied permission to do business at all. Such restrictions are possible under the general rule of a decision of the United States Supreme Court, quoted below, but the "comity" referred to in the quotation keeps the number of restrictions small.

. . . The corporation being the mere creation of local law can have no legal existence beyond the limits of the sovereignty where created. . . . The recognition of its existence even by other states . . . depend purely upon the comity of those states—a comity which is never extended where the existence of the corporation and the exercise of its powers are prejudicial to their interests or repugnant to their policy. Having no absolute right of recognition in other states, but depending . . . upon their assent, it follows . . . that such assent may be granted upon such terms and conditions as those states may think proper to impose. They may exclude the foreign corporation entirely; they may restrict its business. . . . The whole matter rests in their discretion.[17]

Although the comity of the states and reliance on laws of general application have kept the number of restrictions upon foreign corporations small, the added expense alone results in the practice that most corporations incorporate in the state of their principal place of business. On the other hand, several large corporations have chosen as the state of their incorporation some state where the franchise taxes are low or some desired corporate practice is known to be legal.

Table 2–2 shows the state of incorporation and the state in which the general office is located for the 20 largest U.S. industrial corporations (1964).

Financial Contracts

No single corporate characteristic does more to explain the corporation's overwhelming importance in the present-day American economy than its ability to create financial contracts of innumerable types. Any business may be referred to as a "bundle of contracts," for this phrase is used to point out that, as of any moment, the activities of any going concern, no matter what its form of organization, are defined in innumerable ways by the contracts into which it has entered. Such contracts, in fact, define the activities of a business from day to day far more then the basic documents referred to above. The bundle includes contracts of purchase and sale, contracts of employment, real estate lease contracts, and all the other types of business contracts that will be found to be in force in any going concern.

Contracts of the type just referred to do not distinguish a corporation. The distinction is found in the greater variety of financial contracts possible to a corporation because of its long span of existence and its ability to limit the liability of investors. When contrasted with the partnership or any business unit whose life is measured by that of some individual, the corporation offers much greater continuity, and thus the basis for long-term arrangements, such as bond or preferred stock issues. Finally, the entity conferred upon the corporation permits it to make contracts of the nature of mortgages upon its property without the cumbersome detail that attends the use of instruments of this nature in connection with partnerships.

---

[17] *Paul* v. *Virginia,* 8 Wall. (75 U.S.) 168 (1869).

The term *corporate securities*, as used in finance, usually refers to stocks, bonds, and other evidences of contracts for funds.[18] Actually, existing security contracts, as used by corporations, vary in detail almost as widely as the range of the imagination, for there is as little restraint upon the draftsman of corporate securities as upon the draftsman of the articles of incorporation and bylaws that create the corporation. But examination of the innumerable corporate securities that have been issued shows three characteristics prevailing among them. Their terms are made *suitable* to the needs of particular buyers; they provide for the *division* of the contract among many investors; and they permit *transfer* of the benefits of the contract from one investor to another.

Suitability: Debt versus Ownership. Much of the art of financial management is applied to the drafting of corporate financial contracts that are suitable to the circumstances of the corporation and the investor. But although the variety of individual cases is almost infinite, the contracts fall into two main classes: those which create debt and those which recognize ownership. The distinguishing characteristic of debt is that a contract of this nature contains a promise to pay money under stated conditions. The law conveys to the holder of a debt the right to enforce his claim by court action, if necessary. A contract of participation in ownership, on the other hand, does not contain a promise to pay but merely conveys an opportunity to participate in such distributions as shall be voted by the directors of the corporation. Thus, as a minimum, the holder of a debt of a corporation is more certain of receiving payments according to the terms of his debt contract than is the holder of a share in ownership.

Out of this distinction, with all the variety that can be applied in individual cases, arises the possibility of drafting corporate financial contracts that are suitable to a variety of investors. Those desirous of relative certainty of payment will be offered debt contracts, broadly referred to as *bonds* or *notes*. Others, anxious to participate as owners when profits expand, will be buyers of shares of ownership, usually referred to as *common stock* or *capital stock*.

A middle position, that of *preferred stock*, often appeals to investors desiring a larger return than that offered by debt contracts; but in law, this type of contract enjoys none of the certainty of a debt obligation. The dividend, though having priority over common stock, is only paid when voted by the directors.

For example, the life insurance companies of the United States, with investments in the securities of business and industry totaling approxi-

---

[18] Originally, the term may have been restricted to contracts under the terms of which the promises were secured by the pledge of something of value—"the security"—but the use of the term is now far more general.

mately $63.8 billion at the close of 1964,[19] are heavy buyers of corporate bonds. Their investment policy, reflecting the nature of their obligations, calls for an emphasis on safety of return rather than on any prospect of great profit. Corporations obtain funds from this enormous investing industry by creating bonds and preferred stocks which confer a priority of claim on earnings (and perhaps also on assets). In return, the insurance companies agree to take a fixed and limited return on their investment, forgoing the opportunity for greater gain from common stock investment.

Divisibility. Any corporate financial contract may, and usually does, provide that its terms shall apply ratably to each of many fractional parts evidenced by documents that shall be issued to a total representing the entire contract. Such parts may then be sold to as many separate investors as desire to participate in the provisions of the financial contract.

For example, a corporate mortgage contract involving a loan of, say, $20 million, may be evidenced by 20,000 bonds, each of $1,000 denomination. Each bond contains on its face a summary of the contract of debt. It is considered as evidence of a 1/20,000 interest in the benefits of the contract.

The exact mechanism of accomplishing this result varies from case to case, but the essence always is that many investors may participate by buying as much of the total issue as may suit their plans. The result is that a corporation may obtain enormous quantities of funds from the small purchases of many security buyers, including those who are not professional investors. In no other way could one obtain the great aggregations of wealth that have been accumulated by the major corporate businesses of the United States. In fact, the great corporations rely on "OPM"— Other People's Money—to use the designation made famous by Justice Brandeis.

The American Telephone and Telegraph Company, one of the largest corporations in the United States, can be used as an example. At the end of 1964, this corporation published a consolidated balance sheet showing assets totaling $30,906,295,000. It had obtained $2,724,460,000 of these assets by entering a variety of short-term contracts classed as "current liabilities."

The balance was made up in part of debt contracts totaling $8,725,-000,000. This sum represented a considerable number of issues and types of bonds issued by the parent company and its subsidiaries. The total number of bondholders is unknown, but it is undoubtedly very large.

Substantially all of the remainder of the total assets of the company were represented by 522,392,709 shares of stock, owned by 2,674,000 shareholders. The average holding was about 195 shares.

---

[19] Institute of Life Insurance, *1965 Life Insurance Fact Book* (New York, 1965), p. 66.

Such an example serves to explain the essential feature of the financing of large corporations. The corporation, contrasting with the partnership-proprietorship, provides for the building of great sums out of small individual investments.

Transferability. The documents evidencing participation in corporate financial contracts can be made freely transferable, and in the typical case the contract so provides. Details vary from case to case, but the essence is that a holder of a security may transfer it at any time to some person who will take it. If the transaction is a sale, the price is negotiated between the investors. It must be recognized that the corporation is not a party to the transfer. It has received funds from the original investor, and subsequent transfers do not affect this sum. There is merely a transfer of parties on one side of the corporate contract. In fact, the corporation frequently receives no notification of the transfer. By contrast, a member of a partnership cannot sell his interest unless the transaction has the approval of a previously agreed number of the remaining partners.

No corporate characteristic is more responsible than this feature of transferability for the enormous growth of corporate enterprises. *Suitability* provides a variety of investment media; *divisibility* provides the means for the accumulation of a great whole out of many small parts; *transferability* allows the investor to choose the time for his own purchase and sale.

Liquidity through sale is relied on by both small and large investors who would not be willing to commit funds to a single enterprise for as long as the business might need it. Thus is created a paradoxical condition in which businesses receive funds for long-term purposes such as the building of hydroelectric dams, while investors receive securities that may be converted into liquid funds by sale.

As a necessary result of the transfers that take place so frequently, there has developed the whole organization of security dealers and securities exchanges which are a vital part of the system of corporate finance. These institutions will be described more fully in later material.

Transferability, while it is a necessary condition for size, is not always a desired characteristic for small corporations. Frequently, the owners of a closely held corporation may reject the idea that any stockholder should be able to sell his interest to any one at any time. In such a case the solution is provided by the inclusion in the articles of incorporation of provisions restricting transfer. Here, as elsewhere, the ingenuity of the draftsman is the limit to the terms of the limitation. The only general rules are that the limitation must be provided in advance, or imposed with the consent of the security holder, and that the limitation must apply equally to all the holders of any class of security to which it is applied.

An example that is frequently encountered among closely held corporations requires the security holder first to offer his security to the directors of the corporation. A procedure for setting the price for the sale is specified. If the directors do not act favorably within a specified time, the security holder is free to sell in the open market. It is of doubtful legality to forbid the stockholder to sell his holding under all circumstances.

Tax Status

A review of the major considerations that need attention before making the choice of the legal form of doing business must include the topic of income taxation. There is little difference in the treatment of the various types of business units as far as property and similar taxation is concerned. There is some disadvantage to the corporation because it must pay fees to maintain its corporate status in each state wherein it does business, but such payments are minor considerations. On the other hand, there are significant differences between the proprietorship, or the partnership, and the corporation in tax treatment of income derived therefrom, and this can be of real importance in the choice of one or the other of these organizational forms.

For those who have not studied the federal income tax law, a brief introduction to some of its provisions is necessary. The reader is warned that in our attempt to be brief, we shall necessarily describe a complex situation only in approximate terms. First, the law recognizes two types of income: *capital gains* and *ordinary income*. There are also, of course, *capital losses* and *ordinary losses*. Capital gains or losses result from transactions involving the sale of a capital asset, as opposed to a product offered for sale, where the selling price is above (or below) a value based on what was originally paid for the asset. The most important type of capital transaction for the present discussion is the gain or loss resulting from the sale of a corporate security by an investor, who may seek his gain in this way rather than by the receipt of dividends.

Ordinary income and losses result from the ordinary business activities of the taxpayer. This class includes, in the case of an investor, interest and dividends on securities.

The distinction between capital gains and ordinary income is important because capital gains are taxed at rates equal to one half the applicable rate for ordinary income, with a maximum of 25%. When personal rates rise as high as 70% this is a matter of considerable importance.

The tax law treats a corporation, which is a legal entity, as a separate taxpayer and levies taxes on its ordinary income and capital gains without reference to the way in which this income is distributed or retained in the business. Unlike the progressive personal income tax, the corporate income tax since 1965 is a flat rate of 22% on all taxable income plus a surtax of 26% of income in excess of $25,000.

Any distribution to shareholders will then be considered part of their personal income, and will be subject to a personal income tax at a rate determined by the overall income situation of the individual shareholder. There was modest relief from this double taxation of the distributed income of corporations under the 1954 Code. Under that code, the first $50 of dividends received was not included as taxable personal income; and, in addition, a credit of 4% of dividends received in excess of $50 was allowed as a deduction from the tax payable. The 1964 law eliminated the 4% dividend credit. To offset this, but only partially for many taxpayers, the dividend exclusion was increased from $50 to $100.

The idea of a separate tax on business income does not apply to the proprietorship or the partnership. As explained previously, business activity carried on under these forms is considered merely as an extension of the personal activities of the owner or owners; hence, business income is classed as personal income of the proprietor or partners. As personal income it is subject to the personal income tax rates applying to the individual owners.

This basic difference in treatment has given rise to significant variations in the tax burden, depending not only on the legal form chosen for the business but also on the ways in which the income of the business is handled. Whether these variations favor the corporate form or the partnership-proprietorship depends on the particular circumstances of the business and its owners and, at least in part, on circumstances which the owners may not be able to foresee at the time the legal form is chosen. Some of the more generally significant implications of these differences will be outlined in the remainder of this section.

At first glance, it might be concluded that a 48% levy on corporate income added to the personal tax on dividends to shareholders would make the corporate form distinctly unattractive from the tax point of view. This would be particularly true if all or a large part of the corporate earnings were regularly distributed in the form of dividends. On the other hand, if corporate earnings are retained in the business, they do not become personal income and therefore bear only the corporate tax, at least at that point of time. The opportunity of deferring, perhaps indefinitely, the receipt of the business earnings of a given period and the personal income tax associated therewith may be considered a major advantage by shareholders, particularly those whose personal income puts them in a tax bracket which is very high. There is a different opportunity, present only in a closely held company, to pay very high salaries to officers who are also shareholders. If such payments are allowed as "costs" by the income tax authorities, the corporate tax is avoided, although, of course, the personal income tax remains.

One important possible advantage of this aspect of the corporate form is the opportunity of using earnings for business expansion without being first subject to the personal income tax—an advantage which would have particular appeal for the owner whose tax bracket is above 48%. Further, the reinvestment of earnings makes possible their ultimate "withdrawal" as a capital gain rather than as dividend income, thus giving the advantage of the low capital gains tax. This results when there is an appreciation in the value of the stock as a result of reinvested earnings, with the shareholder receiving the benefit of the investment in a higher price for the stock when it is sold rather than in dividends during the time the stock is held.

There may also be some owners who have no desire to benefit from their investment during their lifetime. If the earnings can be reinvested without the depleting effect of the personal income tax and permanently retained in the business, the only tax which will bear on such earnings will be the tax on the value of the estate at time of death, a tax which would be paid in any case if the earnings were withdrawn and retained rather than spent.

It must be stressed, however, that the Internal Revenue Service has no intention of permitting the corporate form to be used simply as a device to avoid the personal income tax. The retention and reinvestment of earnings must have a valid justification in terms of normal and reasonable business practice. Although infrequently used, a special tax is provided by the Internal Revenue Code on the accumulated earnings of a corporation where it can be proved by the government that the purpose is to avoid the personal tax on dividends.

Even where it can be justified, the advantages of the corporate form arising out of the opportunity to defer the receipt of income may not be sufficient to outweigh the disadvantage of the added corporate income tax. There can be other disadvantages as well. The distribution received by the shareholder as dividends is personal income, regardless of its original source. The distribution received by the proprietor or partner retains the character as originally received by the business. Thus, a capital gain to the partnership is also a capital gain to the partners, whereas a capital gain to the corporation passed along as a dividend to its shareholders becomes personal income and is taxed as such. On the other hand, a potential advantage to the corporation lies in the handling of business losses. Because of the way the tax law stands, a net loss for a given year in a partnership could be used by the partners only as an offset against personal income in that year. A net loss to a corporation would have an advantage as a tax offset in certain past and future years.

From the foregoing, the reader can see that very few general statements can be made about the advantages of a corporate form of doing business from a tax point of view. The advantage will depend on the exact nature of the interests involved in the particular case, with emphasis probably being given to the degree of interest the owners may have in cash dividends in the near future, and to the uses the corporation may be expected to have for funds for expansion, debt retirement, and other purposes.

Probably in order to reduce the importance of the tax factor in the decisions of smaller businesses about the form of organization which they will use, the 1954 revision of the Internal Revenue Code provided that certain unincorporated businesses can be taxed as corporations and that certain small corporations can be taxed as partnerships. The reader is referred to Code Section 1361 for details. If a business once elects to be treated in one or another of these ways, it cannot change its choice at a later date without the consent of the Director of Internal Revenue.

The Effect of Size on Choice

The corporation has been said to dominate the business section of the American economy. This is true because large-scale enterprises almost exclusively use the corporate form in order to raise the great amount of funds they need.

Much greater diversity exists among smaller firms. The advantage of security flotation loses much of its force. Instead, the factors of administrative complication, length of life, limitation of liability, centralization of management, fees, and income taxation assume greater importance. The result of such considerations on the selection of the form of organization varies with the details of a particular business and the predispositions of its managers.

PART II

The Management of Assets and the Need for Funds

Chapter 3

Inventory Management and the Need for Funds

As WE noted in Chapter 1, the need for funds to carry on a business typically stems from the need to invest in three major categories of working capital—inventories, receivables, and cash and temporary investments of cash—and in property, plant, and equipment. Decisions relating to investment in these asset categories shape the overall need for funds. In the next four chapters we focus in turn on each of these major uses of funds. In each case we identify the more important considerations that lie behind management decisions as to how large a commitment of funds should be maintained in that asset category. We next are concerned with how buildup or contraction of the commitment affects the funds flows of the firm and its overall financial needs and with techniques of analysis helpful in exposing the significance of changes in the pattern of asset use. Highlighted are distinctive problems in managing and controlling the investment of funds in each of the four major asset categories.

Once we have provided the student with some knowledge of what is behind the bare numbers of the asset (or use) side of the balance sheet, we can focus on techniques of analysis of past financing and of future funds needs. The background of the next four chapters should make it easier for the student confronting financial data to make the figures come alive and tell a meaningful story. In effect this background should help him to think more as a manager than as a figure technician.

The great bulk of business inventories represents goods carried for ultimate sale in the normal course of operations. The overall category also includes stocks of supplies—items that are not intended for sale directly but are needed to operate the business, such as coal for the heating plant, lubricants for machines, and paper for the office. The total value of supplies usually is of minor importance in the inventory total.

Manufacturers, wholesalers, and retailers typically maintain a large investment in inventory, and its management is a highly important function. On March 31, 1965, U.S. manufacturers had $78.0 billion or

43

23.6% of their total assets tied up in inventory.[1] Inventory makes up about 28% of the total assets of wholesale firms and about 32% of retailers' assets.

The importance of the commitment of funds to inventory in relation to total assets in a number of selected industry groups is shown graphically in Chart 3–1. Note particularly how minor the inventory investment is to companies in the fields of transportation, communication, and electric power. Basically, these concerns sell a commodity or service that cannot be stored. Thus, an electric power company sells power virtually as it generates it; its inventory consists almost entirely of fuel for generating plants and other items of supplies.

Another indication of the importance of investment in inventory is given in Table 3–1, which lists the relation of year-end inventories to annual sales in selected industry groups. Here again, differences appear among industries in the amounts of inventories held in stock in order to maintain sales. The turnover rates in the table range from 2.1 in tobacco manufactures to 18.9 for bakery products.

A Focus on Manufacturers' Inventories

In this chapter we shall discuss aspects of inventory management of especial significance to the financial manager. We have chosen a focus on inventory management in manufacturing concerns. Manufacturing firms hold well over half of all business inventories. Moreover, the problems of managing manufacturing inventories are relatively complex. If they can be understood, the basic concepts involved can be applied to inventory problems in retailing and other fields. Further, most manufacturers' operations are subject to rapid change, and the dynamic quality of their inventory problems makes them a particularly interesting subject for study.

The Varied Makeup of Manufacturers' Inventories

Although the inventory investment often is shown on published balance sheets as a single figure, the total "inventory" of the typical manufacturing company is a composite of one minor (supplies) and three major types of inventory:

1. Raw materials.[2]
2. Work in process.
3. Finished goods.

---

[1] U.S. Federal Trade Commission and Securities and Exchange Commission, *Quarterly Financial Report for Manufacturing Corporations; First Quarter, 1965* (Washington, D.C.: U.S. Government Printing Office, 1965), p. 34.

[2] For simplicity of presentation, we shall use the term *raw materials* in a broad sense —that is, to include with basic materials all parts, subassemblies, and components purchased from other firms but not yet put into the manufacturer's own production processes.

TABLE 3–1

INVENTORY TURNOVER, U.S. MANUFACTURING CORPORATIONS,
DECEMBER 31, 1964
(Dollar Figures in Billions)

	Net Sales	Inventories	Turnover Rate*
All manufacturing corporations.............	$443.1	$75.6	5.9
Motor vehicles and equipment..............	40.2	6.5	6.2
Aircraft and parts.......................	15.4	3.8	4.0
Electrical machinery, equipment, and supplies.	36.2	7.4	4.9
Other machinery........................	34.6	7.7	4.5
Metalworking machinery and equipment.....	4.9	1.1	4.4
Other fabricated metal products............	22.6	4.0	5.7
Primary iron and steel....................	22.0	4.1	5.4
Primary nonferrous metals.................	11.6	2.3	5.1
Stone, clay, and glass products.............	12.1	1.6	7.4
Furniture and fixtures....................	5.6	0.8	6.9
Lumber and wood products, except furniture.............................	8.0	1.3	6.2
Instruments and related products..........	6.9	1.5	4.6
Miscellaneous manufacturing, and ordnance..	6.4	1.2	5.4
Food and kindred products................	63.8	8.1	7.8
Dairy products..........................	9.3	0.7	12.8
Bakery products.........................	4.6	0.2	18.9
Alcoholic beverages......................	7.1	1.5	4.9
Tobacco manufactures....................	5.8	2.8	2.1
Textile mill products.....................	16.2	3.1	5.2
Apparel and other finished products........	14.9	2.2	6.7
Paper and allied products.................	14.8	2.0	7.3
Printing and publishing, except newspapers...	10.4	1.1	9.6
Basic chemicals.........................	18.4	3.1	6.0
Drugs.................................	5.4	0.9	6.1
Petroleum refining.......................	37.4	4.1	9.2
Rubber and miscellaneous plastics products....	11.1	2.2	5.1
Leather and leather products..............	4.9	0.9	5.7

* Annual sales divided by year-end inventories.
SOURCE: U.S. Federal Trade Commission and Securities and Exchange Commission, *Quarterly Financial Report for Manufacturing Corporations: First Quarter, 1965.*

Each of the major categories of inventory differs significantly from the others, so that analysis of the inventory investment and its management can be most meaningful if each category is thought of as a separate and distinct "animal."

As can be seen from the breakdown of inventories at the end of June, 1965 (p. 48), for manufacturers as a whole the three major categories are of somewhat similar magnitude.[3] Work in process is particularly important for durable goods producers. For nondurable goods manufacturers (textiles, food, gasoline, and the like), it is of much less consequence than raw materials or finished goods.

[3] U.S. Department of Commerce, *Survey of Current Business,* August, 1965, p. S-6.

CHART 3-1

Investment in Inventory of Corporations in Selected Industry Groups, as a Percentage of Their Total Assets, for Companies with Accounting
Periods Ended July, 1961–June, 1962

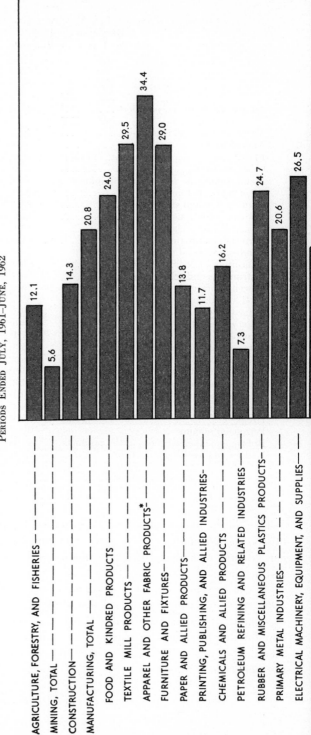

AGRICULTURE, FORESTRY, AND FISHERIES———————— 12.1

MINING, TOTAL———————————— 5.6

CONSTRUCTION—————————— 14.3

MANUFACTURING, TOTAL————————— 20.8

FOOD AND KINDRED PRODUCTS———————— 24.0

TEXTILE MILL PRODUCTS—————————— 29.5

APPAREL AND OTHER FABRIC PRODUCTS*—————— 34.4

FURNITURE AND FIXTURES——————————— 29.0

PAPER AND ALLIED PRODUCTS—————————— 13.8

PRINTING, PUBLISHING, AND ALLIED INDUSTRIES——— 11.7

CHEMICALS AND ALLIED PRODUCTS——————— 16.2

PETROLEUM REFINING AND RELATED INDUSTRIES——— 7.3

RUBBER AND MISCELLANEOUS PLASTICS PRODUCTS—— 24.7

PRIMARY METAL INDUSTRIES——————— 20.6

ELECTRICAL MACHINERY, EQUIPMENT, AND SUPPLIES—— 26.5

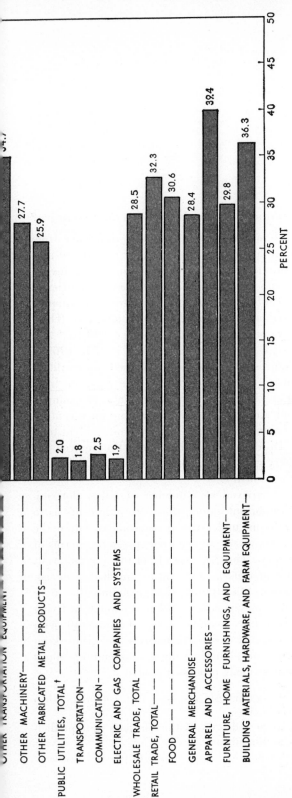

OTHER TRANSPORTATION EQUIPMENT

OTHER MACHINERY— — — — — — — — — — — 27.7

OTHER FABRICATED METAL PRODUCTS— — — — — — 25.9

PUBLIC UTILITIES, TOTAL† — — — — — — — — — 2.0

TRANSPORTATION— — — — — — — — — — — 1.8

COMMUNICATION— — — — — — — — — — — 2.5

ELECTRIC AND GAS COMPANIES AND SYSTEMS — — — 1.9

WHOLESALE TRADE, TOTAL — — — — — — — — 28.5

RETAIL TRADE, TOTAL— — — — — — — — — 32.3

FOOD— — — — — — — — — — — — — 30.6

GENERAL MERCHANDISE— — — — — — — — 28.4

APPAREL AND ACCESSORIES — — — — — — 39.4

FURNITURE, HOME FURNISHINGS, AND EQUIPMENT— 29.8

BUILDING MATERIALS, HARDWARE, AND FARM EQUIPMENT— 36.3

PERCENT

0   5   10   15   20   25   30   35   40   45   50

* Apparel and other finished products made from fabrics and similar materials.

† Total transportation, communication, electric, gas, and sanitary services.

SOURCE OF DATA: U.S. Treasury Department, Internal Revenue Service, *Statistics of Income, 1961–1962: Corporation Income Tax Returns* (Washington, D.C.: U.S. Government Printing Office, 1964), Table 2—"Balance Sheets and Income Statements . . . by Major Industrial Group." The percentage investments in inventory were computed from aggregate balance sheets derived from sampling the income tax returns of the active corporations in each industry group. Some 704,000 corporations in the selected industry groups submitted balance sheets; these corporations accounted for virtually all the corporate sales reported in their industries.

PERCENTAGE OF TOTAL INVENTORY INVESTMENT

	All Manu-facturers	Durable Goods Manu-facturers	Nondurable Goods Manu-facturers
Raw materials......................	34.3%	31.4%	39.0%
Work in process.....................	31.1	41.3	14.6
Finished goods......................	34.6	27.3	46.4
	100.0%	100.0%	100.0%

What Determines the Amount of Funds Invested in Inventory?

As noted earlier, Chart 3–1 makes apparent the wide difference from one manufacturing grouping to another of the inventory investment as a percentage of total assets. Another way of viewing the inventory investment is in relation to sales volume. U.S. manufacturers had inventories of $78.0 billion on March 31, 1965, while sales for the preceding quarter were $114.9 billion or approximately $1.28 billion a calendar day. Thus, the inventories amounted to approximately 61 days' sales. In Chart 3–2 the investment in inventory of U.S. manufacturers from 1947 to 1965 is plotted along with sales figures. A ratio scale is used to facilitate comparison of the movements in inventory and sales. The variation from the overall average figure among industry groups was great. For example, manufacturers of aircraft and aircraft parts were carrying an inventory equal to 90 days' sales while manufacturers of bakery products had total inventories equal to only 18 days' sales. Doubtless the figures for individual firms within industry groups would show significant variations from the average figure for the industry.

Most established firms have arrived at a number of policy determinations affecting inventory. Important among these are judgments as to what levels of stocks are optimum under the circumstances. Often the target levels of inventory the firm works toward are expressed in terms of anticipated rate of usage or sales. Thus, a target level for raw materials might be set at 45 days' anticipated usage and that for finished stocks at, say, 30 days' anticipated sales. Shortly, we shall examine the more important considerations that managements are likely to weigh in fixing or modifying target levels. Basically, manufacturers could operate with almost no raw material or finished goods inventories and a work-in-process inventory representing only that minimum amount of goods necessarily tied up in the manufacturing process provided:

1. Purchased materials were continuously available from suppliers when and as needed and at stable prices.
2. Sales were stable over long periods or variations in sales were predictable with great accuracy well in advance.
3. Manufacturing operations could be counted upon to proceed precisely on schedule at all times.

CHART 3-2

Quarterly Inventories of All U.S. Manufacturing Corporations (Except Newspapers) Compared with Quarterly Sales, 1947-64

(Ratio Scale)

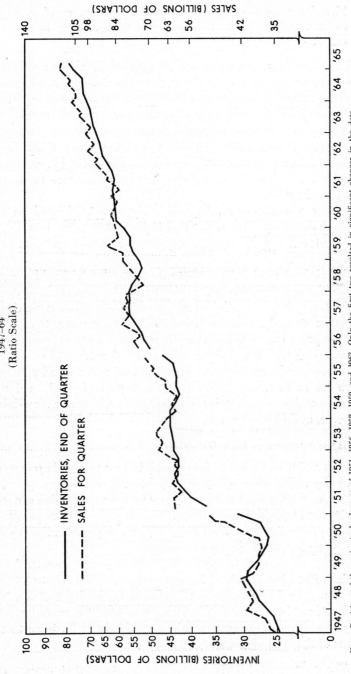

Note: Revisions of the series took place as of 1951, 1956, 1958, 1959, and 1962. Only the first, two resulted in significant changes in the data.

Source of Data: U.S. Federal Trade Commission and Securities and Exchange Commission, *Quarterly Financial Report for Manufacturing Corporations: 1947-First Quarter, 1965.*

4. Manufacturing schedules were subject to easy, cost-free adjustment so that output would mesh perfectly with changes in customer demand.

While some firms can enjoy one or more of the above conditions, few enjoy most or all. Hence, raw materials and finished stocks, and to a degree in-process stocks, serve a buffer or "change-absorbing" function. Thus, management faced with a sudden, unexpected decline in sales volume may elect to continue production at scheduled volumes and let the unsold products accumulate in finished goods inventory. If sales rebound, the additional costs of stop-and-go production involved in a shutdown will be avoided by this use of finished goods inventories to absorb the fluctuations in sales.

In other words, inventories are subject to unplanned as well as scheduled developments, and, at any particular point in time, actual inventory levels may be significantly above or below optimum or target levels.

This brief set of comments about inventory levels should suggest that the financial officer is only one of the men in top management concerned with the levels and fluctuation of the investment in inventories. Obviously, production officials, who are concerned with keeping the production operation going smoothly and at minimum costs, and sales executives, who are concerned with maximizing sales and full service to customers, are keenly concerned with inventory management practices and policies.

Now let us look more closely at the key considerations that shape management decisions relative to inventory levels of raw materials, work in process, and finished goods.

The Investment in Raw Materials

At any point in time, the investment in raw materials represents the sum of the dollar value of all materials, purchased components, subassemblies, or parts owned but not yet put into the productive process. The commitment of funds to raw material inventory swells with purchases and shrinks as materials are issued for entry into the productive process and are taken up in work-in-process inventory.

Virtually all manufacturing concerns must carry some stocks of raw materials. But what is judged enough—supplies for 1 day or 90—is very much a matter for management judgment in the light of a variety of considerations in the particular case. However, for manufacturing industry broadly, several considerations are likely to be important determinants of the level of raw material stocks:

1. The volume of "safety stocks" needed to protect against material shortages that interrupt production.
2. Considerations of economy in purchase.
3. The outlook for future movements in the price of the materials.
4. Anticipated volume of usage.

5. The efficiency of the procurement and inventory control functions.
6. The operating costs of carrying the stocks.
7. The costs and availability of funds for investment in inventory.

The management decision as to how large the safety stocks should be is an especially important one. The basic justification for safety stocks is that they serve a cost-cutting function by avoiding costly interruptions of production due to "out of stocks." Hence, judgment is required as to the likely cost-inflating or revenue-loss consequences of running out of material stocks. In some cases it may be possible to utilize available substitute materials more freely, or the firm may be able to shift production for the time to other products with little strain or cost. Or the marketing situation may be such that the sales seemingly lost through temporary shutdowns may be simply postponed. In such cases it may be feasible to operate with very much lower safety stocks than in the case of firms that might anticipate near-catastrophic results from production stoppages.

Also of basic importance to the determination of optimum safety stock levels are the *conditions of supply,* that is, the speed and reliability with which suppliers can be counted on to fill orders. If suppliers of a particular item are nearby and customarily carry sizable stocks on hand for immediate shipment, the user can safely carry very much smaller stocks of this item than of others requiring a long "procurement lead time." Thus, if a key component is available only on a made-to-order basis from a foreign manufacturer who customarily has heavy order backlogs, the time required for new orders to be filled may be very long indeed, and larger inventories of the item may be desirable.

In recent years New England manufacturers of silverware have been able to get overnight delivery of silver bullion from New York City suppliers who carry large stocks ready for immediate shipments. Consequently, many silverware manufacturers have concluded that 2 or 3 days' stock of silver provides reasonable assurance that operations will not be impeded. Similarly, a New York doughnut maker, whose main plant was located near flour mills, carried only a few days' supply of flour. The same manufacturer, however, who used large quantities of dried egg yolks imported from the Orient, carried several months' supply of egg yolks.

Threats from such events as an industry-wide strike also affect inventory levels. For example, in early 1965, when a strike of steelworkers was in prospect, users of steel built up large stocks against the threat of shortage.

Also, supplies of raw materials may be available only at certain times of the year. The steel mills in Cleveland, Ohio, or Gary, Indiana, which depend on iron ore from the Mesabi Range in Minnesota, find it necessary to build up huge piles of iron ore in the summer and fall in order to continue production through the winter, when ice on the Great Lakes prevents economical water transportation of the ore.

Considerations of purchase economy may affect stock levels. Purchasers of large lots frequently can command favorable prices from suppliers and lower transport costs. For example, small paint manufacturers often buy minor ingredients in economical carload lots, even though a carload may last them several months. This method of purchase is of particular importance to smaller concerns and to processors using small quantities of a wide variety of commodities or purchased parts.

The outlook for changes in the price of important materials may well influence stock levels. Unquestionably, some managements act on their anticipation of price movements, building up commitments when price increases are expected and trimming them when price declines are anticipated. When price trends have been in one direction for an extended period, manufacturers' inventory policies commonly reflect the trend. Thus, manufacturers in countries experiencing continuing inflation typically carry heavy stocks.

In most U.S. companies in recent years, price speculation does not appear to have been a major factor in inventory movements. Many manufacturers would agree with the Texas retailer quoted as saying, "Trying to beat price increases by building up inventories probably costs you more in the long run than simply paying the higher prices when they go into effect. Those who gamble on high inventories can also guess wrong and get stuck with a lot of merchandise they can't sell."[4] He might have added that many speculators have been caught by sudden shifts in price trends, and the anticipated "inventory profits" have turned into sharp losses.

The efficiency of the procurement and inventory control functions in the firm can have a significant effect on raw material inventories, particularly when a great number of different items are carried. If management has full confidence in the accuracy of the stock records and the reliability of replenishment routines, it can work with leaner stocks than if such were not the case. In a number of firms the use of computers in inventory control has been credited with making possible operation with significantly lower levels of stock than would have been feasible under manual methods.[5] On the other hand, many firms have accumulated

---

[4] *Wall Street Journal*, December 1, 1964, p. 1.

[5] The "economic order quantity" (EOQ) is one widely used method for setting order quantities which, when combined with procedures for setting appropriate safety allowances, determine the level of inventory. EOQ is based on the formula $\text{EOQ} = \sqrt{\dfrac{2DC}{PI}}$, where D = demand for the item during the period, C = purchasing cost per order, P = price paid per unit, and I = annual inventory carrying charge as a percentage of the average inventory value. Essentially, this method equates the procurement cost (ordering costs, quantity discounts, freight differentials, etc.) with the inventory carrying costs (interest, risk of price declines, obsolescence, depreciation, insurance, taxes, storage, etc.) as a function of expected demand.

More advanced inventory control techniques, based upon the use of computers employing more sophisticated mathematical models to obtain rules for operating inventory systems, have been developed in recent years and doubtless will be further refined.

unintentionally heavy stocks simply because record keeping was so poor that no one knew the true state of inventories.

As suggested above, of major significance in the determination of optimum inventory levels are the operating costs of carrying raw material stocks. These include the costs of storage facilities, loss of value through physical deterioration, property taxes, insurance, and protection against theft. Less obvious, but often of critical importance, particularly in the case of components of industrial products subject to rapid change in design, are the hazards and costs of obsolescence of particular inventory types. In a recent survey reported in *Purchasing Week*,[6] 70 firms gave their calculations of the cost of carrying inventories. The range was from 12% to 33+% of the purchase price per year with 68% of the firms placing their carrying costs between 18% and 27%. We should add that a figure for "interest on investment" was included in the estimate of costs. Later in this book, we devote close attention to just how capital costs should be measured. Suffice it here for us to note that use of the rate of interest the firm pays on borrowings as a measure of the firm's overall cost of capital usually substantially understates the true cost of capital.

As we have suggested, inventory-level objectives very commonly are set in terms of so many days of sales or, in the case of raw materials, of anticipated usage in production. Once levels are set in these terms, fluctuations in anticipated and actual usage are responsible for much of the change in inventory investment.[7] The common tendency of purchased

---

[6] *Purchasing Week*, Vol. VII, No. 50 (December 14, 1964), p. 1.

[7] This is not to imply that changes in materials availability are of little significance. Note, for example, the following comments from a *Wall Street Journal* article of February 10, 1961, on shifting inventory policies:

" 'Despite a substantial pickup in sales to distributors since the first of the year, we intend to adhere to the policy of getting along with smaller stocks of parts and raw materials,' says a spokesman for Admiral Corp., Chicago-based manufacturer of major appliances and television sets. 'We're simply able to live on smaller stocks and order at more frequent intervals.'

" 'Expected order increases are making us a little more optimistic about putting something on the shelf,' says Paul Fischer, plant manager for Hyster Co., Portland, Ore., lift truck manufacturer. But he indicates the ease of getting steel is leading the company to put off adding to its stocks of this key raw material for the time being. 'Steel mills are operating more or less as warehouses," he says. 'They're giving 10-day deliveries where it would normally take two or three months.' "

Indeed, some observers, commenting on widespread inventory reductions in late 1960 and early 1961, saw evidence of a long-term trend toward greater inventory turnover. Thus, a writer in the November 1960, *Monthly Review* of the Federal Reserve Bank of New York commented:

"Some of the factors underlying the weak demand for inventories thus far this year may prove to be long run in nature. Various structural forces, previously concealed by cyclical movements and strike effects, may be causing a secular downtrend in the inventory level required to support a given volume of sales. Although the evidence for such a trend is not conclusive, inventory-sales ratios during cyclical expansions have been progressively lower in each of the successive postwar business cycles. At the distributive level, where the differences among recent cycles are quite clear, inventory needs have probably been reduced relative to sales, not only by some recent shifts in the urgency of consumer buying, but also by the increasing importance of large-scale self-service stores

materials inventories of durable goods manufacturers to move directly
with sales and new orders is illustrated in Chart 3–3.

So far, this discussion of inventory policies has appeared to assume
that funds are available to support whatever inventory investment is
desired. In the case of many strongly financed firms, this is a valid
assumption. But a great many firms do not enjoy unlimited access to
capital, and heavy use of funds in inventories may well mean that other
opportunities for effective use of funds must be forgone. In still other

CHART 3–3

SHIPMENTS, NEW ORDERS, AND INVENTORIES OF MATERIALS AND SUPPLIES—ALL
MANUFACTURERS OF DURABLE GOODS, 1939–64
(In Billions)

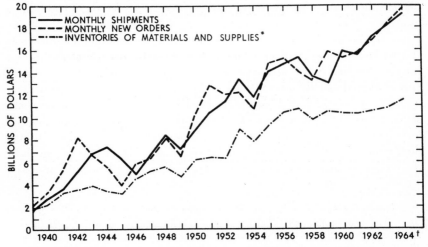

* Book value, seasonally adjusted, end of period.
† Preliminary.
NOTES: Data for Alaska and Hawaii included beginning with 1958. Revisions of these series have been made
recently. The revised data for shipments and new orders begin with 1947; those for inventories in 1953.
SOURCES OF DATA: *Economic Report of the President, 1963* (Washington, D.C.: U.S. Government Printing
Office, 1963), p. 219; and *Economic Report of the President, 1965*, pp. 238–39.

firms, financial resources are so limited and the problems of raising more
funds so great that the need to minimize investment becomes the
dominant consideration in inventory policies.

Thus far, we have talked of size of inventory primarily in terms of
physical volume. The financial burden of these inventories, of course, is
measured in dollars; a general rise in price heightens the dollar

and of chain stores with centralized order procedures and the opportunity to shift stocks
quickly among branches. At both the distributive and manufacturing levels, the more
flexible transportation opportunities offered by combinations of truck, rail, and air
facilities have cut down the relative volume of goods 'in transit.' Some shifts in the
composition of output may also have reduced stock needs; for instance, the rapidly
growing chemical industry reportedly requires a small volume of goods in process relative
to final output. Greater reliance on 'production to order,' increased use of high-speed
computers for inventory control, and development of techniques for determining the most
efficient location of plants and warehouses may all also play some part in a tendency to
conserve inventories."

investment required to maintain a given volume of goods. True, a sustained price rise often increases profits as low-cost materials eventually are sold in the form of higher-priced finished goods.[8] But the added "inventory profits" left after income taxes usually are inadequate to provide funds needed to replenish stocks with the then higher-cost new materials. Conversely, a decline in prices may have the net effect of so reducing the dollar commitment to inventory that the cash account is swelled despite reduced profit inflows.

Clearly, the more obviously financial considerations—the costs of the funds tied up in raw material and the financial problems of raising those funds—are of keen significance in the determination of optimum raw material inventory levels. Since these apply equally to in-process and finished inventories, we shall defer comment on these aspects until later in this chapter.

The Cash Flows Associated with Raw Material Inventories

For purposes of financial planning, the financial officer is particularly concerned with the cash flows connected with inventory. From a cash flow standpoint the crucial dates connected with the purchase of raw materials are the dates by which the invoices for the materials must be paid. Typically, the business concern will not have to pay cash at the time of purchase. Instead, an account payable, due perhaps in 30 days, is created at the time of purchase. The cash outflows resulting from purchases of raw materials can be planned for by setting up a schedule of future payments. In the illustration below, assume accounts payable were $1,500 on December 31 and that purchase terms called for payment in 30 days:

	January	February	March	April	May	June
Expected raw material purchases..........	$2,000	$4,000	$8,000	$7,000	$6,000	$2,000
Cash required to pay accounts payable— raw materials during month.....	1,500	2,000	4,000	8,000	7,000	6,000

[8] During the periods of significant price movements of important raw materials, the choice of accounting method employed to assign costs to particular batches of materials as they are moved from inventory into production may have a noteworthy effect on both the materials inventory figure on the balance sheet and the costs of materials in the income statement. Used most widely is FIFO, the first-in, first-out method. Under FIFO, for costing purposes materials are presumed to be used in the order of purchase. In a period of rising prices, the costs employed under FIFO will be less than the current costs of replacing the materials.

An alternative approach, which has been adopted by a number of firms, is LIFO, the last-in, first-out method. As the name implies, materials put into use are assigned the costs of the most recent purchases. In a period of rising prices, use of the LIFO method results in the reporting of higher costs, lower profits, and lower inventory values than if FIFO were used. On the other hand, in a period of declining prices, reported profits and inventory values will be higher under LIFO than under FIFO.

No cash inflows occur when raw materials are put into production. Instead, cash inflows come only when finished goods are sold for cash or, if sales are on credit, when the related accounts receivable are collected weeks or months later.

Investment in Work-in-Process Inventory

As the name suggests, this category of inventory comprises the goods in the process of being manufactured. From an accounting viewpoint a part of the investment in goods in process at any one time consists of the original cost of the raw materials. Added to the material costs transferred to the work-in-process account are the accumulated cost charges for wages and other direct costs of manufacture applied to these raw materials, together with an allocation of overhead costs such as heat, power, and plant supervision. Thus, the balance sheet value assigned to work-in-process inventory at any particular date is the summation of all costs assigned up to that date to the partially completed products.

What are the main determinants of the amounts of funds locked up in work-in-process inventory? To what extent is the size of the investment dictated by the nature of the operations? And to what degree can managerial policies shape the size of the funds commitment?

The length of the complete productive process clearly has a major influence on the value of the inventory undergoing processing at any one time. An extreme illustration is furnished by a canner of peaches. Less than a day is normally required to pick, grade, process, can, label, and package peaches. Naturally, the canner's work in process at any date will be negligible in relation to annual sales. In contrast, consider the case of a manufacturer of large aircraft. Production and assembly of the complicated aircraft typically will extend over many months; at any one time, once production is well under way, the aircraft company will have accumulated a sizable investment in aircraft in all stages of completion, from raw stampings of parts to aircraft undergoing final tests before being delivered.

Although technological considerations may largely dictate the length of time required for the production process, management policies usually can have significant influence on the process time and hence on the process inventory investment. In the case of durable goods manufacturing, an important decision area is the extent to which parts or subassembly items will be produced in long runs or in shorter runs closer to the time they are needed for assembly. For example, the aircraft manufacturer working on an order for 200 planes with staggered delivery dates might well try to cut production costs by making all of a particular part in one long production run, even though most of the 200 would not be needed for final assembly for many months. Thus, a decision as to the length of production runs for parts, at first thought to be purely a production problem, has decided implications as to the size of in-process inventories.

Actions that speed the production process increase output without proportionately increasing in-process stocks. Thus, adding second or third production shifts should boost output without proportionate boosts in inventories. Conversely, interruptions in the flow of work through the plant—such as would result from unexpected delays in the receipt by the aircraft firm of the engines for installation in the partially completed aircraft—inflate the tie-up of funds in inventories. Many new firms not yet skilled in production scheduling and control have encountered unexpected problems and delays in moving jobs through the plant and have in consequence tied up much larger amounts in in-process inventories than expected, with resulting serious financial problems.

The amount of costs incurred in the particular manufacturing process, often referred to as the "value added in manufacture," also affects the amount of funds converted to work in process. A very simple operation, even if extended over a long period—such as the aging of wines—requires little outlay.

The volume of production is also a major determinant of work in process. If other factors are equal, as production increases, the amount invested in work in process increases. And as volume of production operations is curtailed, the investment in in-process inventory drops. As we noted earlier in connection with raw material inventory, production generally is geared to anticipated sales. Hence, the amount of funds tied up in work in process might also be expected to fluctuate directly with sales expectations and perhaps somewhat less directly with actual sales levels.

Chart 3–4 plots monthly averages of shipments, monthly averages of new orders, and monthly inventories of work in process, for manufacturers of durable goods. As in the case of raw material inventories, the amount of funds tied up in work in process tends to vary with the level of sales and new orders.

The price levels of raw materials used, wages, and other items that enter into production costs also influence the dollar investment in in-process inventories.

Cash Flows Associated with Work in Process

As indicated above, the accounting for work in process involves accumulation of accounting charges for raw materials used and for various expenses of manufacture and overhead, including depreciation charges. The flow of funds out of the company in connection with manufacturing, of course, will not coincide in timing or in amount with these accounting charges. No checks are written or payments made when raw materials are moved from the company's storerooms into production. Rather, the cash payments associated with raw materials occur when the accounts payable generated by the raw material purchases are paid. Further, payment of manufacturing costs—such as those for wages and salaries—seldom takes place at the time when these obligations are

CHART 3-4

Shipments, New Orders, and Inventories of Work in Process—All
Manufacturers of Durable Goods, 1939-64
(In Billions)

* Book value, seasonally adjusted, end of period.
† Preliminary.
Notes: Data for Alaska and Hawaii included beginning with 1958. Revisions of these series have been made recently. The revised data for shipments and new orders begin with 1947; those for inventories in 1953.
Sources of Data: *Economic Report of the President, 1963* (Washington, D.C.: U.S. Government Printing Office, 1963), p. 219; and *Economic Report of the President, 1965*, pp. 238-39.

incurred. One item of expense—depreciation—calls for no cash payment at all. In planning the outflow of cash to support manufacturing, then, it is necessary to determine which of the anticipated expenses will require payment and to schedule these payments according to the time when they will be made.

The Investment in Finished Goods Inventories

Finished goods inventories build up with additions from the production line and are cut down with sales. Finished goods inventories can be minimized if production can be geared only to firm orders in hand. By producing only to order, many manufacturers—particularly those of specialized machines—avoid finished goods inventory, other than of spare parts, almost entirely.

Most manufacturers find it advantageous or necessary to maintain stocks of finished goods ready for shipment when anticipated orders come in. Pressures to carry sizable stocks of finished goods may stem from considerations of production convenience and economy and/or of marketing effectiveness. Where demand for the products is in small or uneven increments, production for stock permits longer production runs and more even and efficient production scheduling. For example, the demand for skis is concentrated in the late fall and early winter. Ski manufacturers can achieve steady production through the year only by building up heavy stocks of finished skis in advance of the selling season.

Some manufacturers must produce for stock, because vital raw materials are available only on a seasonal basis while customers' demand is spread throughout the year. The California canner of peaches, for example, must process the fruit when it ripens in July and build up a huge finished inventory if he is to meet orders spaced throughout the year.

Sales considerations may dictate an ability to fill orders without delay. In many lines competition for sales necessitates maintenance of stocks near customers so that fast delivery can be promised. For example, a number of cement manufacturers have found it necessary to build silos near key market centers.

A number of firms with far-flung distribution systems have reported success in the use of mathematical models and electronic computers to work out distribution patterns and inventory locations and levels that best reconcile considerations of customer service, manufacturing and distribution costs, and inventory turnover.

Under World War II conditions of restricted supply, intense demand, and heavy production against government order, many manufacturers operated with almost no finished inventories. Return to more competitive conditions saw manufacturers rebuild finished goods to a more normal relationship to sales—as is shown in Chart 3–5.

CHART 3-5

Shipments, New Orders, and Inventories of Finished Goods—All Manufacturers of Durable Goods, 1939–64

(In Billions)

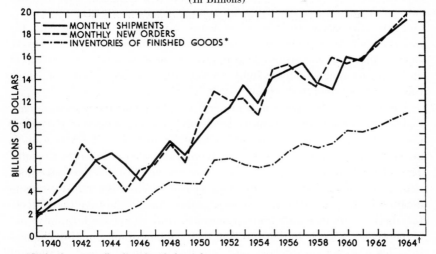

* Book value, seasonally adjusted, end of period.

† Preliminary.

Notes: Data for Alaska and Hawaii included beginning with 1958. Revisions of these series have been made recently. The revised data for shipments and new orders begin with 1947; those for inventories in 1953.

Sources of Data: *Economic Report of the President, 1963* (Washington, D.C.: U.S. Government Printing Office, 1963), p. 219; and *Economic Report of the President, 1965*, pp. 238–39.

In some industries, such as seasonal apparel, manufacturers have attempted over the years to force retailers to carry a larger part of the inventory burden—a burden in terms of space and risk as well as investment—with limited success. Of course, if the manufacturer is in a very strong position vis-à-vis the retailers, he may be able to force inventories on the dealers. Thus, Henry Ford in 1921 was seriously short of funds to meet bank loans; at the same time there were large stocks of unsold Fords at the plant. Mr. Ford simply shipped large numbers of unordered cars to his dealers with drafts calling for cash payment attached to the shipping papers. The dealers were forced to provide cash and accept the inventory burden or yield their dealerships. However, few manufacturers today possess either the commanding position or the willingness to take the risks of such action.

Optimum finished goods stock levels, like those of raw materials, are usually set in terms of so many days' or months' anticipated sales. Thus, over extended periods, finished goods inventories tend to move directly with sales volume.

But in the short run, finished stocks may well vary inversely with sales. If sales fall below expectations and production is not cut back sharply, unsold goods pile up. Despite strenuous efforts to forecast sales accurately, a great many manufacturers (and retailers) are confronted with unexpected, and often inexplicable, declines in sales which pose poignant problems. Seldom can production be cut back or expanded rapidly without severe organizational strains and higher unit costs. If the sales drop proves short-lived, holding production steady and accepting temporarily swollen inventories may well maximize return on investment. But if sales stay off, inventories pile up, and even more drastic production cutbacks ultimately are needed to bring inventories into line with the reduced sales prospects. Many manufacturers have experienced severe cash stringency, sometimes leading to business failure, as a result of allowing too much of their funds to flow into finished goods for which timely orders failed to develop.

Unexpected sales spurts also present inventory management problems. Unless production and inventory levels are boosted, service to customers may suffer, and sales opportunities may be lost. But if production is boosted and the sales surge proves temporary, excess inventory results. The critical relationship of sales forecasting to effective inventory management can hardly be overemphasized. Increasing effort is being devoted by the managements of many companies to improve their "feel" for their customers and their intentions, and to respond rapidly and perceptively to shifts in demand. But the problem of anticipating changes in sales remains a difficult one—especially where a wide range of products is involved.

The impact on cash of an inventory buildup or decline is usually a deferred one. The immediate cash flow impact of a sales decline and inventory buildup is minimal, as cash flows in from collection of the receivables from sales at the old high level. But the decline in sales means fewer new receivables, and a sharp drop in inflows occurs when the smaller volume of receivables comes due and is collected.

Risks in Inventory Investment

The decades since 1945 have been ones of general prosperity and broad commodity price increases. Nevertheless, there have been enough sharp drops in the prices of important commodities to remind businessmen that heavy inventory positions, particularly in standard commodities with free markets, expose their firms to risks of loss through sustained price declines. For example, the market price of cocoa, a basic material for candymakers, fell from a high of $0.263 in January, 1964, to a low of $0.116 in July, 1965.[9] Generally, the vulnerability to price declines has been greatest on standard raw materials and least on differentiated finished goods.

More significant in recent years have been the risks of inventory obsolescence. Changing customer tastes, as in high-style merchandise, may make finished goods, work in process, and even raw materials obsolete and therefore unsalable and nearly worthless. Nor is vulnerability to obsolescence restricted to luxury consumer goods. Changing needs of industrial customers, new production techniques, or product improvements by competitors may force changes in product specifications and design that cut the value of old-model stocks and of components or materials distinctive to the earlier models. An electronics firm responding to the *Purchasing Week* survey reported on page 53 estimated its annual cost of obsolescence on stored products at 10%. As the rate of technical change and product development shows evidence of acceleration, full sensitivity to the hazards of inventory obsolescence becomes more urgent.

Further, those numerous firms whose resources are limited must be particularly wary of the risks to their liquidity—indeed, their solvency— in tying up too much of their limited funds in hard-to-move inventories.

Aids in the Analysis of the Investment in Inventory

The financial and other officers of the company are seldom alone in their interest in the company's inventory investment. Because of the importance of this asset group to the financial condition of the concern, important stockholders, the credit analysts of commercial banks or other lenders, and the credit men of important suppliers are also interested in discovering and understanding significant movements in inventory or its turnover. Unless the "outside" analysts receive more information about

---

[9] *Commodity Year Book, 1965* (New York: Commodity Research Bureau, Inc., 1965), p. 98; and *Wall Street Journal*, July 19, 1965, p. 16.

inventories than is usually available from published financial statements, the degree of penetration of analysis and understanding they can hope to achieve is limited. This is particularly true if only annual statements are available and inventories are reported in a single lump sum. Yet some calculations can be made and often prove useful, especially in raising questions which may indicate the desirability of further inquiry.

The same general methods of analysis used by outside analysts, which we shall discuss below, can be pushed further and used with greater precision by the financial officer of the firm, who has full access to available sources of data. For example, while the outside observer must often work with a single inventory figure, the financial officer of the firm would have figures available for each major type, and indeed for each major item, of inventory and thus should be able to arrive at more meaningful conclusions.

It is often helpful to determine whether changes in inventory investment are in line with changes in the volume of sales. As we have seen, the level of investment in inventory tends naturally and normally to vary directly with the volume of sales. Movements not in line with sales raise questions for further inquiry—for example, an increase in inventory levels substantially beyond that which might be expected from an increase in sales should stimulate the analyst to further investigation. Is the unexplained increase the result of a conscious policy shift to higher stock levels, of unintended accumulation of unsold stocks, of inventory speculation, or simply of stocking in anticipation of an almost certain surge of orders?

Among the more common ratios used to depict the relationship between inventories and sales are the following:

1. Number of average days' sales in inventory.
2. Inventories as a percentage of sales or of cost of sales.
3. Inventory turnover ratios.

Let us use the following facts to illustrate these inventory/sales ratios. Total inventories reported by the XYZ Corporation on December 31, 1965, were $462,000. Reference to earlier balance sheets shows that the inventory investment was $274,000 on December 31, 1964, and $270,000 in 1963. Reference to income statements reveals the following:

1965 Sales	$1,060,000
1964 Sales	830,000
1965 Cost of sales	$ 860,000
1964 Cost of sales	702,000

Quick mental arithmetic indicates that inventories are up in 1965 and that they increased faster in 1965 than did sales. But the extent to which inventories relatively have outrun sales can be made more apparent through the use of ratios.

Let us look first at the inventory in terms of the number of days' sales it represents. Thus, we can note that year-end 1965 inventories amounted to 157 days' sales at the average daily rate of sales in 1965 ($462,000 ÷ $1,060,000/360). In contrast, year-end 1964 inventories amounted to 112 days' sales at the 1964 rate. Some analysts prefer a modification of this ratio, using cost of sales rather than net sales figures. A figure for average daily sales at cost is computed and divided into inventory to derive a figure for average days' sales (at cost) in inventory.

Calculation of inventories as a percentage of sales is simple. In the example above, 1965 inventories are seen to be 43.5% of sales ($462,-000/$1,060,000) while 1964 inventories were 31.1% of 1964 sales. Again, an alternative approach utilizes cost of sales rather than net sales figures.

Turnover calculations portray the relationship between stocks and sales in terms of the number of times inventories are "turned over" in a sales year. Since "turnover" suggests physical movements of goods, and inventories are carried at cost rather than selling price, turnover usually is calculated by dividing inventory into cost of sales rather than net sales. In 1965 goods valued at $860,000 were sold so that year-end inventories of $462,000 can be thought of turning over 1.9 times ($860,000/$462,-000). Similar computations for 1964 show a turnover of 2.6 times. Thus, inventory turnover based on year-end inventories had fallen from 2.6 to 1.9 times.

Some analysts prefer to use the average of beginning and ending inventories in computing turnover ratios. It can be argued that use of average inventory figures gives a more accurate "turnover" figure, but it also plays down the influence of the recent inventory figure, which is generally the item of particular interest to the analyst concerned with the "here and now" as a guide to future developments. Thus, turnover of *average* inventory in 1965 was 2.3 times (860,000/(462,000 + 274,-000/2)) and in 1964 was 2.6 times (702,000/(274,000 + 270,000/2)). It will be noted that the average turnover figures, being an average of beginning and ending inventories, changed less widely (from 2.6 to 2.3 times) than did the ending inventory turnover figure (from 2.6 to 1.9).

If a breakdown of inventory is available, inventory/sales ratios can be calculated for each category of inventory, or indeed for each product line. Thus, changes out of line with sales movements can be pinpointed. For example, the buildup of inventory relative to sales shown in the XYZ Corporation might be found to be entirely in one or two product lines of finished goods, with materials and work in process down substantially.

Of course, if only annual sales and inventory data are available, important movements of sales and inventories within the year will not be discernible and ratios drawn from annual sales totals may have limited value or in some cases may be positively misleading. Certainly, our view of the 1965 year-end inventory position would be very different if the annual sales of $1,060,000 had been achieved according to pattern A rather than pattern B or C, in the accompanying table.

Quarterly Sales, 1965	Pattern A	Pattern B	Pattern C
First Quarter.....................$	175,000	$ 320,000	$ 265,000
Second Quarter..................	220,000	300,000	265,000
Third Quarter...................	300,000	260,000	265,000
Fourth Quarter.................	365,000	180,000	265,000
	$1,060,000	$1,060,000	$1,060,000

In the case of firms that operate under essentially similar conditions, the comparions of inventory/sales ratios of one company with those of its competitors may prove useful in calling attention to distinctive policies of the subject firm.[10] On the other hand, it is extremely difficult to apply value judgments on the basis of summary ratios, and such ratios will usually suggest more questions than answers. As one writer has put it, ratios such as those of turnover provide many clues but few conclusions.

The Financial Officer's Role in Inventory Management

Seldom is the financial officer the corporate officer most directly concerned with inventory policies. Usually, purchasing and production officers are more directly concerned with raw material policies, production officers with work in process, and production and sales officers with finished goods inventories. But it should be clear that inventory policies have a very direct and important impact on the financial needs of the firm. The financial officer can do a good job of anticipating changes in the need for funds only if he thoroughly understands the implications of changing inventory policies and positions. Where finances are a limiting factor, he should be prepared to help directly in shaping inventory policies that are consistent with the realities of the firm's financial position.

But the financial officer's role should be much more than that of an informed observer—or monitor—if funds are short. Good inventory management is good financial management. Levels should be under frequent or constant review. When inventory levels are set, the financial officer can help in applying pressure against practices that slow turnover and debase return. For example, in one outstanding firm the financial officer was instrumental in the establishment of a highly productive program of periodic "turnover audits" in which questions like the following are investigated:

---

[10] Among the sources of information on average inventory/sales and other ratios for different industries are the results of a continuing program of ratio analysis published periodically in Dun's Review and Modern Industry. For example, ratios in the retailing field were published in the September, 1965, issue; for wholesalers in various lines in October, 1965; and for manufacturers in November, 1965.

1. Are we exercising full vigilance against imbalances of raw material and in-process inventory that limit the utility of stocks to that of the item in shortest supply?

2. Are we employing the shortest procurement lead-time assumptions and leanest stock levels consistent with safety, recognizing that complete safety has a prohibitive cost?

3. Do we keep the heat on uncompleted production items held in suspension to get them into salable condition?

4. Do we press hard enough to keep production schedules firm, so that unneeded materials and in-process inventories don't accumulate? Does purchasing get early notification of production schedule changes?

5. Do we move vigorously to dispose of goods that are obsolete, surplus, or for any other reason unusable for production?

6. Are we continually striving to shorten the production cycle? Are we careful to be sure that long production runs are worth the cost and risks of the extra inventory investment?

7. Is design engineering making maximum use of standard materials and components available from suppliers' shelves on short notice?

8. Are we quick enough to use special pricing to move extremely slow-selling finished items?

9. Are we doing all we can to flatten out seasonal sales patterns that bulk up inventories?

To firms short of funds, imagination in exposing, and full vigor in exploiting, opportunities to cut inventory investment can be highly rewarding in reduced capital requirements. The advice of one experienced businessman speaking to a group of small manufacturers, "When you need money, look to your inventories before you look for your banker," deserves more than a smile.

Even if funds are plentiful, the financial officer should be prepared to participate actively and helpfully in the formulation of inventory policies designed to speed turnover and maximize return on investment. Our discussion has indicated some of the key considerations in setting and trying to hold to inventory levels that represent the best reconciliation of profit and turnover objectives and that give appropriate emphasis to the impact on the need and availability of funds for inventory investment.

Chapter 4

Receivables Management and the Need for Funds

THIS CHAPTER is primarily concerned with the management of receivables arising out of the sale of goods and services by business firms on terms other than for cash. Since most business sales are made on credit terms, the investment in receivables represents a major and continuing commitment of funds for most business enterprises. The investment is increased as new credit sales are recorded and is reduced as payments in settlement of purchase obligations are received from customers.

Many nonfinancial firms make loans to other entities or individuals. Thus, a short-term investment in U.S. bonds by a business firm is, in effect, a loan to the government. Such extensions of credit involve considerations that usually are very different from those involved in credit to customers and will not be discussed in this chapter.

U.S. manufacturing corporations, which sell primarily to other firms and almost entirely on credit terms, had $57.5 billion or 17.4% of their total assets tied up in receivables on March 31, 1965. Almost all of this represented *trade credit*—that is, credit extended from one business firm to another arising out of the sale of goods or services. Wholesalers, who also sell primarily on credit and to other businesses, on a recent date had $15.8 billion or 35.6% of their total assets in receivables. Among retailers sales for cash are common. As many readers well know, most retail food chains sell only for cash and avoid an investment in receivables altogether. Nevertheless, data for all retailing corporations showed a receivables investment of $11.0 billion or 23.1% of total assets.

Chart 4–1 portrays the importance of the investment in receivables in relation to total assets in a number of industry groups. The range is wide —note, for example, the great importance of receivables to construction firms and the minor importance to public utilities.

Chart 4–2 pictures the investment of manufacturing firms in receivables and also their sales over a period of years on a ratio scale. While much of the great growth in the commitment to receivables is explained by the growth in sales, a long-term tendency for collection periods to lengthen (that is, for receivables to increase faster than sales) is clearly discernible. If manufacturers during the first quarter of 1965 had collected on sales as rapidly as they did in 1947, the 1965 investment in receivables could have been lower by $24 billion—that is, $33.7 billion instead of the actual figure of $57.5 billion. We shall comment further on the trend toward longer collection periods at the end of this chapter.

Form of Receivables

The bulk of credit sales are made on *open account*. That is, the seller keeps a simple book record of the obligations arising out of sales and does not ask his customers for formal acknowledgment of their debts or for signed promises to pay. In case of dispute the seller has the customer's order, copies of the sales invoice, and shipping papers as evidence of the validity of the debt.

In open-account selling there is no security behind the obligation. The seller enjoys no special rights to recover the goods he has sold if the account is not paid. Moreover, no interest is charged on open-account sales.

At one time, decades ago, it was the common practice of many business firms to ask their customers to sign unsecured *notes*, or written promises to pay by a stated date the amount of credit extended on routine credit sales. This practice was especially common in product lines customarily sold on long credit terms. The holder of an ordinary note receivable does not enjoy any priority of claim to payment over open-account creditors in the event of a debtor's bankruptcy and the subsequent liquidation of his assets for distribution to creditors. But the signed note does provide strong legal evidence of the validity of the debt; and written stipulation of a due date, together with the practice of note collection through banks, provides psychological pressures for prompt payment at maturity. Too, the mechanics of charging interest on notes are simple. Further, usually it is easier to use notes from customers than accounts receivable as security for bank loans. Despite these advantages, the use of notes in routine domestic trade credit by manufacturers and wholesalers has given way in the United States to the currently predominating practice of sale on open account.

In many countries sellers still ask their customers to sign a note or other form of written obligation. In Mexico, for example, many firms send along with shipping papers a form for signature by the customer by which he formally accepts the obligation to pay for the goods on stated terms. After it is signed, the acceptance form is returned to the seller.

Although most retail credit sales in the United States are also made on an open-account basis, "big-ticket items"—durable goods of considerable value, such as automobiles, television receivers, and refrigerators—com-

CHART 4-1

Investment in Notes and Accounts Receivable, Less Reserve, in Selected Industry Groups, as a Percentage of Their Total Assets, for Companies with Accounting Periods Ended July, 1961–June, 1962

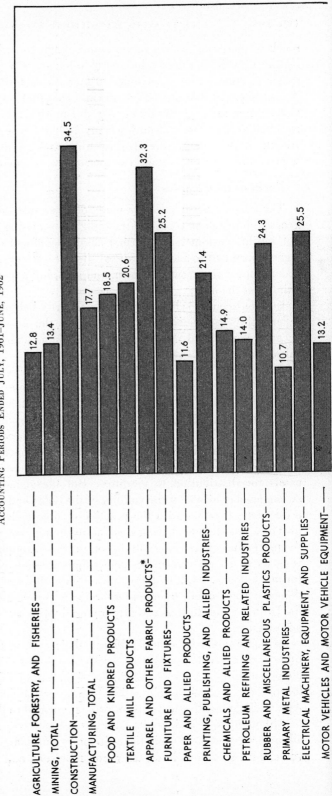

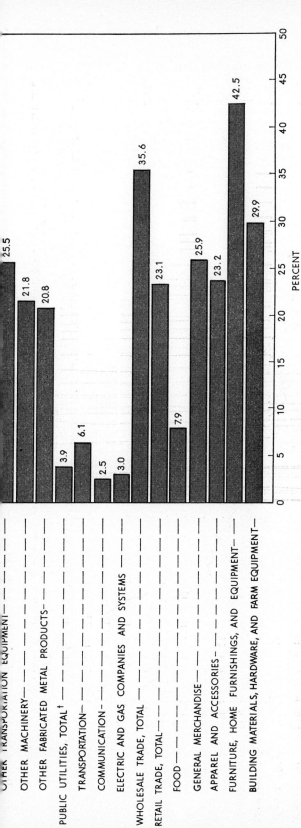

Bar chart with categories (top to bottom) and their percent values:

- OTHER TRANSPORTATION EQUIPMENT — 25.5
- OTHER MACHINERY — 21.8
- OTHER FABRICATED METAL PRODUCTS — 20.8
- PUBLIC UTILITIES, TOTAL† — 3.9
- TRANSPORTATION — 6.1
- COMMUNICATION — 2.5
- ELECTRIC AND GAS COMPANIES AND SYSTEMS — 3.0
- WHOLESALE TRADE, TOTAL — 35.6
- RETAIL TRADE, TOTAL — 23.1
- FOOD — 7.9
- GENERAL MERCHANDISE — 25.9
- APPAREL AND ACCESSORIES — 23.2
- FURNITURE, HOME FURNISHINGS, AND EQUIPMENT — 42.5
- BUILDING MATERIALS, HARDWARE, AND FARM EQUIPMENT — 29.9

PERCENT (axis 0 to 50)

* Apparel and other finished products made from fabrics and similar materials.

† Total transportation, communication, electric, gas, and sanitary services.

SOURCE OF DATA: U.S. Treasury Department, Internal Revenue Service, *Statistics of Income, 1961–1962: Corporation Income Tax Returns* (Washington, D.C.: U.S. Government Printing Office, 1964). Table 2—"Balance Sheets and Income Statements . . . by Major Industrial Group."

CHART 4-2

QUARTERLY ACCOUNTS RECEIVABLE OF ALL U.S. MANUFACTURING CORPORATIONS (EXCEPT NEWSPAPERS)
COMPARED WITH QUARTERLY SALES, 1947–64

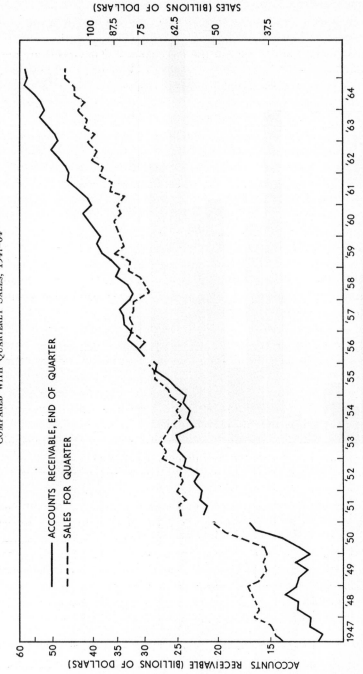

NOTE: Revisions of the series took place as of 1951, 1956, 1958, 1959, and 1962. Only the first two resulted in significant changes in the data.
SOURCE OF DATA: U.S. Federal Trade Commission and Securities and Exchange Commission, *Quarterly Financial Report for Manufacturing Corporations*, 1947–1964.

monly are offered for sale on terms that call for *instalment payments* extended over many months. Such sales are customarily made subject to the terms of *conditional sales contracts,* which give the seller (or his assignee) the right to recover the merchandise if payments are not made as agreed upon in the contract. Usually, a significant cash payment, often 20% to 30% of the retail price, is required. And unlike the case in routine open-account credits, significant interest and other credit charges are added to the cash sales price.

The retailer may retain the instalment sales obligation. More commonly, instalment contracts are sold to banks or specialized sales finance companies. Some retailers, such as Sears, Roebuck and Company, have formed subsidiaries to hold and collect instalment credits. Some manufacturers, who have found easy credit vital to the ability of final users to buy their products, have established sales finance subsidiaries to buy the instalment "paper" of customers of their dealers. Thus, major farm equipment makers, such as Deere & Company, now finance not only the sale of equipment to dealers for inventory but the dealers' sales to farmers as well. Indeed, some farm equipment manufacturers also finance the resale by their dealers of other makes of used equipment acquired as trade-ins on new equipment.

In recent years an increasing number of manufacturers of industrial equipment also have found it necessary or desirable to offer instalment credit terms to their business customers. Most manufacturers of machine tools and of equipment for service industries, such as dry-cleaning equipment, for example, offer credit terms extending over as much as three to four years. A number have formed so-called *captive finance companies* to take over these credits or have arranged their resale to other finance companies. Usually, these credits are extended on conditional sales contracts. Since the instalment credit terms include substantial financing charges, companies whose finances are strong generally prefer to purchase equipment on the normal trade terms and open account.

Although some increase in export selling on an open-account basis has been reported in recent years, the great bulk of the sales to overseas customers is not on an open-account basis. Instead, a number of distinctive credit and financing instruments and practices have been developed in response to the special problems of international commercial transactions. Particularly important among the credit instruments of international trade are the *letter of credit* and the *banker's acceptance.* These will be discussed in Chapter 12.

Objectives in the Management of the Investment in Receivables

In the typical firm the financial officer has operating responsibility for the management of the investment in receivables. Reporting directly to him in most firms is the head of the credit department, which carries out the work of granting credit and supervising the collection of receivables.

In addition to his role in overseeing the administration of credit, the financial officer is in a particularly strategic position to contribute to top-management decisions as to the best credit policies for the firm.

Unless the firm's own finances are closely limited, the basic objective of receivables management, like that of inventory management, should be that of maximizing return on investment. Policies which stress short credit terms, stringent credit standards, and highly aggressive policing of collections clearly should work to minimize bad-debt losses and the tie-up of funds in receivables. But such policies may well restrict sales and profit margins, so that despite the low receivables investment, rate of return on total investment of the firm is lower than that attainable with higher levels of sales, profits, and receivables. Conversely, extremely lenient or sloppy credit extension may well inflate receivables and bad debts without compensating increases in sales and profits. Clearly, the objective of receivables management should be the achievement of that balance which in the particular circumstances of the firm results in the combination of turnover and profit rates that maximizes the overall return on investment of the firm. Mutual understanding and close cooperation of the financial officer with sales executives are essential to full progress toward the objective.

We should recognize, however, that limited financial resources of the particular firm may force greater restraint in receivables than would be ideal from a return-on-investment viewpoint. If the availability of funds is restricted, their use in inventory, equipment, or other areas offering even higher return may dictate severe restraint on credit administration. Or if the financial position of the firm is so precarious that a major bad-debt loss would be disastrous, extreme caution in credit administration, though costly in forgone profit, may nevertheless be wise.

Now let us turn to a consideration of the major determinants of the size of the investment in receivables in the individual firm, with especial attention to those particularly subject to management influence and control.

Major Determinants of the Size of the Investment in Receivables

Of particular importance in shaping the size of the firm's investment in receivables are the following factors:

1. The terms of credit granted customers deemed creditworthy.
2. The policies and practices of the firm in determining which customers are to be granted credit.
3. The paying practices of credit customers.
4. The rigor of the seller's collection policies and practice.
5. The volume of credit sales.

Let us look briefly at each of these factors. In theory each firm is free to specify whatever *terms of sale* best suit its objectives and circumstances. It may sell only for cash on delivery in order to avoid tying up its funds in receivables and risking bad-debt losses, perhaps consciously conceding the added sales that might be achieved through selling on credit. Or it may use the extension of generous credit as an aggressive selling tool. One used-car retailer in Boston has advertised that he would sell cars to any customer "whose credit is good" on terms of "no down payment, 48 months to pay." Further, the seller is free to change his terms of sale when and as he likes.

In actual practice, competitive pressures tend to push the individual firm to offer credit terms at least as generous as those of most of its competitors. Over a long span of years, particular terms of sale have become traditional in many product lines. Buyers have come to expect these terms to such an extent that new suppliers joining an industry usually offer the "customary" terms of sale of the industry as the course of least resistance. Thus, manufacturers of machine tools often sell on terms of "2/10, net 30." This notation means that a discount of 2% is allowed if payment is made within 10 days of invoicing, and payment regardless of discount is expected within 30 days, although sometimes on an "E.O.M." basis, that is, within 30 days after the end of the month of sale. Terms on a few products are quite long; for example, uncut diamonds usually are sold on terms of 6 to 9 months.[1]

A 1958 study of the terms of sales used by 1,600 firms in 145 manufacturing lines and 75 wholesale lines[2] brought out the prevalence of cash discounts. Sixty-five percent of the manufacturers and 93% of the wholesalers surveyed customarily extended prompt-payment discounts. The most common period within which payment was required to earn the cash discount was 10 days among manufacturers and the 10th day of the following month among wholesalers. If discounts were not earned, the period of credit most commonly specified under manufacturers' terms of sale was 30 days.

Most firms make their "customary terms" available to all customers whom they have judged worthy of this credit. Changes in the customary terms of sale generally are made only infrequently; in many firms and industries the customary terms have remained constant over decades. Evidence to support this view is afforded by two broad studies of changes in credit terms during the years from World War II to 1958.[3] Each study reported that only 16% of the firms studied had changed their formal terms of trade during these years. Moreover, among those changing there were no pronounced trends toward tighter or more liberal terms.

---

[1] For a list of customary terms of sale for 161 types of products, see T. N. Beckman, *Credits and Collections; Management and Theory* (7th ed.; New York: McGraw-Hill Book Co., 1962), pp. 639–44.

[2] R. A. Foulke, *Current Trends in Terms of Sale* (New York: Dun & Bradstreet, 1959).

[3] Described in Martin H. Seiden, *The Quality of Trade Credit* (Occasional Paper 87) (New York: National Bureau of Economic Research, 1964), pp. 42–43.

The constancy of formal terms, however, suggests a misleading degree of rigidity toward credit extension by sellers. While few respondents to formal studies have said that they grant special terms freely, it is clear that in many competitive fields suppliers do tacitly extend their terms by permitting selected customers to take much longer to pay than the formal terms allow. As one student concludes:

> . . . in practice credit standards are normally altered through a change in credit policy rather than through a change of terms. . . . Less than vigorous enforcement of the net period [the stated terms of credit] has particular advantages. It facilitates discriminatory price discounts and conceals price changes from competitors. As a result of its flexibility, selectivity, and low cost relative to formal price changes, credit policy is an important factor determining both the quantity and the quality of the trade credit outstanding."[4]

In particular industries, such as the textile industry during especially competitive periods, many firms, while announcing no changes from the traditional terms of sale of the industry, reportedly were granting special terms to so many of their customers that their formal terms had become more nominal than real.

At any rate, it should be clear that the credit terms granted customers are an important determinant of the size of the investment in receivables. If other factors are constant, the longer the credit terms offered, the larger will be the investment in receivables.

It is interesting to note that the outstanding receivables of U.S. manufacturers on March 31, 1965, represented some 45 days' sales at the rate of sales reported for the preceding quarter.

The policies and practices of the individual firm in deciding which of its customers should be granted its customary terms of credit also affect the size of its investment in receivables. The firm's customary credit terms typically are extended only to those customers which are adjudged acceptable credit risks. Terms of cash on order or on delivery, or shorter than usual credit terms, may be used for sales to "poor risks" or to concerns for which available information is insufficient to establish their creditworthiness for the amounts involved. Different firms apply different standards in appraising the creditworthiness of their customers. Speaking generally, the more liberal the standards used in extending credit, the larger will be the investment in receivables. Some firms modify their standards in granting credit with the sales outlook, taking greater risks of bad debts when demand is slack. Most firms, however, appear to change their standards infrequently and then only within relatively narrow limits. We shall have more to say at a later point in this chapter on how credit risks are evaluated and controlled.

The actual paying practices of customers also have an impact on total credit outstanding. As noted earlier, many firms offer customers a

---

[4] *Ibid.*, p. 43.

discount for early payments. Firms offering terms of 2/10, net 30 give their customers the option of taking discounts and paying within 10 days or forgoing the discount and waiting 30 days to pay. The choice exercised by the customers clearly affects the amount of credit outstanding. Further, as we have noted, even where inflexible terms are quoted, customers may take liberties with them. Customers who buy primarily from sellers offering, say, 30-day terms, often ignore shorter terms of minor suppliers and pay all bills on the same basis. In other cases important customers deliberately and habitually take extra time to settle their trade obligations. In such instances, rather than risk losing the valuable sales outlets, the sellers may allow their stated terms to be exceeded. Still other customers, financially hard pressed, may let their debts run as far overdue as their creditors will tolerate.

While many firms are careful to meet all their trade obligations when due, others appear all too willing to take advantage of tolerant suppliers. The closeness with which the supplier follows up on overdue accounts and the degree of pressure he brings for prompt payment have a material effect on the paying practices of many customers and hence on the level of outstanding receivables.

The most important variable affecting the level of the receivables investment is the volume of credit sales. If the other variables we have discussed remain constant, the level of receivables may be expected to vary directly with changes in sales volume. As sales increase, receivables expand, absorbing funds. As sales fall off, the related receivables decline, releasing funds. Unless long credits are granted, the time lag between changes in sales volume and proportionate changes in receivables is short. This behavior is often forgotten by planners, in relation to both expansion and contraction.

Since the determinants of the investment in receivables other than sales volume typically do not change rapidly or drastically, most of the important short-term changes in the amount of outstanding receivables can be traced to changes in sales volume. Conversely, important variations in the outstanding receivables of firms whose sales volume has been constant must be attributed to changes in credit terms, in the standards for granting credit, in the paying practices of customers, or in the rigor with which collections are policed.

The Work of the Credit Department

Since the financial officer usually is responsible for the effective functioning of the *credit department*, it is appropriate that we review the key functions and major problem areas in the effective administration of trade credit.

The work of the credit department consists of three main activities. First, the department must gather and organize the information necessary for decisions on the granting of credit to particular customers. Second, it must police the collection of receivables to ensure that efforts are made to collect the debts when due. Finally, in the case of accounts which appear to have "gone bad," that is, accounts of customers who apparently cannot or do not intend to pay, it must determine and carry out appropriate efforts to collect the accounts and avoid loss.

Sources of Credit Information

Although the usual standards for extension of trade credit are not severe, prospective new customers seldom are automatically extended

EXHIBIT 4–1

KEY TO DUN & BRADSTREET RATINGS

KEY TO RATINGS

ESTIMATED FINANCIAL STRENGTH			COMPOSITE CREDIT APPRAISAL			
			HIGH	GOOD	FAIR	LIMITED
Aᴀ	Over	$1,000,000	A1	1	1½	2
A+	Over	750,000	A1	1	1½	2
A	500,000	to 750,000	A1	1	1½	2
B+	300,000	to 500,000	1	1½	2	2½
B	200,000	to 300,000	1	1½	2	2½
C+	125,000	to 200,000	1	1½	2	2½
C	75,000	to 125,000	1½	2	2½	3
D+	50,000	to 75,000	1½	2	2½	3
D	35,000	to 50,000	1½	2	2½	3
E	20,000	to 35,000	2	2½	3	3½
F	10,000	to 20,000	2½	3	3½	4
G	5,000	to 10,000	3	3½	4	4½
H	3,000	to 5,000	3	3½	4	4½
J	2,000	to 3,000	3	3½	4	4½
K	1,000	to 2,000	3	3½	4	4½
L	Up to	1,000	3½	4	4½	5

CLASSIFICATION AS TO BOTH ESTIMATED FINANCIAL STRENGTH AND CREDIT APPRAISAL

FINANCIAL STRENGTH BRACKET			EXPLANATION
1	$125,000 to	$1,000,000 and Over	When only the numeral (1, 2, 3, or 4) appears, it is an indication that the estimated financial strength, while not definitely classified, is presumed to be within the range of the ($) figures in the corresponding bracket and that a condition is believed to exist which warrants credit in keeping with that assumption.
2	20,000	to 125,000	
3	2,000	to 20,000	
4	Up	to 2,000	

NOT CLASSIFIED OR ABSENCE OF RATING

The absence of a rating, expressed by the dash (—), or by two hyphens (- -), is not to be construed as unfavorable but signifies circumstances difficult to classify within condensed rating symbols and should suggest to the subscriber the advisability of obtaining additional information.

SEE REFERENCE BOOK FOR EXPLANATION OF ABSENCE OF A LISTING AND ADDITIONAL SYMBOLS USED IN REFERENCE BOOK

Dun & Bradstreet, Inc.
Offices in Principal Cities of the United States

SOURCE: Dun & Bradstreet, Inc., *Subscriber's Manual.*

normal credit terms. Typically, before shipment of a sizable order to a new customer, the credit department conducts a quick investigation to determine whether the company is justified in extending its normal credit terms to the new customer. Usually, the investigation must be a rapid one lest the prospective sale be lost as a result of delays in clearing the credit.

In checking on the creditworthiness of the prospective customer, the credit department can take advantage of a widespread network of credit information for data other than those provided by the customer. Particularly valuable sources are *credit reporting organizations* which make a business of collecting and supplying credit information. The largest firm in this field, Dun & Bradstreet, Inc., operates on an international basis, but its files on U.S. firms are particularly comprehensive in coverage.

Subscribers to its services receive the Dun & Bradstreet *Reference Book*, published every two months, listing about three million manufacturing, wholesaling, and retailing firms. Over 70% of the listings are accompanied by an estimate of the financial strength of the firm and a composite *credit rating* assigned the firm by Dun & Bradstreet. The rating seeks to reflect and summarize the information assembled to throw light on the creditworthiness of the subject firm. The key to Dun & Bradstreet ratings is reproduced as Exhibit 4–1, and an illustrative page from the *Reference Book*, with explanations of the symbols used, as Exhibit 4–2.

Unrated firms are those for which insufficient information was available to justify a rating. The *Reference Book* also includes firms "for whom the information available disclosed financial weaknesses of hazardous proportions, an undue moral risk, litigation critical to the business, or other circumstances of similar import."[5]

The "high" rating indicates minimum credit risk. At the other end of the scale, "limited" is applied to firms, usually quite small, with substantial and chronic deficiencies. A sampling of ratings undertaken in connection with the Seiden study showed the following distribution of 1,200 ratings drawn from the editions of July, 1950, and July, 1958:

Rating	1950	1958
High	17.5%	14.0%
Good	71.6	59.3
Fair	10.9	24.9
Limited	–0–	1.8
	100.0%	100.0%

SOURCE: Martin H. Seiden, *The Quality of Trade Credit.*

It is interesting to note the downward shift in quality ratings during the 8-year period, which was overall one of economic progress and prosperity. It should be pointed out, however, that the above distribution of ratings is by number of firms. Smaller and new firms dominate the limited and fair ratings. Large firms, which do a high percentage of total business, are mostly in the high category.

To the firm considering whether to ship an order to a new customer on normal terms, the credit ratings afford a handy, quick screening device. If the customer enjoys a good rating and the size of the order is reasonable in relation to his financial strength, the decision may well be to ship the order on normal terms but to proceed with a more complete investigation for future use.

[5] Seiden, *op. cit.*, p. 66.

EXHIBIT 4–2

SYMBOLS USED IN DUN & BRADSTREET *Reference Book*

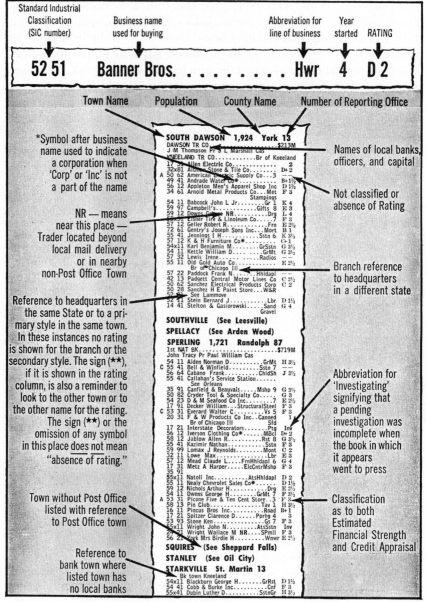

SOURCE: Dun & Bradstreet, Inc., *Subscriber's Manual*.

If the customer is a concern of any size, the department can probably obtain, at moderate cost, a *credit report* from one of the credit reporting agencies. Dun & Bradstreet, for instance, usually is able to supply information about the background and experience of the principal executives of the concern, a summary of its history and methods of operation, notation of any bankruptcies or compromises with creditors on the part of the firm or its executives or owners in the past, and also income and balance sheet data. Further, the credit agency periodically conducts trade checks on concerns on which it maintains files. The agency investigates the collection experience of the major suppliers of the firm and summarizes this experience in the credit report, together with information on present credit outstanding, amount past due, recent high credits, and whether the concern usually pays on time. For an example of a credit report see Exhibit 2 of the "Union Paint and Varnish Company" case (page 658).

In addition to the large national credit information firms, a number of industry associations operate credit information services. Further, local mercantile credit agencies, dealing mainly in information about the credit standing of individuals, operate in almost every city. These are widely used by retail establishments whose potential sales to individual customers hardly justify extensive credit investigations of their own.

Commercial banks serve an important function in the exchange of credit information. Usually, the banks stand ready to help customers carry out credit investigations. If the subject of the credit investigation is not a customer of the bank, upon request the bank will commonly make inquiries of banks that are familiar with the subject's reputation and financial standing.

The company's own salesmen, who may well have visited the subject concern in getting the order, are sometimes helpful. However, sales personnel often are more concerned about the booking of the sale than the collection of the ensuing debt, and their information must be interpreted accordingly.

Where it appears necessary, the credit department can approach the prospective customer directly, either to discuss questionable aspects of the credit or to round out the file of information. In determining how much time and effort to devote to accumulation of credit information and its analysis, credit managers must balance the costs of added information against the benefits from the degree of improvement in the credit decisions that can be expected as a result of the more refined analysis. Usually, the balance indicated is far short of the complete analysis that theoretically could be made.

We should note that the practice of providing credit and financial information and the institutional network for its dissemination in the United States and Canada far exceed those in other countries. Overall, the availability of reliable credit information facilitates credit extension and trade development. Although progress in the area in some other countries appears rapid, the room for further progress is great.

Reference might also be made to the network of information regarding individuals as well as businesses. Many credit organizations are prepared to report on individuals, their background, reputation, payment practices, and financial strength. Men must live with the record and reputation they have formed.

Evaluation of Credit Risk

Once the available sources of information have been utilized and a mass of data accumulated, the data must be interpreted and the credit

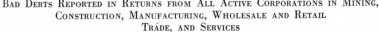

CHART 4-3

BAD DEBTS REPORTED IN RETURNS FROM ALL ACTIVE CORPORATIONS IN MINING, CONSTRUCTION, MANUFACTURING, WHOLESALE AND RETAIL TRADE, AND SERVICES

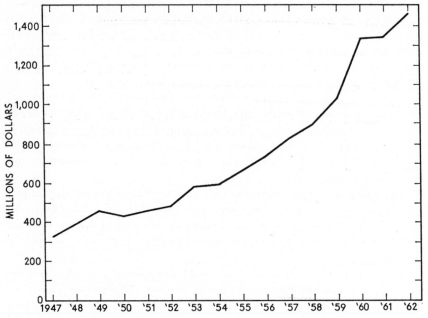

SOURCES: Data for 1947–59 from Martin H. Seiden, *The Quality of Trade Credit*, Table 5, p. 16; data for 1960–62 from U.S. Treasury Department, Internal Revenue Service, *Statistics of Income: Corporation Income Tax Returns* for 1960, 1961, and 1962 (preliminary).

decision made. In digesting the facts and reaching a credit decision, many financial officers more or less explicitly keep in mind as basic criteria the "Four C's of Credit—Capital, Capacity, Character, and Conditions." *Capital* obviously refers to the financial resources of the company, as indicated primarily by the balance sheets. *Capacity* has reference to the experience of the principals and the demonstrated ability of the concern to operate successfully, the latter to a good degree indicated by the profit record of the company. *Character* refers to the reputation of the owners and management for honesty and fair dealing. Information reflecting unfavorably on the integrity of the principals is especially important, because time and cost considerations limit the extent and thoroughness to which investigation can be pushed, and a clever rascal is likely to be able to present an outwardly attractive situation. The criterion *conditions* suggests the possibility of placing special limitations or restrictions on the extension of credit to doubtful accounts.[6]

In most companies a minor fraction of the credit accounts causes a very high percentage of the credit department's headaches. Chronically slow in paying but quick to claim faulty merchandise, these problem accounts dilute turnover and enrich correspondence files. The cost of credit mistakes is not measured by bad debts alone but by the trouble and expense of collection efforts and litigation in the case of accounts that ultimately are collectible.

We do not mean to suggest that business *bad-debt losses* in themselves are trivial; all active nonfinancial corporations reporting for income tax purposes showed aggregate bad-debt expenses of $3,144 million in 1961–62. In relation to total business receipts, the figure was modest— only 0.38%—but the absolute amount, even after allowance for the likelihood that the reported expense exceeded losses actually realized, is not one to be dismissed lightly.

As Chart 4–3 shows, the amount of corporate credit losses has been increasing rapidly in recent years. Chart 4–4 puts the losses in better perspective by expressing them as a percentage of sales and of outstanding receivables.

Analysis of bad-debt losses has shown that smaller firms have suffered a very much higher percentage of losses than have large firms. For example, Seiden's analysis of data from tax returns showed that bad debt losses of all manufacturing concerns from 1947 through 1957 averaged 0.81% of outstanding receivables. When the losses were analyzed by size of firm, the following results were obtained:

Small	1.87%
Medium	1.19
Large	0.80
Giant	0.37

It seldom is difficult for trained credit men, on the basis of information easily gathered, to spot those accounts—both new and already on the books—that are inherently high-risk accounts. The key problem in credit evaluation is to decide which of the admittedly higher-risk accounts are to be given credit, how much, and under what conditions. At one time the ability to avoid credit losses was widely regarded as the complete measure of the success of a credit manager. Measured by such standards, the credit manager had every incentive to turn down the credit requests of questionable customers. This concept of credit evaluation clearly is a gross oversimplification; the credit manager who maintains a credit

---

[6] The term *conditions* is also used by some in a very different sense. Some use the term to stress the importance of the business conditions or level of prosperity of the customer's industry as a factor affecting his creditworthiness.

policy so strict that credit losses never occur is properly suspected of
turning away profitable business.

In deciding what credit risks to accept, the responsible officer should
balance the risks of loss and the burdens involved in possibly tying up
funds in slow-paying accounts against the value to the firm of the
prospective sales involved. Commonly, the value of added business is high
enough to justify a high degree of risk taking in trade credit. But just how

CHART 4–4

BAD DEBTS REPORTED IN RETURNS FROM ALL ACTIVE CORPORATIONS IN
MINING, CONSTRUCTION, MANUFACTURING, WHOLESALE
AND RETAIL TRADE, AND SERVICES, EXPRESSED
AS A PERCENTAGE OF SALES AND OF RECEIVABLES

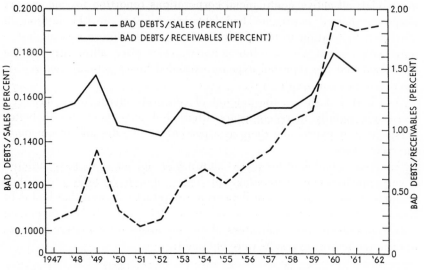

SOURCES: Data for 1947–59 from Martin H. Seiden, *The Quality of Trade Credit*, Table 6, p. 17; data for
1960–62 from U.S. Treasury Department, Internal Revenue Service, *Statistics of Income: Corporation Income
Tax Returns* for 1960, 1961, and 1962 (preliminary).

the value of the added business should be calculated can be open to sharp
differences of opinion. One approach is to value additional business
simply in terms of the average profit rate on sales of the firm. Another
approach measures the contribution of the added volume in terms of the
excess of sales revenue over the additional costs that the company will
incur in producing and selling the added goods. The added costs represent
those costs that will change by virtue of the added volume—the cost of
the materials going into the product, the additional labor necessary,
added freight, added commissions paid on the sales, and so on. Not
included will be costs such as depreciation and general and administrative expense, which are expected to remain fixed in amount despite this
increase in volume. If the firm operates with a high level of fixed costs,
and if it is operating below capacity, additional volume may be handled at

limited "out-of-pocket" or additional expense, and the added profits to the firm from the additional business will be very much more than the average profit on sales of the firm.

An illustration should be helpful. Suppose prospective new customer A promises to buy $10,000 of goods a month, but his financial position is weak and he may take 60 days to pay, disregarding the regular 30-day term. Our firm is operating well below capacity, and if we do not supply new customer A, our competitor will. Our average profit is 10% of sales; however, inquiry reveals that the additional or out-of-pocket costs that will be created in producing and selling the added $10,000 a month will be only $6,000. Thus, our net income before taxes should increase by $4,000 a month, not $1,000, if we take on the account. In return for tying up and exposing to the risk of bad-debt loss an average of $20,000 (if the outstanding receivable balance is held to 60 days' sales) we can expect added net revenues of $4,000 a month or $48,000 a year. If the account were to stay active for only 6 months, the added marginal revenue from $60,000 in sales, which would be $24,000, would more than match complete loss of $20,000, the average balance in this account.

Once an initial credit to a new customer is approved, it is customary for the credit department to approve continued shipments to the customer, provided the shipment does not bring the outstanding balance due from the customer above a designated high limit established for that customer. Shipments on orders that would mean exceeding the high limit or credit line on the account are subject to review by the credit executives. Credit lines usually receive periodic routine review, often on an annual basis, and are revised only if important changes develop.

Policing the Collection of Outstanding Credits

The credit department also has the work of supervising or policing the accounts to see that customers are billed promptly and that slow-paying customers are reminded in effective fashion of their delinquency before it becomes serious. Books have been written on the art of gentle but effective "needling" of slow-paying customers so that prompt payment may be obtained without giving offense and jeopardizing future business.

In getting prompt payment of receivables, credit men are aided by the pressures stemming from the general recognition that failure to pay promptly will receive widespread publicity in trade circles and reflect adversely on the credit standing of the firm. Furthermore, for continuing customers the credit department has a more drastic weapon at hand: it can cut off future shipments on credit unless overdue accounts are given attention.

Once either supplier or customer has ceased active business, the pressure vanishes. The threat of unfavorable publicity is a minor one to customers in severe and well-publicized difficulty. It is also true that liquidators have had disappointing experiences in collecting the accounts receivable of bankrupt concerns.

Collection of inactive and long-overdue (or "sour") accounts involves difficult problems. In such circumstances normal pressures on the debtor to make payment are not likely to be effective, and bad-debt losses or excessive expense and effort in collection can be avoided only through skillful action. Initial efforts should be designed to discover the real reasons for the debtor's delinquency.

If the debtor appears able to pay, vigorous collection procedures are in order. If the account is small, often it is best to turn it over to a specialized collection agency, which, for a substantial percentage of the debt, assumes the task of collection. These agencies typically act with great vigor, and they are set up to handle such operations with a minimum of expense. Direct legal action by the seller in the case of small accounts often involves legal expense and managerial effort disproportionate to the amounts involved. This is especially true since persons seeking to avoid legal obligations frequently challenge quantities or qualities of the goods involved and do anything else they can to make the collection effort so tiresome that it will be abandoned.

In the case of important customers who freely acknowledge the debt but are in such financial difficulties that payment in full is difficult, somewhat different tactics are in order. If the creditor insists on his full legal rights and brings suit to collect the debt, he may only force the company into bankruptcy. When bankruptcy results, the affairs of the company are put in the hands of the courts, usually federal, for reorganization or liquidation under the supervision of court-appointed officials. If liquidation of the company results, the assets left after payment of the legal and administrative expenses of bankruptcy are divided among the creditors. Typically, the net proceeds from asset liquidation permit only a modest partial payment to trade creditors. Further, unless the sales outlet can be replaced, the future sales that might have been made to the customer are lost if he is forced out of business.

Consequently, it is often desirable for the creditor to seek a compromise settlement with an embarrassed customer that will get some payment yet permit the customer to stay in business. Unfortunately, if the customer has many other debts, as is typical, a compromise settlement may not be feasible unless other creditors will join in the compromise, since any unpaid creditor can demand its legal rights and throw the debtor into the courts. To help achieve such concerted action, standing creditors' committees in some industries and cities provide a continuing organization to bring the credit officers of the cooperating concerns together in particular cases as the need arises. Although compromise settlements are difficult to accomplish when many creditors are involved, such efforts have been relatively successful. In fact, experience dictates that a creditor should carefully investigate compromise settlement before it resorts to the more drastic use of full legal remedies, which often prove remedies in name only. Procedures of compromise and of bankruptcy are discussed in some detail in Chapter 30.

Aids to the Analysis of the Investment in Accounts Receivable

We have noted that the level of the investment in trade receivables can be expected to fluctuate in direct relationship with the volume of sales, provided sales terms and collection practices do not change. Naturally, credit officials, financial officers, and others associated with the finances of the concern are interested in detecting any tendency toward more lenient credit extension, as would be suggested by tendencies of collections to slow up and slow-paying accounts to increase. These interested parties look carefully at the relationship of receivables to recent credit sales. The comparison of receivables to sales can take several forms. One comparison simply expresses outstanding receivables as a percentage of sales. Unless sales terms are unusually long, the existing receivables should be the product of recent sales. Consequently, persons within the firm, who have available recent monthly or quarterly sales data, relate reported receivables to these data. As an illustration consider the following data:

Sales fourth quarter, 1965	$1,860,000	
Accounts receivable, Dec. 31, 1965		$967,200
Sales fourth quarter, 1964	1,200,000	
Accounts receivable, Dec. 31, 1964		492,000

Let us assume in this case that the analyst is the financial officer, who knows that sales during each quarter were at a relatively even rate. It can be quickly determined that the 1965 receivables are 52% of the last quarter's sales (967,200/1,860,000 = 52%). Looking back to 1964, he can readily see that receivables then were only 41% of the preceding quarter's sales. Thus, the analyst can see that the large increase in receivables in 1965 is not simply the natural result of the growth in sales, and he is alerted to the need for further inquiry as to the reasons for the slowing of payments.

The relationship between sales and receivables is also expressed in terms of days' sales outstanding or collection period. In 1965, in the approximately 90 days of the last quarter, sales equaled $20,666 a calendar day. The receivables on hand at December 31, 1965, equaled 46.8 days' sales (967,200/20,666 = 46.8 days). Using the same method of calculation, the 1964 receivables represented 36.9 days' sales at the 1964 rate of $13,333 a day. Comparison of 46.8 days' sales currently outstanding against 36.9 last year thus also reveals the apparent slow-up of receivables. The result in days' sales outstanding also permits comparison with stated terms of sale. If the company offers 30-day terms, it is apparent that these terms are being abused significantly.

Outside analysts often have only annual sales totals to compare with year-end receivables. If sales are steady through the year, the comparisons drawn from the data can be meaningful. But if sales fluctuate through the year, a comparison of year-end receivables with sales at the annual rate can be misleading. For example, if a firm sold on net 30-day terms and had monthly sales of $100,000 for January through November and $250,000 in December, it might well have receivables outstanding on December 31 of $250,000. Yet, in comparison with the annual sales of $1,350,000, or average monthly sales of $112,500, the $250,000 in receivables would appear unduly high.

Of course, if monthly sales are known to follow a consistent seasonal pattern year after year, the analyst can compare a year-end receivables/annual sales ratio with those of the same date in earlier years. The results should be comparable in relative if not absolute terms. Yet, as we have suggested earlier, receivables should be compared with recent sales data whenever such data can be obtained.

A useful management control device for review of the condition of receivables is the *aging schedule*. As the name suggests, this is a tabulation of receivables outstanding according to the length of time they have been outstanding. Each account, or a broad sample of accounts, is broken down according to the date of sale, and the results tabulated.

Let us suppose, for illustration, that two firms each have monthly sales of $700,000 on 30-day terms. Each has outstanding receivables of $1,000,000. Aging produces the following schedules:

	Firm A		Firm B	
Outstanding less than 30 days	$ 700,000	70%	$ 700,000	70%
Outstanding 30–59 days	280,000	28	150,000	15
Outstanding 60–89 days	15,000	1.5	60,000	6
Outstanding 90+ days	5,000	0.5	90,000	9
	$1,000,000	100%	$1,000,000	100%

Without the aging schedule, the receivables position of the two firms appears the same. Certainly, receivable/sales ratios and the collection period are identical. But firm B may be encountering serious difficulty in collecting the $150,000 in long-overdue receivables, even though it has a number of customers who are more prompt in paying after 30 days than those of firm A. Thus, the aging schedule, by revealing any tendency for old accounts to accumulate, provides a useful supplement to the various receivables/sales ratios. Since the outstanding receivables are appraised in terms of the associated dates of sale, the tabulation automatically recognizes recent bulges or slumps in sales. Many financial officers have such schedules prepared in routine at periodic intervals, and commercial banks and other lenders to firms with important investments in receivables frequently ask for aging schedules.

Accounting for Accounts Receivable

The accounting for accounts receivable involves a large volume of record keeping, calling for rapid and accurate recording of sales and payments. The accounting theory, however, is simple. When a sale is made, the appropriate amount is added to an account kept for each customer and is thus included in the total of accounts receivable. As payments are received, the fact of payment is noted on each account, and the total of accounts receivables is decreased at the same time cash is increased.

Most concerns recognize the fact that some of their sales on credit will not be paid and set up an account called *Reserve for Bad Debts* or *Provision for Bad Debts*. An amount equal to the portion of sales which it is estimated will prove uncollectible is charged to income as Bad-Debt Expense, and an equal credit is made to the Reserve for Bad Debts. When it is determined that a particular account receivable will not be collected, it is taken off the books by reducing accounts receivable and the Reserve for Bad Debts by an equal amount. Many firms, in reporting their accounts receivable on the balance sheet, show "Accounts Receivable, net"—in other words, after subtraction of the Reserve for Bad Debts.

Cash Receipts from Receivables

In planning when and in what amounts cash will be received as a result of credit sales, the critical dates are the dates when receipts of payment for credit sales can be expected. Thus, forecasts of credit sales must be converted into estimated collections of accounts receivable in order to determine cash receipts from such sales. Usually, an average figure based on past experience is employed as a measure of the time lag between sales and collection of the related receivables. If the average collection experience has been 30 days, for instance, and there is no reason to anticipate a change in this figure, the receipts from future sales on credit can be scheduled a month behind the sales. Appropriate deductions should be made for bad debts if there is reason to believe they will prove significant.

The Trend toward Longer Collection Periods

Earlier we noted with interest the long-term trend made apparent in Chart 4–2 for receivables to grow faster than sales. By way of emphasis we pointed out that manufacturers would have had an investment of only $33.7 billion in receivables rather than the actual $57.5 billion on March 31, 1965, if they had collected for sales as rapidly in 1965 as in 1947. In terms of the collection period, the 1965 receivables represented almost 46 days' sales compared with 26.5 days in 1947.

The growth in receivables relative to sales is in striking contrast to the movement of inventory relative to sales. As noted in Chapter 3, the inventory/sales ratio has declined modestly.

Why have American manufacturers let receivables outpace sales? The discussion in this chapter on management policy toward receivables should suggest some likely explanations. Our listing of contributing factors could almost serve as a summary to this chapter. The factors include:

1. A long-term continuing shift in top-management policy objectives away from a dominant emphasis on minimizing credit losses toward one of maximizing overall firm profits. This latter emphasis balances the gains from more sales attributable to more accommodating credit policies against the larger investment in receivables and the higher credit losses that may be expected from less rigorous credit policies.

2. The fact that the larger suppliers typically have not found it difficult to meet the additional funds requirement stemming from the increased investment in receivables.

3. The existence through most postwar years of excess productive capacity and the related fact that in many industries the incremental costs of producing and selling additional units was small. Thus, the profit reward for additional sales was high.

4. The fact that in many industries competition for sales by covert credit leniency was thought easier to administer selectively and less likely to bring quick competitive retaliation by other suppliers than would price cutting.

5. The general prosperity of recent decades, which has made managers bolder in assuming exposure to bad-debt losses. Thus, the rising volume of losses has been taken in stride by many managements.

Chapter 5

Management of the Money Position

IN EARLIER EDITIONS of this book, this chapter was titled "Management of Cash and Near-Cash Reserves and the Need for Funds." We have concluded that "Management of the Money Position" is more sharply descriptive of the work of controlling and utilizing effectively the liquid resources of the firm. *Money Position* is intended to encompass the cash position of the firm, investments that can readily be converted into cash, and indeed readily available sources of credit that can be drawn upon if and when needed. In many respects the financial officer's job in managing the cash position and in drawing upon or rebuilding short-term investment portfolios or credit lines is like that of the commercial bank officer charged with the day-to-day and hour-to-hour management of the bank's own cash and investment position—its "money position." Like the banker, the alert corporate financial officer wants to minimize unproductive cash balances, to invest temporarily excess cash advantageously, and to make the best possible arrangements for meeting planned and unexpected demands on the company's cash. Although top management can be expected to have a keen interest in the liquidity of the firm and in the shaping of policies governing cash and near-cash accounts, the direct and immediate responsibility for management of the money position of the firm typically rests with the chief financial officer.

The commitment of funds to *cash* and *near-cash investments* (near-cash in the sense that they are readily marketable with little fear of loss) for American businesses generally is a significant one. Thus, U.S. manufacturing corporations on March 31, 1965, had $29 billion in cash and U.S. government securities, an amount almost 9% of their total resources. Since many firms invest surplus funds in securities other than those of the U.S. government, the above figures understate the totals committed to cash and liquid investment.

Chart 5–1 shows the percentage of total assets committed to cash and U.S. securities in a number of manufacturing industries and in a number of nonmanufacturing industry groups. Only in the case of electric and gas utilities was the total in cash and U.S. obligations relatively insignificant

CHART 5–1

INVESTMENTS IN CASH AND U.S. OBLIGATIONS OF CORPORATIONS IN SELECTED
INDUSTRY GROUPS, AS A PERCENTAGE OF THEIR TOTAL ASSETS, FOR COMPANIES
WITH ACCOUNTING PERIODS ENDED JULY, 1961–JUNE, 1962

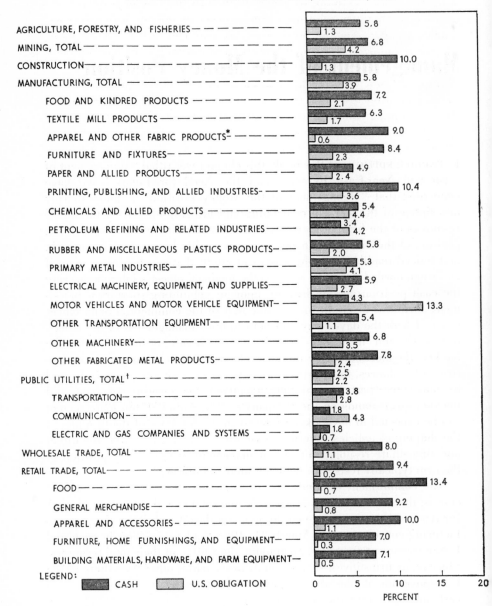

AGRICULTURE, FORESTRY, AND FISHERIES — 5.8 / 1.3
MINING, TOTAL — 6.8 / 4.2
CONSTRUCTION— 10.0 / 1.3
MANUFACTURING, TOTAL — 5.8 / 3.9
FOOD AND KINDRED PRODUCTS — 7.2 / 2.1
TEXTILE MILL PRODUCTS — 6.3 / 1.7
APPAREL AND OTHER FABRIC PRODUCTS* — 9.0 / 0.6
FURNITURE AND FIXTURES— 8.4 / 2.3
PAPER AND ALLIED PRODUCTS— 4.9 / 2.4
PRINTING, PUBLISHING, AND ALLIED INDUSTRIES— 10.4 / 3.6
CHEMICALS AND ALLIED PRODUCTS — 5.4 / 4.4
PETROLEUM REFINING AND RELATED INDUSTRIES— 3.4 / 4.2
RUBBER AND MISCELLANEOUS PLASTICS PRODUCTS— 5.8 / 2.0
PRIMARY METAL INDUSTRIES— 5.3 / 4.1
ELECTRICAL MACHINERY, EQUIPMENT, AND SUPPLIES— 5.9 / 2.7
MOTOR VEHICLES AND MOTOR VEHICLE EQUIPMENT— 4.3 / 13.3
OTHER TRANSPORTATION EQUIPMENT— 5.4 / 1.1
OTHER MACHINERY— 6.8 / 3.5
OTHER FABRICATED METAL PRODUCTS— 7.8 / 2.4
PUBLIC UTILITIES, TOTAL† — 2.5 / 2.2
TRANSPORTATION— 3.8 / 2.8
COMMUNICATION— 1.8 / 4.3
ELECTRIC AND GAS COMPANIES AND SYSTEMS — 1.8 / 0.7
WHOLESALE TRADE, TOTAL — 8.0 / 1.1
RETAIL TRADE, TOTAL— 9.4 / 0.6
FOOD — 13.4 / 0.7
GENERAL MERCHANDISE— 9.2 / 0.8
APPAREL AND ACCESSORIES— 10.0 / 1.1
FURNITURE, HOME FURNISHINGS, AND EQUIPMENT— 7.0 / 0.3
BUILDING MATERIALS, HARDWARE, AND FARM EQUIPMENT— 7.1 / 0.5

LEGEND: CASH   U.S. OBLIGATION

0   5   10   15   20
PERCENT

* Apparel and other finished products made from fabrics and similar materials.
† Total transportation, communication, electric, gas, and sanitary services.
SOURCE OF DATA: U.S. Treasury Department, Internal Revenue Service, *Statistics of Income, 1961–1962: Corporation Income Tax Returns* (Washington, D.C.: U.S. Government Printing Office, 1964), Table 2—"Balance Sheets and Income Statements . . . by Major Industrial Group."

(2½%). It should be emphasized, however, that this chart presents industry averages in which the large companies have heavy weight. The figures for individual companies can and do vary widely from the industry averages—more so generally than in the case of inventory and receivables. Many hard-pressed firms necessarily operate with a very lean money position. On the other hand, at year end, 1964, such a highly regarded company as General Motors Corporation had $2,343 million or 21% of its total resources in "money assets," and another, Standard Oil Company (New Jersey), had $1,326 million or 11%. Nor was a heavy money position restricted to the giants. American Metal Climax, Inc., a leading mining company, reported money assets of $119 million or 25% of total assets, while Dun & Bradstreet, Inc. reported money assets of almost $52 million or 42% of its total assets!

In the chapters just preceding we stressed the importance of managerial efforts toward efficient employment of the funds committed to inventory and receivables. Moreover, we emphasized the potential contribution of the financial officer to policies and practices that speed asset turnover and maximize return on investment. Against this background, the relatively heavy money positions of the companies cited above might well raise such questions in the student's mind as these:

1. Isn't it as important to make economical use of money assets as of inventory and receivables? Should not financial officers practice what they preach?
2. What are the functions served by the money assets? What are the key determinants of the corporate investment in cash and near-cash?
3. What are the key considerations in the effective management of the money position?

The answer to the first question above must be an immediate and resounding affirmative. Money assets *are* susceptible to management; money has a real cost, and failure to utilize money assets efficiently will dilute return on investment—"lazy cash" is just as debilitating to a healthy return as sluggish inventories. Moreover, the financial officer does have a unique opportunity with those assets peculiarly under his dominion to demonstrate skill and drive in achieving judiciously economical use of these resources. As in the case of other assets, the end objective is not simply to minimize the investment in money assets. It is rather to achieve a level of investment that balances effectively considerations of cost of resources and return on investment on the one hand, and on the other the functions served by the money assets and the closely related tangible and intangible benefits of a strong money position.

Let us turn first to an examination of the functions served by the money assets or, put differently, the various reasons why companies carry such assets. Then in the light of these we shall look at the key guidelines to effective management of the money position.

Before going further, we should be clear as to what we include under the classification *money assets*. Basically, we include those assets that management itself regards as a part of, or an adjunct to, the cash position. Along with currency on hand and bank deposits (both *demand deposits—checking accounts*—and *time deposits*), we include those investments which management would not hesitate to liquidate as cash is needed and which in fact are held in a form that makes conversion into cash easy and at little risk of loss of principal. Investments in subsidiaries or in the common stock of concerns believed to represent rewarding, long-term capital gain opportunities would *not* be considered as money assets but rather as long-term investments.

Most companies now show marketable securities as a separate current asset just below the cash account on the balance sheet. Investments in subsidiaries or in stocks for appreciation objectives are normally shown separately and among the noncurrent assets.

The Function of the Investment in Money Assets

Why do well-managed companies, such as General Motors, carry huge amounts in money assets, which earn directly at most a return very low in relation to the rate of return on assets overall? In most firms the money assets serve a variety of needs or purposes. The more important of these functions can be usefully classified and summarized as follows:

1. Meet operational requirements.
2. Provide reserves of liquidity against:

   a) Routine net outflows of cash.
   b) Scheduled major outlays.
   c) Exploitation of possible opportunities for advantageous longer-term investment.
   d) Unexpected drains of cash.

3. Meet bank relationship requirements.
4. Enhance investment image and other such intangibles.
5. Serve as a reservoir for net inflows of cash pending the availability of better uses for the funds.
6. Earn directly.

Operational Requirements for Cash

Most firms find it convenient to keep on hand small amounts of petty cash for making the minor disbursements most conveniently made in cash. Retail firms and service establishments normally keep some currency on hand to make change on cash sales. But the cash account consists primarily of funds on deposit at commercial banks.

For the vast majority of firms, which receive payment predominantly by check, a significant portion of the firm's nominal deposit balance usually is immobilized by *float*—the time required for the bank of deposit to get credit for funds due on checks deposited with it and drawn on other banks. For example, a New York manufacturer receives a check for $1,000 from a California customer, drawn on the customer's account at the Bank of America in San Francisco. The New York manufacturer deposits the check in his New York bank, the Irving Trust Company, on Monday, and it in turn deposits the check at the Federal Reserve Bank of New York for collection and *ultimate* credit to Irving Trust's own reserve account at the New York "Fed." The New York Fed will airmail the check to the Federal Reserve Bank of San Francisco, which will deduct the amount of the check from the deposit account with it of the Bank of America. The check is then turned over to the Bank of America, which in turn deducts the $1,000 from the account of the customer who wrote the check.

The Federal Reserve banks, which handle the mechanics of collection of most out-of-town checks, give depositing banks such as the Irving Trust unrestricted credit for the deposited funds only after an allowance of time for the check to be sent to San Francisco for collection. A set schedule of collection time is followed; normally the "Fed" makes funds available in one day for nearby cities and in two days for more distant points—a much shorter schedule than that used before air shipment of checks came into general use. Thus, the deposit of $1,000 would be credited to Irving Trust's account at the Fed on Wednesday. Naturally, Irving Trust in the above example and other banks of deposit will not let depositing customers draw on uncollected funds that the bank itself cannot yet use. Hence, a part of the New York manufacturer's bank balance is effectively immobilized by being tied up in the process of check collection.

We might add that banks may choose not to make funds available for withdrawal even when nominally collected by the Federal Reserve because the checks may turn out uncollectible—because of improper preparation or, more importantly, because the writer of the check has insufficient funds on deposit to cover the check. The process of getting a bad check to the bank on which it was written and back to the bank where it was deposited may take several days. If the depositor's account is a good one, and the bank can count on him to make good on bad checks he has deposited, the bank may allow him to draw on deposited funds as soon as the scheduled 1 or 2 days' collection time has elapsed. Otherwise, it may well insist that the deposit balances created by checks on other banks should not be drawn upon until enough time has elapsed so it can be confident the deposited checks are good.

The large concern typically has accounts with a number of banks, using some primarily as receiving or collection banks, others as major depositaries where major reserve accounts are held, and still others as paying banks—that is, for payroll check or other disbursement purposes.

In recent years American companies have made much progress in devising techniques to minimize the amounts necessarily tied up in operational requirements. We shall describe some of these later. Many firms appear to have cut operational requirements for cash near to an irreducible minimum—at least under existing banking practices.

Reserves of Liquidity

If the daily cash receipts almost exactly matched the daily outflow, the total cash balances would not have to be very large to meet the purely operational needs described above. Such even flows, however, seldom can be expected. Consequently, the cash account serves the added function of absorbing the normal ebbs and flows in funds through a business from day to day and week to week. For example, most department stores buy from suppliers whose terms call for payment around the 10th of each month, while their major receipts come in more evenly through the month. Unless they are to borrow for midmonth needs, routine cash balances must be sufficient to cover the heavy outflow around the tenth.

Liquid asset balances are also swelled by accumulation of funds in anticipation of major outlays for such items as planned expansion of inventories or receivables, dividend payments, income tax payments, debt retirement, and purchase of major items of equipment. Prudence may suggest that the funds for such purposes be raised well in advance of the scheduled payment date to ensure that payments can be met without strain. For example, if a major building program is to be financed through the sale of securities, the company may well prefer to sell the securities and have the funds in hand before firm contracts for the construction are let, even though the payments for the construction will not be required for many months or even years into the future.

Further, many managements like to keep "extra" cash on hand as an "opportunity fund" to permit rapid exploration of attractive opportunities for investment that may present themselves—exploitation of a research finding pointing up a new product possibility, an unexpected chance to buy another company, and the like.

An additional highly important function of the cash and near-cash accounts is that of providing a defensive or protective reserve against unexpected drains on liquidity. Interruptions to production and sales as a result of a strike, a transportation tie-up, or a fire in a major plant can rapidly deplete cash. A sudden decline in sales or an extremely bad year with heavy losses may create major cash drains at an unpropitious time for borrowing or for selling securities. Further, major adverse changes in the firm's competitive position may call for heavy expenditures at times when new capital is relatively unavailable. Moreover, the adverse developments setting up heavy cash needs may well be linked, so that the pressures on cash are multiple in nature. In uncertain times—and when is the future outlook entirely serene?—it is highly comforting to all those dependent on a business to know that it is "well heeled." To Benjamin Franklin is attributed the observation that in adversity a man can count on only three truly reliable friends: "a faithful dog, an old wife, and money in the bank."

Bank Relationship Requirements

Considerations of bank relationships have an important influence on the size of deposit balances maintained. While some banks are quite willing to provide their services on a cash-fee basis, most prefer to be compensated in the form of demand deposit balances. Deposits are vital to the banks; naturally, large and less active deposit accounts are especially valued by the bankers. And to the firm the favorable regard and active support of its major banks can be valuable in a variety of ways. First, the banks are in a position to supply a variety of tangible services, such as the provision of credit information, beyond the routine ones of servicing deposit accounts. Second, the bankers, by virtue of their experience and wide contacts, often can render important intangible services such as the discovery of attractive merger opportunities or advice as how best to raise needed capital.

Highly important to many firms is the fact that banks will be particularly interested in meeting the credit needs of those customers who have maintained desirable deposit accounts. In some recent years, many banks have had more loan opportunities than money to loan. When credit must be rationed, the value of the deposit account becomes a major, often critical, factor in bankers' decisions as to which of the would-be borrowers (all representing acceptable credit risks) are to be accommodated and on what terms.

Indeed, most banks insist that business borrowers maintain deposit accounts with them. Many require a compensating balance equal to a stated percentage of loan balances or credit lines. In recent years, for example, most banks have required finance companies, which typically borrow from many banks, to carry deposit balances equal to 20% of their loans or to 15% of their credit lines when they are not borrowing. If the firm normally would carry a sizable account with the bank anyhow, the compensating balance requirement is more nominal than burdensome. If not, the balance requirement effectively increases the amount of credit needed and the cost of the usable funds.

Intangible Values

Some business executives attach prestige values to a highly liquid position. Certainly, an illiquid position can adversely affect credit and other appraisals of the firm, and a strong money position may help build an investors' image of solidity. But once an obviously strong position is reached, it is doubtful that further liquidity adds material prestige value. One businessman in North Carolina some years ago took great pride in sending New York and other banking connections annual balance sheets which showed substantial cash and no current liabilities. The reaction was less one of respect than of amusement, of skepticism as to the validity of his accounting, and of sympathy for harried clerks who must have been frantically paying bills on New Year's Eve.

"The Money Just Rolled In"

It should be recognized that the cash balance is to an extent a residual figure—the net result at any time of a multiplicity of inflows and outflows. If unforeseen or unexpectedly heavy inflows swell the account, redundant cash may be carried for a long time before decisions as to its use are made and implemented. Consequently, the level of a firm's cash at any particular time may be as much the result of happenstance as of conscious decision and plan.

Earning a Direct Return

Since 1933 banks have been forbidden to pay interest on demand deposits (checking accounts). During the late 1930's and the war years, short-term interest rates were very low, and there was little incentive for corporate financial officers to invest the bank balances that were in excess of needs for operations and maintenance of banking relationships. However, as interest rates rose in the postwar period, financial officers of cash-heavy firms increasingly undertook to invest currently surplus cash in income-producing securities.

U.S. Treasury bills have been an especially popular vehicle of short-term investment. Weekly issues of Treasury bills of 3-month and 6-month maturities supply the market with a choice of maturities from 1 week to 26 weeks, and bills up to 1 year often are available. The Treasury bill market is extremely active and broad so that trading costs are small and marketability unquestioned in large or small amounts. During the period 1962–64 stated yields on 3-month Treasury bills ranged from a low of 2.65% to a high of 3.88%.[1]

U.S. government tax anticipation bills have been a popular means of reserving funds for tax payments. The Treasury issues these bills with a maturity a week later than the quarterly due dates for payment of income tax liabilities, but the bills have a "bonus feature" in that they can be used at par to pay tax bills.

Early in 1961 the First National City Bank of New York introduced a new money market instrument, the *negotiable certificate of deposit*. These "CD's" are receipts for deposits for a stated period of time and bear interest rates according to market demand at the date of issue. Maturities of less than a year are most common, but CD's are also issued for as much as 5 years. There is a market for these, so that they can be sold readily if the holder needs funds before the stated maturity. Sale of CD's by the banks permits the banks to compete for corporate cash that otherwise would have been invested in treasury bills or other investment media.

---

[1] No interest as such is paid on bills. They are sold at a discount, the amount of which determines the yield on the face amount. Since the actual investment is less than the face amount by the amount of the discount, the true return on the amount invested is somewhat higher than the stated yield figure.

Banks particularly desirous of more funds can attract them by quoting a relatively high rate.

The CD's quickly became a popular money market instrument. By mid-1965 New York banks alone had outstanding more than $6.4 billion negotiable CD's, while the national total was estimated to be over $15 billion. Smaller banks as well as large can compete for CD money, but the failure early in 1965 of two smaller banks, which had sold CD's to a number of corporate investors, emphasized that the CD's were only as safe as the issuing bank and that the small extra yield available from buying the CD's of lesser-known banks might not be worth much risk of loss. Consequently, the CD's of big, highly regarded banks are especially popular.

Since CD's represent a deposit, an investment in CD's is generally shown on the balance sheet as cash, rather than with marketable securities.

Commercial paper—the short-term notes sold by sales finance companies and by industrial concerns of strong credit standing—also has become popular as a short-term investment medium. Many investors have valued the chance to arrange directly with the finance company issuer the amount and maturity desired.

A variety of foreign investment media has been used by more venturesome firms. Canadian finance company paper has been popular. Non-Canadian investors, including The Ford Foundation, The Dow Chemical Company, Minnesota Mining and Manufacturing Company, and National Lead Company, were reported to have held $50 million of the notes of Atlantic Acceptance Corporation, Ltd., when it failed in the summer of 1965.[2]

While the chief financial officer normally has the responsibility for managing the money position, generally the board of directors and top management have established policy guidelines that shape and constrain the investment policies and practices. Commonly, these investment policies are directly concerned with the balance to be struck between the objectives of maximum investment safety or avoidance of principal loss and maximum marketability on the one hand and the maximization of current income from investment on the other. Case studies of the policies of a number of individual firms have suggested that initial investment guidelines emphasized investment safety and marketability to a high degree. For example, many firms gave their financial officers authority only to invest in U.S. government securities of maturities of less than one year.

Over the years many companies have liberalized their investment policies in order to boost income. Available income yields on money market investments reflect a variety of shifting supply and demand

---

[2] *The Financial Post*, Toronto, August 7, 1965, p. 22.

factors including inherent vulnerability to loss. As we indicated earlier, securities of the U.S. government, which to American firms involve no bad-debt risk, enjoy exceptional marketability. The income available on U.S. bills normally provides a base for comparison of other rates available in short-term money market instruments. Table 5–1 shows the spread in investment income, or investment yield, on a selected list of money market instruments on a mid-1965 date. It is obvious that the spread of rates does not provide a large premium for risk in these investments over the rate available in government bills. Should economic conditions turn sharply downward, the spread would doubtless widen. The highly publicized failures of the San Francisco National Bank early in 1965, a $40 million bank that had aggressively gathered funds through issuance of CD's, and the Atlantic Acceptance Corporation, the Canadian finance company, in the summer of 1965, have served to remind corporate investors of the risks inherent in "aggressive search for income" with short-term funds.

Policies regarding choice of appropriate maturities for portfolio investments also involve a reconciliation of the objectives of safety of principal and maximum income. Generally, during postwar years, securities of intermediate or long maturity have offered investors higher yields than have very short maturities. Thus, at the beginning of 1963, 3-month U.S. Treasury bills yielded 2.9%, 1-year U.S. securities, 3.02%, and 5-year U.S. bonds 3.50%. When patterns like these prevail and these interest rates do not change, an investor likely to need cash in a year or two could earn more on his investment in the interim if he were to buy, say, 5-year bonds and sell these bonds when the cash was needed. However, if interest rates should rise, the prices of outstanding securities will fall, and their sale will be possible only at a loss. The vulnerability to loss with rises in interest rates increases as the maturity of the investment instrument lengthens. If interest rates move up from 3% to 4%, a 3% bond will decline to a price level at which buyers are offered a 4% return on the purchase price. If the maturity is short, the price decline to be expected if interest rates rise will be small—to only $995.10 for a $1,000 6-month bond. Yet, as Chart 5–2 demonstrates, a $1,000 bond with a 5-year maturity would drop very much more, to $955.10, while a 30-year bond would fall to $826.20. Thus, exposure to price risk due to interest rate increases is minimized by use of short maturities.

Available evidence suggests a modest relaxation in recent years in many companies of earlier policies that restricted maturities to 1 year or less. For example, in its 1963 annual report, General Motors Corporation for the first time showed an investment in U.S. government securities maturing from 4 to 9 years later. Although GM's investment amounted to $130 million, it represented less than 5% of the total of cash and U.S. government securities with maturity of less than 1 year.

Despite the tendency toward greater emphasis on income, and conse-

SUMMARY DATA ON SHORT-TERM INVESTMENT MEDIA

Short-Term Investment Media	Summary Description	Approximate Amount Outstanding 6/30/65	Marketability	Yield on 9/29/65 6 Months Maturities
U.S. Treasury bills	Direct obligations of U.S. government. Weekly sales of 3- and 6-months maturities so that bills maturing each week up to 6 months are available in secondary market. Treasury also sells 1-year maturities on less frequent basis. Sold at a discount. Amount of discount determines investment return.	Almost $49 billion in hands of public	Extremely good secondary market	4.21
Federal agency issues	Securities issued by agencies of U.S. government, such as Federal Home Loan Bank notes. About one half of total outstandings of agency securities are of maturities less than 1 year. Enjoy an investment standing close to that of direct obligations of U.S.	$13.5 billion	Good secondary market	4.40
Negotiable bank certificates of deposit	Represent receipts for time deposits at commercial banks. Maturities and interest rates are negotiated directly by investors with issuing banks. Maturities most commonly under one year, but can be longer.	$15 billion	Good—for CD's of larger banks	4.49
Prime bankers' acceptances	Bills of exchange usually arising out of international trade transactions, which an "accepting" bank has effectively guaranteed. Bank's backing gives a strong quality standing. Maturities less than 1 year, commonly under 90 days.	$1.7 billion held outside banks	Good secondary market	4.50
Commercial paper—prime industrial names	Unsecured notes of leading industrial firms, normally sold through a dealer. Issued on a discount basis. Maturities generally in 30–120-day range.	$2 billion	No secondary market	4.38
Commercial paper—prime finance paper	Unsecured notes, generally placed directly by sales finance company issuers with investing firms. Usually sold on discount basis. Investor commonly can specify maturity desired in range of 5–270 days.	$7.4 billion	No secondary market	4.25
Short-term tax exempts	Temporary and preliminary notes of local housing authorities, which have quality rating like that of U.S. agencies, and tax and bond anticipation notes of states and municipalities, and other political subdivisions. Usually carry fixed interest rates and interest is exempt from federal income taxation.	Several billion	Fair secondary market	2.50 tax free

quently a growing acceptance of a slightly higher level of risk, it appears that most companies continue to regard the earning of income as a decidedly secondary objective in the overall management of the firm's money assets.

An Example: A.T.&T.'s Money Position

Many of the reasons for carrying large liquid reserves can be illustrated by reference to the American Telephone and Telegraph

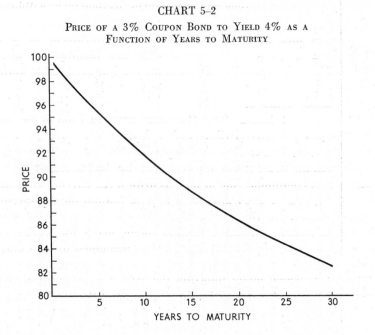

CHART 5-2

PRICE OF A 3% COUPON BOND TO YIELD 4% AS A
FUNCTION OF YEARS TO MATURITY

Company (A.T.&T.), a holding company for the operating telephone companies in the Bell System, which provide telephone service for most of the country. A.T.&T. carries a very large investment in cash and marketable securities. The total cash and marketable securities (primarily short-term U.S government securities) account of the System on December 31, 1964, amounted to $1,972 million or 6.4% of total assets. Since the telephone companies are regulated utilities, their earnings are limited to a *fair return* on total capital employed in their businesses. To the extent that capital is tied up in cash and low-return temporary investments, the return on stockholders' investment may be diluted. Hence, the cost of carrying a sizable investment in cash and low-return securities is significant.

In considering the reasons why A.T.&T. has chosen to carry such large liquid reserves, it should be understood that the parent company acts as a sort of central banker for the operating companies. Certain cash balances must be carried by the parent and the subsidiary companies with banks to compensate them for the activity in clearing checks and drafts and for other services. As bank balances build up above these levels, the excess is withdrawn and added to the central pool of funds with the parent company.

One of the functions of the central pool of funds is to provide funds needed for large payments anywhere in the System, most of which can be scheduled. They include quarterly dividend payments, interest payments on bonds, payments of income and excise taxes, income taxes withheld by law from employees' pay, and social security taxes, which are collected by the companies and turned over to the U.S government at regular intervals. Large payments to contractors for new facilities can also be scheduled. Thus, the central pool covers uneven but predictable outflows of cash for the system.

Certain needs come up which are hard to predict—such as funds needed for repair of damage from Hurricane Betsy in 1965 in the South, the most expensive natural disaster in telephone history. The central funds must be prepared to meet such unpredictable cash needs on call.

In addition, the Bell System in recent years has had to raise huge sums through almost continuous sale of new securities. An offering of common stock in the spring of 1964 amounted to $1.2 billion, the largest single offering in history. The proceeds of such sales are held in the central fund until needed. System expansion to meet public needs for service (Bell System expenditures for construction in 1964 amounted to $3.5 billion) should not be subject to interruption through any demoralization of the capital markets which might interrupt the sale of new securities. While A.T.&T. would doubtless find it hard to "stay out of the market" for new funds for long periods, it is deemed desirable to keep on hand enough funds so that new offerings could be deferred for at least several months if such action seemed urgently desirable.

Finally, as a very large enterprise aware of its great public responsibilities, the Bell System wants to keep in a sound, reasonably liquid condition against the general uncertainties of the times, and in striking a balance between too much in money assets and too little, doubtless would prefer to have been on the safe rather than the sorry side of a theoretically perfect balance.

Approaches to More Effective Management of the Money Position

As we have indicated earlier, the money assets of a great many firms are large enough to warrant, indeed demand, vigorous and thoughtful management. This involves much more than keeping excess cash fully invested. Even if surplus funds are kept invested continuously, the net after-tax return from even the less conservative money market instruments is modest—probably less than 2¼%. Almost certainly the costs of capital to the firm are well above this figure, and the carrying of unnecessarily large money assets will dilute overall rate of return.

We suggest five major approaches to effective management of the money position, which have proved helpful in a number of firms:

1. Exploitation of techniques of money mobilization to reduce operating requirements for cash.
2. Major efforts to increase the precision and reliability of cash flow forecasting.
3. Maximum effort to define and quantify the liquidity reserve needs of the firm.
4. The development of explicit alternative sources of liquidity.
5. Aggressive search for more productive uses for surplus money assets.

Money Mobilization

Many firms have found that the operating needs for cash can be cut sharply through various devices of *money mobilization*. These aim at the reduction of funds tied up in the process of receiving and collecting checks and in the routines of transfer of bank balances to the points where they are most useful. In the absence of special effort, cash equal to several days' sales is likely to be tied up in the process of receiving check payments from far-flung customers and converting them into collected, and hence usable, bank balances.

With the aid of their banks, a number of firms have developed comprehensive programs to cut days off this process and free up the funds in the unnecessarily long process. For example, company X formerly asked its customers all over the country to mail their payments to the company headquarters in New York. The customers regarded their obligations to company X as settled when they put checks in the mail. Yet several days would normally elapse while the check was in the mail to New York, while company X's routines of receiving and accounting for the payment and getting the checks to its New York bank were accomplished, and while the New York bank converted the check into collected funds available for use by company X. In essence, an amount equal to several days' sales was tied up in the "collection pipeline."

Under a program designed to reduce this pipeline, company X opened accounts with a number of regional banks around the country, for instance, Los Angeles. Customers in southern California were asked to remit to company X at a post office lockbox in Los Angeles. Actually, company X's Los Angeles bank maintained the lockbox. The bank was authorized to open the incoming mail, deposit all checks for collection, and send a record of receipts airmail to company X in New York. Since most of the checks were drawn on Los Angeles or area banks, the collection period was very short, with same-day credit on many checks. Arrangements were made to transfer to company X's main depository bank in New York by wire[3] all collected balances beyond a modest amount designed to compensate the regional collecting bank for its services.

A variety of other programs of money mobilization have proved helpful in reducing operational requirements for cash. These are not necessarily elaborate. In the case of smaller firms with predominantly local sales, simple programs such as organized effort to cut the time utilized in office routines of processing incoming checks and getting them into the bank can be rewarding in freeing up otherwise unproductive cash.

The Contribution of Improved Cash Flow Forecasting

As we noted earlier, an important reason for carrying cash balances beyond operating and bank relationship needs was to provide liquidity reserves to take care of intramonth or seasonal periods of net cash outflow. Clearly, the degree of accuracy and reliability with which the amount and timing of these periodic net cash outflows can be predicted will determine the degree of precision of planning how best to meet outflows. In recent decades most well-run companies have instituted programs of cash flow forecasting. Building on study of past patterns of receipts and expenditures and learning from experience, many companies have achieved a degree of forecasting skill and precision once believed impossible.

The improved forecasting has led to improved money management in a variety of ways. First, money position managers are able to keep temporarily surplus funds more fully invested. Where large amounts are involved, the knowledge that it is safe to delay conversion of an investment into cash by a day or two or over a weekend can add materially to income. Second, once future needs are clearly outlined, alternative methods of meeting the outflows can be explored. Some companies, for example, have arranged with their major suppliers to set due dates on bills to coincide with the buying firm's forecasted periods of peak receipts. Other firms have changed their own collection terms in an effort to iron out the differences between patterns of inflow and outflow.

In other cases improved forecasting has shown that normal cash inflows will be adequate to cover major future outlays earlier covered by funding with a special reserve. Thus, many firms have gained sufficient confidence in their forecasting and money management techniques to abandon long-in-advance specific funding of major tax payments.

Of course, efforts to forecast cash needs involve some expense.

---

[3] A private telegraph network between more than 200 larger banks permits telegraphic or "wire transfers" of funds between banks. Thus, a San Francisco investor could direct his San Francisco bank to transfer a given amount of funds to the credit of his broker's account at a New York bank and have the whole transaction carried out in a matter of minutes.

However, we are confident that there is still room for substantial progress in cash forecasting in a great many companies, particularly smaller ones, which will permit closer management of money assets and more than cover the expense involved.

Pinning Down Needs for Protective Liquidity

A third approach to more effective utilization of money assets involves effort to define as crisply as possible and to quantify the needs for liquidity reserves against various kinds of unplanned developments that might well require substantial amounts of cash. Certainly, almost every firm faces a great number of uncertainties and contingencies that might sponge up cash. Yet, to gain absolute protection against cash stringencies from the worst combination of the worst possibilities would require unthinkably large hoards of money assets. Some sort of balance or compromise must be struck between the degree of protection afforded and the cost of holding reserves of protective liquidity. Holding money assets against possible needs has a real and, within limits, calculable cost. It is highly desirable to try to evaluate the protective benefits gained for these costs.

To try to quantify precisely the need for protection against uncertain developments is in some respects to seek "to unscrew the unscrutable." Yet many firms have had some success in gauging the need for protective liquidity. These efforts usually take the form of:

1. Explicit identification of the kinds of contingencies against which protection is desirable—a long strike, a recession, need to reequip major production units, etc.
2. Assessment of the probabilities or odds that each of these will develop within a given period in the future, such as 5 years.
3. Assessment of the probabilities that the developments creating cash drains will occur at the same time.
4. Assessment of the likely amount of the cash drain that will result if each of the contingencies develops. This requires pencil pushing with appropriate assumptions—in a number of cases careful projections have resulted in estimates of the amounts of net drain quite different from management's general impressions.

Assessing Alternative Methods of Providing Protective Liquidity

Once the efforts to identify and measure the potential unscheduled demands for cash have been made, alternative methods of meeting these needs should be canvassed and evaluated. A great many U.S. firms—a very high percentage of these with heavy money positions—have unused borrowing capacity. Many managements regard this ability to borrow as a part of the overall money position of the firm and expect to draw on it to meet unscheduled needs if and when they develop. A strong argument can be made in favor of this approach over that of carrying sizable money assets as precautionary reserves. First and foremost, it can well be a more economical method of dealing with the possible needs, since funds are drawn down from lenders only as and when the possible needs actually develop. It may be years before a major unexpected need does develop. In the meantime, reliance on credit makes it possible to avoid holding low-yielding money assets as a protective reserve of liquidity. Moreover, if the unexpected need for cash proves short-lived, the loans can be repaid and the reserves of borrowing capacity restored.

Those managements that support policies of carrying large precautionary balances of money assets commonly stress the risk that funds will not be available from lenders when needed or else will be available only on unfavorable terms. Banks may be "loaned up" and unable to accommodate the firm's needs when they develop. Or the circumstances that created the need—such as a period of price cutting leading to heavy volume and very low profits or even losses—may damage the credit standing of the firm and make banks hesitant to meet its needs for credit when the needs are more intense. Negotiation of loans with insurance companies or the sale of bonds may be too slow a process to meet rapidly developing needs. Moreover, the need for funds might come at a time unpropitious for the sale of common stock. Altogether, they argue, carrying liquid reserves against possible needs is a useful form of insurance against having to make rushed and possibly unsatisfactory arrangements at unpropitious times. Moreover, in this view, invested money reserves do add something to income so that the "net cost of insurance" against embarrassing cash stringencies or having to make a bad deal is quite tolerable.

Many firms relying on borrowing power as a source of precautionary liquidity do take steps to help assure that loan funds will be available to them when and if needed. These may simply take the form of efforts to cultivate close relationships with a number of strong banks, perhaps by carrying larger deposit balances than otherwise necessary or desirable. In such cases the firm may test its credit standing by arranging lines of credit at several banks. As we shall explain in some detail later, the line of credit does not represent a firm commitment to lend on the part of the bank. However, for a fee of one quarter or one half of 1% of the unused credit, it may well be possible to arrange a definite standby loan commitment with bank or other lenders—if this is judged necessary.

On the whole, it seems to us that the management carrying unused reserves of liquid assets for long periods is properly suspect of striking an unnecessarily comfortable, conservative, and costly balance between risk avoidance and effective utilization of resources.

Aggressive Search for More Productive Uses of Money Assets

Now let us focus on the fifth of the suggested approaches to more effective use of money assets—the desirability of aggressive search for more productive uses for surplus money assets. In recent years many firms have experienced such a heavy inflow of cash from operations that unplanned accumulations of money assets have resulted. Moreover, the condition has been general enough so that in many industries and areas there appears to be more money available for investment than attractive investment outlets. Thus, in recent years many oil companies have been hard put to find promising longer-term investment outlets for their abundant liquid resources.

In these circumstances many firms have found that it took much time and effort to turn up attractive opportunities and to complete the necessary negotiations and arrangements for the investment. Rather than waiting until the funds come in to begin their search for outlets and thus facing a long delay in getting surplus funds into high-return use, many firms have organized for a continuous search for promising acquisitions, mergers, or other long-term uses for funds outside the usual ones generated internally.

Facing up to the fact that continued, vigorous, and organized search is likely to prove necessary if attractive outlets for available funds are to be kept in good supply will help many firms avoid the accumulation of a large pool of funds temporarily invested at low return pending more lucrative permanent investment.

Chapter 6

Fixed Assets and the Need for Funds

IN PRECEDING chapters, we have discussed the necessary commitment of funds in cash, inventories, and trade credit, pointing out the continuing nature of the basic investment of funds in these categories, despite the movement of individual items through the process of production and sale. In this chapter, we turn to the investment of funds in assets where the permanent nature of the underlying need for funds is paralleled by the more enduring characteristics of the assets themselves.

The most important group of these assets is the *fixed assets*, also termed *capital assets*. To quote Kohler:

Included in the fixed-asset family are land, from which the flow of services is seemingly permanent, buildings, building equipment, fixtures, machinery, tools (large and small), furniture, office devices, patterns, drawings, dies. . . . The characteristic fixed asset has a limited life (land is the one important exception), and its cost, less salvage, is distributed over the periods it benefits by means of provisions for depreciation.[1]

Many businesses also have investments of consequence in *intangible assets,* which represent investments having no physical existence in themselves, but rather rights to enjoy some privilege. Examples are patents and investments in the securities of other companies. If the value of the intangible assets is expected to have a limited life, their cost usually is distributed by charges similar to depreciation, known as *amortization.*

Importance of the Investment in Fixed Assets

The technology of the industry in which a company operates largely determines the quantity of funds it must commit to fixed assets. While other factors influence the investment of individual firms in fixed assets, firms in the same industry generally tend to have a similar portion of their total assets in fixed assets. Thus, no electric utility company can avoid a

---

[1] Eric L. Kohler. *A Dictionary for Accountants* (3rd ed.; Englewood Cliffs, N.J.: Prentice-Hall, Inc., 1963), pp. 215–16.

CHART 6-1

INVESTMENT IN NET CAPITAL ASSETS OF CORPORATIONS IN SELECTED INDUSTRY GROUPS, AS A PERCENTAGE OF THEIR TOTAL ASSETS, FOR COMPANIES WITH ACCOUNTING PERIODS ENDED JULY, 1961–JUNE, 1962

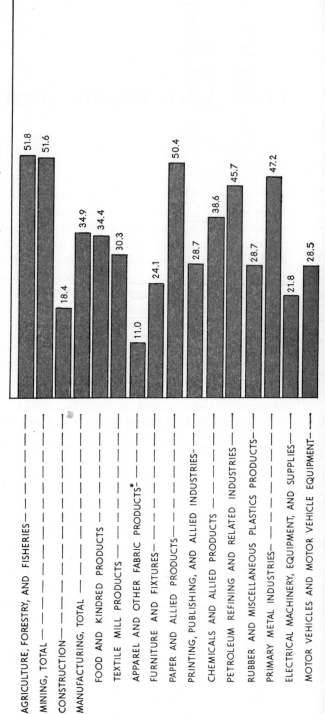

AGRICULTURE, FORESTRY, AND FISHERIES— — — — — —   51.8

MINING, TOTAL— — — — — — — — — — —   51.6

CONSTRUCTION— — — — — — — — —   18.4

MANUFACTURING, TOTAL — — — — — —   34.9

FOOD AND KINDRED PRODUCTS— — — — —   34.4

TEXTILE MILL PRODUCTS— — — — — —   30.3

APPAREL AND OTHER FABRIC PRODUCTS*— — —   11.0

FURNITURE AND FIXTURES— — — — — —   24.1

PAPER AND ALLIED PRODUCTS— — — — —   50.4

PRINTING, PUBLISHING, AND ALLIED INDUSTRIES—   28.7

CHEMICALS AND ALLIED PRODUCTS — — — —   38.6

PETROLEUM REFINING AND RELATED INDUSTRIES—   45.7

RUBBER AND MISCELLANEOUS PLASTICS PRODUCTS—   28.7

PRIMARY METAL INDUSTRIES— — — — — —   47.2

ELECTRICAL MACHINERY, EQUIPMENT, AND SUPPLIES—   21.8

MOTOR VEHICLES AND MOTOR VEHICLE EQUIPMENT—   28.5

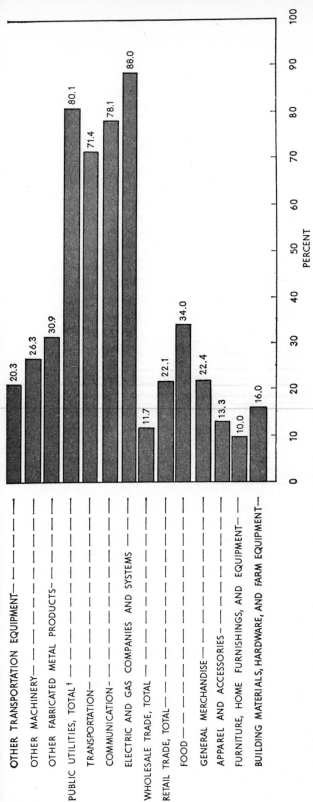

OTHER TRANSPORTATION EQUIPMENT— — — — | 20.3

OTHER MACHINERY— — — — — — — | 26.3

OTHER FABRICATED METAL PRODUCTS— — — | 30.9

PUBLIC UTILITIES, TOTAL† — — — — — | 80.1

TRANSPORTATION— — — — — — — | 71.4

COMMUNICATION— — — — — — — | 78.1

ELECTRIC AND GAS COMPANIES AND SYSTEMS — — | 88.0

WHOLESALE TRADE, TOTAL — — | — — — | 11.7

RETAIL TRADE, TOTAL— — — | — — — | 22.1

FOOD — — — — — — — | 34.0

GENERAL MERCHANDISE— — | — — — | 22.4

APPAREL AND ACCESSORIES — — — — — | 13.3

FURNITURE, HOME FURNISHINGS, AND EQUIPMENT— — | 10.0

BUILDING MATERIALS, HARDWARE, AND FARM EQUIPMENT— | 16.0

PERCENT

0   10   20   30   40   50   60   70   80   90   100

* Apparel and other finished products made from fabrics and similar materials.
† Total transportation, communication, electric, gas, and sanitary services.
Source of Data: U.S. Treasury Department, Internal Revenue Service, *Statistics of Income, 1961–1962: Corporation Income Tax Returns* (Washington, D.C.: U.S. Government Printing Office, 1964),
Table 2—"Balance Sheets and Income Statements . . . by Major Industrial Groups."

heavy investment in generating and/or distributive facilities. Since these utilities have little need for inventories and only moderate receivables, it is not surprising to note from Chart 6–1 that fixed assets represent over four fifths of their total assets.

In the aggregate, U.S. manufacturers' investment in fixed assets was $127.3 billion, or 38.6%, of their total resources on March 31, 1965. Chart 6–1, which is based on earlier but more detailed data, shows the relative importance of fixed assets to manufacturers in various industry groups. As might be expected, primary metal manufacturers, such as the steelmakers, have a relatively high commitment in plant facilities. In contrast, note the low investment in fixed assets of apparel manufacturers. The technology of the garment industry is very simple compared to that of steelmaking. Much of the needed machinery, such as sewing machines, is relatively simple and inexpensive and is available on rental. Specialized buildings are not required, and the "loft space" available for rent in New York and other garment centers meets the needs of many manufacturers.

The reference to the garment industry has indicated another significant determinant of the required investment in fixed assets—the extent to which needed plant or equipment is available on reasonably satisfactory rental terms. Rental of office space is especially common, even among the largest and most affluent concerns. Of 129 new office buildings put into place in Manhattan (New York City) during the fifties, only 28 were owner-occupied. Many retailers, and some manufacturers whose space needs are not distinctive, are able to meet their major building needs through rental. Certain leading manufacturers of office and plant equipment, notably International Business Machines Corporation and Xerox Corporation, have made their products available on rental terms. In recent years an increasing variety of productive equipment—from refrigerator trucks to automatic machine tools—has become widely available on a rental basis, both from equipment manufacturers and from specialized leasing firms. Long-term leasing of industrial and commercial plant also has come to represent a financial alternative to ownership and debt financing. Since most long-term leases deserve to be evaluated as a form of long-term financing, we shall discuss such leasing in the long-term financing section of this book.

Another determinant of fixed asset investment of particular importance to firms with limited finances is the degree to which the need for facilities, particularly highly specialized and expensive equipment, can be avoided through subcontracting of work or outside purchase of parts and components requiring special equipment. For example, if a machinery builder can arrange to have the electroplating of certain parts performed by an outside specialist in this work, he may be able to avoid otherwise necessary ownership of expensive and little-used plating equipment. Or the small wheat farmer may find it wiser to have his wheat harvested by custom combiners than to own a little-used combine. One of the less widely recognized strengths of American industry lies in the extent to which finished product manufacturers can rely on specialized manufacturers for particular parts or components. By virtue of their large volume as suppliers of their specialty items to many end-item manufacturers, these specialty manufacturers can make economic use of highly specialized and expensive equipment that would be burdensome if production of these items were widely diffused.

In some fields used equipment or old plant, available at prices that are far below those of new facilities, may be satisfactory. This is particularly likely to be true in areas where the rate of technological change in production methods has been moderate or slow. Their use can materially reduce the required investment in fixed assets, and firms with limited financial resources should carefully investigate the possibilities of buying used facilities before committing themselves to heavier investment in new fixed assets.

Distinctive Aspects of the Investment in Fixed Assets

In earlier chapters we have stressed the central importance in asset management of concern for overall return on investment, and there should be no need to belabor the point that these same considerations apply with equal force in fixed asset management. Indeed, certain distinctive aspects of investment in fixed assets make it especially important that new fixed assets be acquired only after searching consideration of the impact on investment return. First, proposed additions to fixed assets are commonly in sizable increments which can be considered deliberately and consciously as discrete proposals. Given reasonable foresight, it is usually possible to plan new acquisitions sufficiently far ahead that analysis of their desirability can be deliberate and appropriately organized.

Second, the purchase of plant and equipment (or their long-term lease) represents a financial commitment that will be binding over a period of years. If increases in inventory, receivables, or liquid reserves prove unwise, or if funds stringencies make it necessary, management often can act to cut back these investments and free the funds involved in a matter of weeks or months. But the typical fixed asset investment can be recovered only through operations over a period of years. Further, uncertainty of return, as well as time, is very much involved. For example, demand for the products to be made with a new machine may not develop as expected, so that operations do not return the investment in the form of added profits and coverage of depreciation. Or new methods of production may make the machine expected to have an economic life of 10 years obsolete in 3.

Third, the loss in forced sale of excess or obsolete equipment and facilities typically is great. For example, the automobile manufacturer faced with unsold stocks of an unsuccessful model can usually find economy-minded buyers for the unsold cars coming forward to buy the cars at reductions of 10% or 20%. Buyers for specialized productive equipment and facilities designed especially for manufacturer of this model are likely to be found only at prices that are a small fraction of their book value—if at all.

In brief, investments in plant and equipment are inherently illiquid, that is, retrievable only over years and then only under conditions of uncertainty. Consequently, it is important that purchases of new plant or important items of equipment be made only after particularly careful consideration of the prospects of recovery of the investment from operations, with a profit return that is adequate in the light of the risks, the cost of the funds, and the effect on the financial position of the firm of tying up substantial amounts of funds for long periods.

Analyzing the Attractiveness of Opportunities to Invest in New Fixed Assets

In recent decades there has been a developing recognition of the importance of the points noted above and of the desirability of searching examination of proposals for new asset investment to ensure that they justify the use of capital and that the selection among available opportunities is a keen and discerning one. Many large firms have organized special departments for this work and are engaged in a restless search not only for new opportunities to invest but for better methods of assessing opportunities. In academic circles, interest in what has come to be known as "capital budgeting" has also flourished. The literature on the subject is growing in quantity, in complexity, and, overall, in quality.

To go into the techniques of evaluation of opportunities for fixed asset expansion in any detail at this point in our book would represent a diversion from the primary emphasis of these early chapters on the impact of varying asset management policies on the need for funds. Hence, we shall be content here to briefly identify some of the key features of the newer approaches to investment opportunity analysis. Later chapters will develop this important subject.

Most evaluations of the likely consequences of new asset investment actions, such as the purchase of a large, new machine, seek to quantify the net inflow of funds created by purchase of the asset (stemming from cost savings, higher profits due to higher sales made possible by added capacity, etc.). They then compare the anticipated inflows with the outflow of funds necessary to purchase and install the asset. Assessment of the probable effect on net inflows of introduction of the new machine requires judgments regarding a number of factors well into the future.

Particularly basic are estimates of total demand for the products made with the machine and of the success of the firm in competing for a share of the total demand. Other important questions include: Will the new machine work satisfactorily? Will the projected economies actually be achieved? Will new and better machines be available shortly?

A long-established method of assessing the attractiveness of the inflows in relation to the investment outlay is the payback method, in which estimated annual net inflows stemming from the investment are divided into the investment outflow figure. The result represents the number of years required, on the basis of the estimate used, for the firm to recover its investment. Projects offering quick recovery presumably are preferred over those requiring a longer period.

In many leading firms the payback method has given way to methods promising more accurate measure of the investment return from the proposed projects. These include "the average-return-on-investment method" and related approaches, which attempt to estimate the time span over which the savings or added revenues stemming from the investment will continue—its economic life.

Particularly important in recent years have been the further efforts to incorporate into the methods of assessing the desirability of investment opportunities a means of weighing appropriately differences in the timing of inflows and/or in the investment outflows. As an illustration of this problem posed by timing differences, consider two proposals each calling for a total investment of $10,000. Project A requires outlay of the full $10,000 now. Project B calls for outlay of $5,000 now and $5,000 more in 2 years. Each will have a total life of 8 years. The net inflows from the two projects are as follows:

Year	Project A	Project B
1	$ 2,000	$ 500
2	2,000	500
3	2,000	1,000
4	2,000	1,500
5	2,000	2,000
6	2,000	3,000
7	2,000	4,000
8	2,000	5,000
	$16,000	$17,000

It is clear that the timing of the investment outlays and the timing of the projected inflows differ and that total inflows differ. Since these funds can presumably be put to work elsewhere, the larger inflows in earlier years are an attractive feature of project A, but are they enough to compensate for the deferred outlay and greater total inflows of project B? In the light of the costs of funds to the firm and its other opportunities to put funds to work, which of the two projects offers the higher return? Is either attractive?

Techniques of *time adjustment, discounted cash flow* analysis, and *present-value* analysis, all of which are designed to cope with time-span variations like those in the illustration above, are finding increased use in business. They are explained in some detail in Chapter 20. Other new and promising developments in investment opportunity analysis are discussed in the growing specialized literature of the field. Chapters 21 and 22 will introduce these topics, also.

Major Funds Flows Related to Fixed Assets

From the cash flow viewpoint, the costs of fixed assets take on importance as the funds are actually expended by the firm. A major construction project may well require substantial payments during the period of construction, perhaps as long as several years before any productive activity can be commenced. One of the authors has visited a new rubber plantation on the Amazon River where large expenditures for land clearance, dwellings for workers, and nursery plants were not expected to become productive for at least 10 years. Although this type of project is exceptionally long, the lead time for an ordinary factory building is often 2 years.

On the other hand, fixed assets may be acquired under a time payment contract where (usually after some initial expenditure for a *down payment*) the actual funds are expended during the use of assets. Again, if the use of fixed assets may be acquired by lease, there is no transfer of ownership, and the actual flows of funds take place during the period of use as the rent is paid. The first step in looking at a fixed asset project from a funds flow point of view is, therefore, to ask, "When must payments be made?"

Another flow of funds must also be considered. It is the net effect of inflows and outflows which occurs because the fixed assets have been acquired and put into operation, and can be referred to as *funds provided by operations*. In collecting information to permit the determination of this quantity, the analyst must be careful to choose only those flows of funds whose magnitudes change because the particular capital investment project has been undertaken. Such a search is sometimes easy, as when the project does not displace or compete with some existing operation. Sometimes, the determination is difficult. To illustrate the major cash flows in fixed asset investment, we shall now look at a simple project, a new motel to be added to an existing chain of motels.

Our motel will cost $200,000 and we estimate its useful life at 10 years.[2] In order to determine the funds that will be provided by operation

---

[2] For simplicity we assume that there will be no salvage value at the end of the period.

of the motel, we estimate that all rentals—$40,000 annually—will be collected and that we shall incur and pay for the expenses listed below:

Rental income...		$40,000
Expenses:		
Heat, lights, etc..	$10,500	
Repairs and maintenance.................................	500	
Income and real estate taxes, and all other expenses............	5,000	
Outflow for expenses................................		16,000
Funds provided by operations...............................		$24,000

For the time being, we prefer not to explore the question of how income taxes are determined; the topic gets considerable attention later on. The table above shows that for the year in question, the net inflow of funds from operations is $24,000. How should this quantity be considered by management? Does it constitute funds that can be used for any corporate purpose? Must a portion of it be regarded as tied to the particular investment in some way?

Any business operation that produces a net gain in funds does so throughout a period of time and not in a single sum at the end of the period. Thus, in our example the gain of $24,000 will be simply the cumulative result of the operations of the period. In the absence of special action to that end, the funds will not be segregated as they are received, and there will be no special box or bank account where they can be found at the end of the year. All we can say with assurance is that management will have at its disposal $24,000 more in funds than if the motel had not been in operation. Surely, the funds will be in liquid form immediately after receipt; and they may well be kept in such form, but not certainly. It all depends on how management decides to use the funds, and the possibilities cover all types of transactions.

Having looked at 1 year of operations, let us try to foresee what problems management will face at the end of the 10-year life of the motel. If one of the vital concerns of management is that of *preserving* the earning power of the investment in this motel, much more must be done than simply to try to regain the original investment of $200,000. Let us suppose that in looking forward to the 10th year of the life of this project, management estimates that the earning power of the motel can be extended for a new period of time by the expenditure of $100,000 for extensive alterations. It is then management's task to see to it that the needed funds are available in liquid form, either from accumulated funds provided by operations over the first 10 years, or from available credit, or otherwise. This same task, in different magnitude, would confront management if it found that rising prices made an investment of $275,000 necessary and desirable. It cannot be overemphasized that recovery of the cost of the original investment does not assure the availability or adequacy of funds to provide for its continuation or replacement.

The Impact of Depreciation Accounting on Cash Outflows for Income Taxes

As we shall emphasize, charges to income for depreciation do not in themselves affect the total inflow of cash from operations. However, the allowance of depreciation expense as a deduction from income subject to taxation does have an important effect on the outflows of cash necessary to satisfy tax requirements. For this reason, it is desirable that we devote attention to the accounting for depreciation for tax purposes. As an accountant views the $200,000 investment in the motel at the beginning of the 10-year period, he finds he must record an outflow of funds of that amount. Among the principal concerns of accounting is the determination of income, year by year (or more generally period by period), and for this purpose the expenditure of $200,000 is obviously not an expense to be charged wholly to the first year of the 10. The accountant, therefore, *capitalizes* the expenditure by "booking" $200,000 as fixed assets. There then ensues the procedure referred to by Kohler: "The characteristic fixed asset has a limited life . . . and its cost, less salvage, is distributed over the periods it benefits by means of provisions for depreciation."

A widely used method (known as the *straight-line method*) of providing for the depreciation of the $200,000 motel in 10 years would be to take one tenth of its cost as an expense each year, deducting $20,000 from the gross income (along with the other costs), and reducing the capitalized value of the fixed asset accordingly. If this were done, the income statement of our sample year of operations would become:

Rental income	$40,000
Expenditure of funds	16,000
Funds provided by operations	$24,000
Depreciation	20,000
Net Profit	$ 4,000

While this income statement is decidedly more useful to those who are studying the profitability of the firm, especially from year to year, it must be emphasized that the charging of depreciation, itself, does nothing that alters by as much as 1 cent the amount of funds provided by operations. All that has happened (apart from the income tax effect discussed below) is that the $24,000 has been divided into two accounts, one called Depreciation and the other Net Profit.

Business income taxes in the United States are levied on net profits, so that all allowable expenses are deductible from gross revenues before the "net income subject to tax" is determined. Treasury regulations govern the admissibility of items as deductible expenses. Depreciation is one of the acceptable charges.

The consequence of any allowable expense is a reduction of the tax liability. Taking the annual depreciation of the motel as $20,000 and the income tax rate as 48%, there will be a reduction in net profits of $20,000 and therefore a decline in the tax liability of (0.48) ($20,000) = $9,600. In other words, the depreciation expense permits retaining $9,600 more net funds after taxes than would otherwise be possible. This is referred to as the *tax shield*, which is always the full amount of the deductible item multiplied by the applicable tax rate. How much this shield can be depends, of course, on the amount of depreciation permitted by the tax authorities to be used for tax purposes.

As we have explained, the amount of the annual expense item for depreciation derives from four key elements:

1. The cost of the item—$200,000 in our illustration.
2. The estimate of its economic life—10 years in our illustration.
3. Its salvage value once the economic life is over—estimated at zero in our illustration.
4. The pattern by which the total amount to be depreciated is spread over the years of economic life. So far, in our motel case, we have employed the straight-line method, that is, spread the $200,000 to be depreciated equally over the 10 years of estimated economic life.

Focusing now on the estimate of economic life, it is clear that the use by business of short life estimates will result in larger expense charges over a shorter period of years, and hence in lower income tax payments in these years, than if depreciation charges were spread over a longer period. It is not surprising that federal tax authorities have long been interested in seeing that the estimates of useful life used by taxpaying firms are not unreasonably short. In 1962 the Internal Revenue Service published a list of "guideline lives" for large classes of assets. For example, the guideline life of hotel buildings was put at 40 years, office equipment and fixtures at 10 years, automobiles at 3 years, and metalworking machinery at 12 years. The new guidelines were intended to conform to actual industry replacement experience; generally, they were significantly shorter than the earlier lives specified for a great number of individual items.

Basically, taxpayers may use these rates until and unless a test of their own replacement experience (provided for in the regulations but not to be applied until 1966) shows the guideline lives to be excessively short. Taxpayers are not required to use these life estimates, but they may well be called upon to justify their use of shorter ones. Treasury interest in the matter, however, extends only to the depreciation claimed in tax returns as a business expense deductible before determination of taxable income. Some thoroughly reputable companies go so far as to keep two sets of property records and charge depreciation for their own accounting purposes differently from the charge for purposes of accounting for income tax.[3]

---

[3] Thus, the United States Rubber Company comments in a note to the financial statements presented in its 1964 annual report:

"For financial accounting purposes, depreciation of property, plant and equipment is

Now let us turn to the matter of how the total amount to be depreciated is spread among the years of economic life and look at alternative approaches to the straight-line method. Under liberalized tax laws enacted in 1954 regarding depreciation, two other major methods of allocating depreciation to annual periods were authorized. In effect, these newly authorized methods permit larger amounts of the total depreciation to be charged in the early years of useful life of newly acquired assets. Since the total charged as depreciation under any method cannot exceed the cost of the item to its owner,[4] the new methods do not alter the total depreciation that can be charged off as a business expense, nor is the total life of the asset reduced. Thus, given constant tax rates, the ultimate total of tax liabilities is not reduced by shifts in the timing of depreciation deductions. By advancing the time when much of the depreciation can be taken as an expense, however, the new methods do permit the postponement of part of the tax liability and give the firm the use for a time of the funds that otherwise would have been paid in taxes at an earlier date.

The two alternative methods are the *declining balance* and the *sum-of-the-years'-digits methods*. Under the declining balance method a uniform rate, which may be as much as twice the straight-line rate, is applied to the undepreciated asset balance. In the case of an investment for a 10-year period, the annual rate would be twice the straight-line rate of 10%, that is, 20%; but the charge for each year would be determined from the application of the 20% rate to the declining book value of the asset. At any time during the life of the asset, a shift may be made to the straight-line method for the undepreciated balance. As an example, we give the computation of the depreciation charges for a $200,000 asset as a part of Table 6–1.

The years'-digits method is better explained than defined. The amount that can be taken as depreciation in each year is established by use of a

provided on a straight line basis at rates presently considered adequate to amortize the total cost over the life of the assets.

"For Federal income tax purposes, the Company uses the accelerated depreciation method and the liberalized depreciation 'Guideline' rates. The resultant reduction in current taxes payable, $5,311,000 in 1964 and $8,164,000 for years prior thereto, is included in Deferred Federal and Foreign Taxes on the balance sheet.

"The Investment Credit for 1964 made available under the Revenue Act of 1962, as amended in 1964, representing 7 per cent or less of the cost of certain machinery and equipment purchased for domestic operations, amounted to $1,895,000. This credit and the amortization of 1962 and 1963 credits of $230,000 for a total of $2,125,000 were applied as a reduction of our 1964 provision for Federal income taxes. . . ."

[4] We should take note, however, of the "investment credit" authorized by the Revenue Act of 1962 as later amended. Under the provisions authorizing the investment credit, 7% of the initial outlay for qualifying fixed assets (not buildings) may be deducted from the tax obligations of the firm. By amendment it was provided that the amount of the credit did not have to be subtracted from the cost of the asset to be depreciated. Hence, the investment credit was over and above and separate from allowable depreciation. The precise provisions of the investment credit are detailed and complex. For a detailed explanation see: *Prentice-Hall Federal Taxes, 1965* (Englewood Cliffs, N.J.: Prentice-Hall, Inc., 1965), para. 5898.1.

TABLE 6-1

Comparison of the Results of Three Methods of Allocating Depreciation of a $200,000 Asset over 10 Years with No Salvage Value

	Straight-Line, 10% Rate		Declining Balance, 20% Rate		Years' Digits		
	Allowable Depreciation	Undepreciated Cost, Year End	Allowable Depreciation	Undepreciated Cost, Year End	Rate	Allowable Depreciation	Undepreciated Cost, Year End
At purchase	.....	$200,000	.....	$200,000	.....	.....	$200,000
First year	$20,000	180,000	$40,000	160,000	10/55	$36,364	163,636
Second year	20,000	160,000	32,000	128,000	9/55	32,727	130,909
Third year	20,000	140,000	25,600	102,400	8/55	29,091	101,818
Fourth year	20,000	120,000	20,480	81,920	7/55	25,455	76,363
Fifth year	20,000	100,000	16,384	65,536	6/55	21,818	54,545
Sixth year	20,000	80,000	13,107	52,429	5/55	18,182	36,363
Seventh year	20,000	60,000	13,107	39,322	4/55	14,545	21,818
Eighth year	20,000	40,000	13,107	26,215	3/55	10,909	10,909
Ninth year	20,000	20,000	13,107	13,107	2/55	7,273	3,636
Tenth year	20,000	0	13,107	0	1/55	3,636	0

fraction. In this fraction the numerator is the number of years of useful life remaining and so changes each year. The denominator in all years is the number representing the sum of the digits of years of full life of the property. For a $200,000 asset with a 10-year life, the denominator would therefore be $1 + 2 + 3 + 4 + 5 + 6 + 7 + 8 + 9 + 10 = 55$, and in the first year the depreciation would be as shown in Table 6–1. A graphic comparison of the results of different methods is shown in Chart 6–2.

CHART 6–2

ACCUMULATED DEPRECIATION PER $1,000 FOR AN ASSET WITH 10-YEAR
USEFUL LIFE AND NO SALVAGE VALUE

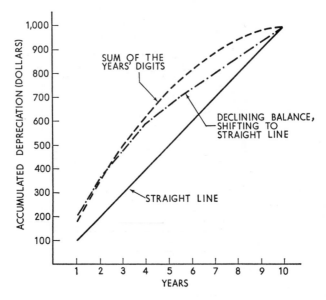

Remembering that it is almost always advantageous for a firm to have funds at its disposal early rather than late, one can see that the newer methods are preferable, and we find it surprising that many firms cling to the straight-line technique.

Business Investment and Depreciation

In this discussion of the funds flows related to fixed asset use, we have stressed the concept that the charging of depreciation does not in itself require or create funds but rather divides the flow of funds from operations into two parts, a net income portion and a portion measured by the amount of the depreciation charge. In order to calculate the funds flow from operations from the income statement, one simply adds to the net income figure the amount of depreciation charged as an expense. For this reason, it has become common in business usage to refer—loosely and erroneously, as we have indicated, but understandably—to "depreciation as a source of funds."

The importance of the depreciation component of the funds flow from operations has grown greatly in recent years. In 1964 total depreciation charges of U.S. corporations amounted to $30.5 billion, while increases in plant and equipment totaled $39.2 billion.[5] As Chart 6–3 shows,

CHART 6–3

Depreciation Charges and Increases in Plant and Equipment,
U.S. Corporations 1946–64

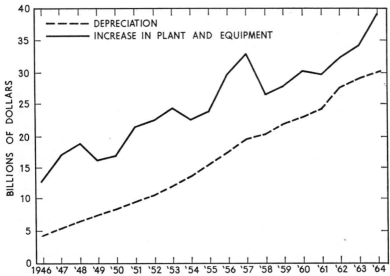

Sources: U.S. Department of Commerce, Office of Business Economics, *U.S. Income and Output* (Washington, D.C.: U.S. Government Printing Office, 1958), Table V-10; *Survey of Current Business*, July, 1962, Table 34; July, 1964, Table 34.

depreciation charges of corporations grew from $4.2 billion in 1946 to $15.7 billion by 1955 and to the $30.5 billion in 1964.

The chart also depicts the annual corporate increase in plant and equipment for the corresponding years. If the size, quality, and cost of the total plant and equipment were to remain constant, and if depreciation charges proved thoroughly accurate, depreciation charges could be expected to match new equipment outlays. It can be seen from the chart that such has not been the case in the postwar period. As the country and the economy have grown, corporate plant investment has grown in size and in complexity—compare the DC-8 jet aircraft with the DC-3—and costs of plant have increased. Consequently, depreciation charges based on the smaller, less complex, and cheaper fixed asset acquisitions of the past have fallen far short of current outlays. However, it can be seen that the gap between depreciation charges and new plant outlays has narrowed in the more recent years. This is in part due to the rise of depreciation

[5] *Economic Report of the President, 1965* (Washington, D.C.: U.S. Government Printing Office, 1965), p. 270.

charges as the heavy postwar plant investment was reflected in the accounts and, in recent years, as more liberalized methods of computing depreciation for tax purposes were used. Also, in recent years the mix of new asset outlays has shifted somewhat toward machinery and equipment, which is subject to rather rapid depreciation, and away from buildings.

Summary of Funds Flows Related to the Ownership of Fixed Assets

Now, let us recapitulate our main points regarding the cash flows related to acquisition and ownership of fixed assets. In planning the outflows related to the acquisition of fixed assets, care should be taken to schedule the outflows in payment for the assets as they actually will be made, since their timing may differ materially from the time at which ownership of the assets is reflected in the accounting records of the firm. Further, funds inflows from operations are *not* reduced by the acknowledgment of depreciation as an expense appropriate for purposes of income determination. The amount of depreciation which can be taken as a deduction from taxable income does, however, have a significant effect on the timing of outflows required to satisfy income tax liabilities. So the firm's pattern of allowable depreciation deductions does affect its depreciation tax shield and hence the timing of its outflows for taxes.

Further, the tax-free recovery through operations of the original cost of fixed assets will not, in a period of rising costs, supply a sufficient inflow of funds, even if segregated and accumulated for the specific purpose, to pay for replacement of the assets with higher-cost physical equivalents. To maintain a constant level of physical facilities over a long period of rising costs, added funds are required to match the excess of replacement over original fixed asset costs.

Since American business has been adding to its stock of fixed assets, acquisition in the postwar years of fixed assets has represented a major use of funds and one well in excess of the operational inflows measured by depreciation. This has continued to be true despite the impact of liberalized tax laws governing the timing of tax-deductible depreciation charges.

The Total Business Outlay for Fixed Assets in Recent Years

The aggregate outlays of business for new fixed assets are great enough to have a major impact on the total demand for funds by business and hence on the conditions of the capital market faced by the individual firm needing external financing. Further, the volume of business spending on fixed assets both influences and is influenced by the overall level of the economy. Consequently, a brief review of aggregate business spending on fixed assets in recent years may be useful.

As can be seen from Chart 6–4, during the period from 1930 through 1941, the expenditures of American business on new plant and equipment were very low—just about equaling the use or depreciation of equipment

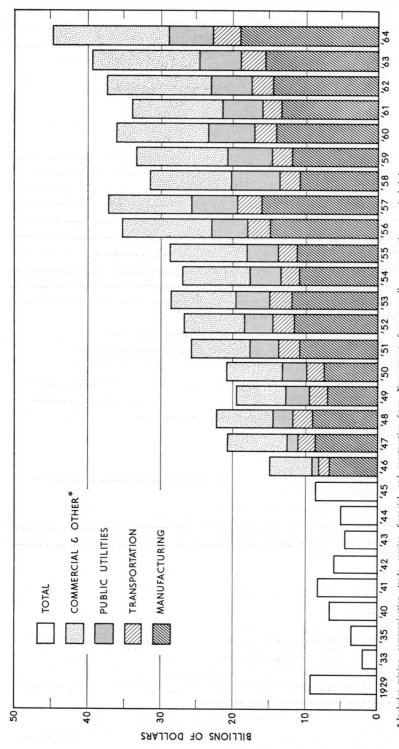

CHART 6-4

BUSINESS EXPENDITURES FOR NEW PLANT AND EQUIPMENT, SELECTED YEARS, 1929–64

* Includes mining, communication, trade, service, financial, and construction firms. Noncorporate firms as well as corporations are included.
Sources: For 1929–44 data, *Moody's Industrial Manual, 1956*, p. a7. For 1945–56 data, *Economic Report of the President, 1958* (Washington, D.C.: U.S. Government Printing Office, 1958), Table F-30. For 1957–64 data, *Economic Report of the President, 1965*, Table B-39.

and plant. During the war years, business expenditures on plant and equipment fell behind the heavy use of physical facilities. For a period of 16 years the *net* investment of American business in fixed assets actually declined.

Since 1945, as is apparent from Chart 6–4, expenditures for plant and equipment have surged sharply upward. Total business outlays for new plant and equipment during the 19 years from 1946 through 1964 amounted to almost $500 billion. Since, as we have noted, the outlay for new plant and equipment outran depreciation and retirements in each of the 19 years by a significant margin, the net investment in plant and equipment for business as a whole has increased substantially.

Several reasons appear to account for the increased outlays on plant. The low rate of capital expenditures during 1930 to 1945, together with rapid technical development and heavy wartime usage, meant that much of the nation's facilities in 1946 were worn or obsolete. A second basic cause has been the rise in population under conditions of general prosperity, in which the effective demand of the population for goods and services has been great and rising. The development of new products—television, jet aircraft, diesel locomotives, synthetic fibers, air conditioning, to mention a few—and radical changes in others, such as the extension of dial telephoning, called for new or expanded facilities. Changes in productive processes and methods, such as the shift to oxygen furnaces in the steel industry, have been important. Further, the rise in labor wage rates and the periodic shortages of labor have accelerated a long-term trend toward greater use of laborsaving machinery. Adding to the costs of new facilities has been a trend toward provision of improved working facilities—for example, air conditioning in plants, offices, and stores. Important also in adding to the dollar cost of new construction and equipment outlays has been the general rise in price levels since 1945.

Finally, it would be most inappropriate for authors of a book on finance to overlook the facilitating role of finance in making possible the huge outlays on plant and equipment. The fact that the necessary cash or credit needed to finance the outlays has been forthcoming on terms judged reasonable must be included among the major reasons for the postwar upsurge in business spending for plant and equipment.

Business spending for new fixed assets falls into one of two broad categories:

1. Expansion of capacity to produce existing or new products.
2. Replacement and modernization of facilities to cut costs or produce other benefits such as higher-quality output.

During certain boom years in the 1950's, spending for new capacity exceeded that for replacement and modernization. Thus, in 1957, 52% of all new spending planned by manufacturers was to increase capacity.[6]

---

[6] McGraw-Hill Publishing Company, Inc., *Business Plans for New Plants and Equipment, 1957–1960* (10th Annual Survey) (New York, 1957), p. 7.

During the years from 1959 through 1965, manufacturers concentrated their new fixed asset investment on replacement and modernization, putting only about one third into expansion. This added about 4% each year to capacity.[7] Nevertheless, the overall rate of expansion of manufacturing capacity since 1950 has been enough to bring 1964 manufacturing capacity to a level more than twice that of December, 1950. Expansion has been especially strong among manufacturers of nonautomotive transportation equipment (aircraft, etc.) and chemicals and electrical machinery.

Rapid growth of demand for the products of many industries during 1964 brought reported rates of operation in manufacturing generally to 88% of capacity. Several industries were operating above their preferred percentages of capacity.[8] The strong demand promised a developing emphasis on adding capacity—this was reflected in the 1965 mix of spending, when 45% of planned investment was for added capacity, and in reported plans for future spending.[9]

Since recession years heighten pressures for cost cutting, the level of outlay for replacement and modernization tends to be much less volatile than that for increased capacity, which is directly affected by changing expectations as to future product demand.

Of total spending by business for fixed assets planned for 1965, a large part—69%—was for machinery and equipment. Seven percent was for motor vehicles, and 24% was for buildings. In manufacturing, the emphasis was even more heavily (79%) on machinery and equipment. Only in the commercial sector (chain stores, mail-order and department stores, insurance companies, and banks) did building account for over half (51%) of the total.[10]

Aids in the Analysis of the Investment in Fixed Assets

As we emphasized early in this chapter, commitments of funds to fixed assets typically are for long periods into the future and usually are difficult and costly to reverse. Often, they are in large increments. Consequently, it is important that the firm carefully establish and apply a valid pattern of analysis of the impact of proposed investments on the rate of return on the investment involved. The importance and inherent complexity of such analysis and selection among opportunities for fixed asset investment appear to us to justify the extended treatment of this subject which we undertake in Chapters 21 and 22.

The impact of fixed asset outlays on the firm's financial needs and position also typically is major. Unduly heavy commitment of available resources to relatively illiquid fixed assets—even ones of promising long-

---

[7] McGraw-Hill Publishing Company, Inc., *Business Plans for New Plants and Equipment, 1965–1968* (18th Annual Survey) (New York, 1965), pp. 3–4.

[8] *Ibid.*, p. 5.

[9] *Ibid.*, p. 3.

[10] *Ibid.*, Table IV.

term earning power—can precipitate major liquidity problems and, indeed, in extreme situations, make it impossible for the firm to meet maturing obligations. In Chapter 7, we shall consider some leading ratios used to measure liquidity and the impact of the firm's fixed asset investment on its liquidity, and Chapter 8 discusses the forecasting of cash needs.

At this point, it may well suffice to note that ratios similar to those applied to the investment in inventory and receivables can also usefully be applied to fixed assets. Thus, net fixed assets can be expressed as a percentage of total assets. Also, the turnover of net fixed assets in sales (sales/net fixed assets) is useful as a quick, if rough, index of the efficiency of use of fixed assets. Those firms which, by the nature of the technology of their industry, can hope to achieve only low turnover of fixed assets, notably utilities, can achieve a satisfactory return for their shareholders only if a high rate of profit can be achieved on sales (or revenues) and/or relatively heavy use can be made of low-cost debt money. Firms, on the other hand, that can achieve a high turnover of fixed assets, such as retail food chains, may well be able to achieve a high return on assets with only a moderate rate of profit on sales.

PART III

Analysis of Past Financing and Future Funds Needs

Chapter 7

Interpreting Financial Statements

OUR EMPHASIS in recent chapters has been on uses of funds, as we looked in turn at the need for funds in inventory, receivables, and money assets and in plant and equipment. In this chapter we are concerned with how to interpret or draw meaning from the basic financial statements. To the uninitiated, balance sheets and income statements represent a confusing jumble of figures. But those skilled in drawing out their meaning can make the financial statements tell a revealing story of what has happened to the needs for financing and how these needs were met. Moreover, to the skilled analyst, the statements provide the raw material for judgments as to the financial condition of the subject firm.

In Chapter 8, the other chapter in Part III of this book, we shall shift attention from techniques of analysis of past developments and the current financial position, as mirrored in the financial statements, to a focus on future needs for funds. In Chapter 8 we introduce the major methods of forecasting funds requirements and discuss the main problems in doing an effective job of forecasting.

In Part IV we turn to issues of where and how to raise needed funds advantageously.

While we shall delay a focus on sources of funds until Part IV, the chapters on interpreting financial statements and forecasting needs necessarily are concerned with the total finances of the firm—that is, with sources as well as uses of funds. Hence, we believe it desirable to provide at this point an overview of the major sources of funds for business. Exhibit 7–1 sets forth in highly capsuled form the more important sources of debt and ownership financing. The exhibit includes references to the pages in the book at which each major source is discussed in some detail. Students who may be confused as to the essential nature of particular sources of funds can refer to the appropriate pages for clarification.

Now let us turn to a consideration of techniques of interpretation or analysis of the basic financial statements. We shall be concerned here with generally useful techniques or tools of analysis and we shall illustrate

129

EXHIBIT 7-1

MAJOR SOURCES OF FUNDS FOR AMERICAN BUSINESS

Broad Classification of Sources	Instruments or Form in Which Funds Are Acquired	B.B.F. Page Reference	Major Suppliers of Funds	Classification by Length of Term
Spontaneous	Normal trade credit	171	Vendors selling to the firm	Short term
	Accrued expenses	174	Miscellaneous creditors	
	Accrued U.S. income taxes	175	U.S. government	
	Special credits from suppliers	227	Major vendors	
	Customer loans and advances	227	Major customers	
	Short-term bank loans	190	Commercial banks	
	Loans from specialized lending companies	222–25	Business finance companies, factors, sales finance companies	
	Commercial paper (short-term notes payable)	220	Nonfinancial corporations, banks and other financial institutions	
Negotiated	Term bank loans	202	Commercial banks	Intermediate term
	Term loans—directly placed with nonbank lenders	205	Insurance companies, pension funds, small-business investment companies	
	Long-term debt instruments (Bonds, Notes, Debentures)	352	Primarily insurance companies, pension funds, savings banks and other institutional investors, (to lesser extent) individual investors	Long term
	Preferred stock	364	Institutional investors, individual investors	
	Common stock	361	Individual investors, institutional investors	
Operational	Inflows from operations represented by retained earnings; noncash charges to earnings (depreciation, etc.)	277; 298	Operations of the business	

their use on the financial statements normally available to persons outside the subject firm.

In business usage, the term *financial analysis* is applied to almost any kind of detailed inquiry into financial data. The specific nature of the financial inquiry or analysis undertaken will be shaped by the following factors:

1. The objective and the point of view of the analyst. A trade creditor considering what action to take on a long-overdue account may well focus his inquiry on the immediate financial condition of the subject firm and the liquid resources it has with which to meet maturing obligations. In contrast, a security analyst considering a purchase of common stock, after a quick check to see that the balance sheet offers no cause for alarm, tends to center his efforts on the profit results in an effort to gain clues as to the future profitability of the firm.

2. The degree of interest in the company and the need for depth of inquiry. An insurance company considering a multimillion dollar loan to a new customer will be justified in devoting a great deal more time and effort to analysis of the company and its finances than will the credit department of a manufacturing firm making a routine annual review of the data on a small customer who has followed satisfactory payment practices. We know of one investment firm which permitted one of its security analysts to spend 6 months investigating the investment merits of a single company. (Happily his reports strongly recommended the purchase, and the stock has quadrupled in value; he is now a vice president, not an ex-employee.)

3. The amount and quality of the data available. Trade creditors in routine seldom are furnished more than summary financial statements, supplemented modestly by credit agency reports. The individual investor usually has little more than the financial information published in the annual report or in a prospectus. In contrast, the commercial banker considering a large loan is usually in a position to get from the company a great deal of additional information, such as breakdowns of inventory, aging schedules of receivables and payables, sales and production plans, product line profitability estimates, and the like.

If a thorough analysis is desired and the full data needed are not available, or if the suspicion exists that the firm involved is trying to hide or confuse its real situation, the financial analyst must be a virtual detective in order to ferret out the full facts and piece together the story they tell.

In Exhibits 7–2, 7–3, and 7–4 we reproduce the financial statements and president's report to stockholders of Cenco Instruments Corporation as presented in its 1960 annual report to stockholders. Cenco manufactures scientific instruments for sale to industry and to educational institutions as aids in the teaching of science subjects. The financial data

EXHIBIT 7–2

cenco *Instruments*

CONSOLIDATED BALANCE

ASSETS	1960	1959
Current assets:		
Cash	$ 773,206	$ 1,270,806
Government securities, at cost which approximates market	—	407,477
Accounts receivable, less allowance (1960, $56,500; 1959, $35,000) for doubtful accounts	3,699,515	1,958,945
Inventories, at the lower of cost (average or first-in, first-out) or market:		
Finished and resale merchandise	4,029,140	3,300,921
Work in process and parts	946,858	775,866
Raw materials and supplies	563,920	315,643
Goods in transit	237,712	175,320
	5,777,630	4,567,750
Total current assets	10,250,351	8,204,978
Property and equipment, at cost:		
Land	71,977	71,977
Buildings	417,901	417,901
Machinery, equipment, and office furniture and fixtures	1,267,223	1,157,120
	1,757,101	1,646,998
Less allowance for depreciation	985,028	903,382
Total property and equipment, net	772,073	743,616
Other assets:		
Prepaid expenses and deferred charges	104,287	114,274
Investment in and receivables from foreign subsidiaries, not consolidated	250,559	56,383
Excess of cost of investment in subsidiaries over net tangible assets acquired	616,406	128,604
Other assets	19,260	1
Total other assets	990,512	299,262
	$12,012,936	$ 9,247,856

See accompanying notes to financial statements.

EXHIBIT 7–2—*Continued*

CORPORATION *and subsidiaries*

SHEET *April 30, 1960 with comparative figures for 1959*

LIABILITIES	1960	1959
Current liabilities:		
Notes payable to bank . . . . $	500,000	—
Accounts payable	872,916	488,002
Accrued expenses	650,016	449,533
United States and Canadian taxes on income	999,456	500,616
Total current liabilities	3,022,388	1,438,151
Long-term debt:		
Fifteen-year 5⅛% notes of Central Scientific Co., payable in annual installments of $100,000, 1961 to 1963; $125,000, 1964 to 1968; $175,000, 1969 to 1972; and $425,000, 1973.	2,050,000	2,150,000
Stockholders' equity:		
Capital stock of $1 par value. Authorized 2,500,000 shares; outstanding: 1,033,504 shares in 1960; 1,013,479 shares in 1959	1,033,504	1,013,479
Capital in excess of par value (note 4)	1,967,428	1,565,482
Retained earnings (note 2)	3,939,616	3,080,744
Total stockholders' equity	6,940,548	5,659,705
	$12,012,936	$ 9,247,856

EXHIBIT 7–3

CENCO Instruments CORPORATION *and subsidiaries*

CONSOLIDATED STATEMENT OF EARNINGS
AND RETAINED EARNINGS

Year ended April 30, 1960 with comparative figures for 1959

	1960	1959
Net sales	$21,107,533	$15,032,904
Cost of sales	13,545,966	9,691,891
Gross profit	7,561,567	5,341,013
Operating expenses	4,958,728	3,753,720
Operating profit	2,602,839	1,587,293
Other charges, net	70,138	53,145
Earnings before taxes on income	2,532,701	1,534,148
United States and Canadian taxes on income	1,364,000	805,000
Net earnings for the year	1,168,701	729,148
Retained earnings at beginning of year	3,080,744	2,654,887
	4,249,445	3,384,035
Dividends paid—30c a share	309,829	303,291
Retained earnings at end of year	$ 3,939,616	3,080,744

Depreciation expense included in the above statement amounted to $192,061 for 1960 and $159,908 for 1959.

See accompanying notes to financial statements.

EXHIBIT 7–3—*Continued*

Notes to Financial Statements

April 30, 1960

(1) The consolidated financial statements include the accounts of all subsidiaries operating in the United States and Canada.

(2) The loan agreement relating to the 5½% fifteen-year notes provides, among other things, for certain restrictions upon the payment of dividends. At April 30, 1960 consolidated retained earnings amounting to approximately $2,135,000 were free from these restrictions.

(3) Under the terms of a restricted stock option plan approved by the stockholders in 1951 options on 2,025 shares were exercised during the year at a price of $12.825 a share. Options to purchase 10,000 shares at a price of $21.375 a share were granted during the year in connection with the acquisition of a subsidiary company.

At April 30, 1960 there remained 56,975 shares under option at option prices of $12.825 and $21.375 a share, of which 20,000 shares are exercisable during the year ending April 30, 1961. At April 30, 1960, 15,000 shares were reserved for the grant of further options under the plan.

(4) The increase of $401,946 in capital in excess of par value represents the excess of market value at date of issuance over par value of shares issued during the year, of which $23,946 was in connection with stock options and $378,000 was in connection with the acquisition of a subsidiary.

(5) The company's subsidiaries are obligated under long-term property leases expiring in 1968, 1976, and 1980 for which the aggregate annual rentals are approximately $93,000.

ACCOUNTANTS' REPORT

PEAT, MARWICK, MITCHELL & CO.

CERTIFIED PUBLIC ACCOUNTANTS

10 SOUTH LA SALLE STREET

CHICAGO 3, ILL.

The Board of Directors
Cenco Instruments Corporation:

We have examined the consolidated balance sheet of Cenco Instruments Corporation and subsidiaries as of April 30, 1960 and the related consolidated statement of earnings and retained earnings for the year then ended. Our examination was made in accordance with generally accepted auditing standards, and accordingly included such tests of the accounting records and such other auditing procedures as we considered necessary in the circumstances.

In our opinion, the accompanying consolidated balance sheet and consolidated statement of earnings and retained earnings present fairly the financial position of Cenco Instruments Corporation and subsidiaries at April 30, 1960 and the results of their operations for the year then ended, in conformity with generally accepted accounting principles applied on a basis consistent with that of the preceding year.

Peat, Marwick, Mitchell & Co.

Chicago, Illinois
June 9, 1960

EXHIBIT 7–4

President's Report to Stockholders:

April 30, 1960 nears the completion of the first five-year reconstruction plan of your company, and the fifth year of consecutive increases in sales and earnings. We finished the year with better than a 40% increase in our volume and a 60% increase in our after tax earnings.

April 30, 1960 showed a record volume for the year of $21,107,533 compared with $15,032,094 the previous year. Earnings advanced from last year's $1,534,148 to $2,532,701 before taxes, or $1,168,701 after taxes, compared with last year's $729,148. The per share earnings this year mounted to $1.13 from last year's 72c. The percentage of net profits on our volume increased to 5.5 as against last year's 4.8 and 2.8 five years ago. Our educational business showed the largest increase over last year, but the industrial division, too, showed a substantial gain.

Much of our growth was attributable to the new proprietary items we brought to market this year. As illustrated in another portion of this Annual Report, Cenco begins the 1961 fiscal year with 35 additional new products developed by our own and our research affiliates.

On the manufacturing side we are on constant vigil to improve efficiency in production and the utilization of the most advanced methods of operation.

To take advantage of increased leverage to our shareholders during this period of growth, your management intends to augment its finances in the near future by the issuance of $5,000,000 in convertible debentures.

An acquisition division has been established and is examining a number of situations that fit into our over-all picture. We are particularly on the alert for the more sophisticated scientific companies available. Naturally, acquisitions will only be made where an attractive deal can be consummated for their inclusion in the Cenco family.

June 2nd will mark the formal opening of our new Breda, Holland plant. After only two months of manufacturing operation, Cenco Instrumenten Maatschappij N.V. is already in the black, and is definitely an active participant in the European Common Market.

Our country has come to realize that it has as much to fear from technological warfare as from missiles, hydrogen and atomic bombs. To help with the war of technology, your company has dedicated itself to the development and the production of the finest educational and scientific research instruments and equipment that the world has to offer. Cenco's technical men are on the alert everywhere for any and every new development that can help us in this monumental effort.

We wish to take this opportunity to again express our gratitude to our management and to our loyal working force, whose efforts and support are speedily molding our dreams into a reality.

Chairman of the Board   President

presented in its annual report are typical of those made available in routine to stockholders, trade creditors, and the public.

Those interested in Cenco's progress during the year can make some significant observations from a quick scanning of these financial statements. Readily apparent, for example, is the sizable increase in sales and in net profits. But the person who is equipped with basic techniques of financial analysis can use these skills to shape up a much more meaningful picture of Cenco's financing. With these tools he can make clearer the changes in Cenco's financial needs during the year and how these needs were met. He can also get a much clearer picture of Cenco's financial position at year end and of how it changed during the year. In short, he can shape the data into a story of what happened.

Let us use the Cenco data as an illustration of the application of techniques of analysis and see what kind of story we can put together. In so doing, we should be alert to the limitations of our data and to the danger of drawing unwarranted conclusions from our analysis. If we had the kinds of detailed information normally available to management, we should be able to make a much more complete and discerning analysis and be in a position to evaluate those developments which we have noted with much keener insight and more confidence than we can when we have only the summary financial statements with which to work.

Let us emphasize again that by *funds* we mean cash or other means of payment. Thus, as we have noted in Chapter 3, an increase in inventory absorbs or "uses" funds. If the increase in inventory was financed by increasing accounts payable, the use of funds was met not with cash outflow but with credit. The increase in a liability, accounts payable, served as a source of funds. Also in Chapter 6 we discussed how funds are provided through operations.

SOURCES AND USES OF FUNDS ANALYSIS

We can draw on both the income statement and the balance sheets in developing a *statement of funds flows,* also known as a *statement of sources and uses of funds*. Various formats are used in developing such statements. We suggest preparation of a statement for Cenco in three steps:

1. Note from the income statement the net cash inflows from operations during the year.
2. Classify the net changes in the asset and liability accounts from the balance sheet at the beginning of the year and that at year end.
3. Bring the statements of funds flows from operations and the balance sheet changes together into a statement of funds flow for the year. In so doing, we must eliminate any double-counting involved in bringing the material together.

Proceeding with step 1, we can note from the Cenco income statement in Exhibit 7–3 that net earnings for the year were $1,169,000. A footnote indicates that the noncash charge for depreciation in 1960 was $192,000. Thus, funds inflow from operations was $1,361,000. However, we must also note that dividends of $310,000 were paid to shareholders.

These funds flows from operations during 1960 will, of course, be reflected in the balance sheet changes. Thus, the net income retained in the business of $859,000 ($1,169,000 of income less the $310,000 paid out in dividends) should increase the retained earnings balance by that amount. And the charge for depreciation should be reflected in the net fixed asset account. We must avoid double-counting in these accounts when we bring together in step 3 the funds flows from operations and those reflected in the balance sheet changes.

Now let us undertake step 2, classification of the net changes in the asset, liability, and net worth accounts according to whether each change represented an absorption or use of funds or alternatively a provision or source of funds. Listed in the *use* column are:

Increases in assets (for example, an increase in inventory).
Decreases in liabilities (e.g., payment of a bank loan).
Decrease in net worth (e.g., payment of dividends).

Conversely, the following changes provide funds and hence are sources:

Decreases in assets (e.g., reduction of inventory).
Increases in liabilities (e.g., increases in accounts payable).
Increases in net worth (e.g., from sale of stock).

Using this approach, let us classify the net changes in the various Cenco balance sheet accounts in its 1960 fiscal year:

USES OF FUNDS

		In Thousands
Increases in assets:		
Increase in accounts receivable, net......................		$1,741
Increase in inventories:		
Finished and resale merchandise........................	$728	
Work in process and parts.............................	171	
Raw materials and supplies............................	248	
Goods in transit......................................	63	
		1,210
Increase in total property and equipment, net..............		28
Increase in investment in and receivables from foreign subsidiaries, not consolidated..........................		194
Increase in excess of cost of investment in subsidiaries over net tangible assets acquired............................		488
Increase in other assets..................................		19
Decreases in liabilities:		
Decrease in long-term debt..............................		100
Total uses...		$3,780

SOURCES OF FUNDS

Decreases in assets:

Decrease in cash......................................	$ 498
Decrease in government securities........................	407
Decrease in prepaid expenses and deferred charges..........	10

Increases in liabilities:

Increase in notes payable to bank.......................	500
Increase in accounts payable............................	385
Increase in accrued expenses............................	200
Increase in accrued U.S. and Canadian income taxes........	499

Increases in net worth:

Increase in capital stock...............................	20
Increase in capital in excess of par value.................	402
Increase in retained earnings...........................	859
Total sources.....................................	$3,780

We can now move to step 3 and bring together the information about cash flows from operations and that drawn from balance sheet changes.

We noted that the net income inflow from operations was $1,169,000 and dividends were $310,000, resulting in an increase in retained earnings of $859,000. Surely these flows are material, and our funds flow statement is made more useful if we show the net income as a source and the dividends as a use of funds, replacing the single figure for the net increase in retained earnings.

We must also bring the figure for funds flow from operations-depreciation into our summary of funds flows. We have shown in our tally of uses of funds only the amounts of increase in the *net* property and equipment accounts. Thus, the net property increased $28,000 after deduction of the reserve for depreciation. We noted earlier that depreciation expense amounted to $192,000, and so a similar amount must have been added to the reserve for depreciation during the year. Thus, if we show "funds provided from operations-depreciation" of $192,000 as a source, we should also add $192,000 to the $28,000 shown as increase in the property accounts and label this $220,000 figure "outlay for new fixed assets."

Our statement of sources and uses, expanded by the items in italics, now appears as follows:

USES OF FUNDS (In Thousands)

Dividends paid		$ 310
Increase in accounts receivable, net.....................		1,741
Increase in inventories:		
Finished and resale merchandise........................$	728	
Work in process and parts............................	171	
Raw materials and supplies...........................	248	
Goods in transit.....................................	63	1,210
Outlays for machinery, equipment, etc.....................		220
Increase in investment in and receivables from foreign		
subsidiaries, not consolidated........................		194
Increase in cost of investment in subsidiaries over net		
tangible assets acquired..............................		488
Increase in other assets...............................		19
Decrease in long-term debt.............................		100
Total uses..		$4,282

SOURCES OF FUNDS

Funds provided by operations:
Net income...*$1,169*
Depreciation charged without outlay.....................*192*   *$1,361*
Decrease in cash.......................................   498
Decrease in government securities.......................   407
Decrease in prepaid expenses and deferred charges........   10
Increase in notes payable to bank.......................   500
Increase in accounts payable...........................   385
Increase in accrued expenses...........................   200
Increase in accrued U.S. and Canadian income taxes.......   499
Increase in capital stock..............................   20
Increase in capital in excess of par value................   402
          Total sources................................... $4,282

Now, we can draw on our funds flow analysis to summarize Cenco's financing in the year. Would the paragraphs below fairly tell the story?

During 1960, Cenco experienced a major need for funds to match sharp increases in receivables and in all types of inventories, apparently related to the big increase in sales. Acquisition of a domestic subsidiary was financed through exchange of a small number of newly issued common shares, but a modest investment in a foreign subsidiary contributed to the need for other funds. No new plant facilities were acquired; and the moderate outlays for machinery, equipment, and office furniture and fixtures were almost matched by operational inflows related to depreciation.

A variety of sources was drawn on to finance the expansion of receivables and inventories. The substantial net income, largely retained, met almost one third of that need. The combined increases in accounts payable, accrued expenses, and in the tax accrual stemming from higher earnings were an almost equally important source. Management also utilized the funds invested in U.S. securities and drew down cash by more than one third. Despite these moves, external funds were needed, and $500,000 was raised through short-term bank borrowing. That management anticipated further and continuing need for external funds in the future was evidenced by the president's announcement of plans to sell a large issue of convertible debentures.

But our opportunities for possibly useful analysis of Cenco's financial data have by no means been exhausted by our review of funds flow management. We have done little to probe profits beyond noting their increase and the funds they have provided. Remaining unanswered are such relevant queries as: Was the profits increase due solely to higher volume of sales or were margins increased? Did management succeed in getting a higher gross margin over cost of goods sold? Did operating expenses increase in line with sales? How was profit return relative to total assets? To owners' investment? Nor have we explored the big increases in receivables and inventory to see whether they were in line with sales increases. Beyond noting the pulldown of liquid assets, we have not looked into the financial condition of the company as revealed by the latest balance sheet. Nor have we devoted attention to the developing capital structure of the firm and the extent to which it is relying on the use of debt relative to ownership funds. Exploitation of the opportunities for further analysis can be aided by purposeful ratio analysis.

But before we turn to a discussion of ratios and their application to the Cenco data, some further general comments on funds flow analysis are appropriate.

Professional accountants making up source and use of funds statements for clients where full facts are available often undertake further refinement of the funds statement to remove from the tabulation any transactions which were merely "paper transactions" not actually involving any flows of funds. Seldom does the outside analyst have enough information on transactions of this sort to attempt such refinements in the source and use of funds statements he constructs.

The reader should appreciate the fact that the source and use of funds statement, as we have constructed it, and as it is generally prepared, does not attempt to picture all the flows of funds through a business during the period. Note that from the income statement, we picked up only *net* profits and the noncash expense depreciation. Left off the source side were the remainder of the sales dollars received, and the cash expenses paid during the year do not show up on the use side. Many other transactions within the year are not shown. For example, Cenco might have borrowed from banks for short periods and repaid the loans several times during the year; these intraperiod flows would not show up in our statement, which deals primarily with *net* changes during the year.

While it is more thorough to bring all known flows during the period into the source and use statement, in practice published statements of sources and uses of funds seldom show more than does our revised one for Cenco. The source and use statement often is put together in somewhat different form, though with essentially the same information.

THE USE OF RATIOS IN FINANCIAL ANALYSIS

Ratios, discriminatingly calculated and wisely interpreted, can be useful tools of financial analysis. Ratios are simply a means of highlighting in arithmetical terms the relationships between figures drawn from financial statements. A great number of ratios can be computed from the basic financial statements—for example, the relationship of Cenco's accrued expenses to its net investment in fixed assets can be readily calculated as 84.2% (650/772). But does this relationship have any significance? None is apparent, so that the 84.2% figure is meaningless and its calculation distracting.

Ratios will be meaningful and useful, then, only to the extent that significant relationships exist between the figures selected for comparison through ratios. And as we earlier pointed out, the viewpoint and particular interests of the analyst will make some relationships of especial interest to him. The more commonly used ratios fall into one of three generic groupings according to their use. These main groups or families of ratios are:

1. Measures of profitability.
2. Measures of asset use.
3. Measures of liquidity and the use of debt.

Let us identify and discuss these ratios in the practical context of their use in the analysis of the Cenco data.

Ratios in the Measurement and Analysis of Profitability

Sales and Profit Comparisons. The absolute figures for profit take on more meaning when compared with sales. Widely used as a measure of profitability is the percentage ratio of net income after taxes to net sales —or to total income if income from sources other than sales is material and repetitive. In Cenco, the 1960 net profit after taxes on sales was 5.54%, calculated as follows:

$$\frac{\text{Net Income after Taxes}}{\text{Net Sales}} = \frac{1,169}{21,108} = 5.54\% \,.$$

The corresponding ratio for 1959 was 4.85%. Thus, it is apparent that Cenco's increased profits in 1960 were not solely the result of higher sales but were attributable also to success in taking down into net profit a higher percentage of total revenues from sales.

Since the burden of income taxation can vary from year to year, operational results often are measured in terms of net income before taxes compared with sales. In Cenco, net profit before taxes was 12% of sales, up from 10.2% in 1959.

Sales and Expense Ratios. Management and those outside analysts particularly interested in profit performance and the control of expenses commonly compute many expense/sales ratios. Outside analysts, who commonly have no breakdowns of expenses beyond the summary ones presented in published income statements, make frequent use of "100% statements"—that is, convert each of the expense and profit items in the income statement into percentages of net sales. The Cenco income statement, in percentages, appears below:

	1960	1959
Net sales	100.00%	100.00%
Cost of sales	64.18	64.47
Gross profit	35.82%	35.53%
Operating expenses	23.49	24.97
Operating profit	12.33%	10.56%
Other charges, net	0.33	0.36
Earnings before taxes on income	12.00%	10.20%
Income taxes	6.46	5.35
Net income after taxes	5.54%	4.85%

The percentage statement makes it apparent that Cenco's higher net profit percentage in 1960 is due in part to an increased gross profit or *gross margin* percentage, but more importantly to control of operating expenses so that they did not increase so fast as sales. These favorable factors more than offset an increased tax burden. With its more complete information about various expense items, management can make a similar but much more detailed expense/profit analysis.

Profits Compared with Assets

In Chapter 1 we discussed measures of profitability which related the amount of profit to the funds employed in the business. We stressed the importance of return on investment ratios as gauges of the ability of managements to make effective use of the resources at their command.

Now let us relate the Cenco profit results to the funds or resources employed in the business. Cenco's return on overall assets in 1960 is found to be 9.73%:

$$\frac{\text{Net Income after Taxes}}{\text{Total Assets, Year End}} = \frac{1,169}{12,013} = 9.73\% \ .$$

The 9.73% return in 1960 represents a sharp increase over the 1959 return of 7.88%.

We can also come to the same rate of return on assets figures by a two-step calculation employing return-on-sales and asset-turnover figures, as described in Chapter 1.

$$\frac{\text{Net Income}}{\text{Sales}} \times \frac{\text{Sales}}{\text{Assets}} = \text{Net Return on Assets} \ .$$

$$5.54\% \times 1.757 = 9.73\% \ .$$

As we pointed out in Chapter 1, management can boost return on assets by either or both the routes of higher profit per dollar of sales or of higher turnover of assets in sales. The two-step calculation highlights the source of improvement. Thus, comparison with Cenco's 1959 results, as set forth below, shows that both a higher profit rate on sales (5.54% versus 4.85%) and a higher turnover of assets in sales (1.757 times versus 1.625 times) contributed significantly to the overall higher return on assets.

$$\frac{729}{15,033} \times \frac{15,033}{9,248} = 4.85\% \times 1.625 = 7.88\% \text{ in 1959} \ .$$

Another measure of profitability of widespread use and keen significance, particularly to shareholders, relates total income after taxes to the total investment of the common shareholders as shown in the balance sheet. This return on owners' investment ratio supplements the return on total assets ratio. The return on owners' investment in Cenco was 16.84% in 1960, up from 12.88% in 1959.

The 1960 figure of 16.84% was derived as follows:

$$\frac{\text{Net Income after Taxes}}{\text{Owners' Investment}} = \frac{\text{Rate of Return on}}{\text{Owners' Investment.}}$$

$$\frac{1,169}{6,941} = \underline{16.84\%} .$$

The much higher return on ownership funds in Cenco than on total assets (16.84% versus 9.73%) reflects the fact that creditors were the source of much of the funds used in the business. The degree to which the return on total assets and the return on owners' investment differ from one company to another will hinge on the relative mix of ownership and creditors' funds in the business. Thus, the figure for return on ownership funds reflects the financial policies of the firm as well as its effectiveness in employing the assets. In later chapters we shall be very much concerned with the considerations bearing on the choice of debt versus equity sources of funds.

The discerning student may have taken note of the fact that we used year-end figures for total assets and for owners' investment in calculating the return on total assets and on owners' investment. Some analysts prefer to use a figure representing an average of the figures at the beginning and end of the year for total assets and/or owners' investment. This, they argue with considerable logic, more accurately depicts the assets or ownership funds in actual use during the year against which to relate the earnings for that full year. In growing firms, use of average figures will result in a higher figure for return than use of the year-end figures. For example, the calculations below of Cenco's return on average ownership funds in 1960 show it to be *18.55%* compared with the figure of *16.84%* on year-end equity as calculated above.

$$\frac{\text{Net Income}}{\substack{\text{Average of Beginning} \\ \text{and Year-End Figures} \\ \text{for Owners' Investment}}} = \frac{\text{Return on Average}}{\substack{\text{Ownership Investment} \\ \text{during Year .}}}$$

$$\frac{1,169}{(5,660 + 6,941) \div 2} = \underline{18.55\%} .$$

Ratios as Measures of Asset Use

In Chapter 3 we emphasized the significance of the relationship between inventories and sales and described key ratios used to depict this relationship. We suggest that the reader review this material. Now, let us apply the ratios discussed there to Cenco. First, we can note that despite the large dollar increase, total year-end inventories as a percentage of sales fell from 30.39% of sales in 1959 to 27.37% in 1960. Similar checks on each type of inventories show that each, except the minor item, goods in transit, increased at a rate less than that of sales.

The same relationship can be expressed in terms of turnover (sales/inventory). Since inventories are usually carried at cost, a more precise measure of physical turnover can be obtained by dividing inventories into cost of sales rather than sales. As might be expected, turnover increased from 2.12 times to 2.34 times.

In Chapter 4 we introduced some ratios useful in appraising the investment in receivables. The first of these simply expressed receivables as a percentage of sales. Cenco's receivables were 13.03% of sales in 1959, 17.53% in 1960. Thus, unlike inventories, receivables went up faster than sales.

The growth in receivables relative to sales is brought out, perhaps more sharply, by calculation of "days' sales outstanding," or collection period. It will be recalled that this ratio is calculated in two steps, the first being determination of an average day's sales:

$$\frac{\text{Annual Sales, 1960}}{360} = \frac{\$21,108,000}{360} = \underline{\$58,633} .$$

In the second step the average day's sales are divided into year-end receivables:

$$\frac{\text{Year-End Receivables, 1960}}{\text{Average Day's Sales}} = \frac{\$3,700,000}{\$58,633} = \underline{63 \text{ days}} .$$

The 63-day figure at the end of 1960 compares with a 46.9-day figure at the end of 1959.

The net investment in plant can also be compared with sales: Cenco's net plant investment in 1960 was only 3.66%; in 1959, it was 4.95%. In terms of turnover (sales/net plant), the very high rates of 27.34 times and 20.22 times call attention to the high volume of sales achieved by Cenco on its very limited fixed asset investment. Partial explanations are suggested in the note that subsidiaries lease property and in the fact that the finished goods inventory is labeled "finished goods and *resale merchandise*"—apparently, some of Cenco's sales are of products made for it by other firms. Yet, the question raised by the ratios as to how Cenco can achieve such high sales relative to plant investment remains one that the analyst anxious to understand fully Cenco's operation will want to investigate further.

Ratios as Measures of Liquidity

Several ratios are used as measures of liquidity—that is, they are concerned with short-term obligations and the assets that are more readily convertible into the means of payment. Outside analysts who lack detailed data about the anticipated cash flows of the business use the liquidity ratios as rough indices of the likely ability of the subject firm to meet its near-term obligations, or of possible need to raise additional funds through borrowing or stock issues.

Perhaps the most widely used ratio is the *current ratio*, which is simply the current assets divided by the current liabilities. Using Cenco's figures, we find the following:

$$\frac{\text{Current Assets, Year End, 1960}}{\text{Current Liabilities, Year End, 1960}} = \frac{10,250}{3,022} = 3.39 \, .$$

The 1960 ratio of 3.39 compares with that of 5.71 a year earlier. The strength of Cenco's current ratio, despite the decline during 1960, reflects the predominance of receivables and inventory in its asset structure and its substantial net worth and long-term debt.

Despite its wide use—which suggests that analysts think it revealing— the current ratio is at best a very crude measure of the financial health of a firm and its ability to meet its debts. An example of the limited conclusiveness of the current ratio as a measure of debt-paying ability arises out of the fact that inventory is included in current assets. Actually, the inventory may be of limited salability, particularly in the short run. Consider the situation of a manufacturer of ice skates at the end of March with the following summary balance sheet and the strong current ratio of 3 to 1:

Cash	$ 10,000	Current liabilities	$100,000
Receivables	10,000		
Inventory	280,000		
	$300,000		

This firm could still be in financial difficulty if the $100,000 of current liabilities were all due within a month, while inventory could be sold without severe loss only over a period of many months.

Recognized for what it is—a very rough and not necessarily conclusive indicator of liquidity—the current ratio can be useful in the absence of better information or as a small part of a more complete and discerning analysis. In the case of Cenco the decline in the current ratio from 1959 to 1960 does call attention to a significant decline in liquidity during the year.

The current ratio is also used by creditors as a measure of the extent that current asset values could shrink in liquidation of the firm and still be adequate for repayment of current creditors—fixed assets and long-term debts left aside. Thus, the current assets of a firm with a 4.0 current ratio could shrink to one fourth and still match the current debts.

Another widely used ratio is one called the *acid test* or the *net quick* ratio. This ratio is like the current ratio except that inventory and prepaid expenses are excluded. Using the 1960 Cenco figures, we see the following results:

$$\boxed{\frac{\text{Cash, Marketable Securities, and Receivables}}{\text{Current Liabilities}}} = \frac{773 + 3,700}{3,022} = \underline{\underline{1.48}} \,.$$

The 1960 figure, 1.48, represents a sharp drop from that of 1959, 2.53. But it indicates that Cenco's cash and receivables, without reference to inventory, still exceed current liabilities by a large margin.

A third ratio used to assess liquidity is one which compares the level of cash and near-cash accounts to average daily cash payments:

$$\boxed{\frac{\text{Cash} + \text{Marketable Securities}}{\text{Average Daily Cash Payments}}}$$

Since no figures for daily outflows are available in the case of Cenco, this ratio cannot be calculated by outsiders. Here again, speaking broadly, the ratio is open to "ifs, ands, and buts." A firm with strong, little-used lines of credit with banks or other creditors can well afford to operate with a lower cash balance relative to the size of its outflows than can a firm without such "credit backstops" in reserve for use if cash stringencies develop.

The accounts payable of firms whose purchase terms and payment practice do not change can be expected to fluctuate with the recent volume of purchases. Hence, a sharp rise in payables may simply reflect a bulge in purchases. A significant increase in *payables relative to purchases*, however, may well indicate developing financial stringency. Firms experiencing a shortage of funds face strong temptation to lean on their supplies by delaying payment of trade obligations. The tolerance of suppliers is not unlimited, however, and an increasing ratio of payables to purchases often is one of the first signs of a developing shortage of funds.

The level of payables can be usefully related to the volume of purchases in either of two ways:

1. Payables are expressed as a percentage of recent purchases. For example, if monthly purchases data are available, the outstanding payables become the numerator in a payables/purchases ratio.
2. Payables are expressed in terms of average day's purchases outstanding:

$$\boxed{\frac{\text{Payables Outstanding}}{\text{Average Day's Purchases}}} \,.$$

Clearly, this figure will be more significant if average day's purchases are based on recent purchase figures. If they are so based, the resultant figure can be compared with the customary terms of sale of the major suppliers. For example, assume purchases in company X were running at a fairly even rate of $120,000 a month during the last quarter, and it was known that its suppliers were reluctant to have customers exceed their 30-day payment terms. Company X's outstanding accounts payable of $300,000 thus are found to represent 75 days' purchases.

$$\frac{\$120,000}{30} = \$4,000 \text{ Average Day's Purchases.}$$

$$\frac{\$300,000}{4,000} = \underline{75 \text{ Days}}.$$

In the light of the usual terms of 30 days, this 75-day figure suggests that company X has stretched the payment terms far beyond a sustainable level or else has arranged for special credit from suppliers.

If full data are available, an aging schedule of payables can be developed using an approach like that used in aging receivables (see page 86).

In the Cenco case, purchase data are not available, and so we cannot assess Cenco's payables in these terms.

The Source of Funds for the Business: Comparisons of Borrowed Funds with Ownership Funds

Of much interest to many analysts is the relative use of debt and of ownership funds in the concern. A useful and simple way of depicting the extent of debt financing is to calculate the percentage of total assets provided by all creditors. As shown by the calculations below, in Cenco, *debt as a percentage of total assets* increased somewhat in 1960:

$$\frac{\text{Total Debts, 1960}}{\text{Total Assets, 1960}} = \frac{5,072}{12,013} = \underline{42.22\%}.$$

$$\frac{\text{Total Debts, 1959}}{\text{Total Assets, 1959}} = \frac{3,588}{9,248} = \underline{38.8\%}.$$

It is interesting to note Cenco's plans to issue $5 million of convertible debentures. If none of the $5 million were used to pay off existing debts, total debt would increase to 59.2% of the expanded total assets.

Also in wide use, particularly in the public utility and railroad industries, are ratios that focus on the relationship between equity and long-term debt. The total of long-term debt and total equity sources (preferred stock, common stock, and surplus accounts) is referred to as the *capitalization* of the firm. A commonly used ratio shows *long-term debt as a percentage of total capitalization*. Using Cenco figures of 1960 we have:

$$\boxed{\frac{\text{Long-Term Debt}}{\text{Total Capitalization}}} = \frac{2,050}{2,050 + 6,941} = \underline{22.8\%}.$$

L-T   STOCK
DEBT   EQUITY

The 22.8% figure compares with one of 27.5% for 1959. Thus, this ratio indicates a modest decline in the importance of long-term debt in the total long-term financing at Cenco. The increased percentage of debt to total assets noted earlier then reflects the short-term bank borrowing and the sharp increases in each of the other current liabilities.

Another ratio used to summarize the relationship between total equity and total debt is the *equity-to-debt* ratio. Computing this ratio for Cenco at year end, 1960, we show the following:

$$\frac{\text{Total Equity, 1960}}{\text{Total Debt, 1960}} = \frac{6,941}{5,072} = \underline{\underline{1.37}}.$$

The 1960 equity-to-debt ratio of 1.37 compares with one of 1.58 for year-end 1959. The decline in the ratio reflects the greater reliance on debt in the total financing of Cenco, which is also highlighted by the figures for total debt as a percentage of total assets.

Speaking generally from a creditor's viewpoint, the lower the percentage of debt financing to total assets the better. The creditor can regard the ownership funds as representing a buffer protecting him from loss. If, for example, debt is only 20% of total assets, the assets could shrink in liquidation to one fifth of the balance sheet values and still be sufficient to cover debt claims, since creditors are entitled to be paid out in full before the owners are entitled to anything. In contrast, if total debts amount to 90% of total assets, a shrinkage of more than 10% would leave the creditors "under water."

Of course, the amount of debt that the business can reasonably carry depends on many factors, to be discussed at length in a later chapter. A public utility with stable earnings and favorable prospects may safely finance a much larger percentage of its assets with debt than can, say, a manufacturer with a past record of erratic profitability who produces a single specialty product of uncertain long-term demand.

As we observed earlier, the conclusion that a particular ratio depicts a good or bad condition may rest with the analyst's viewpoint. One suspects that the holders of Cenco's outstanding long-term debt might well prefer a slower expansion financed predominantly by retained earnings or equity issues to faster expansion with convertible debentures which, if the company's fortunes wane, would remain unconverted as debt. Yet, to the common stockholders the convertible debentures may well represent the most feasible means of financing desirable rapid expansion.

Increasing the Usefulness of Ratio Analysis

In our analysis of Cenco, we have looked only at the balance sheets at the end of Cenco's 1959 and 1960 fiscal years and at operating results for 2 years. We could add depth to our analysis by extending it backward over a much longer span of years. The calculation of ratios for a span of years may bring to light important trends unapparent in analysis focused on short periods. Further, marked changes in the ratios from those characteristic of the past may signal important changes in industry conditions or in management policies deserving further investigation. Thus, data on the use of debt relative to equity financing over, say, a 10-year period would make clearer whether the rise in the debt percentage shown in 1960, and promised for 1961, was in line with a long-standing management policy of gradually expanding reliance on debt or a sharp departure from past debt policies. Similarly, the profit ratios for 1960 would take on more meaning against the background of profit ratios over a longer period. If profit ratios have bounced up and down from year to year in the past, the 1960 improvement would be much less encouraging than if it were found to be in line with a long and steady trend toward wider margins and greater sales.

It can also be helpful to compare the funds flow data and the ratios of the subject firm with those of competitors in the same industry. Many trade associations and other industry groups collect and publish data for firms in the industry, often classified by size or specialized activities within the industry. If the firms within industry groups operated along similar lines and under reasonably comparable conditions, comparison of the subject firm's ratios with industry ratios can add much to the analysis. It should be emphasized that deviations from typical industry ratios should not be judged as being undesirable per se. For example, the firm under study may show a much higher investment in receivables relative to sales than its competitors. At first thought, it might appear that the subject firm was guilty of dangerously lax credit policies. But in fact, the high ratio may be simply the reflection of a conscious management policy of competing for sales through especially liberal credit policies; and this policy might be paying off handsomely to the firm in the form of higher sales and profits, and even return on assets, than it otherwise would have achieved. In other words, deviations from "normal" may mean simply that the firm operates differently, not less effectively. Further, the ratios are drawn from the accounting data of the firm, and differences in accounting policies and practices between firms naturally limit complete comparability between their respective ratios.

In recent years the moves of many firms toward diversification into multiple-product lines that cut across traditional industry groupings has made more difficult comparison of these firms with industry indices. Indeed, a number of firms are sufficiently unique to defy close comparison with any other. However, it may still be possible for management of these concerns to make useful ratio comparisons among certain of their divisions or subsidiaries and of these units with ratios drawn from other firms in the industries in which these units operate.

Since this discussion is already an extended one, we shall concede in our analysis of Cenco the advantages of depth of analysis that might have been gained through comparison with Cenco ratios of earlier years or with industry ratios. Let us see what we can add from our admittedly limited ratio analysis to the interpretative comments on Cenco's statements that were based only on the funds flow analysis. The reader is asked to compare the following with what he would regard as the major points from the analysis worthy of inclusion in a summary commentary. There is abundant room for differences in view as to the more significant points for comment and emphasis.

Cenco's 1960 sales increased 40.4% over 1959; profits were up 60.3%. The disproportionate profit increase reflected a small increase in gross margin and a larger cut in the percentage of the sales dollar consumed by operating expenses, which more than matched an increase in Cenco's effective tax rate. Though heavy inventories are carried (turnover of cost of sales was 2.34), the inventory increases were less, proportionately, than that of sales. Year-end receivables were up much more than sales, the collection period rising from 46.9 to 63 days. This might well warrant inquiry. The high (20.22 times) turnover of plant in terms of sales of 1959 was boosted further to 27.34 times. Profit return on total assets at year end increased to 9.73% from 7.88%, while return on shareholders' investment jumped from 12.88% in 1959 to 16.84%.

Reflecting the various financing moves, liquidity ratios all showed sharp declines, but the acid-test ratio at year-end 1960 still was 1.48. Liquid assets were 25.6% of current liabilities, down from 117%. Management increased its use of debt as shown by an increase in the percentage of debt to total assets from 38.8% to 42.22%. If none of the proceeds of the forthcoming $5 million convertible debenture issue is used to repay existing debts, the debt percentage will rise to some 59% of total assets.

Actually, the above summary of the results of the ratio analysis could well be blended into the earlier comments drawn from the funds flow analysis for a more compact single statement of the results of our financial analysis.

Recognizing the Limitations of Ratio Analysis

At several points in our discussion of ratio analysis, we have counseled caution in the interpretation of ratios. Hasty or overconfident judgments as to the facts behind the ratios can prove dangerously wrong. For example, the increased collection period in Cenco *might* reflect credit or collection difficulties. But other possible interpretations may, upon inquiry, prove the real explanation. For example, public school administrative agencies are notoriously slow in processing and paying bills. A shift in the mix of total sales toward more sales to schools could well explain the change. Or it might simply be due to very heavy sales in the weeks before the fiscal year end. Ratios are mechanical tools of analysis; they never should be used standing alone as arbitrary standards of excellence. As aids to judgment, they can be helpful; as mechanical substitutes for thinking and judgment, they can be worse than useless.

Chapter 8

Forecasting Future Needs for Funds

VIRTUALLY ALL financial managers do some sort of forecasting of the future needs for funds of their business. Yet, in many firms the forecasting is so limited in scope, haphazard, based on rules of thumb of dubious reliability, or on such a short-term basis that many of the potential gains from careful, organized planning of financial needs are lost. As a practical matter, the major issue connected with cash planning in most concerns is not whether any financial planning will be attempted but rather how far the managers should go in putting their funds forecasting into organized, systematic, and careful form.

Effective forecasting of funds needs, like any kind of forward planning, calls for mental effort, cooperation of the nonfinancial executives, and time and energy. The advantages to be gained must justify the effort involved. Actually, in the typical firm the potential benefits from fully effective forecasting of financial needs can be great. The benefits include the following:

1. Pretesting of the financial feasibility of various programs before moves are made that are difficult to retract.
2. Facilitation of the raising of additional funds that may be required.
3. Increased confidence in the firm's management on the part of lenders or other sources of funds.
4. Provision of a control device or check points useful in exposing deviations from plans.
5. Improvements in utilization of funds, particularly of cash balances.

Systematic financial forecasting pushed well into the future provides the necessary data for review by top management as to the advisability of projected plans and programs in the light of their probable impact on the company's finances. In most concerns the supply of available funds is by no means unlimited, and the plans of the company must be shaped to fit the financial capabilities of the firm. Once the needs implicit in proposed programs are set forth, those programs involving undue outlays can be cut back or reshaped before embarrassing commitments are made. For

152

example, a medium-sized manufacturing concern had expanded profitably over the years without particular cash stringencies to signal the need for careful cash planning. Rather casually, management undertook the construction of a new plant and office building, the expansion of civilian sales, and a large government manufacturing contract, all of which, it developed, called for heavy cash outlays at about the same time. Some of the needs for cash, such as the heavy cash outlays involved in moving to the new location, and the extent and timing of the other needs were not calculated or foreseen by top management. Consequently, a serious shortage of cash developed, which had to be met through hasty and improvised borrowing arrangements on highly disadvantageous terms. Very serious embarrassment was narrowly averted. To use a nautical analogy, careful cash planning would have pointed up the financial rocks and shoals ahead before the course of the business was firmly set. Further, in many cases where no major new programs calling for large cash outlays are planned, many diverse and individually small needs can combine to sneak up insidiously and confront management with unexpected cash stringency.

When the cash forecasts indicate that programs desirable on balance will result in the need to raise additional funds, the advance warning gives the company time to turn around in planning and executing programs to raise funds. Many methods of raising funds—sale of common stock, for example—normally require several months in consummation. Unanticipated cash stringencies leading to hasty crash-program efforts to find funds often result in the company's assuming loan repayment or other commitments it subsequently finds difficult to meet.

Furthermore, advance discussion and planning of financial needs with lenders or other sources of money tend to inspire confidence that management is on top of its problems. For example, two young men promoting a new enterprise appeared at a commercial bank to discuss prospective loan needs of their business several months in the future. With them, they brought a full outline of their plans, with schedules showing financial needs under various alternative plans of action. The banker, who was more accustomed to seeing loan applicants only after financial needs had become immediate and urgent, was impressed and offered a substantial credit. The banker was even more impressed (and the young businessmen were almost equally surprised in view of the many variables involved) when their cash forecast for the program selected proved accurate almost to the dollar.

Cash forecasts can be valuable as a control device as well as an aid to planning. Once plans are agreed upon and programs are under way, the forecasted levels of cash can serve as check points against which actual results can be compared. Significant deviations from expected levels serve as signals that the program is not moving along as it should and hence requires top-management attention and action. Alternatively, deviations may indicate that the plans were unrealistic and should be revised in the light of unforeseen or uncontrollable developments.

While cash forecasting is especially important for firms whose financial resources are limited, it can also be useful in affluent concerns by pointing up opportunities to use liquid funds more profitably. For example, in one very large, wealthy, and liquid company, only a modicum of financial planning was done prior to a postwar management reorganization. The new financial management undertook a wide range of planning activities, including cash forecasting. The cash forecasts revealed that existing cash balances were unnecessarily high. Subsequent investment of unneeded cash in income-producing securities reportedly contributed income sufficient to more than cover the costs of a wide range of valuable planning activity.

Techniques of Forecasting the Need for Funds

Two different methods of forecasting future cash needs are widely used. These are the cash flow forecast method and the projected balance sheet method. Naturally, being forecasts of the same thing, they should show the same net results. In this chapter we shall explain the essential nature of each approach and outline for each method the basic procedures in building a forecast of cash needs. Each method will be illustrated by reference to a simple situation, but we do not wish to imply that a single format can be applied mechanically to any business situation. While the essentials of forecasting are broadly applicable, the details of the approach should be adapted to fit the distinctive needs and circumstances of the subject business. The related case problems are relied upon to help the student get a working understanding of how to apply the basic techniques to the requirements of specific business situations. It is suggested that the student use this chapter to get a basic idea of how to go about forecasting cash needs in advance of the case work on forecasting, and then as reference material in handling the cases. Finally, we suggest that the student review the chapter carefully after he has worked with the forecasting cases. Much of the generalized discussion here will have more meaning after the student has struggled with the specifics of the case problems.

The Cash Flow Forecast

The most basic and comprehensive method of predicting the amount and the time of future funds needs is through preparation of a *cash flow forecast* or, as it is often called, a *cash budget*. Essentially, the cash flow forecast is a tabulation of the plans of the firm in terms of their impact on the receipts and expenditures of cash in future periods. The basic theory of the cash flow forecast is simple—it seeks merely to predict when and in what quantity receipts of cash will come into the firm and when and in what quantity payments of cash will be made. It is not much of an oversimplification to think of the cash forecast as a timed prediction of additions to and deductions from the company's bank accounts.

In the cash forecast, all anticipated receipts of cash are included, regardless of whether or not they represent income in the accounting sense. Thus, included along with collection of cash from sales and receivables arising out of sales are cash receipts from such sources as sale of securities or sale of fixed assets. Similarly, the tabulation of payments should include, along with routine payments of accounts payable, wages, salaries, rents, etc., any planned payments of taxes, dividends, loan repayments, or outlays for equipment or buildings. It should *not* include expense items which do not represent outlays of cash, such as the allowance for depreciation and the allowance for bad debts.

Usually, the financial planner is interested in revealing not only the total outflow and inflow over an extended period, such as a year, but also the timing of the cash flows within this period. In most cash forecasts, receipts and payments are broken down by months. If uneven inflow and outgo are anticipated within the monthly intervals, it may be necessary to break the forecast down into weekly or even daily periods if maximum needs are to be brought to light.

Some concerns vary the time period breakdown of the cash forecast according to how far into the future the forecast is projected. One concern, for example, has a program of cash flow forecasting that extends 5 years ahead. Estimates for the next month are broken down by days, for the following 11 months by months, for the next 12 months by quarters, and for the ensuing 3 years only by annual periods. This pattern is based on two arguments, the first being that highly detailed information as to timing is needed only for short periods ahead. The second is that the accuracy of the estimating decreases markedly as the forecasts are pushed out into the future and consequently that the distant forecasts are too uncertain to justify more than general planning for the needs suggested by them.

We have described the cash flow forecast as a tabulation of the plans of the business in terms of the effect of these plans on the cash account. As such, the results of the cash flow forecast will prove only as accurate and as reliable as the underlying planning on which the forecast is based. And as we have seen in earlier chapters, virtually all of the significant activities of the firm affect its flow of funds. Thus, for complete effectiveness in his work the forecaster of funds flows first needs comprehensive and accurate data on what the operations of the firm will likely be.

The task of assembling the background data for the cash flow forecast is made much easier if the firm operates under *profit budgeting*. Under profit budgeting, profit objectives are set for the firm, and operations are planned to produce the desired results. Revenues and expenses are forecasted in detail; and if necessary, the plans are altered so as to produce the desired end results. Some firms employing profit budgeting use the budgets exclusively as planning devices and make no effort to use the estimates as a continuing control device to force actual operations to conform to the plans. Many others go further and do attempt to control operations in such a way that the targeted profit goals actually are realized. Where the budget is used as a control as well as a planning device, provision is typically made for revision of the original targets, if unforeseen or uncontrollable factors make them inappropriate.

Where operations of the firm are closely geared to careful plans, and planning assumptions are revised to reflect changes in the outlook, it is possible for the cash forecaster to maintain cash forecasts that are much more likely to prove accurate and reliable than is possible in other firms that utilize budgets for planning alone or that attempt no formal planning, simply "playing it by ear."

Where profit budgets exist, they supply much of the background information needed for preparation of a cash flow forecast. The task of forecasting cash flows becomes one of simply translating these plans, which are stated primarily in terms of accounting income and expense, into cash flow terms, as described later in this chapter. Actually, although the use of profit budgeting is growing, most firms still do not have a carefully organized profit budget program. Yet, cash flow planning, though on a less solid footing, may still be highly useful to them. Under such circumstances, what information must the financial officer assemble, and how can he organize it into a cash flow forecast?

Probably the most critical estimate in cash flow forecasting is the forecast of sales. Usually, sales represent the primary source of cash receipts. Further, the operations of the business requiring cash outlays are typically geared to the anticipated volume of sales. Particularly closely tied to sales are the purchases of materials and outlays directly related to manufacturing. In compiling sales forecast data, the financial officer must usually rely heavily on the active cooperation of the sales department. Ideally, the sales department will provide a sales forecast in terms of both physical units and dollar value, and this will be checked and approved by top management.

Let us assume, for purposes of illustration, that the financial officer of the Able Company is preparing a 6-month cash forecast beginning in January, to be broken down into monthly periods. Putting ourselves in his place, we shall assume that the best estimate we can get calls for sales of $200,000 per month in the first 3 months, $250,000 per month for April and May, and $300,000 in June. Ten percent of the sales are expected to be for cash, the remainder on credit terms. On the basis of the experience of the firm, we estimate that the receivables arising out of sales will be collected approximately 1 month after sale. It is further estimated that the outstanding receivables on December 31 will amount to $185,000 and that these will all be collected in January. No bad debts are expected. The sales forecast now can be converted into a schedule of cash receipts from sales, expressed in thousands of dollars, as follows:

	Jan.	Feb.	March	April	May	June	Total
Total sales.................	$200	$200	$200	$250	$250	$300	$1,400
Credit sales................	180	180	180	225	225	270	1,260
Receipts from collection of accounts receivable..........	185	180	180	180	225	225	1,175
Cash sales.................	20	20	20	25	25	30	140
Cash receipts—sales.........	$205	$200	$200	$205	$250	$255	$1,315

Note that the collection of the receivables from sales is scheduled to lag 1 month behind the credit sales. Thus, the $225,000 credit sales of April are shown as cash receipts of May.

Now, let us take into account any anticipated receipts from sources other than sales, such as the proceeds of sale of fixed assets or of new security issues. The only cash receipts apart from those arising from routine sales, already tabulated, which are anticipated are from the planned sale for cash of used equipment no longer required, amounting to $40,000 in April and $30,000 in June. With this information, we are ready to put together a summary schedule of forecasted cash receipts, expressed in thousands of dollars:

	Jan.	Feb.	March	April	May	June	Total
Cash receipts—sales ...	$205	$200	$200	$205	$250	$255	$1,315
Proceeds from sale of used equipment.....	...	...	...	40	...	30	70
Total cash receipts.......	$205	$200	$200	$245	$250	$285	$1,385

Now, let us turn to the forecast of cash payments. As we have said, many of the operations of the company are geared to the sales forecast. It serves as the basis for the development of manufacturing schedules that will provide the products needed for sale and inventory. The production schedules indicate the timing and amount of labor, material, and additional equipment needed. On the basis of the material needs established by the production schedules, procurement officials can be expected to prepare schedules of planned purchases of materials and of equipment. A major step in building the forecast of payments is the conversion of the purchase schedules, employing appropriate assumptions as to the terms of sale that will be offered by suppliers, into a schedule of anticipated payments of the accounts payable arising out of these purchases. Any purchases for cash usually are best listed separately.

Let us assume that the purchase schedule drawn up in the Able Company calls for purchase of materials costing $70,000 in each of the first 3 months and $90,000 a month thereafter. All are to be purchased on 30-day payment terms, and the accounts payable will be paid promptly when due. The company is also planning to buy two major items of equipment costing $200,000 each, one for delivery in January and the second in June. Sixty-day terms are expected on these items. In addition, routine replacement of minor equipment items of $5,000 per month is expected, also purchased on 60-day terms. Miscellaneous cash purchases of $1,000 per month are also planned. The outstanding payables together with miscellaneous accrued expenses on December 31 are estimated at $110,000, all due in January.

With these data, we can schedule the planned purchases and, from this schedule, prepare a schedule of planned payment for purchases, expressed in thousands of dollars:

	Jan.	Feb.	March	April	May	June	Total
PLANNED PURCHASES							
Cash purchases	$ 1	$ 1	$ 1	$ 1	$ 1	$ 1	$ 6
Production materials	70	70	70	90	90	90	480
Replacement equipment	5	5	5	5	5	5	30
Special equipment	200	...	...	...	...	200	400
PAYMENT FOR PURCHASES							
Trade payables outstanding on December 31	110	...	...	...	...	...	110
Cash purchases	1	1	1	1	1	1	6
Production materials	...	70	70	70	90	90	390
Replacement equipment	...	...	5	5	5	5	20
Special equipment	...	...	200	...	...	...	200
Total	$111	$71	$276	$76	$96	$ 96	$726

The wage costs established by the production program next are tabulated and brought into a summary schedule of payments when they are expected to be paid. Usually, wages are paid weekly so that the payments closely coincide with the incurring of wage expense. In our illustration, wage payments of $50,000 are scheduled for each of the 6 months. Other manufacturing costs, such as light and power, are estimated to require payments of $10,000 each month.

General and administrative expenses, such as rents, salaries, travel expense, and property taxes, should next be tabulated and included in the summary schedule of payments in the month of payment. The total of these is estimated to call for payments of $25,000 each month.

Income tax payments, scheduled repayment of existing loans, dividends, and other nonroutine items of significance are usually listed separately in the summary payments schedule. The only such payments anticipated in the Able Company are income tax payments of $20,000 in March and again in June, and a dividend payment of $40,000 in January.

Having satisfied ourselves that no prospective payments have been overlooked, we can now bring the anticipated payments together in a summary schedule of payments, expressed in thousands of dollars:

SUMMARY CASH PAYMENT SCHEDULE

	Jan.	Feb.	March	April	May	June	Total
Payments for purchases.............	$111	$ 71	$276	$ 76	$ 96	$ 96	$ 726
Wages paid........................	50	50	50	50	50	50	300
Other manufacturing payments.......	10	10	10	10	10	10	60
Payments of general and administrative expenses....................	25	25	25	25	25	25	150
Payments of income taxes...........	...	...	20	...	...	20	40
Dividend payments.................	40	...	...	...	...	...	40
Total payments.............	$236	$156	$381	$161	$181	$201	$1,316

Now, let us bring the summaries of payments and receipts together and calculate the *net* cash inflows or outgoes for each month by subtracting the total payments from the total of anticipated receipts. An additional calculation of cumulative inflow, or outgo, should next be made. When matched with cash on hand at the beginning of the period, it is then possible to calculate the additional cash needed (or excess cash above minimum needs) in order to maintain the minimum cash balance desired. In our illustration, assume that cash on hand on December 31 amounted to $65,000. Further, let us assume that after consideration of all the aspects bearing on the subject (such as those discussed in Chapter 5), management decided that it wished to maintain at each month-end a cash balance of no less than $50,000:

SUMMARY SCHEDULE OF CASH FLOWS
(In Thousands)

	Jan.	Feb.	March	April	May	June	Total
Total receipts.............	$205	$200	$ 200	$245	$250	$285	$1,385
Total payments...........	236	156	381	161	181	201	1,316
Net inflow or outgo ( )	$(31)	$ 44	$(181)	$ 84	$ 69	$ 84	$ 69
Cumulative inflow or outgo ( )...............	(31)	13	(168)	(84)	(15)	69	69
Beginning cash.............	65						65
Minimum cash.............	50						(50)
Funds above minimum needs or funds shortage ( ) end of month...............	(16)	28	(153)	(69)	0	84	84

It can be seen that a substantial shortage of cash can be expected in March, but that operations of the business should generate enough net cash inflow in April and May so that the need for extra funds should last little more than 2 months. A brief analysis of the data reveals that the shortage is primarily attributable to the payment in March for the

$200,000 equipment item scheduled for January purchase and for March payment. Confronted with our evidence of the forthcoming shortage of cash, management can plan to finance the needs by borrowing or other methods. Alternatively, it can reconsider the plans, perhaps postponing the $200,000 equipment purchase until March or April, in order to reduce the need for funds during this 6-month period.

We should emphasize again that those expenses which do not by their nature require cash outlay are not included in the cash forecast. Thus, we did not include the important expense item for manufacturers, depreciation, among the payments listed in our illustration. On the other hand, appropriately, we did include the payments for equipment purchased (except for the second purchase, for which payment was not due until July) and of dividends, even though they are not treated as expenses.

Our cash forecast illustration was based on a single set of plans for the business. Where alternative plans of operation are under consideration, it will often prove helpful to run cash forecasts based on each alternative plan. This permits the financial officer to determine the cash impact of each plan and to help top management decide on the best alternative in the light of this information.

The Essential Nature of the Projected Balance Sheet Method

The projected or *pro forma* balance sheet method of forecasting funds requirements is built around a forecast of the size of key balance sheet items at a selected date or dates in the future. Four major steps are involved in building a balance sheet forecast. The first involves forecast of the net investment required in each of the assets in order to carry out operations at the level planned on the date involved—say, a date 6 months ahead. Second, the liabilities that can be counted on without especial negotiation are listed. Third, the net worth on that date is estimated. The total of projected assets is then compared with the total sources of funds—debts and net worth. If the total of assets required exceeds the total for expected liabilities and net worth, the difference represents the additional sources that must be negotiated if operations and the buildup of assets to desired levels are to proceed as planned. On the other hand, should the sources exceed the assets required, the excess presumably indicates the additional cash above the desired minimum level that will be on hand.

Put another way, in using the balance sheet approach, the forecaster is reasoning essentially as follows: To carry out our plans, certain predictable investment in assets is required. On the other hand, we can count on certain spontaneous sources of credit. The owners' investment in the business as of the future date can also be predicted. If our indicated sources fall short of meeting the desired investment in the various assets, the amount by which the sources must be expanded or asset investment held down is made apparent. If the expected sources more than cover the needed asset investment, a measure is provided of the cash cushion above minimum working balance needs or of cash available for uses beyond those envisioned in the original planning estimates.

Major Steps in Preparing the Projected Balance Sheet

With this general explanation of the approach in mind, let us now look more closely at each of the key steps in preparation of a projected balance sheet forecast. Let us assume that the subject firm has prepared fairly definite estimates of sales through to the date of the projected balance sheet and that in the light of the sales expectations, manufacturing and procurement schedules have been drawn up in some detail. Let us also assume that profits for the period have been budgeted.

A first item to be estimated is the anticipated investment in accounts receivable on the forecast date. As we have seen, a major determinant of the size of the receivables investment is the volume of sales. From past records of sales and receivables, the forecaster can determine what the relationship of receivables has been to sales in the past. The ratio suggested by past experience then should be adjusted in the light of any anticipated changes in credit terms, in the leniency with which credit will be granted, or in any other factor that might affect the receivables balance. The adjusted ratio then can be applied to the forecasted sales immediately preceding the forecast date.

Inventory needs can also be projected on the basis of "normal" inventory/sales relationships in the past. Alternatively, if purchase, production, and sales plans have been worked out in detail, the value of inventory that will be left on hand at the forecast date can be directly determined, using the approach: Beginning inventory plus purchases plus value added in manufacture less cost of goods sold equals value of inventory left on hand. All inventory values should be in terms of cost rather than selling prices.

The investment in fixed assets should next be forecasted. Planned purchases of new plant or equipment are added to the existing net investment in fixed assets, and planned depreciation is subtracted, in order to arrive at the estimated net investment in fixed assets on the forecast date.

Taking into account the considerations discussed in Chapter 5, the minimum cash balance that the firm would wish to carry is next determined.

Turning to the liability side of the balance sheet, the level of accounts payable on the forecast date must next be calculated. Based on the schedule of planned purchases, the assumed purchase terms, and the policy of the firm in meeting the due dates of trade payables, the purchases for which payment will not yet have been made on the forecast date can be tabulated and entered on the projected balance sheet as the anticipated accounts payable.

Accrued wages and other accrued expenses can also be calculated by reference to the production schedule, allowing for the usual lag between the incurring of the wage and other expense items and the required payment of the accrued expenses. Often it is useful to assume that these items are constant.

The amount of accrued income tax can be estimated directly if the probable profits and income tax rates are known. To the currently outstanding balance of accrued income taxes, the taxes accrued on income to be earned before the forecast date are added. Scheduled payments of taxes are then deducted to arrive at the amount of accrued taxes which will be outstanding on the forecast date.

Next, existing net worth must be adjusted for planned sales of stock, stock retirements, or any other such changes in prospect. Further, the addition to surplus from retained earnings (net profits after taxes less planned dividend payments) must be reckoned. The profits forecast is usually based on a projected income statement.

Let us suppose that when all the anticipated assets and all liability and net worth items are added up, the totals show $1.2 million for assets and $1.05 million for combined liabilities and net worth. Somehow, an additional $150,000 must be secured from owners or creditors if the $1.2 million level of assets is to be reached. Thus, the balancing figure, when planned assets exceed anticipated liabilities and net worth, represents the additional funds needed to permit the planned asset investment—or else the dollar extent by which the investment in assets must be reduced in order to bring it into line with available sources of funds.

On the other hand, if the sources exceed the assets needed, the excess presumably will accrue as cash above the required minimum amount.

It must be emphasized that the projected balance sheet method of forecasting depicts funds requirements as of the particular balance sheet date only. It does not show varying needs in the interim period. In the case of companies whose needs fluctuate sharply from month to month, or seasonally, a forecast of needs based upon construction of a balance sheet as of a single distant date can be highly misleading. Maximum needs during a future period will be brought out only if the dates for projection of balance sheets are carefully selected so as to represent the balance sheet situation at times of maximum strain—that is, dates on which the combinations of heavy asset commitments and below normal liabilities and net worth are most severe.

Some forecasters, using the projected balance sheet approach, attempt to meet the problem of interim fluctuations by setting the minimum level of cash desired at a high enough level to take care of short-lived peak needs within the forecast periods. As indicated earlier, this can be a costly method of meeting peak and temporary needs.

Our outline of procedures useful in fashioning a projected balance sheet was based on the assumption that detailed plans for the business existed and were available to the forecaster—information of a sort that would have permitted preparation of a full-fledged cash flow forecast showing interim needs as well as those on the balance sheet date. But one of the attractions of the projected balance sheet approach is that it can be used (as a cash flow schedule cannot) to make rough—yet often highly useful —forecasts in situations where detailed forward plans of the sort necessary for cash flow forecasting do not exist.

Consider, for example, the following simplified problem. A program of sales expansion was being considered by the Baker Company. The owners of the company said they would be willing to advance any added funds needed to finance the expansion but asked whether they could look forward to the return of these additional advances within a year. Consequently, the question was raised: "If we double sales in the next year, what will be our need for additional funds at the end of one year?"

Let us see if we can answer the query by means of a projected balance sheet a year ahead.[1] The current balance sheet was as follows:

Cash.....................	$ 50,000	Trade payables..........	$120,000
Receivables..............	120,000	Accrued expenses.........	60,000
Inventory................	240,000	Accrued income taxes......	30,000
Net fixed assets..........	400,000	Net worth................	600,000
Total assets........	$810,000	Total liabilities.....	$810,000

In the past year, sales had amounted to $1.2 million and profits were $120,000 before taxes. Income taxes were at the rate of 50%. Production and sales were at a relatively even rate, and the sales at the doubled rate were also expected to be achieved evenly through the coming year. In the past, receivables and inventory had borne approximately the same relationship to sales as currently. Profits of 12% before taxes, 6% after taxes, were expected on the new volume of $2.4 million. No dividends were planned. The Baker Company's productive facilities were adequate for the expanded volume, and new equipment to be purchased would about equal the depreciation to be charged during the year. Since detailed plans did not yet exist, other than for sales, we shall have to draw liberally on the relationships between the various assets and sales in the past as guidelines for estimating the needed investment in these assets at the doubled volume of sales.

Turning first to the estimate of receivables, we note that the current $120,000 figure represents approximately 10% of annual sales at the $1.2 million volume. In the absence of indications that this relationship will not continue at the higher sales volume, we can estimate the receivables on $2.4 million sales at $240,000.

A similar approach to the inventory figure suggests a doubling of the

---

[1] This simplified example disregards the special treatment applicable to the first $100,000 of estimated tax liability as explained in the Tax Table at the end of this book.

current inventory to $480,000. Since the new acquisitions of fixed assets are expected to equal the depreciation to be charged, we can carry $400,000 forward as our net investment in fixed assets.

Now, let us assume that after consideration of all aspects of the problem, it is decided somewhat arbitrarily that $75,000 will provide an adequate minimum level of cash for the expanded operations.

Accounts payable in the past have fluctuated with the volume of purchases, which in turn have varied with sales. Similarly, accrued expenses have tended to vary with the level of production, which also has moved with sales. Consequently, we can forecast with some confidence a doubling of these items with a doubling of sales.

The accrued income tax item is shown by the current balance sheet to be one half of the previous year's income taxes. Since the income tax rate of 50% is assumed to remain constant, our taxes on profits of $288,000 (12% of $2.4 million sales) should amount to $144,000. If the schedule of required payments is assumed to remain the same, then we can expect one half of the $144,000 taxes, or $72,000, to remain outstanding as accrued taxes a year hence.

Net worth should increase by the amount of the profits after taxes, or $144,000, to a projected total of $744,000. Putting these estimates together, we get the following projected balance sheet:

Cash..................	$ 75,000	Trade payables.........	$ 240,000
Receivables.............	240,000	Accrued liabilities.......	120,000
Inventory..............	480,000	Accrued income taxes....	72,000
Net fixed assets........	400,000	Net worth.............	744,000
	$1,195,000		$1,176,000

Desired asset position............$1,195,000	
Anticipated liabilities and net worth....................... 1,176,000	
Additional funds needed.........$ 19,000	

Thus, we see that on the assumptions built into the above forecasted balance sheet, additional funds of $19,000 will be required a year hence to support operations at the $2.4 million sales level. Although, as is true of any forecast, the estimate is only as reliable as the assumptions on which it was based, it does give an approximate answer to the owners' question which prompted this forecast. We can assure the owners that if operations proceed as we expect them to, they will need to keep only $19,000 in added investment in the firm for more than a year.

Upon reflection, it should be apparent that the balance sheet does not picture the maximum amount the owners will have to advance during the coming year if sales are to be built up to the $2.4 million annual volume at once. Receivables and inventory presumably will be doubled almost at once in line with the immediate doubling of sales. While trade payables and accrued expenses also can be expected to increase rapidly, the accrued income tax liability and, more importantly, the net worth account will only gradually be built up through retained earnings to the year hence totals. Thus, the need for additional funds should peak at a high figure soon after the higher sales volume is reached. Our projected balance sheet as of a year ahead, though it supplies an answer to the specific question posed, definitely does *not* show the maximum amount the owners will have to advance the company in the interim months. A further balance sheet projection as of the anticipated date of maximum need or a monthly cash flow forecast will be necessary in order to establish this figure.

So far, we have spoken of the projected balance sheet method primarily as an alternative to the cash flow forecast approach. Actually, when a cash flow forecast has been made, it is a relatively simple matter to round out the forecast data by preparation of projected balance sheets also. If consistent assumptions are used in the two approaches, the cash flow forecast and projected balance sheets should yield identical estimates of cash as of corresponding dates.

Some Basic Problems in Effective Cash Forecasting

An important practical limitation to effective cash forecasting by either method, but especially to cash flow forecasting, is suggested by our earlier discussion. We refer to the fact that virtually all of the firm's operations affect its need for cash; and hence, in order to forecast cash needs closely, comprehensive and detailed planning data are required. Most of these data cover operational areas outside the direct responsibility of the financial officer. It is seldom hard for the financial officer to get his management associates to agree in theory that careful planning is important and desirable. But it often is more difficult, when day-to-day problems are clamoring for their attention, to get other department personnel to devote time and effort to the less obviously urgent task of planning well into the future. Unless top management appreciates the value of good forecasting and insists that planning is given appropriate attention throughout the organization, getting the necessary data on which to base his cash forecasts is likely to be a continuing problem for the financial officer.

Even if top management appreciates the need for careful planning and organizes to do a good job of it, the realistic forecaster knows that no matter how well he does his work, he cannot expect to prove exactly right in his forecasts. Most businesses operate in an atmosphere of change, and predictions of an inherently uncertain future necessarily are subject to error. Of course, the degree of predictability of the future varies among firms. Some are highly vulnerable to sharp fluctuations in sales or to disruptions of their plans owing to such events as strikes or the breakdown of key equipment. For example, firms whose sales are directly dependent on the vagaries of the weather have difficult cash forecasting assignments. Manufacturers of fertilizer being sold in areas where its use by farmers is sharply influenced by the season's rainfall face forecasting problems inherently more formidable than those of firms whose sales are made against firm orders placed long in advance of production.

Yet, even in those firms where the future is hard to predict, the choice is not one of planning or not planning. Rather, it is one of the degree to which the difficult job of planning is thought through and organized. And there is much that the firm whose future operations are inherently difficult to plan can do to make its forecasting as helpful as possible and to reduce management's problems of staying on top of the finances of the firm.

First, in the highly variable situation, it is particularly important that management recognize the likely margins of error inherent in its forecasts. So, at the least, management can avoid the hazards involved in attaching false connotations of accuracy in forecast data based on inherently tenuous assumptions.

Second, in situations where different assumptions as to key variables reasonably can be made, it may be helpful to prepare several different forecasts, each employing a different basic assumption as to the key variable. This, in effect, permits the financial officer to determine, "If this happens, then this will be the effect on cash . . . , etc." For example, a forecaster for the fertilizer concern referred to earlier might well run different forecasts using sales estimates based on normal, on heavy, and on sparse rainfall, and thus be forewarned as to the funds implications of each development. Along the same lines, some firms find it helpful to put together forecasts under combinations of assumptions that would picture likely minimum and maximum, as well as most probable, needs for the future period.

Third, frequent revision of the forecasts as the future unfolds helps to keep them attuned to changing conditions and to provide as much advance notice as possible of developing changes in the need for funds. In the very dynamic firm the forecasts must be adjusted almost continuously if they are to be helpful in detailed financial planning.

Fourth, the organization of the firm and the way its finances are handled can be adjusted to fit the degree of variability of its future needs. For example, the firm subject to sudden, hard-to-predict cash outflows might well plan to carry a much larger cash balance than would be appropriate in a firm whose future needs were subject to more accurate prediction.

Further, experience with forecasting in the firm should lead to development of improved methods, both of preparation of forecasts and of their interpretation, which will reduce to a minimum the inherent margins of error. Learning by trial and error has its place in forecasting.

When forecasts of cash needs are prepared for use by top managers or outsiders such as bank lending officers, the forecaster should include with the forecast data a careful statement of the key assumptions upon which his forecasts were based. This gives the reviewer a better basis for understanding the figures and an opportunity to form his own judgments as to the validity of the key assumptions. Further, subsequent revisions of the forecasts based on differing assumptions can be more readily understood and appraised.

Long-Range Financial Forecasting

Just as financial management in the short term can be made far more effective by the practice of budgeting financial sources and needs, so in the long run it is desirable to have an estimate of the quantity and timing of funds movements. Of course, the farther into the future one looks, the less detail is seen, and the greater is the likely variance of the long-term estimate from the actual event. But, while it must be admitted that in a few cases the outlook is almost completely unpredictable (and a long-range forecast meaningless), in the majority of firms some meaningful specification can be made about the next few years.

There is every reason not to forecast in greater detail than the uncertainties of the situation permit. Early in World War II, one of the authors was shown a 3-year forecast, by months, of the detailed income statements and balance sheets of a company making military aircraft. It had been made with immense labor, and it was worthless, because everyone knew that the product was obsolescent and that any new product would have very different funds flow (as well as airflow) characteristics. A simple forecast, showing a few broad categories of inflow and outflow, was all that might usefully have been made.

On the other extreme, the electric and telephone utilities estimate their financial flows, and plan their expansion and its financing, 5, 10, and even 15 years ahead of actual construction. They are able to do so, of course, both because the demand for their product is related in a very stable way to the growth of production and population and also because (despite technological changes) the capital investment and other funds flow characteristics relative to volume are also stable.

The format for long-range financial forecasts found useful by many firms is one in which funds flows over the near future are tabulated in detail, the intermediate future is pictured in a more generalized way, and the long-term by even fewer categories. The short-term forecast often takes the form of a cash budget, while the longer term will be presented by pro forma funds flow statements with aggregate figures under such captions as: funds provided by operations, working capital changes, plant and equipment expenditures, tax payments, financial burden, and proceeds of new financing. Many of these items can be expected to have a steady ratio to sales, others are matters of contract or law, and the rest will reflect established policies concerning the security issues of the corporation.

PART IV

Short-Term Sources of Funds

Chapter 9

Spontaneous Sources of Credit

In PRECEDING chapters we have discussed at length how continued investment in particular assets is a necessary feature of most business operations. Before we turn to further consideration of sources, we should recognize that successful business operations give rise not only to needs for funds but, happily, to certain significant sources of credit. In the normal course of profitable operations, three major sources of continuing credit tend to develop without especial effort or negotiation. Together, these sources constitute a substantial offset to the gross need for funds in the business. Since they grow out of normal patterns of profitable operation without special effort or conscious decision on the part of owners or managers, they can be thought of as *spontaneous* or *self-generating sources* of credit. They reduce the amounts of funds that the managers must raise from other sources.

NORMAL TRADE CREDIT

The first and most important of these spontaneous sources is the trade credit normally provided by suppliers of the company. As we have seen, most raw materials, supplies, and other items purchased on a recurring basis are available on purchase terms which permit a delay in payment. The credit standards imposed by sellers, which buying firms must meet in order to get credit on their purchases, seldom are severe. Concerns whose purchases bear a reasonable relationship to their capital and scale of operations, and which can show some liquidity, seldom have difficulty in qualifying for the credit terms normally offered by suppliers.

For American business in general, trade credit represents a major source of funds. For all manufacturing companies, total trade credit was $26.0 billion, or 7.8% of all assets, on March 31, 1965. In the case of manufacturers of apparel and related products, trade payables represented 23.3% of all assets—this source almost matching their investment in inventory.[1] In some companies, which buy on very generous credit

---

[1] Federal Trade Commission and Securities and Exchange Commission, *Quarterly Financial Report for Manufacturing Corporations: First Quarter, 1965* (Washington, D.C.: U.S. Government Printing Office, 1965).

terms, have a short and inexpensive manufacturing operation, and sell on short terms, the trade credit virtually finances their entire operations, making it possible for them to do a very large volume of business with a minimum of ownership funds and negotiated credits. For example, we learned of a manufacturer who insisted that he could finance his working capital needs for the manufacture of parachutes under a government contract on an investment of his own funds of only $17 for each $1,000 of annual sales. Making this possible was the combination of generous credit from suppliers, a simple and fast production operation, and fast collection from the government.

In the wholesale and retail fields, trade credit is relied on heavily. Tax data for a recent year showed that accounts payable were more than 23% of the total assets of wholesale firms and almost 15% of retailers' asset totals. In some fields, trade credit is even more important. Thus, in the construction industry accounts payable were 27% of total assets.

Trade credit is a particularly important source of funds for smaller companies. Many financially weak small firms that find it difficult to negotiate loans from banks or other institutional lenders are able to qualify for trade credit. The importance of trade credit to smaller firms is evidenced by available data on manufacturing concerns. On March 31, 1965, manufacturing firms with assets under $1 million relied on trade credit to finance 19.1% of their total assets. In contrast, manufacturers with assets over $1 billion used trade credit to the extent of only 6.1% of their total assets.[2]

Normal credit terms offered by many suppliers leave purchasers the option of earning a discount by paying within a certain period or of having longer credit without the discount. Very common, for example, are terms of 2/10, net 30—that is, the buyer can deduct a 2% discount from payments made within 10 days, or he can take 30 days to pay without discount. Using the full 30 days is quite permissible under such terms, but the buyer pays a high price for the extra 20 days of credit. By taking the extra 20 days on a $1,000 purchase under such terms, the purchaser gets the use of $980 for an extra 20 days at the cost of the discount forgone of $20. In effect, the purchaser is paying 2.04% (20/980) for the use of the $980 for 20 days, or one eighteenth of a year. In terms of annual interest, the cost of continued loss of the discount is almost 37% (2.04% times 18).

Some suppliers let their terms be regarded as somewhat nominal, taking no action to speed collection until payments become well overdue. If the supplier's terms were nominally 2/10, net 30, but he actually permitted payment in 60 days, the buyer then gets credit for 50 extra days, or 50/365ths of a year, bringing the cost of discounts forgone in

[2] *Ibid.*

terms of annual rates down to 14.8%. Failure to take discounts is still expensive, even when nominal terms are stretched considerably.

Firms which are short of funds find it tempting to lean on their suppliers by delaying payment of trade debt well beyond due dates. Where loss of discounts is not involved, the extra credit taken at the expense of suppliers appears to be "cost-free" credit. Further, suppliers are likely to be the most indulgent of the firm's creditors, particularly if they are well financed and are earning a good profit on the sales to the firm. Some managers have become masterful tacticians in stretching their trade credit to a point just short of the breaking point. Tactics used in making full use—or perhaps we should say "abuse"—of trade credit include "selective payment" of trade debts, which is a euphemism for testing and taking full advantage of the limits of indulgence of each major creditor, concentration of purchases with the most lenient suppliers, and periodic cleanup of overdue accounts on a rotating basis as a means of reducing pressures from suppliers. Many firms have been able to stay in business only through continuous heavy use of trade credit over many years.

As a general rule, taking of cash discounts wherever available, and prompt payment of trade debt when due, represent sound long-run business and financial practice. Not taking discounts is expensive. Too, as we indicated, the network of exchange of credit information is sufficiently well organized and extensive in this country that the payment record of firms becomes a matter of widespread knowledge. A record of promptly meeting all its obligations adds much to the general reputation of the firm. Further, the way the firm handles its obligations to trade creditors will have an impact on its ability to get credit from banks and other lenders. Also, in a sellers' market, where demand pushes hard on supply, "slow-pay" customers may find themselves at a real disadvantage in competing for scarce supplies. In the long run, the tangible and intangible benefits flowing from a record of prompt payment of trade obligations are impressive.

Analyzing Changes in Trade Payables

It should be apparent from the foregoing discussion that the three major determinants of the size of the accounts or notes payable are the terms offered by suppliers, the payment practices of the firm, and the volume of purchases. In most concerns the terms offered by suppliers and the firm's policy as to payment of trade debt do not change frequently. Consequently, the major element back of most changes in the level of trade payables is variation in the volume of recent purchases.

Outside analysts are often anxious, however, to detect any evidences of shifts in policy or practice toward "slow pay." Yet, increases in accounts payable in themselves do not suggest "slow pay"—instead, as indicated above, they are as likely the result simply of a larger volume of purchases. Consequently, analysts typically seek to determine whether changes in the amount of payables outstanding are in line with changes in the volume of purchases. The methods by which payables are compared with purchases are similar to those by which receivables are compared with sales, as are the problems of interpreting the results of the comparison. One method of comparison is to express payables as a simple percentage of recent or annual purchases. A second is to convert outstanding payables into a figure of *days' purchases outstanding*. As was the case in computing days' sales outstanding, a single day's purchases are computed and divided into the outstanding payables. A third method of comparing purchases and payables is to compute the *turnover of payables* by dividing the payables, either year end or average of beginning and ending payables, into total purchases for the period.

Each of the purchases/payables ratios should, when compared with similar ratios for earlier periods and with terms of purchase common for the type of goods purchased, bring to light tendencies toward slowing up or speeding up in payment. Of course, as was true of receivable/sales comparisons, it is most desirable to use *recent* purchase figures wherever they are available, since fluctuations in the level of purchases within an annual period will distort a comparison of annual purchases with the payables at the end of the year which relate to relatively recent purchases only.[3]

Analysts particularly interested in the condition of a firm's accounts payable sometime require an *aging schedule* of the payables. This schedule simply breaks down the payables according to the time they have been outstanding. An aging schedule serves to bring to light the existence and extent of overdue accounts.

In forecasting cash outflows of a concern, the dates when payments for purchases are due, rather than the dates of purchase themselves, are of key concern. Consequently, in planning cash outflows arising out of purchases, it is necessary to prepare a schedule of purchases and then, using time lags appropriate to the customary terms of purchase, to construct a schedule of required payments of trade payables.

ACCRUED EXPENSES

The typical concern is supplied with many services on a continuing basis, with the suppliers of such services not expecting payment immediately upon rendering the service. For example, it is common practice in many businesses to pay the labor force weekly, clerical and supervisory

---

[3] In many cases no data on purchases may be available to the outside analyst. In such cases an analyst with some knowledge of the industry may be able to estimate the annual purchases from cost of sales and annual inventory figures. Assuming a constant rate of purchases, a highly approximate but possibly useful appraisal of the condition of the payables can be made.

personnel twice a month, and executive personnel monthly. In the accounting sense, an expense is created when the services are rendered. But since payment is not made at once, a liability is created, usually termed an *accrued expense*. In effect, the company receives some credit from the wage earner and other suppliers of services. A related source of funds of some significance to important employers stems from established patterns of payment to the federal government of old-age benefit and income taxes which employers must withhold from employees' pay. Employers have until the 15th of the month following the month in which these taxes are withheld to deposit them in an authorized bank. Effectively, the employer has the use of these funds for an average of one month. In the aggregate the credit represented by accrued expenses is of some significance. On March 31, 1965, all U.S. manufacturers reported "other current liabilities," which were chiefly accrued expenses, of $20.6 billion, or 6.2% of their total assets.[4]

Normally, there is little opportunity to postpone the outlays connected with accrued expenses. Thus, the volume of accruals tends to vary with the level of operations. However, if wages and salaries are a major item, the size of accrued expenses shown on the balance sheet will be affected by the date on which employees are paid in comparison with the date on which the balance sheet is computed. Just after payday, the amount will be small.

ACCRUED INCOME TAXES

Under our tax laws, corporations operating at a profit are required to share such profits with the federal government and in many cases with state governments. Thus, every time profits are computed, a liability to the government for its share of the profits should be recognized. In accounting for federal income taxation, the claim of the government to a portion of accruing profits is usually recognized each time profits are calculated by adding an appropriate amount to a liability account variously termed *Accrued Income Taxes, Reserve for Income Taxes,* or *Provision for Income Taxes.* Although the government lays claim to a percentage of the profits as they are made, it does not require payment of the taxes due until after the time when the profits are earned and the liability for taxes is created. So long as a company continues to make profits and thus to incur an income tax liability, it will continue to have an outstanding liability to the government for taxes. As new tax obligations are recognized, these add to the liability, while periodic payments to the government to extinguish old tax debts reduce the total tax liability. Thus, the liability to the government represents, in effect, a continuing source of funds for profitable corporations.

Until 1951 the authorized time lag between receipt of income and

---

[4] Federal Trade Commission and Securities and Exchange Commission, *op. cit.*

required payment of taxes approximated 1 year. The Revenue Acts of 1950, 1954, and 1964, and the Tax Adjustment Act of 1966 have provided for progressive cuts in the authorized delay in tax payment so as to move corporations closer to a "pay-as-you-earn" basis. Corporations with an estimated tax liability of over $100,000 must pay in the year earned progressively larger percentages of the total taxes due on the year's income. As Table 9–1 shows, by 1967 corporations must make equal

TABLE 9–1

PAYMENT DATES FOR CORPORATE U.S. INCOME TAXES*

	Percentage Paid in Income Year				Percentage Paid Following Year	
	April 15	June 15	September 15	December 15	March 15	June 15
1965	4	4	25	25	21	21
1966	12	12	25	25	13	13
1967 and subsequent years	25	25	25	25	..	..

*The Tax Table on page 986 gives more detail on changes in payment percentages.

quarterly payments of the estimated tax on income of the current year. This move toward "pay as you earn" will cut down sharply on a major source of credit to American business. During 1964 the income tax accrual of all U.S. manufacturers averaged about $11.5 billion, an amount equal to 70% of their total income taxes due on 1964 income of $16.8 billion.

The amount of accrued taxes outstanding during 1967 and the years thereafter will fluctuate between zero just after the payment date to 25% of the year's taxes just before the payment—or on the average 12½% of the annual tax bill. If the total income tax bill of manufacturing corporations is assumed constant between 1964 and 1967, the tax accrual as a continuing source of funds for these firms can be expected to drop from $11.5 billion to around $2.1 billion ($16.8 billion × 12½%). Using similar assumptions, a very rough estimate of the extent to which the reduced lag in payment will cut the average tax accrual for all corporations is $14.7 billion. In any case this important source of credit will be cut sharply.

So far, we have assumed that the individual corporation continues to make profits and to accrue a liability for new taxes during the year. What happens if a profitable concern ceases to be profitable and just breaks even? Clearly, it must pay off its liability for back taxes on schedule. But it is not adding to the Accrued Income Taxes account, since it is making no profits. The "spontaneous" source that it enjoyed while profitable disappears. So it not only loses the inflow of funds from net profits after taxes but must pay off its liability for back taxes. The squeeze on funds from a shift from profitable to break-even operations is thus a double-barreled one, as many concerns have learned to their sorrow.

If losses are realized, <u>partially compensating relief may be obtained</u> <u>through application for refunds of taxes paid in earlier profitable years.</u> Operating losses may be carried back 3 years, or forward for 5 years. If carried back, the losses reduce the taxable income of the previous years and the taxes due on that income. Provision is made for rapid processing of claims for the difference between the taxes actually paid and the taxes due on the income of the earlier year remaining after deduction of the loss carried back. Of course, the tax refund will in no case exceed 48% of the losses suffered.

<u>In planning cash outflows of corporations related to income taxation,</u> <u>the significant dates are the dates when tax payment must be made.</u> The federal government is not an indulgent creditor, and it is wise to make the required payments strictly on schedule.

In the case of concerns organized as individual proprietorships or as partnerships, the business enterprise in the eyes of the law and of tax regulations normally has no entity apart from that of the proprietor or the partner-owners. Consequently, such businesses incur no income tax liability on their income. Instead, the individual owners are expected to report their share of the business earnings in their personal tax returns and to pay taxes on this income at the rates of personal income taxation applying to their income. Therefore, the income statements and balance sheets of individual proprietorships and partnerships make no provision for income tax obligations.

Provisions have also been made to permit small business corporations to elect to be treated like a partnership for tax purposes—that is, to have the income of the corporation taxed directly to its shareholders. In a recent year, about 8% of all corporations filed returns under this option, but these were typically small and accounted for only about 2% of total corporate income.

Under a relatively recent provision in U.S. tax law, businesses operated as individual proprietorships or partnerships may, if a variety of conditions are met, elect to be taxed as if they were corporations.[5] The number desiring and qualifying for such distinctive treatment has not been large.

---

[5] See Internal Revenue Code, 1954, Sec. 1361.

Chapter 10

The Effective Use of Bank Credit—I

IMMEDIATELY FOLLOWING the attack on Pearl Harbor on December 7, 1941, Rear Admiral Yokoyama, the Japanese naval attaché in Washington, together with two naval officer associates, was interned at Hot Springs, Virginia. For several months there, they had full access to the American press and could add to their knowledge of America and the American Navy. When their diplomatic exchange ship arrived in Japan in August, 1942, they were met at dockside by an officer of the Naval General Staff and taken directly to headquarters. They were allowed to see no one and to read no Japanese newspapers. The idea was that they should use their fresh knowledge of America and the U.S. Navy to play the role of the U.S. leaders in an extended war game. In this game, Admiral Yokoyama was to conduct the war against Japan as he thought the American commanders should and would. Thus, through this and other measures the Japanese sought to know and understand their adversary and to forge their own plans in the light of this understanding.

Fortunately, the negotiations of businessmen are unlike the wars of nations, and the gains of one need not be at the expense of the other. Business relationships *can* be profitable and satisfactory from the viewpoint of *each* party—indeed, if they are to endure, the arrangements must be good ones from the standpoint of each concern involved. But effective business planning and negotiation, just as certainly as military planning, must be grounded in a basic understanding of the circumstances and thinking in the organizations with which a relationship is to be developed. The more that can be learned about how their managers operate, their aims, their procedures, the logics of their operations, and the human prejudices and irrationalities of their managers as well, the more likely it is that arrangements can be made that will meet their needs and situation and yet will be a "good deal" for the initiating firm.

This philosophy certainly is pertinent in the case of the businessman hoping to make good use of potential sources of credit. This chapter and the three that follow are intended to help the reader to gain a basic understanding of banks and other lenders to business, and their lending attitudes and practices.

IMPORTANCE OF BANK CREDIT TO BUSINESS

American business firms depend on their commercial banks for a wide range of important services. Carried on with such smooth routine that it is taken virtually for granted is the service of the banks in handling the mechanics of payment by check. A very high percentage of the nation's business transactions are settled by check, and the number of business checks handled annually by the banks runs into the billions. Business firms in 1960 carried some $64 billion on deposit in more than 6 million bank accounts. But in this chapter we are interested primarily in the nation's banks as sources of credit for business and the manner in which these sources can be tapped effectively by business concerns.

The commercial banks have long been a highly important source of business credit. While banking statistics do not isolate the amount of total bank credit going to business, it is likely that as much as half of the $178.6 billion of commercial bank loans outstanding at the end of 1964 were for business purposes. To the $60.0 billion of commercial loans shown in Chart 10–1, we could appropriately add considerable portions of the amounts in several other loan categories that directly or indirectly were for business purposes. The great growth of bank lending in recent decades is also brought out in Chart 10–1.

Especially rich, though somewhat aging, sources of information on bank lending to business have been the studies of the loans of member banks of the Federal Reserve System. The more recent of these were based on loans outstanding on October 5, 1955, and October 16, 1957; they drew information on the member banks which accounted for some 86% of all commercial bank loans. On the 1957 date business firms had outstanding 1,286,600 loans from member banks. Table 10–1 presents a classification of these loans according to the business of the borrower. Since many firms borrow for short periods, the total number of loans or the amount of bank credit outstanding on a single date substantially understates total business use of bank credit.

The availability of bank credit is of much importance to a great many companies that may not borrow at all for extended periods. To these companies the banks serve as a "backstop" or reserve source of cash. As we have seen, it is often difficult for the businessman to forecast with precision or full confidence the amount of funds his business will need during a substantial period in the future. Many unpredictable events can create the need for cash. If the business has a good credit standing with its bank and knows it can borrow if unexpected needs develop, it can undertake larger scale and more risky operations than would be feasible in the absence of the reserve of borrowing power at the banks. For many

CHART 10–1

LOANS OF U.S. COMMERCIAL BANKS AS OF DECEMBER 31
(In Billions of Dollars)

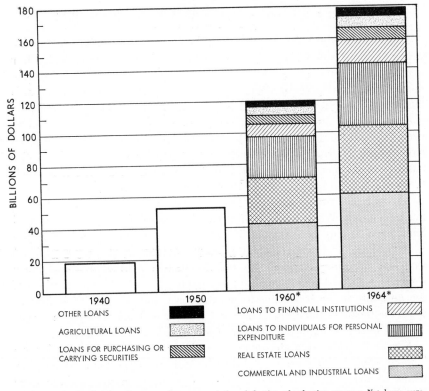

* Figures for detailed loan items are shown gross, before deduction of valuation reserves. Net loans were $117.6 billion in 1960 and $175.6 billion in 1964.
SOURCE: *Federal Reserve Bulletins.*

businesses, it is entirely uneconomical and in some cases impossible for the business itself to hold idle cash in reserve for such possible needs. The value to American business of unutilized but potential bank credit, though inestimable, is unquestionably great.

In the interests of undistorted perspective, we should recognize that bank credit is a much smaller source of funds for business than the spontaneous sources, notably trade credit. But for business generally, the banks represent the dominant source of negotiated short-term credit. For most smaller firms and a large percentage of medium-sized firms, bank loans represent the paramount source of negotiated credit—long, intermediate, and short term. For very strong and larger firms that can sell bonds in the capital markets, bank credit represents one of several important sources of credit open to them.

There is abundant evidence of the relatively great importance of bank credit to small business. As Table 10–2 makes clear, almost 1,000,000 of

TABLE 10-1

Business Loans of Member Banks of the Federal Reserve System, 1957 and 1955, by Business of Borrower
(Estimates of Outstanding Loans)

Business of Borrower	Amount of Loans				Number of Loans*	
	In Millions of Dollars		Percentage Distribution		In Thousands	Percentage Distribution
	1957	1955	1957	1955	1955	1955
All business	40,618	30,820	100.0	100.0	1,317	100.0
Manufacturing and mining, total	16,144	11,283	39.7	36.6	225	17.1
Food, liquor, and tobacco	2,392	1,838	5.9	6.0	36	2.7
Textiles, apparel, and leather	1,683	1,689	4.1	5.5	31	2.3
Metals and metal products	5,527	3,235	13.6	10.5	59	4.5
Petroleum, coal, chemicals, and rubber	3,750	2,646	9.2	8.6	28	2.2
Other	2,792	1,875	6.9	6.1	72	5.4
Trade, total	8,386	6,539	20.7	21.2	517	39.2
Retail	4,589	3,476	11.3	11.3	411	31.2
Wholesale	2,982	2,312	7.4	7.5	96	7.3
Commodity dealers	815	751	2.0	2.4	9	0.7
Other, total	16,087	12,998	39.6	42.2	575	43.7
Sales finance companies	3,095	2,872	7.6	9.3	13	1.0
Transportation, communication, and other public utilities	4,169	2,906	10.3	9.4	44	3.4
Construction	1,980	1,691	4.9	5.5	105	7.9
Real estate	2,976	2,405	7.3	7.8	76	5.7
Services	2,262	1,783	5.6	5.8	239	18.2
Other nonfinancial	1,605	1,340	3.9	4.4	98	7.5

*Comparable data on number of loans were not included in the 1957 survey.
SOURCE: *Federal Reserve Bulletin*, April, 1956; April, 1958.

the 1,280,600 business loans of member banks in 1957 were to firms with total assets of less than $250,000. For most of the smaller businesses, the banks were the only source of negotiated credit open to them. A Department of Commerce study in the mid-fifties showed that bank loans constituted nearly 80% of all negotiated credit for a broad sample of established small and medium-sized firms. For newly established firms in the sample, bank loans accounted for nearly 70% of all loans.[1]

Several factors contribute to the especial importance of bank credit to smaller business. First, banks generally are actively interested in making

TABLE 10–2

BUSINESS LOANS OF MEMBER BANKS, 1957, BY SIZE OF BORROWER

Size of Borrower (Total Assets, in Thousands of Dollars)	Amount of Loans		Number of Loans		Average Size of Loan (In Thousands of Dollars)
	Millions of Dollars	Per-centage Distribution	Thou-sands	Per-centage Distribution	
All borrowers..................	40,618	100.0	1,280.6	100.0	31.7
Less than 50..................	1,456	3.6	504.7	39.4	2.9
50–250......................	5,256	12.9	494.3	38.6	10.6
250–1,000...................	6,302	15.5	157.6	12.3	40.0
1,000–5,000.................	6,775	16.7	48.2	3.8	140.5
5,000–25,000................	5,912	14.6	13.3	1.0	445.7
25,000–100,000..............	4,893	12.0	5.4	0.4	901.6
100,000 or more.............	8,815	21.7	6.5	0.5	1,363.5
Not ascertained.............	1,207	3.0	50.7	4.0	23.8

SOURCE: *Federal Reserve Bulletin*, April, 1958, p. 396.

small as well as large business loans. The borrowers usually are well known to their banks, and the extent of the credit investigation is not so great as to make the costs of extending small business loans prohibitive. Second, there are commercial banks in almost every town in the country, and local firms are likely to find their local bank interested in helping enterprises which contribute to the community's economy. Further, small businesses generally are less strongly capitalized and their internal sources of funds less adequate than in the case of large firms; many, if not most, are chronically short of funds. Apart from the relatively small number of "glamour firms" with outstanding prospects, smaller firms, and many of intermediate size, find the capital markets ill-suited and unreceptive to their needs. The inability to tap other institutional sources makes it especially important that the managers of small and intermediate-sized firms make effective use of the credit facilities of their commercial banks.

That bank credit is not restricted to established firms with demonstrated earning power is indicated by the fact that 107,000, or 8.4%, of

[1] McHugh Loughlin and Jack N. Ciaccio, "Financing Small Business in the Postwar Period," *Survey of Current Business*, November, 1955.

the loans reported in the Federal Reserve study of October, 1957, were to businesses less than 2 years old. The bank loans outstanding to these new firms totaled almost $2 billion.

THE STRUCTURE OF U.S. COMMERCIAL BANKING

U.S. commercial banks are distinguished from the two other major deposit institutions—mutual savings banks and savings and loan institutions—by their ability to accept demand deposits subject to check as well as time and savings deposits. The savings accounts of mutual savings banks and the share accounts of savings and loan associations are invested predominantly in residential mortgage loans and in U.S. bonds. The savings institutions play an important role in the financing of home construction, but their lending to business outside the construction industry is very limited.

Although commercial banks typically accept both demand deposits subject to check and interest-bearing time deposits, the demand deposits of commercial banks as a whole have been greater than time deposits. The deposit accounts of business firms are carried predominantly at commercial banks. While the commercial banks make home mortgage loans, they specialize in loans to business and to individuals. Unless reference to the contrary is made, hereafter when we speak of "banks," we refer to commercial banks.

The federal government and each of the states have enacted specialized legislation governing the operations of commercial banks. Further, banks are subject to continuing supervision of their activities by one or more public agencies. The regulations applicable to a particular bank are governed in part by its decision to incorporate as a *national* or as a *state bank*.

At the end of 1964, about one third of the nation's 13,738 commercial banks were incorporated as national banks and as such were subject to federal banking legislation. The 4,773 national banks, however, held well over half of the total bank assets. The remaining banks have chosen to incorporate under the laws of the states in which they are located.

Primary responsibility for supervision of national banks rests with the U.S. Comptroller of the Currency. The Comptroller has a sizable staff which reviews periodic reports from the banks and conducts field examinations of the banks' affairs. A team of examiners visits each national bank at least once a year to examine the condition of the bank and to check compliance with pertinent laws and regulations. The examiners give particular attention to the bank's investment in loans and securities. Responsibility for supervision of state banks typically rests with a state banking department whose examiners perform a function similar to that of the national bank examiners.

By law, all national banks must be members of the Federal Reserve

System. State banks may apply for membership in the Federal Reserve System. To date, most of the state banks have not sought membership, but enough of the larger state banks have become members so that member banks hold almost 84% of all commercial bank assets. State banks joining the System become subject to Federal Reserve regulations and to supervision and examination by the System.

In addition, all national banks and 97% of the state commercial banks have a portion of their deposits guaranteed by an agency of the U.S. government, the Federal Deposit Insurance Corporation.[2] Since the FDIC assures depositors of the safety of their deposits (up to $10,000 in each account), it naturally is interested in seeing that the bankers manage depositors' money with due regard for avoidance of losses or illiquid investments that would impair their ability to meet their deposit liabilities. The FDIC, too, has a staff of examiners.

A few of the detailed restrictions on bank lending are of general interest to business borrowers. For example, national banks are subject to a "legal limit" on the amount they can lend to a single borrower. Unsecured loans to one borrower may not exceed 10% of the bank's combined capital stock and surplus. Most state banking laws also have provisions aimed at forcing diversification in loan portfolios, but the precise legal limit may well be different from that of a national bank in similar circumstances. Although the regulations governing specific banks may differ in detail, the similarities are more striking than the differences, and the typical business borrower is unlikely to be materially affected in his use of bank credit by the differences.

The most important point for the businessman to appreciate with respect to bank regulation and supervision is that the bankers operate under certain definite and vigorously enforced restrictions on their lending activity.

In terms of numbers, most of the nation's commercial banks operate as unit banks from a single office. Over the years, there has been vigorous and continuing debate in the United States as to whether it is wise public policy to permit individual banks to establish branches. The various states have come to different conclusions. At the end of 1964, 12 states, including Illinois, Texas, and Florida, virtually prohibited branch banking. On the other hand, 17 states, including California and Connecticut, permitted statewide branch banking. The largest bank in the country, the Bank of America National Trust and Savings Association, operated from 891 offices in California cities and towns and 34 foreign offices in 1965. The remaining 21 states permitted some branch banking but restricted it to certain areas within the state.

Branch banking is more completely established in other countries than in the United States. Eight banks dominate the commercial banking

---

[2] At the end of 1964, 235 state commercial banks were not insured by the FDIC. These banks held less than 1% of total commercial bank deposits, however.

business in Canada, as do five in England. A few large banks with many branches also characterize the commercial banking systems of Italy, Belgium, France, West Germany, and Japan.

Commercial Banking as a Business

So much has been written and said about the obligations of banks to their depositors, to their borrowing customers, to their communities, and to the general public that it is easy to overlook the basic fact that our commercial banks are also private businesses, owned by the stockholders, operating to make a profit for the stockholders. They are not charitable institutions or organizations operating exclusively, or even in large measure, for the public welfare as such.

It is true that most banks are operated in the interests of *long-run profitability* rather than for "the fast buck." Few bank shareholders invest in bank shares for quick speculative profit. Most managements identify the long-run interests of their banks with the prosperity of their customers and the long-term economic health of their communities. Further, few broad-minded bankers challenge the social need for substantially more supervision and regulation of bank affairs in the depositors' and the public interest than is appropriate for most other businesses. Nevertheless, *banking is a business*, with profit making the mainspring and basic objective of banking operations.

Banks have been aptly described as "dealers in debts." The basic features of the commercial banking business are relatively simple. When a commercial bank is started, the stockholders, by purchasing common stock, commit capital as a continuing investment in the business. Then the bank receives deposits. The deposits may be on a *checking* or *demand deposit* basis, subject to check and withdrawal on demand without notice. Since 1933 U.S. banks have been forbidden by law from paying interest on demand deposits. Most banks also compete for time and savings deposits on which they can and do pay interest. These deposits are not subject to check, and the bank may require advance notice before withdrawal. For most types of time and savings deposit accounts, however, banks customarily waive their legal right to require advance notice before funds on deposit can be withdrawn. In recent years commercial banks have intensified their efforts to compete with the savings and loan associations, mutual savings banks, and other competitors for the growing volume of savings of the public. And, as we noted in Chapter 5, larger banks have sought to compete for corporations' liquid funds with negotiable certificates of deposit.

The intensified competition for time and savings deposits has contributed to more rapid growth in these interest-bearing deposits than in demand deposits. The growing burden of interest expense associated with the growth of interest-bearing deposits has put increasing pressure on the banks to invest the funds effectively.

Deposits are debts of the bank; if it is to stay in business, the bank must be prepared to meet deposit withdrawals *at all times*. Banks typically get most of their funds from depositors. As can be seen from Table 10–3, depositors provided 88.7% of all commercial bank assets at the end of 1964; the owners, 8.0%. Banks typically earn profits by investing a substantial amount of the deposited funds in interest-bearing loans to individuals and business firms or in income-producing securities. Obvi-

TABLE 10–3

SUMMARY BALANCE SHEET,
ALL U.S. COMMERCIAL BANKS
December 31, 1964

	Total in Millions	Percentage of Total
ASSETS		
Cash and balances with other banks.............\$ 60,032		17.4%
Loans, net of reserve for bad debts.............. 175,096		50.7
Investment in securities:		
U.S. government securities................... 62,588		18.2
Other securities........................... 38,372		11.1
Other assets............................... 9,042		2.6
	\$345,130	100.0%
LIABILITIES		
Demand deposits...........................\$178,691		51.7
Time and savings deposits.................... 127,539		37.0
Other liabilities.............................. 11,462		3.3
Capital...................................... 27,438		8.0
	\$345,130	100.0%

SOURCE: *Federal Reserve Bulletin*, October, 1965.

ously, the banks, in investing the deposit funds, should so invest them that ability to meet potential withdrawals is not jeopardized. Just how much "liquidity" of assets is enough in the particular circumstances of their banks is one of the difficult decisions facing bank managers.

Table 10–4 shows how important the income from loans and investment in securities is to commercial banks generally. Interest from loans accounted for 65.1% of the total operating income of commercial banks in 1964. Interest on investments produced 22.1% of total revenues, while service charges on deposits returned 5.2% and other income the remaining 7.6%.

The net income after taxes of commercial banks in 1964, which was \$2,284 million, represented only 0.70% of average total assets held by the banks in that year. Yet, this was enough to represent a net return of 8.65% on the average investment of stockholders during 1964. It is apparent that banks depend for profitable operations on effective employment of the funds entrusted to their care by depositors as well as stockholders.

TABLE 10–4

SELECTED INCOME DATA, 1964,
ALL U.S. INSURED COMMERCIAL BANKS

	In Millions	Percentage of Current Operating Income
Income from loans..............................	$ 9,785	65.1
Interest on investments...........................	3,325	22.1
Service charges on deposit accounts................	781	5.2
Other current earnings...........................	1,133	7.6
Total current operating income..............	$15,024	100.0
Current operating expenses.......................	10,897	
	$ 4,127	
Losses on security sales, charge-offs of loans, and transfers to reserves less recoveries, profits on securities sold, and transfers from reserves..............	695	
Net profits before income taxes....................	$ 3,432	
Income taxes....................................	1,148	
Net profits after taxes...........................	$ 2,284	
Cash dividends and interest on capital..............	1,088	
Net income added to capital.................	$ 1,196	

SOURCE: Federal Deposit Insurance Corporation, *Annual Report* (Washington, D.C.: U.S. Government Printing Office, 1965).

The rates charged on loans are influenced by a variety of factors. The rates charged by the large metropolitan banks, sometimes termed "money market banks," are more sensitive to changes in the supply and demand for credit than are the rates charged borrowers by smaller banks. Bank loan rates have generally been lower in the east and midwest areas than in the south, southwest and western areas.

Chart 10–2 shows the changes in the "prime rate" in recent years. This is the rate generally accepted by the larger banks throughout the country

CHART 10–2

PRIME BANK RATE ON BUSINESS LOANS

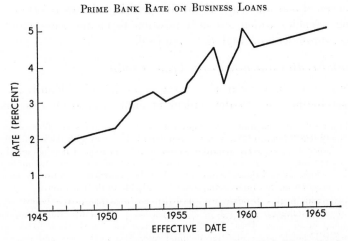

SOURCE: *Bank Stock Quarterly,* December, 1965 (New York, M. A. Schapiro Co., Inc.).

as the "going minimum" rate for short-term loans to larger firms of the strongest credit standing. The charges to other business borrowers generally represent adjustments upward from the prime rate.

BANK LENDING STANDARDS AND PROCEDURES

Basic Economics of Bank Lending

As emphasized earlier, commercial banks are in business to make money for their stockholders. Income from interest on loans is a major source of bank income. But it is _net income from lending_ that counts— income after allowance for losses and for other costs of the lending operation. Naturally, in their effort to maximize their net profits, banks compare loan opportunities with other investment opportunities open to them. In recent years there has been an abundant supply of U.S. government bonds available to banks with cash to invest. It is appropriate for bankers to regard the government bonds as entirely free of risk of nonrepayment. In recent years banks have been able to earn 4% or more on certain government bonds held to maturity. In appraising the risks and return from loans to private businesses, the bankers can appropriately ask that the amount of interest they can receive above the "risk-free" 4% at least compensate for the risk of default by the prospective borrower.[3] Theoretically, banks might appropriately consider making loans of any degree of risk, however great, by simply charging an interest rate high enough to compensate for the estimated risk of nonrepayment and return a profit on the business. In some cases, such a charge might run to 20%, 30%, or even 50%. Actually, for many years in this country, borrower attitudes, custom among bankers, and legal requirements have restricted the maximum interest rates banks charge. Six or seven percent has been the normal ceiling on the interest rates banks have charged business borrowers.[4] Loan applications involving high risk are referred to other lending agencies which are in a position to charge rates more nearly commensurate with the high-risk appraisal.

Bank Credit Contrasted with Trade Credit

The gain to the bank from risk taking on a typical loan is in striking contrast to the gain to the typical manufacturer from risk taking in

---

[3] As a means of cementing close relationships with borrowers and of boosting deposit funds, many banks require borrowers to keep deposit balances with the bank. The amount of the "compensating balance" required is usually 10% to 20% of the amount of the loan. To the extent that the required deposit balances would *not* have been maintained in any case, the compensating balance requirement may be regarded as indirectly boosting the rate of interest on the net funds actually made available to the borrower.

[4] Exceptions to this generalization do exist. For example, in the case of some loans repayable in instalments over a 2- or 3-year period, a 5% or 6% rate is applied to the full amount of the loan. Thus, the effective interest rate on the loan balances actually outstanding is much larger than the nominal rate. Also banks may add service charges related to loans to supplement the interest return.

extending trade credit to a customer. Consider the following illustration. A manufacturer sells on 30-day credit terms to a particular customer. The customer's credit position has deteriorated, and the manufacturer must decide whether or not to grant him 30-day payment terms. Assume that the manufacturer is not selling his full capacity and that the sales involved will be lost if he does not offer the 30-day credit terms. If the manufacturer sells $10,000 a month to this customer and collects the account receivable in 30 days, he will have just $10,000 at risk at any one time, assuming sales at an even rate. In a year he would turn over the $10,000 receivable 12 times, achieving sales of $120,000 while risking no more than $10,000 at any one time. If profit before taxes on the sales is 10%, a not uncommon figure, he will realize $12,000 profit on the $120,000 yearly sales (in addition to any contributions to the manufacturer's fixed costs) in return for his continuing risk of $10,000. On the other hand, if a banker loaned the shaky customer $10,000 at 6% interest for a year, he would get $600, less any cost associated with making the loan. If he could get 4% for his money in "risk-free" government bonds, the banker's return for risking $10,000 would be something less than $200 a year, in contrast to the $12,000 or more return of the manufacturer. Obviously, in his own economic interest the banker must take a very different view of the risk he is willing to undertake in the total relationship than should the manufacturer in his extension of trade credit.

Contrast between Owner's and Creditor's Return for Risk Taking

It is important also to appreciate the very significant difference in the gain from risk taking of a banker whose lending agreement provides only for a fixed and limited interest return for his risk taking[5] and the gain from risk taking of shareholding investors who, as owners, participate fully in the profits of the business. Consider, for example, the position of a banker asked to make a loan to a newly established business which appears highly risky but may be very profitable. If the business proves highly profitable, the bank will get its money back with only the fixed amount of interest as its reward for its courage and capital. The owners, on the other hand, in return for their capital ventured, will get all the profits after taxes of the venture, whether they are 10%, 20%, or even 100% per year. Viewed in this light, it is obvious that the limited and fixed return available to the bank does not justify its taking risks in providing capital that a partner or common stockholder participating fully in prospective profits might well regard as reasonable.[6]

---

[5] Some European banks have invested money in business enterprises on a common stock or ownership basis, but U.S. commercial banks generally have not.

[6] An experienced Canadian banker, Mr. A. B. Jamieson, writing in *Chartered Banking in Canada* (Toronto: Ryerson Press, 1953), makes this same point in these terms:

"In many cases where a banker is approached for a loan, the financial position of the prospective borrower is such that what he really needs is more risk capital. When the banker points this out, perhaps the applicant's response is 'If I get someone to put money

Traditional Theories of Sound Commercial Bank Lending

As we have seen, commercial bankers must limit their risk taking to situations that promise an acceptable return after allowances for the risk of losses and the total relationship with the customer. The bankers also must have regard for investing the banks' funds in such a manner that the demands of depositors can be met at all times. What kind of business loans have bankers regarded as particularly appropriate to their needs and to the nature of their liabilities? Or put most simply, "What sort of loans are the bankers looking for?" Although some pragmatic modern bankers might snort in reply, "Anything we can make money on," over a very long span of years one type of loan has been regarded as especially suitable for commercial bank portfolios. This "ideal bank loan" is a short-term, inherently self-liquidating loan for productive or commercial purposes.[7] *Short-term* is usually interpreted to mean a few months, normally less than 6 and certainly less than 12. *Self-liquidating* indicates

---

in my business, he will expect a proportionate share of the profits; if I get money from the bank, all it will cost is the interest on the loan.' With such an answer the banker can tell the applicant he is showing exactly why the loan should not be made. The bank does not share in the profits of the business; therefore, it should not put up money which might be lost if the business proves unsuccessful."

[7] Adam Smith, writing in 1776, set forth the arguments in favor of short-term, self-liquidating loans in the following terms:

"What a bank can with propriety advance to a merchant or undertaker of any kind, is not either the whole capital with which he trades, or even any considerable part of the capital; but that part of it only, which he would otherwise be obliged to keep by him unemployed, and in ready money for answering occasional demands. . . .

"When a bank discounts to a merchant a real bill of exchange drawn by a real creditor upon a real debtor, and which, as soon as it becomes due, is really paid by that debtor; it only advances to him a part of the value which he would otherwise be obliged to keep by him unemployed and in ready money for answering occasional demands. The payment of the bill, when it becomes due, replaces to the bank the value of what it had advanced, together with the interest. The coffers of the bank, so far as its dealings are confined to such customers, resemble a water pond, from which, though a stream is continually running out, yet another is continually running in, fully equal to that which runs out; so that, without any further care or attention, the pond keeps always equally or very near equally full. Little or no expense can ever be necessary for replenishing the coffers of such a bank. . . .

". . . A bank cannot, consistently with its own interest, advance to a trader, the whole or even the greater part of the circulating capital with which he trades; because, though that capital is continually returning to him in the shape of money, and going from him in the same shape, yet the whole of the returns is too distant from the whole of the outgoings, and the sum of his repayments could not equal the sum of its advances within such moderate periods of time as suit the conveniency of a bank. Still less could a bank afford to advance him any considerable part of his fixed capital; of the capital which the undertaker of an iron forge, for example, employs in erecting his forge and smelting-house, his work-houses and warehouses, the dwelling-houses of his workmen, etc.; of the capital which the undertaker of a mine employs in sinking his shafts, in erecting engines for drawing out the water, in making roads and waggonways, etc.; of the capital which the person who undertakes to improve land employs in clearing, draining, enclosing, manuring and ploughing waste and uncultivated fields, in building farmhouses, with all their necessary appendages of stables, granaries, etc. The returns of the fixed capital are in almost all cases much slower than those of the circulating capital; and such expenses,

that the loan is for a purpose that will generate the funds for repayment in the normal course of the projected operations. Loans to support a seasonal buildup of inventory and receivables are generally of this type. Consider, for example, a fertilizer manufacturer whose sales are heavily concentrated in the spring and early summer months yet who wishes to mix and bag the fertilizer at an even rate through the year. The manufacturer will experience a heavy buildup of inventory in the winter months of slack sales. A bank loan in early winter to provide the funds for the seasonal inventory buildup would meet what is expected to be a temporary need. As the peak inventory is reduced through heavier sales in the spring months, accounts receivable will be increased. When these are collected, cash accumulation will permit repayment of the loan. In this example, then, if operations, sales, and collections proceed as expected, the loan to finance the temporary expansion of inventory and receivables can be regarded as self-liquidating.

The merchant's buildup of inventory for the heavy pre-Christmas sales season, the manufacturer's need to finance production of an unusually large order, and the needs of the farmer who buys cattle in the fall to "feed out" and fatten for sale to the packers in the spring represent other situations in which operations of the enterprise are expected to sponge up, then to release, funds. The short-term, inherently self-liquidating type of loan, which for ease of reference we shall hereafter refer to as "STISL" loans, has several basic attractions as an outlet for commercial bank loan funds. First, the inherently self-liquidating aspect means not only that the borrower's need for bank funds is essentially temporary but also that the timing of the need derives from predictable patterns of the business operations. Once these needs are understood, the banker has a solid basis on which to establish sound loan repayment terms—"sound" in the sense that the terms fit a predictable pattern of developing, and then abating, need.

Second, the fact that STISL loan requests are to meet identifiable, understandable needs permits the banker to make a meaningful evaluation of the risks that the plans of the business will miscarry and that repayment will be jeopardized. Thus, in the case of the farmer's request for credit to finance his cattle-feeding program, the banker can weigh the

---

even when laid out with the greatest prudence and judgment, very seldom return to the undertaker till after a period of many years, a period by far too distant to suit the convenience of a bank. . . . [The] money which is borrowed, and which it is meant should not be repaid till after a period of several years, ought not to be borrowed of a bank, but ought to be borrowed upon bond or mortgage, of such private people as propose to live upon the interest of their money, without taking the trouble themselves to employ the capital; and who are upon that account willing to lend that capital to such people of good credit as are likely to keep it for several years."

Adam Smith, *An Inquiry into the Nature and Causes of the Wealth of Nations* (Modern Library; New York; Random House, Inc., 1937), pp. 288–92. The attention of the authors was directed to this quotation by a similar reference by H. V. Prochnow in his book, *Term Loans and Theories of Bank Liquidity* (New York: Prentice-Hall, Inc., 1949).

risks of unfavorable movements in feed or cattle prices over a known rather than indefinite period of exposure.

Third, lending for needs of short duration also tends to reduce the inherent risk exposure of the bank, since risks and uncertainties tend to increase as the time horizon is extended.

Fourth, in lending only against predictably temporary needs the bank reduces the likelihood of becoming frozen into the financial structure of borrowing customers. In cases where the bank supplies capital to meet a long continuing need, the bank loses mobility in its credit relationship with the borrower. Should the bank believe it necessary to insist on repayment, the borrower may have to make major dislocating changes in his pattern of operations in order to free up funds for loan repayment. Indeed, the borrower's needs for the funds may be so acute that the bank in self-interest may be forced to continue with a loan it would have preferred to terminate. Obviously, such *frozen loan* situations are unsatisfactory to all involved.

Fifth, emphasis on STISL loans gives a high degree of theoretical liquidity to the bank's loan portfolio. The liquidity inherent in an STISL loan portfolio has long been regarded as consistent with and appropriate to the banks' deposit source of funds. However, in recent decades, U.S. bankers have tended to reassess downward the extent of the need for liquidity to be met through the loan portfolio. Moreover, the use of STISL loans provides real liquidity only to the extent the bank does not reloan the funds from loan repayment. Since the bank's lending is likely to be in large measure in response to the needs of valued customers, failure to respond to customers' loan demands can seriously damage the bank's long-term competitive position. Hence, in an environment in which good relations with borrowers are important, STISL loans represent a last resort rather than a routinely utilizable source of liquidity against deposit declines.

In periods when customer demand for loans is heavy relative to the amount of funds available for lending, STISL loans have a further attraction. On a given amount of money to lend, the bankers are able to serve the intermittent needs of many more STISL loan customers than would be possible if the loans were to continuous borrowers.

Despite the attractions, theoretical and practical, of STISL business loans, in actual practice few U.S. banks have restricted their business lending to this type of loan.[8] One basic reason they have not is that the

---

[8] A study by the Federal Reserve Bank of Cleveland of loans in the Fourth Federal Reserve District (Ohio and parts of Pennsylvania, Kentucky, and West Virginia) provided impressive evidence of the extent of continuous bank borrowing through renewal of short-term loans. While only one third of the dollar amount of the notes outstanding of business borrowers were over a year old, nearly two thirds of the business loans were outstanding to business firms who were continuously in debt to the same bank for more than a year. Further, only 6% of the amount of notes were 5 years old or more, but 25% of the outstanding loan volume was to firms continuously in debt to the same bank for 5

demand from business for STISL credit has seldom been sufficient to absorb fully the bank funds available for lending to business. Patterns of seasonality in production and sales still exist in some firms, but most have sought vigorously to iron out or offset peaks and valleys of activity; many have succeeded to a high degree so that their primary need for funds is continuing in character rather than temporary. Banks have had to accommodate lending policies and practices to the need of a great many of their customers for more or other than STISL credit. This accommodation has taken three major forms.

A first form has been the practice of long standing of extending credit on nominally short terms (often 90 days), even though there was little prospect that the business borrower actually would be able to repay the loan at the stated maturity date. Both lending bank and borrower expected that the maturity would be extended by renewal of the note. In defense of the practice, bankers pointed out that the use of short maturities did afford the lending officer an opportunity to review the company's progress and situation before renewal and perhaps the occasion to insist on changes in the terms of the credit (i.e., the interest rate) or in the operations of the business. Also, many banks insisted that the borrower arrange his affairs so as to pay off, or clean up, the loan for a period each year in order to demonstrate that the bank loan did not represent permanent capital. In many cases the need for funds actually was continuous, and the cleanup was accomplished only by letting trade creditors go unpaid for a period or by "rotating the line," that is, shifting the borrowing to another bank for a time. Under a rotating-line arrangement, each bank could have the dubious satisfaction of showing a nominal cleanup of the loan on its books, and the borrower could finance a portion of his continuing needs at the banks. Such arrangements in which neither party means what it says about repayment incorporate a high potential for misunderstanding between bank and borrower. Moreover, the bank risks being frozen into the loan should its own needs for funds or deterioration of the credit make it desirable to terminate the loan. Nevertheless, many business loans continue to be made on this basis.

Banks have also been willing to provide extended or continuing credit to firms able to provide suitable security. Thus, most banks make 2- to 5-year loans secured by industrial equipment and longer loans against plant facilities or commercial real estate. Also, many loans are extended against the security of accounts receivable and/or inventory. Often these are made under *revolving credit arrangements* in which the notes may be of

---

years or longer! Details of this study are described in the *Monthly Business Review* of the Federal Reserve Bank of Cleveland, September, 1956.

The author of a more recent study of New York City bank loans to business estimated that nearly one half of the volume of nominally short-term loans represented credit continuously extended for more than a year. "Turnover of Business Loans at New York City Bankers," *Monthly Review* of Federal Reserve Bank of New York, January, 1962.

short maturities but the bank is committed to renewal over an extended period. The use of security is important not only in facilitating longer-term or continuing accommodation to business, but also as a support to loan requests by firms that might otherwise not be able to qualify for bank credit. The use of security in business borrowing from banks and other lenders is sufficiently important and complex that we devote a separate chapter to the subject.

A third major accommodation of lending practice to business needs has taken the form of *term loans,* credits calling for repayment in instalments over a number of years, sometimes as much as 10. Bank term lending has a relatively short history dating back only to about 1934. In the years after 1934, commercial banks had particular difficulty finding enough STISL loans to absorb available funds. This pressure, along with other factors explained later, led to the new type of loan, the term loan, in which the bank looked to the cash flows from profitable operations over a span of years rather than to reduced needs as the source of loan repayment. While security commonly was not required, the company had to agree to a variety of protective covenants designed to help protect the banks' interests. Bank term lending has grown to great importance; it is discussed at some length in the following chapter.

Differences between Banks and Bankers

So far, we have spoken of the lending policies and practices of commercial banks as a group and perhaps implied a uniformity of approach to lending. Actually, many factors condition the business loan practice of particular banks and bankers. Consequently, while there can be general agreement along the lines suggested above, there are important differences in the lending practices between banks and even between loaning officers in a single bank.

What are some of these factors that make loan officers react differently toward similar loan opportunities? They include:

1. The importance of business loans to the particular bank will influence the reaction. In recent decades, many banks have developed a very important volume of home mortgage loans and consumer instalment loans to cover purchases of automobiles or other such purposes. Where these alternative outlets for loan funds are large and profitable, the interest of the bank in business loans may be very much less intense than that of other banks which depend more heavily on business borrowers.

2. The basic policies of banks toward risk taking differ. Some managements prefer to remain conservative, perhaps in a conscious concession of gross income to peace of mind.

3. Banks have different concepts of appropriate loyalty to borrowing customers. The erstwhile First National Bank of New York for many decades was famous for the care with which it entered into lending relationships with its customers. Once it decided to meet the needs of a

customer, it was equally famous for standing by its customer in good times *and* bad. Other New York banks loaned more freely in good times but felt more at arm's length with their borrowers.

4. Differences in the nature of the deposit liabilities of banks create different liquidity needs. Lending policies of banks with a large number of inactive, stable deposits can differ from those of banks with a few very large but volatile deposits which may be quickly withdrawn. Also, if interest costs on savings or time deposits are high, the pressure for income may well be especially great.

5. Banks tend to specialize in particular types of loans, developing especial experience and confidence in their ability to gauge risks in their specialties. For example, one New York bank has developed a particularly large business in shipping loans. Too, a textile manufacturer would be more likely to find credit in a North Carolina bank, while an oil producer would usually find a Dallas bank more interested in lending against security of oil production runs.

6. The amount of assets a particular bank already has invested in loans obviously affects its willingness to undertake new loans. As general credit conditions tightened during the fifties, and again in the mid-sixties, many banks with substantial loan credit outstanding reviewed requests from new borrowers very severely, preferring to save some lending power to meet the possible additional credit needs of old customers.

7. As indicated earlier, legal regulations to which they are subject, such as the limitation of amounts that can be loaned to a single borrower to a fixed percentage of permanent capital, can make for differences between banks.

8. Perhaps most important are the twin facts that loans are made by men, not machines, and that the appraisal of the risks of most loans is in the last analysis a matter of personal judgment. No bank lending officer has a crystal ball that reveals the future to him. Within a single bank, individuals with different personality, experience, and status frequently form very different judgments on particular loan requests. A lending officer who has just had important loans for which he was responsible "go sour" and is wondering what to do about them is likely to look differently on a new loan request before him than would another more confident colleague. Banking is still an art.

General Procedures in Making New Loans

As we have said, there are many differences among banks and bankers in procedures and practices of lending. However, most banks follow a relatively similar procedure in considering an initial loan request from a prospective borrower. A first formal step consists of a request, often in letter form, by the prospective borrower for a loan of a stated amount. Let us assume that the president of a small manufacturing concern visits his bank and, after a discussion with a bank lending officer, writes him a letter asking for a loan. Immediately, the bank will undertake to accumulate information about the background, experience, business and personal reputation of the company and its management, its record with suppliers for prompt payment of its trade debts, the reasons the company needs the loan, sources of funds for repayment, its record as to profitability in past operations, and recent balance sheets detailing its assets and liabilities.

With the aid of specialized credit techniques, lending officers of the bank review the accumulated information and reach a decision as to whether and on what terms the proposed loan represents a good investment. In most banks the lending officers have authority to make loans within certain limitations of bank policy and according to their own experience and status. In the case of large or complicated loans, the loan officer typically arrives at a recommendation on the loan; but final decision on the request is made by a committee of officers and, in some cases, by the board of directors of the bank. In other words, while particular loan officers have much influence in the final decision on important loans, the ultimate decision often rests with a group of senior officers.

In many instances prospective borrowers do not need a bank loan immediately but would like to determine, perhaps many months in advance, what the viewpoint of the bank will be toward a subsequent request for a loan. In such cases most banks are willing to consider a request for a *line of credit* at the bank. The prospective borrower usually discusses with a loaning officer in detail his anticipated needs for credit in advance of the need, and the request is considered in much the same fashion as if he were asking for an immediate loan. If the borrower's situation is a strong one and the loan looks clearly attractive, the bank may decide to extend a line of credit to the customer. This represents an assurance by the bank that, barring major changes in the borrower's situation, the bank will be willing to lend up to a stated amount to the borrower. Once a line of credit has been opened, when the company wants the money the bank lending officers review the situation of the company primarily to determine that no major changes have in fact occurred. If not, the loan will be granted. While the line of credit is not a contract and does not absolutely guarantee the borrower that the loan will be forthcoming, it does serve to let him know how he stands with the bank. In many cases it permits the prospective borrower to embark on operations that will probably require bank credit with reasonable assurance that such credit will be forthcoming. Lines of credit are usually extended for periods of a year or less.

Banks sometimes are willing to make a firm commitment to lend particularly strong customers a stated amount whenever the borrower wants to borrow, or "to take down" the amount involved. Typically, the borrower is asked to pay a small amount (often one fourth of 1% but up to one half of 1%) in return for the definite commitment of the bank to make the loan when requested.

Form of Loan

In a number of foreign countries, bank credit is extended in the form of authorized overdrafts. That is, the borrowing customer is permitted to overdraw his deposit balance at the bank up to an agreed-upon amount.

EXHIBIT 10–1

TYPICAL PROMISSORY NOTE

$75,000.00 ....   Boston, Massachusetts, ...November 23..., 19 65.

........................Ninety (90) days........ after date,

for value received, the undersigned, which term wherever used herein shall mean all and each of the signers of this note jointly and severally,

promises to pay to NEW ENGLAND MERCHANTS NATIONAL BANK OF BOSTON, or order, at said bank, ...

Seventy-five thousand and 00/100 .... Dollars.

At the option of the holder, this note shall become immediately due and payable without notice or demand upon the occurrence at any time of any of the following events of default: (1) default in the payment or performance of any other liability or obligation of the undersigned, or of any indorser or guarantor of any liability or obligation of the undersigned, to the holder; (2) if the undersigned or any indorser or guarantor hereof is a corporation, trust or partnership, the liquidation, termination or dissolution of any such organization or the appointment of a receiver for its property; (3) the institution by or against the undersigned or any indorser or guarantor hereof of any proceedings under the Bankruptcy Act or any other law in which the undersigned or any indorser or guarantor hereof is alleged to be insolvent or unable to pay their respective debts as they mature or the making by the undersigned or any indorser or guarantor hereof of an assignment for the benefit of creditors, or (4) the service upon the holder hereof of a writ in which the holder is named as trustee of the undersigned.

The undersigned agrees to pay upon default costs of collection including reasonable fees of an attorney.

No delay or omission on the part of the holder in exercising any right hereunder shall operate as a waiver of such right or of any other right of such holder, nor shall any delay, omission or waiver on any one occasion be deemed a bar to or waiver of the same or any other right on any future occasion. Every one of the undersigned and every indorser or guarantor of this note regardless of the time, order or place of signing waives presentment, demand, protest and notices of every kind and assents to any extension or postponement of the time of payment or any other indulgence, to any substitution, exchange or release of collateral if at any time there be available to the holder collateral for this note, and to the addition or release of any other party or person primarily or secondarily liable.

The proceeds of the loan represented by this note may be paid to any one of the undersigned.

All rights and obligations hereunder shall be governed by the law of the Commonwealth of Massachusetts and this note shall be deemed to be under seal.

Edgewater Manufacturing Company...........

No..............................   By: .... _Treasurer_

Often there is no written evidence of the debt except the checks drawn on the account and the account itself, which serve as evidence of the debt. Interest is calculated periodically on the average amount of the overdraft. This arrangement is perhaps the simplest and in some respects the most logical of lending arrangements. In this country the deposit and the loan accounts of a borrowing customer are kept separately by the banks.[9] When a company borrows money, its authorized officers sign on its behalf a written agreement to repay, known as a _note_. The note, typically in the

---

[9] Some U.S. banks have adopted personal loan plans that have many features of authorized overdraft lending.

form shown in Exhibit 10–1, serves as evidence of the debt and states the terms of the credit extension. Except in the case of very large borrowings, it is customary to make the note for a term of at least 30 days, even though the borrower may actually need the funds involved for only a few of the 30 days. From the borrower's point of view, such a note arrangement is obviously less flexible than the authorized overdraft approach.

The interest charged by the bank usually is deducted at the time the loan is made. Thus, on a $10,000, 3-month note at 5% per annum, interest of $125 would be deducted, $9,875 being deposited to the credit of the borrower. This is known as *discounting* the note. Under an optional form commonly used on notes of more than 1 year or on notes payable on demand, the full amount of the loan is advanced, with payment of the interest called for upon repayment of the principal amount of the loan.

If the repayment of the loan is to be secured by the borrower's pledge of valuable assets as specific security for the loan, in addition to the preparation of the note as evidence of the debt, preparation of documents conveying a security interest in the asset pledged will also be involved.

NEGOTIATING A BANK LOAN

The businessman who can be confident that he will never need bank credit is in a position to treat his bank relationship lightly. But the businessman who may need bank credit at some time in the future *can do much* to improve his chances of getting the necessary credit on favorable terms when it is needed.

The earlier discussion of the differences in lending practices among banks and bankers should suggest the wisdom (and the difficulty) of judicious selection of the bank with which to do business. Since it takes time to build the mutual understanding and confidence basic to a good banking relationship, unnecessary change should be avoided. If the firm may want to borrow from the bank, the likely reaction to future requests for credit should be a major factor in selection of a bank.

Paving the Way for Credit Applications

The work of building a favorable climate for loan requests should begin long before the credit is needed. Company officers should devote substantial effort to building up a background of information and goodwill with the bank. They should seek to know well the lending officers with whom they may deal, and to be known well and favorably by the lending officers, before they go into the bank with outstretched palms. Specifically, the banker should be told that credit might be asked in the future, so that he will accumulate a file of basic data on the company. At least annually, preferably quarterly, the bank should be furnished balance sheets and income data along with a verbal fill-in on the current operations and future outlook of the business. Projection of anticipated cash flows will be of special interest to the banker. Unfavorable information, as well as good news, should be discussed candidly. The banker should be urged to visit the company and to meet key officers. A loan officer familiar with a business over a period of years and confident that he has a complete picture of the company will be much more competent in working out a satisfactory loan arrangement, and certainly more comfortable in doing so, than in a situation completely new to him. Such knowledge promotes future confidence.

A further factor has become particularly important in recent years, when loan demands have increased faster than the deposits of many banks, particularly the large city banks which loan heavily to national corporations. We refer to the renewed interest of bankers in deposit balances. Concerns that have kept, and will maintain, sizable collected deposit balances with a bank will find that their requests for loans receive more favorable attention than those of equally creditworthy firms which have favored the bank with smaller deposits.

Supporting the Loan Application

Before applying for credit, the prospective borrower should attempt to analyze his own situation from the perspective and point of view of the bank lending officer. He should anticipate the banker's questions and have careful and convincing answers ready. While the detailed questions will vary with the situation, a number of the following will almost surely be raised:

1. Why has he left his former bank connection?
2. Why does the business need funds?
3. How much is needed?
4. How and when will the loan be repaid?
5. What are the possibilities that the plans of the company will miscarry?
6. If the plans miscarry, what will be the situation of the company, and how will it meet its commitment to the bank?
7. What is the background, character, and experience of the principal executives and/or owners of the business? This question will be particularly pointed and detailed in the case of the small company, where the success of the company is especially dependent upon only a few persons.
8. What is the record of profitability in the company?
9. What is the current financial position of the company?

In general, the better the evidence of careful planning, the more convincing will be the loan application. The banker must be confident that the managers of the borrowing company are and will stay "on top of their business."

Recent financial statements, preferably audited by a certified public accountant, should be submitted with loan requests. Highly desirable as supporting data are carefully prepared cash flow forecasts and projected balance sheets extending beyond the term of the loan requested. These projections should be invaluable in indicating the nature, timing, and amount of the need for funds and the cash inflows that will provide the means of repaying the loan—in other words, properly drawn, they provide ready answers to key questions in the banker's analysis. In those cases where the forecasts are based on tenuous assumptions, alternative forecasts on other assumptions may well be put before the banker so that he can fully understand the more important variables that will affect the borrower's funds requirements.

In emphatically stressing the value of cash flow projections, both in planning loan requests and in supporting loan applications, we recognize that only a moderate, though growing, number of bankers customarily require them. Until the use of projections becomes more universally routine, as we believe will in time be the case, the financial officer who recognizes their value has the opportunity to add especial strength to his firm's credit request by voluntary submission of forecast data to his bankers.

Few bankers will be willing to finance operations or projects that do not promise to succeed. But there are few "sure things" in business, and risks of failure are present in some degree in almost all projects. Consequently, the answers to questions 5 and 6, above, are of particularly keen interest to the bank lender whose return for risk taking typically is small. In a very real sense the investment of the owners in the business serves as a protection or buffer against loss by the creditors should the venture fail. Naturally, the bank lender will be keenly interested in the size of this buffer in relation to the debts of the business and its adequacy to absorb the shrinkage in asset values from operations so unfavorable that failure of the firm results. Again, we can refer to classic and highly pertinent observations of the eighteenth-century writer, Adam Smith:

Traders and other undertakers may, no doubt, with great propriety, carry on a very considerable part of their projects with borrowed money. In justice to their creditors, however, their own capital ought, in this case, to be sufficient to ensure, if I may say so, the capital of those creditors; or to render it extremely improbable that those creditors should incur any loss, even though the success of the project should fall very much short of the expectation of the projectors.[10]

Just how much ownership capital the lender will deem enough to provide the desired protection is a matter of judgment in the light of the circumstances of the particular case. The greater the chances are of failure and of major shrinkage in the asset values should liquidation of the enterprise prove necessary, the greater, generally, will be the ownership capital the lender will require in relation to his and other debts

---

[10] Smith, *op. cit.*, pp. 291–92.

TABLE 10–5

RELATIVE FREQUENCY OF VARIOUS REASONS FOR REJECTIONS
OF SMALL BUSINESS LOAN APPLICATIONS

Reasons for Loan Rejections Involving Small Business	Percentage of All Banks Citing Each Reason as "Relatively Important"
Reasons involving creditworthiness of borrower:	
1. Not enough owner's equity in business	93
2. Poor earnings record	85
3. Questionable management ability	84
4. Collateral of insufficient quality	73
5. Slow and past due in trade or loan payments	69
6. Inadequacy of borrower's accounting system	51
7. New firm with no established earnings record	48
8. Poor moral risk	41
9. Other reasons	6
Reasons involving bank's overall policies:	
1. Requested maturity too long	71
2. Applicant has no established deposit relationship with bank	49
3. Applicant will not establish deposit relationship with bank	36
4. Type of loan not handled by bank	33
5. Line of business not handled by bank	21
6. Loan portfolio for type of loan already full	19
7. Other reasons	4
Reasons involving federal or state banking laws or regulations:	
1. Loan too large for bank's legal loan limit	23
2. Other reasons	9

SOURCE: Federal Reserve System, *Financing Small Business*, report to the Committees on Banking and Currency and the Select Committees on Small Business, U.S. Congress (Washington, D.C.: U.S. Government Printing Office, 1958), Part II, Vol. III, p. 415.

of the enterprise. In virtually all instances the bank lender will give important attention to the size of the ownership investment relative to the borrowings on the enterprise.

In interviews with bankers representing more than 670 banks, members of a Federal Reserve System research group sought to determine the more important reasons for banker rejection of credit requests of small business firms. Each bank was asked to rate the relative frequency with which each of a list of reasons for rejection had occurred. Responses were in terms of "frequent, occasional, rare, or never." In Table 10–5 the percentage of all banks responding either "frequently" or "occasionally" to each of the reasons is presented.

Chapter 11

The Effective Use of Bank Credit—II

IN THE PRECEDING chapter we sought to explain the commercial banks' traditional preference for STISL-type business loans. At the same time we noted that banks have been willing, particularly in recent years, to meet other kinds of loan demand from business. Particularly important has been the development and growth of _term lending_, and in this chapter we focus attention on this form of bank credit. After first identifying the distinguishing characteristics of term credits, we shall briefly review the history and growth of term lending. We then describe recent term loan practice with an emphasis on the measures taken by lenders to control distinctive risks in this type of lending. Assuming the borrower's viewpoint, we next focus on the attractions and disadvantages of this form of financing. Further, we consider how borrowers best can negotiate suitable term credit and maintain good relationships with the lenders.

Key Characteristics of Bank Term Loans

Bank term loans have taken on several distinguishing characteristics. First, they are business loans with an original maturity of more than 1 year. Most bank term loans are written for a maximum term of 5 years or less. However, in recent years, a significant portion (perhaps one third by amount) have carried maturities of from 5 to 10 years. A small percentage have had maturities over 10 years.

Second, repayment in periodic instalments typically is required. Although many term loans call for equal instalments each quarter or year, the schedule of repayment customarily is designed to fit the borrower's projected capacity to repay as well as the needs of the lender. So long as the borrower carries out his commitments under the loan agreement, the lender can require payment only in accordance with the specified maturity schedule. Should the borrower fail to comply with any important provision of the agreement, the agreement typically provides that the maturity of the loan is accelerated so that the lender(s) legally may demand payment of the full amount outstanding.

Third, as suggested above, the credit extension is based on a formal

202

loan agreement that specifies the terms and conditions on which the credit is extended and will be administered as well as various provisions regarding the financial conduct of the borrower. The protective covenants incorporated in the term loan agreement usually are a mixture of customary or "boilerplate" items and ones especially designed to fit the distinctive circumstances of the particular borrower.

Fourth, the terms of the loan are arrived at in direct negotiation between the borrower and the lending bank. In the case of large loans, several banks commonly participate in a single loan with one bank serving as *lead bank* in working up the terms of the loan agreement and in its subsequent administration. The direct contact makes it easy to accomplish modifications of the loan agreement that are mutually acceptable.

Additionally, it can be observed that the term loan typically is for other than a STISL-type need for funds. Commonly, the projected means of repayment are from operational cash flows over an extended period rather than from a lessened asset requirement.

The Development of Bank Term Lending

The history of bank term lending as we have described it is a relatively short one. Banks became term lenders on a significant scale only after 1935, as the country recovered from the Great Depression. As we noted in the preceding chapter, banks long have made many loans on a term nominally short, which really represented an *intermediate term* (intermediate term we consider more than 1 year and less than 15) credit in that both borrower and lender anticipated that the need for the funds would continue and the loan would be renewed rather than repaid at stated maturity.

Nevertheless, the deliberate and definite commitment of loan funds for a period of years represented a noteworthy departure from traditional theory and practice. A variety of factors affecting the supply and demand for bank credit contributed to the initial term lending around 1935 and its subsequent continued growth. Among the factors increasing the willingness of bankers to make term loans, probably the most important was the fact that from the mid-thirties to the mid-fifties the demand from business for short-term credit of the traditional sort was insufficient to absorb the funds the banks had available to lend. Economic recovery from the Great Depression, the success of certain depression-born governmental agencies with longer-term loans repayable in instalments geared to estimates of the borrower's ability to pay, the inauguration of deposit insurance and waning fears of massive deposit contraction, and increasing acceptance by bankers and bank supervisory agencies of the concept that the liquidity needs of the banks would not be compromised by a moderate amount of term lending, all provided encouragement to its growth.

At least equally important was the fact that a great many creditworthy businesses needed and wanted intermediate credit rather than, or in addition to, temporary short-term credit. As particular banks aggressively expanded their term lending, competing banks experienced pressure from their customers for similar accommodation, and many reluctant bankers were forced into term lending to keep their institutions competitive.[1]

TABLE 11–1

OUTSTANDING TERM LOANS TO BUSINESS OF MEMBER BANKS
OF FEDERAL RESERVE SYSTEM
As of October 16, 1957

Business of Borrower	Amount (In Millions)	Term Loans as Percentage of Total Bank Loans to Industry Group
All businesses......................	$15,421	38.0
Manufacturing and mining:		
Food, liquor, and tobacco...........	485	20.3
Textiles, apparel, and leather........	314	18.6
Metals and metal products..........	1,905	34.5
Petroleum, coal, chemicals, and rubber.......................	2,763	73.7
Other manufacturing and mining....	1,067	38.2
Retail trade........................	1,387	30.2
Wholesale trade....................	600	20.1
Commodity dealers.................	88	10.8
Sales finance companies.............	266	8.6
Public utilities.....................	2,839	68.1
Construction......................	596	30.1
Real estate........................	1,307	43.9
Services...........................	1,194	52.8
Other nonfinancial.................	611	38.1

SOURCE: *Federal Reserve Bulletin*, April, 1959.

By 1946, term loans had grown to represent one fifth of the total number and one third of the amount of member bank loans to business. During the great expansion of bank credit to business in the following decade, the proportion of total bank credit in term loans expanded further. The member bank survey on October 16, 1957, revealed that $15.4 billion of the $40.6 billion of total loans to business by these banks, or 38.0%, represented term credit.

The increasing difficulty experienced by a number of banks at various periods in recent years in being able to meet the avid loan demand of their customers has fostered a reluctance to build up their term loan portfolios. When bankers must ration credit among their creditworthy

[1] For an excellent survey of term lending through 1940, see N. H. Jacoby and R. J. Saulnier, *Term Lending to Business* (New York: National Bureau of Economic Research, Inc., 1942).

customers, they can use a given amount of funds for lending to satisfy the needs of a larger number of short-term than of long-term borrowers. Furthermore, bankers point out that if an undue proportion of loanable funds is tied up in term credits to strong, big firms, which could have borrowed through public issues of bonds, other borrowers, who possess no other sources of credit than their banks, are deprived of access to short-term funds. Nevertheless, it is difficult for the bankers to turn down term credit requests of highly valued customers, and data on the lending of large New York banks show that term loans grew from 51% of their business loans in 1957 to about 60% at year-end 1965.

Term lending clearly has become particularly important to big New York City and other large banks, and much of these banks' term credit is to large firms.

For member banks of the Federal Reserve System as a whole, loans to borrowers with assets over $5 million amounted to more than half of the $15.4 billion term credit outstanding in 1957. However, term lending was by no means restricted to large companies; the 1957 study showed that more than 479,000 firms had bank term loans outstanding from member banks.

The industry distribution of member bank term loan borrowers in 1957 is shown in Table 11–1.

While there has been no correspondingly comprehensive study since 1957, various evidence suggests that term credit made up some 40% of the something more than $58 billion total of commercial and industrial loans of member banks in late 1965.

CURRENT TERM-LENDING PRACTICE

The commitment of loan funds directly to a borrower for a period of years has basic implications keenly important to the lender. Recognizing and understanding these implications helps much toward understanding key features of term-lending practice.

A basic fact that the lender must face in considering a loan for a period of years is the near certainty of major change in the situation and affairs of the borrower before the loan is repaid. Five or ten years is long enough in our dynamic and competitive economic environment for material developments to occur in the management of any borrowing enterprise, in its products, its markets, its competitive position, and in the general level of the economy in which it operates. Of course, lenders have always had to cope with change. But the extent, speed, and intensity of change in our present-day economy particularly complicates the job of working out lending arrangements that will stand up for years under rapidly shifting circumstances.

A related and rather obvious point is that risk increases with uncertainty, and that uncertainty increases as the length of the loan commitment is extended. If term lending is to be extended beyond those few companies with particularly outstanding prospects and those seemingly invulnerable to unfavorable developments, while the risks in lending are to be held to proportions consistent with the interest income, lenders must exercise imagination, skill, and vigor in working out provisions that will minimize the risks inherent in the unpredictable but certainly changing future. Furthermore, once a term loan is made, the lender is firmly committed to that investment, since there is no secondary market for term loans corresponding to the active markets that exist for many bonds.

Measures by Lenders to Restrict Risk

During almost three decades of active term lending, lenders have developed a variety of measures to restrict the risks inherent in term credit. As in the case of all bargaining for funds, the final provisions of a credit reflect the bargaining strength of the parties as well as the objectives of each party. When credit was easy and the supply of funds for loan investment exceeded the demand, as was true of most years between 1935 and 1955, competitive pressures commonly forced concessions on the part of the lender that in periods of active loan demand and less avid competition for loans, as in early 1966, were successfully resisted. But regardless of what competing lenders might do, the intelligent lender must at all times keep his risk taking in line with his prospective rewards for risk taking.

Distinctive Aspects of the Credit Analysis

Since most term loans are for sizable amounts, as well as for considerable periods of time, the credit analysis of a typical term loan application is more comprehensive and thorough than for short-term credits. The industry in which the company operates and its vulnerability to downturn in business conditions is the subject of close scrutiny. Industries with a history of vulnerability to cyclical changes in demand are obviously less attractive than those which have stood up well under recession conditions.

Particular emphasis in the analysis is placed on the long-term profit and cash-generating prospects of the borrower's industry and of the company within the industry. Loan repayment over a period of years is highly dependent on profitable operations. The protection afforded by even a very strong asset position can be swept away by only a few years of heavy losses. Looked upon with favor are companies with a diversified line of products which have built-in protections against especially rigorous competition. Such protections include particularly strong quality features in their products, research effective in developing profitable new products, strong consumer brand loyalty, and fixed asset requirements great enough to discourage entry into the field by new competitors.

Established, stable product lines are preferred over high-style or novelty items. It is not surprising that companies in the chemical, oil, and public utility industries, all requiring heavy capital investment and regarded as having favorable long-term profit prospects, have been particularly important term loan borrowers.

Term lenders place much stress on appraisal of the competitive effectiveness of the applicant's management. Certainly, an alert, able, and aggressive management is essential if even those companies most success- ful in the past are to make the adaptations necessary to keep ahead of competition in a dynamic economy. But as intangibles, the character and skill of management are not easy to measure and project into the future. For example, the past success of a particular company may be due largely to a top-management team that is nearing retirement, so that another generation of management, as yet not fully tested, may hold the key to the future. However, if the lending institution has had a long relationship with the would-be term borrower, its officers have had considerable opportunity to get a useful, if inconclusive, size-up of the caliber of those who will guide the borrower's affairs in the future. Put most simply, the question to be answered is: Are these the kind of men able to light on their feet if major problems knock them off balance? or Will these people do all right, come what may?

The emphasis on the outlook for profit and cash flow generation and the relative de-emphasis of balance sheet analysis does not mean that such items as the working capital position or the relationship of debt to ownership funds are ignored. It is more an implicit recognition that even though working capital is adequate for the apparent near-term needs of the company, and the debt/equity position is reasonable, the long-term maintenance of a healthy balance sheet must hinge on profitability, which not only provides funds for debt service but forms the basis for equity or other financing as needed.

As the length of term credit is extended, the analysis becomes closer to that of a reasonably conservative and astute common stock investor and less like that of the typical short-term creditor.

While larger term loans generally have been made on an unsecured basis, lenders commonly take security—typically equipment or land and buildings—in the case of small term loans.

Repayment Provisions

One of the main protections against risk built into term loans is the typical provision for instalment repayment beginning soon after the credit is extended. From the outset of the loan the borrower is forced to think of repayment and to plan for it as an integral part of his financing. Most lenders prefer to set repayment schedules that leave no large *balloon payment* until the final maturity date. Indeed, many see a need by the borrower for deferral of large amounts to the final maturity as a confession of weakness in the loan application. While conditions at final maturity *may* be sufficiently favorable to permit refunding or extension of the unpaid amount, there is no assurance that this will be the case. There is evidence that the percentage of loans with balloon payments has increased in recent years; perhaps bankers have become somewhat more tolerant of the practice.

Provision for instalment repayment from cash provided by retained earnings compensates to some degree for the risks inherent in term loan commitments, inasmuch as the size of the loan is reduced as time goes on. At the same time as repayment is made from cash from retained profits, the ownership equity (in the form of earned surplus) increases, so that the debt/ownership relationship is improved both by reduction of the debt and by the retention, in a balance sheet sense, of the earnings in the business. Some have labeled term loans repaid out of profits as programs of *forced reinvestment of earnings*.

In judging ability to repay and in setting repayment schedules, bankers have been giving increasing attention to estimates of the net cash flows that likely will be available to *service the debt,* that is, to meet interest and principal payments. Gross cash inflows include net income plus noncash expenses such as depreciation, depletion, and amortization. From the gross figure for cash inflows are deducted anticipated outlays for new fixed assets, any additional working capital needs, projected dividends, and other debt service. It is the *net* cash flow or *cash throwoff* on which term loan repayment properly can be programmed. Moreover, the net cash flow figure should be sufficiently greater than scheduled loan payments to provide a reasonable margin of safety. What will be needed for a reasonable margin varies with the circumstances. Clearly, the need for a margin of safety increases as the degree of stability and reliability of the projections decreases. As yet no rule of thumb as to what net cash flow coverage bankers should and do expect has won wide acceptance, but one banker recently put his judgment in these terms, "the amount [of net cash flow] available to service the loan should probably equal 150% to 200% of the amount required, depending on the stability of cash flow and the adequacy of working capital."[2]

Some lenders prefer to build repayment plans only on projected cash throwoff from profits and to treat the projected excess of noncash charges over new asset outlays as providing only a contingent margin of safety should profits prove disappointing. Also regarded as a possibly helpful but not-to-be-counted-upon source of funds for loan repayment is the extra cash that might well be made available if sales declined and funds were released as inventories and receivables were reduced.

Of course, the ironical observation that "them what has gits" applies to loan repayment scheduling. In the case of companies with excellent

---

[2] Dean E. Rogers, "An Approach to Analyzing Cash Flow for Term Loan Purposes," *Bulletin of Robert Morris Associates*, October, 1965.

prospects for large, continuing profits, which could afford fast repayment, the lender is less anxious to get his money back quickly and more prepared to accept the risks of a long loan with smaller repayments. Conversely, lenders are more anxious to keep short the term of loans to companies with more uncertain profit potentials, and shorter term means higher instalment payments. Speaking generally, effort is made to compensate for higher risk by shorter repayment schedules.

Not uncommon is a provision requiring repayment of a percentage of profits in addition to the fixed minimum instalment. This contingent requirement is common where the credit analysis suggests the likelihood of very large but fluctuating profits. From the lender's viewpoint, it provides an opportunity for getting paid "while the getting's good" without embarrassing the borrower if profits prove only moderate.

Since profit and net cash flow forecasts are at best estimates, tailoring repayment to cash throwoff remains an art rather than a science.[3] The repayment schedule frequently is a major bargaining issue during the term loan negotiation, the borrower seeking the most lenient terms the lender is willing to supply.

Typically, provision for prepayment at the option of the borrower is also made in the term loan agreement. Commonly, prepayments are applied to reduce the principal in inverse order—that is, applied against the most distant instalment rather than the one next due, so that they are not a substitute for regular repayments. Usually, lenders insist on provisions calling for prepayment fees, but this is often a matter for bargaining.[4]

Curbing Risks through the Provisions of the Loan Agreement

The direct contact between the business borrower and the bank lender affords the banker an excellent opportunity to try to curb the risks he sees in the commitment by incorporating *protective provisions* in the loan agreement. For example, a rather standard provision in term loan agreements bars the corporate borrower from repurchasing outstanding common stock during the life of the loan. The borrower in turn has the opportunity to identify those proposed provisions he thinks might prove

---

[3] One eminent banker explained his approach to scheduling term loan repayment in the following terms: "My own homely method, over a number of years of term lending, has been to arrive at the term of the loan backwards, which is, perhaps, the way I do a lot of things. Having been satisfied with the desirability of the amount of the loan requested, and then having satisfied myself from a cash flow sheet or forecast as to the actual annual cash throw-off or debt paying ability and having reduced that figure, perhaps arbitrarily, to provide some elbow room for the borrower in the event of unforeseen conditions, I then divide the amount of the loan by the figure thus obtained and the resultant figure is the number of years that the loan should run." Hugh H. McGee, "Term Lending by Commercial Banks," *15th New England Bank Management Conference* (Boston: New England Council, 1945), October 11, 1945.

[4] In actual practice, many commercial banks waive the penalty payments on early repayments by customers with large deposit balances. Insurance companies have become increasingly insistent on significant prepayment premiums and on flat prohibitions of refunding the loan to take advantage of lower interest rates.

unduly restrictive or burdensome. The final terms should reconcile the conflicting needs and desires of each party in the light of their respective bargaining strengths. Because the issues involved in the negotiation of term loan covenants are conceptually similar to those involved in the fixing of terms in longer-term debt financing, we shall leave detailed discussion of protective covenants to a later chapter.

The Costs of Bank Term Loans

The costs of bank term borrowing are of both a direct and an indirect nature. The chief direct costs are the continuing cost of interest and the one-time costs associated with the negotiation of the loan. Except in large or complex situations, the costs of negotiation are small. If the bank engages special counsel to assist in the drafting of the loan agreement, it is customary for the borrower to pay for the bank's counsel as well as for its own. Beyond the legal expense there is usually little direct cost of issue.

The interest rate on term loans commonly has been slightly higher (often 0.25%) above the rate the bank would charge the company on a STISL loan. Since a substantial percentage of total term credit is to strong and large borrowers, the average rate charged on term loans is not very far (less than 0.50%) above the prime rate.

Commonly, provision is made for adjustment of the interest rate if interest rate levels as measured by an index such as the prime rate change.

Some banks have developed special term loan programs for small businesses. Under such a program a bank might well loan a delicatessen $5,000 to cover the costs of rehabilitating the premises and installing new display cases, repayable monthly over a 3-year period. In these special programs, the stated interest rate commonly is applied to the face amount of the loan for the full life of the loan. If this rate were 5% on the $5,000 loan for 3 years, $750 interest would be charged (.05 × $5,000 × 3). Since the loan is to be repaid over the full period, the $750 represents 10% interest on the *average* loan balance outstanding ($2,500 × 10% × 3 years = $750).

Commonly, banks insist on inclusion in the term loan agreement of a compensating balance requirement. To the extent that this requires the borrower to maintain a higher deposit balance than he would have in any case, the income forgone on the extra deposit funds can be regarded as an additional cost of the term loan.

Term Loans from the Borrower's Viewpoint

Now let us take advantage of the background material on bank term lending policies and practice to consider the attractions and shortcomings of bank term loans as a source of funds.

In the actual case, the attractiveness of term loan capital depends on the nature and intensity of the need and the alternative sources available. Most readers have heard of the reply of a careful man to the question, "How's your wife?" The reply was, "Compared with what?"

With what alternative sources of funds can bank term credit be compared? Most large, successful firms have a range of very real, though not directly comparable, alternative sources of debt financing open to them. Such firms could probably place a debt issue with much longer maturities directly with life insurance companies, which are very active buyers of corporate debt issues. Alternatively, they could sell publicly an issue of bonds or they might well be able to secure bank credit on short terms frequently renewed.

Many smaller firms that could qualify for bank term credit have available very limited alternative sources of intermediate credit. The alternative of a public sale of bonds, if it exists at all, is likely to be unattractive; the capital markets are not receptive to the bonds of smaller companies, and the issue costs and the interest rate would have to be high in order to attract buyers. Some life insurance companies and pension funds are receptive to requests for intermediate credit of as little as $100,000. However, the costs of investigating, making, and administering loans of this size have tended to be a high percentage of the interest return on the investment, and for this and other reasons most insurance companies and pension funds are not much interested in issues below $500,000. As we shall see in the following chapter, the Small Business Administration or small business investment companies represent sources of intermediate capital for smaller firms that may be satisfactory, but in each instance some disadvantages attach to use of these sources.

Advantages of Term Credit

To most firms the big attraction of term loan credit is the contractual assurance of continued credit for an extended period so long as the terms of the credit are met. Armed with credit made available under terms explicitly spelled out in writing, the borrower can go forward with plans and projects for the use of the funds for a period corresponding with the duration of the credit. Usually, these plans involve investment of the funds in a continuing expansion of working capital or in plant and equipment that will "pay out" only over a period of years. In other words, term credit fits the nature of their need for funds.

Some borrowers who have been successful in financing medium-term needs with renewed, short-term borrowings are likely to overemphasize the restrictions of the term loan and to overlook the fact that the lender, as he considers each renewal of the short-term notes, has very much in mind certain minimum standards for continued credit, even though these standards may not be discussed with the borrower and renewal seems routine. The requirements spelled out in the term loan are *not necessarily* more stringent than those the lender in fact requires upon renewal of a short-term credit. And lender attitudes are not always constant or, indeed, fully logical; at least, the term loan agreement commits the lender to a definite, constant set of standards and requirements. The borrower can plan accordingly.

The direct negotiation implicit in the bank term loan has a number of advantages to the borrower. Term loans typically can be negotiated faster and at less expense than public issues of debt securities. The major inescapable *issue costs* of term loans are those of legal counsel. In the case of debt issues placed with insurance companies and pension funds, borrowers frequently employ the services of an investment banking firm as an adviser in planning the financing and as an agent in searching for the most suitable lender and in negotiating terms. The usual charge for such services—0.25% to 1.25% of the principal amount—is avoided in bank term borrowing where use of an intermediary is unusual. In term borrowing, disclosure of information is only to the lender(s), not to the general public; and the time and trouble of preparing the registration statement and prospectus necessary in larger public offerings also are avoided. Altogether, the mechanics involved in arranging a term loan are less than those of a typical public issue.

Many borrowers want to make firm arrangements for funds that they will not need in hand for some months or even years. For example, a company planning a new plant may well want to complete the borrowing necessary to finance the expansion before firm contracts are let, even though actual payments to the contractor will be necessary only as work on the plant progresses. Under such circumstances, funds raised from a public issue of securities before construction contracts are signed are likely to remain relatively unproductive for an extended period. Term lenders, however, for a small fee, perhaps 0.25% on the committed but unused funds, will commonly permit the borrower to *take down* or draw against the loan in increments corresponding with his planned needs. This flexibility can mean significant interest savings for the borrower.

As we have indicated, to many firms that can qualify for term loans the alternative of a public issue of debt securities is not available. The cost of term credit to these firms is likely to be very much lower than the cost of funds raised through sale of common or preferred stock. Many owners of smaller companies are extremely reluctant to concede the degree of control over the corporation that might well be involved in a major issue of common stock. The interference by the term lender with the control exercised by the borrower's management is restricted to that explicit in the loan agreement provisions so long as these are met. While it is not prudent, of course, for the borrower to count on the willingness of the lender to agree to any modification of the term loan the borrower might like, the fact that reasonable and appropriate changes can probably be made is a major advantage of the term loan.

One further advantage of term borrowing from banks, and indeed from insurance companies, has been particularly apparent during recent periods of heavy loan demand. That is the fact that most term lenders look upon their borrowers—or at least the ones with whom their experience is favorable—as valued clients whose reasonable needs for money deserve precedence over those of new customers. Consequently, the borrower who has repaid on schedule has available what amounts to an inside track to funds needed in the future. One large insurance company, for example, has reported that 60.7% of the dollar volume of its direct placement loans to business in a recent year was to old customers.

Inherent Disadvantages or Problems in the Use of Term Credit

Earlier we cited, as a basic attraction of borrowing under a term loan agreement, the contractual assurance of credit over the scheduled life of the loan. Yet, it follows clearly from our brief discussion of restrictive covenants typical of term loans that the assurance of credit is a *conditional* one, dependent upon the borrower's meeting fully the terms of the loan agreement throughout the life of the credit. The *accelerated maturity* feature of the loan agreement can be a severe penalty for acts of default by the borrower. Even if the lender does not avail himself of his rights to insist upon accelerated payment of the loan, the lender may well be able to insist upon new terms and restrictions that are very onerous from the borrower's point of view.[5] In effect, the defaulting borrower must "bargain while flat on his back"—an unenviable position.

Consequently, the astute term borrower must appraise the proposed terms with care and foresight. If he plans carefully and bargains skillfully, the restrictions arrived at may be entirely reasonable and represent a quite tolerable risk to assume. But even though they are judged acceptable, it must be recognized that the restrictions do reduce the flexibility of management to some degree.

The major disadvantages of term borrowing, however, are those of any borrowing. Lenders expect debts to be repaid; the penalty for nonrepayment can be severe. Further, loan funds are not like water from an ever-flowing spring—the more a borrower draws on his ability to borrow, the lower is the reserve of additional borrowing power for future expected or unexpected needs. Debt money is "unfriendly money"; it repels other money, unless it is used so profitably as to attract additional equity investment.

The typical term loan involves only one or a few lenders. The term loan borrower is dealing with an informed, sophisticated lender, who can be expected to be vigorous in protecting his sizable investment. Compared

---

[5] Some astute bankers who have read this chapter disagree with this emphasis. They argue that as a practical matter the strong legal position of the bank in the event of default is misleading and that in most cases, exercise of the bank's legal rights is less feasible than efforts to work out the difficulties over a long period. In such efforts, they insist, the cooperation of the borrower's management is almost essential. While recognizing the merits of the point, it seems to the authors only to temper somewhat the points in the text and not to invalidate them.

with the creditors in the form of small investors who buy a widely distributed issue of bonds, the term lender is a fast-moving, informed creditor who has such a big stake in the credit that he can be expected to follow it carefully and to defend his right effectively.

While the bank term lender can usually be presumed to be an intelligent and reasonable creditor who will react sensibly to requests for modification of the loan agreement, it is important that the borrower recognize an inherent or potential conflict of interest between himself and the lender. Many possible modifications, which seem clearly desirable from the borrower's point of view, will not be attractive to the lender. Consider, for example, the situation of a borrower who sees opportunities for expansion into a new field that promises big profits but contains substantial risks. The borrower might well, in view of the profit outlook, be willing to assume the risks to him of more debt and hence want the banker to waive restrictions on further debt. But the term lender, who gains little from extra profits from expansion, may well, intelligently and reasonably, refuse to increase his risks by permitting the expansion of debt.

Many borrowers find the maturities and repayment schedules preferred by the banks unduly restrictive as compared with the 15-year, 30-year, or even longer maturities that they can arrange by public sale of bonds or by a private sale of debt securities to insurance companies. Hence, many larger firms of good credit standing which can sell or place long-term bonds at a reasonable cost prefer such action to term borrowing from their banks. Often these firms turn to use of term credit when capital market conditions are not favorable to a long-term issue, in the expectation that the term loan will be *refunded*, that is, be repaid out of proceeds of a longer issue, when capital market conditions improve.

Concerns that have never come under the full disclosure requirements of the Securities and Exchange Commission and that have borrowed before only on a short-term basis may find irksome the relatively full investigation of a term lender. Certainly, the borrower should expect to have few secrets and should anticipate having any "skeletons in the corporate closet" exposed to the view of the lender. However, term lenders are accustomed to respecting the confidences of borrowers and can usually be counted upon to treat confidential data in proper fashion. And surely, the disclosure of facts to a single lending institution is much less distasteful to a reticent firm than would be the public disclosures involved in public offerings of bonds or other securities subject to the informational requirements of the SEC.

NEGOTIATING EFFECTIVE TERM LOAN ARRANGEMENTS

For most term borrowers, it is highly important that the term loan arrangements be negotiated effectively. What aids to successful term borrowing can be suggested? Our more important suggestions can be grouped under four headings:

1. Top management's role in negotiating term credit.
2. Getting ready for the loan negotiations.
3. Appraisal of provisions and selective bargaining.
4. Keeping a good banking relationship.

Top Management's Role in Negotiating Term Credit

While many financial matters are appropriately delegated to financial specialists, especially in larger firms, term borrowing seldom is one of them. The working-out of a credit arrangement that can stand up over a period of years calls for careful planning of a variety of aspects of the firm's operations. The more clearly the future needs of the business for facilities, for working capital, for dividends, etc., can be formulated, the more effectively can the plans for financing through term credit be brought into harmony with the overall plans and objectives of the firm.

Top management's responsibilities toward term lending are not limited, however, to formulation of the plans which are to serve as the basis for term borrowing that will fit in with those plans. For the desires of the would-be borrower must be reconciled with the needs and demands of the lender. Almost inevitably, the give-and-take of bargaining over specific provisions raises questions that can only be resolved by top management. For example, only top management and the board of directors should assume final responsibility for the reconciliation of dividend objectives with lender proposals for restricting dividend pay-out.

In brief, term borrowing is intertwined with many matters of significance to top management. Top-management understanding and participation in the planning and decision making that is a part of effective term loan negotiation are essential to term borrowing that serves, rather than stifles, management's objectives.

Most business leaders are involved in the planning and negotiation of term loans only infrequently, or the process is entirely new to them. Important term lenders are at it continuously. As even our brief treatment early in this chapter suggests, an important body of theory and practice has developed in term lending. Clearly, a basic understanding of *term loan theory and practice* by would-be borrowers is a prerequisite if they are to be fully effective in tapping term loan credit. Much of this chapter has been devoted to providing such basic background; other more detailed sources of information are also available.[6] The borrower, from study of such material and of his own situation, can help to establish the limits of bargaining within which he must operate and to see ways he can

---

[6] For example, see H. V. Prochnow, *Term Loans and Theories of Bank Liquidity* (New York: Prentice-Hall, Inc., 1949) ; Jacoby and Saulnier, *op. cit.*; and the excellent discussion by George Moore of bank term lending in chap. ix of *Business Loans of American Commercial Banks*, ed. B. H. Beckhart (New York: Ronald Press Co., 1959).

meet the needs of the lender at minimum sacrifice of his own key interests.

As we have noted, many firms who seek to tap insurance company credit—and to a very much smaller extent, bank term loan credit—enlist the advice and counsel of investment bankers in approaching lenders and in working out suitable terms. Legal counsel who are experienced in this area may also be of great assistance. But such advice should supplement rather than substitute for top-management understanding of term lending.

Getting Ready for the Loan Negotiations

Many of our comments in the preceding chapter on the importance of careful selection of the major bank or banks are particularly relevant if term credit is likely to be needed. Several considerations make highly desirable a long-established relationship with the bank or banks which will be asked for term credit. First, these banks will have had more opportunity to build up a depth of knowledge about, and confidence in, the firm. Second, there is a widespread prejudice among lenders against "shopped-around" loan proposals. Many lenders flatly refuse to consider a loan application—and to undergo trouble and expense in the process— if the borrower is engaged in serious discussion of the loan with even one other lender. In other words, custom dictates that the borrower select the lender with whom he wants to do business in advance of serious discussion and exhaust the possibilities of a satisfactory agreement with that firm before turning to other lenders.

As indicated earlier, in periods of tight money, lenders are more likely to accommodate old customers than new applicants to whom they owe no loyalty and with whom they have had no experience. The nature of the credit analysis described earlier further suggests the wisdom of building a good relationship with the most likely term lender well in advance of "putting on the touch." And finally, since the association of term borrower and lender may well become an intimate and extended one, it is well that compatibility be pretested as far as is feasible.

Appraisal of Provisions and Selective Bargaining

The shrewd borrower enters the bargaining conference in which the amount of the loan, the repayment terms, and the various restrictive covenants are to be worked out only after he has considered carefully the provisions the lender may propose and their probable impact on his company and its future operations. Once he has forearmed himself with knowledge of term-lending practice, the major limiting factor on the borrowing management's skill in appraising the terms is the extent and degree of accuracy of the future planning of the company. If plans for the future are vague and uncertain, skillful bargaining is difficult, if not impossible.

Particularly important to the borrower are the terms of repayment.

Some firms are content with the haphazard approach of seeking credit as large and a repayment schedule as lenient as the lender's indulgence will grant. Yet, the borrower has as much (or more) to lose from too much borrowing as the lender. Moreover, he is in a much better position than the lender to appraise his own capacity to carry and repay debt, since he has a depth of internal experience and information bearing on the subject. Few subjects deserve more careful scrutiny and analysis. Speaking generally, the borrower should estimate as carefully as he can, through cash flow forecasting, his future cash throwoff from operations and borrow no more than can be repaid easily—allowing a comfortable margin between his forecasted means of repayment and the contractual repayments. The more uncertain or unreliable the forecast, the greater should be the planned margin of safety. If reasonable margins between the repayment demanded by the lender and the capacity to repay cannot be projected, serious doubt is thrown on the wisdom of borrowing, and curtailment or abandonment of the borrowing plans is suggested.

As we indicated earlier, a critical variable in the assessment of ability to repay is the extent to which operational inflows related to depreciation and other noncash charges will be matched by outflows for new plant or equipment. Management of the borrowing firm can draw on its knowledge and judgment to gauge the degree to which the firm could shelve or postpone desirable outlays without irreparable injury should the need for funds become acute. In this connection it should be appreciated that it is necessary to anticipate a developing shortage of funds many months in advance of the actual need in order to halt normal equipment purchases for a long enough period so that inflowing funds from operations can be accumulated in quantity and made available for debt service. Under certain conditions management may conclude that it can reasonably regard the depreciation flows as routinely available for debt service. In other cases the flows may be regarded as a reliable emergency source, and in still other cases as preempted or highly uncertain.

A related issue concerns the wisdom of counting on, even as an emergency source, the funds that might be expected to accumulate as a result of a decline in sales leading to a reduction of receivables and inventory. There are "catches" here: The reduction-of-inventory assumption is valid only if production is cut back to more than match the decline in sales and if the inventory on hand proves salable. Further, if the funds from current asset pulldown are used for loan repayment, additional funds will be needed to support a recovery in sales, if and when it occurs. Finally, a severe drop in sales may well be accompanied, if fixed costs are high, by heavy losses which eat into the funds created by working capital liquidation. Once again, management is in a good position to make judgments as to how much and under what circumstances its company can plan on net cash inflows from liquidation of inventories and receivables.

Turning now to the appraisal of the restrictive covenants and the need for selective bargaining, the key problem here is to separate those restrictions that may well prove burdensome from those with which compliance is painless—which require policies that the borrower would in ordinary business prudence follow anyway. Separating the onerous from the innocuous again requires forecasts over the life of the loan. A requirement that no dividends be paid during the life of the loan might not appear very objectionable if the company were owned by a few stockholders who had little need or desire for dividends. But should the company want to sell common stock to the public, dividend payments may be essential to the sale of the stock at a good price, and the provision barring dividends would become highly restrictive.

Of course, few borrowers can expect to have the bargaining go all their way. The secret of successful bargaining is to discover and concede those points which are important to the other party but represent relatively minor concessions to you, and vice versa.

The interest rate is a good illustration of a feature which is very important to the lender, yet of lesser significance to many borrowers. The range for bargaining on the interest rate proposed by the lender is usually small—one half of 1% or less. Since the lending institution lives largely on its interest income, the fraction of 1% is important to it. Yet, the cost to the borrower is reduced by the inclusion of interest as a business expense before calculation of income tax—hence the *net cost* is about halved for most companies. More importantly, the borrower typically expects to make 10% or more on the borrowed funds, so that availability of the credit and freedom from onerous restrictions commonly are much more vital than the difference in cost that would result from concentrating his bargaining power on the interest rate.

Keeping a Good Banking Relationship

A good banking relationship, like a good marriage, requires and is worth some cultivation. Moreover, each relationship should be built to last. Well maintained, a good bank relationship should grow stronger over the years and become a priceless, if intangible, asset of the business.

Of course, loan arrangements are only part of the total relationship with the bank. Of great importance to the bank are the deposit balances maintained. Hence maintenance of an attractive collected deposit balance can be regarded as a key ingredient of a strong relationship with the bank.

Another ingredient of a good relationship is provided by continued diligence in meeting all commitments to the bank precisely and scrupulously and in spirit as well as in letter.

It is hard to overemphasize the importance of providing the lender with good and candid information about the company, not only at the outset of negotiations but throughout the loan as well. Since the lender has an important financial stake in the enterprise, his interest in timely notice of major developments affecting it—favorably and unfavorably—should be taken for granted and freely met. Moreover, the bank lending officers prefer to hear of major developments affecting the company promptly and from company officers. In the absence of confidence that they are in complete and continual contact with their borrowing customers, the bank officers must depend on the unreliable and often distorting services of the grapevine.

As suggested above, candor is extremely important in a continuing relationship. It is not very difficult for a glib person to sell a "bill of goods" to a banker once and perhaps twice, but the passage of time will help even an unsophisticated banker recognize a "phony" for what he is. A continuing relationship can be built only on continuing, mutual confidence.

If modifications of the agreement are needed, as is so often the case, the borrower should give the lender as much notice as possible of the impending need for change and carefully work out appropriate modifications to propose. Similarly, as the borrower has unfavorable developments to report, he should have plans worked out to cope with these developments. While the lender wants to know of impending problems, he does not want them thrust in his lap for solution. Instead, he is entitled to evidence that the borrower is making constructive plans to overcome his own problems.

Yet, in the final analysis, there is no adequate substitute for effective performance—the meeting of commitments—as the foundation for a sound and viable borrower-lender relationship.

Chapter 12

Nonbank Sources of Short-Term Credit

IN PRECEDING chapters we have discussed the spontaneous sources of credit normally available to business in routine and the use of bank credit on a short- and intermediate-term basis. In this chapter we shall review the variety of other sources of short or intermediate credit available to business generally. The amount of credit provided to business firms by the other sources is much less than the total credit extended by the spontaneous sources and by commercial banks, but the total is significant, and to many firms these nonbank sources are of critical importance.

Because the nonbank or secondary sources are diverse and heterogeneous, this chapter will appear cut up and digressive. To help the reader keep his perspective as he is introduced in turn to different and less familiar sources, we list below the various sources we shall discuss.

1. The commercial paper market for the sale of unsecured notes.
2. Business finance companies.
3. Factoring firms.
4. Private lenders.
5. Customer advances.
6. Special credits from suppliers.
7. Credit arrangements primarily oriented to international trade.
8. State, regional, or local development credit corporations.
9. U.S. government sources of funds to meet particular needs:
   a) Depression relief.
   b) To fill gaps in private availability of funds.
   c) Special financial aids available to military suppliers.
   d) Special aids to groups adjudged especially deserving.

The Commercial Paper Market as a Source of Short-Term Funds

To several hundred concerns of strong credit standing, the commercial paper market is an important source of short-term funds. *Commercial paper* refers to short-term promissory notes, generally unsecured, which are sold through commercial paper dealers or directly to investors. The investors in commercial paper include banks and other financial institutions; but in recent years, nonfinancial concerns with excess funds to invest on a short-term basis have been the major buyers of commercial paper.

Notes sold in the commercial paper market typically are written in denominations or multiples of $5,000 and with maturities of from 1 to 9 months. Ninety-day maturities are particularly common. Some firms sell commercial paper on a continuing basis; others borrow through its sale only to meet seasonal and other temporary needs.

The setup and pattern of operation of the commercial paper market is such that it is at the disposal only of borrowers with high credit standing. Prospective users of commercial paper must be relatively large, with a net worth of at least $500,000 and commonly $5 million or more. Credit records and pay-out prospects must be excellent. Also, commercial paper borrowers are expected to have open and unused bank borrowing lines which could be drawn on, if necessary, to replace the commercial paper borrowing. Finally, the firm name should be one recognized immediately by investors as an excellent credit risk.

According to one analysis, 371 firms in a wide variety of industries sold commercial paper in 1962. A summary of the industry distribution of these firms follows:

Finance	132
Textiles	55
Food	50
Metals and hardware	18
Lumber and furniture	10
Tobacco products	9
Leather and shoes	7
Chemicals and drugs	6
Building materials	2
Miscellaneous	82
Total	371

SOURCE: Richard T. Selden, *Trends and Cycles in the Commercial Paper Market* (NBER Occasional Paper No. 85) (New York: National Bureau of Economic Research, 1963), p. 100.

Borrowing through commercial paper is an old practice dating back more than a century. Chart 12–1 traces the fluctuation in total volume of commercial paper outstanding in recent decades. The decline in the use of commercial paper during the 1930's will be noted, as well as the post-World War II increase, attributable largely to finance companies. A very large percentage of the total dollar volume of commercial paper since 1945 has been issued by finance companies that use it to supplement other borrowing.

A principal attraction of borrowing through commercial paper lies in the relatively low rates of interest at which this borrowing can be accomplished. If the borrowing firm can meet the exacting standards for

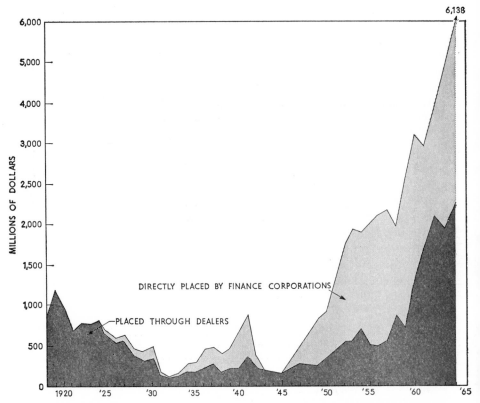

CHART 12–1

COMMERCIAL PAPER OUTSTANDING AT YEAR END, 1918–64

SOURCE: Data for 1918–47 are from Federal Reserve Bank of Chicago, *Business Conditions* (Chicago, August, 1955). Data for 1948–64 are from *Federal Reserve Bulletin*.

use of commercial paper, it can ordinarily obtain short-term funds thereby at effective interest rates significantly below the interest rates charged by commercial banks. Chart 12–2 pictures this rate differential in recent years.

The notes sold in the commercial paper market do not provide for interest as such. Instead, an effective interest rate is established by sale of the notes at a discount from face value. Thus, a 6-month note for $100,000 sold by a *prime name* in June, 1965, at the then prevailing market rate of 4.38% per annum would net the borrower $97,685, which is the amount left after deduction of interest discount of $2,190 and the dealer's commission of 0.25% per year for the 6-month bill, $125.

Finance Companies

The label *finance company* is used loosely in business circles. In the absence of a more crisply definitive term, we use the term *finance companies* to refer to the several thousand firms that are in the business of

CHART 12-2

SELECTED SHORT-TERM MONEY RATES, MONTHLY, 1947–JUNE, 1965

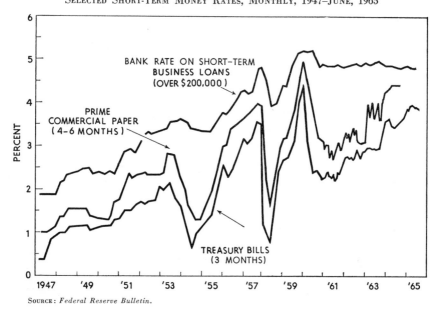

SOURCE: *Federal Reserve Bulletin.*

lending money, yet cannot be classified as banks, insurance companies, or other forms of traditional financial institutions. This rather broad definition includes many companies which specialize in one or more of several widely different types of lending. However, a few of the largest finance companies, such as the Commercial Credit Company and C.I.T. Financial Corporation (C.I.T.), directly, or through subsidiaries, offer a wide range of lending services. Finance companies, regardless of their special lines of business, raise their funds in much the same general fashion. Almost all are corporations with a significant ownership equity, often in the form of both common and preferred stock. On the basis of the equity investment and profitable records, finance companies have been able to borrow relatively large amounts through short-term bank loans and through sale of commercial paper and a variety of long-term debt instruments. For example, the consolidated balance sheet of C.I.T. on December 31, 1964, showed ownership funds of approximately $383 million compared with total debts of $2,404 million. By borrowing at lower rates than they charge on their loans, the finance companies hope to cover their expenses and enhance the return on their stockholders' investment.

Most of the finance companies specialize in direct lending to individuals and are called *personal finance or consumer finance companies*. Household Finance Corporation is the largest company of this type. On June 30, 1965, these firms had outstanding instalment loans of $5,287 million.[1] Another group of firms are known as *sales finance companies*. These firms specialize in the purchase from retailers of the instalment receivables arising out of retail sales of automobiles, household appliances, industrial equipment, farm equipment, mobile homes, boats, and other durable goods sold on the instalment payment plan. The total instalment credit held by sales finance companies at the end of June, 1965, was estimated at $15.4 billion.[2] Given the fact of widespread instalment selling, the sales finance companies in effect supply the funds that firms selling on instalment credit would have to acquire elsewhere if they were to carry the investment in receivables themselves. In addition, these firms do a large volume of wholesale financing; that is, they loan to distributors and retailers of the above items to finance their inventory of unsold merchandise. The inventory serves as security for these loans, which typically are on a continuing basis.

Still another group of firms, variously termed *business finance companies* or *commercial finance companies*, lend directly to a wide variety of businesses, mainly of small and medium size. The bulk of their lending is against the security of assigned accounts receivable, but they also do a significant amount of lending on inventory and equipment. Under special circumstances, these firms also extend unsecured loans to valued clients, but the volume of their unsecured lending is small. Rates charged, translated into annual interest terms, commonly range from 9% to 16% and in some cases may be much higher. Most of their business customers are ones that could not qualify for equivalent bank credit; the borrowing relationship typically is a continuing one over a period of years, ending when the position of the borrower has sufficiently improved so that it can shift to lower cost sources.

Industry sources estimated the combined volume of commercial finance and factoring in 1964 at approximately $20.5 billion, up from $2.67 billion in 1945.[3] In view of the turnover of receivables and other assets against which the total advances were made, the credit extended at any one time was only a fraction of the $20.5 billion annual total. Nevertheless, the volume of such credit is significant and has grown steadily through boom and recession years alike.

A limited number of finance companies specialize in providing a distinctive financing service known as *factoring*. Factoring is essentially the purchase of accounts receivable. It has become sufficiently important to warrant separate discussion later in this chapter.

As we have suggested, the lines between the various types of finance companies often are blurred. A breakdown of the receivables acquired during 1964 and those outstanding on December 31, 1964, in the course

---

[1] *Federal Reserve Bulletin*, August, 1965, p. 1152.

[2] *Ibid.*

[3] National Commercial Finance Conference, Inc., *Annual Convention of the Commercial Finance Industry, 1964* (New York: The Conference, 1964), p. 18.

of the finance company operations of Commercial Credit Company and its subsidiaries indicates the varied kinds of financing supplied by this leading diversified firm:

RECEIVABLES ACQUIRED DURING 1964
(In Millions)

Motor retail	$ 707.9
Farm equipment, mobile homes, and other retail	321.0
Loan receivables	474.3
Motor wholesale	1,257.2
Factoring, open accounts, leases, other wholesale notes, and mortgages	2,280.8
Total	$5,041.2

RECEIVABLES OUTSTANDING ON DECEMBER 31, 1964
(In Millions)

Automobile, retail	$ 774.7
Automobile, wholesale	211.1
Farm equipment, mobile homes, and other retail	444.4
Loan receivables	362.8
Open account and factoring	406.3
Leases and other notes	275.1
Total	$2,474.3

SOURCE: *Moody's Bank and Finance Manual* and company's annual report for 1964.

The diversified lending operations of companies like Commercial Credit Company suggest a characteristic important to many business borrowers. Generally, the better finance companies have won a reputation as venturesome and imaginative lenders. Their willingness to consider lending to companies in difficult situations, and their skill and resourcefulness in setting up lending arrangements that meet the pressing needs of borrowers yet hold the lender's risks to tolerable proportions, have made them an invaluable source of credit for many companies and won them an important role in the economy.

The Use of Factoring

As an alternative method of converting accounts receivable into cash, many firms can look to factoring, a service offered by factoring concerns and a very limited number of commercial banks.[4]

For many decades, factoring has been very important in the textile

---

[4] Among the larger firms active in factoring are two subsidiaries of C.I.T. Financial Corporation, Meinhard-Commercial Corporation and William Iselin & Company, Inc.; a subsidiary of Commercial Credit Company, Textile Banking Company, Inc.; Walter E. Heller and Company; James Talcott, Inc.; John P. Maguire and Company, Inc.; and Mill Factors Corporation.

The First National Bank of Boston, the Trust Company of Georgia, and the Bank of America N.T. and S.A. have for some years operated factoring services on an important scale. During 1965 at least three major banks, First National City Bank of New York, Citizens and Southern National Bank, and United California Bank, entered the field by purchasing factoring firms.

industry, and this industry is still the source of a large percentage of total factoring business. In recent decades its use has spread to many other industries. Factoring perhaps can best be understood if major distinctive aspects of a factoring arrangement are compared with those of a loan secured by assignment of accounts receivable. As we shall see in Chapter 13, under the typical accounts receivable loan arrangement the borrower still holds title to his accounts receivable,[5] and the lender expects him to absorb losses if particular accounts are not paid. The firms owing the accounts normally are *not* notified that their account is pledged and continue to send their payments to the borrower. In contrast, the typical factoring arrangement has the following characteristics:

1. The factor *purchases* accounts acceptable to him without recourse. That is, if the accounts are not paid, the loss is the factor's. The client no longer carries factored accounts receivable on his balance sheet, in effect having converted them into cash.[6]

2. Firms owing the accounts receivable to client firms are notified that the account has been sold to the factor and are asked to remit directly to the factor.

3. As implied above, the factor seldom agrees to buy all of the accounts receivable of a client firm; instead, he retains the right to screen the accounts and select those acceptable to him. The client firm can continue to sell to customers whose accounts are unacceptable to the factor, but it must carry them itself and assume all risks on them.

4. Under the typical factoring arrangement the client maintains a running account with the factor. As receivables are sold to the factor, the proceeds are put at the client's disposal in this account. Often, clients are given the privilege of overdrawing their account with the factor, or, in effect, of borrowing on an unsecured basis, in addition to drawing against the proceeds of the factored accounts. Also, interest is normally credited by the factor on funds left with him.

Usually, the factor's charges are computed and assigned to the client's account once a month. The computation of the factor's net charges, involving a variety of charges and credits, is a somewhat complex one. This complexity, together with the fact that the factor provides certain distinctive services, such as credit investigation, collection, and the absorption of bad-debt losses, makes difficult a clear-cut comparison of the costs of factoring with the costs of alternative methods of raising funds. However, factoring is widely regarded as a relatively high-cost method of financing. Outside the textile industry, factoring has been used

---

[5] The borrower pledging accounts receivable shows the pledged receivables on his balance sheet. Good accounting practice requires note, however, of the fact that they are pledged as security.

[6] Where the factor advances less than 100% of the receivables, the borrower carries his equity in the receivable among his assets. Thus, if $500,000 of accounts are factored but only 90% is advanced, the client would show accounts receivable of $50,000 on his balance sheet.

most widely by firms with annual sales in the $500,000 to $10 million range.

Private Lenders

In past decades a number of private individuals who had accumulated considerable wealth, particularly in the smaller cities and towns of the nation, made a practice of lending money. While most of their loans took the form of long-term notes, they did some short-term lending to businesses, particularly smaller local concerns. While no statistical information is available on the loans of individuals to businesses, there is strong reason to believe that the amount of such lending currently is small.

In the larger cities there are still individuals who make business loans, usually to firms that cannot find enough credit elsewhere. Rates charged are very high, often amounting to annual rates of 24% or more on the funds supplied. The little information that is available about such lenders suggests that they are truly a "source of last resort" and that they should be dealt with most cautiously—preferably not at all.

Customer Advances and Prepayments

Some companies are able to get substantial aid from customers in the form of advances against orders for future production and delivery, or by special arrangements under which partial payments are received prior to completion of an order or contract. Such financial aid from suppliers is most important to producers of large, specialized equipment, where the time and expense involved in production are great. For example, R. Hoe & Co., Inc., which makes high-speed printing presses, reported customer advances of $1.2 million on September 30, 1964, when total assets of the company were $17.5 million.

Most contract builders also depend heavily on customer advances and/or contractual agreements under which they are authorized to bill customers as certain costs are incurred in connection with the partially completed contract. For example, Combustion Engineering, Inc., designs, manufactures, and installs complete steam power plant and other such installations. At the end of 1964, Combustion Engineering showed on its balance sheet advance payments from customers of $47.9 million or 22% of total assets of $217.7 million. In addition, contract terms which permitted billing as progress was made on incomplete contracts helped very materially to reduce the financial needs from what they would have been if Combustion Engineering had not been able to collect from customers in advance of completion of the contracts.

Special Credit from Suppliers

In our earlier discussion of trade credit from suppliers as a spontaneous source, we did not discuss the possibilities of obtaining through negotiation special additional credit from suppliers. Under certain circumstances, sellers are willing to grant somewhat longer terms than those made available in routine to all their credit customers. In a number of instances, buying firms have been able to negotiate with the seller special terms for the financing of an especially large or otherwise unique purchase order. Illustrative of such possibilities was the reported willingness of the Hammond Organ Company in 1960 to offer to new distributors of Hammond's products term credits as large as twice the distributor's equity investment. According to the vice president of finance of Hammond: "We will offer loans up to 200%, to be retired in three years, at an attractive interest rate. This capital financing program will help us put into business those who have expressed interest in owning a studio but who have not had the necessary capital."[7]

Not infrequently, hard-pressed firms are able to arrange with important suppliers to put outstanding overdue open-account payables on a note basis with maturities deferred for a period of months or years. In such cases, it is usually expected that new purchases will be on open account and regular terms and will be paid promptly when due; it is the prospect of further business and an improved relationship that encourages suppliers to accept deferred payment arrangements on old payables. Needless to say, suppliers enter into such deals with reluctance.

Another form of special credit is the use of special credit terms designed to encourage inventory stocking by distributors or retailers well ahead of their normal selling season. In such cases the supplier offers "seasonal datings," that is, special credit terms which require payment only after the retail selling season is well advanced. Special credit terms also are often made available in the case of promotional stocks.

A number of firms have formed finance company affiliates to help dealers finance inventories of their products as well as to take over retail instalment sales contracts. Some firms are willing to support bank borrowing by customers with credit guaranties or agreements to buy back unsold inventories of their products. Suppliers also may provide financial aid to their customers to permit them to acquire specialized equipment necessary to handle their products. A number of dairy products producers help customers acquire refrigeration equipment. Grain companies may finance customers' purchases of bulk feed storage facilities. Oil companies may help finance the construction of filling stations.

Speaking generally, suppliers are most likely to consider granting special credit terms when all or most of the following circumstances exist: The customer is one who can be expected to buy important quantities of goods in the future if the special terms are granted; the customer can get equally satisfactory products from other suppliers; the supplier itself is well financed; the supplier expects to operate at a rate short of full capacity, and marginal production costs are low; and there is evidence

---

[7] *Wall Street Journal*, October 31, 1960.

that the need for special credit will not last indefinitely. If the supplier is making a large profit margin on marginal increments of sales, the chances of his agreeing to a special credit deal are enhanced greatly.

Reliance on suppliers for unusual credit arrangements can have weighty disadvantages, including the loss of bargaining power on price, delivery, and other terms. However, firms hard pressed for funds should not overlook the possibility of negotiating special credit terms for new purchases, extended payment terms on existing payables, or other forms of assistance from major suppliers.

Credit Instruments Used Predominantly in Foreign Trade: The Banker's Acceptance

Certain credit instruments, of which the *banker's acceptance* is the most important, are used primarily in connection with the financing of imports from and exports to foreign countries. The financing of foreign trade involves many distinctive instruments and practices, detailed description of which is best left to specialized books on the subject. We shall briefly discuss here the banker's acceptance and its use, both because of its importance in foreign trade and as an example of the specialized instruments of credit that have been developed to meet special needs.

The banker's acceptance begins as a *draft* or demand for payment, drawn on a bank, asking the bank to pay a stated amount to a stated firm or its assignees at a definite date. When the bank on which it is drawn agrees to make the payment by writing "Accepted" on the draft (along with the signature of an authorized official of the bank), it becomes a banker's acceptance—or an obligation of the accepting bank. Of course, the bank will only accept drafts in behalf of customers who have made the necessary previous arrangements with the bank and convinced it that they in turn will repay the bank upon maturity of the acceptance. The accepting bank charges a commission of at least $1\frac{1}{2}\%$ for the use of its name and credit.

An illustration may help to explain how the banker's acceptance is used as a source of credit by business firms. Let us assume that a New York manufacturer of topcoats desires to import a $20,000 shipment of Harris tweed from a manufacturer in Scotland. The Scottish manufacturer is anxious to make the sale and will be willing to defray the costs of extending the credit the American importer wants on the deal—say, 90 days from shipment.

The New York garmentmaker—who, we shall assume, has a good credit standing with his New York bank—arranges to have his bank open a *letter of credit* in favor of the Scottish tweed manufacturer. This document states that the New York bank will honor—or accept—drafts drawn on the New York firm, provided they are drawn in accordance with detailed terms stated in the letter of credit. When shipment is made, the Scottish firm prepares a 90-day draft on the New York firm in accordance with the letter of credit and presents it to its Scottish bank. That bank will advance the funds—actually, the pound equivalent of $20,000 less interest and fees—to the Scottish company and forward the draft along with shipping papers, the ocean bill of lading, etc., to its New York correspondent bank, which presents it to the New York manufacturer's bank for acceptance. If all papers are found to be in order, the New York manufacturer's bank accepts the draft, and it becomes a *banker's acceptance.*

Since there is an open market in bankers' acceptances based on their very strong credit standing as a result of the bank's acceptance, the Scottish bank could readily arrange its sale and thus recoup the dollar equivalent of the funds it had advanced. The American manufacturer gets the credit he wants, the risks to all parties except the accepting bank are minimal, and the sales transaction is completed. The credit transaction is completed when in 90 days the acceptance is presented to the New York bank and paid by it; and the bank, in turn, looks for repayment to the New York manufacturer.

Of course, the accepting bank depends heavily on the credit of its customer—the New York importing manufacturer. It may release the goods to him upon arrival only under a security arrangement, or it may satisfy itself that it can safely accept the draft without requiring security when the goods are released to the manufacturer.

Since the Scottish firm, or its bank, usually is in a poor position to assess the creditworthiness of the American customer, the use of the letter of credit and the insertion of the American bank's credit into the picture through its acceptance is an important, and often vital, part of the trade arrangement.

Although bankers' acceptances are used predominantly to finance the movement of goods in international trade, they are also used to a modest extent for domestic transactions where goods are used as security. In one field, the domestic storage and sale of raw cotton by cotton dealers, bankers' acceptances are a major method of financing. At the end of June, 1965, bankers' acceptances outstanding were estimated at $3,355 million. Bankers' acceptances, like commercial paper, are bought and sold on a discount basis. Discount rates during July, 1965, averaged 4.22%, a rate approximating that of prime commercial paper, and only modestly above the rate of U.S. government 90-day bills.[8] The low rate reflects the high credit standing of bankers' acceptances as obligations of the banks.[9]

State, Regional, or Local Development Credit Corporations

In a number of states and localities, development credit corporations have been established to support and develop economic activity and

---

[8] *Federal Reserve Bulletin,* August, 1965.

[9] For a more complete description of the use of acceptances and the market for them, see Federal Reserve Bank of Cleveland, *Monthly Business Review,* January, 1961.

employment in their areas by extending financial or other support to firms that cannot secure needed funds from conventional lenders. Most of the development credit corporations operate with local government encouragement; some operate with public funds, but most are privately financed. Although they make short-term loans, their loans are more commonly of intermediate term and call for instalment repayment. One of the first of these, the Massachusetts Business Development Corporation, had in 11 years through 1964 made 223 loans of $20.4 million.

Twenty such corporations, most of more recent origin, reported approving 207 applications (out of 353 received) for $25 million, an average of $120,773 each. Most (71%) of the firms aided were manufacturers; only 13% were new business; 81% were established firms already located in the area, 6% represented established firms relocating from another state.[10] It is interesting to note that in their total experience to date on 1,288 loans involving $114 million, 519 loans had been repaid in full. Losses of $616,000 had been taken on 34 loans, while 29 borrowers owing a total of $2.4 million were delinquent on loan repayments at the end of 1964. A total of 678 loans totaling $59 million were outstanding.

While the above figures cover only a portion of the local development groups in the country, they include a high percentage of the larger and more active ones. While the total amount loaned by the 20 corporations can hardly be called insignificant, the figure does represent a small fraction of 1% of the credit extended by the commercial banks or trade suppliers during the period. But their existence does add a possible alternative to firms having difficulty meeting their needs elsewhere.

U.S. Governmental Sources of Short-Term Funds

In recent decades the United States Congress has enacted a number of laws providing for federal government financial assistance to business enterprise. Most of these programs have been directed at meeting financial needs which have been intermediate or long term rather than short term as we have defined it. In view of the great variety in the provisions for governmental financial assistance, however, a classification of the purposes of federal financial assistance to private concerns may be helpful. The legislation providing for governmental financial assistance seems to fall into four rough categories.

1. Broad-scale government loans to business under depression conditions, in which the normal sources of financial assistance to business are inadequate for business needs, or where the economic welfare of the country suggests the wisdom of lending standards more lenient than those normally considered appropriate by lenders for profit.
2. Legislation under which governmental agencies seek to fill gaps in the

---

[10] Federal Reserve Bank of Boston, *Business Development Corporation Report for the 12 Months Ending December 31, 1964.*

financial structure of the country believed to exist under normal economic conditions.

3. Aids to suppliers to the government of military items.
4. Special aids to particularly deserving groups such as military personnel returning to civilian life and the victims of floods, tornadoes, or other disasters.

Broad-Scale Government Financing to Business under Depression Circumstances

During the depression of the 1930's, several governmental agencies were established to loan public funds to business firms in need of aid because of depressed conditions. The Reconstruction Finance Corporation was the most important agency set up for this purpose, and it granted loans on a massive scale to a wide variety of businesses, both large and small. Most of the RFC loans called for periodic repayment over a period of years. During World War II, this agency also provided much aid to industries vital to the war effort. Finally, in 1953, the RFC was put in the position of winding up its affairs. By that date, it had loaned more than $12 billion. A very large percentage of the RFC loans were ultimately repaid. In the event of general depression the federal government probably would again establish credit facilities of the RFC type.

Government Efforts to Fill Gaps in the Availability of Credit

Even under prosperous conditions, Congress has concluded that private financing agencies have not met fully the needs of all segments of socially desirable business. Most important of the gaps have been in the availability of intermediate loan capital for smaller businesses, in the loan capital available to farmers, and in credit on export sales. Various agencies have been set up to assist small businesses to meet their capital needs. The most recent of these, the Small Business Administration, in 1953 was given the authority both to make direct loans and to guarantee portions of loans to small business by banks and other private lenders. The Small Business Administration has described the business loan program in these words:

Section 207(a) of the Act gives the Small Business Administration authority *to make loans to small business enterprises when credit is not otherwise available on reasonable terms*. The loans are intended to fill a gap in the financing provided small firms by private financial institutions and are designed to stimulate and preserve the initiative, independence and enterprise of small businesses. To the greatest extent possible, the Small Business Administration is striving to provide this credit in cooperation with private lending institutions. Its success in this is evidenced by the fact that about two-thirds of all loans approved are in participation with banks and other financial institutions.

In order to expand financial assistance to small business concerns and to promote a balanced national economy, the Bank–Small Business Administration participation loan plan offers the greatest possible benefit to the participating institution consistent with the intent of the Small Business Act. For example, the plan enables a bank to broaden its lending activities, while maintaining desired liquidity of assets. The bank is assured a fair return on money loaned and is able to give better service to its depositors.

In the administration of its lending program under Section 207(a) of the Small Business Act, the Small Business Administration is governed by the policies established by the Agency's Loan Policy Board and the requirement of the Act that "*loans be of such sound value or so secured as reasonably to assure repayment.*"[11] The Agency applies the most liberal interpretation of these policies and requirements possible, consistent with sound credit principles, but at the same time is fully aware of its responsibility to protect Government funds. Therefore, each loan application is thoroughly analyzed and a loan is never approved or declined without full consideration of all factors concerned. The Agency's lending program is under continual study, and the area in which credit can be provided safely is being constantly reviewed.

Applications and approvals reached all-time highs in 1964. Out of 17,854 applications, 10,707 were approved for $425.8 million. This brought the total number of loans approved by the SBA to 50,754 and the amount to $2,440 million. The average size of the loans approved in 1964 was $39,768; over SBA's full life through 1964 the average was $48,075. Commercial bank participation in the SBA loan program has grown; in 1964 banks participated in almost half of the approved loans. While rates on the bank participations may be higher, the maximum rate that the SBA can charge is set by statute at $5\frac{1}{2}\%$.

Losses, actual and projected, on SBA business loans through June 30, 1964, amounted to $37.4 million or 2.51% of the $1,492.3 million actually disbursed by the SBA to that date. Losses on those loans made directly by the SBA without bank participation were highest at 3.33%.

It is interesting to note the reasons given for loan rejections by this "source of last resort," as summarized in Exhibit 12–1.

Under Section 207(b), as amended, of the Small Business Act of 1953, the SBA is also authorized to make loans to assist in the rehabilitation of homes and businesses which have been damaged by floods, storms, or other natural disasters. In addition, the SBA is empowered to give loan assistance to businesses suffering economic loss as a result of drought conditions where there is any reasonable chance of rehabilitation. In the words of the SBA: "Loans can be made only to the extent of actual losses (apart from those of drought) not covered by insurance, and, as in the case of regular business loans, cannot be approved if the financing is otherwise available on reasonable terms."

Since the disaster loans are intended as a rehabilitation measure, much

---

[11] Italics supplied.

more liberal credit standards are applied to them than would be prudent for the Agency's business loans. Interest rates, too, are lower (3%). Through 1964 the agency had approved a cumulative total of 25,422 disaster loans of all types for $297.6 million. In 1964 alone, principally because of a violent earthquake in Alaska in that year, SBA approved 4,009 disaster loans amounting to $91.7 million.

EXHIBIT 12–1

U.S. SMALL BUSINESS ADMINISTRATION
REASONS FOR DECLINING BUSINESS LOAN APPLICATIONS
January 1 through June 30, 1960

Reasons	Number	Percent of Total
Total reasons*	4,264	100.0
Lack of reasonable assurance of ability to repay loan (and other obligations) from earnings	1,564	36.7
Collateral, considered along with other credit factors, not deemed sufficient to protect the interest of the government	931	21.8
Disproportion of [loan requested and of] debts to [tangible] net worth before and after loan	923	21.6
Need for loan funds not demonstrated	327	7.7
Inadequate working capital after the loan	284	6.7
The result of granting the financial assistance requested would be to replenish funds distributed to the owners	68	1.6
Other—including size, policy reason	167	3.9

* Total number of reasons is in excess of the number of applications declined (1,936) because in most instances, two or more reasons for declination were given.
SOURCE: Small Business Administration, *Fourteenth Semiannual Report for the Six Months Ending June 30, 1960* (Washington, D.C.: U.S. Government Printing Office, 1960).

As might be expected, SBA estimates of ultimate loss on disaster loans were higher at 3.48% of disbursements than on business loans.

The SBA also has important administrative responsibilities under the Small Business Investment Act. This Act provided for certain government tax and financial aids to privately owned investing firms organized under the regulations established for Small Business Investment Companies. At the end of 1964, more than 700 "SBIC's" with combined assets of about $750 million were in operation. These firms make loan or equity investments in small businesses. Usually, the loans are for a period of years. By the end of 1964, SBIC's had invested more than $500 million in more than 10,000 small companies.[12] In a later chapter we discuss further the work of the SBIC's in supplying funds to small business.

Governmental financial aid to farmers has taken a variety of forms. Suffice it for our purpose here to recognize that sizable governmental

---

[12] Small Business Administration, *Annual Report to the President and Congress for 1964* (Washington, D.C.: U.S. Government Printing Office, 1965).

programs exist to help the farmers finance both long-term and short-term needs.

One student of the subject commented that government programs of loans to private business, such as those of the RFC and the SBA, shared the following characteristics:[13]

1. Avoidance of competition with private lenders and the related emphasis on participation arrangements with private lenders. . . .
2. Emphasis on secured loans.
3. Elaborate procedure of loan processing involving counseling on business management matters.
4. Large proportion of loan applications denied.
5. Relative inflexibility of interest rates over time and absence of differentials for varying size, risk, and maturity of loans.
6. Intermediate-term financing for working capital purposes.
7. Large proportion of loan approvals for manufacturing enterprises.
8. Subsidy aspects of programs.

Especially important among the government-sponsored organizations active in the support of export sales by U.S. firms has been the Export-Import Bank of Washington, a government-owned corporation. The Eximbank makes direct loans to foreign governments and private concerns which permit them to purchase machinery and other products from U.S. firms. In addition, the Eximbank has participated with American exporters and U.S. commercial banks in extending short- and intermediate-term credit to foreign buyers on specific export transactions, such as the sale of textile machinery to a Colombian textile manufacturer. Since July 1, 1963, the Eximbank has had an active program of guaranteeing medium-term credits to foreigners by U.S. exporters of capital goods. This has facilitated the efforts of the U.S. vendor firms to have banks take over these credits without recourse to the exporter if the foreign customer failed to complete his payments. The Eximbank has also had an important role in the development of programs of insurance against certain of the risks in extending routine export credit.[14]

The scale of Eximbank lending, guarantee, and insurance activity has been substantial. In the 6 months ended December 31, 1964, Eximbank authorized a total of $882.3 million in loans, guarantees, and insurance. Total loans disbursed over its life through 1964 amounted to $10 billion; on December 31, 1964, outstanding loans were approximately $3.5 billion.[15]

---

[13] Carl T. Arlt, "Government Loan Programs for Small Business," chap. xii in *Financing Small Business* (Washington, D.C.: Board of Governors, Federal Reserve System, 1958).

[14] For an extended exposition of the export financing assistance programs of the Eximbank see *Financing U.S. Exports and Overseas Investment—A MAPI Study and Guide* (Washington, D.C.: Machinery and Allied Products Institute, 1964).

[15] Export-Import Bank of Washington, *Report to Congress for the First Half of Fiscal 1965* (Washington, D.C.: U.S. Government Printing Office, 1965).

Financial Aids to Military Suppliers

During World War II, it was vitally important that production of war goods not be hampered by the financial limitations of otherwise desirable suppliers. Accordingly, a variety of forms of financial aid to military suppliers was developed. Most forms were continued in use after the war, although used more selectively, or were revived during the Korean conflict. As long as defense outlays continue at a high level, the financial aids to military suppliers will continue to be of great importance.

The more important financial devices to help private business assist in the defense effort include the following:

1. *Government Construction and Equipping of Plants with Government Money.* For many important items the government provides the basic facilities and equipment, and private concerns operate the facilities, providing—sometimes with government aid—the necessary working capital and management for operations.

2. *Authorization of Rapid Amortization of New Facilities and Equipment Important Immediately or Potentially for Defense Purposes Which Are Acquired, Owned, and Operated by Private Concerns.* In time of emergency a method of depreciation was available under our federal tax laws to those firms that obtained, for certain new assets, a *certificate of necessity* from a military procurement agency. The certificate stated that the assets in question were necessary for defense purposes and that otherwise they would not be constructed. In such cases *accelerated amortization* was allowed on all or part of the cost of the assets and the investment could be depreciated in 5 years. This was avowedly an incentive plan designed to induce capital investment where desired by the government, and it was effective because of the large size of the tax shields provided in the first 5 years of a project. The certificates could no longer be granted after December 31, 1959.

3. *Government Guaranties of Commercial Bank Loans to Military Contractors.* The program of government loan guaranties, known as the "V-Loan" program, is designed to help private firms get commercial bank credit to aid them in financing working capital needs arising out of performance under specific defense contracts. Under this program the contractor negotiates a loan with his commercial bank. The bank typically agrees to advance a percentage (usually 80% to 90%) of the contractor's inventory and receivables connected with the military supply contract. As a means of encouraging the bank to make the loan through reducing the risks of loss to the bank, the buying agency—Army, Navy, Air Force, or Defense Supply Agency—guarantees repayment to the bank of a percentage, usually between 70% and 90%, of the bank's advances to the contractor. The banks must pay a percentage of the interest charged on the loan to the government for its guaranty, the amount of the payment varying with the percentage of the total loan guaranteed.

From revival of the V-Loan program in 1950 through August, 1965, 1,628 V-Loans were authorized, totaling $3.5 billion. In recent years, use of the program has declined greatly owing in part to the improved financial condition of many defense contractors and in part to the fact that the permissible return on V-Loans has become relatively unattractive to the banks. On August 31, 1965, V-Loans amounting only to $65 million were outstanding.

4. *Progress Payments.* Military contracts may authorize payments to the contractor before any deliveries of finished products are made. Progress payments are made as work proceeds under a contract on the basis of costs incurred or upon accomplishment of stages of completion of the project. They have become traditional for production contracts involving a "long lead time," or preparatory period of 6 months or more between the beginning of work under a contract and deliveries of finished products. Progress payments are widely used in the procurement of aircraft, ships, guided missiles, and a variety of other expensive items that involve lengthy design and production schedules. As of June, 1965, the Defense Department had progress payments of $3.5 billion outstanding under fixed price contracts with a face value of $21 billion. After September 1, 1957, "customary" progress payments on new contracts based on costs were limited to 70% of the contractor's total cost outlays or 85% of his direct labor and materials costs. (Slightly higher percentage payments were permitted small business firms.) Provision was also made for the approval, under exceptional circumstances, of "unusual" progress payments at greater percentages of the contractor's incurred costs.

5. *Advance Payments.* Under certain circumstances, the terms of military contracts may authorize advance payments to prime contractors prior to, and in anticipation of, performance under the contracts. As distinguished from progress payments, advance payments do not require previous work on the contract. It is Defense Department policy to authorize advance payments only if no other method of financing will meet the contractor's needs. As a result, advance payments are seldom used to finance private defense contractors; however, they are frequently used to finance contracts with universities and with nonprofit corporations engaged in government research and development, such as the RAND Corporation.

Advance payments to private contractors require an interest charge of 5% per annum; however, those made to nonprofit institutions may be interest free. Special procedures, including the use of special bank accounts, designed to protect the government's interests, are involved in advance payments.

We should make clear that the government is sparing in its extension of the various financing aids to contractors, and some military suppliers may not be able to qualify. Where financing aid is to be extended suppliers, current Defense Department policy observes the following order of preference: (a) customary progress payments, (b) guaranteed loans, (c) unusual progress payments, and (d) advance payments.

Programs of Aid to Especially Deserving Groups

An example of programs of this sort is the provision by legislation for governmental guaranties of certain loans by banks or other private agencies to ex-servicemen. Greatest use of these loan guaranties by veterans has been for the purchase of homes. However, guaranties of up to 50% and a dollar amount of $2,000 can be obtained for business ventures that have good promise of success. Through 1963, 238,041 loans, totaling $671 million, involving credit for business ventures of veterans, had been made under this continuing but decelerating program. It is interesting to note that defaults were reported on 43,932, or 18%, of these loans through 1963; claims for Veterans' Administration reimbursement were filed on 16,200, or about 7% of the loans.[16]

The disaster loan program of the SBA, discussed earlier, is another example of this sort of government financial aid.

---

[16] Administrator of Veterans' Affairs, *Annual Report, 1963* (Washington, D.C.: U.S. Government Printing Office, 1964).

Chapter 13

The Effective Use of Security in Business Borrowing

A VITAL feature of much business borrowing is the granting to lenders of a security interest in particular assets of the borrower. A large percentage of the commercial bank credit, and virtually all of the credit granted business by commercial finance companies and governmental agencies, is predicated on the granting of security.

The importance of security in bank borrowing is documented by comprehensive studies of business loans by member banks of the Federal Reserve System. Key findings relative to the use of security are summarized in Table 13–1 and in Table 13–2 (page 250). Although the most recent Federal Reserve studies took place in 1957 and 1955, there is no evidence of great change in the use of security in bank borrowing since the dates of the studies.

As Table 13–1 brings out, 66.8% or 856,000 of the 1,281,000 business loans outstanding at these banks were supported by collateral. Comparison with results of earlier studies in 1946 and 1955 indicated that the use of security in commercial bank lending to business had increased moderately in the 1946–57 period.

The use of security is particularly important in the bank borrowing of small and medium-sized firms. This conclusion is supported by the Federal Reserve study, which disclosed that secured loans, while representing 66.8% of the total *number* of business loans, accounted for $20,426 million, or 50.3% of the total *amount* of bank credit to business.[1] The lower dollar amount percentage reflects the fact that most large loans are made on an unsecured basis. As might be expected in view of the general tendency for the financial strength of business firms to increase with asset size, the study showed that the use of security varied inversely with the size of the borrowing firm. Thus, 76.5% of the bank credit extended firms with total assets of between $50,000 and $250,000 was on

---

[1] *Federal Reserve Bulletin*, April, 1958.

TABLE 13-1

RELATION OF SECURED LOANS TO TOTAL BUSINESS LOANS OF MEMBER BANKS, 1957, WITHIN SIZE-OF-BORROWER GROUPS

Size of Borrower (Total Assets, in Thousands of Dollars)	Amount			Number		
	Total Loans (In Millions of Dollars)	Secured Loans		Total Loans (In Thousands)	Secured Loans	
		Millions of Dollars	Percentage of Total for Size Group		Thousands	Percentage of Total for Size Group
All borrowers*	40,618	20,426	50.3	1,281	856	66.8
Less than 50	1,456	1,141	78.4	505	344	68.2
50–250	5,256	4,023	76.5	494	325	65.7
250–1,000	6,302	4,543	72.1	158	104	65.9
1,000–5,000	6,775	4,056	59.9	48	29	60.7
5,000–25,000	5,912	2,661	45.0	13	6	48.5
25,000–100,000	4,893	1,381	28.2	5	2	31.7
100,000 or more	8,815	1,546	17.5	6	2	34.7

* Includes a small amount of loans to borrowers whose size was not ascertained.
SOURCE: Adapted from *Federal Reserve Bulletin*, April, 1958, p. 403.

a secured basis, while only 17.5% of the credit extended firms with assets above $100 million was secured.[2]

As we have seen, commercial finance companies are important lenders to business. A very high percentage of their loans to business is extended against security. Since the finance companies generally have been willing to loan to companies inherently more risky than commercial banks have cared to accommodate, they have been especially vigorous and imaginative in developing ways of taking security as a means of curbing their risks in lending.

The lending to business by governmental and semigovernmental agencies has been predominantly on a secured basis. A major proportion of the Reconstruction Finance Corporation loans were made against specific security. The loans currently made by the Small Business Administration, and loans supported by governmental guaranties to aid in the financing of military contracts, such as those under the V-Loan program, typically are predicated on the grant of a security interest to the lender.

Why Borrowers Offer Security to Lenders

The paramount reason why most borrowers offer lenders a security √ interest in their assets is simply to enhance their borrowing power. Many American concerns, particularly very large ones, enjoy such excellent profit prospects and strong financial positions that they do not need to offer security—they can get sufficient credit on suitable terms on an unsecured basis. But a great many more enterprises are able to boost their attractiveness to lenders materially by skillful concession of security interests in their assets.

To many firms with uncertain prospects or limited ownership funds, little or no credit, other than that from the spontaneous sources described in Chapter 9, is available on an unsecured basis. Only by offering security attractive to lenders are they able to get loans at all. In other words, to these firms, use of security in borrowing is not really a matter of choice but the *sine qua non* of any debt financing. Still other, less weak, concerns could arrange some bank credit on an unsecured basis but can get larger loans by offering security.

In the case of other borrowers, offering security may be desirable primarily as a means of obtaining more favorable credit terms—lower interest rates, longer maturity schedules, or less restrictive covenants— than could be obtained through unsecured borrowing. For example, many railroads use locomotives or other rolling stock as security under equipment trust certificates, a borrowing device referred to later in this chapter. The repayment record of equipment trust certificates over past decades has been so excellent that it is usually possible for even the

---

[2] *Ibid.*

strongest railroads to borrow through equipment trust certificates at lower net interest rates than could be obtained through unsecured borrowing for comparable periods.

Why Security Is Valuable to the Lender

Why do lenders so frequently prefer a *secured position* to the status of an unsecured creditor? As suggested earlier, lenders take collateral primarily as a means of reducing the risk of loss through nonrepayment of their loans. The risks of loss may be reduced by a secured position in several ways:

1. Under many security arrangements, close contact with the borrower is required in order to maintain an effective secured position. As a by-product of the security arrangement, the lender often gains a more intimate, complete, and up-to-date acquaintance with the borrower's affairs than he would have obtained as an unsecured creditor.

2. Under many security arrangements the lender obtains a close and continuing control over assets vital to the borrower's business. This control helps to prevent the sale or diversion of assets that the lender is looking to as an ultimate source of repayment of his loan. Some lenders would be willing to accept an unsecured status *provided* no other creditor could obtain a prior claim. By taking key assets as security, the lender assures himself that these assets cannot be pledged to another creditor who would thereby gain priority over unsecured lenders. If the lender has full confidence in the borrower, he may seek to gain this same objective through an agreement that the borrower will not pledge assets to other lenders. Such compacts, known as *negative pledge* agreements, are used with some frequency.

3. Finally, and most basically, if the borrower encounters serious financial difficulties and cannot meet his obligations, the secured lender expects to enjoy a prior claim to the security and to the net proceeds from its disposition. Under certain circumstances, if the borrower cannot meet his commitments to the secured lender, the lender can seize and sell his security to satisfy his debt without ever becoming a party to developing bankruptcy proceedings. Alternatively, if all of the distressed borrower's assets are placed under the supervision of a bankruptcy court for distribution to creditors or for reorganization of the business, the secured lender expects to be able to establish his prior claim over unsecured creditors to the proceeds of his security.

Taking over security does not necessarily mean the full satisfaction of the debt obligation. In the event that sale of the security does not net enough money to pay off the debt in full, the secured lender usually can obtain a *deficiency judgment* for the unsatisfied portion of the debt. However, for this portion of his debt, the lender ranks as an unsecured or general creditor of the firm and shares pro rata with other unsecured creditors in any proceeds available for them.

As we shall see in a later chapter, most sizable firms that enter bankruptcy do not undergo complete liquidation of their assets. Very often, the total value of the firm as a reorganized, going concern is judged to be greater than the probable net proceeds from liquidation and dispersal of its assets. Consequently, the firm is reorganized and continues in business. The treatment accorded secured creditors in reorganization is influenced strongly by the value of the secured assets under the alternatives of liquidation or reorganization. Secured creditors with claims on assets vital to the operation of reorganized firms frequently have been paid in full while unsecured creditors suffered heavily. Consequently, the priority ranking of creditors strongly influences their vulnerability to loss in reorganization, as well as in bankruptcy leading to complete liquidation. At worst, secured creditors of bankrupt concerns generally fare substantially less badly than unsecured creditors.

It should be emphasized that the legal rights to a security interest in particular assets can be no more valuable than the assets themselves. If the assets prove of limited value in sale or use, the priority that attaches to the proceeds of this security likewise will be of limited value.

What Assets Make Good Security

Not many decades ago, only *real property*—land and buildings—and marketable securities found widespread use as security for loans. In recent decades the situation has changed markedly. Today, every major type of business asset is used as security for loans in significant volume. Accounts receivable, inventory, equipment, and even claims not yet appearing as assets on the balance sheets of borrowers (such as anticipated rental receipts for property rented under long-term leases) now serve as collateral on an important scale.

Back of the broadening security base for business borrowing have been several developments. Important among these have been major improvements in the legislation covering the use of business assets, such as inventory and receivables, as security. Further, lenders have much improved their skills and techniques in taking and administering a secured position. Vitally important, too, has been the increasing conviction on the part of lenders broadly that such assets as accounts receivable, properly handled, can constitute good security against loss to the lenders.

Of course, this does not mean that in a specific situation a potential lender will conclude that all or any of the firm's assets represent good collateral. Rather, it means that lenders increasingly are willing to take a searching look at almost any asset for its possible value as security. If lenders are to regard a particular asset as attractive security, it must meet four basic tests:

1. The lender must be able, under applicable laws (usually state legislation) to obtain a legal security interest in the asset that clearly is valid and sustainable against challenge in the courts.
2. The lender must be able to achieve a reasonable degree of protection

against loss through fraud. This requirement is especially critical in respect to these assets which the lender for practical reasons cannot take into direct and continuous possession.

3. The mechanics of the security device and of supervision of the security interest must be such that they can continue in force without undue expense and trouble to either borrower or lender.

4. The asset must be one that can reasonably be expected to continue to have value over the projected life of the loan. This value must be recognizable and realizable; that is, the lender must be able to forecast with some confidence that even under adverse conditions, he will be able to convert the asset into enough cash to cover his advance.

Establishing a Legally Valid Security Interest

Although certain provisions of federal bankruptcy law may be applicable, the legislation governing the taking of a security interest and the rights and obligations of secured lenders is primarily that of the 50 states. Until recently the state legislation dealing with the granting of security interests was characterized by diversity, complexity, and more than a little obscurity. This was particularly true of the law and practice related to the use of *personal property*—assets other than real estate—as security.

It is pleasing to acknowledge the great progress achieved in recent years toward relative uniformity in state legislation related to many aspects of commercial transactions including the granting of security. This progress has taken the form of adoption by a preponderant number of the states of model legislation called the Uniform Commercial Code. Since the Code went into effect in Pennsylvania in 1954, it has been adopted with limited changes by the more important commercial states, and by year-end 1965 it appeared that the laggard states would soon join in adopting this legislation.

A great deal of effort by outstanding members of the bar and other interested parties went into the drafting of the provisions of the Uniform Commercial Code. Section 9 of the Code was devoted to security interests; its provisions sought to clarify both basic concepts and legal mechanics of granting a security interest. For example, the pre-Code requirements of the various states were particularly diverse regarding the methods by which other interested parties could inform themselves of the fact that particular creditors were being extended a security interest in accounts receivable. Clearly, in fairness, trade creditors and other interested parties were entitled to a warning that a security interest had been granted and that the debtor did not hold the accounts receivable free and clear. While agreeing generally to the need for a warning mechanism, the states disagreed as to what form it should take.

The objectives of notification are served under the Uniform Commercial Code by requirement of *notice filing* at a designated public office, often that of the Secretary of State at the state capitol, to put other creditors on notice that the debtor has given, or may in the future give, to one or more specified creditors an interest in the accounts receivable (or other assets if they are covered). Notice can take the form of filing the signed security agreement between borrower and lender or, alternatively, by the filing of a financing statement which either may relate to a particular transaction or may give generalized warning of present and

EXHIBIT 13-1

ILLUSTRATION OF FORM USED IN FILING A FINANCING STATEMENT IN MASSACHUSETTS UNDER THE UNIFORM COMMERCIAL CODE

UNIFORM COMMERCIAL CODE — FINANCING STATEMENT — FORM UCC-1

INSTRUCTIONS
1. PLEASE TYPE this form. Fold only along perforation for mailing.
2. Remove Secured Party and Debtor copies and send other 3 copies with interleaved carbon paper to the filing officer. Enclose filing fee of $3.00.
3. When filing is to be with more than one office, Form UCC-2 may be placed over this set to avoid double typing.
4. If the space provided for any item(s) on the form is inadequate the item(s) should be continued on additional sheets, preferable 5" x 8" or 8" by 10". Only one copy of such additional sheets need be presented to the filing officer with a set of three copies of the financing statement. Long schedules of collateral, indentures, etc. may be on any size paper that is convenient for the secured party.
5. If collateral is crops or goods which are or are to become fixtures, describe generally the real estate and give name of record owner.
6. When a copy of the security agreement is used as a financing statement, it is requested that it be accompanied by a completed but unsigned set of these forms, without extra fee.
7. At the time of original filing, filing officer should return third copy as an acknowledgement. At a later time, secured party may date and sign Termination Legend and use third copy as a Termination Statement.

This FINANCING STATEMENT is presented to a filing officer for filing pursuant to the Uniform Commercial Code. 3 Maturity date (If any):

1 Debtor(s) (Last Name First) and address(es)	2 Secured Party(ies) and address(es)	For Filing Officer (Date, Time, Number, and Filing Office)
William Brown, Inc. Stoneham, Massachusetts	New England Merchants National Bank of Boston 28 State Street Boston, Massachusetts	

4 This financing statement covers the following types (or items) of property:

Accounts receivable, contracts, contract rights, returned merchandise, and inventory.

Check [X] if covered: [X] Proceeds of Collateral are also covered [X] Products of Collateral are also covered No. of additional sheets presented:

Filed with:

William Brown, Inc. New England Merchants National Bank of Boston

By: Joseph Burke Treas. By: William Brenton

Signature(s) of Debtor(s) Signature(s) of Secured Party(ies)

FILING OFFICER COPY — ALPHABETICAL This form of financing statement is approved by the Secretary of State.

STANDARD FORM — UNIFORM COMMERCIAL CODE — FORM UCC-1 Forms may be purchased from Samuel Narcus, Boston, Mass.

future transactions in receivables or other types of assets (see Exhibit 13-1).

Although widespread adoption of the Uniform Commercial Code promises to reduce much of the pre-Code ambiguities and uncertainty related to taking a security interest, a cautionary generalization still has broad validity: *Lenders must exercise great care in taking a security interest and in maintaining it.* If the borrower gets into financial difficulties and bankruptcy ensues, typically, unsecured creditors also will be in the picture. It will be to the unsecured creditors' advantage to have as much as possible of the proceeds of the bankrupt's assets put in the pool for division among unsecured creditors. Consequently, counsel for unsecured creditors can be expected to exploit any opportunity to challenge the claims of secured creditors to a priority security interest in the more valuable assets. If counsel for unsecured creditors can find significant flaws in the prior claims, they may well succeed in having the court deny the validity of the security interest, so that the secured lender finds himself unwittingly and unwillingly a general creditor. In effect, lenders against security still must walk a legal tightrope in order to ensure that their claim to a security interest can stand up under challenge in the event the claim needs to be asserted.

BORROWING AGAINST RECEIVABLES

Discounting Notes Receivable

In an earlier chapter we noted that it was once common practice for manufacturing and wholesale firms to sell to retailers on credit terms of several months. The credit instrument in such sales was the unsecured promissory note of the customer. Commonly, the seller *discounted* or borrowed against these notes at his bank. The bank held such notes in its possession and presented them, through correspondent banks, for collection at maturity. Since the discounting bank required endorsement of the notes by the seller, they were known as *two-name paper;* and if either buyer or seller had a good credit standing, the notes represented good support for the bank's advance. No priority of claim over unsecured creditors of either firm was involved, however.

In recent decades the volume of business borrowing through discounting of notes receivable has shrunk. The decline in such financing has resulted not from bankers' unwillingness to discount notes of responsible concerns but from changing business practice in terms of sale. As we noted earlier, most businesses now sell on short terms and on open account. Consequently, even though those firms still selling on notes from creditworthy customers have little trouble converting such notes into cash, the overall volume of such transactions in domestic trade now is small.

While the use of notes receivable in routine trade credit has declined, there has been a sharp increase in the sale of machinery and equipment and consumer durable goods on terms which call for monthly instalment payments over a period of several years. Typically, the manufacturer or retailer granting such credit retains legal title to, or a security interest in, the equipment, and the debt is evidenced by notes or sales contracts which are assignable to lenders. The discounting of notes secured by equipment will be discussed later in this chapter under "Borrowing against Equipment."

Borrowing against Accounts Receivable as Collateral

Since most business concerns sell on credit and on open account, the typical firm has a large investment in accounts receivable. The attitude of banks and other commercial lenders toward accounts receivable as security has changed substantially in the last 25 years. In earlier periods, many lenders, particularly commercial banks, hesitated to enter into loan agreements with accounts receivable as security. Generally, they took accounts receivable as security only as a means toward the "working-out" of loans which had "gone sour." As a consequence, the use by a business of its accounts receivable as security for loans was widely regarded as evidence of serious financial weakness on the part of that firm.

Despite this early stigma and the problems involved in lending against accounts receivable, this form of lending has become important in recent decades. Basic to the growth is the solid fact that accounts receivable represent the closest asset to cash timewise and the asset of soundest value of many would-be borrowers. For example, many small, financially weak shoe manufacturers sell on short terms to large retail chain stores or department stores whose credit is excellent. Too, much progress has been made in the development of procedures for efficient and low-cost handling of the extensive paper work necessarily involved in lending against accounts receivable. Aware of fraud hazards in this sort of lending, lenders have had considerable success also in developing policing techniques which reduce the opportunities and temptations for fraud. These include periodic inspection of the borrower's receivables records, selective verification, often through a public accounting firm, of the receivables through confirmation by the customers of the amounts they owe the borrowers, and especial effort to see that the accounting procedures for crediting returned merchandise are adequate and are followed carefully.

Other important measures of curbing the risk in loaning against accounts receivable have come into widespread use. Perhaps most important among these are the following:

1. Lenders reserve the right to select the accounts that will be acceptable to them as security. Effort is made to screen out and exclude from the security base overdue accounts and current accounts from concerns financially weak or with a poor reputation for payment.

2. Accounts typically are accepted *with recourse*. That is, the borrower agrees to replace those accounts that are not paid reasonably promptly with acceptable accounts not overdue, or to reduce the loan accordingly.

3. Perhaps most important is the usual practice of loaning only a percentage of the full face amount of the accounts pledged. For example, if the lender advances only 75% of the face value of the accounts pledged, the 25% margin is available to cover prompt payment discounts, goods returned by the customer for credit, and demands for allowances for faulty merchandise or damaged goods, and accounts that prove uncollectible. If these are expected to be high, a wider margin of safety is sought through establishment of a lower percentage of loan to accounts pledged.

4. Typically, a maximum limit also is established on the total amount that will be loaned, regardless of the total value of the security. This ceiling recognizes that the general credit of the borrower is also back of the loan and that this added protection is diluted when the receivables loan becomes very large relative to the total resources of the borrower.

Now, let us get some idea of the mechanics of receivables borrowing by reviewing typical terms of loan agreements drawn up to cover bank loans against receivables. Points covered in the loan agreement or other papers establishing the loan arrangements commonly include the following:

1. The term of life of the lending arrangements. Although provision often is made that the loan secured by receivables is payable on demand of the lender, there is usually an understanding that the loan will continue for a considerable or indefinite period. Many receivables loans continue for years, terminating only when the company no longer needs to borrow or has prospered to a point where it can get satisfactory credit on an unsecured basis.

2. Agreement that the bank may screen the accounts to determine which represent acceptable security, and an outline of the procedures by which accepted accounts that become overdue are replaced or the loan base is reduced.

3. The percentage that the bank will loan against the face amount of receivables.

4. The maximum dollar amount of the loan against receivables.

5. The evidence that the borrower must submit in support of the validity of the accounts. In some cases, only a simple listing of the customers and the amounts owing from each is required. In other cases the borrower may be required to submit such evidence as original invoices, or signed receipts from shipping companies, for the goods giving rise to the account receivable.

6. Authorization to the lender to inspect the borrower's books upon demand or to undertake other methods of checking up on the validity of the receivables given as collateral.

7. The frequency with which the borrower can bring in new accounts to add to the security base and thus permit greater borrowing, as well as the interval within which he must bring in the money collected from pledged accounts to pay down the loan. In some cases, collections and new accounts added are brought in daily, and a new calculation is made of security base and loan balance. Since most firms make new credit sales and collections each day, both the gross value of the accounts given as security and the loan amount totals are shifting ones. Specific receivables pledged change, and the totals pledged and borrowed rise and fall; but normally, some accounts remain outstanding, and so does the loan against the receivables.

A loan agreement granting a security interest in accounts receivable and inventory is shown as Exhibit 13–4, page 258.

What Lenders Make Accounts Receivable Loans?

Commercial banks, commercial credit companies, and factoring concerns are the principal financial concerns that lend against accounts receivable on a major scale. In commercial banking circles it is now widely recognized that accounts receivable can represent satisfactory security, and most large banks now stand ready to make such loans as part of a well-rounded lending service to business. Since such lending often implies relatively steady lending, requires more paper work and generally more trouble to service than most loans, and necessitates some specialized knowledge and procedures, many smaller banks have shown little interest in making such loans.

As indicated earlier, commercial credit companies pioneered in accounts receivable lending, and such lending still accounts for a substantial portion of their total lending volume. While factoring concerns, as explained earlier, finance receivables primarily on a purchase basis, they also do a certain amount of lending against pledge of receivables.

Costs of Borrowing against Accounts Receivable

Since companies borrowing against receivables tend to be of less than average financial strength, and since the continuing borrowing arrangement involves relatively high expense and trouble to the lender, the costs of such borrowing tend to be higher than on unsecured loans to stronger companies. When the interest rate charged by banks to prime credits on an unsecured basis is around 4%, the interest rate on accounts receivable loans will likely be 6% to 7%; and additional charges for servicing the account, amounting to an annual cost of 1% or 2%, are common. Total charges by nonbank lenders commonly amount to an annual rate of 9% to 16% of the credit supplied, and often may be higher.

BORROWING AGAINST INVENTORY

As we have seen, most business firms have a substantial portion of their resources invested in inventory. And many in need of credit have inventory with characteristics that make it good collateral for borrowing. Of the 799,100 secured bank loans covered in a 1955 Federal Reserve study summarized in Table 13–2, some 47,400 loans representing 9.2% of the total amount and 5.9% of the number were secured by inventory.

What Inventory Makes Good Collateral?

An outstanding characteristic of the investment in inventory of a great many firms is its heterogeneity. The typical manufacturer, for example, has on hand raw materials, work in process, finished goods, and supplies;

and each of these categories consists of a variety of items of different sizes, shapes, and grades. In considering the possibilities of bolstering a credit application by giving the lenders a security interest in particular inventory, it can be helpful to appraise the inventory in terms of the qualities that lenders look for in deciding whether a particular commodity will be good security.

TABLE 13–2

SECURITY PLEDGED ON BUSINESS LOANS AT MEMBER BANKS
OF FEDERAL RESERVE SYSTEM, OCTOBER 5, 1955,
BY TYPE OF SECURITY

(Estimates of Outstanding Loans)

Major Type of Security	Amount of Loans (In Millions)	Number of Loans (In Thousands)	Percentage Distribution	
			Amount	Number
Unsecured	$15,105	386.1	49.0	32.6
Secured	15,700	799.1	51.0	67.4
Total, all loans	$30,805	1,185.2	100.0	100.0
SECURED				
Endorsed, comaker, or guaranteed	$ 2,755	185.9	17.5	23.3
Receivables and other claims	2,813	52.9	17.9	6.6
Inventories	1,448	47.4	9.2	5.9
Equipment	2,194	218.5	14.0	27.3
Plant and other real estate	3,592	164.4	22.9	20.6
U.S. government securities	182	8.5	1.2	1.1
Other bonds	165	2.6	1.0	0.3
Stocks	1,002	39.1	6.4	4.9
Life insurance and savings accounts	447	53.8	2.8	6.7
Other security	1,102	26.1	7.1	3.3
			100.0	100.0

SOURCE: "Security Pledged on Business Loans at Member Banks," *Federal Reserve Bulletin*, September, 1959.

The physical characteristics of the goods are of basic importance. Clearly, lenders prefer products that are not vulnerable to physical deterioration during the terms of the credit. Wheat of low moisture content, properly stored, resists deterioration for long periods, for example, in contrast to fresh peaches, which may go soft, even under refrigeration, in a matter of hours. While conditions of storage can affect perishability risks, it is possible to generalize that lenders are little interested in taking as security those commodities subject to substantial risks of physical deterioration.

Relatively homogeneous products generally are preferred to commodities whose grade or quality is diverse or hard to measure. For example, lumber of a single type, grade, size, and shape would be easier to appraise and keep tallied than lumber of diverse kinds, grades, and shapes.[3]

Although bulk is not necessarily undesirable, commodities of high value relative to bulk generally are preferred.

It is perhaps more important that the commodity be one that reasonably can be expected to continue to have resale value. No lender wants to take over inventory and have to dispose of it. But he wants to be confident that if he must, he can find a ready buyer at a good price. What factors help build such confidence? First is a record of price stability in the past. Some products, such as wool, have records of rapid and wide price fluctuations in contrast to the relative price stability of such items as sheet steel.

Second, the existence of a broad, local market for the commodity heightens the possibility that buyers can be found at a relatively small reduction in price. Such a broad market is more likely to exist if the commodity is a relatively standard one. High-style items with a narrow local market, such as women's high-style dresses in a small midwestern town, could be compared with uncut yard goods of a popular grade and color suitable for men's suits, located in New York City, center of the garment industry. Usually, raw materials have a broader market than semiprocessed or finished goods where the process of manufacture has created distinctive features. Most lenders are very reluctant to lend much on in-process inventories.

Third, the existence of frequent selling transactions in an organized market with published price quotations helps the lender to follow trends in value of the product with minimum effort.

Fourth, as is true of any asset considered as security, the commodity must be such that the borrower can give the lender a clear-cut security interest without undue inconvenience or disruption of his business operation and associated expense. For many would-be borrowers against inventory, this is a major problem area. Consider the highly diverse circumstances under which inventories are held—pulpwood at the paper mill awaiting processing, cattle in the farmer's feed lot for fattening, refrigerators on the floor of the appliance retailer, oil reserves still underground, the food processor's stocks of frozen foods located in cold-

---

[3] At a 1964 convention of the commercial finance industry, a participant on an industry panel was asked, "Do you find, in the event of liquidation, that the inventory mix is different from the going concern's mix?" The answer of the experienced lender was, "I think we will always find that. . . . When you liquidate an inventory, you are always going to find that the less desirable items are on hand. I recall one recently where we thought we had a pretty good mix on a lumber inventory, but when it went into bankruptcy all we had—or at least eighty per cent of it—were moldings, which were very hard to sell. This poor mix occurs even with the finished goods; hence, the only product you can be sure of is probably raw steel." *Proceedings of the Twentieth Anniversary Convention of the Commercial Finance Industry* (New York: National Commercial Finance Conference, Inc., 1964), p. 85.

storage warehouses in a number of cities. These few items suggest the need for a variety of legal procedures and for imagination on the part of lenders if they are to obtain a valid security interest and keep track effectively of their collateral. And indeed, much progress has been made in the development of legal and operational procedures that can offer adequate protection to the lender while minimizing the inconvenience and expense to the borrower.

Several different methods of giving lenders a security interest in inventory are in widespread use. The basic features of the more important types of arrangements will be described briefly.

1. *Borrowing against Inventory Covered by Warehouse Receipts.* Under this well-established method, physical custody of the goods is placed in the hands of a warehousing company which, at the direction of the borrower, issues a *warehouse receipt* made out in favor of the lender. An example of such a receipt is given in Exhibit 13–2. As custodian of the goods, the warehousing firm releases them only upon the instructions of the lender. Properly handled, the warehousing arrangement gives the lender firm control over the collateral. Much of the moral risk inherent in other kinds of inventory financing, where physical control of the goods is

EXHIBIT 13–2

EXAMPLE OF A WAREHOUSE RECEIPT
Front Side of Receipt

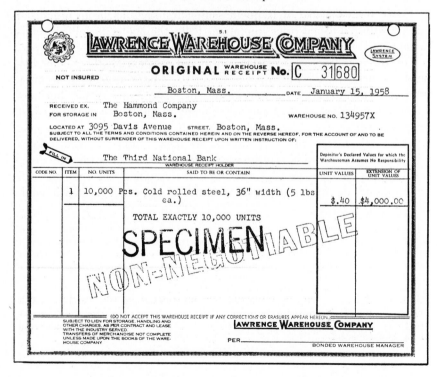

EXHIBIT 13–2—*Continued*

Provisions Stated on the Reverse Side of the Receipt

The face hereof is a copy of original Non-Negotiable Warehouse Receipt bearing the same number and date hereof. This copy is for purposes of certification and record only and is not a Warehouse Receipt. Any references on this copy to the face of such original Non-Negotiable Warehouse Receipt or the face of this copy includes only that portion of the original Warehouse Receipt or this copy above the words "Lawrence Warehouse Company Office Copy" set forth on the face hereof.

* * * * * *

I (We) the undersigned, certify and guarantee that the face hereof is a true copy of the face of the Lawrence Warehouse Company original Non-Negotiable Warehouse Receipt bearing the same number and date hereof and this copy has been compared by us with the original.

I (we), the undersigned, hereby certify and guarantee that I (we) are the legal owners of the commodities set forth on the face hereof and that the quantity and quality stated thereon are correct and that I (we) have delivered the same as of the date hereof to the Lawrence Warehouse Company for warehousing purposes in accordance with the terms of our storage agreement with them. I (we) hereby authorize the Lawrence Warehouse Company to issue a Non-Negotiable Warehouse Receipt bearing the same number and date hereof covering the above mentioned commodities in the name of

The Third National Bank at

Depositor _____ The Hammond Company

By _____ John Doe

* * * * * *

I, the undersigned, certify and guarantee that the face hereof is a true copy of the face of the Lawrence Warehouse Company original Non-Negotiable Warehouse Receipt bearing the same number and date hereof and this copy has been compared by me with the original.

I hereby certify that I received on _____ January 15 _____ 19 58 into my custody as

Bonded Warehouse Manager of the Lawrence Warehouse Company at its _____ Boston,

_____ Mass. Warehouse No. 134957X _____ Warehouse No. _____
the commodities set forth on the face hereof and have issued an original Non-Negotiable Warehouse Receipt covering the above mentioned commodities. Such original Non-Negotiable Warehouse Receipt was issued and signed by me and such commodities will be released by me from the above mentioned warehouse only in accordance with Lawrence Warehouse Company written instructions which I have heretofore received or may hereafter receive. I realize that to issue or sign such original Warehouse Receipt and the copies thereof or to release such commodities otherwise than in accordance with such written instructions violates the terms of my employment by the Lawrence Warehouse Company and constitutes a fraud upon that Company and the holders of its Warehouse Receipts.

Lawrence Warehouse Company Bonded Warehouse Manager

* * * * *

INSTRUCTIONS TO LAWRENCE WAREHOUSE COMPANY BONDED
WAREHOUSE MANAGER

IMPORTANT: The Lawrence Warehouse Company Bonded Whse. Mgr. making out and signing the original Non-Negotiable Warehouse Receipt bearing the same number and date hereof must forward this signed copy of such Warehouse Receipt **ON THE DATE HEREOF** to the Lawrence Warehouse Company office, the address of which is included in its written instructions addressed to such Bonded Warehouse Manager.

---

left with the borrower, is avoided. The legislation of the various states relating to the pledge of commodities under warehouse receipts is relatively uniform and well tested, so that the legal uncertainties that relate to many aspects of secured lending are relatively small in the case of lending against warehouse receipts.

Warehousing arrangements are of two major types—*public* and *field*. In the case of public warehouses the goods are brought to the warehouses for storage—for example, wheat moved into the public grain warehouses that dot the skylines of farm belt towns and cities. Lenders have long looked with favor on the public warehouse receipt security arrangement, and it has worked well from the borrower's viewpoint in the case of commodities that can be left undisturbed in the warehouse for long periods of time—such as whiskey being aged or wheat stored after harvest awaiting processing into flour.

Yet, many firms have their own storage facilities convenient to their manufacturing facilities or markets and want to avoid the trouble and expense of moving inventory to and from the warehouseman's facilities. Further, they wish to add to and draw from warehoused stocks frequently or continuously. To meet such needs, several warehousing firms[4] offer a *field warehousing* service. Under a field warehouse arrangement the warehousing firm leases storage facilities of the borrower and posts signs to signify that goods stored therein are in its exclusive custody, to be used as security. Commodities are put in the custody of the warehousing firm,[5] which issues warehouse receipts covering these segregated goods in the name of the lender. We should make clear that the warehousing firm performs only a warehousing function, making it possible for banks or other lending organizations to advance loans against the security of the goods covered by the warehouse receipt. Under the typical field warehouse receipt loan the lender advances a percentage of the value of the commodities covered by the warehouse receipt. When the borrowing firm wants to withdraw goods for processing or sale, it arranges with the lender to pay down that portion of the loan advanced against the particular goods involved, and the lender authorizes the warehouseman to release the goods to the borrower by surrendering the warehouse receipts.

The field warehousing arrangement is a highly ingenious method of facilitating the extension of credit and has come into widespread use in recent decades. One of the first industries to make heavy use of field warehousing was the California food-canning industry. The typical canner's manufacturing operation was highly seasonal, but sales were spread through the year. Customarily, the canner had a large investment in finished goods at the end of the canning season. The field warehousing arrangement permitted the canners to get substantial bank credit against the collateral of the canned goods and yet fill shipment orders through the year with minimum inconvenience and expense.

Over the years, field warehousing has been used for a wide variety of

---

[4] The leading field warehousing firm is Lawrence Warehouse Company.

[5] Care must be taken that the borrower in fact has no control over the goods. To be legally valid, the warehousing arrangement must put "continuous, exclusive, and notorious possession" in the hands of the warehousing firm.

commodities, including such items as coal in hopper cars on a railroad siding (locked switches into the main railroad line were in the control of the field warehouseman), logs in a mill pond, and watch movements stored in a large file cabinet.

The foregoing paragraphs dealing with borrowing against inventory covered by warehouses receipts have been carried forward exactly as they appeared in the preceding edition of this book (except for footnote 4, which has been revised to reflect the demise through bankruptcy of American Express Field Warehousing Corporation). Note the implicit confidence in the integrity and competence of the field warehousing companies. Our confidence reflected the general attitude of banks and other lenders toward the field warehouse receipts of well-known warehousing companies. It is also interesting to note that a basic commodity such as soybean oil, used in a variety of important products, and for which there is an active market, has the characteristics that make for valuable collateral—as we had listed them.

These basic considerations—widespread confidence in field warehouse companies and the validity of their receipts and confidence in the security value of basic commodities like soybean oil—help to explain how 51 companies and banks lost many millions of dollars in credit extended against field warehouse receipts for soybean and other vegetable oils that proved nonexistent. The total inventory shortage discovered in the wake of the failure of the presumed owner, Allied Crude Vegetable Oil Refining Corporation, in late 1963, was reported to be 1,854 million pounds of oil with a stated value of $175 million.[6] Incorrect or fraudulent warehouse receipts had served as the basis for what appears to have been well over $100 million of credit. The proceeds of insurance and payments from the parent company of one of the warehousing firms, American Express Company, will significantly cut the gross losses but net losses will be huge. Altogether the "Great Salad Oil Swindle" stands as one of the worst of all times and one especially striking because of the nature of the major victims, sophisticated and prominent business, financial, and commercial banking firms.

It is perhaps too early to gauge the long-run impact of the salad oil swindle on the ability of firms to borrow on the security of inventories evidenced by the receipts of third-party warehouses. Probably the near-term negative effect will in time be overcome as tighter procedures and closer surveillance on the part of both warehouse firms and lenders rebuild the confidence of lenders in warehouse receipts.[7]

2. *Borrowing against Inventory Covered by Trust Receipts.* A long-established method of borrowing against inventory that has continued

---

[6] The figures quoted here are from Norman C. Miller's *The Great Salad Oil Swindle* (New York: Coward McCann, Inc., 1965).

[7] Among the interesting articles in banking publications on the subject is John F. Barna's "Assessing the Risks in Warehouse Receipt Lending," *Banking*, June, 1964, p. 40.

under the Uniform Commercial Code involves the use of trust receipts. Lending arrangements under trust receipts typically involve three parties: for example, the manufacturer of automobiles, the automobile dealer, and the commercial bank lending to the dealer. If a shipment of cars to the dealer is to serve as security, the manufacturer transfers title to the cars

EXHIBIT 13–3

ILLUSTRATION OF A SECURITY AGREEMENT
COVERING TRUST RECEIPT FINANCING
Front Side

NEW ENGLAND MERCHANTS NATIONAL BANK OF BOSTON

BOSTON, MASSACHUSETTS, _____October 7,_____ 19 65

SECURITY AGREEMENT
(Trust Receipt)

Credit or Agreement No. 3406/1

Draft or Note Dated September 20, 1965

Face Amount Draft or Note $18,765.13

Bartlett Trading Company, Inc., 685 North Main Street, Braintree, Massachusetts 02184
(NAME)   (NO. AND STREET)   (CITY)   (STATE)

(hereinafter called the "Trustee") hereby acknowledges receipt from New England Merchants National Bank of Boston (hereinafter called the "Bank") of the documents, instruments or goods specified below which, together with any goods represented by said documents or instruments and any improvements or additions to or products of such goods, if any, are all hereinafter called the "Collateral", and the Trustee hereby acknowledges the existence and hereby grants a security interest in the Collateral and in the contract rights relating thereto and proceeds of both in favor of the Bank:

1 in trip.	Commercial Invoice	United States Lines Co. bill of lading No. 86 dated
1 in dup.	Customs Invoice	September 27, 1965, at Bremen, Germany, covering shipment
	Health Certificate	of 12 packages Dial Calipers per S.S. "American Pilot"
1 in dup.	Certificate of Origin	
1 in dup.	Insurance Certificate	from Bremen, Germany, to Boston, Mass., U.S.A.
	Specification	
	Weight Note	
	Declaration of Shipper	12 packages Dial Calipers valued at $18,765.13
	Warehouse Receipt	per Kaufmann & Co. AG. invoice No. 375.
	Delivery Order	
3/3	Bill(s) of Lading	

The security interest granted or acknowledged hereby secures payment of liabilities of the Trustee to the Bank evidenced by or arising in connection with a Letter of Credit, Agreement, Draft or Note noted above, all renewals thereof and also, if permitted by applicable law, any and all other liabilities of the Trustee to the Bank direct or indirect, absolute or contingent, due or to become due, now existing or hereafter arising (all hereinafter called the "Obligations").

In consideration of such receipt and other valuable consideration, the Trustee agrees to hold the Collateral in trust for the Bank subject to its security interest, to be used promptly by the Trustee without expense to the Bank for the purpose(s) checked below but for no other purpose(s) and without liberty to pledge the same or, unless hereafter expressly provided, to sell the same:

☐ 1. To transfer to carrier (land, water or air).
☐ 2. To transfer to warehouse.
☐ 3. To deliver the Collateral to ....

who have/has agreed to purchase the same for $.............................payable in ....
☐ 4. To sell the Collateral.
☒ 5. To manufacture or process and sell the Collateral whether or not manufactured or processed.
☐ 6.

The Trustee agrees to account for the Collateral and to that end to deliver to the Bank immediately upon the receipt thereof by the Trustee, any of the following as indicated by the appropriate number under the purposes for which the Collateral is entrusted as indicated above:
  1. Proper and sufficient negotiable bills of lading to the order of the Bank or airway bill.
  2. Proper and sufficient warehouse receipts to the order of or in the name of the Bank.
  3, 4 and 5. Proceeds of the sale of the Collateral in whatever form received, to be applied by the Bank to the payment of any obligations for which the Collateral is security or was security before this transaction and of any obligations arising as part of this transaction and of any renewals of any such obligations. If such proceeds be notes, bills receivable, acceptances or in any form other than cash, they need not be so applied by the Bank until paid; the Bank, however, to have the option at any time to sell or discount such items and so apply, conditionally upon final payment of such items, the net proceeds thereof. The Trustee will assign or endorse proceeds to the Bank as the Bank may request and the Bank shall have full power to collect, compromise, endorse, sell or otherwise deal with proceeds in its own name or that of the Trustee.

The Trustee agrees that the Bank assumes no responsibility for the correctness, validity or genuineness of the documents released to the Trustee hereunder or for the existence, character, quantity, quality, condition, value or delivery of any goods purported to be represented by any of such documents.

No waiver of any rights or powers of the Bank or consent by it shall be valid unless in writing signed by it and the rights and powers herein given the Bank are in addition to those otherwise enjoyed under applicable law.

All rights of the Bank hereunder shall inure to the benefit of its successors and assigns; and all obligations of the Trustee shall bind his heirs, executors or administrators or his or its successors or assigns. If there be more than one Trustee, their obligations hereunder shall be joint and several.

THIS AGREEMENT IS SUBJECT TO THE ADDITIONAL PROVISIONS SET FORTH AT THE TOP OF THE REVERSE SIDE HEREOF, THE SAME BEING INCORPORATED HEREIN BY REFERENCE.

Bartlett Trading Company, Inc.
TRUSTEE

By ....
AUTHORIZED SIGNATURE   President

21-059

EXHIBIT 13-3—*Continued*

Reverse Side

The Trustee agrees to pay all charges in connection with the Collateral and any proceeds thereof, and will at all times hold the Collateral and proceeds separate and apart from the property of the Trustee and will definitely show such separation in all its records and entries.

The Trustee will at all times keep the goods fully insured at the Trustee's expense in favor of, and to the satisfaction of the Bank against loss by fire, theft and any other risk to which said goods may be subject. The Trustee will deposit the insurance policies with the Bank upon its demand.

The Trustee agrees to permit and allow the Bank by its duly accredited representatives to examine all Collateral in possession of the Trustee at any reasonable time.

The Bank may at any time it deems itself insecure, without notice or demand, declare all Obligations secured hereby immediately due and payable and this agreement in default, and thereafter the Bank shall have the remedies of a secured party under the Uniform Commercial Code or other applicable laws. The Bank may require the Trustee to assemble the Collateral and proceeds and make them available to the Bank at a place to be designated by the Bank which is reasonably convenient to both parties. Whenever notification with respect to the sale or other disposition of the Collateral is required by law, such notification of the time and place of public sale, or of the date after which a private sale or other intended disposition is to be made, shall be deemed reasonable if mailed, postage prepaid, addressed to the Trustee at the mailing address hereinabove given at least seven (7) days before the time of such public sale or the date after which any such private sale or other intended disposition is to be made, as the case may be. The Trustee shall pay to the Bank on demand any and all expenses, including legal expenses and reasonable attorneys' fees, incurred or paid by the Bank in protecting or enforcing the Obligations and other rights of the Bank hereunder including its right to take possession of the Collateral and the proceeds thereof.

The Trustee agrees to join with the Bank in executing one or more financing statements pursuant to the Uniform Commercial Code or statements of trust receipt financing, all in form satisfactory to the Bank, and will pay the cost of filing the same in all public offices wherever filing is deemed by the Bank to be necessary or desirable.

and receives payment for them from the lending bank. The lending bank, in turn, delivers custody of the cars to the borrowing dealer under a *trust receipt agreement,* which specifies what the borrower may do with the cars. In the case of finished goods held for resale, such as the automobiles on the premises of the dealer, the agreement will provide that the goods may be sold but that the borrower will use the proceeds from sale promptly to pay off the loan. An illustration of a security agreement covering trust receipt financing is given in Exhibit 13–3.

The goods in trust should be specifically identified in the trust receipt, and the lender must devote reasonable care to policing the agreement to insure that the borrower carries out his responsibilities under the trust agreement. The fact that the borrower can put the material into process or sell it, as the trust agreement specifies, *before* he makes settlement with the lender can be a major convenience to the borrower, but it also involves risk to the lender. Accordingly, the moral standing and reputation for integrity of the borrower are particularly important to the lender considering a trust receipt financing arrangement—more so than in the case of warehouse receipt financing.

The trust receipt device has been heavily used by distributors and retailers of new automobiles and of major equipment and appliance items, who borrow to finance their working inventories of these items. Since the trust receipts must specifically identify the security, new trust receipts must be prepared as the borrower adds and disposes of particular items of inventory. The problem of specific identification and the burden of paper work in trust receipt financing makes the trust receipt an awkward or unsuitable device for securing highly diverse, fast-moving, or hard-to-identify inventory such as work in process.

3. *Borrowing against Inventory Covered by a Floating Lien under the Uniform Commercial Code.* The Uniform Commercial Code provides that lenders may be given a very broad security interest in inventories of

EXHIBIT 13–4

EXAMPLE OF A SECURITY AGREEMENT
COVERING BOTH INVENTORY AND
ACCOUNTS RECEIVABLE

First Page

NEW ENGLAND MERCHANTS NATIONAL BANK OF BOSTON

INVENTORY AND ACCOUNTS RECEIVABLE SECURITY AGREEMENT

........October 8, 1965........
(Date)

........William Brown, Inc.........................., the debtor hereunder (hereinafter called the "Borrower")
for valuable consideration receipt whereof is hereby acknowledged hereby grants to New England Merchants National
Bank of Boston, the secured party hereunder (hereinafter called the "Bank"), a security interest in Borrower's inventory,
including all goods, merchandise, raw materials, goods and work in process, finished goods and other tangible personal
property now owned or hereafter acquired and held for sale or lease or furnished or to be furnished under contracts of
service or used or consumed in Borrower's business (all hereinafter called the "Inventory") and in all accounts receivable, contract rights, notes, drafts, acceptances and other forms of obligations now or hereafter received by or belonging
or owing to Borrower for goods sold by it or for services rendered by it, all guaranties and securities therefor, all right,
title and interest of Borrower in the merchandise which gave rise thereto, including the right of stoppage in transit,
and all rights of Borrower earned or yet to be earned under contracts to sell goods or render service and in all warehouse
receipts (which with Inventory is all hereinafter called "Collateral") and in the proceeds thereof.

The security interest granted hereby is to secure payment and performance of the liability and obligations of
Borrower to Bank hereunder and also any and all other obligations of Borrower to Bank of every kind and description
direct or indirect, absolute or contingent, due or to become due, now existing or hereafter arising, (all hereinafter
called "Obligations").

BORROWER'S PLACES OF BUSINESS. Borrower warrants that Borrower has no places of business other than
that shown at the end of this Agreement, unless other places of business are listed immediately below, in which event
Borrower represents that it has additional places of business at the following locations and none other:

....

....

and if Borrower has an office in more than one state, the office where Borrower keeps its records concerning accounts and
contract rights is

....

or if left blank, is that shown at the end of this Agreement. All inventory presently owned by Borrower is stored at the
following locations:

....

....

Borrower will promptly notify Bank in writing of any change in the location of any place of business or the location of
any inventory or the establishment of any new place of business or location of inventory which should be shown in this
Agreement if it were executed after such change.

LOANS. Subject to the terms and provisions of this Agreement, Bank will make such loans to Borrower as from
time to time Bank elects to make which are secured by Borrower's inventory and accounts receivable and the proceeds
thereof. The aggregate unpaid principal of all such loans outstanding at any one time shall not exceed..Fifty.............
per cent (.........50....%) of the cost or market value, whichever is lower, of all Inventory (hereinafter called the
"Inventory Value") plus.....Eighty............. per cent (......80.....%) of the unpaid face amount of Qualified Accounts
(as defined below), plus one hundred per cent (100%) of the balance in the special account hereafter referred to, or such
other percentages thereof as may from time to time be fixed by Bank upon notice to Borrower. The sum produced by
applying at any given time the then prevailing percentages to the Inventory Value and to the total of Qualified Accounts
and balance in the special account respectively as of such time is herein called the "Borrowing Base". All such loans
shall bear interest, and where appropriate under the Bank's prevailing policy shall bear a service charge, at the rate
agreed on from time to time by the parties and at the option of Bank shall be evidenced by demand notes in form
satisfactory to Bank, but in the absence of notes shall be conclusively evidenced by the Bank's record of disbursements
and repayments and shall be repayable on demand.

DEFINITION OF QUALIFIED ACCOUNT. The term "Qualified Account" as used herein, means an account
receivable owing to Borrower which met the following specifications at the time it came into existence and continues
to meet the same until it is collected in full:

    (a) The account is due and payable not more than.....30.........days from the date of the invoice therefor, and is not
        more than........60......days past due.

    (b) The account arose from the performance of services or an outright sale of goods by Borrower, such goods
        have been shipped to the account debtor, and Borrower has possession of, or has delivered to Bank, shipping
        and delivery receipts evidencing such shipment.

EXHIBIT 13-4—*Continued*

Second Page

(c) The account is not subject to any prior assignment, claim, lien, or security interest, and Borrower will not make any further assignment thereof or create any further security interest therein, nor permit Borrower's rights therein to be reached by attachment, levy, garnishment or other judicial process.

(d) The account is not subject to set-off, credit, allowance or adjustment by the account debtor, except discount allowed for prompt payment, and the debtor has not complained as to his liability thereon and has not returned any of the goods from the sale of which the account arose.

(e) The account arose in the ordinary course of Borrower's business and did not arise from the performance of services or a sale of goods to a supplier or employee of the Borrower.

(f) No notice of bankruptcy, insolvency or financial embarrassment of the account debtor has been received by Borrower.

(g) Bank has not notified Borrower that the account or account debtor is unsatisfactory.

COLLECTIONS; NOTICE OF ASSIGNMENT; EXPENSES. Borrower will immediately upon receipt of all checks, drafts, cash and other remittances in payment of any Inventory sold or in payment or on account of Borrower's accounts receivable, deliver the same to the Bank accompanied by a remittance report in form specified by Bank, to be credited to a special account maintained by Bank over which Bank alone has power of application or withdrawal. Said proceeds shall be delivered to Bank in the same form received except for the endorsement of Borrower where necessary to permit collection of items, which endorsement Borrower agrees to make and which Bank is also hereby authorized to make on Borrower's behalf. Any funds to the credit of Borrower in said account shall be held by Bank as security for all loans made hereunder and all other indebtedness of Borrower to Bank secured hereby. Bank will, at least once a week, apply the whole or any part of collected funds in the special account against the principal or interest of any loans secured hereby. The order and method of such application shall be in the sole discretion of Bank and any portion of such funds which Bank elects not so to apply and deems not required as collateral shall be paid over from time to time by Bank to Borrower.

The Bank may at any time notify account debtors that Collateral has been assigned to Bank and that payment shall be made directly to Bank. Upon request of Bank at any time, Borrower will so notify such account debtors and will indicate on all billings to such account debtors that their accounts must be paid to Bank. The Bank shall have full power to collect, compromise, endorse, sell or otherwise deal with the Collateral or proceeds thereof in its own name or in the name of the Borrower. Borrower shall pay to Bank on demand any and all expenses including legal expenses and reasonable attorneys' fees reasonably incurred or expended by Bank in the collection or attempted collection of Collateral and in protecting and enforcing the Obligations and other rights of Bank hereunder.

FINANCING STATEMENTS. At the request of Bank, Borrower will join with Bank in executing one or more Financing Statements pursuant to the Uniform Commercial Code or other notices appropriate under applicable law in form satisfactory to Bank and will pay the cost of filing the same in all public offices wherever filing is deemed by Bank to be necessary or desirable.

BORROWER'S REPORTS. At the time of each borrowing hereunder and at other times on demand of Bank, Borrower will give Bank a certificate on a form to be supplied by Bank setting forth the total Inventory Value and the total amount of all Qualified Accounts created since the filing of the last such certificate with Bank or since the filing of the last monthly report of Borrower (as hereinafter provided) whichever last occurred. In addition, if Bank so requests, Borrower shall furnish a list of the names of each account debtor whose account is reflected in such certificate together with the amount of such account so reflected.

On or before the tenth business day after the close of each calendar month, Borrower shall deliver to Bank, in a form satisfactory to Bank a report of all inventory on hand and all accounts receivable as of the close of such calendar month, showing the total Qualified Accounts by month in which created, the total accounts receivable which are not Qualified Accounts, the total amount due from each account debtor, the total Inventory Value, and such other information as Bank shall request.

GENERAL AGREEMENTS OF BORROWER. Borrower agrees to keep all the Inventory insured with coverage and amounts not less than that usually carried by one engaged in a like business and in any event not less than that required by Bank with loss payable to the Bank and Borrower as their interests may appear, hereby appointing Bank as attorney for Borrower in obtaining, adjusting, settling and cancelling such insurance and endorsing any drafts. The Bank or its agents have the right to inspect the Inventory and all records pertaining thereto at intervals to be determined by Bank and without hindrance or delay. Although as above set forth Bank has a security interest in all of Borrower's Inventory and existing and future accounts receivable and in the proceeds thereof, Borrower will at all times maintain as the minimum security hereunder a Borrowing Base not less than the aggregate unpaid principal of all loans made hereunder; and if Borrower fails to do so, Borrower will immediately make the necessary reduction in the unpaid principal amount of said loans.

Borrower will at all times keep accurate and complete records of Borrower's inventory and accounts receivable and Bank, or any of its agents, shall have the right to call at Borrower's place or places of business at intervals to be determined by Bank, and without hindrance or delay, to inspect, audit, check and make extracts from and copies of the books, records, journals, orders, receipts, correspondence which relate to Borrower's accounts receivable, other transactions between the parties thereto and the general financial condition of Borrower and Bank may remove any of such records temporarily for the purpose of having copies made thereof.

The Bank may in its own name or in the name of others communicate with account debtors in order to verify with them to Bank's satisfaction the existence, amount and terms of any accounts receivable or contract rights.

EXHIBIT 13–4—*Continued*

Third Page

This agreement may but need not be supplemented by separate assignments of accounts receivable and if such assignments are given the rights and security interests given thereby shall be in addition to and not in limitation of the rights and security interests given by this Agreement.

If any of Borrower's accounts receivable arise out of contracts with the United States or any department, agency, or instrumentality thereof, Borrower will immediately notify Bank thereof in writing and execute any instruments and take any steps required by Bank in order that all monies due and to become due under such contract shall be assigned to Bank and notice thereof given to the Government under the Federal Assignment of·Claims Act.

If any of Borrower's accounts receivable should be evidenced by promissory notes, trade acceptances, or other instruments for the payment of money, Borrower will immediately deliver same to Bank, appropriately endorsed to Bank's order and, regardless of the form of such endorsement, Borrower hereby waives presentment, demand, notice of dishonor, protest and notice of protest and all other notices with respect thereto.

Bank is authorized to make loans under the terms of this Agreement upon the request, either written or oral, in the name of Borrower of any person whose name appears at the end of this Agreement or of any of the following named persons, or persons from time to time holding the following offices of Borrower:

Borrower agrees that any and all loans made by Bank to Borrower or for its account under this Agreement shall be conclusively deemed to have been authorized by Borrower and to have been made pursuant to duly authorized requests therefor on its behalf.

If Borrower shall fail to pay when due any amount payable on any of the loans made hereunder or on any other indebtedness of Borrower secured hereby, or shall fail to observe or perform any of the provisions of this Agreement, Borrower shall be in default hereunder. When Borrower is so in default, all of such loans and other indebtedness secured hereby shall become immediately due and payable at Bank's option without notice to Borrower, and Bank may proceed to enforce payment of the same and to exercise any or all of the rights and remedies afforded to Bank by the Uniform Commercial Code, under the terms of this instrument, or otherwise.

PROCESSING AND SALES OF INVENTORY. So long as Borrower is not in default hereunder, Borrower shall have the right, in the regular course of business, to process and sell Borrower's Inventory.

TERM OF AGREEMENT. The term of this Agreement shall commence with the date hereof and end on the termination date as herein defined. The termination date means the date when, after written notice from either party to the other that no further loans are to be made hereunder, Borrower pays in full all outstanding loans made hereunder and all other indebtedness of Borrower to Bank secured hereby.

No delay or omission on the part of Bank in exercising any right shall operate as a waiver of such right or any other right. Waiver on any one occasion shall not be construed as a bar to or waiver of any right or remedy on any future occasion. All Bank's rights and remedies, whether evidenced hereby or by any other agreement, instrument or paper, shall be cumulative and may be exercised singularly or concurrently.

The laws of Massachusetts shall govern the construction of this Agreement and the rights and duties of the parties hereto.

NEW ENGLAND MERCHANTS NATIONAL BANK OF BOSTON

By ...*William Brenton*...   ...William Brown, Inc....
    Loan Officer   (Borrower)

                             By ...*Joseph Burke*...
                                      (Title) *Treas.*

                       Address:

                                       (Number and Street)

                    ...Stoneham, Massachusetts...
                                      (City, County, State)

      Dated this___8th___ day of___October___, 1965

the borrower. The security interest can extend to all the stocks of the borrower, raw materials, in-process, or finished goods. Specific identification is not required; indeed, the lien can extend to inventory yet to be acquired. The security interest can extend over long periods of time, during which the actual stocks held by the borrower may turn over several times and the dollar value can rise and fall substantially. Moreover, the security interest can extend to receivables and the proceeds of collection of the receivables, so that the lender can have both inventory en masse and receivables as security. Note particularly the broad coverage of the first paragraph of the "Inventory and Accounts Receivable Security Agreement" shown as Exhibit 13–4.

The floating lien arrangement under the UCC has basic similarities with the *factor's lien* arrangement earlier authorized by the laws of some states, and in time it will probably completely replace the factor's lien.

As in the case of the trust receipt arrangement, the floating lien leaves practical control over the inventory with the borrower and calls also for a strong sense of moral responsibility, as well as accounting care, on the part of the borrower. Too, much of the inventory, particularly if work in process is a large percentage of the total, may have a low value upon forced sale. Consequently, lenders under the floating lien arrangement usually are willing to loan only a modest percentage of the book value of inventory covered. In one case known to the authors, where a factor was lending to a manufacturer of venetian window blinds, the factor determined that he could safely advance only 20% of the cost of the inventory. Since the floating lien arrangement is adaptable to heterogeneous, fast-moving inventory, it is expected to find growing usage by banks, business finance companies, and factoring concerns.

4. *Inventory Pledges under Chattel Mortgage, an Instrument Which Conveys to the Lender a Security Interest in Specifically Identified Goods.* The chattel mortgage is an old, well-established, and widely used legal device. Farmers holding cattle in feed lots for fattening over a period of months have made particularly heavy use of the chattel mortgage in posting such livestock as security for bank loans. As we shall see, however, the chattel mortgage instrument is more widely used for items of machinery and equipment than for inventory.

BORROWING AGAINST FIXED ASSETS

Borrowing against Equipment

The continuing long-term trend toward mechanization in manufacturing, farming, service, and even retailing (use of vending machines, etc.) has been accompanied by increasing investment in equipment by firms in these fields and by growing use of equipment as security for loans.

Much of the credit to businesses secured by equipment is extended initially by manufacturers or sales concerns supplying new machines. Many vendors of important items of new equipment accept from purchasers who make a significant down payment (often 20% to 33%) notes calling for payment of the remainder of the purchase price plus interest and other charges over a period of months, in some cases as many as 60. Generally, the seller requires a down payment and monthly payments sufficiently large so that the outstanding debt over the life of the credit remains less than the estimated net resale value of the equipment if repossession becomes necessary. The seller takes a security interest in the equipment, a common instrument being a *conditional sale contract,* under which the seller retains legal title until the buyer has met all terms of the sale agreement. Under the terms of the conditional sales contract, the seller has the right to repossess the equipment if the contract terms of payment are not met. Alternatively, chattel mortgages are taken on the equipment, but their use is less frequent, partly because the word *mortgage* has undesirable connotations to some borrowers.

Many vendors who offer instalment payment terms to purchasers of their equipment cannot, or prefer not to, maintain a large investment in such instalment receivables. Most finance companies, and in recent years a number of commercial banks, have been willing to extend credit based upon such instalment notes secured by an assignment of the vendor's security interest (the conditional sales contract or chattel mortgage) in the equipment. Usually, financing of the instalment notes receivable is with recourse to the vendor, so that the financing agency has the obligation of the buyer of the equipment, the assigned security interest in the equipment, and the right of recourse to the vendor to support the obligation. In addition, a portion of the payment to the seller is often withheld by the financing agency as a "dealer's reserve" until the note is paid. A conditional sale contract and its related dealer assignment to a lending bank are shown in Exhibit 13–5.

A number of manufacturers and a few large retailers of equipment and consumer durables have set up wholly owned subsidiaries to take over the parent firm's investment in extended receivables. Typically, these "captive finance companies" borrow heavily from banks and through bond issues; frequently, their debts are supported by parent company guaranties.

Concerns purchasing new equipment may find it cheaper or otherwise preferable to borrow directly from banks or finance companies in order to pay the vendor the full purchase price in cash. Such a direct lender often takes a chattel mortgage on the equipment to secure his advance, normally an amount significantly less than the purchase price. Repayment of the notes is scheduled on an instalment basis, again at a rate calculated to keep the loan balance below resale value upon repossession.

Instalment financing is used for a great variety of equipment—from barber chairs to giant diesel earth movers—and by a wide variety of businesses. Large corporations of strong credit standing are less likely to use the device, but many strong railroads are outstanding exceptions to this generalization. For a long time, major railroads have been buying locomotives and other rolling stock through use of *equipment trust certificates,* which can in many ways be regarded as a specialized form of instalment equipment financing. Insurance companies have been major buyers of equipment trust certificates.

Speaking broadly, credit against equipment is restricted mainly to new or highly serviceable used machinery. The rapid obsolescence of many

EXHIBIT 13–5

ILLUSTRATION OF A SECURITY AGREEMENT
COVERING A CONDITIONAL SALE CONTRACT
Front Side

SELLER'S ORIGINAL

NEW ENGLAND MERCHANTS NATIONAL BANK OF BOSTON
SECURITY AGREEMENT — CONDITIONAL SALE CONTRACT
Consumer Goods or Equipment

Contract made at the time and place indicated below between the undersigned Buyer, hereinafter called "Buyer" and the undersigned Seller, hereinafter called "Seller", which term shall be deemed to include any assignee of Seller's interest, whereby Seller has this day delivered and agrees to sell and Buyer has this day received and agrees to purchase on the following terms and conditions the articles of personal property listed below, all hereinafter referred to as the "property":

1 - 1965 Mack 10 Wheel Dump Truck, Model No. BS81,
Serial No. 1965 BS81, with Garwood 12 yard body.

(1.) CASH PURCHASE PRICE (Including Taxes & Extras)	$ 26,382.00
(2.) DEDUCTIONS FROM CASH PURCHASE PRICE	
A. Down Payment in cash	$ 8,382.00
B. Trade-in or other credit allowances (describe)	$
C. Total Deductions	$ 8,382.00
(3.) NET CASH PURCHASE PRICE (Item 1 less Item 2C)	$ 18,000.00
(4.) TOTAL PHYSICAL DAMAGE INSURANCE PREMIUM OR PREMIUMS	$

Coverage included in the policy or policies purchased with the above premium or premiums, written for a term of_____months, is:

Coverage checked above to be placed through broker or agent selected by Seller, unless Buyer has designated broker or agent to be used. If Buyer has designated agent or broker check here ☐. In any event, Buyer is obligated to provide insurance as required herein. CREDITOR LIFE INSURANCE PREMIUM (Will NOT be provided unless a specific premium is inserted on this line, and then ONLY on life of individual Buyer signing FIRST below. Not available to Buyers who have attained 65 years of age.)

(5.) FILING OR DOCUMENTARY FEE	$ 6.00
(6.) CASH BALANCE DUE (Total of Items 3, 4, & 5)	$ 18,006.00
(7.) FINANCE CHARGES	$ 2,430.84
(8.) NET BALANCE DUE SELLER FROM BUYER (Total of Items 6 and 7)	$ 20,436.84
(9.) TOTAL TIME PRICE (Total of Items 8 and 2C)	$28,818.84

Buyer agrees to pay to Seller, or order at the office of New England Merchants National Bank of Boston the net balance due (Item 8), in 48 consecutive monthly instalments of $ 567.69 each and one final instalment of $; the first instalment to be paid on November 20 , 1965 or one month from the date of this contract if not otherwise specified, and the remaining instalments on the same day of every month thereafter until paid.

DELINQUENCY CHARGES. There shall be assessed a delinquency charge of five cents (5c) for each dollar or fraction thereof of any principal instalment in arrears more than ten days, but it shall rest in the discretion of Seller whether to reinstate the contract upon payment of instalments in default and such delinquency charges and all other charges lawfully due, or to demand the entire unpaid balance of the Total Time Price.

PREPAYMENT ALLOWANCE. In the event of prepayment at any time when the contract is not in default, Seller will grant a prepayment allowance in accordance with Section 128 of Chapter 255 of the General Laws of the Commonwealth of Massachusetts, or other applicable law.

Seller has a security interest in the property, including all additions and accessions thereto, to secure payment and performances of all Buyer's obligations hereunder and title to the property shall be and remain in Seller until the entire net balance due and all other sums due hereunder are paid in full and Buyer has fully complied with all his obligations under this contract. The Seller may examine or inspect the property at any time, wherever located.

BUYER HEREBY WARRANTS AND COVENANTS:
1. That the property is bought or used primarily for
   ☐ Personal, family or household purposes.   ☒ Business use (including a profession),   ☐ Farming operations use.
2. That the property will be kept at

Prudential Center	Boston	Suffolk	Massachusetts
Street	City	County	State

or, if left blank, at the address shown at the end of this agreement; that Buyer will promptly notify Bank of any change in the location of the property within said State, and that Buyer will not remove the property from said State without the written consent of Bank.
3. If the property is attached or is to be attached to real estate, the name of the record owner of the real estate is_____. Buyer will on demand of Bank furnish Bank with a disclaimer or disclaimers signed by all persons having an interest in the real estate of any interest in the property which is prior to the Bank's interest.
4. If the property is bought or used primarily for business use, the Buyer's principal place of business is in the city or town of Boston , county of Suffolk , and State or Commonwealth of Massachusetts ; and that the Buyer has the following other places of business located in Massachusetts:

"None"

(if more than two list only two — if none, write "none");
or if Buyer has no place of business in Massachusetts but resides in Massachusetts, his residence is in the city or town of_____. Buyer will immediately notify Bank in writing of any change in or discontinuance of Buyer's place or places of business listed above.
5. If the property is bought or used primarily for personal, family or household purposes or for farming operations use, the Buyer's residence is

Street	City	County	State

The Seller shall have the right to enforce any remedies hereunder successively or concurrently. Delay in the exercise of any of Seller's rights shall not constitute a waiver thereof. The waiver of any default of Buyer shall not be a waiver of any subsequent default. No promises, agreements or representations shall be binding upon Seller unless set forth herein.
Buyer represents that no other extension of credit exists or is to be made in connection with this purchase except as expressly indicated here_____

All obligations of Buyer, if more than one person, are joint and several.
THE FINANCE CHARGES PROVIDED HEREIN ARE NOT REGULATED BY LAW. THEY ARE A MATTER FOR AGREEMENT BETWEEN THE PARTIES. SELLER MAKES NO WARRANTY OF THE PROPERTY EXPRESSED OR IMPLIED, INCLUDING WARRANTY OF MERCHANTABILITY, AND BUYER TAKES DELIVERY UNDER THE WARRANTY (IF ANY) OF THE MANUFACTURER ONLY. BUYER ACKNOWLEDGES RECEIPT OF A TRUE COPY OF THIS CONTRACT AT THE TIME OF EXECUTION THEREOF.
THIS CONTRACT IS SUBJECT TO THE ADDITIONAL PROVISIONS SET FORTH AT THE TOP OF THE REVERSE SIDE HEREOF, THE SAME BEING INCORPORATED HEREIN BY REFERENCE.
PRINT BUYER'S NAME AND ADDRESS: Buyer's address being place of principal garaging or location of property unless otherwise shown.

Massachusetts Sand & Gravel Co., Inc.; Prudential Center, Boston, Massachusetts
(Name)   (Street and No.)   (City)   (State)

Executed at Boston, Massachusetts   October 27   , 1965
(City and State)   (Date)

Signature of SELLER { A E L TRUCK SALES, INC. (Seal)
{ By Robert O'Smith, Pres.
(Owner, Officer or Firm Member, and Title)

Signature of BUYER { MASSACHUSETTS SAND & GRAVEL CO. (Seal) INC.
{ Joseph Gravel, Pres.

15-015

EXHIBIT 13–5—*Continued*

Reverse Side

Buyer agrees to join with Seller in executing one or more Financing Statements pursuant to the Uniform Commercial Code in a form satisfactory to Seller and will pay the cost of filing the same in all public offices wherever filing is deemed by Seller to be necessary or desirable and Seller is hereby appointed Buyer's attorney-in-fact to do at Seller's option and at Buyer's expense, all acts and things which Seller may deem necessary to perfect and continue perfected the Security Interest created by this Agreement and to protect the property; to pay promptly all taxes and assessments upon the property and for its use or operation and on this contract; to keep the property free from liens; not to sell or encumber the property or use it illegally; to keep the property insured with coverage and in amounts satisfactory to the Seller, loss payable to Buyer and to Seller as their interests may appear, but in the event that the property is not kept so insured the Seller may at its option purchase such amount of insurance coverage (single interest or other) at the Buyer's expense for which the Buyer expressly agrees to reimburse the Seller.

Buyer hereby assigns to the Seller any moneys not in excess of the unpaid balance hereunder which may become payable under any insurance, including return or unearned premiums, and directs any insurance company to make payment direct to the Seller to be applied to said unpaid balance and appoints the Seller as attorney-in-fact to indorse any draft. In the event of any default under this contract, Seller is authorized to cancel said insurance and credit any premium refund against said unpaid balance.

Time is of the essence of this contract. The entire unpaid balance of the Total Time Price and all other sums due hereunder shall, at the option of Seller, become immediately due and payable upon default in any payment or obligation of Buyer to Seller under this Contract, or if proceedings in bankruptcy are instituted by or against Buyer under any of the provisions of the Bankruptcy Act or any other law, or if Buyer makes an assignment for the benefit of creditors, or if Seller in its sole judgment deems itself insecure; thereupon Seller may repossess the property without liability for trespass or responsibility for any article left in or attached to the property, and shall have the remedies of a secured party under the Uniform Commercial Code or under other applicable law. Seller will mail to Buyer, postage prepaid, at the address shown at the end hereof, not less than ten days prior thereto, notice of the time and place of any public sale or of the time after which any private sale or other intended disposition of the property is to be made and such notice shall be deemed reasonable. Expenses of retaking, holding, preparing for sale or selling of the property shall include Seller's reasonable attorneys' fees and legal expenses. The Seller will account to the Buyer for any net surplus remaining after repossession and sale of the property. Any deficiency remaining after repossession and sale of the property by the Seller shall be paid by the Buyer to the Seller immediately upon demand, together with interest thereon and reasonable fees of any attorney employed by the Seller to collect such deficiency. Buyer waives any defenses, set-offs or other claims Buyer may be entitled to assert against Seller and all claims, damages and demands against Seller arising out of the repossession, removal, retention or sale of the property.

DEALER'S ASSIGNMENT

For value received, the undersigned hereby assigns all undersigned's right, title and interest in and to the within instrument and the property covered thereby to New England Merchants National Bank of Boston, and authorizes it to do every act and thing necessary to collect and discharge the same, either in the name of the undersigned or in its own name. The undersigned warrants that the person, firm or corporation described as Buyer had legal capacity to execute the contract, both by reason of age (being, if an individual, 21 years of age or older) and otherwise, and that the Buyer's true name is signed thereto; that all the information given is complete, accurate and correct; that to undersigned's knowledge and belief said Buyer has never violated any laws concerning liquor or narcotics; that the down payment made by the Buyer, except to the extent expressly shown in the contract to have been by trade-in of property therein described, was in cash and that no part thereof was loaned by the undersigned to the Buyer; that the undersigned has full power and right to assign this instrument and its rights in the property free and clear of all claims, liens and encumbrances whatsoever except the within contract; and that the within contract is genuine and in all respects what it purports to be. If any of the above warranties should be untrue, undersigned agrees to buy the within contract from New England Merchants National Bank of Boston upon demand and to pay thereof not less than the amount then owing and unpaid thereon plus all costs and expenses. The undersigned hereby waives all notices of default and repossession of the property and agrees that the assignee may grant extensions of time to the Buyer without notice to and without affecting the liability of the undersigned hereunder. This assignment is also subject to the terms and conditions of any purchase agreement that may be in force between the undersigned and the assignee.

....
(Seller)

DATE..   BY..(SEAL)
(Officer, owner or partner, and title, if seller other than an individual).

DEALER'S SPECIFIC REPURCHASE AGREEMENT

In the event New England Merchants National Bank of Boston as assignee shall repossess the property, the undersigned agrees upon demand to repurchase the property for cash in an amount equal to the balance unpaid upon the within contract, provided the property is offered to the undersigned within ninety (90) days after maturity of the earliest instalment unpaid at the time of such offer; expressly waiving notice of the acceptance of this agreement.

....
(Seller)

DATE..   BY..(SEAL)
(Officer, owner or partner, and title, if seller other than an individual).

DEALER'S ASSIGNMENT AND FULL GUARANTY

For value received, the undersigned hereby assigns all undersigned's right, title and interest in and to the within instrument and the property covered thereby to New England Merchants National Bank of Boston, and authorizes it to do every act and thing necessary to collect and discharge the same, either in the name of the undersigned or in its own name. The undersigned guarantees payment of the amount due on the within contract as and when the same shall become due, hereby waiving any extension of time made by assignee and waiving presentment for payment, protest and notice of protest, and non-payment and notice of the acceptance hereof.

..............A E L TRUCK SALES, INC...............
(Seller)

DATE.....October 27, 1965.....   BY.....*Robert O'Smith*.....(SEAL)
(Officer, owner or partner, and title, if seller other than an individual)

---

types of equipment reduces the resale value of much used, though serviceable, equipment to near scrap values. Consequently, a would-be borrower will find it much easier to get substantial credit on new than on old equipment, even though the used equipment is physically sound and is carried on the owner's books at substantial value.

Costs of credit against equipment vary widely. Equipment trust certificates of strong railroads have long carried low interest rates, while financially weak concerns buying equipment subject to rapid depreciation in value may well pay fees amounting to an annual interest rate on the balance owed of from 12% to 24%.

More than 27% of the secured commercial bank loans covered in the 1955 Federal Reserve analysis were secured by equipment. Since the equipment loans were typically for small amounts, they were about 14% of the total dollar amount of secured loans.

Borrowing against Plant or Other Real Estate

Businessmen are inclined to regard their investment in brick and mortar—in plant and built-in or fixed equipment—as excellent potential security under mortgage arrangements.[8] Particularly is this impression likely to be strong if the plant facilities are handsome, costly, and built to last for a long time. Yet, our earlier observation that few lenders are willing to make a loan against security if they really expect to have to take over and liquidate the security in order to settle the loan is particularly valid in the case of loans against plant as security.

Industrial plants have, in the view of many lenders, particular weaknesses as loan collateral. A first weakness is that firms wanting to borrow against fixed assets often want the money to finance added investment in fixed assets. Since recovery of this investment by the borrower through depreciation or added profits normally takes many years, his investment is relatively illiquid. Further, action to seize and sell, or *foreclose,* a company's productive establishment is indeed a drastic step, often fatal to the company, and hence one taken by lenders with real reluctance. Third, the process of foreclosure is, in many states, a time-consuming one, with the debtor retaining rights to reclaim his property over a considerable time. Fourth, and most basic, is the high degree of uncertainty regarding resale value upon foreclosure. If the difficulties of the borrower that lead to default and foreclosure are the result of generally depressed conditions in his industry, as frequently is the case, the number of firms interested in buying the foreclosed plant may be limited indeed. Prosperous and expanding companies which might be buyers often prefer to build a new plant designed and located to meet their particular requirements. In such circumstances the added expense of building to their own needs may result in lower operating costs and in long-run economy, so that they are not interested in the older, foreclosed plant at any price.

Furthermore, relatively few plants are truly general-purpose facilities. Most contain much built-in equipment or special features for a particular

---

[8] The mortgage device of granting to lenders a security interest in real estate is a very old one. Since ownership of residential property is so commonly financed by borrowing, with the home used as security under a mortgage (or a similar form, used in several states, called a deed of trust), mortgage law has become detailed and complicated in all of the states. Generally, commercial or industrial real estate is mortgaged under the basic mortgage laws applying to residential property.

EXHIBIT 13-6

A TYPICAL PROMISSORY NOTE WITH SECURITIES AS COLLATERAL

C19-A

NON-PURPOSE "STOCK" COLLATERAL TIME LOAN

BOSTON, MASSACHUSETTS _____ January 5, _____ 19 58 _____ $5,000.00

Ninety days _____ after date, for value received, I/we promise to pay to the order of

at said Bank _____ THE FIRST NATIONAL BANK OF BOSTON

Five thousand - Dollars

having deposited with said Bank, as collateral security for payment of this and any and all other liabilities, direct or indirect, absolute or contingent, due or to become due, now existing or hereafter arising, of mine/ours or either of us to said Bank, its successors or assigns, the following property, viz.:

Fifty (50) shares American Telephone and Telegraph Company - common stock

I/We agree to either deliver to the holder additional security or make payments on account, to the holder's satisfaction, should the value of the security at any time held decline, or should the holder or any officer or anyone acting in behalf of the holder deem such security to be insufficient by reason of the decline in the market value of any part thereof.

This note and any or all of the liabilities above mentioned shall, at the option of the holder, become immediately due and payable without notice or demand upon the occurrence of any of the following events: (a) failure of the undersigned with or without demand or notice, to deliver additional security or make payments on account to the holder's satisfaction as above agreed; (b) default in the payment or performance of any liability or obligation of any of the undersigned, or of any maker, endorser or guarantor of any liability or obligation of any of the undersigned, to the holder; (c) failure to pay when due any premium on any life insurance policy held as collateral herefor; (d) death, dissolution, termination of existence, insolvency, business failure, appointment of a receiver of any part of the property, of assignment for the benefit of creditors by, or the filing of a petition in bankruptcy, or the commencement of any proceedings under any bankruptcy or insolvency laws or any laws relating to the relief of debtors, readjustment of indebtedness, reorganization, composition or extension, by or against, any maker, endorser, or guarantor hereof.

The undersigned do hereby fully authorize and empower the holder, on the non-performance of any promise made herein, or the non-payment of any of the liabilities above mentioned, or the occurrence of any of the events specified in the next preceding paragraph, or at any time or times thereafter, to sell, assign and deliver all of the security herefor or any part thereof, or any substitutes therefor, or any additions thereto, at any Broker's Board, or at public or private sale, at the option of the holder, or any officer or anyone acting in behalf of the holder, without advertisement or any notice to the undersigned or any other person, and the holder, its officers or assigns may bid and become purchasers at any such sale, if public, or at any Broker's Board. Right is expressly granted to the holder at its option to transfer at any time to itself or to its nominee any securities pledged hereunder and to receive the income thereon and hold the same as security herefor, or apply it on the principal or interest due hereon or due on any liability secured hereby.

Any deposits or other sums at any time credited by or due from the holder to any maker, endorser or guarantor hereof and any securities or other property of any maker, endorser or guarantor hereof in the possession of the holder may at all times be held and treated as collateral security for the payment of this note and any and all other liabilities, direct or indirect, absolute or contingent, due or to become due, now existing or hereafter arising, of said respective maker, endorser or guarantor to the holder. The holder may apply or set off such deposits or other sums against said liabilities at any time in the case of makers, but only with respect to matured liabilities in the case of endorsers or guarantors.

The holder may at its option, whether this note is due or not due, demand, sue for, collect, or make any compromise or settlement it deems desirable with reference to collateral held hereunder. The holder shall have no duty as to the collection or protection of collateral held hereunder or any income thereon, nor as to the preservation of any rights pertaining thereto beyond the safe custody thereof. No delay or omission on the part of the holder in exercising any right hereunder shall operate as a waiver of such right or of any other right under this note. A waiver on any one occasion shall not be construed as a bar to or waiver of any such right and/or waiver of any such right and/or remedy on any future occasion.

Every maker, endorser and guarantor of this note, or the obligation represented hereby, waives presentment, demand, notice, protest, and all other demands and notices in connection with the delivery, acceptance, performance, default or enforcement of this note, assents to any extension or postponement of the time of payment or any other indulgence, to any substitution, exchange or release of collateral, and/or to the addition or release of any other party or person primarily or secondarily liable. Nothing in this paragraph shall be construed to prevent any maker, endorser or guarantor from paying this note on its stated maturity.

The undersigned will pay all expenses of every kind of the enforcement of this note, or of any of the rights hereunder, and hereby agree to pay to the holder on demand the amount of any and all such expenses incurred by it. After deducting all legal or other expenses and costs of collection of this note and all legal or other expenses and costs of collection, storage, custody, sale and delivery of collateral held hereunder, the residue of any proceeds of collection or sale shall be applied to the payment of principal or interest on this note or on any or all of the other liabilities aforesaid, due or to become due, in such order of preference as the holder shall determine, proper allowance for interest on liabilities not then due being made, and any overplus shall be returned to the undersigned.

As herein used the word "holder" shall mean the payee or other endorsee of this note, who is in possession of it, or the bearer hereof, if this note is at the time payable to the bearer.

Under the provisions of Regulation U issued by the Board of Governors of the Federal Reserve System pursuant to the authority of the Securities Exchange Act, I/we certify that this loan is not made for the purpose of purchasing or carrying any stock registered on a National Securities Exchange.

Address	3095 Davis Avenue	Signed by	The Hammond Company
	Boston, Massachusetts		Alexander Hammond
			President

productive activity that limit the potential market for the property. Highly specialized plants such as foundries have attraction and value only to other foundry companies, and they may well share the slack business or other unfavorable developments that led to the trouble of the borrower.

This is not to say that industrial facilities have no value as collateral. There is widespread mortgaging of plants as security—almost 21% by number and 23% by volume of secured loans in 1955 were secured by plant and other real estate. But much of their use as security is not due to the attractiveness of plants as collateral. Lenders often take the security as a means of added control over a borrower for a loan they are making essentially on an unsecured basis. That is, many loans that are nominally against plant security are in fact regarded by the lender as primarily unsecured, with some possibility of added security in the plant because of its value to the borrower. If the property is essential to the borrower, or to a reorganized company in the event of bankruptcy, the lender may get better treatment at the hands of the court owing to his claim against the vital, if nonresalable, plant.

BORROWING AGAINST SECURITIES AND LIFE INSURANCE

For various reasons, concerns owning government bonds or other securities may prefer to raise needed funds by borrowing against the securities rather than by selling them. The mechanics of pledging securities are relatively simple and easily accomplished. Although the borrower retains ownership of the securities, he assigns an interest in them to the lender, who holds physical possession as security for the loan. The note or other debt instrument specifies the terms upon which the lender can dispose of the securities and apply the proceeds toward the debt. A typical 90-day note against securities as collateral is shown in Exhibit 13–6.

If the securities are marketable government bonds or corporate securities traded actively on national security exchanges, the borrower seldom will have difficulty finding lenders willing to loan a high percentage of the market value of the securities.[9] If the securities are those of little-known subsidiaries or other companies whose securities have limited markets, prospective lenders can be expected to consider carefully the factors that will probably affect the future value and marketability of the securities, and to loan only a portion of their appraisal of the value of the securities. In 1955, 6.3% of the total number of secured member bank business loans and 8.6% of the total amount were against pledged securities.

Many firms carry life insurance policies on key personnel of types that

---

[9] Full freedom to use listed stocks as security for loans may be subject to the restrictive provisions of Regulation U of the Board of Governors of the Federal Reserve System. These restrictions are designed to curb speculative buying of stocks "on margin."

in time accumulate considerable cash surrender value. The rights to matured or cash surrender value can be assigned to bank or other lenders as security for loans. Much of the lending against securities or cash surrender values of life insurance policies is by commercial banks, ordinarily at near prime interest rates.

USE OF COMAKER, ENDORSEMENT, OR GUARANTY OF LOANS

Over 23% of the secured member bank loans to business in 1955 were secured in the sense that other concerns or individuals accepted direct or contingent obligations for the loans. As will be noted by reviewing

EXHIBIT 13–7

ILLUSTRATION OF A GUARANTY AGREEMENT

NEW ENGLAND MERCHANTS NATIONAL BANK OF BOSTON

Agreement of Guaranty

For valuable consideration, receipt of which is hereby acknowledged, the undersigned, jointly and severally if more than one, hereby guarantees due payment and fulfillment to New England Merchants National Bank of Boston, its successors and assigns, of all liabilities, obligations and undertakings of ....

.............................Northeastern Fisheries Corporation...
to said Bank, whether direct or indirect, absolute or contingent, due or to become due, now existing or hereafter arising or acquired, expressly including, without limiting the generality of the foregoing, obligations upon notes whether as maker or indorser, upon acceptances, upon agreements relating to acceptances, upon obligations incident to the issuance of letters of credit, upon security agreements and upon guaranties of the liabilities and obligations of others.

The liability of the undersigned hereunder shall continue, regardless of payments by any other person or from any other source, until each and all of said liabilities, obligations and undertakings have been paid in full.

The undersigned agrees to the provisions of any notes or other instrument and agreements evidencing the liabilities, obligations and undertakings hereby guaranteed; waives presentment, protest and all demands and notices of every kind in connection with this guaranty and the liabilities, obligations and undertakings hereby guaranteed; and agrees that any renewal, extension or postponement of the time of payment or any other indulgence, any substitution, exchange or release of collateral security and the addition or release of any person or persons primarily or secondarily liable may be effected without notice to and without releasing the undersigned.

This guaranty is to continue in effect until receipt by said Bank of notice of revocation from the undersigned in writing, and thereafter until all liabilities, obligations and undertakings guaranteed hereunder have been paid and discharged.

This guaranty is under seal and is dated   December 9   , 19 65 .

Walter G. Jackson

Exhibit 10–1 (page 197), a plain note can be signed by several parties, each party becoming a *comaker* of the note, and all parties jointly and severally assuming the obligations of the promise to pay. As another technique of security, a lender may ask for an *endorsement* of a borrower's note by a third party. The third party, by signing a note on the reverse side, grants to the lender full recourse to his resources (unless otherwise stated) in case the borrower fails to honor the debt. In a third and more flexible arrangement, a third party signs a guaranty agreement covering all debts of the borrower to the lender and thereby obviates the necessity for each note or other debt instrument being individually endorsed. Guaranty agreements are particularly common in the case of closely held corporations whose owners have substantial personal resources and are willing to put these resources behind the firm's borrowing. An example of a guaranty agreement of this nature is shown in Exhibit 13–7. Also, it is common for parent companies to guarantee loans to their subsidiaries.

Obviously, the value to lenders of any of these arrangements varies with the financial resources of the comaker, endorser, or guarantor. It is interesting to note that lenders, by obtaining endorsement or guaranty of corporate debts by share owners, in effect break through the limited liability feature of the incorporated business.

We should make it clear that the comaker, endorsement, or guaranteed loans are not secured loans in the sense that the lender gets any priority over the other general creditors of either the comaker or endorser of the note. The use of the comaker simply gives the lender a general claim on two persons or firms, rather than one.

SUBORDINATION OF CERTAIN DEBT CLAIMS TO OTHER OBLIGATIONS

In recent years the practice of subordination by a creditor or group of creditors of certain of their rights as creditors to another creditor or class of creditor has become sufficiently important to deserve attention here. Subordination is accomplished through contract between the interested parties and as such can take whatever form the interested parties can agree upon.

One of the most common uses of subordination is by stockholders of closely held corporations who are also creditors of their corporations. Tax considerations have been especially important in recent years in stimulating stockholders to make part of their investment in their company in the form of loans to the company. In negotiating bank credit, agreement by the stockholder-creditors to subordinate their own loans to those of the bank may materially improve the chances of getting bank loans. In such cases the subordination is usually stated both in terms of maturity (for example, agreement that no debt to stockholders will be repaid so long as the bank loan is unpaid) and in terms of bankruptcy leading to reorganization or liquidation. The subordination agreement often is drawn to provide that in the event of bankruptcy the favored creditor—in this case, the bank—is entitled to stand in the place of the subordinated creditors when assets are distributed and thus be entitled to payment in full before the subordinated creditors are entitled to anything. An example of a subordination agreement between an important stockholder and creditor of a borrowing company and its bank is shown in Exhibit 13–8.

Often it is said that such subordination agreements, from the viewpoint of the favored creditor, make the subordinated debt money the equivalent of equity funds as a protective cushion in the event of bankruptcy. Actually, from the viewpoint of the favored creditor, debt subordinated to his debts may be better than equity because the favored creditor acquires, for his exclusive benefit, the subordinated creditor's rights as a *creditor* of the company.[10]

Consider the following simplified examples:

BALANCE SHEETS, IN SUMMARY, BEFORE BANKRUPTCY

Company A		Company B	
Total assets	$500,000	Total assets	$500,000
Bank loan	$100,000	Bank loan	$100,000
Due trade and other creditors	200,000	Due trade and other creditors	200,000
Loan from stockholders, subordinated to bank	100,000	Common stock and surplus	200,000
Common stock and surplus	100,000		
Total liabilities	$500,000	Total liabilities	$500,000

Note that the only difference between the two balance sheets is that $100,000 of the owners' investment in company A is in the form of debt which has been subordinated to the loan to the company from the bank. Now, assume that each company found it impossible to meet maturing obligations and was forced into bankruptcy leading to liquidation. Assume that in each company, enough cash was available to pay the expenses of bankruptcy and to pay certain preferred creditors in full, leaving thereafter $220,000 in cash for all other creditors.

In company A, a 55% distribution to creditors ($220,000 divided by 400,000) is sufficient to pay the bank in full, since it is entitled to $55,000 on its debt directly and, under the subordination agreement, is entitled to enough (in this case, $45,000) of the subordinating creditor's share to permit repayment of the $100,000 due the bank in full.

In company B, however, a similar net amount for distribution to all creditors, $220,000, would permit a 73.3% pay-out to each creditor

---

[10] A disadvantage is that the holder of the subordinated debt may have greater power than the holder of an equity of the same amount to initiate bankruptcy proceedings at a time when the favored creditor would prefer to avoid such proceedings.

EXHIBIT 13-8

ILLUSTRATION OF A SUBORDINATION AGREEMENT

SUBORDINATION AGREEMENT

For valuable consideration receipt whereof is hereby acknowledged and in consideration of the loans, advances, discounts, renewals or extensions now or hereafter made by the NEW ENGLAND MERCHANTS NATIONAL BANK

OF BOSTON (hereinafter called the "Bank") to or for the account of ....

Edgewater Manufacturing Company .... (hereinafter called the "Borrower")

having a usual place of business at 120 School Street, Boston, Massachusetts 02107 ....,
the undersigned (both jointly and severally if more than one) agrees with the Bank as follows:

1. The undersigned represents to the Bank that the Borrower now owes the undersigned the sum of

Fifteen thousand dollars ....without counterclaim or offset, and that the indebtedness
is not represented by any notes or other negotiable instruments, except such notes or negotiable instruments, if any, as have been, as hereinafter provided, endorsed and delivered by the undersigned to the Bank at the time of the execution of the agreement. The undersigned further agrees that at no time hereafter will any part of said indebtedness be represented by any notes or other negotiable instruments except such as exist at the time of this agreement and except such notes or other negotiable instruments as the Bank shall request to be executed and delivered for the purpose of evidencing said indebtedness or any part thereof, and in that case the said notes or other negotiable instruments shall either be made payable to and delivered to the Bank, or, if payable to the undersigned, shall be endorsed by the undersigned and delivered to the Bank.

2. The undersigned hereby subordinates all present and future indebtedness of the Borrower to the undersigned, to any and all indebtedness now or hereafter owing by the Borrower to the Bank, and agrees not to demand, accept or receive any payment of principal or interest upon account of the indebtedness so subordinated, or any collateral therefor, until all such indebtedness of the Borrower to the Bank has been paid in full.

3. As security for any and all obligations of the Borrower to the Bank and in order to effectuate the foregoing subordination the undersigned has endorsed and delivered to the Bank simultaneously with the execution of this agreement all notes or other negotiable instruments representing indebtedness presently existing from the Borrower to the undersigned, and the undersigned hereby transfers and assigns to the Bank all claims or demands of the undersigned against the Borrower, with full right on the part of the Bank, in its own name or in the name of and as attorney in fact for the undersigned, to collect and enforce said claims by suit, proof of debt in bankruptcy, or other liquidation, reorganization or insolvency proceedings or otherwise. Should any payment or security be received by the undersigned for or on account of any of said notes, claims or demands, prior to the satisfaction of all said obligations of the Borrower to the Bank, the undersigned will forthwith deliver the same to the Bank, in precisely the form received (except for the undersigned's endorsement where necessary) for application on account of the Borrower's obligations to the Bank and, until so delivered, the same shall be held in trust by the undersigned as the property of the Bank. In the event of the failure of the undersigned to endorse any instrument for the payment of money so received by the undersigned, payable to the undersigned's order, the Bank is hereby irrevocably constituted and appointed attorney in fact for the undersigned, with full power to make such endorsement, and with full power of substitution.

4. In order to carry out the terms and the intent of this agreement more effectively, the undersigned will do all acts and execute all further instruments necessary or convenient to preserve for the Bank the benefit of this Subordination Agreement.

5. No action which the Bank, or the Borrower with the consent of the Bank, may take or refrain from taking with respect to any indebtedness of the Borrower to the Bank, or any note or notes representing the same, or any collateral therefor, or any agreement or agreements (including guaranties) in connection therewith, shall affect this agreement or the obligations of the undersigned hereunder. If all indebtedness of the Borrower to the Bank is at any time hereafter paid in full and thereafter Borrower again becomes indebted to the Bank, the provisions of this agreement shall apply to said new indebtedness unless before the same is incurred the undersigned notifies the Bank in writing of the cancellation of this agreement.

6. No waiver shall be deemed to be made by the Bank of any of its rights hereunder unless the same shall be in writing and as a waiver, if any, shall be a waiver only with respect to the specific instance involved and it shall in no way impair the Bank's rights or the undersigned's obligations to it in any other respect or at any other time.

7. This agreement shall bind the undersigned and the undersigned's successors, assigns and legal representatives and shall inure to the benefit of the Bank and its successors and assigns.

IN WITNESS WHEREOF, the undersigned has/have hereunto set his/their hand(s) and seal this

23rd day of   November , 1965   ....

Signed and Sealed in the presence of: ....

Notice is hereby acknowledged of the terms of the foregoing Subordination Agreement and of the rights of the Bank thereunder.

25-066

Edgewater Manufacturing Company ....

By...... Albert Samson ....
                                    President

($220,000/$300,000). In this instance the bank is able to collect only $73,333 on its $100,000 credit. Trade and other creditors fare better than in company A, getting paid $146,666 in comparison with $110,000 in company A. The owners get nothing in either case.

In the discussion and examples above, we have considered only one of the important types of subordination agreements. Other circumstances in which subordinations are used include subordination by an entire class of creditors, such as trade creditors, as a means of encouraging new credit to keep a valued customer in business. Further, in nondistress circumstances, many concerns, particularly finance companies, have succeeded in selling to the public subordinated debentures which by their terms subordinate certain rights of the holders of these securities to those of other creditors.

Some Cautions Regarding the Giving of Security

Earlier in this chapter, advantages that borrowers might obtain from effective use of their assets as security for loans—greater credit, lower interest rates than on unsecured borrowing, etc.—were discussed. It is appropriate at this point to consider the serious disadvantages that can result from injudicious giving of security.

First, the increased availability of credit by giving security may encourage excessively heavy use of debt. Any borrowing involves risk to the borrower—financial risk added to the normal risks of doing business. The increased risks of debt should be appreciated and accepted only after careful and full consideration.

Second, for many firms, there is great advantage (not to say comfort) in retaining reserves of borrowing power for use in financial extremity or to finance particularly desirable investment opportunities that may develop. Obviously, security, once committed, no longer is available as the basis for further credit; and the firm that ties up all of its attractive security is in the same exposed position as the general who has committed all his reserves to battle. When secured borrowing is undertaken, the borrower should appreciate that if he concedes more security than really is required and further credit subsequently is needed, it may be hard indeed to get the old lender to release security or to dilute his own cushion by lending more against the same security.

Third, most firms depend heavily on continued trade credit from suppliers, extended on an unsecured basis. As the firm commits more and more of its best assets as security for loans, the trade creditors increasingly depend on the shrinking and poorer assets left unpledged. While it is difficult to determine in advance the exact extent to which pledging of assets can be carried without jeopardizing the continued availability of trade credit, excessive pledging of assets *can* result in impairment or loss of credit from alert suppliers and other unsecured creditors.

PART V

The Sources of Long-Term Corporate Capital

Chapter 14

Reinvestment of Earnings and Dividend Policy

FROM OUR discussion up to this point of sources of capital for business, the reader has become aware of the fact that the typical business is financed through a variety of sources and under a variety of conditions. We have considered the substantial source described as spontaneous credit, which arises in the normal course of business because actual payment of obligations usually occurs a number of days or weeks later than the date on which the obligation to pay is incurred. We have also considered certain negotiated sources of funds—short- and medium-term debt where capital is made available for periods of time conditional on certain predetermined commitments, including a fee which reflects the relative bargaining conditions of borrower and lender at the time the contract was made. Similarly, although we have not yet discussed it in detail, the reader is aware of the investment made by the owners through the purchase of ownership certificates, and equally if not more importantly, through the retention of some portion of corporate earnings.

An itemization of the particular mix of sources in use by a business at any given point in time is, of course, shown on the right-hand side of the company's balance sheet. A comparison of company balance sheets will show that this mix of sources varies considerably among companies, even within the same industry, and also within the same company over extended periods of time. The rationale behind a particular set of sources in use by a given company is not likely to be apparent from the bare statistics, and it might appear that a random selection of sources within a rather broad range of choice would do equally as well as any other, provided the desired number of dollars was obtained for the desired interval of time.

Before we turn to the consideration of the issues involved in determining an appropriate mix of the various debt and equity sources, which will be the subject of Part VI, we feel it would be helpful to provide an informational base for the analysis. In Part V we will deal first with internal sources of funds, centering on the legal, organizational and policy issues of dividend payments, and then present information on the external capital markets and the approaches to these markets.

In these chapters we refer constantly to "long-term capital." To most financial people this brings to mind the major sources of funds, contractual and noncontractual, which are itemized on the balance sheet below the "Current Liabilities." In fact, we shall be primarily concerned with these sources.

However, if this interpretation were followed literally, it would include any source negotiated for a time period in excess of 1 year and would exclude those sources like commercial bank loans which, though carrying a maturity date within the 1-year period are as a matter of practice renewable for more extended periods of time. Since our primary purpose is to bring under review all major sources which may be expected to continue in use over a company's planning horizon (usually 3 to 5 years and upwards), it is desirable that we do not let ourselves be bound by an arbitrary definition. For the most part we will be focusing attention on the decisions relating to retained earnings, negotiated debt sources, and new equity issues which, singly or in combination, make possible the future continuity of business operations.

In considering these decisions, there will be differences of opinion as to where to begin. Since they are unavoidably interrelated, it is a somewhat arbitrary choice. We have chosen to begin with the question of dividend policy, simply because this is usually the starting point of corporate planning. The consideration of new negotiated sources of capital is preceded by a long-term projection of funds flows which shows a gap between planned expenditures and internal sources of funds. The projection will have been constructed on the basis of an assumed dividend policy—likely the one most recently in effect. When it becomes apparent that the related retained earnings are inadequate, new sources must be considered in order to balance the budget without cutting back on essential expenditures. These sources may be external—new debt or equity—or they may be internal, taking the form of a change in dividend policy or some reallocation of existing capital. In any case a dividend policy must have been determined before action is taken on additional external financing. We now turn to some factual information about dividend payments before taking up the issues of dividend policy.

The Nature and Form of the Dividend

A *dividend payment* is a distribution to the shareholders of something belonging to the corporation, and specifically belonging to the stockholders themselves as owners of the corporation. If a company has more than one class of shareholders, a dividend might be declared to one class and not to another, or different amounts of dividend might be paid to each class. However, all shareholders of one class of stock must be treated alike, according to the number of shares they hold. Cash payments are the most frequently used method of distribution.

The material in this chapter concentrates upon the determination of policy for the payment of cash dividends. Before doing so, however, we shall give brief consideration to the other forms a dividend payment may take. Whatever the type of payment may be, it has the effect of reducing some of the value of the business. In the accounting sense, this means that the transaction has the effect of reducing the net worth of the business, specifically the surplus. The fact that all forms of dividend payment have this effect in common has led legislators to define the legality of dividends in terms of this surplus. It must be recognized that surplus is not itself a tangible thing which can be distributed. The debit to Surplus merely records the fact that a portion of the stockholders' equity in the business has been withdrawn, usually in the form of cash. The credit to Cash records the withdrawal of the tangible asset itself. We are already well aware of the fact that this withdrawal is not a cost of the business in either the economic, the accounting, or the income tax sense.

If cash is not distributed, the most common asset which is used is stock of another corporation held by the company. Beginning in 1948, Standard Oil of Indiana began to distribute shares in Standard Oil of New Jersey along with its cash dividend. The stock being distributed had been acquired in 1932 as a part of a sale of certain foreign properties. At the outset the distribution was on the basis of 1 share of New Jersey stock for each 100 shares of Indiana stock held. The company continued to make a distribution of this stock along with its cash dividend in each year through 1963. Some companies which have decided to divest themselves of a portion of their activity incorporate it separately and then distribute the resulting shares to their shareholders. This is referred to as a *spin-off*. An example of a dividend of this type is seen in the case of Textron Inc. In the year 1953 this company suspended its cash dividend and instead distributed 1 share of Indian Head Mills, Inc., for every 10 shares of Textron Inc. held by its shareholders. The cash dividend was resumed in the following year.

On occasion, other types of assets have been distributed as a dividend, such as the company's own products. It will be apparent, however, that the necessity of making the distribution on a per share basis puts practical limitations on the use of assets other than cash.

The definition of a dividend which has been adopted here, namely, that the payment must be one which reduces the value of the business, excludes the *stock dividend*, which has been frequently used in recent years. Such a distribution is not correctly termed a dividend. In this case the company distributes unissued shares of its own stock to the existing shareholders in proportion to the number of outstanding shares they hold. Normally, the stock which is distributed is of the same class as that held by the recipients. If so, then the proportion of ownership held by each shareholder in the business remains exactly as before, except that he has more pieces of paper as evidence of this. If the stock distributed is of a class other than the one held by the recipients, then the relative position of these two classes will be affected. In either case, however, the total assets of the business remain unchanged—nothing of value leaves the business.

Such distributions of the company's own stock have come to be known as dividends because in many instances the transaction is recorded by reducing Earned Surplus by the par value of the new shares issued, the other side of the entry being an increase in Capital Stock outstanding. Since it is the authors' opinion that the stock dividend is a type of voluntary recapitalization similar to the stock split, it will be discussed in detail in Chapter 26, and no further reference to it will be made here. We turn now to the problems of practice and policy relating to cash dividends.

Dividend Payments a Matter for the Board of Directors

The power to declare dividends rests in all cases in the discretion of the directors of the corporation. It cannot be made into an obligation of the corporation by contract or otherwise. As we have seen previously, this is one of the basic distinctions between debt instruments and equity instruments. Even the strongest preferred stock will not receive dividends unless the directors take action to vote them. A decision not to pay a dividend may have unpleasant consequences, such as a change in the membership of the board of directors or some other change provided for in the contract creating a preferred stock; but as long as the directors have used their judgment in good faith, there is no way to force a dividend by direct legal action.

On the other hand, business practice often tends to make certain dividend payments relatively secure. As a result, investors are justified in expecting the regular payment of dividends on the better grade of preferred stocks and even on some common stocks. But since this condition is the result of a management decision and not of legal obligation, it is more useful for us to leave elaborations of the reasons why such regular dividends can be expected from certain companies until after a study of the determinants of policy.

Although, as we have just said, the law does not force dividend payments, there are well-established legal rules defining precisely under what circumstances dividends must not be paid. The provisions of the corporation laws of the various states differ in detail on this matter, but the general rule is clear that dividends may be paid only out of realized earnings and only if the paid-in capital of the business is not "impaired."[1]

---

[1] Special provisions exist for corporations with wasting assets, such as mining corporations, and for the exceptional cases when ordinary corporations wish to pay liquidating dividends.

The historical origin of all these legal provisions is the desire to protect creditors; that is to say, that they are to be free to assume, first, that the owners of a corporation will not reduce by dividends the amount of its original paid-in capital, and, second, that the owners will not distribute "paper profits"—that is, those arising from transactions like upward revaluations of property not yet sold by the company.[2]

There is a financial rule of thumb which expresses the foregoing in deceptively precise and rather dangerous terms: "Dividends may be paid out of surplus." If this were to be rephrased as follows: "The measure of the maximum dividend a corporation can pay is the amount of the earned surplus," the rule would be more safely stated. One must always avoid giving any basis for the dangerous inference that a balance sheet surplus is the *source of payment* for anything.

In the precise legal language of the Model Business Corporation Act,[3] the rule is expressed as follows. We add also part of the section on the liability of directors with respect to payment of dividends. Note that these provisions merely establish the amount that *may* be distributed.

Section 40. Dividends

The board of directors of a corporation may, from time to time, declare and the corporation may pay dividends on its outstanding shares in cash, property, or its own shares, except when the corporation is insolvent or when the payment thereof would render the corporation insolvent or when the declaration or payment thereof would be contrary to any restrictions contained in the articles of incorporation, subject to the following provisions:

(a) Dividends may be declared and paid in cash or property only out of the unreserved and unrestricted earned surplus of the corporation, except as otherwise provided in this section.

.   .   .   .

(c) Dividends may be declared and paid in its own shares out of any treasury shares that may have been reacquired out of surplus of the corporation.

(d) Dividends may be declared and paid in its own authorized but unissued shares out of any unreserved and unrestricted surplus of the corporation upon the following conditions:

(1) If a dividend is payable in its own shares having a par value, such shares shall be issued at not less than the par value thereof and there

---

[2] Accountants never tire of pointing out that the quantities of paid-in capital, and the amounts of earnings, both realized and unrealized, are extremely difficult to determine, so that the actual decision of the precise quantities involved may be very difficult.

[3] *Model Business Corporation Act* (revised 1959), prepared by the Committee on Corporate Laws of the American Bar Association (Philadelphia: Joint Committee on Continuing Legal Education of the American Law Institute and the American Bar Association, 1961), pp. 32–37.

See also *Model Business Corporation Act, Annotated,* Committee on Corporate Laws of the American Bar Association (ed.) (St. Paul, Minn.: West Publishing Co., 1960).

See also Commerce Clearing House, Inc., *Corporation Law Guide* (Chicago: 1965) (2 vols.; looseleaf; kept current) for the laws of individual states.

shall be transferred to stated capital at the time such dividend is paid an amount of surplus at least equal to the aggregate par value of the shares to be issued as a dividend.

(2) If a dividend is payable in its own shares without par value, such shares shall be issued at such stated value as shall be fixed by the board of directors by resolution adopted at the time such dividend is declared, and there shall be transferred to stated capital at the time such dividend is paid an amount of surplus equal to the aggregate stated value so fixed in respect of such shares; and the amount per share so transferred to stated capital shall be disclosed to the shareholders receiving such dividend concurrently with the payment thereof.

Section 43. Liability of Directors in Certain Cases

In addition to any other liabilities imposed by law upon directors of a corporation:

(a) Directors of a corporation who vote for or assent to the declaration of any dividend or other distribution of the assets of a corporation to its shareholders contrary to the provisions of this Act or contrary to any restrictions contained in the articles of incorporation, shall be jointly and severally liable to the corporation for the amount of such dividend which is paid or the value of such assets which are distributed in excess of the amount of such dividend or distribution which could have been paid or distributed without a violation of the provisions of this Act or the restrictions in the articles of incorporation.

Payment of Dividends Greater than Earnings

Since the law in the United States permits the payment of dividends as long as there is an amount of earned surplus large enough to absorb the payment, it is possible for companies to pay more than the amount of current earnings in a period of low activity, if earned surplus was retained in previous profitable years. It is interesting to note that in some countries, companies are not permitted to draw upon past earnings in this way. In other countries, such as Italy, in addition, corporations are required to transfer a certain percentage of each year's earnings to a paid-in reserve account before dividends can be considered.

In the United States, if by operation during economic depression or for other reasons companies find themselves without any surplus on their balance sheet to support the payment of a dividend, yet desire to make payments, some states permit an adjustment of the corporation's capital structure to transfer values from the stated or paid-in capital account to distributable surplus. This must be done after due notice to stockholders, followed by a vote taken at a meeting of stockholders entitled to vote. The publicity given to the move is considered to give adequate protection to creditors, in place of the absolute rule otherwise in force.

Contractual Limitations on Dividend Payments

Since most companies would not be permitted, nor would they consider, the payment of dividends under conditions which would impair their capital, it is much more important to discuss the self-imposed restrictions on freedom to pay dividends out of existing surplus which managements accept by contract in the bargain for funds. Many times, companies find it desirable to limit the ability of the directors to make dividend payments. As we have already seen, such promises are often made in loan agreements, and the same situation exists in many preferred stock contracts with reference to dividends on common stock. It is the existence of such provisions in the contracts of senior securities or in the charter or bylaws of a corporation that often leads to considerable restriction in the possibility of declaring dividends upon common shares. Anyone studying the position of a stock of a company must therefore include in his study reference to the *protective provisions* in senior securities.

The type of contractual limitation which restricts the freedom of a company to declare dividends is usually expressed in terms of the necessity to maintain a certain financial position or a certain level of earnings. This type of provision has already been referred to in previous material, but it is useful to quote an example of a term-loan restriction here: "Company may not pay cash dividends on common or acquire stock in excess of consolidated net income after December 28, 1957, plus $2,500,000 and provided consolidated net working capital is not less than $10,000,000. At December 26, 1959, $4,073,247 of retained earnings were not so restricted."[4]

In the preferred stock contract the most frequently encountered provision defining when dividends may not be paid is that which requires the accumulation of unpaid preferred dividends. A typical provision of this type might read as follows:

The holders of the $6 preference stock shall be entitled to receive, if and as declared by the board of directors, dividends from the surplus of the company or from its net profits at the rate of $6 per annum, per share, and no more, payable quarterly on the first days of January, April, July, and October in each year. Such dividends shall be paid or declared and set apart for payment before any dividends shall be paid upon, or declared and set apart for, the common stock of the company, and shall be cumulative from and after January 1, 19—, so that if in any quarterly dividend period thereafter dividends at the rate of $6 per annum per share shall not have been paid upon, or declared and set apart for, the $6 preference stock, the deficiency shall be fully paid or declared and set apart for payment before any dividends shall be paid upon, or declared and set apart for, common stock of the company.

Taxation and Dividend Policy

Before we leave the topic of the legal rules imposed by statute and contract which limit freedom in the area of dividend policy, we should

---

[4] Term loan of General Baking Company, as stated in *Moody's Industrial Manual,* *1960,* p. 1136.

make brief reference to the laws of taxation, for there one can find examples of provisions which give strong incentive either to pay dividends or not to pay them, depending upon the law and the particular circumstances of a company. For example, frequent reference is made in financial journals to the paradoxical situation of the stockholder who does not want to receive dividends because he must pay a higher rate of personal income tax upon the dividends that he might receive than on the capital gains he may realize by selling the stock later on. Publicly owned corporations with scattered shareholders may not have to worry about stockholders of this kind, but closely held companies do sometimes give consideration to this factor in determining the amount of cash dividends to be distributed. In view of this fact, there exist Sections 531–37 of the United States Revenue Code (1954), to which we have referred previously. It will be recalled that this provision of the Code may be used to penalize those corporations which unnecessarily retain earnings for the purpose of benefiting the personal income tax position of their shareholders. There exists a considerable body of specialized knowledge about how this provision must be regarded, but it will not be discussed here because of the narrow range of companies to which in fact it might be applied.

Laws of general applicability also exist which apply the power of taxation in such a manner as to give incentives to pay or not to pay dividends. From 1936 to 1939 the United States had in force a Surtax on Undistributed Profits, which in 1936 and 1937 caused many companies to increase their dividend payments (because of the extra tax which was levied on profits retained). In later years the rates of surtax were reduced, and the effect was much smaller, although in the same direction. On the other hand, beginning in 1947, Great Britain imposed a special tax on *distributed* profits. This had, of course, exactly the opposite effect to the American law.

Procedure in Voting and Distributing a Dividend

In the United States it has become customary to consider the question of dividends quarterly. In fact, when a company has been paying dividends regularly, a certain meeting of the board comes to be recognized as the *dividend meeting,* at which the matter of dividends comes up on the agenda. There are only a few companies in America which pay dividends at other intervals, such as monthly or annually. In other countries this is not always the case. Particularly in those countries where the law requires that a corporation shall not pay more than it has earned in a particular year, it is not uncommon for companies to make payments on an annual basis after the determination of the earnings has been made by the company's accountant. Concerns in these countries which are rather sure of their earnings estimates may make advance payments, but they leave the bulk of the dividend to be paid at the end of the year. The relative infrequency of such payments and their unequal amounts make the ownership of stocks a little less attractive to the average investor than is the case in the United States.

At the dividend meeting the board of directors considers not only the amount of the dividend but also the form it will take. In describing the procedure here, we shall concern ourselves only with cash dividends. The vote which the board takes will specify the amount, the date of payment, and the *record date*. Just after the dividend meeting a formal notice is often given to the financial journals in words like these:

"The board of directors has this day declared a quarterly dividend of 25 cents per share on the capital stock of this corporation, payable September 15, 1965, to shareholders of record August 30, 1965. Checks will be mailed." (Published August 16, 1965.)

The record date is established because it is necessary for dividend checks to be prepared for all the shareholders, and time is needed to make up these checks from an address list which will not change. Hence, a record date is established which is commonly a week or two weeks before the payable date. In the days before the development of fast-moving clerical machinery, the *transfer books* were *closed* for the period between the record date and the payable date, and no transfer of securities could take place, although, of course, sales and purchases did take place with the new owner waiting for formal transfer until the transfer books were reopened. At present, the closing is not necessary.

In the case of securities which are traded on registered exchanges, an *ex-dividend date* is established by the rules of the exchange. It is calculated from the record date with a time advance from that date to allow for the usual mechanics of delivery and transfer of securities that have been sold. On and after this ex-dividend date a stock is sold to the buyer without any right on his part to claim the dividend that has been declared. It goes to the former owner. Therefore, the market price of the stock should drop by the amount of the dividend involved between the closing price of the previous day and the opening price of the ex-dividend day. In fact, however, other market forces tend to obscure this change.

Beginning on the record date the dividend-paying agency or officer of the corporation prepares checks for the correct amount of the dividend to be sent to each shareholder. Oftentimes, the corporation takes advantage of this mailing to include *dividend stuffers:* letters to shareholders which contain information about the company and its affairs—quite frequently the most recent interim financial reports. The checks are placed in the mails either on the payable date or according to a schedule which will cause the checks to arrive at the address of record on the day the checks are payable.[5]

---

[5] Every corporation with any sizable list of shareholders always finds that a few checks are not cashed from each dividend payment, and these are accumulated in a special liability fund for later claim by the stockholders when they discover their right.

The Elements of a Dividend Policy

In considering what we mean by the term *dividend policy*, we should take note of the fact that there are many companies which do not pay any dividends. This may be the result of an inability to realize the earnings which are the legal and financial prerequisite to such payments. It may also result from a deliberate policy of retention of all earnings for the purpose of financing growth. In both cases it is usually anticipated that the nonpayment of dividends reflects a certain stage in the company's history which will ultimately give way to conditions which will permit the payment of dividends. Few companies will assert that nonpayment is an inflexible long-term policy. For companies in a stage of rapid development, commonly known as *growth companies*, it may be expected that there will ultimately be a slowdown in the rate of growth, but it is hoped that at the same time earnings flowing from past growth will set the stage for cash dividend payments. During the period of nonpayment, stockholders will be looking to the capital gains which will result from improving earnings performance. These situations are particularly attractive to investors in a high personal income tax bracket. For purposes of discussion here, however, we assume that the choice we are considering is not whether to pay a cash dividend but how much to pay, since this is the most common problem. Obviously, nonpayment is one of the alternatives open but an extreme one for most companies having some maturity and experiencing some degree of success.

The concept of a dividend policy implies that businesses through their boards of directors evolve a recognizable pattern of cash dividend payments which has a bearing on future action. Undoubtedly, some businesses do not have a dividend policy in this sense but rather act as if each dividend decision was completely independent of every other such decision. However, the results of a study of dividend policies in large industrial corporations in the United States strongly suggest that in the majority of cases, current dividend decisions are intimately related to previous dividend decisions.[6] In this study, cited below, Professor Lintner has concluded that management typically takes the existing dividend rate as its starting point and views the dividend decision as a question of whether or not to change this rate in the current period. He further concludes that while there is a feeling of responsibility to share increased earnings with the stockholders, there is a general resistance on the part of management to any change which may only be temporary and consequently a certain inertia which favors the continuance of the existing rate unless there are strong and persistent reasons to change. At this point we simply report these findings without making any comment as to whether

---

[6] See John Lintner, "Distribution of Incomes of Corporations among Dividends, Retained Earnings and Taxes," *American Economic Review, Papers and Proceedings* (May, 1956), pp. 97–113.

or not such action appears to be a rational and sensible policy. It is clear that this action produces a strong tendency to regularity of dividend payments.

The term _regular dividend_ has been used to mean a variety of things. It may mean simply that a company has paid *something* in each year over a certain period. More significantly, it may mean regularity in dollar amount, for example, American Telephone and Telegraph's $9 per year paid without interruption from 1922 to 1959 (at which time the stock was split and the dividend increased). The term may also refer to a regular *pay-out* as a percentage of earnings or a regular pattern of change in dollar amounts. Obviously, from the shareholders' point of view, there is a great deal of difference among these different forms of regularity.

It should be noted that in the usage of the securities market the term _regular dividend_ is employed in certain situations to draw a distinction between that portion of a cash dividend which is expected to continue from year to year and an additional payment, known as an *extra* dividend. An example of the use of such terms is seen in the following excerpt from the 1956 annual report of Standard Brands, Inc.:

> Dividends totalling $7,331,731, equivalent to $2.25 per share, were declared and paid on the common stock during 1956. This total, which compares with $2.15 per share paid during 1955, comprised quarterly dividends of $0.50 each, plus an extra dividend of $0.25 in December.
>
> A regular quarterly dividend of $0.50 per share was declared on the common stock, payable on March 15, 1957.

The significance of this distinction is that there is not the same implied commitment to continue the extra dividend as there is on the regular dividend. If and when the time comes when the added earnings upon which the extra dividend has been based prove to be permanent, the extra dividend is likely to become a part of the regular dividend, and the distinction would then be dropped.

When dividend payments in the past have shown a certain regularity, this becomes a basis for confidence in forecasting what future dividends will be. Unfortunately, regularity as applied to dividend payments is rarely if ever an absolute term, and what we really mean is that the business in question is more regular than some other businesses. Thus, a degree of uncertainty remains; and the vital question as to what may be expected in the future has—for the shareholder, at least—no sure answer.

In this situation it is natural that shareholders of a public corporation search for clues as to the basis upon which management approaches the dividend question. Speaking generally, management is deliberately noncommittal on its future plans for dividend payments. The typical annual report dismisses the topic of dividends with a brief statement such as: "Quarterly dividends on the common stock totaled $1.20 per share." Most managements shy away from any statement which remotely resembles a promise for the future, and this is consistent with a literal interpretation of the traditional concept of a common shareholder as a guarantor of payments to others rather than the recipient of a guaranteed or promised payment. On the other hand, there are some companies which make comparatively forthright statements of intent as, for example, that which is found in the 1955 annual report of the Standard Oil Company (Indiana): "On June 30 we announced that our present intention for the next several years is to continue to supplement regular cash dividends by a special dividend in an amount sufficient to bring our total dividend declaration in any year to about 50 per cent of that year's earnings." This policy has been adhered to in the years since 1955.

Some companies come very close to a statement of dividend policy by the somewhat oblique method of commenting on past performance. Thus, for example, the annual report of General Electric for 1959 commented that dividends for the year were "62% of net earnings for the year, compared with 71% in 1958, and this compares with an average rate of 66% for the past 61 years." Other annual reports make similar, if somewhat less encouraging, comments on policy. Thus the Sperry Rand Corporation annual report for 1962 stated: "Stockholders will remember that at the time of the stock dividend paid on March 30, 1961, the Board of Directors pointed out the advisability of conserving cash and forgoing the former cash dividend. The Board based its judgment in the fact that the long-range interests of the stockholders would be served best by the retaining of earnings of the Company in order to finance expected growth, particularly in the electronic data-processing equipment field."

The Determinants of Dividend Policy

In the comprehensive study of dividend policy to which we referred earlier (see footnote 6), the typical established business was observed to take as its starting point the dividend rate of the preceding period and to be reluctant to depart from this rate (up or down) unless there were clear and compelling reasons to do so. This followed from a strong desire to avoid an erratic pattern of payments symptomatic of hasty decisions based on incomplete knowledge of the future. We now quote from Professor Lintner's article:

. . . The principal device used to achieve this consistent pattern was a practice or policy of changing dividends in any given year by only part of the amounts which were indicated by changes in current financial figures. Further partial adjustments in dividend rates were then made in subsequent years if still warranted. This policy of progressive, continuing "partial adaptation" tends to stabilize dividend distributions and provides a consistency in the pattern of dividend action which helps to minimize adverse stockholder reactions. At the same time it enables management to live more comfortably with its unavoidable uncertainties regarding future developments. . . .[7]

At the same time, this study indicated a general agreement on the part of management that dividends should be related to current earnings. This was evidenced by widespread acceptance of some specific ratio of dividends to earnings as being reasonable for the company concerned. This pay-out ratio varied widely from company to company, but remained relatively fixed for a given company over time. On the face of it, the idea of a fixed pay-out ratio runs contrary to the observed deep-rooted reluctance to change. In practice the reconciliation is brought about by the use of the pay-out ratio as a target, toward which the established dividend rate will be partially adjusted period by period.

The reader will observe that in this brief summary of a portion of the report on dividend practices we have only begun to touch on the basic determinants of dividend policy. Given that current business practice is generally appropriate (or, at least, is generally accepted by business as appropriate), there remain the unanswered questions as to how and why a company selects a particular target pay-out ratio and determines its rate of adjustment toward this target. Since we have been talking only about going concerns with an established record of dividend payments, there is also the question of how a company which is planning its first dividend payment will make this decision.

The fact is that we cannot arrive at a specific answer to any policy decision on a general basis, since in the last analysis the decision must take into account the special circumstances of the individual case. On the other hand, careful observation and intelligent interpretation of general practice is of real assistance in narrowing down the area of study and in confirming the analysis in the individual case. Our next step, therefore, is to consider in general terms those determinants of dividend policy which are observed to be of major importance in the typical business situation. We shall then leave it to the reader to assess their applicability in the individual case and to fill in whatever additional considerations he may find to have a bearing on the decision.

1. *Relation of Dividends to Earnings.* As previously indicated, the starting point of dividend policy is the earnings of the business. We have seen that a business is legally entitled to pay dividends up to an amount equal to the net accumulated earnings of the business to date. Practically speaking, the upper limit on dividends tends to be set by the earnings of the current period, since the retained earnings of previous years generally become a part of the permanent investment of the business upon which current earnings are based. On the other hand, we have noted the

---

[7] *Ibid.*, p. 100.

observed inertia in dividend payments and the widespread reluctance to reduce, as well as to increase, dividends. In fact, it appears that the reluctance to reduce dividends is greater than the hesitancy in increasing them. It is also apparent, however, that a company cannot continue to pay dividends in excess of earnings over extended periods of time without impairing the future earning capacity of the business and therefore future dividends.

As a consequence, a rational dividend policy must take account of the amount and behavior of year-to-year earnings. Since dividend policy is by definition forward-looking, it must be based not only on earnings already realized, which provide the funds for the current dividend distribution, but also on anticipated earnings. The reader will be well aware of the fact that the pattern of change in earnings varies widely among industries and individual companies. Earnings may be so variable as to be largely unpredictable, or they may show a definite trend which may be up, down, or generally stable. They may be influenced by heavy leverage of senior securities, or there may be no leverage at all. Change from year to year may be abrupt or very gradual. The specific characteristics applying to a particular case are of obvious importance to a plan for the distribution of these earnings.

2. *The Alternative of Reinvestment.*   In any dynamic business, there will be many alternative uses for the funds which are available to it. This applies to the funds provided from operations equally as much as to any other source. Consequently, dividend payments will be competing with other possible uses for the current earnings dollar. The basic choice that must be made by the board of directors is whether the earnings will be distributed to the shareholders or whether they will be reinvested in the business for strengthening of the existing earning capacity and for growth. Table 14–1 clearly indicates that with the possible exception of periods of general business recession, the large majority of businesses consistently reinvest a substantial fraction of current earnings. In view of the natural desire of the owners for an immediate income from their investment, there must be compelling reasons which would lead business to follow a regular practice of turning a substantial fraction of the earnings back into the business.

The obvious question presents itself as to which is the governing consideration—dividends or the needs of the business for new capital. This question brings up the issue of the balance of sources from which new capital will be obtained. Later chapters will deal with this subject at length. It will be found that common equity capital is generally a high-cost source of funds as compared to debt sources. On the other hand, businesses must have a balance of these sources; and if this balance is to be maintained, new financing means new equity capital sooner or later. Given this need, the alternatives are new common stock issues or retained earnings.

TABLE 14–1

CORPORATE INCOME AND DIVIDEND PAYMENTS IN THE UNITED STATES,
ALL INDUSTRIES, 1935–63
(In Billions of Dollars)

Year	Corporate Income before Tax	Corporate Income after Tax	Net Corporate Dividend Payments	Retained Earnings	Percentage of Income after Tax Retained
1935	3.1	2.2	2.9	− 0.7	−32%
1936	5.7	4.3	4.5	− 0.2	− 5
1937	6.2	4.7	4.7	0.0	0
1938	3.3	2.3	3.2	− 0.9	−39
1939	6.4	5.0	3.8	1.2	24
1940	9.3	6.5	4.0	2.4	37
1941	17.0	9.4	4.5	4.9	52
1942	20.9	9.5	4.3	5.2	55
1943	24.6	10.5	4.5	6.0	57
1944	23.3	10.4	4.7	5.7	55
1945	19.0	8.3	4.7	3.6	43
1946	22.6	13.4	5.8	7.7	57
1947	29.5	18.2	6.5	11.7	64
1948	33.0	20.5	7.2	13.3	65
1949	26.4	16.0	7.5	8.5	53
1950	40.6	22.8	9.2	13.6	60
1951	42.2	19.7	9.0	10.7	54
1952	36.7	17.2	9.0	8.3	48
1953	38.3	18.1	9.2	8.9	49
1954	34.1	16.8	9.8	7.0	42
1955	44.9	23.0	11.2	11.8	51
1956	44.7	23.5	12.1	11.3	48
1957	43.2	22.3	12.6	9.7	43
1958	37.4	18.8	12.4	6.4	34
1959	47.7	24.5	13.7	10.8	44
1960	44.3	22.0	14.5	7.5	34
1961	44.2	21.9	15.2	6.7	31
1962	48.2	25.0	16.5	8.5	34
1963	51.3	26.7	18.0	8.7	33
1964	57.6	31.8	19.8	11.9	37

SOURCES: Office of Business Economics, Department of Commerce, *U.S. Income and Output: A Supplement to the Survey of Current Business* (Washington, D.C., 1958), Table 1–8, pp. 126–27, for figures through 1955; *Survey of Current Business* (National Income Number), July, 1964, Table 2., p. 8, for figures for 1956–63; U.S. Bureau of the Census, *Statistical Abstract of the United States: 1965* (Washington, D.C., 1965), p. 496, for 1964.

In Chapter 21 we shall develop an approximation of the cost of retained earnings and of new common stock issues. Some of the conclusions of that chapter are of significance here. One is that from a profit standpoint new investments should not be made unless they are expected to earn a return which is at least equal to the cost of the funds which will be used to finance them. As a potential source of such funds, retained earnings are found to have a cost which is measured in terms of alternative investment opportunities of comparable risk outside the business, and this cost is incorporated into the general standard for a cutoff point on new investment. Obviously, if there are no investment opportunities which meet this standard, the source would not be used, and the earnings should be distributed as dividends.

On the other hand, we observe that where there are such opportunities, which must be financed in part by equity capital, there is strong pressure for the use of retained earnings rather than new common stock issues. In defining the cost of retained earnings, it is commonly concluded that, although normally high relative to debt, this cost is significantly less than that for new stock issues. It is therefore quite conceivable that under circumstances of abundant opportunities for profitable expansion, all of the current earnings could be usefully retained in the business. In this situation the distribution of earnings to shareholders would appear to be contrary to their best (economic) interests, and any dividend policy which favored the maintenance of some dividend payment would be under considerable pressure.

There are also certain practical reasons why retained earnings appeal to management as a source of funds. As compared to other external sources, retained earnings have the advantage of being immediately available to the business as they are realized, and the decision is merely one of whether or not to continue to use them. There is no problem of negotiation with sources of supply and no uncertainty, at least as regards earnings realized to date. There is also the fact that the cost of retained earnings, in terms of alternative investment uses forgone, is less tangible than that for bonds or stocks, does not involve immediate and obvious cash drains, and therefore may tend to be given less weight by a management preoccupied with day-to-day financial problems.

The line of reasoning based on our discussion of corporate investment decisions would appear to lead us to the conclusion that, given the current level of earnings, dividend policy would be a by-product of the capital budget. The dividends paid would fluctuate from year to year, depending on investment opportunities within the company as compared with those without, and would be that portion of current earnings which could not be profitably reinvested.

The reader will note that this does not appear to square with observed business practice, previously cited, which shows a strong preference for stability and regularity in dividend payments. However, the observed practice regarding dividends is not necessarily inconsistent with the idea of adjusting the proportion of retained earnings in accordance with investment opportunities. Viewed over a period of years, the policy of partial adjustment toward a fixed target pay-out ratio means that in a period of developing prosperity, rising earnings will always have a lead over rising dividends. As a consequence, there is increased earnings retention at a time when investment opportunities are becoming more numerous and more profitable. In a period of recession the same reluctance to change means that dividend payments tend to take an increasing proportion of current earnings and may even exceed them. Since this is a period when investment opportunities are few or nonexistent, the resultant decline in retained earnings is unlikely to be in serious conflict with management's investment objectives.

3. *The Effect of Dividends on the Investment Worth of the Company's Stocks.* A matter of primary interest to management, especially shareholder-oriented management, is the relationship of dividends and dividend policy to the investment worth of the common stock. This would appear to be directly related to the preceding discussion of reinvestment versus distribution because—in theory, at least—the investment worth of a stock at any given time would be the present value of the stream of earnings which is expected to flow from the investment. Since a dividend is by definition a distribution of something of value, it would seem that by reducing the earning assets of the business, the payment of a dividend would thereby reduce the investment worth of the stock below what it would have been if the funds had been retained.

Unfortunately, observation of the securities market fails to show an easy and uncomplicated relationship of this nature; in fact, the precise effect on market value of reinvestment and dividend policies is not at all clear. The analytical task of measuring the impact on market prices of any given consideration such as dividend payments is one of unusual complexity in view of the wide variety of possible considerations and the difficulties involved in translating these into quantitative terms. When we add to this the fact that the market is made up of many different kinds of investors with substantially different objectives and that emotion as well as reason has its influence, there is little reason to wonder that clear-cut answers are hard to come by.

However, there are some things that can be said by way of useful generalization to set the limits on this relationship between dividends and market prices. Let us first be clear that our primary interest is in the effects of dividend policy rather than the effects of any particular dividend payment. We have already noted that there is an observed pattern of market price in response to the periodic dividend payment, which involves a buildup to the date when the list of dividend recipients is drawn up and a drop on the ex-dividend date by the amount of the dividend. Our interest here is in such policy questions as the probable effects on market price of regular versus fluctuating dividends, high versus low dividend pay-out, and changes in dividend pay-out.

These questions are of obvious importance to the common shareholders, whose opportunities for gain (or loss) include changes in market price of the securities as well as dividend income. They are also vital to management, even though it may not be closely identified with the common shareholder, for the equally obvious reason that these questions bear directly on the salability of new issues of common stock and on the number of shares which must be sold or exchanged as new investments are made.

One thing is clear, and that is that the market does not uniformly accept the line of reasoning we suggested at the outset, which implied that the more paid out in dividends, the less the value of what remained in the business. On the contrary, observation suggests that an increase in the dividend payment normally acts to raise market price rather than lower it, and there are several reasons why this should be expected. First, let us note that while there are some shareholders whose income tax bracket might lead them to prefer no dividends at all, the great majority of shareholders attach some importance to income as well as capital gains, and that a substantial number of individual and institutional shareholders consider dividends as all-important. The latter shareholders would, as a result, tend to discount to some extent the capital gains potential of reinvested earnings.

To these shareholders, reinvested earnings would be of interest primarily as a basis for the preservation of and increase in the current dividend rate. Expectations as to future dividends are normally based on the dividend record of the immediate past. If a company has had a record of regularity in dividend payments and the dividend rate has been recently increased, investors may very naturally expect that this increased rate will continue and thus be prepared to pay a higher market price for the stock. In view of the fact that such increases are usually small relative to the existing earning assets of the business, the market may well ignore the effect on earning capacity which might follow from reduced earnings retention. It is possible, of course, that extreme changes in dividend pay-out over short periods of time might raise questions as to future earnings and dividend-paying capacity. However, changes are frequently small enough, the remaining margin of earnings over dividends large enough, and the level of earnings sufficiently uncertain in any event that this aspect may be discounted completely.

It is not our intention here to leave the reader with the impression that dividends are all-important in market price determination but rather to bring out that they may be more important than has often been suggested in writings on the subject. We must continue to remind ourselves of the wide variations in shareholder objectives and among company share-holder groups, and remember that this has a major bearing on how they will respond to various dividend policies. There are, for example, the growth companies, which over long periods have paid out little or nothing in dividends and yet have experienced a steady rise in the market price of their stock and a flattering price-earnings ratio.

If, however, we conclude that there is the possibility, if not the probability, of raising the level of the market price by raising the dividend rate, this is of real significance in management decisions. For example, it has a bearing on the question of new financing. Here, management may find itself in something of a dilemma. By raising the dividend rate, it may be possible to make a new issue more attractive, raise the issue price, and lower the number of shares required to be sold, thus reducing the dilution of equity and control. On the other hand, increased dividend payments mean less funds available from internal sources. The issue may turn on the extent of the response in market price which is expected to follow from the change in the dividend. In addition to the difficulty of forecasting the precise effect of the increase in dividend on market price, there is an ethical question as to whether it is appropriate for management to attempt to "manipulate" the market in this manner, particularly if it knows that the increase in dividend cannot or will not be maintained.

So far, we have been focusing on market price responses to changes in dividend pay-out. There is also the question of the relative desirability of stable dividend payments versus payments which follow closely the swings of business earnings. From the dividend study cited earlier, it would appear that the majority of established businesses have followed a dividend policy with the built-in assumption that shareholders prefer stability. If this is so, then we might conclude that the market price of a stock with a stable dividend payment should be higher than that of a similar stock with payments which fluctuate about an average of equal amount. In contrast to this, there are some who maintain that a stable dividend policy is often attained at the cost of a comparatively low dividend pay-out, thus working to the long-term disadvantage of the shareholder.

While it might be assumed that a company's dividend policy would be determined by its stockholders, it is sometimes claimed that the reverse is true, namely, that the company's dividend policy determines the stockholder group. Thus, a company with low pay-out and heavy reinvestment attracts stockholders interested in capital gains rather than current income subject to a personal income tax. A company with a stable dividend policy is said to attract those who look to it as a source of regular income. Likewise, a company with a high pay-out attracts those who emphasize immediate income. While there is undoubtedly some truth in this, the idea carries the questionable implication that any policy which suits the management is all right, since those shareholders who do not like it will sell out to those who do. Such an approach would have a certain appeal for professional management, particularly in those companies where a diverse stockholder group makes it difficult to develop a policy that suits everyone.

4. *The Relation of Dividend Policy to Cash Flows and Liquidity.* Whatever the considerations which dominate its thinking in the setting of dividend policy, management must take account of the obvious fact

that dividends involve an outflow of cash and therefore that dividend payments must be fitted into the company's cash budget. Even when dividend policy is carefully tied to a capital budget which makes adequate provision for needed funds through retained earnings and other sources, the precise matching of cash inflows and outflows remains a problem.

The reader should now be well aware of the fact that a given number of dollars of earnings in a period does not automatically produce an equivalent sum in cash at the end of the period. In a dynamic business, profit as an element of the selling price is almost immediately subject to reinvestment in the working capital stream. Thus, the payment of a dividend at the end of the period usually constitutes a diversion of funds from active use.

Because of seasonal, cyclical, or random variations in cash inflows and outflows, the cash position of the business must be subject to constant reappraisal. At any point in time there will be many needs competing with dividends for the cash inflows which are expected over the forecast period. Some of these needs are mandatory, others optional and in varying degrees of urgency. Increases in working capital, replacement of productive equipment, payments to a pension fund, retirement of debt—these are typical of alternatives which may have high priority. Shareholders may view dividends as a distribution of what is rightfully theirs, but the corporate officer responsible for the management of funds sees them as a reduction in usable cash, and it is an unusual company that could not usefully employ the cash in other ways.

In a business with a strained cash position due to any one of a number of possible reasons, dividends are likely to have low priority because of their noncontractual nature. Here, we can hardly justify the use of the term dividend policy, since dividends are likely to have been the result of a series of *ad hoc* decisions, each of which was dominated by the circumstances at the time. On the other hand, a business which is able to preserve a margin of liquidity at all times—through one or a combination of bank balances, highly liquid short-term investments, and reserve borrowing capacity—is in a better position to put into practice a dividend policy which has a degree of consistency over time. The company is then able to draw on its reserves of cash, or their equivalent, to meet a temporarily unbalanced budget instead of using the alternative of cutting out planned expenditures of low priority.

5. *Other Considerations.* In any dividend policy decision, there may be a variety of considerations in addition to those already mentioned.[8] To suggest that those we have emphasized are more fundamental than some others is not to imply that they will be dominant at all times and in all situations. When one becomes familiar with the details of a particular business situation, other considerations will undoubtedly emerge; and in

---

[8] The reader may wish to read the list of considerations given by Professor Lintner on page 104 of the article cited earlier in this chapter.

the last analysis, they may dominate the decision, at least for a time. Such factors as the dividend policy of other similar businesses in the same industry, restrictions on dividend policy imposed by debt contracts, the extent to which management identifies itself with the common share-holders, the nature of the capital structure, the existence of influential shareholders with special investment objectives, and other considerations must be weighed in the balance.

In view of the variety of considerations which may bear on the dividend question, it is unlikely that any one dividend policy will be completely satisfactory in all respects. Whatever course of action is chosen is likely to be a compromise of conflicting objectives. Thus, management is found in the familiar position of having to assess the relative importance of the relevant factors and choose that course of action which is of maximum advantage in the light of the circumstances of the business and the objectives of its shareholders. The task is sometimes complicated by the fact that this is one of those critical deci-sions which tends to bring into the open latent conflicts of interest between management per se and the shareholders, or between one shareholder group and another.

Dividends on Preferred Stock

In this chapter we have been discussing dividend policy as it relates to the basic equity issue—common stock. We have not considered the special aspects of dividend policy on preferred stock. The preferred stock contract grants to the owners certain priorities which normally mean that management will treat preferred dividends differently. Since we have not discussed these characteristics as yet, we shall defer reference to dividend policy on preferred until a later chapter.

Chapter 15

External Sources of Long-Term Capital

IN THIS chapter we shall consider first the extent to which American corporations raise funds through the sale of new securities. Then we shall focus our attention on the markets for corporate securities. It is axiomatic in marketing that selling programs should be built on a foundation of knowledge about the potential customers. We shall present basic information about the major buyers of corporate securities, indicating the types of securities they buy and their relative importance in absorbing new issues of securities. In the following chapter we shall discuss the major means by which corporate sellers of securities can tap these markets—the principal methods of distributing new issues and the major institutions, particularly the investment banking industry, which exist to facilitate distribution of new issues. Finally, we shall review the markets for outstanding securities and how they relate to the sale of new securities.

The Use of Long-Term External Capital in Perspective

To what extent have American corporations turned to the long-term capital markets for funds to meet their expanding total need for funds? And how does the total amount provided by the sale of long-term debt and by issues of preferred stock and common stock compare with the amounts provided by internal sources, bank borrowing, expanded trade credit, and other sources of financing? Helpful in answering these questions and thus in putting the use of external long-term sources into proper perspective are the data on corporate sources and uses of funds during the post-World War II years presented in Table 15–1. Strikingly apparent from the table is the dominant importance of the operational sources—retained earnings, depletion, and depreciation, which together supplied almost 60% of the total. Also apparent on closer examination is the particularly great growth, both in absolute and relative terms, of the flows related to depreciation. Even though overshadowed by the operational sources, external financing through sale of securities did provide 16.8% of the

TABLE 15-1

SOURCES AND USES OF CORPORATE FUNDS
(In Billions)

Uses	Annual Averages of 1946–55	Annual Averages of 1956–60	1961	1962	1963	1964	Total 1946–64	Percentage of Total
Increases in:								
Cash and U.S. government securities	$ 1.37	$ –0.14	$ 3.6	$ 2.0	$ 2.0	$ –1.0	$ 19.6	2.6%
Inventories	4.35	3.28	1.3	4.4	3.7	3.4	72.7	9.7
Receivables	5.40	7.90	9.9	11.3	12.9	13.9	141.5	18.9
Gross plant and equipment	19.60	29.50	29.6	32.0	33.8	39.4	478.3	63.9
Other assets	0.20	2.76	4.3	4.7	5.9	5.6	36.3	4.9
Total uses	$30.92	$43.30	$48.8	$54.4	$58.4	$61.3	$748.4	100.0%
SOURCES								
Increases in:								
Trade payables	$ 2.81	$ 4.30	$ 7.4	$ 5.6	$ 6.8	$ 5.8	$ 75.2	9.6%
Federal income tax liabilities	0.83	–1.18	0.7	0.9	1.2	0.7	5.9	0.8
Short-term bank loans	1.17	1.76	0.4	3.0	4.3	2.6	30.8	4.0
Long-term bank loans and mortgage loans	1.07	1.90	2.2	4.2	5.0	4.4	36.0	4.6
Other liabilities	1.40	2.74	2.3	3.2	2.5	2.0	37.7	4.8
Retained earnings and depletion	8.72	8.16	5.6	7.7	8.0	11.6	160.9	20.6
Depreciation	9.04	20.24	24.1	27.5	28.8	30.5	302.5	38.8
Net new security issues*	5.55	8.74	9.6	7.1	5.8	9.0	130.7	16.8
Total sources	$30.59	$46.66	$52.3	$59.2	$62.4	$66.6	$779.7	100.0%
Statistical discrepancy	0.33	–3.36	–3.5	–4.8	–4.0	–5.4	–31.3	
	$30.92	43.30	$48.8	$54.4	$58.4	$61.3	$748.4	

*The discerning reader will note that the figures for net new security issues shown in Tables 15–1, 15–2, and 15–3 differ somewhat. The differences are due to variations in the treatment of such items as sales of securities to foreigners, sales of securities by investment companies which in turn are invested in other corporate securities, and the treatment of cash received when securities such as convertible bonds are exchanged for common stock and additional cash is paid into the company. For our purposes, we have been content to keep the tabulations in their original form.

SOURCES OF DATA: U.S. Department of Commerce, *Survey of Current Business*, September, 1957, and July, 1961; and U.S. Department of Commerce, Bureau of the Census, *Statistical Abstract of the United States, 1965* (Washington, D.C.: U.S. Government Printing Office, 1965), p. 502.

total inflows into corporate coffers, and the hardly insignificant amount of $130.7 billion, in the years from 1946 through 1964. Clearly, for American business in general, this outside capital has been an important source, and its availability on acceptable terms has helped to make possible the great postwar expansion of the U.S. economy.

The Volume of Funds Raised through Sale of New Securities

Data on new issues of corporate securities in 1934, 1940, and 1945 through 1964 are presented in Table 15–2. Retirements of outstanding securities are also shown. There is much of significance to the student of finance in these data. Especially notable is the upswing in net new issues over the period from the earlier years when corporations were supplying rather than drawing long-term funds from the capital markets. In the earlier years, much of the sale of bonds was for the purpose of refunding old issues at the very low interest rates which prevailed in the late thirties and the forties. Total new issues peaked at $18.6 billion in 1964.

As can also be seen from Table 15–2, corporations have made particularly heavy use of debt securities in tapping the capital markets. In recent years, however, the sale of stocks has become more important; and in 1961, stock sales contributed slightly more than half of the total net inflow from sale of securities. Doubtless, the rise in the sale of stocks was due, at least in part, to the relatively high levels of common stock prices in these years. While the data do not separate common and preferred stocks, other sources indicate that common stocks accounted for the bulk —and in recent years the predominant portion—of the proceeds from stock sales; in 1964, common stocks represented 86.7% of the total, preferred stocks the remaining 13.3%.[1]

While the data in Tables 15–1 and 15–2 give an idea of the role of sale of securities in the financing of corporations generally, it should be recognized that these are aggregate figures for corporations as a whole. As such, the aggregate figures conceal such important differences as those between various industries, between groups of companies by size, and between individual concerns. For example, the electric utility industry has made particularly heavy use of the sale of new securities in financing its expansion. In recent decades the electric utilities as a group have paid out a relatively high percentage of their earnings in dividends; hence, retained earnings have been of less importance than in the case of manufacturing companies, which have made less heavy use of the capital markets through sale of stocks or bonds.

For reasons discussed in more detail later, the typical small corporation finds the problems in effective sale of securities much more formidable than does its large counterpart. Consequently, smaller concerns have relied more on internal and short-term sources than have large

---

[1] Securities and Exchange Commission, *Statistical Bulletin*, October, 1965, p. 11.

TABLE 15-2

Net Changes in Outstanding Corporate Securities
(In Millions of Dollars)

Year	Bonds and Notes			Stocks			Total		
	New Issues	Retirements	Net New Issues	New Issues	Retirements	Net New Issues	New Issues	Retirements	Net New Issues
1934	391	635	− 244	154	78	76	545	713	− 168
1940	2,477	2,814	− 337	324	260	64	2,801	3,074	− 273
1945	4,924	5,996	−1,072	1,533	910	623	6,457	6,906	− 449
1946	4,721	3,625	1,096	2,459	1,173	1,286	7,180	4,798	2,382
1947	5,015	2,011	3,004	1,867	512	1,355	6,882	2,523	4,359
1948	5,938	1,283	4,655	1,632	400	1,232	7,570	1,683	5,887
1949	4,867	1,583	3,284	1,865	292	1,572	6,731	1,875	4,856
1950	4,806	2,802	2,004	2,418	698	1,720	7,224	3,501	3,724
1951	5,682	2,105	3,577	3,366	667	2,700	9,048	2,772	6,277
1952	7,344	2,403	4,940	3,335	348	2,987	10,679	2,751	7,927
1953	6,651	1,896	4,755	2,898	533	2,366	9,550	2,429	7,121
1954	7,832	4,033	3,799	3,862	1,596	2,265	11,694	5,629	6,065
1955	7,571	3,383	4,188	4,903	2,216	2,687	12,474	5,599	6,875
1956	7,934	3,203	4,731	5,267	1,836	3,432	13,201	5,038	8,162
1957	9,638	2,584	7,053	4,712	1,024	3,688	14,350	3,609	10,741
1958	9,673	3,817	5,856	5,088	1,479	3,609	14,761	5,296	9,465
1959	7,122	3,049	4,073	6,216	1,796	4,420	13,338	4,845	8,492
1960	8,072	3,078	4,994	5,413	1,884	3,529	13,485	4,962	8,523
1961	9,194	4,024	5,170	8,309	2,975	5,334	17,503	6,999	10,503
1962	8,613	3,749	4,864	5,593	2,707	2,886	14,206	6,457	7,750
1963	10,556	4,979	5,577	4,997	3,733	1,264	15,552	8,711	6,841
1964	10,715	4,077	6,637	7,895	4,212	3,683	18,610	8,290	10,320

Source: *Federal Reserve Bulletin*, based on Securities and Exchange Commission's estimates of cash transactions only. New issues exclude foreign and include offerings of open-end and closed-end investment companies, sales of securities held by affiliated companies or the RFC, special offerings to employees, and also new stock issues and cash proceeds connected with conversions of bonds into stocks. Retirements include the same types of issues and also securities retired with internal funds or with proceeds of issues for that purpose.

corporations. Indeed, the hundred largest corporations account for a very substantial portion of the sale of new securities each year. A.T.&T. and its operating subsidiaries alone raised almost $1.8 billion through security issues in the single year 1964.

A few companies have been able to grow to great size without recourse to the sale of securities to the public. The Ford Motor Company, which from its inception through 1955 drew no funds from the capital markets through stock or bond issues, and yet amassed total assets of almost $2.6 billion, is a striking example of a large enterprise that long relied entirely on internal and short-term sources of funds for expansion. And even Ford found it necessary to finance part of the major expansion program in 1956 and 1957 through a large private placement of debt securities.

The External Sources of Funds for Purchase of Corporate Securities

This chapter has been headed "External Sources of Long-Term Capital." It should be emphasized that there is no single homogeneous market for new issues of corporate securities. Instead, it is more useful to think of the buyers of corporate securities as being grouped in a number of more or less tightly compartmented segments with differing investment objectives and operating under distinctive investment policies and practices. For some of the segments or individual markets, available information permits fairly precise, summary description; in other segments, few data are available, and our comments must be more general and tentative.

The savings of individuals are the most basic source of funds for investment in corporate securities. If individuals in the United States spent all their income for current consumption, few corporate securities could be sold. Indeed, in many of the less developed countries, the inability or unwillingness of the people to forgo current consumption makes it extremely difficult for private industry to accumulate the long-term capital necessary for large-scale and expensive industrial development. In other less developed countries, such as India, the problem of raising funds for private industrial development is further accentuated by a long-standing preference on the part of many of those who have been able to save and accumulate capital for investment in gold, precious jewels, real estate, or other material wealth rather than in intangibles such as stocks and bonds of corporations.

In the United States the people have turned over much of their savings to financial institutions, which have invested the funds entrusted to them. Thus, financial institutions, including insurance companies, savings banks, etc., have been the actual buyers of many of the new securities issued by corporations. Since the financial institutions, other than commercial banks, do not create funds, they must be thought of rather as conduits or intermediaries in the flow of savings from the people into effective investment.

As we shall explain in detail later, a large and generally increasing share of the financial savings of the people reaches the capital markets through financial institutions. But by no means all of the savings flow into institutions for investment by them. Many individuals, particularly the more affluent, buy corporate securities for their own account.

Competing Demands for Savings

Corporations seeking capital through the sale of securities do not represent the only ultimate outlet for savings seeking investment. Instead, corporate demand for capital must compete with several other sectors of demand for the public's savings. The demand from four major noncorporate users of funds, as shown in Table 15–3, has resulted in strong competition for the saver's—or his institutional intermediary's—dollars in recent years.

The demand for mortgage credit to finance individuals' purchases of homes has been particularly strong. The purchase of the record-breaking volume of new homes constructed since World War II has been financed by the buyers largely through borrowing secured by mortgages on the homes. Total mortgage debt outstanding on one- to four-family homes increased from $18.6 billion at the end of 1945 to $205.0 billion on June 30, 1965.[2]

Increasing use by consumers of instalment debt, primarily to finance the purchase of automobiles and other durable goods, has been a smaller but important basic source of demand for credit. New borrowing by consumers has far exceeded their repayment of such debt in most recent years. The net increase in the use of credit by consumers has come to represent a significant but sharply fluctuating demand for capital. In the 10 years 1955–64, consumer credit grew by over $44 billion.

State and local governments have also stepped up their borrowing through bond sales. Capital outlays for such facilities as new public schools and highways are typically financed by bond issues, and the heavy activity in these two fields has been the source of much demand for long-term capital by states, cities, toll road authorities, and other public agencies. Interest income on the bonds sold by the state and local governmental units, unlike the interest on U.S government bonds issued since 1941, is essentially exempt from federal income taxation; and this feature of *municipal securities*—the term applied to securities issued by states and any other governmental unit, other than the federal government—makes them particularly attractive to some investors.

During most of the years since 1945 the U.S. government has operated

---

[2] *Federal Reserve Bulletin*, November, 1965, p. 1589.

TABLE 15–3

MAJOR SECTORS OF THE ECONOMY ABSORBING INVESTMENT AND COMMERCIAL BANK FUNDS, 1955–64

(In Billions of Dollars)

	1955	1956	1957	1958	1959	1960	1961	1962	1963	1964 (Estimated)
Increase in mortgage debt..........	16.2	14.6	12.0	15.3	19.0	16.0	19.5	25.3	29.3	29.5
Increase in consumer credit..........	6.4	3.6	2.6	0.2	6.3	4.5	1.6	5.5	6.7	6.9
Increase in net debt of state and local governments..........	3.4	3.3	4.5	5.5	4.7	3.9	5.2	5.6	7.0	6.5
Increase in publicly held debt of U.S. government and agencies..........	1.6	– 6.1	– 0.0	6.2	10.5	– 2.7	5.9	6.0	2.5	3.0
Net new issues of securities by non-financial corporations..........	6.1	7.2	9.7	8.0	6.4	6.7	7.8	5.6	5.3	8.1

SOURCE: Bankers Trust Company, *The Investment Outlook for 1965* (New York, 1965).

at a cash deficit and issued bonds to raise funds. In other years, notably 1956 and 1960, it operated at a cash surplus and supplied funds to the capital market through retirement of debt held by the public. When the federal government and its agencies were heavy borrowers in periods when the demand for funds from other sectors also became strong, as in 1959, the pressure of total demand for funds was intense. Since financial savings tend to be relatively stable from year to year, total demand can be met only through expansion of the credit supply through the commercial banks, which have a unique capacity to create credit. If the Federal Reserve System, which controls the expansion of commercial bank credit, believes it important to restrain credit expansion for anti-inflationary or other reasons, it may allow interest rates to rise and money to become "tight." Thus, even though a sizable increase in bank lending was permitted, credit tightened and interest rates rose in late 1959. Lesser demands for funds in 1960, particularly from the federal government, and Federal Reserve easing of restraint contributed to much lower interest rates and easier money market conditions in the latter part of 1960.

The main point to be drawn for our purposes from the brief review of data on the demand for capital funds from various sectors of the economy is that corporations, to be successful in raising capital through the sale of securities, must compete with other major claimants for funds. When demand is great and supply is not unlimited, corporations naturally must sweeten the terms of their security wares in order to get the funds they want. At the same time, when funds are harder to get and more costly, the projects calling for more funds can be rigorously scrutinized by business managers and expansion plans curbed in order to lessen the need to raise capital funds under unattractive capital market conditions.

The Institutional Market for Corporate Securities

As we noted earlier, much of the financial savings[3] of the people flows into institutions which have the task of putting it to work. The major financial institutions fall into two main groups—the deposit type, such as commercial banks, savings banks, and savings and loan associations; and the contractual type, such as life insurance companies, corporate pension funds, and governmental unit pension funds. Estimates placed total personal financial savings during the 1950's at $220 billion. Of this total, some 40% was estimated to have flowed into deposit-type institutions, 40% into the contractual type, and the remaining 20% to have been invested directly in securities or through investment companies or personal trust funds.[4] Fortunately, rather reliable data are available as to

---

[3] Investment of savings in tangibles, such as homes and consumer durables, is not included in "financial savings."

[4] Jules I. Bogen, "Trends in the Institutionalization of Savings and in Thrift Institution Policies," *Proceedings of 1960 Conference on Savings and Residential Financing* (Chicago: U.S. Savings and Loan League, 1960).

how the more important institutional investors employ the funds entrusted to them, so that it is possible to assess the importance of the various institutions as suppliers of long-term corporate funds. Further, while the various individual institutions of a particular type do not follow identical investment policies and practices, there is considerable similarity among firms of each type. The various life insurance companies, for example, are subject to much the same governmental regulation and other basic constraints and pressures bearing on the investment of funds under their control.

Institutional investors currently or potentially important as buyers of corporate securities include the following:

1. Life insurance companies.
2. Fire and casualty insurance companies.
3. Private noninsured pension funds.
4. State and local government pension funds.
5. Investment companies.
6. Commercial banks—as investors of deposit funds and as trustees for private trust funds.
7. Mutual savings banks.
8. Savings and loan associations.
9. Religious, educational, and charitable funds.

The Life Insurance Companies as Buyers of Corporate Securities

The life insurance companies of the country represent a large and ever-growing segment of the institutional market for corporate securities. The total assets of the U.S. life insurance companies grew from $19 billion in 1930 to $150 billion on December 31, 1964. This great growth in assets was the result not only of the increase in outstanding policies as more life insurance was sold but, even more importantly, the accumulation of premiums paid in over a period of years before the maturing of the obligation of the insurance company to pay at the death of the insured (or maturing of annuities) on an ordinary life policy. The young man of 30, on an actuarial average, will pay into the insurance company annual premiums which the company can use over the years until his death calls for the policy to be paid. One insurance company executive has estimated that if no further policies were sold, the assets of his company would continue to increase for more than 12 years.

Due to the continued growth, stability, and predictability of their funds, the life insurance companies have been able to invest a major portion of their huge assets, which represent largely reserves held against policy obligations to millions of policyholders, without primary emphasis on liquidity. Since only a small portion of these policies is expected to mature during any year or at any single time, the insurance companies hold only a small percentage of their assets in cash and feel free to invest the bulk of their funds in income-producing securities on a long-term basis.

TABLE 15-4

Distribution of Assets of U.S. Life Insurance Companies
(Dollar Figures in Millions)

	December 31, 1940		December 31, 1950		December 31, 1960		December 31, 1964	
	Amount	Percentage	Amount	Percentage	Amount	Percentage	Amount	Percentage
Cash	*	*	$ 1,005	1.6%	*	*	*	*
U.S. government bonds	$ 5,767	18.7%	13,459	21.0	$ 6,427	5.4%	$ 5,594	3.7%
Foreign government bonds	288	1.0	1,060	1.7	437	0.3	842	0.6
State and local government bonds	2,392	7.8	1,547	2.4	4,576	3.8	5,639	3.8
Railroad bonds	2,830	9.2	3,187	5.0	3,668	3.1	3,327	2.2
Public utility bonds	4,273	13.9	10,587	16.5	16,719	14.0	17,216	11.5
Industrial and other corporate bonds	1,542	5.0	9,526	14.9	26,728	22.4	35,345	23.7
Stocks	605	2.0	2,103	3.3	4,981	4.2	7,938	5.3
Mortgage loans	5,972	19.4	16,102	25.1	41,771	34.9	55,152	36.9
Real estate	2,065	6.7	1,445	2.2	3,765	3.1	4,528	3.0
Policy loans	3,091	10.0	2,413	3.8	5,231	4.4	7,140	4.8
Miscellaneous assets	1,977	6.3	1,586	2.5	5,273	4.4	6,749	4.5
Total assets	$30,802	100.0%	$64,020	100.0%	$119,576	100.0%	$149,470	100.0%

* Included with miscellaneous assets.

Source: Institute of Life Insurance, *1960 Life Insurance Fact Book* (New York, 1960) for years 1940 and 1950; *1965 Life Insurance Fact Book* (New York, 1965) for 1960 and 1964.

In their investment policies, however, the life insurance companies are subject to certain legal restrictions imposed by the states in which they operate. The restrictions are designed to insure protection of principal, and tend to limit investment primarily, although not exclusively, to low-risk debt instruments.

Table 15–4 presents a breakdown of the assets of U.S. life insurance companies as of December 31, 1940, 1950, 1960, and 1964. Especially noteworthy, along with the almost fivefold growth in assets during the 24 years, was the great increase in the life insurance companies' investment in "industrial and other corporate bonds." Total corporate bondholdings

TABLE 15–5

Sources and Uses of Funds, Life Insurance Companies, 1955, 1960–65

(In Billions of Dollars)

	1955	1960	1961	1962	1963	1964 (Estimated)	1965 (Projected)
Sources of funds:							
Increase in admitted assets*...5.7		6.0	6.3	6.9	7.3	7.9	8.4
Uses of funds:							
Mortgages.................3.5		2.6	2.4	2.7	3.6	4.6	4.8
Corporate bonds............1.9		1.4	2.0	1.8	2.1	1.9	2.3
Corporate stocks*..........0.1		0.4	0.4	0.4	0.2	0.5	0.2
All other assets............0.2		1.6	1.5	2.0	1.4	0.9	1.1
	5.7	6.0	6.3	6.9	7.3	7.9	8.4

* Net of appreciation or depreciation in market value.

Source: Bankers Trust Company, *The Investment Outlook for 1961* (New York, 1961), Table 12, and *The Investment Outlook for 1965* (New York, 1965), Table 14.

amounted to nearly $56 billion, or 37.4% of their total assets. In addition, some of the mortgage loans represented intermediate credit to business firms.

The life insurance companies also are seen to have a significant and growing investment in common stocks.

Perhaps even more revealing as to the continuing importance of life insurance companies as buyers of corporate securities are the data on their sources and uses of funds over several years since 1955, presented in Table 15–5. These show only the *net* new funds the insurance companies have to invest. Actually, their annual inflow of funds for investment is swelled as payments are received on outstanding mortgages and other debt securities, and as particular security holdings are sold, mature, or are called for redemption by the issuers. There is compelling evidence that life insurance companies will continue to grow in the future, although at a slower rate; and they should continue as a strong and relatively constant source of demand for those corporate securities which they regard as suitable for their portfolios. For certain types of corporate securities, principally higher-yielding debt issues offered privately, the insurance companies very probably will continue to be the *major* market. Consequently, corporate designers of a bond issue of this type must tailor such security issues in a way that meets the needs and tastes of the investment officials of the insurance companies, for their approval can be the *sine qua non* of a successful placement of the issue.[5]

Fire and Casualty Insurance Companies

Fire and casualty insurance companies are also important investors in corporate securities. Total assets of these companies amounted to $37.1 billion at the end of 1963, up sharply from $5.1 billion in 1940 and $7.9 billion in 1945. In general, these companies are subject to much less rigid legal restrictions in their investment policies than the life insurance companies, and they have invested relatively heavily in common stocks. A breakdown of the holdings of companies representing about 99% of the industry assets showed holdings of corporate bonds of $1.7 billion, or 4.6% of total assets; corporate preferred stocks of $0.9 billion, or 2.4%; and common stocks of $12.0 billion, or 32.3%. Holdings of government bonds were also large.[6]

In recent years, these companies have added to their holdings of common stock at an average rate of about $400 million a year. Additions to corporate bondholdings have been much smaller but significant.[7]

Corporate Pension Funds

Corporate pension funds, which accumulate funds paid in by corporate employers and to a lesser extent by employees, are largely a post-World War II development. The assets being accumulated against present and future obligations to pay pensions to retired employees have grown from a modest figure in 1947 to an estimated $77.2 billion in 1964. A significant portion of these funds, $25.2 billion at the end of 1964, was held by life insurance companies under "insured plans" and generally were commingled for investment purposes with their other assets. A larger amount, $47.3 billion at year-end 1964, was held and administered by trustees, frequently banks, appointed for the purpose.[8] Strictly speaking, it may be inaccurate to classify funds so managed as "institutional"; but to the extent that the pension funds are run by full-time

---

[5] In recent years, some of the largest life insurance companies have confined almost all of their new acquisitions of debt securities to "private placements" and have bought few public issues.

[6] *Best's Fire and Casualty Aggregates and Averages 1964* (New York: Alfred M. Best Co., Inc., 1964).

[7] Bankers Trust Company, *The Investment Outlook for 1965* (New York, 1965), Table 17.

[8] Securities and Exchange Commission, *Statistical Bulletin*, June, 1965, p. 33. This amount includes $4.6 billion in noninsured and mostly noncorporate funds, including those of nonprofit organizations and multiemployer funds.

investment managers on a continuing professional basis, in operation they are handled much like institutional funds, and so we discuss them under the institutional heading.

Most pension fund managers believe that they can, like life insurance companies, invest appropriately in long-term corporate securities. The investment income of pension trusts is free of federal income tax. Table 15–6 shows the distribution of assets of noninsured pension funds on

TABLE 15–6

DISTRIBUTION OF ASSETS OF PRIVATE NONINSURED
PENSION FUNDS, DECEMBER 31, 1964

(In Millions of Dollars)

	Book Value*	Percentage of Total	Market Value	Percentage of Total
Cash and deposits............	$ 892	1.7%	$ 892	1.4%
U.S. government securities......	3,069	5.9	3,039	4.8
Corporate bonds...............	21,206	40.9	20,536	32.4
Preferred stock...............	654	1.3	668	1.0
Common stock................	20,836	40.1	32,859	51.9
Mortgages...................	2,746	5.3	2,773	4.4
Other assets..................	2,509	4.8	2,585	4.1
Total assets............	$51,912	100.0%	$63,352	100.0%

* Book value usually equals cost.
   Figures include all private pension plans other than those administered by insurance companies. They include multiemployer plans, nonprofit organizations, and deferred profit-sharing plans, but not health, welfare, and bonus plans.
   SOURCE: Securities and Exchange Commission, *Statistical Bulletin,* June, 1965, p. 32.

December 31, 1964. Note the heavy emphasis on corporate securities, including common stocks.

The chief significance of the pension funds as investors in corporate securities lies not so much in the size of their present holdings as in their impressive growth in recent years and the currently large additions to their holdings through new purchases each year. The noninsured pension funds alone between 1960 and 1964 added more than $5.5 billion to their holdings of corporate bonds and $10.0 billion to their investments in corporate stocks. In 1964 alone, these funds increased their corporate bond portfolio by $1.6 billion and their common stocks by $2.7 billion.[9]

Most corporate pension funds were established as a result of collective bargaining with labor unions, and pressures from unions should tend toward increasing the long-term importance of the pension funds. For this and other impressive reasons, we anticipate that the pension funds will continue to grow robustly and that they will represent a continuing, important source of funds for investment in corporate securities. If the

[9] *Ibid.,* p. 32.

trends of recent years continue, these funds will be especially important buyers of common stocks.

State and Local Government Retirement Funds

Like the corporate pension funds, the retirement funds of state and local governments are accumulated in order to meet obligations to pay pensions. The total amount of such funds at the end of 1964 was estimated at $29.9 billion.[10] In 1964, payments into such funds and investment income were estimated to total $5.2 billion, while benefit payments amounted to only $1.9 billion.[11] Until relatively recent years, their assets were invested predominantly in U.S. government and state and municipal bonds. More recently, the investment managers of many funds have taken advantage of eased restrictions on their investing policies to seek the higher investment returns available from corporate bond issues. In 1964 these funds added $2.6 billion of corporate bonds and notes to their portfolios.[12] There is every reason to expect that these funds will continue to be an important and growing source of demand for corporate debt issues.

Some funds have begun to buy common stocks, but their total holdings of stocks were still small at year-end 1964.

Parenthetically, social security and retirement funds administered by the U.S. government can be acknowledged as representing a huge and growing accumulation of savings. These funds are invested exclusively in U.S. government securities. As of September 30, 1965, these funds, along with other U.S. government agencies and trust funds, held $63.6 billion of U.S. government securities.[13] This compares with a total figure for such holdings of $27 billion at the end of 1945. Since they have absorbed U.S. government bonds that otherwise might well have been sold in competition with corporate securities, these funds have had a significant, though indirect, effect on the markets for corporate securities.

Investment Companies

On June 30, 1964, 731 companies engaged primarily in the business of investing in securities, including 72 small business investment companies, were registered with the Securities and Exchange Commission as investment companies.[14] Of these 617 were active. Known also as investment trusts, these firms have grown sharply in recent years, primarily through

---

[10] Ibid., p. 33.

[11] Bankers Trust Company, The Investment Outlook for 1965 (New York, 1965), Table 16.

[12] Securities and Exchange Commission, Statistical Bulletin, June, 1965, p. 34.

[13] Federal Reserve Bulletin, November, 1965, p. 1580.

[14] Securities and Exchange Commission, Thirtieth Annual Report, 1964 (Washington, D.C.: U.S. Government Printing Office, 1965), p. 110.

CHART 15–1

ᴇꜱᴛɪᴍᴀᴛᴇᴅ Mᴀʀᴋᴇᴛ Vᴀʟᴜᴇ ᴏꜰ Iɴᴠᴇꜱᴛᴍᴇɴᴛ Cᴏᴍᴘᴀɴʏ Aꜱꜱᴇᴛꜱ ᴀꜱ ᴏꜰ Jᴜɴᴇ 30
(In Millions of Dollars)

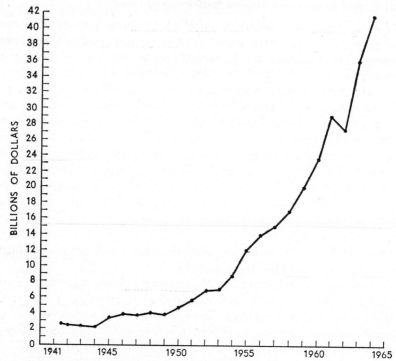

SOURCE: Securities and Exchange Commission, *Thirtieth Annual Report, 1964* (Washington, D.C.: U.S. Government Printing Office, 1964), p. 112.

the appreciation in value of their holdings but also, in the case of the *open-end* companies,[15] through sale to the public of their own securities— the proceeds of which are in turn invested in other corporate securities. Chart 15–1 shows the growth in the market value of their assets over recent years. The market value of the assets of registered companies

---

[15] Investment companies are of several types, two of which, the *open-end* and the *closed-end* types, are of especial importance. The open-end companies, of which Investors Mutual, Inc., with assets of $2,674 million on December 31, 1964, is the largest, have no fixed number of shares of common stock. Instead, they offer new common shares for sale continuously. The price of the shares is established by the current per share value of the company's assets plus a "loading" to cover sales commissions and other expenses of selling the new shares. The open-end companies typically contract to repurchase their shares at the per share asset value of the investment company on the date they are presented for redemption. In recent years the sales of new shares of the open-end companies have far exceeded the redemptions, so that the assets available for investment have grown for this reason, as well as because of market appreciation of holdings over the years.

The closed-end trusts operate with a fixed number of shares. These shares are traded on the stock exchanges or over the counter and may sell at wide discounts or premiums over their asset values. Tri-Continental Corporation, which had assets with market values of $545 million on December 31, 1964, is an example of a closed-end investment company.

amounted to some \$41.6 billion on June 30, 1964, compared with \$2.5 billion on June 30, 1941. In contrast to the policies of other institutional investors, American investment companies consistently have placed the bulk of their assets in corporate common stocks, primarily those of large, prospering companies—the "blue chips" of the market.

Table 15–7 gives a breakdown of the portfolios of 11 important investment trusts at the end of 1954, 1959, and 1963.

TABLE 15–7

AVERAGE DISTRIBUTION OF THE PORTFOLIOS OF
11 INVESTMENT COMPANIES AT YEAR END

Type of Investment	1954	1959	1963
Cash................................	5.3%	3.8%	3.9%
Bonds and preferred stock...............	8.7	5.1	3.6
Common stock........................	86.0	91.1	92.5
	100.0%	100.0%	100.0%

The leading open-end investment companies have developed aggressive sales outlets for their own securities and—barring a major, continuing decline in the market values of common stocks—should continue to represent a growing sector of demand for common stocks of higher investment quality.

The Commercial Banks

The commercial banks of the country have long been important investors in bonds. Most of the banks' bond portfolio has consisted of U.S. government issues. On December 31, 1964, the banks had invested in U.S. government and federal agency bonds \$66.6 billion of their total assets of \$348.4 billion. The banks also were major holders—\$33.6 billion—of tax-exempt securities. Banks have legal sanction to invest in corporate bonds, and during the 1920's and certain other less recent periods, they represented an important market for corporate bonds. At year-end 1964 the banks had only \$900 million of their total assets in corporate bonds, and there was nothing to indicate an upsurge of bank interest in corporate bonds as an outlet for their own funds.[16]

Speaking generally, the commercial banks are not permitted to invest bank funds in common stocks.

Earlier we referred to the fact that banks administer as trustees a very substantial portion of noninsured corporate pension funds.

The assets at market value held in personal trusts administered by commercial banks have grown sharply in recent years—from \$49.7

---

[16] Federal Deposit Insurance Corporation, *Annual Report, 1964* (Washington, D.C.: U.S. Government Printing Office, 1965), Table 105.

billion at year-end 1958 to $82.2 billion at year-end 1963. The distribution of the assets of these funds is shown in Table 15–8.

The very large and increasing investment of personal trust funds in common stocks is strikingly apparent in Table 15–8. Banks buying for trust accounts represent the largest institutional investment source of demand for common stocks, outstripping even the investment companies.

Also especially noteworthy from Table 15–8 is the very heavy use made of the tax-exempt bonds of states and municipalities. This reflects

TABLE 15–8

ASSET HOLDINGS IN PERSONAL TRUST ACCOUNTS
ADMINISTERED BY COMMERCIAL BANKS
(In Millions of Dollars)

Type of Asset	December 31 1958		December 31 1963	
Common stock	$30,664.5	61.7%	$54,017.1	65.7%
State and municipal securities	7,791.2	15.7	11,644.0	14.1
Participation in common trust funds	2,122.8	4.3	4,749.3	5.8
Corporate bonds and debentures	2,335.3	4.7	3,032.5	3.7
U.S. government securities	2,513.1	5.1	2,772.7	3.4
Preferred stock	1,290.9	2.6	1,315.6	1.6
Mortgages	671.0	1.3	941.7	1.1
Cash	384.6	0.8	552.0	0.7
All other assets	1,906.9	3.8	3,215.9	3.9
Total	$49,680.3	100.0%	$82,240.8	100.0%

SOURCE: Gordon A. McLean, "Report of National Survey of Personal Trust Accounts," *The Trust Bulletin*, published by the Trust Division of the American Bankers Association, Vol. XLIV, No. 4 (December, 1964), p. 9.

the fact that the income beneficiaries of trusts commonly are in high income tax brackets and they can net more income after taxes from the tax-exempt interest available from municipal bonds than on the higher-yielding but taxable return available from governments and corporates. In other words, investors in a high tax bracket normally find tax-exempt bonds more attractive investments than U.S. government or corporate bonds.

The banks have had some success in devising trust arrangements especially for persons with a small or moderate amount of capital for management. If continued progress along these lines can be made, the growth of bank-administered trust funds will be very much greater than if the banks are forced, for cost and other reasons, to restrict their interest to trust accounts of $100,000 or more.

Mutual Savings Banks

The mutual savings banks, largely concentrated in New England, New York, and Pennsylvania, had assets amounting to nearly $54.2 billion on

December 31, 1964. The mutual savings banks have invested primarily in home mortgage loans and in U.S. government bonds. Although subject to close legal restriction in their investment in corporate securities, a breakdown of their assets at the end of 1964 showed holdings of $3.8 billion in corporate bonds and $1.3 billion in corporate stocks.[17] Should the recently abundant opportunities for investment in home mortgages decline importantly, the savings banks may well prove a more important market for corporate securities, mainly high-quality bonds of intermediate and long maturities.

Savings and Loan Associations

In recent years savings and loan associations have been particularly effective in competing for individuals' savings. Their total assets on June 30, 1965, amounted to almost $124.5 billion.[18] Regarded by many savers as the approximate equivalent of savings banks, the savings and loan associations have invested predominantly in home mortgages and to a much lesser extent in government bonds. To date, their investment in corporate securities has been negligible, but they represent a possible source of demand for corporate securities should the supply of mortgage investments available to them shrink greatly.

Religious, Educational, and Charitable Funds

The assets of the various nonprofit institutions of the country are largely invested in corporate securities. They are relatively free of income taxation and of legal restrictions on their investment policies, and their security holdings include substantial amounts of common and preferred stocks as well as bonds. An analysis of the investment portfolios of 67 college and university endowment funds on June 30, 1964, showed 27.8% of the total market value of the endowment funds invested in bonds, 1.1% in preferred stocks, and 58.2% in common stocks. The total market value of the 67 endowment funds was $5.67 billion.[19]

The assets of other nonprofit organizations total several billion dollars and also include a substantial amount of corporate equities.

The inflow of funds to the nonprofit funds is relatively slow, so that they are net buyers of corporate securities only in moderate amounts.

Summary of the Institutional Market

Before turning to a review of the noninstitutional, or individual, investor segments of the market, we can appropriately summarize some key points about the institutional markets for corporate securities. We have reviewed briefly the investment practices of the institutions with

---

[17] National Association of Mutual Savings Banks, *National Fact Book* (New York, 1965).

[18] *Federal Reserve Bulletin*, November, 1965, p. 1577.

[19] Boston Fund, *The 1964 Study of College and University Endowment Funds* (Boston, 1964), p. 5.

important amounts of funds to invest in corporate securities along with other segments—pension funds and institutionally administered personal trust funds—of the market that are professionally managed. We have seen that the institutions, broadly considered, represent a very important market for corporate bonds. Further, the institutions are continuing to buy a dominant portion of new issues of debt securities, and there is evi-

TABLE 15–9

ESTIMATED OWNERSHIP OF CORPORATE SECURITIES
BY U.S. INVESTORS, DECEMBER 31, 1961

(In Billions of Dollars)

	Bonds and Notes		Common and Preferred Stock	
	Market Value	Percentage of Total	Market Value	Percentage of Total
Life insurance companies	$ 50.6	47.2%	$ 6.3	1.2%
Other insurance companies	1.6	1.5	9.3	1.7
Noninsured private pension funds	15.0	14.0	21.0	3.9
State and local government pension funds	9.0	8.4	0.7	0.1
Investment companies	1.7	1.6	29.2	5.3
Commercial banks	0.8	0.7	0.2	—
Mutual savings banks	3.7	3.4	0.9	0.2
Personal trust funds	3.4	3.2	53.1	9.7
Fraternal orders	1.5	1.4	0.1	—
Institutional investors	$ 87.3	81.4%	$120.8	22.1%
Foreign	0.6	0.6	11.9	2.2
Domestic individuals and nonprofit institutions	19.3	18.0	413.5*	75.7
Total	$107.2	100.0%	$546.2	100.0%

* Includes $29.9 billion of investment company shares.
† SOURCE: *Report of the Special Study of Securities Markets of the Securities and Exchange Commission* (Washington, D.C.: U.S. Government Printing Office, 1963), Part 2, p. 960.

dence to support the view that they will continue to be the principal purchasers of new issues in the future.

Table 15–9 presents estimates of the holdings of corporate bonds and notes and of stocks by the institutions we have described, at the end of 1961. It should be noted that the holdings of colleges and other nonprofit institutions are lumped with the holdings of "domestic individuals." This tabulation highlights the importance as bond buyers of life insurance companies (which hold nearly one half of the total), noninsured private pension funds, and state and local government pension funds. Each of these has continued to absorb large quantities of corporate bonds in the years after 1961.

Individual investors are shown to hold a significant ($19.3 billion) amount of bonds and notes, but this represented only 18% of the total outstanding.

The pattern of ownership of stocks is shown to be very different. The stockholdings of individuals are of dominant weight—$413.5 billion, or 75.7% of the $546.2 billion total. Institutions were estimated to hold $120.8 billion, or 22.1% of the total. This is generally in line with more recent New York Stock Exchange estimates of institutional holdings of stocks listed for trading on that Exchange. At year-end 1964, institutions, excluding bank-administered personal trust funds, were estimated to hold 20.4% of the total listed stocks.

The table brings out the particular importance of personal trust funds, investment companies, and pension funds as owners of stock. The life and the fire and casualty insurance companies also are shown to be important investors in common stocks.

As we pointed out earlier, the value of the stockholdings of personal trusts, investment companies and pension funds, and other of the institutions, has increased sharply in recent years. The rise in value is in part a reflection of the general rise in the level of stock prices, but it also reflects the investment of substantial amounts of new money in stocks.

Other evidence from a variety of sources also suggests that institutional investors have been absorbing an increasing percentage of equity issues in recent years and that their role as current buyers of equities is greater than that suggested by data on their existing holdings.

Individual investors, on the other hand, appear to have been net sellers of stocks in recent years. Consequently, institutions are increasing in relative as well as absolute importance as buyers of corporate equities.

The Noninstitutional Market for Corporate Securities

Now, let us turn to what can be loosely termed the "individual investor" segment of the market. As we said earlier, much investment in corporate securities is made by individuals directly, using their own funds. Unfortunately, fully reliable and detailed statistical data on this important part of the market for corporate securities do not exist; and since it is very difficult to assemble such data, the deficiency of precise information in the area will probably continue, despite some helpful studies in prospect. Consequently, the data—and the conclusions gingerly drawn—that will be presented must be regarded as tentative and highly approximate.

One inescapable characteristic of the individual investor segment is its heterogeneous nature. The investment objectives of the various individual holders of corporate securities, for example, are widely varied, running all the way from the needs of the almost impecunious widow, who desires most the protection of her small principal but who also needs income, to that of the speculator, who is willing to risk his money on the most hazardous issue in hope of large return through capital gains.

The degree of investment sophistication and skill is also extremely varied. The Kansas farmer with a large supply of extra cash from the last wheat crop obviously is a prospective investor quite different from the seasoned speculator who has survived many years on Wall Street. The diverse character of the individual market in this respect contrasts with the institutional market, in which it is presumed that most important firms have the resources and personnel for careful, informed investment management.

Table 15–9 brought out the importance of individual investors as owners of equities. Now let us look at data regarding the extent to which

TABLE 15–10

ANNUAL ADDITIONS TO THE CORPORATE SECURITY HOLDINGS OF INDIVIDUALS
(In Billions of Dollars)

	Bonds and Notes	Investment Company Shares	Other Stocks	Total
1955................	1.0	0.8	0.4	2.2
1956................	0.4	1.0	0.6	2.0
1957................	1.3	1.1	0.4	2.8
1958................	1.3	1.6	−0.3	2.6
1959................	0.1	1.7	−0.9	0.9
1960................	1.5	1.5	−1.9	1.1
1961................	0.1	2.7	−2.3	0.5
1962................	−0.2	1.8	−3.8	−2.2
1963................	0.2	1.2	−4.1	−2.7
1964................	0.3	1.8	−2.7	−0.6

SOURCE: Securities Exchange Commission, *Statistical Bulletin*, July issues, 1959, 1961, 1964, and 1965.

individuals have been net buyers or sellers of stocks in recent years. Table 15–10 gives SEC estimates of individuals' net investment or disinvestment in recent years. Particularly noteworthy has been the continuing acquisition of investment company shares and the net selling of other stocks by the public. Note the particularly heavy disinvestment in and after 1962—a year in which a market decline hit individual speculators in smaller and newer issues especially hard.

At the same time that individuals have been sellers of common stocks on an overall net basis, individuals have been the initial buyers of a high percentage of new common stock issues. A study of purchase transactions in the case of new common issues totaling $784 million in January–March, 1962, showed that individuals purchased directly 72.6% of the total amount. The average purchase transaction by individuals was only $2,200.[20]

Now let us look more closely at the stockholding public. One of the more recent studies is that of the New York Stock Exchange. On the basis of a study in early 1965, it concluded that some 20 million individuals

[20] Irwin Friend, *Investment Banking and the New Issues Market: Summary Volume* (Philadelphia: University of Pennsylvania, 1965), Table 12, p. 51.

held shares in publicly held corporations. One out of every six U.S. adults owned common stock. The total number of shareholders represented more than 13% of the population in New England and in the Middle Atlantic states, but only 5.8% in the South Central region.[21]

While the total number of shareholders sounds impressive, stock-holders represent just 10.2% of the total population; in contrast, about 62% of the total population owned life insurance policies in 1965.

Further, the total number of shareholders includes many whose holdings are very small. Available data indicate clearly that the bulk of

Spending Units with Income of:	Approximate Percentage of All Spending Units	Cumulative Percentage of Marketable Stock Owned by Private Investors
$50,000 and over	0.1%	35%
$25,000 and over	0.5	50
$15,000 and over	1.0	65
$10,000 and over	3.0	75

the stockholdings of individuals is held by a relatively small number of investors in corporate securities is shown in the brief table on this page, estimated that in 1949, family spending units with incomes of $50,000 and over, which represented only 0.1% of the family spending units in the country, held about 35% of all the marketable stock owned by private investors. Further evidence of the importance of high-income groups as investors in corporate securities is shown in the brief table on this page, taken from data in this study.

The study, while recognizing that taxes have substantially cut into the incomes of upper-income groups, did not find evidence to support the view that these taxes prevent upper-income groups from investing current savings in equity securities.

Much more recent evidence that high-income groups continue to be the major holders of corporate stocks is available in data based on income tax returns. Such data, in the form of the percentage of dividend payments received by various income groups, are given in Table 15–11. Note that taxpaying units with incomes of over $20,000 received 56.2% of total dividend payments in 1963, though their total income was but 12.0% of the total adjusted gross income.

Perhaps significant was the correlation of share ownership with

---

[21] *Shareownership U.S.A.: 1965 Census of Shareowners* (New York: New York Stock Exchange, 1965).

[22] J. Keith Butters, Lawrence E. Thompson, and Lynn L. Bollinger, *Effects of Taxation: Investments by Individuals* (Boston: Division of Research, Harvard Business School, 1953), p. 25.

TABLE 15-11

DIVIDENDS AND INTEREST RECEIVED BY INDIVIDUALS IN VARIOUS INCOME GROUPS, AS REPORTED IN INCOME TAX RETURNS FOR 1963

(Dollar Figures in Millions)

Adjusted Gross Income Group	Adjusted Gross Income	Percentage of Total	Cumulative Percentage	Dividend Income (after exclusions)*	Percentage of Total	Cumulative Percentage	Interest Received	Percentage of Total	Cumulative Percentage
Under $5,000	$ 79,491†	21.6%	21.6%	$ 1,213	10.6%	10.6%	$2,857	31.0%	31.0%
$5,000–$10,000	156,702	42.5	64.1	1,512	13.2	23.8	2,523	27.4	58.4
$10,000–$20,000	88,240‡	23.9	88.0	2,291‡	20.0	43.8	2,073‡	22.5	80.9
$20,000–$50,000	29,916	8.1	96.1	2,781	24.3	68.1	1,195	13.0	93.9
$50,000–$100,000	8,651	2.3	98.4	1,598	13.9	82.0	365	4.0	97.9
$100,000–$500,000	4,537	1.2	99.6	1,519	13.3	95.3	175	1.9	99.8
$500,000–$1,000,000	537	0.2	99.8	243	2.1	97.4	13	0.1	99.9
$1,000,000 or more	704	0.2	100.0	295	2.6	100.0	11	0.1	100.0
Total	$368,778	100.0%		$11,452	100.0%		$9,212	100.0%	

* Taxable and nontaxable returns.

† Gross income of $80,983 million less gross deficit of $1,492 million.

‡ May include some nontaxable returns in groups over $20,000.

SOURCE OF DATA: U.S. Treasury Department, Internal Revenue Service, *Preliminary Report, Statistics of Income—1963: Individual Income Tax Returns*, Table 2.

educational achievement, revealed in the NYSE study. Of the total population of college graduates, 59.1% were shareholders, while only 5.6% of the adults who had not finished high school owned shares.

As might be expected, share ownership was most common among individuals in the 45- to 54-year age group. Of the population in this age group, 21.8% owned stock.

Interestingly enough, and for whatever significance it has, women shareholders outnumbered the men, 51% of the adult shareholders being women, mostly housewives.

Chapter 16

Tapping the Sources of Long-Term Capital

EARLIER, we pictured the relative importance to American corporations in recent years of capital raised through the sale of new issues of securities and sketched in broad-brush terms the nature of the ultimate market for these securities. In this chapter we shall discuss the major means by which corporations issuing new securities reach buyers for their securities and thus avail themselves of long-term capital. Although numerous methods of distribution of corporate securities have been developed, our discussion will center on the few basic methods that are of particular importance.

Relation of the Markets for Outstanding Securities to the Distribution of New Issues

It is important at this point that the reader carefully distinguishes between the sale by corporations of newly issued securities, or *primary* distribution, and the trading of *outstanding*, or "old" issues in the *secondary* markets like the New York Stock Exchange. Our major focus in this chapter is on primary distribution of securities, but later in this chapter we shall look briefly at the secondary markets and their somewhat distinctive activities, institutions, and mechanisms.

The existence and operations of the secondary markets are important to, though distinct from, the primary distribution of securities. Each new issue of securities competes, directly or indirectly, with outstanding securities for the ultimate investor's favor and dollars. The terms and price of new offerings must be made temptingly attractive in comparison with those of outstanding securities which can be bought in the secondary markets. Also, the attractiveness of a newly issued security to potential investors is enhanced by the prospect that a good secondary market for the securities will develop. In other words, good secondary markets add the valuable feature of potential marketability to securities purchased upon initial or primary distribution.

Major Types of New Offerings

Most new securities for cash sale are sold through one of three basic methods of distribution:

1. *A public offering involving the issue of subscription rights to existing shareholders.* The rights to subscribe to the new offering, typically at a price well below the market for outstanding shares, are extended pro rata to existing shareholders. The subscription rights typically are transferable, so that a shareholder who does not want more shares can sell his rights to someone who does want to subscribe.

2. *A public offering without rights,* in which the new issue is offered for sale to the public.

3. *Private placements,* which represent the offering of an entire issue to a single or limited number of investors who buy as ultimate investors rather than for early resale. This method is used primarily for new issues of debt securities.

Corporations have used the public offering method predominantly in marketing new issues of equity securities. According to Securities and Exchange Commission data, about 91% of all corporate equity issues[1] between January 1, 1960 and June 30, 1964 were public offerings. We shall defer further discussion of recent practice in the public sale of common stock with and without subscription rights until a later point in this chapter.

Corporations have made heavy use of private placement in selling debt issues. Chart 16–1 shows the amount of corporate debt issues sold in recent years and the portions placed privately. As can be seen from the chart, private placements of debt have grown particularly sharply since 1960, and have exceeded public sales in each year since 1960. Through December 28, 1,074 private sales of bonds amounting to $6,791 million were reported in 1965, along with 69 private sales of preferred stock ($321 million) and 8 private sales of new common ($11 million).[2]

Industrial concerns have made especially heavy use of direct placement. The growth of private placements has been facilitated by the continued growth and importance of institutions—notably life insurance companies, state and local pension funds, and noninsured private pension funds—as buyers of debt securities. The larger of these represent an identifiable, relatively concentrated market, and, in recent years an especially approachable and receptive one, as these institutions have been eager to garner the somewhat higher yields of private issues over public issues.

Why have corporations been willing to offer higher yields to private

---

[1] The term "equity issues" encompasses both common stock and preferred stock. The amount of preferred issues was a small part of the total.

[2] *Investment Dealers' Digest,* December 27, 1965, p. 11.

CHART 16–1

Private Placement and Public Offerings of New Corporate Debt Issues

(In Millions of Dollars)

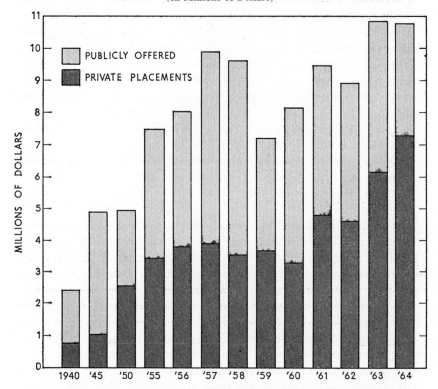

Source: Securities and Exchange Commission, *Thirtieth Annual Report, 1964* (Washington, D.C.: U.S. Government Printing Office, 1965), p. 179; and Securities and Exchange Commission, *Statistical Bulletin,* August, 1965.

buyers than they would have to offer if bonds were sold publicly?[3] Several advantages of private sale appear of importance to corporate issuers. First, the registration and disclosure procedures of the Securities and Exchange Commission, which are a necessary part of public offerings, are not required if the securities are sold privately. Avoiding these procedures may save time, trouble, and some expense. Second, the issuer may be able to arrange more satisfactory covenants in direct negotiation with the informed and sophisticated institutional buyers than would be the case in a public offering. Third, the mechanics of making agreed changes in the terms of private placements are not difficult; in contrast it may be extremely difficult to garner the necessary consents of scattered public

[3] The public offering also may afford the issuing corporation opportunities over the life of the issue to buy up and retire bonds at favorable prices. Depressed market prices are likely if the level of interest rates rises above the interest rate of the bond. In the case of bonds placed privately, there is no market for the securities, and so parallel opportunities do not exist.

bondholders to even minor changes. Fourth, the costs of issue are usually significantly smaller under private placement, since the costs of distribution involved in issues to the public are largely avoided. While the costs of public bond issues are less than those of public common stock offerings, they can be material. We shall speak later in more detail regarding costs. Fifth, under private placement there is somewhat more flexibility in arranging for instalment or deferred takedowns or for other special needs. For example, in December, 1965, Southland Paper Mills, Inc., with the agency help of Lehman Brothers, arranged the sale to institutional investors of $35 million of 5¼% notes due in 1986. Of the total, $15 million was to be taken down in the third quarter of 1966 and another $15 million in the first half of 1967. In addition, Southland had the option of borrowing an additional $5 million from the institutional buyers of the other notes.[4]

The Role of Investment Bankers in Distribution of New Issues

The issuing corporation usually is free to undertake without outside help all aspects of the job of designing a new security issue and selling it to investors; in most cases, however, it has enlisted the help of investment bankers who are specialists in the marketing of new security issues. Basically, investment banking firms perform a distributive function, acting as middlemen between issuing corporations and the ultimate buyers of new securities. In recent years investment banking firms have been willing to make their services available on a variety of different arrangements, although several are of particular importance.

In outline form the major arrangements under which investment bankers assist in the distributive functions are:

1. Underwritten issues:
   a) Fully underwritten public issues.
      (1) Negotiated underwritings.
      (2) Underwritings won under competitive biddings.
   b) Standby underwriting of issues offered with subscription rights.
2. Issues in which investment bankers work on an agency basis:
   a) Nonunderwritten agency basis on sales to the public.
   b) Agency basis in private placements.

Particularly complete and reliable data concerning the relative importance of the various major arrangements are available for the years 1935–49, and these are summarized in Table 16–1. It will be noted that more than half of the issues in these years were on an underwritten basis.

While equally complete and parallel data are not available for the years since 1949, the basic pattern of investment banking activity has not changed greatly from that reflected in Table 16–1.

---

[4] *Investment Dealers' Digest,* December 20, 1965, p. 14.

TABLE 16-1

NUMBER OF NEW SECURITY ISSUES BY TYPE OF TRANSACTION, 1935-49

	Bonds*		Preferred		Common		All Securities	
	Num- ber of Issues	% of Total Number	Num- ber of Issues	% of Total Number	Num- ber of Issues	% of Total Number	Num- ber of Issues	% of Total Number
Total...........	3,215	100%	973	100%	718	100%	4,906	100%
Underwritten negotiated......	856	26.6%	706	72.6%	438	61.0%	2,000	40.8%
Underwritten public sealed bidding........	502	15.6	89	9.1	32	4.5	623	12.7
Total Under- written.....	1,358	42.2%	795	81.7%	470	65.5%	2,623	53.5%
Nonunderwritten agency.........	32	1.0%	47	4.8%	62	8.6%	141	2.9%
Nonunderwritten, no investment banker.,.......	42	1.3	45	4.6	162	22.6	249	5.1
Total Nonun- derwritten...	74	2.3%	92	9.5%	224	31.2%	390	7.9%
Private placement agency.........	818	25.4%	52	5.3%	6	0.8%	876	17.9%
Private placement, no investment banker.........	965	30.0	34	3.5	18	2.5	1,017	20.7
Total Private Placements	1,783	55.5%	86	8.8%	24	3.3%	1,893	38.6%

* Including bonds, debentures, notes, etc.
SOURCE: *United States of America* v. *Henry S. Morgan, Harold Stanley, et al., Doing Business as Morgan Stanley & Co., et al.*, U.S. District Court for Southern New York, Civil No. 43–757, Defendants' Preliminary Memorandum for the Court, p. 24.

Underwritten Public Issues—Negotiated Deals

In underwritten issues, one or a group of investment banking firms working together on an issue assure the issuing firm a definite sum of money for the issue at a definite time. The underwriting investment banking firms are willing to back their judgment as to the marketability of the issue at the proposed public offering price by agreeing to purchase the entire issue at a firm, agreed price, assuming the risks that they will be unable to resell the issue to the public. In other words, they assure, or *underwrite*, the success of the issue, and add the function of risk taking to their selling function.

At this point, it is well to distinguish between underwritten issues in which the arrangements between issuer and investment bankers as to price and other key factors are arrived at by *negotiation* between the parties and those other underwritten issues in which the terms of the new security issue are drawn up by the issuer and the issue is placed with underwriting investment bankers on the basis of *public sealed bids.* Under the public sealed bid arrangements, commonly known as *competitive bid* deals, the issue is, in effect, put up for sale to the highest responsible bidder. Use of competitive bidding is confined almost exclusively to security issues of regulated industries or governmental units.

Investment banking sources reported that 75 issues of bonds, including 28 issues of debentures convertible into common stock, totaling $1,640 million, were sold publicly through negotiated underwritings in 1964. In the same year 50 underwritten bond issues totaling $1,439 million were sold at competitive bid. The amount of negotiated public bond offerings in 1963 also exceeded the amount sold through competitive bid.[5]

The negotiated arrangement is the traditional form of underwriting and is favored by investment bankers generally. In a negotiated underwritten public offering, the services of the investment bankers may be utilized, to the extent the issuer wishes, in every stage of the process from the design of the security through its actual distribution to the public. An investment banking firm, which will act as manager of the syndicate of banking firms it selects to assist in the underwriting and sales operation, will be chosen at a very early stage. Morgan Stanley & Company, for example, from 1935 through 1964, served as manager or comanager in public offerings totaling more than $23 billion. The firm selected as manager or comanager undertakes a searching and detailed investigation and analysis of the affairs of the issuer, with especial emphasis on its current and future financing needs. Working with company officers, the managing firm attempts to work out details of an issue which effectively reconcile the objectives of the issuer and the requirements of investors under the anticipated market conditions upon offering of the security. Typically, the investment bankers assist corporate management in reaching decisions as to the type or types of securities to be offered, their provisions, and the timing of the offering. The banker and his counsel also help in the drafting of the registration statement and prospectus usually required by the Securities and Exchange Commission, and in the filing of other documents necessary to qualify the issue legally for sale. Since most companies undertake public issues only infrequently, the market *expertise* of the investment bankers can be highly valuable to the issuer.

About the time the prospective new security takes tentative form, the investment banker undertakes to line up other investment banking firms to join in a group of firms or *syndicate* to share the risks of underwriting and the job of selling. In a large issue the syndicate will usually include many firms. The size of the syndicate formed and the number of selling dealers enlisted tend to increase with the size of the issue. In the huge offering of Ford Motor Company common stock owned by The Ford Foundation—10.2 million shares sold to the public at $64.50 for a total of $657.9 million—in January, 1956, seven firms served as comanagers of the underwriting syndicate, which was composed of 722 firms. In

---

[5] Investment Bankers Association of America, *Statistical Bulletin*, March, 1965.

addition, the syndicate employed the services of 1,000 security dealers in selling the issue. The issue was quickly oversubscribed.

Firms joining the syndicate as underwriters also act as selling firms; in large deals, additional firms commonly are brought in only as selling dealers, as was the case in the Ford issue. Because the security issues often are large in relation to the capital resources of individual investment banking firms[6] and because it is helpful in tapping as wide a market as possible to have a number of firms with customers throughout the country, syndicate arrangements under which various firms band together on a single issue have become typical for all but the smallest issues. The composition of the syndicates and the percentage participation of each firm differ from one issue to another, but certain firms tend to work together on many issues.

Tentative understandings as to probable price both to the company and to the public (thus approximating the anticipated *banker's spread*, or gross margin of profit, on the deal) may be reached early in the discussions. Just before the registration statement becomes effective and the issue legally can be sold, definite prices and terms of the issue are established in final negotiation between bankers and issuer.

To be fully satisfactory to all concerned, such a pattern of operation requires a high degree of mutual confidence and trust on the part of all parties. One of the prime assets of a successful investment banking firm is its reputation for fair and effective operation over the years, and such reputations are jealously guarded. This feature also helps to explain why many issuing firms have developed close relationships with particular investment banking houses and continue to do business with them in successive issues over long periods of years.

The investment bankers make strenuous efforts to sell new issues quickly—both to achieve rapid turnover of their capital and to minimize the risk that a downturn in the market will leave the securities "on the bankers' shelves" at what become unattractively high prices. Despite the bankers' best efforts at close pricing, relatively minor downturns in the market may leave an issue unsold at the issue price, necessitating either sale at reduced prices or holding for an upturn in prices, which may not materialize, and in any case ties up the investment bankers' capital. The spread between the price that the bankers pay the issuers and the resale price to the public is usually so small that even a small break from planned prices may result in losses to the bankers.

---

[6] This is not to imply that the capital resources of the larger investment banking firms are small in absolute terms. Thirty-nine firms were reported to have, in 1962, capital in the firm of over $10 million. These firms accounted for 31% of the retail sales and 20% of the sales to dealers of new issues publicly offered. These large firms also did 63% of the private placement agency work done by investment bankers.

Source of Data: Irwin Friend, *Investment Banking and the New Issues Market: Summary Volume* (Philadelphia: Wharton School of Finance and Commerce, University of Pennsylvania, 1965), Table I.

It is common practice for the syndicate manager to retain a portion of the securities for sale to institutional buyers for the "pot," that is, the account of the whole underwriting syndicate. This is in addition to the managing firm's own selling commitment.

In compliance with regulations that control the practice, the manager for the syndicate generally is authorized to—and when the occasion requires, does—undertake buying and selling in the market designed to *stabilize* the market price of the security during the period in which the new securities are being sold by the syndicate. Profits and losses stemming from the stabilizing operations are for the account of the whole syndicate.

Important prospective buyers are supplied with copies of the prospectus describing the issue, complete except for final price and a few other terms, for their study well before the offering date. Many make their decision to buy, contingent on the final price, before the actual offering. Consequently, if the issue is to be a successful one, it usually "goes out the window," that is, it is entirely sold out, in a matter of hours or a few days after the initial offering—and the syndicate is quickly terminated. When sales are slow, the syndicate typically continues in operation for a longer time with sales only at the agreed, announced price. If the offering is not sold out in a few weeks, by agreement the syndicate usually breaks up, stabilization activities are abandoned, and each investment banking underwriter is free to hold or dispose of his inventory of securities as he sees fit.

Underwritten Issues under Competitive Bidding

Security issues under public sealed bidding generally follow this basic pattern: The issuing firm offers an entire issue, generally of bonds or preferred stock, for outright purchase by the bidder offering the highest price—in terms of the lowest cost of money to the issuer. Bidding typically is by investment banking syndicates formed for the purpose of bidding on the specific issue. Unlike the pattern in negotiated underwritings, the investment bankers come into the picture at a late stage in the financing process. The investment bankers who bid on the issue do not act as consultants to the company in designing the issue—in fact, they are forbidden by administrative regulation to do so. The issuer and its counsel, or other expert advice, design the issue entirely by themselves and solicit by advertisement sealed bids for the definitively designed issue. (See Exhibit 16–1.)

The process of bidding and sale under competitive bidding has been described in the following terms:

Normally, numbers of bankers associate together to form accounts to bid for a specific issue. The reason for such association is the same as in the case of a negotiated transaction—to spread the risk and to accomplish distribution of the securities. After analyzing the registration state-

EXHIBIT 16–1

ILLUSTRATION OF INVITATION FOR BIDS FOR A NEW ISSUE OF BONDS

General Telephone Company
of California

PUBLIC INVITATION FOR BIDS

For the Purchase of

$40,000,000 First Mortgage Bonds, Series R, Due December 1, 1995

General Telephone Company of California, a California corporation (hereinafter called the "Company") hereby invites bids, subject to the terms and conditions herein stated or referred to, for the purchase from it of $40,000,000 principal amount of its First Mortgage Bonds, Series R, Due December 1, 1995 (hereinafter called the "Bonds"). Copies of the Statement of Terms and Conditions Relating to Bids for the purchase of the Bonds, and of other relevant documents referred to therein may be examined, and copies of certain of such documents may be obtained, at the office of the Company, 2020 Santa Monica Blvd., Santa Monica, California 90406, or at the office of GT&E Service Corporation, 730 Third Avenue, New York, N.Y. 10017.

Sealed written bids will be received by the Company at the office of GT&E Service Corporation, 730 Third Avenue, New York, N.Y. 10017, up to 11 A.M., Eastern Standard Time, on December 8, 1965, or such later date as may be fixed by the Company as provided in the Statement of Terms and Conditions Relating to Bids.

Prior to the acceptance of any bid the bidder or bidders will be furnished with a copy of the Prospectus relating to the Bonds as contained in the Registration Statement at the time it became effective. Bids will be considered only from persons who have received copies of the Prospectus and only if made in accordance with and subject to the Statement of Terms and Conditions Relating to Bids.

The Company hereby further advises prospective bidders that representatives of the Company, counsel for the Company, a representative of Arthur Andersen & Co., and a representative of Messrs. Milbank, Tweed, Hadley & McCloy, who have been requested by the Company to act as counsel for the successful bidders, will be available at the office of GT&E Service Corporation, 730 Third Avenue, New York, N.Y. 10017, on December 6, 1965, at 3:45 P.M. Eastern Standard Time, to meet with prospective bidders for the purpose of reviewing with them the information contained in the Registration Statement, in the Prospectus, and in the Statement of Terms and Conditions Relating to Bids. All prospective bidders are invited to be present at such meeting.

GENERAL TELEPHONE COMPANY
OF CALIFORNIA

By R. Parker Sullivan,
President

December 2, 1965

---

ment, prospectus and other general data available as to the issuer and the issue to be offered, and after meeting with the issuer at a prebidding information session, the bankers comprised within each account meet together just before the bidding date to determine a bid. In the light of their estimates of the highest price at which the securities can be sold to the public based on then current market conditions, prices of comparable securities, and other relevant factors, each account determines the bid it will make for the entire issue. It frequently occurs that underwriters withdraw from the [syndicate] account because their views of the proper bid are lower than the bid price set by the other members of the account, or for other reasons. If the number of such "drop-outs" is large, it may be impossible for that account to submit a bid at all, in which case it disbands without further action unless other bankers will come in.

Each bid submitted indicates that the members of the account, as then constituted, offer to purchase the entire issue on a several basis[7] at the bid price.

---

[7] Purchase by the underwriters on a "several basis" means that each member of the syndicate is legally obligated to the issuer to take only that portion of the issue subscribed to by it. [Authors' note.]

The underwriters in the winning account then determine by themselves, and without reference to the issuer, the public offering price, the method of sale, and any concessions or reallowances, subject, where and to the extent required, to the approval of the proper regulatory authority. The difference between the public offering price and the bid price establishes the level of anticipated gross compensation for the underwriters of the issue.

The offering to the public in public sealed bidding issues usually differs from that of a negotiated underwritten public offering in the extent of distribution. Since the winning account knows that it has been successful only a very short time in advance of the public offering and has had no assurance that it would win the issue, there has been little time and no assurance of reimbursement for the advance work of educating dealers or investors in the special characteristics of the prospective issue. As a result, and in view of the fact that such issues are generally of the higher grades permissible or suitable for institutional investment, the underwriters frequently sell much of the issue in large blocks to institutions. The underwriters have no undertaking to the issuer to try to place the securities with any particular class or classes of investors or in a particular or widespread geographical area, and the cost of organizing selling efforts through dealers may not be warranted by the spread which may exist for the particular issue, so that wide distribution is often not achieved.

If the issue is successful the compensation received may (although not always, even in a successful issue) cover the function of carrying the risk of the issue, the distribution function and the services of the manager in managing the distribution. Since no services have been performed in the design of the issue, and in view of the nature of the distribution, the services of the manager are much less than in a negotiated issue and the compensation, if any, is substantially less.[8]

Use of competitive bidding has been restricted largely to firms in the public utility and railroad industries, which are required to use it by administrative agencies—chiefly the Securities and Exchange Commission, the Interstate Commerce Commission, the Federal Power Commission, and various state agencies regulating public utilities.[9] Use of competitive bidding received a great boost in April, 1941, when the SEC issued Rule U–50, which required its use, subject to certain exceptions, for issues by public utility holding companies under its jurisdiction under the so-called "Death Sentence Act"—the Public Utility Holding Company Act of 1935. In announcing the new rule, the SEC argued:

After weighing the evidence and considering all aspects of the problem, the Commission concluded that there was no way short of competitive bidding that would afford it satisfactory means of determining the reasonableness

---

[8] This description is taken from the Defendants' Preliminary Memorandum for the Court in the case of *United States of America* v. *Henry S. Morgan, Harold Stanley, et al., Doing Business as Morgan Stanley & Co., et al.*, U.S. District Court for Southern New York, Civil No. 43–757, pp. 89–90.

[9] Most new bond issues by state and local governmental units are sold to investment bankers through competitive bidding.

of spreads [investment banker's gross margins] or the fairness of prices [of new issues bought by investment bankers], assure disinterested advice in financial matters to the companies concerned, and effectively control their dealings with affiliates.[10]

Whatever the merits of competitive bidding from the issuer's viewpoint, the investment bankers generally have taken a dim view of its merits relative to those of negotiated bidding. And it is significant that competitive bidding has been little used by issuers who are not under pressure from regulatory agencies to use it. Indeed, the record in recent years shows that public utilities that have come out, through reorganization, from under SEC jurisdiction as holding company units or subsidiaries and that had had experience with competitive bidding, have generally chosen not to use it when they subsequently have had free legal choice in the matter.

An example of competitive bidding under somewhat difficult conditions is provided by the sale of a $40 million mortgage bond issue by General Telephone Company of California in early December, 1965. The company's public invitation to bid (Exhibit 16–1) appeared in the papers on December 2, one day before the Federal Reserve Board raised the discount rate to 4½%. The General Telephone issue was the first large issue to be brought out in the still unsettled markets following the discount rate increase. The results of the bidding were described as follows in the *Wall Street Journal* of December 9, 1965:

General Telephone Co. of California, a unit of General Telephone and Electronics Corporation, obtained a 5.02% annual net interest cost in selling $40 million of single-A rated 5% first mortgage bonds, due Dec. 1, 1995. That rate is significantly above the 4.53% the communications unit is paying annually for $35 million it raised last Feb. 25 on 30-year first mortgage 4½% bonds.

Yesterday's 5.02% rate came on a bid of 99.7097 for the bonds from an underwriting team managed by Paine, Webber, Jackson & Curtis and Stone & Webster Securities Corp. A group led by the same two managers also won the February issue.

The successful bidders planned to release the new 5s to the public market, after compliance with Securities and Exchange Commission requirements, at 100.3097, to yield 4.98%.

The new bonds will be nonrefundable by the Santa Monica–based utility for five years.

Other bids for the bonds, all specifying 5% coupons, came from Lehman Brothers, Blyth & Co., Merrill Lynch, Pierce, Fenner & Smith, Inc., and Salomon Brothers & Hutzler, jointly, 99.6011; First Boston Corp. and Equitable Securities Corp., jointly, 99.5799; White, Weld & Co. and Kidder, Peabody & Co., jointly, 99.46, and from Halsey, Stuart & Co. 99.459.

---

[10] Securities and Exchange Commission, *Seventh Annual Report, 1941* (Washington, D.C.: U.S. Government Printing Office, 1942), p. 101.

The company will use the proceeds from yesterday's sale of bonds to discharge short-term bank loans incurred in connection with its 1965 construction program and the redemption of its 5½% cumulative preferred stock in August.

The difference between the price at which the winning syndicate offered the bonds to the public, $1,003.097 for each $1,000 of face value, and the $997.097 it paid the company, provided a gross margin, or *spread*, of $6 a bond or $240,000 for the $40 million issue.

The yield near 5% appealed to buyers; the issue sold rapidly and moved up in price in the secondary market to 102⅜ the following day.

Investment Bankers' Activities in Nonunderwritten Public Issues

In some public issues the issuing company is willing to stand the risk of an unsuccessful offering but desires to use the services of investment bankers on an *agency* basis. Under such arrangements the investment banking firm, for a fee, typically assists the issuer in surveying and gauging the market for the issue, in the design of the security, in setting fees the issuer will pay for distribution services, and in organizing dealers to distribute the securities for the account of the issuer. Under the usual agency arrangement the dealers receive a commission based on the amount they are able to sell. The bankers may also assume greater responsibility by agreeing with the issuer that they will use their *best efforts* to sell the entire issue and will receive commissions for the sales made as a result of their efforts.

Sale of New Issues to Existing Security Holders

The existing security holders represent a significant and identifiable potential market for further issues of securities; and a substantial percentage of new issues of common stock, and of bonds and preferred stocks convertible into common stock, is offered first to existing common stockholders. Some corporations have free choice in deciding whether or not to offer new common shares first to present stockholders, but in many companies the present common shareholders possess a legal right to receive *privileged subscriptions* to new issues of common stock. The legal right to privileged subscriptions is termed a *preemptive right*. Where it exists, corporations have no choice but to offer new issues of securities for cash pro rata to the security holders having the preemptive right. We shall discuss this further in Chapter 25.

A corporation that has decided to offer a new issue of stock to its stockholders usually distributes to them purchase warrants known as *rights*. The rights state the privilege of the holder to subscribe at a specified subscription price to a stated number of the new shares. Usually, such stock purchase rights must be exercised within a limited period of time, seldom more than 30 days. Such shares as remain unsubscribed on the date the rights expire may then be offered to the public at the same or at a higher price.

In most instances the rights are freely transferable, so that a stockholder who does not care to exercise his rights can sell them to someone who does want to use them to buy the stock at the subscription price. When the issue of rights relates to an actively traded stock, active trading in the rights usually develops and continues until the date the rights expire. In trading, the price of a right is the price of the subscription privilege derived from ownership of one old share.

Illustrative of the process of selling new shares through a rights offering was the offering by the Chrysler Corporation in April, 1965, of 5,611,360 new common shares to existing shareholders on the basis of one new share for each seven held of record on April 23. At the close of the market on April 23, the Chrysler stock sold at 54⅞. Subscription rights were issued to common stockholders entitling them to buy new shares for $48 plus seven rights per share. The rights were transferable, and active trading in the rights on the New York Stock Exchange continued until the announced terminal date of May 12, 1965.

During the April 23–May 12 subscription period when the rights were effective, anyone wanting to invest in Chrysler could have bought the common shares directly in the market; alternatively, he could have purchased the necessary rights (seven per share) and subscribed to the new stock at $48 a share. During the offering period the new issue would be attractive at $48 and the rights would have much value only if the current market price stayed above $48. A decline below $48 for a protracted time during the offering period would have jeopardized sale of the new issue. The setting of the subscription price, therefore, in such offerings to stockholders involves prediction of likely market prices for the security during the life of the rights. Some companies attempt to set the subscription price close to the market; others price the new issue well below the market in order to provide maximum inducement for use of the rights and successful sale of the issue. In the Chrysler case the market sagged somewhat during the offering to a low of 51⅞ for the stock and ½ for the rights on May 11. As might be expected from the fact that the market price stayed well above the $48 subscription price, the issue was more than 98% taken up, leaving only 97,562 shares unsubscribed.

In offering securities to existing shareholders, the issuing company frequently elects to dispense entirely with the services of investment bankers and absorb any risks that market declines will cause the offering to fail. For example, A.T.&T. and its subsidiaries commonly set low prices on new issues of common shares offered with rights and do not arrange for underwriting. In other cases, such as the Chrysler offering, the issuer employs investment bankers on a *standby underwriting* basis. In the Chrysler instance, a syndicate of 310 investment bankers headed by the

First Boston Corporation agreed to buy all unsubscribed shares at the subscription price. The underwriting fees were reported to be $1.10 a share.

Relatively seldom are nonconvertible bonds and preferred stocks offered through rights to existing shareholders of sizable concerns. As indicated above, this method is quite important in the sale of common shares or securities convertible into common stock.

The Investment Banker as Agent in Private Placements

As private placement has grown, investment bankers have demonstrated increasing interest in working with corporate clients on an agency basis in placing new issues. Some corporate financial officers prefer to deal directly with institutional buyers without use of investment bankers, particularly in cases where they are going back to institutions with whom they have had long-standing relationships. A great many issuing firms do enlist the assistance of investment bankers in planning the offering, in finding likely buyers, and in taking over, or helping in, the negotiation of the final terms of an issue.

Investment bankers argue, with great justification in many cases, that they are in a position to more than earn their fee. First, they point out that they are in virtually continuous contact with the state of the market and with prospective buyers. Thus, they can closely gauge market conditions and the terms the company should get. Moreover, they can get to know well the various preferences, prejudices, and money positions of the different institutions and hence are in a good position to find buyers for the issue. As one young banker put it, "I know key investment officers in seventy-five or a hundred top insurance companies and pension funds. I am learning a great deal about what each of these fellows does and doesn't want and what kind of a reaction I can get from them on a given deal." In contrast to the investment banker's continuing, intimate contact with the market, the corporate financial officer may have a major financing only every few years and hence have been only in loose contact with the market.

Second, the investment bankers bring a degree of objectivity to each transaction and can help the issuer define the limits within which bargaining is possible and recognize when he has gotten the best price and terms he is likely to get. Sometimes the banker can suggest changes in the policies or practices of the issuing firm that make their securities more attractive.

Third, they argue that the usual fees for direct placement work are not large except in unusually difficult or time-consuming issues. Fees of one-half of 1% of the amount involved are common and in many cases fees are lower. Hence, it is not hard, they say, for them to get the company a deal enough better than it could have gotten alone to cover the fee.

In any case, work as agents in private placements has become a major activity for many investment bankers.

Direct Sale of Common Stock to Employees, Suppliers, or Other Special Groups

Although the total amount of new issues sold to employees and other special groups is not such as to make it a major means of raising capital, it does deserve brief mention. Many companies make stock available to key employees on an option basis, and some have special plans on a continuing basis to permit employees to buy new shares. Usually, the motives of the issuer in such security issues are not primarily financial—that is, not primarily to raise capital—but rather to provide additional incentive compensation or to encourage or cement employee loyalties to the company. In a few instances, however, amounts of capital raised thereby have been quite consequential—as in the case of A.T.&T., where 44,593,000 shares had been purchased by employees up to the end of 1964, and instalment payments, carried at $349 million at December 31, 1964, were being made on 15,103,000 shares.

During the 1920's a number of companies, especially public utilities, made strenuous efforts to sell securities to employees and to customers, largely with the aim of increasing the goodwill of these groups toward the companies. Many found, however, that subsequent declines in the market values of the securities sold these groups resulted in ill will rather than good feeling toward the company. Another objection to this practice is grounded in the fact that employees are, in effect, being asked to compound their risks when they are asked to invest their savings in the same enterprise on which they are dependent for a livelihood.

Costs of Sale of New Security Issues

So far we have referred to the costs of direct placement and of underwriting in specific cases. Fortunately, considerable data are available which permit a useful general view of the costs to issuers connected with the public sale of new issues.

Underwriting compensation or *underwriting spread* is the term applied to the compensation of investment bankers and security dealers for their participation in public issues. This spread is measured by the difference between the price the bankers pay the issuing firm and the price at which they sell to the public. It is a gross figure and must cover a variety of expenses.

In Table 16–2 we present data regarding underwriting spreads on underwritten issues registered with the SEC in 1951–53–55 and in 1963.

One of the striking features to be noted from the data is the relatively low spreads on debt securities sold to the public in comparison with those of common stock. In all size groups, bonds were sold at lower spreads than

TABLE 16-2

WEIGHTED AVERAGE UNDERWRITING SPREADS, AS A PERCENTAGE OF GROSS PROCEEDS, ON UNDERWRITTEN SECURITIES REGISTERED WITH THE SECURITIES AND EXCHANGE COMMISSION, 1951-53-55 AND 1963*

Size of Issue (Millions of Dollars)	Debt Issues		Preferred Stock Issues†		Common Stock Issues	
	(Number of Issues in Parentheses)		(Number of Issues in Parentheses)		(Number of Issues in Parentheses)	
	1951-53-55	1963	1951-53-55	1963	1951-53-55	1963
Under 0.5					20.99 (13)	10.42 (2)
0.5-0.999	7.53 (5)	4.73 (2)			17.12 (43)	7.53 (4)
1-1.999	5.80 (15)	7.89 (7)			11.27 (60)	8.18 (15)
2-4.999	2.37 (29)	3.87 (9)			8.47 (62)	6.30 (10)
5-9.999	1.01 (44)	1.61 (17)	2.93 (21)	1.24 (4)	5.31 (24)	6.20 (2)
10-19.999	0.88 (72)	0.89 (24)	2.40 (19)	1.36 (6)	4.20 (17)	4.27 (4)
20-49.999	0.85 (79)	0.80 (41)			4.98 (11)	....
50 and over	0.88 (21)	0.79 (24)			....	....
Total (dollar amount in millions)	$5,900 (265)	$3,907 (124)	$850 (120)	$133 (15)	$1,000 (230)	$134 (37)
Weighted average spread	0.92	0.87	2.98	1.52	6.54	5.65

* Data for 1963 include only new issues of domestic corporate securities. Not included are issues in intrastate sales, Registration A exemptions, exempted industries, and issues registered with the Interstate Commerce Commission. Data for earlier years are from the Securities and Exchange Commission, *Cost of Flotation of Corporate Securities, 1951–55* (Washington, D.C.: U.S. Government Printing Office, June, 1957).

† The number of issues in other categories was too small for useful comparisons.

SOURCE: Investment Bankers Association of America, *Statistical Bulletin*, June, 1964.

were common stocks. Preferred stock spreads fell between those of bonds and common, tending to be closer to the costs of bonds than of common stock.

Reference to similar material on spreads for earlier postwar years, not presented here, indicates no marked trend in the spreads on public sales during this period. Comparison with data for the decades of the twenties and thirties shows that spreads for the post-World War II years were significantly lower than for the earlier decades.

Why are the spreads in sale of common stock so much higher than those for bonds? A basic reason is the difference in the nature of the markets. As indicated in the preceding chapter, a large percentage of the new bond issues is sold to the relatively concentrated, easily reached institutional market. In the case of common stock a much higher percentage must be placed with the diffuse individual buyer market. Hence, typically, it is much easier and cheaper for investment bankers to sell bonds than common stocks.

Generally, more selling effort is required for common stocks than for bonds, where institutional buyers pretty much decide for themselves whether or not to purchase. Except in the case of "hot" issues, the investment bankers have to "sell" new issues of common stock aggressively. Further, their selling largely takes the form of recommending the issue to their customers as a "good buy." For their efforts and for "putting on the line" their own reputations as shrewd analysts of value, they expect more compensation.

It will be noted also from Table 16–3 that the percentages of costs of sale of securities are very much higher for small issues than for large. The costs of selling small issues of common stock are particularly high in comparison with those of large issues. There are several reasons for the higher costs of smaller issues. First, many of the costs of investment bankers in investigating an issue, in preparing an issue for sale, and in selling it are relatively fixed. Since the absolute amount of the costs does not increase proportionately as the amount of the issue is increased, the costs in percentage terms of the smaller issues are much greater. In addition, the larger issues tend to be of firms that are well known to investors and hence require less selling effort. Institutional buyers are more likely to represent an important potential market, easily reached, in the case of issues of strong, large companies. The investment quality of the security generally *tends* to be higher with size of the issuer. Small issues of companies with uncertain futures tend to involve considerable price risk to investment banker-buyers. Again, when an investment banker with a fine reputation takes on the job of selling the securities of a small, little-known firm, the banking firm is selling its reputation as much as, or more than, that of the issuing firm—so the banker expects a compensating margin for his contribution and risks.

Issuing concerns also encounter significant other expenses in addition

TABLE 16-3
Costs of Sale as Percentage of Proceeds*
Securities Offered General Public†
in Selected Years: 1951, 1953, 1955

Size of Issues (In Millions of Dollars)	Bonds, Notes, and Debentures			Preferred Stock			Common Stock		
	Compensation	Other Expenses	Total Costs	Compensation	Other Expenses	Total Costs	Compensation	Other Expenses	Total Costs
Under 0.5	...	...	...	...	...	...	20.99%	6.16%	27.15%
0.5–0.9	7.53%	3.96%	11.49%	8.67%	3.96%	12.63%	17.12	4.64	21.76
1.0–1.9	5.80	2.37	8.17	5.98	2.09	8.07	11.27	2.31	13.58
2.0–4.9	2.37	1.41	3.78	3.83	1.05	4.88	8.47	1.50	9.97
5.0–9.9	1.01	0.82	1.83	2.93	0.79	3.72	5.31	0.86	6.17
10.0–19.9	0.88	0.64	1.52	2.40	0.52	2.92	4.20	0.46	4.66
20.0–49.9	0.85	0.48	1.33	2.84	0.35	3.20	4.98	0.38	5.37
50.0 and over	0.88	0.32	1.19	2.12	0.38	2.51	...	...	...

* Data on compensation do not include the ultimate burden involved in the granting to underwriters of additional but contingent compensation in the form of options or warrants to purchase common stock at what may prove to be bargain prices. Options are particularly common in the case of small issues of common stock.

† Only securities registered with the Securities and Exchange Commission are included. Bank stocks and railroad equipment trust certificates are the major types of public sales excluded.

Source: Securities and Exchange Commission, *Cost of Flotation of Corporate Securities, 1951–1955* (Washington, D.C.: U.S. Government Printing Office, June, 1957).

to the compensation of the underwriters. These include legal and accounting fees, printing costs, certain federal and state taxes and fees and, in the case of bond issues, trustees' fees. The SEC has estimated the expenses of public issue, other than compensation, for an "average debt issue" of $15.5 million at about $110,000, broken down as follows:[11]

```
Legal fees.............................................$16,700
Printing and engraving of the bonds, prospectus, etc........  30,500
Accounting fees........................................   5,300
Engineering fees, etc..................................   9,100
Federal and state stamp taxes and fees.................  21,400
Trustees' fees.........................................  16,300
SEC fees...............................................   1,600
Miscellaneous costs....................................   9,900
```

Table 16–3 shows the total costs of sale of new issues publicly offered in selected years. The "total costs" do not include warrants and other indirect compensation given investment bankers in some common issues. As can be readily noted, "other expenses" are a much higher percentage of small issues than of large and are significant in all size categories.

As will be seen from Table 16–4, the costs of issuing common stock

TABLE 16–4

Costs of Sale as Percentage of Proceeds*

Registered Common Stock Offerings through
Rights to Existing Stockholders, 1955

Size of Issue (In Millions of Dollars)	Compensation†	Other Costs	Total Costs
Under 5.0.	3.81%	1.81%	5.33%
5.0–19.9	4.24	2.48	7.26
20.0–99.9	2.48	1.04	3.45
100.0 and over	1.50	0.85	2.82

* Median percentages in each size group.
† Primarily to investment bankers for standby underwriting and services in aiding the sale.
Source: Securities and Exchange Commission, *Costs of Flotation of Corporate Securities, 1951–1955* (Washington, D.C.: U.S. Government Printing Office, June, 1957), p. 60.

through first offer to existing shareholders typically are smaller than those of selling common stock to the general public. The chief saving is in the compensation paid investment bankers. As we have seen, in some offerings to stockholders, standby underwriting is avoided altogether. Where used, standby underwriting fees and other investment banking charges typically are smaller than in the case of underwritten issues sold to the general public.

The costs of placing securities privately include certain accounting, legal, and other expense in addition to the fee paid investment banks

[11] Securities and Exchange Commission, *Cost of Flotation of Corporate Securities, 1951–1955* (Washington, D.C.: U.S. Government Printing Office, June, 1957), p. 11.

when they are used as agents. Cost data covering a large number of private placements during 1951, 1953, and 1955 are shown in Table 16–5.

We should caution the reader that the costs of sale, as we have discussed them here, include only the costs of getting the new issue out and sold. They do not include the continuing costs associated with the issue once it is outstanding. Thus, the concern that must pay a higher interest rate on bonds sold privately than it would have had to pay on bonds sold to the public may well use up in higher interest costs over a

TABLE 16–5

Costs of Sale as Percentage of Proceeds*

Securities Placed Privately in Selected Years:
1951, 1953, 1955

Size of Issue (In Millions of Dollars)	Bonds, Notes, and Debentures†	Preferred and Common Stock†
Under 0.3	1.49%	1.25%
0.3–0.4	1.06	0.13
0.5–0.9	0.83	0.53
1.0–1.9	0.59	0.61
2.0–4.9	0.43	0.50
5.0–9.9	0.34	0.38
10.0–19.9	0.32	0.14
20.0 and over	0.22	. . .

* Median percentages in each size category.
† Data are drawn from 1,846 issues of bonds, notes, and debentures and from 108 issues of preferred and common stock.
Source: Securities and Exchange Commission, *Cost of Flotation of Corporate Securities, 1951–1955* (Washington, D.C.: U.S. Government Printing Office, June, 1957), p. 66.

period of years any savings in issue costs achieved through private placement.

The Secondary Markets for Corporate Securities

As we indicated earlier, the existence of good markets where investors can buy or sell outstanding securities has an *important, though indirect,* effect on the ability of corporations to raise new capital through the sale of securities. In this section we shall briefly review the secondary markets for corporate securities.

The Organized Security Exchanges. Much of the secondary trading in corporate securities takes place on organized security exchanges such as the New York Stock Exchange (NYSE). The exchanges essentially provide central market places where individual and firm members execute buying and selling orders for securities admitted for trading. Member brokers act primarily as agents of customers wishing to trade particular securities, executing buying or selling orders in their behalf. In return for executing the orders and related services, the broker charges a commission, the amount of which is determined by reference to a standard schedule of fees established by the exchange.

Trading on the organized exchanges is conducted on what can be termed a "two-way auction" basis. Members with buy orders compete with each other to purchase the shares at the lowest possible prices. At the same time, sellers compete to get the highest possible price. A transaction is made when the highest bidder and the lowest offerer get together. The prices at which sales are made are recorded and immediately publicized. Consequently, the prices for exchange transactions reported in the newspaper represent actual transactions, and the person for whom orders to buy or sell are executed can assure himself that the prices reported to him by his broker represent reasonable prices, given the state of the market at the time of the transaction.

Obviously, the exchange and its member brokers do not create the prices at which securities are traded; instead, the prices arrived at by buyer and seller are the reflection of relative supply and demand for the security at the time it is traded.

Issuing firms must take the initiative in getting their securities listed for trading on the exchanges. To qualify its securities for listing, the corporation must meet certain requirements of the exchange and of the SEC. The NYSE requires that the concern be a going business with substantial assets and earning power. The company's stock should have sufficiently wide distribution and potential activity that a reasonable auction market may be expected to develop.[12] In addition, the company must conform to various SEC or stock exchange rules requiring independent outside audit, publication of financial statements, and the like. The other exchanges also have rules relative to the listing of stocks for trading but, in addition, permit trading in stocks not fully listed under certain conditions, which include the permission of the SEC. There has been a marked tendency over the years toward stricter requirements for listing.

---

[12] With respect to the specific requirements of the NYSE for initial listing of securities, the Exchange commented as follows:

Initial Listing

While each case is decided on its own merits, the Exchange generally requires the following as a minimum:

1. Demonstrated earning power under competitive conditions of $2 million annually before taxes and $1.2 million after all charges and taxes.
2. Net tangible assets of $10 million, but greater emphasis will be placed on the aggregate market value of the common stock, where $12 million or more applicable to publicly-held shares at the time of listing is looked for.
3. One million shares outstanding, of which at least 700,000 common shares are publicly-held among not less than 1,700 round-lot shareholders, and a total of 2,000 shareholders of record.

This is quoted from *New York Stock Exchange Fact Book, 1965* (New York: The Exchange, 1965), p. 8.

At year-end 1964, 1,221 U.S. and 25 foreign corporations had common stock listed on the NYSE. These 9.1 billion listed shares had a total market value of $466 billion. In addition, 359 preferred stock issues and 1,186 bond issues were listed for trading.[13] Some 1,350 other security issues were listed for trading on other exchanges.

Thirteen stock exchanges registered with the SEC and subject to its regulations account for virtually all the trading on exchanges. Table 16–6 shows the volume of stock traded on each of the registered exchanges in 1964. The dominant position of the NYSE, where 84% of the trading in stocks on exchanges took place, will be noted. The importance of New York City as a trading center for stocks is also readily apparent. The

TABLE 16–6

SALES OF STOCKS ON REGISTERED EXCHANGES DURING 1964*

Exchange	Market Value (In Thousands)	Percentage of Total
New York	$60,424	83.7%
American	5,923	8.2
Midwest	2,286	3.2
Pacific Coast	1,790	2.5
Philadelphia-Baltimore-Washington	828	1.1
Detroit	481	0.7
Boston	310	0.4
Cincinnati	46	0.1
Pittsburgh	45	0.1
Spokane	9	..
Salt Lake City	3	..
National	1	..
San Francisco Mining	1	..
	$72,149	100.0%

* The Chicago Board of Trade, a registered securities exchange, had no trading in securities in 1964.
SOURCE: Securities and Exchange Commission, *Statistical Bulletin*, March, 1965, p. 9.

NYSE and the American Stock Exchange (formerly the New York Curb Exchange), also located in the New York City financial section, together accounted for 92% of all stock trading on exchanges.

What is the extent of market turnover for all stocks listed on the NYSE? The total market value of all equity shares listed on the NYSE was $411.3 billion on December 31, 1963, and $474.3 billion on December 31, 1964. The market value of shares traded in 1964 was $60.4 billion, or 13.6% of the average market value of the listed shares. Total value of all bonds listed for trading on the NYSE at the end of 1964 amounted to $133.8 billion; but trading in bonds on the NYSE was very light—only $2.5 billion in 1964—most of the trading in bonds being done in the over-the-counter market, discussed later. In other words, the

[13] *New York Stock Exchange Fact Book, 1965*, p. 9.

NYSE is a very important market for stocks and relatively unimportant for bonds.

The Over-the-Counter Markets

Like the organized exchanges, the over-the-counter markets (OTC) perform the basic economic function of promoting liquidity—or more accurately, transferability—for investors in securities. In contrast to the exchanges, the OTC does *not* represent auction markets where buying bids and selling offers of many customers are brought together. Instead, prices are arrived at by negotiation between dealers and between dealers and investors. In this trading the dealers usually act as principals for their own accounts rather than as broker-agents for customers. Publicity of prices is limited to the furnishing of bid and asked quotations rather than the public reporting of actual sales prices. Many OTC dealers specialize in a limited number of selected issues and "make a market" for these securities by carrying an inventory of the securities and standing ready to buy or sell the securities to customers or other dealers.[14]

As suggested above, the size of markups (or markdowns) in principal transactions and commissions in agency transactions is not governed by a

---

[14] It may be of interest to some readers to review how an order might be handled for purchase of an over-the-counter security. Suppose you wished, on December 15, 1965, to buy 100 common shares of Cabot Corporation, a firm manufacturing principally carbon black and oil field equipment and producing and distributing natural gas. Since there is some trading in this stock, you noted in the morning *Wall Street Journal* that data on the current market for this stock are available under the headings, "Over-the-Counter Market," "Industrial and Utility Stocks." The data are prefaced by the notation: "These quotations, supplied by the National Association of Securities Dealers, are bids and offers quoted by over-the-counter dealers to each other as of approximately 3 P.M. (Eastern time). The quotations do not include retail markup, markdown or commission, and do not represent actual transactions."

Having been cautioned that the quotations provide a guide only as to the price at which you can expect to buy, you noted that Cabot common was listed as of December 14 at 39¼ bid and 40¼ asked (dollars per share). Suppose you lived in Scranton, Pennsylvania, and dealt with the local office of Carl M. Loeb, Rhoades & Co.—a large brokerage and investment banking firm with offices in 18 cities. If you wished definitely to buy, provided you had to pay no more than 40¼, the local office of Carl M. Loeb, Rhoades would take your order on that basis. Since the firm operates as an over-the-counter dealer as well as a broker on national exchanges and makes a market in Cabot stock, it probably would carry an inventory of Cabot and could sell you shares out of its inventory. If not, it would consult data that indicate the 10 or more dealer firms customarily making a market in Cabot and ask for firm offers on 100 shares from several of these firms. If it accepted the lowest of these offers—say, 39½—and bought as your agent, it would charge you $39.50 a share plus a regular brokerage commission. If Carl M. Loeb, Rhoades made a market in Cabot shares and carried a dealer's inventory in these shares, it would probably price the shares to you at 39¾ or 37⅞—or whatever amount above the prevailing dealer's market price it regarded as providing an appropriate dealer's margin. In this case the report of the transaction to you would make clear that the transaction was with Carl M. Loeb, Rhoades as principal. Since it made its profit as principal, it would charge no brokerage commission. If you did not have confidence that its offer was a good one, you would be free to ask Carl M. Loeb, Rhoades only for a quotation and could seek quotations from other firms.

fixed schedule in the OTC markets. Principal markups usually are higher than agency commissions.

The OTC markets are very heterogeneous in character and in technical quality. An SEC report commented,

> . . . the securities and markets constituting the broad over-the-counter category range from well-known, established companies with a substantial number of dealers making a close and competitive market at one extreme, to obscure, recent issues with a single dealer dominating the market, quoting widely spread bid and asked prices, and combining wholesale and retail trading at the other extreme, and with many variations and gradations between the two extremes.[15]

What securities are traded over the counter? The answer is a bit involved. A very important segment of the market is composed of U.S. government bonds. Although some U.S. bond issues are listed on the NYSE, an overwhelming percentage of total trading in governments is carried on in the over-the-counter markets, with 17 dealer firms handling the bulk of the volume. Trading in U.S. bonds has often been very heavy. In one period of active bond trading, the early weeks of 1961, *daily* trading in U.S. government securities in the OTC markets ran between $1.2 and $1.7 billion, or about six times the value of stocks traded on the New York Stock Exchange during this period.[16] Traded over the counter exclusively are the bonds of some 150,000 state, municipality, school district, and other local governmental units, known as *municipals*. A number of dealer firms specialize in municipals, a few firms dealing exclusively in them. It is interesting to note that commercial banks have authority to act as dealers in government bonds and in certain classes of municipal bonds, and a few large commercial banks are among the leading dealer firms in this activity. Trading in corporate bonds is also accomplished mainly in the OTC markets, although many are listed on the NYSE.

The common stocks of almost all commercial banks are traded in the OTC market, and the shares of insurance companies are predominantly traded in the OTC market. The industrial and utility issues traded over the counter are typically those of small or medium-sized companies whose securities are narrowly distributed and whose trading is relatively inactive. Since the securities of a large number of the corporations in the country are so characterized, the total number of issues of corporate stocks traded in the OTC market in the course of a year is large. The National Quotation Bureau, a private concern circulating quotations for OTC stocks, reported about 26,000 security issues in its October, 1965,

---

[15] Securities and Exchange Commission, *Report of Special Study of Securities Markets* (Washington, D.C.: U.S. Government Printing Office, 1963), Part 5, p. 123.

[16] *Boston Herald*, March 31, 1961, based on Federal Reserve Bank of New York data.

volume, which is a cumulative record covering a period of years. The daily quotation sheets, or *Pink Sheets*, of the Bureau carry some 9,000 separate issues of stocks and bonds, many of which are listed on a U.S. or Canadian stock exchange. That many of these are small or closely held is suggested by SEC estimates for 1963 that there are about 4,400 stocks of U.S. corporations, exclusive of investment companies, with 300 or more stockholders each, whose stocks are quoted only over the counter. These stocks were estimated to have a total market value in 1963 of about $98.8 billion. This figure included bank stocks valued at $26.7 billion and insurance stocks at $25.3 billion.[17]

In addition to the trading in corporate stocks not admitted for trading on organized exchanges, there is considerable trading over the counter in stocks that are also traded on the exchanges. Many large blocks of listed stocks are traded in negotiated deals off the exchanges, despite progress by the exchanges in developing specific techniques for handling effectively large block transactions on the exchanges.

The total dollar volume of trading in corporate stocks unquestionably is large. A major study of the OTC markets estimated OTC sales of common stocks in 1961 at 2.5 billion shares valued at $38.9 billion, or 61% of the sales on organized exchanges in that year. The $38.9 billion figure compared with an estimate of $4.9 billion for 1949. The growth reflected an increase in the number of issues traded, and very active individual speculative interest in OTC stocks in 1961, an interest that was very much dampened by sharp downturns in many OTC shares in 1962. Some 3,303 dealers participated in OTC trading in 1961, but 56 broker-dealers accounted for over half of the business.

On a sample day in early 1962, individuals were responsible for 89% of the number of shares bought and sold by the public and 73% of the value.[18]

A Look at the Firms Doing Business in the Primary and Secondary Security Markets

The piecemeal references to financial houses in this chapter, variously speaking of "investment bankers," "brokers," "broker-dealers," "traders," etc., has probably been confusing to the reader. At this point, clarity may be served by a recapitulation of the major functions served by financial houses and a brief elaboration of their patterns of operation.

We have at various points identified several major functions performed by financial firms:

1. Participation as underwriters of new issues and related activity in selling new issues.

---

[17] Securities and Exchange Commission, *Thirtieth Annual Report, 1964* (Washington, D.C.: U.S. Government Printing Office, 1965), p. 55.

[18] Securities and Exchange Commission, *Report of Special Study of Securities Markets*, Part 2, chap. vii.

2. Selling of new issues without underwriting participation.
3. Brokerage activity as agents, for a commission, in the buying and selling of outstanding securities.
4. Trading as principals in the buying, holding for trading, and selling of securities in the over-the-counter market.

Not noted earlier are additional roles assumed by many firms. For example, some firms invest in securities for continued holding as investors rather than for early resale. Related but distinct are the activities of some firms in trading for their own account for short-run gains. This may take the form, for example, of *arbitraging*—taking advantage of aberrations of the market which present opportunities for profitable two-way simultaneous transactions in equivalents, in which one security is bought and its equivalent sold at about the same time, as in the case of stock purchase rights and the security they can be used to buy.

Some large firms, such as Merrill Lynch, Pierce, Fenner & Smith, or Carl M. Loeb, Rhoades & Co., although best known as brokers, actually are engaged in all the major types of activity summarized above. Other firms specialize, a few exclusively, in performing one of the above functions. Thus, Morgan Stanley & Co. specializes in underwriting and, indeed, in the management of underwriting syndicates; while Aubrey G. Lanston & Co., Inc., operates as a dealer in U.S. government and federal agency bonds in the over-the-counter market.

Some 700 securities firms—out of several thousand registered securities dealers—are members of the Investment Bankers Association of America and presumably do a significant amount of investment banking. While they may refer to themselves as investment bankers (this activity appears to carry more prestige than does brokerage or trading), most of these firms derive the bulk of their revenues from the brokerage and other functions described earlier.

Secondary Offerings through Investment Bankers

Throughout this chapter we have tried to emphasize the distinctions between the primary and secondary markets. In so doing, we have implied that investment bankers are involved only in primary distributions. Perhaps without confusing the reader, we now can acknowledge the developing importance of a kind of security sale that technically is a secondary distribution but is commonly handled by investment bankers much as they handle primary issues. We refer to the sale of large blocks of stock by their owners through investment bankers. For example, a syndicate of investment bankers headed by Paine, Webber, Jackson & Curtis underwrote the sale in December, 1965, of 250,000 shares of Swingline, Inc., manufacturers of staplers and other office equipment. This issue was registered with the SEC and a prospectus was issued, but the shares were sold, not by the company, but by a stockholder, the wife of the chairman and president.

In many cases in recent years, company and leading shareholders have joined in a public offering of shares. Investment banking sources reported 78 underwritten issues totaling $392 million for the account of shareholders in 1964 and 47 combination new and secondary issues aggregating $78 million.[19]

---

[19] Investment Bankers Association of America, *Statistical Bulletin*, March, 1965.

PART VI

The Long-Term Capital Structure

Chapter 17

The Basic Security Types

HAVING NOW considered the primary source of funds for the going corporation—the earnings of the business itself—and the nature of the market for external capital, we are in a position to turn our attention to the basic contractual arrangements by means of which these external funds are obtained from time to time. Because it is one of the most critical aspects of financial policy, the question of the optimum mix of securities in new financing will occupy our attention over the next three chapters. As we shall see, the choice of dividend policy is not separate from this decision, since it must be considered along with new equity issues in the balance of debt and equity funds. However, we shall approach the problem as the corporate management normally does; namely, on the expectation that predicted needs will at times exceed internal funds flows (under the existing dividend policy), and therefore a new security issue must be brought into the financial plan. This chapter is designed to provide the background of information about these securities which will enable us to carry forward the analysis upon which a decision will be based.

Earlier in this book it was pointed out that corporate securities fall into two main classes: contracts of debt and participations in ownership. Three main types were named: bonds or notes in the first class and preferred stock and common stock in the second. The reader may already be aware that there are in common use a great many different kinds of debt contracts as well as a variety of preferred and common stock forms. To the beginner in finance, it would be a very difficult assignment to get this confusing array of securities clearly fixed in mind.

Fortunately, this is not at all necessary or desirable, at least at this stage of our study. As will be brought out in this chapter, the first step is to gain a clear understanding of the fundamental characteristics of the three basic security forms—the bond, the preferred stock, and the common stock. It is these characteristics which are of primary importance in decisions relating to long-term finance. Later, when the basic analysis has been well established, we shall introduce the subject of the bargaining

351

process between issuer and investor and the many special kinds of bonds and stock which have been produced in an effort to meet special needs and circumstances. It will be seen that the concepts and analytical approaches developed in this chapter and the two which follow will be directly applicable to the many different forms of long-term debt and equity contracts which show up in our illustrative examples.

The Bond: The Basic Promises

The responsibility of a company to those who have supplied funds through the purchase of its bonds is essentially the very simple obligation of anyone who has borrowed money, namely, to repay the sum at the promised time and to compensate the lender for the use of his money by the payment of an interest charge while the debt is outstanding. A formal statement of this obligation is found on the face of the bond certificate held by each individual or institution participating in the loan. The precise details of the legal contract between the issuing company and the bondholders is to be found in a document known as the *bond indenture*. A copy of this document is held and enforced by a *trustee under the indenture*, who represents the bondholders as a group.

The following is a condensed version of the wording of a typical bond certificate:

The A.B.C. Corporation . . . for value received, hereby promises to pay to bearer on the first day of August, 1975, the principal sum of—ONE THOUSAND DOLLARS—and to pay interest on said principal sum at the rate of three and three-quarters per cent (3¾%) per annum semiannually on the first day of February and the first day of August in each year until payment of said principal sum. . . . This is one of a duly authorized issue of bonds of the Company . . . of the aggregate principal sum of $5,000,-000. . . .

To cite a current bond issue, we may take the case of the Allied Chemical Corporation. In April of 1953, Allied Chemical raised the sum of $200 million through the sale of bonds. In exchange for the use of these funds for a period of 25 years, the company contracted to pay interest to the bondholders on April 1 and October 1 of each year to 1978 (3½% annually) and to repay the principal amount by April 1, 1978. The semiannual amount of interest at the time of issue was, therefore, $3.5 million.

There are no qualifications to this time series of payments. The certificate does *not* say "if earned" or "if the financial condition of the company permits"—but simply, "hereby promises to pay." To fail to do so at any point constitutes a breach of a legal contract, which act (under almost all bond contracts) entitles the bondholders to declare the entire sum due and payable and to take court action to recover the loan. This process is known as *acceleration of maturity*.[1] It is clear that if the

---

[1] Debtors are not permitted to default willfully in order to pay off burdensome debt.

business is to continue without a financial crisis, there is no alternative to a literal adherence to its promises. Herein lies the hazard of debt financing to the issuer and the advantage of bond ownership to the investor. A bond will not be well regarded unless both sides see a considerable margin of safety to assure the performance of the promises in the bond contract even if events turn out badly.

To a company such as Allied Chemical, with sales of $545 million in the year in which the bonds were sold, the addition of $7 million to annual costs of operation may seem unimportant. It must be remembered, however, that this is a charge against the remaining income after making payment of the year's costs of operation. In the year 1953 the *net earnings* of Allied Chemical *before interest and federal corporate income taxes* were $89 million. This relationship between net income available for the payment of fixed charges ($89 million) and the fixed charges on the debt ($7 million) is a significant ratio in financial analysis. Analysts often refer to this ratio as *times interest earned*—in this case, 12.7 times.[2] Another way of expressing this relationship is to divide $7 million by $89 million, thus to measure the fraction of income needed to carry the interest. In this case it is 7.9%.

The reader is reminded that the debtor must meet each promise to pay at the time it becomes due. Therefore, in viewing this margin of net income over fixed charges on debt, it must be borne in mind that corporate gross revenues fluctuate from year to year and that net earnings fluctuate even more to the extent that the costs of operation are inflexible. Thus, it is possible that a margin of earnings such as that shown by Allied Chemical could shrink rapidly, although perhaps only temporarily. The range of possible fluctuation varies, of course, from one industry and one company to another.

Sinking Funds

In modern practice, corporate debt contracts usually provide for partial repayment of the debt at intervals, usually yearly. Such requirements are generally referred to as *sinking funds*. In the case of the Allied Chemical issue, the bond indenture required that in addition to interest payments the corporation must make the following sinking fund payments to the trustee, who will call bonds by lot, pay them, and thus cancel the corporate liability to that extent:

1959–63	$ 7 million annually
1964–68	9 million annually
1969–73	11 million annually
1974–77	13 million annually

Such payments do not always provide for complete retirement of the debt by maturity; and often, there is a substantial final payment on the

---

[2] Note that we recommend that the earnings used in this ratio be taken before both interest and taxes. Where there is more than one bond issue, it is better practice to relate total charges to total income available for such charges, rather than taking each issue separately.

maturity date, commonly known as a *balloon payment*. However, to the extent that the sinking fund provision requires a portion of the debt to be repaid prior to the official maturity date, these funds must be provided by the debtor out of earnings or other sources.[3]

It is to be noted that these repayments of the principal are just as mandatory as the payments of interest, and any failure to pay on the dates specified will accelerate the maturity of the whole issue. The indenture for the Allied Chemical bonds contains a typical provision on this point, as follows:

SECTION 6.01. In case one or more of the following Events of Default shall have occurred and be continuing, that is to say:

(*a*) default in the payment of any installment of interest upon any of the Debentures as and when the same shall become due and payable, and continuance of such default for a period of thirty days; or

(*b*) default in the payment of the principal of (or premium, if any, on) any of the Debentures as and when the same shall become due and payable either at maturity, upon redemption, by declaration or otherwise; or

(*c*) default in the payment of any mandatory sinking fund payment as and when the same shall become due and payable, and continuance of such default for a period of thirty days; or

.   .   .   .

then and in each and every such case, unless the principal of all the Debentures shall have already become due and payable, either the Trustee or the holders of not less than twenty-five per cent, in aggregate principal amount of the Debentures then outstanding here-under, by notice in writing to the Company (and to the Trustee if given by debentureholders), may declare the principal of all the Debentures to be due and payable immediately, and upon any such declaration the same shall become and shall be immediately due and payable, anything in this Indenture or in the Debentures contained to the contrary notwithstanding. . . .[4]

It is obvious that management must consider the sinking fund, as well as the annual interest payments, when deciding whether or not to issue bonds. Times interest earned is, therefore, often an incomplete measure. A more inclusive measure will be suggested below.

---

[3] The bond indenture may provide, as an alternative to a cash payment, the equivalent in par value of bonds repurchased by the issuing company. If these are available on the market at less than par, the cash drain involved will be somewhat less than the indicated sinking fund obligation. In other cases the company must expend a set amount of money, leaving the number of bonds acquired to be determined by the market price.

In some issues a corporation has the option to use funds to retire some of the debt or to buy new assets of specified types. It is argued that the new investment serves to protect the debt by adding value and earning power.

[4] For examples of other indentures, see *Bond Indentures* (Michigan Business Cases, Financial Management Series, No. 20) (Ann Arbor: Bureau of Business Research, School of Business Administration, University of Michigan, 1935).

The Flow of Funds Related to the Bond

Stripped to its purely financing implications, a bond is an instrument which commits the corporation to certain outflows of funds at specified times. The combined amounts of interest, sinking fund, and final maturity payments are referred to as the *burden, service,* or *cash drain* of the bonded debt. In addition to the obligation to meet the burden annually, there is also the obligation to repay at maturity that portion of the original issue which has not been redeemed by the application of the sinking fund. This would not present a problem in the Allied Chemical case, since no more than 6.5% of the original issue of $200 million will remain outstanding in the year of maturity. There are, however, many bond issues which either have no sinking fund provision or provide for only a partial retirement by this means. As a result, the sum outstanding and due for repayment at the maturity date is of an entirely different order of magnitude from that required for annual servicing of the debt. For example, the U.S Plywood Corporation's $25 million issue of 5¼% debentures, dated April 1, 1960, and due in 1985, carries a semiannual sinking fund payment rising to a maximum of $455,000. If no bonds were redeemed except as required by the sinking fund provision, $7 million would be due and payable on April 1, 1985. This is, clearly, a major fraction of the original borrowing.

The fulfillment of this obligation might well appear to present an impossible strain on the earnings and cash position of the company in the year 1985. It is obvious that since the maturity date is known at the time of issue, a management which intended to eliminate the debt would be guilty of negligence if it left plans for repayment of this sum until the final year. Actually, management may have no intention of terminating its borrowings at that point but rather may expect to find the solution in a new issue of bonds, the proceeds of which will be used, in whole or in part, to repay the holders of the old bonds. This process, known as refunding, will be discussed in more detail in Chapter 26. It can, however, be noted that one of the major immediate causes of business failures is the inability to pay maturing obligations. Usually, there are other underlying causes, but a large maturity is often the event that makes continuation impossible.

The Tax Implications of Debt Service

In observing the role played by debt and other basic security types in the long-term financing of individual companies, it is necessary to develop one or more simple measures of significance so that objective comparisons can be made among companies and over time. Before we turn to a description of these measures, however, it will be helpful to identify one of the important elements of such comparisons, namely, the effect of the associated payments on the company's corporate income tax position.

With regard to debt, it is particularly important to have a clear understanding of the differences between interest and sinking fund payments in this respect. The reader will be aware that in the United States, income taxes are levied on *net income*, that is, on the sum remaining from gross income after the deduction of all costs. Among the expenditures accepted as "costs" for tax purposes, and thus deductible in computing the income upon which the tax is based, is interest on debt.

In order to bring out the significance of this, we present a revised and simplified version of the Allied Chemical income statement for 1959, the first year in which the sinking fund requirement took effect. These figures, adjusted to the then applicable 52% federal corporate income tax rate and assuming no prepayment of the debt (which, in fact, there was) are as follows:

		(*In Thousands*)
Net sales..		$720,000
Cost of goods sold and operating expenses............	$499,000	
Depreciation and depletion.........................	55,000	
Selling, general, and administrative expenses..........	69,000	623,000
Gross income from operations......................		$ 97,000
Other income....................................		5,000
Earnings before interest and income tax..............		$102,000
Bond interest....................................		7,000
		$ 95,000
Federal income tax (@ 52%).......................		49,400
Net income after taxes............................		$ 45,600

Now, let us suppose that instead of financing by bonds, the company had raised the $200 million by the sale of stock. The relevant portion of the income statement would then have appeared as follows:

Earnings before interest and income tax.........	$102,000
Federal income tax (@ 52%)...................	53,040
Net income after taxes.......................	$ 48,960

A comparison of these two sets of figures shows that the use of debt has reduced taxes by $3.64 million, or 52% of $7 million. Thus, it can be said that the *after-tax cost* of the debt is $3.36 million, because this is the net increase in costs caused by the debt.

Since we are constantly relating interest and other payments associated with corporate securities to the company's taxable income, it is frequently desirable to identify the exact amount of the tax which would be payable on an equivalent amount of taxable corporate income. This we will call the *tax related*. In the example above, the tax related to the bond interest of $7 million is $3.64 million.

It must be emphasized that the privilege of deducting debt costs for purposes of income tax computation does not extend to sinking fund payments. Although such payments involve a cash drain similar to the payment of interest, the sinking fund payment is in fact a repayment of part of the liability, which is the principal of the bonds, and cannot be counted as a cost any more than the original proceeds of the loan received by the company would be counted as income. A sinking fund should therefore be regarded as a contractual commitment defining how earnings, or a part of earnings, shall be used. That is to say, they must be retained in the business to permit the repayment of a portion of the debt. Interest, on the other hand, is an expenditure necessary to have the use of the funds, just as wages are an expenditure necessary to obtain the services of employees.

The reader is reminded that this line of reasoning does not apply to dividends on stock. In contrast to the treatment of bond interest as a cost, dividends are considered as a distribution of the net income of the business to the owners and, as such, are not deducted when computing the corporate income tax. This applies to dividends on preferred stock as well as to dividends on common stock.

The Burden of Debt: Measures of Significance

In the analysis of the capital structures of individual companies, there are two commonly used methods for measuring the importance of debt. One is the simple and obvious statement of total debt as a *percentage of total capitalization* (often referred to as the *debt ratio*). In the case of Allied Chemical the year-end balance sheet related to the income data of 1953, previously cited, shows capital stock and surplus of $344 million. Adding this to the long-term debt of $200 million gives total capitalization of $544 million. The debt is 36% of this. The other method is that which was described on page 353, namely, *times interest earned,* which relates total bond interest to the earnings from which bond interest must be deducted in arriving at net profit for the period. Both of these measures have the advantage of simplicity and clarity, and both can readily be derived by external as well as internal analysts from conventional financial statements.

Throughout this book, however, we have emphasized that numerical values are of little use unless they are meaningfully related to the objectives of the analysis. In this respect the two measures cited above, although widely used by borrowers and lenders alike, have some serious limitations. These will be discussed more fully in Chapter 19. At this point, it is sufficient to state that our primary concern regarding the burden of debt is with the capacity of the borrower to make the cash payments required by the debt contract. It makes sense, therefore, to derive a measure of significance which relates more directly to the total cash flows of debt servicing: *times burden covered*. The reader has already been told the elements of the cash flow which represent the burden of a debt. These are:

1. The interest.
2. The sinking fund.
3. The final payment at maturity.
4. The tax related to the above items.

A table describing the burden of debt may be prepared in the following form (see Table 17–1). We have filled in the initial information from the Allied Chemical example, using boldface type. The data are for the year 1959, cited previously. The reader should note carefully that some of the

TABLE 17–1
(Figures in Thousands)

		Amount before Tax	Amount of Tax related @ 52%	Amount after Tax
Interest................(A)		**$ 7,000**	$ 3,640	$ 3,360
Sinking fund............		14,580	7,580	**7,000**
Total contractual burden...(B)		21,580	11,220	10,360
Earnings before interest		(E.B.I.T.)		
(1959)................(C)		**102,000**	53,040	48,960
Depreciation charged......		**55,000**		
Net funds inflow from operations.............(D)		157,000		

initial information appears in the column headed "Amount before Tax," and some in the column for "Amount after Tax." Great care must be taken to assign the initial information its proper class, for any combination of before-tax with after-tax figures is as meaningless as the familiar example of adding oranges and apples.

The next step is to complete the table. The formula for converting before-tax to after-tax amounts, or vice versa, where r is the applicable tax rate, as a decimal, is (Before $)(1 − r) = (After $).

In Table 17–1, the reader should observe the meaning of the figures in each line. Starting with the before-tax amount of interest, the sum actually paid the bondholders, the tax related represents the actual reduction in taxes payable, or *tax shield*, provided by the use of debt, and the after-tax amount is the net cash drain on the company. In the case of the sinking fund, the before-tax amount is what the company has to earn in order to have after taxes a sum equal to the required sinking fund, and the tax related is what the name implies. Thus items (A) and (B) of the table picture the financial burden which is obligatory under debt contracts. We refer to this as the *contractual burden*. (In order to avoid possible confusion, it should be noted here that the term *tax shield* represents an actual reduction in taxes payable, whereas the term *tax related* is a broader concept which shows the amount of taxes related to any given sum expressed in before-tax terms.)

As we have pointed out, the amount of burden cannot be judged to be large or small except as it is compared with the inflows available to meet it. The figure of earnings before interest and taxes (E.B.I.T.) is widely used for this purpose, and it has been entered on line (C), first column, in Table 17–1. The tax related to the E.B.I.T. is computed from this before-tax figure; the after-tax figure shows what the net income would have been if there had been no tax shield from the use of debt. We have already entered this tax shield in the line for interest; to use it again would be double counting.

We now have figures for inflow and outflow that are consistently measured, and we can use either the before-tax or after-tax column to calculate the following ratios.

$$\text{Times Interest Earned} = \frac{C}{A} = \frac{102,000}{7,000} = \frac{48,960}{3,360} \qquad = 14.6$$

$$\% \text{ Income Required for Interest} = \frac{A}{C} \qquad\qquad\qquad\qquad = 6.9\%$$

$$\text{Times Burden Covered by Earnings} = \frac{C}{B} = \frac{102,000}{21,580} = \frac{48,960}{10,360} \quad = 4.7$$

$$\% \text{ Income Required to Carry Debt} = \frac{B}{C} \qquad\qquad\qquad = 21.2\%$$

The ratio of times interest earned is one that has been most frequently used by analysts in the measurement of the safety of bond issues. It is presented by every standard financial manual; and it is embedded in the laws of those states which regulate the investment practices of certain types of investors, such as trustees, insurance companies, and savings banks. Despite this use, it is now becoming clear that a more comprehensive analytical test is that which confronts all the burden of a debt in a year with the inflows available to meet it. The comparison of burden with earnings makes such a test.

The reader is already familiar with the fact that the charge for depreciation, which reduces reported earnings, does not represent a use of funds. Therefore, one can obtain the amount of the *net funds inflows*, (N.F.F.) or "*funds provided by operations*" by adding the depreciation to the E.B.I.T. While no firm can, over the long run, avoid the need to make expenditures to replace depreciating equipment, the expenditures can often be deferred, and so the ratios:

$$\text{Times Burden Covered by N.F.F.} = \frac{D}{B} = \frac{157,000}{21,580} = 7.30$$

$$\% \text{ Funds Flow Required to Carry Debt} = \frac{B}{D} = 13.7\%$$

provide a measure of the margin over the contractual burden that might be available in relatively short emergency periods. It is to be noted that this ratio can only be reached from before-tax figures.

We shall have more to say later on about these ratios and the others we shall encounter in this chapter. The reader should be sure that he understands what they are, how they are computed, and what lies behind them. May we emphasize that no method which gives unequal ratios from before-tax and after-tax figures is properly designed. It is also to be remembered that before-tax and after-tax figures cannot be combined. A very common error, for example, is to add interest and sinking fund without taking account of the tax-related items. Thus, it would be a mistake to calculate the burden of the Allied Chemical debt as being the sum of the interest charges of $7 million and sinking fund payments of $7 million, since one is in before-tax dollars and the other is in after-tax dollars.

There are reasons which lead us to recommend that the reader make it a practice, where possible, to use the before-tax basis for these ratio comparisons: (1) In comparisons of different companies, there can be significant differences in the tax levy which are not apparent in the information available. (2) For the same company over a period of time, there will surely have been significant changes in the basis and rate of tax from one year to another, which will affect the results and again may not be apparent in the data used. (3) Finally, if the company should sustain a loss in any year, the full interest payment must still be met. (Of course, to the extent that the bond interest increases the deficit for the year, a tax credit may be taken later against earnings of other years.) For these reasons, our comparisons will be made primarily in terms of burden before taxes, earnings before interest and taxes (which we abbreviate to E.B.I.T.), and depreciation charged.

Summary: The Bond

Let us now summarize briefly what has been said about a bond. The typical bond contract requires the repayment of the principal amount on a specified maturity date and regular interest payments while the bond is outstanding. The consequences of default at any time are that the debt matures at once. The bond contract may also require payments into a sinking fund in partial or total anticipation of the repayment of the principal amount. The total annual payments required by the bond contract, referred to as the burden, service, or cash drain of the debt, may be measured in terms of their effect on corporate income only after allowance for the corporate income tax. Times interest earned is a frequently used test of the safety of a debt, but it pictures only one element of the burden. Times burden covered is a more inclusive test.

The Common Stock

In contrast to the bondholders, the common shareholder has no promise from the company to which he may turn for an assurance of income or the return of his investment. The absence of any specific financial commitment on the part of the corporation to the shareholder is reflected in the wording of the stock certificate, an example of which appears below:

This is to certify that _____ is the owner of _____ fully paid and nonassessable shares of the par value of $20 each of the common stock of the A.B.C. Company, Inc. . . . A statement of the designations, preferences, privileges and voting powers, and the restrictions and qualifications thereof, of the Preferred Stock . . . and of the Common Stock . . . is printed on the reverse side hereof, and this certificate . . . shall be subject to all the provisions of the Certificate of Incorporation . . . to all of which the holder by acceptance hereof assents.

Dated _____ Signed _____

The basic purpose of the certificate is simply to indicate that the person named is a shareholder of the company and to indicate the extent of his participation as measured by the number of shares owned. No payment in the form of dividends is promised or implied. No repayment of the original principal is anticipated, since the money supplied by the common shareholder is considered to be an investment for the life of the business. The principal assurance given the holders of the common stock is the basic right of ownership—the right to decide matters of corporate policy either directly, by vote at regular or special meetings of the shareholders, or by delegating their powers of control to a board of directors of their own choosing.[5]

Thus, the corporation has no specific financial commitments to its shareholders of a nature that would make the expenditure of cash at any point of time mandatory. Of course, profits which are not paid out in cash dividends remain in the business; and if wisely used, they will add to the value of the common shareholders' residual claim on the assets and earning power of the business. The realizable value to the shareholder of reinvested earnings depends on the extent to which they are reflected in a higher market price for the stock.

It is this absence of specific financial obligations which makes common stock so attractive and necessary as a basis of long-term finance in the business corporation, characterized as it is by fluctuating earnings in greater or lesser degree. Dividend payments can be adjusted year by year to the financial circumstances of the moment. This is not to imply that the management is free from pressures of a nonlegal sort for payment of

---

[5] Stock records show the name and address of the "holder of record," while most bonds are payable to the bearer. A company may not be able to communicate directly with its bondholders!

dividends. It is apparent that a board of directors elected by the common shareholders will probably be sensitive to the wishes of those shareholders. Even when the directors are representative of the shareholders in name only, significant pressures are likely to exist. The most important of these relates to future financing. Companies which face a long-range program of growth, or even just the possibility of such growth, must keep in mind the fact that at some time in the future they may have to supplement existing equity capital with a new issue of stock. In order that the new stock be readily marketable, the outstanding stock must have an attractive record of stability and strength. A pattern of stability and growth in dividend payments is often the foundation for stability and growth in the market price of the stock. Obviously, then, the necessity for a sale of stock at a favorable price in the future can be a very practical and powerful incentive to pay dividends in the present.

However, the essential feature of stock remains, namely, that management can, if necessary, disregard these urgings and reduce or suspend dividend payments without breaking a legal contract or interfering in any way with the continuity of the business. This gives management a flexibility which it does not possess with fixed charge debt obligations.

In view of the absence of assured income in the case of common stock, it may seem surprising that many investors prefer to invest in stocks rather than in bonds. The reason is, of course, that the residual claim of the shareholders has its advantages as well as its disadvantages. The holder of a bond of Allied Chemical, cited earlier, will never under any financial circumstances receive for each bond more than $35 per annum interest income nor more than $1,000 at maturity. There is a limit to his gains which goes along with protection against loss. The shareholder, on the other hand, has no limit placed on possible participation in earnings. If the business prospers, it is quite likely that he will receive dividends which pay him a rate of return substantially above that which is paid to the bondholder; and if he liquidates his investment, he may also realize a capital gain over and above his original investment. Counterbalancing the uncertainty associated with a return which is dependent on earnings and the policy decisions of the directors is the prospect of greater rewards than can be obtained when the return is guaranteed.

The advantages of owning common stock seem all the greater in periods of general inflation, when the fixed income of bondholders becomes less and less attractive from the point of view of purchasing power. Many companies enjoy not only increasing profits in such periods but also increasing monetary values of their fixed assets, so that their common stocks are considered especially attractive investments.

The Flow of Funds Related to Common Stock and Its Measurement

In the case of bonds, we identified certain outflows of funds as committed because the corporation had entered into the bond contract.

Although no such enforceable commitments are made to the common stockholder, two kinds of funds flows must be identified with this type of security. The first of these is an actual outflow of funds to the shareholder, in the form of such cash dividends as may be paid. This flow is of the same nature as the burden of a bond, and it is on an after-tax basis because the law does not regard it as a cost. The amount of the dividend is, therefore, an important measure. It is usually computed and expressed as the *dividend per share*.

The special nature of the common stock interest brings another flow into consideration. Since the common shareholder has the residual equity, he is entitled to consider as his all the earnings after prior charges, whether or not they are to be distributed as dividends. Funds earned but not paid out serve to add to the value of the stockholder's interest. A measure of equal importance to *dividend per share* is, therefore, *earnings per share*.

These two measures can be illustrated by referring to the Allied Chemical financial statements on page 356. The per share figures are arrived at as follows:

(In Thousands)

Earnings before interest and income tax (E.B.I.T.)	$102,000
Deduct: Bond interest	7,000
	$ 95,000
Deduct: Federal income taxes @ 52%	49,400
Net earnings on total common stock (19,906,318 shares)	$ 45,600
Dividends on common stock	$ 31,352
Net earnings per common share (E.P.S.)	$ 2.29*
Dividend per share	$ 1.57½

* For purposes of our example, we have used a 52% tax rate rather than the actual taxes shown on Allied Chemical statements. Actual E.P.S. for 1959 was $2.51.

Note that the figures of $2.29 and $1.57½ per share are on an after-tax basis and that they may also be considered on a before-tax basis. Thus, in this case, it takes $95 million of before-tax earnings to produce the $45.6 million of earnings after taxes to which the common shareholders have claim. On a similar basis, it takes $65.32 million of before-tax earnings to enable the company to pay $1.57½ per share of dividends.[6]

A measure of the same nature as the ratio of earnings coverage for bonds or preferred stock is computed for common stock in the form of the *pay-out ratio*, which is the amount paid in dividends divided by the earnings:

$$\frac{\text{Dividend per Share}}{\text{Earnings per Share}} = \frac{1.575}{2.29} = 69\%.$$

[6] In making calculations or projections of earnings data where the exact tax is not known, our practice is to assume that the full federal corporate income tax applies, which in 1959 was 52% of taxable income.

It is a common practice of investors to relate earnings per share and dividends per share to the market price of the stock. Thus, *dividend yield* is the dividend expressed as a percentage of the market price at whatever point of time is significant in the analysis. The average market price for Allied Chemical common stock during 1959 was $58. Thus, the yield based on this price would be:

$$\frac{\text{Dividend per Share}}{\text{Average Price}} = \frac{1.575}{58} = 2.71\%.$$

The relationship between earnings per share and market price is most commonly expressed in terms of the *price-earnings ratio*, which in the Allied Chemical example would be:

$$\frac{\text{Market Price}}{\text{Earnings per Share}} = \frac{58}{2.29} = \frac{25}{1}.$$

Thus, the stock is said to be selling at 25 times earnings. This also can be expressed as an *earnings yield* similar to the dividend yield, as follows:

$$\frac{\text{Earnings per Share}}{\text{Market Price}} = \frac{2.29}{58} = 3.94\%.$$

Summary: Common Stock

In summary of this section on common stock, we can say that the holder of this stock has no enforceable promises relating to monetary payments. He shares in the residual values of the company, and benefits or loses as the company prospers or declines. The value of the stock depends not on promises to pay but upon the ability of the company to grow in value, and thus reinvested earnings will influence the price of the stock. Dividends depend upon management decisions, but there are several reasons why management will consider paying dividends when earnings exist. Useful measures of the position of a common stock include earnings per share, dividends per share, and ratios of earnings or dividends to price.

The Preferred Stock

The preferred stock represents a type of corporate financing which is somewhat paradoxical as between its nominal characteristics and its practical application. On the surface, it appears to provide the corporation with a security which couples the limited obligation of the bond with the flexibility of the common stock—a combination which would be unusually attractive to the issuer. Unfortunately, general experience does not bear out such expectations.

From the purely legal point of view the preferred stock is a type of ownership certificate and thus takes a classification similar to that of the common stock. Accounting practice recognizes this by placing preferred stock along with common stock in the net worth section of the balance sheet, and tax laws interpret preferred dividends as a distribution of net profits to the owners rather than a cost of the business, as in the case of bond interest. The preferred stock certificate is much the same as that for the common stock, stating that the named individual is the owner of a number of shares of preferred stock with such "designations, preferences, privileges, and voting powers, and the restrictions and qualifications thereof," as are shown on the face and reverse side of the certificate. Unlike the bond, the preferred stock does not contain any promise of repayment of the original investment; and as far as the shareholders are concerned, this must be considered as a permanent investment for the life of the company. Many preferred issues give the corporation the right to call in the stock and pay off the shareholders at a predetermined price, but there is no obligation to do so.[7] Further, there is no legal obligation to pay a fixed rate of return on the investment.

The special character of the preferred stock lies in its relationship to the common stock. When a preferred stock is used as a part of the corporate capital structure, the rights and responsibilities of the owners as the residual claimants to the asset values and earning power of the business no longer apply equally to all shareholders. Two types of owners emerge, representing a voluntary subdivision of the overall ownership privileges. Specifically, the common shareholders agree that the preferred shareholder shall have "preference" or first claim in the event that the directors are able and willing to pay a dividend. In the case of what is termed a nonparticipating or straight preferred stock, which is the most frequent type, the extent of this priority is a fixed percentage of the par value of the stock or a fixed number of dollars per share in the case of stock without a nominal or par value.

For example, in May, 1965, the Allis-Chalmers Manufacturing Company issued a new 4.20% preferred stock. According to the terms of the issue, the preferred shareholders were entitled to $4.20 annually in dividends on each $100 par value share before the common shareholders would be allowed to receive a cash dividend. The issue was cumulative, which is true of most preferred issues, and which means that before any common dividends can be paid, not only must the current preferred dividend have been paid but also the preferred dividends of previous years which have remained unpaid. The issue was also made convertible at the option of the shareholder into common stock at a prescribed rate of exchange and callable at the option of the company at predetermined prices. A discussion of the significance of these latter features will be reserved for a later chapter in the book.

It must be emphasized that the prior claim of the preferred stock does

---

[7] Some preferred issues are subject to sinking funds, but the annual payments are usually a small fraction of the amount outstanding.

not guarantee a fixed and regular rate of return similar to that on a bond —it merely establishes an order of priority in which the board of directors will pay dividends *if* it decides to do so. At the same time, it establishes a definite upper limit to the preferred shareholders' claim on earnings. Whatever the profitability of the Allis-Chalmers Company, the preferred shareholders of this issue will never receive more than the $4.20 per share per annum dividend.

In most cases the prior position of preferred stock extends to the disposition of assets in event of liquidation of the business. Again, the priority is only with reference to the common stock and does not affect the senior position of creditors in any way. It has meaning and value only if asset values remain after creditors have been fully satisfied—a condition which is by no means certain in the event of liquidation following bankruptcy. In the preferred issue cited above, the shareholders are entitled to receive $100 per share plus accrued dividends, in the event of involuntary liquidation, before the common shareholders participate in the remaining assets.

So far, we have considered the preferred stock in terms of the formal rights and responsibilities inherent in this type of security. The impression created is that of a limited commitment on dividends coupled with considerable freedom in the timing of such payments. In reality, experience with preferred stocks indicates that the flexibility in dividend payments is more apparent than real. The management of a business which is experiencing normal profitability and growth desires to pay a regular dividend on both common and preferred stock because of a sense of responsibility to the corporate owners and/or because of the necessity of having to solicit further equity capital in the future. The pressure for a regular common dividend in many cases assures the holder of a preferred stock in the same company that his regular dividend will not be interrupted, even in years when profits are insufficient to give common shareholders a comparable return, for it is very damaging to the reputation of a common stock (and therefore its price) if preferred dividend arrearages stand before it. The fact that most preferred issues are substantially smaller in total amount than the related common issue means that the cash drain of a preferred dividend is often less significant than the preservation of the status of the common stock.

The result is that management comes to view the preferred issue much as it would a bond, establishing the policy that the full preferred dividend must be paid as a matter of course. The option of passing the dividend still exists, but it is seen as a step to be taken only in case of unusual financial difficulty.[8] Under such a circumstance, the obvious question presents itself: Why, then, use preferred stock as a means of raising

---

[8] The experience of the 1930's is evidence of the fact that such periods do occur; and it must be recognized that in such conditions of severe economic recession, large numbers of preferred issues will stand in arrears.

permanent capital? Why not use bonds instead? The primary advantage of the preferred stock becomes identical with that of a bond, namely, the opportunity to raise funds at a fixed return which is less than that realized when the funds are invested. On the other hand, the dividend rate on preferred stock is typically above the interest rate on a comparable bond and is not allowable as a cost for tax purposes. Of course, the bond is more likely to have a sinking fund, so that the *burden* of bond and preferred may not be greatly different.

The differential in cost between a preferred stock and an alternative debt issue may be considered a premium paid for the option of postponing the fixed payments. If management is reluctant to exercise this option, it is likely that the premium will be considered excessive. However, the closer a company gets to its recognized debt limits, the more management is likely to appreciate the option to defer the dividend on a preferred stock issue and be willing to pay a premium for this potential defense against a tight cash position.

The Flow of Funds Related to Preferred Stock

It is our opinion that for planning purposes, management should regard preferred dividends (and sinking funds, if any) as a fixed charge. This concept of preferred stock should therefore be reflected in quantitative analysis except when the viewpoint is that of senior creditors. The recommended management approach is seen in the following calculations. In the Allis-Chalmers Company example the total annual dividend payment on 300,000 shares of the new preferred stock would be $1,260,000. Like common dividends, preferred dividends are (except for certain older utility issues)[9] treated for tax purposes as a distribution of profits and not as a cost. Consequently, the sum of $1,260,000, which is a payment after taxes, may also be considered in terms of the before-tax income necessary to cover this payment. Assuming a 48% federal corporate income tax, the figure would work out approximately as follows:

Preferred dividends......................$1,260,000
Tax related at 48% rate.................. 1,163,076
Required before-tax income..............$2,423,076

As a measure of the degree of assurance which the investor may place in the continuity of this dividend, we may use the same criterion suggested for bonds, namely, coverage. In discussing the ratios of times interest earned and times burden covered in connection with bonds, it was suggested that whatever particular issue happens to be under consideration, the calculation should include in the denominator the interest and sinking fund charges on all fixed debt.

---

[9] Internal Revenue Code, 1954, Sec. 247.

Likewise, in considering preferred stock, our calculations should include the total burden of all securities which are equal or senior to the issue in question, because all must be paid if this class is to be. Thus, the ratio of times burden covered for preferred stock should have earnings before interest and taxes and depreciation in the numerator and in the denominator the total of the following, where they apply:

1. Total bond interest.
2. Total sinking funds on bonds plus tax related.
3. Total preferred dividends plus tax related.
4. Total sinking funds on preferred stock (if any) plus tax related.

In the case of Allis-Chalmers, the company had four long-term debt issues outstanding plus a senior preferred as of December 31, 1964. The pertinent information for Allis-Chalmers' 1965 capital structure, assuming net earnings at the 1964 level and including the new preferred stock issue and a new debenture issue at the full annual rate of servicing, is as follows (in thousands):

	Amount before Tax	Amount of Tax Related @ 48%	Amount after Tax
Total interest on debt	$ 5,078	$ 2,437	$ 2,641
Sinking funds on debt	7,058	3,388	3,670
Total preferred dividends*	3,163	1,518	1,645
Total burden	$15,299	$ 7,343	$ 7,956
Earnings before interest at 1964 (E.B.I.T.) level	$26,675	$12,804	$13,871
Depreciation charged	18,980		
Net funds inflow from operations	45,655		

*There was no sinking fund on preferred stock.

Times Burden Covered, including Preferred Stock: $\dfrac{45,655}{15,299} = 3.0$.

It is often useful, especially where management regards a common dividend as a part of an established financial policy, to extend the calculation of burden to include the amounts related to the dividend on the common stock. For example, the table just above can be extended as follows (in thousands):

	Amount before Tax	Amount of Tax Related @ 48%	Amount after Tax
Total burden (preferred)	$15,299	$ 7,343	$ 7,956
Common dividends (1964 level)	8,633	4,144	4,489
Total burden (including common)	$23,932	$11,487	$12,445

$\left[\text{Times Burden Covered, including All Dividends: } \dfrac{45,655}{23,932} = 1.9.\right.$

On page 363 we illustrated a form for calculating the effect of an existing or proposed capital structure on the position of the common shareholder as measured by earnings per share. This can be modified to take account of preferred stock, as seen in the following example based on Allis-Chalmers income data at the 1964 level:

	(In Thousands)
Earnings before interest and taxes	$26,675
Deduct: Bond interest	5,078
	$21,597
Deduct: Federal income taxes @ 48%	10,366
Net earnings after interest and taxes	$11,231
Deduct: Preferred dividends	1,645
Net earnings on common stock	$ 9,586
Net earnings per common share (E.P.S.) (9,101,382 shares outstanding)	$ 1.05

Summary: The Preferred Stock

To summarize what has been said about preferred stock, it is a security that offers no contractual guaranty of dividends, although it does define the amounts that may be received and usually provides for the accumulation of dividends that are not paid. In fact, most preferred stocks are issued with the intent of management to pay the dividends on time; and for analytical purposes, they should be treated as a kind of debt, although they are not legally so considered. Preferred dividends cannot be considered as costs, and the income tax related to the dividend is part of the burden of the issue. If there is a sinking fund, it is part of the burden, too.

General Summary

As mentioned at the beginning of this chapter, we have confined our attention to the basic security types—bonds, straight preferred stock, and common stock. This has enabled us to examine the fundamental characteristics of these securities free of the distractions which would result if the discussion were extended to include the many modified forms of bonds and stocks. Later, in Chapters 24 and 25, it will be seen that these modified security forms evolve in the bargaining process between issuer and investor as variations in, or modifications of, the normal distribution of risk, income, and/or control found in the basic types.

We have in this chapter illustrated certain quantitative measures which we have found most useful in appraising the financial significance and effects of these basic security types. In particular, we have emphasized the ratios of times interest earned and times burden covered for senior securities and the measures of earnings per share, price/earnings ratio, and dividend and earnings yields for common stock. Throughout, a careful distinction has been drawn between before-tax and after-tax comparisons. Whether or not the reader accepts our preference for before-tax comparisons, it is essential that the calculations be consistently on one basis or the other and that the analyst be ready to use either. Finally, the analysis of this chapter has been confined to data available to both the external and the internal analyst. In the chapters which follow, we will develop ideas for a more detailed analysis by the internal financial staff, which is made possible by access to privileged financial information.

Chapter 18

The Use of Securities to Allocate
Risk, Income, and Control

IN CHAPTER 17 we described important characteristics of the basic security types taken separately. We shall now begin to consider how these securities relate to one another when they are used in combination in the financing of a single corporation. It is in the power of management to decide from time to time what type or types of security shall be used. It might be desirable to use debt, preferred stock, new common stock, or retained earnings—most often, in fact, some combination of these. It is therefore one of the tasks of financial management to decide on the "mix" of securities most suitable to the policies of the company.

As we begin to explore the determinants of the management decision about the most desirable capital structure, we shall find that the types of securities available permit the allocation of certain attributes of business activity to security holders in varying proportions. Chief among these attributes are risk, income (or cost, depending on the point of view), and control. In this chapter we shall see how these elements have been subdivided in a specific corporation, from which we can draw facts for illustration. We have chosen a company that makes use of long-term debt (notes), preferred stock, and common stock in a relatively uncomplicated capital structure. It is Standard Brands Incorporated, and our data are taken from its financial statements for the year ended December 31, 1964.

At the time of our example, we see a company with total assets of $292 million and annual earnings before interest and federal income taxes of $46 million. The assets, of course, are funds which have been invested in the properties of the business. From our knowledge of the makeup of a balance sheet, we know that the liabilities and stockholders' equity side shows the sources from which the investment of $292 million has come (see Table 18–1).

It is apparent from the balance sheet that with the exception of the current liabilities, which by definition are due within a period of less than

1 year, and the amounts payable to the International Division subsidiaries, these sources are all on a long-term basis. In Table 18–2 we have made a more detailed statement of the sources of long-term funds, including several calculations that will be referred to later in this chapter. The $217 million total shown is referred to collectively as the *capitalization* or the *invested capital* of the company. When we speak of the capitalization of a

TABLE 18–1

STANDARD BRANDS INCORPORATED
CONSOLIDATED BALANCE SHEET
As of December 31, 1964
(In Thousands)

ASSETS

Current assets:

Cash		$ 13,751
Accounts receivable, less reserve		45,135
Inventories		104,611
Prepaid expenses		1,253
		$164,750
Investments, at cost		2,880
Plant and equipment, net		118,925
Goodwill		5,788
Total assets		$292,343

LIABILITIES AND STOCKHOLDERS' EQUITY

Current liabilities	$ 55,593
Payable to International Division subsidiaries	4,890
Reserves	14,651
Long-term debt	30,357
Cumulative preferred stock	20,000
Common stock	26,544
Capital surplus	6,478
Retained earnings	136,180
Less: Common stock held in treasury, at cost	(2,350)
Total liabilities and stockholders' equity	$292,343

company, we are therefore talking about the funds provided by the long-term creditors and the owners—the latter through stock subscription and reinvested earnings.

The first on this list of long-term sources is long-term debt, $30,357,-000 of 3.7% promissory notes, which were privately placed in 1946 in the amount of $45,000,000. The agreement called for annual payments of $2,250,000 to be made on April 1, 1962–1975, with the balance payable on April 1, 1976. This debt makes up 14% of the capitalization, a relationship often referred to as the *debt ratio*. The terms of this issue reflect the results of the bargain made between Standard Brands Incorporated, which was the issuer, and the lenders. They also reflect the market conditions at the time the debt was issued.

The funds provided by direct shareholder investment came in part from a preferred stock issue as well as from the sale of common stock. The preferred shareholders of Standard Brands have made their funds available to the management on the promise of limited dividends of $3.50 on a share with no par value but a stated value of $100. This series of preferred stock, which is cumulative and callable, was offered in 1946 on the basis of an exchange of 1.1 shares for each $4.50 preferred share then outstanding. This issue makes up 9% of the total capitalization, and the _debt and preferred ratio_ is 23%.

TABLE 18–2

DETAILS OF CAPITALIZATION OF STANDARD BRANDS INCORPORATED
As of December 31, 1964

(Dollar Figures in Thousands)

	Amount	Capitalization Ratios
Long-term debt—3.7% notes, 1976............	$ 30,357	14%
Preferred stock—$3.50 no par.................	20,000	9%
Total of debt and preferred stock........	$ 50,357	23%
Common stock equity		
Common stock: Subscribed value, less stock		
held in treasury........................	$ 30,671	
Retained earnings (excluding reserves)........	136,180	
Total common stock equity.............	$166,851	77% = S
Total capitalization....................	$217,208	100%
Earnings before interest and taxes........	$ 46,028	21.2%

BURDEN, DECEMBER 31, 1964

	Before Tax of 48%	After Tax of 48%
Interest, long-term notes.....................	$ 1,123	$ 584
Preferred dividend...........................	1,346	700
	$ 2,469	$1,284
Sinking fund due 1965........................	4,327	2,250
Total...............................	$ 6,796	$3,534

Times Interest and Preferred Dividend Earned $= 18.6 = T$.

The rest of the equity capital came through the sale of common stock. This stock, a no-par value issue, is the current distribution of the ownership interest and has altered over time in both form and amount as new shares have been issued and changes in the capital structure have occurred. The shareholders, both preferred and common, invested without promised maturity and hence for an unlimited period so far as they were concerned. These issues make up an investment base which can be as permanent as the business itself.

The remaining item is the total of _retained earnings_. The figure of $136,180,000 is the sum total of those profits which have been realized over the years since incorporation (net of any losses) and which have been reinvested in the business rather than distributed in the form of dividends. These earnings stand to the credit of the common shareholders, and the common shareholders' equity therefore includes them. Unlike the investment in stock, the earned surplus is an amount which the board of directors is legally entitled to distribute to the shareholders at any time. In practice, however, such action is unlikely to take place, since most, if not all, of the funds provided by profits have long since become a permanent part of the asset structure upon which the present earning capacity is based. The reader is reminded that surplus represents a surplus of historical values, not of liquid assets, as some ill-informed people believe. Seventy-seven percent of the capitalization is represented by the common stock equities in this corporation. This is sometimes referred to as the *equity ratio*.

With the details of the capitalization of Standard Brands before us, we now turn to the ways in which certain of the characteristics of the company have been allocated to the three types of securities that have been used.

The Distribution of Risk

Under a private enterprise system the prospects for individual gain are inevitably associated with the possibility of loss, and this hazard rests on those who have supplied the capital. The hazard shows itself in the uncertainty both of the income to be received and also of the recovery of the original principal invested. It is to these uncertainties that we turn under the heading of "risk."

If a firm fails to realize a profit and continues to spend more money than it takes in, the time will come when it is unable to meet its current obligations. When there is no longer enough to go around and some legal claims against the business remain unsatisfied, the company is said to be *insolvent* or *bankrupt*. If this occurs, certain legal procedures are instituted to assure a fair and orderly distribution of the remaining assets (in liquidation) or revision of claims (in reorganization), following a pattern of priorities established by the terms previously negotiated for the outstanding obligations of the company.

All debts are to be settled in full before any equity claim can be paid. Among the debts, there are certain claims which have top priority over all others. These are established by law and include tax liabilities and the legal expenses that arise because of the bankruptcy. All other debts have equal priority unless some specific collateral has been provided. Let us assume that the values of the assets of the bankrupt company amount to 90% of the debts after paying the special types mentioned above. Then all debts in this general category should receive 90% of their amount, regardless of their form. The open account payable to a supplier ranks equally with the formal bond.

As we saw in Chapter 13, persons negotiating debt contracts can improve their position against the prospect of bankruptcy by arranging to have a secured position. In the field of long-term debt, a real estate mortgage is a common type of such a pledge, though many other forms exist, as will appear in a later chapter. We have already discussed the limits to the significance of collateral—the claim has priority only as to the value of the specified assets; and if the asset has ceased to produce a return on investment, that value may be seriously in question. Nevertheless, properly selected collateral can add substantially to the relative position of a debt claim in a bankruptcy.

The existence of such priorities as those just mentioned further strengthens the position of a creditor as contrasted with any holder of any equity security and further contributes to a creditor's willingness to lend funds and to take a fixed rate of return in the form of interest instead of requiring a proportionate share in the profits. The relatively low cost of raising money by the use of debt comes from the more certain position of the investor derived from his creditor position, supplemented in some instances by collateral.

It may be emphasized at this point that the position of creditor is a negotiated one, the result of a bargain between the firm obtaining funds and the person or institution supplying them. The division of risk, therefore, is voluntary on both sides and must be consistent with the established policies of management. The management of a firm has a large amount of choice as to whether or not to permit debt and to give priorities, as an alternative to raising funds by the issuance of equity securities.

The preferred stock contract is like a debt contract in that it confers a priority on its owner, but this is only superior to the common equity. All debts must be fully settled before any claim arising from a preferred stock can be met. In the previous chapter we suggested that management should, for planning purposes, view preferred stock as if its claims were debt claims. While this is the appropriate posture for management, the preferred holder should always be aware that he does not have the protection against the ultimate risk of bankruptcy that any holder of a debt has. The intermediate position of preferred stock as to risk is normally reflected in a dividend rate somewhat higher than the interest rate on a bond of the same company issued at the same time.

Although financial failure occurs in only a minority of instances, and hence may seem unimportant, a priority position also influences the market value given to the securities of going concerns. Since the future is never wholly certain, the bonds of strong firms enjoy better markets than those of weak ones, and the bonds of any firm can be expected to exhibit more stable prices than the equity issues of the same firm, both in periods of poor economic results and in days of prosperity.

It is, therefore, within the power of a firm to increase the stability of the market price of some of the securities it issues, but only within the limits of the firm's capacity to stabilize, given its inherent cash flow characteristics, and only by creating a greater risk for the junior issues of the company.

Little needs to be added about the position of common stock with reference to the allocation of risk, because the matter is implicit in the preceding paragraphs. Management can weaken the position of common stock with reference to claims on assets for advantages which will appear below, but it cannot strengthen it, since the common stockholder is last in line, and there is no one to whom he may turn for greater assurance of income or principal.

While the market price of a security is the result of many forces, it reflects in its stability or instability the degree of confidence that investors have in the security. In illustration of the effect of the uneven distribution of risk on the market prices of bonds, preferred stock, and common stock, we have chosen the 1957 record of three issues of the Erie Railroad and plotted them in Chart 18–1. The first is one of the bond issues under the consolidated mortgage. Not only is it a debt instrument, containing firm promises to pay interest and principal, but it is secured by the existence of a mortgage of property whose value is directly tied to these bonds, whatever happens to the Erie Railroad corporation.

Erie's preferred stock comes below a number of issues of bonds, so far as priority of claim for dividends is concerned. It would receive nothing in liquidation until every debt of any nature had been settled in full. Thus, it is not surprising to find that its price was more responsive to the developing pessimism in 1957.

Erie's common stock, which bore not only the risks of the railroad business but also those created by the promises made to bond and preferred issues (those *senior* to it), was considered much more risky, as Chart 18–1 shows.

For the same basic reasons, if the outlook in 1957 had been for growing railroad prosperity, one could expect the common stock to rise as steeply as it fell. The preferred and bond issues would respond in a less pronounced upward movement.

From the point of view of management in a going business, what happens in the event of failure is secondary to the question of what needs to be done to avoid failure. The practical concern of management at the time of signing a debt contract, as far as risk is concerned, is the extent to which the increase in the total of fixed cash payments resulting from the new interest and sinking fund commitments makes the task of avoiding failure (cash insolvency) more difficult. A rational appraisal of the risk element would relate expectations on the magnitude and timing of cash flows to cash outflows, particularly to mandatory cash outflows, in an effort to anticipate the chances of being "out of cash" at some time in the future and to determine how these chances are affected by the additional fixed cash commitments. In this regard, the principal amount of the debt is meaningful only when it is translated into the terms of repayment. Since there are wide variations in these terms as between different debt contracts, it is necessary to examine the sinking fund requirements in detail for each debt issue of the company.

CHART 18–1

ERIE RAILROAD COMPANY
Relative Changes in Market Price of Three Securities, Weekly, 1957
Prices of Week Ended January 4, 1957 = 100*

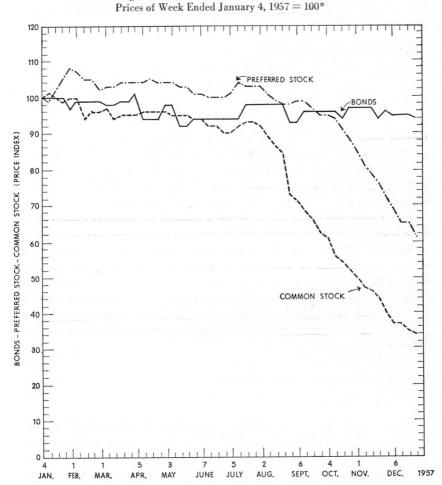

* Prices for week ended January 4, 1957, were as follows: bonds, 92; preferred, 72½; common, 20.
SOURCE: *Commercial and Financial Chronicle*, issues for 1957.

To illustrate this point, we return to the Standard Brands case. The lower half of Table 18–2 (page 373) translates the $30,357,000 of long-term notes into the annual cash outflows which Standard Brands must provide for the repayment of this debt, as defined by the contracts. Remember that sinking fund payments are made in after-tax dollars.

Since the terms of repayment illustrated in Table 18–2 are negotiated and are open to a considerable range of variation, it can be seen that the degree of risk presented by a debt of any given principal amount can be altered somewhat by management if it chooses to give priority to this in its negotiations with the creditor before the signing of the contract. Thus, for example, extending the life of the loan by 10 years could substantially reduce the annual cash drain required to retire the debt by the maturity date. Naturally, the opportunity to modify the risk in this manner will depend heavily on the bargaining position of the borrower and the risk standards of the lender.

The Allocation of Income

Standard Brands reported for 1964 the amount of $46,028,000 as earnings before interest and taxes. This can be related to the year-end capitalization of $217,208,000 to show a return on invested capital of 21.2%. Despite the fact that the corporation earned this return, it paid only 3.7% on the funds raised by its long-term debt. The preferred dividend of $3.50 a share, when translated to a before-tax basis, required 7% on the stated value of this issue. Clearly, the holders of the senior securities of this company were satisfied with relatively low returns on their investment. They preferred to receive fixed incomes and to enjoy stable market values rather than to participate in all the risks of the business.

The safety granted to these holders of senior securities was obtained by increasing the risk of the investment of the common equity shareholders, who promised fixed returns and granted priorities in liquidation to the holders of the bonds and preferred stock. By this acceptance of greater risk, the common equity created for itself the expectation of greater return on the investment of the common stock. This process has long been known as *trading on the equity,* a term which indicates that a bargain has been made between the classes of securities, as is indeed the case. It is also referred to as *leverage.*

Trading on the Equity

A diagram will serve to indicate the nature of the bargain as far as the allocation of income is concerned. Chart 18–2 has been drawn with the horizontal axis representing the $217,208,000 invested capital of Standard Brands. The line has been subdivided into the amounts provided by the various classes of securities, as tabulated in Table 18–2. The vertical axis represents rates of cost or return, so that the area of the rectangle *ABCD* is the product of the rate of return on capital, 21.2% and of the capital itself, or the $46,028,000 earnings before interest and taxes.

On the base representing the capital contributed by each of the senior securities, rectangular areas are shown which represent the amounts of cost required to support these securities. These claims must be met before the common equity can receive anything, thus adding some risk to the equity position. On the other hand, the amount of the senior claims is fixed, and any earnings above these fixed amounts benefit the common shareholders. We have shown this in our diagram by transferring the irregular area above the fixed charges to an equal area based on the amount of the common equity. It will be seen that the effective return on

CHART 18–2

Effects of Trading on the Equity in Standard Brands
Incorporated, 1964

(Dollar Figures in Thousands)

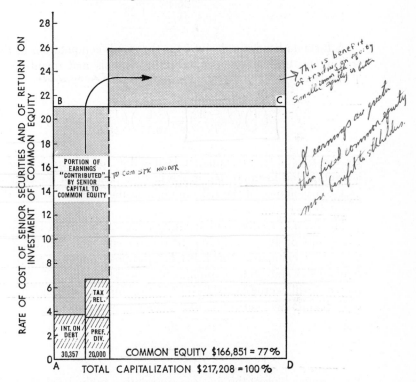

the amount of common equity capital has been increased by trading on the equity from 21.2% to 26.1%. These rates are, as will be recalled, on a before-tax basis.

By comparing these two percentages we have a precise measure of how the use of debt and preferred stock has worked to the benefit of the equity holders of Standard Brands in the year 1964. In everyday business usage, the terms *trading on the equity* and *leverage* are used rather loosely and interchangeably to refer to the substitution of low-cost fixed charge securities in place of common equity capital in the hope of the beneficial effects seen above. One of the authors of this book has suggested that a distinction be drawn between the effect this form of financing has at a point in time and the effect it has over time with respect to the rate of change in earnings on the common equity. Whether or not the reader accepts his use of terms, the distinction is important to recognize.

Following his suggested usage, trading on the equity is defined as: the use of fixed charge securities in the capitalization of a company, measured by the ratio of (1) the rate of return on the existing common stock equity to (2) the rate of return on the entire capitalization as it would have been if there were only common stock outstanding. In this instance the amount is:

$$\frac{26.1}{21.2} = 1.23 .$$

accruing to existing stockholders if >1 is benefit to stockholders

A formula has been derived for the quick computation of the ratio of trading on the equity, using certain symbols and quantities shown in Table 18–2:

times interest + preferred divid. earned.

$$\left(\frac{1}{S}\right)\left(\frac{T-1}{T}\right) = \left(\frac{1}{0.77}\right)\left(\frac{17.6}{18.6}\right) = 1.23 .$$

By the use of this formula, it is possible to determine precisely what advantage has been created in the income position of the common equity by the acceptance of the risks implicit in the promises to pay the charges for senior securities.

The ratio of trading on the equity relates to a certain level of earnings, which obviously is not going to remain constant. What happens when there is a change in the E.B.I.T.? Suppose that the earnings rate on Standard Brands' total capitalization should rise by 2%. Clearly, all the increase will accrue to the benefit of the common shareholders, i.e., 77% of the capital will get 100% of the change, or a growth of

$$\frac{2.0\%}{0.77} = 2.59\% .$$

We can now look at this increase in relation to the level of earnings from which the growth took place. A growth of 2% on 21.2% is an increase of 9.4%. For the common stock equity alone, the growth is 2.59% on 26.1%, or 9.9%. It will be seen that trading on the equity results not only in higher levels of return for the residual equity but also *in higher rates of change* that will occur in the basic earnings of the company.[1]

---

[1] The author suggests that the term leverage be reserved for this effect of debt on the rate of change in earnings. The formula for its measurement, using the symbols of Table 18–2 is

$$\left(\frac{T}{T-1}\right) .$$

For further discussion, see Pearson Hunt, "A Proposal for Precise Definitions of 'Trading on the Equity' and 'Leverage,' " *Journal of Finance*, September, 1961, pp. 377–86.

So far, we have presented the use of senior securities in a favorable light, when seen from the point of view of the holders of the common stock. If this be so, why do corporations not adopt the policy of borrowing all that anyone can lend? There are two important reasons for reluctance, although the second is only a reflection of the first.

Effects on the Cost of Capital

In considering the effect of variations in debt proportions on the cost of capital to the corporation concerned, it is necessary to take account of some differences which appear to exist between rational expectation and observed behavior. To begin with, it is generally agreed that as the proportion of debt increases, the capacity of a business to service that debt without default decreases (all other things remaining equal), the debt becomes a more risky investment in the mind of the lender, and he will expect a higher interest rate to compensate for the increased risk. If the debt is sold publicly and the increase in the debt is large enough, this change will be apparent in a lower rating for the bonds, and there will be the dual effect of rising interest costs on new issues and a narrowing of the market interest in the issue. The latter will be particularly apparent when the rating slips below the "A" rating required for certain institutional investments.

Increased proportions of debt may also be expected to have an effect on the cost of the underlying security issues, particularly the common equity. As we have just illustrated, the volatility, and therefore the riskiness, of the common stock is increased, and reason would lead us to expect an adverse effect on the market price of the common stock, a decline in the price-earnings ratio and a consequent rise in the earnings yield on this stock. And so it would appear that any change in the debt ratio will, in theory at least, be reflected in the cost of each of the elements of the capitalization.[2]

The net effect of these changes and the ultimate implications for the market value of the common stock of leveraged companies is currently a matter of hot debate in the academic literature and, on a much reduced scale, in the business community. In particular, the now-famous Modigliani-Miller thesis that the total market value of all the securities in the capitalization of a company will not change despite the particular debt-equity mix has challenged a very common assumption in business that borrowing lowers the overall cost of capital.[3] Their argument, in simple terms, is that the advantage in improved earnings on the common stock derived by using higher proportions of low-cost debt is exactly offset by the deterioration in the price-earnings ratio due to the increased risk.

[2] For further discussion, see Eli Schwartz, "Theory of the Capital Structure of the Firm," *Journal of Finance*, March, 1959, pp. 18–39.

[3] See Franco Modigliani and M. H. Miller, "The Cost of Capital, Corporation Finance, and the Theory of Investment," *American Economic Review*, June, 1958, pp. 261–97.

Whatever the theoretical merits of this thesis—and one can find able theorists in both opposing camps in this debate—there are certain practical limitations on its application to business decisions. Experience strongly supports the view that there are in practice certain debt levels which are regarded by investors as "reasonable" for certain industrial or commercial categories. It follows from this that the adverse market reaction to higher levels of debt is largely reserved for those companies which are clearly out of line with what is regarded as reasonable or normal. This is consistent with the generally observed phenomenon that market behavior in practice is less continuous than market behavior in theory. It is also relevant that whatever the theoretical or logical facts, if a large segment of the business community *believes* debt is a means of reducing the overall cost of capital, this is a factor to be taken into account. Nor is this necessarily "irrational" behavior, since in practice the decision makers may be concerned about aspects of the decision which lie beyond the maximization of the market value of common stock at a point in time.

We therefore conclude that the debt-equity mix is not a matter of indifference so far as management and the stockholder are concerned and that there are opportunities for lowering the overall cost of capital which should be explored—even though there are theoretical and practical limits on the extent of the expected benefits.

A final note concerns the reference above to debt level norms. It is generally recognized that there are different norms for such industry categories as public utilities, retail food chains, finance companies, oil and gas companies, and so on. There is some tendency to lump manufacturing companies together in this respect, where there is a familiar 30% of capitalization debt standard commonly applied. However, such generalizations must not be taken too literally, and practice clearly shows a wide range of behavior. The following debt-equity ratios, by industry aggregates for the end of the first quarter of 1965,[4] may be of some interest:

All manufacturing corporations, except newspapers..................26.5%
Manufacturers of motor vehicles and equipment.....................11.3
Manufacturers of lumber and wood products, except furniture........48.5
Manufacturers of textile-mill products............................32.6
Manufacturers of apparel and other finished products..............41.0
Manufacturers in petroleum refining and related industries..........17.2

The Location of Control

In Chapter 2 we said that the control of a corporation can be considered as being in the hands of those who have the voting power to elect the board of directors of the corporation. Such power is obviously

---

[4] Based on data in U.S. Federal Trade Commission and Securities and Exchange Commission, *Quarterly Financial Report for Manufacturing Corporations, First Quarter, 1965* (Washington, D.C.: U.S. Government Printing Office, 1965), pp. 12–27.

centralized when a person or group holds a majority of the voting stock. On the other hand, many corporations, even among those of small size, have issued some voting shares to holders who are not part of the management group, so that a threat to control may develop if new issues of voting shares are created or, perhaps, if a preferred stock dividend is passed.

In many cases, therefore, the location and distribution of voting power is an important part of the planning of security issues. There must always be a voting stock outstanding.[5] Sometimes, however, the common stock is "classified," with one class having all the rights of such stock and the other class having all of them except voting power. Many investors are not interested in participating in management, even to the minute degree of making use of a proxy; so there is a market for nonvoting common shares. In 1926, however, the New York Stock Exchange adopted a rule against accepting any future nonvoting common stocks; and although other exchanges have not been as rigid in this respect, nonvoting common has tended to become a device that is adopted with hesitation.

There are rare instances where voting power is not proportionate to the number of shares held. Most cooperative corporations allow but one vote to each stockholder, for example. A "reform" of corporate voting power, which has strong proponents and opponents, is the scheme of *cumulative voting*, where all the nominees for office are voted for at once, and a shareholder is allowed the number of votes resulting from his number of shares multiplied by the number of persons to be elected to the board. The reader will see that this system allows minorities to elect members to the board roughly in proportion to their relative shareholding. The argument rages as to whether such minority representation assists or hinders the proper working of a board of directors. The right to vote cumulatively is assured by a number of states, namely:[6]

Arizona	Kansas	Nebraska	South Dakota
Arkansas	Kentucky	North Carolina	Washington
California	Michigan	North Dakota	West Virginia
Hawaii	Mississippi	Ohio	Wyoming
Idaho	Missouri	Pennsylvania	
Illinois	Montana	South Carolina	

All national banks also have cumulative voting.

---

[5] For many years (1890–1954) the Great Northern Railway Company had only one class of stock outstanding, designated as a $6 noncumulative no-par preferred stock. Each share had one vote. In 1954 the stock was split two for one and reclassified as a common stock. There is also the unique case in Virginia where a corporation acquired all its voting stock from a bank which had taken it over as collateral from the owner, who had defaulted on a loan. Although sympathizing with the management for its efforts to "bail out" the former owner, the probate court ordered the transaction rescinded. It is beyond the powers of a company to extinguish all its voting stock.

[6] C. M. Williams, *Cumulative Voting for Directors* (Boston: Division of Research, Harvard Business School, 1951), p. 8; and Commerce Clearing House, Inc., *Corporation Law Guide* (Chicago, 1965).

In recent years preferred stocks have not received general voting power, although there are still outstanding many older issues with full voting privileges. Instead, it has become customary to confer voting power on the preferred in the event that its dividends or sinking funds fall into arrears for longer than a specified period. Provisions range from the transfer of all voting power from the common to the preferred, a most rare case, to the power to elect a minority of the board of directors to represent the interests of the preferred stock. Such a power in the case of nonpayment of the preferred dividend is very different from the acceleration of maturity which occurs upon the default of a bond, and it has led one of the authors to say that a preferred stockholder has a pillow while a bondholder has a club with which to threaten management.

Before one can take into account the question of the location of voting power, one must have a thorough understanding of the way in which the holders of voting power can be expected to use it. Many corporations have well-established managements whose direct supporters have very few votes. Yet, their nominees are regularly elected to the board of directors through the operation of the proxy system, as described in Chapter 2. A successful proxy fight could unseat the existing management; but if the nonmanagement shareholders are widely scattered, and if there are no large blocks held by persons ready to take leadership, the proxy system can be relied on to provide the necessary support for management.

There is risk in minority control, however, and many managements holding majorities find it almost impossible to consent to any plan which endangers the "absolute" control which they have. (It is not in fact "absolute," for minority interests must always be considered fairly when policies are made.) In our view, small and growing corporations have too often chosen to borrow rather than to sell voting shares because of excessive fear of the risks to management of a public holding of voting control. But the actual appraisal of the risks is too complicated for a general statement. The matter must be studied on a case-by-case basis.

Bondholders, like other creditors, do not have a vote; and as long as the corporation lives up to the terms of the debt contract, they can take no action. The actual situation, however, is less permissive than it seems to be at first glance, for both bond indentures and preferred stock contracts usually contain clauses known as protective provisions specifying what the corporation will do (affirmative covenants) or will not do (negative covenants) during the time the particular security is outstanding. To cite a few examples: corporations may promise not to pay dividends, even on preferred stock, unless earned; they may promise to set aside certain funds for the replacement of assets; and so on. The existence of such clauses leads us to suggest supplementing the definition of control, given in Chapter 2, so that it reads: ". . . We may say for practical purposes that control lies in the hands of the individual or group who has the actual power to select the board of directors (or its majority). In most corporations a measure of control is exercised by the promises that have been made in contracts in force at any moment."

We now return to the instance of Standard Brands to cite examples of major ways in which the control of its policies has been determined by the terms of senior security issues.[7]

1. Term loan (3.7% serial promissory notes).
   Company agrees not to pay cash dividends on common or acquire any stock in excess of consolidated net income after Dec. 31, 1955, plus $15,000,000.

2. $3.50 cumulative preferred; no par (stated value $100).
   Voting rights—Has one vote per share, and in addition whenever equivalent of annual dividend is in arrears preferred, voting separately as a class, is entitled to elect two directors.
   Consent of a majority of preferred necessary to (1) amend provisions to affect rights of preferred adversely; (2) increase authorized preferred; (3) create or increase authorized amount of equal stock or reclassify any stock to rank equal to preferred or any security convertible into preferred or equal stock; (4) dissolve or liquidate, or dispose of (except to subsidiaries) substantially all assets; or (5) merge or consolidate, if thereby any class of stock would rank equal to preferred.
   Consent of 66⅔% of preferred necessary to (1) create or increase authorized amount of any stock or any security convertible into stock prior to preferred; or (2) merge or consolidate, if thereby any class of stock would rank prior to preferred.

There are many types of protective covenants found in security issues. It is one of the places where the limit of possibility is set only by the ingenuity of the draftsman. The actual terms of issues are reached by bargaining between the issuing corporation and some agency representing the investors' interests. We deal further with this subject in the chapters on the bargain for funds. Suffice it to say here by way of summary that questions of control enter into the selection of corporate securities not only with reference to the powers granted to vote at annual meetings, but also in terms of the detailed contractual provisions that may be agreed upon for specific issues.

Summary Grid

The contrasting characteristics of bonds, preferred stock, and common stock with respect to the distribution of income, risk, and control may be summarized in the form of an analytical "grid." We recommend that students use such a grid in getting an overall appraisal of the balance of security types in the capital structure of a corporation. After a time the

---

[7] *Moody's Industrial Manual, 1964*, pp. 1108–9.

TABLE 18-3

Basic Security Types	Income	Risk	Control
Bonds or notes	Fixed payment of 3.7% annually on outstanding notes through April, 1976. Fourteen percent of capitalization.	Contractual obligation to pay interest and repay principal on specified dates. Total outstanding debt as of December 31, 1964, $30,357,000 (plus $2,-250,000 carried in current liabilities). Sinking fund payment April, 1965, $2,250,-000.	No voice in management other than through terms of loan (see p. 385).
Preferred stock	Prior claim to earnings of $3.50 per share before payment of dividends on common. Dividends cumulative. Nine percent of capitalization.	Board has power to suspend dividends without penalty other than (1) suspension of common dividends and (2) election of two directors by preferred shareholders. No sinking fund.	One vote per share (200,000 preferred shares as against 6,635,829 common shares), and in addition, when the equivalent of an annual dividend is in arrears, preferred as a class may elect two directors to a 13-man board. Terms of issue control some policies (see p. 385).
Common stock	Entitled to all earnings remaining after all prior claims deducted. In 1964, this amounted to $3.48 per share, of which $2.25 was paid out in dividends. Ratio of trading on the equity 1.23 (based on 1964 charges and earnings).	Basic risks of the business rest on the common shareholder, who has no legal claim except to the ownership of whatever remains after all other claimants have been satisfied. Debt/equity proportions at the end of 1964 were 14% debt, 9% preferred, and 77% common equity.	Common shareholders elect the board of directors on the basis of one vote per share.

scheme of classification will become habitual and need no longer be done on paper, unless the structure is very complex. The grid in Table 18–3 is illustrated with reference to Standard Brands' capitalization as of December 31, 1964 (see Table 18–2, page 373).

Chapter 19

The Analysis of Alternative Security Issues

In the two preceding chapters, we have focused attention on the basic contracts by means of which a corporation acquires the use of external funds on a long-term basis. The reader is now familiar not only with the nature of these contracts—the common stock, the preferred stock, and the bond—but also with the effect each has on the incidence of the fundamental elements of investment—risk, income, and control. Up to this point, we have considered these securities in a general context as an important part of the institutional framework within which every business corporation operates.

We are now ready to move from the general to the particular and to view these securities through the eyes of the individual corporation facing a need for external funds at a point in time. Considered in this way, these basic security types are seen as alternatives in the solution of a specific financial problem; and we now turn to the analytical methods by which their potential effects may be compared as a preliminary stage in the decision-making process. As we proceed through the analysis, it will become clear to the reader, if it is not clear already, that a decision on the "right" balance of security types can be made only within the context of the individual corporation at a specific stage in its history, in full knowledge of its special circumstances, of the attitudes and objectives of its owners and management, and of the current condition of the capital markets.

Before the reader becomes involved in the details of analysis, it may be helpful to provide him with a little perspective on business practice in this regard. The extent to which the choice of security types occupies the time and attention of the financial officer and the board of directors varies greatly from one company to another and within a single company from period to period over its life span. Obviously, the problem is presented when the company is first organized, though the choice may be simplified by the fact that one or more of the security types may not be available at that time. Subsequently, the frequency with which this type of decision has to be made depends on the rate of growth of the business, the capital requirements of growth, and the extent to which the needed funds can be generated internally. In some companies, even large and successful ones, the treasurer may never face a decision of this type during his period of office. In many businesses, new securities may be floated no more than three or four times over a 20-year period. Obviously, in such companies the growth rate and capital requirements are such that they are substantially or entirely covered by retained earnings. In contrast, there are some companies which are issuing new securities every year.

Even where this problem is presented infrequently, however, it is of critical importance, with long-term financial implications. Usually, the need for additional external funds can be anticipated well in advance, so that there is time for a careful weighing of all relevant considerations. Further, it should be pointed out that although by far the largest proportion of funds for new business investment comes from internal sources, the choice between internal and external sources is an ever-present aspect of long-term financial planning. Every management has some control over the corporate rate of growth and the rate of earnings retention and therefore over the extent to which the need for external funds presents itself. Many managements consciously work to avoid the need for selling new securities; but in so doing, they are making a deliberate choice between equity capital generated internally and capital provided by the sale of stock or bonds. This choice is rational only if it includes a careful analysis of the effects of new external sources of funds.

Establishing a Point of View

For the individual company whose circumstances or policies require it to turn periodically to the external capital market for new long-term funds, there is a necessity for achieving a proper balance of the basic debt and equity sources in its capital structure. What is a "proper balance," however, cannot be determined before we define a point of view from which the use of securities will be assessed. In studying what has occurred in actual cases, one can recognize several distinctly different viewpoints—such as those of the creditors, the management, "the company," the existing shareholders, and the prospective shareholders. It is clear that the relative advantages and disadvantages of securities in the corporate capital structure will appear very differently to individuals with varying relationships to the corporation. What is considered "best" by the bondholders may be viewed as less than best from some other point of view. Thus, for example, the sale of a new block of common stock would be welcomed by bondholders, since they would have prior claim to the earning power and residual values of the funds so acquired. The existing common shareholders, on the other hand, could be strongly opposed, particularly if the stock was sold below market price, because the new shares would dilute their participation in future earnings. Specific illustrations of such effects will be found in the pages to follow. For management to reach a meaningful decision in a given situation, a point of view must be adopted and adhered to consistently.

In the analysis that follows, we adopt the viewpoint of the holder of common stock. It is his interests which are most clearly and intimately connected with the long-term prospects and objectives of the business. It is he who accepts (knowingly or not) the basic risks of ownership and whose resources are committed for the protection of others, including senior security holders. In contrast to this, the interests of the bondholder and preferred shareholder are negotiated and limited by contract. It is the common stockholders, acting as a group, who have the power to elect the board of directors, thus making the board—legally, at least—responsible to them. It seems reasonable to expect that the basic objectives of management will normally be identical with the objectives of the common shareholder and that management in its decisions should reflect this identity of interest.[1]

Of course, this is not to say that in practice management will always take this point of view, nor that it should be interpreted so narrowly as to exclude from consideration the valid interests of others toward whom the company has important responsibilities—creditors, employees, customers, the general public. It is, however, an appropriate starting point for the consideration of problems such as the one posed in this chapter. It should be emphasized that if a new stock issue is in prospect, we narrow the point of view still further by identifying the company's interests with those of the *existing* common shareholders as opposed to the *new* common shareholders where a possible conflict of interest may develop (as, for example, in the pricing of the new issue).

With this point of view, the problem of balance in the capital structure can be brought into focus, though the solution is by no means obvious. Bonds normally offer the best alternative for maximizing earnings per share and do not affect the existing distribution of control. On the other hand, they involve more risk because of the fixed annual burden on cash, a burden which may well be substantially larger than that of other securities because of a sinking fund requirement. The preferred stock will normally appear less attractive than the bond in terms of the income consideration but, on the other hand, may be less risky as a result of a smaller annual burden on cash and more flexible terms of payment. There may also be a possible disadvantage in the voting feature written into many preferred stock issues. Common stock will appear least attractive to existing common shareholders because of the effect on earnings per share and the dilution of control that always takes place if new common shares

---

[1] For a discussion of some points of difference see G. Donaldson, "Financial Goals: Management vs. Stockholders," *Harvard Business Review*, Vol. XLI, No. 3 (May–June, 1963), pp. 116–29.

are issued. On the other hand, since the new stock would be equal in status to the old, it does not add anything to the risks already present except, perhaps, to the risk of the continuity of the common dividend.

It will be apparent that the choice of securities is a problem which cannot be solved in general terms or by any simple formula. There are pros and cons for each alternative, and the final choice must be left to individual judgment in each particular case. At the same time, however, if the analysis of these considerations is carried out in a thorough and objective manner, the resulting capital structure should, within limits, fit into a general pattern suited to the character of the industry in which the business operates.

A Problem for Analysis

The process of analysis of alternative security issues will be most meaningful if illustrated with reference to an actual company. In order to take full advantage of the knowledge built up in the two preceding chapters, we shall continue with the case of Standard Brands Incorporated. To do so, however, requires us to set up a hypothetical situation. Previous references to this company related to its capital structure as of the end of 1964. In order to preserve the time sequence, it will be assumed that the company developed a need for external funds in the early months of 1965 and was considering alternative sources. (In fact, the company financed its 1965 operations entirely through internal sources.) It is further assumed that the funds required amounted to $30 million and that the company was confining its consideration to the basic security types already outstanding—bonds, preferred stock, and common stock.

The market for the securities of Standard Brands during the early months of 1965 continued to be relatively stable. This stability gave some support for the assumption that current market values could be used as an adequate guide for the immediate future when the new securities would be offered. The common stock price appeared to fluctuate within a range of ± $6 around an average price of $78 a share. The $3.50 preferred stock was selling around $84 to yield 4.16% to the new investor. Yields on the bond market had moved upward since the company's last debt issue in 1946. Working against this trend was the fact that the company was now a much larger and presumably more stable company, a factor which should place it in a lower risk category in the minds of prospective lenders.

While much of the challenge and excitement of new security issues lies in the uncertainty surrounding the price at which the securities will actually be sold, we shall for the moment bypass the important step of market analysis and assume that the following conclusions have been reached: new common stock can be sold at $75 a share, a new $4.50 preferred series can be sold at $100, and a 20-year bond issue bearing a coupon rate of 4.25% can also be sold at par. Underwriting, legal, and other costs incidental to the flotation of these issues will be ignored for the sake of simplicity. We now proceed to consider the implications of these three alternative methods of raising $30 million for Standard Brands and its common stockholders, particularly with reference to the effects on the allocation of risk, income, and control.

Comparisons of Alternatives: The Effect on Income

It will be apparent to the reader that in order to consider the income effect of a $30 million issue of one of these three security types, it is necessary to make some estimate of what the basic earning capacity of Standard Brands will be in the foreseeable future when the new securities will have become a part of the company's capital structure. Since few businesses are able to make meaningful detailed forecasts of earnings and cash flows beyond the period of a year, it seems appropriate to start with earnings expectations for the year 1965. Management's expectations, as revealed in the company's annual report for 1964, reflected confidence in the continuation of the growth and profitability shown in 1964.

This, then, becomes our starting point. Table 18–2 (page 373) showed that earnings before interest and taxes (E.B.I.T.) in 1964 were 21.2% of total capitalization. Let us assume that in 1965 the company will earn just over 21% on the total permanent funds invested, including the $30 million of new funds. (This is, of course, somewhat optimistic, since it will take time for the new funds to find their way into profitable employment and earn at their full potential.) If this is the case, the effect on the earnings per common share resulting from the three alternatives will be as shown in Table 19–1.

It can be seen that on the basis of the anticipated effect on earnings per share—the criterion which we believe is of greatest immediate concern to the existing common stockholders—the most favorable result is produced by an issue of bonds, an E.P.S. of $3.84. This represents an improvement of 40 cents a share over the 1964 E.P.S. The improvement follows from the fact that the new investment is expected to earn 21% before taxes, as compared with the effective cost of the debt, which is expected to be 4.25% (before taxes). The preferred stock ranks second in terms of a favorable income effect, with an expected E.P.S. of $3.73. The increase in preferred dividends more than makes up for the lower level of interest payments under this alternative, so that the net result is less favorable to the common stockholder. The result is again more favorable than the 1964 E.P.S., since the 21% return on the new investment exceeds the cost of the new preferred stock. Note here, however, that the comparison is not with the 4.5% dividend rate, but with the rate of before-tax earnings (8.65%), which must be realized in order to pay the preferred dividends out of after-tax earnings without depleting what is left for the common shareholder. The least attractive from the income point of view is the common stock alternative, where the anticipated E.P.S. is $3.71—27 cents a share above 1964 level.

Two points are worth noting about the results in this particular example, both relating to the peculiarities of the market at this time. One is the relatively narrow differential between the interest rate on the debt and the dividend rate on the preferred stock—a quarter of a percent would hardly appear adequate to compensate for the significant difference

TABLE 19-1

(Dollar Figures in Thousands)

	1964 Capital Structure and Earnings	1965 Earnings @ 21% of Capitalization, Assuming $30 Million Expansion Financed by		
		Bonds	Preferred Stock	Common Stock
Earnings before interest and taxes......	$46,028	$52,328	$52,328	$52,328
Interest on debt.....................	1,123	2,398	1,123	1,123
	$44,905	$49,930	$51,205	$51,205
U.S. federal income tax @ 48%........	21,554	23,966	24,578	24,578
Net profit after taxes.................	$23,351	$25,964	$26,627	$26,627
Preferred dividends..................	700	700	2,050	700
Net earnings on common stock........	$22,651	$25,264	$24,577	$25,927
Number of common shares outstanding (in thousands).....................	6,585	6,585	6,585	6,985*
Earnings per share..................	$3.44	$3.84	$3.73	$3.71
Chart 19-1 reference point............		(3)		(4)

* Assuming new stock sold at $75 a share: 400,000 new shares.   *shows benefit of trading on equity*

in risk between these two security forms. The larger difference in the resultant E.P.S. is primarily due to the difference in tax treatment. The other point to be noted is the relatively high market price for the common stock, which means that even when the expansion is financed by common stock, there is an improvement in E.P.S. over the 1964 level. Unfortunately, this is not always the case. It is quite usual to find the results of a common issue much less beneficial to earnings than the bond and preferred stock alternatives—even to the point where it may actually *reduce* E.P.S. below the previous level.

In spite of these market circumstances for Standard Brands securities at this time, however, the bonds, preferred stock, and common stock come out in a normal 1, 2, 3 ranking as far as the income effect is concerned. The question arises: Would this be true if corporate earnings in 1965 or any subsequent year prove to be different from the 1964 level? It is inherent in the nature of a dynamic economy that they will be. The critical question is, therefore, not whether the E.P.S. will differ from that shown in Table 19-1, but rather whether it will change so much and in such a manner that the ranking will change. We can, of course, test for this by substituting another earnings assumption in place of the 21% return in Table 19–1. If this is done, the most sensible approach would be to estimate an upper and a lower limit for anticipated earnings and work out an E.P.S. calculation for each alternative at these two extremes. If the results show the same ranking at the extremes, then from an income point of view one of these long-term sources will be clearly preferable to the other two.

It is possible, however, that the ranking may differ so that, for example, common stock would have the more favorable income effect at the lower level of earnings and bonds the more favorable effect at the upper level. In such a case, we need more information. This is best provided by the analytical device of a range-of-earnings chart, which will be the subject of the next section.

The Range-of-Earnings Chart

In considering the potential effects on earnings per share of alternative security types under varying assumptions with respect to future earnings, it is desirable to be able to observe these effects over the entire range of expected earnings and not merely at one or more points, the selection of which is bound to be somewhat arbitrary (as in Table 19–1). Given the assumptions of the case in question, there is a simple mathematical relationship between E.B.I.T. and E.P.S. for each one of the alternative security types. This can be represented graphically in what we call a range-of-earnings chart. Chart 19–1 presents a graph of the relationship for Standard Brands bond and common stock alternatives in accordance with the assumptions outlined in the preceding section. For the sake of simplicity, the preferred stock alternative has not been included, but it would be drawn in exactly the same manner.

The two lines show what the E.P.S. on the common stock would be for any level of E.B.I.T. from zero up to $64 million (a) if bonds were used to finance the new investment and (b) if common stock was used. It will be observed that in each case, there is a simple straight-line relationship. For this reason the line can be drawn merely by determining any two points on the line. We have already provided one point on each line; they come from Table 19–1, where the E.P.S. was calculated at the E.B.I.T. level of $52.33 million. These are shown as points (3) and (4) on Chart 19–1.

The second set of points may be established by answering the question: What level of E.B.I.T. would result in exactly zero E.P.S. under each alternative? The obvious answer is: that level of E.B.I.T. which exactly equals the total dollar amount of bond interest plus preferred dividends and their tax related. This gives two points along the base line of the chart, which will be joined to the related points derived from Table 19–1.

The levels of E.B.I.T. which will produce zero E.P.S. in the Standard Brands example are shown in Table 19–2 and are plotted as points (1) and (2) on Chart 19–1.

The most significant feature of all such charts is the difference in slope of the two lines, resulting in an intersection point at some level of E.B.I.T.

CHART 19–1

RANGE-OF-EARNINGS CHART SHOWING COMPARISON OF BOND AND COMMON STOCK ALTERNATIVES AT DIFFERENT LEVELS OF E.B.I.T. IN TERMS OF EARNINGS PER SHARE

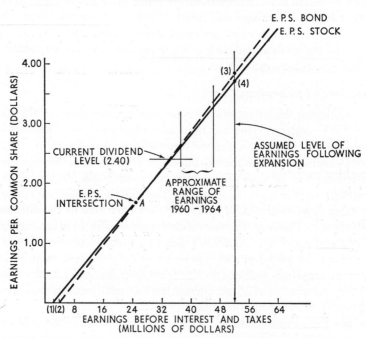

Graph based on following data: points (1), (2)—Table 19–2 (p. 395), points (3), (4)—Table 19–1 (p. 392).

At this point the E.P.S. is the same for both alternatives ($1.66 in the Standard Brands case, Chart 19–1). For levels of earnings below this point, the common stock has the more favorable income effect; for levels of earnings above this point, the bond alternative has the more favorable income effect. The difference in slope is due to the fact that under each alternative the number of outstanding shares of common stock is different. The chart serves to illustrate a point made earlier (see page 380) that the dilution caused by increasing the number of common shares reduces the rate of growth in E.P.S. as the level of earnings increases.

In the Standard Brands case the anticipated dilution (change in slope) under the common stock alternative is relatively modest, thanks to the high market price for the company's common stock that prevailed in

1965. For example, if the market price had been \$35 rather than \$75 (i.e., an earnings yield of 10%), the E.P.S. in the last column of Table 19–1 would have been \$3.48, which means that virtually all of the gain in earnings from the \$30 million investment would have been canceled out by the dilution effect.

TABLE 19–2

(Dollar Figures in Thousands)

| | 1965 Earnings Assuming \$30 Million Expansion Financed by: | | |
	Bonds	Preferred Stock	Common Stock
Preferred dividends and tax related (48%)....	\$1,346	\$3,942	\$1,346
Bond interest............................	2,398	1,123	1,123
E.B.I.T. necessary to cover interest and preferred dividends.........................	\$3,744	\$5,065	\$2,469
Chart 19–1 reference point.................	(2)		(1)

Looking at the bond alternative in Chart 19–1, we can see that unless E.B.I.T. is above \$24,734,000 (point A), the positive leverage of debt on earnings per share will not be realized.[2] This point becomes significant in relation to the range of earnings expected in the future. If it is expected that the lower limit of this range may fall below the intersection point, then the use of bonds may not give the desired leverage and therefore may not have the income advantage which we have assumed to be associated with this type of financing. If, on the other hand, the intersection point appears well below even the lower limit of future earnings, then the income advantage of bond financing seems assured.

---

[2] This "break-even" point on earnings per share between the bond and the common stock alternatives can be calculated algebraically, as follows:

Let
x = Break-even level of E.B.I.T.
I_1 = Dollar amount of interest without new bonds
I_2 = Dollar amount of interest with new bonds
PD = Dollar amount of dividends on preferred stock now outstanding
S_1 = Number of common shares if new stock is sold
S_2 = Number of common shares if new stock is not sold
TR = Tax rate

Then:

$$\frac{(x - I_1)(1 - TR) - PD}{S_1} = \frac{(x - I_2)(1 - TR) - PD}{S_2}$$

In our example:

$$\frac{(x - 1123)(1 - .48) - 700}{6985} = \frac{(x - 2398)(1 - .48) - 700}{6585}$$

$$x = \$24,734,000$$

This appears to be the case for Standard Brands if the earnings of 1960–64 can be taken as a guide for the foreseeable future. The lower limit of this range is well above the intersection point. Thus, the impressions of Table 19–1 are confirmed.

The Comparison with Respect to Risk

In view of the comparatively low interest rates on the modest amounts of long-term debt carried by many business corporations and the fact that interest is treated as a cost for tax purposes, it is frequently found that bonds are the most beneficial alternative among long-term security types as far as the income effect is concerned. However, this is only one of several considerations, even in a company which stresses profit maximization. A dimension of comparable importance is the effect these securities have on the risks of the business. This, we shall find, not only requires ranking the alternatives in this respect—a relatively simple matter—but also requires some method of measuring incremental risk and of deciding how much risk is "too much." This latter problem turns out to be very difficult indeed.

As we have already explained in the two preceding chapters, the risk associated with debt derives from the contractual periodic payments that are due the bondholder regardless of the company's earnings or financial circumstances. Since bond interest is to be found on the income statement as a deduction from current earnings, it is not surprising to find that one of the most common measures of risk is a calculation of the excess or *margin of safety* of earnings available for bond interest over the amount of the interest payments. Of course, now that our focus has shifted from measuring the "cost" of debt to the size of mandatory payments, we must recognize that the periodic repayment of principal through a sinking fund provision poses just as much of a threat to corporate solvency as does interest. Failure to meet either payment would constitute a default of the contract. Thus, when measuring risk, our attention shifts to the total burden of debt represented by interest *and* sinking fund payments.

One way of measuring the adequacy of earnings for this purpose follows the form of analysis used in the section on income. Table 19–3 continues the Standard Brands example where Table 19–1 left off, namely, at the point where net earnings on common stock had been derived. In order to take account of the drain on currently generated funds caused by the sinking funds on outstanding debt, we now proceed to deduct this amount and derive what we call uncommitted earnings on common stock and *uncommitted earnings per share* (U.E.P.S.). In this connection, it has been assumed that the new bonds are to be fully retired by maturity (in 20 years) through equal annual payments. The substantial annual burden which this imposes is seen in the fact that the bond alternative on a U.E.P.S. basis is only a modest improvement over the

TABLE 19–3

(Dollar Figures in Thousands)

	1964 Capital Structure and Earnings	1965 Earnings, Assuming $30 Million Expansion Financed by:		
		Bonds	Preferred	Common
Net earnings on common stock (Table 19–1)....................	$22,651	$25,264	$24,577	$25,927
Sinking fund requirements on bonds....	2,250	3,750	2,250	2,250
Uncommitted earnings on common stock...........................	$20,401	$21,514	$22,327	$23,677
Uncommitted earnings per share......	$3.10	$3.27	$3.39	$3.39
Chart 19–2 reference point...........		(3)		(4)

1964 level and is actually inferior to the preferred and common stock alternatives in this respect.

The significance of the comparison of the burden of these securities is seen even more clearly in a range-of-earnings chart. Chart 19–2 is similar to Chart 19–1 except that the lines now represent U.E.P.S. rather than E.P.S. Points (1) and (2) at the base of the chart indicate, for Standard

CHART 19–2

RANGE-OF-EARNINGS CHART SHOWING COMPARISON OF BOND AND COMMON STOCK ALTERNATIVES AT DIFFERENT LEVELS OF E.B.I.T. IN TERMS OF UNCOMMITTED EARNINGS PER SHARE

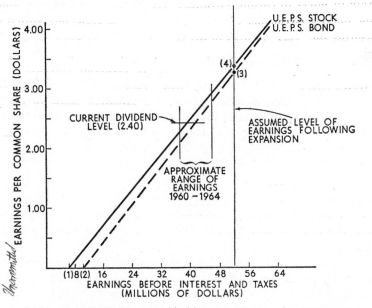

Graph based on following data: points (1), (2)—n. 3, p. 398; points (3), (4)—Table 19–3, p. 397.

Brands under the bond and common stock alternatives, the level of E.B.I.T. which just equals the total of bond interest and sinking fund payments plus preferred dividends on a before-tax basis.[3] Points (3) and (4) are taken from Table 19–3.

The chart brings out very clearly that the reversal of the positions of the bond and common stock alternatives when measured in terms of U.E.P.S. rather than E.P.S. applies not only for the level of earnings selected in Table 19–3 but throughout the entire range of earnings under consideration. Thus assuming the market conditions prevailing in early 1965, the common stock alternative provides more of a margin over the current common stock dividend level than does the bond alternative. From the viewpoint of those who value the continuity of this dividend, U.E.P.S. is an important criterion of safety. The chart also shows that the level of U.E.P.S. needed to cover the common dividend lies within the 1960–64 range of earnings, suggesting possible difficulty in covering dividends out of current earnings if these levels of earnings persist in the future. (Let us remember, of course, that we are now dealing with a hypothetical financing and not the real Standard Brands.)

In comparing Chart 19–2 with Chart 19–1, the reader will note the absence of an intersection point. There does not appear to be any range over which the bond alternative would give superior results. Close observation shows, however, that the two lines do have a different slope and that they are converging to the right. A calculation similar to that shown in the footnote at the bottom of page 395 produces the information that U.E.P.S. for the two alternatives are equal at the E.B.I.T. of $79.4 million. Beyond that level the bond alternative will give superior results, but this is far beyond current expectations.

Conventional Standards for Risk Bearing

Our first approach to the measurement of risk, then, has been in terms of the total burden of debt servicing and the impact this has on uncommitted earnings per share. However, the basic problem of risk is still to be solved. It is apparent from Chart 19–2 that, as debt increases,

---

[3] Points (1) and (2) on Chart 19–2 are obtained as follows: points (1) and (2) from Table 19–2, plus the sinking funds from Table 19–3, plus the tax related to the sinking funds:

	(In Thousands)	
	Bonds	Common Stock
E.B.I.T. necessary to cover interest and preferred dividends (Table 19–2)	$ 3,744	$2,469
Sinking funds (Table 19–3)	3,750	2,250
Tax related to sinking funds	3,461	2,077
	$10,955	$6,796
	(1)	(2)

the level of E.B.I.T. required to cover the burden of the debt and the common dividends moves closer to the current range of earnings, and the chances increase that E.B.I.T. will be deficient in a recession period. How does a business decide on the point at which further use of debt to increase E.P.S. must be resisted because the risk has become "excessive"?

In practice, business resolves this problem in a variety of ways. There are many people in management positions who believe that any debt is too much debt. Few, however, are able to impose financial policies that exclude long-term debt entirely from the capital structure. Of the majority of businesses that do borrow at one time or another, many follow the practice of letting the creditor decide. Established financial institutions— commercial banks, insurance companies, investment bankers—have evolved what are generally considered to be conservative standards of debt capacity for a given industry. The simplest solution to debt policy is to stay within the requirements or recommendations of a trusted financial institution. A variation of this approach is to borrow as much as possible at the prime rate or within the requirements of an "A" rating, thus assuring some margin of unused borrowing capacity for unanticipated needs.

A second approach to debt capacity is to follow what appear to be the conventions of the industry by observing the debt policies of comparable companies. Here again, the borrower is passing the responsibility for a judgment on appropriate risk levels to someone else—in this case, his competitors. The argument in favor of such an approach is that the practices of the industry reflect a pooling of extensive experience, and widely accepted decision rules are time-tested rules. There is the additional consideration that investors apply this test of comparability, and any company seriously out of line with comparable companies may be penalized in the capital market. However, in most industries the variations in corporate debt and other financial policies are broad enough to leave a considerable range within which individual choice can be exercised without being obviously out of line. Further, the definition of an "industry" is not always easy to come by.

Thus, most borrowers have some type of operating debt capacity rule which they think of as being tailored to their individual circumstances. These rules commonly take one of two forms. The most common is the *percentage-of-capitalization* rule, which states that no new debt will be incurred if it raises long-term debt as a percentage of total capitalization above x percent. The other, more frequently used by lenders than by borrowers, is the *earnings coverage* standard, which sets a minimum required ratio between net earnings available for annual debt servicing and the total amount of the debt servicing. This latter standard relates directly to Chart 19–2, being the ratio of (a) the distance from the origin to the current (or an average) E.B.I.T. to (b) the distance from the origin to point (2). As the debt proportion increases, point (2) moves to the right, and the ratio decreases.

Where such standards as "30% of capitalization" or "3 to 1 earnings coverage" come from is usually rather obscure. Evidence suggests that these so-called "individual" company standards merely reflect some widely accepted financial conventions or what may be described less reverently as financial folklore. The 30%-of-capitalization rule is widely quoted in a variety of industrial and competitive situations. Oftentimes, the rules relate to individual circumstances only in the sense that they have been honored for many years by the company in question and have stood the test of time—*so far.*

It would be incorrect to say that such uncomplicated guides to debt usage do not have a useful place in business practice. They are frequently appropriate as a quick and crude test of "normalcy" for external analysts who may lack the incentive, the time, or the information to do anything better. On the other hand, they are seriously deficient as an adequate guide to long-term capital structure policy in the individual firm. The next section will suggest an approach to risk analysis for use by corporate management that offers the prospect of more meaningful information.

The Analysis of Risk in the Individual Company

In our initial approach to risk via the criterion of burden coverage and uncommitted earnings per share, we were taking earnings as defined by accounting practice as a reasonable approximation of ability to pay debt servicing charges. In fact, of course, debts are serviced by cash payments, and it is cash flow and cash reserves that determine whether a problem of servicing exists. We know that it is the variations in cash inflow unmatched by compensating changes in outflow that create problems for management. The more management adds to the fixed element of outflows, the greater the threat from unexpected and prolonged declines in inflow. Thus, a serious approach to analysis of the risks of indebtedness must be expanded to include consideration of *all* those factors that significantly influence the behavior of cash inflows and cash outflows over extended periods of time. This information is accessible to the internal analyst, and it should be used as a means of coming to an independent judgment on capital structure policy.

The cash flow approach to the analysis of the risk of different debt levels begins by identifying the underlying determinants of inflow and outflow and determining how they behave over time and why they behave as they do. Debt servicing is only one of many items of outflow and the simplest to describe. Of considerably greater complexity are such expenditures as purchased materials and direct labor. There will, of course, be a good deal of interdependence which must be taken into account. When the various inflows and outflows have been described as to individual behavior, the next step is to formulate their combined behavior in a form such that the effects on net cash flow of various assumptions about external and internal conditions can be observed.

The precise form of cash flow analysis can vary considerably from crude approximations to very refined models. A computer model of cash flows can be developed to serve many purposes in corporate financial analysis, including the consideration of debt policy. In any case, crude or refined, the description of the corporate system of cash flows has as its objective the simulation of a range of adverse conditions so that the effect on net cash flows and cash reserve position can be measured. In the more refined models a considerable array of results can be developed over a wide range of recession conditions and can be used to develop a measure of the probability of cash insolvency or inadequacy for any given level of debt. The analysis will also show how this probability of insolvency is increased for any given increase in debt level.

Although it is not accustomed to receiving such data, management could make a decision on the debt-equity balance more objectively with estimates of the risk magnitudes before it—estimates developed from the specific circumstances of its own company and industry and reflecting its own financial priorities. This is something generalized debt standards cannot provide. But it must be recognized that an objective measure of risk magnitude does not provide the final answer. There is also the subjective dimension of the debt-usage decision—willingness to bear risk. This is a choice to be reserved solely for those who bear the risk—the common shareholders—or their duly elected or appointed representatives —the board of directors and top management. They alone can say whether any given level of risk of insolvency is acceptable to them. Here is the clearest evidence that generalized debt capacity rules must always be viewed with suspicion.

Before concluding this brief reference to risk analysis in the individual firm, we must add that there are serious practical restraints on carrying it to its theoretical limit. These restraints relate to the availability of the data, analytical competence to handle the data, the cost of the analysis in terms of time and money, and, not the least of these, the attitude and motivation of management in substituting an elaborate analysis for rules of thumb that have kept the company out of trouble in the past. Fortunately, there are various compromises in refinement of the cash flow analysis which produce useful results with a moderate investment of time and relatively simple analytical tools. These are in use by some businesses today as an important supplement to the more conventional debt capacity criteria, and we believe that in time the approach we describe here will be more widely used in practice.

Balancing Income and Risk

Before continuing with the question of control and other aspects of the capital structure decision, we shall find it helpful to stop and review the results of our analysis of the basic security types as regards income and risk. To refer to the Standard Brands example, we see that the choice of debt to finance the $30 million expansion will, if the earnings assumptions hold, produce 13 cents per share more than the common stock method ($3.84 versus $3.71) and that this differential will expand uniformly as earnings increase. We also see that uncommitted earnings available for the payment of common dividends are 12 cents per share *less* under the bond alternative ($3.27 versus $3.39), meaning greater exposure of this dividend and more risk of cash inadequacy generally. This differential increases uniformly as earnings decrease.

Thus, at any point of earnings or over any range we wish to consider, we have a precise measure of the effects, and if we were to do a complete cash flow analysis for Standard Brands, we would have a measure of the chance of cash inadequacy or insolvency for whatever adverse circumstances we might wish to consider. Given this information, how is the prospective gain in earnings per share resulting from debt to be weighed against the concomitant increase in risk?

Financial theory would answer this question with deceptive simplicity. It would say that having taken the viewpoint of the common shareholder, its objective would be to adopt that capital structure which maximizes the market price of the common stock. Since this price is sensitive to both earnings prospects and the anticipated certainty or uncertainty of those earnings, debt proportions should be increased until the beneficial effects of rising E.P.S. are outweighed by the deterioration of the price-earnings ratio as the market reacts to the growing uncertainty of those earnings.

Unfortunately, this simple answer immediately plunges us into some very difficult theoretical and practical problems, the answers to which will ultimately lie, in practice, in the mature judgment for which the financial officer, the chief executive, and the board of directors are paid. We have already referred to the continuing theoretical debate as to whether the use of debt does in fact lower the overall cost of capital (see page 381) and have indicated our position, which lies with those who believe that, within limits, it does. With this as a starting position, we can then suggest a sequence of considerations to which the mature judgment referred to above may be applied.

First, let us recognize that there are in fact definite limits to the amount of fixed payment securities that will be accepted by the segment of the capital market to which a business will have access or with which it chooses to deal over the long run. These are the banks, the insurance companies, the investment bankers, the pension funds, and so on which make up the established capital market. This limit is not clearly stated anywhere, but must be sensed and negotiated by the financial officer in terms of his own market contacts.

Second, there are limits on normal debt usage imposed by the company itself in terms of its own willingness to bear risk—the willingness of its stockholders or, in the larger corporations, the willingness of top management acting for the stockholders (and themselves). If it is argued that this willingness should be flexible, depending on the rewards to be gained from the use of debt, the answer would be that in practice it is somewhat flexible—but not completely so—and tends to have a definite limit for normal or nonemergency purposes. In other words, there is customarily a point beyond which management becomes distinctly uncomfortable with the risk magnitudes imposed by debt, particularly when the anticipated rewards (earnings) from the investment of the funds are only average.

Given both the willingness of the market to lend and of the management to borrow—one of the two limits will be the controlling one—then the question is one of how much of this debt capacity to use at a point in time. Here again, judgment must be exercised, for the problem is then one of sensing the reaction of the stock market to determine whether, as debt approaches the prescribed limit, the price-earnings ratio will be substantially affected by the risk consideration. Here customary debt levels are important—what the industry does; but the market also considers the quality of management and other factors in the nature of its response, and the outcome is very difficult to predict.

Finally, we reach the point where we are working with a debt limit that is acceptable to both the market and the company and that promises incremental gains in market price. Then the decision becomes whether to use debt rather than equity at this particular time for this particular financing. We are now ready to consider some of the other considerations that will influence this capital structure decision.

The Comparison with Respect to Control

Turning to the consideration of control, we can state the implications of the three alternatives briefly. Neither a new bond issue nor a preferred stock issue would alter the control of the business as exercised through shareholders' meetings and the board of directors. As suggested by the outstanding preferred issue, a new issue of this class of stock might join in the election of a minority of directors in the event of a lapse in dividend payments. The exercise of the existing provision will not involve a major upset in control but merely representation on the board (2 directors to be added to a 13-man board). The issue of common stock, however, does involve the problem of control directly, since each new share adds one new vote. To the extent that the stock is sold to new shareholders, there is a dilution of the control of the existing shareholders, the magnitude of which will be measured by the amount of new stock in comparison with the amount of stock presently outstanding.

A convenient measure of dilution may be made as follows: Divide the old number of shares by the total of old and new to be outstanding under the proposed plan. In the case of Standard Brands, this would be:

$$\frac{6,585,000}{6,985,000} = 94\%.$$

The figure of 94% is the proportion of voting power that would remain for the old holders after the dilution. It is a factor that can be used by any holder to determine his future position. Thus, if a group held 51% of the voting stock before the dilution, it would have (0.51) (0.94) = 48% afterwards.

The analysis of alternatives so far as the issue of control is concerned is so simple and direct that it hardly warrants description. It is for this reason that the theoretical discussions of capital structure virtually ignore control, and focus on the more analytically complex issues of income and risk. It is not to be inferred, however, that control is therefore unimportant in the actual choice between voting and nonvoting securities. On the contrary, control often is the dominant consideration. Even in companies with widely dispersed stockholder groups, management is always sensitive to the effect of new common stock issues on actual or potential loci of voting power.

The Question of Marketability

While the considerations of income, risk, and control are basic to the problem of achieving a balanced capital structure, they are by no means the only considerations. In our initial presentation of the Standard Brands expansion, we very conveniently assumed away one of the major determinants in the choice of securities, namely, the ability of the company to market successfully $30 million of bonds, preferred stock, or common stock at this time. It must be remembered that the wishes of the prospective security holder are just as important as the wishes of the issuer in bringing the two together successfully. So far, we have considered only the interest of the latter.

In spite of the size, maturity, and reputation of the company concerned, we have no basis for assuming that Standard Brands could market with equal ease $30 million of a 4.25% bond, a 4.5% preferred stock, or a common stock priced at $75. The securities market is at best highly complex and constantly changing. The services of men experienced in the ways of the market and in constant touch with it are required to approach a statement of the possibilities at a given point of time; and even then the statement will be tentative. The acceptable type, amount, and terms of security to be offered will vary from time to time. This is not to suggest that Standard Brands could not have marketed all three types of securities in 1965 on the terms indicated but simply to indicate that the market could not be taken for granted. In a given situation, the factors considered of primary importance to the company and the common shareholders may be overshadowed by the consideration of what is acceptable to the prospective security holder.

Timing the New Security Issue

Related to the question, "Can the issue be sold?" is the question, "Is this the best time to sell it?" In prosperous times the large and successful business can usually sell an issue, provided it is willing to meet the investors' terms. In our Standard Brands example, we assumed these terms to be a 4.25% interest rate on the bonds, a 4.5% dividend rate on the preferred stock, and a price of $75 for the common stock. However, we know that the securities market is dynamic, and a month or a year later the investors' terms on any or all of these securities might have changed significantly.

How this affects our decision depends entirely on our expectations as to the future trends in the securities market. If a consideration of risk, income, and control in this case pointed to the choice of common stock, for example, as the desirable medium for financing current needs, management might still pause in its decision if it felt that by waiting for, say, a year, the stock could be sold substantially above $75. Since we started by assuming that the company could sell any of the three security types, such an expectation could lead to a decision to finance through debt on a temporary basis until a more advantageous price for the common stock could be obtained. Far-thinking management recognizes that financing in the long run will be a combination of debt and equity sources, and its ideal is so to time its approaches to the market as to minimize the cost of senior securities and minimize the dilution resulting from new common stock issues.

There are, of course, certain obvious limitations to the achievement of this ideal. The most basic is the dynamic nature of the market and our very limited capacity to anticipate trends. Obviously, there are considerable risks in waiting a year for this hoped-for-rise in the market price of common. The company's expectation could be entirely wrong, and it might ultimately be forced to sell the common below $75. This brings up a second limitation, namely, that the issuing company cannot postpone equity financing indefinitely, since it must maintain a certain balance of debt and equity at all times. The opportunities for taking advantage of market trends have certain time limits placed upon them by these circumstances.

The question of timing is equally relevant with respect to the preferred stock and bond alternatives. Yields on corporate bonds had shown a clear upward trend through 1964, and, except for a slight faltering in February and March, the trend appeared to be continuing into 1965 at the time our assumed financing would be under consideration. This situation might tend to reinforce an inclination to postpone the stock issue on the grounds that debt was about as cheap as it was going to be for some time. Indeed, if this trend in bond yields was expected to continue for a year or two, there might be a desire to take advantage of what would later appear as low interest rates and "freeze" these in through a medium-term or long-term contract.

Thus near-term market conditions and expectations tend to push the decision one way or another, particularly when the debt versus equity choice is a borderline one. On the other hand, every experienced financial executive knows how transitory market conditions can be and how dangerous it is to try to make long-term decisions on the basis of short-term market advantage. There are, therefore, severe limits on the extent to which the issue of timing can or should influence basic long-term capital structure policy. Normally, the timing issue is a major factor only when the market indications are clear and strong.

The Need for Flexibility

Although the matter of flexibility is involved in some of the considerations already discussed, it requires special emphasis. By flexibility, we mean the capacity of the business and its management to adjust to expected and unexpected changes in circumstances. Another way of expressing the idea would be to say that management desires a capital structure which gives it maximum freedom to maneuver at all times. Thus, this must be a consideration each time management changes its capital structure by a new issue of securities.

Of course, a goal of "maximum freedom to maneuver at all times" is an ideal never attained, short of holding all resources in cash and never taking any action or position. Every act to commit resources to specialized use means a denial of these resources to other uses and therefore a reduction in maneuverability. And as management presses for maximum return on capital through full utilization of resources, it is reducing its capacity to shift quickly if its judgments prove to be less than optimum. This is the essence of business risk, and it is part of the game of business that the use of funds for one purpose today is a restriction on their use for another purpose tomorrow—a use that may turn out to be more profitable or even vital to survival.

Financial flexibility or mobility is a much broader issue than the question of capital structure. As suggested above, it pervades the whole spectrum of uses and sources of funds. In its most obvious form it is concerned with liquid balances—cash and marketable securities. However, of greater importance in most companies than the "stocks" of liquid funds are the flows of these funds—the rate of conversion into and out of specialized use and the variability over time. In addition to those assets that are quickly convertible into cash as a matter of business routine, there are assets that are potentially convertible into cash, and these also are part of the picture of mobility. Finally, there are the various short-term and long-term sources of funds and their potential role in providing new capital when an unexpected need arises. An adequate strategy for financial flexibility must bring all of these into balanced consideration.

In this chapter we are concerned only with the question of how flexibility influences or should influence the capital structure decision—the use or conservation of sources of funds tapped through the basic security contracts. It will be recalled that our analysis of risk dealt with the question of the unexpected need for funds, and the analysis of cash flows was an effort to explore the range of possible future circumstances and determine the magnitude of the chance of a cash deficiency. Since this dealt with all elements of cash flow and was used to observe the impact of various debt levels on the cash position, it can be argued that we have already included the consideration of flexibility in our analysis. In other words, we have explored the unexpected, we have assessed the probability of being unable to meet cash needs, and we have decided we are willing to live with whatever probability is associated with the approved debt limits. Implicit is the acceptance of some degree of inflexibility, and the choice of degree is up to management.

However, the determination of debt capacity in this sense does not necessarily mean that the company will rush out to use debt to the full immediately. In practice, most financial officers prefer to hold some of their debt capacity in reserve. Along with excess cash this forms the first line of defense in their strategy of flexibility. These are the funds they can lay their hands on confidently and quickly when the unexpected need suddenly presents itself. The questions arise: Is this widespread practice of hoarding debt capacity rational, particularly if we can assume that a comprehensive risk analysis has been made and debt limits have been based on a recognition of apparent risk magnitudes? If management knows its limit of debt and debt is in fact the low-cost source, why not push to the limit and stay there?

Without an attempt at an exhaustive answer to this important set of questions, some points should be made. One is that there is a potential element of inconsistency in asserting on the one hand that we are willing to live with a given level of risk and on the other that we need to keep some idle resources to protect ourselves if that risk materializes. We can be guilty of creating the appearance of risk bearing while at the same time carrying an "insurance policy" to cover it.

At the same time, from a practical viewpoint one can see rather persuasive arguments for not being fully "borrowed up" at all times. One obvious one is that in practice financial analysis, including the analysis of debt capacity, is a crude and imperfect art, and even the analysis we propose must not be considered an exact science. Experience teaches that one's best judgment can be wrong. Beyond this, however, is a concern which is perhaps the essence of the practitioner's view of flexibility. It is that the stream of investment needs or opportunities includes some which prove to be critical in the growth and development of a company, and the timing of these is often beyond management's ability to predict. In the face of this, there is a natural reluctance to fully commit the company's most reliable and readily available external source, debt, on investments which, even though profitable, are not critical to the company's future. The critical need or opportunity may be just around the corner and that may be the very time when other means of financing, such as the common equity market, may be very unattractive and uncertain alternatives.

Hence comes the common practice of a dual debt limit: the one reflecting the amount of debt available at an acceptable level of risk and the other the amount of debt the company is willing to commit to "normal" investment opportunities.

PART VII

Capital Budgeting

Chapter 20

The Evaluation of Cash Flows

THE OBJECTIVE of the capital budgeting procedure is to provide guide-lines for the managers of a firm so that they may allocate its financial resources to the activities that promise the most value and so that they may select among the ways to obtain the needed resources those that have the least cost—in the sense that they provide funds under contracts that require the least sacrifice on the part of the equity owners. This two-part goal may be simply stated, for at the highest level of abstraction, capital budgeting theory follows the path of marginal analysis in value theory that is familiar in economics. One continues to expand the activities of the firm until the marginal project offers no further gain in the firm's value.

Given a ranking of alternatives according to a value scale and a cutoff point to apply to remove alternatives below the margin, we can easily make a list of approved capital investment projects. Given the costs of various ways to raise funds and maximum limits to the use of each of them, we can select a mix of financing which can raise the desired funds at the lowest cost. By selecting the most valuable projects and financing them in the least costly way, managers create the greatest possible value for the ownership of the firm.

It is in the application of this abstract principle to the real world that one encounters difficulties. For example, many of the quantities that the theorist assumes can be estimated accurately prove in reality to be difficult, if not impossible, to obtain with acceptable certainty. Since we propose to describe the theory in a way that makes its application possible, we have been forced to combine theoretical and practical matters in the following pages, drawing on the information in earlier pages of this book as we go.

There is general agreement that the structure of a capital budgeting decision requires that the following things be considered. The order in which they are obtained is not vital.

1. For each of the alternative uses of funds under consideration, an esti-mate of the funds required to establish it and the change in funds flows which it will bring about. This is the subject matter of the first part of this chapter.

411

2. A procedure to evaluate the funds flows of each alternative, so that each may be placed in a rank order of desirability. This is the presentation of the last part of this chapter. For those needing it, the middle section of the chapter presents the essential mathematics, which is simply that of compound interest.

3. A procedure to estimate the cost of providing the needed funds, so that the benefits of proposed uses can be compared with their costs. Chapter 21 is devoted to this subject, so far as individual security issues are concerned.

4. A standard of comparison, or criterion, which represents the minimum level of desirability the firm will accept. This may well be the cost of capital, but it need not be, as will appear below. This topic is dealt with in Chapter 22.

I. INFORMATION NEEDED

The first steps in the capital budgeting process require that an estimate of future events be made and expressed in a schedule of cash flows. Thus, if new assets are needed to establish the capacity to introduce a new product, there must be estimates both of the costs to buy, install, and put the assets into production and of the results of the selling, manufacturing, and other operations that will take place. All such estimates are uncertain, and some may be recognized to have wide margins of error.

In order to postpone questions of dealing with uncertainty, we have chosen as our example a possible use of funds through the purchase of a high-grade corporate bond. All of the procedures of "capital budgeting" can be brought to bear on such an investment opportunity. In fact, "bond valuation," using time adjustment, has been a regular part of the work of investment analysts for many years. In recent years financial analysts have learned how to apply the same type of evaluation to the more complex and uncertain investment opportunities that exist outside the bond market, but there has been no change in the kinds of information needed, nor in the essential mathematics. Our choice of a possible purchase of a corporate bond is, therefore, a good example to use when introducing the basic procedures, and we shall use it as a "project" for the analysis known as "capital budgeting."

Perhaps we should say to those of our readers who are already somewhat familiar with the subject that our presentation does not employ all the timesaving shortcuts that are familiar in practice. They add nothing to the quality of the results, and we have avoided them deliberately, in order to be sure that the structure of the logic of analysis is not concealed by any combination of steps that might easily confuse the inexperienced reader.

Basic Quantities to Be Estimated

A firm is assumed to have available to it at any time a number of alternative ways to invest its funds. These are termed *projects*, and the purpose of the capital budgeting procedure is to obtain an indication of the value each might contribute to the firm, so that the ones offering greater value can be chosen as the most desirable from the financial point of view.

Since this value indicator cannot be chosen without quantitative information, the first step in the work of capital budgeting is the projection of the amounts of cash flows, both in and out, related to the project, together with the time dimension of each flow. Such a schedule is referred to as a *schedule of cash flows.* Six quantities must be estimated to make up such a schedule. Three are in terms of quantity of money, two are in terms of time, and one is a rate of return.

1. The amount of the net capital investment required to acquire the project.
2. The amount of value expected to remain at its termination.
3. The change which is anticipated in the operating funds flows of the firm as the result of the project.
4. The times at which the amounts in the preceding classes can be expected to flow in or out.
5. The terminal time at which the project may be expected to be discontinued as a part of the firm's activity.
6. The benefit which may be obtained by placing the investment in an alternative project.

Initial and Later Investment. An *investment* takes place whenever an economic unit devotes some of its funds to the establishment of a project. By doing so, it removes resources from other possible uses and supplies them to the project in question. The amount that has been devoted to a project until the time it commences to receive net cash inflows from operations may be termed the *initial investment.*

We are not concerned here with the accountant's separation of "invested capital" from "expense." All movements of funds, no matter what their nature, having a net negative influence are part of the investment. Not only the cash outlays associated with the initial price of some property are needed, but also such terms as installation costs for equipment must be included. Also (although frequently forgotten), there must be a determination of the addition to permanent working capital necessary to support the output of the new assets at the desired capacity. This may include, for example, the added inventory of materials in process related to a machine and the added accounts receivable related to an estimated increase in sales.

The desired figures are net of all related movements. If, say, a new machine has been intended as a replacement for an existing machine, certain variations in the calculation would occur. On the outlay side, change-over costs would be included. But there would probably be an inflow from the proceeds of disposing of the old machine.

Further investment in a project may take place later on, if a period of cash losses occurs for any reason. Thus, if a particular division of a firm falls temporarily into a condition causing net cash outflows, it can only continue by drawing funds away from alternate uses, and the process of investment is again taking place. It is important to search for all these later investments, because it is fundamental that a firm cannot enjoy income from a project until it is assured that all of the investment will be returned to it by the time the project ends. But at the moment it is the initial investment which concerns us.

Much of the detailed questioning we have just suggested is intended for use on projects that are less simple than in the case of a corporate bond. Yet, even in this case, there are payments that make the net investment different from the quoted price.

Our "project" is the possibility of buying a 6% corporate bond, par value $1,000, due in 10 years, at the market price of $1,077.95. If this bond were purchased on the New York Stock Exchange, the firm would make an initial investment of:

Market price	$1,077.95
Broker's fee	2.50
Delivery charge	2.15
Total	$1,082.60

A corporate bond is a contract that specifies that certain funds are to be paid at certain times. It is the contractual specification that makes such a project easier to deal with than a type of project where both time and amount are uncertain. Here, the potential investor is assured of payments of $60 per year (we assume their receipt at the end of each year of the 10-year period) and $1,000 at the end of the 10th year. The prospect of this large payment at the end of the period leads us to write in general terms about the problem of recovering invested capital.

Terminal Values. At the end of a project's productivity, the firm must have received and retained the amount of the funds that were devoted to investment in the project, for investment anew. If this were not the case, and the situation repeated itself, the firm would ultimately have no resources to invest. Only after this return of capital has been provided for can one speak of "income" from the project.

A firm looks for the recovery of its investment from two sources: (1) the liquidation of the assets assigned to the project as they exist when it ends, (2) the retention of enough of the proceeds from operations to make up differences between final values and the amounts invested. Speaking of projects in general, one can say that nondepreciable assets, such as elements of working capital, should preserve their value during the project so that they can return funds equal to those invested in them. Depreciable assets, especially special-purpose equipment, are usually liquidated for much less than cost. In a small number of cases, where great appreciation in price can be anticipated (as might in a few instances be expected of strategically located real estate or of an investment in a "growth stock"), the liquidation may not only return the initial investment but contribute to the income. What the analyst must remember (many forget) is that the exploration of *"terminal value"* or "residual value" must never be omitted.

In the case of the bond, the terminal value is $1,000. Since the initial investment was $1,082.60, we see that the depreciable portion of the initial investment is $82.60. The facts concerning the investment may be summarized as follows:

Time		Amount
Beginning.......	Initial investment	$1,082.60
	Intermediate investment	none
End year 10.....	Terminal value	1,000.00
By end year 10..	To be supplied from operations	$ 82.60

The Change in the Operating Cash Flows. As we have said, six quantities must be estimated to provide the basis for a time adjustment. The first, the amount of the capital investment required, and the second, its terminal value, were presented above, together with the needed time dimension. We now turn to the quantity which results from the investment, namely, the change in the firm's operating cash flows.

It cannot be overemphasized that, as was the case for investment amounts, we are searching for the incremental change in cash—the difference between what the total cash received from the operations of the business would be if the change is not made and what cash the firm is expected to receive if the project is adopted. The desired number, it must be emphasized, is not an accounting figure, and it must not include any item which is not a cash movement. Also, we strongly recommend excluding at this stage any flows related to the financing which may be proposed to provide the needed investment. Financial devices can affect the final value put on a project, but value cannot be created by financial means if there is no value in the underlying project itself, and that is what we are now trying to estimate.

In the case of the projected investment in the corporate bond, the increase in cash flows is $60 per year for 10 years. This amount, however, is subject to income tax, and grave errors in capital budgeting can be (they have been, all too frequently!) committed if this factor is forgotten. We shall return to this point a few paragraphs further on.

The certainty and regularity of the estimate in this instance should not obscure the fact that the estimate of operating flows is difficult to make in most of the cases that require study. One proceeds from the great certainty associated with financial contracts, with their precise terms, through a variety of classes of projects where estimates are possible but uncertain.

Many investment projects cannot be expected to produce funds at an even rate over the length of life which it is reasonable to assume for their use. A project to introduce a new product is often slow in coming into profitability, if only because a growing market has been anticipated and the demand has yet to be experienced. A period of the collection of know-how, during which income is often reduced for some time, also often occurs in the early part of the project's life. Following a central period of profitability, toward the close of its life, a project can be expected to produce somewhat less than it did earlier, because of increased mainte-nance if nothing else. On the other hand, a project which revives the profitability of an existing operation, such as pumping an oil well where the natural flow has slowed, can be expected to show high net inflows at once, tapering off as time goes by. In the interests of financial analysis it is essential to attempt to describe irregularities and their timing, even though all must recognize that estimates of this kind are sure to be inaccurate.

Finally, there are some investment projects where one cannot set down an estimate of benefit in terms of the direct effect on cash flow. Some research work falls into this category, as well as the often-quoted example of the project to air-condition the factory lunchroom. While in recent years new techniques have been devised to obtain useful quantitative estimates from some of these cases and the number of exceptions is therefore narrowing, some investment proposals will not permit the use of the procedures we are presenting here.

The Anticipated Length of Life.   The third quantity to be estimated is the total time the project is expected to be productive. By the term *economic life* we refer to the period over which the equipment (or other investment) remains economically superior to alternative equipment that might be purchased for the same purpose—the period before it becomes obsolete. It is often difficult to estimate this time; yet, the effort must always be made, since the period of time within which a project must justify itself is extremely critical. An estimate based on the experience of persons who have spent considerable time in the business is often more useful than some technical estimate by either an engineer or a tax accountant.

Thus, there is uncertainty both in estimating income in years far removed from the time of making the forecast and in estimating the length of the economic life of productive assets. These combined uncertainties lead many firms to select for application as a general rule some term of years within which a project must justify itself—leaving possible gains in later years to be hoped for but not relied upon. Some analysts refer to this terminal date as a *horizon*—a happy choice of terms since we are dealing with operations requiring foresight.

Here again, experience is usually the ultimate guide. One can merely ask that those who have experience use it as carefully as possible. Too many managers use horizon times which are arbitrarily shorter than experience would seem to justify, as shown by the continued desirability of many projects years after the horizon has been passed or the high terminal values at the horizon date. When this occurs, we have evidence that decisions were based on erroneous assumptions. However, we expect to find a horizon time often used in practice and to find it often an arbitrary figure.

Effect of Tax Laws on Funds Flows.   Few economic units enjoy freedom from taxation. In fact, the forces of taxation are too large to ignore, and the analyst must recognize them, giving particular attention to the options his firm faces that may permit lessening the adverse effects of

TABLE 20–1

BEFORE AND AFTER-TAX FUNDS FLOWS,
FROM PROPOSED INVESTMENT IN 6%, 10-YEAR BOND
(Tax Rate 48%)

	Time 0	Years 1–10		Year 10	
		B.T.	A.T.	B.T.	A.T.
Net investment.........	$1,082.60				
Annuity...............		$60.00	$31.20		
Principal..............				$1,000.00	$1,039.65*

* Tax credit for capital loss added to principal: ($82.60)(0.48) = $39.65.

the tax claim on the project he is studying. This may be a most complex matter. It usually is, when the new project calls for the liquidation of some present activity and some of the new assets are of the kind that permits the "Investment Credit" provided by the Revenue Act of 1964. We chose the corporate bond in order to stay as far as possible from such details, and we shall take the simplest way out for the particular case. This chapter is already too complex for us to do otherwise. Thus, we assume an unchanging income tax rate of 48% and tabulate and chart the net funds flows in Table 20–1 and Chart 20–1.

The Opportunity Rate.   We have still one more quantity to find before our work is done. We have referred to it at page 413 as "the benefit to be obtained from alternate uses of the funds," and we may call it, following the language of economics, *the opportunity rate.* We shall, from time to time, refer to it as "the criterion."

In capital budgeting work, as elsewhere, the value of a promised benefit can be measured only by comparison with an alternative that must be given up in order to choose the one offered. We shall have much to say in Chapter 22 about the need for realistic judgment in selecting an alternate opportunity that is suitable for comparison, but at the moment it is quite realistic to assume that our analyst is told that an assortment of bonds of this quality can be bought to yield 2½% after corporate taxes of 48%. So the alternate opportunity offers the rate of 2½%.

The Problems Created by Uncertain Estimates

With these quantities estimated, we have provided ourselves with the basic estimates needed for capital budgeting procedures, but for a type of investment where uncertainty is at a minimum.

One can always question the accuracy of estimates of the quantities which we have specified must be available to evaluate a project. The future is inherently uncertain, and we need to recognize the fact.

CHART 20–1

CHART OF AFTER-TAX FUNDS FLOWS, PROPOSED
INVESTMENT IN 6%, 10-YEAR BOND

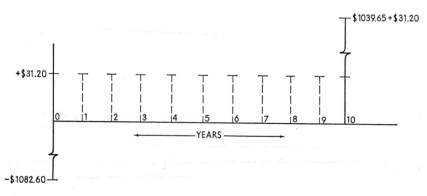

Professor Joel Dean has suggested the following four-part classification, which is very useful in dealing with the problem of uncertainty.[1] We are glad to accept it, while adding a fifth part. The distinctions among the classes are based upon differences in certainty of estimating the basic data to appraise the desirability of the investment. As Dean says, ". . . it is important to note that most capital expenditures have mixed objectives . . . and thus do not fit neatly into any single category."

1. Replacement investments, where the new project is proposed to replace an existing investment, perhaps simply because of wearing out, but more often because of technical obsolescence. Savings in cost are usually anticipated. Estimates of the net flow of funds for the investment and of the savings are usually sufficiently accurate.

2. Expansion investments, where increased earnings rather than reduced costs are anticipated. If the demand for the new capacity is real, estimates in this area are also reliable.

3. Product line investments, where improvements to existing products

---

[1] Joel Dean, *Capital Budgeting: Top Management Policy on Plant, Equipment, and Product Development* (New York: Columbia University Press, 1951), chap. v.

or new products are planned but the demand is not assured. In this area the uncertainties of estimation are much greater, and judgment must have great weight. In no area is this more true than that of maintaining competitive position.

4. Strategic investments, where the benefits are so spread through the firm that their effect on income is almost impossible to measure. Examples of such projects would be a new locker room for the staff, air conditioning, or new elevators in a store. For most such projects the numerical procedures described in this chapter cannot be applied, although the relevant quantities should be estimated to the extent possible.

5. We would add a category, "contractual change," where most of the flows of funds are determined by contracts, and alternative contracts are to be considered. For example, the exact terms and times of payment under construction contracts, loan agreements, leases, etc., often play a major part in the choice of a project or its financing. Whenever they do appear, the relevant figures are usually not only easily determinable but precise, and time-adjusted methods are particularly appropriate.

The growing availability of methods of quantifying uncertain estimates, and of applying probability mathematics to these quantities, supplies the financial analyst with ways to give the inputs to the procedures we have described more meaning. "Estimated monetary values" may be substituted for "most probable" forecasts, or "simulation" may be undertaken to permit the analyst to select from a table of "cumulative probabilities." Whenever such things are done, the confidence of the user of the figures may rise in contrast to his doubts of a few years ago.

Our field work leads us to say that, pending the dissemination of the better methods, many managers allow a margin for error in the form of an adjustment to the opportunity rate. Thus, a company that has selected 12% as its opportunity rate will perhaps accept a "sure thing" at that rate, while requiring that a risky project promise 20%. This is a rough "judgmental" adjustment that is perhaps better than none at all.

II. BACKGROUND MATHEMATICS

We have now accumulated, for the project to buy the corporate bond, the six estimates that are necessary to permit considering one project as an alternative to another. We need one more thing to answer the question: Does the investment promise more value to the firm than other ways to use the same funds? It is a procedure to bring the quantities that have various dates to a single number for comparative purposes. Here enters the mathematics of time adjustment, so we turn away from the example so far used to explain the mathematics required. We hope that even the reader with background in this technique will skim the following paragraphs, to refresh his memory and to see the order in which the procedures are introduced.

The Procedure of Time Adjustment

Compounding a Single Sum. We first turn to *compounding*, that is, the subsequent growth in the value of funds initially invested at a certain time, because this process is one with which most readers will be familiar from such well-advertised operations as savings accounts on which interest is compounded. We shall then be better able to understand *discounting*, which looks in the other direction along the time scale. Discounting is the procedure more often used in financial analysis.

Four quantities must be specified:

1. *The rate of return:* In the following exposition we shall use 4% and 10%, in order to see the changing results from using different rates.
2. *The frequency of compounding:* In the following examples (and throughout this chapter) annual compounding will be used.
3. *The amount of funds in question:* It is convenient to use the sum of $1 to develop the formulas, since if one knows how the values of this sum are affected by time, one can compute the values of any other sum by simple multiplication.
4. *The length of time from the chosen date:* This may be measured in days, weeks, etc., so that for the sake of generality, one refers to the *period* rather than to some specific unit of time. One warning is necessary here. The rate of return used must be stated consistently with the actual length of the time period. Thus, 6% per year becomes 0.5% per month, and so on.

At present we are searching for an answer to the question: How much will a sum increase over a stated time interval if it is invested at the present time at compound interest?

The growing amount that will be found at later times from an investment at the present time is referred to as the *compound amount* (of a single sum). Interest is computed on the original sum and then added to the original sum at the end of the first period. The new and larger principal is then the base for the interest calculation in the second period, and so on. Jumping over the detailed mathematics, we can turn to almost any set of tables for business computations, among which we shall find values for the compound amount of a single sum invested at a given time. Table 20–2 is a portion of such a table. Note how the higher rate produces values that are increasingly greater than those obtained from the lower rate.

In Table 20–2 the present time is designated by a zero, and may be called "time zero." It can also be read "beginning of year one," with 1 designating "end of year one," 2 "end of year two," and so on.

Discounting a Single Sum. The process of compounding discloses how the value of an investment made at the present time grows in later time.

TABLE 20–2

COMPOUND AMOUNT OF $1

Periods	Rate 4%	Rate 10%
0...................	1.000	1.000
1...................	1.040	1.100
2...................	1.082	1.210
3...................	1.125	1.331
4...................	1.170	1.464
5...................	1.217	1.611

We now turn to discounting, a process which in financial analysis also looks at times following the present but answers the question: How much must be invested at the present time to produce a desired sum at a specified time in the future?

The answers to such questions are determined by using the reciprocals of the values in the table of compound amounts, for the reasons exemplified in the following instance. Let us use for our example four periods and 4%. Table 20–2 shows that if $1 is compounded for this time and rate, it will increase to $1.17. Therefore, to have only $1 at the end of four periods of compounding, we obviously need to invest less than $1, in proportion to the ratio of 1.00 to 1.17, as follows:

If an investment of: $\dfrac{1.000}{}$
will produce: 1.170 in 4 years at 4% $\left. \begin{array}{} \\ \\ \end{array} \right\} \dfrac{1}{1.170} = x$

Then an investment of: $\dfrac{x}{}$
will produce: 1.000

And $x = 0.855$ (which is the reciprocal of 1.170).

The number so produced is known among financial analysts as the *present value* (at the selected time and rate) which if invested now at compound interest will produce $1 at a specified date in the future. The term *"discounted value"* is also used, although less frequently. Specifically, the investment of $0.855 at 4% compounded annually will produce $1 at the end of the fourth year.

Since discounted values are often used in financial calculations, a table of present values is provided in this book (Table A, at page 984). For convenience, we reproduce a portion of it in Table 20–3.

Examples of Compounding and Discounting. We shall now present two simple examples of how problems of compounding and discounting arise in business, and briefly indicate the nature of their solution.

EXAMPLE 1. A firm with a major debt maturity at the end of 2 years set aside $500,000 for investment in tax-exempt bonds at 4% to help meet the maturity. How much will be available from this source when the debt matures?

TABLE 20–3

PRESENT VALUE OF $1
(Reciprocals of Table 20–2)

Periods	Rate 4%	Rate 10%
0....................	1.000	1.000
1....................	0.962	0.909
2....................	0.925	0.826
3....................	0.889	0.751
4....................	0.855	0.683
5....................	0.822	0.621

The problem is one of compounding. The initial date is the present and the period is 2 years. From Table 20–2, we find 1.082 as the compound amount of $1 at 4%. Multiplying by $500,000 gives us $541,000, which is the sum that will be on hand.

EXAMPLE 2. A firm has granted a license to another firm to use one of its patented processes, upon a promise to pay $1 million 5 years in the future. The licensing firm now advises the licensee that it would prefer payment at present and that it is ready to negotiate a settlement. What price should the licensee suggest?

The problem is one of discounting, the difficulty being the selection of a rate. Suppose the licensee learns that the licensor could, as an alternative to making the settlement, borrow at 4%. Surely it would not accept a price computed at a higher rate. Using 4%, and Table A, we find the discounted value of $1 over 5 years to be $0.822. The suggested value for a settlement "on a 4% basis" is, then, $822,000.

EXAMPLE 3. A factor often given importance when a firm is deciding whether to own or lease land and buildings is the residual value of the property that the firm would own if it bought rather than leased. Suppose that a certain property now costing $1 million is expected to be worth $2 million (after allowance for taxes on the capital gain) at the end of 25 years. How much importance should this terminal value have on a decision now, when the company has the option to buy or to lease?

The problem is one of discounting. Let us assume that the firm averages 10% return (after taxes) on assets invested in the business. One way to obtain $2 million at the end of 25 years is by holding the real estate. An alternative way would be to invest some funds now and use them at 10% to produce $2 million.

A calculation is necessary to find what present investment at 10% will produce $2 million 25 years hence. From Table A we find that at 10% the present value of $1 to be received after 25 periods is 0.092. Multiplying by $2 million, we obtain $184,000. Thus, the desired value can be obtained either by using $184,000 in the business, allowing profits to compound, or by spending $1 million to buy the property. Obviously, the latter choice requires a much larger commitment of present funds to reach the desired results. It is therefore less valuable than the alternate opportunity that calls for $184,000 now.

The Behavior of Values over Time

Before we apply our newfound skill to make a time adjustment of the figures so far accumulated, let us pause to consider some generalizations about the behavior of values over time. Chart 20–2 has been designed to show the continuity of the mathematics of compounding and discounting.

CHART 20–2

EFFECTS OF TIME ADJUSTMENT: SINGLE SUM

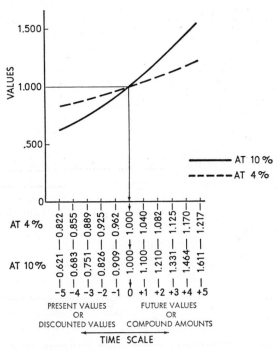

Time zero is represented in the center of the horizontal scale. The effects of compounding are shown to the right and of discounting are shown to the left. The basic relationships to be observed are simple but very important:

1. The value of a sum invested at any time grows as time passes.
2. The necessary investment to produce a future sum decreases as the time allowed to produce it is increased.
3. Both these effects are magnified as the rate of return increases.

Discounting an Annuity

We have now equipped ourselves with the mathematics necessary to bring the promised flows to our investment project to a common figure, the present value, but we can save time in this and later work by pausing to note the fact that the $31.20 of after-tax net flows from operations is the same for each of 10 years. This is a kind of situation which occurs frequently in business. It fits the definition of an *annuity, which is: a series of equal payments at fixed intervals.*

When we introduced discounting, we said that the procedure answered the question: "How much must be invested at the present time to produce a desired sum at a specified time in the future?" The parallel question for an annuity is to ask: "How much must be invested at the present time to produce an annuity of a desired amount over a certain series of time periods in the future?

The answer can be found by considering each payment separately and computing its individual present value. Let us take 4% and 5 years for the purposes of our example. Table 20–3 can be used. From it we see that:

> It takes 0.822 to produce $1 in 5 years,
> It takes 0.855 to produce $1 in 4 years,
> It takes 0.889 to produce $1 in 3 years,
> It takes 0.925 to produce $1 in 2 years,
> It takes 0.962 to produce $1 in 1 year.
> Total 4.453, value of annuity at period −5

This example shows how the desired present values of annuities can be obtained by accumulating values from the table of the present values of a single sum. Such a table has been included in this book as Table B at page 985; but for convenience, we reproduce a portion in Table 20–4.

TABLE 20–4

PRESENT VALUE OF $1 RECEIVED PERIOD-
ICALLY FOR *n* PERIODS

Periods	Rate 4%	Rate 10%
0	0	0
1	0.962	0.909
2	1.886	1.736
3	2.775	2.487
4	3.630	3.170
5	4.452*	3.791

* The difference between this figure and 4.453, the value of the annuity given above, is due to rounding.

When we were dealing with the changing values of a single sum over time, we ended our explanation with a diagram. A similar one, Chart 20–3, can be presented for annuities, although the situation is more complex, so that the values get larger as one proceeds away from the present. This is because of the periodic payments of $1 that are involved.

The reader will also note here, as in the simpler case, that changing the rate of return has considerable influence on the values, especially as time becomes more remote. In each instance the higher the rate, the greater the advantage to a person who invests funds to purchase the annuity. That is, if 10% is applied, an annuity will cost less than if the 4% rate were applied.

CHART 20–3

EFFECTS OF TIME ADJUSTMENT: ANNUITY

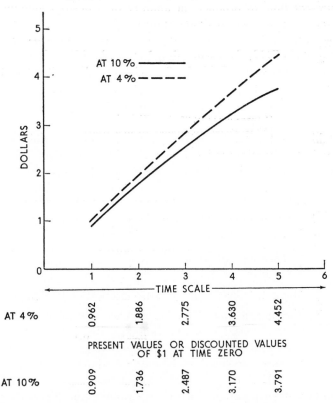

| AT 4% | 0.962 | 1.886 | 2.775 | 3.630 | 4.452 |

PRESENT VALUES OR DISCOUNTED VALUES
OF $1 AT TIME ZERO

| AT 10% | 0.909 | 1.736 | 2.487 | 3.170 | 3.791 |

Examples. As before, we conclude our explanation of the derivation of tables of present value for annuities with examples taken from business situations.

EXAMPLE 1. Analysis of a certain investment project indicates that it will produce $50,000 a year, before taxes, for 10 years. How much could the company justify investing in this project if other investments are available at 4%? At 10%?

The problem is the evaluation as of now of an annuity whose terminal date is 10 years from the present. Using Table B we find the present value factor of $1 a period for 10 periods to be 8.111 for 4%, and 6.145 for 10%. Multiplying each factor by $50,000, we find $405,550 for

4% and $307,250 for 10%. These are the sums that could be invested at the specified rates to produce $50,000 a year for 10 years.

EXAMPLE 2. Taking the figures as developed in Example 1, assume that the firm finds that $350,000 is required as an investment to establish the project. Since this number is more than the present value at 10%, the firm should not undertake the project if it has other opportunities on which 10% can be earned. The firm should, however, consider the project an excellent one if the alternative opportunities are offering 4% return.

Amortization of Loans

With increasing frequency in business practice, the terms of payment of long-term loans are designed so that the debtor makes a *level payment* of the same sum each time, the sum being large enough to cover the interest due and leave the necessary balance to be applied to the reduction of principal. The problem can be stated: given the present value, the term of the arrangement, and the rate of interest, how does one arrive at the annuity?

The table of present values gives us the value of an annuity of $1 per year. For instance, at 10% for 5 years, the present value is 3.791. The following calculation derives the annuity that $1, invested now, will buy.

$$
\begin{array}{c}
\left.
\begin{array}{l}
\textit{If} \text{ an annuity of:} \quad \dfrac{1.000}{} \\
\text{has a present value of:} \quad 3.791
\end{array}
\right\rbrace \dfrac{1}{3.791} = x \\[2em]
\left.
\begin{array}{l}
\textit{Then} \text{ an annuity of:} \quad \dfrac{x}{} \\
\text{has a present value of:} \quad 1.000
\end{array}
\right\rbrace 3.791 \\[2em]
\textit{And } x = 0.264 \text{ (which is the reciprocal of 3.791).}
\end{array}
$$

So, knowing the specification of an annuity, you multiply by the factor in Table B to get the present value. Or, knowing the amount at hand, you divide by the factor in Table B to get the annuity.

We have already presented in Example 1 above an instance of the former operation. Here is an example of the latter.

EXAMPLE: A corporation borrows $5 million for 20 years at 6%. What is the level of payment that will pay principal and interest on an annual basis?

From Table B we find the present value of an annuity of $1 for 20 years at 6% to be 11.470. Dividing $5 million by 11.470, we obtain $435,920, the desired amount.

Problems

1. What amount will be accumulated by a present investment of $4,100 at 4% compounded annually in 5 years?

2. At what rate will a present investment of $4,100, compounded annually, amount to $6,805 in 5 years?

3. What is the present value of $9,000 to be received 12 years from now with interest compounded annually at 8%?

4. What is the present value of the receipt of $700 a year for 14 years with interest at 6% compounded annually?

5. At what rate of annually compounded interest would an investment of $2,979 at the present time produce an annuity of $500 per year for 11 years?

6. What equal annual payments are necessary to repay $7,000 over 12 years if interest is compounded at 4% annually?

III. THE COMPUTATION AND COMPARISON OF VALUES

The Present Value of the Cash Flow Schedule

Part I of this chapter gave us the quantities needed if the value of a proposed investment is to be estimated. Part II explained the necessary mathematics. At last we are equipped to obtain a single number that will represent the schedule we presented in Table 20–1 and Chart 20–1, and that will be commensurable with numbers similarly obtained for alternate projects. It is obtained by using the opportunity rate and discounting all the quantities from their estimated time to the present. The appropriate discount factors are taken from tables like Tables A and B and one proceeds as in Table 20–5.[2]

TABLE 20–5

CALCULATION OF PRESENT VALUE AT 2½%
OF THE FLOWS SHOWN IN TABLE 20–1

Time	Amount	Factor for 2½% Discounting	Present Value
1–10 annuity	$ 31.20	8.7521 (Table B)	$ 273.065
10 terminal value	1,039.65	0.7812 (Table A)	812.174
			$1,085.240

The present value of the future funds flows is $1,085.24. This number may be taken as a figure which represents the more complex schedule which lies behind the single amount. It is the mathematical equivalent of the schedule, "on a 2½% basis." If there were a computer whose output were cash, one could set it at 2½%, and put $1,085.24 into it. Then it would produce the scheduled amounts at the appointed times, and no more or less.

The number also tells us that if one begins with an investment of

---

[2] To avoid confusion due to rounding, we have calculated to more decimal places than are available in the abridged tables that we publish in this book. This precision is seldom necessary in solving actual business problems.

$1,085.24, and receives the schedule offered by the bond, he may take away income on the principal at 2½%, and still find the sum of $1,085.24 at the end of the 10th year, ready for reinvestment. In Table 20–6 the process is shown in detail. For example, in the first year the

TABLE 20–6

RECEIPT OF INCOME AND AMORTIZATION
OF PRINCIPAL, $1,085.24 INVESTED IN $1,000,
10-YEAR, 6% BOND.*

Year	A Principal Invested	B = A × 0.025 Income for Year	C Received during Year	D = C − B Balance Reducing Principal
1............	$1,085.240	$27.131	$ 31.200	$ 4.069
2............	1,081.171	27.029	31.200	4.171
3............	1,077.000	26.925	31.200	4.275
4............	1,072.725	26.818	31.200	4.382
5............	1,068.343	26.709	31.200	4.491
6............	1,063.852	26.596	31.200	4.602
7............	1,059.250	26.481	31.200	4.719
8............	1,054.531	26.363	31.200	4.837
9............	1,049.694	26.242	31.200	4.958
10..........	1,044.736	26.118	31.200	5.082
Subtotal..........				$ 45.586
Terminal values....			1,000.000	
			39.650	1,039.650
Total........				$1,085.24

* Calculated to three decimal places for accuracy.

income (2½% of $1,085.24) is less than the receipt by $4.069. This balance reduces the principal invested to $1,081.17, on which income for the second year is calculated, and so on, until at the end of the 10th year the sums used to retire principal have equaled the original investment. By the test shown, it is clear that the firm can take income at 2½%, but only *on the declining principal*, since despite this withdrawal, the firm will have regained, to invest in other ways, the resources that were assigned to this project.

The Implicit Sinking Fund. We have already seen that the purchaser of the corporate bond at the price of $1,085.24 would get his capital back. Now let us look a little further into the details of the mathematics. In this instance, much of the capital is returned at the end of the 10th year, by the receipt of $1,039.65. Only the difference, $45.59, needs to be made up from the annual receipts. This sum is exactly akin to the "depreciable portion" of any investment project, so what we shall say about the way it is regained applies equally to the problem created by any asset which has a lower terminal value than its initial investment.

In Table 20–6 the right-hand column shows the sums assigned each year to reduce principal. We present these numbers again in Table 20–7 in the left-hand column, omitting the terminal values, so the total is $45.586.

The analysis of the figures in columns A, C, and D shows that the amount withheld by the firm (column A) can be divided into two parts: one is a constant sum, 4.069 in the example (column D), and the other is

TABLE 20–7

FURTHER ANALYSIS OF THE PROCESS OF
REGAINING A DEPRECIABLE INVESTMENT*

Year	A Balance Re- ducing Prin- cipal from Table 20–1 (End of Year)	B = ΣA Cumulative Figure of Reduction (End of Year)	C = B × 0.025 Lagged 1 Year. 2½% Interest on Accumulated Fund at Begin- ning of Year	D = A − C Balance of Annual Reduction
1	$ 4.069	$ 4.069	....	....
2	4.171	8.240	$0.102	$4.069
3	4.275	12.515	0.206	4.069
4	4.382	16.897	0.313	4.069
5	4.491	21.388	0.422	4.069
6	4.602	25.990	0.533	4.069
7	4.719	30.709	0.650	4.069
8	4.837	35.546	0.768	4.069
9	4.958	40.504	0.889	4.069
10	5.082	45.586	1.013	4.069
Total	$45.586			

* Calculated to three decimal places for accuracy.

annual interest on the accumulated sums previously withheld (column C). In other words, we are observing the same accumulation of values as occurs where annual deposits are made to a savings account drawing compound interest—except that in this case the interest is not drawn from another source but from the project itself.

It is correct to say of the investment in the corporate bond, bought at $1,085.24, that it yields 2½%, because if a sinking fund is established at 2½% compound interest and taken from the receipts annually, it will be sufficient to restore the depreciation of the investment. Then the balance of the annual receipts will be found to represent income at 2½% on the declining principal not yet covered by the sinking fund or anticipated terminal values.

The implicit assumption that is revealed is the process of compounding that goes on to achieve the return of capital. It can be called the *sinking fund assumption*, and it is implicit in every calculation using discounting procedures to arrive at present value. The sinking fund that is implicitly established always accumulates at the rate chosen for the discounting process.

Net Present Value, and Reasoning Therefrom

We may now return to the computations in Table 20–5.

With this work completed, what judgments concerning the value of the proposed investment are suggested? If it is indeed true, as has been assumed, that the firm can invest in other bonds of equal quality at $2\frac{1}{2}\%$, then it has two ways to buy the equivalent of the flows tabulated for the particular project. One way is to buy the bond whose net price is $1,082.60; the other is to take the alternative opportunity and pay $1,085.24. The project consumes $2.64 less of the firm's funds than the alternative, and this shows that it will make a more economical use of the resources at the disposal of the firm.[3] That is, the firm obtains greater value for the dollars it will invest by accepting the project to buy the bond than by taking the alternative route.

When, as in the examples used so far in this chapter, the schedule of cash flows is given, and the rate is obtained from an alternative opportunity, the analyst computes the present value of the schedule of funds flows, as we have shown. The firm is guided in this way toward the maximum price it could justify paying for the precise flow of funds that it is considering, for it can always shift to the alternate opportunity rather than pay more. The method of computing present values, in other words, leads to a signal whether the proposed investment is desirable or too expensive.

Many analysts compute a *net present value* by subtracting the net investment required for the project from the present value they have computed. (In this case $1,085.24 - 1,082.60 = +2.64$). If the answer is positive, the conclusion is favorable to purchase; if it is negative, the opposite is indicated. The analysts who use this system feel that it gives the desired indication with the least confusion; it is a logical last step from the comparison described above.

Desirability Ratios

Another way of presenting the same finding, which has the advantage of reducing the result to a basis that can be compared with other possible investments of different size, is to state the ratio of the present value of the alternate opportunity to the net investment of funds required for the project, or in this case:

$$\frac{1085.24}{1082.60} = 1.0024 \ .$$

---

[3] It might be remarked that only when all flows are fixed by contract could so small a difference as the one shown be considered a definite signal. But such small differences do cause action in the bond market.

Clearly, a ratio of 1.00 or more indicates the acceptability of the investment at the price quoted. Such a ratio is known as the *index of desirability*.

While all persons who practice capital budgeting agree on the need for the six estimates that were described in Part I of this chapter, there is not general agreement that the calculation of net present value is the best technique of comparing alternative projects. We shall, therefore, present three more techniques and then comment on their relative merits.

Yield, or the Internal Rate of Return

The calculation of the present value of the net funds flows has shown us that the project to buy the bond is slightly superior to an investment offering $2\frac{1}{2}\%$. But it has not told us what rate of return, or *yield* as it is known in the bond market, the project will give. Such information is often desired, and it can be obtained. Instead of yield, it may be termed *"the implicit rate of interest,"* the *"discounted cash flow rate"* (D.C.F.), or *"the internal rate of return"* (I.R.R.). These terms are synonomous, as the method is the same.

The objective is to find the rate whose use in a discounting calculation will cause the net present value of the future funds flows to equal the initial investment. The method involves trial and error computations, which are time-consuming but not difficult conceptually. We have tried $2\frac{1}{2}\%$ and have seen that the present value of the net funds flows slightly exceeds the net investment required. Since higher rates cause lower present values, let us try the next higher rate, 3%.

In Table 20–8 we repeat the $2\frac{1}{2}\%$ calculation of Table 20–5, and add

TABLE 20–8

CALCULATION OF PRESENT VALUE AT $2\frac{1}{2}\%$ AND 3%
OF THE FLOWS SHOWN IN TABLE 20–5

Time	Amount	Factor at $2\frac{1}{2}\%$	Present Value	Factor at 3%	Present Value
0 net investment........	$1,082.60	1.0	$1,082.60	1.0	$1,082.60
1–10 annuity...........	31.20	8.7521	273.07	8.5302	266.14
10 principal...........	1,039.65	0.7812	812.17	0.7441	733.60
			$1,085.24		$1,039.74
Net present value...			+2.64		−42.86

the work at 3%. It can be seen that we have "straddled" the desired zero amount of the net present value, with a range from plus 2.64 to minus 42.86, totaling 45.50. The position we want is $\dfrac{2.64}{45.50}$ of the way from $2\frac{1}{2}\%$ to 3%, or $(0.058)\,(0.50\%) = 0.03\%$. Therefore the rate of 2.50% plus 0.03% would yield the desired equality, and the yield is 2.53%.

The analyst who prefers to use the internal rate of return instead of the net present value finds his signal of desirability when the internal rate of return equals or exceeds the rate that was taken to represent the alternate opportunity. Here again, we see that the bond in question is slightly better as our investment project.

An index of desirability can be computed from this method by dividing the yield of the project by the opportunity rate. In this case, $2.53 \div 2.50 = 1.012$.

An approximate method to estimate a yield is often used, as follows. The method assumes that it is not important when the income of the project will be received, that is, that a dollar of inflow or outflow in any year is worth as much as in any other year. On this assumption the rate of return for our example is:

$$\frac{\text{Average Net Annual Income}}{\text{Average Investment}} = \frac{31.20 - \frac{1}{10}(82.60 - 39.65)}{\frac{1}{2}(1,082.60 + 1,039.65)} = 2.53\% .$$

Putting the fraction into words suitable for all types of possible investments, the numerator is the averaged accounting net income after depreciation, and the denominator is the average of the initial investment and the terminal value.

Although the approximate method will not always come as close to the accurate method as in our example, it is useful in a number of ways. Sometimes it results in a figure so high in comparison with an opportunity rate that approval is indicated without further work. Or the result can be so low that disapproval follows at once. Finally, it is a way to find a possible rate to begin with as one attempts the "straddle" to find the yield by the discounting procedure.

Future Value at the Terminal Date

Another method of combining the basic facts that have been gathered is coming into favor, because it seems to be more understandable to many top executives who have to use the results of evaluation procedures but who have not studied the subject in detail. Looking once more at the schedule of funds flows that the corporate bond offers us, let us assume that the opportunity rate of $2\frac{1}{2}\%$ will continue from the present until the terminal date of the project, in this case the maturity of the bonds. We can then calculate how much value could be made available at the terminal date, if each time there were a receipt of cash it was promptly invested to obtain the $2\frac{1}{2}\%$ rate, compounded to the terminal date. The computation is as follows:

Time		Factor to Compound to End of Year 10	Future Value
1–10 annuity.............	31.20	11.483	$ 358.27
10 principal..............	1,000.00	1.000	1,000.00
10 tax refund............	39.65	1.000	39.65
			$1,397.92

Just as the total present value shown on page 427 is a single number having the same effect as the detailed schedule, so the total future value of $1,397.92 is a single number with that effect, but at the terminal date instead of time zero. We now have the following information, and can ask the question: "What rate of interest will produce the growth in value that is shown?"

Time		
10	Future value obtained............	$1,397.92
0	Net price of bond...............	1,082.60
	Growth in value................	$ 315.32

The reader is equipped to answer this question, and we leave it as a problem for him to verify that the rate is 2.59%. Again, we have a signal that to buy the bond is slightly better than to use alternative opportunities at 2½%.

The index number derived from these two rates is 1.036.

Annualizing

Knowing how to find the annuity that a present value will buy permits one to "smooth" an irregular schedule into a level annuity that has the same value as the irregular scheme. One first computes the present value of the irregular flows, which we have done already, and then finds the level payments that are associated with this present value. The corporate bond offers an irregular flow consisting of 10 equal payments of $31.20 capped by one payment of $1,000 and a tax credit of $39.65 at the end of the fifth year. What level annuities have the same present value as this flow? The calculation is:

	At 2½%
Present value of expected flow...............	$1,085.25
Factor, 10-year annuity....................	8.5721
Result of division: 1,085.25 ÷ 8.5721........	126.60

The annual "smoothed" flow is $126.60. "Annualizing," as this is called, sometimes helps one to compare the desirability of one irregular flow with another. Here, we learn that an annuity of equal payments of

$126.60 per year for 10 years is equivalent in value to the bond, with its smaller annual amounts and large final payment, when the applicable rate is $2\frac{1}{2}\%$. By dividing $1,082.60 by the same factor, we obtain $126.29 per year, which is all that one can expect at the opportunity rate of $2\frac{1}{2}\%$. Thus, the project is superior to the standard, in the ratio of desirability of $126.60 \div 126.29 = 1.0024$. The reader should note that this is the same ratio as that derived from net present value, as is a mathematical necessity.

The Choice among Procedures

We have gathered below the results of each of the procedures we have described. They give signals of slightly different force, but all of them are in favor of the purchase of the bond over the $2\frac{1}{2}\%$ opportunity.

	Project		Criterion	Index
Present value..........$1,082.60			$1,085.25	1.0024
Net present value.......		$+2.65		
Yield.................	2.53%		2.50%	1.012
Rate to reach future				
value...............	2.59%		2.50%	1.036
Annualizing............$ 126.60			$ 126.29	1.0024

One may ask, which is the best? It would take many pages to bring out the differences in the implicit assumptions in these methods that explain why they produce slightly different numbers on the same basic figures. We have decided not to introduce this material into this book. Instead, we may say that the choice among methods depends in part on their intelligibility to the user, and that depends on his background.

We can also say with assurance that the calculation of the yield is one that every worker in finance has to do frequently. This is certainly the first procedure to be mastered. We can add that, in the United States, the net present value procedure appeals to the majority of authors who specialize in capital budgeting, so that the person intending to read further must also master it. Our own preference is for the index number derived from net present value, but the point remains that any of the methods we have shown will give satisfactory results in most situations.

Problem

1. A business firm is attempting to decide which of three investments should be undertaken. Each requires the same initial investment of funds. One alternative involves a new product which should return an increasing amount of revenue in each of the next 5 years, as shown in column A. The second alternative is an addition to an existing facility which, while increasing revenue temporarily, will gradually decline in the future, as shown in column B. A third possible choice is to buy a piece of new

equipment which will add a relatively small amount of revenue in each of the next 4 years but has a high sale value in the fifth year, as shown in column C.

NET ANNUAL INCREASE IN INCOME TO THE FIRM

Year	A	B	C
1.....................	500	630	262
2.....................	550	616	276
3.....................	600	600	290
4.....................	650	575	304
5.....................	700	545	2,010

a) If the firm requires a 5% return on its investment, which alternative is the most desirable?

b) If an initial investment of $2,800 were required for each of the three alternatives, which, if any, should be undertaken?

c) What other considerations would enter into such a decision for the firm?

Chapter 21

The Cost of Security Issues

In the previous chapter we specified that the cash inflows of projects should be estimated without the inclusion of any charges for financing. Now we must turn to the various measures of the cost of providing the funds which investment projects require. In Chapter 17 we presented the outflows of cash that are called for by certain types of security arrangements and called them "burden." Here, we wish to examine burden again, but this time as the burden of a particular security is related to the amounts of funds that can be raised by issuing that security, that is to the cost of the security issue.

Introduction—And Definition

The example of a short-term loan made by a bank to a corporation can be used to show more clearly the focus of our interest and to introduce some of the quantities involved. Let us say that the XYZ Corporation needs $10,000 for a month to cover some seasonal need. A bank makes the loan, quoting the interest rate of 6% per year. Following the usual practice in such short-term arrangements, the bank would *discount the loan*, deducting interest in advance for the duration of the loan. Thus, the company at the outset of the loan would have *net proceeds* of $9,950 at its disposal; and it would be required to pay $10,000 one month later, a sum which we defined in Chapter 14 as the burden of the debt.

The *cost of capital* contained in a financing arrangement may be determined in amount by finding the difference between the net proceeds actually made available to the company and the total burden incurred during the arrangement. In terms of a rate of interest, it may be defined as the rate that must be earned on the net proceeds to provide the cost elements of the burden at the times they are due.[1] Having computed this rate, management may use the cost of capital to select from among alternative financial arrangements, or to decide whether promised gains

---

[1] We have worded this definition carefully so as to omit questions of the sources of funds necessary to retire the net proceeds themselves.

436

from some operation are sufficient to justify the costs of raising the needed funds.

Even in considering the bank loan, unfortunately, the complications begin. The cost is not the rate of 6% per year, for that rate was applied to $10,000, a sum that was not received by the borrower. The net proceeds were $9,950. The cost of capital is the rate that must be earned on this sum to provide the $50 interest that will be due in a month: $\dfrac{\$50}{\$9,950} =$ 0.503% in one month, or at the rate of 6.036% per year, before tax.

Another example from short-term financing will be taken. A company can often obtain extended use of funds by paying its accounts payable on a delayed basis. If $10,000 is owed on a 2/10, n/30[2] basis, the company has the option of paying $9,800 within 10 days or $10,000 at the end of 30 days. If the second option is taken, the funds provided are $9,800, and the cost is $200. Again, the determination of the rate that must be earned (before tax) to produce the needed $200 is: $\dfrac{\$200}{\$9,800} = 2.04\%$ for 20 days, or at the rate of 37% per year.

If we consider these two examples as alternatives available to a company, it is clear that great advantage lies in choosing the bank loan, because of its much lower cost. Here, we see one of the important uses of the cost-of-capital calculation, for it is a basis for a choice among alternative ways of raising funds.

If we assume that the XYZ Corporation does not have bank credit available, we can see another use of the computation of the cost of capital, for it would take a most promising opportunity (or a great necessity) to justify carrying the account payable beyond the discount period. That is, the cost of capital can be used as a criterion in comparison with anticipated rates of profit for the acceptability of projects requiring funds.

We now turn to a description of how the cost of capital can be determined for each of the basic financial contracts taken separately. In doing so, we shall draw the needed quantities from the experience of the Long Island Lighting Company, which in 1953 obtained funds from the public by using bonds, preferred stock, and common stock at various dates during the year. It is, of course, easy to determine what such figures are after the financing has taken place. The precision thus given to our figures was not present when management was making its decisions; but the reader, we feel, will have troubles enough at this introductory stage without the need to worry about the accuracy of his forecasts. Suffice it to say here that cost-of-capital figures used in planning are based on estimates and that the results of calculations made during the planning

---

[2] To be read "2% discount may be taken if paid within 10 days; otherwise the net amount is due in 30 days."

period are regarded as approximations rather than precise amounts. In practice, estimates are first based on the observation of the fate of similar issues made by other companies and/or the market behavior of the outstanding securities of the particular company. Later, the estimates can be refined as quotations are received from potential distributors in the process of discussing an issue with them.

Costs of Fixed Return Types of Securities

The easiest costs to determine are those related to contracts which have the outlay fixed at the time they are issued: preferred stock, bonds, and leases. Preferred dividends cannot go above a known limit (in the usual case of a nonparticipating issue), and bond interest is rigidly set so that it cannot vary up or down, and a majority of leases also call for amounts that are defined in the original contract. We shall proceed to explain how the costs of each of these types of financing can be computed, taking them in the order named above.

The principal types of cash costs associated with the acquisition of funds through financial contracts may be classified as follows:

a) Periodic payments to the contract holder in the form of interest, dividends, or rent.

b) Any payment to the distributor of the issue as compensation for his services in marketing the issue and for assuming the risks associated with a public offering. The distributor deducts from the price received from the investor an amount which he has agreed is adequate compensation and then remits the net proceeds to the company. The difference between the price to the investor and the price to the company is referred to as the *spread*.

c) Other costs incidental to the making of the contract which are paid by the issuing company, such as legal and printing costs.

d) Any payment to the contract holder at the retirement of an issue in excess of the amount originally provided by the investor. This *discount* applies only to securities which have a definite maturity, or which may be redeemed at the option of the company, and only when the issue is sold at a price less than the amount payable at retirement. This amount may be amortized over the life of the issue and considered as an addition to the periodic interest or dividend cost. According to similar reasoning, a security sold at a *premium* would involve a downward adjustment of the interest or dividend cost.

1. *Preferred Stock.* The case of a "straight" preferred stock, one without a sinking fund, is relatively simple, for two reasons. First, the security is a fixed income type, where compensation to the investor in the form of dividend payments is rigidly limited to the amount specified at the time of issue. While this annual payment is not mandatory, as in the case of bonds, it is appropriate that management assume it to be, as has been explained before. The other simplifying feature is that the ordinary

straight preferred stock does not have a fixed date for the repayment of the principal sum; therefore, the costs which may be associated with repayment (item [d]) are ruled out.[3]

For our purposes, it is desirable to express the cost of capital as an annual percentage outlay on the dollars provided. As the issuer views it, the dollars provided are the net proceeds available for investment in corporate activity—the sum provided by the investor, less the costs of issue, including the amount retained by the investment banker handling the issue and the expenditures incurred directly by the issuer. These are, of course, items (b) and (c) in the foregoing list.

An illustration of this process in the case of preferred stock will be helpful. The prospectus on Long Island Lighting Company's Series C preferred stock, offered during 1953, gave the following information:

Amount: 100,000 shares, par $100:
  a) Cumulative dividend.............................5.25%
     Price to public...................................$100
  b) Spread...$2
     Proceeds to company (from underwriter)............$98
  c) Other costs of issue paid by company...............$45,000
     Other costs as a percentage of total issue............0.45%
     Net proceeds to company...........................$97.55

It will be seen that although the public was to pay $100 per share, the company would have only $97.55 per share available for investment. For the use of this sum of money the company would pay the investor $5.25 per year. Under these circumstances, the annual cash payment, expressed as a percentage of the investable funds, would amount to 5.38%; and this will be taken as the cost, on an after-tax basis:

$$\frac{\text{Payment to Holders}}{\text{Net Proceeds to Issuer}} = \frac{\$5.25}{\$100.00 - (2.00 + 0.45)} = 5.38\% .$$

The reader already knows how to convert this figure to a before-tax basis. At a tax rate of 48%, the before-tax cost is 10.35%.

2. *Bonds.* The measurement of the annual cash obligation on bonds runs in a pattern similar to that for the preferred stock but is complicated by the facts that bonds must be repaid at a specific future date and that the amount originally received by the company is likely to differ from the amount repaid to the investor at maturity. Thus, for example, if we are considering a 15-year, 3% bond with a face value of $1,000, which brought the issuer $980 net, we must take into account not only the $30 annual interest payment but also the $20 which must be paid to the investor at the end of 15 years in addition to the $980 actually received and used by the company. As was shown in the previous chapter, these amounts can be tabulated with proper attention to time, and the "yield"

---

[3] It is true that a redeemable preferred may be repaid eventually at the option of the management, but this would normally be a possibility so uncertain at the time of issue as to rule it out of consideration at that time.

or internal rate of return may be computed. Since a calculation of this sort with reference to bonds is needed many times a day by specialists in bond financing, "bond value tables" have been published to which one may make reference. The section of a bond value table applicable to the problem at hand is reproduced in Table 21–1. It will be seen that for a

TABLE 21–1

THREE PERCENT BONDS

Yield to Maturity	14½ Years	15 Years	15½ Years
2.75%............	$102.97	$103.06	$103.14
2.80.............	102.37	102.44	102.50
2.90.............	101.18	101.21	101.24
3.00.............	100.00	100.00	100.00
3.10.............	98.84	98.81	98.78
3.20.............	97.69	97.63	97.57
3.25.............	97.13	97.05	96.97

3% 15-year bond which nets the company $98 per $100 of bond, the actual cost lies between 3.1% and 3.2%. A more precise figure may be gained by interpolation. It is 3.17%.[4]

The difference between this calculation of the effective cost to the user of funds and the yield calculation of an investor may be noted. The bond above might have been sold by the underwriter to the investor at a premium—say, at $1,020. The difference of $40 was used to compensate the distributor and pay other costs. As far as the investor is concerned, the yield to him is less than 3%, since he must make allowance for the fact that he will not receive $1,020 at maturity but only $1,000. His effective return (from a yield table) at this price would be 2.84%. It will be apparent that the difference between the yield to the investor and the cost to the company results from the use of a portion of the proceeds to cover the costs of issue. And obviously, the yield to the investor is normally less than the cost to the issuer.

We may now proceed to consider the case of the Long Island Lighting Company bonds offered during 1953, comparing them with the preferred stock. The facts of the issue, as given in the prospectus, follow:

```
    Total amount....................................$25,000,000
    Term...........................................30 years
        a) Coupon rate...............................3½%
           Price to public...........................100.929%
        b) Spread...................................0.719
           Proceeds to company......................100.210%
        c) Other costs of issue......................$195,000
           Other costs as a percentage of total issue.........0.780%
           Net proceeds to company....................99.430%
        d) Discount..................................0.570%
           Maturity value.............................100.000%
```

---

[4] If bond value tables are not available, the cost may be approximated by using the method introduced at page 432.

Following the method of computation suggested above, we note that the company must pay $35 of interest per year on each $1,000 bond and, in addition, amortize one thirtieth of $5.70—the excess of the amount to be repaid over the amount received on a $1,000 bond. The effective cost in this case is 3.53%. Since we are dealing with a bond, this figure represents a before-tax cost. On an after-tax basis, at a 48% rate, the cost is 1.84%.

Readers who are watchful of details will note that we have made no allowance for the effect of periodic retirement of the bond through sinking funds, although methods do exist for this refinement. The usual calculations for the cost of bonded debt are based on the assumption either that the bonds in question are not to be retired by sinking fund or (another way of saying the same thing) that sinking fund purchases and the ultimate maturity will be priced so as not to incur further costs or to create further income. For most purposes, the values given by bond value tables or by the approximate method presented earlier in this chapter are sufficiently accurate.

In Chapter 17 we specified that any method of calculation of burdens and costs must give consistent results. We have achieved the desired result here; and the following table shows the cost of the preferred stock to be 2.9 times that of the bonds, whether one looks at before-tax or after-tax costs.

COSTS OF CAPITAL AS COMPUTED

	Before Tax	After Tax (48%)
Bonds	3.53%	1.84%
Preferred stock	10.34%	5.38%

Coverage Requirements as Limits to Borrowing at Established Rates

If the Long Island Lighting Company, with all other things equal, had tried to raise twice as much money with its bond issue, would it have been able to obtain the same terms as to cost? Almost certainly not, since the investors would have insisted upon higher rates to compensate for higher risk. In appraising a particular security for possible investment, the investor is concerned not only with the amount of the prospective income to be derived but also with the certainty of that income. It is common knowledge that even in the case of a senior mortgage bond, the terms of which are legally enforceable, there is an element of uncertainty about the periodic interest payments and the repayment of principal at maturity. This uncertainty comes from the possibility that at some time over the life of the issue the issuing company may find itself with a cash position so weakened that it cannot fulfill its obligation to the security holder.

There are various ways in which investors may take steps to protect themselves against this risk. The primary safeguard is considered to be a demonstrated capacity to earn, in normal times, an income substantially in excess of the total contractual or assumed obligation on the securities. It is recognized that however well managed a business may be, it cannot escape the influence of a general business recession, should such occur. It is, therefore, necessary to be assured that the earnings available for payments to senior security holders in prosperous times are large enough so that the possible shrinkage in bad times will not endanger these payments, either in fact or in the minds of investors. Suppose it is assumed that a recession might cut net earnings available for bond interest to one half the level of prosperous times; then the ratio of such net earnings to total bond interest in normal times would have to be more than 2/1 for the bondholder to feel any real protection. This "cushion" of excess earnings capacity will be referred to in this discussion as the *earnings coverage* on a security.

It may be helpful to illustrate how these considerations apply in practice. Let us compare two railroad bonds whose contractual terms seem to offer a similar investment opportunity:

1. Atchison, Topeka & Sante Fe Railway Company general 4%, due 1995.
2. Missouri-Kansas-Texas Railroad Company first 4%, due 1990.

Although the two companies concerned are not comparable as to size, the securities have a number of aspects in common. They are both bonds, secured by a first mortgage on the same type of property, and both have distant maturity dates. They are both accepted for listing on the New York Stock Exchange.

However, in spite of these similarities, *Moody's Transportation Manual* for investors, 1965 edition, rated the "Atchison" issue as Aaa, the highest rating given, and the "Katy" issue as B, five grades below the former. It is instructive to note the general statements in *Moody's Transportation Manual* concerning these ratings:

> Aaa—Bonds which are rated Aaa are judged to be of the best quality. They carry the smallest degree of investment risk and are generally referred to as "gilt edge." Interest payments are protected by a large or by an exceptionally stable margin and principal is secure. While the various protective elements are likely to change, such changes as can be visualized are most unlikely to impair the fundamentally strong position of such issues.
>
> B—Bonds which are rated B generally lack characteristics of the desirable investment. Assurance of interest and principal payments or of maintenance of other terms of the contract over any long period of time may be small.[5]

On closer examination, the most striking difference between these two securities is the extent to which annual earnings have, or have not,

---

[5] *Moody's Transportation Manual, 1965*, p. vi.

exceeded bond interest. In the case of Atchison, the times fixed charges earned ratio (see p. 399) was 10.9 times in 1964,[6] whereas the same ratio could not be computed for the Katy's, which experienced a loss in 1964. In 1963 the Katy's ratio was 1.01.[7] A similar contrast is found over a period of recent years. This difference in coverage was certainly a major factor in the ratings of these bonds given by Moody's Investors Service.

Since the market in general agrees with Moody's ratings, one can predict that owners of the Katy issue, in order to find buyers, must offer some attraction to overcome the greater degree of risk. The terms of the contract fix the quantities to be received from the ownership of the bond, so the adjustment must be in the price. In November, 1965, when this paragraph was being written, the Atchison bonds were selling at 90¾ ($907.50 per $1,000. bond) and Katy bonds at 63½.

Use of the approximate method explained above shows that the rate of interest to a purchaser of these bonds at the prices indicated is 4.52% for the Atchison bonds, and 6.70% for the Katy issue. Furthermore, if this condition exists for outstanding bonds of the two companies, it is certain that in 1965 any bond financing by Atchison would cost far less than in the case of Katy. Unquestionably, this higher cost was directly related to the greater risks of default on the bond's promises, which investors have come to associate with the weaker company.

To return to the Long Island Lighting Company example, cited earlier, earnings which merely covered the direct cash outlay of 3.53% on the bonds would not be sufficient to satisfy a bond buyer's concept of a safe investment. It is clearly a part of the overall financial obligation associated with new security issues that a business meet the minimum earnings coverage necessary to induce the bondholder or stockholder to invest at the current rate of return. This aspect is difficult to pin down quantitatively, however, because of the lack of uniformity of investment standards in the securities market. We term this kind of requirement the *coverage requirement* and emphasize that the outlay cost of any security always has behind it a coverage requirement which is larger. Without such coverage and the assurance it gives, the specific rate of outlay cost would not have been acceptable to the investor.

For purposes of illustration, we have chosen to use the standard used by a major insurance company, because it is a standard which has actually been applied by this investor to our case in question, the Long Island Lighting Company. We emphasize that this is an example and is not intended to suggest a general rule.

For public utility bonds, the desired earnings coverage rates applied by this particular investor are measured by a times interest earned ratio of 3½:

---

[6] *Ibid.*, p. 1310. "Fixed charges" include rentals in the ratio used.

[7] *Ibid.*, p. 120.

$$\frac{\text{Earnings before Interest and Taxes}}{\text{Interest on Long-Term Debt}} = 3\frac{1}{2}.$$

If the Long Island Lighting Company bonds are to meet this test without drawing on the general earning power of the company, the investment that will be financed by the proposed issue must earn something like three and a half times its cost—or the issue will be rated as more risky and will become more costly, if it will be sold at all. In some cases, failure to meet the standard could mean that the investors would not buy the bond on any terms. At all events, the question of earnings coverage is one that must be considered by management whenever any fixed charge type of financial contract is proposed.

Elements to Consider in the Cost of Common Equity

We have seen in the previous section how the cash outlays on senior securities can be measured precisely and expressed as a percentage of the net proceeds made available for investment. We also have just indicated the existence of not so clearly defined coverage requirements which must also be met if the issuer wishes to continue to sell these senior securities at the same quality rating.

In considering these two aspects of the financial obligation associated with senior securities, it is apparent that there is a clear line of distinction between what the security holder actually receives in earnings and the earnings he asks the company to provide as a margin of protection against the effects of adverse circumstances, protection which has the twofold significance of demonstrated coverage and a growing equity base to the extent that these earnings are reinvested.

There is an all-important difference in the case of common stock, in that the retained earnings, although not received at the moment, nevertheless belong to the shareholder. On the surface the relation of a corporation to the holders of common stock appears to have the same components as in the case of preferred stock and bonds. The common shareholder, like the preferred shareholder, receives his dividend as a cash outlay and looks to an excess of earnings per share as his assurance that this dividend will continue in the future. In fact, in some countries the dividend of a company is seldom mentioned without a statement of its "cover," which is the number of times the earnings of a period exceed the dividend paid out. This cover, of earnings retained, may be expected to provide growth of dividends through their productive use in the firm in the future. It is this hope of growth in value through retained earnings that distinguishes the common stockholder's position from that of the holders of nonparticipating senior issues. But the common stockholder's direct interest in the value of earnings in excess of his dividend greatly complicates any estimate of the cost of this type of security.

The context of this chapter requires that we define a "cost" for equity capital which is commensurable with the cost of other forms of financing. This requires a number expressed as a percentage of the amount to be obtained from the owners (either by retention or new shares). It can be derived from the fraction:

where

$$C = \frac{V}{P}$$

cost of new equity

Earnings yield

> C = The desired ratio.
> V = The benefits expected by the investor.
> P = The net investment of new or retained funds.

The reader will easily see that this fraction has the same form as those used for senior securities, but he may note that, in place of the precise elements of cost that we set for bonds or preferred stock, we have substituted the vaguely defined symbol V.

So far, in discussing the cost of securities senior to the common equity, it has been unnecessary to distinguish between the corporation and its owners when we defined the cost of the issue. But grave errors have been made by financial managers who neglect this distinction when they consider the cost of the common equity.

The policies to be set with reference to the common equity should be those that maximize the value of the shares that have been issued to the owners of the corporation. This requires a particular point of view on the part of the manager when he considers how to deal with the owners. It is appropriate for the financial managers of a corporation to minimize the cost of borrowings and similar prior-charge arrangements precisely because (as explained in Chapter 18) the benefits of using low-cost senior securities may be passed on to the equity interest. On the other hand, when attention is turned to policies that relate to the treatment of the common shares, it is entirely inappropriate to set policies that reduce the "cost" from the firm's point of view. In the determination of dividends, for instance, the probable effect of the dividend on the value of the shareholders' interest must be the central concern. It certainly would be indefensible for the directors of a corporation to vote the lowest dividends that they believe are possible without producing a revolt on the part of the stockholders—and yet this attitude of economizing on funds paid out is correct when the managers negotiate with lenders.

dividend yield + normal ratio of earnings growth

The question: "Will this proposal increase or decrease the value of the stockholders' interest?" needs constantly to be kept in mind.

The Concept of Free Transferability

Some help in reaching a cost for equity funds can be obtained by using the concept that the owners of a firm are supplying funds to it only because they see more value in this investment than in alternatives that are available to them on comparable conditions of amount, time, and uncertainty of the funds flows they anticipate receiving from their stockholding. It they foresee a change which will make their holding in one firm less desirable than it has been in comparison with alternatives, they will move out of the holding. If they foresee a relative improvement, they will acquire more of the shares of the firm in question. And, when the company's plans promise no change in the relative position, they will be "indifferent" (in the sense in which the term is used in economics).

The concept just stated assumes that shareholders have complete freedom to withdraw, or to invest, funds in a corporation. In the real world, the decisions are largely those of the corporation's management, which may retain funds without consulting the shareholders and which decides whether or not to invite new investment by offering new shares. Nevertheless, the concept that the firm holds funds by the consent of the owners is a valuable guide to policy, and the question for management becomes: "Would the investor, if he were given the funds, do better elsewhere?"

The investor is assumed to look at the benefits the company offers him through its use of equity funds and to reach a conclusion about the value of these benefits. He compares the value he reached in this manner with the value offered by the benefits of alternate investments and makes his choice. There is no question that investors do reach conclusions about relative values, so the query arises: "How do shareholders evaluate their holdings?" This question, unfortunately, has yet to be answered, despite the best efforts of many investigators. The mind of the shareholder remains a "black box," and the process of "value generation" that takes place as he observes dividends, earnings, and other factors can only be approximated. It is surely a complex process that varies from investor to investor and as each investor views the industry, the company, the general environment, and recent events. There is no easy answer.

Yet financial managers continually face the necessity to use equity funds if new assets are to be acquired, and some of them wish to do so as far as possible by economic criteria. Needing some guidelines, they turn to various quantities which they think may be used as an index of the value in the stockholders' minds, because the fluctuation of the chosen quantities correlate with observed prices in the stock market.

The Earnings Yield

For many years the amount of net earnings available for common stock has been assumed, in the United States, to correlate satisfactorily with the value of the stock. Many firms make decisions concerning the investment of equity funds solely by studying the effect of their plans on this number. Thus, it is widely held that if new investments can produce earnings at the same rate per dollar of investment as has been the firm's experience, the investor will see that the value of his holding is unchanged, and not take action. Using the assumption that earnings correlate with value, the *earnings yield* (obtained by dividing the earnings per share by the price of the share) is the condition which leaves the investors' position unchanged. It then serves as the "cost" of the equity capital.[8]

The argument runs as follows: The market value of the stock represents the stockholders' current assessment of the value of a share, reached after comparison with the benefits offered by alternative shareholdings. On the assumption that this evaluation is directly correlated with earnings, the ratio of earnings to price expresses the results of the comparison. If the firm's use of new funds is not expected to produce earnings at least at the same rate per dollar invested as the existing earnings yield, the average rate of return on previously invested funds will fall, thus making investment in this firm less attractive than investment in the other firms that represent alternative opportunities for the stockholders' use of funds. Such a result is undesirable.

On the other hand, if the new money can be invested at a higher rate of return than the present earnings yield, the average value will rise, and the owner may be expected to approve. The point of indifference, or marginal point is, then, when:

$$\frac{\text{Existing Earnings}}{\text{Existing Investment (at Market Value)}} = \frac{\text{Increment in Earnings}}{\text{Funds Devoted to New Investment}}.$$

While this test may be applied both to test the desirability of retaining internal funds or of obtaining new funds, it appears in slightly different guise to the existing owner, depending on whether the funds are to be retained or raised by the sale of new shares.

In the first case, that of retention, there will be no change in the number of shares. Then the test for acceptability of expansion in the amount of equity is that the value of the shareholding must rise in the same proportion that the amount of retained funds bears to the previously invested equity.

In the second case, when new shares are to be issued, the existing owners are concerned that the value of their existing interest be preserved. This occurs under the same condition as in the case of retention, but it can be expressed as occurring when the proportionate increase in the number of shares is the same as the proportionate increase in value to be expected.

Improvements on the Earnings Yield

But it is now generally accepted by analysts that the earnings-price ratio must be modified by other information in order to get a closer

---

[8] The reader will recognize the earnings yield to be the reciprocal of the "price-earnings ratio," as described on p. 364. We often refer to it as the "earnings-price ratio."

correlation between "the independent variable," V, and the dependent variable P. Elaborate formulas have been developed by some observers, but here it is enough to say that at least two other factors need attention. One, which appears to have considerable force, is the anticipated rate of growth in earnings. The other factor results from the fact that the size of any dividend and the outlook for future dividends are undoubtedly of great significance in the determination of market price at any point of time (even when the amount of the dividend is zero!).

In terms of the problem before us, which is how the proposed use of funds will affect the value of the existing shares, we can describe the point where this value is unchanged and thus define *the cost of new equity capital* as that combination of earnings, growth, and dividends which must be produced by the incremental investment in order that the market value of an existing stockholder's existing proprietary interest be neither increased nor decreased. This condition can be expected, we suggest, when the promised growth rate will be unchanged and the increase in earnings and dividends will be proportional to the increase in the equity of the firm.

If, for example, an investor in the XYZ Corporation feels that it should pay him a dividend of 3% of the value of the shares, yet grow in earning power at a compound rate of 5%, it is necessary that the firm earn 8%, in order that the 3% can be paid out while 5% is retained to provide the year's increment of growth.[9] This line of reasoning leads to estimating the cost of capital as: dividend yield plus rate of growth in earnings. Many analysts now prefer to use a cost of capital built up in such a manner rather than the simple earnings-price ratio.[10]

To be more explicit, let us refer again to the case of the Long Island Lighting Company. The prospectus for a common stock issue during 1953 gave the following information:

Amount: 685,648 shares	$10 par
Price to public	$16
Spread	$0.29
Proceeds to company	$15.71
Other costs of issue	$128,000
Other costs as percentage of total issue	1.17%
Net proceeds per share	$15.52
Expected dividend per share	$0.90

The most recent annual earnings per share figure on the outstanding common stock at this time was $1.15 (after taxes).[11]

---

[9] This statement has behind it the implicit assumption that earnings growth is directly correlated with the amount of earnings retained.

[10] Theorists who assume perfect certainty of the necessary forecasts can show that the total of dividend yield and rate of growth will be the same number as the ratio of earnings to price. But as soon as growth is recognized as less certain than current dividends, the equality disappears.

[11] *Moody's Public Utilities Manual, 1954*, p. 1371.

To express the cost measured by a rate of return on the dollars invested, we must recognize the fact that each new share of the new issue will produce only $15.52 of investable funds and not the currently quoted price.

If the earnings yield is to be used as the cost of the equity capital to the corporation, the rate is:

$$\frac{1.15}{15.52} = \quad \text{7.41\% after tax, or 14.25\% before tax when the tax rate is 48\%.}$$

On the other hand, the dividend of $0.90 per share related to the proceeds of the new issue of $15.52 per share, requires a rate of earnings of 5.80%. The authors have computed the rate of growth of earnings on the common equity established over the previous 5 years as a guide to the future. It is at the rate of 2.71%. The sum of the two rates is 8.51%, and the cost of capital may be estimated to be this total, after tax. On a before-tax basis, the figure (at 48% rate) becomes 16.35%.

It may be concluded from these two ways of figuring that the before-tax cost of equity capital for the Long Island Lighting Company at the time it sold shares in 1953 was somewhere in the neighborhood of 15½%, as the earnings-price test gives 14.25%, and the more complex test gives 16.35%.

The following table brings together the before- and after-tax costs of the Long Island Lighting financing, as we have computed them. It shows the usual relationships, bonds being less costly than preferred, and common "costing" the largest figure.

	Before Tax	After Tax (48%)
Bonds........................	3.53%	1.84%
Preferred stock.................	10.34	5.38
Common Equity...............	15.50*	8.00*

* Figures chosen by the analyst after observation of the results of two calculations.

What Ratio to Choose?

At the present state of our knowledge, no one can claim that any model to obtain a cost of equity capital can give infallible results. The analyst must choose a method that gives acceptable[12] results in the case he is considering. Where it is possible to assume, as often it may be, that a

---

[12] Acceptable in this context means "less likely to produce results that one rejects intuitively," as in the case of an earnings-price ratio of 2% for a "growth stock" of a company whose prospects are highly uncertain, but include the possibility of enormous growth, or in the case of stocks in depression periods, where the earnings-price ratio has risen to 25% or higher.

firm's growth rate will be maintained by the new investment, and that dividend pay-out ratios are the basis of dividend policy (see pages 288 to 297), then the earnings-price ratio may justifiably be used.

What the reader is asked to remember, as he reads further in the literature, is that any figure for the cost of equity capital, however it may be reached, is an estimated one. We will remain in this fix until we learn far more about the things that actual shareholders actually recognize as conferring value on their holdings.

Another Route to the Cost of New Equity Capital

Since our endeavor to establish a cost for new equity capital by studying the particular company has led to results that are not entirely satisfactory, it is interesting to review another procedure of estimation. Let us now remember that the holder of the particular shares chose them from other shares of the same type and say that the additional capital of this particular firm shall be raised in a way which will offer at least as good results as the average stock of the industry. That is, we require that a company must earn on its investments at least what its shareholders could earn on the money if they invested it elsewhere at similar risk.

We are beginning to have the results of extensive studies of investment results from holdings of common equities which offer figures that might be used, at least to check the results obtained from the test derived from figures about the particular company in question.

The Center for Research in Security Prices at the University of Chicago has at its disposal the most detailed record of security prices ever assembled. Its findings are just beginning to be published, but figures like the following are pertinent to our problem of setting a cost for the equity capital of the Long Island Lighting Company.

The Center has calculated the rate of return on an investment in all the stocks on the New York Stock Exchange, for 22 various time periods of holding. Included in the calculation as income were all cash dividends received and the capital gain or loss experienced at the time of sale. Rates of return were calculated to give the yield, on a compound interest basis, by the same method as that described in the previous chapter. In 54% of the periods, the before-tax return to the stockholder exceeded 10% per year. The rate exceeded 6% in 64% of the periods.[13]

Even when the choice of stock and the period of holding were completely randomized, the median before-tax rate of return was 9.8%, and 69% of the investments had a return of over 4%.[14]

It is greatly to be hoped that this informative research will continue,

[13] Lawrence Fisher and James H. Lorie, "Rates of Return on Investments in Common Stocks," *Journal of Business*, Vol. XXXVII (January, 1964), pp. 1–21. The figures used above were taken from Table 2.

[14] Lawrence Fisher, "Outcomes for 'Random' Investments in Common Stocks Listed on the New York Stock Exchange," *Journal of Business*, Vol. XXXVIII (April, 1965), pp. 149–61.

and that we shall soon have results by industry groups. For the present, we can only point out that the results should prevent any one from using as cost of equity the very low percentages that are observed in a boom market when price-earnings ratios are very high.

Summary: Costs of Individual Classes of Securities

The cost of raising funds from fixed return types of securities can be obtained from the relationship of the outlays required to support them to the net amounts obtained from these securities during the period they are outstanding, but it must be remembered that the particular cost that is actually observed depends upon the investors' quality rating of the issue. This, in part, depends upon the degree of coverage in excess of the precise burden that must be met. In this chapter methods of determining the cost are given, but the determination of the coverage requirement is indicated only by an example.

The cost to be considered for equity capital is derived from the argument that existing stockholders will wish additional investments of equity funds to produce values which do not reduce the values of their existing holdings. We believe that this test should be applied not only when new money is to be raised by the sale of shares, but also as an important consideration whenever it is to be decided how much earnings should be retained.

Although the costs of each class of security can be determined separately, it must be recognized that there is an interrelationship among the costs of the types of capital of a particular company. If a management chooses to increase significantly the proportion of bonds in the company's capitalization, the effect will be not only to increase the cost of debt, but also—because of the increased risk to the equity—to change the cost of equity financing. Until recently, this interdependence of costs has been too much ignored. We shall have more to say of it in Chapter 22, where ways to obtain a single figure to represent the effect of combining securities with various costs will be presented.

Among the uses for computed costs of capital are (1) selection for lowest cost among alternative ways of raising desired funds, (2) testing the adequacy of estimated profits from a project against the cost of financing it, and (3) comparison of the cost of a proposed financing at a certain time with historical levels of cost for the type of security being studied.

It is also sometimes desirable to combine the costs of the individual issues of a company into a single figure to represent the cost of capitalization as a whole. But this process requires some introductory material, and we leave it to the next chapter. We now turn to a presentation of some questions that are frequently asked as one looks more deeply into the vexing question of the proper number to use for the cost of equity capital.

Do Retained Earnings Have a Cost?

Despite our argument that the "cost of equity capital" may be derived without distinction as to whether the new capital uses retained earnings or newly sold shares, practice indicates that many firms consider retained earnings to be essentially a cost-free source of funds. It has been a well-accepted company policy to reinvest a portion of annual earnings, even though the amount reinvested apparently bears no relation to the prospective return on investment opportunities from year to year.

In view of the great importance of retained earnings as a source of corporate capital, the question whether such sums should be regarded by management as having a cost has great importance. It is a matter about which managers and theorists have differed for many years. In the treatment which follows, we shall try to indicate the reasons why some of the earnings reported by accountants need to be retained regardless of cost, because they are not real earnings. When it comes to the real earnings, we side with the theorists who claim that a cost should be assigned to retained funds when financial policies are considered.

It is argued that some earnings must be retained in order to support the established appraisal of the dividend and that—for these earnings, at least—their "cost" has no significance. Management people recognize the fact, as we have done above, that an investor's appraisal of the value of a dividend is related to the relative certainty of the payment. This, in turn, depends in part on the coverage. A cushion of retained earnings is needed to assure the likelihood that in a bad year the dividend payment can be maintained without reduction.

If, for example, a firm that has had the practice to pay 60% of its average earnings should suddenly adopt the policy to pay 100%, the investor could not appraise each $1 of dividend as highly (from the viewpoint of certainty) as before, and the price paid per dollar of dividend would fall. In other words, the yield (dividend ÷ price) would rise.

It is also pointed out, and we agree, that some of the earnings that are computed according to the rules of accountancy are fictitious, because, in fact, the amounts charged for depreciation are too low to cover the using-up of assets in terms of the funds required to maintain profit levels. Therefore, since this portion of the "earnings" is not real, it should be retained as an addition to the depreciation. We have no objection to this procedure, but we should require that the sums involved be estimated with some care.

These arguments have value. We shall, nevertheless, counter with the argument that we have made before, namely, that it is always a possibility that the shareholder's funds might earn more if they had been put into his hands and he had invested the money elsewhere. We feel that management must view the investment in a particular business as one of several investment opportunities open to the stockholder. If the stockholder had free access, funds could be withdrawn and used wherever they could be more profitably invested. Every investment, including reinvested earnings, viewed in this way has its opportunity cost, that is, the benefit forgone by not investing elsewhere. For a fair comparison, of course, the alternative investment must offer the same degree of uncertainty.

Thus, one is led to the conclusion that the test to be applied to projects that would use earnings in the business and thus deny them to the shareholders must be the same as is applied for new issues of common shares, refined perhaps by changing the price used in the calculation to the market price quoted, instead of the net price obtainable after the costs of issuing new shares.

A frequently noted problem arises, in the case of earnings retention, from the fact that if a firm is to pay out funds to the shareholders, the amount in the shareholder's hands will be reduced by taxation, so there would be less available for investment by him than there would have been if the funds were retained by the firm. We have argued in previous editions that this fact justifies the firm in reducing the rate of opportunity cost it will apply to a number that is lower than the one used for new share issues. We are no longer of the opinion that this can be done as a general rule.

Because of the personal tax on dividend income, it is obviously true that the firm can retain more than the stockholder can invest. But if the funds are retained, they are still in the hands of the firm. The question of the relative values of retention or dividend is not settled from the stockholder's point of view before we have followed the alternatives through time, until the stockholder receives proceeds from the investment (either the firm's or his own). Or, stated in another way, we must avoid the implicit assumption that the addition of a dollar to retained earnings will be reflected by an increase of a dollar in the market price of equity.

What was forgotten is that the personal tax that was avoided by the firm's retention of earnings at the start is experienced later, when the stockholder receives the benefits that have been accumulating for him within the firm. If no tax rates change in the interim, and the firm does precisely as well as the stockholder in its use of funds, there is no tax advantage from the owner's point of view to the retention of the earnings, and therefore there is no reason to lower the size of the cost of capital. The cost of retained earnings may therefore be taken to be the same as that of new equity money.

Only when one can foresee with confidence that the shareholder can reduce his future tax burden below that applicable at present can one justify a firm in setting a criterion for the retention of earnings that is less demanding than that established to test the desirability of raising new money. In the United States the possibility of receiving "capital gains treatment" is a very real one. But unless the facts of a particular case permit a reliable forecast that capital gains treatment is to be expected, one cannot lower the opportunity cost for reinvested funds below the cost of new equity capital.

Do Funds Earmarked as Depreciation Have a Cost?

The process of depreciation, in a profitable firm, results in the setting aside of some of the net inflows of funds to compensate for a shrinkage in the value of the assets which are used in the business. What we are observing is a gradual return of the funds once invested in specialized assets back to liquid form.

What must be recognized is that there is no obligation for the managers of a firm to devote these liquid funds to replace specific assets, or even to buy any assets at all. Only if projects are found that meet the criteria of the firm, should these funds be used. It is to such criteria that we will turn in the following chapter, where ways to combine the individual costs will be discussed.

Historical Behavior of Costs of Capital

An alert financial manager will recognize that the costs of various types of securities are constantly changing. This fact can be observed not only from the terms that his company obtained whenever it did issue new contracts but also and more continuously from the behavior of the issues of his company and similar issues in the market. As was pointed out earlier, the historical costs of a particular issue are not so important to the management as the likely costs of the next issue; and costs in the near future may be inferred, as a first approximation, from the present level and historic behavior of the market. For this reason, we present in Chart 21–1 certain measures of cost since the end of the second World War.

The data for the chart were taken from the tabulations which show the "yield" of various issues to a buyer. In order to make these statistics useful from the point of view of a corporation considering an issue, the yield rate on debt instruments was reduced to an after-tax figure, using a 52% rate until 1964, 50% for that year, and 48% thereafter. The costs of stocks and bonds were thus made comparable for our purposes, and no longer useful to potential buyers.[15]

With this presentation, we see that the ordering of costs is what our theoretical descriptions would suggest; short-term debt is normally the cheapest and bonds come next. Costs do not change greatly in these categories. The fact that the dividend yield on common stock has been below that of preferred stock since 1954 is worthy of note. It confirms our argument in this chapter that the buyer of common stocks is finding value in something in addition to his dividend.

---

[15] Actually, since these data were taken from seasoned issues, they slightly understate the cost of new issues, which often are offered at favorable prices and always bear registration and other costs.

CHART 21-1

INDICATORS OF COSTS OF
CORPORATE ISSUES, 1946–65
(After Tax on Debt Instruments)

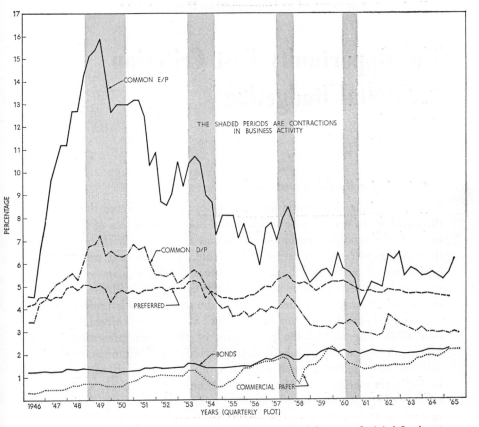

SOURCES OF DATA USED: Office of Business Economics, Department of Commerce, *Statistical Supplements to Survey of Current Business* for stock data to December, 1951; *Federal Reserve Bulletins*, for all other data.

The major change to be noted is the movement downward of the common stock earnings-price ratio, and its relatively stable relationship to the dividend yield on common stock since 1958. Certainly there is evidence that the attitude of buyers toward common stocks has changed greatly. The "rule of thumb" that common stock can be sold only in a few months of the business cycle can certainly be challenged from the facts shown in the chart.

As we are writing this chapter, in December, 1965, the "spread" between the yield to buyers of common stock and the yield to buyers of bonds is very close. But, viewed from the issuers' position, borrowing is still notably less costly than stock financing, because of the tax deductibility of interest.

Chapter 22

The Opportunity Cost Criterion in Capital Budgeting

Criteria for Ranking and Cutoff

IN THE previous chapter the investment opportunity offered the firm was the purchase of a corporate bond. When the criterion rate of $2\frac{1}{2}\%$ was applied, the proposed purchase was found to be slightly more desirable than the opportunity to invest at that rate. By this work, we made the beginning of a capital budget. As other possible investments were proposed and tested, the managers of the firm could evaluate each, and thus obtain a ranking of the projects in the order of their preference one over another, or in other words a "ladder" of possible projects. With rare exceptions, any one of the procedures of evaluation presented in the previous chapter will be adequate to provide a ranking, once a criterion rate has been selected. Such a result is an essential part of the capital budgeting process, since firms in fact must make choices among a number of opportunities, and they need to know their relative desirability, in terms of the value they offer.

The opportunity to buy other bonds to yield $2\frac{1}{2}\%$, while real, may nevertheless not be the appropriate alternative to consider when a project of a different nature comes up for analysis. It is a real alternative, and therefore an appropriate criterion, when we limit ourselves to the question of buying one bond or another. A theorist might describe the limited choice we have illustrated as "suboptimization," because the decision maker has constrained his choice to only one type of the possible alternatives that a firm might develop.

A criterion that would be applicable generally and still be a real alternative use for the firm's funds is what is also required. We shall try to satisfy the requirement, but first let us point out that many decisions are in fact made with constraints and that in such cases serviceable opportunity costs, within the limits of what is possible, may be obtained quite quickly. We would not take the trouble to make this point if it were not true that to reach a precise quantity for a general criterion is a task of

456

unusual complexity, which continues to occupy the attention of experienced financial theorists and practitioners without sufficient agreement. Therefore, when the constraints permit the identification of a specific alternate opportunity, there is much to be said for such procedure, although it contains the danger of narrowing the alternatives too much.

For example, we feel that the firm's values will still be maximized if on occasion in situations like the following, the specific alternatives as indicated were recognized instead of a more generalized alternative.

Nature of Project	Alternative Opportunity
1. Buy a bond with excess funds	Buy another bond
2. Borrow money to buy goods at bargain prices	Do not borrow
3. Offer liberal credit to increase sales	Buy short-term bonds
4. Make an investment to replace an inefficient machine	Keep the old machine, and buy short-term bonds

Despite this fact, that many projects may be given their place in a rank order by the use of a specific alternative of similar nature, the managers of a firm need a criterion, expressing an alternative that is generally available to the firm in place of any particular project. Then it will be possible not only to rank the possible projects in their order of desirability but also to show which among the alternatives is less promising than the general alternative. Such a rate, so used, serves as a *cutoff criterion* (or "cutoff rate"), since no specific project less desirable than the general alternative offers as much value as the alternative itself.

It is now necessary to suggest ratios which will be useful as general criteria. We shall present the most frequently encountered alternatives, so that the reader may see the nature of the choices he must make if he is to recommend a criterion for a firm.

Historical Profitability as a Criterion

The most popular criterion in use among practicing managers is a rate which reflects the average level of profitability of the business in the recent past. Such a number offers a number of attractions. It changes slowly over time, since the bulk of the firm's assets at any time have already established their earning power. Therefore it may be used as an expectation for the near future. It is made from internal data and thus avoids the gyrations that characterize ratios that use quotations from the security markets.

Finally, it is argued that the investors who own the firm's securities have appraised it in terms of its earning power, as demonstrated by the historical evidence, so that the established rate of return is correlated with the value of securities. This latter argument will remind the reader of the similar argument which was presented in the last chapter when the level of earnings was presented as an index of the value of the common equity. It follows from this position that new investments should offer at least the established average rate of return. While this conclusion is not valid for an individual project (because the average will move upward if all new projects do better than the criterion), it does have merit when projects are considered in groups.

Let us look at this suggested ratio more closely. The *return on invested capital* is a ratio which requires a figure for earnings in the numerator and a value for the "earning assets" of the firm in the denominator. The latter number may be found by deducting from the total of the assets the following:

1. Current liabilities other than those borrowings which are regularly renewed. This deduction is made because "self-generating" sources of funds usually are noninterest bearing and do not need to be provided in the long-term capital program.
2. Intangible assets. This deduction is made because intangible assets are very unlikely to have the value at which they are shown on the books. The result of deducting these two items from the total assets is known as *net tangible assets*.
3. Any assets which clearly are not needed to support the earnings being used as the numerator in the ratio. The holding of vacant land by a manufacturing company will serve as an example of such an asset. Another example is found in many companies which hold unnecessarily large accounts of liquid funds.

Some analysts adjust upward the values of fixed assets to reflect their observation that much old plant could not be replaced without the recognition of increased construction costs since the plant was built. This practice is widely used in the utility industry, wherever public utility commissions can be persuaded to consider "fair value" instead of "historical cost." The issue is a very important one in this context, since the permitted earnings of a regulated utility depend as much on the value given to the "base" of capital necessary to the business as on the prescribed rate of return.

The earnings figure for the ratio, it is generally agreed, should be before interest and dividends. We prefer that it should be presented after taxes, though there is difference of opinion also on this point.

Here again, we find no unanimous opinion among the experts. It is very difficult to figure a ratio for a single time period that can be defended against criticism, but it is easier to defend an average if made consistently, since many of the adjustments to income named above represent transfers of amounts from one period to another.

Our own preference among ratios of this kind is for the accountant's figure of net earnings before interest and dividends but after taxes, related to the net tangible assets. But we hasten to add that this is a general rule, open to exception whenever a strong case for adjustment can be made. The need for such an adjustment is seen, for example, when measuring the efficiency of two plant managers, if one operates in an old plant of low book value and the other in the newest gem of factory architecture that has yet to be depreciated.

Marginal Analysis and the Cost of Capital

On the other hand, most economists and a growing number of managers argue that such a standard as the retention of past averages will not serve to maximize gains. A "marginal" analysis, as performed at many points in economic theory, will show that projects should be accepted as long as they promise a rate of return that will exceed the cost of financing. The needed figure for "cost of capital" is estimated in a number of ways, as discussed below.

The difference may be illustrated as follows. Assume a company with a capitalization of $1 million and profits of $120,000 (12%) after taxes. The cost of capital for the company is 8%, also after taxes. This capitalization, profit and cost can be expected to continue. Projects for expansion have been analyzed, with rates of return as follows:

Project	Capital Outlay	Profit after Taxes	Rate of Return
A	$25,000	$3,750	15%
B	25,000	3,250	13
C	25,000	2,500	10
D	25,000	2,250	9

A 12% cutoff rate would be used if the return on invested capital is the chosen criterion. An 8% rate would be used if the cost of capital is taken. These alternates give the results shown below:

	12% Cutoff	8% Cutoff
New investment............................	$50,000	$100,000
Profit from new investment.................	$ 7,000	$ 11,750
Cost of raising new funds..................	4,000	8,000
New profit allocable to old capitalization......	$ 3,000	$ 3,750
Return on total investment................	12.100%	11.977%
Return on old capitalization..............	12.300%	12.375%

This example shows that the profits for the existing owners of the firm will be maximized by accepting all projects with returns above the cost of new capital. One very important condition exists, which is that the cost of capital has been properly estimated with consideration of the effect of the way the money is raised upon the cost itself. If so, the new investor has been satisfied, and the management is maximizing the results from the previous owner's point of view within the conditions thus established.

If it is possible to find a figure for the cost of capital, it can serve both as a criterion for ranking and combining the alternative projects and as a cutoff criterion which will require submarginal projects to justify themselves from other than financial points of view, if they are to be accepted. But there is no obvious answer to the question of the cost of capital, because most firms have various types of securities open for their use, and we have already seen that the costs of these securities in a single firm are different—usually equity has the highest cost and borrowing with fixed interest has the lowest.

Such considerations, using the marginal procedure, would lead to the maximum use of low-cost instruments, such as bonds, a practice which, if not restrained, could ultimately be very damaging to the interests of the owners because of the degree of risk that such financing would create. Any scheme of ranking capital costs must deal with this problem. We propose to do so by using a weighted average of the costs of individual parts of the capitalization, a procedure which will permit maximization of the value of the equity interest in the long run.

We have not forgotten that the "mix" of fixed charge and equity securities affects the cost of each element. For most companies, however, any particular financing should be regarded as a part of a continuing program. If we assume for the moment that a business has a satisfactory balance among its securities, then new debt cannot be contemplated at a certain time unless there is the definite expectation that new equity will be provided later (from reinvested earnings and otherwise) in order to restore and preserve the balance in the capital structure. From the long-range point of view, relatively low-cost debt goes hand in hand with high-cost equity capital in the proportions set by business experience and the standard of investors. If the proportions for a certain firm were to be altered significantly, both the cost of debt and the cost of equity would change.

A failure to recognize this relationship may lead to mistakes in investment planning, as in the following illustration. Suppose a management considers that the current securities market is unusually receptive to a new bond issue. If the projects for expansion are related solely to the cost of the bond issue used to finance them, it might appear that any investment which earns over, say, $2\frac{1}{2}\%$ after taxes would result in a net gain in earnings per share and therefore would be financially acceptable to the shareholders. The new bond issue, however, may push total debt up to or beyond the upper limit of risk, so that the next round of expansion would necessarily be financed by common equity capital at a cost made higher by the new element of risk. If the same short-run approach were then taken, new investment would have to earn a very high rate in order to add anything to the value of the existing shareholders' interests. An investment yielding less than this would be rejected. This piecemeal analysis could result in acceptance of a 2½% addition to the earning assets of the business at one stage and the rejection of a 15% addition a year or two later.

A more rational long-range approach to the setting of minimum earnings standards for new investment would be to depart from a rigid marginal approach and calculate an average cost of capital, weighted according to the proportions of debt to equity which preserve the desired balance. Another complication now arises. Before one can compute the weighted average cost, as we suggest must be done, one must have some idea of the proportions of the various sources which the particular company will use. Ideally, each firm should consider the proper balance of income, risk, and control for the nature of the company and its particular stockholders. The costs of the permissible securities would then be combined according to the proportions indicated by this analysis.

Few such studies have been made explicitly, but most firms do have a pattern for the proportions of the various sources of capital. The patterns can be derived from the financial statements of the firms, and the records of recent financing, with proper attention to financial leases, where they exist (page 487). In the Long Island Lighting Company (to return to the example used in Chapter 21), the invested capital at the end of 1953 was made up as follows:

	In Thousands	
	Book Value	Market Value*
Bonds with market values.........$	70,000	$ 67,856
Bonds closely held...............	76,125	76,125†
Preferred stock..................	30,000	30,144
Common stock...................	78,126	93,503
Total.................... $	254,251	$267,000

* Average of year's high and low
† Book value used in absence of market prices

The reader will recognize the danger in assuming that the proportions of new financing provided by various sources in the past necessarily coincide with what these proportions will be or should be in the future. On the other hand, an alert management will have recognized the basic characteristics of risk in the industry in which it operates, and this awareness tends to be reflected in the existing debt-equity balance of the company. Thus, for example, relatively stable industries, such as the one to which Long Island Lighting belongs, show an average proportion of senior securities substantially higher than those of industries exposed to a more variable earnings experience. Let us assume, for the sake of our example, that the management of the Long Island Lighting Company considers its December 31, 1953, condition to be a balance appropriate to the company's circumstances and one which it wishes to preserve in future financing.

The preceding table shows book and market values. Which should be used? From all that has been said concerning the concept of free access to funds by investors, we hope it is clear that market values should be used. Market prices, and not book values, show the investors' current evaluation of their holding in comparison with other investment opportunities. But any one who has looked at the instability of prices in the security markets, which is greatest in the market for common stocks, intuitively rejects the quotation of a moment as a satisfactory figure. He searches for a figure which is representative of a "normal" price. Often this requires more than a cursory survey of recent prices. The quotations of a particular stock must be studied in the light of developments in the market as a whole, as well as in relation to particular events in the trading of the stock in question.

A common practice, given these difficulties, is to accept book values instead of market values for bonds and preferred stocks, unless they are observed to be selling far from their stated values, and to choose some sort of an average price for the stock. One well-known investors service averages the high and low price of the preceding 12 months. Another first computes the average of the high and low of each month, and then averages these averages for the preceding year.

Accepting the book value of bonds and preferred, and the former method of averaging, we find the proportions of value in the capitalization of the Long Island Lighting Company to be:

	Amount in Thousands	Percent of Total	Basis of Valuation
Bonds	$146,125	54.0%	Book
Preferred stock	30,000	11.2	Book
Common stock	93,503	34.8	Average of year's
Total	$269,628	100.0%	high and low

Using the percentages of capitalization as weights, and the costs of the security issues as tabulated on page 449, we may compute a weighted average cost of capital of 4.38%, on an after-tax basis, as follows:

	Weights	Individual Costs	Product
Bonds	54.0	1.84%	99.36
Preferred stock	11.2	5.38	60.26
Common stock	34.8	8.00	278.40
Total	100.0		438.02
Weighted average			4.38%

In order that a firm may avoid the dangers of becoming committed to certain investment opportunities with relatively low return to the exclusion of later opportunities offering a higher return, the marginal approach suggests that all investment opportunities should earn at least the weighted average cost of capital. It follows that each financing decision, whether it be to sell bonds, preferred stock, or common stock, or to retain earnings, will be regarded as one of a series that includes both debt and equity capital. At any point in time the current condition of the market and the expectation as to future trends will determine the specific security to be used. If the market is judged accurately, this will keep the average cost of capital for the desired mix of sources at a minimum. Noting that stock prices fluctuate considerably more than do bond prices, the issuing company should aim to time its issues of high-cost equity capital to coincide with periods of minimum earnings-price ratio,[1] thus minimizing its cost and the number of shares issued.

In following this policy, the managers of the Long Island Lighting Company can be advised to rank its projects using as a basis the rate of 4.38%, and to realize that projects offering less than this rate cannot be justified purely on financial grounds.

Criteria Are Approximate Figures

This is a point at which we should remind the reader that neither of the procedures to quantify the return on investment or the marginal cost of capital which we have been describing can give correct answers. Each is an endeavor to find a useful number to represent the concept that investors will place their funds in a firm only if it offers opportunities equal or superior to alternatives of the same kind. We have been careful to point out many of the judgments which have to be made in order to express the criterion as a percentage rate. There are also others, which experienced readers have doubtless thought of as they have read these pages.

The reader must have recognized that we have departed from pure marginal thinking by relying on averages, and need accept only the conclusion that we have arrived at a useful estimate of the general level of the alternate opportunity that surrounds specific projects to be considered by the Long Island Lighting Company.

In fact, we are content if we have given the reader a choice between often-used ways to reach a number of about the right size. The job to be done is to use the criterion rate to rank and combine projects from the viewpoint of their economic value and to indicate a level at which questioning about other than financial justifications would become more intense. It is unnecessary for such a purpose to go into the fine points of procedure to find a perfect criterion number.

---

[1] Equivalent to maximum price-earnings ratio.

Available Funds as a Cutoff Criterion

The attraction of low-cost financing in the form of bonds is that the proper use of such an element as a source of funds reduces the average cost of capital while conferring a benefit (through "trading on the equity" as described in pages 378 to 381) on the holders of the common stock of the firm. It is our observation that, although rates will rise as the extent of borrowing increases, the managers of a firm seldom get a signal from increasing costs to stop borrowing. Instead, they observe reluctance on the part of lenders to supply funds without tight restrictions, or they reach their own conclusion about the degree of burden that the nature of the business permits their company to undertake.

Field studies indicate that instead of using a rate as a cutoff criterion, a great number of firms establish a total amount of funds as the basis for deciding how much capital investment will be undertaken in a period of time. To establish this quantity, the dividend pay-out (if any) is first set, leaving a certain quantity of undistributed earnings to be invested. To this sum will be added the amount of the depreciation, giving a total of internally generated funds. The managers of some firms stop there, having adopted the policy to restrict the firm's expansion to internal sources. Or, if policy permits using external sources, they take their place in the total to be raised in a ratio of debt and equity which reflects the managers' decision about the degree of risk which can be undertaken.

Whenever the total of investible funds is set as a limit to the total to be invested, the criterion rate is used only to establish the necessary ranking of projects in the order of their desirability. The cutoff point is reached when the available funds are exhausted.

The widespread use of this procedure in practice should not be overlooked. It can lead to the failure to take advantage of many value-creating opportunities, unless the managers of the firm have studied carefully the real capacity of the firm to provide itself with funds. But if this has been done, a criterion of this kind is hard to challenge.

The Payback Criterion Rejected

We have omitted from previous paragraphs any reference to the "payback" test for the acceptability of a proposed investment, although it has long been used and is still widely encountered in business practice. It is also to be encountered in many books on the subject, and therefore deserves a brief discussion here, although it is a test that we cannot recommend.

As usually defined, the payback period is the period within which the project is expected to produce enough funds to restore the total depreciable cost associated with it, if it earns no taxable income and all the funds are devoted to retirement. In other words, this criterion poses the question: "How soon can we get back our investment in depreciable assets if all the funds inflow of the project is devoted to this purpose and tax liabilities are ignored?" The period is usually computed without allowance for any costs required by financing.

Some firms use a payback criterion exclusively in selecting investment projects. The justification might be expressed in these words: "The future is too uncertain. Let's confine ourselves to short periods. Once we have our money back, all further gains are gravy."

Let us look at the payback figure a little more closely. We see that if the project operates as planned for the period computed, and then suddenly becomes worthless, the firm will have its investment back. Payback ratios do not tell us how the funds might actually be regained if, say, depreciation were charged as planned and taxable income were reported from the beginning. This is in itself a weakness of the criterion.

The greatest weakness of the payback period as an investment criterion is that it does not recognize the duration of anticipated earning power. For any projects with the same payback, the criterion would give the same result regardless of the duration of earnings beyond that time. We think this omission is so great that payback cannot be used as a sole criterion for investment analysis.

The matter of prompt return of invested funds is, however, not one that can be ignored completely, for the funds so received can be invested elsewhere to produce new earnings while the original project continues to operate. But the time-adjusted methods described in Chapter 21 are designed to recognize precisely this type of situation, and they do so more effectively than is possible with only payback information.

Uncertainty and the Usefulness of Capital Budgeting Procedures

Uncertainty accompanies almost every figure used in capital budgeting. Yet we are convinced that the introduction of time adjustment, marginal thinking, and valuation procedures into financial analysis has contributed greatly to wise decision making in an area most needing it— the choice among ideas for future development. It is not that precise numbers are obtained so that judgment no longer needs to be exercised. Far from it. But the judgment of managers can be greatly improved if they recognize that rates of return do exist in projects, and train their minds to use the procedures we have been describing. Then the financial portion of the firm's work will be done more effectively.

In contrast to our feeling that it is important to assign quantities to the elements of every investment project, we must admit that various field studies of actual business decision making show that a majority of managements do not make their selections with so much care. In particular, we can refer to the field survey made by one of the authors of this book in 1958, in which it was found that managements tend to divide proposals into two groups. The first group includes all projects which will continue the company in its established business, increase its efficiency, and help it to hold its accepted "market share." Such projects as new facilities for warehousing, cost-reducing equipment, and "normal" increases in capacity would come into this group. The second group contains projects outside the area of activity that has become the accepted one for the particular management.

The finding of the field research is that projects in the first group are given far less searching analysis of a financial valuation nature than are projects in the second group. That is, a project believed to be in the natural course of development is often undertaken without any test of whether its profitability is as great as that of a project in a less familiar area. There are many reasons for this expression of preference on the part of management; yet, there is a growing group of observers and managers who feel that the study of all projects should include an estimate of financial return. In what we have said above, we are trying to increase the size of this group. And it is growing.

More important than purely financial considerations, of course, is the flow of ideas and suggestions from which projects may be developed. They will come from time to time from all levels of responsibility in an organization if it is sensitive to opportunities—from workers and foremen for projects that increase productivity, from plant engineers and others in contact with technical developments inside and outside the firm, from the sales department, from top management, even from existing or potential customers. The first task of a management is to stimulate such a flow of ideas and to prevent their being cut off from consideration by rigid rules or by unimaginative persons at intermediate levels in the organization. To handle such a flow of ideas, at least two administrative procedures are necessary. There must be rules for preliminary screening of projects, to select those deserving of further study. Then, as promising ideas are accumulated, there must be a more precise scheme for the study of individual projects, including some way of ranking them in the order of their desirability. What we have been presenting is a precise scheme for the financial part of the necessary study.

Each project must be studied from many points of view, any one of which might be the most important in a particular case. The availability of personnel, the need for specialized know-how, the extent of the market, the effect of the particular project on others, the desire to maintain certain activities of the firm, the possible reactions of competitors are only a few of the many factors to be studied. We are well aware of their diversity and importance. On the other hand, we feel that the question of the value of a project is always important, and we have shown how this quantity can be estimated, for use with the other criteria that need also to be considered.

Summary of the Capital Budgeting Process

A summary can now be presented of what has been said in many pages about the valuation process in capital budgeting. It is a process that assists managers to select among various ways of using a firm's funds those which promise the greatest value. The results of this analysis can only assist in the final decision, because its procedures use only quantities relating to funds movements, and there are many other factors to be considered as the managers of a firm set its policies. Moreover, almost every quantity entering into the procedure is uncertain to some degree, so the results of computations must be taken as approximations, not precise numbers.

Nevertheless, there is great value to management in the procedure, because (1) it concentrates on cash flows, (2) it brings time systematically into consideration, and (3) it requires explicitly the observation of alternative opportunities.

The quantities that must be estimated for capital budgeting are (1) the amount of the initial investment, (2) the terminal values, (3) the change caused by the investment in the operating funds flows, (4) the times of each outflow or inflow, (5) the duration of the project and (6) a possible alternative use of the funds in question.

The procedure of capital budgeting calls for a ranking of projects in the order of their desirability, and the application of a cutoff criterion to this ranking, to establish the list of projects which will add the most to the value of the owners' interest in the firm.

Several techniques to accomplish this result have been presented, including net present value, yield, compounding to terminal date, and annualizing. Each gives adequate results under most business circumstances. They differ in result because of certain assumptions about how the firm will handle its net receipts of funds, which need not concern us at this point.

Opportunity Cost and the Selection among Securities to Be Issued

We can now leave the subject of selecting among investment opportunities and observe what can be done with similar procedures to assist managers as they raise funds to guide their choice among various types of security issues that will be available to them. So far in this book we have limited the choice to one type of debt, one type of preferred stock, and the common equity. In fact, there are many types of arrangements possible under each of these catagories, and it is time to explore what can be done to guide the choice among them.

As an example to illustrate the possibilities, let us assume a firm which uses 10% after taxes as its opportunity rate. It has decided to buy land and build a warehouse at a certain distribution point. The required investment is $100,000, and the treasurer has developed two ways to finance this sum, both of the nature of bonds.

One alternative is a loan for 10 years, payable in equal annual instalments of $20,000 a year, beginning at the end of the sixth year, with interest at 4% on the outstanding balance. (We shall state costs throughout this example on an after-tax basis.)

The other alternative is a "level-payment" loan, calculated at 3% cost, requiring $11,723 per year of payment combining principal and interest.

Although these alternates have different rates of cost and different patterns of payment, one thing is certain. *Each has a present value of $100,000 in the eyes of the lender,* or he would not have offered to provide this sum in return for the borrower's promise to pay the schedule shown.

By the rules of accountancy, of course, the borrowing firm will show a liability of $100,000 whichever alternative it selects, and it will be tempted to select the one offering the lower rate. But let us look further. The managers of the borrowing firm believe that they can earn 10% with funds at their disposal. Each alternative offers $100,000 for investment by the firm but calls for its return with interest in a different time pattern. Let us regard each outflow as causing a loss of 10% in earning power from the firm's point of view, and bring each schedule to comparability by computing the present value, at 10%, of the burdens shown. This work is presented in Table 22–1, with the result that alternative 2, the level-payment loan, despite its lower interest rate, has the larger present value, $72,038, to be compared with the present value of alternative 1, $63,308.

Since the firm wishes to minimize its burden, the choice of the deferred payment plan is indicated, although its interest rate is higher,

TABLE 22–1

CALCULATION OF PRESENT VALUES OF
ALTERNATIVE DEBT BURDENS AT THE
BORROWER'S OPPORTUNITY RATE

Time	Alternative 1	Factor at 10%	Present Value	Alternative 2	Factor at 10%	Present Value
1............	$ 4,000			$ 11,723		
2............	4,000			11,723		
3............	4,000	3.7910	$15,844	11,723		
4............	4,000			11,723		
5............	4,000			11,723		
6............	24,000	0.5644	−13,545	11,723	0.6145	$72,038
7............	23,200	0.5132	11,290	11,723		
8............	22,400	0.4665	10,450	11,723		
9............	21,600	0.4241	9,161	11,723		
10............	20,800	0.3855	8,018	11,723		
Total....$132,000			$68,308	$117,230		$72,038

because it leaves funds longer with the company to enjoy at 10%. Perhaps the reader's appreciation of this point will be aided by Chart 22–1, which shows the way in which borrowed funds are reduced by the two schemes of outflows.

The chart is to be read as follows: Either plan initially provides $100,000 to finance the purchase of the property. As the firm makes the required payments, it substitutes its own funds for portions of the

CHART 22–1

CUMULATIVE AMOUNTS OF BURDEN OF
ALTERNATIVE LOAN ARRANGEMENTS

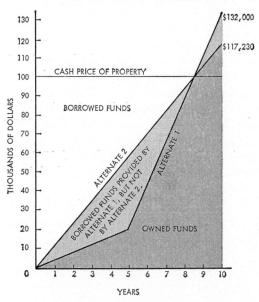

borrowing, so that the amount of borrowed funds decreases as the owners' investment increases. Alternative 1 is more desirable because it provides borrowed funds (on which the firm may earn 10 percent) longer than alternative 2, despite the larger cumulative total burden it calls for.

The similarity of procedure to the ranking process in studying investment opportunities is exact. One chooses an opportunity rate and evaluates the outflows of each alternate method of financing. Thus, one can make a ranking and choose the least burdensome arrangement.

In the figures used so far, we have assumed that the borrowing firm will meet the debt obligations by assigning funds to the purpose from the general resources of the firm. A growing number of firms, however, have made studies of their debt capacity and have established a policy to maintain a certain part of the capitalization in one form of debt or another. If this were the case for the firm we have been considering, the opportunity rate would no longer be 10%, because the real alternative to using one or another of the two schemes we have described would not be to use the general funds of the firm, but rather to borrow in another way. From this line of thinking comes the quantity of the *borrowing opportunity rate,* a figure representing management's judgment of the typical interest cost at which it can borrow long-term funds. When this number is available, it can be substituted for the general rate we have used so far. It is a better figure, to be used when managers can accept the idea of constant borrowing. It will lead to different choices whenever it is less than at least the cost of one of the alternatives. The reader is asked to think what the choice in the assumed situation would be if the company had a borrowing opportunity rate of $3\frac{1}{2}\%$.

PART VIII

The Bargain for Funds

General Introduction to Part VIII

EACH CORPORATE security issue is made up of a number of rights and duties running between *the issuer*, the corporation that offered the security, and the person who owns the security. Some of these are established by law and apply to all securities of a certain type. For example, interest on bonds may be deducted by the issuer among the tax-deductible expenses, while the dividends on preferred stock may not. Or, common stockholders may hold corporate directors responsible to make decisions in their interest, while bondholders can ask for no more than strict accordance with their contract.

The greater part of the conditions of a security issue, despite the increasing complexity and volume of legislation in this area, is set by the terms of its particular contract, which is drafted while negotiations progress. It is, therefore, correct to say that the specific terms under which a group of investors makes funds available to a business are the result of a bargaining process between the investors and the management of the corporation. As in any bargain, the final terms represent a workable compromise which embodies the essential objectives of both parties. For example, it is obvious that any investor will want to have the highest possible return on his investment and at the same time have the maximum assurance that his income will be received and his principal protected. The issuing company, however, will wish from the point of view of its common shareholders, to minimize the costs associated with the financing and to preserve maximum flexibility in the payments and terms to which it becomes committed. The terms of the actual security issue must somehow reconcile these conflicting objectives.

Despite the fact that all categories of investors are anxious to achieve a "maximum" return on their investment, an agreement is possible because different kinds of investors want their position guaranteed by safeguards of varying strength. An investor who is concerned about steady, moderate income and the safety of his capital, for example, might easily furnish funds with adequate safeguards to a risk taker who is willing to run a substantial chance of losing all his capital if he can

473

double his money in a short time. The first man might accept relatively low rewards if the venture was a success in return for the safety given by first claim on certain valuable assets if it failed. The risk-taking investor would gain the majority of the fruits of success but, in return for assistance in financing this opportunity, would stand to lose much more heavily in the event of a failure. Needless to say, each category of investor is anxious to secure his objectives as much as possible by placing limitations on the positions of the other classes of investors. Over the years a large variety of investment forms and terms have been developed to define these relationships, and it is in the negotiation of the specific terms that the bargaining takes place.

In a sense the bargaining process does not stop when the terms are set and the issue sold but can continue on in the form of negotiations for modification of the terms of the agreement to meet changing operating conditions and financial needs. With respect to this process, there is a major difference between a private sale to a few institutional investors (or a term loan from a bank or a lease) and a public issue of bonds. The direct relationship between the company and its security holders implicit in the private placement affords greater opportunities for the borrower to renegotiate any terms that have been found unduly burdensome. The investment officers of the institution, which perhaps may be eager for future business from the company, can examine the situation and relatively quickly determine what modifications are reasonable. The two parties can thus understand each other's positions quickly and reach a decision on the action required.

In a public issue, on the other hand, a change in the provisions may require soliciting the vote of hundreds or thousands of individual security holders. With unregistered securities the task of merely identifying the owners can be staggering, requiring a major expenditure of corporate managerial resources. The investment banker can help in the process of solicitation, but unlike his role of "representing the investor" in the initial negotiations, he himself cannot commit the investors to a position. Because changes in the terms of a public issue are so difficult, corporations issuing such securities are wise to seek the maximum flexibility in the construction of the agreement which the investment banker believes investors will accept.

It should not be inferred from the concept of security planning as a negotiated procedure that each and every term of the issue is carefully weighed and debated before it is included. In fact manuals exist in which many standard clauses are to be found. We start with the three basic and considerably standardized security forms of bonds, preferred stock, and common stock, the primary features of which have been well established in company law, corporate charters, and investors' standards. The precedent of accepted corporate practice in a given industry has a great deal to do with the form which new issues take. There are also the regulations of government agencies such as the Securities and Exchange Commission, which have an influence on the terms that shall be included or excluded, as well as the regulations of the organized exchanges. The general economic and business conditions at the time of issue have a bearing. All these things tend to narrow the range of security features which may be negotiated before the precise form of the security is finally decided.

It is important to recognize that when company officials make some concession in price, income, or other terms to a group of security holders in order to have a successful offering, what they concede is a portion of what would otherwise belong to other security holders. It is a process of allocating the benefits that exist, not of creating values out of nothing. The tangible gain to the company resulting from a security sale on unusually favorable terms is a gain to the other security holders. A sale of bonds at a relatively higher interest rate means lower net earnings per share of common stock. A preferred stock which has the cumulative feature means a greater hazard to common dividends than would be the case if it was noncumulative. A further common issue offered to new stockholders and priced at an unusual discount from market price in order to assure ready sale means added dilution of the investment of existing common shareholders. Thus, the ultimate bargain is not between the new security holders and management as such but rather between one class of security holders and another. In this connection, we remind the reader that we have consistently emphasized the essential responsibility of management to act as the representative of the common shareholder. Despite the inability to create something out of nothing, one can bring a greater part of the benefits to each equity dollar received, and this increases the value of the equity holding.

We are now ready to extend our consideration of long-term finance to take account of the influence which variations in the circumstances and objectives of both issuers and investors have on the terms of the investment contract. Over a period of many years the basic security types have been subject to a considerable variety of modifications in an effort to have them meet more precisely the special needs of particular investors and business corporations. A complete catalog of kinds of securities would be almost endless and never quite up to date, for the possibilities of special arrangements are limited only by the imagination of the draftsman.

Our purpose is to show, by reference to the more commonly used variations, how these features come into being in the bargaining process between issuer and investor. A review of these features should stimulate the reader to invent new terms when necessary to suit the conditions of particular problems that he one day comes to face.

We shall first introduce the form of financing known as the lease, so far not described in this book. It serves as a special form of debt. In

Chapters 24 and 25 we shall return to the variations in the details of bonds, preferred stock, and common stock as they may be negotiated at the time of issue. In Chapter 26 we shall describe how changes may be made in issues after they have become outstanding. Finally, we shall take up the influence on corporate financial practices of the federal regulatory agency known as the Securities and Exchange Commission, and other agencies.

Chapter 23

Leasing as an Alternative to Ownership

THE COMMON purpose of the various types of security contracts is to raise funds which are used to acquire the assets used by a firm. But since the use of assets for a desired period of time can often be made fully available through rental rather than ownership, financial managers often have the option to arrange contracts of rental rather than being limited to ways to finance ownership. We shall deal with the advantages and disadvantages of this alternative in this chapter.

Long-term rental arrangements are usually called leases. From the points of view of finance and accounting, the unique feature of a leasing contract is that although the lessee is entitled to the use of the asset, legal title is retained by the lessor, who continues to own it. Thus arises the term *off-the-balance-sheet financing*, for under present accounting conventions the user of the property cannot show it among his assets, and the periodic obligations to pay rent are not shown as liabilities until they become due.

There are many types of rental arrangements which are of short duration, or cancelable, or otherwise not important as alternatives to long-term ownership. A *financial lease*, with which we are now concerned, has two distinguishing characteristics. The first is the fixed nature of the obligation. Whenever a lease is noncancelable and runs over a long period of time, it produces a financial burden on the lessee similar to that of a debt. Second, under a financial lease a lessee promises payments which, in total, exceed the purchase price of the assets that are leased. Usually also, though not necessarily, a financial lease is a "net" lease. That is, the tenant agrees to pay property taxes, maintain the property, etc., as if he were the owner. Thus, a financial lease can be described as "a practicable alternative to ownership of the asset by the company, with the decision between owning and leasing turning on financial rather than operating consideration."[1]

---

[1] D. R. Gant, "Illusion in Lease Financing," *Harvard Business Review*, March–April, 1959, p. 122.

Thus, once more, we see that the scope of finance is broader than the confines of a balance sheet. Management must provide the firm with the use of properties needed for its activities, either by ownership or by rental. We are familiar with the idea that assets are acquired by the creation of securities which appear as liabilities. The promises made under leases are just as binding as those under security contracts, although no asset or liability appears. In fact, we regard payments under long-term lease arrangements to be part of the burden of financing and in the same category as the servicing of a bond issue. In doing so, we assume that obligations should be compared as they are seen by solvent, going concerns.

Nevertheless, the reader should know that the ultimate consequences of default under a lease are different from those if bonded debt exists. In case of breach of contract (known in the financial world as *default*), the lessor may repossess his property,[2] but he may claim damages only for 1 year's future rent if a liquidation results from the failure, or 3 years' rent if the company undergoes reorganization, no matter how long the lease had to run. The holder of a bond, on the other hand, is a creditor for the entire principal of his claim against a defaulting debtor. But even if the bond is secured by a mortgage, the property cannot be taken away without a court order, which is seldom forthcoming unless a complete liquidation has been decided upon. He is "locked in" to the situation, although the value of the mortgaged property is recognized as assigned to him.

Examples of Leasing Arrangements

The parties to contractual relationships that are found in a financial lease can be diagrammed as in Chart 23–1. In studying this chart, the reader should remember that the functions of selling, titleholding, and investing may be performed by one company, two companies, or three.

A variant on the use of a private company as titleholder is found when a corporation leases a property from a municipality, which bor-

CHART 23–1

RELATIONSHIPS IN A TYPICAL FINANCIAL LEASE

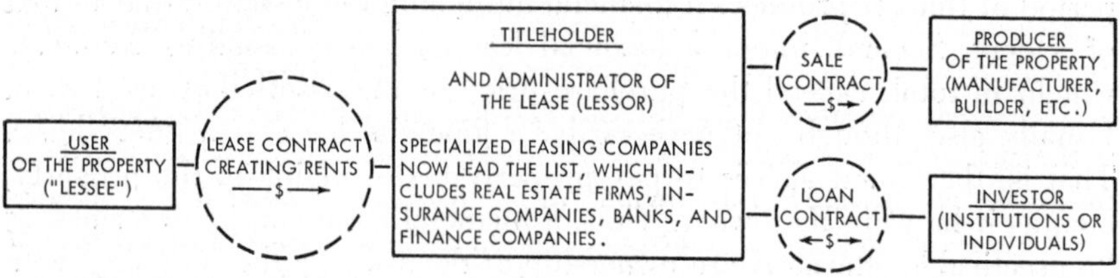

---

[2] If the tenant, although in default on other obligations and bankrupt, continues rental payments, the landlord may not repossess the property.

rows the funds needed to build the plant by issuing Revenue Bonds, whose interest is tax-exempt.

For example, we refer to the financing arranged by American Airlines, Inc., to provide the engines for its jet fleet. The producers, to use the term in the chart, were the manufacturers of the engines. Each of these producers established a leasing subsidiary to act as titleholder of the engines. The engines were purchased by these subsidiaries, using funds provided by investors, and leased to the airline on terms that amortized the purchase price and provided interest at about $41/8\%$ per year. The transaction "saved" the airline a capital investment estimated at $67 million at a time when public placement of stock would have been possible only at depressed prices, and when the company, because of existing loans, would probably have had to use subordinated debt if it had attempted to borrow in the investment market. Other airlines have followed this initiative. Some of them were able to negotiate very favorable terms by consenting to the use of the Investment Credit by the lessor, in circumstances where the airline's tax liability was not large enough to benefit from it.

No doubt this arrangement was developed from the model provided for many years by the "equipment trust," widely used to supply rolling stock to railroads. It is one of the earliest examples of a specialized financial lease. Today, the varieties of leasing arrangements are almost endless, with new variations being heard of frequently, as the use of this extremely flexible form of financing is extended. It is in the extension of its use that one sees the change. One can now find leasing arrangements offered for such items as office equipment, large and small computers, all kinds of production tooling, engines for aircraft, the aircraft themselves, entire corporations, general-purpose buildings, buildings built to the tenant's specification, and very many fleets of cars and trucks. In fact, leasing companies are ready to offer terms for consideration almost any time a firm is studying how to finance the acquisition of a specific property.

A great advantage of the leasing arrangement is that it is available to finance amounts too small to be of interest to major institutional lenders or the public market. It is an important device in the expansion period of a small business and a very convenient one for larger companies when their needs are small and a specific asset is to be purchased.

Immensely popular in the thirties and forties, and still a device in use, is the *sale and leaseback* arrangement. This is a device which exists if company A, already the owner of a property, sells it to B and immediately leases it for continued use. The new lessee, A, then has in his possession the use of the property as well as the cash received from the sale. For a time this seemed like magic to many people in the financial world, but it is now recognized that the device has the same essential feature as any lease: namely, the granting of the use of a property in return for a series of rental payments. It is more dramatic to see an existing property exchanged for cash, but it is really the same thing as to obtain the use of a property in which the firm has not previously invested funds.

The Avoidance of Investment

By surrendering the benefits of holding title to a property, a lessee may avoid the need to buy it. In order to be concrete, we shall use the actual problem of a chain of variety stores which projected a new branch to cost $225,000, a sum made up of land, $25,000; building, $150,000; and certain basic equipment, $50,000. The financial officers of the chain store company found a group of investors who operated in the area of the proposed store. This group offered to build the store to the tenant's specifications and to lease it for 25 years, with annual rentals as follows: first 10 years, $22,035; next 15 years, $11,583. If this lease were accepted, the variety chain would not have immediately to pay out $225,000 to establish the new outlet.

But the belief that the company in this example has "released" $225,000 for other business purposes by using a lease is quite superficial.[3] Such an idea contains the implicit assumptions both that the funds in question exist in the business already and that we can ignore the way in which they were obtained. We cannot. The lease should be regarded as a case of a loan of 100% of the needed funds—$225,000. The outflows to meet the obligations of the lease are fixed and represent the burdens of financing just as much as the promises which accompany borrowing. Surely, the acceptance of the proposed lease will consume a portion of the company's total capacity to arrange debt financing. In purely logical terms the debt capacity that is consumed must be equal to that of borrowing to raise the same amount of funds. If the advantages of the lease are to be tested against alternatives, the comparison should be made between the obligations of the lease and those of a debt contract that might actually be arranged. The latter financing would create a balance sheet asset of $225,000, balanced by a debt of the same amount.

Further on in this chapter we shall describe an analysis to determine whether it is better to borrow or to lease the property. Here, it is sufficient to point out that a lease uses up credit. One might expect that it would use up as much of the company's borrowing capacity as a loan of equivalent terms. Altogether too many leases have been signed without recognition of this matter, as evidenced from time to time by the bankruptcy of a firm with small debts but heavy rental obligations.

The frequent appearance of a prohibition of leasing as well as of

---

[3] Much of the literature, however, reflects this opinion.

further borrowing among the protective provisions of loan contracts is additional evidence that the financial world is recognizing the essential similarity of lease obligations to those incurred by long-term borrowing. Thus, in the case of the variety chain, the firm will obtain $225,000 in funds (in the form of the desired store) in return for fixed contractual obligations to pay rent, as stated above.

Effect on Borrowing Capacity

Two factors exist, however, which sometimes permit a company to raise more funds by leases than by debt. One of these factors is that the title to leased property remains in the control of the lessor. It cannot be touched by the creditors of the lessee. If, instead, the property in question had been bought and financed by a mortgage and there were a default, the investor would have to await foreclosure, which is at best a slow and expensive process. In fact, if the property can be expected always to have a value to others, a lease may be the only way a financially embarrassed corporation can obtain the use of new equipment. For example, the financially weak Northeast Airlines, Inc., recently obtained the use of new jet-powered equipment through a leasing arrangement, and many a weak manufacturer has leased new tools when its general credit was exhausted. In order to obtain such a result, however, the criterion that the property is sure to be valuable to others must be met without any possibility of doubt. The more the leased property becomes special purpose, the more the general credit of the company limits its power either to lease or to borrow.

A second factor that may sometimes permit a company to raise more funds by lease than by debt is that the burdens the lease creates are not evidenced by liabilities on the balance sheet. The result may be that certain grantors of credit will not take the leasehold obligations fully into account and thus will be more liberal than if an equivalent debt were to appear. There is evidence that this situation does exist, despite the efforts of accountants, the Securities and Exchange Commission, and others to provide full disclosure.[4] As time goes on, however, this condition will dwindle in importance. What is perhaps more important to say in this book is that no financial manager who contemplates a lease obligation

---

[4] The Accounting Principles Board of the American Institute of Certified Public Accountants, in *Opinions of the Accounting Principles Board*, No. 5 (September, 1964), recommends that "financial statements should disclose sufficient information regarding material, noncancelable leases . . . to enable the reader to assess the effect of lease commitments upon the financial position and results of operations, both present and prospective, of the lessee." This information is to be given in the statements themselves, or in accompanying notes.

While this statement is the latest guide to good accounting, it is by no means binding on all accountants in their work. Compliance with the spirit of the statement, though increasing, still leaves much to be desired.

should allow himself to be deceived. Contractual rental obligations from his point of view are charges as fixed as the elements of the burden of bonds.

The Question of Terminal Values

The lease is a device which separates the possibility to use the property from its ownership for the period of the lease. At the expiration of the lease, the property is returned to the lessor together with all permanent improvements installed by the lessee. Thus, the managers of the variety chain must recognize that the lease gives them less than full ownership would. An argument favoring ownership over leasing that is frequently heard is, therefore, that the values that will exist at the terminal date of a lease are too great to give up. Certain types of property may enjoy a high sale value at the time the lease expires, and it may be desirable to hold title for the purpose of gaining from this residual value. The argument is especially attractive for well-situated real estate, since it is well known that substantial profits are often made in this way. While conceding the attractiveness of this line of thinking, we urge the reader to note carefully the fact that money which may be received in the distant future has far less value in the present than its future amount makes it seem to have. It is often far better to conserve funds for immediate purposes, as the earnings thus obtained will be more than the expected long-run windfall. Such would be the case, evidently, for the variety chain in our example, since its financial reports show us that it can earn 9% or more on current funds, after taxes.

It is also to be noted that the terms of many leasing contracts are now being written with an allowance for a terminal value which alters the required lease payments in favor of the lessee, implicitly or explicitly. It is our conclusion that careful negotiation of the terms of a lease can overcome the disadvantage of loss of title, unless major capital gains are very certain. We shall discuss this matter further, later on in this chapter.

Tax Advantage in Leasing

While the owner of property must suffer taxes on the income it produces, he has depreciation expense and the newly granted Investment Credit available to create tax shields. The person using property belonging to another must also suffer taxes on the income it produces, but tax shields are created by the rental payments he must make, and it is possible for the lessor and lessee to agree that the benefits of the investment credit may be enjoyed by either one or the other.

There is little doubt that the lease came into popularity in the 1930's largely because it would permit a far more favorable schedule of tax shields than was available to owners under the then existing laws and regulations.

For example, when straight-line depreciation was substantially the only method owners could use for tax purposes, and a commercial building was often required to be depreciated over 67 years, the maximum tax shield in any year, per thousand dollars of such an investment, was ($1,000 ÷ 67) (0.48) = $7.20, given a tax rate of 48%. With such constraints on ownership, it was easy to set up a lease obligation under which the rental payments produced larger tax shields in the early years of the life of the property. For example, a 25-year lease with equal payments of the capital value would create a tax shield on $1,000 invested in a building of $19.20 instead of $7.20.

Today, when the term of depreciable life has been shortened by the new "guidelines" and one may select a scheme of depreciation with heavy charges in early years, it is much less likely that a lease will offer tax-shield advantages that preempt any consideration of other advantages and disadvantages of leasing. Advantage may remain in favor of the lease when the property contains a good proportion of land, which is not depreciable, or when some asset must be depreciated more slowly than over the period of the lease. But even these advantages are small, if any terminal values for the land or slowly depreciating property have been allowed for in the terms of the lease.

Substantial tax advantages still exist for certain types of lessors, but this side of the matter will not be explored here.

The Cost of the Arrangement

It is as necessary to have some idea of the cost of raising funds by leasing as it is to have a figure for the cost of borrowing. In the first place, it is an important part of the average cost of capital (page 461) which is too often forgotten. Sometimes, the cost is explicitly stated. If not, it is useful to know that studies show that the interest cost of funds provided by lease runs from a minimum of the same rate to 2% higher than could be negotiated on a loan of equivalent amount and terms. The discrepancy varies according to several factors, including the general credit standing of the lessee and the ease with which the leased property could be transferred to other use following a default.

The implicit cost of a lease may be computed, as in the case of a bond, by tabulating the outflows it requires, considering the initial value provided and the terminal value to be expected, and working out the internal rate of return (page 431). But this is sometimes easy to say and hard to do, because some of the required quantities may be difficult to obtain. The schedule of rents is not always absolutely fixed, it is often not possible to know the terminal value that should be used for the value of the remaining property, and it may even be difficult to learn the price at which the property could be acquired for cash—a number which to most analysts represents the value provided by the lease financing.

The variety store in our example knows the cash price of the property it may lease; it is $225,000. To avoid paying out this sum, the firm accepts the schedule to pay $22,035 annually at the end of each of the first 10 years, and $11,583 at the ends of years 11 through 25. The "internal rate of return" worked out from these figures is 6% before taxes, which reduces to 3.12% after a 48% tax shield is taken into account. The calculation ignores the question of terminal values, which will be dealt with below.

Years	Amount	6% Factor	Present Value
1–10.............$22,035		7.3601	$162,180
11–25............ 11,583		5.4233	62,818
			$224,998

Ownership versus Leasing, an Example

If the reader has accepted our position that a lease, because of its fixed obligations, must be regarded as a form of borrowing by a potential lessee, its desirability can only be tested against the alternative of borrowing an equivalent amount of funds. In practice one compares with alternatives that are possible. They may call for payments on slightly different terms. Here, in order to focus only on the two distinguishing features of leases, we assume the alternative of a debenture debt for the whole $225,000 with the same repayment terms and interest rate as the lease. This gives us the opportunity to compare ownership with leasing in an instance where the differences are confined to the tax treatment which is afforded the lease payments, as contrasted with the depreciation which is granted with ownership, and to the ownership of the terminal value. We shall deal with these in the order named.

The schedule of cash flows demanded by the lease is easily derived, for if the lease is used, all of the annual rent is a tax-deductible expense. In each of the first 10 years, the payment of $22,035 results in a tax shield of $10,577 (at 48% rate) so that the net cash flow is $11,458. In the ensuing period, the annual rent is $11,583, and the net cash flow is $6,023. These net cash outflows called for by the lease are pictured cumulatively, in Chart 23–2. The total of the yearly after-tax figures over the 25-year period is $204,925.

To make a schedule of the cash flows for the borrowing is more difficult, because not all the annual payment is to be treated as expense for tax purposes. Instead, a tax shield must be computed from the total of the interest paid on the loan plus the allowable depreciation expense. This total is then deducted from the before-tax payment to produce the after-tax cash outflow to be compared with the lease. The authors have done this work for each of the 25 years, and the cumulative figures appear in Chart 23–2. We shall give the details from our table only for the first 2 years, to show the way the numbers change.

The assumed loan, following the payment pattern established by the lease, contains two parts. One part is a fixed loan for the first 10 years of $112,500. It is amortized in years 11–25 by the annual payment of $11,583. In each of the first 10 years, it requires interest expense at 6% of $6,750.

When this amount is deducted from the annual payment of $22,035 in each of the first 10 years, we have $15,285, which is sufficient to amortize the second part of the loan financing, a loan of $112,500 to be amortized over 10 years at 6%. In the first year, interest is $6,750 and the balance of the payment, $8,535, is applied to reduce the principal from $112,500 to $103,965. Thus, the total payment the first year of $22,035 is treated as $13,500 of tax-deductible interest and $8,535 of principal reduction. The second year's interest is $6,238 on this portion of the loan and remains at $6,750 for the other portion. One proceeds similarly to obtain the interest expense of each of the 25 years.

We now turn to the calculation of the depreciation expense. In the case of ownership of the $225,000 investment, the $25,000 cost of land may not be depreciated. The new "guidelines" permit a 10-year schedule for the equipment and 40 years for the building. The greatest tax advantage likes in using one of the accelerated methods now available, and we have chosen to use the "double-declining-balance-shifting-to-straight-line" scheme. On this basis, the depreciation for the first 2 years is $10,000 and $8,000 on the equipment costing $50,000. It is $7,500 and $7,125 for the $150,000 building.

The tax-deductible expenses for the first 2 years are tabulated below, together with a computation of the tax shield and the net after-tax cash outflow related to the loan.

	Year	
	1	*2*
Interest...................	$13,500	$12,988
Depreciation...............	17,500	15,125
Total expense........	$31,000	$28,113
Tax shield, 48%...........	$14,880	$13,494
Before-tax payment.........	22,035	22,035
After-tax payment..........	$ 7,155	$ 8,541

Having completed work of this kind for each of the 25 years, we find the total of the outflows to be $236,282, which is $31,357 larger than the total of after-tax outflows demanded by the lease. It is interesting to ask ourselves why this difference exists. It must be due to the difference in tax shields, because other possible variables, such as the rate of interest and the schedule of payments, were assumed to be the same. The lease permits the tenant to take as expense all of the $225,000 invested in the property. But in the case of ownership, only the equipment is fully depreciated. Therefore, only the first 25 years of the 40-year schedule for the building has been used, totaling $109,672. And the land is not depreciated at all. These figures show that ownership will develop a tax shield of ($159,672) (0.48) = $76,643, or $31,357 less than the tax shield the lease provides, ($225,000) (0.48) = $108,000.

Chart 23–2 shows that the lease payments are more demanding than the bond payments during the first 10 years, but that the opposite is true during the second period, after the rental rate falls. Since the eye is not able to perform "time adjustment" calculations, it is necessary to find a present value for each of the two schedules in order to have commensu-

CHART 23-2

ACCUMULATED AFTER-TAX CASH OUTFLOWS IN BOND VERSUS LEASE
METHODS OF FINANCING AN INVESTMENT OF $225,000

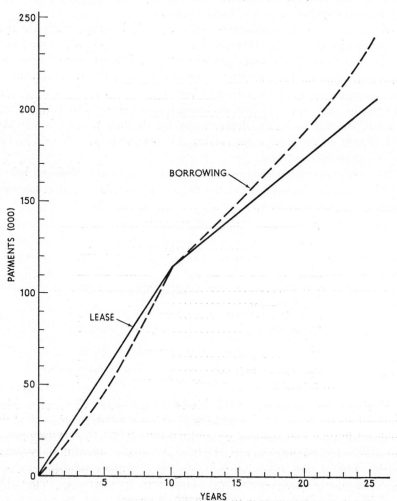

rate figures for our use. We have done this work at the rate of 3.12%, which is the after-tax cost of a loan at the before-tax rate of 6%. This is taken as the opportunity cost of credit for the case at hand (see page 470). The total of the present values of the annual outflows under the lease is $149,421, and under the borrowing, it is $164,784. From this we learn that the initial advantage of the borrowing is more than overcome by the later advantage of the lease.

But we cannot leave the matter at this point. The question of terminal value still faces us. By accepting the lease arrangement, the management of the variety chain would be giving up whatever the terminal values may be, and we need to know whether these values are less than or greater than the difference that, so far, favors the lease. The difference in the present values is $15,683, but this is a number evaluated at the outset of the financing. It tells us that the lease form of providing its needs will leave the firm with funds for other uses that are the equivalent of the immediate investment of $15,683. We have gone to the statements of the variety chain in question and found that it can be expected to earn 9% after taxes. By compounding at this rate, we find that $135,236 is the equivalent sum, the present value of $15,683, at the end of the 25th year.

Although there are reasons behind the ruling of the tax authorities that land does not depreciate, and also reasons why store buildings are depreciated over 40 years, it would be hard to predict that these assets, with a book value of $65,000, will have a realizable value over twice as much at the end of the 25th year. We would feel safe in advising the managers of the variety chain to take the lease arrangement.

Nevertheless, we must remind the reader that the question of terminal values is always present. Where the tax advantages of a lease are not as great as in our example, some bargaining over the matter can be expected, resulting in terms of a lease more favorable to the lessee. It is more and more being recognized that the $225,000 in funds provided by the lease is only for the use of the property and that a lessee who gives up ownership is in reality adding the forgone terminal value to the more easily seen costs of his lease.

Lease Obligations, Burden Coverage, and Debt Ratios

In Chapter 17, at page 355, we defined the burden of a debt and we suggested certain ratios that are useful to relate the burden to the earnings or cash inflows of the borrower, and to measure the degree of trading on the equity. For analyzing a company with large lease obligations, we recommend including these lease payments as part of the financial burden and relating the burden thus found to earnings before interest, lease payments, and taxes (E.B.I.L.T.) instead of earnings before interest and taxes (E.B.I.T.). The necessary amounts can be determined from most published statements, and will, of course, be available to the management of a specific company.

Suppose, for example, we are to analyze the debt position of a company that reports an invested capital of $65,000, made up as follows:

Long-term debt...............................	$15,000
Capital stock and surplus...................	50,000
	$65,000

The income statement shows:

E.B.I.T.................................	$14,000
Interest expense........................	750
Taxable income..................	$13,250

We also learn from footnotes to the company's statements that there are long-term lease payments of $3,000 a year and that assets with a cost of $50,000 were provided under the lease. The figures above can be adjusted as follows:

Long-term debt and leasehold value......	$ 65,000
Capital stock and surplus...........	50,000
	$115,000

E.B.I.L.T.............................	$ 17,000
Burden of debt and leases..............	3,750
Taxable income.................	$ 13,250

We then find:

Burden coverage:

$$\text{Unadjusted} \ldots\ldots\ldots\ldots\ldots\ldots \frac{14,000}{750} = 18.7$$

$$\text{Adjusted} \ldots\ldots\ldots\ldots\ldots\ldots \frac{17,000}{3,750} = 4.5$$

Equity ratio:

$$\text{Unadjusted} \ldots\ldots\ldots\ldots\ldots\ldots \frac{50,000}{65,000} = 77\%$$

$$\text{Adjusted} \ldots\ldots\ldots\ldots\ldots\ldots \frac{50,000}{115,000} = 43\%$$

Ratio of trading on the equity:

$$\text{Unadjusted} \ldots\ldots\ldots\ldots\ldots \left(\frac{1}{0.77}\right)\left(\frac{17.7}{18.7}\right) = 1.2$$

$$\text{Adjusted} \ldots\ldots\ldots\ldots\ldots \left(\frac{1}{0.43}\right)\left(\frac{3.5}{4.5}\right) = 1.8$$

If one is inside a firm, the alternate purchase price of leased property is usually available for such a purpose as that just mentioned. Analysts "on the outside looking in" may be forced to capitalize annual lease payments at some rate in order to get a figure to use. Controversy rages over the rate to be used, but the present authors feel that the yield on debenture debt in the industry is a rate that will serve for most cases. It should, however, be applied to the payment schedule over the time of the lease, through the use of present-value factors.

Summary

We can summarize the place of the financial lease in the area of bargaining for funds by saying that its obligations are to be regarded as a form of debt, treated in financial analysis in the same way as the burden of a bond issue. Leases are used for both small and large transactions, and their variety is great. The tax treatment accorded to lease payments may make them less burdensome than an equivalent borrowing, although this is not always the case. Leases often assist in financing small or financially weak companies. They are often used by large companies to finance specific projects where the property is available on favorable terms, or when for some reason the time is not deemed propitious for the issue of new securities.

Perhaps this is the place to point out that the special advantages of leases in the tax field have led to very careful scrutiny of the real situation that lies behind the formal lease. Expert legal counsel is required for the complex task of drafting lease arrangements that will stand up against possible legal attacks either from creditors of the lessee (who would like to have the value of the property declared an asset of the lessee) or from the tax authorities (who would prefer to have the lease payments taken as instalments for an ultimate purchase). It is no game for the superficial or the unwary.

Chapter 24

Modifications of the Distribution of Risk

We ended Chapter 18 by showing how a grid, or cross-classification, could be made, showing for each security type how it affected the allocation of risk, the distribution of income, and the location of control. We now turn to exploring the relationship between the terms of security issues which may result from the bargaining process and these three categories. As with most classifications, the approach has its limitations. The security known as a subordinated income bond represents a modification of risk as well as income and could fit with equal justification under either category. This is not a serious problem, however, provided the classification is recognized as secondary to the objective of a clear understanding of the security in question.

By the term "risk" we refer to uncertainty both with respect to the receipt of income and to the return of the principal invested. It would be impossible to guarantee absolutely either of them, but much can be done to bring assurance through contractual provisions. In this chapter we shall deal with attempts to assure the ultimate repayment of the principal value of a particular issue despite the possibility that the issuer might at some future time be unable to meet all its obligations.

Types of Protection

The terms of a security may provide the security holder with any or all of three major types of protection. First, the company may agree to a variety of *controls over the creation of additional obligations*. These will limit the amount and/or the form of other securities which the firm may issue. Second, the provisions may grant the security holder some *control over funds flows* within the company and between the company and its external suppliers of funds. Such controls may prevent actions that otherwise might bring insolvency. The final type of protection, one which most security purchasers hope they never have cause to use, provides *protection in case of default* by creating for one class of security some

490

JUCK COCK

priorities of claim over specific assets. These terms can provide additional bargaining strength in the event of failure. We shall discuss each of these methods of allocating risk, bearing in mind that specific provisions often can be placed in more than one category. Before turning to these details, however, it is necessary to look more specifically at the nature of default.

The Nature of Default

A company is surely in *default* when it is unable to make payment on contractual obligations. These obligations may range from accounts payable to long-term bonds. In the case of bonds, default will normally occur when the company is unable to meet either interest or principal payments. At the time of default (or after a grace period of a few weeks), the creditors may begin to take formal action to secure the funds due them, and the company must pay or be declared bankrupt (Chapter 30).

Some security holders, of course, are not guaranteed fixed payments by their relationship with the company. When payments are suspended upon a preferred stock, the stock is said to be in *arrears*, but the actions the owners of the stock can take do not include the right to sue for their dividends. Their contract may provide for some change in their relationship with the company, such as giving them the right to elect directors. But it will not allow them to bring bankruptcy. Common shareholders are even more restricted in the actions they can take when payments to them are terminated. Usually, their rights do not change.

Once a business has been forced into formal bankruptcy, its relations with creditors, suppliers, and customers become complicated. Legal expenses rise. The company's ability to act rapidly is reduced, and it may ultimately be forced to discontinue its business and liquidate. Consequently, security holders who are concerned about the protection and return of their capital often wish to have a voice in the company's operations *in advance* of a liquidity crisis. Bondholders' contracts with a corporation do not permit them to vote on corporate actions. Therefore, whatever controls they require must be written into the agreement at the time it is drawn up.

Technical Default

Acceleration of principal is a device used frequently to protect the senior security owners. The bond covenant will provide that if the company takes certain actions or if certain events should occur, a *technical default* will have taken place and the principal of the security will become due immediately (or within 30 to 90 days). Few firms would be able to meet such accelerated maturities, and therefore, unless revisions could be negotiated with the bondholders, default of payment on the principal of the bond would occur.

The purpose of these terms, however, is not to force the company into bankruptcy but to put the lender in a position to insist on measures he thinks will help the situation *before the financial position of the company has become desperate*. The terms are thus written with an expectation that they will become effective while a margin of safety still exists. At this point the senior creditors may still have time to improve their position by negotiation. Management and the more junior creditors will probably still be willing to work toward a negotiated agreement. At the time of technical default they should have something promising to negotiate toward rather than accepting immediate bankruptcy.

The terms which define technical default are subject to infinite variation. We shall discuss three major categories:

1. Change in the nature of the business.
2. Diversion of assets.
3. Degeneration of corporate financial position.

1. *Change in the Nature of the Business.* The first set of provisions represents assurance against changes that could substantially alter the nature of the borrower's business and hence the position of the senior securities. These terms might include prohibitions during the life of the security of the following:

1. Sale of the assets of the company other than in the normal course of business—for example, sale of an obsolete machine would be permitted; sale of a plant would not.
2. Merger of the company with other companies.
3. Major changes in the management of the company except by normal processes such as retirement.

If any of these actions in a particular case were found to be consistent with sound operation of the firm, the debtholders would undoubtedly agree to modifying the prohibitions or to granting waivers for specific actions. But they, by providing the limitation, give themselves the right to review the scheme.

2. *Diversion of Assets.* The second group of restrictions guards against undesirable diversion of the assets of the firm. One of the most common and direct of such clauses is explicit limitation of the salaries or other benefits paid top management. Such a limitation is particularly common in the case of small, closely held companies where major stockholders are also employees and could, in the absence of restrictions, siphon off funds required for the protection of the senior creditors through excessively large salary withdrawals.

Potentially more important in the case of larger companies is the restriction of dividend payments, particularly to common stockholders. The restriction of dividends takes various forms and degrees of severity, depending largely on the strength and bargaining power of the borrower. Even for the strongest borrowers, lenders frequently insist that future dividends be paid only out of future earnings, so that the surplus cushion at the time the loan is granted is not reduced. In other instances, dividends may be prohibited entirely until repayment of a debt has been completed or has reached a lower level. Dividends may also be restricted to a certain proportion of each year's income.

The precise form of such restrictions varies, but the following example of Sperry Rand Corporation sinking fund debenture 5½'s, issued in September, 1957, and due in September, 1982, is typical:

Company may not pay cash dividends on or acquire any stock unless consolidated net income after Mar. 31, 1957 plus $35,000,000 and net cash proceeds after that date from stock sold, exceed such payments after Mar. 31, 1957.[1]

The effect of the clause quoted is to freeze surplus at the time of issue. Nevertheless, the situation in which the issuing company would find such a clause seriously restrictive is likely to be unusual. For this reason, and also because this feature has become so common since the thirties, it is not often a major bargaining consideration. Where it is likely to be a problem, as in the instance when a smaller, family-owned company is bargaining with a financial institution, it may well be worth substantially more attention than is usually the case.

3. *Financial Degeneration.* The last group of provisions seeks to encourage management to prevent certain events and actions which would be harmful to the lenders. Many of these terms are written to ensure that the corporation maintains a strong current position. The long-term profits looked to for loan repayment may be jeopardized if the borrowing firm does not maintain sufficient working capital and credit standing to permit normal conduct of its business. Furthermore, in the event of serious trouble, when the lender may be forced to look for repayment from liquidation of the borrower's assets, the lender would like to have the prospect of substantial pay-out from current assets. These are typically the most liquid and often the highest-yielding assets in bankruptcy, and heavy current borrowings would dilute the lender's prospects of repayment from their liquidation.

With these points in mind, many lenders rely on a requirement that the current ratio of the borrower be maintained above a minimum figure, such as 2 to 1, counting on this requirement for protection against excessive reduction of working capital. A minimum "net quick" ratio is also frequently included. These restrictions may be stated alternatively (or concurrently) in absolute dollar amounts or in terms of some multiple of the long-term debt outstanding. Usually, the lender's desires in this area can be expressed in a clause which expresses what a prudent borrower would plan to do anyway.

Definitions of the sort described can be quite effective in maintaining control over short-term borrowing. At the same time, a frequent source of

---

[1] *Moody's Industrial Manual, 1960,* p. 1761.

strain on working capital is the investment of funds in fixed assets. Undue diversion of cash into plant, equipment, or long-term investments may hamper normal operations and jeopardize repayment of the senior securities. Consequently, holders of long-term debt may also require restrictions on the amount of fixed assets acquired each year. For example, the corporation may be limited to investing the amount supplied by annual depreciation charges. Such limitations are often the subject of vigorous bargaining and, over the full life of the loan, are among the provisions most frequently modified by mutual agreement.

Senior lenders may also wish the protection of a clause providing that a default on any of the company's obligations, including rental of leased property, will accelerate the maturity of the issue.

Because provisions of the type mentioned are intended as guides and to give the company's debtholders an opportunity to strengthen their position early in case of difficulty, the provisions may be modified by joint consent when sound business reasons exist for changes. A company with good reason to sell its assets or to merge would undoubtedly get permission to do so, although in return the lender might well wish to have his protection increased. If a major asset were sold, for example, permission for the sale might require the company to use part of the proceeds to repay a portion of the loan. If a company wished to invest more heavily in fixed assets because sales and profits were rising rapidly, the lenders might agree on the condition that the term of the debt be reduced or the interest rate be increased, or the dividend restriction be tightened.

Sinking Funds

It is undoubtedly obvious that many of the provisions defining the conditions of technical default also exert control on the flow of funds. Those terms apply generally to internal operations of the company or protect one set of security holders from actions harmful to them but favoring another set. The terms discussed in this section relate more directly to regulating the flow of funds between the firm and a specific set of its creditors.

It is characteristic of uncertain conditions that the longer the period of his contract, the greater the risk to the bondholder. The longer he has to wait for the repayment of principal, the more difficult it becomes to forecast with accuracy ability to pay, and the less meaningful is the record of the immediate past upon which confidence is usually based. It follows from this that the risk to the bondholder may be modified by varying the timing and method of repayment of the debt. It also follows as a consequence that a significant lengthening of the maturity date of an issue will probably require a somewhat higher yield to the bondholder or some other concession in order to induce him to accept the increased risk.

Bondholders may attempt to reduce their risk by requiring periodic repayment of principal over the life of a loan, an arrangement which reduces the principal exposed to default. A number of these provisions will be discussed below. It is worthwhile mentioning, however, that bondholders' desires for income may occasionally conflict with their concern for orderly retirement of their principal. When interest rates are high, lenders may want relatively deferred payments so that they may earn high interest rates on their funds for a longer time. In particular, investors may insist on terms preventing the company from retiring the debt when the company's purpose is to refinance the loan at a lower rate. Because debt issues which cannot be retired may put the firm in a relatively inflexible financial position, management must be careful to insure that covenants designed to protect the lender's interest rate do not interfere with arranging a sound financial structure.

The basic bond is repayable in a lump sum at a single known future date, which may be 15 or 20 years from date of issue. A very common modification of the lump-sum repayment of a bond issue is found in the *sinking fund bond*. Previous chapters have made the reader aware that some bonds require the issuing company to set aside a sum of money each year for the repurchase and retirement of some of the outstanding bonds instead of leaving repayment to the uncertain financial capacity in the year of maturity. In the past, most bonds were written to remain outstanding until maturity, and the sinking fund was accumulated elsewhere. This practice still continues in many countries, but it is open to the consequences of mismanagement of the accumulating fund. Experience in the United States has counseled the present practice of retiring some of the debt itself with each sinking fund payment.

Sinking funds may be set up in various ways. The terms of United States Plywood Corporation debenture 5¼'s, issued in April, 1960, and due in April, 1985, include the following sinking fund provisions:

Cash (or debentures) to redeem at par following amounts of debentures each A & O: $335,000, 1963–66; $375,000, 1967–70; $420,000, 1971–76; $455,000, 1977–84; plus optional payments equal to minimum requirements. Payments are estimated sufficient to retire 72% of issue by maturity. Callable at 100 for sinking fund.[2]

A company such as United States Plywood, which has the option of buying in bonds for the sinking fund on the open market or calling them by lot, naturally will take that alternative which offers the lowest price. In any case the effect is to reduce the debt outstanding, provide some

---

[2] *Ibid.*, p. 2746.

support for the market for the remaining securities when the issue is selling below call price, and increase the certainty of total repayment. The decrease in risk to the bondholder resulting from a sinking fund is a significant bargaining point when setting up the terms of a bond issue and one which should give the issuer a more favorable bargaining position in other respects. The disadvantage of such a feature to the common stockholders stems from the fact that the retention of earnings to meet the sinking fund requirements means, in effect, a gradual substitution of high-cost equity capital for low-cost debt. Alternatively, the earnings could have been applied to new investments within the company or withdrawn and invested elsewhere. However, the practical significance for the stockholder may be small if the company is maintaining a continuous debt position through new bond issues which overlap the old.

Variations on the sinking fund principle occasionally require separate establishment of additional special accounts such as a *maintenance and replacement fund*. Cash, in an amount determined by the bonds outstanding, total capital investment, or some other figure, is deposited with a trustee. The trustee may release the money back to the company to spend on certain specified types of assets, which then become security for the bonds already outstanding. In the event that the fund is not exhausted by these withdrawals, the money is applied to the repurchase of debt. These techniques give the lenders additional control over company expenditures without necessarily removing the money from the company. At the same time, the provisions can be made quite flexible from the company's standpoint.[3]

Another type of bond which has an effect somewhat similar to a sinking fund requirement is the serial bond, where specific groups of bonds, all of which are covered by the same indenture, are repayable at predetermined dates. The significant difference between this bond and the sinking fund bond is that the bondholder knows in advance the exact life of his particular bond and can take this into account in the price he pays for it. The serial feature is not nearly so common as the sinking fund provision, but it continues to fill a need in certain situations and is frequently used in municipal finance. An example of a public utility issue is Indiana and Michigan Electric Company's 3.25% serial notes, due in 1957–67 (issued on January 1, 1952). These notes were floated "for construction" and were sold to yield 2.75% for the nearest maturity to 3.2% for the farthest maturity. The various series were due as follows: $250,000, 1956–60; $500,000, 1961–62; $750,000, 1963–67.[4]

A variation on either the serial or the sinking fund bond requires that additional retirements of debt be made depending on the income of the

---

[3] For example, see St. Joseph Light & Power Co., *ibid.*, p. 573, or Southern California Edison Co., *ibid.*, p. 1093.

[4] *Moody's Public Utility Manual, 1960,* p. 1248.

company. For example, the Erie Forge & Steel Corporation first 5¾'s of 1977 has a _contingent sinking fund_ provision which requires the company to make sinking fund payments equivalent to 40% of earnings in excess of $550,000.[5] These payments would usually be credited against the most distant maturities so that the company's more immediate obligations are not reduced by the contingent payments.

Preferred Stock

Because preferred shareholders, like bondholders, desire greater certainty, the sinking fund provision has, with increasing frequency, been written into the terms of preferred issues. As mentioned previously in connection with bonds, the sinking fund presents a possible disadvantage from the common shareholder's point of view. Nevertheless, investors— especially the casualty insurance companies which are major buyers of preferred stock—have demanded it. The reason lies in part in the unhappy experience of "default" on many oversized preferred issues in the thirties. It is also recognized that the market price of the stock benefits from some compulsory buying on the part of the issuing company.

The payment may be required as a flat sum annually or may be tied to earnings on a percentage basis, thus automatically relieving the company of payments in years of losses. The following is the sinking fund provision of the St. Regis Paper Company 4.4% cumulative first preferred, series A, par $100:

Sinking Fund—Annually, and cumulative to extent of net income (after deduction of dividends on preferred and prior or equal stock, and sinking fund for any funded debt not to exceed the lesser of 3% of such debt or $1,200,000) for succeeding years, sufficient to retire by purchase or redemption at $100 per share and dividends, for (_a_) first 2 years, 2½%, (_b_) next 20 years, 4%, and (_c_) succeeding 3 years, 5%, of greatest number of shares of preferred at any time outstanding.[6]

It should be noted again that if the provision is in the form of a flat sum, failure to pay will not precipitate bankruptcy but may affect the relative voting position of the preferred and common shareholders. This is distinctly different from the effect of default of the sinking fund provision on a bond. The terms of the American Cement Corporation class A cumulative preferred stock 6.25% series sinking fund provision illustrate the relatively weak position the preferred shareholder holds in contrast to a typical bondholder:

The Company will have no obligation or liability with respect to the sinking fund or the redemption of shared of the 6.25% Series. Holders of shares of the 6.25% Series will have no remedy whatsoever in the event of the

---

[5] _Moody's Industrial Manual, 1965_, p. 2086.

[6] _Ibid._, pp. 851–52.

Company's failure to make sinking fund payments or to redeem shares of said series, their rights being limited solely to the restriction on declaration and/or payment of Common Stock dividends, the restrictions on the purchase of Common Stock and the majority voting requirements set forth above.[7]

As in the case of bonds, the risk to management and to the common shareholder which preferred stock presents in the form of a rigid prior claim to earnings may be reduced by making the preferred callable or redeemable. This is essential in the issue where a sinking fund is required and is desirable in any case to give the company needed flexibility. The possible effect of this provision on market price of the preferred is the opposite of that of the sinking fund. The general effect of purchases for the sinking fund is to support the market price. The effect of a call feature, where the possibility of call appears a reality, is to hold the market price down to the call price when the general condition of the market might push it higher. An investor is seldom willing to pay more than the call price, even were yield attractive at the higher price, if the company might pick his number for redemption.

Control over Other Obligations

Debt Issues.   Since the terms of a security issue establish the rights and responsibilities of the parties to the agreement, the owners of a security will want to prevent the company from modifying those terms by the act of issuing other securities whose rights jeopardize previous agreements. For this reason, holders of senior securities will usually insist on terms which limit the ability of the company to issue additional obligations.

Two types of clauses are quite effective in this respect, so we shall mention them briefly at this point. Their primary characteristics, however, dictate deferring a full discussion until the section on protection in the event of default. The first provision is that of taking a *pledge of specific assets* as security for a loan. This agreement limits the firm's ability to secure additional debt by making some assets unavailable as prime security for additional debt issues. To the extent that the limitation is successful, it acts to hold down the overall proportion of debt in the capital structure, thereby improving the earnings coverage of the outstanding bonds beyond what it would be otherwise. This reduces the risks assumed by the existing bondholders. From the company's viewpoint the acceptance of such limitations may be a means of gaining advantages in other ways, such as a lower interest rate and/or a better selling price for the bonds.

A second form of protective provision is found in some debt contracts which provide that property acquired after the securities are issued will

---

[7] American Cement Corp., Listing Application to New York Stock Exchange (Common Stock), December 6, 1962.

also become part of the collateral against which the lenders may take a claim in the event of default. This provision, known as the *after-acquired property clause* not only provides protection for the lender against additional issues of debt but increases the strength of his position by adding to the property against which his claims are secured.

Another way of preventing claims from rising to dangerous levels is to forbid further borrowing. Clauses of this type are known as *negative pledge clauses*. The prohibition against additional debt may be as direct, specific, and complete as the company is willing to accept. Additional pledges of assets can be prohibited. The company can be prevented from entering into sale and leaseback agreements. It is even possible to forbid additional borrowing of any type.

In cases where all parties agree that the company has capacity and needs for further borrowing (or is likely to have in the future), the terms of the debt agreement can be made more flexible. Then the agreement can define the circumstances in which more debt might be raised rather than strictly prohibiting all additional loans. Then, if the company continues to prosper and remains strong, more money can be raised without having to renegotiate the outstanding debt agreements. For example, the terms of a loan might permit the company to borrow on a short-term basis, either a specified amount or as much as needed, provided certain working-capital ratios are not violated. If longer-term funds are a possible requirement, the agreement might permit the company to pledge certain assets or to issue subordinated loans up to a specified amount. Subordinated debt could, for instance, be limited to the smaller of 200% of senior, secured debt or 300% of tangible net worth. Terms of this kind can also be used to control the nature and amount of borrowing by subsidiaries. The lenders and the corporation could negotiate any of a wide variety of specific terms that would permit additional borrowing while controlling its amount and form.

It is often the case that a *debenture, an unsecured form of bond*, is the only bond issue of a particular company. In order to protect against the hazard of a subsequent bond issue secured by a lien on assets, which would then take precedence over the debenture as to these assets, the terms of the debenture normally prohibit a future pledge of assets or outline the conditions under which such a pledge would be acceptable. For example, the Allied Chemical debenture 3½'s, due in 1978, are covered by the following provisions, known as the *equal and ratable security clause* (with, in this case, certain exceptions as mentioned above):

Company and any subsidiary will not mortgage property unless debentures are equally and ratably secured therewith, except for (1) purchase money or existing mortgages up to 66⅔% of lower of cost of fair value of property, as provided and (2) other permitted liens. If on any consolidation or sale of substantially all properties, any property would become subject to a mortgage, debentures will be secured by direct prior lien thereon except for any existing lien.[8]

Ownership Control over New Obligations. Preferred and common shareholders, having been willing to accept greater risk in hopes of greater income, receive less specific control over the additional obligations their company can issue. Within the ownership position itself, of course, the major redistribution of risk occurs when a preferred stock is created. Unless the preferred is issued as part of a corporation's initial capitalization, most states require a two-thirds vote by the common stockholders to amend the company's charter to create a new preferred stock. The common shareholders are protected in this way against dilution of their ownership without the consent of a large majority.

1. *Preferred Stock.* One of the potential hazards associated with preferred stock is the creation of additional securities at a later date which have an equal or senior position in the capital structure. Protection against this hazard in preferreds is a relatively new idea, but many issues currently outstanding contain restrictive provisions in this regard. These vary in the degree of limitation placed on management. They may apply only to a new stock issues, or they may apply to new debt as well. The following example of the Kendall Company $4.50 cumulative preferred A illustrates the latter type:

> Consent of two-thirds of preferred necessary to (1) issue or assume any funded debt . . . if thereafter consolidated funded debt plus involuntary liquidating value of outstanding preferred of subsidiaries and of preferred and of any stock having priority or on a parity with preferred exceeds 75% of excess of consolidated tangible assets over consolidated current liabilities, (2) create or issue any stock having priority over preferred (3) alter or amend provisions of preferred.
>
> Consent of a majority of preferred necessary to create or issue additional preferred or any stock on a parity therewith. . . .[9]

2. *Common Stock.* To the extent that the risks borne by senior security holders are lessened by the specific terms attached to their securities, the risks associated with the junior securities are likely to be increased, since the modification does not normally remove the risk but merely shifts it. Because the common stock stands last in line, there is no opportunity for a favorable shifting of the basic risks by qualifications in the terms of the issue.

There is, however, one respect in which the risk may be reduced, and that is with regard to the dilution of equity values through additional issues of the same class of stock. The feature aimed at safeguarding the interests of existing stockholders is the preemptive right. This is the right to buy any additional issues of common stock on a pro rata basis, before

---

[8] *Moody's Industrial Manual, 1960,* p. 2814.

[9] *Ibid.,* p. 763.

it is offered to new stockholders, on terms which are at least as favorable as those offered to the new shareholders. If dilution is involved in the offering price, the old shareholder can protect his position by buying a block of the new stock in proportion to his present holdings. This right may be required by state law, or it may be left to the bargaining process between the company and the shareholders. For common stock which does not have the preemptive right, new issues of common may or may not be first offered to existing shareholders before being offered to the public at large, depending on the decision of management. If the new common is priced substantially under the market, then it may result in lowered market value and earnings per share on the outstanding stock. We shall give further attention to various aspects of rights offerings of common stock in the following chapter.

The Call Provision

In contrast to the serial and sinking fund bonds, which work to reduce the risk to the bondholder, the *call provision* provides a means by which the terms of a particular debt can be canceled. The call feature gives the company the option of repaying all or some portion of the debt prior to maturity, as in the following example of Texas Company debenture 3⅝'s, issued in May, 1958, and due in May, 1983:

Callable—As a whole or in part at any time on 30 days' notice to May 1 incl. as follows:

1961	104½	1964	104
1967	103½	1970	103
1972	102½	1974	102
1976	101½	1978	101
1980	100½	1981	100¼
1983	100		

Optional redemption is also permitted up to $5,000,000 of debentures during each 12 months' period ending May 1, beginning with period ending May 1, 1969, at 100 and interest.[10]

The call feature gives the company the very real advantage of greater flexibility in its capital structure so that it can time repayment to suit its needs and objectives as they develop. It also enables the company to take advantage of lower market interest rates, should they occur prior to maturity, by calling in the old bonds and replacing them with new bonds at the lower rate. In this respect the company's gain is the bondholder's loss; thus, the question of having a call feature may be hotly debated issue. The small call premium may be quite inadequate to compensate the bondholder for having to reinvest his funds for the balance of the period at a lower rate of return. It is apparent that the call feature is one which may affect the distribution of income as well as risk.

[10] *Ibid.*, p. 2894.

The call provision is a good example of an indenture clause which is subject to change over time as the condition of the money market and the bargaining position of the borrower and lender change. In the period of declining interest rates which prevailed for many years, an unrestricted call provision was considered highly desirable by the borrower and was almost invariably included in the indenture as long as a strong demand for bonds by investors persisted. However, whenever their bargaining position permits, and this is likely to be strong when interest rates are high, lenders are inclined to demand that limitations be placed on calls so as to slow down their turnover of investments and to preserve higher yields for a longer period of time.

Having observed many occasions where the absence of the call feature has forced firms to continue obligations that there is every reason for them to avoid, the authors urge all who bargain for funds not to give up the call feature entirely. One may agree on noncallability for a few years, or accept a high premium cost if call is decided upon, but to approve a completely noncallable arrangement is a sign of lack of foresight. The only exception, in our view, for which argument can be made may exist in term loan agreements of short duration where there is no reason to foresee either having excess funds on hand or being embarrassed by one of the contract clauses.

Protection after Default: Priority

If a company does encounter severe and prolonged difficulty, advance efforts to protect the position of the security holders may fail. It is possible that the company would then go into bankruptcy proceedings and be liquidated. Even if this event is avoided, the company's creditors may have to agree on a settlement in order to keep the firm operating. In either case the holders of the firm's securities will find themselves in quite different positions according to how they secured their advances against the assets of the company. For example, a lender whose loan is secured by the primary productive assets of the company not only has his principal protected by first claim on the proceeds of those assets in the event of liquidation, but he is also in a very strong bargaining position during the settlement negotiation.

Thus, the effect of a pledge is to give a certain priority to one group of creditors over the claims of others.[11] The obvious reason for a pledge of, or a lien against, *specific* assets is to decrease the risk to the bondholder, which may mean that the issue is salable at a somewhat lower interest rate as a result. On the other hand, the primary protection for any bond lies in the earning capacity of the issuing company, so that the debenture of one company may involve less risk to the investor than the secured bond of another.

---

[11] *Moody's Public Utility Manual, 1960*, p. 481.

Pledges do not come into action until after default, which is avoided through favorable operations and not through the pledge. The pledge merely confers on the privileged creditor a priority of claims on the value of the assets pledged to him. There is no way in the United States to create a general priority over other creditors. The pledge is of a specific asset.

The Mortgage. Almost any corporate asset may be pledged, but the laws are intricate, and so the forms of contract differ according to the type of property. The most common form of secured bond is that secured by a mortgage on all or some of the fixed assets of the business—in the form of real estate; land and buildings. This type of issue is known as a mortgage bond and is frequently found in industries which combine relatively stable earnings with a high proportion of the total investment in fixed assets, such as public utilities and railroad or companies owning income-producing real estate. The mortgage will contain a detailed description of the property pledged, so that it can be accurately identified in event of default. An abbreviated statement of such security is seen in the following example of Inland Steel Company's first 4½'s, Series L, issued in February, 1959, and due in February 1989:

Secured equally and ratably with other series by first mortgage on (1) Indiana Harbor and Chicago Heights plants, (2) certain iron ore properties in Iron and Marquette Counties, Mich., and St. Louis and Crow Wing Counties, Minn., (3) coal properties of company, subject to certain exceptions, and (4) approximately 800 acres of vacant land in Porter County, Ind.[12]

It is a recognized fact that in the event of liquidation, business assets generally undergo shrinkage in value. This is particularly true of specialized fixed assets, where the cash realized in sale is likely to be considerably below the book value. In view of this, it is a general rule that the value of fixed assets pledged as security for a bond issue will be substantially larger than the amount of the debt. The usual upper limit for mortgage loans is two thirds of the cost of the pledged assets; and in some cases, it may be as low as one half.[13] Obviously, this is one of the ways in which the creditor seeks to limit the risks involved in investment.

There are occasions when a bond issue is secured by a *second mortgage* on assets which have already been pledged on a previous issue. As the term implies, the holders of such securities take a secondary position to the holders of the first-mortgage bonds in the event of

---

[12] *Moody's Industrial Manual, 1960,* p. 1059.

[13] Some investors, such as insurance companies, often have maximum loan ratios set by law. At the same time, however, the value against which the loan is made is frequently subject to negotiation. If the value is not determined by the cost of the building but by appraised valuation, it is possible for several appraisers to place quite different values on the property.

foreclosure and sale of the particular assets. On the other hand, they rank before other creditors as regards these assets. It will be apparent that a second mortgage has an appeal to the potential bondholder only when the value of the pledged assets is substantially in excess of that necessary to provide protection under a first mortgage.

Some security provisions include property "hereafter acquired" as well as property in existence at the time of the mortgage. This is known as an after-acquired property clause and is found in many such mortgages as a feature to increase further the confidence of the investor by adding new assets to the pledge. More significantly, the effect of the clause would be to exclude additional first-mortgage debt, which would otherwise increase the fixed charges against earnings and thereby the risk to existing bondholders. The mortgage may also include a statement of certain exceptions to this clause in the case of property which bears a prior lien at the time of acquisition.

As an instance of the type of bargaining which is appropriate when a bond contract is being designed, let us look at the consequences to a debtor of accepting the after-acquired clause. It prevents borrowing on mortgage when new property is acquired. Therefore, if this clause is requested, an alert management will suggest that the terms should also include some degree of permission to increase the amount of the borrowing under the existing mortgage to finance additional assets. This is usually arranged by some type of an *open-end clause* which permits additional issues of bonds under the same mortgage provided certain conditions are met. An example of this is the Michigan Consolidated Gas Company first-mortgage 3½'s, series due in 1969. These bonds have an open indenture with the following provision regarding further issues:

Additional bonds may be issued (unlimited except as provided by law) equal to (1) 60% of lower of cost or fair value of net property additions after December 31, 1943, not theretofore bonded . . . (2) bonds issued hereunder and prior lien bonds returned but not theretofore bonded; (3) cash deposited with trustee for such purpose, but only if net earnings available for interest and depreciation for 12 out of 15 months next preceding are at least 2½ times annual interest on bonds to be outstanding and on all prior lien bonds outstanding; except that, in general, no earnings test is required to issue bonds (*a*) for refunding bonds issued by company or prior lien bonds, or (*b*) to reimburse company for monies expended or repay loans incurred for such refunding.[14]

Even an open-end mortgage bond issue usually contains provisions designed to preserve a certain minimum protection of asset values and earning power for the bondholder. At the same time, the clause gives the issuer a degree of flexibility in the further use of debt. The specific terms of this provision are of obvious importance to both parties and would be

---

[14] *Moody's Public Utility Manual, 1960*, p. 1609.

a subject for negotiation in discussions preliminary to the sale of the issue.

Other Forms of Pledge.   A second type of property which may become security for long-term debt is movable physical assets such as equipment, commonly referred to as chattels. The mortgage which cover such assets are broadly classified as *chattel mortgages*. This form is widely used in the transportation industry. An example of a straight chattel mortgage is Trans World Airlines, Inc., equipment mortgage sinking fund 3¾'s issued in 1954, due in 1969, and secured by a general mortgage on aircraft and engines owned as of December 31, 1957, with the exception of certain specific aircraft and engines pledged under a bank loan or purchased under a conditional sale contract.[15]

A third type of property frequently pledged by certain types of businesses is investments in stocks and bonds or other instruments such as notes receivable. A bond secured by a pledge of such securities is known as a *collateral trust bond*. This type of collateral may be more or less effective as protection against the risk of default, depending on the character of the pledged securities and the strength and stability of the market for them. Such bonds would not normally be used by industrial companies, since few of them carry a sufficient investment in marketable securities to support a bond issue. On the other hand, they are a natural form of bond issue for finance companies, which have large portfolios of notes receivables from those to whom they have made advances.

The features mentioned so far have been designed to reduce the risk to the investor. On occasion a feature is introduced which acts to increase the risk to the investor. Such is the case of the *subordinated debenture*. As we indicated previously in Chapter 13, a subordinated debt is one which would in the ordinary course of events be equal to or have priority over other debt but which for some reason has been placed in a secondary position to such debt. An example of the subordinated debenture is W. R. Grace and Company convertible subordinate debenture 3½'s, due in 1975, which were sold in 1955 for additions to plant, facilities, and working capital, and were "subordinated to all senior debt, including bank borrowings, current loans, etc."[16] Such subordination is necessary for new debt when existing debt contracts prohibit additional debt having equivalent or senior claim on assets and earnings. In order to make such bonds acceptable to the prospective holders, a higher interest rate may be necessary.

The Floating Charge.   In countries which have modeled their laws on the British statutes, the floating charge appears. This is just the opposite of subordination, since it is an arrangement by which groups of assets are pledged by categories to a certain creditor. They are not

---

[15] *Moody's Transportation Manual, 1960,* p. 1387.

[16] *Moody's Industrial Manual, 1960,* p. 2929.

pledged specifically with detailed descriptions, as in the United States, but by kind. Thus a certain secured issue may have a floating charge on all the real estate and/or other categories as each may exist at the time of default. The floating charge "fixes" at that time, so that to speak of "fixed charges" in London is to raise images in the hearers' minds quite different from those that would result from the use of the term in New York.

In our view there is a great deal to be said for this device, which permits the bargainers to confer priorities of claim without reference to particular assets. Those who are interested in the improvement of commercial law in the United States would do well to study it. We mention it here as an example of the fact that not all the best practices in finance are to be found in the United States.

Unsecured Debt, Subordination. As we progress down the list of priorities, we must not forget the many kinds of unsecured debt, from the formally engraved debenture bond to the verbal contract that created a purchase on credit. Any of these ranks equally as a claim on the values of the unpledged assets. Nor should we forget subordination, which was described in pages 270–273.

Preferred Stock. Preferred shareholders usually, but not necessarily, receive a preferred position ahead of common shareholders but after all forms of debt in the event of liquidation of assets. The terms may be stated, for example, as a certain dollar amount to which will be added any accrued dividends. At times the amount assigned to the preferred shareholders will be larger if the liquidation is voluntary than if it is involuntary. On the other hand, the preferred shares are seldom secured against any particular assets, which makes their claim relatively weak. Countless cases suggest that preferred shareholders may receive the least satisfactory treatment of any security holders in a liquidating company as compared with the agreed terms of their security.

The common shareholders are in the position of having to take what is left in event of a liquidation. They have invested in the company with the objective of increasing their wealth by receiving the major portion of the benefits of success and at the risk of losing their investment in the event of failure. It is appropriate for their claims to be for leavings, be they large or nonexistent.

Chapter 25

Modifications of the Distribution of Income and Control

WE MAY regard the earnings before interest and taxes (E.B.I.T.) as the contribution made by efficient use of the assets at the disposal of the firm and therefore as the source of the values of these assets as they are used in the going concern. When the managers of a firm cause it to issue securities with special claims to income, they are allocating the E.B.I.T. and thus allocating value among the securities the firm issues. If this process is wisely done, the result will be increased return on each dollar invested by the common shareholder without a corresponding increase in risk. The process will, therefore, provide greater value for the common shareholder. This result is in accord with the obligation of management to the owners of the common equity: to arrange the terms of security contracts with the goal of maximizing the value received by the holders of the common stock, as that holding exists at the time a choice of financing is under consideration.

Commitments to Fixed Payments

The complement of a desire for greater security of principal is a willingness to accept less income. Security holders who are averse to risk are also interested in insuring the safety of that income, however small. This can be accomplished by the establishment of fixed payments with priority over disbursements to other security holders. The fixed obligations of interest owed bondholders, lessors, and the like fall at one end of the spectrum with the dividends paid common shareholder, which are declared at the discretion of the directors, at the other. Dividends on preferred shares are also paid at the discretion of the directors. Nevertheless, because preferred dividends are often cumulative and failure to make payments can frequently have unattractive repercussions upon the common shareholders' position, management usually considers preferred dividends as fixed requirements.

Given that interest payment is to be granted priority, the problem of setting an interest rate on a specific issue is an extremely important one. In fact, in the bargain between the corporate borrower and the bondholder, there is no issue more vital to both than the interest rate which will be necessary to market the issue completely and quickly. In a private placement this can be settled by direct negotiation, whereas in a public offering the issuer and his investment banker must estimate in advance of the offering what will be the minimum yield acceptable to the bondholder. In either case, however, once the coupon rate is accepted by both parties, the specific terms of payment follow a standard pattern—typically, a regular semiannual payment of fixed amount of maturity. The only way to make a change after the issue is to call the issue and replace it, unless the issue is closely enough held to permit a negotiated adjustment. Replacing or amending an issue is an expensive operation, assuming that it is even possible.

The primary determinant of the interest rate (or preferred dividends) which a firm must concede to its lenders (or preferred shareholders) is the general level prevailing at the time of issue for companies whose risks are adjudged to be approximately the same as those of the issuing corporation. Small changes in the rate can sometimes be arranged if concessions are made elsewhere in the contract. Generally speaking, lower rates can be obtained by including clauses which reduce risk (such as the variety of pledges, covenants, and maturity arrangements described in the Chapter 24). On the other hand, the preservation of some freedom (permission to borrow further, smaller sinking fund) can often be arranged by concession on the rate. One large corporation, for example, was told that its insistence on a call feature in its issues was costing it an additional $3/8\%$ to $1/2\%$ on the rate.

Convertibility

It is often desirable to provide part of the income to senior holders on a contingent basis. For example, it may be possible to raise funds less expensively (from the existing common shareholders' point of view) by offering a security containing some elements of both a bond and a stock rather than selling securities which are pure examples of either type. Alternatively, it may be necessary to concede additional, contingent income in return for terms of the contract which management believes to be essential. In some instances lenders may refuse to make a risky loan unless they are provided with a share in the anticipated profits. Traditional or legal restraints may also prevent them from requiring fixed interest compensation adequate to allow for the risks they accept. A wide variety of instruments have been developed to meet the demand for protected securities with contingent compensation. Two basic types exist: issues providing convertibility and issues whose rewards depend on participation in the earnings.

A significant modification of the normal fixed income position of the bondholder and preferred shareholder is to be found in the convertible issue. The convertible bond gives the bondholder the option of retaining his normal contractual claim or exchanging his security for another security, usually common stock, on a ratio fixed at the time of issue of the bonds. The terms may be illustrated by Continental Baking Company convertible subordinated debenture $3\frac{5}{8}$'s, issued on March 1, 1955, and due in 1980. The provision for conversion into common stock was stated as follows: "The basic conversion price shall be $34.50 per share of Common Stock to and including February 28, 1958, $37 thereafter to and including February 28, 1961, and $39 thereafter to and including February 28, 1965." Cash was to be paid in lieu of fractional shares, and there was to be no adjustment for interest or dividends. The conversion privilege was protected against dilution. As a result, when a stock dividend was paid on the common stock in September, 1955, the conversion prices were changed to $32.50 to February, 1958; $34.85 to February, 1961; and $36.73 to February, 1965.[1]

It will be apparent that this privilege has no realizable value to the bondholder unless and until the earnings and/or dividend performance of the common justifies a market price of the stock in excess of the conversion prices quoted. At that time the bondholder is able to acquire common stock at a bargain price and either take an immediate capital gain by selling the common or hold it for income and further appreciation. Thus, the bondholder has the option of retaining his contractual but limited claim on earnings or of taking advantage of the more favorable income position of the stockholder if and when this becomes a reality. It would appear that if there is any real prospect of conversion under favorable terms, the holder of the convertible bond has "the best of all possible worlds"—the protection of a bond plus the speculative opportunities of a stock. In this respect the bondholder's gain is the common shareholder's loss. When conversion takes place, high-cost equity capital is substituted for low-cost debt, and the common shareholder's equity is diluted by the addition of stock "sold" at a (conversion) price below market.

There are two principal reasons why companies are willing to consider a convertible bond. One is that circumstances may make it difficult to market a particular bond (for example, a subordinated debenture) at a reasonable coupon rate and the speculative feature is added to put the issue across. Thus, the conversion feature is often a sign of weakness, and convertible bonds often are found to have relatively low ratings. The other and perhaps more justifiable reason is found in the case of a company which prefers to finance by stock rather than bonds but finds the current stock market unfavorable. Being unwilling to sell stock at the price dictated by the existing market and at the same time able to sell a

---

[1] *Moody's Industrial Manual, 1956,* p. 1090.

bond which is convertible into stock at a higher price, the company sells
the convertible bond in the expectation that it will be fully converted in
the near future. If conversion takes place, the company has, in a sense,
sold common at the higher price in an indirect manner.

To illustrate, the range of Continental Baking common in the year
preceding the debenture issue of March 1, 1955 was 20¾–33, with the
high prices being recorded in March. At the time the decision to float this
issue was made, it was highly uncertain whether a common issue could be
sold at or near $34.50. On the other hand, it was quite within the realm of
possibility that even within the year the market price of the common
could rise above this figure and thus make conversion attractive to the
bondholders.

In practice, it is possible for the bondholder to realize his capital gain
without actual conversion. The reason for this is that once the market
price of common stock rises above the conversion price, the market price
of the bond tends to rise along with it. The bond is no longer valued as a
bond but rather on the basis of its conversion value. As a consequence,
the bondholder can take his capital gain simply by selling the bond. This
market result tends to prevent the issuing company from realizing its
objective of replacing debt with common equity capital. In order to
assure that this objective will be realized, convertible bonds must be
made callable.

For example, the Continental Baking convertible debentures were
callable at 105 to February 28, 1958, and thereafter at 104¾ to February
28, 1961. If the hoped-for rise in the price of the common stock occurred
(above $32.50 after September, 1955) and the price of the debentures
began its corresponding rise but no conversion actually took place, the
company could precipitate conversion at any time that the debentures rose
above 105 by issuing a call for redemption. The bondholders would then
convert to avoid being paid off at the lower call price.

At the beginning of 1958, about $3.8 million of the $13 million issue
of Continental Baking debentures already had been converted. The
common stock price began a steady rise from 27¾ early in 1958, and the
debentures were called for redemption on October 1, 1958, at 104¾. At
the time of call the common price was 41½. Almost $9.2 million deben-
tures were converted during 1958, and only $36,000 were redeemed.[2]

The critical decision in establishing the terms of a convertible issue is
setting the conversion ratio or conversion price. Normally, this price is
above the current market price of common, although there have been
issues where the convertible bond had an immediate value in conversion
(for example, the A.T.&T. 4¼% convertible debentures offered to
shareholders of record as of January 24, 1958, convertible at $142 per
common share, market price of stock on January 24, $172⅞). It is in the

---

[2] Continental Baking Company, Annual Report, 1958.

interests of the existing common shareholders to set the price as high as possible; but on the other hand, it must not be so high as to make conversion very remote and therefore valueless in the mind of the prospective bondholder. The setting of the conversion price on the Continental Baking issue is an example of an attempt to achieve both objectives.

It will be remembered that the terms of the Continental Baking issue included protection against dilution. This term means that the basis of conversion will be adjusted in the event of a subsequent stock split or stock dividend so as to preserve the original advantage. Thus, if the common stock is split 2 for 1, the conversion price offered to the bondholder will be cut in half.

A *convertible preferred* stock is occasionally placed on the market. Since the characteristics of this security are very similar to those of the convertible bond as far as this feature is concerned, it will be discussed very briefly. Like the bond, it gives the senior security holder an opportunity to profit from his investment in the business beyond the fixed limits of his security type. To the extent that he does, it is at the expense of the common shareholder. If the security is issued as an intermediate stage in a plan for ultimate common stock financing, it will be necessary to include the call feature in order to be able to force conversion when the time becomes appropriate.

Typical of the terms of such an issue is Abbott Laboratories 4% convertible preferred, par $100:

Convertible into common at any time to Dec. 31, 1961 incl., on basis of 1.7 common shares for each preferred share, with no adjustment for dividends and with scrip for fractional shares. Conversion rights subject to adjustment in certain events. Right to convert preferred called for redemption prior to Jan. 1, 1962 will terminate not earlier than seventh day prior to redemption.

Callable as a whole or in part on not less than 30 days' mailed notice at any time at $105 per share and dividends.[3]

It is interesting to note that the 1960 price range for Abbott Laboratories common stock was 69½–50 and for the convertible preferred, 114½–98¼. At the high for the common of 69½ the gain from conversion would have been $18 over the par value of the preferred and $13 over the call price.

Convertible preferred stock has been used in recent years as a vehicle for effecting mergers. One advantage is that an exchange of common stock for a preferred stock is not considered a taxable transaction at the time of the exchange. The exchange of stock for a bond is taxable. More important, however, a convertible preferred provides a chance to negotiate a mutually satisfactory merger in conditions where the earnings per

---

[3] *Moody's Industrial Manual, 1960*, p. 698.

share, dividends, and market price of the two companies are not in the same relationships. For example, on June 1, 1965, the *Wall Street Journal* reported a proposal for merging Beneficial Finance Co. and Spiegel, Inc., a Chicago mail-order house. In exchange for each share of his company's common stock a Spiegel shareholder would receive ⅓ share of Beneficial common stock and ½ share of a new Beneficial $50 par cumulative convertible preferred stock with a $2.15 dividend. Each full share of the new preferred could be converted into 0.7 share of Beneficial common stock at any time during a 12-year period. Beneficial could not call the stock for 5 years. Thereafter, Beneficial could call the stock at prices which gradually declined to $52.50 a share.

At the time of the announcement, earnings, dividends, and price of the common stocks of the two companies were as follows:

	Market Price May 28, 1965	1965 Indicated Dividend	1964 Earnings per Share
Spiegel, Inc.	$36.625	$1.50	$2.61
Beneficial Finance Co.	60.125	1.40	2.92

The terms of the merger gave Spiegel shareholders an increased dividend rate of $1.61 if they did not convert their preferred stock. To have provided them a similar income from Beneficial common stock would have required more than one share of Beneficial for each share of Spiegel and would have entailed dilution of Beneficial's earnings per share. Under the terms suggested, Spiegel shareholders (assuming immediate conversion) would in fact have their per share earnings diluted but would receive stock with a market price of about $41 to compensate them for the earnings drop. Although neither set of shareholders received all the benefits, as befits a satisfactory negotiation, they each improved their position in some respect to compensate for their concessions in others. The flexibility of the convertible preferred was apparently an extremely important factor in permitting a satisfactory distribution of the benefits of the merger.

Warrants, Units

Occasionally, the opportunity for capital gains is offered a senior security holder in a manner that does not require him to give up his preferred position. This is accomplished by attaching to the senior security stock purchase warrants, which entitle the holder to acquire common stock at a fixed price, intended to be favorable. If and when the warrants are exercised, the senior security remains outstanding—in contrast to the convertible security. Once again, to the extent that the senior security holder gains, the common stockholder loses.

An example of warrants is seen in Mack Trucks, Inc.'s, subordinated debenture 5½'s, issued in September, 1956, and due in 1968:

Warrants, detachable and transferable by delivery. Holders have right to purchase one and one-third $5 par common shares at following prices per share to each September 1 inclusive: 1959, $40; 1961, $43; 1963, $45; 1965, $47.50; thereafter at $50 to September 1, 1966, when privilege expires.[4]

The market price range for Mack Trucks common stock during 1956 (until the 4-for-3 stock split in December) was 42⅜–26¼.

Another technique for providing a security purchaser with a mix of protection and income is to offer a *unit* composed of two or more securities. These may be any combination of debt, preferred stock, and common stock of several classes. In some respects a unit issue of securities gives the purchaser a preconverted issue for which there is no clearly separable cost or a warrant which requires no additional payment to be exercised. For example, in 1960 the Mid-America Pipeline Company offered to the public $20.5 million of 6½% subordinated debentures in units of a $50 debenture and 3½ shares of common stock for a total price of $73.50 a unit.[5]

Contingent Payments

Another form of senior issue with a contingency clause are securities whose provisions relate payments to the security holder with the income of the company. The *income bond* is one example. Briefly stated, an income bond is one in which the interest payment is made contingent on earnings. The payments may be cumulative or noncumulative. It differs from a preferred stock in the respect that the payment is mandatory if earned, whereas the preferred dividend is still at the discretion of the board of directors.

There has been a growing interest in income bonds by solvent and profitable businesses. The primary reason is that under current conditions of heavy corporate income taxation, the security offers the elements of flexibility found in a preferred stock, combined with the tax advantage of interest payments deductible as a cost. The result has been that the income bond has taken on a new respectability. This is another example of how attitudes toward security forms are modified as circumstances change.

The following terms of the Security Banknote Company convertible subordinated income debenture 5's, dated June 1, 1956, and due in 1976, illustrate the principal features of this type of security:

Interest payable . . . at 5% per annum, to extent earned; noncumulative.

---

[4] *Moody's Industrial Manual, 1957*, p. 2312.

[5] *Moody's Transportation Manual, 1965*, p. 1038.

Sinking Fund—Annually, April 30, 1957–75, cash (or debentures) equal to 10% of consolidated net earnings, for redemption of debentures at 100.

Security—not secured; subordinated to prior payment of senior indebtedness, including bank borrowings.

Dividend Restrictions—Company may not pay cash dividends on common while interest, principal or sinking fund installment is in default.

Issued—Series A . . . in exchange for preferred at rate of $20 of debentures for each preferred share; series B issued in payment for preferred dividends in arrears.[6]

Price Range (over-the-counter bid) 1959: 86–80.[7]

Note that in this particular case the bond issue is further weakened by subordination.

In recent years the Interstate Commerce Commission has authorized a number of railroads to issue income debentures for the purpose of retiring preferred or class A common stock. The Commission commented on these developments as follows, in 1957:

There was a continuance of the trend which began several years ago for railroads to substitute interest-bearing obligations for preferred stock, with payment of interest generally contingent upon earnings, in order to reduce Federal income taxes. Interest on debentures is deductible whereas dividends on preferred stock are not.[8]

A preferred stock offering a shareholder an opportunity to participate in income beyond the stated dividend is known as a *participating preferred*. Unlike the income bond, which places a ceiling on the income the bondholder can expect, the maximum income of the participating preferred shareholder is often unrestricted. The terms of the Virginia-Carolina Chemical Corporation 6% cumulative participating preferred illustrate this form:

Dividend Rights—has preference over common as to cumulative dividends of 6% annually. . . . After common has received $3 per share in any fiscal year entitled to participate share for share with the common in any additional dividends in such fiscal year.[9]

It is obvious that such a feature can result in a major income concession to the preferred shareholder at the expense of the common shareholder; and for this reason, it is not found very frequently in preferred stock issues. Its presence indicates that at the time of issue the company and/or the common shareholder were in an unusually weak bargaining position.

---

[6] *Moody's Industrial Manual, 1960,* p. 992.

[7] Standard & Poor's Corporation, *Standard Corporation Descriptions*, P-S, August–September, 1960 (New York, 1960), p. 8853.

[8] *Interstate Commerce Commission, Seventy-First Annual Report* (Washington, D.C.: U.S. Government Printing Office, 1957), p. 57.

[9] *Moody's Industrial Manual, 1960,* p. 245.

The Cumulative Preferred Dividend

Almost all the preferred stocks now issued contain the cumulative feature. While it must be recognized that any dividend must be declared by the directors of the corporation before it becomes an enforceable financial obligation, it is possible to arrange by contract that if a dividend on preferred stock is not declared, no dividend on the junior stocks of the company will be paid until all *dividends in arrears* have been made up. This is the *cumulative feature*. In addition, in situations where dividends are not declared on a preferred stock, the preferred stockholder is usually put in a position where his representatives have more direct control over the use of funds than the provisions of the security would allow in normal circumstances. The degree of influence may vary from the right to elect only one or two members of the board of the directors to the right to elect all the directors until such time as the arrears have been completely eliminated. On the other hand, the terms of this power can define it very narrowly. A case is known where, despite the accumulation of substantial dividends in arrears on a preferred, the common shareholders have remained in control by virtue of paying every fourth preferred dividend. The terms of the preferred issue provided for preferred voting power only in the event four *consecutive* dividends had been passed.

Classified Common Stock

Generally the common shareholders exercise their control over the funds of the company, on which they have the last call, through their ability to elect the directors. In a few companies, however, two classes of common stock have been created where the burden of risk is divided unequally. Such stock, referred to as classified common, may differ only in respect to voting privileges and may be equal in all other respects. On the other hand, one class may be set up with a prior claim to dividends, in which case it becomes in essence a type of preferred stock, even though not so named. Such a provision obviously effects an uneven distribution of risk among the common shareholders. An example of this is Crown Cork International Corporation's $1 cumulative participating class A stock: "Has preference as to cumulative dividends of $1 per share and participates in any further distribution equally, share for share, with class B stock after latter has received noncumulative dividends of $1 per share in any year."[10]

Another interesting example of classified common stock is the A and B common issues of the Citizens Utilities Company. Both A and B stock carry one vote per share. However, the dividends on class A stock are paid only in stock, whereas the dividends on B stock are paid in cash.

---

[10] *Ibid.*, p. 2219.

Class A stock is convertible into B at the holder's option, share for share, except at the time of cash dividend payments. The two classes were issued as a part of a stock reclassification plan.

Dilution and the Position of Common Stock

Aside from the very important ways in which the income and control position of the common equity can be affected by the terms of securities senior to it, the value of an existing stockholder's interest is challenged every time new shares are to be issued. If an expanding corporation proposes to issue new shares, it inevitably creates a situation where those who formerly held all the equity must either invest additional funds to maintain their position, or concede a portion of the equity to others. Under such circumstances even actions that promise to increase the value of the equity may sometimes reduce the portion of it that represents the present investment of the present ownership group. In this, we are only saying again what was said in the discussion of the cost of equity capital.

Let us look at the situation this time in terms of numbers of shares, recognizing that any increase in the number of shares is a value-reducing event from the viewpoint of the existing ownership. Only when positive factors exist to offset the effect of increasing the "number of mouths to feed" should the new issue be considered.

First, we see a negative force, termed *immediate dilution*, which can be defined as the relative loss or weakening of the equity position caused by the issuance of new shares. The degree of this dilution can be measured precisely by the fraction

where:
$$\frac{N}{N + \Delta N}$$

N = Existing number of shares.
ΔN = Proposed added number of shares.

This tells us the proportion of the total shares that the former owners of the equity will hold after the new shares are issued (unless they commit additional resources to the corporation).

The same fraction, therefore, indicates the percentage of control, through voting power in stockholder meetings, which will remain with the group that had a certain fraction of these votes. For instance, suppose a management group controls a corporation by holding 60% of the 100,000 shares of common stock. If the corporation issues 20,000 more shares to new investors, the 60% interest becomes:

$$0.60 \left(\frac{100,000}{120,000} \right) = 0.50 \ .$$

This is barely enough to retain unquestionable control, and the controlling group may not wish to consent to any larger issue, no matter what the attractiveness of the opportunity in terms of its contribution to value.

Putting questions of control aside, despite their importance, and dealing solely with value, the existing shareholders will not find their value position protected unless some value-creating event results from the issue of the new shares which at least offsets the effects of the initial dilution. New stock should only be issued, to repeat the words of Chapter 21, "when the proportionate increase in the number of shares is at least the same as the proportionate increase in the value to be expected." To use the numbers just assumed, there must be a 20% increase in the total value of the equity if 20,000 shares are to be added to a 100,000 share base. This condition is theoretically necessary even if rights are issued to the existing shareholders. Since this important point is overlooked by many experts, we shall discuss it at length.

Privileged Subscriptions: Rights

The existing security holders represent a significant and identifiable potential market for further issues of securities; and a substantial percentage of new issues of common stock, and of bonds and preferred stocks convertible into common stock, is offered first to existing common stockholders. Some corporations have free choice in deciding whether or not to offer new common shares first to present stockholders, but in many companies the present common shareholders possess a legal right to receive *privileged subscriptions* to new issues of common stock. The legal right to privileged subscriptions is termed a *preemptive right*. Where it exists, corporations have no choice but to offer new issues of securities for cash pro rata to the security holders having the preemptive right.

What determines whether a particular security issue has this preemptive right? In most cases the status of the preemptive right is governed by specific provisions on the subject in the charter or bylaws of the corporation. If the status of the right is not clearly established in this way, the laws on the subject of the state of incorporation must be studied. In the absence of both charter and statutory definition of the preemptive right, reference must be made to the common law.

A number of states have enacted specific legislation in regard to the status of the preemptive right for corporations incorporated under their laws. Under the statutes of many of these states, corporations are empowered to write into their charters and bylaws clauses granting, limiting, or denying the preemptive right to any or all classes of their securities. In the absence of charter statements, certain broad rules are stated to apply. Some states, including Indiana, California, and Delaware, have enacted legislation providing that the preemptive right does *not* exist unless it is specifically called for in corporate charters. For example, the California law provides: "Unless otherwise provided in the articles [of incorporation] the board of directors may issue shares, option rights, or securities having conversion or option rights, without first offering the same to stockholders of any class or classes."[11]

Where the status of the preemptive right is not established clearly by state legislation or the terms of corporate charters or bylaws, the legal status of the preemptive right has been evolved from common-law decisions on the subject. The courts have recognized the fact that the issue of new stock may well mean dilution of the voting power, asset values, earning power, and market values of the holdings of existing stockholders and have concluded that the stockholders are entitled, in justice, to the protection against such a dilution of voting power and other interests afforded by the preemptive right. Consequently, the common-law decisions on the preemptive right have established the principle that a stockholder is entitled to the preemptive right in the absence of charter or statutory provisions to the contrary, with the following restrictions:

1. The preemptive right is restricted to common stockholders and applies only to common stocks or securities convertible into common stocks.
2. It does not apply to stock issued for property.
3. It does not apply to treasury stock or to stock originally authorized under the corporate charter and issued in a "reasonable time" after incorporation.

Whether conferred by law, corporate charter, or as a privilege extended at the discretion of management, the right to subscribe to new securities has important implications for income and potential capital gains. In many instances the right to subscribe to a given number of new securities is made at a price below the normal market price, and this means that those who hold the rights have a measurable advantage over those who do not.

It will be the primary purpose of this section to describe the effect of rights on the market price of the outstanding stock. The privilege of subscribing to new securities on favorable terms may be offered to any class of security for the purchase of the same or another class of security. The most common example, however, is a right extended to common shareholders for the purchase of additional shares of the same stock. We deal with this situation here.

We shall use as an example the National Aviation Corporation, which in 1956 offered its stockholders the privilege of subscribing to one new share for each four old shares held. In this case, one right was the privilege to subscribe to one-quarter share. In practice, while this right could be sold independently, it could only be exercised in conjunction with three other rights, to permit subscription to one share of the new issue.

If the stock is traded on an exchange, the exchange typically

---

[11] California Civil Code, Sec. 297.

designates a date after which the stock will be traded free of the rights, or *ex rights*. Until that date, trading is on a *cum-rights* basis (also termed *rights on* and *with rights*). When stock is sold cum rights, the seller of the stock agrees that the buyer is to receive, in addition to the shares of stock, any rights that have been or are being issued on that stock.

Referring again to the National Aviation Corporation illustration, stock rights to expire on May 22, 1956, were mailed to stockholders of record as of May 8, 1956. The stock was traded on the New York Stock Exchange cum rights through May 9, and thereafter on an ex-rights basis. During the ex-rights period the stock and the rights were traded separately with independent quotations.

But before we look at the period when the rights are traded, let us look at the likely behavior of the market price cum rights, after the announcement of the plan to undertake rights financing and before the ex-rights date. Suppose it were generally believed that the new money was to be used on projects which would not contribute proportionately to future earnings. We have shown that, under such conditions, the average value of all the shares will fall. In a perfect market this fall will take place in anticipation of the ex-rights date. Nothing in the rights procedure can overcome such a loss. *Thus, an implicit assumption of thinking about rights must be that the proposed expansion meets the criterion already stated.* If so, the price, cum rights, will hold steady. Specifically, we assume that the proposed use of funds by National Aviation was justified.

During that time that rights are effective, the ex-rights period, any person planning to invest in the stock of the company has alternative ways to acquire it. He may buy a share on the market at the current market price, or he may buy the proper number of rights and then subscribe at the subscription price. In the latter case his total cost is the price of the rights plus the subscription price.[12] It is clear that investors will not be attracted to the new issue unless the subscription price is less than the going market price of the outstanding stock. Consequently, the setting of the subscription price contains the problem of predicting likely market prices for the security during the life of the rights. Some companies attempt to set the subscription price close to the market in order to minimize dilution. Others price the new issue well below the market in order to provide maximum inducement for use of the rights and to protect against the possibility that downward pressure on market price during the offering period will render the rights valueless.

In practice, the question of dilution of market values arises in every case, because the subscription price for the new stock is at least somewhat lower than the recent market price for the existing issue. In fact, it will appear from the following discussion that the market value of a right represents (approximately but not fully) the amount of the dilution of

---

[12] We ignore brokerage.

the previous market values which is implicit in the new offering at favorable subscription prices.

Effect on Market Value of Issue of Stock at Less than Old Market Price. Perhaps the effect on market value can be pictured best by first examining the theoretical effect on market value of a *stock split;* for in a stock split the number of shares of stock is increased, but the net worth of the company does not change. From the standpoint of the stockholder, his total values remain the same; and in theory, he has gained or lost nothing as a result of the split.

For example, a 4-for-1 stock split is announced for a stock selling at 120. Since the corporation will acquire no new money as a result of the split, its stock will have gained or lost nothing in value. A total value of 120 is now represented by four shares. Hence, the new stock would be expected to sell at

$$\frac{120}{4} = 30 .$$

(Further reference to the stock split will be found in Chapter 26 on refunding and recapitalization.)

Now, let us return to the National Aviation illustration of the sale of new stock. Although the old stock was selling at about $41\frac{1}{4}$ cum rights, stockholders received rights to purchase at 30 one new share for each four shares held. What dilution of market value of the old shares results from the issue at 30? In answering, let us consider a stockholder who owns four old shares. Before the stock went ex rights, his four shares represented a value of 165 ($41\frac{1}{4}$ times 4). In exercising his rights to purchase one new share, he added an investment of 30 in cash, making a total investment of 195 now represented by five shares. One new share, then, could be expected to have a value of

$$\frac{195}{5} = 39 .$$

Actually, the first sale on the first day of trading ex rights was $39\frac{1}{8}$, and the market closed at 39.

A formula incorporating this reasoning is widely used as a rough measure of the theoretical effect of issuance of stock at less than the market on the ex-rights market price of the stock. In the formula the following notations are used:

M = Market value of one share cum rights .
N = Number of old shares that entitle the holder to purchase one new share .
P = Theoretical market value of one share ex rights .
S = Subscription price .

Using the above notations, the formula is:

$$P = \frac{MN + S}{N + 1} \text{ (Theoretical Market Price after Exercise of Rights) .}$$

Substituting the facts from the National Aviation illustration:

$$P = \frac{(41\frac{1}{4} \times 4) + 30}{4 + 1}$$

$$P = \frac{195}{5}$$

$$P = 39 .$$

Valuation of Stock Rights. If the stockholder does not care to exercise his right to purchase, at what price will he be able to sell the right in the market? Once the stock is selling ex rights, the calculation of the value of one right is relatively simple. The value of one right is the difference between the ex-rights market price of one share and the subscription price, divided by the number of rights necessary to purchase one share. In the National Aviation case the first market price on the first day of trading ex rights was $39\frac{1}{8}$. With four rights an investor could buy one share at an effective discount of $9\frac{1}{8}$, since the subscription price was 30. Hence, one right had a worth of about $2\frac{1}{4}$.

Expressed in a formula, this relation is:

$$\frac{P - S}{N} \text{ (Theoretical Market Value of One Right, Ex Rights)}$$

$$= \frac{39\frac{1}{8} - 30}{4}$$

$$= 2\frac{1}{4} .$$

Before the ex-rights date, when the stock is still selling cum rights, the value of one right can be predicted by use of the following formula:

$$\frac{M - S}{N + 1} \text{ (Theoretical Value of One Right, Cum Rights) .}$$

Using the National Aviation illustration again, with the cum-rights market price of $41\frac{1}{4}$:

$$\text{(Theoretical Value of One Right)} = \frac{41\frac{1}{4} - 30}{4 + 1}$$

$$= \frac{11\frac{1}{4}}{5}$$

$$= 2\frac{1}{4} .$$

It will now be apparent that the value of one right, in theory, will equal the anticipated dilution of market value of one old share. Hence, if brokerage fees and income tax questions involved in sale of the rights are ignored, the stockholder who sells his rights theoretically receives enough cash from the sale so as to sustain no net loss or gain in total market value of his holdings. From this point of view, a privileged subscription, if exercised or sold, prevents dilution of the market value of the total interests of the existing shareholders.

As a matter of interest, the following is the actual record of National Aviation Corporation common stock during the period (taken from the *Wall Street Journal*):

Date	Price of Common*		Price of Right
	Cum Rights	Ex Rights	
May 7, 1956	41⅜	...	...
May 8, 1956	41½	...	...
May 9, 1956	41¼	...	...
May 10, 1956	...	39	2⅛
May 11, 1956	...	38⅜	2¼
May 14, 1956	...	38⅜	2⅛
May 15, 1956	...	38¼	2
May 16, 1956	...	38⅜	2
May 17, 1956	...	38⅜	2⅛
May 18, 1956	...	38½	2⅛
May 21, 1956	...	38	2¼
May 22, 1956	...	38½	2⅛

* Closing prices only.

The discussion above was based on an issue of common stock. In valuing rights to subscribe to issues of straight preferred stock or bonds (an event much less frequent than in the case of common stock), the ex-rights formula given above, $\dfrac{P-S}{N}$, may be used in all instances, since dilution is not involved. If a valuation of the rights to buy preferred stock or bonds in advance of the establishment of a market price for the issue is desired, a probable market price, P in the formula, must be assumed.

Rights offerings are generally made with the presumption that a large proportion of the new shares will be subscribed for: 90% subscription is regarded by many financial analysts as the lower limit of a "successful" rights sale. Under such circumstances, the issuing company can either withhold the few unsubscribed shares from the market or sell them to the general public. In order to increase the chances that a large part of the issue will be taken up by stockholders, a number of companies offer *oversubscription* privileges, sometimes known as *the second bite*. Under this arrangement, stockholders are allowed not only to subscribe to the new issue on a pro rata basis but also to oversubscribe any shares not bought on the initial subscription.

The use of rights in connection with new issues gives an existing shareholder two types of protection. He may preserve his proportionate control, but only by buying the shares offered to him. He may overcome the effect of the discount that is used to assist in the sale of the new shares, either by subscribing to the new shares or by selling rights. But there is *no way for him to overcome the loss created by expansions which do not create new value in proportion to the increase in the number of shares.*

Before leaving the subject of rights, we call the reader's attention to the widespread use of executive stock options which grant executives, and sometimes other employees, the right to purchase a specified number of the company's common shares at a fixed price within a certain time period. This practice must be considered not as an aspect of the bargain for funds but rather as an aspect of the bargain for executives. Nevertheless, from a strictly financial viewpoint the effect on the common shareholders is the same as if the right to buy common stock had been extended to another group of security holders. It has been estimated that as of 1957, well over 50% of the companies with common stock listed on the New York Stock Exchange offered a plan of this sort to their employees. The average amount of stock set aside for this purpose was approximately 5% of the shares outstanding prior to the offering.

Of course, the attractiveness of such plans depends on a rising market price, and it is not surprising that some of the enthusiasm wears off in periods of recession. This was evident in the period of declining profits and uncertain market prices of stock during 1960 and extending into 1961.

Stock Purchase Warrants

Earlier in the chapter we mentioned the function of *stock purchase warrants* as a device for providing potential capital gains to holders of senior securities. Warrants, which threaten the common shareholder with the same sort of dilution that any type of new issue does, need not be issued only to purchasers of bonds. They can serve other purposes, but of course should be used only after careful exploration has indicated they provide the best way for protecting the common shareholder's position. For example, warrants are sometimes issued to individuals in return for their services to the company. Lawyers, underwriters, and promoters may be granted warrants as part of the remuneration for their efforts to found a company or to secure new capital for it. Executive stock options are a form of warrant. In one instance, a corporation has sold warrants directly to the public. In 1964 Mid-America Pipeline Company offered warrants at 9 cents each to its common shareholders on the basis of one warrant for each six common shares held. Each warrant entitled the holder to purchase a share of Mid-America common stock at $9 through March 31, 1972.[13]

---

[13] *Moody's Transportation Manual, 1965,* p. 1038.

Modification of the Distribution of Control

In Chapter 18 the normal distribution of control among the basic security types was discussed. It was brought out that normally, voting power rests in the hands of the common shareholders alone, although certain contingent voting privileges may be reserved for the preferred shareholders in event of suspension of dividend payments.

In a few cases the preferred stock does have a share of the voting power at regular shareholders' meetings. The extent varies from one issue to another. The holders of Sperry Rand Corporation $4.50 cumulative preferred have full voting rights of one vote per share along with the common. The holders of Mead Johnson & Company 4% cumulative preferred are entitled to one vote per share, to use these votes cumulatively in voting for directors, and on some issues, to vote as a group. Under certain circumstances, the voting power of the preferred shareholders could be a major consideration in the minds of the common shareholders and hence an important issue in setting the terms of the preferred.

It has been mentioned previously that some companies have subdivided their common stock into two classes. Usually, the primary purpose of this is to reserve the voting power for one class and use the other class as a means of raising capital from the investing public. Obviously, such nonvoting stock can be sold only to shareholders who are first and foremost investors and therefore attach only secondary importance to the voting privilege. It is a significant fact that nonvoting common stock is not accepted for listing by the New York Stock Exchange.

Although bondholders and most preferred stockholders do not have a direct voice in management, they nevertheless influence the actions of management by means of positive or negative covenants in the bond indenture or in charter provisions relating to preferred stock (described in the previous chapter). Further, if the issue is in default and/or the company in bankruptcy, these investors or their representatives will have a strong influence on management decisions, and this influence may be perpetuated in a reorganization under which old securities are exchanged for new securities with voting power. The full implications of reorganization will be taken up in a later chapter.

Summary

In this and the preceding chapter we have developed the idea of the security form as a product of the bargaining process between the corporate user of funds and those individuals and institutions which supply the funds. It has been seen how certain security features are to the advantage of the issuing company and its common shareholders and that other features are to the advantage of the senior security holder. The resultant security is basically a compromise of objectives which is acceptable to both parties to the contract. We have stressed that the fundamental give-and-take of this process is not really between management as such and a group of security holders but rather between one group of security holders and another—between the common shareholders, on the one hand, and the senior security holders, on the other.

Because of the wide variation of circumstances and objectives, it is not surprising that this bargaining process has produced a complex of special security types. We have reviewed the major variations in general use; but as we stated at the beginning, this is by no means a catalog of all possible types. The reader is referred to the appendix of the first edition of Graham and Dodd's *Security Analysis* for a list of illustrations of unusual variations of the common security forms.[14] This list includes such securities as bonds payable at the option of the bondholder, noninterest-bearing bonds, preferred issues with little or no claim as to assets, preferred stock with a mortgage lien, and common stock with a claim to income senior to another issue. The perusal of such a list brings home the importance of judging a security not by the name which the company has applied to it but rather by the specific terms which determine its true nature.

---

[14] B. Graham, and D. L. Dodd, *Security Analysis* (1st ed.; New York: McGraw-Hill Book Co., 1934), Appendix, Note 3, pp. 618–35.

Chapter 26

Refinancing

Definitions

IN CONSIDERING the management of long-term finance, it is natural that
our attention should have been concentrated on the issuance of securities
for the purpose of acquiring new capital. This is a primary concern of
both new and growing businesses. In prosperous times the purpose of
raising new money is the dominant one in corporate security offerings, as
is shown by Table 26-1.[1]

However, as the table indicates, there are other reasons why corporations issue securities. For the more mature business, there is likely to
come a time when new securities will be issued not to add to the funds
invested but rather to replace some portion of the existing investment.
When a new issue of securities is sold to a new group of security holders
and the proceeds are applied to the retirement of an existing issue of
securities, the company is said to be engaged in *refinancing*. The most
common form of refinancing is the sale of a new bond issue to replace an
existing bond issue, and this is known as *refunding* the debt. The similar
process of retiring a preferred stock with the proceeds of a borrowing is
known as *funding*. There are also those situations where a group of
existing security holders accepts a new issue in voluntary exchange for
the issue it now holds. This process of modifying the capital structure is
referred to as *recapitalization*.

In our discussion in this chapter, these distinctions will be preserved,
although in practice, new financing, refinancing, refunding, and recapitalization may be linked together in some degree in one operation. For
example, a new issue of securities may be in part new money and in part
refinancing. Similarly, the refunding of a bond at maturity may be
accomplished in large measure by the existing bondholders taking new
bonds in exchange for the old, thus coming under the definition of
recapitalization. However, the problems associated with each of these

---

[1] Securities and Exchange Commission, *Thirtieth Annual Report* (1964), p. 174; and
Statistical Bulletin, November, 1965, p. 14.

526

TABLE 26–1

PROPOSED USES OF ESTIMATED NET PROCEEDS FROM
OFFERINGS OF CORPORATE SECURITIES
(In Millions)

	1961	1962	1963	1964
Total net proceeds........	$12,885	$10,501	$12,081	$13,792
New money..............	10,715	8,240	8,993	11,233
Plant equipment........	7,413	5,652	5,405	7,003
Working capital........	3,303	2,588	3,588	4,230
Retirement of securities...	868	754	1,528	754
Other purposes..........	1,302	1,507	1,561	1,805

types of capital structure changes are sufficiently different to warrant separate treatment.

Refunding Bonds at Maturity

The reader is now well aware that a corporate bond involves the contractual obligation to repay the face value of the bond in cash at a fixed maturity date. The setting of the life period of a bond is determined more by convention than by the issuer's long-range plans. At the time of issue the conditions and needs 15 or 20 years hence cannot be foreseen with any degree of accuracy. Thus, it will normally be mere coincidence if the maturity date coincides with a time when disinvestment or a change in the debt-equity balance is desired. On the contrary, it will frequently be true that a business finds it continues to need the funds supplied by the bondholders and is confident that the existing debt-equity balance is one that can and should be preserved.

Under these circumstances, the company will desire to refund the old issue. The normal procedure is to create a new issue of bonds approximately equal in amount to the maturing issue. It may be sold generally or offered to the present bondholders in exchange for the maturing bonds. Bondholders are, of course, entitled to receive cash and will be paid in cash if they so desire. On the other hand, it is likely that if they have been satisfied with the bonds of this company up to the present, they too will be interested in continuing the investment. Provided the new bonds are offered on terms which are attractive to the investors, a large percentage of them are likely to take advantage of the exchange. The balance can then be paid off in cash provided by the sale of the unexchanged refunding bonds.

It is almost certain that the refunding bonds will not contain precisely the same terms as the bonds they are replacing. Both the company and the investment market will have changed significantly between time of issue and time of maturity. Whether the net result will run toward more favorable terms for the issuer or for the bondholder depends on the individual circumstances. Normally, it is to be expected that the financial condition of a successful and profitable business would improve over a period of 15 or 20 years to the point where the company's bargaining position in the market would be reflected in an upgrading of its bonds. Thus, it might be expected that the new bonds could be offered at a lower interest rate or with other terms more favorable to the issuer. On the other hand, the company must reckon with the general market trends and with the general demand for and supply of investable funds at the time of maturity. It may well be that a weakness in the market at that time could more than offset any improvement in the company's financial position and risk status. Such is certainly the case at the time of writing (winter, 1965–66) when long-term rates are reaching high levels (Chart 21–1).

It would appear that the occurrence of a maturity is an event which involves considerable uncertainty for the issuing company and, at the same time, one in which the outcome is largely outside the discretion of management. It is quite conceivable that a large bond issue could come due in a very soft bond market, which would make it very difficult to refund except, perhaps, on unfortunate terms. It would also appear that there is little management could do about this, in view of the fact that it cannot influence the timing of refunding or the market conditions.

In practice, both the hazard and the limitation of management discretion may be considerably reduced. In various ways the amount of the debt may be substantially diminished by the time of ultimate maturity. As previously mentioned, many bond issues today carry sinking fund provisions which make retirement of a substantial portion of the debt prior to maturity mandatory. Further, there is nothing to prevent a company from acquiring its own bonds on the open market at any time before maturity, with or without a sinking fund provision, thus reducing the outstanding obligation.

Refunding after Call

We have noted that a call, or redemption, privilege is one that is included in the terms of most of the corporate bonds and preferred stocks issued in the United States. The existence of this feature enables management to choose its own time to retire an issue and thus to take advantage of favorable conditions to revise its bargains with investors by replacing the called security by a refunding issue. The call feature adds great flexibility to managerial discretion, since a bond may be retired before maturity, and a preferred stock, which has no maturity, may also be retired. Thus, a management may consider a refunding at any time it feels that the terms of financing can be significantly improved.

Although it is sometimes decided to retire an issue to stop the effect of some burdensome protective provision, the most significant incentive to refunding is to gain a lower cost of funds for the issuer. Apart from changes within the firm which might change favorably the quality rating of its bonds and preferred stocks, shifts in the structure of interest rates sometimes make refunding very attractive. In the late 1940's there was such a period, but there has been little opportunity since so far as bonds are concerned.

During the summer of 1965 the officers of the General Telephone Company of California, who were considering the issue of bonds for a number of purposes, decided to raise $16.5 million more by borrowing in order to call and retire the 750,000 shares of outstanding $5\frac{1}{2}\%$ cumulative preferred stock. The redemption price was, at the time, $22 on shares with $20 par value. This call was made, effective August 31, and the stock was retired.

It happened that, after the call had been announced (and therefore could not be rescinded), conditions in the bond market seemed unfavorable, and the company chose to borrow temporarily from banks. On December 8, the funding was accomplished by the successful issue of $40.0 million of 5% first-mortgage bonds due December 1, 1995. The prospectus accompanying the issue stated that $16.5 million of the proceeds was to be used to repay the bank loans referred to above.

Despite this passage of time, which serves as an example of the problems of timing that are sometimes encountered when one attempts to raise funds, we have an example of a recent funding. The interest cost of the new issue, calculated from the price paid by the banking syndicate to the telephone company, is 5.02%. The cost of the retired preferred, based on the redemption price of $22, is 5%.[2] But bond interest is tax deductible while preferred dividends are not. With taxes at 48% taken into account, we have the following comparison, which shows a significant saving.

	Before Tax	After Tax
Preferred, $5\frac{1}{2}\%$ @ 22............... .9.65%		5.00%
Bonds, 5's @ 99.7097.................5.02		2.61

The comparison can also be made in terms of outflow of funds. The 750,000 shares of preferred stock required the payment of dividends amounting to $825,000. To raise $16.5 million by bonds priced at 99.7097 requires a par value of $16,548,039, on which 5% interest is $827,402. The tax shield on this interest is $827,402 × 0.48 = $397,153. So the after-tax cost of the bond interest is $827,401 − $397,132 = $430,249.

In the language of capital budgeting, the "net funds inflow" of this refunding is $825,000 − $430,249 = $394,751 per year. We may ignore the funds flows related to the sinking fund on the new bonds, because for purposes of comparison with a preferred that had no sinking fund, we should assume that any bonds retired would be replaced by new borrowing at the same rate.

[2] The fact that the stock was sold in 1957 at a cost of 5.77% is of no significance in 1965.

One is tempted to calculate a rate of return on the investment, because apparently there has been an investment of the call premium that the preferred stock required, $1.5 million. But such a calculation is misleading. The fact is that the telephone company has increased its debt capacity by the funding, despite the apparent increase in its obligations. It has the same assets as before, and it has less to pay for the financing that provides them. Our thesis is that what we have named "burden" is the significant measure of the obligation of a bond or preferred stock, not the

TABLE 26–2

Comparison of Funds Flows, 1965–66
5½% Preferred vs. 5.02% Bonds

Time	Event	Preferred	Preferred Present Value @ 2.61%	Bonds	Bond Present Value @ 2.61%
1–30....Dividend on preferred		$ 825,000	$17,019,750	...	...
1–30....Interest on bonds		...	...	$ 430,249	$ 8,876,037
30....Call in 1995		16,500,000	7,623,000	...	...
30....Maturity of bonds		...	...	16,548,039	7,645,194
			$24,714,750		$16,521,231

book values on the balance sheet. The burden has been reduced and that is the important fact. The total sum paid out over the life of the bonds and at their maturity is less than would have been required by preferred stock over the same period plus a call of the preferred in the year 1995. In detail, the comparison appears in the Table 26–2, which shows the actual dollar amounts and their time adjusted equivalents at 2.61%, the after-tax cost of the borrowing (following the method described on page 468). What these figures tell us is that the company can carry the obligation for 30 years and then retire it with a present commitment which is $8.2 million less if the bonds are used.

We may emphasize the point of recent paragraphs by saying that a successful refunding operation should never be regarded as competing with a project to acquire new assets. The success of the refunding makes it easier to finance the desired assets, because the total financial burden of the company is made lower. Any call premium (and other expenses of the refunding operation) is not to be regarded as an investment at the time, but rather an increase in the ultimate repayment at maturity.

Recapitalization

The term *recapitalization* normally refers to the voluntary exchange of one security for another. While the term is broad enough to cover a variety of different exchange combinations, certain forms of recapitalization have been more common than others, and these will be given special attention in this section. The use of the adjective *voluntary* is designed to exclude from the discussion those exchanges which take place under conditions of bankruptcy and receivership where the choice on the part of the existing security holders can hardly be described as free. Such exchanges of securities will be discussed in Chapter 30, which deals with this subject. Also excluded here are those exchanges of the securities of one company for another which are covered in the chapter on mergers and acquisition, Chapter 29.

Unless a specific procedure for change has been agreed upon and made a part of a legal contract, its terms are binding during its life. Therefore, for a corporate issuer to attempt to modify the terms of an issue or to make a substitution of a new security without the consent of the holder would not only be without legal foundation but would also justify a legal action for enforcement of the original contract and recovery of damages, if any. But in practice the need for change has been foreseen. For example, most of the existing preferred stock contracts provide for change, if approved by a large majority (frequently two thirds) of the shares. Modern bond indentures also make provision for change, if approved by a similarly large majority in amount of the issue. Such privileges are, however, almost never extended to the basic conditions of the issue, such as the rate of interest, the maturity date, the priority of claim over other creditors, the call premium, etc. Nevertheless, especially since many new bond issues are issued in registered form so that the issuer knows who the holders are, and can reach them, it can no longer be said absolutely that the terms of senior securities are unalterable without unanimous consent.

Since common stock is the voting stock, it is normally considered that the power to elect the board of directors is sufficient protection of the best interest of this stockholder group. The one specific right which may be attached is the preemptive right, which is intended to protect the individual shareholder against dilution of the voting privilege and of the value of his investment (see page 517).

The need to obtain the necessary consent in recapitalization presents a phase of the problem which was absent in the cases of refinancing previously discussed. Through maturity or by exercising the call provision, the company legally discharged its obligation to the old security holders and replaced them with a new group of security holders who were prepared to accept the terms of the new issue. In such cases there was no need to consult the holders of the redeemed securities. In other cases where the privilege to change with the consent of a specified majority has not been provided, there is a question of what becomes of the stockholder who refuses to go along with the proposal. As a general rule, those who do not consent remain with their previous holding. Many corporate balance sheets show small amounts of such issues. But the corporation law of many states now provides the alternative that such dissenting stock-holders must be paid off in cash at a price to be set by independent appraisal or arbitration. Since there is no quick answer to the problem of valuation, the value which will finally be set as a basis for compensation is difficult to estimate in advance.

In order to keep recapitalization in perspective, it should be borne in mind that the typical industrial corporation has a relatively simple capital structure made up of some combination of bonds, preferred stocks, and common stocks, and that if this structure is changed at all by recapitalization during the life of the corporation, it is only at infrequent intervals and under unusual circumstances.

In August, 1965, the United States Steel Corporation announced that a special meeting of shareholders would be held November 24 to obtain approval, among other proposals, of a plan to create a new issue of subordinated debentures to be offered to the holders of the existing 7% preferred stock. Concerning the details of the new issue, the chairman of the board of the corporation said only that they would be priced "some-what in excess" of the current market value (about $152 per share).

The 7% preferred stock of the United States Steel Corporation was one of the last of a group of "noncallable" preferred stocks that had been created by corporations in the early years of this century when the non-callable feature had been considered necessary to attract investors. In view of this protection against call, the high 7% rate, and the financial standing of the issuer, the stock sold well over par, and the yield fol-lowed that of the less highly rated industrial bonds. At 150, for example, the yield was $4\frac{2}{3}\%$.

Over the years, often attracted by the fact that preferred dividends are not allowed as expenses for tax purposes, most of the noncallable pre-ferreds had been retired, or reduced to small amounts, by exchange offers and other devices. Now the United States Steel Corporation made its move by requesting the shareholders to approve a recapitalization.

On September 29 the exact terms of the exchange were made public. Each $100 par value share of the 7% preferred could be exchanged for $175 par value of $4\frac{5}{8}\%$ subordinated debentures of 1966, with no call permitted for 10 years and then callable at a small premium. The preferred holder might well expect that the market price of his holding of the new bonds would be greater than recent levels of the preferred, and his new income would rise to $8.09\frac{3}{8}$ per year. It was, however, expected that the transaction would be taxable as a capital gain, measured between the market price of the new bonds and each preferred shareholder's cost.

The United States Steel Corporation received a large favorable vote at its meeting in November, and it proceeded to make the exchange offer as described. "When issued" trading opened in the new bonds as soon as the vote was taken. Thus the preferred holders were given more definite information about the terms. The opening quotations of the bonds were 95½, and the preferred stock, of course, traded at 167⅛. Only one stockholder gave notice of dissent to this refinancing and he did not pursue his claim.

It is perhaps worth nothing that, while most of the opinions the authors heard "on the Street" were to the effect that the move was a constructive one for the corporation because it would create new tax shields, there were a few "old-timers" who grumbled because the debt ratio of the United States Steel Corporation was almost doubled, and the fixed charge coverage fell from about 7 times to about 4 times. There was also a substantial reduction in the corporate surplus, due to the creation of $175 in debt for each $100 of stock.

We present here the history of two recent recapitalizations within the same company.

On January 30, 1964, Litton Industries, Inc., offered to its common shareholders a share-for-share exchange of the common stock into a new $3 dividend cumulative preference stock (par $5 per share, involuntary redemption price after 1972, $100). The preferred stock was convertible at the option of the holder into one share of common stock, and this privilege was protected against dilution. Only 428,141 preferred shares of a larger authorization were offered for exchange. Convertible preferred stocks are coming into fashion as a means of accomplishing acquisitions (page 511). In such negotiations it is desirable to know the likely market value of what is being offered, so it is not surprising that Litton stated as its purpose for offering the new shares in exchange for common: "to create an ascertainable market value for the preferred and a ready market therefor."[3] It is also not surprising, in view of the intended use of the unissued portion of the preferred stock, that it was provided that shares reacquired in any manner, including those surrendered for conversion, may be reissued.

The offer was a great success, as about 7.6 million common shares out of 10.7 million were tendered for the exchange. The actual issue was distributed in proportion to all those tendering, each holder receiving about 4% of the number of shares he requested.

During the year 1964, among other acquisitions, Litton Industries acquired the Fitchburg Paper Company by issuing Litton common and preferred stock, and the Royal McBee Corporation by issuing Litton preferred in return for Royal McBee common stock. Negotiations to acquire the Streater Corporation in return for cash and Litton preferred were reported.[4] So the new preferred proved very useful.

---

[3] *New York Stock Exchange Listing Statement*, No. A 21504 (January 14, 1964).

[4] *Wall Street Journal*, April 3, June 12, September 9, 1964.

It is of interest to note that, at the shareholders' meeting of December 4, 1965, a new preferred with many novel features was approved.[5] It will be offered for exchange to existing common shareholders on a share-for-share basis, and to the holders of the cumulative preference stock on a 3-for-1 basis. The new preferred is a unique security. It is nondividend paying but redeemable on a schedule which guarantees a 3% compound interest rate of growth over the initial value. It is convertible into common stock, with the ratio of conversion rising at the rate of 3.09% compounded annually. At the time of writing, the success of this new exchange offer cannot be recorded, but clearly a strange new stock is on its way to the market.[6]

Recapitalization and the Bargain for Funds. We have now seen that there are a number of ways in which a business corporation may modify its capital structure from time to time. The usual methods by which this comes about and the immediate and potential benefits have been illustrated. It is clear that the basic objective of refinancing and recapitalization is to improve the position of the company and (usually) its common shareholders through a modification of the terms of the existing security forms.

Properly considered, these activities on the part of the issuing company are a continuation and extension of the bargaining process we discussed in the preceding two chapters. Such changes usually would not be initiated by the company unless an advantage, through a change in the market and/or the bargaining strength of the company, was anticipated. On the other hand, it must also be true that if there is to be a change at all, it must be generally acceptable to the other security holders and realistic in terms of existing market conditions.

Stock Splits

A stock split is a type of recapitalization designed to increase the number of shares outstanding. There is also a reverse split, in which the number of shares outstanding is reduced. In a stock split the shareholders receive more shares of the same class of stock (for example, $1\frac{1}{2}$ to 1, or 2 to 1) for each old share previously held. Thus, the number of certificates of ownership outstanding is increased by a multiple without any change taking place in the total value of the investor's holding. It will be apparent, however, that the one thing that is affected is the value of one share. Since no new funds have been added and nothing has happened to the basic determinants of the value of the business as a result of this exchange of paper, reason would suggest that the value of one share after a stock split will be that fraction of the value before the split which is the inverse of the increase in the number of shares. If it is a 3-for-1 split, for

---

[5] The reader must not confuse this approval, which authorized the issue, with the exchange offer. They are separate matters.

[6] *Ibid.* December 5, 1965.

example, three new shares for one old, then the value of the new shares would be one third the value of the old shares, so that the total valuation "per stockholder" of the stock after the split is exactly equal to the total valuation before the split. It should be noted that when a company splits its stock, it is usual to make a parallel downward adjustment in the per share dividend, so that the total payment is the same as before.

The reason usually advanced for a stock split (or stock "split-up") is that of providing a broader and more stable market for the stock. It is argued that a larger volume of lower-priced securities should make for a more continuous market and therefore one which is less subject to erratic fluctuations. Officials of the New York Stock Exchange have estimated that the most satisfactory price to induce active trading is between $18 and $25 per share.[7]

The pressure for a stock split is usually found in a company which has demonstrated consistent profitability over a number of years. As a result of this, the market price of the stock has appreciated considerably. There may be a feeling that the price of the stock has moved out of the price range of many investors and that this is detrimental to the future growth of the stock. In fact, it is often seen that the number of shareholders increases after a split.

Although it is not always explicitly stated, there is often the additional hope that the market reaction to the split will be irrational to the extent of giving the three new shares a combined market value in excess of one old share. As a result, some capital appreciation will have been realized by the holders of the old shares. The one valid reason for expecting such a result holds if the old stock has been somewhat undervalued in a market which is "narrower" because of its relatively high price. This line of reasoning would argue that the split restores the stock to the full impact of market demand and thus to "proper" valuation.

Whether or not stock splits actually increase the overall market valuation is a hotly debated issue. This would seem to be a debate easily resolved by reference to the facts of market price. However, the problem is one of isolating the effects of the split from the many factors which can have a cause-and-effect relationship with market price. Those who see a capital gain advantage can point to cases where a higher overall valuation obtained after the split; but to prove the precise cause is difficult, if not impossible. Those who oppose the stock split claim that if there is any benefit at all, it is only a temporary one resulting from speculative activity.

The problem may be illustrated by the case of the American Telephone and Telegraph Company. Between 1936 and 1959 the common stock of A.T.&T. did not sell below $100, and there was a steady upward trend, which brought the price to the 224–65 range in early 1959. In recent

---

[7] N.Y.S.E. *Company Manual*, § A 15.

years there had been strong pressure on management to split the stock, pressure which management resisted. This activity culminated in a vote on the issue in 1957, at which time the split was rejected by a substantial majority. At the annual meeting of the previous year, 1956, the president of the company commented on the stock split proposal, in part, as follows:

> When there is an announcement of a stock split, the price of stock goes up, there isn't any question about that at all. You will get a flurry in the stock market and a rise in the price of the stock. But if there is no substantial dividend increase . . . at the time of the stock split, or shortly thereafter, that stock goes down in the market. And in almost every case it goes down below where it was before. . . . So I think if the telephone company were to split without a dividend increase, you would see our price go up on the market temporarily. That would benefit some people who bought our stock on a short-term basis. It would not benefit you people that want to keep your stock on a permanent investment.[8]

In 1959, however, the management split the stock 3 for 1, and at the same time increased the cash dividend. The following explanation of the change was given by the president at the annual meeting in 1959:

> Conditions have changed from two years ago. The Company has consistently opposed a stock split with no dividend increase, and at the time referred to an increase could not be justified. Recently our growth in share owners has slowed down—it is important to encourage more people to invest in the business—an increased dividend is needed to maintain investors' confidence—and the Company's improved financial situation permits us to pay it. . . .[9]

Previous to the 1959 split, the dividend had been $9 per share, unchanged since 1922. The dividend rate at the time of the split was established at $3.30 per share. It was made $3.50 in 1962 and $3.60 in 1964. In that year the stock was again split, 2 for 1, and the dividend rate of $2 per share was established. The reader is asked to calculate what is a proper adjustment to make to compare the present rate of $2 per share with the old $9 rate.

Stock Dividends

An alternative to the stock split as a means of increasing the number of shares outstanding is the stock dividend. For example, the number of shares in a company could be doubled without an increase in the funds invested in one of two ways: (1) by splitting the company's Capital Stock so as to have twice as many shares representing the same total nominal or

---

[8] American Telephone and Telegraph Company, *Report of the Annual Meeting of Share Owners, April 18, 1956,* pp. 7–8.

[9] American Telephone and Telegraph Company, *Report of the Annual Meeting of Share Owners, April 15, 1959,* p. 12.

par value as shown on the balance sheet; or (2) by declaring a 100%
dividend in stock, issuing each shareholder one new share for each share
now held and transferring from the Earned Surplus account to the
Capital Stock account an amount equal to what is now in that account.

The difference in accounting procedure may be illustrated. Suppose a
company to have the following net worth:

Capital stock:
    Common, $10 par, 100,000 shares...............$1,000,000
Earned surplus................................. 3,000,000
                                               $4,000,000

After a 2-for-1 split, this would appear as follows:

Capital stock:
    Common $5 par, 200,000 shares................$1,000,000
Earned surplus................................. 3,000,000
                                               $4,000,000

After a 100% stock dividend the net worth would show as follows (using
par value as a basis for the transfer):[10]

Capital stock:
    Common $10 par, 200,000 shares...............$2,000,000
Earned surplus................................. 2,000,000
                                               $4,000,000

While the accounting procedure is different and the balance sheet will
appear differently in each case, the net effect is the same, namely, to
double the number of shares by a paper transaction with no increase in
funds invested or in earning capacity as a result of these changes. Thus, a
stock dividend can be a means of bringing about this type of recapitalization without the trouble of arranging for the exchange of stock, provided,
of course, that the authorized capital stock permits and earned surplus is
large enough to cover the transfer.

Since it has been argued in terms of logic that a stock split should
bring a reduction in per share market value which is exactly the inverse
of the increase in the number of shares, so it would appear to follow that
a stock dividend will bring a similar lowering of market price. If all that
has happened as a result of the dividend is that the shareholders hold
twice as many certificates as before, each certificate should be worth one
half of what it was worth before the dividend with no net increase in the
total market valuation of the company. An important distinction must be
made, however, between the large-scale stock dividend, illustrated above,

[10] The New York Stock Exchange requires that the transfer be at "fair value" instead
of par value. N.Y.S.E. *Company Manual* § A 13. Such a transfer is also the recommendation of the Accounting Practices Board. American Institute of Certified Public Accountants,
Accounting Research and Technology Bulletins (Final Edition, 1961), p. 51.

which is basically a stock split in a different form, and the small-scale stock dividend which is in the range of 1%, 2%, or 5% of the outstanding stock.

Stock dividends on a modest scale have become quite popular with management in recent years. In some companies such dividends have been issued as a supplement to cash dividends on a regular basis over a period of several years. The argument usually advanced for such stock dividends is that in this way, management is recognizing the shareholders' additional contributions through retained earnings in a tangible form which can be either retained or sold, as the individual shareholder chooses. The inference is that the declaration of the stock dividend has, in and of itself, added something to the value of the shareholder's existing investment. Thus, if he sells the stock received as a dividend, the remaining investment will be as valuable as it was before the stock dividend.

The facts of the situation run contrary to this argument. If any value has been added, it is the result of the earnings which have been realized and retained, and this will be reflected on the balance sheet and in the market price of the existing shares without any assistance from the formalities of a stock dividend. Rationally, the effect of a small stock dividend should be the same as that of a large one—simply to spread existing values over a larger number of shares, thus leaving each shareholder exactly as he was before, with the exception that he has certificates for more shares of stock. If he sells the shares received as a "dividend," he is in fact liquidating a portion of his investment. This is not "income" but rather a conversion of principal into cash.

Having recognized this basic point, we can now proceed to note how a stock dividend may have some real meaning and value to the shareholder. It will be recalled in the reference to A.T.&T. that the president qualified his criticism of a proposed stock split in saying "if there is no substantial [cash] dividend increase." In the case of a stock split or large stock dividend, it would be an unusual company which could maintain the per share cash dividend paid before the split or stock dividend. However, in the case of a small stock dividend of, say, 2% or 5% of the outstanding issue, it is quite possible that the company could maintain the existing per share cash dividend, thus increasing the dollar dividend pay-out in the period following the stock dividend payment.

Thus, if a person held 100 shares and was receiving a $2 per share cash dividend, a 5% stock dividend would give him 105 shares and a total cash dividend in the following year of $210 rather than $200. A number of companies which have a stable cash dividend policy declare periodic small-scale stock dividends with this in mind. The stock dividend becomes, in effect, a promise of increased cash dividends in succeeding years. Of course, the same result could be obtained by raising the cash dividend on the old number of shares.

In view of our suggestion in Chapter 21 that dividends may play an important part in a shareholder's appraisal of the value of his shares, the small periodic stock dividend may have real future value in the eyes of the shareholder; and this, coupled with the conflicting evidence regarding the reaction of the market price, gives the stock dividend considerable appeal among shareholders. In addition, for management, there is a possible advantage in a lower market price and a wider and more stable market for the stock.

Conversion as a Means of Recapitalization

Significant changes in the capital structure can be effected by the exercise of the conversion privilege attached to bonds or preferred stock. However, unlike the forms of recapitalization already mentioned, conversion is not initiated by management at a time of its own choosing but rather is negotiated when the security was first issued and is at the discretion of the security holder, if and when he finds reason to do it. These forms are similar in that they involve a voluntary exchange of securities and bring about the replacement of one type of security by another of distinctly different form. The factors involved in conversion have already been discussed in Chapter 25.

While it is true that management cannot "make" a favorable market price or decide for the shareholder whether he wants to be in a preferred position or a common equity position, it can nevertheless have a great deal to do with the timing of conversion. By having a call provision in the terms of the convertible security, management is in a position to precipitate a mass conversion at an early date, by calling the security at a time when the market price is above the call price. Of course, a company's managers cannot guarantee a rising market price of the common stock. Nevertheless, many issues of convertible securities are sold by companies which have a definite plan for forcing conversion at the earliest favorable opportunity.

The Repurchase of Outstanding Common Shares

In this final section of the chapter on refinancing we shall turn to a process that does alter the proportions of an existing capital structure, but by reducing the amount of the outstanding equity interest instead of by rearranging security contracts.

The corporation laws in the United States permit corporations to buy their own outstanding shares, and the rules of the national stock exchanges and of the Securities and Exchange Commission only require that corporations make public the number of shares they have purchased after the purchase has taken place. Many firms have availed themselves of this privilege, though most of them have advised their shareholders of their intention in advance of the purchasing.

The privilege to repurchase shares has long been used to buy small amounts of outstanding shares, for example to supply shares for stock options being exercised or, in the case of a closely held company, to assist a stockholder who desires to liquidate his interest.[11] In recent years, however, the amount of repurchasing by major corporations has made this activity one of great importance. For example, such companies as General Motors, General Electric, and the Standard Oil Company (New Jersey) have themselves accounted for over 14% of the annual volume of trading in their securities, and over 125 of the companies listed on the New York Stock Exchange have purchased over 5% of their volume. It has been estimated that, since 1962, the money spent for such purchases (over a billion dollars a year) has exceeded the net amount of cash funds raised by new common stock issues to the public in the same years.)[12] Here is a phenomenon worthy of far more attention than it has yet received in the legislative and academic worlds.

Most of the countries around the world have prohibited the retirement of corporate capital without a finding by some tribunal that the proposed retirement does not (1) damage creditors by unduly reducing the equity base, (2) represent an attempt to avoid the taxation that would fall on a dividend distribution, and (3) represent an attempt by "inside" interests to buy out other shareholders who are not fully informed of the firm's prospects. These are the three principal dangers that must be avoided in the United States by other means than a governmental review, if the practice is to be endorsed. To quote Guthart:

At the present time, the SEC has no specific requirements concerning share repurchases, and the body of corporate law concerning this particular activity is not clear regarding the potential conflict of interest that may exist. Conclusive definitions of responsibility in this area are urgently needed.[13]

In this brief presentation we shall concentrate on the questions that arise from the point of view of the company's shareholders. What does repurchase mean to the "typical" shareholder who must rely only on the information that will be made public? Our first point here is the assumption that the repurchases are decided upon by the managers because they believe that the repurchasing will benefit the firm. If so, it seems reasonable to suggest that the persons who decide for the action expect that the value of the shares which will remain outstanding will increase, relative to the value at which the purchased shares are obtained. Whether the expectation will prove correct, of course, is a very important

---

[11] In one of the developing countries, Ghana, the new corporate law specifically provides power to repurchase shares in order to encourage the spread of stock ownership that would otherwise be limited by the fear of being unable to liquidate the holding.

[12] The information in this section is drawn from an unpublished thesis of Leo A. Guthart, and his article "More Companies Are Buying Back Their Stock," *Harvard Business Review*, Vol. XLIII No. 2 (March–April, 1965), pp. 39–58 ff.

[13] *Ibid.*, p. 53.

question as to which a shareholder might well reach an opposite conclusion. But the shareholder who does not know of the proposed action has no chance to make his decision.

Such reasoning has led the great majority of persons who have considered the matter to recommend that all shareholders be put on notice of the company's intentions before purchases begin. The argument that, if the corporation buys through a broker it can only obtain shares from someone who has decided to sell anyway and who therefore is not damaged, does not hold water, because the fact is that the company is reducing its outstanding shares to increase the value of each remaining share. It is thus a very "material fact" (using the words of the Securities Act) and it must be disclosed.

The principal reasons given by corporations for the retirement of their shares are as follows:

1. To use liquid funds that have accumulated beyond the level necessary for the conduct and expansion of the business.
2. To have treasury stock which can be used instead of the new shares otherwise necessary when shares are needed:
   a) For acquisitions.
   b) For satisfying stock options as exercised.
   c) For meeting the conversion of convertible issues.
   d) For regular or occasional stock dividends.
   e) For meeting obligations under employee stock purchase plan.
3. To improve the record of earnings per share.

The diversity of these reasons, in Guthart's words, leads "unmistakably to the conclusion that no comprehensive theoretical solution exists to the problem of when, and at what price, a corporation should buy back its own shares. Furthermore, no attempt has been made to solve the problem of how to allocate funds among share repurchase, dividends, and new investments in plant."[14]

Two methods of accomplishing stock repurchase are prevalent. We shall do no more than name them here, because they are well described in the case of the Extone Chemical company, at page 885. One method, which assures that every shareholder has a notice of the program sent to his address, is the invitation to shareholders to *tender* their shares. In this method the prospective buyer announces its intention of making purchases under specified terms and invites owners to indicate their acceptance, that is, to tender their securities. The terms offered may be fixed in price and quantity, as in the example at page 888. Or, they may be dependent on the demand which develops, as in the procedure announced by the Universal Leaf Tobacco Company. This is very similar to a procedure that has been used to offer new issues of securities in England.

---

[14] *Ibid.*, p. 172.

Universal Leaf is letting shareholders name their own price for the shares and is reserving the right to reject all offers that exceed a maximum price—a price which hasn't yet been set by company officials.

The Company will pay stockholders of all shares accepted the same maximum price per share, with stockholders tendering their shares at the lowest price to be the first in line, according to Gordon L. Crenshaw, president.

Thus, a stockholder who offers to sell his preferred stock at $100 a share may be first to get paid $250 a share if the company decides to pay $250. He also may get paid $150 a share, if officers set the price at that level. Another shareholder asking $250 for each of his shares may get turned down if the company sets the price at $225 a share.

"We are going to set one price at which we're willing to pay and everybody who tenders their stock at that price or under will get paid the same price, with the lowest prices offered us getting first considerations," said Mr. Crenshaw.[15]

The second method of acquiring shares is simply to buy them through brokers in the ordinary way. Some firms issue elaborate instructions to minimize the effect of this special source of demand on the price (no one is so naïve as to think that there is no effect). Others are less careful. With reference to the possibility that the corporation might, with "inside" knowledge, take advantage of the outside shareholders, some firms cease buying when such information comes to light until it has been made public. Other firms, again, are not so meticulous. Surely Guthart is right in his conclusion that, "Conclusive definitions of responsibility in this area are urgently needed."

In this connection, we might quote one of the authors of this book, although others would not go so far:

I must admit that I share some of the questionings [which others have expressed] about the current wave of stock repurchasing. I know that I would favor any kind of regulation that would make it certain that companies would inform their shareholders of their intentions before they start purchasing, and I would even consider the possibility of limiting the methods of acquiring the shares to such procedures as an invitation to tender, or even of making a distribution of surplus funds equally to all shares in lieu of purchasing shares at all. . . .

. . . Concentrating the number of shares does of course distort the record of earnings per share. In fact, some companies seem to be expecting that the increase in earnings per share will be received with the same enthusiasm as if it represented growth. On the whole, I think they have been disappointed—since investors are not quite as gullible as one sometimes assumes. . . .

In fact, I am critical of those companies which for too long hold large amounts of liquid funds invested at low returns. . . . Many of the compa-

---

[15] *Wall Street Journal*, December 7, 1965.

nies which are now embarrassed with excess funds might avoid the embarrassment if they reconsider their dividend policy!

Like almost everything else in finance, the fine points of a decision seem to rest on the facts of a particular case. We have collected instances where it seems obvious that the accumulation of funds was due to a stingy dividend policy, and, on the other hand, we have cases where some sort of a nonrecurrent capital disinvestment has created funds that can quite properly be returned through repurchase. With sufficient notice, on such facts as the latter, I cannot criticize the action.[16]

---

[16] Pearson Hunt, letter to the editor, *Harvard Business Review*, Vol. XLIII, No. 4 (July–August, 1965), pp. 36–37.

Chapter 27

The Nature and Effects of Government Regulation on Long-Term Finance

IN CONSIDERING the subject of long-term corporate finance, it is necessary to take account of the very considerable and increasing influence which government has come to exert on this aspect of business activity. This influence has always existed in some degree because of the fact that the corporation is a creature of the state and derives its characteristics from a charter issued in accordance with the provisions of state laws. As indicated in Chapter 2, however, the control exerted by government through the laws of incorporation is in the main more potential than actual, and it has been through other devices and in other ways that the real teeth of state and federal intervention have been displayed.

Except for the railroads, most of the effective regulation of corporate issues and the security markets had its origin in the collapse of the stock market in 1929 and in the severe depression which followed in the early thirties. The widespread collapse of confidence was nowhere more apparent than in the financial aspects of the economy, and direct governmental action here came early and took a vigorous form. From the nature of this action, certain objectives were apparent. One was to modify the form of certain key financial institutions—notably, the commercial banks and the securities exchanges—with the intention of eliminating the weaknesses which had led to their breakdown under pressure and which had contributed to the general decline in economic activity and employment. Another objective was to protect the investor, particularly the small-scale unsophisticated investor, from what were considered to be unnecessarily severe losses in the collapse of stock market values. Beyond this, there was the intention of restoring the investors' confidence in the securities markets, so that savings would again flow into productive activity. Still another objective, which appeared in regard to certain key industries, such as the public utility industry, was that of protecting the public as consumers against the (4) actual or potential decline in efficiency and increase in costs resulting from weaknesses in or abuses of corporate financial policy.

If the 1929–32 debacle brought losses to an estimated 10.0 million stockholders,[1] any similar event in the 1960's would affect a much larger proportion of the population of the United States. The *Census of Shareholders* of the New York Stock Exchange has recorded a great growth in the number of stockholders, from 8.6 million in 1956 to 29.1 million in 1965.[2] This growth has increased the importance of security regulation in our society.

Federal Regulation of New Issues

The principal federal agency for achieving the objectives sought through government regulation has been the Securities and Exchange Commission, established in 1933. A series of acts and amendments from 1933 to the present have given the Commission power to regulate many matters related both to security issues and to trading in securities.[3] The first two in this series were the Securities Act of 1933 and the Securities Exchange Act of 1934. They are sometimes referred to as the "full disclosure laws," because great reliance is placed on the informed investor to make his decisions wisely. "The Commission has no authority to control the nature or quality of a security to be offered . . . or to pass upon its merits."[4] The 1933 Act requires registration with the SEC of all securities offered for sale to the public through the mails or "other instrumentalities of interstate commerce." It is nearly impossible to escape such control. However, the Act provides certain exemptions. Several classes of corporations are exempt, including railroads. Also excluded are those issues of any corporations which are placed privately. Private placements have supplied a growing proportion of new financing and in 1964 made up 40.2% of new corporate securities offered for cash.[5] Finally, the amount of required details of information is reduced for firms that raise publicly less than $300,000 in one year.

Companies that propose to issue securities coming under the provisions of the 1933 Act must file a *registration statement* containing detailed information. In addition to stating the purposes for which the funds are to be raised and presenting audited statements of financial position and of recent operations, "the registration statement of an issuer . . . must describe such matters as the names of persons who

---

[1] Edwin B. Cox, *Trends in the Distribution of Stock Ownership* (Philadelphia: University of Pennsylvania Press, 1963), p. 33.

[2] New York Stock Exchange, *Census of Shareholders, 1965*.

[3] Each annual report of the Commission summarizes its powers under the current statutes.

[4] Securities and Exchange Commission, *Thirtieth Annual Report* (1964), p. 26.

[5] *Ibid.*, p. 179.

participate in the direction, management, or control of the issuer's business; their security holdings and remuneration and the options of bonus and profit-sharing privileges alloted to them; . . . payments to promoters made within 2 years or intended to be made; . . . [etc.]⁶ This registration statement, as soon as filed, is open to public inspection. Accompanying it must be a copy of the *prospectus, the document to be sent to prospective or actual buyers of the proposed issue*. It contains most of the information in the registration statement and must be sent to anyone requesting it.

The registration statement and the prospectus are reviewed by the Commission to determine whether all material facts have been disclosed. If the Commission is satisfied on this point, the registration will be allowed to become effective; but if not, amendments or additions will be requested. The SEC is empowered to issue a *stop order* either before or after the registration becomes effective if it is apparent that the circumstances under which the securities are being offered to the public are contrary to the Act. In the event of continued violation of the Act the Commission may request a court injunction. It is to be repeated here that the responsibility of the Commission does not extend to the consideration of investment quality and the risk to the investor; these are matters which remain the responsibility of the investor himself, but it must be conceded that the manner in which the SEC insists that facts be stated (including the exact wording in some cases) often comes very close to stating the conclusion that an intelligent investor should reach. For example, the Commission has ruled:

In many instances the securities to be offered are of a highly speculative nature. . . . In such instances, and particularly where a lengthy prospectus cannot be avoided, there should be set forth immediately following the cover page of the prospectus a carefully organized series of short, concise paragraphs summarizing the principal factors which make the offering speculative.⁷

The median lapse of time between the date of filing a registration statement and the date it became effective, during the 1964 fiscal year, was estimated by the SEC at 36 days.⁸ The law provides a minimum time of 20 days as opportunity for the public to become adequately informed on the issue before it is offered for sale. In practice, the time is taken up with the analysis by the SEC of the registration statement and prospectus, the preparation and delivery of a letter of comment, and the filing of amendments. Once the registration becomes effective, the issue may be offered to the public subject to the provision that each investor must be supplied with a copy of the prospectus.

⁶ *Ibid.*, p. 27.

⁷ Securities Act of 1933, Release No. 4666 (February 7, 1964), par. 18.

⁸ Securities and Exchange Commission, *Thirtieth Annual Report* (1964), p. 28.

There are, of course, significant benefits to corporate enterprises generally resulting from government pressure for honest reporting of the facts about new security issues. Publicity under the auspices of a disinterested agency builds public confidence in the securities markets and strengthens the demand side by reducing the chance of misrepresentation or fraud. On the other hand, such measures have their price—not only in the time and expense of formal registration but, more importantly, in introducing an element of rigidity in the procedure of issue at a point where maximum flexibility is desired. In a highly volatile securities market, time is of the essence in assuring a successful sale, in terms of both volume and price. It is only fair to say, however, that the Commission is fully conscious of this problem and does its best to reduce to a minimum its interference with the normal processes of the market.

Regulation of the Securities Markets

The second major piece of legislation administered by the SEC is the Securities Exchange Act of 1934. This Act was designed to complement the regulation of the purchase and sale of new securities, first, by requiring for many companies whose securities are widely held the same type of information as described above, and second, by controlling the activities of security exchanges and investment brokers or dealers. The companies covered include all those whose securities are listed for trading on national exchanges and, since the Securities Acts Amendments of 1964, all other companies having over 750 shareholders and assets in excess of $1 million.

Since the registration provisions are similar to those already described, we shall turn to the second purpose, that of control. In this case the SEC exerts its control both directly and through the rules and regulations of the securities exchanges and of the National Association of Securities Dealers, Inc., which the SEC has the power to review.

The Act requires that all national exchanges be registered with the SEC. In the year 1964, 14 exchanges were so registered, but 93% of the total value of stocks listed was in those listed on the New York Stock Exchange and the American Stock Exchange in New York City.[9] Failure to provide requested information or to comply with the Act or the rules of the Commission may bring denial or suspension of trading privileges. This threat is a powerful weapon against dishonesty in the national securities markets and on the part of the security issuer.

In recent years, as a result of the facts developed in its special study of the securities markets,[10] the Commission has taken the initiative in working out with the two principal national exchanges (New York Stock

---

[9] Securities and Exchange Commission, *op. cit.*, p. 48.

[10] Securities and Exchange Commission, *Report of Special Study of the Securities Markets* (House Document 95, 88th Cong., 1st sess.). (4 vols.; Washington, D.C.: U.S. Government Printing Office, 1964).

Exchange and American Stock Exchange) new rules concerning the activities of floor traders and specialists. The new rules restrict the activities of these persons but are designed to cause their work to assist in the creation of an auction market in the general interest. Recently, also, new rules were adopted to improve the accuracy of the quotations made public concerning trading in the over-the-counter markets.

The 1934 Act also provides for the licensing of brokers and dealers in the over-the-counter market, so that the SEC is fully equipped to take aggressive action against manipulative practices in the nation's securities markets. The Commission is continuously on the alert for evidence of such practices. It is authorized to instigate private investigations, may subpoena relevant material, and may take testimony under oath. Action to stop any undesirable practices may be taken directly by the Commission or through the courts, with loss of license the most frequently applied form of discipline. Unhappily, the Commission has had to be very active in this way, so that almost any week one may read of disciplinary action against some person or firm in the investment business. The percentage of dishonesty is a very small part of the total, but it is a matter of constant concern. The get-rich-quick speculator has his counterpart among brokers and dealers!

In addition to its control over individual dealers, the SEC also exerts control over national securities associations, which at the present time means the National Association of Securities Dealers, Inc. By requiring the Association to register with the SEC and report regularly on its rules and membership action, the Securities Exchange Act puts the Commission in the position of being able to determine whether the Association's activities are in accord with the letter and spirit of the Act. Since it has authority over both rules and membership, the SEC has all the power it needs to enforce compliance with its decisions.

Another of the abuses which the Securities Exchange Act was designed to eliminate is the misuse of a position of influence for personal gain on the part of corporate officers, directors, and major shareholders. The primary regulating device here is the requirement that such individuals (including all shareholders holding more than 10% of a listed stock) report to the Commission their holdings of securities in the company concerned and report any subsequent changes in these holdings. Such information is made available to the public. In addition, the Act provides for the recovery by the issuing company of profits realized by an "insider" in the purchase and sale of securities of the company within a period of 6 months. The intention here is to prevent the use of inside information for personal gain by such individuals.

The SEC has also been concerned with the exercise of voting power at stockholders' meetings. As we have seen previously, the large-scale corporation generally draws its equity funds from a large number of shareholders. Although, as owners, they represent the ultimate control in the corporation, many of these shareholders are not in a position to attend the annual shareholders' meeting. The only alternative, if their vote is to be exercised, is to designate someone who will be in attendance as their proxy. Possible abuse of the proxy device arises because shareholders are often indifferent to or ill-informed on management matters. It has become common practice for the existing directors regularly to solicit the proxies of the shareholders and for many shareholders either to sign these as a matter of course or to ignore entirely their privilege to vote. In this way the existing management can often perpetuate itself indefinitely without ever really rendering full account to the shareholders who elect them.

The SEC has been given authority to regulate proxy solicitation by all the companies that must register under the 1934 Act, namely those whose securities are traded on the national exchanges and the larger companies traded over the counter. The same principle of full disclosure applies here as well, so that the stockholder may be informed about the persons managing the company, its directors, etc., in addition to receiving the notice of the matters to come before the meeting for which proxies are solicited.

In addition, the regulation provides:

. . . that when a management is soliciting proxies, any security holder desiring to communicate with other security holders for a proper purpose may require the management to furnish him with a list of all security holders or to mail his communication to security holders for him. [He] may also require the management to include in its proxy material any appropriate proposal which such security holder desires to submit to a vote. . . . Certain additional provisions of the regulation [chiefly calling for details about the persons soliciting] are applicable where a contest for control . . . is involved."[11]

Although stockholder proposals seldom gain the necessary majority, the fact that they are possible is important, for managements would rather negotiate an agreement with dissenting groups than have evidence of disagreement go to all shareholders.

This is an appropriate point at which to raise the issue of one of the most publicized phenomena of current business life—the proxy fight. It is a rare but exciting event.[12] To the extent that shareholders become alerted to their actual or potential influence as the electors of top management, with or without the assistance of the SEC, the possibility that the existing management may be challenged from without grows in significance. In recent years there have been some spectacular battles between the

---

[11] Securities and Exchange Commission, *Thirtieth Annual Report* (1964), p. 60. During fiscal 1964, 45 stockholders submitted 211 proposals to 125 companies. In total, there were 2,530 proxy statements submitted during the year, of which 17 were not management solicitations.

[12] Eighteen in fiscal 1964 came under SEC jurisdiction (*ibid.*, p. 63).

established board of directors and a rival individual or group seeking to take its place. Both groups actively solicit the proxies of the masses of independent shareholders in advance of the annual meeting at which directors are elected. Depending on the form of voting used by the corporation, the persuasiveness of the rival parties, and the size of the "independent vote," the "outsiders" may fail completely, elect a minority of directors, or sweep the "old guard" out of office. The outcome may be highly uncertain until the vote has been actually counted.

To the disinterested observer, the event of a proxy fight raises some significant questions. On the one hand, the fact that it can happen may help to keep the management alert and responsive to the interests of the shareholders. It provides an occasion on which shareholders are made very conscious of their responsibilities as the ultimate authority in the business. It is entirely possible that the existing management should be replaced. On the other hand, the experience can be seriously damaging to the morale and efficiency of the business as a whole. Competent management, as well as incompetent management, may be challenged in this way, and by outsiders whose capacities and motives may be in doubt. Many shareholders are not really equipped to choose. Revisions of the proxy rules in the last 2 years have, however, assured existing managements against surprise, and required considerably more detail about the persons soliciting in opposition to management.

State Regulation of Security Issues

Prior to the enactment of the Federal Securities Act, many states had laws on the statute books relating to the sale of securities. The primary purpose of these laws was to prevent the sale of fraudulent security issues to unsuspecting investors. They came to be known as blue-sky laws, a term descriptive of the extravagant and unfounded representations made by the promoters of such securities.

The immediate pressure for federal regulation in this area came from the market collapse of the thirties, but behind this lay a general dissatisfaction with state regulation. The laws were not uniformly good, nor was the enforcement uniformly effective. Of greater significance, however, was the basic inadequacy of intrastate law in combating what was basically an interstate and even at times an international problem. The misuse of securities markets did not stop at state borders. As a consequence, federal regulation, once in existence, rapidly assumed a dominant role.

Nevertheless, the jurisdiction of the states over issuers, brokers and dealers continues, and it has been used effectively in some instances. Most interesting to students of security regulation are those states whose laws reject the theory that full disclosure is an adequate goal, and empower state officials to pass judgment upon such things as the merits of the proposed issue as an investment, or the fairness of the fees paid or anticipated by "insiders" and dealers. California is regarded as the leader in this type of regulation, with Texas, Illinois, and Wisconsin also important. Unfortunately, we do not have the space to go further into the pros and cons of such regulation, but we can say that under able administrators many questionable activities have been stopped sooner than they would have been under federal law. On the other hand, it may be argued that desirable initiatives have been discouraged, and it is certainly true that an administrator with poor judgment could do considerable damage to the delicate but valuable mechanism that channels investors' funds to productive use, especially in new (and therefore speculative) ventures.

Investment Companies and Advisers

Because of the complexities involved in the selection of a group of securities for investment, many investors feel incapable of making their own selections. In these circumstances the investor may seek the advice of a professional investment counselor to guide his decisions, or he may sidestep the problem entirely by placing his money in the hands of an investment company, which then applies its own investment standards and policies. In either case the inexperienced investor is potentially at the mercy of the adviser or the investment company. The opportunities for misuse of this position of trust in the past have been considered so significant that the federal government has enacted legislation which empowers the SEC to oversee these activities. The basic legislation is the Investment Advisers Act of 1940 and the Investment Company Act of 1940.

The objective of the Investment Advisers Act is to assure that those who seek investment counsel get advice which is honestly given and free from the influence of self-interest on the part of the adviser. For example, the Act prohibits an adviser from basing his compensation upon a share of the appreciation of his client's funds. The Commission watches for other evidences of conflict of interest and may revoke the adviser's license for cause. On the other hand, the SEC is not required to assume any responsibility for the professional competence of the adviser or the soundness of the advice given, nor does the SEC assume such responsibility. The legislation fits the general regulatory pattern of getting the important facts out in the open and then leaving the investor to use them as he wishes and to make his own decisions. As of June, 1964, there were 731 investment companies registered, including 72 small business investment companies. Of these, 617 were "active," with assets at market value approximating $41.6 billion.[13] All these numbers have been increasing rapidly. Obviously, the managements of these companies exercise control over a major segment of the investment market and hold the fortunes of a

---

[13] *Ibid.*, p. 110.

great many investors in their hands. In the early days of investment company growth, serious abuses of management responsibility developed, which contributed to the heavy losses and investment company liquidations of the early thirties. In addition to the requirement of registration, which provides the SEC with a tool of control and brings important facts of company operation out into the open, the regulation has the further objectives of strengthening the control of the shareholders over company policy, assuring the integrity of management by prohibiting or supervising practices which would give rise to a conflict of interest between management of the investment companies and their shareholders, and improving the capacity of such companies to survive recessions by regulating the issuance on their part of senior securities. Of particular interest is the close watch kept by the SEC on transactions between the company and its directors and officers. Another possible conflict of interest is minimized by the rule that underwriters, investment bankers, and brokers may not hold a majority position on the boards of directors of investment companies.

SEC Investigations under Way

Not content with the administration of its existing powers, the SEC initiates studies which lead to revisions of its regulations as well as to requests for changes in the governing laws. Congress has from time to time made amendments, the most comprehensive being the law known as the "Securities Acts Amendments of 1964." This law followed the "Special Study of the Securities Markets," made by the SEC upon Congressional request. The major effects of the amendments were, first, to extend registration provisions into the over-the-counter markets, and, second, to strengthen qualification standards for entrance into the securities business and permit more effective disciplinary action.

Three major studies may be productive of action in the near future. One, of long standing, is considering the most desirable standards for the debt-equity proportions of public utility capitalization. Another, which was done at the Wharton School of Commerce and Finance of the University of Pennsylvania, is a thorough study of mutual investment companies.[14] The third, also done at Wharton, is the study of the operations of the over-the-counter markets.[15]

The attitude of the SEC toward such studies can be found in the following quotation from the Transmittal Letter which accompanied the text of the "Special Study of the Securities Markets" when it was sent to Congress.

---

[14] Irwin Friend et al., A Study of Mutual Funds (Report of the Committee on Interstate and Foreign Commerce) (Washington, D.C.: U.S. Government Printing Office, 1962).

[15] Irwin Friend et al., The Over the Counter Security Markets (New York; McGraw-Hill Book Co., 1958).

At the outset we emphasize that, although many specific recommendations for improvements in rules and practices are made . . . the report demonstrates that neither the fundamental structure of the securities markets nor of the regulatory pattern of the securities acts requires dramatic reconstruction. . . . At the same time the Report makes very clear that important problems do exist, grave abuses do occur and additional controls and improvements are much needed.[16]

Government Regulation of Corporate Financial Policy

The regulation which has been outlined up to this point has been concerned with the development of a sound market for new and outstanding securities which is free from manipulation and deceit and in which the investor's basic rights are assured and his decisions informed. It is likely that most businessmen would agree that such regulation is desirable and that, on balance, it has facilitated the task of raising long-term funds for the legitimate business enterprise. Of course, it is inevitable that regulation will interfere with the free process of the market to some extent, and this may be counted as the cost to be set off against the gains from such regulation. In the main, however, government regulation of the securities markets has only touched the fringes of the corporation's financial activities and has not constituted a serious encroachment on freedom of action in corporate financial policy. There is, nevertheless, an area of government regulation which does invade what was once considered the private area of internal financial policy, and it is this with which we shall now be concerned.

In one sense the powers of the SEC to regulate corporate financial policy by direct intervention in the policy-making process are confined entirely to a relatively small segment of business, namely, the electric and gas utility industry. However, they have considerably broader implications. To the extent that the Commission's standards become formalized and are known and accepted by the investing public, they may become the model for investment standards in other industries.

The Role of the SEC under the Public Utility Holding Company Act. The Public Utility Holding Company Act was passed in 1935 in an effort to put a stop to certain corporate practices which had had free play in the electric utility industry during the preceding decade. By means of the parent-subsidiary device and the creation of nonoperating (holding) companies, which existed merely as a means of concentrating the ownership of operating companies, vast electric utility pyramids were developed, with control concentrated in the hands of a relatively few men. Because of the widespread indifference of investors to their ownership responsibilities, it was possible for determined individuals to gain voting control of a utility with a comparatively small investment and then proceed to issue large quantities of nonvoting senior securities. With

---

[16] Securities and Exchange Commission, *Twenty-ninth Annual Report* (1963), p. 3.

the funds so produced, the utility in question could then be used as a base for the acquisition of voting control in other utilities; and they, in turn, would become the means of bringing more companies within the orbit of the central organization. Such pyramiding of control was theoretically without limit, and so it must have appeared to those who attempted to use it for personal gain.

In an industry which by its very nature has distinct monopolistic characteristics, the integration of a number of operating companies and the concentration of control in the hands of a few at the top of the pyramid presented the federal government with a challenge it could not ignore indefinitely. While it was recognized that integration per se was not a bad thing, these practices had in some cases resulted in serious abuses of the consumer and the investor. In these situations, efficiency of operating companies became a secondary consideration; corporate funds and corporate earnings were drained off to purchase stock in other companies; and top-heavy capital structures were created which became a burden to earnings and a threat to solvency. Companies and managements were linked together where there was no conceivable economic advantage to be gained.

The public utility holding company having had more than a decade in which to develop its maximum potential, drastic governmental action was required to check and reverse the trend. The authority for this action was contained in the Public Utility Holding Company Act of 1935, which conferred almost unlimited powers on the Securities and Exchange Commission, the agency which was to administer the Act. The regulation was limited to electric and gas utilities doing an interstate business and covered both the holding companies themselves and their operating subsidiaries. Under the "death sentence" provisions, the SEC was given the power to require holding companies to divest themselves of subsidiaries which, in the opinion of the Commission, were not an integral part of a geographic and economic unit. As the result of such action, as of June 30, 1964, there remained in existence 18 active registered holding company systems involving a total of 155 system companies.[17]

The continuing task of simplifying public utility systems has been paralleled by efforts to simplify the capital structures of the remaining holding companies and their operating subsidiaries. Through a gradual process of retirement and consolidation of issues, it was intended that the confusing maze of senior security issues characteristic of these systems in the twenties would be replaced by an uncomplicated and clear-cut bond, preferred stock, common stock relationship. Important as this simplification process was for public utility financing, it represented only a part of what has amounted to total supervision of long-term financial practices and policies by the SEC. A detailed study of the standards which have

---

[17] Securities and Exchange Commission, *Thirtieth Annual Report* (1964), p. 87.

guided the SEC in this regard is of real significance far beyond the public utility industry itself. It provides a sample of what government regulation can mean in the area of corporate finance. It is a measure of the attitudes and thinking of this administrative body, which is accepted by many as the "financial conscience" of the nation. Because of the great influence of the SEC in the general securities markets, the criteria of sound corporate finance it applies directly to one important industry "affected with the public interest" may well have an indirect but significant impact on corporate practices generally.

Debt-Equity Balance. In setting standards of sound financial practice for electric and gas utilities, the SEC has had as one of its major preoccupations the debt-equity balance in the capital structure. Its concern in this regard derived from the fact that many of the companies which the Commission set out to regulate had a capital structure so top-heavy with senior securities that it threatened profitability, stability, and even solvency. The severe depression of the thirties demonstrated that even a public utility could experience a significant shrinkage in earnings and that the consideration of safety of investment in both the bonds and the stocks of such companies required a limitation on the proportion of securities bearing a fixed commitment to the investor. A further reason for such a limitation was to provide for some reserve of borrowing power in anticipation of future financing and the need for flexibility in the timing of new issues.

An expression of this general objective and its hoped-for results is found in the Commission's annual report for 1950:

. . . By insisting that parent holding companies undertake common stock financing periodically to match increases in system debt financing, the Commission seeks to prevent a return of the high-leveraged, unwieldy structures which led to the legislation it now administers. Many holding companies have recognized their responsibilities in this respect and a number . . . have already reached a point where the market receptivity to their common stock offerings is almost comparable with that accorded to the stock of good quality operating companies.[18]

The standards which have been evolved in this regard have taken various forms, but all have the common objective of keeping senior securities within "reasonable" limits. The most common form is in terms of a maximum percentage of debt in the capital structure. An indication of SEC thinking is found in a decision on an issue of debentures by the Columbia Gas System, Inc., in 1949. A report of this decision by the Commission reads, in part, as follows:

The indenture . . . permits the company to issue debt to the extent of 60 percent of its total capitalization. Columbia Gas indicated that while . . . a debt ratio of not more than 50 percent is desirable, it felt that . . .

---

[18] Securities and Exchange Commission, *Sixteenth Annual Report* (1950), p. 104.

additional borrowing capacity might be necessary in periods of heavy construction which would temporarily bring the debt ratio above this level. The Commission recognized the desirability of such flexibility. . . . It indicated, however, that it considered 50 percent to be the desirable proportion of debt for the system and noted that its approval was not to be construed as an indication that the issuance of debt to the full limit permitted by the indenture would be approved under all circumstances.[19]

Limitations on debt have also been expressed in terms of earnings coverage—the extent to which earnings available for the payment of fixed charges should exceed these fixed charges. The annual report of the Commission for 1947 expressed such a standard in an unusually general and unqualified form. The statement of this and other standards was preceded by these significant remarks:

> During recent years the Commission has evolved comprehensive protective provisions relating to bonds and preferred stock. . . . The extensive refunding program of the last few years has accelerated the pace at which these provisions have been put into effect. However, because many operating companies are being removed, under section 11, from the jurisdiction of this Commission, much of the prospective new financing . . . will not contain these provisions unless they are accorded the support of other regulatory bodies as well.[20]

The report then proceeds to set up certain standards, among which is found the following relating to earnings coverage: "Issuance of additional bonds is also conditioned upon the adequacy of the earnings coverage for the entire amount of bonds to be outstanding. This coverage is computed on the basis of earnings before income taxes and a coverage of at least two times in usually required."[21] It must be noted that these standards were prefaced by a statement which emphasized the need for flexibility in individual cases and also for continuous reexamination. Nevertheless, it does indicate a standard which has evolved from experience and which has widespread application.

The use of debt has also been limited by a standard expressed in terms of the value of new property acquisitions financed by this (and other) means:

> The issuance of additional bonds is limited to 60 percent of the cost or fair value of net bondable additions to fixed property. While the Commission endeavors to limit the amount of debt initially outstanding to 50 percent of new fixed property, the standard of 60 percent with reference to additional bonds is designed to give the issuer sufficient flexibility to meet future emergencies while at the same time requiring it to provide a reasonable proportion of junior capital in meeting its growth requirements.[22]

---

[19] Securities and Exchange Commission, *Seventeenth Annual Report* (1951), p. 95.

[20] Securities and Exchange Commission, *Thirteenth Annual Report* (1947), p. 88.

[21] *Ibid.*

[22] *Ibid.*

Because of the heavy preponderance of fixed assets in the asset structure of public utilities, the above standard bears a close similarity to the standard cited earlier in the Columbia Gas case.

Concerned that the value of a mortgage bond should not be eroded by the depreciation of mortgaged property, the Commission has insisted that all mortgage indentures either provide a sinking fund or an obligation requiring the company to use new funds in renewal or replacement investments that will be covered in the mortgage. This obligation is sometimes expressed as a percentage of the cost of the property originally mortgaged and sometimes as a percentage of earnings. For some years the SEC has not approved any mortgage debt proposal of a utility under its jurisdiction without some provision of this nature.

The possibility that improvident payments of dividends might endanger the solvency of a company has also received attention:

> As an additional means of protecting senior security holders, the Commission has continued to insist upon restrictions on the payment of dividends where common stock equity was considered inadequate. For example, in the case of Western Light & Telephone Co. the declarant agreed that— "If at any time the aggregate of the common stock and surplus . . . is or becomes less than 20 percent of the total capitalization, dividends on common stock in any fiscal year shall be limited to 50 percent of net income available . . . and whenever such ratios shall be 20 percent or more but less than 25 percent, then not more than 75 percent of the earnings accumulated . . . shall be used therefor. No dividends shall be paid on common stock which will reduce such ratio to less than 25 percent.[23]

Likewise, standards with regard to sinking fund provisions on bond issues may be used to reduce gradually the outstanding debt, relying on retained earnings or new stock offerings to maintain the level of investment. The Commission's views have been stated as follows:

> The primary function of a sinking fund is to improve the ratio between debt and net property. . . . The Commission ordinarily requires a sinking fund of 1 percent of the largest principal amount of the issue at any time outstanding; where the initial ratio is unfavorable, this percentage is increased.[24]

In these various ways the SEC has sought to force the electric and gas utility industry to accept a set of objective yardsticks by which to measure the limits of a sound and, at the same time, flexible debt-equity balance in the capital structure. For those utilities which come directly under the regulatory powers of the Commission, such standards virtually become "law," since their acceptance by the utility is a prerequisite to Commission consent to reorganization plans, new security issues, and

---

[23] Securities and Exchange Commission, *Twelfth Annual Report* (1946), p. 77.

[24] Securities and Exchange Commission, *Thirteenth Annual Report* (1947), p. 89.

new indentures. This control is made complete through authority over short-term borrowing as well. For example:

> . . . the Commission approved a credit agreement under which Middle South [Utilities, Inc.] may borrow up to $15 million from banks. . . . However, no loan renewal may be made . . . without further application to the Commission. . . . These loans are to be subsequently replaced with permanent financing.[25]

We must also mention the powers of the Commission under the Trust Indenture Act of 1939. This law applies to all new issues registered under the 1933 Act, not only to public utilities. The terms of the contract between an issuer and its bondholders are expressed in the *indenture*. Actually, the parties to the contract are the issuer, on one side, and an *indenture trustee*, on the other. The trustee accepts a trust to administer the contract in the interest of those who will be holders of the bonds.

It is the intention of the legislation to make certain that the trustee is completely independent of the indebted company or the underwriter and acts with a sense of responsibility to the bondholder. To this end, the Act requires that the indentures of all issues coming within its scope be submitted to the Securities and Exchange Commission. Before an issue can be offered for sale, the Commission must rule that the indenture qualifies as being in conformity with the provisions of the Act. This procedure ties in to the registration procedure under the Securities Act, and registration will not be permitted to become effective without a favorable ruling on the indenture.

Financial Flexibility.   As previously indicated, one of the objectives of the Commission in limiting the use of senior securities was the establishment of a "reserve" of borrowing power which would give the companies concerned a desired degree of flexibility in the timing of new issues. "Public utilities, unlike most other industries, are usually faced with the problem of expanding plant facilities in periods of depression as well as prosperity. A high degree of financial flexibility is therefore essential in order to insure maintenance of adequate service to consumers."[26] In order to add to this flexibility, the SEC has insisted that all new issues of senior securities have a redemption clause, so that the issuer is not unavoidably bound to a given amount of debt for the life of the issue. This policy is seen in the following quotation: ". . . in the light of its [the SEC's] established policies under which it has almost uniformly required that senior securities be fully redeemable at the option of the issuing company upon payment of a reasonable premium."[27] It will be recalled that in the chapter on the bargain for funds, we noted a growing resistance to this clause on the parts of investors.

---

[25] Securities and Exchange Commission, *Eighteenth Annual Report* (1952), p. 118.

[26] Securities and Exchange Commission, *Seventeenth Annual Report* (1951), p. 105.

[27] Securities and Exchange Commission, *Twenty-first Annual Report* (1955), p. 54.

Cost of Financing. Another set of standards which has been developed for utility financing has had as its objective the minimization of costs in the issuance of new securities. The most widely publicized Commission ruling in this connection has been its insistence, in the large majority of cases, on competitive bidding by investment houses seeking to handle new utility issues. Studies undertaken by the SEC have satisfied it that this results in a significantly improved price to the issuing company as compared with private negotiation of issues.

The objective of greater economy in financing has been one of the reasons why the Commission has encouraged the application of the preemptive right and rights offerings in further issues of outstanding stock. A new issue which is taken up largely if not entirely by the existing shareholders minimizes or eliminates the services and costs of the investment banker as "middleman." This policy has been expressed as follows:

It is, and has long been, our opinion that when holding companies and public utility companies subject to our jurisdiction sell additional shares of common stock, their own interests, as well as the interests of their common shareholders are, absent special circumstances, best served by allowing common shareholders the right to purchase their proportionate shares of the new issue.[28]

Further, the Commission has reported, with apparent approval, a trend away from the underwriting of rights offerings as, presumably, an avoidable cost:

Probably the most significant development in this group of issues was the growing importance of the non-underwritten rights offering. Only five offerings . . . were made with the aid of firm underwriting commitments. Four issues . . . were offered without underwriting, but had the benefit of dealer solicitation. The remaining five rights offerings . . . were sold without the benefit of underwriting or dealer solicitation assistance. All five were subscribed in percentages ranging from 106 to 188. In each of these cases the oversubscription privilege made an important contribution to the success of the sale.[29]

The attitude of the SEC on the matter of rights offerings has been subject to some modification in recent years. During 1952 a study of recent rights offerings was undertaken; and shortly after this was completed, the following statement was made: ". . . it is our view that, while there are many advantages to a rights offering, these advantages are not so conclusive as to warrant a strict policy in favor of rights. . . . Accordingly it will be the policy . . . not to insist upon a rights offering where management can make a showing that an underwriting by

---

[28] Securities and Exchange Commission, *Holding Company Act Release No. 9730*, as quoted in the Commission's *Eighteenth Annual Report* (1952), p. 128.

[29] Securities and Exchange Commission, *Seventeenth Annual Report* (1951), p. 109.

competitive bidding without an offer to stockholders would be preferable.[30]

Preferred Stock. Although the Commission has been primarily concerned with the control of debt in public utility capital structures, it has also developed a set of standards for preferred stock. Preferred stock has presented a special problem because of its somewhat paradoxical position halfway between a fixed charge security and a true equity security. The opinions of the Commission reflect the difficulty of a satisfactory classification for the stock, at one time treating it as a part of equity capital and at another time treating it as a senior security which has a fixed claim on earnings and which results in a mandatory drain on cash. This conflicting interpretation is seen in the following commentary of the Commission, made in 1948, regarding an observed trend toward sinking funds as a requirement of new preferred issues:

> Since institutions were no longer under any particular pressure to buy preferred issues, they were in a position to demand certain concessions in the terms of security. In this way the sinking fund came into use in connection with utility preferred stocks. These provisions were initially set up on a 2 percent basis. . . . Thus preferred stock ceases to be permanent capital . . . [the sinking fund] places an additional cash requirement upon the issuer and has undoubtedly led some companies to seek other means of financing.
>
> The declining interest in preferred stock has rendered more difficult the problem of maintaining an adequate proportion of equity security in the capital structure.[31]

In spite of the inference in the above quotation that preferred stock normally lies on the equity side of the debt-equity balance, the Commission has formulated standards which treat preferred stock as a senior security akin to bonds. Note the following decision which applied to a convertible preferred issue:

> Subsequent to this offering [the New England Electric System] submitted a general financing program proposing the sale of $7,500,000 of convertible preferred stock and $5,000,000 of debentures by the parent company. . . . the Commission found that the proposal was faulty in failing to provide for additional common equity to balance the large amount of senior securities proposed to be issued. It indicated that a minimum acceptable position might be reached if the $7,500,000 now proposed to be raised through convertible preferred stock were raised instead through the sale of additional common shares.[32]

The idea of preferred stock as a senior security and therefore subject to limited usage in the interests of financial safety and flexibility is well

---

[30] Securities and Exchange Commission, *Nineteenth Annual Report* (1953), p. 78.

[31] Securities and Exchange Commission, *Fourteenth Annual Report* (1948), p. 78.

[32] Securities and Exchange Commission, *Sixteenth Annual Report* (1950), p. 95.

established in certain SEC standards, notably in the one cited on page 557 regarding dividend policy and in the minimum proportions for common stock and surplus. (From our treatment of preferred stock in earlier chapters the reader will be aware that we share this view.) A rule similar to the one cited for the maintenance of a minimum cushion of common equity in the capital structure was included in a list of specific provisions prepared by the Commission to be included in corporate charters of utilities about to issue new preferred stock.[33] Another rule in the same list requires that preferred stocks be redeemable at the option of the issuer, thus again recognizing the need for flexibility in the use of a semifixed security type.[34]

The ambivalence of the Commission toward preferred stock is seen in cases where a utility plans to increase the amount of its debt while reducing its outstanding preferred stock. There is obvious tax advantage in such a step, but the SEC has said: "The desirability for tax purposes of interest on debt capital should not be employed as a basis for permitting an excessive debt ratio. . . . The stock equity of a company should be sufficient to enable it to withstand economic adversity."[35]

Yet in this case, a debenture issue was approved partly because the company announced its intention to abandon further issuance of preferred and to give "early consideration" to the feasibility of retiring the system's outstanding preferred.

Financial Planning. A natural by-product of the SEC's careful probing of utility capital structures has been an emphasis on careful planning for future needs. Where it appears necessary, the Commission insists on a forecast of future capital expenditures and a plan for financing these expenditures which preserves the desired balance of debt and equity sources. Recognizing the long-term growth characteristics of the utility industry and the uncertainties of the capital market over the years, the Commission has stressed the desirability of a margin of borrowing power in existing capital structures as a necessary prerequisite to financial planning and to the appropriate timing of new issues.

An example of the role of the Commission in the area of financial planning is seen in the following SEC commentary:

. . . Before granting approval of $18,000,000 of bank borrowings . . . the Commission . . . gave careful consideration to the over-all financing program of [American Gas and Electric Co.] . . . and devoted particular attention to the responsibility and intentions of the holding company to preserve the balance of underlying equity in the system.

American, in response to this inquiry, placed before the Commission the

---

[33] Securities and Exchange Commission, *Holding Company Act Release No. 13106* (February 16, 1956), p. 3.

[34] *Ibid.*, p. 2.

[35] Securities and Exchange Commission, *Holding Company Act Release No. 14451* (May 25, 1961).

details of its 3-year construction and financing program. . . . The Commission observed that the financing program ". . . appears feasible and sound in the light of the standards of the Act."[36]

Shareholders and Management. In its efforts to strengthen the financial structure of the electric and gas utility industry, the SEC aims to benefit directly or indirectly all who are associated with the industry, including the stockholders. In a sense the Commission has been attempting to protect ownership from its own shortsightedness and neglect. Of course, the existence of the large numbers of shareholders who do not have any effective voice in management decisions leads to the conclusion that special safeguards are necessary if their somewhat defenseless position is not to be abused. In line with this the SEC has advocated a number of corporate practices which are designed either to strengthen the voice of the shareholders or to protect them where they are voiceless.

As a protection for preferred shareholders, the SEC has presented the following provision for inclusion in corporate charters as a part of a formal statement of policy on preferred stock:

If and when dividends on any series of the preferred stock shall be in arrears in an amount equal to four full quarter-yearly payments or more per share, the holders of all series of the preferred stock voting together as a class shall be entitled to elect the smallest number of directors necessary to constitute a majority of the full board of directors until such time as all dividend arrears on the preferred stock shall have been paid or declared and set apart for payment.[37]

As a means of giving a voice to minority groups of common shareholders, the Commission has advocated the adoption of cumulative voting rules for the election of directors of electric and gas utilities. Commission rules have also included protection of preferred shareholders against the creation of additional securities with an equal or prior claim without the consent of a majority of the preferred shareholders, and it has also encouraged the use of the preemptive right as a means of protecting the common shareholder against some of the effects of dilution.

Finally, the SEC has been pressing for the elimination of publicly held minority interests in the voting stock of subsidiaries. Where the rest of the votes are held by the holding company, the voting power of the minority provides nothing. This problem remained, as of June 30, 1964, in only three systems.[38]

---

[36] Securities and Exchange Commission, *Sixteenth Annual Report* (1950), p. 88.

[37] Securities and Exchange Commission, *Holding Company Act Release No. 13106* (February 16, 1956), p. 3.

[38] Securities and Exchange Commission, *Thirtieth Annual Report,* p. 89, n. 8.

The Role of the SEC under Chapter X of the Bankruptcy Act

There is also another way in which the Commission makes its influence on financial policy felt beyond the limits of the public utility industry. Under the provisions of Chapter X of the Bankruptcy Act, the SEC may act in an advisory capacity in proceedings leading to the reorganization of corporations in bankruptcy. The specific nature of this activity of the SEC will be treated in some detail in Chapter 30 on corporate reorganization. At this point, it is sufficient to note that there is a natural carry-over of concepts and standards developed in the public utility field into the more diversified applications of the bankruptcy courts.

It is also interesting to note that in practice the role of the SEC under the Bankruptcy Act has not been the passive one which might be inferred from an "advisory" role. Rather, it has assumed the role of "watchdog" and moves with obvious determination when the situation appears to warrant its participation. During the 1964 fiscal year the Commission participated in 93 proceedings involving the reorganization of companies with aggregate assets of $748 million. To quote the Commission, it "seeks to participate principally in those proceedings in which a substantial public investor interest is involved."[39]

Regulation by Other Agencies

Although our attention has been centered on the SEC, it must not be forgotten that many other agencies have powers affecting the financial decisions of business firms. Each state has a utility commission, but its primary responsibility is toward the setting of reasonable prices for the utilities' services. Generally speaking, state commissions have either followed the SEC or given less direction over the policies that have been under discussion.

The powers of the Interstate Commerce Commission, over railroads and other land transport, and of the Civil Aeronautics Board, over airlines, include the right to approve or disapprove of the terms of security issues. Their regulation, however, shows a disinclination to become involved in the details of the financing of solvent companies. After bankruptcy, it is another story.

The following brief survey of the major issues which the ICC has raised in its supervision of the issuance of new railroad securities will suggest the nature of these differences in approach. One of the primary concerns of the Commission, which reflects the financial condition of many segments of the industry, has been to avoid or reduce overcapitalization. The desired objective is to have a full value of tangible assets standing behind every dollar of outstanding securities. This is achieved by requiring that new issues of securities represent actual expenditures. A

---

[39] Securities and Exchange Commission, *Thirtieth Annual Report* (1964), pp. 98–99.

related requirement is that the Commission will set the minimum price at which new issues will be sold. In this way the Commission seeks to assure that the issue will produce the maximum of funds possible under the circumstances.

With the exception of these two aspects of railroad finance, neither of which would appear to infringe on the freedom of action of management to any serious extent, the Commission generally takes a more flexible position and is more inclined to "suggest" than to "require." On the subject of competitive bidding, the ICC has backed away from a universal requirement, except for equipment trust certificates. Although it has sometimes required competitive bidding on interest-bearing securities, the Commission has clearly recognized that exceptions are often justified.

Perhaps the most significant area of intervention by the ICC has been in regard to debt-equity proportions in the capital structure. Here, its actions are far less precise than those of the SEC, reported earlier in this chapter. Note the general tone of the following statement:

It is our view that railroads with weak financial structures, and those just emerging from receivership or reorganization proceedings . . . should be encouraged to use their earnings . . . to build up and improve their property, retire their funded debt, and create corporate surpluses in amounts sufficient to meet their emergency needs, support their borrowing powers, and afford insurance against obsolescence."[40]

The principal means by which the ICC has attempted to bring about a more conservative capital structure in railroads has been through the sinking fund requirement, initiated in 1933. In 1936 the Commission reported on this requirement as follows: "In all cases where we have been called upon to approve the actual issue of bonds we have insisted that the applicant make provision for the retirement of all or a part of the bonds before maturity and have required that sinking funds be provided, unless good and sufficient reasons appeared for not doing so."[41]

It is undoubtedly true, of course, that the more restrained regulation of the ICC has been conditioned by the characteristics of the industry and also by the fact that its responsibilities were only in part financial. On the matter of the balance of debt and equity in the capital structure, for example, the Commission has considered it a fact of life in the railroad industry that improvement in the ratio through new equity issues is often out of the question:

Few railroads are in a position to reduce their indebtedness through the sale of capital stock. Most railroads must look entirely to their earnings for necessary funds. . . .

At present a large proportion of the outstanding railroad bonds can be

---

[40] Interstate Commerce Commission, *Fiftieth Annual Report* (1936), p. 19.

[41] *Ibid.*, p. 17.

bought at large discounts. This affords a most favorable opportunity to eliminate debt and to cut fixed charges. . . .

In our last report we again discussed the importance of debt reduction. We suggest that the present favorable earnings be used as largely as is practicable for that purpose. We are convinced that both the public interest and the interests of the carrier shareholders will in the long run be served by that policy.[42]

It is apparent that under these circumstances, the Commission feels that all it can or should do is to suggest and encourage action toward the desired objective.

Before we leave this subject, it is interesting to note that the ICC in recent years has permitted the substitution of income bonds for preferred stock as a means of reducing the tax burden on the railroads concerned.[43] This reflects the general trend away from preferred stock as a source of funds and the growing respectability of the income bonds as a security combining the flexibility of equity capital with the tax advantage of debt.

Summary

In this chapter, we have been considering the various ways in which government, particularly the federal government, exercises an influence over the long-term financing of private enterprise. It will now be apparent that government regulation has extended far beyond its initial objectives of protecting the unsophisticated investor from fraud and his own ignorance. Much of this necessary kind of regulation continues today. It is, however, in the area of regulation of long-term financial policy where the most significant recent developments have come. In focusing on the detailed regulations of the SEC and looking at other agencies, we have attempted to serve two purposes: (1) to present for consideration and discussion a set of specific standards of financial practice which have been imposed on private enterprise on an industry-wide basis and which have implications for business generally, and (2) to illustrate what government intervention can mean in restricting the area of decision making in long-term finance.

---

[42] Interstate Commerce Commission, *Fifty-sixth Annual Report* (1942), p. 29.

[43] Interstate Commerce Commission, *Seventy-third Annual Report* (1959), p. 65.

PART IX

Financing Growth and Development

Chapter 28

Financing the New Small-Scale Enterprise

IN FINANCING the new small-scale business enterprise, certain variations in the financial problems and practices occur which are peculiar to a business at this stage of its development. This chapter is designed to bring out the nature and significance of the more important of these variations. A primary objective will be to draw a distinction between the problem of smallness in business and the often related but different problems of newness, inexperience, and incompetence.

In view of the large numbers of new businesses that are being formed every year, it is obvious that each year a substantial percentage of the business owner-manager population is going to be preoccupied with the special problems of a business in formation. When these figures are considered in relation to those on business termination, it is also apparent that a great many businessmen cope with these problems unsuccessfully. A study on business turnover was prepared by the Department of Commerce relating to the period 1946–54.[1] This study indicated that about half of the businesses formed in this period were sold or liquidated within 2 years. Only one in every three survived a 4-year life, and only one in every five survived for 10 years. The Department of Commerce figures indicated that the turnover was greatest in the retail trade, where only three out of five new ventures survived beyond the first year and only one in six reached an age of 10 years.[2]

Statistics such as these, which have been available and widely circulated for many years, are not likely to encourage an attitude of optimism toward new businesses on the part of those who are asked to supply capital to such businesses. Of course, aggregate statistics cannot

---

[1] "Age and Life Expectancy of Business Firms," *Survey of Current Business,* December, 1955, pp. 15–19.

[2] *Ibid.,* p. 15.

provide a satisfactory basis for judgment in the individual case. Unfortunately, however, a new business is by definition a business without a record of performance by which potential can be measured; consequently, there is little if any basis for differentiating it from what is assumed to be typical. A new and small business must have some unusual appeal before it can be considered an exception from the general expectation of great risk and probable failure, an expectation which continues to be supported by experience even in times of high-level prosperity.

Newness as a Financial Problem

A new business which is well conceived and well planned possesses certain inherent competitive advantages. At the same time, the fact of its newness may have significant financial disadvantages. One of these comes in financial planning. The starting point of any program for the financing of a business is a careful estimate of requirements. The usual starting point in business forecasts is the record of the immediate past, modified for foreseeable variations during the forecast period. Without the advantage of a period of actual performance upon which to base assumptions, it is exceedingly difficult to anticipate such vital information as the amount and timing of customers' orders, credit experience with customers, and profit margins with the degree of accuracy necessary to make the forecast useful. The possibility of substantial errors of forecast is great. Unfortunately, the spirit of optimism which is a necessary accompaniment of new ventures in business tends to produce underestimates rather than overestimates of the needed funds.

Take, for example, the problem of forecasting the absorption of funds into working capital in a business manufacturing children's clothing which is commencing its first season of operations. First, there is the problem of customers' orders—amount and timing. Typically, samples would be made up in advance of the season and shown to buyers. Then comes a waiting period while buyers delay their commitments as long as possible as a precaution against sudden changes in consumer buying. The manufacturer may lay in cloth in expectation of the hoped-for sales, but the question is: How much? What kind and grade of material? What colors? To misjudge in any direction may mean that funds are unnecessarily tied up in unusable inventory. Even if he judges correctly, he does not wish to invest earlier than necessary, since the cost of funds is a function both of the amount and of the period of time over which it is needed. On the other hand, to invest too late may mean that inventory is not available at reasonable prices and/or that delivery dates cannot be met.

Eventually, the actual buying time arrives, and orders are placed by various customers within a matter of weeks in varying amounts and with varying delivery dates. Even this does not completely answer the question of sales volume, since there remains the possibility of reorders of successful items at a later date. The anticipation of demand in such an industry is difficult even for a business of long standing, but it becomes an almost impossible task for a new one. Added to this are the uncertainties of the production process. The costs and capacities of workers and machines individually and as a productive unit are to a considerable extent unknown until an actual run has been experienced. Workers prove incapable of doing their jobs, machines break down, scheduling proves inefficient and must be changed. An interruption at one point may well affect the whole operation. The usual result is more money invested for a longer period of time than was anticipated.

When the garments are finally produced and the order shipped, there comes a further waiting period over which the new manufacturer has little control—the time it takes for each customer to get around to paying his bills. Here, some information may be available on the experience of others; but there is no way of knowing how the customer will view this particular supplier, particularly when it is obvious that he is anxious to build up business. Every additional day that a customer uses the manufacturer as a source of short-term funds (by delaying payment) means another day during which the manufacturer is prevented from using those funds for a new cycle of working capital investment, and therefore means a net addition to his total financial need.

To the inherent difficulty of forecasting the need for funds may be added another problem. New businesses frequently involve new and inexperienced management. Since the idea which sparks the drive for independence in business normally grows out of experience in areas other than finance, the basic problem of forecasting the need for funds is often complicated by a lack of understanding of the means by which business transactions are translated into financial terms. Errors in projecting needs which result from inexperience are particularly common in the calculation of absorption of funds into working capital as production and sales develop.

Incompetence in the financial area may not be disastrous. The effects of ignorance depend on the nature and magnitude of the errors, the circumstances which may either magnify or cushion the effects, and the rapidity with which management can recognize and correct its mistakes. On the other hand, managerial incompetence is considered to be the primary cause of failure among new and small businesses. In Chapter 30 we cite the study of Dun & Bradstreet in reference to this. It is difficult in practice to separate incompetence in the financial area from incompetence in other areas of managerial responsibility, since most important decisions have their financial implications. Thus, "receivables difficulties" may have resulted from overenthusiastic selling, inadequate credit control, or an inability to anticipate the working capital requirement of credit to customers. There is no doubt, however, that the typical manager of a new business is much better prepared for his responsibilities in the areas of production or sales than he is in finance.

The disadvantage of newness is also to be found in relations with suppliers of capital. For those suppliers who are motivated by purely business considerations (as distinct from friends and relatives who play an important part in financing many new ventures), the principal guide to future performance is again the record of the immediate past. In the absence of operating statements, balance sheets, and credit and other records which lend some degree of objectivity to a judgment of future prospects, the prospective creditor or shareholder lacks a firm basis for the assumption of the very considerable risks involved. The inevitable result is that many sources, particularly institutional sources, refuse to assume these risks or insist on protective provisions such that the extent of their participation is seriously limited. Thus, a bank may be prepared to make a limited short-term loan, provided it is well protected by high-grade collateral with a value substantially in excess of the amount of the loan. A loan which is only a fraction of the value of inventory or accounts receivable will not solve the working capital problem of a new and growing business.

One business source of capital which frequently departs from the attitude suggested above is trade credit from suppliers. Primarily because suppliers wish to develop new customers, they often show a very tolerant attitude toward the new business, provided the management gives evidence of good faith in its dealings. In this regard, openness about financial difficulties in discussions with suppliers usually yields better results than secretiveness. It is because of this policy on the part of suppliers that trade credit ranks as one of the major sources of short-term funds in new and small businesses. It is unfortunately true that many new businesses under financial pressure will abuse trade credit, going on the assumption that the supplier will not get tough because he is anxious for business and will wait for his money (and even ship more inventory on credit) when a bank or finance company would not.

A partial substitute for lack of a performance record in the new business is to have management which has had a record of satisfactory performance in other business situations. If such is the case, the persons in question know and are known by suppliers of debt and equity capital and may be able to overcome their suppliers' natural reluctance by the confidence they personally inspire. Confidence inspired by individuals must, of course, be supported by early indications of strength in the new venture.

As a result of one or more of these disadvantages of newness, the founder of the new business may well find himself in an unusually weak bargaining position until such time as he is able to give clear proof of profit potential. If the founder needs further capital in the intervening period (which may last several years) and is not able to supply it himself or obtain it through normal channels such as trade credit, he may not be able to obtain the extra funds except on unfavorable terms. On the one hand, he himself is committed to the business and cannot withdraw at this stage without the chance of serious loss. On the other, there is little by which independent investors can be attracted to the business except the enthusiasm of those who need the money. The prospective creditor or shareholder is in a position to drive a hard bargain.

The Related Problem of Smallness

In the large majority of cases the new business is also a small business —small in the sense that the entire responsibility of management rests on one or two men. How far this statement is true can be seen from Table 28–1, which shows the results of a study of the formation of new

TABLE 28–1

Number of New Businesses in the United States, by Size of Firm, 1945–55
(Thousands of Businesses)

Year	Total of All Industries	Breakdown by Number of Employees			
		0–3	4–7	8–19	20 or More
1945	422.7	372.1	33.1	12.3	5.3
1946	617.4	533.0	56.5	20.9	7.1
1947	460.8	397.6	43.1	15.3	4.9
1948	393.3	337.7	38.3	13.0	4.3
1949	331.1	286.9	30.4	10.3	3.6
1950	348.2	298.3	34.3	11.7	3.9
1951–55 (total)	1,798.0	1,560.9	161.0	55.0	21.1

Source: *Survey of Current Business*, May, 1954, Table 6, p. 20, for 1945–50; and September, 1959 Table 4, p. 18, for 1951–55.

businesses by size, measured in terms of number of employees. The figures indicate that about 99% of all new businesses had fewer than 20 employees at the time of their origin and that 86% had fewer than 4 employees. Thus, consideration of the problems peculiar to the new business must be supplemented by a consideration of those associated with smallness of scale of operations.

One of these problems is the highly personal character of businesses of the size indicated above. The business typically stands or falls on the experience, intelligence, and initiative of one man. This can be a very real asset, and it is this which makes the small business so well suited to certain types of business activity. It can also give rise to difficulties. A business at this stage is merely an extension of an individual's personal activities, and its business decisions—particularly financial decisions— may be strongly influenced by purely personal considerations. So, for example, the absence of debt in the capital structure may result from a deeply rooted personal feeling against borrowing in general, although the circumstances of the business may indicate that a limited use might be highly desirable and financially sound. In the larger business with a management group and possibly with a separation of ownership and management, personal considerations are more likely to be subordinated to the common goals of the business.

The attitude of suppliers of capital may be influenced adversely by the fact of one-man management. The possibility of death or withdrawal of this individual presents a significant risk. Here, insurance can be of some help, but continuity of the business as a profitable unit independent of particular persons is much to be desired in financial contracts. The corporate form provides the legal fiction of continuity of life, but it becomes a reality only through the development of a competent and reliable management group capable of reproducing itself.

Another aspect of one-man management is the pressure of time, which frequently bears down on one individual who is attempting to discharge all the demands made on him as owner-manager in addition to the many operating tasks which others in the business are not capable of doing. The inevitable result is to give low priority to those things which appear to him to be less important at the moment, less interesting, or by nature more postponable. Financial matters often fall into this category. Insufficient time is given to keeping informed on the financial implications of action, to careful projection of needs, and to the cultivation of sources of capital so important in the rather informal capital market in which the small business often operates.

This raises another aspect of the small-scale business—the peculiarities of its market for funds. Since the depression of the thirties, the organized capital market has been under attack for being insensitive to the needs of small business. There are good and obvious reasons why financial institutions are likely to be less interested in the small business than in the large business. Banks and insurance companies have a primary responsibility to depositors and policyholders to maintain high standards of safety in their investments. The record of solvency in small business has not been encouraging; and while this does not mean that large-scale business is necessarily a safer investment, these investors tend to be wary of heavy involvement in new and small-scale businesses. Further, there is the obvious point that the return to be derived from the small account is less interesting than that from the large account, particularly in view of the relatively fixed costs of servicing the account. It is for this reason that the machinery which has been developed in the capital market for such tasks as the marketing of securities is primarily designed for the larger sums required of large-scale enterprise.

This does not mean that a small business cannot satisfy its need for funds in the normal capital market. Many mature and profitable small businesses are more than adequately supplied in this way. What it does mean is that the small-scale businessman may have to spend considerable time and effort cultivating this market before the desired results are obtained.

New businesses are typically small for two reasons: The scale may be that which is best suited to the particular activity, or the resources of the founders are such that a larger and more efficient scale is not possible at the outset. Through either ignorance, impatience, or sheer venturesomeness, many businesses are started on a scale far below that which the industry and the market require as a prerequisite for permanence, stability, and profitability. For such a business, rapid growth is vital to survival. There is a great sense of urgency to obtain the break-even point of profitability in the shortest possible time; and if the business has promise, there may be the opportunity to grow as rapidly as financial, physical, and human capacities permit. It is not unusual to find a business in its early years doubling or tripling sales volume from one year to the next. Such a rate of growth gives the business an almost insatiable appetite for new capital. Until it reaches and passes the break-even point, however, the business has little appeal to outside investors and little, if any, throwoff of funds from internal sources. Operations in this early period may constitute a drain on funds because of a net excess of costs over revenues. A business in these circumstances has little staying power, and the slightest reverse creates a major financial crisis.

The Sources of Funds for New Enterprise

In many respects, the financing of a new small-scale business is no different from that of business in general. By calling attention to certain peculiarities which have widespread occurrence among such businesses, there is a danger of leaving the impression that they exist in a financial world of their own. On the other hand, it is important to be alerted to the fact that certain variations in the normal pattern of business finance can be traced to the age and size of the business unit.

The primary source of equity capital in the new small-scale business is the personal savings of the founders and the earnings of the business. In a study made by the Office of Business Economics of the Department of Commerce of the initial financing of wholesale and retail businesses, it was found that two thirds of the total investment came from personal savings.[3] Further, it was indicated that in the sample under consideration, 45% of the firms financed the initial investment entirely through savings. Chart 28–1 shows the sources of the initial capital for the sample of retail businesses. In many cases the personal savings of the founder were supplemented by the personal savings of relatives and friends. The comparative importance of this source reflects a desire for independence of ownership and control, and also the basic difficulty of raising initial

---

[3] "Capital Requirements of New Trade Firms," *Survey of Current Business*, December, 1948, pp. 19–20.

CHART 28-1

SOURCES OF INITIAL INVESTMENT FUNDS—600,000 RETAILERS
PERIOD OF ORIGIN: 1945–47*

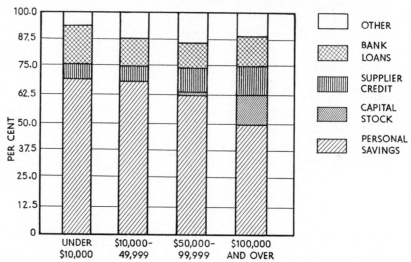

* Office of Business Economics, Department of Commerce, "Capital Requirements of New Trade Firms,"
Survey of Current Business, December, 1948, Table 1, p. 23.

capital from impersonal sources except on a relatively minor scale and only when the owners are themselves heavily committed.

The other side of the same picture is the very minor role played by public offerings of stock. The study quoted above showed that for businesses with sales up to $50,000, this source was practically non-existent. In businesses with sales over $100,000, it provided a modest 13% of the total. This situation exists primarily for two reasons. One is the widespread reluctance among founders of new businesses to share the hoped-for profits and control of the business. The other is that public offerings of stock involve considerable overhead-type costs, as well as substantial risks, which make the costs of flotation of new and small issues almost prohibitive. A study made by the Securities and Exchange Commission for the years 1951, 1953, and 1955 of costs of flotation of new issues of common stock for cash sale through investment bankers showed that for issues under $500,000, commissions and discount averaged 20.99% of gross proceeds and other expenses averaged 6.16%, giving a total cost of 27.15%. On the other hand, issues of $2 million to $5 million cost 8.47% in commissions and discount and 1.50% in other expenses, totaling 9.97% of gross proceeds.[4]

---

[4] Securities and Exchange Commission, *Cost of Flotation of Corporate Securities, 1951–1955* (Washington, D.C.: U.S. Government Printing Office, June, 1957), Table 1, p. 37.

Table 16–2, on page 337 of this book, adds data on underwriting spreads in 1963 to those in the SEC study. On common stock issues under $500,000 the underwriting spread was 10.42% in 1963, compared with 20.99% in 1951–53–55; on issues of $2 to $5 million the spread was 6.30% in 1963, against 8.47% in 1951–53–55.

The remaining means by which the owner-manager can contribute to the capital of the business is by plowing back all earnings of the business except for a modest salary. Unfortunately, it is often true that the earnings of a business in the early years, when need is greatest, are small or nonexistent. Among other causes, this may result from a volume of sales below the break-even point for the industry or because of the inevitable time lag in reaching maximum efficiency. This situation will be particularly serious if it has not been anticipated or if the reverse has been expected and plans made accordingly. All too frequently, the optimism of the founders leads to the hope of large profits immediately, profits which are counted on to contribute essential capital for stabilization and growth.

Whatever one may think about the appropriateness of trading on the equity in the new small-scale business, it is a fact that debt capital plays a major role in the financing of this type of business. This is supported by the figures on retail stores previously cited (page 576). A more recent study of debt financing in small business (by the Office of Business Economics, Department of Commerce) gives more detailed information which bears out what others have observed in individual cases.[5]

This study gives information on the financing of newer firms with respect to both funds obtained and funds not obtained. The figures in Table 28–2 are for the year 1954. It can be seen that the primary demand, whether satisfied or not, was for debt capital. It is interesting to note, however, that the businesses concerned had better success in obtaining debt capital than equity capital.

The same study provided an analysis of the character of the loans sought and obtained by these newer firms. The statistical data are shown in Table 28–3. Certain features stand out. One is the dominant place of banks as a source of loan funds and the very minor role played by other established financial institutions, such as insurance companies. Another feature is the absence of collateral in over 50% of the loans made. It is also significant that, with respect to the duration of the loan, most of the loans obtained were of the seasonal type, but most of the unsatisfied need for debt capital was in the categories of 1 to 3 years and longer. Finally, it is perhaps not surprising to find that the loans wanted but not obtained were for larger amounts than was the case for loans obtained.

The importance of trade credit as a source of funds for the new and small business has already been mentioned. The magnitude of its contribution to small businesses in general is indicated in Chart 28–1. The place of trade credit in the financing of a particular business depends on its particular group of suppliers, the customary credit terms of the industry, and the general state of the market. As a source of short-term debt capital, trade credit has a special appeal not only because of its

---

[5] See "External Financing of Small- and Medium-Size Business," *Survey of Current Business*, October, 1955, pp. 15–22.

TABLE 28-2

CAPITAL FINANCING BY NEWER FIRMS* FOR YEAR ENDED JUNE 30, 1954
(Percent)

```
All firms—total...................................100.0%
    No outside funds wanted........................ 46.8
    Outside funds wanted........................... 53.2

    Obtained all funds wanted..................25.3
    Did not obtain all funds wanted.............27.9

    Obtained some funds...................19.2
    Obtained no funds..................... 8.7
Aggregate demand—total............................100.0%
    Loans......................................... 87.0
    Equity........................................ 13.0
Funds obtained—total..............................100.0%
    Loans......................................... 92.0
    Equity........................................  8.0
Funds wanted but not obtained—total...................100.0%
    Loans......................................... 74.0
    Equity........................................ 26.0
Loan demand—total.................................100.0%
    Obtained...................................... 75.0
    Not obtained.................................. 25.0
Equity demand—total...............................100.0%
    Obtained...................................... 45.0
    Not obtained.................................. 55.0
Aggregate demand—total............................100.0%
    Obtained...................................... 71.0
    Not obtained.................................. 29.0
```

* Newer firms defined as firms with one or more paid employees, which started new businesses after March, 1951.

SOURCE: Office of Business Economics, Department of Commerce, "External Financing of Small- and Medium-Size Business," *Survey of Current Business*, October, 1955, pp. 18–19.

magnitude but also because of the comparative flexibility in the enforcement of credit terms by suppliers.

A development in recent years that may hold considerable significance for new and small-scale businesses is the interest shown by insurance companies and some other lenders in an equity type of participation as a part of a loan agreement. The option to purchase a block of common stock at a favorable price is regarded as an inducement to make a loan that would otherwise be considered unattractive at fixed interest rates within the customary range. This suggests a possible formula whereby some conservative financial institutions which are not now considered as a primary source of capital for small business may be induced to divert some funds into this market. So far, however, loans of this type form a very modest part of the portfolios of the lending institutions making use of them.

A point which has been observed to be significant to many new and small businesses is the time and effort required in the cultivation of capital sources. When a business must supplement regular sources such

TABLE 28-3

Statistics on Loans Obtained and Not Obtained by Newer Firms*
for Year Ended June 30, 1954

	Source of Loans				Type of Collateral Required			
	Bank	Individual†	Other‡	None	Current Assets	Equipment	Other Fixed Business Assets	Personal and Other
All firms	68.8%	15.7%	15.5%	54.1%	11.1%	14.8%	11.5%	8.5%
Construction	70.5	13.4	16.1	50.4	10.6	12.0	18.4	8.6
Manufacturing	67.9	12.2	19.9	53.5	10.0	22.3	12.3	1.9
Wholesale trade	70.6	16.4	13.0	60.0	20.7	9.0	4.8	5.5
Retail trade	67.7	18.7	13.6	54.7	8.3	14.8	8.9	13.3

Duration of Loans

	Loans Obtained				Loans Not Obtained			
	90 Days or Less	91–364 Days	1–3 Years	3 Years or More	90 Days or Less	91–364 Days	1–3 Years	3 Years or More
All firms	43.5%	19.1%	30.0%	7.4%	3.2%	9.2%	52.8%	34.8%
Construction	40.1	24.4	25.6	9.9	1.2	11.0	63.4	24.4
Manufacturing	45.1	20.0	28.8	6.1	2.4	7.1	47.6	42.9
Wholesale trade	62.6	16.3	18.4	2.7	6.3	12.5	40.6	40.6
Retail trade	37.5	16.1	38.2	8.2	4.3	7.4	50.0	38.3

Median Amount of Borrowed Funds

	Obtained	Wanted but Not Obtained
All firms	$ 4,500	$10,000
Construction	5,000	10,000
Manufacturing	7,300	10,000
Wholesale trade	10,000	15,000
Retail trade	3,100	7,000

* Newer firms defined as firms with one or more paid employees, which started new businesses after March, 1951.
† Partner, corporate official, acquaintance, or relative.
‡ Insurance companies and other financial institutions, supplier, equipment dealer, factor, government, and other.
Source: Office of Business Economics, Department of Commerce, "External Financing of Small- and Medium-Size Business," *Survey of Current Business*, October, 1955, pp. 20–21.

as trade credit and bank loans by recourse to the secondary capital market of relatives, friends, business acquaintances, customers, finance companies, and the like, there are very few reliable guides. Each source must be explored carefully and exhaustively to pin down the precise terms upon which the money will be made available. Even when terms are established, the reliability of the lender may be in doubt, especially if the agreement extends over a considerable period of time. In such situations the negotiations for capital can consume a great deal of time and effort, and the task cannot be delegated by the owner-manager.

Special Assistance to Small Businesses

The widespread acceptance of the idea that small business is confronted with unusual problems peculiar to it has resulted in efforts on the part of government and private agencies to diminish or eliminate these problems. For many years, government has assumed the role of custodian of the competitive system, and one of the key elements in such a system is a business climate favorable to the formation of new competitive units where the need exists. It is natural, therefore, that the government would take it upon itself to keep the opportunities for new and small business alive. Whether or not such governmental activities are appropriate may be open to debate; but they are a fact of life for small businesses, a vital fact for many, and must therefore be taken into account.

All levels of government have hastened to pay at least lip service to the needs of small business, but the most noteworthy service has been that offered by the federal government. The principal agency for this activity is the Small Business Administration. The work of the SBA has very significant financial implications for the small business which seeks and qualifies for its assistance. One of the responsibilities of the SBA has been to assist small businesses in getting their share of government contracts. This it does by acting as a source of information for government purchasing agencies, as well as potential suppliers, by certifying businesses as being financially and technically competent to undertake government contracts, by helping to form production pools, and by setting aside certain government purchases for competitive bidding by small firms.

The SBA is also authorized to assist in the financing of small business either by making direct loans or by participating with banks or other private credit institutions. The loan may be for the purpose of financing plant and equipment or working capital. There are a number of restrictions as to the circumstances under which a loan will be made, one of which is that all other reasonable sources, internal and external, must first be exhausted. The SBA is a lender of last resort—a possible alternative to the high-cost secondary money market so frequently used by small businesses.

Some statistics on SBA loans will give a more precise idea of the nature and extent of this activity.[6] From the beginning of its loan program through December 31, 1964, the SBA approved 50,754 business loans for a total of $2,441 million. This is exclusive of disaster loans. Of the loans made during 1964, 51% were made directly by the SBA, 42% involved immediate participation with banks, and 7% involved either deferred participation by the SBA or a guarantee to the lender by the SBA. As a measure of the size of the loan, 31% of the loans approved in 1964 were for amounts of $10,000 or less, 34% were in the $10,000 to $25,000 range, 26% were $25,000 to $100,000, and 9% were over $100,000. These figures reflect an increase in the number of very small loans encouraged by a liberalized Small Loan Program directed at retail and service businesses.

The SBA loss experience on business loans has been reported through June 30, 1964. Up to that date the SBA had experienced losses on 803 loans and had charged off approximately $9 million of principal due. An additional 910 loans representing $18 million were under suspicion of loss at that time. The total of actual and estimated losses represented 1.8% of the loan funds disbursed through that date. There was insufficient evidence to indicate the effect on loss experience of the stepped-up efforts on very small loans.

A third function of the SBA is to provide financial counseling and other management and technical assistance where it is needed and requested. The criteria as to what businesses may qualify for these various forms of assistance are not completely rigid. The business must be independently owned and operated and not dominant in its field. For contract assistance a firm with fewer than 500 employees is small. The measure for financial assistance is more complex. In manufacturing, a firm with fewer than 250 employees is small, and a firm with more than 1,000 employees is considered large. For companies between these limits, acceptability varies with the industry. A retail business with annual net sales of $1 million or less is considered small scale, and in wholesaling the limit is set at $5 million. It is clear that these limits in terms of number of employees and sales volume are arbitrary, but it is also clear that a line must be drawn at some point.

In 1958 the SBA was made the channel through which a new form of federal assistance became available to small business. In this year the Small Business Investment Act was passed. This Act provided for the licensing and incorporation of investment companies to supply equity as well as debt capital to small business. Minimum initial capital required for such an investment was $300,000, half of which might be provided by the federal government through a long-term loan and at least half by private investors through the purchase of stock. The intent of the Act was

---

[6] Small Business Administration, *1964 Annual Report* (Washington, D.C.: U.S. Government Printing Office, 1965).

to encourage private investment in small business and to recognize the critical need for equity funds as well as debt capital.

The response to the Small Business Investment Company (SBIC) concept was substantial. By the end of 1964 there were 700 such companies in operation with an investment of $500 million in 10,000 small businesses. Their performance, however, was less impressive than some of the founders had been led to expect. A problem in identifying investment opportunities having the appropriate risk and profit characteristics led to delays in reaching full employment of resources and profitability in the SBIC's. Inevitably there was some mismatching of investors, SBIC management, and small business investment opportunities.

In 1964 the federal government moved to relieve some of the problems which had emerged. The changes which were instituted included a higher initial investment hurdle for new SBIC's (now $300,000 of private capital), increased opportunity for investment by the government itself through the SBA in the form of direct loans to SBIC's (maximum raised from $400,000 to $700,000) and guarantees, and more freedom for the SBIC's in the risk and profit characteristics of their investments. In general, the problems of the SBIC's for which these moves were designed as a partial solution merely reflect the basic difficulties of equity investment in the new and small business, to which we have already referred.

Another and quite different means by which governments have sought to assist small-scale business is through relief from taxation. The primary tax on business income is the corporate income tax. Since many small and new businesses are not incorporated, they escape this tax. Whether or not this is an advantage depends on circumstances. The owner escapes the business income tax but must pay the personal income tax on all business income, whether withdrawn or not. The problem comes down to a comparison of corporate and personal income tax rates for the sums involved.

Within the federal corporate income tax, there is presently a degree of relief for the small business in the breakdown between the so-called "normal" tax and the surtax, which applies only to income in excess of $25,000. Under the tax reduction introduced in 1964, the normal tax rate to be applied in 1965 and later years is 22% and the surtax is 26%. This compares with the previous rates of 30% and 22%. For the very small corporation the advantage of this provision can be significant. It is interesting that, to date, tax concessions of this type have been solely in terms of size of a business (measured by taxable income) rather than some combination of size and age of the business. There is reason to believe that if tax relief is justified in the broad economic sense, it would be for the new business rather than the small business as such. Greater competitive stimulus might well result from substantial but temporary relief for the new business rather than permanent shelter for the small business.

An expression of the fiscal concepts which underly the approach to small business is seen in the following excerpt from a speech by the Undersecretary of the Treasury in 1953:

The broad objective of providing a tax system under which small business will flourish has three major aspects: First, small business must be permitted to grow. An ample supply of available funds from the business' own earnings and from outside sources is essential to finance expansion. In this connection the structure and rates of the corporate and individual income taxes, the definition of income, the allowable deductions and the treatment of undistributed corporate income are all of great importance. Second, the continued independent existence of established small business must be encouraged. Those features of the law and regulations which relate to financing the estate taxes due when important members of the business die are of particular interest. The tax effect of the recapitalization which occurs in connection with the partial withdrawal of investment of the original owners is also of special importance. The third major approach . . . is concerned primarily with lightening the burden of the compliance for small business through simplification of the tax laws and regulations and improvement in administrative attitudes. . . .[7]

While generally less ambitious in scope, programs have been established by state and local governments in aid of the small-scale business. Such programs generally have the twofold objective of helping existing businesses to become more efficient and profitable and of attracting new business ventures, large and small, to a particular area. For many years, New York State has been one of the leaders in encouraging better-informed and better-qualified small business management. Through various publications the State Department of Commerce gives general advice on starting and operating small business, specific counsel and information on the operation of many different types of small businesses, such as restaurants and electrical appliance stores, a variety of pertinent business statistics for the state as a whole and by districts, and other information which is not readily available to the small-scale operator. In addition, personal counsel is available through regional offices of the Department and by the operation of regional workshops and forums.

As a general rule, state and local governments refrain from becoming involved in financial assistance to small business. They have, however, lent encouragement to the establishment of an institution of some real significance in this respect—the business development corporation. These corporations have as their primary objective the encouragement of

---

[7] From a speech by Marion B. Folsom before the House Committee on Small Business, May 21, 1953, as quoted in the *Journal of Accountancy*, July, 1953, p. 106.

industrial growth in an area, working on the assumption that one of the chief obstacles, particularly for smaller businesses, is a lack of medium- and long-term debt capital. An example of this type of institution is the Massachusetts Business Development Corporation. Its capital is derived from loans from banks with which it is associated and from the sale of stock. The loans made by this corporation are primarily of a long-term character, with maturities ranging to 10 years. For the most part, they have been secured by one or more of the following types of collateral: first or second real estate or chattel mortgages, liens on accounts receivable and inventories, and assignments of life insurance policies and leases.

In summary, it may be said that at the present time the presence of various governmental and private agencies in the small business capital market has not made a radical change in the general financial position of the new and small business. However, for particular businesses, they have often meant the difference between continued operation and liquidation. Further, they appear to have become a permanent part of the financial scene.

The Conservation of Scarce Funds

Because the typical new and growing enterprise is faced with a persistent shortage of funds, which places serious restrictions on management's freedom of action, it is necessary not only to explore all possible sources of capital but also to consider ways and means of making available funds go as far as possible. In every business, there are certain physical facilities, stock-in-trade and personal and other services which must be provided in order to operate at all. On the other hand, these requirements normally have some element of flexibility, and there may be two or even several ways of providing some requirement which have significantly different financial implications. Hard-pressed small business managers must of necessity use as much persistence and originality in managing the productivity of each dollar raised as they do in raising it.

Without attempting to provide a complete catalog of the ways in which the business investment dollar may be made to go farther, the job of conservation can be illustrated by reference to several approaches which are in common use by small business managers. The investment in the physical facilities necessary for a given scale of operations may be minimized as follows:

1. Rent factory or store space, and rent equipment rather than purchase. Store or office space is usually easier to find on a rental basis than is factory space, because the former is a more standardized commodity. The opportunity for rental of machinery and equipment depends a great deal on the industry, since practices differ.
2. Purchase secondhand rather than new machinery and equipment. The availability of good secondhand equipment varies with the degree of

standardization of the equipment to be used and the size and character of the industrial area in which the new business is to be located. For example, it is quite feasible to pick up suitable secondhand equipment for a garment factory in the New York City area, where the industry is well established.

3. Purchase an existing business in financial difficulties. The opportunity to begin business in this way depends a great deal on the patience and flexibility of the individuals involved and the timing of the misfortunes of others. The individual who cannot or will not delay his start and who is strongly wedded by experience or prejudice to one line of activity is unlikely to find a favorable opportunity just when he wants it.

4. Build rather than buy ready-made. Many small business owners have saved scarce dollars by undertaking to construct their own physical facilities and, at least to some extent, make their own equipment. The possibilities here obviously depend on the capacities of the people involved and the nature of their business.

5. Assemble rather than manufacture. It is very common to find new businesses in the manufacturing area doing what is essentially an assembly operation. This helps to minimize the initial investment in plant and equipment. As they prosper and grow, they tend to take on more and more of the manufacturing, with the timing largely influenced by the growth of their financial resources.

6. Substitute labor for equipment. The initial financial burden in a new business may be minimized by purchasing only that equipment which is absolutely necessary and using labor wherever possible. Labor-saving equipment may then be added at a later date as funds permit.

In other ways the basic investment in working capital may be reduced by:

1. Keeping inventory down to what is absolutely necessary for continuous operation—and running some risk of inability to meet customer orders or of work stoppages.

2. Handling product lines which are available on favorable credit terms and avoiding lines which are not.

3. Restricting sale to those customers who are prepared to pay cash on delivery or within a brief credit period.

4. Scheduling production so as to produce salable products in the shortest possible time. The objective here is to produce an account receivable in the shortest possible time. Efficient production scheduling is not necessarily based on individual customers' orders, but it may be forced into this pattern if the need for release of cash is great.

5. Operating in whole or in part as a subcontractor to a larger business which may be willing to ease the financial burden by such means as supplying the raw materials for the operation out of its own inventory.

These devices are examples of what may be termed legitimate efforts to pare down the financial requirements of the business. It must be added that under extreme financial pressure, businesses sometimes resort to tactics which have a similar end result but which hardly qualify as sound financial practice. One of these is to abuse trade credit by allowing obligations to remain outstanding well beyond the limits set by the supplier. This practice is based on the assumption that because the supplier wants the business, he will not react by cutting off the supply and enforcing payment. A little experimentation along these lines shows up the soft spots. Another practice is to rely on the "float" of issued but uncashed checks to extend the usefulness of the bank account. Checks may be issued without being covered at the moment by cash in the bank in the hope that they will not be cashed immediately and that, by the time they are, deposits will have covered the amount. It is hardly necessary to say that this kind of "shoestring" financing is at best a questionable device for getting over the occasional tight spot and cannot be a part of a sound long-run financial policy.

In a review of the various ways of effecting some reduction in the need for funds during the initial stages of business life, it becomes apparent that the ultimate financial implications are not always the same. Four distinctly different effects can be observed:

1. A genuine reduction in the capital required to conduct the business—as illustrated by the purchase of assets at distress prices or the sale of products for cash rather than on extended credit terms.
2. Illusory economies of capital which simply defer the outlay—as illustrated by the purchase of secondhand plant or equipment which requires drastic overhaul or replacement in the near future.
3. The exchange of one financial problem for another—principally the exchange of a large initial outlay for a series of smaller payments over a period of time. This is illustrated by the "rent versus buy" alternative and the substitution of labor for machinery.
4. A reduction in the initial capital required in exchange for some loss of efficiency and profitability. This is seen in the subcontracting of aspects of a manufacturing process, in small and frequent purchases of raw materials, and in the scheduling of production in terms of orders rather than economical runs (when these conflict).

In taking a course of action that postpones an expenditure or changes its form from a lump sum to a series of smaller payments, the manager is primarily motivated by a desire to buy time. Such a step may be based on a careful projection of the future financial position of the business or may merely reflect an impatience to get under way and a blind optimism that things will work out somehow if only a start is made. If, as often happens, the shortage of funds is solved by "economies" which reduce efficiency, increase costs, and lower profit margins, the business manager may merely be postponing the evil day. The immediate financial relief is bought at the cost of lower profits in the future—profits which are a vital source of funds for consolidation and expansion. The hazards of such an approach to a shortage of capital are heightened by the fact that many men new to the role of the independent business operator may be ignorant of the effect on profit or, if aware of this possibility, are unable to assess its magnitude and tend to ignore it.

Summary and Conclusion

In this chapter we have outlined some of the financial problems and practices commonly associated with the new and small-scale business. It would be unfortunate if, in doing so, we overstated the differences between small-scale and large-scale business. In fact, businesses on both sides of this rather arbitrary classification are faced with the same basic financial problems involved in planning, raising, managing, and conserving the capital necessary to carry on their activities. In general, the approach to and analysis of the problems we have described throughout this book can be applied with equal advantage to both small-scale and large-scale business. Thus, for example, the usefulness of a detailed cash budget has nothing to do with the size of the operation.

It is true, of course, that much of our discussion, particularly as it relates to long-term finance, has been in terms which are more familiar to the large business. Even here, however, the careful reader will observe that, for example, the public stock offerings and privately placed bond issues of the multimillion-dollar corporation have their modest counterpart in the equity and debt arrangements of the one-man business and present the same basic questions as to the proper apportionment of risk, income, and control. Similar parallels could be drawn in regard to such problems as capital budgeting, the bargain for funds, and income administration. It was the major purpose of this chapter to assist the reader in making the necessary modifications of his analysis when dealing with a new or small-scale business problem.

Chapter 29

Business Mergers: Valuation and Other Financial Aspects

Definition of Terms

THE TERM *merger* implies a combination of two or more formerly independent business units into one organization with a common management and ownership. In business practice the term is loosely used to cover a variety of legal and financial devices by which this union of ownership and management is achieved. Other terms—*consolidation, amalgamation, acquisition*—are used in a similar context, and the lines of distinction are often unclear. Since an event of this sort has major legal implications, it might be helpful to begin with the legal concept. The statement which follows covers the basic legal framework. It is not intended to cover all the variations which have come into existence, the use of which has been strongly influenced by tax considerations.

Formal statutory provision for corporate mergers is to be found in the corporation laws of the various states. To choose a prominent example, the corporation law of the state of New York makes specific provision for both mergers and consolidations. According to this law, a *merger* takes place when two or more corporations merge into a single corporation which is one of the constituent corporations. A *consolidation,* on the other hand, takes place when two or more corporations consolidate into a new corporation to be formed pursuant to the consolidation. In both mergers and consolidations the plan usually must be authorized by vote of holders of two thirds of all outstanding shares entitled to vote thereon. However, a parent company owning 95% of the stock of a subsidiary may merge with the subsidiary without a shareholder vote. In a merger the certificate of incorporation of the surviving corporation, as amended by the merger plan, becomes the certificate of incorporation of the merged company. In a consolidation a new certificate of incorporation must be drawn up for the consolidated corporation. Both surviving and consolidated corporations possess all the rights, property, and the like, of the constituent corporations, and assume all their liabilities. In both cases,

588

provision is made for the appropriate treatment of those shareholders who formally protest the decision within the stated time limit.[1]

In contrast with the rather narrow and precise legal definition, we have the relatively loose and all-inclusive concept of a merger as used by the Federal Trade Commission. With an obvious interest in the monopolistic implications of mergers, the FTC is concerned with any act which causes the disappearance of a formerly independent business. It prefers to use the term *acquisition,* which includes "all business and corporate organizational and operational devices and arrangements by which the ownership and the management of independently operated properties and businesses are brought under the control of a single management."[2] Accordingly, this term includes mergers which are defined as acquisitions of large companies, as contrasted with those where the acquired company is small compared to the acquiring company. In this sense, mergers are numerically less important than acquisitions.

Within the framework of this book, we are primarily concerned with the financial implications of mergers. Thus, definitions which are useful for legal or regulatory purposes are not completely satisfactory for our purposes. A statutory merger of company A with company B, where A already owns 100% of the stock of B, is largely a legal formality with no major financial implications at this time. Similarly, there could be acquisitions which appear highly significant to the FTC, in terms of potential control of output or markets, which do not give rise to major financial problems for the businesses concerned. It will therefore suit us best to use an all-inclusive definition of a merger and ignore those forms which are of a nonfinancial character. Such a broad definition was suggested at the outset: the concept of a merger as a union of two or more independent business units into one organization with a common ownership and management.

The Merger Movement

What is termed *the merger movement* refers to the periodic rise and fall in the number of mergers taking place, roughly corresponding to cyclical swings of prosperity and depression. The Federal Trade Commission has brought up to date a statistical study of mergers which was begun by the Temporary National Economic Committee. A graph showing the number of mergers taking place in the years from 1919 through 1964 is reproduced in Chart 29–1. As indicated by the FTC, certain limitations of the study make the absolute figures unduly conservative, but the relative changes in merger activity are unmistakable. As can be seen, the first wave of merger activity came following

---

[1] See *The Corporation Manual* (1965 ed.; New York: U.S. Corporation Co., 1965), Vol. II, New York, pp. 53–57.

[2] Federal Trade Commission, *Report on Corporate Mergers and Acquisitions* (Washington, D.C.: U.S. Government Printing Office, May, 1955), p. 8.

CHART 29-1

MERGERS AND ACQUISITIONS IN MANUFACTURING AND MINING

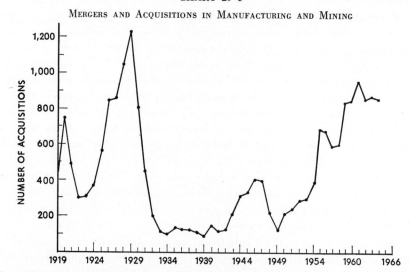

SOURCES: U.S. Federal Trade Commission, *Report on Corporate Mergers and Acquisitions* (Washington, D.C.: U.S. Government Printing Office, 1955), Appendix Table 1, p. 33, for 1919–54; U.S. Department of Commerce, Bureau of the Census, *Statistical Abstract of the United States, 1965* (Washington, D.C.: U.S. Government Printing Office, 1965), p. 503, for 1955–64. This series covers only actions reported by Moody's Investors Service and Standard & Poor's Corporation. Many smaller acquisitions are not reported; partial acquisitions, when they comprise whole divisions of other companies, are included. The series covers only part of the mergers and acquisitions now reported by the Federal Trade Commission but is carried on to keep up the data started by the Temporary National Economic Committee.

World War I, to be followed by a second peak in 1929—an all-time high. The third upsurge came toward the end of World War II, subsiding in 1948 and 1949, to be followed by another increase in activity which had not as yet subsided by the final date of the study. As of the present moment, substantial numbers of mergers are still taking place, in spite of rumblings from federal regulatory bodies, which read into the trend monopolistic implications.

A significant rise in the number of mergers such as we have experienced in recent years naturally leads to questions as to why mergers take place. In a broad sense the answer lies in the fact that mergers are basically a form of expansion, and therefore it is to be expected that periods of prosperity would be accompanied by increased merger activity. This, however, is not particularly informative in arriving at the answer as to why a decision was made to merge companies A, B, and C at some particular point in time.

On the subject of causes of corporate mergers the studies which have been conducted[3] reveal that there may be several factors in a given

---

[3] See J. K. Butters and J. Lintner, *The Effects of Taxation on Corporate Mergers* (Boston: Division of Research, Harvard Business School, 1951); also Federal Trade Commission, *op. cit.*; also M. L. Mace and G. G. Montgomery, Jr., *Management Problems of Corporate Acquisitions* (Boston: Division of Research, Harvard Business School, 1962).

situation and that it is often difficult to rank these in order of importance. It is also pointed out that there are at least two sides to every merger, and the reasons for acquiring a company may be very different from the reasons for offering the company for acquisition. As mentioned above, the primary drive on the part of the acquiring company is the desire for expansion and the conclusion that this can be done more effectively by purchasing a going concern than by internal growth. Such expansion may be encouraged by the existence of surplus funds. It may take the form of expanded capacity in existing product lines, integration back toward basic raw materials or forward toward the production of the ultimate end product, diversification of product lines, acquisition of marketing facilities, or any other form which expansion of corporate activities may suggest. There may be the expectation of improved competitive position, higher gross earnings or lower costs, improved financing, or better management. It may be possible to achieve these advantages more rapidly and with greater assurance through merger than through the development of additional facilities within the acquiring company.

The Butters-Lintner study indicates that the primary reasons for the sale of the business being merged fall into three basic categories: management considerations, investment considerations, and taxation.[4] Under the heading of management considerations are the problems of weak management, death or impending retirement of key personnel, and internal disputes. There are many such situations where the best alternative appears to be to sell out if a favorable price can be obtained. Investment considerations include the desire to make the most of an investment opportunity by selling when its value is considered to be at a maximum, and the desire to become less vulnerable to risk through greater diversification.

The tax implications of corporate mergers appear to relate almost entirely to the interests of those who are selling out. Although there often is a tax advantage for a profitable company in absorbing an unprofitable one with a record of recent losses which can be used as a tax offset, the study previously mentioned did not find this to be a significant motivation for purchase. On the other hand, tax considerations were found to be of considerable importance in the sale of closely held companies. One of these is the desire to liquidate in advance of the death of the principal owner, so that the cash will be available to pay the estate tax. For the man whose resources are tied up in one company which is without a public market for its stock, the risks of financial embarrassment to his heirs and of loss in a forced sale of the business after his death are very real. The other important tax consideration on the part of those whose business is being merged concerns the basis upon which the profits of a business are to be taxed at the time they are withdrawn. If profits are withdrawn as

---

[4] See Butters and Lintner, *op cit.*, esp. chap. viii, pp. 201–32.

dividends, they are taxed as personal income, and the rate can be as high as 70%, depending on individual circumstances. If the profits are successfully reinvested in the business and the business is ultimately sold, they are reflected in the selling price and are withdrawn as a capital gain, taxable at a maximum of 25%. If the merger is effected by a tax-free exchange of stock in the acquired company for stock in the surviving company, then the tax is avoided entirely at that point of time.

As mentioned previously, there are often several factors which provide the justification for a merger of two companies. For our purposes the quest to determine which of these factors is the most important in a given situation is not particularly necessary or useful. It is important, however, to recognize when financial considerations are involved—the present and future demand for funds, profitability, cash savings, marketability of securities, to name some of the more common ones—and to evaluate their significance as objectively as possible.

The Procedure of Mergers

We have already mentioned the formal procedures which have been prescribed by state law for the effecting of corporate mergers and consolidations. Such *statutory mergers,* as they are called, represent one of the ways in which businesses are brought together under common management and ownership. The steps taken under corporation law for the dissolution of the merged company may in fact be merely giving formal recognition to a union which has been in effect for some years. It is the purpose of this section to describe how mergers commonly come about and how the financial aspects are worked out.

Mergers may be initiated by either of the parties to the merger or by an outside organization such as an investment banking firm which sees in it some direct or indirect advantage to itself. Negotiations may be conducted between or among the top managements concerned or directly with the owners. At times, top management may be deliberately bypassed where it is expected to be antagonistic to the change. The most frequently used procedure for bringing ownership and management together is for one company to acquire ownership of all or a substantial portion of the voting stock of the other. In the initial stages, therefore, the company to be merged retains its identity, and the two companies are in a parent-subsidiary relationship. This relationship may continue for a very brief period or sometimes for years before actual merger takes place. If the acquiring company does not gain 100% ownership in the original transaction, it may find it necessary or desirable to add to its ownership before initiating merger proceedings. Even if it has the majority necessary to vote approval of the merger by the company to be merged, it may wish to reduce further the minority interest, which will have to be reimbursed in cash at an arbitrated price. In the meantime, the fraction of the stock originally acquired may be quite sufficient to operate the two companies as if they were parts of a single organization.

The voting stock of the company to be merged may be acquired in several ways. It may be obtained in a private negotiation between the acquiring company and a single owner or small group of owners. In the case of a publicly owned company the stock may be purchased gradually on the open market at the market price in effect at the time. It may be purchased by a public offer to buy all or a stated number of shares of the company at a price which is usually above the market price. This offer may be made with or without the knowledge and blessing of the management of the company to be merged. As an alternative to the payment of cash for the stock, the acquiring company may offer its own stock in exchange at a ratio which is expected to be attractive. In this way the shareholders of the merged company become shareholders of the surviving corporation. Apart from the possible advantages of the exchange itself, there may be considerable attraction in becoming a part of a larger and more diversified organization.

The other alternative to the acquisition of the stock of a going concern is to purchase its assets. This might appear to be a more direct and therefore more satisfactory procedure for the acquiring company, since the ultimate purpose in acquiring stock is to have the use of these assets. Instead of the shareholders receiving the payment directly, the acquired corporation receives it and ultimately disburses it to the stockholders as a liquidating dividend when they dissolve the company. The acquiring company is thus relieved of the formal merger proceedings and the problems of minority interests. However, in practice, the purchase-of-stock route often proves to be the quicker and more effective procedure, as evidenced by its use in a majority of cases. Where there is an established market price for the stock, the key problem of valuation is greatly simplified. Further, the purchase of stock is a way of bypassing antagonistic management, and it may be done with a minimum of publicity through the impersonal medium of the stock market.

When a company is acquired through the purchase of stock, the acquiring company indirectly takes on responsibility for its liabilities as well as its assets, since it has assumed the responsibilities of ownership. When a direct purchase of assets is made, there is no necessity for the acquiring company to assume the liabilities as well, although this may be a part of the deal, especially where the merged company is in a weakened financial condition.[5] Otherwise, the company concerned is simply converting earning assets into cash, and it retains responsibility for discharging its own obligations before it is dissolved and any cash disbursed to its shareholders.

---

[5] Federal Trade Commission, *op. cit.*, p. 101.

As an illustration of the varied procedures in corporate mergers, we may use the experience of one company, Textron Inc., during the year 1956. The annual report of the company for that year reported the following acquisitions:

On April 2 we acquired all the stock of General Cement Mfg. Company of Rockford, Illinois on a part fixed price and part contingent installment purchase plan. This division manufactures radio, television, and electronic parts and tools, liquid cements and certain chemicals.

On April 2 we purchased on a part fixed price and part contingent installment purchase plan all the stock of Benada Aluminum Products Company of Girard, Ohio. This division is a leading producer of extruded aluminum products consisting primarily of storm windows, doors, awnings, and siding.

On April 2 we purchased for cash and short term notes all the assets, subject to certain liabilities, of Myrtle Point Veneer Company, Norway, Oregon, and on June 20, for preferred stock, the assets, subject to certain liabilities, of Bandon Veneer and Plywood Association, Bandon, Oregon. Both these plants have been integrated with Coquille Plywood Division.

On April 20 we acquired for cash substantially all the assets, subject to certain liabilities, of Campbell, Wyant and Cannon Foundry Company of Muskegon, Michigan. C.W.C. is a leading producer of alloy iron and steel castings for the automotive, railroad, agricultural implements, refrigeration, marine and other industries.

On May 1 we acquired for cash all the stock of Carolina Bagging Company, Henderson, North Carolina, as an addition to the F. Burkart Manufacturing Company Division to supplement its six other plants with an operation in the rapidly-growing South-East.

On June 29 we purchased for cash all the assets, subject to liabilities, of Hall-Mack Company of Los Angeles, California, and at the same time we acquired the business of its affiliate, Peat Manufacturing Corporation of Norwalk, California. Hall-Mack manufactures and distributes a distinctive line of bathroom accessories and fixtures.

On July 10 the company purchased the S.S. LaGuardia, which has since been rechristened the S.S. Leilani. This is a 18,500 ton, single class, tourist passenger liner with accommodations for about 650 persons. She has been bare boat chartered to Hawaiian Steamship Company, Limited on a long term net lease over which all costs and responsibilities of operation are borne by Hawaiian Steamship. Regular sailings between the West Coast and Honolulu started February 5, this year. Three quarters of the purchase price and reconstruction costs have been paid for through non-recourse mortgage notes held or insured by the government.

On August 31 we acquired, on a common stock for assets basis, the business of the Federal Leather Company (now Federal Industries) of Belleville, N. J. Federal Industries manufactures vinyl resin coated fabrics for automotive interiors, as well as for use in railway cars, planes and ships, and for luggage, handbags, shoes, furniture upholstery and wall coverings.[6]

---

[6] Textron Inc., *Annual Report*, 1956, p. 4.

VALUATION

The issue of valuation is one which pervades the whole of financial management. From the stockholder viewpoint the end product of successful financial management is the creation of value and its growth over time. The ultimate measure is the change in the market price of the ownership certificate as compared with other similar equity investments. This is now a familiar concept to the reader, and we have raised the issue many times and in a variety of contexts. However, we have deferred a summary of concepts of valuation until this chapter for two reasons: one is that it is the central issue of the financial aspect of mergers and acquisitions; and the other is that it is a very appropriate core around which to summarize the many dimensions of financial management discussed throughout this book.

It should be stated at the outset that a review of the literature of finance as it refers to the question of valuation leaves one with a feeling of disappointment at the apparent lack of objective and definitive treatment of the subject. Further, it is unlikely that this chapter will do much to change that impression. The subject remains as one of the great challenges to financial practitioners and theorists. The reasons are not hard to find. Economic value is something which has little if any meaning in the abstract. The concept of value has practical meaning only when the parties concerned have been identified and the circumstances of the need for valuation spelled out. There is a great deal of truth in the statement that "value is what people agree it is," and this opens up the whole elusive dimension of opinion and judgment and bargaining position.

Thus, one may easily conclude that value cannot be generalized and that it is objective only in the historical sense of what was agreed upon by particular individuals at a point in time. Nevertheless, even where value is being set by the give and take of direct negotiation between two parties, there is usually an attempt to appeal to the impersonal arbiter of objective criteria. Each party will seek to support his position by such evidence as appears at least to remove the elements of opinion and bias and substitute therefor fact. As we shall see, however, when we review the commonly accepted bases of valuation, it is impossible to escape from a degree of subjectivity, since value relates to an individual (or group) and his (their) participation in unknown future events.

When two or more independently owned businesses are merged, a problem of valuation is inevitably involved. If it is done by the purchase of stock or of assets, the cash equivalent must be established. If the merger is accomplished by an exchange of stock, then the relative value of each component part must be determined in order to find the share which each of the formerly independent stockholder groups will have in the surviving corporation. It will be apparent that this valuation will be the key issue in negotiations between or among the parties to the merger. It is appropriate, therefore, that we take up the problem of the valuation of a going business concern in some detail at this point.

While valuation is of special significance in business mergers, this is not by any means the only situation in which this problem arises. The question of the value to be placed on a going business, either as a whole or on a fraction thereof (a share or block of shares), also comes up in the pricing of new issues of securities; in the purchase, sale, taxation, or pledge of existing securities; in recapitalization; and in reorganization and liquidation. Because of this, the following discussion of valuation should be read not only in relation to the question of mergers but also in terms of its wider application to these other situations.

Kinds of Value

The term *value* is used in economic, business, and legal phraseology with a wide variety of meanings. Some of the many kinds of value confronting the student of finance are *assessed value* for purposes of property taxation; *condemnation value* awarded as payment in takings by right of eminent domain; *book value*, as derived from accounting statements; *reproduction value* of existing fixed tangible business assets; *going-concern value* of assets of at least potentially profitable business enterprises; *liquidating value* of assets on dissolution of a business; *collateral value*, representing the amount that may be borrowed on the pledge of an asset; *fair value*, used as a base for public regulation of utility rates; *sale value*, representing the anticipated realization upon sale under various conditions; *market value*, usually determined from actual prices, or bids and offerings in some sort of "market" (which implies the existence of potential buyers and sellers), though it may be imputed by estimate; and *fair market value* that adds to the concept of market value the assumption of the existence of a large number of buyers and sellers and sometimes the assumption that those buyers and sellers are well informed and entirely rational in their evaluations. The value derived under this last assumption is also called *intrinsic value* or *investment value*, distinguishing it from market price.

Despite the variety of the concepts of value indicated above, most of the methods of security valuation fall into three main categories: those based on the capitalization-of-earnings concept, those that emphasize asset values, and those that stress actual or imputed market prices. The outlines of each major approach will be drawn in succeeding pages. For purposes of simplicity, each approach will be discussed in terms of the valuation of a single share of stock. It will be apparent that whether we are placing a value on the business as a whole or on a fractional interest in the business, the concepts will be the same, and there will be a direct relationship between the two.

The reader will soon become aware of the fact that there is no single, always reliable method of determining *the* value of a business or its securities that can be applied to all situations. Often, several methods of getting at an answer, or various combinations of methods, will be useful in a particular situation. As we said earlier, valuations are undertaken for a definite purpose and from a definite point of view, and the choice of approach and the final appraisal will inevitably reflect that purpose and point of view. For example, a businessman who is considering the purchase of the majority stock of a street railway company with intentions of liquidating the company for the scrap value of its property would obviously approach the problem of placing a dollar value on the stock differently from an investor who plans to acquire the stock for the income it may produce from continued operation.

The Capitalized Earnings Approach

The capitalized earnings approach to the evaluation of common stocks rests on the philosophy that the current value of property depends on the income it can be made to produce over the years. Hence, it is argued, ownership shares in the assets of a business concern are properly valued on the basis of the earning power of the business. It is the earning power that will provide income to the shareholder, and it is income that he values rather than the physical assets themselves. The basic validity of the concept that value rests on earning power, or potential earning power, is seldom challenged. It is in the application of the concept to actual situations that major questions arise.

In other chapters of this book, particularly the chapters which deal with capital budgeting, the reader is introduced to the idea and method of establishing a present value for a stream of earnings (or savings) extending into the future. In those chapters, however, we were primarily concerned with the internal investment opportunities commonly available to a going concern in a period of growth. The required investment was generally taken as given, and the question was one of determining the time-adjusted rate of return to be realized from the expected earnings or savings. This was then compared to a standard set by the company's cost of capital or some other criterion.

The problem we now take up is largely an extension of this line of reasoning, although the form of the question has changed. Attention shifts from the determination of an expected rate of return on a given investment of capital to the determination of what this investment of capital should be. From the point of view of the one acquiring the investment, the question is: What is the maximum amount I am willing to pay for this stream of earnings? From the point of view of the one selling the investment, the question is: What is the maximum amount I can reasonably expect to get for this stream of earnings? Unlike the capital budgeting problems, the problem we are now considering involves an investment which is an entire business entity (or group of entities);

consequently, the "earnings" in this case are the total net profits of the business (after taxes).

There are two basic problems involved in arriving at an earnings valuation of a business. One of these is the determination of the annual earnings (or earnings per share) which the business can be expected to produce in the future. The other basic problem is the determination of the rate of return to be applied to these earnings. We shall discuss these in order.

Estimate of Earnings.   Before considering the problem of estimating earnings, we should note another difference between our analysis here and our capital budgeting problems. There, specific investment opportunities are considered to have an income stream of limited duration. A business entity, on the other hand, must, in the absence of evidence to the contrary, be considered as having an unlimited future; therefore, its income stream must be treated as if it will continue to infinity. Thus, it is natural that we think of earnings figures in terms of earnings per unit of time—the amount per year.

In assessing future earning power, the starting point is obviously the record of the past, and the first step is to get this record straight—or as straight as is possible and useful. The obstacles to reliable data we have discussed many times before, particularly in the chapter on interpreting financial statements. They derive from the fact that the person making the valuation may not have access to all the data he would like and even when he has, he is somewhat at the mercy of the whims of accounting practices. The inevitable adjustments will be a part of converting earnings data to a basis appropriate for the comparisons that are to be made. Where companies are being merged, it is essential that comparability of treatment of cost and revenue terms be established. Obviously, a great deal rests on the good faith of the parties concerned, since there is both an opportunity to conceal and/or distort the data and the temptation to do so.

Given a reasonable approximation of recent earnings performance, there is then the perplexing problem of how to allow for apparent trends. If the earnings are reasonably stable or fluctuating around a more or less horizontal trend line the meaning of an annual earnings rate is fairly clear. If, on the other hand, there is an apparent trend upward or downward, an allowance must be made, and although the direction of the allowance is clear the magnitude is not. The problem is one of identifying the extent to which a rate of increase in the earnings level is inherent in the particular business entity being acquired (and therefore an asset commanding a price) or simply a function of the general industry environment or of the efforts of the new ownership and management. It is obvious that you won't pay for results you will produce yourself. On the other hand, the prospect of rising earnings which results from a unique product, market position, or management team is a salable asset and one which will strongly influence negotiated value.

As a practical matter, what the latter case suggests is an estimate of future earnings over an arbitrary time horizon as supported by the apparent trend in the past and present expectations. The horizon would presumably be a period short enough to justify a reasonable degree of confidence in the expected earnings and the resultant estimate of earnings would be an upper limit for bargaining purposes. In practice, there is a strong correlation between eagerness to acquire certain earning properties and the willingness to pay for tomorrow's earnings rather than today's or yesterday's.

Let us assume that the analyst, as a result of a reasonably complete consideration of the various factors affecting the profitability of company X, forecasts annual earnings of $3 a share. How much is the probable earnings stream of $3 per share worth? What value should be placed on a share of this stock?

Rate of Capitalization. Once we have an annual earnings rate for the company as a whole or per share—or possibly a range of earnings rates— the next step is to apply *a capitalization rate* to arrive at the prospective investment value. This is the sum which, if invested at the assumed capitalization rate, will yield the expected annual earnings in perpetuity. This assumes, of course, that the earnings rate has been calculated net of whatever capital expenditures are necessary to assure their perpetuity. Thus, if the capitalization rate is taken as 10%, the $3 of earnings per share are worth $30 and presumably this is what someone who accepted these data would describe as the "value" of the share.

However, all this is deceptively simple; and in fact, the determination of the appropriate rate of return is the most difficult and subjective aspect of the problem. In general, the selection of a rate of capitalization is determined by the relative certainty of the estimated earnings actually being realized. The more certain the prospective buyer is that the earnings will materialize, the more he will pay for the claim to the earnings. On the other hand, where uncertainty is great—or in other words, where the risk is believed high—the buyer will insist on a high rate of return. For example, in the case of a small concern producing a highly competitive item of uncertain demand, the buyer of stock may insist on a price which will yield a return of 25% on his investment. That is, he would capitalize estimated earnings of $5 a share at 25% and reach a valuation of $20 for one share of the stock. Another commonly used way of expressing this is to say that the risk justifies a value of "four times earnings." If, however, the business in question were a very stable one with every prospect of steady earnings at the $5 level, the buyer might well be willing to accept a capitalization rate as low as 5%, in which case he would value one share of stock at $100, or "20 times earnings."

In the example of the high-risk situation above, the analyst might prefer to adjust for the risk by writing down the estimate of earnings to, say, $2.50. To the extent that he has thus made allowance for the risk factor through a conservative estimate of earnings, a duplicate allowance for the uncertainty would not be made through the capitalization rate. In other words, if the earnings estimate were written down from $5 to $2.50 to allow for the risk, then a capitalization rate of 12½% rather than 25% would be in order. This, however, seems to us to be an undesirable way to approach the problem. It makes for a "cleaner" analysis to separate so far as possible the measurement of earnings magnitudes from the assessment of the variability or certainty of those magnitudes as expressed in the multiplier or capitalization rate. In any case care must be exercised not to double-count the risk allowance as may well happen particularly when several people are involved in the evaluation process.

Since the factors that go to determine the risk in a particular situation are complex and the weighing of them is a matter of judgment, it is apparent that the selection of a capitalization rate appropriate to the risk is subjective. It is also clear that a small change in the rate of capitalization applied will make a substantial change in the final valuation figure. In practice, many analysts tend to classify industries by groups and to develop rules of thumb governing appropriate rates, however questionable on theoretical grounds. Thus, for many years, it was widely felt that the more stable industrials with good prospects were "worth" about 10 times conservatively estimated earnings.

Before concluding this section on the capitalized earnings approach to value, we remind the reader of the growing body of theoretical literature concerning the determinants of value in the securities market and in particular of the continuing debate regarding the relative impact of earnings and dividends on market price (see Chapter 14). Since our discussion here has been in the context of value for corporate acquisitions, the focus has been on earnings alone. When one company buys another, it buys sales and earnings, and dividend payments, to the extent that they enter the picture at all, are more likely to detract from rather than add to value, since they represent a cash drain which must be assumed. However, it is recognized that the dividend aspect is of very real and positive significance to the individual investor in securities. This merely emphasizes once again how the concept of value changes as the beneficiary and circumstances change.

Asset Approaches to Valuation

Several methods of valuation can be termed *asset approaches*, since they center attention more on the assets to which the shares of stock have claim than on income data. Among the more significant of these concepts of value are book value, reproduction value, and liquidation value.

As the terminology suggests, *book value* is derived from the asset values shown on the company's own books and presented in its most recent balance sheet. The excess of assets over debts represents the accounting net worth of the business and hence the book value of the stockholder's investment. Where preferred stock is outstanding, a value for the preferred shares must, of course, be deducted to determine the net worth applicable to common. The net worth available to common stock divided by the number of common shares outstanding yields book value per share.

Many refinements on this direct method of computing book value are in use. Some analysts prefer to exclude from net worth some or all of such intangible assets as goodwill, patents, bond discount, organization expense, and deferred charges. Others analyze reserve accounts and add to net worth those reserves which are felt to be essentially segregations of surplus. A few inject a measure of the capitalized earnings approach by allowing goodwill (or even adding it when none is shown on the books) if the earnings have been large enough to support a contention that the concern has a "going-concern" value in excess of the stated value of the tangible assets.

Despite the variance in method of computation, book values are relatively easily and simply determined. To the unsophisticated, they are exact and clear cut and, until relatively recent times, were widely accepted as standards of security value.

The student of accounting, however, will immediately recognize the fact that the figures for book value for a particular company will be influenced by the accounting policies of that company. The variations between companies in accounting for current assets are relatively small, with the possible exception of inventories. The lack of standardization of accounting practice is particularly significant in the valuation of fixed assets and in the treatment of intangibles such as patents and goodwill. Hence, a concern with a rigorous depreciation policy would show lower net fixed assets and thus lower book values than would a similar concern that had charged less depreciation. When book values are used in valuing the security of one company against that of another, the analyst must attempt the often difficult task of reconstructing reported figures so as to get them on a comparable basis.

Even if a concern follows "conventional accounting practice" in all respects, it will arrive at its balance sheet values by reference to conventions rather than sheer logics of value. Hence, inventories are generally carried at cost or market, whichever is lower. More important, fixed assets are typically carried at historical cost less depreciation rather than at current values.

An even more important weakness than the influence of vagaries of accounting convention and practice is the failure of the book value approach to give consideration to the earning power of the assets as the real test of their worth. For example, the Coca-Cola Company of Delaware reported earnings averaging $6.79 per share of common stock over the 10 years ended 1959. Yet, the net tangible assets in 1959 only amounted to $42.15 per share.[7] Clearly, the book figures, even with the

---

[7] *Moody's Industrial Manual, 1960*, pp. 1031–32.

inclusion of the goodwill on the books of the company, are no reasonable indication of the worth of the Coca-Cola stock. On the other hand, there are companies—for example, certain railroads—where book values substantially overstate the worth of the company if earnings are taken as the standard.

Book values are most useful in appraising companies whose assets are largely liquid and subject to fairly accurate accounting valuation (i.e., banks, investment trusts, and insurance companies); but even in these instances, book values used alone are seldom reliable standards of value.

Reproduction value, or the cost of reproducing the assets of a concern at current prices, is of significance mainly in the case of public utilities, where it sometimes becomes a factor in the determination of rate schedules by governmental regulatory bodies. As a single standard of value, it is seldom used. A major objection lies in the inescapable fact that the typical business is much more than the sum of its physical assets. While costs of replacing physical properties can be calculated with some exactness by painstaking appraisal, the cost of duplicating the business organization, its experience, know-how, and reputation, apart from the physical assets, is most difficult of determination.

When physical assets are the principal things of value to a concern, however, and when they can be readily reproduced, the cost of reproducing the assets will tend to serve as a ceiling on valuations reached by other methods. For example, in the case of a concern the principal asset of which is a residential apartment house, few buyers would pay more for the shares of the apartment house concern than the cost of erecting and getting into operation a similar apartment house, regardless of the earnings of the present concern.

On the other hand, *liquidation values* tend to put a floor under valuations reached from other approaches, since there are many firms which will purchase concerns when valuations placed on the business become so low as to create an opportunity for worthwhile profits through their liquidation. During depression periods, when earnings are low or nonexistent for a number of firms, liquidation values may become widely significant.

It might be noted at this point that even in the liquidation approach the valuation of the assets is based indirectly on their potential earning capacity. Unless they are to be sold for scrap value, the assets will ultimately find a market in someone who feels that he can use the assets effectively—that is, make them earn him a profit.

In certain cases in which the business as a whole is being valued, a combined capitalized earnings and asset approach may be appropriate. The appraiser may find, after valuing the shares on the basis of the earning power of the business, that the concern owns certain assets which may be sold or distributed to security holders without impairing the earning capacity of the company. Unneeded cash, government securities, or unused plant may fall in this category. These "extra" assets may properly be valued without reference to the earning power of the business and their net realization value added to the capitalized earnings value in the final determination of the worth of the stock. This is known as the *redundant asset* method.

Conversely, when additional investment by the purchasers is needed in order to realize the estimated earning power, the additional investment required may appropriately be subtracted from the value arrived at by capitalized future earnings based on the assumption that the additional investment will be made.

Asset approaches to valuation, particularly book value, have come under severe criticism as unrealistic measures of value except for the rather limited purposes of law and accounting. At the same time they persist as important guides to the determination or negotiation of value in practice. One reason is that book value is a matter of record—a number independently derived and precisely stated. In an uncertain world precise and apparently unbiased numbers are highly prized— however invalid they may be.

Another and perhaps more important reason for the appeal of book value is that it represents the commitment once made, and particularly in deteriorating situations investors are naturally inclined to cling to the notion that if they can recover what they originally invested they will be satisfied. Anything less represents "loss"—loss of money and, perhaps equally important, loss of face as a measure of bad judgment or bad management. These are some of the human factors which in practice have a strong influence on the positions taken by parties negotiating a value. They tend to lie in the gray area between what is rational and what is a rationalization.

Market Value Approach

Another major approach to value looks to the prices set for the security in actual transactions between buyer and seller—to "the blood-less verdict of the market place." Proponents of this approach argue that actual market prices are set by buyers and sellers acting in basic self-interest. Thus, they are appraisals of supposed experts who are willing to support their opinions with cash. Therefore, it is maintained that the prices at which sales take place are practical expressions of value which are definitely to be preferred to theoretical views of value.

Supporters of market price as a standard argue that the market price at any particular time reflects the value of the security sold in relation to all other securities or opportunities for investment and that all values are basically relative. Hence, the price of a security in a free market serves as an effective common denominator of all the current ideas of the worth of a security as compared to other investment opportunities. Also, market price is a definite measure that can readily be applied to a particular situation. The subjectivity of other approaches is avoided in favor of a known yardstick of value.

Whatever truth is embodied in these arguments, there are many problems in applying market price as a standard of value. In the first place, recent market prices are available for the common stocks of only the larger companies. In the period July, 1962–June, 1963, there were 1,268,044 corporate income tax returns filed for active corporations in the United States.[8] Yet, even in 1964, only 2,467 issuing companies had securities listed on national registered exchanges.[9] Further, "listing" does not in itself create an active group of buyers and sellers, and many listed stocks are traded on a very desultory and infrequent basis.

Where there are few prospective buyers and sellers for a security, a "thin market" is said to exist. Markets are particularly thin for many securities traded in the over-the-counter market, where one will often find such wide spreads between bid and asked prices as "16 bid, 19 asked." The release of a relatively small number of shares on such a thin market may be enough to depress market prices substantially. Further, the market price for a particular stock on a given date may be influenced by artificial means. Stabilization, or price-support activity, is legal in a number of instances and is typical during the period in which a new issue is being marketed by the underwriters.

Another question often arises in the valuation of large blocks of securities. Recorded sales prices for the date in question may be based on the sale of one or two hundred shares. Is it fair and appropriate to apply the price set on a small scale to a large block of shares?

A more basic objection frequently raised is the contention that the market itself tends to exaggerate major upward and downward movements in stock prices. For example, it is argued that speculative influences pushed common stock prices for certain widely traded stocks in the historic boom of 1929 far beyond "reasonable" levels. Conversely, it is claimed that prices in 1932 were so depressed by purely psychological factors and by technical pressures for liquidity as to be manifestly poor standards of long-run value. Other, though perhaps less dramatic, examples could be cited from more recent experience of market and individual company price fluctuations.

Partially in answer to some of the objections above noted, the theory of *fair market value* or *intrinsic value* has been developed. Under this approach, fair market value is the value at which a sale would take place if there were willing buyers and willing sellers actually in the market,

---

[8] Internal Revenue Service, U.S. Treasury Department, *Statistics of Income, Corporation Income Tax Returns with Accounting Periods Ended July, 1962–June, 1963* (preliminary) (Washington, D.C.: U.S. Government Printing Office), p. 1.

[9] Securities and Exchange Commission, *Thirtieth Annual Report, 1964* (Washington, D.C.: U.S. Government Printing Office, 1964), p. 46.

each equipped with full information on the security and prepared to act in an entirely rational manner. This concept does meet most of the objections stated; yet, per se, it raises a need for other standards of valuation than market quotations and suggests recourse to something like capitalized earnings as a more valid appraisal of "intrinsic worth."

At any rate, largely because of their ease of application, market prices are widely used by the courts and by tax authorities, although not to the exclusion of other standards where they are deemed appropriate. Regardless of theoretical weaknesses of market price as a measure of intrinsic value, where a market price exists for even one share of stock, it will inevitably affect the appraisal of a prospective buyer or seller, however large the potential transaction. The seller will, in ordinary human nature, hesitate to take a price much less than the price label established in the market, and the buyer will resist evaluations substantially higher than the market quotations.

Valuation in Practice

These three approaches to valuation represent attempts to remove the problem from the realm of personal opinion and to place it on an objective basis. In this respect they are only partially successful; and in each, some element of individual judgment remains. It must be remembered, also, that in mergers and in most other valuation situations, the final determination of value is a part of a bargaining process and that a compromise value is therefore likely to result. In such cases it would be largely a matter of coincidence if the agreed-on value corresponded exactly to that indicated by any of the objective approaches. This does not mean that they are therefore of no value in practical situations, for they will normally play a significant role in setting rational limits within which the negotiated value will fall. It is not surprising to find that each party to the negotiation will champion the method of valuation most favorable to its interests.

A study of the bases of valuation used in corporate mergers during the years 1953–54 indicated that present and future earnings were of "overwhelming importance."[10] At the same time, it indicated that book values were comparatively unimportant, except in cases where liquidation was a definite possibility. These conclusions are helpful in suggesting the nature of recent precedent in the "court" of corporate practice. In addition, they lend support to the observation that a negotiated price does not necessarily imply one based on nonrational considerations. It must not be interpreted, however, to mean that capitalized earnings value will, or even should, govern every valuation decision. Each case must be considered on its own merits. Without a

---

[10] C. C. Bosland, "Stock Valuation in Recent Mergers," *Trusts and Estates,* June, July, and August, 1955.

careful analysis of the particular circumstances, there is no way of distinguishing the exception from the rule.

The Effect of Mergers on the Capital Structure of the Acquiring Corporations

In some cases a merger is effected by the formation of a new corporation, which takes over the assets and liabilities of the merged companies and issues new stock in exchange for the old. In most cases, however, one of the companies involved survives the merger by "buying out" the others. It is important to note the possible effects of a merger on the capital structure of the acquiring company. Unlike internal growth, which tends to be gradual, growth by merger comes suddenly and often in relatively large "bites," and this may give rise to some manifestations of financial indigestion.

One of these may be a significant shift in the debt-equity balance. If the acquiring company does not possess adequate amounts of surplus cash, it will be necessary either to sell new securities in order to provide cash or to issue new securities for purposes of an exchange. In either case the former balance of debt and equity is likely to be changed and normally in the direction of increased equity. Offsetting this, at least in part, will be the assumption of the liabilities of the merged company by the acquiring company. The net effect and its significance will depend on several factors, among which will be the capital structures of the companies being merged, the price paid for the acquired company, and its size relative to the acquiring company.

There are other aspects as well. It is often the case that the earning capacities of the companies being merged differ significantly as to the certainty of annual profits. The merger may serve either to increase or to decrease the risk inherent in the acquiring company and thus to cause investors to revise their concepts of margins of safety in the market price-earnings relationship. There is also the related question of the effect on earnings per share and dividend policy. The immediate effect on the E.P.S. of the old shareholders of the acquiring company depends directly on the earnings of the newly acquired assets and the price that was paid for them either in cash or by exchange of stock. A factor which is usually somewhat uncertain at the outset is the added earnings or savings which may be generated by the merger itself. If the two companies have had different dividend policies, at least one of the shareholder groups will experience a change in dividend pay-out following the merger, since it is obvious that all must be treated alike.

It should also be noted that there are significant organizational and managerial problems in harmonizing the internal financial operations on such matters as cash balances and liquidity and credit policy. Of course, some of these problems can be worked out gradually, but it should be apparent that the formal aspects of a corporate merger are only the beginning of the process of full and effective integration.

PART X

Business Failure

Chapter 30

Liquidation or Reorganization

Definitions

THE DECISION to terminate a business venture may be reached under a variety of circumstances and for a variety of reasons. It is customary to associate terminations with *failure*—with *insolvency* and *bankruptcy*. While insolvency and bankruptcy will be a primary concern of this chapter, it is necessary to keep in mind that many businesses are terminated while they are still quite solvent and even profitable. Disregarding personal reasons, which are of considerable importance as a cause of termination in closely held businesses, the circumstances surrounding the decision may vary considerably. In the financial sense a specific business is an investment opportunity to be considered in relation to other alternatives. It may cease to be the most attractive alternative long before profits turn into losses. In a sense, it has failed if and when this fact becomes apparent. However, in everyday business usage, we apply the term *failure* only to those cases of termination where it is financially impossible to continue normal business activities. Dun & Bradstreet, Inc., the primary source of statistics on business failures, uses the term to mean "a concern that is involved in a court proceeding or a voluntary action that is likely to end in loss to creditors."[1] It is in this sense that we shall be using the term in this chapter.

Before proceeding, it is necessary to explain the meaning of two other terms which are used in conjunction with failure—*insolvency* and *bankruptcy*. A firm is *insolvent* when either of two conditions exist. (1) It is unable to pay its maturing obligations, or (2) its liabilities are in excess of the fair and realizable value of the assets available. The former situation is easy to see, while the latter test may require proof of the values involved. Strictly speaking, a firm is not *bankrupt* unless it has been found to be so by a federal court, which applies the tests listed in the Federal Bankruptcy Act, among which are the existence of insolvency

---

[1] U.S. Department of Commerce, Office of Business Economics, *1963 Biennial, Business Statistics, Edition: A Supplement to the Survey of Current Business* (Washington, D.C., 1963), p. 212.

as defined above. Other "acts of bankruptcy" include giving preferences to certain debtors in anticipation of insolvency and undertaking action under a state insolvency statute.

A debtor may petition the court himself, admitting that one of the "acts of bankruptcy" has taken place. If so, the action is termed a *voluntary bankruptcy*. If, however, the creditors must petition the court and prove the existence of an act of bankruptcy, the proceeding is termed *involuntary*. In fact, the great majority of bankruptcy proceedings are voluntary.

Many persons use the term "bankrupt" more generally, to refer to any firm which has "failed," but it is well to remember that bankruptcy has a narrow meaning in the legal world. To refer again to Dun & Bradstreet's usage of the term failure, it includes:

All industrial and commercial enterprises which are petitioned into the Federal Bankruptcy Courts. . . . Also included . . . are: Concerns which are forced out of business through such actions in the State courts as foreclosure, execution, ann attachments with insufficient assets to cover all claims and, in addition voluntary discontinuances with known loss to creditors; and voluntary compromises with creditors out of court.[2]

Statistics of Business Failure

Businesses are terminated for many reasons, but the terminations coming under Dun & Bradstreet's broad definition of failure have been relatively insignificant in recent years, as shown in Table 30–1, approximately 0.53% of the total business population in the year 1964. Even in the depths of the depression of the thirties, the failures only reached the 32,000 level (1932), as compared with 13,500 in 1964. It has been estimated that the average annual failure rate for the years 1900–1960 was 0.7% of the total population.[3]

TABLE 30–1

TOTAL INDUSTRIAL AND COMMERCIAL FAILURES IN THE UNITED STATES,
1955–64

Failure Rate per 10,000 Concerns

1955	41.6	1960	57.0
1956	48.0	1961	64.4
1957	51.7	1962	60.8
1958	55.9	1963	56.3
1959	51.8	1964	53.2

SOURCE: U.S. Department of Commerce, Office of Business Economics, *1963 Biennial, Business Statistics, Edition: A Supplement to the Survey of Current Business* (Washington, D.C. 1963), p. 36, for figures through 1962; *Survey of Current Business*, for later figures.

---

[2] U.S. Department of Commerce, *loc. cit.*

[3] Small Business Administration, *Fourteenth Semiannual Report, for the Six Months Ending June 30, 1960* (Washington, D.C.: U.S. Government Printing Office, 1960), p. 12.

The obvious conclusion from a review of these statistics is that the subject of this chapter, narrowly defined, is a problem experienced by only a small minority of business owners and managers. However, the statistics also bring out that in a broader sense the liquidation or sale of a business under unfavorable circumstances is a common occurrence. Further, as statistics of actual failures and terminations, they understate the number of times the prospect of liquidation has entered the minds of management as a very real alternative, under distressing circumstances which were later proved to be temporary.

The Causes of Business Failure

It is a question as to how much can be said usefully by way of generalization on the causes of failure in business. The best-known continuing study of causes of business failure is that made by Dun & Bradstreet. For the year 1964 the breakdown of apparent causes was as shown in Table 30–2.

TABLE 30–2

WHY BUSINESSES FAIL—YEAR ENDED DECEMBER 31, 1964

Apparent Causes	Manufac- turing	Whole- sale	Retail	Construc- tion	Commercial Service	Total
Neglect	2.3%	3.1%	2.9%	2.9%	2.7%	2.8%
Fraud	1.9	3.4	1.4	1.9	2.2	1.9
Inexperience, incompetence	93.6	91.9	91.5	92.2	91.1	91.9
Inadequate sales	50.7	46.0	51.2	25.8	45.4	45.5
Heavy operating expenses	11.1	5.3	3.1	32.0	10.4	10.4
Receivables difficulties	15.3	21.8	6.3	13.4	5.8	10.6
Inventory difficulties	6.4	11.9	9.5	1.9	1.9	7.2
Excessive fixed assets	7.1	3.1	3.9	4.0	9.7	4.9
Poor location	0.5	1.8	5.3	1.0	3.6	3.2
Competitive weakness	15.8	19.8	23.3	21.5	23.3	21.4
Other	4.7	4.1	3.6	4.8	5.4	4.2
Disaster	1.3	0.6	1.1	0.2	0.9	0.9
Reason unknown	0.9	1.0	3.1	2.8	3.1	2.5
Total number of failures	2.254	1,392	6,241	2,388	1,226	13,501

SOURCE: *Dun's Review and Modern Industry*, March, 1965, p. 14. Compiled by Dun & Bradstreet, Inc. Classification based on opinion of creditors and information in credit reports. Since some failures are attributed to a combination of causes, percentages do not add up to 100%.

In March, 1965, *Dun's Review and Modern Industry* commented:

There has been a gradual ebbing in the percentage of bankruptcies attributed to lack of knowledge of the line; 8.8% in 1964 compared with 24% in 1949. At the same time, however, a growing number of failures have stemmed from lack of managerial experience; 20.9% in 1964, 12.4% in 1954. This rise prevailed in all types of operation, but was sharpest among retailers.

A more significant set of ideas on business failure is found in Kaplan's book on small business[4] and is summarized below:

---

[4] A. D. H. Kaplan, *Small Business: Its Place and Problems* (New York: McGraw Hill Book Co., 1948), pp. 66–68 (by permission).

1. Deficiencies in management combined with unfavorable external circumstances.
2. Lack of preparation in organizing the business.
3. Weaknesses in financial management.
4. Preoccupation with business details.
5. Personality difficulties.
6. Severe competition.
7. External factors beyond the influence of management.

It is probably a mistake to try to establish a single dominant cause of failure in each case, as is attempted in the Dun & Bradstreet studies. Invariably, there are several facets to each case of failure, and an attempt to say which is primary tends to lead one into a "chicken and egg" type of dilemma. This is especially apparent in the so-called "financial" causes of failure. An analysis of unsuccessful businesses shows evidence of such weaknesses as insufficient working capital, overextension of credit, overinvestment in inventory, excessive debt, and excessive withdrawals of profits. Yet, each of these may be traced back at least one step: for example, insufficient working capital to lack of intelligent planning, overextension of credit to a tough competitive situation, or overinvestment in inventory to a misjudgment of future trends in demand. They may also be interrelated: for example, a possible relationship between excessive debt, excessive withdrawals of profits, and insufficient capital.

It is not the intention here to suggest that it is either impossible or undesirable to search for causes of failure, even though to the parties involved in liquidation this research may appear purely academic. In a broad sense it is desirable in order that there may be a useful transfer of experience regarding avoidable hazards. In the specific case it may also be of vital importance. When a business is to be reorganized rather than liquidated, it is obvious that the new company must know—and as far as possible, correct—the mistakes of the past in order to have any prospect of surviving. For these purposes, it is important to know all the important contributing factors.

Insolvency without Bankruptcy

It is a rare case where a healthy business is turned into a bankrupt one overnight. It is more usual to find that insolvency (the inability to meet obligations as they come due) is the termination point of a period of struggle to preserve profitability and solvency which has lasted for months or years. During this period the business has gradually exhausted the various means of preserving solvency, in the vain hope that a turning point would be reached.

If a business is experiencing a gradual depletion of its resources resulting from an inability to show a profit, it is likely to turn to any one of a number of courses of action which will enable it to stay in operation. Setting aside the alternative of direct negotiation with creditors for the moment, the more common courses of action for this purpose are summarized below:

1. Convert nonessential assets into cash (what is considered "essential" depends on the severity of the situation). For example:
   a) Sale of idle plant and equipment.
   b) Scaling-down of inventory.
2. Cut back or defer all payments which are not absolutely required by contract, e.g.:
   a) Defer accounts payable.
   b) Cut preferred and common dividends.
3. Replace debt of imminent maturity with debt of more distant maturity, particularly by recourse to the high-cost types of loans.
4. "Extract" new capital from those who have a reason for preserving the company's existence—officers, shareholders, suppliers, and customers.

For some companies, any or all of these steps may serve to preserve the company long enough to enable it to reverse the trend and establish itself on a sound financial footing. For others, they will prove to be only temporary expedients which merely postpone the day of reckoning.

If and when the time comes that a business finds it impossible to continue to meet its obligations on time, even after the kind of emergency action suggested above, the only remaining hope for preserving the business lies in a direct appeal to the creditors in the expectation of some concessions from the rigid terms of the existing contract. The prospects for a permanent or even temporary solution by this means depend very much on all the circumstances of the case. If the debtor continues to hope for a change of fortune, he may seek an *extension* on any or all of his obligations. Extensions usually involve a plan of repayment as well as a postponement of the due date. Apart from humanitarian considerations, there may be valid reasons why creditors, in their own self-interest, may be willing to accept less than that to which they are legally entitled. Formal bankruptcy proceedings are costly and time-consuming, and there is strong likelihood that they will not produce full satisfaction of claims. On the contrary, liquidation under court supervision is almost certain to involve loss to at least some of the creditors. In addition, there is the unpleasant publicity associated with bankruptcy proceedings, which is avoided by creditors and debtors alike if at all possible. Thus, if the creditor has any reason to share the hope of the debtor for an improvement in his circumstances and trusts his basic integrity, he may be willing to go along with the arrangement and may in the long run be better off by so doing.

Another alternative, which usually has less appeal for the creditors, is what is termed a *composition*. The composition is an agreement which takes the form of a legal contract, whereby the debtor pays an agreed-upon percentage of what he owes, and this is accepted by the creditors in full discharge of the debt. The debtor is then free to pursue his normal business activities. Such an arrangement may appeal to creditors, particularly suppliers, who have an interest in preserving the business of the debtor and see no hope of its getting out from under the existing debt. Except where the provisions of Chapter XI of the Bankruptcy Act (which will be discussed in the following pages) apply, the composition must be purely voluntary on the creditors' part. Once accepted, however, the arrangement is final. Because of this finality, it is normally less desirable from the creditors' point of view than the extension, though it may still be preferable to liquidation in bankruptcy.

These arrangements may be carried out in an informal manner where the creditors are few in number and/or can be readily brought together for united action. The detail of the arrangement may be worked out by direct negotiation with the creditor or a creditors committee or through the services of a trustee or outside agency such as a credit bureau. There is no necessity for court proceedings in order that any agreement shall be binding on all who willingly participate. At the same time, any creditor who refuses to go along with the arrangement must be satisfied according to the terms of his original contract, or the debtor runs the risk of his filing a petition for bankruptcy proceedings. Satisfaction in full of certain creditors' claims may be a part of any agreement that is worked out. Full payment of employee and small commercial claims is almost a standard arrangement. The larger creditors approve this step in order to reduce the number of persons who will be party to negotiations.

In considering insolvency without bankruptcy, mention should be made of the role of the *creditors committee.* It sometimes happens that creditors may be willing to work out an arrangement which will preserve the business of the debtor on condition that a creditors committee is allowed to play an active, if not dominant, role in management during the period of rehabilitation. The desire for a part in management may stem from a lack of confidence in existing management with respect to either its ability or its willingness to fulfill its obligations. Any arrangement of this type must be consented to by the existing ownership, but in view of the unpleasant alternatives the wishes of the creditors are likely to be recognized. Once the claims of the creditors have been fully satisfied, they will withdraw, and full control will return to those who own the company.

In these various ways a business which becomes insolvent may avoid bankruptcy and liquidation. Obviously, this cannot be accomplished without the consent, if not the active support, of the creditors. Generally speaking, creditors heartily dislike liquidation as a means of realizing their claims and will give serious consideration to any alternative which offers real hope of ultimate return of their investment. Trade creditors, especially, are apt to be lenient because of the expectation that future sales to the debtor will produce profits enough to justify any immediate sacrifice that an "arrangement" may call for.

Congress established Chapter XI of the Bankruptcy Act to give a formal method to supervise the making of arrangements between a debtor and the creditors. This was done so that, where possible, the more expensive and long-drawn-out proceedings of Chapter X could be avoided. For instance, in the fiscal year 1964, 1,088 cases were initiated under Chapter XI, and 125 under Chapter X.[5] Some of the Chapter XI cases may later be transferred if the situation is found to be complex, but the proportion shows a strong preference for Chapter XI.

Very briefly stated, the procedure involves a petition by the debtor for consideration of a specific plan for extension or composition. Upon receipt of the petition the court will bring the creditors together for consideration of the proposal. In the process, arrangements are made for any necessary supervision of the assets and for verification of the claims of the creditors. Unanimous acceptance by the creditors is desired but is not a prerequisite for confirmation of the proposal. An application for confirmation made by the debtor and backed by acceptance in writing by a majority of the creditors may be approved by the court if in its judgment the proposal is "fair and equitable and feasible" and in the best interests of all concerned. The arrangement will then apply to all creditors alike. Section 771 states: "The confirmation of an arrangement shall discharge a debtor from all his unsecured debts and liabilities provided for by the arrangement, except as provided in the arrangement. . . ."

Liquidation

At the outset of this chapter it was pointed out that the termination of a business either through sale as a business unit or through sale of its several assets separately is not necessarily an event forced on the owners by insolvency. In many cases liquidation takes place with no loss to creditors or even to owners. Ideally, investment in a business which has failed to come up to expectations should be withdrawn long before profits have turned into losses and the assets have become so depleted that creditors, as well as owners, fail to recover their investment.

It is a fact, however, that it is usually not easy to find a market for an unsuccessful business or its assets. It is also true that many businessmen, once committed to a course of action, will pursue it unswervingly, despite the odds, holding to the hope that next year will somehow be different. Such businessmen do not stop until they have either succeeded or literally run out of cash. With creditors pressing for payment and no cash either to pay them off or to finance further sales, there is no alternative but to liquidate.

---

[5] U.S. Administrative Office of the United States Courts, *Tables of Bankruptcy Statistics, with Reference to Bankruptcy Cases Commenced and Terminated in the United States District Courts during the Fiscal Year Ending June 30, 1964* (Washington, D.C., 1965).

Liquidation may take the form of an informal settlement between owners and creditors in which the assets are sold and the proceeds distributed among the creditors. It may also take the form of a more formal assignment of assets to a third party, a trustee, who liquidates and distributes the proceeds. The assignee may be any person or organization willing to perform the function and acceptable to the creditors, for example, a lawyer or a credit bureau. The great advantage of these informal arrangements is their relative speed, efficiency, and economy.

It is important to note, however, that for informal liquidation to work, the debtor must be trusted by the creditors, and the creditors must be in general agreement among themselves. According to bankruptcy law, an assignment on behalf of creditors is one of the acts of bankruptcy, and any dissatisfied creditor may institute formal court bankruptcy proceedings in spite of whatever informal arrangement may be in process. Although there are state bankruptcy laws as well, we shall confine our attention here to the Federal Bankruptcy Act, as amended, to illustrate what is involved in formal liquidation under court supervision.

Before we do so, however, it will give some perspective if we review a few statistics on the federal bankruptcy courts. During the year ended June 30, 1964, a total of 171,719 bankruptcy cases, personal and business, were commenced in federal courts. Of the total, only 16,510 were business bankruptcies, and of these, 92% were voluntary. Of the 16,510 business failures coming under federal jurisdiction all but 1,213 were destined for liquidation.[6] It must not be forgotten that liquidation is the usual result of business failure, and reorganization is the exception.

Even liquidation is an expensive process. The sorting out of claims, the search for all possible assets having value, and the handling of these assets so that they produce the greatest possible amount of funds requires the skillful services of the Referee and the Trustee, both court-appointed officers. We show in Table 30–3 how much of a bankrupt's assets go to others than the creditors of the business. A similar, or greater, sum is consumed in the reorganization process, to be described below. Small wonder that both debtors and their creditors strive to avoid the courts!

The procedures in bankruptcy center around the basic tasks, namely, the preservation of asset values pending liquidation, conversion into cash as rapidly as possible, and the distribution of cash through what are called liquidating dividends to creditors whose claims have been established, recognizing whatever priorities may exist. In this the court is assisted by a *referee*, who oversees the administrative details, such as preparing lists of assets and creditors, declaring liquidating dividends, and so forth; and by a *trustee*, whose primary duty is to "collect and reduce to money the property of the estates." The general creditors will be represented by a creditors committee in any negotiations between them and the court or its representatives. Secured creditors will not be a

---

[6] *Op. cit.* (Note XX), p. 4.

TABLE 30–3

BANKRUPTCY CASES IN THE U.S. COURTS, FISCAL YEAR 1964

Distribution of Total Realization in Asset Cases $73,197,759 = 100%	Distribution of Administrative Expenses $19,481,268 = 100%
Paid priority creditors:	Attorneys.................41.0%
Taxes.................12.3%	Referee and trustee's fees.....23.7
Wages................. 2.1	Trustee's or receiver's
Other................. 1.3	expenses.................16.6
Administrative expenses......26.6	Auctioneer's fees and
Paid secured creditors........28.8	expenses................. 7.1
Paid unsecured creditors......25.5	Rental..................... 6.0
Other..................... 3.4	Miscellaneous.............. 5.6

SOURCE OF DATA: U.S. Administrative Office of the United States Courts, *Tables of Bankruptcy Statistics, with Reference to Bankruptcy Cases Commenced and Terminated in the United States District Courts during the Fiscal Year Ending June 30, 1964* (Washington, D.C., 1965).

part of this activity unless it is apparent that their claims will not be satisfied from the specific assets which have been pledged. To the extent that they do remain unsatisfied, they become general creditors for the balance.

The creditors of a bankrupt business normally fall into three general categories: (1) priority creditors, (2) secured creditors, and (3) unsecured or general creditors. The Bankruptcy Act states that certain creditors, called priority creditors, are entitled to prior payment in full before any liquidating dividends are distributed to other creditors. The principal priority claims, in their order of priority, are (Section 104):

1. The costs and expenses of preserving the estate.
2. Wages earned within three months, up to $600 per claimant.
3. Federal, state, and local taxes.
4. Debts given priority by federal or state law—e.g., rent to a landlord.

The general unsecured creditors will therefore rank after these priority claims as well as after secured creditors with respect to those assets which have been pledged. It can be readily seen why unsecured creditors may find themselves in the position of receiving only a fraction of their legitimate claims.

The adjudication of a person as bankrupt by the court constitutes an application for a discharge of his debts except in the case of a corporation, when an application for discharge may be filed within 6 months of adjudication. Provided the bankrupt has not been granted a previous discharge within a 6-year period and has not engaged in fradulent acts or acts contrary to the provisions of the Act, the court will grant the discharge.

Corporate Reorganization

The term reorganization, as applied to business corporations, means a reconstruction of the financial structure, particularly the debt-equity relationships, in order to permit the resumption of normal business activity. It generally involves a more radical readjustment than does the recapitalization of solvent companies, described in an earlier chapter. Further, corporate reorganization, taking place under court jurisdiction, loses some of the voluntary aspects which are inherent in recapitalization.

With the exception of adjustments under Chapter XI of the Bankruptcy Act mentioned previously, the means of preserving insolvent businesses described so far take place outside a court of law. Such procedures are well suited to smaller businesses where ownership as well as creditors' claims are concentrated in the hands of a few, thus making informal negotiation a practical possibility. In the case of larger corporations the involvement of large numbers of shareholders and creditors makes a formalized procedure supervised by a court of law almost mandatory.

We have noted that Chapter XI of the Bankruptcy Act provided for court supervision of arrangements in the case of insolvent corporations or individuals whose obligations were entirely unsecured. It was the intention of the Act that wherever possible the rehabilitation of insolvent businesses would take place under the provisions of this chapter, and the numbers cited above show that this goal is being accomplished. However, in those corporations which have secured as well as unsecured debt, rehabilitation must take the form of reorganization under the provisions of Chapter X. Apart from the matter of secured versus unsecured debt, the distinction between an arrangement and a reorganization under the Bankruptcy Act is not a sharp one in principle. Both involve a reconsideration and adjustment of creditors' claims. However, the application of Chapter X is confined to corporations and deals specifically with the problem of groups of shareholders as well as groups of creditors. It is, therefore, of greatest interest to students of finance.

A reorganization under Chapter X is initiated, voluntarily or involuntarily, in the same manner as described for a liquidation in bankruptcy. Sometimes it is not known, when a bankruptcy proceeding is initiated, whether reorganization or liquidation will ensue. The *trustee,* whom the judge appoints, will make an investigation and a report to the court. Reorganization will be ordered only if it is shown that the *creditors* (not the stockholders) will receive greater value by the reorganization than by liquidation.

When a bankruptcy petition is approved by the court, procedure under Chapter X takes precedence over any other action. Section 548 states: "Until otherwise ordered by the judge, an order approving a petition shall operate as a stay of a prior pending bankruptcy, mortgage foreclosure, or equity receivership proceeding, and of any act or other proceeding to enforce a lien against the debtor's property."

Following approval of the petition, the judge will proceed to appoint a *trustee* for the property of the debtor, except in cases where the indebtedness is less than $250,000, where he may choose to continue the debtor in possession. The primary function of the trustee is to assemble the facts of the various claims against the corporation and to take certain initiatives. He makes the study, referred to above, concerning the advantages of reorganization over liquidation. He studies the record and begins legal proceedings on behalf of the debtor against any former officers, directors, or others whom he believes to be legally liable for negligence or fraud. He studies the claims and the possibilities of the firm, and drafts a plan of reorganization.

At the same time the trustee operates the business. Two things characterize his administration. First, he may "disaffirm" burdensome contracts entered into by the debtor. These usually include contracts of employment, leases, and long-term contracts of sale or purchase at fixed prices. But, although by this means the trustee may relieve the debtor of the consequences of past errors, each of those parties whose contracts have been broken is entitled to damages, in the usual way. Such damages are added to the unsecured debts of the bankrupt and serve as an additional reason why unsecured debts are seldom paid in full.

The trustee also assembles data concerning all of the debts of the bankrupt and estimates the values available to meet them. If it can be proved that a certain class of claimants has no hope of any payment, the court will order that that group will no longer be heard in the proceedings. Such a fate often befalls the common stockholders.

When the plan of reorganization submitted by the trustee has been prepared, the court then calls a hearing of shareholders and creditors so that the judge may consider any objections or amendments. In the case of companies where the schedule of indebtedness exceeds $3 million, the judge must submit the plan to the Securities and Exchange Commission for its consideration and recommendations. In the case where indebtedness is less, submission to the SEC is optional; and in any case, its recommendations are advisory only.

Extensive and time-consuming hearings and negotiations are often necessary before the conflicting interests of the claimants can be reconciled into a plan that meets the standards set by the law. Whenever this seems to have occurred, the court, if it also approves, will transmit the plan to the claimants who are still parties to the proceeding. The court confirms the plan if and when the plan is accepted (in writing) "by or on behalf of creditors holding two-thirds in amount of claims filed and allowed of each class" (Section 579). If the company involved has not been found to be insolvent, the plan must also be approved by shareholders holding a majority of the stock. When confirmed by the court, the plan becomes binding on all, including the dissenters—quite a different result, it will be noted, from a voluntary recapitalization of a solvent firm.

Fairness and Feasibility in Reorganization. The primary responsibility of the court in giving its approval to a plan of reorganization is to assure that the plan is "fair and equitable and feasible" (Section 621 [2]). It is inevitable that the new capital structure will change somewhat the claims the various classes of investors have in the business and the value of such claims. In a sense, it may be said that certain of these investors will be arbitrarily dispossessed of values which were theirs by legal right (although the real substance of such values will have been lost in the deterioration preceding bankruptcy). It is obvious, then, that the court has a serious responsibility in formulating the new capital structure embodied in the reorganization plan, with little guidance to be found in the words *fair* and *equitable*. It is also necessary that the court give consideration to the *feasibility* of the plan. There is little point to reorganization unless the financial burden imposed by the new capital structure is one which makes possible a permanent return to solvency.

It has already been noted that in seeking a solution to this problem, the court is assisted by the trustee, the advice of shareholders and creditors, and in some cases by the SEC. In order to get a clearer idea of what is implied by the terms *fair, equitable,* and *feasible,* it is helpful to refer to some of the published statements of the SEC in regard to those reorganization proceedings in which it has participated. In Chapter 27, on government regulation, mention was made of the fact that although the role of the SEC is advisory only, the Commission has performed its functions with considerable vigor and made the most of its opportunities in seeking the adoption of reorganization principles it considered proper.

The terms "fair and equitable" refer to the treatment of the various classes of claimants against the debtor. The objective of fair and equitable treatment of investors is obviously at the heart of the whole program of the SEC activities, so that the extension of this interest to include bankruptcy is a natural one. On this point the stand of the SEC is clear, as reflected in the following statement:

> Basic to the Commission's approach to questions involving the fairness of reorganization plans under Chapter X is the fixed principle, firmly established by Supreme Court decisions, that full recognition must be accorded to claims in the order of their legal and contractual priority either in cash or in the equitable equivalent of new securities and that junior claimants may participate only to the extent that the debtor's properties have value after the satisfaction of prior claims or to the extent that they make a fresh contribution necessary to the reorganization of the debtor.[7]

This is the rule known as the rule of *absolute priority*. It will be noted, however, that a question of judgment comes in through the use of the

---

[7] Securities and Exchange Commission, *Seventeenth Annual Report, 1951* (Washington, D.C.: U.S. Government Printing Office, 1952), p. 130.

term *value*.[8] The reader is already well aware of the different approaches which may be taken in arriving at the valuation of a business, and of the absence of universal standards. The position taken by the SEC on this point is again quite clear:

Concomitant to this rule [the rule of absolute priority], it is clear that a sound valuation of the debtor is essential to provide a basis for judging the fairness as well as the feasibility of proposed plans of reorganization. The Commission has continued to urge that the proper method of valuation for reorganization purposes is primarily an appropriate capitalization of reasonably prospective earnings.[9]

Thus, the Commission endorses a forward-looking concept of value, as opposed to the alternatives of book or liquidating value, but one which is at the same time highly subjective, particularly under the circumstances of bankruptcy.

In the application of the rule of absolute priority the SEC has under certain circumstances sought to draw a distinction between shareholders who have a voice in management and those who have not:

In connection with the fairness of plans . . . the Commission has been concerned with situations where mismanagement or other misconduct on the part of a parent company or a controlling person required that the claim of such person be subordinated to the claims of the public investors or that participation be limited to cost. Such matters must be given full consideration since they form an integral part of the concept of the "fair and equitable" plan.[10]

As a part of its concern with fair treatment of investors, the Commission makes a practice of reviewing the charter of the reorganized company. Its announced standards with regard to the provisions of such charters show a close similarity to those developed for public utilities under the Holding Company Act, as might be expected. This is seen in the following statement:

Frequently, the plan of reorganization contains provisions relating to the terms to be incorporated in corporate charters, bylaws, trust indentures, and other instruments. . . . the Commission pays careful attention to these matters and endeavors to obtain the inclusion of protective features and safeguards for investors. Among numerous other matters, the Commission has urged and generally favored provisions for cumulative voting for directors, pre-emptive rights for stockholders, provisions making lists of stockholders available for inspection, the ratification by stockholders of the

---

[8] Some observers have commented that while the law appears to be rigid on the rule of absolute priority, its operation in effecting actual reorganizations does not always bear this out. The result in such cases may be more accurately described as the application of *relative priority*—where priority is still recognized but not to the point of excluding junior claims from receiving some consideration.

[9] Securities and Exchange Commission, *Eighteenth Annual Report* (1952), p. 156.

[10] Securities and Exchange Commission, *Fifteenth Annual Report* (1949), p. 144.

selection of auditors, and, in certain instances, a limitation upon compensation for management. . . . Unless justified by the special and unusual circumstances of the case, the Commission has opposed the voting trust because it disenfranchises stockholders. . . .[11]

The term "feasible" refers to the requirement of the Bankruptcy Act that a court shall not approve a plan, even if it has unanimous approval, unless the capital structure of the reorganized company is one that assures the new company of adequate sources of funds and no danger of a repetition of the bankruptcy. Thus, the SEC's stand on feasibility has great bearing on corporate financial policy.

It has at least as important a bearing on corporate financial policy as does its stand on fairness. In view of the fact that bankruptcy and reorganization involve such a diverse group of businesses and industries, it is not to be expected that the Commission would come up with as precise a set of standards as those applied to the electric and gas utilities. At the same time, however, the thinking of the Commission is obviously influenced by the general concepts of appropriate financial practice developed in and for its public utility work. This is to be seen in the following statement of considerations which the Commission takes into account when assessing the feasibility of a plan of reorganization:

. . . In order to assure a reorganization which will not result in the debtor's return to Chapter X because of financial difficulties, the Commission gives a great deal of attention to the various factors affecting feasibility. Generally speaking these factors involve the adequacy of working capital, the relationship of funded debt and the capital structure as a whole to property values, the type and characteristics of the securities to be issued, the adequacy of corporate earning power to meet interest and dividend requirements, the possible need for capital expenditures, and the effect of the new capitalization upon the company's prospective credit.[12]

In this connection, we might note the consistent objection of the SEC to the creation of securities whose value is contingent upon better than average performance on the part of the reorganized company. The Commission, wherever it has influence, seeks to prevent the issuance of securities that have highly speculative characteristics. Especially is this true when voting power goes with the issue in question. Then, a group might obtain control of a large group of assets by making a nominal investment.

For example, in the one formal advisory report published in the 1964 fiscal year, the SEC disapproved of a proposed issue in the following

---

[11] *Ibid.*, pp. 146–47.

[12] Securities and Exchange Commission, *Eighteenth Annual Report* (1952), p. 156.

words: "it is not appropriate under the auspices of the court to effect a public distribution of securities whose market prices may reflect in large measure uninformed or speculative appraisals of the conjectural possibilities."[13]

It is interesting to note that the interest of the Commission does not necessarily cease when it has stated its views on the plan of reorganization. In this regard the Commission has had the following to say: "The Commission's interest in the entire reorganization process includes not only the consummation of the plan and the winding up of the affairs of the trusteeship (which may occur many years after a plan has been consummated) but may also extend to the execution of the terms of the plan by the reorganized company."[14]

Failure as a Management Problem

At the beginning of this chapter, we drew a distinction between the concept of failure as it is usually presented, with its attendant distress and loss to owners and creditors, and the termination of and/or withdrawal of investment from a business because it has failed to meet the original expectations of its owners. It is true, of course, that once a business has reached the point of insolvency, the initiative shifts from its owners to the creditors or the courts. When a business has reached this stage, management, if it has any role at all, becomes more of a participant than a dominant force directing events.

If, however, management is able to recognize the hard facts of an unfavorable business environment before it has exhausted its resources in a vain attempt to overcome this environment, then it is in a position to retain the initiative. This, of course, is easily said and unusually difficult to do. On the one hand, the handwriting on the wall may only be partially apparent, even to the unbiased observer. This uncertainty about the future becomes the basis for continued hope for recovery. On the other hand, businessmen, being human, become emotionally involved in the situation and personally identified with their particular business ventures so that, like the captain steeped in naval tradition, they would never consider abandoning a sinking ship. It is also true that there are situations where, however willing the management may be to abandon ship, it may be impossible to withdraw without heavy losses.

Nevertheless, there are many situations where a realistic look at the facts in the early stages of decline and a willingness to admit defeat will enable the owners to minimize their losses and shift what remains of their investment to a more promising opportunity. This also implies a full discharge of obligations to creditors and the preservation of the intangible but valuable asset of a good credit record.

---

[13] Securities and Exchange Commission, *Reorganization Release No. 213* (May 25, 1964).

[14] Securities and Exchange Commission, *Sixteenth Annual Report* (1950), p. 128.

Cases

Case 1

Weber Markets, Inc.

IN JUNE, 1956, Mr. G. C. Scarlatti, general manager of Weber Markets, Inc., was considering an offer of Elgar Fisheries Company to sell 10,000 cases of frozen fish sticks at a substantial discount provided that Weber Markets would make payment for and accept delivery of the entire shipment by June 30. A smaller discount was offered if the delivery and payment were made during July.

Weber Markets, Inc., operated a chain of 34 supermarkets in a major northwestern city and its suburbs. The company had been founded in 1925 with the opening of a single small food store. From time to time, other units had been added until 73 stores were in operation in 1937. All but three of these were small combination grocery and meat markets with an average area of less than 2,000 square feet. In these stores, customers were served by clerks who waited upon them from behind counters.

Beginning in 1936, certain significant changes in the company's operations were initiated in keeping with trends in the retail food industry. No new small units of the traditional type were opened. Additions to the chain took the form of large supermarkets.

Together with the construction of supermarkets, a policy of gradually closing the small stores was adopted. The result was a decrease in the number of units in the chain, from 73 in 1937 to 34 in 1956.

Later, larger amounts of space had been used for frozen foods. By 1953, frozen food display cases extended along the entire length of the two sides of each market. The meat department and checkout counters occupied the back and front of the store, respectively.

In 1948 the company had reached a decision to integrate its operation vertically by constructing its own warehouse to service the chain. A modern, centrally located, one-story building with an area of 300,000 square feet had been completed in 1950, and a fleet of six trucks had been acquired for distribution purposes. A feature of the warehouse was a large freezer room for the storage of frozen foods. It covered 25,000 square feet of land at the rear of the warehouse.

On June 1, 1956, Weber Markets, Inc., held cash and government securities totaling $2,860,000. Of these funds, $2,000,000 was earmarked for initial costs in connection with the construction of five new supermarkets, scheduled to begin during the summer, and was thus unavailable for other purposes. The company had a $500,000 line of credit with Rainier-Hood National Bank, of which $84,000 was drawn down on June 1, 1956. This loan carried interest at 6%. Additional borrowings could be made at the same rate, and it was likely that the bank would agree to a loan substantially in excess of the $500,000 credit line. The bank expected that any loan of this type be paid up during at least one month of the year, although this requirement had been waived on one occasion in the past. The company had no plans to sell new issues of securities during 1956 or 1957.

Elgar Fisheries Company supplied fresh, frozen, and processed fish to food jobbers and directly to large retailers. It operated a fleet of seven fishing vessels in the waters off the northwestern United States. The bulk of its fish, however, was purchased from independent fishermen at public auctions in seaport towns. In recent years, the processed fish segment of its business had grown rapidly to a point where it accounted for over 70% of total dollar volume in 1955.

By far the most important item in the Elgar line of processed fish was a relatively new item, fish sticks. These were breaded, precooked fillets of cod, haddock, or ocean perch. They were frozen and packed 10 to a package. Following the introduction of this product in late 1953, national sales had increased quickly, aided by extensive promotion by processors made possible by their margins, which averaged approximately 31% of the wholesale price. By 1955 industry production exceeded 65 million pounds, or over six times the rate of production in late 1953. The number of producers of fish sticks had increased in the same period from 13 to 55. Subsequently, several smaller firms had dropped out of the fish stick business as national consumption appeared, at least temporarily, to level off. Between December, 1953, and January, 1956, the wholesale price of fish sticks in the Northwest had declined from $4.75 per case to $3.85 per case. By June, 1956, this price had recovered to 4.25 per case.

An increasingly pressing problem to Elgar Fisheries was the seasonality of its fish stick business. The fish were caught and processed mainly in the late spring and summer months. On the other hand, the periods of peak consumption of this product occurred in October and during the Lenten season. Accordingly, Elgar was faced with the problem of financing the purchase, processing, and stocking of fish sticks for several months before sales to retailers and jobbers took place in any volume. It was the practice of most of Elgar's customers, including Weber Markets,

Inc., to buy fish sticks on a "hand-to-mouth" basis; that is, purchases were made in relatively small amounts shortly in advance of need. The usual terms of sale were cash within 24 hours of delivery. Elgar therefore rented storage space for its summer production of fish sticks in a commercial frozen storage warehouse located near its processing plant at a rate equivalent to an annual charge of $2.50 per square foot.

In order to finance the production and carrying of its fish stick inventory, Elgar borrowed seasonally from its bank of account, Evergreen Trust Company. Interest at the rate of 6% was charged by the bank on such borrowing. During 1955 these bank loans had reached a peak of $3,400,000.

In an effort to alleviate its problems of seasonality with respect to fish sticks, Elgar's management had decided early in 1956 to offer a 14% discount to customers willing to pay for and accept delivery on "large orders" of fish sticks during the month of June. "Large orders" were defined as orders of 10,000 cases or above. A discount of 10% was to be offered for purchases during July.

Accordingly, on June 10, 1956, Mr. Franck, Elgar's sales manager, had called upon Mr. Scarlatti and offered to sell 10,000 cases or more of frozen fish sticks at $3.655 per case, provided that delivery was accepted and payment made by Weber Markets before June 30, 1956. This price represented a 14% discount from the prevailing wholesale price of $4.25. A price of $3.825 was offered if payment and delivery were made before July 31.

In considering these offers, Mr. Scarlatti recalled that Weber Markets' sales of fish sticks in 1955 had amounted to 11,200 cases. There were presently 200 cases on hand. Gross profit on this item had averaged 30% of wholesale price. He estimated that the storage of 10,000 cases would require 5,000 square feet of warehouse freezer space. Checking with the chief accounting officer, Mr. Scarlatti learned that total costs attributed in 1955 to the 25,000 square foot warehouse freezer area had been $56,000, or $2.24 a square foot. At no time during 1955 had more than 75% of the capacity of the freezer area been utilized; and under current plans, apart from the possible use for frozen fish sticks, increased utilization in 1956 appeared unlikely.

With this information at hand, Mr. Scarlatti was considering how to use it in reaching a sound decision on the Elgar proposal. Mr. Scarlatti knew that Elgar rented frozen storage space. Consequently, he was also considering the likelihood that Mr. Franck would be willing to negotiate a somewhat larger discount than 14%.

As he turned to the figure work which he felt would be helpful, Mr. Scarlatti decided that he would use 1955 sales data as if they would apply to 1956 and early 1957.

Exhibit 1

WEBER MARKETS, INC.

MONTHLY SALES OF FISH STICKS IN 1955

	Cases	Cumulative %
January	810	7.2
February	1,520	20.8
March	2,490	43.0
April	1,710	58.3
May	820	65.6
June	150	67.0
July	90	67.8
August	60	68.3
September	220	70.3
October	1,630	84.8
November	930	93.1
December	770	100.0
Total	11,200	

Exhibit 2

WEBER MARKETS, INC.

COST OF FISH STICK SALES, MONTHLY, 1955*

	Cases	Average Wholesale Price	Cost
January	810	$4.56	$ 3,693.60
February	1,520	4.48	6,809.60
March	2,490	4.42	11,005.80
April	1,710	4.35	7,438.50
May	820	4.41	3,616.20
June	150	4.27	640.50
July	90	4.33	389.70
August	60	4.25	255.00
September	220	4.10	902.00
October	1,630	4.12	6,715.60
November	930	4.01	3,729.30
December	770	3.90	3,003.00
Total	11,200		

* It may be assumed that purchases and sales were made in the same month.

Case 2

The Hintz Company

On May 10, 1954, Mr. Samuel Hintz, president of The Hintz Company, noted that the company's accounts receivable balance had increased to $93,000 as of April 30, 1954. Since this was $19,000 higher than it had been on March 31, 1954, Mr. Hintz decided to investigate the reasons for the increase to see whether it might have significance in determining the company's future plans.

The Hintz Company, located in New York City, manufactured baseball, basketball, and other athletic uniforms. The company's 20 employees cut and sewed fabrics to color and size specifications. The uniforms were sold directly to retail sporting goods shops in the New York metropolitan area. As there were several other small manufacturers of uniforms in New York City, competition for the business of these retail outlets was keen.

Since Hintz's founding in 1946, it had operated profitably, and sales volume had reached a peak of $350,000 in 1951. In the fall of 1952, sales failed to recover from the seasonal low of the summer months. In July, 1953, when a new sales manager, Mr. Katz, was employed, sales volume began improving. By May, 1954, Mr. Katz had secured 50 new accounts for the company.

After reading trade papers, Mr. Hintz believed that the prospects of the athletic uniform market looked promising for the remainder of 1954. It was reported that there were a large number of newly organized athletic teams in the New York area and that schools and other regular purchasers were buying new uniforms more frequently. Since Mr. Katz's more detailed experience in the market tended to confirm this information, Mr. Hintz was looking forward to the best year in the company's history. On this basis, he projected sales and profits by months for the remainder of 1954 as follows:

	1953	Sales *1954*	Profit before Taxes
May......................	$ 50,000		$ 4,000
June......................		40,000	2,000
July......................		40,000	2,000
August...................		40,000	2,000
September................		50,000	4,000
October..................		55,000	5,000
November................		60,000	6,000
December................		60,000	6,000
Total........	*338,000*	$395,000	$31,000

PROFIT 1953
$2000

PROFIT 1954
$43,000
of projection table

Hintz's customers were, for the most part, small sporting goods stores. Of 450 accounts, only six purchased more than $10,000 worth of uniforms in a year. Most of the remainder made periodic purchases of approximately $100 per order. Hintz sold on terms of net 30, but only the large stores paid consistently within 60 days of billing. Bad debt losses were 1% of sales in 1953. A substantial portion of the retail stores' sales of athletic uniforms was made to schools that paid their accounts slowly, and Hintz's collections also tended to be slow. Mr. Hintz believed that many of the smaller stores were operated without adequate capital investment.

Mr. Katz received a salary of $6,000 and a 2% commission on his personal sales. He sold one third of the company's accounts as well as supervising the company's two other salesmen. Each salesman was paid a straight commission of 5%. No attempt was made to charge a salesman for bad-debt losses resulting from his sales efforts.

Neither Mr. Hintz nor the company's bookkeeper, Mr. Stein, had abundant time to devote to credit management. As a result, the following general policies had been established for guidance in credit matters. Before selling to a new account, a company salesman, on the basis of his observations at the store, was expected to appraise the storekeeper's character and abilities, and to judge the financial condition of the store as best he could. If these appeared satisfactory, a line of credit of $200 was extended to the store. After a year a salesman was authorized to increase the line of credit to $500 if the store had made all its payments within 90 days of billing. After 2 years of satisfactory credit experience, open lines of credit were granted when necessary. If a specific case warranted exception to these rules, Mr. Hintz reviewed the information available and made the final decision.

Billings were prepared by Mr. Stein when shipment was made. If payment was not received within 60 days, a form letter was sent to the customer calling his attention to this omission. After 90 days a warning letter was sent, requesting payment within 10 days. Mr. Hintz phoned all store owners who had not made payment within 100 days of billing; and unless he received a firm promise for immediate remittance, he threatened to turn the account over to his lawyer. If payment was not received after 120 days, the receivables were given to a law firm for collection, and the account was written off as a bad debt.

On April 30, 1954, $2,200 in outstanding receivables were in the hands of lawyers pending settlement. Legal fees on these collections amounted to 25% of the amount collected or $50, whichever was the larger. Mr. Hintz considered the company fortunate if it received as much as 50% on a receivable after it had been turned over to a law firm. In several instances final settlement took as long as a year.

Although sales tended to fluctuate from month to month, Mr. Hintz maintained raw material and finished goods inventories at even levels. As the company's production facilities were adequate to support a substantial increase in sales volume, no additions to fixed assets were contemplated. Mr. Hintz noted that with the exception of the bank loan, current liabilities tended to remain relatively constant.

On May 10, 1954, when Mr. Hintz received the April 30, 1954, balance sheet shown in Exhibit 1, he was disturbed by the sharp increase in accounts receivable. He thought several questions important: (1) whether the increase indicated larger bad-debt losses might be incurred in the future; (2) whether the current policies of credit administration needed alteration; and (3) whether the receivables balance might increase in the future to the point where the company would require more funds from the bank. To help answer these questions, he had requested Mr. Stein to prepare the information contained in Exhibits 2 and 3. Profit and loss statements are given in Exhibit 4.

Exhibit 1

THE HINTZ COMPANY

BALANCE SHEETS, DECEMBER 31, 1952–53; APRIL 30, 1953–54
CHANGES IN BALANCE SHEET AMOUNTS, SELECTED PERIODS
(Dollar Figures in Thousands)

	Balance Sheets				Changes	
	Dec. 31 1952	April 30 1953	Dec. 31 1953	April 30 1954	Dec. to April 1953–54	April to April 1953–54
ASSETS						
Cash	$10	$10	$10	$ 4	$ −6	$ −6
Accounts receivable (net)	41	37	68	93	+25	+56
Inventory	23	22	25	22	−3	—
Total current assets	$74	$69	$103	$119	$+16	$+50
Machinery and equipment (net)	20	20	19	19	—	−1
Other assets	4	3	4	3	−1	—
Total assets	$98	$92	$126	$141	$+15	$+49
LIABILITIES						
Accounts payable	$20	$19	$ 21	$ 21	$ —	$ +2
Taxes payable	4	—	4	5	+1	+5
Accrued payroll	6	8	5	8	+3	—
Bank loan	—	—	25	32	+7	+32
Total current liabilities	$30	$27	$ 55	$ 66	$+11	$+39
Common stock	35	35	35	35	—	—
Surplus	33	30	36	40	+4	+10
Total liabilities and net worth	$98	$92	$126	$141	$+15	$+49

[handwritten note:] proprietary ratio has gone from 71% to 53%

Exhibit 2

THE HINTZ COMPANY

Summary of Transactions in Accounts Receivable, January, 1953–April, 1954

(Dollar Figures in Thousands)

1953	Accounts Receivable Beginning	Sales (+)	Collections (−)	Bad Debts (−)	Accounts Receivable Ending	Collection Period (Days)
January	$41.5	$ 30.6	$ 30.7	$0.5	$40.9	34*
February	40.9	32.4	37.1	0.6	35.6	40*
March	35.6	24.1	21.4	0.6	37.7	44*
April	37.7	26.3	26.4	0.6	37.0	43*
May	37.0	25.4	24.7	0.6	37.1	38*
June	37.1	22.0	28.0	0.7	30.4	38*
July	30.4	24.6	22.7	0.5	31.8	40*
August	31.8	27.6	17.7	0.5	41.2	47*
September	41.2	24.6	23.1	0.5	42.2	47*
October	42.2	31.7	28.0	0.4	45.5	48*
November	45.5	30.1	13.3	0.5	61.8	60*
December	61.8	38.2	31.2	0.5	68.3	60*
Total	$41.5	$337.4	$304.3	$6.3	$68.3	73†
1954						
January	68.3	33.7	40.8	0.5	60.7	51*
February	60.7	38.1	28.4	0.6	69.8	58*
March	69.8	45.8	41.0	0.5	74.1	53*
April	74.1	54.9	35.1	0.6	93.3	55*
Total 1954 to date	$68.3	$172.5	$145.3	$2.2	$93.3	65†

* Based on most recent 60-day sales period.
† Based on year, or year to date.

Exhibit 3

THE HINTZ COMPANY

ANALYSIS OF COLLECTIONS, APRIL, 1953–54, AND ACCOUNTS RECEIVABLE, APRIL 30, 1953–54

(Dollar Figures in Thousands)

Month of Sale	Age April 30 (Days)	Amount of Sales		Amount Collected in April	
		1953	1954	1953	1954
Collections in April					
April..........	0–30	$26.3	$54.9	$ 1.0	$ 2.7
March........	31–60	24.1	45.8	2.1	5.5
February......	61–90	32.4	38.1	22.7	26.3
January.......	91–120	30.6	33.7	0.6	0.5
Earlier........	121+	....	....	0.0*	0.1*
				$26.4	$35.1

				Amount of Outstanding Receivables by Month of Sale	
				1953	1954
Age of accounts receivable on April 30					
April..........	0–30	26.3	54.9	$25.3	$52.2
March........	31–60	24.1	45.8	9.5	37.7
February......	61–90	32.4	38.1	2.0	2.7
January.......	91–120	30.6	33.7	0.2	0.7
Earlier........	....	....	....	0.0*	0.0*
				$37.0	$93.3

% of accounts
1953   1954
68%   56%
25   40
5   3.7
.6   0
0   0

* Charged off, in hands of attorneys.

Giving easier terms up to 60 days, quality hasn't gone down

Exhibit 4

THE HINTZ COMPANY

PROFIT AND LOSS STATEMENTS

(Dollar Figures in Thousands)

	Year		Four Months Jan.-Apr.	
	1952	1953	1953	1954
Sales...............................	$335	$338	$114	$173
Cost of goods sold.....................	213	215	75	120
Gross profit...........................	$122	$123	$ 39	$ 53
General selling and administrative expenses..........................	101	103	36	40
Bad debt loss.........................	3	3	1	1
Operating profit.......................	$ 18	$ 17	$ 2	$ 12
Provision for taxes.....................	4	4	0	3
Net profit............................	$ 14	$ 13	$ 2	$ 9
Dividends............................	10	10	5	5
Retained earnings.....................	$ 4	$ 3	$ (3)	$ 4

Case 3

James W. Saxton Company

THE JAMES W. SAXTON COMPANY, manufacturer of fine home furniture in Rocky Mount, North Carolina, distributed its products directly to department stores, independent home furnishing retailers, and a few small regional furniture chains. Early in April, 1951, the credit manager of the Saxton Company, Mr. Frank Preston, received from his assistant, Mr. Richard Rossi, pertinent information on two accounts in Missouri—Bauman's, Inc., of St. Louis, and Vardon's Emporium of Kansas City. Mr. Rossi believed changes in these companies warranted Mr. Preston's attention.

Bauman's retailed quality home furnishings from four locations, one in the downtown section of St. Louis and the others in nearby suburban areas. The company also manufactured custom upholstered furniture on special order. Since Bauman's handled a complete line of home furnishings, sales were fairly steady throughout the year and were approximately 75% for cash and 25% by 30-day charge or 12-month instalment terms. Instalment terms called for 25% down and the balance in equal monthly payments over a 12-month period.

The store had been established in 1915 as a partnership and was incorporated in 1946. In June, 1950, two of the four original partners sold their shares in the company to the two remaining owners.

Bauman's had been a customer of the Saxton Company since 1918 and had previously handled its affairs in a most satisfactory manner. Vardon's Emporium was a comparatively new customer of Saxton's, having been sold since 1946. A medium-sized department store in downtown Kansas City, it was well known for its extensive lines of home furnishings. Its account with Saxton's had been satisfactory through 1950.

Both accounts were sold on terms of 1/10, net 30 and, although not discounting, had been paying invoices promptly until December, 1950. Mr. Preston had previously established a $10,000 limit on Bauman's and a $15,000 limit on Vardon's.

The Saxton Company advertised its lines nationally and attempted to maintain intensive coverage of trading areas by distributing through stores strategically located within a particular marketing area. Beginning in 1949, activity in the furniture market had become sufficiently spotty that quality of product and service were not the only bases for competition among manufacturers for outlets. Credit terms and financing of dealers became equally important; thus, the Saxton Company, in Mr. Preston's words, was "backed into the position of supporting numerous customers in order to maintain adequate distribution for its products."

Because of this requirement for the extension of fairly liberal credit, Mr. Preston had since 1949 adhered strictly to a policy of obtaining current reports on the financial status of customers. These reports, obtained as annual balance sheets and profit and loss statements, for customers that were considered satisfactory risks, were supplied directly by the customers. Under certain circumstances, wherein Saxton's was working very closely with a particular customer who was trading actively on a small investment, Mr. Preston received quarterly and at times monthly statements in order "to keep on top" of the credit situation.

In early April, 1951, Mr. Richard Rossi, assistant credit manager of the James W. Saxton Company, received the annual reports of Bauman's, Inc., and Vardon's Emporium. After reviewing these statements and checking the accounts receivable ledger for both customers, Mr. Rossi felt that the accounts should be reviewed by Mr. Preston. Accordingly, he furnished Mr. Preston with the information found in Exhibits 1 through 5.

When reviewing the accounts, Mr. Rossi kept in mind that 1950 had not been a particularly good year for retail furniture stores. It was generally known that stores such as Vardon's, carrying low-priced furniture lines, were the first to suffer the declines which had come in the late summer and early fall. This situation was followed by signs of a relaxing demand for furniture of higher quality and higher price toward the end of 1950. The drop in volume and the subsequent price cutting hit the profit margins of some retailers to such an extent that their losses in the latter part of the year equaled or more than offset profits gained in the earlier part of the year.

In the early months of 1951 the "softness" of the furniture business continued. Although there was no severe drop in the buying of furniture at the retail level, there was an indication that "scare" buying and purchasing in anticipation of potential shortages had been curtailed. Accordingly, retail stores reduced orders of new lines and reorders of established lines in February, March, and April. Throughout the country, orders for shipment in April were down about 30% from March; March had itself shown a drop of about 10% from February. Thus, credit managers among furniture manufacturing concerns were placed in the unhappy position of trying to please sales managers who wanted to maintain volume while they were aware that the shipment of furniture to customers who had already overextended their financial positions was potentially dangerous in such a period.

Exhibit 1

JAMES W. SAXTON COMPANY

BAUMAN'S INC., BALANCE SHEETS AS OF JANUARY 31, 1949–51

(In Thousands of Dollars)

ASSETS	1/31/49	1/31/50	1/31/51
Cash	$ 14	$ 11	$ 8
Accounts receivable, net	231	261	268
Inventory	304	303	304
Total current assets	$549	$575	$580
Land	59	59	59
Buildings, fixtures, and equipment	225	228	263
Less: Reserve for depreciation	31	48	66
Net buildings, fixtures, and equipment	$194	$180	$197
Investment	11	11	11
Due from stockholders	....	36	48
Deferred charges	7	3	3
Total assets	$820	$864	$898

LIABILITIES			
Accounts payable	$144	$145	$154
Notes payable—employees	12	13	13
Estimated federal income tax	11	....	....
Current maturities on long-term debts	26	60	37
Miscellaneous accruals	36	34	11
Total current liabilities	$229	$252	$215
Notes payable—bank*	91	150	145
Mortgage notes payable	376	375	438
Preferred stock—5% noncumulative	32	32	32
Common stock	60	60	60
Capital surplus	....	....	19
Earned surplus	32	5[d]	11[d]
Total liabilities	$820	$865	$898

* Secured by pledged accounts receivable.
[d]Deficit.

Exhibit 2

JAMES W. SAXTON COMPANY

INCOME STATEMENTS OF BAUMAN'S, INC., FOR YEARS ENDED JANUARY 31, 1949–51

(In Thousands of Dollars)

	1/31/49	*1/31/50*	*1/31/51*
Sales	$1,945	$1,583	$1,502
Less returns and allowances	175	186	122
Net sales	$1,770	$1,397	$1,380
Cost of goods sold	1,077	854	859
Gross profit	$ 693	$ 543	$ 521
Less operating expenses	595	515	498
Operating profit	$ 98	$ 28	$ 23
Other income	67	11	14
Net after other income	$ 165	$ 39	$ 37
Other deductions	40	41	43
Net profit (loss) before tax	$ 125	$ (2)*	$ (6)
Dividends paid	$ 35	$ 35	.....

* Parentheses denote losses.

Exhibit 3

JAMES W. SAXTON COMPANY

VARDON'S EMPORIUM—BALANCE SHEETS AS OF JANUARY 31, 1950–51

(Dollar Figures in Thousands)

ASSETS	*1/31/50*	*1/31/51*
Cash	$ 123	$ 79
Notes and accounts receivableᴾ	917	884
Inventory	895	821
Tax carryback claim	.....	74
Total current assets	$1,935	$1,858
Fixed assets, net	244	221
Leasehold improvements, net	598	577
Cash value life insuranceᴾ	47	46
Investments	9	9
Notes receivable—officers and employeesᴾ	18	23
Prepaid and deferred items	25	26
Total assets	$2,876	$2,760

LIABILITIES		
Notes payable—Industrial Finance Corporation	$ 885	$ 717
Accounts payable	407	443
Miscellaneous accruals	98	113
Total current liabilities	$1,390	$1,273
Common stock	570	570
Surplus	916	917
Total liabilities	$2,876	$2,760

ᴾ Pledged to secure 30-day renewable notes to Industrial Finance Corporation.

Exhibit 4
JAMES W. SAXTON COMPANY

VARDON'S EMPORIUM—INCOME STATEMENTS FOR YEARS ENDED JANUARY 31, 1950–51

(Dollar Figures in Thousands)

	1/31/50	1/31/51
Gross sales..	$5,210	$4,828
Less: Returns and allowances............................	478	369
Net sales...	$4,732	$4,459
Cost of goods sold.......................................	2,975	3,064
Gross profit...	$1,757	$1,395
Operating expenses.......................................	1,499	1,630
Operating profit...	$ 258	$ 235ᵈ
Adjustments:		
Elimination—reserves for inventory losses...............	...	135
Reduction—bad debt reserve............................	...	18
Tax carryback...	...	84
Federal income tax....................................	108	...
Net before dividends....................................	$ 150	$ 2
Dividends paid..	100	1
Net to surplus..	$ 50	$ 1

ᵈ Deficit.

Exhibit 5
JAMES W. SAXTON COMPANY

AGING OF ACCOUNTS RECEIVABLE BALANCES
AS OF MARCH 31, 1951

Due from	Prior	Dec.	Jan.	Feb.	Mar.	Totals
Bauman's, Inc............		$ 913.30	$3,524.37	$1,028.01	$5,803.14	$11,268.82
Vardon's Emporium	$380.84* (October)	4,883.96	1,025.55	4,352.00	9,124.77	19,767.12

* Represents invoice on disputed shipment; customer claimed damaged merchandise.

Case 4

The O. M. Scott & Sons Company

BETWEEN 1955 and 1961 management of The O. M. Scott & Sons Company launched a number of new programs aimed at maintaining and increasing the company's past success and growth. Largely in response to these activities, Scott's field sales force grew from 6 to 150 men, several entirely new and expanded production facilities went on stream, and the number of products in the company's product line tripled. Sales increased from about $10 million to $43 million. In late 1961 company officials were preparing to review the results of all these changes to ascertain how, if at all, Scott's plans and financial policies should be changed.

The O. M. Scott & Sons Company commenced operations in 1868, when it began processing the country's first clean, weed-free grass seed. Scott's early business came from a small but rapidly growing local market in central Ohio. Later, however, the company went through several stages in its growth. At about the turn of the century the company turned from supplying its local market to selling grass and other farm seeds over a wider geographic area by mail. As its success with its mail-order business increased, the company began to advertise extensively and in 1927 added a free magazine called *Lawn Care*, which has been widely distributed ever since. In all of these early promotional activities, the company sought to sell the Scott name and products as well as the idea of improved care of lawns. In the 1920's a special lawn fertilizer developed for home use was added to the company's product line. During the 1930's the company began to distribute its products on a small scale through selected retail stores and garden centers. Sales and profits grew steadily throughout these years. Scott continued to grow along these same general lines until 1945, by which time sales reached $2.7 million and net profits after taxes were about $30,000.

Over the decade immediately following the war, pioneering research by Scott led to the development and introduction of a wide range of new chemical weed and garden pest controls and special-purpose lawn fertilizers. In addition, the company's grass seed lines were upgraded and supplemented. Largely in response to the success of this research, sales increased to $11.4 million and profits to over $210,000 in fiscal 1955.

By 1955, however, despite the company's impressive postwar record of growth in sales and profits, management was convinced that neither Scott nor its competitors had begun to develop and tap the potential inherent in the national lawn care market. In Scott's own case this failure to develop and tap the national market was attributed to the fact that Scott's customers could not buy its products easily where and when they expected to find them. The company's distribution system had not evolved adequately in response to developing market opportunities, and in many instances the company's dealers either were poorly stocked or were not the right kind of dealer for the company's products.

Thus began a new stage in Scott's development. Early in 1955 the company launched a program to build a national field sales organization with the objective of increasing the number, quality, and performance of its distributors so as to capitalize more fully on the success of its product research and development efforts. When this program started, the company had six field salesmen. But 1960 Scott had a field sales force of 150 men serving almost 10,000 retail dealers across the country. These dealers were mainly department stores and small hardware stores and garden supply centers. The company's salesmen spent most of their time training the dealers how to do a better selling job with Scott products and were paid a salary plus a bonus based on factory shipments to dealers.

Scott's product development program continued apace with the buildup in the direct selling force, so that by the end of the 1950's the company was engaged in the purchase, processing, and sale of grass seed, and the manufacture and sale of fertilizers, weed and pest control products, mechanical spreaders, and electric lawn mowers. In 1959 sales increased to $30.6 million and profits to $1.5 million. A large proportion of these sales comprised new products that had been developed and patented by the company within the past few years.

Reviewing the company's progress again in early 1959, management was still not satisfied that the company was marketing its products as effectively as possible. For one thing, it was estimated that an annual market potential of at least $100 million existed for Scott products. Another important consideration was that several nationally known chemical firms had either begun, or were expected to begin, competing against Scott in certain lines. These facts led management to conclude that the most effective way for Scott to preserve its preeminent market position would be to push for immediate further market penetration. If successful such a strategy would enable Scott to eclipse competition as completely as possible before its competitors could establish a firm market position against the company. In this context an annual growth rate in sales and profits of up to 25% was thought to be a reasonable goal for the company over the next few years.

Apart from the need to continue strengthening the company's field sales force and dealer organization, management thought in early 1959 that the most important factor standing in the way of further rapid growth and market penetration was the inability of the typical Scott dealer to carry an adequate inventory of Scott products. Because of the highly seasonal character of sales at retail of the company's products, it was essential that dealers have enough inventory on hand to meet local sales peaks when they came. Experience showed that in many parts of the country a large percentage of dealer sales were made on a few weekends each season. Failure to supply this demand when it materialized most often resulted in a sale lost to a competitor, although sometimes a customer simply postponed buying anything. The problem of assuring adequate dealer inventories had become more of a problem in recent years. The effectiveness of Scott's product development program meant that the dealer was expected to carry many more products than in the past. In addition, Scott had shifted its marketing emphasis from selling individual products to one of selling complete lawn and garden programs. And in order to sell a full lawn maintenance program, it was necessary that the dealer carry the complete Scott line and have it on hand when needed by the consumer.

Because of their small size and often weak working capital position, most of Scott's dealers could not realistically be expected to increase their inventory investment in Scott products. This meant that any desired buildup in dealer inventory levels would have to be financed in some way by Scott itself. In the past the company had extended generous seasonal datings to its dealers, as was industry practice. As a normal pattern, winter and early spring shipments became due at the end of April or May, depending upon the geographical area. Shipments during the summer months were due in October or November. The purpose of these seasonal datings was to enable and encourage as many dealers as possible to be well stocked in advance of seasonal sales peaks. Anticipation at the rate of six tenths of 1% a month was offered on payments made in advance of these seasonal dates, although few dealers availed themselves of this opportunity. With purchases made outside the two main selling seasons, dealers were expected to pay on the 10th of the second month following shipment.

The company's past experience with seasonal datings suggested certain changes in the event Scott proceeded to finance a higher level of dealer inventories. Because of the seasonal nature of the business and the fact that most dealers were thinly capitalized, payment was not often received by Scott until the merchandise involved was sold, irrespective of the terms of sale. This meant that many dealers were continually asking for credit extensions. Another problem inherent in the seasonal dating policy was that Scott retained little or no effective security interest in the goods involved. A final problem was that in the past Scott had followed a policy of not selling to dealers that could not be relied upon to maintain prices at reasonable levels. It was thought that widespread selling at discount prices would undermine the company and the market image it was trying to project. Thus, in any decision to expand dealer inventories, management hoped to contrive a procedure whereby Scott would retain the right to reclaim goods from third parties in the event any of its dealers began selling at wholesale to a discounter.

After considerable study it was decided to continue the traditional seasonal dating plan and to introduce a new trust receipt plan as well. This combination was thought to fulfill all of the requirements outlined in the previous paragraph. As the particular trust receipt plan adopted by Scott worked, a trust receipt dealer was required to sign a trust receipt that provided for (1) immediate transfer to the dealer of title to any Scott products shipped in response to a dealer order, (2) retention of a security interest by Scott in merchandise so shipped until sold by the dealer acting in his capacity as a retailer, and (3) segregation of a sufficient proportion of the funds received from such sales to provide for payment to Scott as billed. Among other things, these provisions made it possible for Scott to move in and reclaim any inventory held by third parties that had been sold by a trust receipt dealer acting illegally as a wholesaler. Exhibit 5 (page 652) shows the trust receipt form used by Scott. In addition to obtaining the trust receipt from its dealers, the company also was required to file a statement of trust receipt financing with the secretary of state in each state where a trust receipt plan dealer was domiciled. Such a statement is shown in Exhibit 6 (page 652). Dealers using the trust receipt plan were charged an extra 3% on the cost of purchases from Scott. They also had to place all purchase orders directly through Scott's field salesmen, inasmuch as these account executives were held responsible by the company for controlling dealer inventories in connection with the trust receipt plan.

This last-mentioned role of Scott's sales force was absolutely central to the proper functioning of the trust receipt plan. Apart from simply policing the level and character of dealer inventories, the account executives also periodically inventoried the trust receipt dealers so that Scott could bill the dealers for merchandise sold. During the two peak retail selling seasons, these physical inventories were taken once a month and even oftener in the case of large dealers. In the off seasons the inspections occurred much less frequently. In any event, the terms of payment associated with the trust receipt plan required that the dealer pay Scott within 10 days of receipt of an invoice from the company for goods sold since the last physical inventory date.

After introduction of the two payment plans in 1960, about half of Scott's sales were by seasonal dating and half by trust receipt. The trust receipt dealers were for the most part local garden centers and hardware stores, whereas the seasonal dating dealers were the larger chain garden centers and department stores. The company's overall collection experience with both plans was that about 75% of receivables were collected in the month due, another 16% in the following month, an additional 6% in the next month after that, and the balance thereafter.

The rapid growth in outstanding receivables resulting from the trust receipt program was financed largely by a combination of subordinated notes, a revolving line of bank credit, and increased use of supplier credit arising out of special deferred payment terms extended by the company's chemical suppliers. The company also retained almost all of its earnings each year as had been its policy in the past.

At the end of fiscal 1961 Scott and its subsidiaries had $16.2 million of long-term debt outstanding, of which $12 million comprised renewable 5-year subordinated notes of the parent company held by four insurance companies and a trustee and $4.2 million was publicly held bonds owed by Scotts Chemical Plant, Inc., a wholly owned subsidiary. The key terms associated with the $12 million of subordinated notes are summarized in the footnotes to Exhibits 1 and 2. The governing loan indenture limited the unconsolidated parent company's maximum outstanding debt at any time to an amount not greater than three times what was termed the company's "equity working capital" as of the preceding March 31. What was meant by equity working capital and the calculation of maximum allowed debt are shown in Exhibit 7 (page 656). The note indenture restricted outstanding subordinated notes to only 60% of maximum allowed debt as determined by the above equity working capital formula. The agreement also required that Scott be out of bank debt for 60 consecutive days each year and that the company earn before taxes 1½ times its fixed financial charges, including interest on funded and unfunded debt, amortization of debt discount, and rentals on leased properties.

In addition to the long-term debt just described, Scott also had a $12.5 million line of credit at the end of fiscal 1961 with a group of seven commercial banks. The purpose of this line was to provide for seasonal funds needs, and in recent years the maximum line had been used at some point during each year. An informal understanding covering this seasonal financing arrangement required that Scott maintain average compensating balances with the banks involved of 15% of the line of credit.

As far as accounts payable were concerned, Scott had negotiated an arrangement with its principal chemical suppliers whereby the company settled with these suppliers just once or twice a year. It had been possible to negotiate these favorable terms because the suppliers were persuaded that it was in their best interests to help Scott develop and expand the home lawn market. Generally, no interest or other charges were levied on these amounts.

As fiscal 1961 drew to a close, management was generally pleased with what appeared to have been the results of the trust receipt program, although final figures for the year just ending were not yet available. Company sales had increased from $31 million in 1959 to over $43 million in 1961. At this level of operations the company's break-even point was estimated at between $27.5 million and $30 million.

By the end of 1961, when company officials were reviewing the results of fiscal 1961 and preparing plans for the 1962 selling season, the audited statements shown in Exhibits 1 and 2 were available, as well as the unaudited and unconsolidated quarterly statements in Exhibits 3 and 4. In addition, on the basis of a physical inventory taken by the company's sales force, combined standard and trust receipt plan dealer inventories were estimated to be at a level of about $28 million at the end of calendar 1961. This compared with roughly $17 million at the end of 1960. On the basis of these and other data Scott's sales department estimated that in terms of cost of sales, dealer sales in fiscal 1961 reached an all-time high of over $30 million. The recent record of earnings, dividends, and market price range is shown in Exhibit 8 (page 653).

It was against this background that company officials began their review and evaluation of recent operations and current financial position. They were particularly anxious to formulate any indicated changes in company plans and financial policies before the new production and selling seasons were upon the company.

Exhibit 1

THE O. M. SCOTT & SONS COMPANY AND SUBSIDIARY COMPANIES

CONSOLIDATED BALANCE SHEETS FOR THE YEARS ENDED SEPTEMBER 30, 1957 TO 1961

(Dollar Amounts in Thousands)

	1957	1958	1959	1960 (a)	1961 (e)
Cash	$ 533.9	$ 1,232.0	$ 1,736.4	$ 2,328.7	$ 1,454.3
Accounts receivable (f)	2,640.0	4,686.5	5,788.4	15,749.7	21,500.5
Inventories	2,340.3	3,379.8	6,993.2	3,914.3	5,590.5
Total current assets	$5,514.2	$ 9,298.3	$14,518.0	$21,992.7	$28,545.3
Land, buildings, equipment	$2,253.5	$ 2,439.5	$ 7,364.6	$ 8,003.4	$ 8,370.2
Less: Accumulated depreciation	544.0	650.0	1,211.3	1,687.1	2,247.1
Net fixed assets	$1,709.5	$ 1,789.5	$ 6,153.3	$ 6,316.3	$ 6,123.1
Investment in and advances to affiliates	1,165.6	28.9	232.3	462.0	133.6
Other assets	488.5	376.6	837.5	1,132.0	937.8
Total assets	$8,877.8	$11,493.3	$21,741.1	$29,903.0	$35,739.8
Accounts payable	$1,540.8	$ 2,134.6	$ 4,140.2	$ 2,791.0	$ 6,239.2
Notes payable—banks	300.0		1,000.0		
Accrued taxes, interest, and other expenses	674.3	1,437.7	1,900.7	1,941.2	1,207.7
Current sinking fund requirements	77.0	173.9	324.3	382.5	512.5
Total current liabilities	$2,592.1	$ 3,746.2	$ 7,365.2	$ 5,114.7	$ 7,959.4
Long-term debt:					
Of parent company (c) (h)	$2,186.7	$ 2,059.7	$ 1,777.2	$ 9,000.0	$12,000.0
Of subsidiary			5,162.6	4,649.5	4,170.4
Total liabilities (d)	$4,778.8	$ 5,805.9	$14,305.0	$18,764.2	$24,129.8
Preferred stock (i)	$1,757.2	$ 2,432.2	$ 2,392.5	$ 2,347.5	$ 2,254.3
Common stock and surplus (b)	2,341.8	3,255.2	5,043.6	8,791.3	9,355.7
Total liabilities and net worth	$8,877.8	$11,493.3	$21,741.1	$29,903.0	$35,739.8

See Notes to Financial Statements following Exhibit 2, at page 650.

Exhibit 2

THE O. M. SCOTT & SONS COMPANY AND SUBSIDIARY COMPANIES

CONSOLIDATED INCOME STATEMENTS FOR THE YEARS
ENDED SEPTEMBER 30, 1957 TO 1961

(Dollar Amounts in Thousands)

	1957	1958	1959	1960	1961
Net sales (b) (g)	$18,675.9	$23,400.2	$30,563.7	$38,396.4	$43,140.1
Cost of sales and operating expenses					
Cost of products sold, including processing, warehousing, delivery and merchandising (including lease rentals of $872,577)	$15,500.9	$18,914.7	$24,119.5	$30,416.8	$34,331.7
General and administrative, research and development expenses	1,817.2	2,134.1	2,499.3	2,853.6	3,850.7
Depreciation and amortization	263.2	185.9	377.6	584.2	589.6
Interest charges	199.8	212.7	410.6	881.6	1,131.5
Total cost of sales	$17,781.1	$21,447.4	$27,407.0	$34,736.2	$39,903.5
Earnings before taxes on income	894.8	1,952.7	3,156.7	3,660.2	3,236.6
Federal and state taxes on income	443.5	1,051.6	1,671.2	1,875.2	1,665.9
Net income after taxes	$ 451.3	$ 901.1	$ 1,485.5	$ 1,785.0	$ 1,570.7

See Notes to Financial Statements, following.

Exhibits 1 & 2 (Continued)

THE O. M. SCOTT & SONS COMPANY

NOTES TO FINANCIAL STATEMENTS

(a) *1960 Auditor's Statement*

THE BOARD OF DIRECTORS
THE O. M. SCOTT & SONS COMPANY
MARYSVILLE, OHIO

We have examined the statement of consolidated financial position of The O. M. Scott & Sons Company and its subsidiaries as of September 30, 1960, the related consolidated statements of operations, capital surplus, and retained earnings for the fiscal year then ended, and accompanying notes to financial statements. Our examination was made in accordance with generally accepted auditing standards, and accordingly included such tests of the accounting records and such other auditing procedures as we considered necessary in the circumstances.

In our opinion, the accompanying statements, together with the explanatory notes, present fairly the consolidated financial position of The O. M. Scott & Sons Company and its subsidiaries at September 30, 1960, and the results of their operations for the year then ended, in conformity with generally accepted accounting principles, except as described in note (b), applied on a basis consistent with that of the preceding year.

PEAT, MARWICK, MITCHELL & CO.

COLUMBUS, OHIO
November 23, 1960

(b) *Sales*

For several years the company has followed a prebilling system to obtain more efficient and economical control of production through the medium of unappropriated inventory. Under this system, the invoicing of customers predates shipment. Consequently, both fiscal 1960 and 1959 sales stated in the operating statement include firm orders received, billed, and costed out in late September which were shipped early in the immediately following October. Prior to September 30, 1960, the amounts involved were not significant, but toward the end of that month shipment was delayed by the company to facilitate the taking of physical inventories at storage warehouses as of the month end. The results of the foregoing is to include an additional amount of approximately $343,000 in net earnings for the year 1960. In management's opinion, the earnings on these sales are properly earnings of the year 1960.

(c) *Long-Term Debt*

All long-term obligations of the parent company at September 30, 1959, were retired prior to December 31, 1959.

In fiscal 1960 the parent company sold 5-year subordinated promissory notes, principally to certain insurance companies, at the principal amount of $9 million, maturing October 13, 1964. The notes bear interest to October 10, 1960, at $6\frac{1}{2}\%$ per annum and thereafter to maturity at (a) 6% per annum, or (b) the New York prime commercial rate plus $1\frac{1}{2}\%$, whichever is higher.

The loan agreement provides, among other things, that (a) payment of principal and interest on the notes is subordinated to repayment of bank loans due within one year, (b) new or additional notes may be sold on October 28 of each future year, and (c) any holder of the notes may, before October 15 of each year, require payment by October 10 of the immediately ensuing year of all or part of the notes held.

All holders of the notes at September 30, 1960, surrendered the notes then held in exchange for new notes having exactly the same terms but maturing October 28, 1965, at an interest rate of 6% per annum to October 10, 1961. Interest after October 10, 1961, accrues at the rate determinable under the provisions of the loan agreement.

Long-term obligations of subsidiary outstanding on September 30, 1960:

Exhibits 1 & 2 (Continued)

20-year 5¾% first-mortgage bonds due March 15, 1977	$1,026,000
18-year 6% secured sinking fund debentures due Feb. 1, 1977	2,840,500
10-year 6% sinking fund notes due March 15, 1967	178,000
10-year 6% subordinated debentures due Dec. 15, 1957	950,000
	$4,994,500
Less: Current sinking fund provision	345,000
	$4,649,500

The above obligations of a subsidiary are secured by property mortgages, and/or assignment or lease rentals payable by the parent company.

(d) Long-Term Leases

The main production, warehousing, and office facilities used by the company are leased from affiliated interests not consolidated, namely, the company's Pension and Profit Sharing Trusts, and also from a consolidated subsidiary, Scotts Chemical Plant, Inc. These leases, all having over 10 years to run, required minimum annual rentals in fiscal 1960 of $872,577. This represented less than 17% of net taxable profit before deduction for rentals, depreciation, and expenses based on net profits. It is anticipated that, in fiscal 1961, the fixed rentals under these leases will approximate the same amount.

(e) 1961 Auditor's Statement

BOARD OF DIRECTORS
THE O. M. SCOTT & SONS COMPANY
MARYVILLE, OHIO .

We have examined the statement of consolidated financial position of The O. M. Scott & Sons Company and its subsidiaries as of September 30, 1961, and the related statements of consolidated operations, capital surplus, and retained earnings for the year then ended. Our examination was made in accordance with generally accepted auditing standards and accordingly included such tests of the accounting records and such other auditing procedures as we considered necessary in the circumstances.

In our opinion, the accompanying statements of financial position, operations, capital surplus, and retained earnings present fairly the consolidated financial position of The O. M. Scott & Sons Company and its subsidiaries at September 30, 1961, and the consolidated results of their operations for the year then ended, in conformity with generally accepted accounting principles which, except for the changes (in which we concur) referred to in Notes (f) and (g), have been applied on a basis consistent with that of the preceding year.

ERNST & ERNST

DAYTON, OHIO
January 6, 1962

(f) Accounts Receivable

Accounts receivable are stated net after reserve of $740,000 for dealer adjustments, allowances, and doubtful accounts.

In 1959 the company adopted a plan of deferred payments for certain retail dealers. Accounts receivable include $16,033,093 for shipments under this plan which are secured by trust receipts executed by the dealers. The trust receipt arrangements provide for (1) immediate transfer to the dealers of title to the merchandise shipped in response to the dealers' orders, (2) retention by the company of a security interest in the merchandise until sold by the dealers, and (3) payment by the dealers to the company as the merchandise is sold at retail. The dealers, whether trust receipt or other, do not have the right to return any part of merchandise ordered by them and delivered in salable condition, but they may tender merchandise in full or part payment of their accounts in the event of termination by the company of their dealerships. To provide for possible adjustments and allowances in the liquidation of dealer accounts receivable, the company has provided an increase in reserve by a charge to net earnings of the current year of $150,000 and a charge to retained earnings at October 1, 1960, of $530,000.

Exhibits 1 & 2 *(Continued)*

(g) Sales

In the financial statements for the year ended September 30, 1960, attention was directed by the company's policy of including in the operating statement firm orders received, billed, and costed out in late September which were shipped early in the immediately following October. During 1961 this policy was discontinued. In order to reflect this change in policy, prebilled sales at September 30, 1960, together with related costs and expenses included in operations of the year then ended, have been carried forward and included in the operating statement for the year ended September 30, 1961, with a resulting charge to retained earnings at October 1, 1960, of $429,600. This change in accounting principle did not have a material effect on net earnings for the year ended September 30, 1961.

(h) Long-Term Debt: Five-Year Subordinated Promissory Notes

The notes bear interest to October 10, 1961, at 6% per annum and thereafter to maturity at a rate which is the higher of (a) 6% per annum, or (b) the New York prime commercial rate plus 1½%. The loan agreement provides, among other things, that (a) payment of principal and interest on the notes is subordinated to repayment of bank loans due within one year, and (b) elections may be exercised annually by the holders to (1) exchange the notes currently held for new notes having a maturity extended by one year, (2) purchase additional notes if offered for sale by the company, or (3) require payment of all or part of the notes held, such payments to be made in four equal annual instalments beginning on October 10 of the immediately ensuing year.

All holders of the notes at September 30, 1961, except for $1 million, surrendered the notes then held in exchange for new notes having exactly the same terms but maturing October 28, 1966, at an interest rate of 6% per annum to October 10, 1962. Subsequent to September 30, 1961, arrangements have been made for the note for $1 million not exchanged to mature September 1, 1962, and to issue a note for $1 million to another lender maturing October 28, 1966.

Obligations of Subsidiaries:

5¾% first-mortgage bonds, due March 15, 1977	$ 964,000		
6% sinking fund notes, due March 15, 1967	147,500		
6% subordinated debentures, due December 15, 1967	819,000		
6% secured sinking fund debentures due February 1, 1977	2,620,500		
	$4,551,000		
Less: Classified as current liability	414,000	$4,137,000	
Real estate mortgage notes ($252 payable monthly for interest at 6% per annum and amortization of principal)	$ 34,383		
Less: Classified as current liabilities	1,000	33,383	
		$4,170,383	

The above long-term obligations of subsidiaries are secured by mortgages on property, plant, and equipment, and/or assignment of lease rentals payable by the parent company.

(i) Preferred Stock

There were 22,460 shares of $5 cumulative preferred stock.

Exhibit 3

THE O. M. SCOTT & SONS COMPANY

UNCONSOLIDATED QUARTERLY BALANCE SHEETS OF PARENT COMPANY
FOR FISCAL YEAR 1961*

(Dollar Amounts in Thousands)

	12/31/60	3/31/61	6/30/61	9/30/61
Cash	$ 1,810	$ 2,140	$ 1,760	$ 2,070
Accounts receivable				
Standard plan	$ 1,500	$ 6,540	$ 3,110	$ 4,400
Trust receipt plan	8,660	15,880	11,890	16,830
Total receivables	$10,160	$22,420	$15,000	$21,230
Inventories				
Finished goods	$ 7,390	$ 5,850	$ 6,420	$ 4,040
Raw materials and supplies	2,380	2,520	1,890	1,460
Total inventories	$ 9,770	$ 8,370	$ 8,310	$ 5,500
Total current assets	$21,740	$32,930	$25,070	$28,800
Land, buildings, equipment	$ 2,130	$ 2,190	$ 2,270	$ 2,290
Less: Accumulated depreciation	800	830	870	910
Net fixed assets	$ 1,330	$ 1,360	$ 1,400	$ 1,380
Other assets	$ 1,990	$ 1,730	$ 1,720	$ 1,240
Total assets	$25,060	$36,020	$28,190	$31,420
Accounts payable	$ 1,390	$ 3,680	$ 3,150	$ 7,040
Notes payable—bank	6,250	12,000	5,750	—
Accrued taxes, interest, and other				
expenses	(390)	950	110	1,170
Total current liabilities	$ 7,250	$16,630	$ 9,010	$ 8,210
Subordinated promissory notes	9,000	9,000	9,000	12,000
Total liabilities	$16,250	$25,630	$18,010	$20,210
Net worth				
Preferred stock	$ 2,380	$ 2,380	$ 2,350	$ 2,250
Common stock and surplus	6,430	8,010	7,830	8,960
Total liabilities and net worth	$25,060	$36,020	$28,190	$31,420

* Excluding items relating to certain nonoperating subsidiaries. Unaudited and unpublished. For these reasons, Exhibit 3 does not correspond exactly with Exhibit 1.

Exhibit 4

THE O. M. SCOTT & SONS COMPANY

UNCONSOLIDATED QUARTERLY INCOME STATEMENTS OF PARENT COMPANY
FOR THE YEAR ENDED SEPTEMBER 30, 1961*

(Dollar Amounts in Thousands)

	Quarter Ended 12/31/60	Quarter Ended 3/31/61	Quarter Ended 6/30/61	Quarter Ended 9/30/61	Year
Net sales	$ 1,300	$15,780	$9,570	$14,740	$41,390
Cost of sales and operating expenses					
Cost of products sold including processing, depreciation, warehousing, delivery and merchandising	$ 3,250	$11,730	$8,670	$10,790	$34,440
General and administrative, research and development expenses	660	800	940	1,000	3,400
Interest charges	150	240	260	200	850
Total cost of sales	$ 4,060	$12,770	$9,870	$11,990	$38,690
Earnings (losses) before taxes on income	$(2,760)	$ 3,010	$ (300)	$ 2,750	$ 2,700
Federal taxes on income	(1,440)	1,570	(160)	1,390	1,360
Net income (loss) after taxes	$(1,320)	$ 1,440	$ (140)	$ 1,360	$ 1,340

* Excluding items relating to the operations of certain nonoperating subsidiaries. Unaudited and unpublished.

Exhibit 5

THE O. M. SCOTT & SONS COMPANY

TRUST RECEIPT

The undersigned Dealer, as Trustee, and Entruster agree to engage in Trust Receipt financing of the acquisition by Trustee of seed, fertilizer, weed controls, pest controls, applicators, mowers and other lawn and garden products, all bearing the brands and trade marks of The O. M. Scott & Sons Company. Entruster will direct said company to deliver said products from time to time as ordered by Dealer.

(*a*) Dealer agrees to hold said products in trust for the sole purpose of making sales to consumers, functioning as a retailer and not as a wholesaler.

(*b*) Dealer agrees to hold a sufficient proportion of the funds received from such sales for payment to Entruster as billed.

(*c*) Either party may terminate this Trust Receipt on notice. In such event Dealer will surrender to Entruster his complete stock of The O. M. Scott & Sons Company products, proceeds thereof to be credited to Dealer.

Official Business Name
of Dealer as Trustee:

Accepted at Marysville, Ohio

—————————————————————   ——————————————————————, 19—

Street & No.———————————————

City————Zone——State————   THE O. M. SCOTT & SONS COMPANY
                                              (*Entruster*)
Authorized
Signature———————————————

Date————————Title————————   *President*

Exhibit 6

THE O. M. SCOTT & SONS COMPANY

STATEMENT OF TRUST RECEIPT FINANCING

The Entruster, The O. M. Scott & Sons Company, whose chief place of business is at Marysville, Ohio, and who has no place of business within this state, is or expects to be engaged in financing under trust receipt transactions, the acquisition by the Trustee whose name and chief place of business within this state is:

of seed, fertilizers, weed controls, pest controls, applicators, mowers and other lawn and garden products, all bearing the brands and trade marks of The O. M. Scott & Sons Company.

Entruster: THE O. M. SCOTT & SONS   Date——————————————————, 19—
              COMPANY   For the Trustee   (Dealer)

By:———————————————   By:———————————————
         President

Exhibit 7

THE O. M. SCOTT & SONS COMPANY

EXAMPLE SHOWING CALCULATION OF EQUITY WORKING CAPITAL AND MAXIMUM
ALLOWED DEBT OF PARENT COMPANY FOR THE 12 MONTHS FOLLOWING
MARCH 31, 1961*

(Dollar Amounts in Millions)

Calculation of equity working capital:

Current assets		$32.9
Current liabilities	$16.6	
Long-term debt	9.0	
Total debt	$25.6	25.6
Equity working capital		$ 7.3

Calculation of maximum allowed parent company debt:

300% of equity working capital	$21.9
Actual parent borrowings—March 31, 1961	21.0
Available debt capacity	$ .9

Calculation of maximum allowed subordinated debt of parent:
60% of maximum allowed total debt ($21.9 million × 60%)... $13.1

* Calculations based on figures taken from Exhibit 3.

Exhibit 8

THE O. M. SCOTT & SONS COMPANY

RECORD OF EARNINGS, DIVIDENDS, AND MARKET PRICE RANGE, 1958–1961

Fiscal Year	Earnings per Share	Dividends per Share	Market Price Range*
1958	$0.69	10% stk.	$6\frac{1}{8}$–$1\frac{1}{2}$
1959	1.15	10% stk.	$32\frac{7}{8}$–$6\frac{1}{8}$
1960	1.21	10% stk.	51 –$31\frac{7}{8}$
1961	0.99	10¢ + 5% stk.	$58\frac{3}{4}$–30

* Calendar year; bid prices. Closing prices September 29 and December 29, 1961 were $49 and $32¼ respectively. Stock first sold publicly in 1958 and traded over the counter since then. The company had about 4,100 common shareholders in 1961.

Union Paint and Varnish Company

On April 14, 1952, in Los Angeles, Mr. Robert Maple and Mr. Harry Hill, the credit manager and the regional sales manager, respectively, of the Union Paint and Varnish Company, met with Mr. Sidney G. Snider, president of Suburban Auto Stores Corporation, to discuss possible credit arrangements for sales of Union products to Suburban. After extensive discussion concerning the current financial position and future prospects of Suburban, Mr. Snider asked if Mr. Maple would approve 3-year terms on an initial order, amounting to some $35,000, for a basic inventory of the complete line of Union products. If such an arrangement could be made, Mr. Snider also wanted to know upon what credit basis "fill-in" orders to replace goods sold could be placed.

Union Paint (see Exhibit 1 [page 658] for 1951 financial statements) was operating near capacity in the spring of 1952, but with the anticipated return to a buyers' market, Union began to prepare for increasingly keen competition. Accordingly, Union was aggressively seeking new outlets through which to sell the company's expanding volume. In this connection, Mr. Hill had pointed out that Suburban, whose account he had sought for several years, had an excellent reputation for being an aggressive merchandising organization; he stressed to Mr. Maple the fact that Union's weakest market coverage was "right in its own backyard," Los Angeles.

For about a year the sales department had been pursuing a nationwide promotional and merchandising program addressed to consumers. In addition, missionary salesmen worked to develop new dealerships, which frequently were excellent market outlets but financially undercapitalized. Although typical terms to retail accounts were 1/10, n/60, terms up to 5 years had been granted to enable new accounts of this type to purchase permanent display and backup stock. Such arrangements were believed necessary to get adequate market coverage and to continue large volume operations.

Mr. Hill told Mr. Maple of the opportunity at Suburban on April 2, 1952. The previous day, Mr. Hill had visited the offices of Suburban and talked with Mr. Snider, its president. Mr. Snider had said that he desired a 3-year payment plan to enable him to acquire the initial stock. Mr. Hill had replied that he could make no commitment, but believed that an extended payment plan could be arranged to cover the initial stock of paints and varnishes.

After this meeting, Mr. Hill concluded that Suburban could now be sold, and thought that steps should be taken promptly to "sew up" the potential account, for he realized that Union's competitors might also recognize Suburban's readiness to drop its current line. He asked Mr. Maple to act as promptly as possible to determine the credit standing of Suburban. Mr. Maple ordered a credit agency report and called his company's bank of account, Golden Gate Trust Company, in San Francisco, requesting information regarding Suburban.

On April 7, Mr. Maple received the credit report (see Exhibit 2, page 661) and a telephone call from John Farmer, an officer of the bank, who reported that the company was indebted to three Los Angeles banks for a total of $345,000, each bank participating equally. These loans, he said, were unsecured but endorsed by Mr. Sidney Snider, president of Suburban. Mr. Farmer said that the loans, which had been made on a 90-day renewable basis, matured on March 31, 1952, but that a temporary extension on a demand basis had been granted to permit the corporation to raise approximately $150,000, the estimated amount which Suburban had lost through operations for the fiscal year ended January 31, 1952. Although no specific time limit had been set for raising the $150,000, it was generally understood that this was to be accomplished by the end of May, 1952. The banks were not willing to comment on how long they would continue "to go along with" Suburban. Such action appeared to depend upon the company's ability to raise funds from outside sources to replace the operating loss.

The total cash balance among the three banks was reported to be slightly more than $60,000 at the moment. A few trade creditors in 1952 indicated a slow manner of payment, which had not been experienced previously. All, however, considered Suburban a desirable account.

Suburban's inventory position in March was reported to be in excess of $1 million despite vigorous attempts to liquidate a surplus of television sets and major appliances in late 1951. The banks were reported to be dissatisfied with this inventory, having concluded that substantial investment rested in types of goods which were moving too slowly. Furthermore, Mr. Farmer stated that the banks were unhappy about a new store opened in November, 1951, when funds were known to be needed to bolster a weak working capital condition. Nevertheless, Mr. Farmer added that the three banks unanimously agreed that they held the

Suburban management in high regard as an aggressive merchandising organization.

On Tuesday morning, April 8, Mr. Maple met with Mr. Hill and the Union sales manager, Mr. Joseph Carton, to discuss Suburban as a potential account. Mr. Maple said that it appeared to him inadvisable to make a definite decision regarding a deferred payment plan with Suburban until its financial status, especially the relationships with the banks, could be clarified.

Mr. Carton reported that he had learned that Suburban was interested in changing its line of paints because it was dissatisfied with the selling arrangements made by its current supplier, another nationally known manufacturer. Suburban was required to purchase paint products on a consignment basis, a procedure that was both bothersome and embarrassing.

Mr. Carton was anxious to get a decision on this account because he estimated, based on Suburban's sales of paint products in past years, that Union's sales should run in excess of $150,000 annually. He reemphasized that all Suburban's sales would be in territory new to Union, since only a few small hardware stores were handling Union's line in Los Angeles.

Mr. Hill commented that, although Mr. Snider had not mentioned it, he had learned through others in the trade that two other national paint manufacturers were currently attempting to sell Suburban their complete line. He further noted that Dun & Bradstreet, Inc., had rated the firm AA1 on January 16. Mr. Maple replied that nevertheless the company was short of working capital, was at that time negotiating with its banks regarding future loans, and that the Dun & Bradstreet report did not reflect the as yet unpublished January 31, 1952, statement.

The credit department of Union Paint and Varnish Company had classified its accounts in three categories: (A) well-financed customers—virtually no risk of loss; (B) moderately financed customers—average risk of loss; and (C) financially weak customers—great risk of loss.

As of April 1, category C accounts totaled nearly $440,000 for accounts sold on regular terms. In addition, about $75,000 of $750,000 receivables on extended terms (averaging 3 years) were in category C. Since Mr. Maple believed that the proposed account would be in the C group, he pointed out to Messrs. Carton and Hill that a decline in general business activity might bring substantial bad-debt losses. The fact that Union's bad-debt losses had been less than one half of 1% of credit sales since 1945 did not measure possible losses in a depression.

Mr. Carton quickly countered that since about one fifth of the company's total expenses continued regardless of sales, he was obliged continually to get more volume in order to spread those fixed charges as thinly as possible. Thus, Union had to take certain calculated risks to break into the Southern California market, where there was potentially great volume. Finally, Mr. Carton said that even if the Suburban account resulted eventually in a loss, in the meantime enough volume could well have been accomplished to more than offset the loss.

On April 10, Mr. Hill, at the request of Mr. Maple, had visited two of Suburban's banks of account to get the most recent information on the company. Officers in both banks expressed considerable faith in the management of Suburban. They indicated that, although the company had suffered a loss of more than $100,000 as a result of a drop in television and major appliance sales, this was typical of the retail trade during 1951. Both officers told Mr. Hill that they were willing to continue accommodating Suburban at least until July of 1952, when they could review operating results for the first 6 months of the year.

On April 11, Mr. Hill, concerned about the possibility of losing a large potential customer, arranged for Mr. Maple to visit Mr. Snider on the 14th in Los Angeles. At this meeting, Mr. Snider showed Mr. Maple summary figures as of January 31, 1952, stating that he wished to keep the statement confidential until it was made public in about a week. These figures are shown below:

SUBURBAN AUTO STORES CORPORATION
BALANCE SHEET AS OF 1/31/52

Cash	$ 64,975	Due banks	$ 345,000
Accounts receivable	102,695	Accounts payable	347,645
Inventory	1,227,760	Reserve for taxes	32,555
Total current assets	$1,395,430	Other current liabilities	117,875
Equipment, fixtures	185,725	Total current liabilities	$ 843,075
Prepayments	23,000	Reserve	64,170
Total assets	$1,604,155	Net worth	696,910
			$1,604,155

Mr. Snider said that, although the television inventory had reached a high point during the last year of $500,000, the inventory position in April amounted to only $125,000. He also stated that the gross profit on television sales throughout the country dropped considerably between 1950 and 1951. For Suburban, this drop was from 22% to 16%, thus causing a $148,000 loss in spite of the fact that sales volume and gross profit on most other items sold by the company remained at very even levels. It was Mr. Snider's opinion that rapid progress could be made, since the newest store of the chain was just getting established.

Mr. Snider asked Mr. Maple whether 3-year terms might be given his company on an initial order of about $35,000. He said he understood that fill-in orders were usually offered on a 1/10, n/60 basis. It was his estimate that Suburban should be able to do an annual volume with Union of over $200,000 if such terms were offered.

Exhibit 1

UNION PAINT AND VARNISH COMPANY

Balance Sheet and Income Statement for Year Ending December 31, 1951
(Dollar Figures in Thousands)

current ratio 3.6

Balance Sheet

CURRENT ASSETS		CURRENT LIABILITIES	
Cash	$ 14,991	Accounts payable	$ 5,675
Accounts receivable* (net)	22,317	Federal and state income taxes	10,790
Inventories	35,777	Miscellaneous accruals	1,516
Total	$ 73,085	Current portion term loan	1,725
		Total	$ 19,706
Real estate, plant and equipment	61,188		
Less: Reserve for depreciation	25,659	Term loan—banks†	14,950
	$ 35,529	Common stock	29,587
Prepaid and deferred charges	1,641	Surplus	46,012
Total assets	$110,255	Total liabilities	$110,255

* Bad-debt reserve, $601,831.
† Term loan with five banks at 3%, payable at rate of $1,725,000 each January 15 to 1961, when final payment is $2,875,000.

Income Statement

Net sales	$262,801
Cost of sales	214,282
Gross profit	$ 48,519
Selling, general and administrative expense	30,224*
Operating profit	$ 18,295†
Provision for federal income taxes	8,314
Net profit	$ 9,981

proprietary ratio 69%

* Includes $152,725 for bad debt expense.
† Total costs were composed of approximately 20% fixed costs, with 80% variable with volume of production.

Exhibit 2

UNION PAINT AND VARNISH COMPANY

West Coast Credit Reports, Inc.

October 15, 1951

Suburban Auto Stores Corporation   Los Angeles, California
Sidney G. Snider—*President and Treasurer*
Jack Binstein—*Exec. Vice President*
Laura B. Goode—*Secretary*

SUMMARY

CORPORATION FORMED 1932; HOLDS A PROMINENT POSITION LOCALLY IN RETAIL TRADE. OPERATIONS HAVE SHOWN A PROFITABLE TREND IN RECENT YEARS ON AN EXPANDING VOLUME. FINANCIAL STATEMENTS OF JANUARY 31, 1951, SHOWED TANGIBLE NET WORTH $855,000 AND A GENERALLY SATISFACTORY FINANCIAL CONDITION. SUBSTANTIAL UNSECURED BANK ACCOMMODATION AVAILABLE, WITH ACTIVE USE MADE OF BORROWING FACILITIES. TRADE PAYMENTS SATISFACTORY.

Exhibit 2 (Continued)

PERSONNEL

Sidney G. Snider, born 1898, married; started business in this line in 1921 with his older brother, Julius Snider, operation under the trade name of Julius Snider Company, Inc. On May 4, 1932, a 50% settlement was made with creditors on an indebtedness of $168,000. Julius Snider Company, Inc., continues active in the automobile supply line with Julius Snider, President and Treasurer, and Sidney G. Snider as Executive Vice President of this corporation.

Jack Binstein, born 1906, married; was elected Executive Vice President in June, 1949. He was formerly employed as an accountant for the company.

Laura B. Goode was appointed Secretary of Suburban Auto Stores in 1947, having been employed by Sidney Snider as his personal secretary since 1936.

HISTORY

INCORPORATED: Under California laws, October 10, 1932, as a new business. *Authorized Capital Stock:* 250,000 shares of Common Stock.

General Background Information: From its inception, this organization grew rapidly, opening new stores from time to time; and by the end of the fiscal year of 1941, the chain operated a total of 32 stores. During the war years, 17 of these stores were closed as the results of war shortages. In the postwar period, 5 of the original stores have been enlarged and modernized and 4 stores added. Until 1941, the company was engaged exclusively in the retailing of automobile accessories and equipment. Since 1942, new lines have been added from time to time, so that the automotive merchandise now constitutes less than 50% of the total volume. Merchandise now carried includes radios, television sets, major electrical appliances and minor appliances, work clothes and related apparel, hardware, housefurnishings, unpainted furniture, house paints, glassware, automobile supplies, tires and accessories, batteries and supplies, toys, luggage and sporting goods.

Locations: All the store locations are leased. Executive offices are maintained at South Flower Street, Los Angeles, where the corporation leases approximately 50,000 square feet of floor space.

Number of Employees: Total 335 employees.

Terms of Sale: Cash sales account for approximately 95% of total volume, this percentage including instalment sales, which are financed by a bank, without recourse. Suburban receives full cash payments from the bank as soon as the latter has approved credit for the account. The remaining 5% of sales are on a deferred payment plan, payments being scheduled up to a period of three months, with notes on certain sales being secured by a chattel mortgage on automobiles. This paper is carried by Suburban.

Exhibit 2 (Continued)

COMPARATIVE FINANCIAL STATEMENTS

	Jan. 31, 1949	Jan. 31, 1950	Jan. 31, 1951
Cash	$ 121,305	$ 130,361	$ 157,402
Accounts receivable	49,628	49,128	86,598
Inventory	1,291,778	1,293,516	1,347,799
Total current assets	$1,462,711	$1,473,005	$1,591,799
Equipment, fixtures	132,574	144,712	129,578
Prepaid and deferred	22,005	29,775	24,048
Total assets	$1,617,290	$1,647,492	$1,745,425
Due banks	$ 345,000	$ 345,000	$ 345,000
Accounts payable	285,963	323,615	291,062
Reserve for taxes	120,518	96,295	101,835
Television service contract	......	44,759	75,183
Customers' deposits	......	14,778	19,864
Total current liabilities	751,481	824,447	832,944
Reserve unrealized profit on instalment sales	51,633	41,700	57,524
Common stock	433,838	400,833	394,422
Surplus	380,338	380,512	460,535
Total liabilities	$1,617,290	$1,647,492	$1,745,425
Net sales	$6,800,228	$7,304,935	$8,292,551
Net profit*	......	......	......
Dividends*	......	......	......

* Not made public.

GENERAL COMMENTS

Management has declined to furnish complete operating particulars, but points out that during fiscal year ended January 31, 1951, company realized satisfactory profit from operations. This profit was offset to a large extent through inventory writedowns.

Financial condition at January 31, 1951, continues to show relatively large current debt as the result of transacting a sizable volume in relation to net working capital, but at the same time the figures reflect a favorable improvement over the preceding year.

Notwithstanding the fact that company trades quite actively in relation to the net investment, it has been able to finance operations and to meet maturing obligations in a satisfactory manner by reason of the fact that fully 95% of sales are on a cash or close to cash basis, plus the fact that substantial bank lines are utilized in order to enable the company to carry representative lines of merchandise at each of its stores. During periods of lower than average inventories (which usually occur in the early months of the calendar year), bank loans are rotated in order to give each bank a full cleanup. During the remaining months of the year, full use is made of borrowing facilities at all of the company's banks.

Television service contracts payable, amounting to $75,183 at January 31, 1951, are liquidated at monthly intervals during the life of each service contract, which runs for a period of one year.

Exhibit 2 (Continued)

Reserve for unrealized profit on instalment sales, $57,524, is a surplus reserve transferable to earned surplus on a percentage basis, upon collection of each monthly payment on respective instalment basis.

BANKING RELATIONS

Accounts are maintained at three local banks. Satisfactory average balances are reported. Accommodation is granted on corporate note, endorsed by Sidney G. Snider. In addition, one of the banks also discounts customers' paper on a nonrecourse basis. Active use is made of loan facilities, but each of the banks was given a full cleanup during the current year.

Exhibit 2 (Continued)

CREDIT INTERCHANGE BUREAUS
OF THE
NATIONAL ASSOCIATION OF CREDIT MEN

Report on SUBURBAN AUTO STORES CORP.

Los Angeles, California
South Flower Street
Los Angeles County

March 16, 1952

The accuracy of this Report is not guaranteed. Its contents are gathered in good faith from members and sent to you by this Bureau without liability for negligence in procuring, collecting, communicating or failing to communicate the information so gathered.

Business Classification	How Long Sold	Date of Last Sale	Highest Recent Credit	Now Owing Including Notes	Past Due	Terms of Sale	Paying Record			Comments
							Discounts	Pays When Due	Days Slow	
SOUTHERN CALIF. 220–2										
AutoA	yrs.	1–52	12,310	5,900		2–10 EOM		x		
Hdwe.	yrs.	12–51	1,855	712	712	2–10–30			30	Slower
Inds.	1 yr.	12–51	26,475	12,575		60–1–10	x			
Tool	yrs.	1–52	175			2–10–30		x		
I & S	2 yrs.	1–52	19,400	7,300		Special		x		
Elec.	yrs.	11–51	28,940			2–10–30		x	30	
Elec.	yrs.	12–51	1,940	1,940	1,940	2–10–30			45	
AutoA	10–51	1–52	1,058			2–10	x			
Chem.	yrs.	12–51	838	838		2–10px		x		
Rdo.	yrs.	12–51	8,125			2–10 EOM	x			
Equip.	6–51	11–51	3,084	1,550	1,550	3–5px			60	
Tex.	yrs.	10–51	24,600	18,600	16,500	2–10 EOM			90	
NORTH & CENTRAL CALIF. 221–14										
AutoA	yrs.	1–52	28,375	28,375	500	2–10 EOM		x	30	First time slow
Elec.	10–51	12–51	940			5–10–30	x			
Hdwe.	yrs.	10–51	19,529	19,529		2–10–30			30	
Plstc.	yrs.	12–51	7,500	7,500		2–10px		x		
Rbr.	yrs.	1–52	22,478	22,478		Regular		x		

ARIZONA 222–12									
Chem.	yrs.	9–51	250		2–10px		x	30	
Elec.	yrs.	11–51	24,490		2–10–30		x	45	
Equip.	6–51	1–52	2,845	2,845	2–10px				
ROCKY MTS. 223–106									
Chem.	yrs.	11–51	28,464	6,464	2–10–30			60	Slower
AutoA	yrs.	10–51	21,495	21,475	2–10–30			90	First sale
Elec.	1–52	1–52	7,050		2–10–30	x			
I & S	yrs.	1–52	22,310		2–10 EOM		x		
Inds.	yrs.	11–51	27,400		Special		x		
CHICAGO 223–18									
Elec.	yrs.	12–51	490	490	2–10 EOM			45	
Hdwe.	yrs.	1–52	26,400	12,400	2–10–30		x		
Hdwe.	yrs.	1–52	9,410	9,410	2–10–30		x		
Equip.	6 mos.	9–51	3,000		2–10–30			45	
Tool	yrs.	1–52	18,650	18,650	2–10–30		x		
CLEVELAND 223–28									
Elec.	12–51	1–52	5,100	5,100	2–10–30	x		30–60	
Chem.	yrs.	9–51	3,400		2–10–30		x		
TOLEDO 223–19									
Rbr.	yrs.	12–51	23,540	18,500	Regular			90	
Rbr.	yrs.	1–52	7,500	7,500	2–10px		x		
NEW YORK–PHILADELPHIA 224–225									
Elec.	1–51	12–51	16,538	8,538	2–10–30			45	
Chem.	yrs.	1–52	250			x			
Tex.	yrs.	1–52	1,812	800			x		
Hdwe.	yrs.	12–51	6,540		2–10–30	x			
BU 95 LM									

Case 6

The Case of the Unidentified Industries

DESPITE VARIATIONS in operational and financial policies and practices and in operating results between firms in the same industry, the nature of the industry has an important impact on the general patterns of the need for funds (asset allocation), the methods of meeting these needs, and the financial results of most firms in the industry. Presented in Exhibit 1 are balance sheets, in percentage form, and selected ratios drawn from the balance sheets and operating statements of 10 firms in 10 different industries. Recognizing the fact of certain differences between firms in the same industry, each firm whose figures are summarized is broadly typical of those in its industry.

See if you can identify the industry represented. Then, be prepared as best you can to explain the distinctive asset structures and ratios of each industry.

1. Basic chemical company.
2. Electric and gas utility.
3. Supermarket chain.
4. Hotel chain.
5. Maker of name-brand, quality women's apparel.
6. Meat packer.
7. Retail jewelry chain.
8. Coal-carrying railroad.
9. Automobile manufacturer.
10. Tobacco manufacturer.

Exhibit 1

THE CASE OF THE UNIDENTIFIED INDUSTRIES

*Balance Sheet Percentages**	A	B	C	D	E	F	G	H	I	J
Cash and marketable securities	8.1	13.9	8.2	15.1	2.3	1.7	1.9	17.4	4.1	6.1
Receivables	2.8	11.7	16.2	21.6	53.7	4.6	6.5	2.9	36.6	7.6
Inventories	1.1	22.4	14.8	28.6	32.7	2.1	79.4	35.8	39.1	3.0
Other current assets	1.3	1.0		0.3	0.6	0.4		1.2	0.5	
Plant and equipment (net)	78.2	40.1	49.0	34.0	6.8	89.9	10.9	40.0	19.1	78.4
Other assets	8.5	10.9	11.8	0.4	3.9	1.3	1.3	2.7	0.6	4.9
Total assets	100.0	100.0	100.0	100.0	100.0	100.0	100.0	100.0	100.0	100.0
Notes payable	3.5		7.1		23.0		3.4	0.3	17.2	6.5
Accounts payable	3.8	14.6	5.3	28.5	6.9	2.9	1.6	22.7	21.0	5.7
Accrued taxes	2.1	5.6	4.8	4.3	4.2	3.5	6.5	4.0	5.2	0.2
Other current liabilities		10.5	3.4	0.5	1.3	3.3	2.5	9.1	8.5	3.5
Long-term debt	25.0	3.5	18.8		14.9	46.5	8.3	8.3	6.6	61.6
Other liabilities	4.1	1.2			10.1	1.3	0.2	7.9	0.4	1.0
Preferred stock	1.2					4.7	6.4	4.8		0.6
Capital stock and capital surplus	17.3	10.7	47.8	13.7	33.6	30.2	24.8	10.9	13.1	16.9
Retained earnings and surplus reserves	43.0	53.9	12.8	53.0	6.0	7.6	46.3	32.0	28.0	4.0
Total liabilities and stockholders' equity	100.0	100.0	100.0	100.0	100.0	100.0	100.0	100.0	100.0	100.0

Selected Ratios	A	B	C	D	E	F	G	H	I	J
Current assets/current liabilities	1.64	1.59	1.89	1.98	2.52	0.93	6.38	1.57	1.55	1.05
Cash, marketable securities, and receivables/current liabilities	1.16	0.83	1.18	1.10	1.58	0.66	0.62	0.57	0.78	0.86
Total debt/total assets	0.393	0.382	0.399	0.333	0.601	0.573	0.224	0.526	0.581	0.885
Long-term debt/capitalization	0.290	0.051	0.237		0.274	0.523	0.097	0.148	0.165	0.740
Net sales/total assets	0.28	1.50	0.85	5.20	1.11	0.35	1.46	4.69	2.22	0.88
Net profits/total assets	0.051	0.078	0.074	0.072	0.024	0.044	0.089	0.056	0.090	0.015
Net profits/total net worth	0.083	0.126	0.123	0.108	0.061	0.103	0.115	0.119	0.218	0.068
Net profits/net sales	0.182	0.052	0.087	0.014	0.022	0.128	0.061	0.012	0.041	0.017

* Without adjustment for lease obligations and other items not generally shown on the balance sheet.

Case 7

Cenco Instruments Corporation

MR. ROSCOE GILES settled down on Sunday evening to review the annual report he had just received from Cenco Instruments Corporation, a company in which he had a moderate-sized investment. Mr. Giles worked for a large commercial bank and considered himself a continuing student of finance. As much in gratification of this interest in finance as because of his investment in the stock, Mr. Giles began with pleasure the task of "seeing what he could get out of the financial statements." These financial statements are reproduced in Exhibits 1 through 4.

Exhibit 1
CENCO INSTRUMENTS CORPORATION
CONSOLIDATED BALANCE SHEET, AS OF APRIL 30, 1965 AND 1964

ASSETS	1965	1964
Current:		
Cash	$ 2,180,684	$ 1,932,872
Marketable securities, at cost (approximately market)	150,598	76,379
Accounts receivable, less allowance for possible losses of $181,000 in 1965 and $197,031 in 1964	9,576,964	8,359,118
Inventories	17,345,375	15,607,275
Prepaid expenses	363,375	388,426
Total current assets	29,616,996	26,364,070
Investments in and advances to unconsolidated foreign subsidiaries:		
Investments	70,842	76,409
Advances	775,542	678,795
Total investments and advances	846,384	755,204
Fixed and other:		
Plant and equipment	4,490,482	4,203,529
Cost in excess of book amount of net tangible assets of businesses acquired	3,898,108	2,965,026
Deferred charges and miscellaneous	716,440	265,503
Total fixed and other assets	9,105,030	7,434,058
Totals	$39,568,410	$34,553,332

Exhibit 1 (Continued)

LIABILITIES	1965	1964
Current:		
Notes payable to banks	$ 1,005,795	$ 901,059
Accounts payable	2,721,225	2,570,883
Accruals:		
Federal and Canadian income taxes	1,585,994	1,249,555
Other taxes and expenses	1,360,962	1,028,814
Current maturities of long-term liabilities	399,025	327,989
Dividend payable August 26, 1965	356,670	....
Total current liabilities	7,429,671	6,078,300
Long-term	13,750,482	13,993,237
Total liabilities	21,180,153	20,071,537
SHAREHOLDERS' EQUITY		
Common stock	2,400,700	1,143,033
Additional paid-in capital	4,459,602	4,107,431
Retained earnings	11,527,955	9,231,331
Total shareholders' equity	18,388,257	14,481,795
Totals	$39,568,410	$34,553,332

Exhibit 2

CENCO INSTRUMENTS CORPORATION

CONSOLIDATED STATEMENT OF EARNINGS

Years Ended April 30, 1965 and 1964

	1965	1964
Net sales	$51,045,681	$44,782,971
Cost of sales	34,510,319	30,259,100
Gross profit on sales	16,535,362	14,523,871
Operating expenses	10,901,811	9,669,911
Operating income, after allowance for depreciation of $585,861 in 1965 and $490,312 in 1964	5,633,551	4,853,960
Other charges (principally interest), less other income	625,670	599,886
Earnings before taxes on income	5,007,881	4,254,074
United States and Canadian income taxes (after application of operating loss carryovers of certain subsidiaries)	2,243,000	1,950,000
Net earnings for the year	$ 2,764,881	$ 2,304,074

Exhibit 3

CENCO INSTRUMENTS CORPORATION

CONSOLIDATED STATEMENT OF SHAREHOLDERS' EQUITY

Year Ended April 30, 1965

	Common Stock— $1 par	Additional Paid-in Capital	Retained Earnings
Amounts at May 1, 1964............$1,143,033	$1,143,033	$4,107,431	$ 9,231,331
Add:			
Proceeds from sale of shares under stock option plan..............	8,000	163,200	....
Shares issued, or to be issued, to effect two-for-one stock split in the form of a 100% stock dividend........................	1,151,033	(1,151,033)	....
Shares issued (52,128) and required to be issued (1,900) for subsidiary's stock acquired and company's assets purchased during year.....	54,028	1,340,004	....
Shares issued (40,606) and required to be issued (4,000) for the acquisition during year of subsidiary under the "pooling of interests" concept......................	44,606	....	528,591
Net earnings for the year..........	....	....	2,764,881
	2,400,700	4,459,602	12,524,803
Deduct:			
Cash dividends paid—$.425 per share........................	....	....	996,848
Amounts at April 30, 1965...........$2,400,700	$2,400,700	$4,459,602	$11,527,955

Exhibit 4

CENCO INSTRUMENTS CORPORATION

NOTES TO CONSOLIDATED FINANCIAL STATEMENTS

Year Ended April 30, 1965

Principles of preparation and consolidation—The consolidated financial statements include the accounts of all subsidiaries operating in the United States and Canada. The accounts of other foreign subsidiaries have been excluded. The underlying net assets (excluding advances by the company as liabilities) as reported by foreign accountants, were $82,000 less at April 30, 1965 than the cost of the company's investments in and advances to these foreign subsidiaries. The retained earnings of acquired subsidiaries to the date of acquisition have been eliminated in the consolidation. The consolidated statement of earnings for the year includes the results of operations from dates of acquisition of companies acquired under the purchase concept; and the excess of cost over the book amounts of underlying net tangible assets of these companies have been considered as intangibles with an indefinite life and in consolidation were charged to "cost in excess of book amounts of net tangible assets of businesses acquired." The cost of the investment in and the excess of cost over the book amounts of underlying net tangible assets of companies acquired during the year were as follows:

Exhibit 4 (Continued)

Company	Cost of Investment and Related Expenses ($)	Excess of Cost over Net Tangible Assets ($)
Vacuum Research Company...........	268,125	128,557
Perry Manufacturing Co. (subsequently liquidated into parent company)......	301,926	147,773
Doerr Glass Company and affiliates (net assets acquired in exchange for stock)...........................	1,062,183(a)	407,486
Lab Glass of Tennessee, Inc. and affiliates (subsequently merged into Lab Holding Company, a subsidiary)..........	416,141	247,634

(a) Represents initial consideration; see note "commitments and contingent liabilities."

During the 1965 year, the company also acquired all of the outstanding stock of Lab Holding Company (name subsequently changed to Lab Glass, Inc.) in exchange for 44,606 shares of its common stock. Lab Holding's consolidated figures for the twelve months ended April 30, 1965 have been consolidated with those of the parent company under the pooling of interest concept. Lab Holding's financial statements for the twelve months ended April 30, 1964 were not audited and have not been consolidated with those of the parent company for the 1964 year. Had such figures been consolidated, the consolidated net earnings for the year ended April 30, 1964 would have been increased by $150,064. See note "commitments and contingent liabilities" for the possible issuance of additional shares of the company's common stock with respect to this acquisition.

Intercompany investments, transactions and balances (other than in or with unconsolidated foreign subsidiaries) have been eliminated in the consolidation, including elimination of intercompany profits in inventories. Minority interests have been recognized.

Inventories—are stated primarily at the lower of cost (first-in, first-out, or average) or market and consisted of the following:

	1965	1964
Finished and resale merchandise................	$13,364,142	$11,851,863
Work in process and parts....................	2,779,464	2,396,591
Raw materials and supplies...................	1,201,769	1,358,821
Totals....................................	$17,345,375	$15,607,275

Plant and equipment—are stated at cost and are summarized as follows:

	1965	1964
Land.....................................	$ 778,039	$ 577,904
Buildings.................................	2,399,500	2,110,794
Machinery and equipment.....................	2,989,993	2,626,264
Educational films...........................	777,534	860,461
Totals....................................	6,945,066	6,175,423
Less accumulated allowances for depreciation.....	2,454,584	1,971,894
Net plant and equipment.....................	$ 4,490,482	$ 4,203,529

Long-term liabilities—consisted of the following:

	1965	1964
4½% subordinated convertible debentures maturing August 1, 1980; sinking fund payments due $300,000 annually beginning in 1970...........	$ 4,997,000	$ 4,997,000
4½% bank term notes convertible into 4¾% term loan at December 15, 1966, maturing ⁶⁄₈ths semiannually in 1967 and ⁷⁄₈ths semiannually in 1968–1971................................	3,400,000	3,400,000

Exhibit 4 (Continued)

4⅞% insurance company term loan maturing $200,000 semiannually in 1972–1977 and $275,000 semiannually in 1978	2,950,000	2,950,000
Fifteen year 5⅛% notes payable $125,000 in 1966–1968, $175,000 in 1969–1972 and $325,000 in 1973	1,400,000	1,525,000
4% installment contracts payable maturing $184,600 on June 2, 1965–1968	738,400	923,000
2% installment contract payable $95,000 on August 15, 1965–1968	341,114	390,773
4½% mortgage on real estate (costing $290,000) payable $962 monthly including interest	122,886	128,762
Mortgage on real estate (costing $175,000) payable December 31, 1966	115,000	
Other	85,107	6,691
	14,149,507	14,321,226
Less current maturities included in current liabilities	399,025	327,989
Total long-term liabilities	$13,750,482	$13,993,237

Under the various loan agreements relating to the 4½% convertible subordinated debentures, the 4½% bank term notes, the 4⅞% insurance company term loan and the 5⅛% notes, the company has agreed, among other things, (1) to maintain consolidated working capital of at least $12,000,000 (2) to maintain net tangible assets of at least 150% of consolidated long-term indebtedness (3) not to pay cash dividends or purchase any of its capital stock or optionally retire subordinated debt in excess of $1,200,000 plus consolidated net income earned after April 30, 1963 (under these provisions $4,712,897 of retained earnings were available at April 30, 1965 for cash dividends, purchase of stock and optional retirement of subordinated debt).

The 2% installment contract payable arose from the 1962 acquisition of the capital stock of the U.S. Hospital Supply Companies. The final amount payable on these notes is contingent upon earnings of these companies from February 1, 1963 to April 30, 1968, under which the total price may be increased by $200,000 or decreased by $300,000.

Commitments and contingent liabilities—The company has guaranteed the indebtedness of an unconsolidated foreign subsidiary in the amount of approximately $200,000.

The company and subsidiaries are obligated under long-term leases expiring at various dates 1969–1983 under which the total annual rentals range from $133,000 to $21,000.

The company's subsidiaries are contingently liable for customers' notes and conditional sales contracts totalling approximately $209,000 which were sold with recourse.

Federal income tax returns of the company have been examined and settled through its 1961 year. A revenue agent's report has been received for the 1962 and 1963 years proposing deficiencies aggregating approximately $80,000 which will be contested. No provision has been made in the accompanying financial statements for the proposed deficiencies and interest thereon. The returns of the subsidiaries have been examined through various years from 1956 to 1962.

The company may be required to issue additional shares of its common stock under the acquisition agreements with respect to several companies (Phoenix in 1964 year; Doerr and Lab Holding in 1965 year) based on the earnings of these companies from the dates of acquisition through April 30, 1966, 1970 and 1972, respectively. The number of such shares to be issued, if any, is not presently determinate. In the case of Lab Holding, the maximum number of shares to be issued is 19,184. Should the shareholder die or become disabled prior to April 30, 1972, the shares are to be issued notwithstanding the failure to meet the earnings formula.

Common stock—During the year, the board of directors and shareholders approved an amendment to the certificate of incorporation for the increase in authorized common stock from 2,500,000 shares to 5,000,000 shares of $1 par value. Also, on action of the board of directors and shareholders, an additional share of the company's common stock was issued for each share of such stock held of record at the close of business on January 4, 1965 to effect a two-for-one stock split in the form of a 100% stock dividend.

Exhibit 4 (Continued)

Authorized common stock at April 30, 1965 consisted of 5,000,000 shares of $1 par value of which 2,377,800 shares were issued and outstanding and of which 22,900 shares, in the aggregate, (to be issued in 1965 and 1966 under certain acquisition agreements) were treated as if issued and outstanding.

Authorized common stock at April 30, 1964 consisted of 2,500,000 of $1 par value of which 1,126,033 were issued and outstanding and of which 17,000 shares, in the aggregate, (to be issued in 1964 and 1965 under certain acquisition agreements) were treated as if issued and outstanding.

Incentive stock options—At May 1, 1964, options to certain officers and executives were outstanding expiring in 1964 to 1969 for 47,600 shares at 95% of the market price at the time the options were granted, namely, $10.6875 to $29.212 per share. During the year options on 16,000 shares were exercised at $10.6875 per share. New options were granted during the year ended April 30, 1965 for 15,000 shares at $22.50 per share, expiring in 1970.

Reserved shares—180,072 shares of common stock were reserved for issuance upon conversion of outstanding 4½% convertible subordinated debentures and 131,600 shares of common stock were reserved for the issuance of shares under the incentive stock option plans.

Subsequent events—Up to July 31, 1965 the company made additional short-term borrowings from banks of $1,000,000.

On July 1, 1965, the directors of the company approved, subject to stockholder approval, an agreement of merger under which Chemsol, Incorporated would be merged with and into the company. If the merger becomes effective, the company will issue .1424 of a share of its authorized but unissued common stock or treasury stock in conversion of each share of Chemsol stock at the effective date of the merger (at April 30, 1965 this would approximate 100,000 shares of the company's stock). Additional shares (27,770) contingent on Chemsol's earnings for the three years ended April 30, 1968 may be required to be issued, and such number of shares are to be reserved for issuance. Such additional number of shares may be increased or decreased dependent on the market price of Cenco's stock, all as defined in the agreement.

Case 8

Shin Mitsubishi Financial

"CHRIS, Joe Fowler of Winkle, Brown & Company called me yesterday afternoon. He wanted to sound us out on an issue of new securities of a Japanese firm, Shin Mitsubishi Heavy Industries, Ltd. Although he wasn't positive, he thinks the underwriters and the company will agree on some sort of a convertible security.

"When I told him I'd barely heard of Shin Mitsubishi and didn't know anything about Japanese business, he likened the company to our General Electric. He said it wasn't entirely comparable but was as similar to GE as to any other U.S. company.

"I told him I'd take a look at it so we could give him an indication of any interest on our part in securities they might have to sell. Could you look into this? From the point of view of relating Shin Mitsubishi to what we're familiar with, why don't you begin with a comparison of its financial statements with those of GE? From what I do know about Japanese business, I understand some of their firms have pretty wild balance sheets. I'd really like to see what you turn up. Maybe I can learn something!"

With these comments, Mr. Alexander Peters, senior vice president in charge of investments of the Sun Rise Mutual Life Insurance Company asked Mr. Christopher Corbett, an analyst in his department, to do some staff work for him.

Sun Rise Mutual Life had in its files annual reports of General Electric Company, and the investment banker had sent along financial data on Shin Mitsubishi. Mr. Corbett thought he would begin with these. Exhibit 1 includes excerpts from recent published materials describing Shin Mitsubishi. Exhibits 2 and 3 show financial statements of Shin Mitsubishi; Exhibits 4 and 5 depict financial statements of General Electric Company.

Exhibit 1

SHIN MITSUBISHI FINANCIAL

Excerpts from Materials Describing Shin Mitsubishi's Product Line

The activities taken over by Shin Mitsubishi from its predecessor in 1950 included shipbuilding and ship repair and the production of various kinds of industrial machinery, motor vehicles, steel structures, and rolling stock. Most of the company's products at that time were products which the predecessor company had manufactured in prewar years, but they also included a limited number of new products (such as motor scooters, three-wheel trucks, and beverage bottling machines) which had been introduced by the predecessor in its process of reconverting to civilian production after the war.

Since 1950 Shin Mitsubishi's manufacturing operations have undergone a continuing process of diversification. A large number of new products have been added to the company's product lines, with the result that the importance to the company's business of the operations in which its predecessor historically was engaged, such as shipbuilding and ship repair, has substantially decreased and the importance to its business of the manufacture and sale of new products has substantially increased. In 1953 the company commenced the manufacture of pulp and paper equipment. In 1955 it began the production of jeeps and reentered the field of aircraft manufacture. In 1959 it began to produce four-wheel trucks and small passenger cars. In 1960 it started to manufacture construction machinery. Over the years, it has undertaken to make various new kinds of industrial machinery. The company's diversified operations are summarized in the table following, which shows net sales by major product categories for each of the fiscal years ending March 31, 1958 to 1962.

In recent years Shin Mitsubishi has commenced development work and production of a series of new products, none of which has so far materially contributed to sales. Under a licensing agreement with Vendo Company of the United States, Shin Mitsubishi has commenced the manufacture of vending machines for, among other products, bottled beverages, hot and cold beverages, foods, ice cream, and cigarettes.

The company has been active in the atomic energy field and is a partner with 26 other Mitsubishi companies in the Mitsubishi Atomic Power Industries, Inc., which was established in 1958. The Mitsubishi Atomic Power Industries was the general contractor in the manufacture of two 10,000 KW thermal research reactors for which Shin Mitsubishi as subcontractor manufactured doors, piping, heavy water circulating pumps, and thermal shields. The Mitsubishi Atomic Power Industries is also active in design studies and investigation of power reactors both for power generation and for marine propulsion.

Shin Mitsubishi has undertaken development work for the Japan Defense Agency in the field of medium range air-to-air and surface-to-air missiles for military purposes and has, out of its own resources, undertaken development work of a weather rocket.

The company has recently commenced production of gas turbines, reversible pump turbines, plastic injection molding machines, plastic extruders,

Exhibit 1 (Continued)

finishing machines, and offset presses and intends to commence the sale of compressors for home refrigerators in fiscal year 1963. In February, 1963, Shin Mitsubishi expects to commence the sale of four-wheel diesel engine tractors for agricultural use.

The company has developed and sold a few small hydrofoil boats and is presently developing a design for larger hydrofoil boats. Shin Mitsubishi is also active in the design of flight simulators for jet planes and high-speed wind tunnels and linear accelerators for research purposes.

Exhibit 1 (Continued)

SHIN MITSUBISHI FINANCIAL

BREAKDOWN OF NET SALES BY PRODUCT, 1958–62

(Dollar Figures in Thousands)

Year Ended March 31	1958		1959		1960		1961		1962		Fiscal Year 1962 Net Sales as a Percentage of Fiscal Year 1958 Sales
Industrial machinery	$ 21,239	11%	$ 13,884	7%	$ 25,260	11%	$ 44,940	16%	$ 50,970	17%	240%
Power generating equipment	16,657	9	25,777	14	53,073	23	50,517	18	19,965	7	120
Small engines and agricultural machinery	11,321	6	12,057	7	15,098	6	22,489	8	28,439	10	251
Other machinery	12,527	7	9,517	5	11,452	5	17,409	6	26,096	9	208
Total machinery	$ 61,744	33%	$ 61,235	33%	$104,883	45%	$135,355	48%	$125,470	43%	203
Motor vehicles	45,094	24	47,121	25	47,653	21	72,674	26	96,704	33	214
Shipbuilding and repair	54,531	29	46,943	25	47,274	20	30,404	11	35,330	12	65
Aircraft	10,986	6	23,955	13	21,316	9	26,354	9	15,771	6	144
Rolling stock	10,058	5	6,202	3	7,805	3	11,759	4	12,074	4	120
Steel structures	5,809	3	2,659	1	4,048	2	5,617	2	6,836	2	118
Total	$188,222	100%	$188,115	100%	$232,979	100%	$282,163	100%	$292,185	100%	155%

Exhibit 2— SHIN MITSUBISHI FINANCIAL

BALANCE SHEET OF SHIN MITSUBISHI HEAVY INDUSTRIES, LTD.
(Dollar Figures in Thousands)

ASSETS	March 31, 1962
Cash and marketable securities	$ 47,217
Notes and accounts receivable net of allowance for bad debts	130,725
Inventories, less advances received on contracts*	92,303
Other current assets	13,764
Total current assets	$284,009
Long-term notes and accounts receivable	$ 43,991
Sundry investments and advances	10,228
Property, plant, and equipment	
Land	5,828
Buildings	50,683
Machinery and equipment	102,628
Construction in progress	24,253
Less: Accumulated depreciation	(54,123)
Property, plant, and equipment, net	$129,269
Other assets	7,111
Total assets	$474,608

LIABILITIES

Notes and accounts payable	$125,773
Bank loans†	101,811
Current portion of long-term debt	13,925
Other current liabilities	37,603
Total current liabilities	$279,112
Long-term debt‡	
Mortgage debentures	$ 21,748
Secured loans from banks and insurance companies	27,303
Unsecured loans	35,751
Less: Portion due within one year	(13,925)
Total long-term debt	$ 70,877
Other liabilities	25,191
Total liabilities	$375,180
Common stock	$ 55,556
Capital in excess of par value	1,282
Revaluation surplus§	9,878
Retained earnings	32,712
Total equity	$ 99,428
Total liabilities and shareholders' equity	$474,608

* Inventories, at the lower of cost or market, include a substantial amount of in-process machinery and equipment for which customers are not billed until delivery.

† Represented by unsecured short-term notes bearing interest principally at 7.3%, generally 90 days, maturing at various dates to June 30, 1962. The company has in the past experienced no difficulty in renewing such notes upon maturity, if it considered such renewals advisable. Substantially all of these notes are with banks which have written basic agreements with the company to the effect that with respect to all present or future loans with such banks the company shall provide collateral or guarantors therefor immediately upon the bank's request if such action is deemed necessary by the bank; the company has never received such a request from the banks.

‡ Long-term debt bears interest rates of 3.55%–9.85% and matures from 1962–96. Aggregate annual maturities of long-term debt during the 5 years ending March 31, 1967 are:

Year Ending March 31	Thousands of Dollars
1963	$13,925
1964	18,220
1965	15,779
1966	11,703
1967	7,645
	$67,272

§ Property, plant, and equipment is stated principally at cost. Under Japanese laws, companies have been permitted to recognize, to some extent, the loss in purchasing power of the yen by revaluing their property, plant, and equipment on the basis of coefficients established under such laws, the last of which was enacted in 1953. The company's property, plant, and equipment accounts were increased by ¥8,371 million ($23,253 thousand), principally prior to March 31, 1955, as a result of revaluation made under these laws; corresponding amounts were credited to a revaluation surplus account.

Exhibit 3

SHIN MITSUBISHI FINANCIAL

INCOME STATEMENTS OF SHIN MITSUBISHI HEAVY INDUSTRIES, LTD.

Years Ended March 31, 1958–1962

(Dollar Figures in Thousands)

	1958*	1959*	1960	1961	1962
Sales and other income					
Net sales	$188,222	$188,115	$232,979	$282,163	$292,185
Other income, principally interest	2,118	3,256	4,167	5,031	8,846
Total revenue	$190,340	$191,371	$237,146	$287,194	$301,031
Expenses					
Cost of sales	$147,622	$145,369	$179,582	$233,388	$233,491
Depreciation	5,812	7,263	8,217	9,008	11,996
Selling, general and administrative	9,576	10,925	12,697	16,759	21,426
Interest	5,042	5,949	6,303	9,192	13,053
Other, including research	2,646	3,191	3,961	5,468	7,589
Typhoon loss			5,407		
	$170,698	$172,697	$216,167	$273,815	$287,555
Income before income taxes	$ 19,642	$ 18,674	$ 20,979	$ 13,379	$ 13,476
Income taxes					
Current	$ 8,916	$ 7,459	$ 9,591	$ 7,176	$ 5,090
Estimated future	1,333	1,131	217	(104)	1,497
	$ 10,249	$ 8,590	$ 9,808	$ 7,072	$ 6,587
Net income	$ 9,393	$ 10,084	$ 11,171	$ 6,307	$ 6,889

*Unaudited.

Exhibit 4

SHIN MITSUBISHI FINANCIAL

BALANCE SHEET OF GENERAL ELECTRIC COMPANY

(Dollar Figures in Millions)

ASSETS	*December 31, 1961*
Cash and marketable securities..	$ 305
Notes and accounts receivable net of allowance for bad debts...........	671
Inventories, less advances received on contracts.......................	476
Total current assets..	$1,452
Long-term notes and accounts receivable............................	130
Sundry investments and advances...................................	272
Property, plant, and equipment, at cost............................	1,673
Less: Accumulated depreciation..................................	(956)
Property, plant, and equipment, net........................	717
Other assets..	132
Total assets...	$2,704

LIABILITIES

Notes and accounts payable....................................	$ 210
Other current liabilities...	572
Total current liabilities.....................................	$ 782
Long-term debt: 3½% debentures due May 1, 1976.................	229
Other liabilities..	90
Total liabilities...	$1,101
Common stock..	447
Capital in excess of par value....................................	152
Retained earnings...	1,004
Total equity...	$1,603
Total liabilities and equity..................................	$2,704

Exhibit 5

SHIN MITSUBISHI FINANCIAL

INCOME STATEMENTS OF GENERAL ELECTRIC COMPANY

YEARS ENDED DECEMBER 31, 1959–61

(Dollar Figures in Millions)

	1959	*1960*	*1961*
Sales..	$4,350	$4,198	$4,457
Operating costs			
Inventories at January 1.........................	$ 610	$ 626	$ 655
Wages and salaries.........................	1,696	1,755	1,798
Materials and supplies......................	1,997	1,970	2,063
Depreciation..............................	120	116	118
Taxes except those on income...............	38	37	39
Less: Inventories at December 31..........	(626)	(655)	(648)
Total operating costs...................	$3,835	$3,849	$4,025
Operating earnings...........................	$ 515	$ 349	$ 432
Nonoperating income.........................	51	54	63
Interest expense............................	(11)	(10)	(9)
Earnings before income taxes.................	$ 555	$ 393	$ 486
Income taxes...............................	275	193	244
Net earnings.........................	$ 280	$ 200	$ 242

Case 9

American Motors Financial

"THESE FIGURES you've worked up look interesting. But now I'd like you to back away from the figures and list the main points your figures seem to bring out as to where American Motors seems to be going, how it's like GM and the rest of the industry, and how it's different.

"While I'm out in Chicago, I'll be talking to Shares, Unlimited, the big mutual fund, about American Motors and the rest of the industry; so be sure that you cover points a common stock investor would be interested in. And as I pointed out, for years we've been after American Motors for a deposit account and some of their loan business. So, of course, we want all the insight we can develop about them and their financing. Also, point up any questions I ought to ask the treasurer when I see him. I'd like to have what you can pull out of your figures before I shove off tomorrow afternoon."

With these words, Gordon Olds, vice president of Northeast National Bank, tossed a folder containing the materials in Exhibits 1 through 4 to his young assistant, Weldon Dunn, and turned to other preparations for his forthcoming trip to the Midwest.

Exhibit 1
AMERICAN MOTORS FINANCIAL

CONSOLIDATED BALANCE SHEETS, AS OF SEPTEMBER 30, 1964 AND 1965

ASSETS	1964	1965
Cash	$ 34,778,575	$ 29,381,662
Marketable securities	15,985,946	6,491,170
Accounts receivable, net	54,974,011	54,880,694
Accounts receivable from affiliated companies	10,362,279	14,557,573
Inventories—at lower of cost (first-in, first-out method) or market	136,757,141	151,239,450
Prepaid insurance, taxes, and other expenses	5,335,113	8,773,590
Total current assets	$258,193,065	$265,324,139
Investments	45,870,355	50,842,297
Property, plant, and equipment	$239,288,590	$251,561,645
Less: Accumulated depreciation	102,414,114	110,726,041
Net property, plant, and equipment	$136,874,476	$140,835,604
Total assets	$440,937,896	$457,002,040

LIABILITIES		
Notes payable	$ 2,706,824	$ 52,040,472
Accounts payable	94,307,070	85,034,154
Salaries, wages, and amounts withheld from employees	14,532,269	10,788,891
Accrued expenses, including excise and miscellaneous taxes	31,650,294	30,337,440
Taxes on income	9,594,459	2,796,547
Total current liabilities	$152,790,916	$180,997,504
Other liabilities	6,450,285	5,681,321
Minority interests	2,978,466	3,074,209
Total liabilities	$162,219,667	$189,753,034
Capital stock, par value $1.66⅔ a share	31,774,774	31,775,774
Additional paid-in capital	50,062,865	50,069,529
Earnings retained for use in business	196,880,590	185,403,703
Total equity	$278,718,229	$267,249,006
Total liabilities and equity	$440,937,896	$457,002,040

Exhibit 2
AMERICAN MOTORS FINANCIAL

CONSOLIDATED STATEMENT OF NET EARNINGS
YEAR ENDED SEPTEMBER 30, 1965

Sales	$1,044,079,873
Less: Excise taxes	53,461,164
Net sales	$ 990,618,709
Equity in net earnings of unconsolidated subsidiaries	833,247
Interest and miscellaneous	6,108,181
Total revenue	$ 997,560,137
Cost of products sold	$ 835,033,863
Selling, advertising, and administrative expenses	102,225,244
Amortization of tools and dies	28,317,705
Depreciation and amortization of plant and equipment	15,292,980
Cost of pensions for employees	9,197,895
Minority interest in net earnings of Kelvinator of Canada Limited	136,878
Total expenses	$ 990,204,565
Earnings before taxes on income	$ 7,355,572
Taxes on income	2,150,000
Net earnings	$ 5,205,572

Exhibit 3

AMERICAN MOTORS FINANCIAL

SALES AND PROFIT FIGURES FOR FOUR AUTOMOBILE MANUFACTURERS
FIRST, SECOND, AND THIRD QUARTERS OF 1965

(Dollar Figures in Millions)

	General Motors	Ford	Chrysler	American Motors
Sales, 1965				
First Quarter................	$ 5,558	$ 2,912	$1,266	$ 215
Second Quarter.............	5,657	3,086	1,370	240
Third Quarter..............	3,743	2,308	1,046	228
Net profit (loss), 1965				
First Quarter..............	636	201	57	2
Second Quarter.............	638	237	62	7
Third Quarter..............	264	102	18	(13)
Sales, 12 months to				
9/30/64..................	17,973	9,672	3,935	1,095
9/30/65..................	18,796	10,849	5,118	991
Net profit, 12 months to				
9/30/64..................	1,866	545	187	26
9/30/65..................	1,913	642	224	5

Exhibit 4

AMERICAN MOTORS FINANCIAL

COMPARATIVE FINANCIAL RATIOS OF FOUR AUTOMOBILE MANUFACTURERS

	General Motors Corporation Years Ended December 31					Ford Motor Company Years Ended December 31				
	1960	1961	1962	1963	1964	1960	1961	1962	1963	1964
Total assets (in $ millions)	7,838	8,273	9,169	9,641	10,293	4,701	5,120	5,416	5,949	6,459
Net sales (in $ millions)	12,736	11,396	14,640	16,495	16,997	6,798	6,709	8,090	8,743	9,671
Current assets, year end/Current liabilities, year end	3.2x	3.1x	3.2x	3.3x	3.0x	1.7x	1.6x	1.7x	1.7x	1.6x
Cash, marketable securities and receivables/Current liabilities	1.8x	1.9x	1.9x	1.9x	1.5x	1.0x	0.9x	1.0x	1.0x	0.8x
Inventory, year end/Sales	14.2%	15.8%	13.7%	13.5%	15.8%	13.1%	14.7%	13.4%	13.7%	14.9%
Sales/Inventory, average of beginning and ending	7.1x	6.3x	7.7x	7.8x	6.9x	7.6x	7.1x	7.8x	7.7x	7.3x
Receivables, year end/Sales	4.8%	8.7%	7.3%	7.6%	8.2%	3.1%	8.7%	7.1%	7.5%	7.8%
Receivables, year end/Average day's sales	17.4 days	31.6 days	26.7 days	27.7 days	29.8 days	11.3 days	31.8 days	25.9 days	27.4 days	28.5 days
Sales/Net plant	4.2x	3.8x	4.6x	4.9x	4.4x	3.4x	3.2x	3.8x	3.8x	3.7x
Sales/Total assets, year end	1.6x	1.4x	1.6x	1.7x	1.7x	1.4x	1.3x	1.5x	1.5x	1.5x
Net profit before taxes/Net sales	16.0%	15.5%	20.0%	20.3%	19.3%	13.0%	12.3%	12.4%	11.7%	10.3%
Net income after taxes/Net sales	7.5%	7.8%	10.0%	9.7%	10.2%	6.8%	6.3%	6.1%	5.7%	5.3%
Net income after taxes/Total assets, year end	12.2%	10.8%	15.9%	16.5%	16.9%	9.8%	8.2%	9.0%	8.4%	7.9%
Net income after taxes/Owners' investment, year end	16.5%	14.8%	21.9%	22.4%	22.8%	14.8%	13.1%	14.0%	13.1%	12.5%
Total debts (excluding reserves)/Total assets	23.1%	24.5%	25.1%	23.8%	24.0%	32.0%	35.4%	33.1%	33.6%	34.2%
Long-term debt/Total capitalization	5.0%	5.7%	4.9%	3.5%	3.0%	7.7%	7.8%	6.2%	5.2%	5.3%
Total equity/Total debt (excluding reserves)	3.2x	3.0x	2.9x	3.1x	3.1x	2.1x	1.8x	1.9x	1.9x	1.9x

Exhibit 4 (Continued)
AMERICAN MOTORS FINANCIAL

	Chrysler Corporation Years Ended December 31					American Motors Corporation Years Ended September 30				
	1960	1961	1962	1963	1964	1961	1962	1963	1964	1965
Total assets (in $ millions)	1,369	1,400	1,525	2,125	2,421	333	375	440	441	457
Net sales (in $ millions)	3,007	2,127	2,378	3,505	4,287	876	1,056	1,132	1,095	991
Current assets, year end/Current liabilities	2.2x	2.3x	2.3x	1.7x	1.4x	2.0x	2.0x	1.7x	1.7x	1.5x
Cash, marketable securities and receivables/ Current liabilities	1.2x	1.5x	1.6x	1.2x	0.8x	1.1x	1.1x	0.9x	0.8x	0.6x
Inventory, year end/Sales	10.7%	13.5%	11.7%	11.0%	13.1%	10.7%	9.1%	11.2%	12.5%	15.2%
Sales/Inventory, average of beginning and ending	9.1x	7.0x	8.4x	10.6x	9.1x	8.4x	11.1x	10.2x	8.4x	6.9x
Receivables, year end/Sales	4.1%	5.7%	6.1%	5.5%	5.4%	4.6%	4.7%	4.7%	5.9%	7.0%
Receivables, year end/Average day's sales	15.1 days	21.0 days	22.5 days	20.1 days	19.9 days	16.7 days	17.2 days	17.1 days	21.7 days	25.6 days
Sales/Net plant	5.9x	4.8x	5.9x	6.3x	4.9x	10.2x	11.9x	10.7x	8.0x	7.0x
Sales/Total assets, year end	2.2x	1.5x	1.6x	1.6x	1.8x	2.6x	2.8x	2.6x	2.5x	2.2x
Net profit before taxes/Net sales	2.2%	1.0%	5.3%	9.2%	9.4%	5.8%	6.9%	6.6%	4.1%	0.8%
Net income after taxes/Net sales	1.1%	0.5%	2.8%	4.5%	5.1%	2.7%	3.2%	3.3%	2.4%	0.5%
Net income after taxes/Total assets, year end	2.4%	0.8%	4.3%	7.4%	9.0%	7.1%	9.1%	8.6%	6.0%	1.2%
Net income after taxes/Owners' investment, year end	4.6%	1.6%	8.5%	16.5%	18.6%	10.4%	13.7%	13.8%	9.4%	2.0%
Total debts (excluding reserves)/Total assets	45.4%	45.4%	44.8%	50.5%	47.3%	31.2%	32.0%	36.6%	34.7%	39.6%
Long-term debt/Total capitalization	26.2%	26.0%	23.6%	21.1%	17.3%	0	0	0	0	0
Total equity/Total debt (excluding reserves)	1.1x	1.1x	1.1x	0.9x	1.0x	2.2x	2.1x	1.7x	1.8x	1.5x

Case 10

Ross Corporation

Mr. H. J. Dart, treasurer of the Ross Corporation, a medium-sized manufacturing and distributing firm, had called Mr. William Kidd, assistant treasurer, to his office to review some material (Exhibits 1–7) that Mr. Kidd had assembled for him.

"As you know, Bill," said Mr. Dart, "we have never included a funds statement in our annual report to stockholders. I've received suggestions from security analysts that we publish such a statement. As your material indicates, there doesn't seem to be much uniformity to the funds statements published by other corporations, and there seems to be some ambiguity about what the term 'funds' means.

"I'm aware, also, of the confusion that exists in some quarters of the financial community about the significance of 'cash flow,' which seems to be defined as 'net income + depreciation.' Some people seem to believe that this 'cash flow' is the best measure of the true economic income of a corporation. Others contend that it is neither 'cash' nor 'flow,' and that it doesn't make sense to use 'cash flow' as an income indicator.

"I'd hate for us to publish a funds statement that would be confusing or misleading to our stockholders. At the same time, we shouldn't hold back information that might be useful to them.

"You've done a good job, Bill, in getting these different examples of funds statements together for me. I should like you to continue working on this problem. Give this whole question some serious study; decide on the best form of presentation; and then prepare a funds statement for Ross Corporation in the form you think best tells the story. I can see some important advantages to presenting a statement of the sources and uses of *cash;* however, most other corporations seem to favor a statement of the sources and uses of *working capital.* Or maybe we ought to show the full story, beginning with net sales and carrying the statement through from that point, as you did in the draft statement [Exhibit 3] you showed me."

Exhibit 1

ROSS CORPORATION

CONSOLIDATED BALANCE SHEETS, AS OF DECEMBER 31, 1964 AND 1965

(Dollar Figures in Thousands)

	1965	1964	Change
Cash	$ 5,120	$ 2,758	+$ 2,362
Accounts receivable	29,520	20,733	+ 8,787
Inventories	38,764	30,048	+ 8,716
Prepaid expenses	468	475	− 7
Total current assets	$73,872	$54,014	+$19,858
Net property, plant, and equipment	24,027	19,267	+ 4,760
Long-term receivables and other assets	990	976	+ 14
Deferred charges	894	705	+ 189
Total assets	$99,783	$74,962	+$24,821
Accounts payable	$15,410	$ 6,815	+$ 8,595
Notes payable to banks	14,567	7,593	+ 6,974
Accrued expenses	7,629	7,065	+ 564
Accrued federal income taxes	9,249	6,063	+ 3,186
Current maturities of long-term debt	400	400	—
Total current liabilities	$47,255	$27,936	+$19,319
Long-term debt	4,279	4,688	− 409
Common stock	5,905	5,891	+ 14
Additional paid-in capital	11,000	10,839	+ 161
Retained earnings	31,344	25,608	+ 5,736
Total liabilities and stockholders' equity	$99,783	$74,962	+$24,821

NOTES TO CONSOLIDATED FINANCIAL STATEMENTS

(All Dollar Amounts Stated in Thousands)

1. Inventories consisted of the following:

	1965	1964	Change
Finished goods	$15,273	$ 9,435	+$5,838
Work in process	9,381	10,487	− 1,106
Raw materials and supplies	14,110	10,126	+ 3,984
Totals	$38,764	$30,048	+$8,716

2. During the year ended December 31, 1965, options covering 14,000 shares of common stock were exercised by employees. Proceeds from the sale of these shares amounted to $175.

Exhibit 2

ROSS CORPORATION

CONSOLIDATED STATEMENTS OF EARNINGS AND CAPITAL

(Dollar Figures in Thousands)

CONSOLIDATED STATEMENT OF EARNINGS, YEARS ENDED DECEMBER 31, 1964 AND 1965

	1965	1964
Net sales	$181,778	$139,571
Cost of sales	138,490	103,263
Gross profit on sales	$ 43,288	$ 36,308
Operating expenses	20,876	17,672
Operating income, after allowance for depreciation of $3,229 in 1965 and $2,309 in 1964	$ 22,412	$ 18,636
Other charges (principally interest)	1,217	921
Earnings before federal income taxes	$ 21,195	$ 17,715
Federal income taxes	10,156	8,656
Net earnings for the year	$ 11,039	$ 9,059

Exhibit 2 (Continued)

CONSOLIDATED STATEMENT OF CAPITAL, YEAR ENDED DECEMBER 31, 1965

	Common Stock ($1 par)	Additional Paid-in Capital	Retained Earnings
Amounts at January 1, 1965..............	$5,891	$10,839	$25,608
Add:			
Proceeds from sale of shares under stock option plan.........................	14	161	11,039
Net earnings for the year.................	$5,905	$11,000	$36,647
Deduct:			
Cash dividends paid....................	—	—	5,303
Amounts at December 31, 1965...........	$5,905	$11,000	$31,344

Exhibit 3

ROSS CORPORATION

CASH FLOW STATEMENT, YEAR ENDED DECEMBER 31, 1965

(Dollar Figures in Thousands)

Net sales.......................................			$181,778
Deduct increase in accounts receivable during year			− 8,787
Net inflow of cash from net sales................			$172,991
Deduct: Net outflow of cash associated with operations:			
Cost of sales (excluding "noncash" expenses—depreciation of $3,229)........................		$135,261	
Add increase in inventories during year.........+		8,716	
Deduct increase in accounts payable during year..−		8,595	
Cash outflow associated with goods produced during year...................................		$135,382	
Operating expenses and other charges..........		$ 22,093	
Deduct decrease in prepaid expenses during year −		7	
Add increase in deferred charges during year......+		189	
Deduct increase in accrued expenses during year −		564	
Cash outflow associated with operating expenses		21,711	
Federal income taxes........................		$ 10,156	
Deduct increase in accrued federal income taxes..−		3,186	
Cash outflow associated with tax payments......		6,970	
Net outflow of cash associated with operations...			164,063
Net cash flow from operations..................			$ 8,928
Add: Other inflows ("sources")			
Increase in notes payable to banks.............		$ 6,974	
Proceeds from sale of shares under stock option plan......................................		175	
			7,149
			$ 16,077
Deduct: Other outflows ("uses")			
Cash dividends paid..........................		$ 5,303	
Acquisition of property, plant and equipment....		7,989	
Increases in long-term receivables and other assets		14	
Decrease in long-term debt....................		409	
Other..			13,715
Increase in cash and marketable securities during year.......................................			$ 2,362

Exhibit 4

ROSS CORPORATION

EXAMPLE OF FUNDS STATEMENT

AMERICAN MACHINE & FOUNDRY COMPANY AND CONSOLIDATED SUBSIDIARIES

Statement of Source and Disposition of Funds	*1964*	*1963*
SOURCE OF FUNDS:		
Net income...............................	$ 18,524,779	$ 9,510,102
Depreciation and amortization................	24,192,818	23,743,877
Federal income taxes deferred................	3,721,000	5,713,000
Common stock options exercised..............	252,740	253,274
Short-term borrowings......................	—	25,000,000
Long-term borrowings......................	102,011,977	—
Amortization of debt expense................	60,197	54,486
Total............................	$148,763,511	$64,274,739
DISPOSITION OF FUNDS:		
Leased machines...........................	$4,851,897	$8,871,618
Property, plant and equipment (net)..........	20,628,538	11,339,359
Patents and developments capitalized.........	2,446,084	3,893,846
Deferred charges..........................	6,996,838	—.
Investments...............................	1,199,239	2,356,010
Preferred stock redeemed...................	222,294	441,735
Long-term debt retired.....................	60,500,000	—
Long-term debt transferred to current liabilities..	1,159,000	4,859,000
Repayment of short-term borrowings...........	25,000,000	2,000,000
Dividends paid............................	15,713,832	15,603,474
Increase in working capital other than cash......	7,669,209	23,165,136
Other items (net)..........................	5,733	93,153
Total............................	$146,392,664	$ 72,623,331
INCREASE (DECREASE) IN CASH................	$ 2,370,847	$ (8,348,592)
CASH:		
At beginning of year.......................	$ 17,283,685	$ 25,632,277
At end of year............................	19,654,532	17,283,685
Increase (Decrease) as above...........	$ 2,370,847	$ (8,348,592)

Exhibit 5

ROSS CORPORATION

EXAMPLE OF FUNDS STATEMENT

ALLIED CHEMICAL CORPORATION

Statement of Funds

	1964	1963
	(In Millions)	
Funds Provided:		
From earnings		
Sales and operating revenues...................	$1043.1	$963.1
Other income................................	8.3	4.9
	1051.4	968.0
Deduct cash items		
Cost of goods sold and operating expenses...........	694.2	650.0
Selling, general and administrative expenses..........	103.3	92.2
Pension costs charged to income....................	22.8	8.7
Income taxes—current...........................	37.2	36.2
Interest and expenses on long-term debt.............	8.7	9.1
	866.2	796.2
	185.2	171.8
From other sources		
Common stock issued...........................	12.5	1.8
Salvage value of retired property..................	6.9	3.6
Increase (decrease) in long-term debt...............	5.9	(13.1)
Total funds provided.........................	$ 210.5	$164.1
Funds Applied:		
Property additions...............................	$ 143.7	$ 99.1
Cash dividends paid..............................	47.3	47.7
Increase (decrease) in cash and short-term securities......	(19.8)	15.6
Increase in other working capital....................	20.4	6.3
Goodwill acquired................................	9.2	—
Pension costs charged (credited) to pension reserves......	4.3	(2.7)
Other items—net................................	5.4	(1.9)
Total funds applied..........................	$ 210.5	$164.1

Exhibit 6

ROSS CORPORATION

EXAMPLE OF FUNDS STATEMENT

CABOT CORPORATION

Consolidated Sources and Applications of Funds and Changes in Working Capital,
Years Ended September 30, 1964 and 1963

Sources and Applications of Funds (Working Capital)	Thousands of Dollars 1964	1963
SOURCES OF FUNDS:		
Net income and special items...................\$	6,243	\$10,750
Charges against income not requiring current expenditure of funds:		
Depreciation and depletion......................	8,959	8,628
Deferred income taxes..........................	(660)	1,163
Loss on abandoned oil and gas leases.............	626	869
Provision for possible loss on investment...........	3,286	
Excess of proceeds (\$3,720 in 1964 and \$7,234 in 1963) from disposal of investments and plant assets over gains included in net income and special items......	2,380	1,210
Sale of capital stock.............................		153
Total sources of funds........................	20,834	22,773
APPLICATIONS OF FUNDS:		
Property, plant and equipment....................	18,643	9,837
Investments.....................................	8,311	5,550
Reduction of long-term debt......................	1,388	763
Reacquisition of common stock...................	1,366	
Cash dividends..................................	1,532	1,414
Notes receivable—noncurrent.....................	3,421	105
Miscellaneous...................................	(28)	684
Total applications of funds....................	34,633	18,353
INCREASE (DECREASE) IN WORKING CAPITAL............\$(13,799)		\$ 4,420

Changes in Working Capital

INCREASE (DECREASE) IN CURRENT ASSETS:		
Cash, time deposits and short-term securities........\$(13,652)		\$ 1,103
Accounts and notes receivable.....................	3,051	1,105
Inventories......................................	1,544	1,608
Increase (decrease) in current assets.............	(9,057)	3,816
(INCREASE) DECREASE IN CURRENT LIABILITIES:		
Notes payable to banks...........................	(4,309)	(732)
Current portion of long-term debt.................	(625)	
Accounts payable and accruals.....................	57	244
U.S. and foreign income taxes.....................	135	1,092
(Increase) decrease in current liabilities..........	(4,742)	604
INCREASE (DECREASE) IN WORKING CAPITAL............\$(13,799)		\$ 4,420
WORKING CAPITAL AT SEPTEMBER 30........ \$27,101		\$40,900

Exhibit 7

ROSS CORPORATION

EXAMPLE OF FUNDS STATEMENT

W. T. GRANT COMPANY

Statement of Source and Disposition of Funds

(Amounts in 000's)

(*Years Which End January 31 of Subsequent Years*)	1964	1963	1962	1961	1960	*Total 5 Years*
WHERE FUNDS CAME FROM						
Sales	$769,921	$698,673	$686,262	$574,501	$512,687	$3,242,044
Less:						
Merchandise costs, supplies, outside services, etc.	530,790	491,938	496,149	407,539	356,860	2,283,276
Wages and salaries, including miscellaneous benefits	143,901	132,756	123,462	107,224	97,336	604,679
Retirement plan contributions	418	619	875	648	908	3,468
Social security taxes on payrolls	7,473	7,430	6,868	5,249	4,459	31,479
Rents to landlords less rentals on subleases	31,542	29,703	27,825	23,854	21,401	134,325
Federal, state and local taxes, excluding social security taxes	27,139	18,250	15,297	15,087	16,262	92,035
Depreciation and amortization	6,998	6,983	6,782	6,541	6,263	33,567
Net Income from Operations (excluding increase (decrease) in equity in Zeller's Ltd.)	$ 21,660	$ 10,994	$ 9,004	$ 8,359	$ 9,198	$ 59,215
Add charges against income which involve no cash outlay:						
Depreciation and amortization	6,998	6,983	6,782	6,541	6,263	33,567
Net increase in reserves	352	237	215	317	123	1,244
Deferred federal income tax	6,610	6,238	2,221	432	310	15,811
From sale of common stock to employees	1,723	1,094	929	1,214	1,487	6,447
From sale of debentures	. . . . .	. . . . .	. . . . .	35,000	. . . . .	35,000
From sale of land and buildings	219	. . . . .	18	146	. . . . .	383
From decrease in sundry accounts—net	76	1,435	880	. . . . .	. . . . .	2,391
Total Funds Provided	$ 37,638	$ 26,981	$ 20,049	$ 52,009	$ 17,381	$ 154,058

Exhibit 7 (Continued)

ROSS CORPORATION

(Years Which End January 31 of Subsequent Years)	1964	1963	1962	1961	1960	Total 5 Years
HOW FUNDS WERE USED						
For dividends to stockholders	$ 7,672	$ 7,611	$ 7,560	$ 7,502	$ 7,429	$ 37,774
For investment in land and buildings	.....	.....	.....	.....	318	318
For investment in furniture and fixtures	4,807	5,306	7,272	7,577	7,596	32,558
For investment in improvements to leased properties	366	346	.....	71	284	1,067
For investment in Zeller's Limited	158	67	42	.....	.....	267
For purchase of common stock for deferred compensation plan	186	82	136	6	126	536
For increase in sundry accounts—net	.....	.....	.....	877	620	1,497
Funds added to working capital	24,449	13,569	5,039	35,976	1,008	80,041
Total Funds Used	$37,638	$26,981	$20,049	$52,009	$17,381	$154,058

Case 11

Big City Trust Company

"Dick, Monday morning I'm flying out to Halley, Nebraska, to spend a couple of days with the people at the Auto-Drive Company. I hope to be able to come away with a fairly intimate feeling for the company's future. From what my friends in the automobile industry tell me, these people are about to perfect their Auto-Drive, a sort of automatic pilot for cars. Installed in a car, the pilot makes it impossible for the car to run off the road or into another car.

"When they get the Auto-Drive into cars, if it's accepted at all, the company will take off. Just think of the lives that would be saved! I'll bet consumers will insist that it be put in every car! If it looks good, I surely want the pension funds managed by Big City Trust to buy Auto-Drive common now."

Mr. Samuel Cooper, a senior trust officer at Big City Trust Company, enthusiastically addressed Mr. Richard Brainard, an analyst in the trust department. "I just wonder how much the stock can grow, though. It seems to me that the way Auto-Drive chooses to finance this growth in sales will be very important. If it has to issue a lot of new stock, much of the benefit of expanded earnings may be dissipated by the added shares. I wonder whether the methods used by other glamour companies, such as Xerox and Polaroid, to finance their growth would throw some light on the options open to Auto-Drive. In fact, before I fly out to Nebraska, I'd like to have the facts on just those two companies fresh in my mind. Dick, could you gather the financial statements for Xerox and Polaroid and summarize for me what their growth has meant in terms of funds requirements and how they have met these needs in the past four or five years?"

To prepare his analysis of how Polaroid and Xerox had acquired and used their resources, Dick Brainard gathered the material shown in Exhibits 1–8.

Exhibit 1

BIG CITY TRUST COMPANY

BALANCE SHEETS FOR XEROX CORPORATION, AS OF
DECEMBER 31, 1960 AND 1964

(Dollar Figures in Thousands)

ASSETS	1960	1964	Net Change 1960–64
Cash	$ 1,779	$ 5,868	$+ 4,089
Accounts receivable	5,536	35,400	+ 29,864
Inventories	5,966	22,860	+ 16,894
Other current assets	1,276	21,809	+ 20,533
Total current assets	$14,557	$ 85,937	$+ 71,380
Investments	1,376	25,556	+ 24,180
Property, plant and equipment*	38,520	262,678	+224,158
Less: Depreciation	(9,241)	(92,628)	(+ 83,387)
Net property, plant and equipment	$29,279	$170,050	$+140,771
Intangible assets	10,643	36,346	+ 25,703
Other assets	572	2,658	+ 2,086
Total assets	$56,427	$320,547	$+264,120
LIABILITIES			
Accounts payable	$ 1,907	$ 6,099	$+ 4,192
Notes payable, bank	3,500	4,600	+ 1,100
Accrued liabilities	3,574	42,531	+ 38,957
Other current liabilities	2,117	7,780	+ 5,663
Total current liabilities	$11,098	$ 61,010	$+ 49,912
Deferred income tax	—	5,712	+ 5,712
Long-term debt	4,666	102,514	+ 97,848
Due for patents processes (in stock and cash)	11,018	22,435	+ 11,417
Deferred executive compensation	949	1,608	+ 659
Rental income—prepaid	353	—	− 353
Total liabilities	$28,084	$193,279	$+165,195
Cumulative preferred stock	1,880	—	− 1,880
Common stock	4,676	20,519 †	+ 15,843
Paid-in surplus‡	13,218	34,774	+ 21,556
Earned surplus§	8,569	71,975	+ 63,406
Total equity	$28,343	$127,268	$+ 98,925
Total liabilities and equity	$56,427	$320,547	$+264,120

* Includes leased machines valued in 1960 and 1964 at $18 million and $85 million.

† Of the increase of the common stock account $15,256 thousand is due to a transfer from "Paid-in surplus" of that amount to effect a change of each previously issued share of $1.25 par value into 5 shares of $1 par value.

After adjustment for the 5 for 1 split in 1963 there were 18,004,575 shares outstanding on December 31, 1960, and 20,518,956 on December 31, 1964.

During the period new shares were issued for the following purposes (adjusted for split): (*a*) Conversion of debentures—717,254; (*b*) Acquisition of other companies—483,435; (*c*) Payment for patents—437,500; (*d*) Employee stock options—176,592.

‡ See Exhibit 3.

§ See Exhibit 4.

Exhibit 2

BIG CITY TRUST COMPANY

Income Statements for Xerox Corporation for 1960, 1964,
and for the Period from 12/31/60–12/31/64
(Dollar Figures in Thousands)

	1960	1964	Total 1961–64
Operating revenues			
Rentals, service on royalties	$10,841	$184,157	$394,990
Net sales	26,233	83,870	225,078
Total operating revenues	$37,074	$268,027	$620,068
Costs and expenses			
Costs of sales and other operating expenses	17,777	88,314	218,718
Selling, service, administrative, and general expenses	12,376	88,866	199,396
Profit-sharing, retirement, and pension plans	516	10,264	21,480
Total costs and expenses	$30,670	$187,444	$439,594
Operating income	$ 6,404	$ 80,583	$180,474
Other income	54	440	1,210
Other deductions			
Interest	$ 253	$ 3,934	$ 9,276
Other	189	381	2,145
Total other deductions	$ 442	$ 4,315	$ 11,421
Income before income taxes	$ 6,016	$ 76,707	$170,264
Income taxes	3,418	38,177	89,323
Net income	$ 2,598	$ 38,530	$ 80,941

Exhibit 3

BIG CITY TRUST COMPANY

Statement of Additional Paid-in Surplus for
Xerox Corporation for the Period
12/31/60–12/31/64
(Dollar Figures in Thousands)

Balance 12/31/60	$13,218
Plus:	
Excess of par value of shares issued	36,812
	$50,030
Less:	
Transfer to common stock accounts as a result of change of each of previously issued shares of $1.25 par value into 5 shares of $1 par value	15,256
Balance 12/31/64	$34,774

Exhibit 4

BIG CITY TRUST COMPANY

STATEMENT OF EARNED SURPLUS FOR XEROX CORPORATION
FOR THE PERIOD 12/31/60–12/31/64

(Dollar Figures in Thousands)

Balance 12/31/60.............................	$ 8,569
Plus:	
Net income.................................	80,941
Credits to earned surplus....................	380
	$89,890
Less:	
Debits to earned surplus.....................	$ 468
Dividends on preferred stock.................	34
Dividends on common stock..................	17,413
	$17,915
Balance 12/31/64.............................	$71,975

Exhibit 5

BIG CITY TRUST COMPANY

BALANCE SHEETS FOR POLAROID CORPORATION, AS OF
DECEMBER 31, 1960 AND 1964

(Dollar Figures in Thousands)

ASSETS	1960	1964	Net Change 1960–64
Cash.......................................	$11,864	$ 41,062	$+29,198
Receivables................................	26,222	37,557	+11,335
Inventories................................	13,980	13,177	− 803
Other current assets........................	379	834	+ 455
Total current assets....................	$52,445	$ 92,630	$+40,185
Properties, buildings and equipment...........	27,421	51,075	+23,654
Less: Depreciation.......................	(9,639)	(20,747)	(+11,108)
Net property, buildings and equipment........	$17,782	$ 30,328	$+12,546
Investment................................	277	146	− 131
Total assets.........................	$70,504	$123,104	$+52,600

LIABILITIES			
Payables...................................	$10,731	$ 11,204	$+ 473
Provision for taxes..........................	7,089	14,212	+ 7,123
Total liabilities.......................	$17,820	$ 25,416	$+ 7,596
Cumulative first preferred stock...............	900	—	− 900
Cumulative second preferred stock.............	35	—	− 35
Common stock*............................	3,871	15,750	+11,879
Paid-in surplus†...........................	14,414	16,359	+ 1,945
Retained earnings‡.........................	33,464	65,579	+32,115
Total equity..........................	$52,684	$ 97,688	$+45,004
Total liabilities and equity...........	$70,504	$123,104	$+52,600

* Stock split 4 for 1 in 1964. Further increases in "Common stock" due to exercising of stock options.
† See Exhibit 7.
‡ See Exhibit 8.

Exhibit 6

BIG CITY TRUST COMPANY

INCOME STATEMENTS FOR POLAROID CORPORATION FOR 1960, 1964,
AND FOR THE PERIOD 12/31/60–12/31/64

(Dollar Figures in Thousands)

	1960	1964	Total 1961–64
Net sales and other income.........	$99,446	$139,350	$468,026
Cost of goods sold.................	$50,304	$ 65,235	$231,125
Selling, administrative, distribution, research, and engineering expenses	27,039	32,761	119,932
Depreciation and amortization......	2,871	5,240	16,780
Total expenses..............	$80,214	$103,236	$367,837
Earnings before taxes..............	$19,232	$ 36,114	$100,189
Taxes on income..................	10,420	17,791	52,571
Net earnings after taxes...........	$ 8,812	$ 18,323	$ 47,618

Exhibit 7

BIG CITY TRUST COMPANY

STATEMENT OF ADDITIONAL PAID-IN SURPLUS FOR
POLAROID CORPORATION FOR THE PERIOD 12/31/60–12/31/64

(Dollar Figures in Thousands)

Balance 1/1/61...................................... $14,414
Plus:
   Proceeds in excess of par value from stock options
     exercised...................................... 1,877
   Other proceeds................................... 68
Balance 12/31/64.................................. $16,359

Exhibit 8

BIG CITY TRUST COMPANY

STATEMENT OF RETAINED EARNINGS FOR POLAROID CORPORATION
FOR THE PERIOD 12/31/60–12/31/64

(Dollar Figures in Thousands)

Balance 1/1/61...................................... $33,464
Plus:
   Net income... 47,618
   Prior year's tax adjustments (1961).................... 131
                                 $81,213
Less:
   Premium on redemption of preferred stock (1963)........ 331
   Amount transferred to "Common Stock" to effect stock
     split (1964).. 11,814
   Preferred dividends (1961–63)........................ 156
   Common stock dividends............................. 3,333
                                  $15,634
Balance 12/31/64.................................. $65,579

Case 12

Clarkson Lumber Company

FOLLOWING a rapid growth in its business during recent years, the Clarkson Lumber Company in the spring of 1940 anticipated a further substantial increase in sales. Despite good profits, which were largely retained in the business, the company had experienced a shortage of cash and had found it necessary to borrow $48,000 from the Suburban National Bank. In the spring of 1940, additional borrowing seemed necessary if sales were to be increased and purchase discounts taken. Since $48,000 was the maximum amount which the Suburban National would lend to any borrower, it was necessary for Mr. Paul Clarkson, proprietor of the Clarkson Lumber Company, to look elsewhere for additional credit.

Through a personal friend who was well acquainted with one of the officers of a large metropolitan bank, the Northrup National Bank, Mr. Clarkson obtained an introduction to the officer and presented a request for an additional bank loan of $80,000. Consequently, the credit department of the Northrup National Bank made its usual investigation of the company for the information of the loan officers of the bank.

The Clarkson Lumber Company was founded in 1930 as a partnership of Mr. Clarkson and Mr. Henry Stark, a brother-in-law of Mr. Clarkson. Six years later Mr. Clarkson bought out Mr. Stark's interest and continued the business as sole proprietor.

The business was located in a suburb of a large midwestern city. Land and a siding were leased from a railroad. Two portable sheet metal storage buildings had been erected by the company. Operations were limited to the wholesale distribution of plywood, moldings, and sash and door products to lumber dealers in the local area. Credit terms of net 30 days and net 60 days on open account were usually offered customers.

Sales volume had been built up largely on the basis of successful price competition made possible through careful control of operating expenses and by quantity purchases of materials at substantial discounts. Almost all of the moldings and sash and door products, which amounted to 40% and 20% of sales, respectively, were used for repair work. About 55% of total sales were made in the 6 months from March through August. No sales representatives were employed, orders being taken exclusively over the telephone. Annual sales of $313,646 in 1935 and of $476,275 in 1936 gave net profits of $32,494 and of $34,131, respectively. Comparative operating statements for the years 1937 through 1939 and for the three months ending March 31, 1940, are given in Exhibit 1.

Mr. Clarkson was an energetic man, 39 years of age, who worked long hours on the job, not only handling management matters but also performing a large amount of the clerical work. Help was afforded by an assistant who, in the words of the investigator of the Northrup National Bank, "has been doing and can do about everything that Mr. Clarkson does in the organization."

Other employees numbered 14, of whom 11 worked in the yard and 3 drove trucks. Mr. Clarkson had adopted the practice of paying union dues and all social security taxes for his employees; in addition, bonuses were distributed to them at the end of each year. In 1939 the bonus amounted to 40% of annual wages. Mr. Clarkson was planning to incorporate the business in the near future and to sell stock to certain employees.

As a part of its customary investigation of prospective borrowers, the Northrup National Bank sent inquiries concerning Mr. Clarkson to a number of firms which had business dealings with him. The manager of one of his large suppliers, the Barker Company, wrote in answer:

The conservative operation of his business appeals to us. He has not wasted his money in disproportionate plant investment. His operating expenses are as low as they could possibly be. He has personal control over every feature of his business, and he possesses sound judgment and a willingness to work harder than anyone I have ever known. This, with a good personality, gives him an excellent turnover; and from my personal experience in watching him work, I know that he keeps close check on his own credits.

All of the other trade letters received by the bank bore out the statements quoted above.

In addition to the ownership of his lumber business, Mr. Clarkson held jointly with his wife an equity in their home, which was mortgaged for $12,000 and which cost $20,160 to build in 1927. He also held a $16,000 life insurance policy, payable to Mrs. Clarkson. Mrs. Clarkson owned independently a half interest in a home worth about $8,000.

The bank gave particular attention to the debt position and current ratio of the business. It noted the ready market for the company's products at all times and the fact that sales prospects were particularly favorable. The bank's investigator reported: ". . . it is estimated sales may run from $1,280,000 to $1,600,000 in 1940." The rate of inventory turnover was high, and losses on bad debts in past years had been quite small. Comparative balance sheets as of December 31, 1937, through 1939 and as of March 31, 1940, are given in Exhibit 2.

The bank learned, through inquiry of another wholesale lumber company, that the usual terms of purchase in the trade were 2%, 10 days after arrival. Suppliers took 60-day notes when requested but did this somewhat unwillingly.

Exhibit 1
CLARKSON LUMBER COMPANY
OPERATING STATEMENTS FOR THE YEARS ENDING DECEMBER 31, 1937, THROUGH 1939 AND FOR THE THREE MONTHS ENDING MARCH 31, 1940
(Dollar Figures in Thousands)

	1937	1938	1939	1st Quarter 1940
Net sales	$740	$880	$1,179	$310*
Cost of goods sold:				
Beginning inventory	111	97	141	180
Purchases	611	846	1,069	336
	$722	$943	$1,210	$516
Ending inventory	97	141	180	244
Cost of goods sold	$625	$802	$1,030	$272
Gross profit	$115	$ 78	$ 149	$ 38
Operating expenses	38	48	73	20
Net operating profit	$ 77	$ 30	$ 76	$ 18
Add: Purchase discounts taken	5	5	5	0.6
	$ 82	$ 35	$ 81	$ 19
Deduct: Sales discounts allowed	16	18	28	8
Net profit†	$ 66	$ 17	$ 53	$ 11*
Drawings by proprietor	...	...	$ 28	$ 6

* In the first quarter of 1939, net sales were $252,000 and net profit was $13,000.

† This item is stated before any provision for federal income tax liabilities. As distinct from corporations, no federal income taxes are levied on the profits of proprietorships and partnerships, as such. The owners of a proprietorship or partnership, however, must include in their personal income their proportionate share of such profits and must pay taxes on them at the regular personal income tax rates.

Exhibit 2
CLARKSON LUMBER COMPANY
COMPARATIVE BALANCE SHEETS AS OF DECEMBER 31, 1937, THROUGH 1939, AND AS OF MARCH 31, 1940

ASSETS	1937	1938	1939	March 31 1940
Cash	$ 56	$ 282	$ 3,560	$ 1,338
Accounts receivable—net of reserve for bad debts	57,322	89,387	109,686	128,893
Inventory	97,005	141,416	179,557	243,658
Total current assets	$154,383	$231,085	$292,803	$373,889
Property—net of reserve for depreciation	5,963	7,608	11,430	10,361
Deferred charges	...	...	...	2,594
Total assets	$160,346	$238,693	$304,233	$386,844

Exhibit 2 (Continued)

LIABILITIES	1937	1938	1939	March 31 1940
Notes payable—bank.....................	...	...	...	$ 48,000
Notes payable—employees for bonuses......	...	...	...	4,840
Notes payable—Henry Stark...............	$ 32,000	...	...	...
Notes payable—trade....................	...	...	...	65,767
Accounts payable.......................	57,460	$136,723	$173,439	138,336
Accrued expenses.......................	...	3,440	7,194	902
Total current liabilities.............	$ 89,460	$140,163	$180,633	$257,845
Net worth.............................	70,886	98,530	123,600	128,999
Total liabilities....................	$160,346	$238,693	$304,233	$386,844

Case 13

Power Mowers, Inc.

IN EARLY January, 1957, Mr. Harold Harman, treasurer of Power Mowers, Inc., was working on a loan request to be presented in the following week to the company's bank of account, Hudson-Security Bank. Mr. Harman had to determine how large a loan to ask for, as well as the duration and type of the loan, and to appraise the likelihood of the bank's granting the loan.

Power Mowers, Inc., was a manufacturer of power lawn mowers for home and institutional use. The company had been founded in 1946 and had experienced a rapid growth in sales. Operations had been profitable in each year since 1948. Recent balance sheets and income statements are shown in Exhibits 1 and 2. Power Mowers, Inc., distributed its products through appliance and general line wholesalers and sold directly to large retailers. In addition, approximately 10% of annual production was sold under contract to a major mail-order house.

The power mower industry had become highly competitive in postwar years. There were over 200 manufacturers of power mowers in the country, but approximately 40 of them accounted for nearly 90% of industry sales in 1956. Numerous firms had failed in the past few years; and competitive conditions, if anything, were expected to intensify during the next few years.

During the last 3 years, Power Mowers, Inc., had undertaken a major expansion and modernization program aimed at providing the efficient production facilities that management considered vital to the company's survival in view of the competitive situation. Plant capacity had already been increased to a point sufficient to handle a volume of $25 million per year in anticipation of rapid growth in the demand for power mowers. It was expected that the company's expansion program would be completed in March, 1957, with the installation of new equipment costing $400,000.

The expansion program had been timely, inasmuch as forecasts indicated a 20% increase in the demand for power mowers in 1957. The management of Power Mowers, Inc., estimated that company sales would reach $18 million in 1957, an increase of approximately 21% over 1956 volume. Further sales growth of between $1 million and $2 million per year was expected in 1958–60.

The company's sales, like those of the industry as a whole, were highly seasonal. Over two thirds of annual sales commonly were made during the first 6 months of the year. Exhibit 3 shows the forecasted monthly pattern of sales in 1957 based upon the sales pattern of previous years. On the other hand, production was generally held relatively steady throughout the year. This policy was necessary to retain and give regular employment to the highly skilled workers required in the company's manufacturing operations. In 1956 the company had been able to maintain production at nearly an even rate throughout the year.

Power Mowers, Inc., had borrowed seasonally from Hudson-Security Bank for several years. These loans had been made under a line of credit arranged annually in January. The bank required that the loan be completely repaid and "off the books" for at least one month during the year.

In previous years, Power Mowers, Inc., had not experienced difficulty in obtaining seasonal loans and meeting loan requirements. Hudson-Security Bank had always readily granted the company's seasonal needs, which in 1956 had amounted to $3.5 million at the peak. Normally, the company began borrowing in early January and repaid its loans by mid-July.

However, in 1956 the company had been unable to liquidate its loan until mid-September and by late October had again required bank funds. At the end of 1956, the bank loan outstanding amounted to $1,620,000. Although the bank had not hesitated to extend this credit, its officers expressed disappointment at not being given greater forewarning of the continued need, particularly at a time when bank credit was in tight supply. They suggested that it would be helpful if Mr. Harman could plan his requirements during 1957 more carefully.

Mr. Harman was also disturbed by the unexpected increase in borrowing and what it might mean in terms of future requirements. Therefore, he began collecting data that might prove helpful in making his plans for 1957.

The company's nominal terms of sale were net 30 days. However, for competitive reasons, these terms were not strictly enforced, and invoices frequently were outstanding for considerably longer periods. Moreover, seasonal swings were experienced in collections, owing to fluctuating cash requirements of customers. Projected accounts receivable balances by months for 1957 are shown in Exhibit 3. In making these projections, Mr. Harman took into account the facts that additional smaller customers were expected to be added and that existing accounts were growing somewhat more lax in their payment schedules. The effect of these factors was difficult to calculate precisely; however, Mr. Harman included in his accounts receivable estimates some allowance for a probable slowing of payments.

Production was scheduled to be level throughout 1957 except for the 2 weeks beginning Monday, August 5, and Monday, August 12, when it was planned to shut down the plant for the annual paid-for vacation period. Materials purchases were scheduled at $750,000 per month, except for August, when purchases of $500,000 were scheduled. The company purchased its materials on terms of net 30 days. Depreciation expense of $500,000 was forecast for the year. Disbursements related to other overhead and labor were planned at $500,000 per month throughout 1957. Operating expenses were estimated at a total of $912,000 in 1957. Disbursements for operating expenses were expected to run fairly evenly throughout the year. Under current tax regulations, the accrued taxes outstanding on December 31, 1956, of $646,000 would be due and payable in equal instalments of $323,000 in March and June of 1957. In addition, payments each equal to 15% of the estimated federal income taxes on 1957 income were due in September and in December, 1957.

The new equipment, costing $400,000, was to be delivered in March. It would be paid for in four equal monthly instalments, beginning in March. Other smaller and recurring equipment expenditures were forecast at $20,000 per month throughout 1957.

In 1957 sales were forecast at $18 million, cost of goods sold at $14.9 million and operating expenses at $912,000. Mortgage loan interest of $172,000 was also anticipated. Profits before taxes were estimated at $2,016,000. Mr. Harman based his plans upon the expectation that a tax rate of 50% would apply during 1957.

In 1953 Power Mowers, Inc., had borrowed $4 million from a life insurance company under a 16-year mortgage loan secured by the entire plant and equipment. This loan was repayable in equal semiannual instalments in June and December in each year. Interest at the rate of 5% per annum on the unpaid balance was also payable at these dates. In his financial forecasting, Mr. Harman planned to treat differently the interest payments on the mortgage loan and on the bank loan. The two mortgage interest payments, totaling $172,000, due in 1957, would be shown separately in the cash flow and income projections. In contrast, bank loan interest payments had been roughly estimated and included in the total operating expense estimate of $912,000.

In 1956 the company had raised its annual dividend to stockholders to $1 per share, payable semiannually in March and September. Mr. Harman knew that the directors of Power Mowers, Inc., would be extremely reluctant to reduce the dividend as they wished to enhance the investment standing of the stock with a view to possible future equity financing. The directors regarded the company as too little known to sell stock at the present time. However, they hoped that another 2 or 3 years of profitable operation and growth might make an equity issue feasible.

As chief financial officer of the company, Mr. Harman had given considerable thought to the optimum cash position of his company. He had concluded that a cash balance of at least $500,000 should be maintained at all times. Furthermore, he believed that the deposit balances of $500,000 or more would satisfy the increasingly strong insistence of the bank that large business borrowers maintain substantial deposit balances at the bank.

On the basis of the plans outlined above, Mr. Harman asked an assistant to prepare a monthly cash flow forecast for 1957, which he hoped would indicate the amount and timing of the bank credit that Power Moters, Inc., would require. He also asked his assistant to prepare an estimated balance sheet for the company as of December 31, 1957. He suggested that his assistant assume no change in "other assets" or "miscellaneous accruals" from their year end, 1956, levels.

Exhibit 1
POWER MOWERS, INC.
BALANCE SHEETS AS OF DECEMBER 31, 1954–56
(Dollar Figures in Thousands)

	1954	1955	1956
Cash	$ 3,188	$ 729	$ 508
Accounts receivable	1,170	1,292	1,680
Inventory	1,972	2,280	2,960
Total current assets	$ 6,330	$ 4,301	$ 5,148
Plant and equipment (net)	6,341	8,483	9,439
Other assets	302	355	370
Total	$12,973	$13,139	$14,957
Bank loan	—0—	—0—	1,620
Accounts payable—trade	690	720	780
Reserve for federal income taxes	472	583	646
Miscellaneous accruals	79	121	138
Mortgage, current	250	250	250
Total current liabilities	$ 1,491	$ 1,674	$ 3,434
Mortgage payable	3,750	3,500	3,250
Common stock (500,000 shares @ $12.00 par)	6,000	6,000	6,000
Earned surplus	1,732	1,965	2,273
Total	$12,973	$13,139	$14,957

Exhibit 2

POWER MOWERS, INC.

INCOME STATEMENTS, 1954–56
(Dollar Figures in Thousands)

	1954	1955	1956
Net sales	$11,546	$12,791	$14,822
Cost of goods sold*	9,875	10,870	12,372
Gross profit	1,671	1,921	2,450
Operating expenses	727	755	834
Profit before taxes	944	1,166	1,616
Federal income taxes	472	583	808
Net profit	472	583	808
Common dividends	350	350	500
Retained earnings	122	233	308

* Includes straight-line depreciation of:
    1954...........$355
    1955...........$370
    1956...........$470

Exhibit 3

POWER MOWERS, INC.

ESTIMATED MONTHLY SALES AND MONTH-END
ACCOUNTS RECEIVABLES FOR 1957
(Dollar Figures in Thousands)

	Net Sales	Accounts Receivable End of Month
January	$ 1,240	$2,610
February	1,750	3,290
March	2,470	4,730
April	2,550	5,720
May	2,850	6,180
June	1,610	5,240
July	1,340	3,300
August	1,120	2,730
September	640	1,820
October	600	1,310
November	630	1,320
December	1,200	1,980
	$18,000	

Case 14

Trivett Manufacturing Company

In JULY, 1946, Eldon Brigham, treasurer of the Trivett Manufacturing Company, was reviewing the working capital position. It was his custom to calculate working capital needs for the next 6 months in January and July of each year and to formulate plans for meeting such needs.

The Trivett Manufacturing Company, which had been founded in 1934, operated a small machine shop in a Philadelphia suburb. The company had originally manufactured lapping plates and made gauges and special tools on order. In 1941 a newly designed industrial stapling machine was added to its line.

Operating losses and poor financial management had kept the company in financial difficulty during the greater part of its early history. Matters were made worse by a conflict which developed between the common and preferred stockholders. Inability of these two groups to agree had prevented the taking of corrective measures.

In the spring of 1942, this situation came to the attention of Mr. Brigham, a businessman who specialized in rehabilitating financially weak concerns. He analyzed the company and found that it had in its employ a number of skilled machinists and possessed good equipment suitable for precision work. Mr. Brigham was also impressed by postwar prospects for the company's stapling machine, which was far superior to competitive products. As a result of his analysis, Mr. Brigham concluded that with competent management the company could be operated profitably. The two stockholding groups were approached, and an agreement was worked out whereby Mr. Brigham became, in effect, head of the company. For his efforts, he was to receive a fixed salary plus a percentage of profits. Mr. Brigham, who was an officer of a number of other concerns, was to devote only part of his time to the Trivett Manufacturing Company.

During the war, Mr. Brigham concentrated on obtaining fixed fee Army contracts for the manufacture of precision instruments. Because of rigid economies which he instituted, these contracts proved highly profitable, even after renegotiation. Wartime profits and Mr. Brigham's skillful financial management soon rehabilitated the company. By the end of 1944 the deficit accumulated during many years of unprofitable operations had been eliminated.

The ending of hostilities in August, 1945, brought cancellation of the company's Army contracts. Mr. Brigham immediately took steps to curtail overhead and administrative expenses, but he retained the company's skilled machinists.

Sales and production efforts were concentrated on the industrial stapling machine. Prewar prices on the company's lapping plates had been about 50% less than for standard makes. As a result, the prices which the Office of Price Administration would permit the company to charge currently were set at a level that Mr. Brigham considered too low. Until a better price could be obtained, he did not intend to manufacture plates. Furthermore, since there was sharp price competition for gauge and tool work in the locality after V–J Day, Mr. Brigham decided that no effort should be made to seek this type of business for the time being.

Demand for the stapling machines was good. Monthly shipments during the first half of 1946 averaged about 75 units priced at $200 each. More units could have been sold and shipped, but Mr. Brigham did not wish to risk overextending the company while conditions were so unsettled.

Balance sheets and operating statements for 1944, 1945, and the first 6 months of 1946 are shown in Exhibits 1 and 2.

Early in May an invitation was received to bid on an Army contract for the manufacture of 301 gun sights. Mr. Brigham thought that a good profit could be made on the sights, and so he decided to submit a bid. His first bid of $720 a unit was rejected, but a second bid of $615 was accepted. One "pilot" sight was to be produced during August for the purpose of testing design and production methods. It was to be retained at the plant but invoiced on September 1 at $615. This experimental unit was to be manufactured from materials on hand. Direct labor for this model was estimated at $500. The lessons learned during the making of the first unit were expected to enable the company to start gun sight production at full scale about September 1. Production was expected to be maintained at a fairly constant rate until November 30. Delivery of the sights was to start the first week in October and was to be made at the rate of 100 units a month during October, November, and December.

Estimated per unit direct costs of producing the gun sight were as follows: labor, $242; material, $128.

In addition to the estimated direct labor cost of $242 per unit, Mr. Brigham estimated that the buildup of the additional labor force needed for gun sight production would require $2,500 in extra wage expense during August. Similarly, $3,000 of additional wage expense was budgeted for December so as to permit less abrupt reduction of the work force upon completion of the contract. Virtually all of the $3,000 would be paid out in the first 3 weeks of December.

To ensure against delays in delivery, Mr. Brigham intended to keep a minimum of one month's supply of raw material for the gun sight on hand at all times during the production period. Work-in-process inventory for gun sight production was expected to average $20,000 during the period of full-scale production. The great majority of the company's purchases were made on terms of net 30, and invoices were paid promptly when due. Wages were paid every Friday.[1] The production process from raw material to finished product was estimated to take a month. The Army would accept shipments in lots of 25 units, and payment would be received about 60 days after shipment.

Estimated per unit direct costs of producing the stapling machine were as follows: materials, $40; labor, $36. A minimum inventory of a 3 months' supply of raw material was currently considered necessary because of unsettled conditions. Work-in-process inventory for stapling machine production was expected to continue at the present level. All current inventory was usable. The length of the production process was 4 weeks. Units were shipped as soon as produced, and terms of sale were net 30. The company had a backlog of orders for 350 machines. Production and shipments, however, were expected to continue at the rate of about 75 units a month through the first quarter of 1947.

Monthly indirect expenses were currently running as follows: depreciation, $540; other factory overhead, $3,500; administration, $2,350. Tooling for the gun sight contract started in July. During July and August, tooling expenses and experimental manufacture of the pilot gun sight were expected to increase factory overhead by about $1,200 a month. Starting in September, when full-scale production of the gun sight was to begin, factory overhead was expected to become about $4,500 a month until the end of November. Administration expense was expected to increase to about $3,000 a month from September 1 to the end of December.

The Army contract had made necessary the purchase of $2,000 of special tools. Delivery of these tools was expected in August; payment terms were C.O.D. Upon completion of the contract, these tools would be scrapped. An additional $5,000 might also have to be spent for the replacement of old machinery which appeared to be nearing the end of its useful life. There was no way of knowing, however, when this machinery would finally break down. Mr. Brigham was confident that he could find replacements within a few days in the event of an emergency. The machinery to be retired was fully depreciated.

Mr. Brigham worked out a tentative purchase schedule for the various

---

[1] There were four paydays in July, five in August, four each in September and October, five in November, and four in December. At each payday, wages were paid for the current week.

material requirements. The schedule is reproduced as Exhibit 3. It shows the amounts of purchases in the months that they were expected to be booked.

The company maintained a small deposit account with a local bank and kept the remainder of its cash in an account with the Fourth National Bank of Philadelphia. The company had originally banked with the Farmers and Merchants Bank, a small local institution, from which it had borrowed from time to time during the war to help finance production on government contracts. Toward the end of the war, however, Mr. Brigham sensed that Mr. Appleseed, the bank's president, was becoming apprehensive about lending money to the company. Mr. Brigham attributed this reluctance to the fact that Mr. Appleseed had had little experience in lending money to industrial concerns; the greater portion of the bank's commercial loans were to local storekeepers. Therefore, Mr. Brigham withdrew his account from the bank. A small account was opened at another local bank, and the remainder of the company's funds were deposited with the Fourth National Bank of Philadelphia, a medium-sized bank with a legal loan limit of $150,000. Mr. Brigham had discussed the company's prospects in general terms with the bank's officers on a number of occasions, but he had never requested a loan.

Mr. Brigham considered his current cash balance of almost $28,000 to be in excess of operating needs. He was willing to reduce cash to a minimum of $5,000. No dividend payments were scheduled for the remainder of 1946.

It was Mr. Brigham's policy not to plan more than 6 months in advance, since he believed that it was impossible to predict with any accuracy what was going to happen for a longer period. The company's plans for the first half of 1947 would be made in the light of conditions as they developed and of the company's prospective financial condition at the end of 1946.

Exhibit 1

TRIVETT MANUFACTURING COMPANY

BALANCE SHEETS

ASSETS	Dec. 31, 1944	Dec. 31, 1945	June 30, 1946
Current assets:			
Cash	$ 12,982	$ 16,066	$27,753
Accounts receivable, net	48,107	29,583	19,593
Inventory	45,514	34,016	...
Raw material	...	...	13,134
Work in process	...	...	6,636
Prepaid items	725	1,179	325
Total current assets	$107,328	$ 80,844	$67,441
Fixed assets:			
Property account	$ 46,507	$ 47,153	$47,776
Less: Reserve for depreciation	14,534	19,916	21,057
Property account, net	$ 31,973	$ 27,237	$26,719
Total assets	$139,301	$108,081	$94,160

Exhibit 1 (Continued)

LIABILITIES AND CAPITAL	Dec. 31, 1944	Dec. 31, 1945	June 30, 1946
Current liabilities:			
Accounts payable	$ 27,668	$ 17,338	$ 9,066
Accrued liabilities	9,592	1,836	4,777
Reserve for previous year's federal taxes	8,172	4,891	12,095*
Reserve for current year's federal taxes	8,451	24,649	4,486†
Accrued taxes	6,381	2,736	1,812*
Total current liabilities	$ 60,264	$ 51,450	$32,236
Fixed liabilities:			
Due officers	13,834	...	...
Due U.S. government on contract advances	21,996	...	...
Capital:			
Preferred stock, 6%	21,000	21,000	21,000
Common stock, $100 par	17,000	17,000	17,000
Surplus	5,207	18,631	23,924
Total liabilities and capital	$139,301	$108,081	$94,160

* Payable in equal instalments, September 15 and December 15, 1946.
† Payable in equal instalments, March 15, June 15, September 15, and December 15, 1947.

Exhibit 2
TRIVETT MANUFACTURING COMPANY
OPERATING STATEMENTS

	Year 1944	Year 1945	6 Months Ending June 30, 1946
Sales, net	$282,888*	$331,575*	$86,966
Cost of sales:			
Material	$ 36,548	$ 97,065	$21,680
Direct labor	116,366	85,758	15,279
Depreciation	6,515	5,382	3,242
Factory overhead	52,842	47,940	20,514
Gross profit	$ 70,617	$ 95,430	$26,251
Less: Administration expense:			
Shipping expense	$ 9,561	$ 5,886	$ 235
Selling expense	10,442	7,480	...
Other expense	31,533	43,300	14,775
Net operating profit	$ 19,081	$ 38,764	$11,241
Other charges	308	521	
Net gain before federal taxes	$ 18,773	$ 38,243	$11,241
Less: Federal taxes	8,450	24,183	4,486
Net profit	$ 10,323	$ 14,060	$ 6,755

* After adjustment for renegotiation.

Exhibit 3
TRIVETT MANUFACTURING COMPANY
TENTATIVE SCHEDULE OF PURCHASES
July–December, 1946

	July	Aug.	Sept.	Oct.	Nov.	Dec.
Raw material—stapler	...	$ 1,994	$ 3,000	$ 3,000	$3,000	$3,000
Raw material—gun sight	...	12,800	12,800	12,800	...	...
Special tools—gun sight	...	2,000	...	...	...	...
Total	...	$16,794	$15,800	$15,800	$3,000	$3,000

Replacement machinery....$5,000 (uncertain date)

Case 15

Progressive Plastics, Inc.

In April, 1965, Mr. I. M. Handy, a former marketing manager of the Extruded Plastics Division of a large diversified chemical company, had succeeded in persuading friends to invest in a new firm, which he would call Progressive Plastics, Inc. As Mr. Handy put it, "I wanted to run a company myself, to oversee the full range of operations, not just marketing. Besides, from my previous vantage point, I had noticed attractive opportunities to produce plastic dinnerware—opportunities too small for my old company to bother with." Total commitments from friends amounted to $260,000, and Mr. Handy planned an additional $40,000 investment of his own. He decided to try to make this amount suffice, although two large investors had indicated that together they could supply an additional $50,000.

Fixed Asset Requirements

After an extended search, Mr. Handy had located a large industrial building in which two floors adequate for his needs could be leased. The necessary electric power and basic facilities already were available there.

Mr. Handy determined that his new firm could expect to achieve a sales level of approximately $200,000 a month by the end of the first year of the operation. He expected sales to remain at about this level for the next 2 or 3 years.

Mr. Handy sought to minimize equipment needs by planning to procure only three new compression molding machines. A fourth machine would be purchased in the used machinery market for a cost no more than half that of a new machine. The used machine would provide standby capacity to cover peak load requirements and breakdowns in the new machinery. To minimize investment in equipment, Mr. Handy planned to operate the new molding machines on a three-shift, 24-hour basis, even though labor on the second and third shifts would be paid somewhat higher hourly wages than for the first shift. Other fixed asset requirements consisted primarily of polishing and grinding machines for the finishing operation, materials handling equipment, and office equipment. Since the costs of the polishing and grinding machines for the finishing operation were modest, Mr. Handy determined to buy enough of these so that this part of the operation could be accomplished through single-shift operation, inasmuch as the prospective employees for this operation would be women who preferred to work daytime shifts. He estimated the total outlays for equipment would come to $263,000.

After intensive negotiation, Mr. Handy was able to arrange for deferred payment terms on the new molding equipment, so that a large percentage of the purchase price could be repaid over a 36-month period.

Working Capital

Mr. Handy decided to forecast his working capital requirements as of a date just after the company had reached its anticipated level of sales volume, which he believed would represent the time of greatest financial strain for the firm. Since this sales volume would be reached in approximately one year, he chose to project requirements as of one year after the company began operation. It would take some 3 months to get ready to begin production; so the balance sheet forecast would be made approximately 15 months in the future.

Mr. Handy wanted to operate with a level of inventory that would provide reasonable protections against both interruption in raw material flows and sudden spurts in sales. With this policy, he hoped to avoid production stoppages. No marked seasonal pattern in sales was anticipated, and he hoped to produce at a level rate once sales had plateaued.

Mr. Handy estimated that raw materials would amount to about 40% of the total cost of goods manufactured, which in turn would amount to about $150,000 a month once the $200,000 sales level was reached. Consequently, raw materials purchases would approximate $60,000 a month. After consideration, Mr. Handy decided to try to maintain a supply of raw materials equal to one month's usage.

The requirements for in-process inventory appeared small. In order to ensure that the labor in finishing the dinnerware would not be left idle by interruptions in molding, Mr. Handy resolved to carry an in-process inventory of about 3 days' output of the molding machines, representing about $12,000 in total value.

Mr. Handy planned to sell his tableware in sets of 30–60 pieces. Several different designs were to be employed, in each of which six basic colors would be used. These marketing requirements appeared to dictate a considerable stock of finished goods, inasmuch as the competitive situation demanded that the company have finished merchandise on hand for immediate shipment as orders were received from retail outlets. Mr. Handy first planned to carry a finished goods inventory equal to about one month's sales at cost, or $150,000. After consideration of the financial burden, however, he had to accept a lower target figure of 3 weeks' supply, or $113,000.

It was the custom in the trade to offer retailers 30-day credit terms. Even though most of the prospective customers were well-established, well-financed firms, some customers might be expected to be slow in payment. Accordingly, Mr. Handy projected his receivables investment as $1\frac{1}{3}$ month's sales, or $267,000.

Other asset requirements were expected to be minimal; Mr. Handy decided to make a $5,000 allowance for these.

Mr. Handy was conscious of his earlier assumption that there would be no seasonal fluctuation in sales. However, from experience he had learned that there would be some fluctuation in the rate of incoming orders and that unexpectedly slack periods of sales might well occur. To provide for such contingencies and also for routine fluctuations, Mr. Handy determined to maintain a bank account of $75,000, a figure equal to approximately 2 weeks' projected, normal expenditures. He would have felt much more comfortable with a larger figure, equal, say, to one month's expenditures. However, he had secured the categorical agreement of two investors to invest an additional $50,000 when, as, and if needed by the firm; so he had chosen to rely on this additional commitment as a contingent reserve of financial strength.

Source of Funds

The tabulation (Exhibit 1) of anticipated investment at the end of 15 months totaled $795,000. Armed with this estimate of likely gross requirements, Mr. Handy turned to the task of generating sufficient funds. First, he undertook a projection of profit and loss for the 3 months of organization and the 12 initial months of operation. After detailed calculation, he determined that the company would become profitable after about 6 months of operation and that in the second 6 months of operation the profits would be sufficient to recoup organizational costs and the losses of the first 6 months. Hence, the owners' investment would be intact by the time of the projected balance sheet. As indicated earlier, Mr. Handy had negotiated a special credit on the new equipment. After allowance for the down payment and for payments during the first year, an amount of $100,000 would be outstanding on the projected statement date. Accounts payable were expected to consist predominantly of payables for raw materials, but some additional supplies would also be bought on credit. The terms of purchase of the principal materials were net 30 days, so that Mr. Handy projected a figure of $70,000 as a normal level for accounts payable. Accrued expenses would consist largely of accrued rental and accrued wages. While these figures would fluctuate somewhat within the month, they would be generally at a level of about $25,000.

The projected sources totaled nearly $500,000, leaving approximately $300,000 of needs unmatched by sources.

Mr. Handy then investigated the possibilities of bank credit. He found that the local commercial banks were unwilling to make unsecured loans that would be outstanding continuously over a long period, but one bank was willing to make a revolving credit loan arrangement under which the bank would advance 80% of new receivables of firms of good quality. Since Mr. Handy planned to sell to only firms of good credit, he felt justified in projecting bank credit at $200,000, a figure almost 80% of the total receivables outstanding. Combining the "sources of funds" in the projected balance sheet, Mr. Handy found that he was still short $100,000. At this point, he had to face some unpalatable choices. He was reluctant to reduce the scale of the enterprise, since a smaller operation could expect to have little impact in the market and could not carry an adequate amount of advertising to support sales. Consequently, he resolved to take the chances of operating with a 2 weeks' stock of finished goods, thus reducing the finished goods investment by $38,000 to $75,000. Next, he considered other possibilities for credit. After investigation, he located a leading supplier of plastic powder, his principal raw material, who was willing to grant 60-day terms instead of the normal 30-day terms, provided Progressive Plastics' purchases were concentrated with his firm. This made possible an additional $60,000 of continuing credit, or a level of accounts payable of $130,000. A recasting of the projection of sources brought the total to $755,000. At this level, if the cash balance was reduced to $73,000, sources and uses would be equal.

On the face of the matter, it appeared that Mr. Handy had a feasible financial program. Yet he queried whether his financial plans made adequate allowance for unexpected needs and unforeseen problems.

Exhibit 1

PROGRESSIVE PLASTICS, INC.

PROJECTED BALANCE SHEETS, AS OF END OF FIRST YEAR OF OPERATION
(Dollar Figures in Thousands)

	Initial Projection	Revised Projection
Cash	$ 75	$ 73
Inventory:		
Raw materials	60	60
In-process	12	12
Finished goods	113	75
Accounts receivable	267	267
Plant and equipment	263	263
Miscellaneous assets	5	5
	$795	$755
Bank loan	$ —	$200
Accounts payable to suppliers	70	130
Accrued expenses	25	25
Notes payable—equipment supplier	100	100
Paid-in capital	300	300
Earned surplus	–0–	–0–
	495	755
Shortfall	$300	$–0–

Case 16

Illuminated Tubes Company

"HOWARD, it looks now as though they're really going to strike the set makers. Leonard Moore, head of purchasing over at Television Corporation of America (TCA), called me this morning. He said the union people walked out of the bargaining session last night. The way everyone's mad at everyone else, this could be a long, bitter strike. And I'm afraid we stand to lose more than anyone else. With our new rectangular color tube nobody can touch us. If sales kept on as they have recently, we could be the top picture tube maker in a couple of months. This strike couldn't have come at a worse time!"

On April 1, 1965, the day before an expected strike of the North American Electrical Workers against all the major television set manufacturers, Mr. Robert Morse, executive vice president of Illuminated Tubes Company (IT), expressed his irritation to an assistant, Howard Jones. In April, 1965, IT was one of three principal producers of color television picture tubes. (One of the others was also a major set manufacturer.) All of IT's sales were to the set makers for use in new sets. Since 1963 IT had increased its share of the market from 25% to 35%. IT's competitors had 50% and 15% of the market.

"There's just one thing that will save us," Mr. Morse continued. "We've got to hope that the set makers will try hard to settle early, in order not to miss out on this current sales boom. If they hold out long, the Japanese might improve their color sets and flood the market. If that happened, lost sales would be permanently lost, not just postponed.

"When I spoke to Len Moore, he said that as of the end of this week he'd have to temporarily cancel TCA's open order for color picture tubes. I'm sure we can expect the same word from the other makers, too, before the day is out. That means for the duration of the strike there will be virtually no sales at all. We're certainly going to have to reconsider our production plans.

"The big question in my mind is, how long will the strike last? If it doesn't go too long and no foreign sets enter the market, as soon as the set

716

manufacturers can start producing again they'll really want to push to make up lost sales. If that's the case, we're going to have to have the tubes ready, or we'll lose any chance of improving our market share. In fact, since we're operating near capacity now, if the set makers push up volume and we don't have the inventory, we could actually lose some of our market share. Our competitors still have a good deal of unused capacity.

"I'd like to continue operating at full capacity for other reasons, too. It can be very expensive to lay workers off. I'd hate to think of trying to get back to capacity if we had to recruit and train new glass workers. These people are pretty skilled, and there are other jobs in the glass industry. If our workers did not wait to be rehired by us, we'd have to look for new people.

"Then too, shutting down would hurt relations with our suppliers. We're the only customer some of them have, and if we shut down they might go out of business for good. We have a 30-day supply of materials on hand now and another 30 days' worth on order. We could cancel the outstanding orders, but there would be considerable expense in doing so in terms of financial penalties and damaged supplier relations."

"All you say sounds reasonable," Mr. Jones interjected, "so much so that I'm not sure there's any choice. The risks and costs of shutting down are too great; we've got to keep producing!"

"Howard, you're right, we've got to, but I'm not sure we can, or at least I'm not sure how long we can. That's why I said the length of the strike is crucial. I don't know how long an inventory buildup our finances can stand.

"Of course, if we were really in straitened circumstances, we might be able to borrow from our banks, but I shouldn't want to depend on that. We could never be sure until we actually needed it how much money we could get. Besides, by borrowing we might use up our last reserve of financial strength to meet possible future difficulties. In making our decisions, I think we'd better not consider borrowing money. Let's leave borrowing for when we really need it.

"Look, here are financial statements [Exhibits 1 and 2] for the last 2 years as well as for the quarter just ended. I wish you would try to figure how our cash position and overall financial position would be affected by continued operations. If we were to continue to operate at full capacity, see what would happen if the strike lasted 1, 2, or 3 months. Also, for those same time periods, see what our financial position would look like if we were to shut down immediately. Why don't you also determine our balance sheet position one month after the strike ends, after accounts receivable have had a chance to build up again? To begin, you can use these rough profit and loss statements I've worked up for a month's operations [Exhibit 3]; as long as the strike lasts, one month will look pretty much like the next. As you can see, I've forecast continued selling and administrative expenditures. Since strikes get settled, I can't see firing salesmen and secretaries and ruining the organization we've so painfully built up.

"Besides salary payments we can expect a cash drain from income tax payments of about $100,000 in April and $600,000 in June. However, we'll be able to claim a tax refund from the government equal to about half of our operating loss. I don't know how quickly the government will credit us with the cash, though. Until we check with our tax lawyers, we had better not count this tax loss as a source of funds."

With a sense of urgency, Howard Jones began to peruse IT's financial statements. Besides the suggestions Mr. Morse had made, he realized that if the strike lasted 3 months, the situation might be made more difficult by special cash needs in July. On July 1, $200,000 of the long-term debt would come due. In addition, it had also been the custom of IT's board to declare a dividend payable on the 15th of January, April, July, and October; for the last two quarters, IT had paid 25 cents a share. For his first projections he decided to assume that both the debt payments and dividends would be paid.

Exhibit 1
ILLUMINATED TUBES COMPANY

BALANCE SHEETS, AS OF DECEMBER 31, 1963 AND 1964, AND MARCH 31, 1965

(Dollar Figures in Thousands)

ASSETS		December 31, 1963	December 31, 1964	March 31, 1965
Cash		$ 2,012	$ 1,994	$ 1,718
Accounts receivable		1,543	1,829	2,128
Inventory				
Raw materials	$ 319		$ 372	$ 431
Goods in process	191		233	238
Finished goods	337		391	409
Total inventory		847	996	1,078
Total current assets		$ 4,402	$ 4,819	$ 4,924
Plant and equipment	$11,263		$12,741	$13,256
Less: Depreciation	2,010		2,792	3,082
Plant and equipment, net		$ 9,253	$ 9,949	$10,174
Total assets		$13,655	$14,768	$15,098
LIABILITIES AND NET WORTH				
Taxes payable		$ 830	$ 1,010	$ 1,050
Accounts payable and accruals		992	1,242	1,285
Dividends payable		150	250	250
Other current liabilities		429	372	220
Total current liabilities		$ 2,401	$ 2,874	$ 2,805
Long-term debt		2,700	2,300	2,300
Total liabilities		$ 5,101	$ 5,174	$ 5,105
Common stock, $5 par		5,000	5,000	5,000
Paid-in capital		2,659	2,659	2,659
Retained earnings		895	1,935	2,334
		$13,655	$14,768	$15,098

Exhibit 2

ILLUMINATED TUBES COMPANY

INCOME STATEMENTS, YEARS ENDED DECEMBER 31, 1963 AND 1964, AND 3 MONTHS
ENDED MARCH 31, 1965

(Dollar Figures in Thousands)

	Year Ended December 31, 1963	Year Ended December 31, 1964	3 Months Ended March 31, 1965
Net sales..............	$17,743	$21,175	$5,942
Cost of sales			
Materials.............$3,921		$4,734	$1,321
Direct labor.......... 3,038		4,104	1,236
Other................ 3,025		3,162	720
Total cost of sales..	9,984	12,000	3,277
Gross margin......	$ 7,759	$ 9,175	$2,665
Selling and administrative expenses*.............	4,424	5,000	1,413
Operating profit....	$ 3,335	$ 4,175	$1,252
Income tax.............	1,734	2,088	599
Net income........	$ 1,601	$ 2,087	$ 653

* Includes depreciation:
  $ 875 thousand in 1963
  $1,036 thousand in 1964
  $ 341 thousand for the first 3 months of 1965.

Exhibit 3

ILLUMINATED TUBES COMPANY

PROJECTED MONTHLY INCOME STATEMENTS

(Dollar Figures in Thousands)

	During Strike		After Strike	
	If Tubes Are Produced	If Factory Shuts Down	If Tubes Were Produced for Inventory	No Finished Goods Inventory Buildup
Sales........................	...	...	$2,500*	$2,000*
Cost of sales†				
Materials..................	...	...	$ 560	$ 450
Direct labor...............	...	...	520	420
Other....................	...	$300	310	300
Total cost of sales.....	...	$300	$1,390	$1,170
Gross margin................	...	($300)	$1,110	$ 830
Selling and administrative expenses‡..................	$400	400	400	400
Operating profit............(($400)		($700)	$ 710	$ 430
Income tax................	(200)	(350)	350	210
Net income................	($200)	($350)	$ 360	$ 220

* Assumes that sales with large finished goods inventories are 25% greater than they would be were
there no significant finished goods inventory to sell from.
  † Approximately $3.6 million of cost of sales at an annual rate is fixed no matter what volume is pro-
duced. If IT produces tubes for inventory, this $3.6 million is charged to inventory and is not an expense.
If nothing is produced, the $3.6 million cannot be charged to inventory and must be expensed.
  ‡ Includes $100 thousand of depreciation.

Case 17

Sprague Machine Tool Company

On September 20, 1951, Mr. Harry Greenwood, vice president of the Wolverine National Bank of Detroit, was examining the company's credit file on Sprague Machine Tool Company, a customer located in a nearby small city. Renewal of a $350,000 loan made to that company was to be considered by the loan committee the next day, and Mr. Greenwood was reviewing what had happened since the bank had taken on Sprague's account, so that he could decide what action he should recommend to the committee. The note had originally been a 9-month loan made in December, 1950, but the Sprague management was requesting a 90-day extension.

Since its establishment in 1900, Sprague had successfully weathered the cyclical fluctuations characteristic of the machine tool manufacturing business. Its peak production had been achieved during World War II, sales reaching $7,300,000 in 1943. From that year, however, sales had declined, reaching a low of $1,765,000 in 1947, and the sales volume had been below $3 million in each subsequent year through 1948. Sprague had come out of World War II with a strong working capital position; with volume reduced in subsequent years, it had had no need to borrow prior to December, 1950.

Mr. Greenwood recalled that in December, 1950, Mr. Robert G. Murray, president of Sprague, requested a loan of $350,000 to assist in purchasing the stock interests of several dissident stockholders. While Sprague Machine Tool Company at that time had some excess cash over that required for normal operations, even more cash was required for the stock purchase, and Mr. Murray had, therefore, requested the Wolverine National Bank to lend Sprague Machine Tool Company $350,000 for a period of 9 months. To justify the credit, Mr. Murray had submitted a monthly forecast of shipments for 1951 (Exhibit 1) and a balance sheet dated November 30, 1950 (shown in the first column of Exhibit 2). The Wolverine National Bank had agreed to make the loan, and in December,

1950, the company had retired 24,300 shares of its $10 par value stock purchased from its stockholders at an aggregate cost of $936,100. After this, there remained several hundred stockholders.

After the loan was made, Mr. Murray regularly sent the bank profit and loss statements and balance sheets. Mr. Greenwood selected the figures given on Exhibits 2 and 3 for use in his analysis.

The company manufactured machine tools which were sold to several metalworking industries but principally to automobile manufacturers and some aircraft manufacturers. These products were largely made to order; their sales prices ranged from $20,000 to $500,000 per installation. Sprague's selling terms were 30 days net. Occasionally, a customer placing a large order would make Sprague an advance payment to help finance the construction of the machines involved, which covered periods up to 5 or 6 months for some of the more complex types of machines. Upon completion and shipment of orders against which advances had been obtained, Sprague deducted the amount of the advance from the amount billed the customer.

On September 19, 1951, Mr. Greenwood had received a letter from Mr. Murray requesting a 90-day extension of Sprague Machine Tool Company's note. Mr. Murray's letter commented at some length on the company's financial condition and stated that the management expected to be able to pay off the note in full within 90 days. Mr. Murray's letter is set forth in full as Exhibit 4.

Exhibit 1
SPRAGUE MACHINE TOOL COMPANY
SHIPMENTS AT SELLING PRICE
(Dollar Figures in Thousands)

1951	As Forecast December, 1950	Actual	As Forecast September, 1951
Jan.	$434	$287	
Feb.	624	224	
Mar.	545	622	
Apr.	351	522	
May	431	291	
June	493	540	
July	496	241	
Aug.	599	169	
8 months' total	$3,973	$2,896	
Sept.	433		$721
Oct.	449		435
Nov.	437		468
Dec.	766		655

Exhibit 2

SPRAGUE MACHINE TOOL COMPANY

Balance Sheets

(Dollar Figures in Thousands)

	11/30/50	12/31/50	3/31/51	6/30/51	7/31/51	8/31/51
Cash	$ 855	$ 155	$ 214	$ 507	$ 652	$ 602
Accounts receivable, net	415	664	657	631	423	228
Inventories	867	883	1,158	1,092	1,208	1,588
Total current assets	$2,137	$1,702	$2,029	$2,230	$2,283	$2,418
Fixed assets	$1,301	$1,301	$1,301	$1,302	$1,302	$1,308
Less: Reserve for depreciation	998	1,002	1,011	1,018	1,018	1,022
Net fixed assets	$ 303	$ 299	$ 290	$ 284	$ 284	$ 286
Prepaid expenses	21	20	13	8	8	14
Total assets	$2,461	$2,021	$2,332	$2,522	$2,575	$2,718
Notes payable—bank		$ 350	$ 350	$ 350	$ 350	$ 350
Accounts payable	$ 116	117	227	133	207	316
Accruals	140	249	283	179	148	137
Reserve for federal taxes*—1950	138	154	108	63	63	63
—1951			112	218	242	277
Customer advance payments	280	280	280	522	522	522
Total current liabilities	$ 674	$1,150	$1,360	$1,465	$1,532	$1,665
Common stock	380	137	137	137	137	137
Surplus	1,407	734	835	920	906	916
Total liabilities	$2,461	$2,021	$2,332	$2,522	$2,575	$2,718

* 1950 federal income taxes payable in 1951: 30% of total on each of March 15 and June 15; 20% of total on each of September 15 and December 15. 1951 federal income taxes payable in 1952: 35% of total on each of March 15 and June 15; 15% of total on each of September 15 and December 15.

Exhibit 3
SPRAGUE MACHINE TOOL COMPANY

INCOME STATEMENTS

(Dollar Figures in Thousands)

	Year Ended 12/31/50	1950 Dec.	Jan.	Feb.	Mar.	Apr.	1951 May	June	July	Aug.	Eight Months Ended 8/31/51
Net sales.	$2,618	$517	$287	$224	$622	$522	$291	$540	$241	$169	$2,896
Cost of sales*	1,684	374	158	123	454	379	189	399	170	92	1,964
Gross profit.	$ 934	$143	$129	$101	$168	$143	$102	$141	$ 71	$ 77	$ 932
Selling and administration expenses.	564	107	49	32	97	83	47	68	40	31	447
Net profit before taxes.	$ 370	$ 36	$ 80	$ 69	$ 71	$ 60	$ 55	$ 73	$ 31	$ 46	$ 485
Provision for federal and state taxes.	154	16	41	35	36	29	28	46	24	36	275
Net profit.	$ 216	$ 20	$ 39	$ 34	$ 35	$ 31	$ 27	$ 27	$ 7	$ 10	$ 210
Dividends paid.	$ 14	.....	$ 7	.....	.....	.....	.....	.....	$ 21	.....	$ 28

* Includes depreciation charges of $28,000 in 1950, $4,000 in December, and $3,000 per month in 1951.

Exhibit 4

SPRAGUE MACHINE TOOL COMPANY

DEARBORN, MICHIGAN

September 18, 1951

MR. HARRY GREENWOOD, VICE PRESIDENT
WOLVERINE NATIONAL BANK
DETROIT, MICHIGAN

DEAR MR. GREENWOOD:

I enclose the company's August 31 financial statements. While our cash balance currently is $602,000, you will note that we have an obligation to a customer for cash advances of $522,000, and we expect to ship this order over the next 2 months. With respect to our note for $350,000 due September 25, we request that you renew our loan for another 90 days. At the end of that period, as you can see for yourself, we expect to be able to have enough cash on hand to retire our obligation in full.

For the past month or more, we have been producing at capacity and expect to continue at that rate through the end of the year. On August 31, our backlog of unfilled orders amounted to about $5,500,000. Our shipment schedule has been upset, particularly the last month or two, because we have had to wait on our suppliers for shipment of electrical control mechanisms; at August 31, we had seven machines with an accumulated cost of about $440,000 completed except for the installation of these electrical components. The components were finally received last week and will enable us to complete a number of machines in the next few days. The remainder of our work in process will probably stay at present levels for the foreseeable future because of our capacity rate of production. Our finished goods inventories are negligible at all times, since we ship machines within a day of completion.

We bought raw materials beyond our current needs in July and August to be assured of completing our orders scheduled to be shipped by December 31. Our purchases were $220,000 in July and $330,000 in August. We have, therefore, accumulated about $140,000 worth of scarcer components above our normal raw material inventories. The extra $140,000 will be used up by the end of the year, bringing our raw material inventories back to normal levels for capacity production. Because we have bought ahead this way, we expect to cut our purchases to about $200,000 a month in each of the four remaining months of 1951.

Our revised shipment estimates are as follows:

	(At Selling Prices)
September	$ 721,000
October	435,000
November	468,000
December	655,000
	$2,279,000

The shipment estimates include the $700,000 order for the Giant Automobile Company. We are now scheduled to ship against this order as follows: September $280,000, October $280,000, November $140,000. Since we obtained a $522,000 advance from Giant on this order, we will be due nothing on these shipments until their $522,000 credit with us is exhausted.

You will probably note the decline in our accrued expenses. As I mentioned to you last month when you visited us, we have been paying off commissions due our two principal salesmen (who are also large stockholders in the company). Last year when we needed funds to redeem part of our capital stock, these men agreed to defer their commissions until the funds could more easily be spared. In August, we paid off the last of these back commissions. This has been the principal cause of the decline in this item, which normally does not change much from month to month. Our outlay each month for all expenses other than materials should be around $136,000. This assumes that accruals will stay about the same as on August 31.

The business which we expect to ship in the next 4 months is on our books on profitable terms. While our profit, as you know, varies with the item involved, our engineering estimates indicate we will probably make a net profit (before taxes) of about 15% of sales on these items. Unfortunately, we shall be working mostly for Uncle Sam—we have already exceeded our excess profits tax credit and as a result our profits earned during the next four months will be taxed at 77% (normal tax plus excess profits tax).

We have spent very little on new equipment in the last 8 months. We will avoid buying new equipment in the next 4 months, unless breakdowns make it necessary to replace existing equipment.

Our profits for the year to date have been quite satisfactory, and toward the end of December we plan to pay a dividend to our stockholders. Our dividend disbursements in 1951 have been quite modest so far, and we want to be sure that those stockholders who stood by us last December have no cause to regret their action. Under the circumstances, we feel that a $50,000 dividend payable in December is the least we can do in view of our high earnings.

If there is anything further you need to know, please do not hesitate to write or phone.

Sincerely yours,
ROBERT G. MURRAY
President

Case 18

Storkline Shops

IN EARLY JANUARY, 1958, Mr. Barnes, the president of a small bank in Houston, Texas, was reviewing the latest loan request from Storkline Shops, a chain of retail stores specializing in maternity clothes and accessories. Mr. Barnes had handled the Storkline account since Mr. Richard Klein, owner and president of the business, first approached the bank in August, 1955, requesting $15,000 to finance the fall's seasonal needs. The initial loan request had been granted, and since that time the firm had experienced a persistent and increasing need for funds. This need had been met in part by the bank; and in early January, 1958, the proprietorship was borrowing $30,000. From the granting of the initial request to the present time, Storkline Shops had been in steady debt to the bank. Mr. Klein's most recent request was for an additional $10,000 to finance "unexpected inventory requirements" in the coming weeks. Before reaching a decision on this latest request, Mr. Barnes wanted to review developments in the account since it was opened in August, 1955.

Establishment of Storkline Shops—August, 1954

Mr. Klein founded Storkline Shops in the fall of 1954 with an initial investment of $15,000. Though he had no direct experience in the retailing of women's clothing and accessories, he had extensive experience in the merchandising and distribution of various other consumer goods. This experience, at both retail and wholesale levels, was gained with numerous companies throughout the Southwest. Deciding to enter a retail business of his own, he surveyed the many available alternatives and selected the maternity clothes line because he believed there was a unique and unfilled demand for a specialty shop in this field.

Mr. Klein started his business by opening three shops in the Houston area. Within the next 6 months, he added five more shops, one in Houston and four in other large Texas cities. Mr. Klein performed all the buying for his shops by visits to Eastern fashion shows. He also planned all the merchandising, pricing, and advertising programs for the chain as a whole, as well as working out in detail the specific interior design and merchandising plans for each shop location. Each shop was staffed by one or two women, selected by the owner himself for their experience, appearance, and sales ability. Storkline shops owned no store locations; each store was leased on a 2- to 3-year basis at annual rentals averaging about $3,300.

As was typical in the ladies' ready-to-wear business, sales mounted seasonally during the spring and during the fall. Sales were on a cash-and-carry basis, and there was little investment in fixed assets. The main investment of the business was in retail inventory; a broad line of clothing and accessories had to be maintained to service the seasonal buying habits and changing fashion requirements of customers. In preparation for peak selling seasons, retail inventories were usually built up by March 15 and September 30 of each year. Mr. Klein also carried a line of accessories in his chain of stores, with such items amounting to approximately 15% of retail sales and inventory value. Most maternity garment makers sold to Storkline on terms 8/10 E.O.M. or a negotiated net price due 10 days E.O.M. Accessories were typically purchased on terms ranging from 2/10, net 30 to 8/10, net 30.

The Initial Loan—August, 1955

In his initial request for a loan in August, 1955, Mr. Klein reported that his operations were very satisfactory for the first 6 months of 1955 and submitted to the bank his most recent operating statement and balance sheet (see Exhibits 1 and 2). The early operations were attributable primarily to the first three Houston stores, as the other stores had been in operation for only 2 or 3 months. In addition to his proprietorship in Storkline Shops, Mr. Klein owned a building in the Houston area with a market value of $60,000, against which he had a mortgage of $40,000. He also had other miscellaneous assets of an approximate value of $15,000. Mr. Klein emphasized the unique appeal of a maternity wear specialty shop and the limited competition in this line of retailing. After some study, Mr. Barnes decided that his bank could accommodate the young and growing organization and granted the company a $15,000 loan, with the understanding that it was to be repaid by the end of 1955. Recognizing Mr. Klein's aggressiveness and zest for expansion, Mr. Barnes obtained his assurance that he would open no new outlets without first consulting the bank.

Developments during the First 6 Months of 1956

On a visit to the bank in January, 1956, Mr. Klein brought with him the company's financial statements for the full year 1955 (see Exhibits 1 and 2). Mr. Klein explained that the year-end inventory was $8,000 greater than anticipated, because sales in November and December had not been up to expectations. Looking ahead to the first half of 1956, Mr. Klein expected that sales would reach $223,000, earnings before drawings and taxes would be $35,000, and the inventory would peak in March at about $75,000 and be reduced to $29,000 by June 30. Though the loan balance as of the end of the year had remained at $15,000, as shown in Exhibit 3, it was paid down to $10,000 on January 2. In order to pay personal income taxes coming due, Mr. Klein requested renewal of the $10,000 and that an additional $10,000 be loaned to the proprietorship. Based on his 6-month estimates, Mr. Klein felt there would be no problem in paying all indebtedness by June 30. Mr. Barnes granted this loan request with the understanding that a cleanup would be accomplished as planned.

During the following month, Mr. Klein again visited the bank and requested an added $5,000. The proprietor of Storkline Shops reported that he had opened an additional Houston store during the latter part of January and was interested in another location in a Dallas suburb. He wanted the added $5,000 to purchase the inventory presently stocked at this suburban location and to take over operation of the shop. Mr. Klein said that his earlier estimate of net profits for the first 6 months of 1956 now appeared very conservative. The request for an additional $5,000 was granted, but Mr. Barnes cautioned that the notes had to be paid by June 30 and no new shops were to be added until figures for the first half of the year were available.

Developments during the Last 6 Months of 1956

By late July the chain of stores and locations had increased to 13 with an aggregate annual lease expense on these locations amounting to approximately $39,000. In a visit to the bank during July, Mr. Klein stated that the minimum basic inventory to support the present sales level of his company amounted to about $50,000. Though the business was unable to clean up its bank debt by June 30, it had been able to meet $9,000 of a $10,000 note, and thus had reduced the loan balance to $16,000 by June 30 (Exhibit 3).

Financial statements for the first 6 months of operations in 1956 were received by the bank in mid-September (see Exhibits 1 and 2). Shortly afterward, Mr. Klein requested a renewal of the $16,000 loan and asked for an additional $9,000 to finance the rising seasonal inventory, which he estimated would reach $75,000 at the end of September (see Exhibit 2). He reported that profits before drawings for July through October were running some $5,000 to $8,000 per month. Mr. Barnes granted the request for additional funds on a promise that a cleanup would be made before December 31.

Developments during the First 6 Months of 1957

In early January, 1957, Mr. Klein again visited the bank, bringing an estimated balance sheet as of the end of 1956. Though his inventory had been up to about $87,000 at the end of October, Mr. Klein believed he had reduced it to about $56,000 by the end of the year. A year-end audit was currently under way in each store. Though he had been unable to clean up his bank debt, as earlier arranged, Mr. Klein pointed out that his profits had been better than expected, and that net working capital had increased since June 30 by $18,000. Mr. Klein also volunteered information about the small manufacturing operation he had started in late 1956 in order to reduce his cost of purchases. The proprietor said that he was doing his own design and cutting work but that sewing was being contracted with a local concern. Mr. Klein estimated that during the fall of 1956, his manufacturing operation netted about $3,700 before drawings and taxes. The proprietor said he planned to manufacture only for the retail side of his business and that he hoped to provide perhaps three fifths of his retail needs for spring sales from this source. Since he was doing this manufacturing, he would need to borrow earlier than would have been necessary with a pure retail operation. As a result, the proprietor wanted to renew the outstanding $10,000 note and to borrow an additional $10,000 to finance the purchases of the piece goods inventory. Since Mr. Klein had continued to generate a growing profit, Mr. Barnes granted this request for funds.

In mid-February, 1957, the bank received the operating and financial statements for 1956 (see Exhibits 1 and 2), accompanied by a memo from Mr. Klein that he had opened up three new locations, one in Houston and two in suburban areas of other Texas cities, bringing the total number of locations to 16. After discussing the 1956 results with Mr. Barnes a few days later at lunch, Mr. Klein asked for an additional $15,000 to finance peak inventory needs for the spring season. He reported that his present inventory amounted to about $80,000, of which $50,000 was staple retail merchandise. The added $15,000 would bring borrowings to a new high of $35,000 (see Exhibit 3), but Mr. Klein believed this amount was required to get over the seasonal hump. With the agreement that all notes would be repaid by June 30, the request was granted.

In mid-April Mr. Klein called to report that his 3-month operations to March 31 had been very successful; sales had been $155,000, and profits before drawings and taxes were $11,700. Of this profit, $2,000 was from retail operations and $9,700 from manufacturing. Retail sales for the coming 3 months were estimated at $180,000, which, in combination with tight control of purchases, would draw down retail inventory to $60,000 by June 30. Upon inquiry, Mr. Klein said that his present inventory amounted to $101,000, of which $17,000 was in piece goods (see Exhibit 2). Mr. Klein said that he still believed there would be a cleanup of his notes by June 30, 1957, as agreed to earlier.

Developments during the Last 6 Months of 1957

In July, 1957, Mr. Barnes noted that Storkline had reduced its notes only to $15,000 at midyear (see Exhibit 3). In discussing the plans for the fall season with Mr. Klein in early September, Mr. Barnes learned that the company had now expanded to 18 locations and operations for the fall season were mounting. Retail sales for August had reached about $40,000; and for September and October together, Mr. Klein expected volume to reach $100,000. Mr. Klein said he was also selling manufactured products to a few select outside customers. Mr. Klein expected his retail inventory to peak by the end of August, and a request for an additional $5,000 was granted. Financial statements for the seven months ending July 31 were recorded during this visit (see Exhibits 1 and 2).

In mid-October, the bank received a financial statement as of September 30, indicating inventory had mounted to $130,900, of which $98,600 was in retail goods (see Exhibit 2). Mr. Klein appended a note to this statement, stating that he expected his retail inventory to be reduced to $65,000 by the end of the year.

In talking with Mr. Barnes in mid-December, Mr. Klein argued that a $65,000 minimum inventory level was unrealistic for the present size of his business. Mr. Klein considered a more appropriate figure to be in the vicinity of $90,000. During this visit, Mr. Klein requested an additional $10,000 loan to finance the acquisition of piece goods inventory for the manufacturing operations and early purchasing for spring retail needs. Mr. Klein emphasized how very profitable the manufacturing operations were becoming and considered this part of his business to have special promise. Storkline's proprietor assured Mr. Barnes that the $10,000 note, bringing the company's indebtedness to $30,000, would be adequate for seasonal requirements, and the request was granted.

The Latest Request—January, 1958

In mid-January, 1958, Mr. Klein brought to the bank a report of his 5-month operations since August 31, 1957, and a year-end balance sheet (see Exhibits 1 and 2). In discussing future operations, Mr. Klein predicted that the manufacturing side of the business would have sales of $300,000 during the first 6 months of 1958. Storkline's spring line was being very well received, and many additional customers were actively interested in purchasing the line. He said he was now manufacturing 60% of his own requirements, in addition to selling to a few leading department stores and chains. He added that he was able to do a much larger volume in the manufacturing side of the business than at present but that in compliance with the bank's suggestion he was moving slowly in accepting orders from outside concerns. He further reported that although national retail sales of maternity clothes during 1957 had dropped some 20% from the 1956 level, Storkline Shops had maintained sales at the 1956 level. Because of the exceptional progress since the beginning of his business in 1954, and the cooperation the bank had given him throughout that period, Mr. Klein hoped that the bank would be pleased to meet his current needs. In this regard, the proprietor wanted an additional $10,000 to finance payment of some maturing bills for piece goods.[1] Mr. Klein believed that he would have no difficulty in completely liquidating his bank debt by midsummer. Whereas in previous years his profits had depended heavily upon the retail side of the business, Mr. Klein pointed out the keen buyer interest and lucrative profits being generated in the designing and manufacturing operation. He added in parting that the added credit would very much improve his ability to repay all notes by midsummer. Since total loans of $40,000 would permit expansion of the highly profitable manufacturing operations, Mr. Klein thought that the cash generated from these operations in the next 6 months would be more than enough to liquidate all bank debts.

[handwritten margin note: Unrealistic / would have / to cut invent / & not pay A.P. / to meet loan.]

---

[1] Garment makers usually purchased piece goods on terms of 2/10 E.O.M. or on the basis of a negotiated price due net 60.

Exhibit 1

STORKLINE SHOPS

Operating Data for Selected Periods

(Dollar Figures in Thousands)

	First 6 Months 1955	12 Months 1955	First 6 Months 1956	12 Months 1956	First 7 Months 1957		Last 5 Months 1957	
					Retail	Manufacturing	Retail	Manufacturing
Net sales	$107.5	$260.1	$199.0	$425.7	$283.0	$96.0†	$231.1	$117.0‡
Cost of goods sold	58.0	135.0	107.2	226.1	n.a.	n.a.	115.0	75.0
Gross profit	49.5	125.1	91.8	199.6	n.a.	n.a.	116.1	42.0
Operating expenses*	37.2	97.1	77.7	163.4	n.a.	n.a.	85.1	17.0
Net profit	12.3	28.0	14.1	36.2	13.8	17.4	31.0	25.0
Withdrawals during period	6.2	8.5	6.2	18.5	$20.3	...	...	...
Reinvestment of withdrawals, end of period	6.0	1.0	0.1	13.1	...	...	$3.0	...
* Includes: Depreciation	n.a.	3.4	n.a.	6.9	n.a.	n.a.	n.a.	n.a.
Store rentals	n.a.	15.2	n.a.	37.5	30.4	...	26.0	...

† $3,000 to outside customers in the first 7 months of 1957.

‡ $47,000 to outside customers in the last 5 months of 1957.

Exhibit 2

STORKLINE SHOPS

Selected Balance Sheets

(Dollar Figures in Thousands)

ASSETS	Audited 6/30/55	Audited 12/31/55	Audited 6/30/56	Estimated 9/30/56	Audited 12/31/56	Estimated 4/15/57	Audited 7/31/57	Estimated 9/30/57	Estimated 12/31/57
Cash	$ 4.6	$ 8.6	$10.9	$16.0	$ 4.4	$ 6.0	$ 8.4	$ 14.0	$ 8.0
Accounts receivable	…	…	…	…	2.8	…	2.2	8.3	30.1
Inventory									
Retail	27.0	48.2	57.9	75.0	64.5	84.0	77.2	99.9	105.0
Piece goods	…	…	…	…	1.0	17.0	25.0	31.0	41.0*
Current assets	$31.6	$56.8	$68.8	$91.0	$ 72.7	$107.0	$112.8	$153.2	$184.1
Machinery, fixtures, equipment (net)	13.6	17.7	20.7	n.a.	30.6	n.a.	32.3	31.2	35.0
Miscellaneous assets	2.1	2.7	7.7	n.a.	4.1	n.a.	4.1	4.3	2.1
Total assets	$47.3	$77.2	$97.2	n.a.	$107.4	n.a.	$149.2	$188.7	$221.1
LIABILITIES									
Notes payable—bank	…	15.0	16.0	25.0	10.0	35.0	15.0	20.0	30.0
Notes payable—others	3.1	1.1	2.6	…	1.7	…	…	…	…
Accounts payable	10.7	11.0	22.2	26.0	15.1	22.0	35.2	42.6	40.1
Accruals	2.7	4.9	3.2	2.0	4.5	3.0	12.0	14.5	11.0
Current liabilities	$16.5	$32.0	$44.0	$53.0	$ 31.3	$ 60.0	$ 62.2	$ 77.1	$ 81.1
Net worth	30.8	45.2	53.2	n.a.	76.1	n.a.	87.0	111.6	140.0
Total liabilities	$47.3	$77.2	$97.2	n.a.	$107.4	n.a.	$149.2	$188.7	$221.1
Data received and recorded by the bank	8/16/55	1/25/56	9/13/56	9/21/56	2/17/57	4/18/57	9/2/57	10/11/57	1/13/58

* Includes $15,000 finished goods held by manufacturing operation against firm orders.

Exhibit 3

STORKLINE SHOPS

RECORD OF BALANCE OF NOTES PAYABLE—BANK
(End of Month)
(Dollar Figures in Thousands)

	1955	1956	1957
January	—	$20	$20
February	—	25	35
March	—	25	35
April	—	25	35
May	—	25	25
June	—	16	25
July	—	16	15
August	$11	16	15
September	15	25	20
October	15	25	20
November	15	16	20
December	15	10	30

Case 19

Long Beach Electronics Company, Inc.

On September 19, 1962, Mr. Roy Johnson, an assistant vice president of the Community National Bank of Long Beach, California, was considering the position he should adopt on the request of Long Beach Electronics Company, Inc. (LBEC) for additional funds. The following day, Mr. Arthur Smith, LBEC's treasurer, was due at the bank at Mr. Johnson's invitation to discuss the company's prospects and financial requirements for the coming year. A week earlier, Mr. Smith had explained that he expected at least a 20% sales increase in fiscal 1963, provided Community National was willing to increase the existing $200,000 short-term credit by no less than $25,000 and perhaps as much as $50,000.

Mr. Johnson had only recently taken on the LBEC account, along with several other loan situations, after the promotion of one of his colleagues, Mr. Jack Ray. In order to get an overall understanding of the situation, he had scanned the material in the company's credit folder and had talked briefly with Mr. Smith. As he prepared to examine the LBEC loan situation in greater depth, Mr. Johnson planned to consider particularly carefully his predecessor's repeatedly expressed view that, ultimately, the bank would be forced to take a firm position against further credit extensions to a company which he considered undercapitalized. While Mr. Ray acknowledged that such action would almost certainly choke off the company's rapid growth and might even place LBEC in a disadvantageous position vis-à-vis equally rapidly growing competitors, he had stressed his conviction that sound banking practice precluded the indefinite substitution of bank debt for equity in a growing company. Mr. Johnson wondered whether the time to take such a firm position had arrived.

Company Background

LBEC had been incorporated in 1932 as La Salle Radio Co., Inc., owned equally by Mr. James La Salle and Mr. Howard Fiske. Through

735

World War II, the company had functioned primarily as a retailer of radios, radio tubes, and parts, and related electrical equipment, with sales being made to the general public and to a growing number of individuals interested in radio as a hobby. With the purchase of Mr. La Salle's ownership interest by Mr. Arthur Smith late in 1946, the complexion of the company, whose annual sales had hitherto never exceeded $100,000, began to change. By 1962 sales to the general public accounted for a very minor portion of the company's revenues, which now were derived primarily from the industrial distribution of nationally known lines of such electrical and electronic parts and supplies as semiconductors, vacuum tubes, capacitors, and laboratory test equipment. LBEC's 1962 industrial catalog listed more than 25,000 individual items within 12 broad product lines. Sales were made to both very large and very small electronic and aerospace companies in the greater Los Angeles area on the customary terms of 2% 10 net 30 days.

LBEC's president, Mr. Howard Fiske, 53, took an especial interest in the areas of purchasing and inventory control. Prior to founding the company in 1932, Mr. Fiske had been a purchasing agent for a medium-sized electrical parts producer. Mr. Smith, 60, had the title of treasurer but was active in general management and sales as well as in finance. In addition to their investment in LBEC, both men had some assets outside LBEC. Mr. Fiske's liquid savings, the equity in his home, and the cash surrender value of his life insurance were estimated to total $75,000. A June, 1962, statement showed Mr. Smith's "outside" net worth as approximately $100,000 in marketable securities, savings, equity in his home and one other piece of property, and cash surrender value of his life insurance. LBEC carried $100,000 worth of "key man" life insurance on each of the partners under a program instituted in 1954. Community National's files contained a notation by Mr. Ray that the amount of insurance currently carried would be inadequate for full payout of one of the two ownership interests.

LBEC's year-end figures were audited by Harold Wadsworth & Co., a small but very reliable firm of CPA's. The firm also assisted in the compilation of quarterly financial figures. In addition, Mr. Harold Wadsworth, the senior partner, was frequently consulted by Mr. Fiske and Mr. Smith on major financial decisions.

Bank Relationship

The borrowing relationship between LBEC and Community National began in 1952 with a $2,500, 30-day loan to help the company finance an unexpected and very temporary inventory buildup. Following the prompt repayment of this initial loan, the company began to borrow regularly from the bank in relatively small but ever increasing amounts as working capital needs outstripped its cash generation ability. Borrowing by LBEC took the form of 90-day renewable notes up to a maximum amount established on a yearly basis by the bank. Borrowings were guaranteed by Mr. Smith and Mr. Fiske. The interest rate was usually $1\frac{1}{2}\%$ above prime, and in 1962 was 6%.

In early 1955 LBEC asked Community National to participate in the financing of the construction of a new warehouse on land adjacent to the company's existing facilities. Title to the new $90.000 property ($30,000 for land and $60,000 for the building) would be held by a wholly owned LBEC subsidiary, Long Beach Realty Co., to which LBEC would pay rent sufficient for maintenance, taxes, interest, other expenses, and debt retirement. After considerable negotiation, Mr. Fiske and Mr. Smith agreed to invest an additional $22,500 in the form of subordinated debt in LBEC, whereupon Community National agreed to a $45.000, 10-year 6% mortgage loan to Long Beach Realty Co., which had only a nominal capitalization, and to lend $22,500 at 5% on a 5-year term basis to LBEC. Both the mortgage and the term loan were fully guaranteed by Messrs. Fiske and Smith. The bank also agreed to continue to make short-term advances to LBEC, over and above the $22,500 term loan, as necessary.

Through fiscal 1959, the total amount owed to Community National by LBEC never exceeded $30,000 (see Exhibit 1, page 744). In the fall of 1959, however, Mr. Smith had advised that the company might require as much as $90,000 of additional bank financing during fiscal 1960. Mr. Smith attributed this need to two factors. First, LBEC's sales had increased steadily in the past several years to slightly less than $1 million in 1959 (see Exhibit 2) and Mr. Smith anticipated a further growth to as much as $3 to $4 million annual volume within the next 4 to 5 years. Second, the prices quoted by electronics parts distributors within the greater Los Angeles area for any given item tended to fall within a relatively narrow range, since most industrial customers, particularly the larger companies, obtained quotations periodically from a number of sources in order to obtain the lowest possible price. With virtual price equality among distributors, then, individual suppliers were forced to compete primarily on the basis of prompt delivery and were therefore required to maintain large inventories. Recently, LBEC's management had completed an exhaustive study of the relative profitability of each of the 20 product lines traditionally carried by the company, and the decision had been made to concentrate exclusively on the 12 most profitable lines. Nevertheless, Mr. Smith stated, given a continuation and very probable intensification of present competitive pressures, LBEC would almost certainly be forced to increase its inventory investment substantially, perhaps by as much as $50,000.

Mr. Smith had explained to the bank that, despite the very technical nature of the material involved, the danger of inventory obsolescence was relatively slight. As he explained LBEC's arrangements, most suppliers would either take back inventory at cost price if it had not moved for 6 months or would take it back at any time if twice as much new inventory, in dollar terms, was ordered at the same time. Mr. Smith explained that it was always possible to follow the latter approach by ordering fast-moving items. The small part of the inventory not covered by these arrangements did occasionally show losses, but Mr. Smith pointed out that LBEC obtained considerable public relations value from its policy of giving away such merchandise to radio enthusiasts and hobbyists.

After careful consideration of Mr. Smith's presentation, Community National had agreed to increase the company's borrowing line, not to $120,000 but to $90,000, on the basis of a year-end fiscal 1959 net worth of slightly more than $175,000 and an approximately equivalent amount in working capital. At the same time, Mr. Smith acknowledged the importance of making some paydown of the loan. In view of his expectation that the concentration on the more profitable product lines would boost the company's profit from approximately $15,000 in 1958 and 1959 to a $40,000 to $50,000 level within the next year or so, he agreed to a bank proposal that at the end of 6 months (i.e., in March, 1960) the outstanding bank debt would be put on a demand basis with equal monthly instalments sufficient to pay out the loan over a 3-year period.

In actuality, despite a close watch over expenses, the anticipated profit level failed to materialize, and LBEC was not able to begin a payout of the loan. Since the loan limit of $90,000 was insufficient to permit LBEC to take account of purchase discounts, Community National agreed in December, 1960, to allow the company to borrow an additional $25,000. At this time, the bank indicated its willingness to continue lending to LBEC on 90-day renewable notes, reviewing the situation periodically, with the understanding that the company would not be in a position to go out of debt for several years.

Late in 1961 LBEC approached Community National with a twofold loan request. In a memorandum to the bank, Mr. Smith explained that for the past several months, LBEC had been stretching its trade payables in order to support a sudden bulge in its receivables. He reported that it had become the custom in the trade to carry customers' accounts beyond the formal credit terms, and LBEC was reluctantly following this practice in order to remain fully competitive with other distributors in the area. Accordingly, LBEC was losing substantial income by passing discounts. As an example, Mr. Smith pointed to approximately $40,000 in bills outstanding on which $700 in discounts could have been earned had they been paid on the December 10 discount date. In addition, concluded Mr. Smith, overdue payables presently amounted to $60,000, of which $10,000 were over 30 days past due, so that LBEC's credit rating was in danger of serious deterioration.

Mr. Smith also explained that the big expansion in volume since 1955 was seriously taxing LBEC's existing warehouse space, and if adequate financing could be arranged, he and Mr. Fiske would construct a $70,000 addition to the existing facility in the spring of 1962. Mr. Smith wondered if it might not be possible to combine this expansion with LBEC's continuing working capital problem and to arrange a $150,000, 10-year term loan to Long Beach Realty Co. This would let Long Beach Realty repay the outstanding balance of the original $45,000 mortgage to Community National, construct the new facility, and still, according to Mr. Smith's calculations, advance approximately $40,000 to LBEC. As security, Long Beach Realty Co. could offer the original building, which had recently been assigned an "available market value" of $110,000 and a "reasonable market value" of $70,000 by an independent appraiser, plus the $70,000 addition, or a possible total value of $180,000. According to Mr. Smith, a major insurance company had expressed a willingness to consider such a term loan, incorporating an 18- to 24-month delay in the initiation of sinking fund repayments.

In view of LBEC's pressing working capital needs and in anticipation of more permanent financing, Community National agreed on January 6, 1962, to increase the company's borrowing capacity by $60,000 to $175,000. Shortly thereafter, the insurance company decided against a term loan. However, a regional business development corporation expressed an interest in the situation provided Community National was willing to participate in the credit. After a week of intensive study and negotiation, the bank agreed to participate equally with respect to both amount and maturity in a $100,000, 10-year 6% first mortgage on the property, and the business development corporation agreed to supply alone an additional $50,000, secured by a second mortgage on the property.

Shortly after the new facility was started, construction costs spurted because of the need to protect the building's foundation against an unsuspected structural fault in the underlying rock. By the time the "$70,000 facility" was completed in April, 1962, it had cost well over $95,000. Accordingly, the amount which Long Beach Realty could advance to LBEC dwindled from the original figure of $40,000 to roughly $15,000. At a May meeting with representatives of Community National and the regional business development corporation, it was decided to retain the $15,000 of "excess" funds in the Long Beach Realty corporate entity to provide a reserve against any future contingencies arising out of the rock fault. At the same meeting, Community National agreed to increase LBEC's borrowing capacity by an additional $25,000 to $200,000 to alleviate the company's continuing cash shortage.

Mr. Johnson's Preliminary Impressions

As he scanned the material in the company's credit folder, Mr. Johnson noted that his predecessor, Mr. Ray, had repeatedly cautioned Mr. Smith that ultimately the bank would be forced to a firm position of "this much credit—no more!" with LBEC. In an August, 1962, meeting, for instance, Mr. Ray had pointed out that while working capital had grown over the past 5 years, the company's indebtedness had more than tripled, and that this was as far as Community National would like to see it go. Putting it another way, Mr. Ray had explained to Mr. Smith that, in 1958, LBEC's indebtedness was $124,000 and working capital was $149,000. At that time, only $0.25 would have had to be realized on each dollar of inventory in order to repay the company's total indebtedness. At the end of fiscal 1962, however, total indebtedness was $360,000 and net working capital was only $226,000. At this time, $0.47 would have to be realized for each dollar of inventory in order to liquidate total indebtedness.

Mr. Smith and Mr. Ray had explored the possibility of an additional equity investment in the company, in the form of either common stock or subordinated debt. Mr. Smith had explained that he and Mr. Fiske had agreed upon equal ownership interests in LBEC. While Mr. Smith was willing to contribute additional equity, Mr. Fiske was not yet in a position to do so, primarily as a result of having incurred exceptionally heavy medical expenses during his wife's recent serious illness. With Mr. Fiske unable to convert any of his remaining personal assets at the present time, an equity contribution by Mr. Smith would result in an imbalance in the ownership interests and would almost certainly cause personal friction between the two men.

In recognition of the bank's cooperation over the years, both Mr. Smith and Mr. Fiske were willing to discuss with a well-known investment banking firm the possibility of raising additional equity through a small public offering. At the meeting Mr. Smith had explained that the 1962 income statement contained a number of nonrecurring expenses caused by the installation of the enlarged warehouse operation, rearrangement of the inventory, and the establishment of an improved system of inventory control. Mr. Smith was fully confident that 1963 and succeeding years would see a net profit of well over $50,000 on a 10% to 20% sales increase. Noting these expectations and LBEC's rather erratic earnings record during recent years, the investment banker had strongly advised that any public offering be postponed for several years in order to give LBEC an opportunity to establish a favorable earnings trend.

After this meeting, Mr. Smith had acknowledged the bank's reasonableness in terms of conservative loan policy but had urged Mr. Ray to go along with the existing loan, pointing out that the company's receivables were from such high-quality names as Lockheed and General Dynamics and that operations had been moderately profitable for a number of years. During one conversation Mr. Smith mentioned that, on the basis of recent experience, he was confident that a large Los Angeles bank would be happy to take over the entire loan, but that this was the last thing he wanted after so many years of harmonious relations with Community

National. Mr. Ray had acknowledged that the bank valued highly the fine relationship through the years with the company and with Mr. Fiske and Mr. Smith personally, but stressed again that LBEC must realize that sound banking practice precluded the indefinite substitution of bank debt for equity in a growing company.

Mr. Johnson noted that for the past several years corporate and personal balances arising from the loan to LBEC had averaged as follows:

Year	Average Balance
1962	$28,300 (8 months)
1961	26,600
1960	18,500

In order to sharpen his thinking on this problem, Mr. Johnson gathered some financial data from published sources, primarily *Standard & Poor's Corporation Records,* on companies which appeared to be roughly comparable to LBEC (see Exhibit 3). While he did not expect to find any definitive answers to his own problem in the financial statistics of other companies, he hoped to gain some clues on the question of a reasonable debt limit for a company such as LBEC.

Exhibit 1

LONG BEACH ELECTRONICS COMPANY, INC.

COMPARATIVE BALANCE SHEETS

AS OF JULY 31, 1957–62

(Dollar Figures in Thousands)

ASSETS	1957	1958	1959	1960	1961	1962
Cash	$ 2	$ 12	$ 6	$ 11	$ 20	$ 17
Accounts receivable (net)	79	71	79	105	135	159
Inventory	153	168	200	285	316	394
Other	1	1	1	2	3	7
Total current assets	235	252	286	403	474	577
Furniture and equipment (net)	9	8	7	9	11	11
Cash value life insurance	6	8	11	15	20	25
Loans to subsidiary	34	18	14	11	11	8
Total assets	$284	$286	$318	$438	$516	$621
LIABILITIES						
Accounts payable	$ 68	$ 64	$ 71	$114	$113	$113
Due banks	18	18	30	65	115	200
Accrued taxes	16	10	11	26	28	24
Other accruals	11	11	8	10	12	13
Total current liabilities	113	103	120	215	268	350
Notes to banks	9	4	—	—	—	—
Due officers*	15	17	21	18	13	10
Total liabilities	$137	$124	$141	$233	$281	$360
Capital stock	15	15	15	15	15	15
Earned surplus	132	147	162	190	220	246
Total capital	147	162	177	205	235	261
Total liabilities and capital	$284	$286	$318	$438	$516	$621

* Subordinated to bank debt in event of bankruptcy.

Exhibit 2

LONG BEACH ELECTRONICS COMPANY, INC.

SUMMARY INCOME STATEMENTS (YEARS ENDED JULY 31)

(Dollar Figures in Thousands)

	1957	1958	1959	1960	1961	1962
Sales						
Industrial............................	$778	$745	$ 963	$1,117	$1,289	$1,567
Service............................	39	37	28	24	27	13
Retail............................	77	77	95	110	100	83
Total sales............................	894	859	1,086	1,251	1,416	1,663
Cost of sales*............................	677	647	842	948	1,059	1,269
Gross profit............................	217	212	244	303	357	394
Expenses						
Selling............................	$ 76	$ 84	$ 103	$ 122	$ 139	$ 158
Administrative†............................	67	66	75	82	110	131
Operating............................	40	39	43	50	55	60
Total expenses............................	183	189	221	254	304	349
Profit before taxes............................	34	23	23	49	53	45
Taxes............................	13	8	8	21	23	19
Net profit............................	$ 21	$ 15	$ 15	$ 28	$ 30	$ 26
* Beginning Inventory....................	$ 152	$ 153	$ 168	$ 200	$ 285	$ 316
Purchases........................	678	662	874	1,033	1,090	1,347
Ending inventory....................	153	168	200	285	316	394
Average inventory..................	152	161	184	242	300	355
† Including executive salaries totaling	$ 36	$ 36	$ 38	$ 40	$ 46	$ 46

Exhibit 3
LONG BEACH ELECTRONICS COMPANY, INC.
COMPARISON SHEET
(Dollar Figures in Thousands)

	Bell Electronic Corporation		Gem Electronic Distributors, Inc.		Harvey Radio Company		Lafayette Radio Electronics Co.	
	1961	1962	1961	1962	1961	1962	1961	1962
Sales	$4,406	$4,854	$3,110	$3,638	$3,755	$3,920	$21,209	$22,442
Net income	274	281	127	183	183	210	711	608
Bank debt								
Short term	630	675	144	45	2	2	1,122	2,970
Long term	76	1,125	....	....	49	47	2,166	1,799
Total	$ 706	$1,800	$ 144	$ 45	$ 51	$ 49	$ 3,288	$ 4,769
Debt								
Current liabilities*	$1,883	$1,301	$ 791	$ 464	$ 417	$ 540	$ 2,942	$ 5,008
Long term	75	1,125	....	....	49	47	2,166	1,799
Total	$1,958	$2,426	$ 791	$ 464	$ 466	$ 587	$ 5,108	$ 6,807
Net worth	$1,237	$1,333	$ 437	$ 996	$1,125	$1,335	$ 3,183	$ 4,212
Bank debt/net worth	57%	135%	34%	4%	4%	4%	103%	113%
Total debt/net worth	158%	182%	185%	44%	41%	44%	161%	162%

* Including short-term bank debt.

NOTES:

Bell Electronic Corp.: Company and subsidiaries distribute electronic parts and components made by others. Products include more than 25,000 items: semiconductors, tubes . . . transformers; connectors; cables; relays; . . . test equipment; and precision gears. Sales are made to more than 3,500 industrial and institutional customers who use products mainly for defense contracts. Company located in Southern California area. . . .

Gem Electronic Distributors, Inc.: Company markets a wide line of electronic components; parts and equipment . . . all made by others. It carries more than 30,000 items purchased from 160 suppliers for each of which it is an authorized or franchised dealer. . . . Company operates in New York City area.

Harvey Radio Co., Inc.: Company and subsidiaries market in New York City and upstate New York electronic components, parts, supplies, and equipment made by others. . . . About half of sales are to industrial customers and the remainder to retail customers.

Lafayette Radio Electronics Co.: Company and its subsidiaries distribute an extensive line of electronic parts and equipment and high fidelity sound components. . . . Company located primarily in the Northeast.

Case 20

Santos Coffee Company

EARLY IN JULY, 1947, Mr. John Richards, a credit officer of the Free State Bank of Baltimore, Maryland, was considering what action the bank should take regarding a large unsecured loan to the Santos Coffee Company. In recent months a series of undesirable developments in connection with the loan had convinced Mr. Richards that the present situation was highly unsatisfactory from the bank's viewpoint. It seemed to him that unless the loan could be covered by adequate security, the bank would have to insist on payment of the loan, even though such action might result in liquidation of the company. Since the company owned little real property, the only possible collateral was the company's accounts receivable and inventory.

The Santos Coffee Company had been founded in 1929 by four salesmen who had worked previously for a large coffee roasting firm in Baltimore. The new company operated as an importer, roaster, and wholesaler of coffee.

The company customarily ordered its principal raw material, green coffee in bean form, from Brazilian exporters. Shipment was made from Santos, the principal coffee exporting port of Brazil. The method by which payment for the coffee was accomplished is outlined as follows: When a shipment was loaded aboard ship, the Brazilian exporter drew a draft on the Santos Coffee Company for the agreed dollar value of the shipment. The draft usually called for payment "on sight," that is, within 3 days after presentation of the draft to the company. With "shipping papers"[1] attached, the draft was then deposited for collection by the Brazilian exporter at its bank. This bank forwarded the draft and attached papers to its correspondent bank in the United States, which in turn sent it on to the Free State Bank, which paid the draft as instructed by the Santos Coffee Company. Upon payment of the draft, the Free State

---

[1] Consisting typically of invoices, ocean bill of lading, marine insurance certificates, and consular certificates.

Bank turned over the shipping papers to Santos, so that it could claim the coffee upon arrival in Baltimore.

Soon after the Santos Coffee Company moved its account to the Free State Bank in 1934, it arranged to borrow up to $30,000 from the bank to meet drafts for shipments of coffee. As the bank advanced the funds to pay for a particular shipment, it prepared a demand note for the amount of the advance. Papers accompanying the note gave the bank legal title to the coffee until the note was paid. Although the bank held title to the coffee, it released the coffee to the company for storage under a legal arrangement known as a "trust receipt." It was the customary practice of the company to pay the note secured by a particular shipment of coffee when it removed that coffee from storage for processing. Each trust receipt identified the particular shipment involved by reference to distinctive marks on the coffee bags in that shipment.

During the 10 years from 1934 to 1944, the company's sales gradually increased, and the amounts of money advanced for the company by the bank against coffee also increased. The bank also made additional unsecured advances to the company on a demand basis from time to time. By 1944 total advances to the company amounted at times to as much as $40,000. Since the company continued to show modest profits and sales increased somewhat, and since the company had only small debts owing to other creditors, the bank had taken no steps to see that the company was fully carrying out its obligations under the trust receipt arrangements. For example, the bank made no inspections of the inventory outstanding under the various trust receipts to make sure that it could be readily identified and that the company had reported promptly all withdrawals from storage. In the absence of these precautions, the bank regarded the advances against coffee under the trust receipts as, in fact, unsecured loans.

In 1944 Mr. John Stone, who had served as president of the company since its inception, died. Mr. Stone was succeeded by Mr. R. H. Sager, formerly sales manager for the company. At the time the bank was somewhat concerned about the future management of the company, since all of the remaining officials were experienced primarily in the sales aspects of the business. Operations continued satisfactorily, however, and a profit of more than $5,000 was recorded in 1945. Late in 1945 the bank learned that Mr. Pierre LeBlanc, one of the salesmen, had purchased Mr. Stone's shares of common stock from his estate. This gave Mr. LeBlanc 385 shares out of the total of 890 shares outstanding. Consequently, Mr. LeBlanc assumed direction of the company with the title of vice president and general manager.

Under Mr. LeBlanc's leadership the company undertook a program of aggressive sales promotion. Sales were made principally to independent retailers and to restaurants and hotels. In 1946 the company had more than 3,400 accounts in Maryland, the District of Columbia, Virginia, and southern Delaware. Late in 1946, subsequent to the removal of OPA price restrictions on coffee, there was a sharp increase both in the price of green coffee and in the company's selling prices. However, the increase in prices accounted for only a portion of an increase in net sales from $432,000 in 1945 to $781,000 in 1946. Profits increased from $5,472 to $9,537.

During the latter part of 1946 the bank agreed to increase the amount of credit granted to the company in view of the increased working capital requirements resulting from higher sales and higher prices. A tentative maximum line of credit of $80,000 was established.

Early in January, 1947, Mr. LeBlanc requested that the line of credit be increased further. He explained that the company was currently spending large amounts on advertising and expected a further increase in sales. Mr. Richards had agreed to the increase in the line of credit in late 1946 to $80,000 with considerable reluctance, since he felt that the additional sales should more properly be financed by increased capital investment by the owners. Therefore, he declined to advance the line beyond $80,000 but promised to lay the matter before the officers' loan committee of the bank.

Shortly thereafter, in late January, 1947, Mr. Richards had a telephone call from an officer of the Chesapeake Trust Company, who informed him that the Santos Coffee Company had opened a borrowing account with the Chesapeake Trust Company in the fall of 1946 and was currently borrowing some $35,000 from that bank. The other banker expressed some dissatisfaction with his new account, particularly when Mr. Richards told him that this was the first news the Free State Bank had that Santos was borrowing from another bank. Shortly thereafter the Free State Bank received a copy of the audited annual report as of December 31, 1946, which confirmed the fact of outside borrowing. The balance sheet of the company on December 31 showed "notes payable to banks" of $105,000. Since $70,000 was outstanding from the Free State Bank, $35,000 was apparently owing the Chesapeake Trust on that date. Other payables also showed a substantial increase over the 1945 figures. Accordingly, Mr. Richards asked Mr. LeBlanc to come in and see him. In an ensuing discussion, he expressed dissatisfaction with Mr. LeBlanc's action in borrowing from another bank without informing the Free State Bank. He further stated that the Free State line of credit of $80,000 was based on the assumption that the company would not borrow from any other bank. He stated flatly that if Mr. LeBlanc did not accept this arrangement, he would have to pay off all the Free State loans and seek other banking accommodations. Mr. LeBlanc agreed to pay off the loans from the Chesapeake Trust Company and to reduce the scale of his operations so that $80,000 would be sufficient bank credit for the company's needs.

Despite the previous understanding, Mr. LeBlanc soon requested a temporary increase in the loans above $80,000 on the ground that he needed at least 2,200 bags of coffee in stock to meet his sales requirements and that the financing of this much inventory, together with the other needs of the business, would require an increase in the loan above $80,000. Mr. Richards replied that $80,000 was the bank's top limit and suggested that the company build up its capital through earnings and through the sale of preferred stock. Mr. LeBlanc agreed to undertake to find additional capital.

Early in May a representative of the bank visited the company and made a brief inspection of the inventory. A classification of the inventory of the company on April 30 was obtained. This was as follows:

	Thousands of Dollars
Green coffee	37.6
Roasted coffee	12.6
Tea	15.9
Groceries and miscellaneous supplies	6.8
Manufacturing supplies	38.6
	111.5

Upon inquiry it was learned that the manufacturing supplies consisted largely of glass containers, which had been purchased in quantity during a shortage period. Very recently, adequate supplies of tin containers had become available. Since tin containers were regarded as much more satisfactory, the company had shifted back to use of tin. There were more than five carloads of surplus glass containers. When pressed for an appraisal of the value of these containers, Mr. LeBlanc conceded that a loss of as much as $14,000 might be expected when they were sold.

In addition, it was learned that recent operations of the company had not proved profitable, although sales were large. In another conversation with Mr. LeBlanc, based on this information, Mr. Richards urged him to reduce the currently large expenditures for advertising and to try to reduce the loan to $55,000. Mr. LeBlanc agreed to do so. He also agreed to make available to Mr. Richards the financial statements of the company as of June 30 as soon as they were available.

Copies of the balance sheet and profit and loss statement for the first 6 months of the year were received by the bank on July 10. (See Exhibits 1 and 2.) Mr. Richards found the statements highly disturbing. Net working capital amounted to only $39,000, compared with total debt of $140,000. In addition, although the first half of 1947 had been a period of general prosperity and good corporate earnings, the Santos Coffee Company showed a loss of $34,000 for the period. At this stage, Mr. Richards was convinced that drastic action was necessary if the bank's interests were to be fully protected and possible loss prevented. While he was determining what action to recommend to the officers' loan committee, he received a call from Mr. Sager, one of the original founders of the firm and the manager during the year intervening between the death of Mr. Stone in 1944 and Mr. LeBlanc's assumption of the job late in 1945. Mr. Sager informed Mr. Richards that the stockholders had determined that a change in management was desirable. Mr. LeBlanc had agreed to resign as general manager and to resume his old duties as salesman. Mr. Sager was assuming the job of treasurer and with other stockholders would assume active management of the company. He agreed that the affairs of the company were in poor shape but expressed the strong hope that the bank would give the new management a chance to pull the company out of its current difficulty. He explained that the large expenditures for advertising had been terminated, that pressure was being put on overdue accounts receivable, that the recent practice of cutting profit margins to get additional sales would be stopped, that salaries were being reduced, and that every step to conserve funds was being taken. He asked Mr. Richards to tell him within a few days what the bank would do in regard to meeting the credit needs of the company.

Mr. Richards was impressed with the earnestness of Mr. Sager's appeal and with his apparent grasp of the management mistakes which appeared to be the cause of the company's difficulties. In view of all the facts, however, Mr. Richards decided that the Santos Coffee Company account should no longer be carried on an unsecured basis. In general, the Free State Bank had followed a policy of trying to work out of difficult situations, where there seemed a reasonable opportunity to do so, rather than forcing liquidation of borrowing customers.

Mr. Richards first centered his attention on the possibilities of securing a pledge of accounts receivable. In order to get a better idea of the company's accounts receivable, a representative of the bank was asked to undertake an aging of the accounts outstanding on June 30. He reported that the company had several thousand accounts, so that the average balance and the individual invoices were small. Of the $75,000 of receivables outstanding on June 30, $52,000 were current or no more than 30 days overdue. Of the remaining $23,000, $15,000 of the accounts were over 90 days overdue. Returns and allowances were very small.

Mr. Richards next focused his attention on the value of the company's inventory as collateral. Upon investigation he found that the green coffee used by the company consisted primarily of common grades of Brazilian coffee for which there was a continuous and rather wide market in Baltimore and in the neighboring cities. At any one time, part of the coffee was in ocean transit to the company. Green coffee actually on hand, preparatory to being roasted, was stored in vacant space in the building which the company rented. The company felt that it was essential to carry a substantial supply of green coffee, either on hand or en route to it, in order to insure no interruption in its supplies. Such a supply would at current prices amount to between $35,000 and $55,000 in total value. As a part of the retrenchment program, the new management planned to concentrate on the sale of coffee, reducing the June 30, 1947, inventory in tea and other lines.

Upon investigation, Mr. Richards verified his opinion that coffee in the green state could be held for many months without substantial deterioration, provided clean, dry storage was available and no other commodities of strong aroma were stored near by. He also investigated recent movements in green coffee prices. The results of the investigation of prices are shown in Exhibit 3. Mr. Richards learned that the government of Brazil, the country which accounted for more than 70% of world production of coffee, had for a number of years made strenuous efforts to maintain the price of coffee at what it considered reasonable levels. These efforts largely took the form of restriction on coffee exports so that they did not exceed world demand. When necessary, substantial stocks had been destroyed in Brazil in order to reduce supply in the world market. Consequently, some observers currently felt that the Brazilian government would take energetic steps to try to prevent any substantial decline from the current high prices.

Mr. Richards also investigated the possibility of getting a secured position in regard to the green coffee which would be unquestionably valid against general creditors in the event of bankruptcy of the firm. The trust receipt method of taking security on the coffee left some doubts on this score. He learned that there was an independent public warehouse across the street from the building in which the company operated, which had surplus space available at reasonable charges. He then conceived the following plan for loaning against the inventory: When drafts covering the new shipments of coffee were received, the bank would advance the agreed loan value, and Santos Coffee would supply the balance necessary to meet the drafts. Immediately, trust receipts describing the bags in the shipment would be prepared and executed by the company. Thus, the bank would have a secured position on the coffee while it was in transit. Marine insurance would be carried and made out so as to recognize the bank's security interest in the coffee in transit. When the coffee arrived in Baltimore, it would be moved immediately to the public warehouse. The warehouser would issue a warehouse receipt naming the bank as owner of the coffee. The warehouse receipt would be held by the bank, which would then return the trust receipt to the company. When the company needed the coffee for roasting, it would pay the bank the full amount of the loan advanced against the coffee. Thereupon, the bank would direct the warehouse company to release the coffee to Santos.

Such a procedure, Mr. Richards felt, would ensure that the bank could properly identify the security back of the inventory loan and establish beyond challenge the bank's ownership of the coffee. The warehouseman was bonded to perform his duties properly; and the coffee, while in the warehouse, would be covered by fire and other insurance. The proposed procedure would involve some expense and trouble for the company, since it now stored its green coffee in otherwise useless space in its rented building. The company would be required to pay the storage charges of the bonded warehouse and, in addition, would incur expense for trucking and handling charges in and out of the warehouse.

After careful study, Mr. Richards concluded that the bank could probably escape with little or no loss if it demanded payment of its loans now and liquidation of the company resulted. Therefore, the major alternatives now open to the bank seemed to boil down to the following:

1. Demand payment of the loans.
2. Continue to loan to the company reasonable amounts on the basis of a pledge of accounts receivable.
3. Continue to loan to the company by advancing reasonable amounts of funds against drafts for shipments of coffee only if the coffee was moved into the public warehouse immediately upon arrival and warehouse receipts pledged as security for the loan.
4. A combination of 2 and 3.

Exhibit 1

SANTOS COFFEE COMPANY

Balance Sheets

(Dollar Figures in Thousands)

	Dec. 31 1944	Dec. 31 1945	June 30 1946	Dec. 31 1946	June 30 1947
Cash	$ 21	$ 12	$ 14	$ 12	$ 16
Accounts receivable, net	37	47	62	87	75
Inventory	46	65	97	129	88
Total current assets	$104	$124	$173	$228	$179
Machinery and fixtures, net	7	13	18	17	18
Other notes and accounts receivable	2	2	2	2	2
Goodwill	28	28	28	28	28
Prepaid expenses	1	1	2	2	3
Total assets	$142	$168	$223	$277	$230
Notes payable—trade	...	...	...	...	$ 10
Notes payable—banks	$ 21	$ 28	$ 37	$105	74
Accounts payable—trade	2	11	48	26	46
Accrued expense	1	5	3	13	4
Reserve for taxes	4	4	7	4	6
Total current liabilities	$ 28	$ 48	$ 95	$148	$140
Common stock ($100 par)	89	89	89	89	89
Surplus	25	31	39	40	1
Total liabilities	$142	$168	$223	$277	$230

Exhibit 2

SANTOS COFFEE COMPANY

INCOME STATEMENTS

(Dollar Figures in Thousands)

	Year 1944	Year 1945	6 Months 1946	Year 1946	6 Months 1947
Net sales......................	$310.7	$431.8	$323.7	$780.7	$361.7
Gross profit....................	55.5	84.2	75.1	180.9	67.2
Administrative and selling expense......................	51.7	78.4	60.3	161.9	97.2
Operating profit.................	3.8	5.8	14.8	19.0	30.0*
Other income (purchase discounts)......................	1.2	2.8	0.9	1.4	0.2
Charges against income..........	4.8	3.1	7.3	10.9	4.2
Net income....................	0.2	5.5	8.4	9.5	34.0*
Common dividends..............	0.9	...	...	...	4.0

* Loss.

Exhibit 3

SANTOS COFFEE COMPANY

AVERAGE SPOT PRICE OF COFFEE IN NEW YORK*

(In Cents per Pound)

	Jan.	Feb.	Mar.	April	May	June	July	Aug.	Sept.	Oct.	Nov.	Dec.
1937	11.3	11.8	11.2	11.2	11.7	11.7	11.6	11.4	11.4	11.5	9.4	8.8
1938	8.6	8.1	7.5	7.3	7.6	7.4	7.6	7.9	7.8	8.0	8.1	8.0
1939	7.7	7.8	7.4	7.2	7.3	7.4	7.3	7.6	7.7	7.8	7.4	7.3
1940	7.5	7.4	7.3	7.3	7.2	7.3	7.0	6.8	6.8	7.0	7.2	7.4
1941	7.8	8.3	9.0	9.9	10.8	11.5	12.2	13.4	13.4	13.2	13.1	13.3
1942†	13.4	13.4	13.4	13.4	13.4	13.4	13.4	13.4	13.4	13.4	13.4	13.4
1943†	13.4	13.4	13.4	13.4	13.4	13.4	13.4	13.4	13.4	13.4	13.4	13.4
1944†	13.4	13.4	13.4	13.4	13.4	13.4	13.4	13.4	13.4	13.4	13.4	13.4
1945†	13.5	13.6	13.6	13.6	13.6	13.6	13.6	13.6	13.6	13.6	13.6	13.6
1946†	13.4	13.4	13.4	13.4	13.4	13.4	20.6	22.1	22.1	24.1	26.3	26.4
1947	26.9	27.2	27.7	25.8	23.7	25.3	...	...	...	...	...	...

* Santos No. 4. Source: Bureau of Labor Statistics.
† United States price controls on coffee were in effect during 1942–46.
SOURCE: *Commodity Year Book, 1948*, "Coffee," p. 165.

Case 21

Custom Plastics, Inc.

IN THE LAST WEEK of July, 1956, Mr. Stanley Ebanson, vice president and loan officer of the Tradesman National Bank of Milwaukee, was introduced to Mr. Charles Miller, newly elected president of Custom Plastics, Inc. Mr. Miller, who with an investment group had purchased control of Custom Plastics 2 months earlier, was requesting short-term credit accommodation for the company from the Tradesman Bank. Though Custom Plastics was an old and reputable firm in the custom molding field, the company had suffered financial difficulties since 1953. In view of the company's continuing management and operating problems, the former owners accepted the offer of Mr. Miller's group to acquire immediate control of the company and pay out the former owners over a 5-year period. The company had been extended short-term bank credit for many years by the Manufacturers Bank; but by mutual agreement between the former owners, Mr. Miller, and the officers of the Manufacturers Bank, the new president was to arrange the company's short-term credit needs with a new financial institution as soon as possible.

Custom Plastics was a manufacturer of custom molded plastic products. Manufacturing facilities were located in Milwaukee, Wisconsin, where the company leased a four-story plant for $50,000 per year, the current lease to expire in 1958. The company employed about 300 personnel and currently was operating on a two-shift basis. Custom Plastics was equipped with a complete line of molding machines, both compression and injection, capable of producing items of all sizes and shapes typically required by an industrial customer. Though the machinery was old and less efficient than new equipment on the market, the management believed the company's technical and engineering skills were of greater importance to profitable operation.

As was typical for a custom molder, Custom Plastics helped design a plastic product, obtained the specially cut mold from a local toolmaker, and manufactured the end product in its own molding machines. The

752

company had a wide reputation for its ability successfully to undertake tricky mold design and product manufacturing assignments. The full cost of mold design and purchase was borne by the customer and paid to Custom Plastics in the initial purchases of the special plastic item. Custom Plastics was fully responsible for the quality of a finished plastic component, and most customers had rigid inspection procedures and quality standards. To obtain physical custody of a mold, the customer was required under a "mold contract" to pay Custom Plastics an additional 30% over the reimbursement price previously agreed to and paid Custom Plastics in the initial purchases.

In 1952 the company entered the plastic dinnerware business under a design and brand name licensing agreement with a nationally known designer. The line of dinnerware provided about 20% of the total sales volume in 1955. Two separate sales forces were maintained to contact the company's 175 customers, no one of which accounted for more than 10% of the company's volume. On the other hand, the list of the company's 15 most important customers in 1954 accounted for over half of that year's volume and included large, nationally known manufacturing, service, and retail distribution companies, each with a top credit rating.

Having been founded in 1905, Custom Plastics had "grown up" with the plastics industry and over the years had established a reputation for quality and service. Except during the depression years, the financial position of the company had always been healthy and operations profitable. Ownership was concentrated in the Saunders family; the senior member of the family had been active in the company management until the late 1940's. Though in many years a high proportion of earnings was paid out in dividends, the owners had retained adequate working capital and had established a substantial equity in the business as of the end of 1952.

During 1952 the production manager died; in his long association with the company, this man had become a key figure in the control and profitability of the manufacturing process. In his absence, cost control procedures were relaxed, and cost estimates and pricing decisions were less firmly based on adequate information. In an effort to lessen the impact of pricing decisions based on underestimated costs, material specifications were sidestepped, and some customers began to reject and return merchandise. At the same time, the coordination between engineering and production personnel began to weaken. Finally, productivity and morale among the employees reached a low point after a profit-participation plan promised them over the years was withdrawn from consideration in mid-1953. This incident, in combination with generally deteriorating morale conditions in the plant, led to a 4-month strike in the early part of 1954 and continued management-labor friction thereafter.

As a result of these management and operating complications taking effect in 1953, the company's net profit before federal income tax fell from $238,000 in 1952 to a loss of $91,000 in 1953 (Exhibit 1). In 1954 the company suffered heavy losses due to a large reduction in revenues and excessive costs due to the strike and the heavy, unexpected returns of merchandise. At the time, however, the magnitude of these losses was not clearly known because of faulty accounting procedures in effect at the company.

During this period, financial strain developed, and the company began to rely heavily on trade and bank credit. Since the late 1940's the company had been borrowing from the Manufacturers Bank moderate amounts, $10,000–$50,000, on unsecured notes to finance working capital needs arising from slight seasonality or unusually large orders. As the unfavorable operating results and the heavy demand for funds developed in late 1953, the management arranged a line of credit with the bank, pledging as security the company's accounts receivable in bulk. The bank agreed to loan up to 90% of the receivables balance. During the same year, added reliance was placed on trade credit, with trade payables increasing from $85,000 at the end of 1952 to $205,000 at the end of 1953 (Exhibit 2). Of this amount, $107,000, which was payable to five important suppliers, was placed on a deferred basis in early 1954 and secured by a chattel mortgage on certain machinery and equipment. Repayment of these notes in 18 monthly instalments with interest at $4\frac{1}{2}\%$ was to commence in January, 1956. These financing arrangements permitted the company to remain current on new material purchases during 1954 and early 1955.

Owing to turnover in management personnel and almost complete loss of accounting and manufacturing cost control, the extent of the losses taking place in 1954 and early 1955 was not fully recognized until mid-1955. Upon the recommendation of the Manufacturers Bank, the owners of the business discharged the accounting manager and replaced him with an experienced CPA. After a thorough audit, losses before taxes in 1954 were calculated to have been $495,000, of which some $150,000 had been obscured by a failure to reflect returns and allowances as deductions from outstanding accounts receivable and from the period's sales. Losses for the first 4 months of 1955 were estimated at $85,000 before taxes.

When the scope of unprofitable operations became clear, the owners of the company decided to sell their interest in Custom Plastics rather than attempt its rehabilitation. This decision was stimulated, at least in part, by the vigorous suggestion of the bank, and by the recommendation of the five trade-note creditors, whose prospects of receiving payment on schedule seemed dim. While the owners were looking for a buyer, losses mounted to $109,000 before taxes by the end of 1955 (Exhibit 1). Working capital was squeezed to a minimum, and cash was drawn down to below $5,000. By the end of 1955 the Saunders family had invested an additional $53,000 in the company on unsecured notes, with the hope of tiding operations over until a buyer with an acceptable plan of purchase could be located. As the Saunders family wanted to withdraw entirely from the operations of the company, it expected a prospective buyer to pay out these notes as a part of the purchase plan. The deferred notes due trade creditors starting January, 1956, were renegotiated in late 1955 to postpone the payment schedule 6 months. At the same time, it again was becoming difficult to pay for current purchases.

Based on the unfavorable disclosures in 1955 regarding the company's receivables, the Manufacturers Bank asked Custom Plastics to pledge the cash surrender value of life insurance on certain officers and to give a chattel mortgage on the machinery not mortgaged to trade creditors as additional security behind its loan. In addition, the bank raised the interest rate from 5% to 6% on its loan and required the Saunders family to subordinate the company debt held by them to the bank obligations. Also, the bank became much more selective in the receivables against which it would lend, accepting only receivables under 60 days of age of the better credit risks. Finally, the bank hinted to Mr. Saunders that it would terminate its credit to the firm unless a prospective buyer of the business would be willing to bring substantial new equity funds into the company. Upon the completion of transfer of ownership to the new owners, the bank considered its obligation to the Saunders family and the company had been fulfilled and thought a fresh look by a new creditor might be beneficial to all parties.

In early 1956 Mr. Charles Miller, the president of Louisville Desk Company, a small but prosperous manufacturer of metal furniture, became acquainted with Custom Plastics' situation and went to Milwaukee to investigate the company. Mr. Miller had a varied background in investment banking and light industry and with the aid of a group of friends had purchased the Louisville Desk Company in 1948. Though this company had a record of unprofitable operations and poor future prospects, Mr. Miller quickly revived the organization, reorganized its management, shifted product emphasis, and within a few years had built it into a quite successful small enterprise. Having completed this task, he sold his interest in the company at a substantial capital gain and was again looking for a "sick" company to purchase and rehabilitate.

Through the early months of 1956, Mr. Miller investigated the Custom Plastics operation rather thoroughly. Convinced that the company's former profitability could be restored under new ownership and management, he arranged in May, 1956, to buy the company, with payment over a 5-year period. The Miller syndicate first purchased $150,000 of newly issued debentures, convertible into a new and second series of common stock. These debentures were secured by a second mortgage on all machinery and by an assignment of the company's mold contracts. Notes payable to the former owners of $53,000 were retired with cash received from the sale of the first $50,000 in new debentures. The existing and first series of common stock was placed in a voting trust with syndicate members as trustees. In each of the next 5 years, 15% of the company's after-tax profits in each year were to be used to repurchase this stock for cancellation, with the proceeds going to the former owners. Any stock not repurchased by the fifth year was automatically transferred to the company and canceled. Furthermore, the total of the five annual repurchase transactions was limited to $98,000. In summary, the obligation under this agreement was contingent upon profits and limited in aggregate amount and period of liability. The monthly balance sheet and operating statements of the company throughout the period of and following the negotiations are shown in Exhibits 3 and 4.

Though Mr. Miller brought additional funds into the Custom Plastics business and presented a plan for regaining profitable operations, the Manufacturers Bank decided to terminate its lending relationship with the company. Upon assumption of control of Custom Plastics, Mr. Miller had quickly organized a board of directors from among prominent Milwaukee businessmen, one of whom was the treasurer of an equipment manufacturer in Milwaukee. This new director was very much impressed with the plans and managerial skill of Mr. Miller, and he offered his assistance to Mr. Miller in finding new credit accommodations for the company. As his company was an important depositor at the Tradesman National Bank and had a long and successful relationship there, the new director introduced Mr. Miller to Mr. Stanley Ebanson, a vice president and loan officer at this bank.

At a meeting with Mr. Ebanson in early August, 1956, Mr. Miller outlined his program for rehabilitating Custom Plastics. In order to utilize the full capacity of the machinery and to push operations well above a break-even level, Mr. Miller believed that sales volume had to be increased quickly. Mr. Miller thought break-even operations currently would result at a sales level of $200,000 per month; and to surpass this level, he intended to push aggressively for new business as well as regain the confidence and orders of lost customers. Though the backlog of orders stood at about $400,000, it consisted of many older and less profitable orders which had been deferred by the previous management in order to process the more profitable, cash-generating orders. Many customers, promised delivery in March, had not received shipment in July, and Mr. Miller considered it vital that this work receive first priority. To encourage salesmen to push profitable new projects, the president was offering bonuses for selected types of orders. In addition, he was personally trouble-shooting problems of rejections and returns which were causing direct losses and poor customer relations. Finally, selective price increases were being made to some customers who had been receiving merchandise on unreasonably good terms.

The second part of Mr. Miller's program was designed to increase the company's gross margin. Whereas the company's margin had been running from 10% to 14%, the industry range was 15% to 18%. The margin on the dinnerware line was about 23%. In reviewing the manufacturing costs, Mr. Miller was especially concerned with the low worker productivity at Custom Plastics. He intended gradually to put in a piecework system wherever possible, and some incentives had already been installed and well received by the employees. To assume much of the direct control of manufacturing operations which he was presently handling, the new president had just hired an able and experienced production manager from a competing molding firm. This new man would be expected to work quickly in expediting old orders, accurately estimating costs on new business and making sound pricing recommendations, increasing labor and machinery productivity and worker morale, and reducing wastage of raw materials.

Mr. Miller expected that operations in July and August would probably show a loss, due primarily to the backlog of unattractive orders which he had inherited. He believed September and October would be break-even months, and profits could be expected in October and thereafter. The new president said that if sales of $200,000 to $250,000 per month could be reached and gross margins increased as planned, the earnings of the company could be restored to 1951–52 levels. He hoped to have his accounting people make a more thorough cost study of the industrial versus the dinnerware lines; his own tentative studies indicated the profits from the dinnerware line were being offset by the losses in the industrial line. Mr. Miller pointed out also that the company had a federal income tax loss carry-over in the next 4 years of over $500,000 and that no taxes would have to be paid on earnings in this amount made during that period.

In light of these plans, Mr. Miller asked the Tradesman Bank to loan Custom Plastics 80% on net receivables up to a loan limit of $200,000. The company would pledge these assets, maintain accurate aging records, adequately provide for returns and adjustments, screen new credit with care (but with full knowledge of the need for additional business), and present the bank with timely monthly reports of the condition of receivables and the month's operating results. Mr. Miller planned to redeem the cash proceeds of the life insurance to supplement working capital. Pointing out the substantial investment he and his associates already had placed in Custom Plastics, Mr. Miller said he would not consider personally endorsing the company's bank indebtedness. The president added that the company's five main trade creditors were confident of the company's future, because they agreed again to defer their notes, now totaling $98,000, and accept repayment at about $5,000 per month (including interest) beginning in September and extending for 22 months.

Mr. Ebanson was impressed with Mr. Miller's seeming insight into the problems at Custom Plastics. From the Louisville banker who was closely familiar with Mr. Miller's handling of the Louisville Desk situation, Mr. Ebanson received a strong recommendation of the new president of Custom Plastics. Mr. Miller was described as unimpeachable in integrity, venturesome in spirit, able to accomplish plans and deal with emergencies, and frank and open in his relations with creditors. Also, the associates of Mr. Miller were reputable businessmen, well-known in their separate communities and fields. Finally, although money and credit conditions were currently tight, the Tradesman Bank was actively interested in seeking new customers and establishing relationships which would prove attractive in the long run.

As Mr. Miller would want to know in a day or so whether the Tradesman Bank would be able to meet the company's loan request, Mr. Ebanson set about immediately to evaluate the company's financial needs and the basis, if any, upon which the Tradesman Bank would be willing to accommodate Custom Plastics.

Exhibit 1
CUSTOM PLASTICS, INC.
OPERATING STATEMENTS, 1951-55
(Dollar Figures in Thousands)

	1951	1952	1953	1954	1955
Gross sales	$2,051	$2,335	$2,306	$1,687	n.a.
Returns and allowances	$137	$168	$ 50	$239	n.a.
Amortization of dies	22	48	3	2	n.a.
Discounts	17	19	14	15	n.a.
	176	235	67	256	
Net sales	$1,875	$2,100	$2,239	$1,431	$1,944
Materials	$601	$477	$692	$556	n.a.
Direct labor	372	462	513	385	n.a.
Indirect labor	223	261	328	278	n.a.
Overhead	278	318	366	316	n.a.
	1,474	1,518	1,899	1,535	
Gross profit	$ 401	$ 582	$ 340	$ (104)	182
Officers' salaries	$ 53	$110	$115	$111	n.a.
Sales salaries and commissions	130	119	192	192	n.a.
Other general and administrative	92	133	169	106	n.a.
	275	362	476	409	300
Operating profit	$ 126	$ 220	$ (136)	$ (513)	$ (118)
Other income—net	33	18	45	18	9
Net profit before tax	$ 159	$ 238	$ (91)	$ (495)	$ (109)
Federal income tax	34	165	(90)	(75)	n.a.
Net profit after tax	$ 125	$ 73*	$ (1)	$ (420)	n.a.

* After renegotiation.

Exhibit 2

CUSTOM PLASTICS, INC.

BALANCE SHEETS AS OF DECEMBER 31

(Dollar Figures in Thousands)

ASSETS	1950	1951	1952	1953*	1955*
Cash	$ 59	$ 52	$163	$116	$ 3
Accounts receivable	114	164	199	321	198
Inventory	201	271	219	265	192
Total current assets	$374	$487	$581	$702	$393
Machinery and equipment, net	146	131	117	129	94
Cash value life insurance	28	29	30	31	34
Miscellaneous receivables	4	6	18	25	6
Secret process	27	27	27	27	...
Total fixed assets	$205	$193	$192	$212	$134
Total assets	$579	$680	$773	$914	$527

LIABILITIES					
Notes payable—banks	$ 45	$ 25	...	$125	$212
Notes payable—equipment	8	...	...	...	...
Notes payable—vendors	...	...	...	...	63
Accounts payable	124	70	$ 85	205	172
Accrued taxes	...	50	75	67	...
Other accruals	30	44	58	60	75
Total current liabilities	$207	$189	$218	$457	$522
Notes payable—equipment	...	...	...	...	7
Notes payable—vendors	...	...	...	...	44
Notes payable—officers	...	...	...	...	53
Total long-term liabilities	...	...	...	...	$104
Common stock	$263	$263	$263	$263	263
Earned surplus	109	228	292	193	(362)
Total net worth	$372	$491	$555	$456	$ (99)
Total liabilities	$579	$680	$773	$913	$527

* No data available for 1954.

Exhibit 3

CUSTOM PLASTICS, INC.

MONTHLY OPERATING STATEMENTS, 1956

(Dollar Figures in Thousands)

	Jan.	Feb.	Mar.	April	May	June
Net sales	$140	$191	$200	$192	$195	$173
Material	n.a.	n.a.	n.a.	n.a.	68	60
Direct labor	n.a.	n.a.	n.a.	n.a.	43	38
Indirect labor	n.a.	n.a.	n.a.	n.a.	34	32
Overhead	n.a.	n.a.	n.a.	n.a.	29	28
Cost of sales	$127	$157	$168	$167	$174	$158
Gross profit	$ 13	$ 34	$ 32	$ 25	$ 21	$ 15
Officers' salaries	n.a.	n.a.	n.a.	n.a.	3	5
Other general and administrative	n.a.	n.a.	n.a.	n.a.	19	21
Operating expense	$ 25	$ 22	$ 23	$ 23	$ 22	$ 26
Operating profit	(12)	12	9	2	(1)	(11)
Other income—net	3	1	2	1	6	2
Net profit before tax	(9)	13	11	3	5	(9)

Exhibit 4

CUSTOM PLASTICS, INC.

MONTH END BALANCE SHEETS, 1956

(Dollar Figures in Thousands)

ASSETS	Feb. 29	March 31	April 30	May 29	June 30
Cash	$ 1	$ 6	$ 5	$ 9	$ 26
Accounts receivable	198	224	178	162	160
Inventory	186	209	222	238	230
Current assets	$385	$439	$405	$409	$416
Machinery and equipment, net	89	87	90	89	89
Cash value life insurance	34	34	34	34	34
Prepaid expenses	31	34	35	23	30
Fixed assets	$154	$155	$159	$146	$153
Total assets	$539	$594	$564	$555	$569

LIABILITIES	Feb. 29	March 31	April 30	May 29	June 30
Notes payable—bank	$176	$202	$156	$128	$111
Notes payable—vendors	63	58	83	83	56
Accounts payable	184	204	203	172	131
Other accruals	97	102	118	102	77
Customer advances	16	18	20	7	...
Current liabilities	$536	$584	$580	$492	$375
Debentures	...	...	53	50	150
Notes payable—officers	54	53	53	...	...
Notes payable—vendors	38	35	6	31	74
Notes payable—equipment	6	6	6	6	6
Long-term liabilities	$ 98	$ 94	$ 65	$ 87	$230
Common stock	263	263	263	263	263
Earned surplus	(358)	(347)	(344)	(287)	(299)
Net worth	$(95)	$(84)	$(81)	$(24)	$(36)
Total liabilities	$539	$594	$564	$555	$569

BREAKDOWN AND AGING OF ACCOUNTS RECEIVABLE—JUNE 30, 1956

Type	Amounts	Current	Last Month	Previous Month	Prior Months
Industrial	$113	$ 79	$24	$ 8	$ 2
Dinnerware	47	27	7	3	10
	$160	$106	$31	$11	$12

Terms: Industrial ... 1%—10; net 30
Dinnerware ... 2%—E.O.M.

Case 22

The Dunning Cabinet Company

ON SEPTEMBER 3, 1950, Mr. Dunning, 68-year-old president and sole owner of The Dunning Cabinet Company, called on Mr. Vines, vice president and loan officer of the Jefferson National Bank of Richmond, Virginia, to discuss the renegotiation of a $140,000 term loan arranged in March, 1950, to finance the expansion of the Dunning Company's plant capacity.

The Dunning Cabinet Company, located in Roanoke, Virginia, manufactured wooden television cabinets against firm orders on hand. It was not a large producer and was best suited for production runs of about 5,000 units. Its high-priced, quality cabinets were sold to large manufacturers of television sets for their console models.

The Jefferson National Bank, a medium-sized bank with a legal loan limit of $1 million, was actively attempting to build a reputation as a progressive bank. To help achieve this goal, the bank's loan officers were encouraged to use originality, whenever the risks did not seem insurmountable, in arranging suitable credit for companies that showed promise of developing into good accounts. It was hoped that, by extending credit to companies in situations where other banks might be hesitant in offering support, sound bank-customer relationships would be established that would prove beneficial to the bank over the long run.

In March, 1950, Mr. Dunning was contemplating a $140,000 addition to the company's single-story plant which would double its production capacity. The company's customers were pressing for production many times the operating capacity of a $1 million annual sales volume. In the period from January 21, 1950, to March 15, 1950, orders totaling $3,700,000 from six major television set manufacturers were declined. These represented initial orders only; and Mr. Dunning estimated that if these orders had been accepted, repeat business would have easily tripled these initial orders.

When Mr. Dunning visited the small Roanoke bank where the company had maintained its account since 1932, he was informed that a $140,000 loan was above the bank's legal limit. Although the loan officer of the local bank expressed his willingness to introduce Mr. Dunning to a loan officer at a large metropolitan bank in Washington, D.C., Mr. Dunning preferred to see Mr. Vines, whom he had known casually for several years. When he went to the Jefferson National Bank on March 17, 1950, to discuss the required loan, Mr. Dunning brought the balance sheets and income statements reproduced in Exhibits 1 and 2.

While at the bank, Mr. Dunning told Mr. Vines that the company had always operated profitably since its founding in 1932 and that it had never failed to have a substantial backlog of firm orders from at least one radio or television set manufacturer during its entire history. Mr. Dunning thought that the company's trade reputation was excellent and that with adequate production facilities the Dunning Company could easily double its sales volume. Since a number of the company's expenses, such as sales and administration, were fixed, he believed that the proposed expansion would more than double profits and would pay for itself within a little more than a year's time. He foresaw no problems in doubling plant capacity, for there appeared to be an ample supply of skilled woodworking labor in the Roanoke area. However, to finance the plant expansion, Mr. Dunning estimated the company would require a 2-year loan of $140,000. He also thought additional funds would be needed to increase the working capital to a level that would support the expected increase in sales volume.

Subsequent to Mr. Dunning's visit, Mr. Vines made several checks with television manufacturers regarding Dunning's trade reputation. A typical response was: "We feel very close to Dunning and think highly of them. They are reliable in their dealings, and Dunning makes a high-quality, high-price article that cannot be obtained in the mass production cabinets usually put out by larger woodworking concerns. Our purchasing department is highly pleased with Dunning's performance, and as long as we need cabinets, we will give Dunning consideration." These sources also confirmed newspaper articles which predicted that television sales would continue to grow in the foreseeable future. The Dunning Company's previous bank of account, which was not a correspondent bank of Jefferson, informed Mr. Vines that the company in recent years maintained a moderate five-figure bank account and properly attended to small seasonal loans which were required occasionally.

In reviewing the balance sheet and income statements provided, Mr. Vines noted that the company had nearly doubled its sales volume within the last 3 years without creating financial imbalance. Whereas only $12,000 principal repayments were required on the $78,000 first mortgage on the company's plant, the outstanding balance had been reduced by $24,000 in 1949. On the whole, Mr. Vines was impressed with Mr.

Dunning as an individual, and an examination of the company's financial development in recent years strengthened his confidence.

When Mr. Vines visited the Dunning plant in late March, 1950, he noted that the production process was orderly and inventories appeared well controlled. He was favorably impressed with several younger officers he met during his tour.

On March 30, 1950, Mr. Vines completed a 2½-year term loan agreement for $140,000 with the Dunning Company. In addition, a $160,000, 4%, open line of credit was extended to cover increased working capital requirements. When the loan agreement was signed, Mr. Vines briefly discussed the covenants of the term loan with Mr. Dunning.

Bearing interest of 4½%, the term loan was to be repaid in quarterly amounts of $16,000 beginning February 28, 1951, with the final maturity on February 28, 1953. Prepayments without penalty were permitted in whole or in part at any time prior to final maturity date and would be applied against instalments due in inverse order. However, there was a ¼% penalty fee if the loan was repaid by means of outside financing. The positive and negative covenants of the term loan agreement are set forth below:

Positive: The company agrees to . . .
1. Maintain net working capital of greater than $100,000 after excluding the current portion of the term loan from current liabilities.
2. Supply the bank with monthly balance sheets and income statements.

Negative: The company will not without prior permission from the bank . . .
1. Merge; consolidate; sell; or lease any asset.
2. Create a pledge or mortgage against any asset with the exception of the present $78,000 first mortgage on the "old" plant.
3. Replace or acquire more fixed assets in any year than can be purchased from the annual depreciation allowance, except for the proposed plant expansion totaling $140,000.
4. Pay dividends.
5. Purchase securities other than U.S. government bonds.
6. Repurchase the company's capital stock.
7. Increase the salaries of the company's officers.

Subsequent to the signing of the loan agreement, Mr. Vines received the monthly financial statements reproduced in Exhibit 3. As developments in the account seemed normal, he found no reason to inquire further about Dunning's progress. On August 31, he had noted that $80,000 of the term loan had been borrowed by the company but that its deposit balance exceeded $60,000.

On September 3, 1950, Mr. Dunning came to the bank to inform Mr. Vines of a change in the company's expansion plans. Instead of rebuilding the plant for a total capacity of $2 million sales volume, the enlarged plant would increase production capacity to an annual sales volume of $3,500,000. This change, Mr. Dunning explained, had been forced by increased pressure from the company's customers for more cabinets. Construction was well under way, and Mr. Dunning expected the new plant to be completed by the end of 1950. He said that $53,000 of the building program had been paid, but that construction costs were now estimated at $470,000. Because the $140,000 term loan was inadequate to meet the new requirements, Mr. Dunning requested that the bank negotiate a new loan for $400,000 to replace the original loan.

Sales during the first 6 months of 1950 had been $679,000, with profits before taxes equal to $123,000. In July, despite closing the plant for a 2-week vacation, sales had amounted to $83,000, and Mr. Dunning estimated August volume was $138,000. Sales for the last 4 months of 1950 were estimated at $700,000. Of this amount, he had accepted firm orders as follows:

September	$146,000
October	232,000
November	171,000
December	28,000

By the end of September he expected to be fully committed for the remainder of 1950. Sales in 1951 were expected to approximate the plant's capacity of $3,500,000. Although a portion of the new plant was already in operation, Mr. Dunning was still turning down orders at the rate of $800,000 per month.

Mr. Dunning estimated that profits before taxes would continue at the level of 18%, the actual results for the first 6 months of 1950. Income taxes payable in 1951 were estimated at 42%. He anticipated the unused $160,000 line of credit extended by the bank would adequately cover the expected increase in working capital requirements.

Mr. Vines was shocked at the action taken by Mr. Dunning, particularly in view of the fixed asset covenant in the original term loan. When asked about this restriction, Mr. Dunning said he had forgotten about it. Mr. Vines replied that such negligence was certainly not conducive to good bank-customer relations. However, he reluctantly agreed to consider a new term loan agreement.

When Mr. Vines inquired about the effect on the company's business of the Korean conflict, which had begun in June, Mr. Dunning said that it did not appear likely there would be any major cutback in television production. If there was a cutback, however, he was not much concerned, since the company had had sufficient woodworking business to operate the plant 24 hours a day during the last war. Mr. Dunning expected to do as well during the Korean War if it became necessary to convert to war production in the future.

After Mr. Dunning had left, Mr. Vines phoned several of Dunning's customers to determine the company's outlook. A typical response was: "We consider Dunning an important supplier of high-quality cabinets. They are fine people to deal with; and if war or another unexpected economic development does not interfere with production of television sets, we expect our orders with Dunning will undoubtedly run higher in 1951. However, they are not one of our major suppliers due to their inability to produce in volume. In the event of an all-out war necessitating a cutback or discontinuance in television production and a resumption of war orders requiring woodworking jobs, Dunning will receive consideration."

With this information at hand, Mr. Vines began reviewing Dunning's financial requirements to determine whether the bank should grant the request for a $400,000 term loan.

Exhibit 1

THE DUNNING CABINET COMPANY

SELECTED BALANCE SHEETS

(Dollar Figures in Thousands)

ASSETS	December 31, 1947	December 31, 1948	December 31, 1949	February 28, 1950*
Cash	$ 19	$ 22	$ 25	$ 40
Accounts receivable	62	30	62	56
Inventory	114	144	147	98
Total current assets	$195	$196	$234	$194
Plant and equipment (net)	210	254	279	285
Other assets	6	3	6	6
Total assets	$411	$453	$519	$485
LIABILITIES				
Accounts payable	$ 14	$ 33	$ 53	$ 18
Taxes payable	53	22	43	43
Accrued payables	22	39	30	17
Total current liabilities	$ 89	$ 94	$126	$ 78
Mortgage	108	108	84	78
Common stock (800 shares— par value $25)	20	20	20	20
Surplus	194	231	289	309
Total liabilities and net worth	$411	$453	$519	$485

* Unaudited.

Exhibit 2

THE DUNNING CABINET COMPANY

INCOME STATEMENTS

(Dollar Figures in Thousands)

	1946	1947	1948	1949	Jan. and Feb. 1950
Sales.........................	$505.0	$716.2	$778.5	$981.9	$181.4
Cost of goods sold*...........	338.9	499.5	598.4	754.2	
Gross profit..................	$166.1	$216.7	$180.1	$227.7	
Operating expenses............	89.4	91.0	121.8	123.5	
Operating profit..............	$ 76.7	$125.7	$ 58.3	$104.2	
Other income (net)...........	0.6	2.9	2.1	0.8	
Profit before taxes...........	$ 77.3	$128.6	$ 60.4	$105.0	20.0
Taxes........................	32.3	53.2	21.8	43.2	
Net profit....................	45.0	75.4	38.6	61.8	
Dividends....................	0	0	2.0	4.0	

```
* Includes depreciation of:
    1946.......$12,000
    1947........ 13,000
    1948........ 15,000
    1949........ 15,000
```

Exhibit 3

THE DUNNING CABINET COMPANY

SELECTED UNAUDITED BALANCE SHEETS

(Dollar Figures in Thousands)

ASSETS	March 31, 1950	April 30, 1950	May 31, 1950	June 30, 1950	July 31, 1950
Cash.........................	$ 25.8	$ 25.6	$ 22.2	$ 10.7	$ 18.2
Accounts receivable............	102.6	114.3	106.4	60.3	73.6
Finished goods.................	10.3	10.1	2.2	1.9	1.8
Work-in-process...............	20.8	19.7	22.4	120.1	138.5
Raw materials.................	48.9	85.4	111.4	42.3	37.5
Supplies......................	4.3	3.9	9.5	11.3	14.3
Total current assets......	$212.7	$259.0	$274.1	$246.6	$283.9
Net plant and equipment........	282.9	290.4	293.8	316.7	331.5
Other assets....................	5.3	7.2	6.8	6.6	6.5
Total assets.............	$500.9	$556.6	$574.7	$569.9	$621.9
LIABILITIES					
Accounts payable...............	$ 29.5	$ 39.0	$ 45.1	$ 27.5	$ 23.7
Taxes payable..................	26.4	26.4	26.4	17.6	17.6
Accrued payables..............	17.6	18.6	24.0	20.4	20.2
Total current liabilities....	$ 73.5	$ 84.0	$ 95.5	$ 65.5	$ 61.5
Mortgage.....................	78.0	78.0	72.0	72.0	72.0
Term loan....................					40.0
Common stock—(800 shares— par value $25)...............	20.0	20.0	20.0	20.0	20.0
Surplus.......................	329.4	374.6	387.2	412.4	428.4
	$500.9	$556.6	$574.7	$569.9	$621.9
Sales........................	$108.0	$143.8	$ 96.9	$148.8	$ 83.0
Profit before taxes.............	20.2	45.2	12.6	25.2	16.0

Case 23

Central Broadcasting Company

ON THE MORNING of June 29, 1961, Mr. Toby Stone was reviewing the highlights of his tour through the operating departments of Cook County National Bank, a large multifaceted Chicago bank aggressively competing for corporate deposits and loans on a national scale. Mr. Stone was currently working in the credit department, the final phase of his training program. He remembered with particular pleasure several projects of the past year which had required him to draw on research and writing skills and insights he had gained during graduate work in business administration.

One of these assignments had been a comprehensive study of the radio-television broadcasting industry undertaken at the request of Mr. Albert Roth, a senior lending officer. Mr. Roth believed that many sound loan situations in the industry were being overlooked or turned down by the banking community because traditional yardsticks were used to measure debt capacity and because bankers had not adequately analyzed key elements in this relatively young industry. Mr. Stone knew that the few bank loans made to broadcasting companies were on a patently conservative basis and hoped that his study would enable Cook County National Bank to pioneer in more aggressive lending to this industry.

While Mr. Stone was speculating on how long he would remain in the credit department before permanent assignment, Mr. Roth approached his desk. "Toby, you're the expert on radio-TV loans; I've got an interesting situation here I'd like your opinion on. Central Broadcasting Company (CBC) wants to borrow $23.5 million to finance the purchase of KMOC and KMOC-TV in Kansas City, and radio station WSUB here in Chicago. As the lead bank, First Cincinnati Trust has agreed to take $7 million of the $16 million bank portion of the loan and has asked us to take $6 million. I believe they are trying to place the remaining $3 million at a New York bank. Several insurance companies have indicated a possible interest in taking the $7.5 million long-term segment of the loan.

"I haven't checked the figures yet, but the principals are well connected and highly regarded. As you'll see in the file, there are collateral business possibilities here. Incidentally, our good neighbors at the Loop National turned this one down.

"Whether or not you think this loan is do-able, I hope you'll take this as an opportunity to dig deeper into this situation and come up with some guidelines we can use in evaluating future broadcasting credits. How much can you lend to a company with good cash flows but a negative tangible net worth? Specifically, how much would you be willing to lend CBC against their current operations and proposed purchases, and on what basis?

"I have a luncheon meeting tomorrow with Mr. Carter of First Cincinnati, so I'd like to have your report by 10 A.M."

THE BROADCASTING INDUSTRY

In the course of his recent study, Mr. Stone had gathered a variety of facts about the broadcasting industry. By December, 1960, there were 530 TV stations and 3,688 radio stations operating in 226 metropolitan markets. The TV industry had grown rapidly in the middle fifties from 122 stations in 1952 to 501 stations in 1957; however, in the following few years the total had shown only a nominal increase. This leveling trend was due to several factors:

1. Uhf stations, which operated on channels 14–83, had not fared well. Whereas 40% of TV sets produced in 1953 were equipped to receive uhf channels, only 15% were so equipped in 1960. The number of uhf stations operating in 1960 was 91, down from 121 in 1953.
2. The Federal Communications Commission was increasingly reluctant to grant coveted vhf licenses in the face of opposition from stations serving the area where the applicant planned to broadcast and in light of adequate coverage in most areas.
3. The industry was approaching saturation. Of the 226 metropolitan markets, 84 were served by three or more stations, 21 by four or more. Since there were only three major networks, it had become increasingly difficult for an applicant to show that the approval of his license would be "in the public interest," a phrase the FCC used often in defining its responsibilities.

The number of radio stations in operation had shown a similar leveling trend. This was believed attributable more to declining opportunities for profit, resulting from competition from TV and other media, than to difficulty in obtaining licenses to operate.

Profitability

Data collected by Mr. Stone, which showed a wide difference in profit performance of TV stations versus radio stations, are given in Exhibit 1 (page 778). Total TV sales and earnings had more than doubled between 1954 and 1960, while the number of stations had increased by only 29%. During the same period the number of radio stations had increased by 38%, and although sales kept pace, aggregate earnings stabilized at a relatively low level.

In both the radio and the TV industries, profits varied over a wide range between stations. Return on equity figures were available only for a few publicly owned companies, but Mr. Stone gathered from a variety of sources that in many cases profits had been quite substantial. Unlike public utilities, broadcasting companies were not restricted by the government as to rates or profits.

Operations

Mr. Stone believed that broadcasting could be characterized as the business of selling to advertisers the markets reached by the stations' transmitting facilities. Advertising revenues were attracted in two ways. Some revenues came through the national networks, which sold programs such as "Bonanza" (or in the case of radio, "Mary Noble, Backstage Wife") to the agencies of national advertisers, then passed along approximately 25% of the revenue to those of their affiliated stations that contracted to broadcast the program. The stations also received revenue directly from national and local advertisers, which sponsored nonnetwork programming such as a film series ("Playboy Penthouse," for example), a cartoon series, or a movie. The rights to broadcast these films were purchased by each station from independent producers. National and local advertisements were also aired during station breaks and locally produced programs.

A recent industry breakdown of these revenues was as follows:

	TV	Radio
Network	21%	6%
National	55	31
Local	24	63

Profitability was affected to an unusually great extent by variations in revenues, since the direct costs associated with incremental revenues were minor, consisting primarily of sales commissions. Network hourly rates were fixed by agreement between the station and the network and were generally subject to change by the network; national spot and local rates were determined by each station and publicly quoted in its rate card. Network and national spot revenues were relatively stable and were to some extent beyond the control of the station sales manager. Local sales were less stable, and while a heavy percentage of local revenues may have been a sign of good sales effort, it was also considered an indication that cash flows and profits were vulnerable.

Local and national spot rates were based on independent estimates of population and number of sets in use in the service area of the station and were affected by appraisals made by various rating agencies of the number of sets tuned into the station. The basis for determining rates was quite consistent across the country, and in the TV industry rates had increased from time to time as a result of the effectiveness of TV as an advertising medium.

Mr. Stone was impressed with the prime importance of network affiliation to a TV station; the network was a major source of revenue and an important factor in the station's relative popularity in its market area. The affiliation was a freely negotiated arm's-length transaction subject to cancellation by either party.

Each station was required to have its license renewed every 3 years by the FCC. Although this was normally a formality, the FCC had on rare occasions refused to renew licenses because of programming or other actions "not in the public interest."

Purchases of Broadcasting Stations

Transfers of existing licenses were subject to the approval of the FCC, but approval was routinely granted. As a result of the great profitability of TV stations and the limited number of new licenses being granted, the price of successful stations had risen substantially above cost. Thus many recently acquired stations had a high intangible value on the asset side of their balance sheets, frequently entitled "Network Affiliation Contracts." These intangibles were not depreciable for tax purposes.

CENTRAL BROADCASTING COMPANY

CBC began operations in the fall of 1954 with the purchase of TV station WTLO in Toledo. In August, 1957, CBC was purchased outright by a group of businessmen headed by Mr. Simon J. Becker, who became the new president, bringing with him an experienced management team.

Mr. Becker had been active in radio since 1935 and in TV since 1946 and was widely regarded as one of the most capable executives in the broadcasting industry. He had excellent connections with the National Broadcasting Company, and was very close to First Cincinnati Trust Company, a bank with which Cook County National Bank had been trying for years to establish an important correspondent relationship but with little success. His business associates, some of whom had their offices in Chicago, were successful men with ample personal bank accounts and a variety of business interests. In a recent discussion with Mr. Roth, Mr. Becker had talked about his plans for CBC:

As you know, because they are not regulated as to return on equity, broadcasting companies under capable management have a unique opportunity to be quite profitable compared with the average manufacturing enterprise. We feel that we can purchase stations and, through our know-how and experience, add profits to existing revenues by cutting operating costs and bring in new business to increase profits even further. Since advertising outlays by major corporations are projected to reach all-time highs in 1962, the outlook for CBC looks really promising.

When Mr. Roth had asked him about possible clouds on the horizon, Mr. Becker had replied, "Despite well-publicized problems[1] of the mass communications industry, we do not feel threatened by any particular legislation or disruption of any existing business relationship. We feel that our principal future problem is the economy itself since advertising budgets are subject to rapid reappraisals."

Of his plans for future acquisitions, Mr. Becker had said, "It's definitely a seller's market. The scramble for stations for the past 10 years has bid prices up to the point where good stations at any price are now hard to find."

Acquisitions

Shortly after the acquisition of CBC by Mr. Becker's group, CBC purchased TV station WCAP in Champaign, Illinois. As reflected in CBC's December 31, 1958, balance sheet (included in Exhibit 2), the cost of these properties ($2.6 million) plus working capital needs were financed by $2.8 million equity and $1.4 million bank debt.

In early 1959 CBC purchased WCNO-AM and WCNO-TV in Cincinnati at prices of $1.0 million and $4.0 million respectively. This purchase and the additional working capital requirements were financed by a term loan of $6 million and subordinated debentures of $1.5 million. The loan, from First Cincinnati Trust, called for repayment in quarterly instalments of $125,000 for 4 years with a $4 million balloon. All the cash flows stemming from depreciation, amortization of intangibles, and earnings in excess of $500,000 a year were to be applied to the balloon portion of the loan. The $1.5 million subordinated debentures, held privately, were due on April 15, 1964. Warrants attached to the debentures entitled the holders to purchase 214,286 common shares at $7 a share until that date. Thus by the end of 1959, CBC had succeeded in obtaining debt-equity leverage of almost three to one.

Under Mr. Becker's leadership significant improvement was shown for each property (see Exhibit 3). Both revenues and operating margins of each station were boosted. According to Mr. Carter of First Cincinnati

---

[1] Among the vocal critics of television programming practices was the newly appointed head of the Federal Communications Commission, Newton Minow, who labeled TV programming "a vast wasteland."

Trust, CBC's performance had exceeded the detailed cash flow projec- ʌ
tions submitted by Mr. Becker prior to the 1959 term loan.

These results, in conjunction with the rising market for broadcasting properties, caused the market value of CBC stations (as appraised by
an industry expert at the request of Mr. Carter) to be substantially in
excess of book value, as shown below:

	Cost	Market Value, 1961
WTLO, Toledo................	$1,000,000	$ 9,000,000
WCAP, Champaign.............	1,600,000	6,500,000
WCNO-TV, Cincinnati.........	5,000,000	10,000,000
WCNO-AM, Cincinnati........	1,000,000	2,000,000
	$8,600,000	$27,500,000

Condition of Stations

The appraisal of CBC properties certified that all broadcasting towers
and equipment were up to date, in good condition, and equipped for
color, and that CBC's film contracts were in good condition and not
immediately subject to unusual decline in value. CBC's fund flows
resulting from earned depreciation would not be needed for capital
expenditures, which in the case of less well-equipped stations could be
major. Installation of color transmitting facilities, for example, often
required an outlay of over $250,000. Film contracts consisted of film
series, usually bought a year in advance, for 39 shows plus 13 reruns;
cartoons, for which the normal contracts ran for a period of 4 years; and
films, which were purchased up to 5 years in advance. Outstanding film
contracts could be a negative factor in the appraisal of a TV station if they
were judged to be overvalued, too large, or for too long a maturity.

Markets

In a ranking of the 226 metropolitan markets by size in *TV Factbook*,
a leading trade publication, markets served by CBC stations were rated as
follows:

Cincinnati..........................	16th
Toledo...............................	39th
Champaign–Decatur–Springfield........	65th

According to census estimates, these areas promised better than average
growth potential. In each of the three areas, CBC was considered to be
more aggressive than its competitors and gaining on them. Currently,
WCNO-TV was ahead of two Cincinnati competitors; WCNO-AM was
fourth of seven; WCAP was even with two competing stations in
Champaign; and WTLO was second of three in Toledo.

Sources of Revenues

Long an advocate of concentrating sales effort on national rather than
local advertisers, Mr. Becker regarded the distinctive mix of CBC's

revenues shown below as lending an element of stability to his operations:

	Sources of CBC Revenues	
	TV	*Radio*
Network	21%	1%
National	61	64
Local	18	35

The Loan Proposal

After reading the CBC credit file, Mr. Stone turned to Mr. Roth's memorandum describing the proposed loan and the attached cash flow projections submitted by CBC. The $16 million bank portion of the $23.5 million loan was divided into two parts: $12 million at 5¼% payable to November 15, 1967, in 12 semiannual instalments of $1 million each; and a $4 million, 5½% balloon due January 1, 1968. Under the proposed terms, each year 75% of the total cash generated from depreciation, amortization, and earnings in excess of $2 million would be applied to the balloon until fully paid. The $7.5 million, 5¾% long-term portion of the loan was to be payable in semiannual instalments of $1 million due May 15, 1969, to May 15, 1972, with the balance of $500,000 due on November 15, 1972. This portion of the loan was to be issued with warrants to purchase 75,000 common shares at $20 per share until November 15, 1972.

The loan proceeds were to be used as follows:

To purchase KMOC and KMOC-TV in Kansas City	$14 million
To purchase radio station WSUB in Chicago	5 million
To repay the outstanding balance of the 1959 term loan	4.5 million

KMOC and KMOC-TV

Stations KMOC and KMOC-TV had begun operations on September 30, 1958. Despite unimpressive management and a mediocre rating as compared with competition in the Kansas City area, the stations showed an operating profit of over $1.2 million for the year ended May 31, 1961. In addition to the normal improvements they could expect to attain, CBC executives saw two special plus factors in the Kansas City situation. First, competition, though fairly competent, was notably unaggressive. Second, the market reached by Kansas City stations was underrated at present; the forthcoming 1961 market appraisal by the American Research Bureau was expected to move Kansas City from 29th to 22nd in the ranking of metropolitan markets, which would allow an upward adjustment of rate cards. Exhibit 4 shows KMOC-TV's 1960 operating results as compared with those of KCM, the larger of its two competitors.

not aggressive, CBC will be → will be able to charge more

WSUB

WSUB, a station located on the northwest fringe of Chicago, had had for years the image of a suburban station, although its signal covered the Chicago metropolitan area. Becker planned to compete vigorously with the major midtown radio stations by means of aggressive rock-and-roll programming and saw an opportunity thereby to add substantially to local advertising revenues.

Cash Flow Projections

CBC's 6-year projections are presented in Exhibit 5. Mr. Stone noted that according to the projections, the balloon portion of the bank loan would be retired at the beginning of 1967, and that if the "Cash Retained" by CBC were applied to the balloon, it could be retired shortly after the end of 1965.

could easily pay off loan

Mr. Stone's Report

For the purpose of evaluating the CBC credit and generalizing his analysis to cover a range of broadcasting credits, Mr. Stone decided to use a checklist he had roughed out during his study of the broadcasting industry. As he started to write his report, he noted that the pro forma balance sheet submitted by CBC showed a debt to stated equity ratio of about 6:1 (see Exhibit 2). That, he mused, would raise a few eyebrows around the bank.

must restate assets at market value

Mr. Stone's report is presented in Appendix A (page 782).

balance sheet ratios are meaningless to Stone

Exhibit 1

CENTRAL BROADCASTING COMPANY

Trends in the U.S. Broadcasting Industry, 1954–60

(Dollar Figures in Millions)

	Number of Stations	Total Revenues	Total Expenses	Pretax Earnings
TV				
1954	410	$ 593.0	$ 502.7	$ 90.3
1955	437	744.7	594.5	150.2
1956	475	896.9	707.3	189.6
1957	501	943.2	783.2	160.0
1958	514	1,030.0	858.1	171.9
1959	521	1,163.9	941.6	222.3
1960	530	1,268.6	1,024.5	244.1
Radio				
1954	2,598	$ 449.5	$ 407.7	$ 41.8
1955	2,742	453.4	407.4	46.0
1956	2,966	480.6	431.4	49.2
1957	3,164	517.9	463.3	54.6
1958	3,290	523.1	485.8	37.3
1959	3,528	560.0	517.6	42.4
1960	3,688	597.7	551.8	45.9

Exhibit 2

CENTRAL BROADCASTING COMPANY

CONDENSED BALANCE SHEETS, AS OF DECEMBER 31

(Dollar Figures in Thousands)

	1958	1959	1960	1961 Pro Forma, after Proposed Acquisitions and Financing
Cash	$ 173	$ 506	$ 1,313	$ 1,804
Receivables	342	874	1,228	1,260
Inventory	28	71	58	107
Film contracts	172	433	416	957
Total current assets	$ 715	$ 1,884	$ 3,015	$ 4,128
Fixed assets	2,294	4,844	4,362	7,779
Prepaid expenses	85	147	155	176
Film contracts	326	968	770	2,132
Network affiliation contracts	641	3,860	3,860	17,933
Total assets	$4,061	$11,703	$12,162	$32,148
Payables and accruals	$ 505	$ 552	$ 541	$ 1,163
Federal taxes	...	...	686	935
Current term debt	635	1,131	1,332	2,807
Total current liabilities	$1,140	$ 1,683	$ 2,559	$ 4,905
Term debt	794	6,011	4,793	21,966
Subordinated debt	...	1,500	1,500	1,500
Common stock	1,150	1,150	1,150	1,150
Capital surplus	1,634	1,634	1,634	1,634
Earned surplus	(657)	(275)	526	993
Total liabilities	$4,061	$11,703	$12,162	$32,148

Exhibit 3

CENTRAL BROADCASTING COMPANY

SELECTED STATION OPERATING RESULTS

(Dollar Figures in Thousands)

Station	Year	Gross Sales	Net Sales*	Operating Profit	Percent to Gross Sales
WCAP	1955	$ 640	$ 548	$ 99	15.5
	1956	928	789	232	25.0
	1957†	549	473	(59)	...
	1958	735	631	17	2.3
	1959	1,056	894	228	21.6
	1960	1,398	1,187	483	34.5
WTLO	1955	$ 477	$ 416	$ (173)	...
	1956	1,102	940	126	11.4
	1957†	1,533	1,314	332	21.7
	1958	2,141	1,773	751	35.1
	1959	2,127	1,752	599	28.1
	1960	2,277	1,869	737	32.4
WCNO-TV	1958	$1,939	$1,587	$ 870	44.9
	1959†	2,474	1,984	1,147	46.4
	1960	3,951	3,131	1,900	48.1
WCNO-AM	1958	$ 476	$ 352	$ 170	35.7
	1959†	411	310	(6)	...
	1960	795	607	195	24.5

* After agency commissions.
† Year acquired by CBC.

Exhibit 4

CENTRAL BROADCASTING COMPANY

OPERATING RESULTS OF KANSAS CITY TV STATIONS, 1960

	KMOC-TV	KCM-TV
Gross revenue	$2,960,000	$4,674,000
Agency and representatives	468,000	842,000
Net revenue	$2,492,000	$3,832,000
Operating expense	1,718,000	2,094,000
Operating profit	$ 774,000	$1,738,000

$$\frac{1961}{\frac{OE}{TA}} = 11.7\%$$

Exhibit 5 CENTRAL BROADCASTING COMPANY

CASH FLOW PROJECTIONS

(Dollar Figures in Thousands)

	(12 months to 5/31/61) Actual	1962	1963	1964	1965	1966	1967
Net revenue:							
CBC	$ 6,795	$ 7,300	$ 7,850	$ 8,436			
WSUB	1,321	1,523	1,774	1,903			
KMOC-TV	2,492	2,930	4,386	4,646			
KMOC	687	1,020					
Total	$11,295	$12,773	$14,010	$14,985			
Operating expenses:							
CBC	$ 3,580	$ 3,800	$ 3,990	$ 4,190			
WSUB	969	915	960	1,008			
KMOC-TV	1,559	1,740	2,200	2,200			
KMOC	402	490					
Total	$ 6,510	$ 6,945	$ 7,150	$ 7,398			
Operating profit:							
CBC	$ 3,215	$ 3,500	$ 3,860	$ 4,246			
WSUB	352	608	814	895			
KMOC-TV	933	1,190	2,186	2,446			
KMOC	285	530					
Total	$ 4,785	$ 5,828	$ 6,860	$ 7,587	$ 7,587	$ 7,587	$7,587
Other deductions:							
Corporate expense	$ 503	$ 570	$ 630	$ 675	$ 675	$ 675	$ 675
Depreciation	916	1,414	1,321	911	911	911	911
Interest	421	1,349	1,249	1,082	959	859	759
Total	$ 1,840	$ 3,333	$ 3,200	$ 2,668	$ 2,545	$ 2,445	$2,345
Profit before taxes	$ 2,945	$ 2,495	$ 3,660	$ 4,919	$ 5,042	$ 5,242	$5,242
Income tax (54.64%)	1,451	1,363	2,000	2,688	2,755	2,810	2,864
Net profit	$ 1,494	$ 1,132	$ 1,660	$ 2,231	$ 2,287	$ 2,332	$2,378
Add: Depreciation	916	1,414	1,321	911	911	911	911
Cash available	$ 2,410	$ 2,546	$ 2,981	$ 3,142	$ 3,198	$ 3,243	$3,289
Payments on loan:							
Fixed		$ 2,000	$ 2,000	$ 2,000	$ 2,000	$ 2,000	$2,000
75% of remaining cash available		410	736	857	898	934	165*
Cash retained		$ 136	$ 245	$ 285	$ 300	$ 309	$1,124
Beginning loan balance‡		$25,000‡	$22,590‡	$19,854	$15,497	$12,599	$9,665
Payments		2,410	2,736	4,357†	2,898	2,934	2,165
Ending loan balance		$22,590	$19,854	$15,497	$12,599	$ 9,665	$7,500

* Balance of balloon portion of term debt due banks.

† Assumes that $1,500,000 subordinated debentures due 1964 would be offset by exercise of attached warrants, entitling holders to purchase 214,286 common shares at $7 per share, which expired on due date. Current market for CBC stock (1,168,223 shares outstanding) was 22¾.

‡ Includes $1.5 million subordinated debentures.

APPENDIX A

Memorandum

To: Mr. Albert V. Roth

Re: Central Broadcasting Company

I have taken the CBC situation as an opportunity to go deeper into the thinking that lies behind credit evaluations in this type of business. The television checklist is an attempt to break down the general conclusion on a TV credit into its various components, and develop a method of looking at and evaluating these components individually, rather than relying on a general "feel" for the situation.

Inasmuch as the $23.5 million loan request comes within CBC's debt capacity as determined by use of the checklist, I recommend that CCNB agree to participate in this loan.

Toby M. Stone
Credit Department

June 30, 1961

Guidelines for Lending to the Broadcasting Industry

The following checklist was prepared to clarify and substantiate the financial analysis of the CBC loan. However, the overall purpose of the analysis is to determine standards for establishing the minimum amount of equity required in the ownership of any broadcasting properties, or more exactly, the maximum amount of bank debt that can be put into any television broadcasting situation with a reasonable amount of risk.

The guidelines are the result of an attempt to form a summary checklist of significant factors which must be taken into consideration in evaluating the creditworthiness of a loan to the owner, or prospective owner, of a television station or group of stations. It is an attempt to formalize the thinking and underlying considerations which make up the final analysis and mathematically come up with a guideline figure which will approximate the amount that can be safely loaned against the properties involved. This should help to provide uniformity and consistency to these evaluations. However, it should be emphasized that this system, which involved the use of a confidence index, is no more than a weighted average use of probabilities, and the results of the analysis will be no better than the individual evaluations which go into the final figure.

It is most important to recognize that this procedure is primarily designed to insure that the lending officer will: (1) consider *all* the factors appropriate to the loan, and (2) keep these factors in their *proper perspective.*

Establishment of Base Figure

To establish the base figure against which the loan will be made, it is necessary to have as accurate an appraisal as possible made of the company, so that the equity base may be restated and a revalued figure for the net worth of the company established. Balance sheet figures in this business *have very little meaning*, unless the property has been recently traded or purchased. Consequently, if the book value of the stations owned is considerably less than their market value, the stations must be realistically reevaluated and placed on the balance sheet at a conservative figure for their current market value. In some cases the stations may even be overvalued on the balance sheet, and in these cases their value must be discounted and the best estimate of their worth used. In this manner the equity of the corporation will be restated, and it is this "Restated Asset Base" that will be used in the subsequent calculations. It is against this figure that the composite ratio will be applied, thus making the composite ratio a form of a debt/equity ratio. CBC's Restated Asset Base will be $27.5 million, the market value of presently owned properties, plus $19 million, the purchase price of the stations being acquired, or a total of $46.5 million.

Use of Composite Ratio

The final composite ratio is determined from the checklist by utilizing the accompanying explanations for each category to assist in applying a reasonable confidence index. The maximum composite ratio that could possibly be obtained is .66 which in effect would allow a 2 to 1 debt/equity ratio. This would appear to be the farthest the bank should extend itself in any loan of this nature. However, to reach this ratio, it would be necessary for the lending officer to have 100% confidence in each aspect of the analysis; consequently, the officer may find it is extremely difficult to justify even a 1 to 1 debt/equity ratio. The use of these guidelines prevents the lender from completely discounting or overlooking the significant aspects of the credit and, it is hoped, will guide him to a more realistic evaluation of the situation.

If the figure reached by the lending officer in making this analysis is satisfactory to him, the checklist will then provide a detailed and inclusive means of substantiating his conclusions.

EXPLANATION OF CHECKLIST FACTORS

(The remainder of Mr. Stone's report covered material presented in the body of the case.)

GUIDELINES FOR LENDING TO THE TELEVISION BROADCASTING BUSINESS

TELEVISION CHECKLIST

Central Broadcasting Company Loan Proposal	Column I Weight Factor*	Column II Confidence Index† 0–100%	Column I × Column II
Cash flow			
1. Reliability			
Historic figures (available used)	6	80%	4.8
Degree of optimism	5	60	3.0
Depreciation—Tax estimated (basis for)	5	90	4.5
Capital expenditures estimates (Height of tower, color facilities, condition and quality of broadcasting equipment)	5	90	4.5

2. Length of payout........................10   30% ·-   3.0

    Cash Flow Subtotal....................31   19.8

Management

    1. Track record in industry and supporting per-

       sonnel............................... 6   100%   6.0 ✓

    2. General reputation, integrity, etc........... 4   100   4.0 ✓

Markets

    1. Size.................................... 5   90%   4.5 ✓

    2. Growth potential....................... 5   70   3.5 ✓

Network Affiliations and License............... 7   90   6.3 ✓

    1. Number of stations in market (also overlap)

    2. Number of stations owned

    3. Station position in market and strength of

       other stations

    4. Ownership of license and history

Outside Influences........................... 8   100%   8.0 ✓

    Balances

    Other relationships

    New business potential

    Interest rate

Film Contracts—if significant minus (up to   ✓

    minus 5)

Composite Ratio............................66   52.1

Restated Asset Base × Composite Ratio = Debt
    Capacity ($46,500,000) × (52.1)/100 =
    $24,227,000.

* Subject to modifications based on experience and the dictates of common sense, these weight factors should be applicable to *any* broadcasting loan.

† These percentages apply only to CBC and reflect the author's judgment based on available information.

Case 24

Price Textiles, Inc.

In PREPARATION for a board of directors meeting on June 5, 1952, Mr. Daniel Randall, treasurer of Price Textiles, Inc., had decided to recommend the payment of the regular quarterly dividend, totaling $41,000, to the holders of the company's 4½% cumulative preferred stock. He had yet to decide what dividend, if any, should be paid to the company's common stockholders in the second quarter of 1952.

Price Textiles operated several cotton and rayon textile mills in four northern states. Like many other textile companies, it had experienced a number of difficult years during the 1930's. It had staved off insolvency only by means of strong bank support. Profits improved later, were high during World War II, and had remained high through 1950.

Following World War II the company's management had taken several actions to improve the company's ability to produce efficiently and to strengthen the company's financial position. In 1946 a new issue of cumulative preferred stock provided funds to retire outstanding bank loans of $5,400,000. From 1946 through the first 16 weeks of 1952, $14,700,000 had been spent by the company in modernizing productive facilities. In addition, $21,600,000, largely written off as expense, had been used to repair existing machinery, buildings, and equipment. The capital expenditures and a working capital increase of $15,500,000 had been financed largely through retained earnings. Exhibits 1 and 2 present the company's balance sheet and income statements for selected years from 1945 to March 22, 1952.

In April, 1951, the company's profits began to decline. Increased wages, declining textile prices, and smaller quantities sold had adversely affected Price Textiles' profits over several months, as shown in Exhibit 3. From April, 1951, to June, 1952, spindle hours per workday declined 40%, loom hours fell off 35%, and total yards produced dropped 30%. By the beginning of May, 1952, order backlogs had shrunk 70%, and on June 1 the company had almost no business booked for the third quarter. On June 5, 1952, Mr. Randall felt that there had been little to indicate any immediate recovery from what he still expected to be a short-run rather than a long-term decline in sales.

With regard to the prospects for the textile industry in 1952, Standard and Poor's *Industry Surveys* carried the following article on May 15, 1952:

. . . textile production in the first quarter of 1952 held at about the same rate as in the final quarter of 1951. . . . A further drop in output is expected in the second quarter as the result of additional cutbacks made in April and seasonally slow demand.

.   .   .   .

The favorable outlook for consumer income, and the probability of greater spending for soft-good lines, point to better business for retail stores later this year. While retailers are likely to be conservative in making forward commitments, inventory positions should permit somewhat more active orders for textile producers during the final half of 1952.

With inventories at most other trade levels in fairly good balance, improved ordering by retailers should stimulate greater activity within the textile industry. More active demand would lift prices from their current depressed levels.

The survey said the following about Price Textiles' prospects:

Although earnings were down in the first quarter of 1952, gradual improvement in Price Textiles' profits is likely, particularly in the final half, and 1952 earnings may not be too far below 1951 earnings. Dividends will probably hold at $0.40 per share in the second quarter. . . .

As indicated in Exhibit 4, dividend payments on the common stock by the company had varied considerably in the past. From December, 1946, to December, 1950, the company had paid a "quarterly" dividend of $0.30 per share, with extras during the course of each year. In 1951 a dividend of $0.70 per share was paid in each of the first three quarters of the year, plus an extra dividend of $0.40 per share in March. The dividend was reduced to $0.50 per share in the last quarter of 1951 and to $0.40 per share in the first quarter of 1952. Each dividend, when announced, was called a "quarterly" dividend or an "extra" dividend. Although the company had carefully avoided any statements which might imply that a minimum dividend rate would be maintained whenever possible, Mr. Randall felt that some stockholders had come to regard the $0.30 dividend as regular.

Mr. Randall had already decided to recommend the payment of the regular quarterly dividend on the company's 4½% cumulative preferred stock, which had been kept current since its issue in 1946. Although this issue had an obligatory sinking fund of $216,000 per year, the company had already bought and retired enough preferred stock to cover the sinking fund through 1955.

Price Textiles' common stock was owned by 8,203 individuals in most of the 48 states. On the other hand, studies of the stockholder list indicated that many stockholders were employees and local businessmen. Management holdings were not significantly large. The influence of the only large stockholder, Mr. Gustaveson, is discussed below.

In late 1950 a small group of southern textile manufacturers headed by Mr. Arthur Gustaveson had attempted unsuccessfully[1] to secure enough Price Textiles' common stock to elect a representative to the board of directors. Mr. Gustaveson and his associates had purchased on the open market 132,700 shares of Price Textiles, or about 17% of the outstanding stock. Price Textiles' stock was not listed on any exchange; however, it was actively traded in the over-the-counter market. In December, 1950, Mr. Gustaveson failed in an attempt to secure an additional 220,000 shares when Price Textiles' stockholders rejected his exchange offer of shares in Mr. Gustaveson's southern textile companies. The company had actively opposed this exchange offer because management believed that the election of the proposed director would benefit neither the company nor the communities in which Price Textiles operated plants. Although unsuccessful, Mr. Gustaveson intimated he might again enter the open market to increase his holdings in Price Textiles.

In the 1951 annual report the company said to its stockholders: "Your loyal support has been one of our strong assets. This loyalty has been rewarded by increasing dividends—a return for the funds which have been so necessary in Price Textiles' expansion program." The company also pledged to its stockholders "to continue its policy of reinvesting earnings for plant improvements so that the company might continue to grow."

The 1950 annual report to the company's stockholders had explained the company's reinvestment of earnings as follows:

In 1950 we spent $1,740,000 for new machinery and equipment. The money used to purchase this required equipment came from our profits. If we had made no profits we would have had to borrow money to purchase this equipment, which we believe is necessary to guarantee a permanent future investment for our stockholders. Next year we plan to spend $1,500,000 on machinery if our earnings provide the cash necessary to pay for it.

Because new equipment has increased so much in price, ordinary depreciation will not provide sufficient funds to replace worn-out equipment when the need arises. We have set aside part of the 1950 profits in a reserve account, thus recognizing the inadequacy of present depreciation rates.

Furthermore, additional funds are needed to finance the increased working capital requirements resulting from higher prices and larger inventories.

---

[1] The company's charter did not provide for cumulative voting in the election of directors.

Mr. Randall felt that two of the seven members of the board of directors, who were investment bankers, might be especially inclined to oppose a reduction in the dividend rate below $0.30 a share. However, a recent report from one of the over-the-counter dealers handling transactions of Price Textiles' common stock ventured the opinion that the market might already have discounted the possibility of lower dividend payment in the second quarter. In May, 1952, other cotton and rayon textile manufacturers were priced on the market to yield about 7%, based on current dividend rates. Market price ranges for Price Textiles' common stock in 1948 to June 2, 1952, are shown in Exhibit 5.

Mr. Randall felt that dividend action of other textile companies might temper or accentuate the market's reaction to any change in the dividends paid by Price Textiles, Inc. Exhibit 6 presents recent dividend action taken by several major textile companies.

On March 5, 1952, the company had to resort to borrowing for the first time in 5 years. It obtained $1,800,000 from the Allen National Bank of Boston on a 3%, 90-day unsecured note. Although Mr. Randall had negotiated a 90-day renewal of the note, he hoped to begin retiring this debt before the new maturity date. If necessary, Mr. Randall believed Price Textiles could borrow several million dollars more, since the company had a strong current position and no long-term debt. He thought that additional borrowings might increase the interest rate slightly. Furthermore, if additional borrowing was necessary, he believed it would be desirable to extend repayments over a longer period than 90 days.

The only sources of cash that Mr. Randall could be assured of during the next 3 months other than borrowing would be from profits, if any materialized, and from depreciation, if earned; this would run at the rate of $66,000 for each 4-week period. There might also be a cash gain of about $30,000 for each 4-week period as a result of writing off prepaid expenditures against income.

On June 4 the company had a book cash balance amounting to $2,880,000. The company had accrued state and city taxes of $1,040,000, payable on June 15, and accrued annual vacation pay of $560,000, due employees on June 27. Outstanding commitments for new capital assets to be purchased in the next 3 months totaled $60,000. No new orders for machinery had been placed during the last 7 or 8 months, and management had made every effort to curtail expenditures other than those incident to normal operating experience. Federal income tax payments of $460,000 were payable on the 15th of September and December.[2] The finished goods inventory had remained at about the same

---

[2] Mr. Randall decided it would not be advantageous to deduct the income tax carry-backs, resulting from the company's recent losses, from the current income tax liability because subsequent profits might offset these losses. If the company's operations for the year resulted in a net loss, it would receive a tax rebate check in 1953. Thus, for short-run planning purposes, Mr. Randall considered that net losses before taxes represented the actual cash drain on the company.

level through 1952. Work-in-process inventories were down, reflecting the lower production levels in 1952; and Mr. Randall felt that as much as $1,800,000 of additional cash would be necessary to finance increased work-in-process inventories and accounts receivable should a rapid and substantial pickup in orders develop. The increase in total inventory between December 31, 1951, and March 22, 1952, was largely the result of forward purchases of cotton. No reduction in this raw material inventory was likely until September.

Technological improvement in textile machinery had been rapid after World War II. Recently one leading textile machinery manufacturer had placed on the market a revolutionary new spinning frame, and other textile machinery companies were continuously developing new machines and new techniques. Although the company's modernization program had been completed, the management of Price Textiles, Inc., realized that additional expenditures would be necessary in the future to keep their company competitive. Mr. Randall believed these expenditures would be resumed at the high level of the previous few years as soon as operations became profitable enough to finance them.

In an effort to reduce labor costs, the company had reopened discussions of its labor contract in late April, 1952. The company officials had argued that the current $0.30 per hour wage differential between their company and southern companies had seriously affected the company's ability to operate profitably. Mr. Randall estimated that each $0.01 reduction in hourly wage rates would save the company $160,000 per year before taxes. With lower costs, he believed the company could compete more favorably for textile orders and thus increase sales volume. Management argued that this would allow it to begin rehiring workers previously laid off. The union opposed any reduction in wages, and the dispute had been submitted to an arbitration board. The company did not expect to know until late June how much, if any, reduction in the $0.30 per hour wage differential the arbitration would grant.

The question of moving entire mills to the South was under study. Mr. Randall did not know what the outcome of this study would be; but should the company decide to move even one mill to the South, he believed relocation expenses would be several million dollars.

Exhibit 1

PRICE TEXTILES, INC.

SELECTED BALANCE SHEETS

(Dollar Figures in Thousands)

ASSETS	1945	Dec. 31 1949	1950	1951	Mar. 22 1952
Cash	$ 2,462	$ 3,144	$ 1,789	$ 2,566	$ 2,701
U.S. treasury notes (in excess of tax liability)	232	245	284	....	....
Accounts receivable	1,045	4,713	6,355	6,460	4,666
Inventories	8,694	17,872	18,946	20,037	22,790
Prepaid expenses	....	348	456	485	786
Total current assets	$12,433	$26,322	$27,830	$29,548	$30,943
Land, building, and machines (net)	5,908	13,686	14,549	15,204	15,817
Other assets	497	113	93	62	69
Total assets	$18,838	$40,121	$42,472	$44,814	$46,829
LIABILITIES					
Accounts payable and accruals	$ 2,120	$ 3,041	$ 3,175	$ 1,494	$ 2,901
Provision for federal income tax (less U.S. treasury notes)	....	....	....	3,210	2,234
Total current liabilities	$ 2,120	$ 3,041	$ 3,175	$ 4,704	$ 5,135
Notes payable—bank	5,400				1,800
Reserve for property replacement	10	1,142	1,426	1,560	1,560
Preferred stock (par value $100)	....	3,956	3,741	3,650	3,650
Common stock (783,000 shares)	10,242	10,242	10,242	10,242	10,242
Earned surplus	1,066	21,740	23,888	24,658	24,442
Total liabilities	$18,838	$40,121	$42,472	$44,814	$46,829

Exhibit 2

PRICE TEXTILES, INC.

SELECTED INCOME STATEMENTS

(Dollar Figures in Thousands)

	1946	1947	1948	1949	1950	1951	Jan. 1–Mar. 22 1952
Gross income	$58,050	$76,822	$84,904	$66,433	$76,589	$72,192	$15,574
Cost of goods sold:							
Materials					40,358	38,671	9,019
Wages and salary					25,224	24,653	5,627
Depreciation					790	846	204
Other					1,824	1,955	449
Total cost of goods sold	$46,240	$61,395	$68,878	$61,195	$68,196	$66,125	$15,299
Profit before taxes	$11,810	$15,427	$16,026	$ 5,238	$ 8,393	$ 6,067	$ 275
Federal taxes	4,666	6,027	6,107	2,058	3,569	3,115	133
Income tax return	.....	.....	.....	.....	.....	440	.....
Net income	$ 7,144	$ 9,400	$ 9,919	$ 3,180	$ 4,824	$ 3,392	$ 142
Distribution of net income:							
Preferred stock dividends	$ 84	$ 220	$ 194	$ 181	$ 171	$ 166	$ 41
Common stock dividends	940	1,835	2,819	1,408	2,232	2,340	317
Reserves	882	1,243	1,123	283	283	134	.....
Retained in business	5,238	6,102	5,783	1,308	2,138	752	(216)
Total dividends as percentage of net income	14%	22%	30%	50%	50%	74%	252%

Exhibit 3

PRICE TEXTILES, INC.

SALES AND INCOME DATA

(Dollar Figures in Thousands)

Four-Week Period Ending	Sales	Income (or Loss) before Tax	Income (or Loss) after Tax
March 24, 1951	$7,590	$1,055	$506
April 21, 1951	5,151	458	221
May 19, 1951	6,037	812	392
June 16, 1951	5,539	512	245
July 14, 1951	4,448	219	104
August 11, 1951	4,426	258	122
September 8, 1951	3,868	120	54
October 6, 1951	4,145	125	67
November 3, 1951	4,949	153	74
December 1, 1951	5,763	(46)	(23)
December 29, 1951	4,960	121	61
January 26, 1952	5,220	164	84
February 23, 1952	5,324	141	70
March 22, 1952	5,001	(39)	(19)
April 19, 1952	4,692	(113)	(52)
May 17, 1952	5,217	(720)*	(360)

* This figure includes an inventory write-down of $540,000. A semiannual physical inventory and adjustment of inventory values to cost or market, whichever is lower, indicated that market values were $540,000 less than shown on the perpetual inventory record.

Exhibit 4

PRICE TEXTILES, INC.

COMMON STOCK DIVIDENDS PER SHARE
1946—MARCH, 1952

Period		Dividends/Share
1946		$1.20
1947		2.40
1948		3.60
1949		1.80
1950		2.85
1951	First quarter	$1.10
	Second quarter	0.70
	Third quarter	0.70
	Fourth quarter	0.50
	Total 1951	3.00
1952	First quarter	0.40

Exhibit 5

PRICE TEXTILES, INC.

MARKET PRICE RANGES FOR PRICE TEXTILES' COMMON STOCK
1948—JUNE 2, 1952

	High	Low
1948	22⅞	13⅞
1949	17½	12¼
1950	39¾	15⅞
1951	49½	33
1952		
January	33½	29
February	31⅝	28⅝
March	31¾	29
April	29	24⅜
May	31⅝	22½
June 2, 1952	25¼ (asked)	24¾ (bid)

Exhibit 6

PRICE TEXTILES, INC.

RECENT DIVIDEND ACTION TAKEN BY OTHER
MAJOR TEXTILE PRODUCERS

Company	Date	Dividend per Share	Date	Dividend per Share
American Woolen Company	2/20/52	passed	5/20/52	passed
Bates Manufacturing Company	1/16/52	$0.20	4/16/52	$0.15
Berkshire Fine Spinning Assoc.	3/1/52	0.35	6/2/52	0.25
Burlington Mills	1/24/52	0.25	4/25/52	0.25
Cone Mills	2/5/52	0.40	4/1/52	0.40
Fruit of the Loom	1/10/51	2.00	1/17/52	1.00
Gustaveson Textiles	1/15/52	0.25	4/15/52	passed
Pacific Mills	1/21/52	0.50	4/21/52	0.50
Pepperell	1/31/52	1.25*	4/24/52	0.75
J. P. Stevens	1/8/52	0.50	4/10/52	0.50
Textron	12/12/52	0.50	3/12/52	0.25

* Includes $0.50 extra.

Case 25

Lesmer Electronics Corporation

ON JANUARY 26, 1956, the board of directors of Lesmer Electronics Corporation was to meet to declare the quarterly dividend on the common stock. Two years earlier, the same board had voted to reduce the quarterly rate from 50 cents to 25 cents per share and to supplement these payments with an annual stock dividend of 5%. The president of the company, Mr. R. K. Patterson, had been the prime advocate of the change on the grounds that the lower cash distribution was better suited to both the needs of the rapidly growing company and the desires of its stockholders. A minority of the directors had dissented from this view, however, and periodically since had proposed the restoration of the 50-cent dividend. The president, in a memorandum to the directors in mid-January, 1956, indicated that he hoped the forthcoming meeting would lead to a unanimous viewpoint on the company's future dividend policy.

Lesmer Electronics Corporation was a medium-sized manufacturer of a variety of specialized electronic products, most of which were developed by the company's research department. Its growth since 1950 had been both rapid and steady, stemming from the defense requirements of World War II and the Korean situation, the postwar development of television, and latterly the specialized applications of electronics to business data processing. Sales, earnings, and other financial data for 1945 through 1955 are given in Exhibit 1.

The board of directors formulated the major policies and programs of the company. The board was composed of the president, four vice presidents, and four outside directors. The latter were all active officers of large, noncompeting industrial firms. They had been invited by Mr. Patterson to serve on the Lesmer board and had done so for periods extending from 6 to 11 years. The directors as a group owned almost 7% of the outstanding common stock as of December 31, 1955.

Apart from the directors' holdings, no stockholder of record owned more than 2% of the outstanding stock. There were over 6,200 stockholders at the end of 1955, which was a record high for the company. Stockholders were geographically dispersed and comprised both individual and institutional investors. The company did not have a stock purchase program for its employees but did have a stock option plan for its key officers. Under the provisions of this plan, an aggregate of 25,000 authorized but unissued shares were reserved for the participants at a price equal to 95% of the market price on the date the option was granted. The options had been granted in May, 1953, when the stock was selling at $50 and could be exercised at any time within the following 5 years.

The board had authorized management to use various methods of financing the company's decade of substantial growth. Two issues of the common stock, which had been listed on the New York Stock Exchange in 1943, were sold to the public. The first offering, in March, 1946, was 30,000 shares, issued at $36⅝ per share with net proceeds to the company of $1,006,000. The second issue was made in January, 1951, when 100,000 shares were sold at $45 to provide the company with $4,180,000. Both issues had been underwritten and were quickly sold.

A second avenue of financing which the management followed was the private placement of debentures in 1950 and 1954. Prior to 1950 the company's policy had been to incur no long-term debt. The officers relinquished this policy, however, when they realized that its consequence would be the indefinite postponement of various projects that promised returns of more than 10% after taxes. Accordingly, the company arranged the placement with the Hamilton Life Insurance Company of a $5 million, 4% debenture issue with a full sinking fund of $250,000 per annum commencing in 1951 and terminating in 1970. Management negotiated a second placement of a $5 million debenture issue in June, 1954. On this occasion, the terms were 4½%, and payments to the sinking fund were deferred until 1959, when yearly amounts of $250,000 would commence. The 1954 debenture issue restricted the company in paying cash dividends on the common stock to "an amount no greater than the aggregate amount of net income after December 31, 1953, plus $2 million."

Management utilized stringent controls over the working capital employed by the company, as a further method of facilitating its growth. Since 1950 various improvements of the inventory control system had permitted the company to reduce its inventory requirements relative to sales to a level which management regarded as the absolute minimum. Similarly, the cash position of the company had been reduced to a reasonable working balance.

Although the various measures mentioned above aided significantly in financing the company's growth, the major sources of funds in the postwar period were depreciation and the retention of earnings. The company's depreciation policy was to depreciate its assets, both for accounting and income tax purposes, over the shortest period of time and on the most favorable basis permitted by the Internal Revenue Service. The company's policy on earnings retention, of course, was the complement of its dividend policy.

Dividend Policy through 1953

Although the directors of the company had not formulated a definite dividend policy prior to 1954, a number of practices had gradually evolved. Foremost of these was the practice of changing dividend payments roughly in proportion to changes in earnings. The directors desired to distribute about 30% to 40% of earnings in any single year. These payout ratios had become accepted as being fair to the stockholders in view of opportunities for profitable investment of almost any amount of retained earnings. Although this practice determined the general level of dividend payments, one other consideration influenced the specific amounts and timing of payments within the year. The directors would not increase the amounts of quarterly payments unless they believed the earnings position of the company could support the higher payments within the desired payout ratio range in future years. Therefore, in years such as 1947 and 1950, a portion of the total payments represented a year-end "special" dividend. Despite this approach, the directors had never formally represented the quarterly payments as constituting a "regular" rate, since they had desired to retain maximum flexibility in dividend determination. Exhibit 2 presents information on the company's earnings, dividends, and stock prices from 1945 to 1955.

Dividend Policy Change, January, 1954

At the meeting of the board on January 24, 1954, the directors voted to reduce the quarterly dividend payment from 50 cents to 25 cents per share and to supplement this payment with a 5% stock dividend. This action culminated discussions which had extended over several months about the best manner to finance the company's future growth.

Commencing in 1953, the company had accelerated its expansion program in order to participate fully in the greatly enlarged markets for its electronic and specialized data processing equipment. Capital expenditures in that year had exceeded $4 million, and final authorizations for 1954 were almost $7 million. Moreover, management's estimates indicated that the demand for the company's products probably would double by 1960 and that, to satisfy this rate of growth, expenditures beyond 1954 might well range from $6 million to $9 million per annum.

This great increase in the need for funds had not, of course, been unforeseen. Mr. Patterson already had received the assurance of Hamilton Life that they would be willing to purchase a $5 million debenture issue in 1954. The projected cash budget, in summary, for 1954 was as follows:

Estimated Receipts

Debentures....................................	$ 5,000,000
Earnings.......................................	4,000,000
Depreciation...................................	2,200,000
	$11,200,000

Estimated Expenditures

Capital expenditures............................	$ 6,800,000
Increased working capital requirements.............	2,600,000
Sinking fund...................................	250,000
Dividends, at 1953 level........................	1,100,000
	$10,750,000
Uncommitted funds, Dec. 31, 1954.................	$ 450,000

Despite the surplus of funds indicated by the cash budget for 1954, Mr. Patterson believed that immediate action should be taken to conserve funds for the expansion program. Accordingly, he moved that the quarterly dividend be reduced to 25 cents per share. He said that these lower payments would increase the uncommitted funds at the end of 1954 to about $1 million but that this amount and more would be needed in subsequent years to finance the company's growth.

In particular, Mr. Patterson believed that the company likely would have to issue common stock within the next few years, because it already would have drawn heavily on debt financing. Previous issues of common had been at prices substantially below the January, 1954, price range of $60 to $63 per share. With further substantial growth in earnings probable, he thought that the amount of future common stock issues should be minimized and should occur at the latest possible dates, so that the benefits of further capital appreciation would accrue largely to present stockholders. An immediate reduction in cash dividends would be in accord with this objective.

An opposing viewpoint was expressed by another director, Mr. F. B. Kugel, himself the president of a large machinery equipment company. He believed that a reduction in the quarterly cash dividend, unlike that of the year-end dividend, would be interpreted by the investment community as the signal of major financial difficulties in the company. The price of the common stock, therefore, in his opinion would decline. A lower market price in turn would adversely affect the company when it went to the market in later years, by requiring the sale of a greater number of shares to realize any needed amount of funds. He proposed, as an alternative, the continuation of the existing 50-cent rate and the granting to stockholders of preemptive rights on all future equity financing, so that their share in the company's growth need not diminish.

Mr. Patterson conceded that the market might react adversely to the proposed dividend reduction but believed that any such decline would be short-lived. As soon as investors could see that the company's program continued to be sound and successful, their confidence in the company would be fully restored. He also argued that the possibility of the temporary market reaction was an added reason for reducing the dividend now, so the market would be back to normal before any common stock was issued.

As for preemptive rights on future issues, Mr. Patterson said that this approach was less desirable than a dividend reduction because of the impact of personal income taxes on stockholders. If the company halved the cash dividend rate, the whole $550,000 of added retention would be available for investment. On the other hand, if it paid this sum to stockholders, perhaps only $300,000 would be left in their hands, for use in exercising rights, after they had paid their tax bill at the marginal tax rates.

Finally, Mr. Patterson said that the use of a stock dividend to supplement the lower cash dividend would be of considerable consequence to those stockholders who needed income from their investments. If the board voted the 5% stock dividend, as he advocated, and the market price remained around $60 per share, stockholders could realize about $3 on each share owned by selling their stock dividends. This sum, moreover, would be subject only to the capital gains tax rates. Thus, under the new policy a stockholder could both obtain and retain more cash than he could have under the previous policy.

Although Mr. Kugel and two other directors believed that Mr. Patterson had overstated the advantages of the new policy, they agreed to vote for its adoption, at least for a trial period. Accordingly, the board unanimously voted a 25-cent cash dividend per share and a 5% stock dividend, both payable to stockholders of record on February 25, 1954. They further authorized Mr. Patterson to announce as the reasons for the change in policy, the needs for the expansion program and the benefits to stockholders of the stock dividend.

Further Developments, 1954–55

Following the announcement of the new dividend policy, the market price of Lesmer common stock declined from 59¾ to 46⅝ and then began to rally. By December, 1955, the price had risen to 80⅞. Exhibit 3 shows the annual market prices and other data for Moody's 125 Industrial Stocks and also for companies comprising Standard and Poor's Index of Radio, Television, and Electronics Companies. Exhibit 4 gives the monthly market prices for Lesmer common stock and these two indexes.

The company received criticism of the new policy from some stockholders, either through letters or through casual personal talks with directors. One investment fund, which sold its holdings of 1,000 shares in February, 1954, wrote that it "could not justify holding the stock at its lower yield." Other stockholders commended the company for instituting stock dividends, but stated that the $2 cash dividend should not have been reduced. Some cited the 15% payout ratio in 1954 as being "by far the lowest in your industry." Many of these protesting stockholders attributed the initial decline in market price to the dividend reduction, and some complained later that Lesmer common stock had not participated fully in the unprecedented bull market of 1955.

These views were shared on the board by Mr. Kugel and, at times, by two other directors. In July, 1954, Mr. Kugel urged the board to restore the 50-cent quarterly payment, in order to bolster the depressed market price. At that time, however, the other directors felt that the new policy had not yet had time to work itself out. Quarterly payments of 25 cents in cash were continued through 1954 and 1955, and a 5% stock dividend was voted in January, 1955.

In October, 1955, Mr. Kugel again proposed the restoration of the 50-cent payment and, on that occasion, was supported by two others. He contended that the preliminary cash budget for 1956 indicated the need for some external financing, probably common stock. Although Lesmer common had risen substantially since 1953, Mr. Kugel believed that even greater appreciation should have resulted, in view of the general market rise and the outstanding sales and earnings records of Lesmer in 1954 and the first half of 1955. Furthermore, a study of the stockholders' list had indicated that less than 10% of shareholders had sold their stock dividends, thus suggesting that stock dividends were generally not an effective means of supplementing cash income.

Mr. Patterson agreed with Mr. Kugel that a common stock issue might be necessary in 1956, and, if not, almost certainly would be in 1957, in view of the foreseeable needs for funds and the reluctance of the board to incur further long-term debt in the near future. He said, however, that his previous position on minimizing the amounts of such financing remained unchanged and that he was not at all sure that the market price would rise significantly if the old policy were restored. At any rate, he urged the directors to defer consideration of a major change in dividend policy until January, 1956, when the final budget for 1956 and the long-range forecasts for 1957–60 would be available. This viewpoint gained general acceptance and the board then voted a 25 cents per share quarterly dividend.

Board Meeting, January, 1956

About one week prior to the meeting of the board on January 26, 1956, each director received a copy of the 1956–60 cash budget for his study. A summarized version of that document was as follows:

CASH BUDGET, 1956–60

(Dollar Figures in Millions)

	1956	1957	1958	1959	1960
Estimated expenditures					
Capital expenditures.....................	$ 7.50	$ 7.50	$ 7.50	$ 8.00	$ 8.00
Net working capital requirements.........	2.00	2.00	2.00	2.50	2.50
Sinking fund requirements...............	.25	.25	.25	.50	.50
Dividends, at 105% of previous year......	.65	.68	.72	.76	.80
	$10.30	$10.43	$10.47	$11.76	$11.80
Estimated receipts					
Earnings.............................	$ 5.20	$ 5.50	$ 6.00	$ 6.50	$ 7.00
Depreciation.........................	2.90	3.30	3.70	4.20	4.80
	$ 8.10	$ 8.80	$ 9.70	$10.70	$11.80
Net need.............................	$ 2.20	$ 1.63	$ .77	$ 1.06	$ 0

Accompanying the budget was an explanation of the assumptions on which it had been constructed.

1. Dividends have been projected on the assumption that annual payments will continue at $1 per share with a 5% stock dividend. No allowance has been made for the dividend requirements arising from issues of common stock, if any, during this period.
2. Sinking fund projections are based solely on the requirements of the outstanding debenture issues. No allowance has been made for sinking fund requirements arising from debenture placements, if any, during this period.
3. Capital expenditures and net working capital requirements have been projected on the basis of a 60% increase in sales from 1955 to 1960.
4. Earnings have been projected for somewhat less than a 60% increase to allow for starting-up costs, promotion, and other initial expenses associated with increasing sales.
5. Net needs are calculated as the difference between estimated expenditures and receipts, there being no uncommitted funds available at January 1, 1956.

Accompanying the cash budget was a memorandum from Mr. Patterson to the directors. In it, he stated his hope that the forthcoming board meeting would lead to general agreement on a dividend policy for the company to follow in the years ahead.

Exhibit 1

LESMER ELECTRONICS CORPORATION

SELECTED FINANCIAL DATA, 1945–55

(Dollar Figures in Thousands)

Year	Sales	Net Income after Taxes	Deprecia- tion	Net Working Capital	Capital Expendi- tures	Common Stock Cash Dividends	New Financing
1945	$14,498	$ 586	$ 440	$ 2,537	$1,382	$ 354	
1946	12,302	513	526	2,519	1,716	354	$1,006
1947	21,159	1,808	655	2,912	1,047	476	
1948	29,864	1,757	813	3,745	1,261	476	
1949	32,920	2,150	938	5,106	985	725	
1950	54,683	3,411	1,067	8,552	4,898	1,134	5,000
1951	62,417	3,419	1,181	12,594	3,382	1,106	4,180
1952	58,962	3,452	1,652	13,840	2,556	1,106	
1953	63,896	3,778	1,959	13,997	4,170	1,106	
1954	69,551	4,165	2,240	17,608	6,963	581	5,000
1955	81,178	5,093	2,547	17,894	6,494	610	

Exhibit 2

LESMER ELECTRONICS CORPORATION

Selected Data on the Common Stock,* 1945–55

Year	Earnings per Share	Dividends per Share	Book Value per Share	Number of Shares Outstanding (In Thousands)	Market Price High	Market Price Low	Average of Monthly Prices	Price-Earnings Ratio, Based on Ave. Mo. Price	Yield, Based on Ave. Mo. Price
1945	$1.45	$ .80	$16.31	423	33⅜	16⅝	27	18.7	3.0%
1946	1.12	.80	18.07	453	38½	21⅜	28	25.3	2.8
1947	3.97	1.20	20.84	453	27⅝	19¾	23	5.9	5.2
1948	3.86	1.20	23.50	453	30¼	24⅞	24	6.2	5.0
1949	4.74	1.60	26.64	453	37⅛	21	26	5.5	6.2
1950	7.51	2.50	33.18	453	46⅞	26⅝	37	4.9	6.7
1951	6.19	2.00	39.89	553	53¾	39½	45	7.2	4.4
1952	6.08	2.00	43.97	553	56⅝	38⅛	46	7.6	4.3
1953	6.81	2.00	48.78	553	63½	42¼	51	7.5	3.9
1954	7.15	1.00 + 5%	52.90	581	67¾	46⅝	56	8.0	1.8
1955	8.32	1.00 + 5%	57.85	610	84⅜	62¼	76	9.1	1.3

* Per share data are as calculated at year end and have not been adjusted to reflect the 5% stock dividends in 1954 and 1955.

Cash Dividends Paid by Quarters, 1945–55

Year	1Q	2Q	3Q	4Q	Year End	Total
1945	$.20	$.20	$.20	$.20	—	$ .80
1946	.20	.20	.20	.20	—	.80
1947	.20	.20	.30	.30	$.20	1.20
1948	.30	.30	.30	.30	—	1.20
1949	.40	.40	.40	.40	—	1.60
1950	.40	.40	.40	.50	.80	2.50
1951	.50	.50	.50	.50	—	2.00
1952	.50	.50	.50	.50	—	2.00
1953	.50	.50	.50	.50	—	2.00
1954	.25	.25	.25	.25	—	1.00
1955	.25	.25	.25	.25	—	1.00

Exhibit 3

LESMER ELECTRONICS CORPORATION

MOODY'S COMMON STOCK AVERAGES, 125 INDUSTRIAL COMPANIES
AS AT DECEMBER 31, 1945–55

Year	Market Price per Share	Price-Earnings Ratio	Yield
1945	$ 43.94	16.15	4.00%
1946	49.84	14.12	3.75
1947	46.10	8.67	5.06
1948	47.50	6.76	5.87
1949	46.88	7.10	6.82
1950	57.83	6.84	6.51
1951	70.72	9.60	6.29
1952	75.63	10.53	5.55
1953	76.05	9.86	5.51
1954	95.81	11.43	4.70
1955	130.66	12.43	3.93

RADIO, TELEVISION, AND ELECTRONICS COMPANIES

	Standard and Poor's Price Index* (1935–1939 = 100)	Average Price-Earnings Ratio of Stocks in Index†	Average Yield of Stocks in Index‡
1945	168.0	20.4	2.5%
1946	164.1	17.6	3.1
1947	111.3	7.0	5.9
1948	140.7	6.5	5.3
1949	139.9	8.2	5.6
1950	199.5	5.1	5.9
1951	237.4	6.8	5.5
1952	296.1	9.0	5.0
1953	285.2	8.0	5.4
1954	332.8	10.2	5.5
1955	454.1	11.4	4.3

* Index includes 11 stocks between 1951 and 1955, 5 between 1945 and 1950.

† Simple average of price-earnings ratios, as reported by Value-Line of companies included in Standard and Poor's price index. Companies with deficits were omitted in computing the average for years in which deficit occurred: 2 companies in 1945; 1 in 1948 and 1952; 2 in 1955.

‡ Simple average of dividend yields, as reported by Value-Line. Companies which did not pay dividends are omitted in years when dividends were passed; 1 company in 1946–47, 1949 and 1951–55.

Exhibit 4

LESMER ELECTRONICS CORPORATION

RANGE OF MARKET PRICES OF LESMER ELECTRONICS CORP. COMMON STOCK, STANDARD & POOR'S PRICE INDEX OF RADIO, TELEVISION AND ELECTRONICS COMPANIES AND MOODY'S PRICE INDEX OF 125 INDUSTRIAL COMPANIES, 1945–55

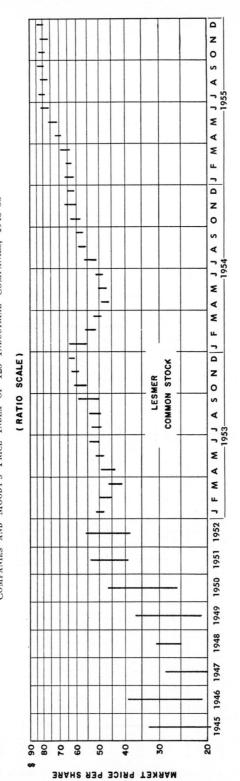

Exhibit 4 (Continued)

STANDARD & POOR'S PRICE INDEX
(1935 - 39 = 100)

MOODY'S PRICE INDEX

PRICE INDEX

MARKET PRICE PER SHARE

Case 26

The Sabbath Container Company

In November, 1952, Mr. Callahan, treasurer of The Sabbath Container Company, was considering the question of how best to determine the relative costs and advantages of two alternative methods of financing the company's expansion program, the sale of bonds or common stock. The question had been precipitated by a disagreement among the company's directors at a recent meeting. Following the meeting, Mr. Callahan had been asked by Mr. Rocco, the president of the company, to assess the logic of the arguments presented by the various directors and outline a position to be taken by the company's management at the directors' meeting the following month.

The Sabbath Company manufactured containers for industrial and commercial use. Although the level of sales and profits fluctuated considerably with the level of business activity, the company's operations had been profitable in almost all years. Originally founded in 1896 to manufacture kerosene cans, the company's product line had changed considerably over the years; metal snuffboxes, cigarette "flat 50" tins, and a variety of other containers had proved profitable. During World War II, the company had concentrated its efforts in the manufacture of first-aid kit containers for the armed forces. Currently a considerable volume of sales was being obtained from the manufacture of small aluminum cans for the shipment of delicate instruments, particularly those used in aircraft. The company also had contracts to supply several pharmaceutical firms with tins for pills and small bandages. The latter line had contributed a needed element of stability to demand.

Management had customarily followed the policy of avoiding long-term debt. Apart from war periods, when working capital requirements had been unusually heavy, the company had met its needs by retained earnings, supplemented from time to time by short-term bank loans. In 1952 the capitalization of the company consisted of common stock and surplus, with no fixed indebtedness of any sort.

803

Although descendants of the founders still retained sizable holdings, ownership of the stock was widely distributed; there was no dominant interest, and the shares, which were traded over the counter, were transferred infrequently. *NO ACTIVE MARKET HARD TO UNLOAD STOCK*

Late in 1952 the management of the Sabbath Company decided that a small plant in Los Angeles, which had been acquired in 1932, should be modernized and enlarged. In recent years this plant had proved inadequate to meet the rising demand for aluminum containers for aircraft instrument firms, and it had become clear that fundamental changes were required. Management estimated that the larger plant and additional working capital needed to finance expanded operations would require $10 million in new funds. Originally it had been planned to provide these funds from retained earnings, but a general increase in working capital requirements and a lowered balance of earnings after higher income and excess profits taxes made this plan inadvisable. It was, therefore, planned to seek capital from outside sources.

BETTER FOR BONDS ONE SHOT NEED?

The proposed investment was expected to net $2 million in annual earnings before interest and taxes as soon as the plant was in operation. The added investment would increase the tax base of the corporation for purposes of excess profits tax computation, so that it was assumed that the 1951 overall tax rate of 58% would apply also to the added income from the new investment. Consequently, the net incremental income after taxes was forecast at 8.4%, or $840,000.

A preliminary investigation of the price record of Sabbath common stock led Mr. Callahan to the opinion that, barring a general market decline, common stock could be sold to the public through investment bankers at $26.50 per share. After underwriting expenses and other fees, net proceeds to the company would be $25 per share. Thus, if common stock were used, the proposed financing would require the issuance of 400,000 shares.

For some years, both Mr. Rocco and Mr. Callahan had been disappointed in the market prices of Sabbath common stock (see Exhibit 1). For this reason, they had decided to reexamine the company's established policy of avoiding long-term debt. Circumstances had changed, and they believed that a new policy might be justified by the prospect of more stable future earnings. Inquiry in financial circles established the likelihood that the company could raise $10 million through the sale of bonds. It appeared that the interest rate on a 15-year issue would be 4%. If such securities were sold directly to insurance companies or other institutional investors, they undoubtedly would insist upon some sinking fund arrangement. It seemed likely that they would require retirement of at least $500,000 of the issue annually, leaving $2.5 million outstanding at maturity. While such terms would create a sizable annual requirement for cash, they were regarded by the company's management as about as good as could be expected.

In view of the tax deductibility of bond interest and the current income tax experience of 58%, the 4% rate was regarded by Mr. Callahan as the equivalent of 1.68%. In contrast, he considered that the stock at $25 per share and a $2 dividend rate would cost the company 8%. This comparison made the bond issue seem very desirable to Mr. Rocco.

Early in November, 1952, Mr. Rocco decided to submit the expansion proposal to the Sabbath board of directors for its formal approval. The proposal to increase the Los Angeles plant had been discussed previously by the board; after reconsidering it briefly, the board voted unanimously to authorize the president to go forward with the project, assuming satisfactory financing could be arranged. At this point, Mr. Rocco decided to sound out board sentiment to see if the possibility of debt financing as an alternative to common stock financing should be explored further. He presented the cost comparison given above. Somewhat to his surprise and concern, an active and at times acrimonious discussion developed, in which all of the directors participated.

Mr. Rocco was immediately challenged as to the cost of the bond issue, since his figure did not include the annual payment to the sinking fund. One director figured this as 8% of the average size of the bond issue over its 15-year life; to him, the cost of the stock issue was less than that of the bonds. Furthermore, he emphasized the cash outlay called for in the bond program and the $2.5 million maturity. The use of debt thus added risks to the company, and he argued that this would make the common stock more speculative and cause greater variation in its market price.

Another director argued for a stock issue because "simple arithmetic" showed that the company could net 8.4%, or $840,000, per year after taxes on the new investment. Yet if 400,000 shares of common stock were sold, the dividend requirements at the current rate of $2 per share would equal only $800,000 per year. Since there was no thought that the $2 dividend rate should be changed, he could not see how the sale of the new common hurt the interest of present stockholders. Further, if there were any immediate sacrifice, he argued that it would be overcome shortly as the expansion of the company continued. Under such circumstances, there could be no thought of the bond issue, for it would place much greater obligations on the company.

On the other hand, one director argued vigorously that common stock was a "giveaway" at $25. He pointed out that the retention of a substantial percentage of past profits in the business had built up the book value of the stock to roughly $45 last December and $47 in November. Moreover, this value substantially understated the true worth of the business, because at today's prices the company could not begin to replace properties and inventories at balance sheet cost. He concluded that the sale of common stock at $25 would give new buyers a substantial part of the value held by the company's present stockholders.

Two other directors agreed that the sale of stock at this price would dilute the value of the stock, but they measured the dilution in terms of earnings per share rather than book or market value. At the level of earnings currently anticipated, about $13 million before interest or income taxes, they maintained that income per share of existing common stock would be diluted to $3.03 per share, if common stock were sold to net $25. In contrast, these directors asserted that the sale of bonds would raise earnings per share to $3.78. These directors said it was unimportant that the annual sinking fund would amount to $0.36 per share.

As discussion of these and other arguments related to cost of financing continued well past the usual hour for adjournment with no signs of developing agreement, Mr. Rocco finally interrupted the discussion to explain that he had not expected the board to go this far into the matter at this meeting. "Obviously," he said, "management must do more thinking about this matter of the costs of the two financing methods." He promised that a careful review of the costs aspects, including all those raised by the directors, would be prepared before the next meeting of the board and asked that decision on the matter be held over. The directors agreed to this proposal, and the meeting was thereupon adjourned.

Exhibit 1

THE SABBATH CONTAINER COMPANY

SELECTED INCOME AND DIVIDEND DATA, 1945–52

(Dollar Figures in Thousands)

	Net Sales	Income before Taxes	Income after Taxes	Income per Share	Divi- dends per Share	Market Prices per Share of Common Stock	
						High	Low
1945..........$	83,562	$ 9,150	$2,366	$1.69	$1.20	$29⅝	$19⅜
1946..........	51,434	4,742	2,802	2.00	1.20	40	21¾
1947..........	81,503	7,225	3,844	2.75	1.20	27⅛	18¼
1948..........	89,822	9,560	5,071	3.62	1.20	25¼	16¾
1949..........	70,662	4,100	3,109	2.22	1.20	19⅛	15½
1950..........	77,736	5,802	3,495	2.50	1.20	22½	17
1951..........	105,640	10,790	4,464	3.19	2.00	26¾	24
1952..........	.....	....	....	...	2.00*	28½†	23⅞†

* Annual rate.
† To November 6 (November 5 prices were 28⅜–28¼).

Exhibit 2

THE SABBATH CONTAINER COMPANY

SUMMARY BALANCE SHEET
DECEMBER 31, 1951
(In Thousands of Dollars)

ASSETS

Cash	$ 8,924
Accounts receivable	15,146
Inventory	32,492
	$56,562
Plant	18,821
Goodwill	5,000
Other	3,676
Total assets	$84,059

LIABILITIES

Accounts payable	$ 8,888
Accrued federal taxes	5,831
Accrued expenses	5,995
	$20,714
Common stock ($10 par)	14,000
Surplus	49,345
Total liabilities	$84,059

Case 27

Viking Steel Corporation

In January, 1960, at the conclusion of a long steel strike, the board of directors of the Viking Steel Corporation decided to raise $10 million for expansion and modernization by selling a new issue of common stock in May, 1960. Subsequent to this decision, the market price of Viking's common stock fell from $49 to $38 per share. At the mid-February board meeting, Mr. Togni, one of the outside directors, noted the downward trend in market prices and posed the following question: "At what market price would it be more desirable to issue debt rather than continue with the proposed sale of equity?" After a brief discussion, the question was referred to Mr. O'Hearth, financial vice president and director, for further study and recommendations. As a first step in this analysis, Mr. O'Hearth planned to investigate the relative desirability of selling stock at current price levels instead of the $45 originally expected.

The Viking Steel Corporation was founded by a small group of businessmen in 1900. Operations began in 1902, with the completion of four open hearth furnaces, a blooming mill, a billet mill, and two hot strip mills. Prior to 1930 the company began production of cold rolled strip steel as well as stainless and other alloy strip steels. In 1930 and the years which followed, the company suffered severe operating losses. Sales in 1932 amounted to only 27% of 1929 sales, and finishing mill operations averaged under 30% of capacity. The company incurred sizable losses during 6 of the 9 years from 1930 to 1938 (the largest loss was $2 million). At the close of the war in 1945, the company resumed its long-run program of development. During the postwar period, negotiations were completed for the acquisition of seven formerly independent concerns. The company also joined with another firm to set up a subsidiary which produced and fabricated titanium, zirconium, hafnium, columbium, and thorium. In 1960 the company and its subsidiaries produced a wide range of products, including: steel bar and plates; carbon, alloy, and stainless hot and cold rolled strip; coal, coke, and chemical by-products; strapping; and various specialty metals. Exhibits 1 through 4 show some of the company's recent financial development.

During 1958 the company's board of directors installed a new management to help strengthen Viking's competitive position. The new president, Mr. Rab Dellor, realized the company's production facilities were badly in need of modernization, since Viking was one of the highest cost producers in the industry. The company's sales organization also needed attention if Viking was to capitalize fully on available market opportunities. Mr. Dellor recognized that Viking was still largely a producer of basic steel products and that further vertical integration toward the market was required. Management believed the solution of these problems would enable Viking both to reduce the cyclical character of sales and increase profitability.

Mr. Dellor and his new management team first concentrated on improving the sales organization and, although it was too early to measure the results of their efforts, they were pleased with the progress made. In particular, it was thought that the company would henceforth operate closer to capacity due to improved selling and that it would be somewhat less subject to cyclical sales fluctuations.

Executives of the company had prepared a detailed modernization plan involving the expenditure of $12 million in 1960 and early 1961. This expenditure was expected to increase finishing capacity by 15%, to raise operating profit by nearly $4 million at the operating level envisioned for 1960, and to improve efficiency at lower levels of activity. For example, Mr. Dellor anticipated that the modernization program would ensure a minimum operating profit (EBIT) of $3.5 million in the future, even under such severely depressed sales conditions as Viking had experienced in 1958.

Although Viking's sales and profits had demonstrated considerable instability during the postwar period, as shown in Exhibit 2, the company had always maintained a strong current position. During the most recent 5 years, for example, net working capital had ranged between $33.4 and $38.6 million, and total current assets between $51.1 and $54.3 million. To maintain this relatively strong current position, management had adopted a firm policy of maintaining a minimum $4 million reserve in marketable securities to cushion sudden changes in financial requirements.

Mr. Dellor also recommended that the board change Viking's dividend policy. In the past, dividends had been closely related to profits and consequently had undergone frequent change despite a determined effort on the part of the board to maintain a minimum $2 annual dividend rate. Mr. Dellor believed the frequent changes in dividend payments had hurt the reputation of the Viking Steel Corporation in the financial community. In view of this situation, the board recently had approved an annual dividend rate of $2.40 per share, to be paid, insofar as possible, during both profitable and unprofitable years. This new stable dividend rate was regarded as a minimum by the board but would be continued until the long-term earnings outlook changed materially. When this new dividend policy was announced publicly in December, 1959, there were favorable comments from investment houses.

In planning the financing aspect of the proposed modernization program, Mr. O'Hearth projected operating profits of $11 million during the first half of 1960, followed by $7 million in the second half of the year. This prediction assumed a relatively strong level of demand throughout the year, with some decline during the last half of the year, once customers' inventories were rebuilt from the depleted levels resulting from the steel strike in late 1959. Retained earnings (before considering the effect of the proposed financing) had been forecast at $5.8 million in 1960, with depreciation remaining at $3.8 million. These internally generated sources of funds and the proposed sale of $10 million in stock would be used as follows: $12 million modernization program, $3.5 million increase in inventories and receivables, $500,000 sinking fund payment, and $3.6 million added to Viking's cash balance, for use in subsequent expansion programs.

In view of the considerable sales and profit uncertainties associated with the future, Mr. O'Hearth did not believe the company could forecast fund flows beyond 1960 with a useful degree of accuracy. Since experience indicated that funds generated through depreciation charges would be required to support the company's existing capacity, funds requirements for expansion and diversification would have to be financed with retained earnings and new external capital in the foreseeable future. The total of all capital expenditures probably would average about $7 million per year after 1960.

In planning the financing of the proposed modernization program, company officials considered a number of alternative debt and common stock proposals. After careful analysis they narrowed the choice to either a privately placed issue of debentures or common stock.

A large pension trust had agreed to buy a $10 million debenture issue from Viking. The 5¾% debentures would mature in 20 years and would involve no sinking fund payments during the first 5 years. Thereafter there would be a $500,000 annual repayment with a balloon maturity of $2.5 million. (The currently outstanding debentures carried a 4½% interest rate and a $500,000 annual sinking fund payment.) The proposed debentures would be subject to the following restrictions: (1) long-term debt would be limited to 75% of net working capital; and (2) dividends could not be paid in excess of profits earned subsequent to 1959. Additional covenants appeared normal and in no way restrictive or threatening.

The exact terms on the proposed common stock issue could not be set until just prior to issuance. In January, 1960, when the market price was

$49, the company was told by investment bankers that it probably could net $45 per share. Sale of common stock would involve additional expenses of about $70,000. On the basis of this information, Mr. Dellor had prepared a detailed analysis of these alternatives. Excerpts from this analysis are shown in Exhibit 5. After careful review of all the available information, management had recommended, and the board had approved, the common stock alternative on the following grounds: the sacrifice in earnings per share appeared justified in view of the greater risk associated with the debt alternative; the timing of an equity sale seemed "right" in view of the high market price of the stock, whereas interest rates on debt were at a postwar high; and the stock alternative allowed for greater financial flexibility by keeping Viking's debt to total capitalization ratio below the industry's average of 18.7%.

After this decision was reached, stock prices on the New York Stock Exchange broke sharply downward and by mid-February were a full 10% below January's highs. Viking's market price had also fallen from $49 to $38 per share. Following this experience, leading investment bankers expressed considerable uncertainty regarding the likely movement of the market over the next few months. In view of this uncertainty, Mr. O'Hearth was unable to get any firm estimate about the level of the stock market, or the likely price of Viking's stock, during the period preceding the proposed midyear stock sale.

This situation led Mr. Togni, an outside director, to question whether the decline in the price of the company's stock justified a reappraisal of the alternative methods of financing the modernization program. Mr. Togni pointed out that, in view of the basic market uncertainties, the board would quite likely have to examine the same proposition after every major market movement up to the proposed date of issue in mid-May. Mr. Togni suggested, therefore, that the board determine the lowest acceptable issue price for common stock (below which the debenture would look more attractive than a new issue of common stock). In this way, he argued, the board would have a firm basis for action until the day preceding the offering date, when a final decision would be made. Mr. Dellor admitted that he had never looked at the question in this way but, because it seemed a useful approach, agreed to have Mr. O'Hearth prepare such an analysis prior to the next scheduled board meeting in early March. As a preliminary step in this investigation, Mr. O'Hearth planned to explore the implications of selling the stock to net $30 per share as compared with the $45 previously considered (see Exhibit 5).

Exhibit 1

VIKING STEEL CORPORATION

BALANCE SHEET, DECEMBER 31, 1959

(Dollar Figures in Thousands)

ASSETS		LIABILITIES	
Cash.........................$	5,641	Accounts payable...............$	5,544
Mkt. securities.................	5,121	Accrued wages..................	3,360
Accounts receivable...........	13,496	Accrued taxes..................	3,474
Inventories...................	30,042	Other current liabilities..........	3,358
Total current assets......$	54,300	Total current liabilities....$	15,736
Investments in affiliates........$	7,000	4½% debentures of 1970........$	12,000
		Total debt...............$	27,736
Net fixed assets...............$	43,697		
Other assets..................	502	Common stock (1.1 million shares	
		outstanding).................$	33,312
		Earned surplus................	44,451
		Total equity.............$	77,763
Total assets...........$105,499		Total liabilities..........$105,499	

Percentage long-term debt to total capitalization:
1. December 31, 1959...13.4%
2. Pro forma (assuming debt alternative).........................22.0%

Exhibit 2

VIKING STEEL CORPORATION

SELECTED DATA FROM INCOME STATEMENTS FOR THE YEARS ENDING
DECEMBER 31, 1947 TO 1959

(Dollar Figures in Thousands)

Year	Sales	Profits before Taxes	Profits after Taxes	Dividends	Depreciation	Capital Expenditures
1947...	$ 89,307	$11,147	$6,722	$2,200	$1,471	$ 2,901
1948...	118,462	15,609	9,234	3,520	1,965	11,418
1949...	89,543	5,065	3,325	2,200	2,247	3,497
1950...	135,409	19,611	9,284	3,300	2,469	2,371
1951...	168,958	28,041	8,861	4,190	2,603	4,667
1952...	131,305	8,045	5,120	4,400	3,024	5,674
1953...	167,240	14,309	6,709	4,400	3,617	4,834
1954...	98,219	5,084	3,134	2,750	3,973	5,766
1955...	171,180	16,187	7,987	3,025	4,714	9,443
1956...	178,682	13,378	6,905	3,300	4,070	9,381
1957...	150,361	7,652	4,048	3,300	4,038	11,276
1958...	99,591	550	220	2,200	3,678	4,053
1959...	119,760	4,462	2,409	2,310	3,811	5,942

Exhibit 3

VIKING STEEL CORPORATION

SEMILOG GRAPH OF EARNINGS, DIVIDENDS AND MARKET PRICE

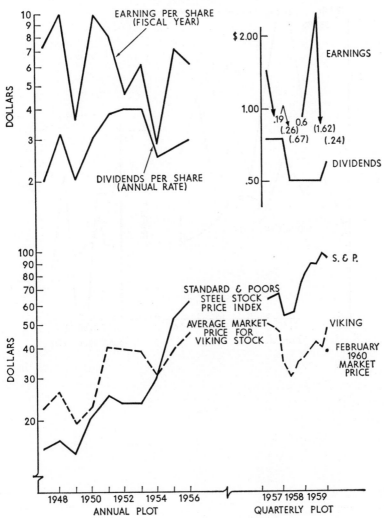

Exhibit 4

VIKING STEEL CORPORATION
GRAPH OF EARNINGS AND DIVIDEND YIELDS

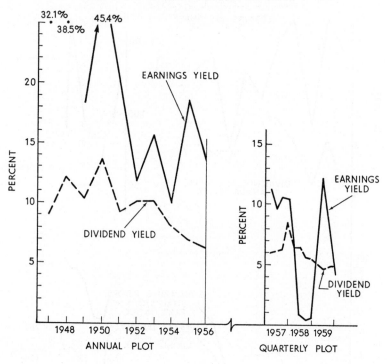

Exhibit 5

VIKING STEEL CORPORATION

EFFECT ON INCOME OF FINANCING ALTERNATIVES
AT EBIT LEVELS OF $6 AND $18 MILLION

	$6 Million EBIT			$18 Million EBIT		
		Common Stock*			Common Stock*	
	Debt	*$45*	*$30*	*Debt*	*$45*	*$30*
EBIT......................	$6,000	$6,000	$6,000	$18,000	$18,000	$18,000
Interest...................	1,115	540	540	1,115	540	540
PBT.......................	$4,885	$5,460	$5,460	$16,885	$17,460	$17,460
Taxes (@ 52%).............	2,540	2,840	2,840	8,780	9,079	9,079
PAT.......................	$2,345	$2,620	$2,620	$ 8,105	$ 8,381	$ 8,381
Sinking fund...............	1,000	500	500	1,000	500	500
UPAT.....................	1,345	$2,120	$2,120	$ 7,105	$ 7,881	$ 7,881
Number of common shares (million).................	1.100	1.322	1.434	1.100	1.322	1.434
EPS ($ per share)...........	$2.12	$1.99	$1.83	$ 7.37	$ 6.34	$ 5.84
UEPS ($ per share)..........	1.22	1.62	1.48	6.46	5.96	5.49
Coverage of interest and sinking funds†.............	1.88x	3.80x	3.80x	5.64x	11.40x	11.40x

* Net proceeds per share under various issuing conditions.
† Calculated as follows for debt alternative:

Thousands of Dollars

Interest................................$1,115
Sinking fund (before taxes)................ 2,080
    Total burden..................... $3,195
EBIT.................................. 6,000
Coverage ($6,000/$3,195)................. 1.88x

NOTE: If no financing were undertaken in 1960, EPS would be $7.61 at an EBIT level of $18 million.

Exhibit 6

VIKING STEEL CORPORATION

Financial Analysis of the Steel Industry

Company	Year	Ingot Capacity Net Tons (Millions)	Ingot Production Net Tons (Millions)	Percent of Capacity Operated	Net Sales (Millions)	Net Income (Millions)	Net Income Percent of Sales	Capitalization: Percent Long-Term Debt	Percent Sales to Total Assets	Percent Net Income to Total Assets	Percent Net Income to Net Worth
Armco Steel Corporation	1958	6.3	4.5	70.5	$867	$57	6.6	14.4	96.7	6.4	9.0
	1957	5.9	5.4	90.9	776	55	7.1	15.8	102.4	7.6	10.8
	1956	5.1	5.2	101.4	761	65	8.6	10.7	124.3	10.2	14.6
	1955	4.9	5.0	103.0	692	64	9.3	12.9	123.0	11.4	16.6
	1954	4.9	4.4	90.8	532	41	7.7	15.9	108.5	8.4	12.1
Inland Steel Company	1958	5.8	4.7	81.3	661	47	7.3	28.3	95.6	7.0	11.5
	1957	5.5	5.5	100.0	772	58	7.7	30.2	115.2	8.9	14.5
	1956	5.2	4.9	94.5	731	52	7.3	25.9	127.0	7.3	14.4
	1955	5.0	5.1	103.8	663	52	8.0	20.2	128.4	10.2	15.8
	1954	4.7	4.5	96.2	537	41	7.7	25.2	115.7	8.9	14.4
Viking Steel Corporation	1958	1.9	.7	39.7	99	0.2	.2	13.2	94.6	0.002	0.003
	1957	1.8	1.2	63.5	151	4	2.7	14.3	141.2	3.8	5.1
	1956	1.7	1.5	85.6	180	6	3.8	5.6	164.2	6.4	8.8
	1955	1.5	1.5	98.6	173	7	4.6	6.8	184.9	8.6	11.7
	1954	1.5	.8	54.6	99	3	3.2	9.1	117.2	3.7	5.0
Kaiser Steel Corporation	1958	1.5	1.4	95.5	181	5	3.0	60.0	37.6	1.0	3.0
	1957	1.5	1.5	103.5	208	21	10.3	61.9	46.4	4.7	14.6
	1956	1.5	1.6	105.3	201	23	11.7	48.5	68.7	7.9	18.2
	1955	1.5	1.4	93.3	136	5	4.2	52.1	50.6	1.9	4.7
	1954	1.5	1.3	90.0	128	7	6.2	55.2	49.0	2.7	6.7
Detroit Steel Corporation	1958	1.5	.4	30.0	61	1	1.9	26.9	56.3	0.9	1.7
	1957	1.5	.5	37.0	82	3	3.6	28.3	75.6	2.8	4.9
	1956	1.2	1.0	80.0	123	8	7.1	29.6	108.0	7.0	13.0
	1955	1.2	.8	68.9	101	6	6.2	32.7	95.2	5.7	10.4
	1954	.6	.4	67.1	51	1	2.3	46.5	56.9	1.1	2.5

Case 28

Dedham Hotel Corporation

IN JULY, 1959, the management of the Dedham Hotel Corporation was studying three alternative arrangements for financing an addition of 42 units to its property, Hotel 128. The cost of building such an addition was estimated at $240,000. The alternatives being considered for raising the funds were as follows:

1. Sale of approximately 10,000 shares of Dedham Hotel Corporation common stock at an estimated price of $24 a share.
2. Sale of $240,000 of 20-year debentures, payable in full at the end of the period (no sinking fund) and bearing 6% interest, payable annually. As an added inducement to investors, 10 shares of the company's common stock would be issued cost-free with each $1,000 debenture purchased.
3. An increase of $140,000 in a first mortgage outstanding against the property, and an unsecured $100,000 loan from a trust company. The first mortgage would be increased from $460,000 at 6% on the unpaid balance—principal and interest payable in equal monthly amounts over the next 13 years beginning in July, 1960—to $600,000 at 6½% on the unpaid balance—principal and interest payable in equal monthly amounts for a 15-year period. The unsecured loan ($100,000) from a trust company would bear interest at 6% on the full amount, principal and interest payable in equal monthly amounts for a period of 13 months.

Background

Hotel 128 was a motel of contemporary architectural design situated at the intersection of Routes 1 and 128 in Dedham, Massachusetts. It comprised 101 air-conditioned rooms, a lobby, swimming pool, main dining room and kitchen, cocktail lounge, large ballroom, smaller dining rooms for private gatherings, and other related accommodations. It was the principal, and only revenue-producing, asset of the Dedham Hotel Corporation and had been in operation for just over one year—since June, 1958.

The motel's history dated back to December, 1956, when the Dedham

Industrial Commission, composed of town officials and one member each from the chamber of commerce, the board of trade, a realty firm, and the New Haven Railroad, had sponsored a dinner to promote the idea of building a hotel on Route 128 in Dedham. The commission, whose function was to bring in selected industries without changing the residential character of the community, had invited to the dinner a group of hotel and real estate developers, among whom was Mr. Arthur L. Lee, representative of a large hotel chain. Sufficiently impressed by the commission's presentation of a need for a hotel in the area, particularly to accommodate customers and representatives of companies located in the Dedham industrial center, Mr. Lee tried to interest his firm in the project. When the hotel chain did not respond favorably, Mr. Lee decided to undertake the project himself.

In early 1957 he proceeded to interest a group of other young men (most were in their thirties) with whom he was personally acquainted, including John D. Young, an investment banking house broker; John J. Flynn, the Dedham controller; Patrick Grant, a certified public accountant; William B. Tyler, an attorney; and H. Holten Wood, a member of an investment management firm. The members of this group combined their efforts to study the prospects and organized to build a hotel in Dedham. Traffic was counted, and companies in the area were interviewed in an effort to predict the demand; interviews were conducted to sample the interest of investors; locations were checked for availability and convenience; architects were retained to prepare preliminary sketches; an option was taken on the land selected; construction and furnishings estimates were made; pro forma income statements were drawn up.

On May 23, 1957, convinced of the potential profits of the enterprise and with the preliminaries behind them, the promoters held a press conference at a well-known hotel in Boston and announced their decision to go ahead. A number of prominent citizens and investors from the Dedham community were invited to the conference, where plans, sketches, and estimates were revealed.

During the months that followed the press conference, until construction was begun on October 4, 1957, Mr. Lee and his associates in the venture completed their plans. They engaged architects to make final drawings, solicited bids on construction, raised the necessary funds, and consummated financial arrangements. Construction was completed in the spring of 1958, and Hotel 128 opened for business on June 13.

Financing Arrangements

The Dedham Hotel Corporation obtained its first money from the promoters by issuing to them a total of 1,000 shares of common stock at $10 a share. To provide the rest of the "promotion" money required by the project, a plan was then drawn up which potential investors received enthusiastically in the preliminary surveys and at the press conference. It consisted of combined issues of 20-year, 6% debentures and common stock. Investors would be offered 10 shares of stock with each $1,000 debenture purchased. The common stock would carry the same stated value per share ($10) as the stock issued to the promoters. Since a selling price of $1,000 was set for each unit, composed of a $1,000 debenture and 10 shares of common stock, the debentures were, in effect, issued at a 10% discount from face value. The debenture issue had no sinking fund requirement.

A debenture issue of $400,000 was sold by September, 1957; and the proceeds, which had been placed on a "called as needed" basis, were fully realized in early 1958. In accordance with the objectives of the promoters, the issue was sold to 123 individual investors, all residents of the Dedham community.

During the summer of 1957 the promoters approached several savings banks and commercial banks in a search for first-mortgage money. The institutions were not interested in providing funds on this basis. The promoters then turned to a large life insurance company, which agreed to furnish $500,000 on a first mortgage with interest at 6% on the declining balance. Principal and interest were to be amortized in equal monthly payments over a 15-year period. On the basis of this commitment a large Boston bank agreed to furnish up to $500,000 of construction money at 6% per annum, plus a 1% fee ($5,000). The insurance company drew up a mortgage, assigned it to the bank during the period of construction, and later obtained a reassignment by taking the bank out when construction was completed.

To round out the major financing needs, the promoters searched for second-mortgage money and found an individual investor with substantial funds available for purchasing second mortgages. The investor advanced $200,000, bearing interest at 6% on the unpaid balance. The face amount of the second-mortgage liability assumed for this money, however, was $236,000. Principal was payable at the rate of $3,000 a month for 35 months, with a balloon payment of $131,000 due in the 36th month. Interest was payable monthly. Under the terms of this mortgage, payment of principal could be delayed up to 6 months, but the full amount of delayed payments would be due and payable at the end of the delay period.

As the project progressed, it was discovered that the original financing arrangements were inadequate to cover fully the cost of construction, furnishings, and equipment. The remainder of necessary funds was raised from several sources. For example, the contractor agreed to carry $30,000 of construction costs for one year at 6%; Mr. Lee put up $26,500 of his own money on a 5-year note at 6%; part of the furniture, fixtures, and equipment was financed on time payments.

The following figures summarize the original financing of the land, motel, equipment, and furnishings:

SOURCES OF FUNDS

Stock purchased by promoters*................................$	9,000
Sale of 20-year debentures.............................	400,000
First mortgage......................................	500,000
Second mortgage, net received in cash..................	200,000
Note payable—officer...............................	26,500
Note payable—contractor.............................	30,000
Note payable—supplier (furnishings and equipment).....	40,000
	$1,205,500

* One of the promoters received 100 shares of stock as partial consideration for a temporary advance of funds to purchase the building site.

The Decision to Build an Addition

During its first complete year of operations, ended June 30, 1959, Hotel 128 exceeded the promoters' expectations. Although net profit was somewhat nominal in relation to total investment, it was considered unusual that this kind of project had shown a profit during its first year. Despite heavy charges for organization and start-up in June of 1958, only a small deficit remained as of June 30, 1959. Gross revenues for the year exceeded earlier estimates by about 12%. Room rentals (on 101 bedrooms) averaged approximately $3,060 a unit; and revenues on banquet facilities, dining room, and cocktail lounge averaged approximately $4,475 on a rental unit (bedroom) basis. Telephone, valet services, and other miscellaneous revenues totaled approximately $22,000, or $218 a unit. (See Exhibits 1 and 2 for statements of financial condition and operations.)

On the basis of recent demand for accommodations, Mr. Lee was confident that existing facilities would show an increase in revenues and profits in the year ahead. He estimated that average annual revenue from rentals would be at least $3,820 a unit and that average revenue, on a rental unit basis, from dining room, cocktail lounge, and banquet facilities would be $4,920 (including valet services and telephone), increases of 25% and 10%, respectively. Departmental expenses and cost of sales were expected to rise proportionately with increases in revenue, and general expenses and fixed charges were expected to be about the same in total.

Most important to the financial success of the operation was the motel's ability to generate cash. Depreciation and other noncash charges, added to profits, resulted in a substantial cash flow during the first year. This enabled the corporation to meet its financial obligations with little or no difficulty. Exhibit 3 presents a cash earnings statement for the year ended June 30, 1959, and estimated cash earnings for the year ended June 30, 1960.

Prompted by results of the first year and expectations for the second, the promoters began considering an addition to Hotel 128. A count taken by Mr. Lee revealed that 400 to 500 people were being turned away each week. On this basis, it was decided that demand would support an addition of 42 rental units, and estimates and plans were drawn up. It was expected that construction would begin some time in the fall of 1959 and that the new units would be completed in May or June of 1960.

The promoters then turned to the question of financing. Approximately $30,000–$40,000 was needed, of course, for furnishings, fixtures, and equipment. This probably would be financed on time payments through a local bank or trust company. An adjoining acre of land was purchased for the addition at a price of $41,000, one third down and the balance payable over a 2-year period, with interest at 6% on the unpaid balance. The remaining problem was how to raise the estimated $240,000 to pay for the building.

A key factor in the decision was the average rate of occupancy that could be expected. Mr. Lee thought that the overall average was certain to decline, at least temporarily, when the addition was finished. The number of people being turned away weekly, however, led him to believe that a decline in average occupancy would be small and only temporary. He estimated that after completion the average would be about 15% less than otherwise during the first month, 10% in the second month, 7% in the third, with a return to normal expected in the fourth or fifth month.

Great interest in Hotel 128 had been expressed by many persons who were now seeking an opportunity to acquire an equity interest in the corporation. Mr. Lee thought that the possibility of raising funds through a sale of common stock would be rejected early, however, owing to the dilution involved for existing stockholders who did not invest more. Members of the promoting group who were connected with the investment banking field believed that a price-earnings ratio of 10/1 on the year's projected earnings was probably an upper limit. On this basis a common stock issue of at least 10,000 shares, at a price of approximately $24 a share, would be required to raise $240,000.

The promoters were confident that a new 20-year debenture issue, plus stock, could be sold to raise the money. In fact, part of a new issue could be sold to the original investing group, a number of whom had expressed a desire to invest more on the same basis as the original issue. This method of raising the money, however, would also involve a dilution of the equity interest held by those who did not invest more. The promoters wanted to avoid any dilution, if possible, but were ready to accept it if the risks and costs of the alternatives were determined to be too great.

The insurance company holding a first mortgage on the property was approached to see what amount it would be willing to furnish. It agreed to raise the balance outstanding on the mortgage ($460,000) to $600,000, and to start the 15-year amortization period running anew. The interest rate on the unpaid balance, however, was to be increased from 6% to 6½% on the full amount of the mortgage. To complete the financing, a trust company agreed to provide the additional $100,000 for 13 months. Interest would be computed at 6% on the full amount for the entire period. Principal and interest would be payable in equal monthly amounts.

Exhibit 4 is an amortization schedule of long-term financial obligations, including current maturities, at June 30, 1959. Exhibit 5 presents an incremental cost and amortization schedule for each of the debt alternatives under consideration for financing the addition.

Mr. Lee thought that one final factor must be given some consideration before a decision was reached. The promoters were so enthusiastic about the results of the entire undertaking that they were thinking of starting a chain of motels. Since this appeared to be a distinct possibility for the future, it was important not to restrict flexibility unnecessarily by any action taken at this time.

Exhibit 1
DEDHAM HOTEL CORPORATION
BALANCE SHEET, AS OF JUNE 30, 1959

ASSETS

Cash...		43,660
Accounts receivable, trade.............................$	16,328	
Less: Reserve for doubtful accounts..................	1,127	15,201
Accounts receivable, other................................		1,095
Inventories, at lower of cost or market...................		9,741
Prepaid expenses.......................................		8,079
Real estate tax suspense deposit (tax liability funded to date, funds invested in commercial paper)..................		16,000
Total current assets.............................		$ 93,777
Noncurrent investment and receivable....................		250
Plant and equipment, at cost...........................$1,169,691		
Less: Reserves for depreciation........................	46,728	1,122,963
Deferred charges.......................................		99,318
Total assets.....................................		$1,316,308

LIABILITIES

Bank loan..		$ 4,200
Accounts payable, trade...............................		71,854
Accounts and notes payable, other......................		40,383
Accrued liabilities:		
State and local taxes................................$	21,189	
Other..	12,336	33,525
Mortgage payments, due within one year.................		58,302
Total current liabilities...........................		$ 208,264
Noncurrent liabilities:		
Notes payable for equipment, due after one year.........$	5,713	
Note payable, officer, due August 16, 1963...............	26,500	
First mortgage payable, due after one year (Note 1)......	460,105	
Second mortgage payable, due after one year (Note 2)....	170,000	
6% debentures, due October 15, 1977..................	400,000	$1,062,318
Stockholders' equity:		
Capital stock (authorized 10,000 shares, no par value; issued, 5,000 shares)...............................$	50,000	
Deficit..	(4,275)	45,725
Total liabilities.................................		$1,316,308

NOTE 1. First mortgage loan, 6%, is payable in monthly instalments of $4,220 on account of interest and principal.

NOTE 2. Second mortgage loan is payable in monthly instalments of $3,000 on account of principal until August, 1961, when balance of $131,000 is payable. Interest at 6% is payable monthly.

Exhibit 2

DEDHAM HOTEL CORPORATION

INCOME AND DEFICIT STATEMENT
FOR THE YEAR ENDED JUNE 30, 1959

Revenue from sale of rooms, food and beverages, and other hotel income.............................			$784,105
Departmental salaries and wages, cost of sales, and other expenses..............................			468,190
Departmental gross profit......................			$315,915
General expenses:			
Administrative.............................	$78,802		
Advertising and promotion...................	24,023		
Heat, light, and power......................	23,169		
Repairs and maintenance....................	14,542	$140,536	
Fixed charges:			
Real estate tax............................	$15,000		
State tax.................................	1,100		
Insurance................................	8,959		
Interest..................................	70,766		
Amortization of debt discount................	14,428		
Depreciation..............................	46,728		
Amortization..............................	6,243	163,224	303,761
Income before federal income taxes..............			$ 12,154
Federal income taxes (none required because of net operating loss carry-forward).................			...
Net income for year...........................			$ 12,154
Deficit, June 30, 1958.........................			(16,429)
Deficit, June 30, 1959.........................			$ (4,275)

Exhibit 3

DEDHAM HOTEL CORPORATION

CASH EARNINGS STATEMENT

	Year Ended June 30	
	1959	*1960 (Estimated)*
Net income before interest and federal income taxes...	$ 82,920	$126,000
Less: Federal income taxes (adjusted for loss carry-forward).............................	...	23,000
	$ 82,920	$103,000
Noncash charges:		
Depreciation..............................	46,728	45,000
Amortization of debt discount.................	14,428	13,000
Amortization of organization and financing expenses...............................	6,243	6,500
Net cash earnings before interest and after taxes*....	$150,319	$167,500
Interest charges deducted for purposes of tax computation..................................	$ 70,766	$ 66,000

* Cash available for interest payments, debt repayment, and other purposes.

Exhibit 4

DEDHAM HOTEL CORPORATION

AMORTIZATION SCHEDULE OF MAJOR LONG-TERM FINANCIAL OBLIGATIONS, INCLUDING CURRENT MATURITIES, AT JUNE 30, 1959

(Dollar Figures in Thousands)

Year Ended June 30	Note Payable to Officer Principal	Note Payable to Officer Interest	First Mortgage Principal	First Mortgage Interest	Second Mortgage Principal	Second Mortgage Interest	Debentures Principal	Debentures Interest	Total Principal	Total Interest	Total Cash Outlay Before Tax	Total Cash Outlay After Tax*
1960		$1.6	$ 22.3	$ 28.3	$ 36.0	$11.4		$ 24.0	$ 58.3	$ 65.3	$ 123.6	$ 91.0
1961		1.6	24.3	26.3	36.0	9.2		24.0	60.3	61.1	121.4	90.9
1962		1.6	25.8	24.8	134.0	1.3		24.0	159.8	51.7	211.5	185.7
1963		1.6	27.3	23.3				24.0	27.3	48.9	76.2	51.8
1964	$26.5	0.2	28.8	21.8				24.0	55.3	46.0	101.3	78.3
1965			30.8	19.8				24.0	30.8	43.8	74.6	52.7
1966			32.8	17.8				24.0	32.8	41.8	74.6	53.7
1967			34.3	16.3				24.0	34.3	40.3	74.6	54.5
1968			36.8	13.8				24.0	36.8	37.8	74.6	55.7
1969			38.8	11.8				24.0	38.8	35.8	74.6	56.7
1970			41.2	9.4				24.0	41.2	33.4	74.6	57.9
1971			43.8	6.8				24.0	43.8	30.8	74.6	59.2
1972			46.2	4.4				24.0	46.2	28.4	74.6	60.4
1973			49.2	1.4				24.0	49.2	25.4	74.6	61.9
1974								24.0		24.0	24.0	12.0
1975								24.0		24.0	24.0	12.0
1976								24.0		24.0	24.0	12.0
1977								24.0		24.0	24.0	12.0
1978							$400.0	7.0	400.0	7.0	407.0	403.5
Total	$26.5	$6.6	$482.4	$226.0	$206.0	$21.9	$400.0	$439.0	$1,114.9	$693.5	$1,808.4	$1,461.9

* Tax rate assumed at 50%.

Exhibit 5

DEDHAM HOTEL CORPORATION

INCREMENTAL COST AND AMORTIZATION SCHEDULE—COMPARISON
OF ALTERNATIVE DEBT-FINANCING PLANS

(Dollar Figures in Thousands)

*Alternative 2, New Debenture Issue**

Year Ended June 30	Principal	Interest	Cash Outlay Before Tax	Cash Outlay After Tax†
1961		$ 14.4	$ 14.4	$ 7.2
1962		14.4	14.4	7.2
1963		14.4	14.4	7.2
1964		14.4	14.4	7.2
1965		14.4	14.4	7.2
1966		14.4	14.4	7.2
1967		14.4	14.4	7.2
1968		14.4	14.4	7.2
1969		14.4	14.4	7.2
1970		14.4	14.4	7.2
1971		14.4	14.4	7.2
1972		14.4	14.4	7.2
1973		14.4	14.4	7.2
1974		14.4	14.4	7.2
1975		14.4	14.4	7.2
1976		14.4	14.4	7.2
1977		14.4	14.4	7.2
1978		14.4	14.4	7.2
1979		14.4	14.4	7.2
1980	$240.0	14.4	254.4	247.2
Total	$240.0	$288.0	$528.0	$384.0

* Twenty-four hundred shares of common stock would be issued with the new debentures.

† Tax rate assumed at 50%.

Exhibit 5 (Continued)

Alternative 3

Year Ended June 30	New First Mortgage		Loan from Trust Co.		Total			Cash Outlay under Existing First Mortgage	Net Cash Outlay	
	Principal	Interest	Principal	Interest	Principal	Interest	Cash Outlay		Before Tax	After Tax†
1961	$ 24.6	$ 38.2	$ 92.3	$6.0	$116.9	$ 44.2	$ 161.1	$ 50.6	$110.5	$101.5
1962	25.8	37.0	7.7	0.5	33.5	37.5	71.0	50.6	20.4	14.1
1963	28.2	34.6			28.2	34.6	62.8	50.6	12.2	6.5
1964	30.0	32.8			30.0	32.8	62.8	50.6	12.2	6.7
1965	31.2	31.6			31.2	31.6	62.8	50.6	12.2	6.3
1966	34.2	28.6			34.2	28.6	62.8	50.6	12.2	6.8
1967	36.0	26.8			36.0	26.8	62.8	50.6	12.2	6.9
1968	38.4	24.4			38.4	24.4	62.8	50.6	12.2	6.9
1969	41.4	21.4			41.4	21.4	62.8	50.6	12.2	7.4
1970	43.8	19.0			43.8	19.0	62.8	50.6	12.2	7.4
1971	46.8	16.0			46.8	16.0	62.8	50.6	12.2	7.6
1972	50.4	12.4			50.4	12.4	62.8	50.6	12.2	8.2
1973	53.4	9.4			53.4	9.4	62.8	50.6	12.2	8.2
1974	56.4	6.4			56.4	6.4	62.8	...	62.8	59.6
1975	59.4	3.4			59.4	3.4	62.8	...	62.8	61.1
Total	$600.0	$342.0	$100.0	$6.5	$700.0	$348.5	$1,048.5	$657.8	$390.7	$315.2

† Tax rate assumed at 50%.

Case 29

Economy Shipping Company

I

In the spring of 1950 the controller of the Economy Shipping Company, located near Pittsburgh, was preparing a report for the executive committee regarding the feasibility of repairing one of the company's steam river boats or of replacing the steamboat with a new diesel-powered boat.

The Economy Shipping Company was engaged mainly in the transportation of coal from the nearby mines to the steel mills, public utilities, and other industries in the Pittsburgh area. The company's several steamboats also, on occasion, carried cargoes to places as far away as New Orleans. The boats owned by Economy were all steam powered. All were at least 10 years old, and the majority were between 15 and 30 years old.

The steamboat the controller was concerned about, the *Cynthia*, was 23 years old and required immediate rehabilitation or replacement. It was estimated that the *Cynthia* had a useful life of another 20 years provided that adequate repairs and maintenance were made. Whereas the book value of the *Cynthia* was $39,500, it was believed that she would bring somewhat less than this amount, possibly around $25,000, if she were sold in 1950. The total of immediate rehabilitation costs for the *Cynthia* was estimated to be $115,000. It was estimated that these general rehabilitation expenditures would extend the useful life of the *Cynthia* for about 20 years.

New spare parts from another boat, which had been retired in 1948, were available for use in the rehabilitation of the *Cynthia*. An estimate of their fair value, if used on the *Cynthia*, was $43,500, which was their book value. Use of these parts would, in effect, decrease the immediate rehabilitation costs from $115,000 to $71,500. It was believed that if these parts were sold on the market they would bring only around

827

$30,000. They could not be used on any of the other Economy steamboats.

Currently, the *Cynthia* was operated by a 20-man crew. Annual operating costs for the 20-man crew would be approximately as follows:

Wages	$110,200
Vacation and sickness benefits	1,880
Social security payments	2,400
Life insurance	1,800
Commissary supplies	15,420
Repairs and maintenance	24,400
Fuel	34,500
Lubricants	550
Miscellaneous service and supplies	12,000
Total	$203,150

It was estimated that the cost of dismantling and scrapping the *Cynthia* at the end of her useful life after the overhaul would be offset by the value of the scrap and used parts taken off the boat.

II

An alternative to rehabilitating the steamboat was the purchase of a diesel-powered boat. The Quapelle Company, a local boat manufacturer, quoted the price of $325,000 for a diesel boat. An additional $75,000 for a basic parts inventory would be necessary to service a diesel boat, and such an inventory would be sufficient to service up to three diesel boats. If four or more diesels were purchased, however, it was estimated that additional spare parts inventory would be necessary.

The useful life of a diesel-powered boat was estimated to be 25 years, at the end of which time the boat would be scrapped or completely rehabilitated at a cost approximating that of a new boat. The possibility of diesel engine replacement during the 25-year life was not contemplated by the controller, since information from other companies having limited experience with diesel-powered river boats did not indicate that such costs needed to be anticipated; but a general overhaul of the engines, costing at current prices $60,000, would be expected every 10 years.

One of the features the Quapelle Company pointed out was the 12% increase in average speed of diesel-powered boats over the steamboats. The controller discounted this feature, however, because the short runs and lock-to-lock operations involved in local river shipping would prohibit the diesel boats from taking advantage of their greater speed, since there was little opportunity for passing and they would have to wait in turn at each lock for the slower steamboats. In 1950 only two diesel boats, out of about 40 boats, were operating on the river. The controller felt it would be many years, if at all, before diesel boats displaced the slower steamboats.

After consulting the Quapelle Company and other companies operating diesel-powered boats, the controller estimated that the annual operating costs of a diesel-powered boat would total $156,640, broken down as follows:

Wages, for a 13-man crew	$ 77,300
Vacation and sickness benefits	1,320
Social security payments	1,680
Life insurance	1,170
Commissary supplies	10,020
Repairs and maintenance*	21,700
Fuel	28,800
Extra stern repairs	2,000
Miscellaneous service and supplies	12,650
Total	$156,640

* Excluding possible major overhaul of diesel engines.

Although the Economy controller had not considered the matter, the user of this case may assume that at the end of the 20th year the diesel boat would have a realizable value of $32,500 and the inventory of parts of $37,500.

III

The controller was also concerned at this time with a city smoke ordinance, which had been signed in 1948 to take effect in 1952. To comply with the regulations of the ordinance, all hand-fired steamboats had to be converted to stoker firing. Several of the Economy's steamboats were already stoker-fired; the *Cynthia,* however, was hand-fired. The additional cost of converting the *Cynthia* to stoker firing was estimated to be $40,000, provided it was done at the same time as the general rehabilitation. This $40,000 included the cost of stokers and extra hull conversion and was not included in the $115,000 rehabilitation figure. The controller also knew that if $115,000 were spent presently in rehabilitating the *Cynthia* and it was found out later that no relief or only temporary relief for one or two years was to be granted under the smoke ordinance, the cost of converting to stoker firing would no longer be $40,000, but around $70,000. The higher cost would be due to rebuilding, which would not be necessary if the *Cynthia* was converted to stoker firing at the time of her general rehabilitation.

Conversion would reduce the crew from 20 to 18, with the following details:

Wages	$100,650
Vacation and sickness benefits	1,650
Social security payments	2,200
Life insurance	1,620
Commissary supplies	13,880
Repairs and maintenance*	24,400
Fuel*	34,500
Lubricants*	550
Miscellaneous service and supplies*	12,000
Total	$191,450

* These costs would remain the same, whether the crew was 20 or 18 men.

IV

All operating data the controller had collected pertaining to crew expenses were based on a 2-shift, 12-hour working day, which was standard on local river boats. He had been informed, however, that the union representing crew members wanted a change to a 3-shift, 8-hour day. If the union insisted on an 8-hour day, accommodations on board the steamers or the diesels would have to be enlarged. The controller was perturbed by this fact, because he knew the diesels could readily be converted to accommodate three crews whereas steamers could not. How strongly the union would insist on the change and when it would be put into effect, if ever, were questions for which the controller could get no satisfactory answers. He believed that the union might have a difficult time in getting acceptance of its demands for three 8-hour shifts on steamers, since it would be very difficult, if not impossible, to convert the steamers to hold a larger crew, because of space limitations. The controller thought that the union might succeed in getting its demands accepted, however, in the case of diesel-powered boats. One of the diesel boats currently operating in the Pittsburgh area had accommodations for three crews, although it was still operating on a 2-shift basis. The diesel boats that the Quapelle Company offered to build for Economy could be fitted to accommodate three crews at no additional cost.

V

Another factor the controller was considering at this time was alternative uses of funds. In the spring of 1950 Economy had sufficient funds to buy four diesel-powered boats; however, there were alternative uses for these funds. The other projects which the management was considering at this time had an estimated return of at least 10% after taxes. The income tax rate at the time was 48%.

The company was conservatively managed and, in 1950, had no long-term debt outstanding. Its net worth exceeded $2 million. The company occasionally used unsecured bank loans to provide working capital during seasonal periods of peak need. In the spring of 1950 the company's liability for bank loans amounted to $150,000, which had been borrowed at 3% interest. The "prime" loan rate in New York City at the time was 2%.

VI

As a further inducement to have a contract to build a diesel boat, the Quapelle Company offered to rent a diesel boat to Economy. The rental terms offered by the Quapelle Company called for annual payments of

$21,700 for 15 years plus $5,700 per year for an interest charge. At the end of 15 years, when the Quapelle Company had in effect recovered the value of the boat, it would charge a nominal rental of $2,850 a year. Title to the boat would continue to remain in the hands of the Quapelle Company. Economy would incur all costs of operating and maintaining the boat, including general overhaul every 10 years, and would still need to invest $75,000 in a basic spare parts inventory.

Case 30

Molecular Compounds Corporation*

THE MOLECULAR COMPOUNDS CORPORATION (MOCOM) manufactured a wide variety of products in the chemical field and related areas, ranging from industrial chemicals through consumer goods. During the 1950's, MOCOM's sales had grown over 60%, reaching a level in excess of $700 million in 1962. Net income had withstood the pressures of competition within the chemical industry, with the result that per share earnings had also risen about 60% during this time. This rise occurred despite additional profit erosion caused by increased depreciation charges and higher allocations for research and development. The corporate executive group was extremely anxious to match or exceed this growth record in the decade from 1960 to 1970. Toward this end, it had instructed the Central Financial and Planning Staff to reevaluate the methods of financial analysis to insure that adequate investments were being made.

The fundamental objective of the company's current capital budgeting process was to maximize corporate growth and especially the growth of earnings per share. This objective would permit the payment of a fair and, it was hoped, growing dividend to stockholders; and, subject to the vagaries of the stock market, it would create conditions favorable for significant capital appreciation.

Developments in the chemical industry had contributed to executive concern about MOCOM's growth prospects. Recently, a number of successful, large firms (e.g., Standard Oil Company (New Jersey), Goodyear Tire and Rubber Company, W. R. Grace and Company, and the Borden Company) had entered the field and had aggressively sought to share in the chemical and allied products market, which had sales of $30 billion in 1961. There were already 10 firms, primarily in chemicals, with sales of over $300 million and numerous smaller firms with

* Abridged.

832

significant sales in narrower segments of the market. Each of these firms was tending to diversify further. Some of the substantial postwar expansion had led to overcapacity. All this meant increased competition among giants for available demand. In particular, price cutting in established products had squeezed margins considerably without generating much new volume. Sales and earnings also seemed likely to become more volatile, especially as foreign competition became more important. The greatest hope for the achievement of corporate goals was seen in the development and rapid exploitation of new products (including product improvement).

At the same time, the industry was becoming increasingly mature. Some segments still retained the dynamic growth patterns that had been evident during the introduction of petrochemicals and plastics. However, more firms were spending more on research to achieve a strong position in these fields, and existing competitive advantages were proving more tenuous. In total, the balance had shifted toward a higher proportion of products with limited prospects for growing demand.

These factors led MOCOM's top management to conclude that it would be necessary to secure full and effective utilization of available capital resources if the firm was to achieve continued rapid growth. The increased size and complexity of MOCOM's operations, however, made such an objective all the more difficult to achieve. A recent drop in the amount of capital expenditures submitted for approval had thus been the cause of considerable concern.

Partially because of these considerations, the members of MOCOM's Central Financial and Planning Staff were considering a revision in the company's budgeting procedure in early 1962. In their judgment, the most significant revision would eliminate the 12% (after-tax) minimum return on investment criterion or "cutoff" rate. This rate had been used to evaluate all projects since the existing procedures had been introduced in the middle 1950's. The essence of the argument for elimination of the rate was that the existing system was overstructured. For example, some executives argued that a cutoff rate tended to discourage submission of low-return but relatively riskless projects in which MOCOM could profitably invest. In short, the elimination of the artificial restraint of a cutoff rate might encourage operating personnel to submit any project that appeared worthwhile.

Other members of the Planning Staff, however, thought that a cutoff rate (preferably 12%, but certainly no lower than 6% or 7%) was essential as a management tool. They believed that with no formal guideline the divisions would create their own rules and procedures, many of which would be more stringent than the 12% rate currently set by the corporation. There remained, however, considerable disagreement as to just what cutoff rate should be used and how it should be administered in order to stimulate satisfactory growth.

Decentralized Management

MOCOM was organized into 11 autonomous divisions. Each division was self-supporting and contained its own staff groups, including a Financial and Planning Staff. Division executives were held responsible for planning the course of their divisions and for operating them successfully. Although plans and problems were discussed regularly with headquarters personnel, central management's greatest influence arose through performance appraisal. Performance was evaluated by a number of financial methods as well as by less formal factors. Top corporate management considered, for example, a division's return on investment (operating income, less an allocation for corporate overhead and for depreciation on the division's assets, divided by the sum of gross fixed investment and gross working capital), its operating percentages (income as a percentage of sales, etc.), and growth trends.

Through these evaluations, top management communicated its desires and criticisms in ways, sometimes subtle, that appeared to have a profound effect upon divisional attitudes and orientations. While unquestionably misinterpretations and other misunderstandings arose, top management considered that this planning system worked more successfully than would a more formal set of policies, goals, and operating directives. Nevertheless, the influence of performance evaluations on subsequent actions was a cause for modest concern because of the difficulty of comparing actual success against relative differences in available opportunities.

Any adjustments in the capital budgeting process would have to take existing division-headquarters relationships into account.

Existing Capital Budgeting Procedures

Although each division was responsible for generating projects, all divisions were expected to abide by the 12% cutoff rate, which was applied by the divisional financial analyst following procedures set by the Central Financial and Planning Staff. Projects below that rate were actively discouraged and usually rejected, even though they required less than $150,000 and could consequently be approved by division management without central management review.

About 40% of the corporation's total capital expenditures were included in the division budgets and were not reviewed by headquarters, although this percentage varied from division to division. Only projects requiring an investment of more than $150,000 were forwarded to the Central Financial and Planning Staff, which reviewed the request on behalf of the Capital Budget Review Committee. This committee, consisting of the corporation's president, the executive vice president, two divisional managers (including the originator of a project under discussion), and two Central Staff vice presidents, gave final[1] approval to

---

[1] In certain instances approval by the board of directors was also required.

projects in excess of the size divisional management could approve. In addition, if any project smaller than $150,000 and returning less than 12% seemed particularly attractive, division management could request the Capital Budget Review Committee to waive the cutoff requirement.

The 12% cutoff rate had been selected after an extensive investigation by the Central Financial and Planning Staff, which considered a wide variety of possibly relevant considerations. The four most important were:

1. *Growth expectations.* Over the previous 50 years the company's earnings per share had increased 7% to 8% a year. It was assumed that the stockholders expected that this rate of growth would be maintained and in addition that a dividend yield of at least 3% would be provided. A combination of these two figures (dividends per share divided by market price, plus "growth") yielded a cost of equity capital of 10% or 11%. Twelve percent was selected to allow a slight margin for error in the budgeting process.

2. *Cost of capital.* From an actual balance sheet, a weighted average cost of capital, including debt (estimated interest charges) and equity (estimated earnings per share/market price), was calculated (see Exhibit 2). This measurement turned out to be substantially lower than 12%.

3. *Industry standards.* Cutoff rates used by other companies in MOCOM's industries were investigated and found to be roughly around 12%.

4. *Feasibility.* Management believed that the 12% rate was quite practical, since it would not generate more projects than the firm could absorb. As there seemed to be no sound, rigorous basis for making the necessary final judgment, a 12% cutoff rate (after taxes) was accepted because it seemed about right.

The corporation also had installed a standard method of computing return on investment. After experimentation with several financial measures, management chose a net after-tax present-value technique. In this measurement present-valued cash outflows were subtracted from present-valued cash inflows (including an estimate for recovery) to arrive at a net present-value figure. From alternative investments, the one showing the highest net present value was selected, all other factors being equivalent. Other measurements, such as internal rate of return (that rate which makes the net present value equal to zero), after-tax return on gross investment, payback years in present-value dollar terms, and profits as a percentage of sales, were used as supplementary guides.

Forecasts were sometimes measured on an expected value basis. Division Planning Staff personnel were supposed to consider various alternative outcomes and calculated related cash flows. They then assigned probabilities to the flows and used the probabilities as weights to obtain an expected present-value figure. This adjustment was used to correct the "most likely" estimate when skewed probability distributions were observed.

Problems with the Existing System

The Central Financial and Planning Staff acted as consultants to the divisions in their planning and capital budget preparation, in addition to reporting to the corporate headquarters and providing the reports, plans, and analyses top management needed. Many of the analysts had worked in one or another of the divisions before they transferred to the Central Staff group. The members of the Staff thus considered themselves fairly familiar with the attitudes of the divisions and with the informal methods that existed on local levels to supplement the formal capital budgeting procedure.

As a result of their visits and work in the field, the Central Planning Staff began to suspect that the existing capital budgeting system was possibly choking off investments at the extremes of the opportunity spectrum. At the least, the planning group believed that too few low-risk, low-return and too few high-risk, high-return projects were being submitted to the Capital Budget Review Committee. For example, very few projects were ever submitted that were as low as the cutoff rate of 12%. The average internal return rate seemed to be between 17% and 20% on low-risk projects and went up much higher for any request that had a major risk associated with it.

Moreover, the Capital Budget Review Committee rarely rejected a project. "When one is rejected," an executive of the Central Staff remarked, "you can hear the anguished cries through the whole building." Some members of the financial and planning group considered this situation evidence that few borderline projects were being submitted for top-level consideration. As a consequence top corporate management was unable to exercise significant influence on the allocation of funds within the company. "It's not the obvious investments that top management should consider," commented one analyst, "since anyone can decide these. They should be concerned with the marginal projects which are at present being screened out all along the line."

While it was less clear-cut, there was also evidence that very few projects were being rejected at lower echelons. This condition further suggested that only those projects which were relatively certain to receive final approval were even flowing into the beginning of the decisional pipeline. The criteria used by the divisions to screen possible attractive opportunities were not always known, but they appeared to be, oftentimes, more cautious than top management wished. The negative decisions, then, were commonly made at the source of the idea, at a level in the organization quite removed from direct communication with the Capital Budget Review Committee.

Equally important, screening criteria at intermediate levels were known to differ from division to division and probably from person to person. For example, a number of executives were known to use a cutoff rate of 15% based upon after-tax return on gross investment (a cutoff criterion used within the company prior to 1956) in evaluation of projects. Unquestionably, other standards were employed wherever they seemed appropriate to individuals.

In composite, these negative decisions were probably quite significant. First of all, some executives were afraid that MOCOM might be underspending relative to its ability. MOCOM's top management believed that the company had sufficient sources of funds to support a substantial increase in the rate of plant expenditures. The company's debt-to-capitalization ratio ranged between 25% and 30%, well below levels considered safe. Management believed that the firm could borrow nearly $100 million more at favorable interest terms. This potential source of funds, combined with a large after-tax income and a substantial depreciation throwoff, practically ensured that even extremely large capital budgets could be sustained over a number of years without recourse to common stock financing. Indeed, in recent years internally generated funds alone had proved adequate to meet normal dividend and capital expenditure demands for funds.

There was good evidence that many favorable opportunities were never submitted. For example, the question of the effectiveness of the capital budgeting system was raised in a dramatic way in 1960, when the limit on projects that could be included in division budgets changed from $75,000 to $150,000. The number of projects included in the division budgets increased substantially, and it appeared that the dollar volume of projects requiring investments of between $100,000 and $150,000 would be about four times its previous level.

Top management's influence on the strategic balance of overall expenditures was limited. While they might suggest directions for expansion or encourage increased outlays for certain divisions, top executives were perforce limited to selecting from projects submitted. Their lack of familiarity with the specific details of projects lost in the screening process made it difficult for them to offer suggestions.

Finally, several types of projects were clearly being overlooked. One category included very safe projects promising a return of between 5% or 6% and 12%. These investments typically were in the cost reduction area and generally promised to continue producing savings long after the nominal 15 years used in calculating the economic value of the project. For example, this type of project would include such installations as power plants, plants for producing basic materials, and improvements in basic heavy equipment. An increase in outlays for these projects might tend to dampen existing cyclical earnings swings.

There seemed to be an equal lack of projects at the other extreme, the high-risk and high-return ventures. In this category were new products which faced great uncertainties in the market but which, if they succeeded, could provide MOCOM with handsome profits.

The problem with the high-risk projects, as the financial and planning group saw it, was the extent of the risk to the division or plant managers. "It is hard to get a division manager," noted one of the central staff analysts, "to commit himself and his division to a project which requires new assets equal to a major percent of the assets he has allocated to him at present. The risk [probability of success or failure] to him and to his division is the same as the risk to the corporation, but the extent of the risk [the seriousness of failure] is greater. If he guesses wrong and the project is a dud, he's got to do some explaining to show why his return on assets has dropped. But the potential returns are so great that the company could afford to have a bunch of duds for each one which pans out and still come off ahead." In essence, the planning staff believed that the utility curves of the division managers were quite different from the utility curve of the corporation as a whole. At lower organizational levels, this problem appeared even more severe.

Exhibit 1

MOLECULAR COMPOUNDS CORPORATION

MARKET PRICE, EARNINGS AND DIVIDENDS PER SHARE

1947–MARCH, 1962

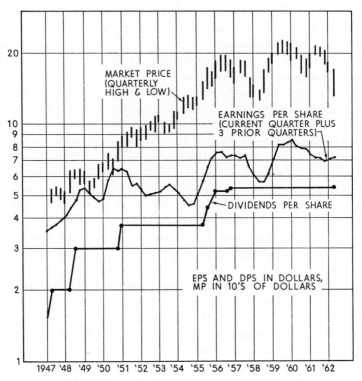

Exhibit 2

MOLECULAR COMPOUNDS CORPORATION

Earnings-Price Ratio

1947–March, 1962

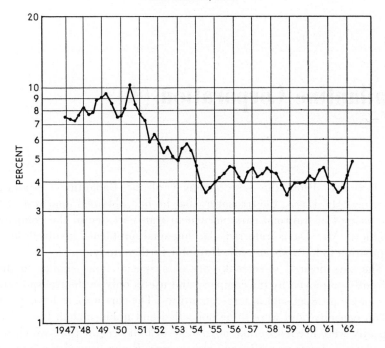

Case 31

Ballantine Corporation (A)

IN JANUARY, 1966, the sales manager of the Ballantine Corporation informed Mr. Davis, the treasurer, that he had obtained approval of the purchase of 35 railroad cars, needed to transport one of the company's products. Mr. Davis referred the financial problems involved in the acquisition to his assistant, Mr. Haig, for further study.

The cars desired were tank cars of a special type, similar to those currently employed by the company and useful only in the transportation of a single product sold in large quantities. The cars were to have 20,000-gallon capacity, and were to be noncoiled and noninsulated. Cars of this capacity were needed to take advantage of bulk freight rates which were in existence for large gallonage movements. Regardless of the financing plan adopted, the cars would be built to the Ballantine Corporation's specifications. If it ever was desirable, however, the cars could be modified at small expense to meet the specifications of other manufacturers of the same product or manufacturers of similar products.

The company had found itself in serious difficulties at times of high seasonal demand during the past year because of its inability to meet delivery requirements. Various alternatives had been investigated, including the use of storage facilities at selected geographical points. None was found to be more satisfactory than the acquisition of additional rolling stock.

The sales department had estimated the losses in profits that would be sustained without the proposed increase in the fleet. The analysis indicated that the proposed investment of $609,000 easily exceeded the company's average 15% return on investment after taxes. In fact, the project ranked high on the list of investment opportunities currently available, when the assumption was made that the existing manufacturing processes would be continued indefinitely and that the cars could be used for 20 years.

There were new processes in the research and development stage, however, which could, if perfected, greatly reduce the company's need for the type of tank cars under consideration. Although the final outcome of the research was still uncertain, the Ballantine executives felt that there was reason to give emphasis to a plan that would minimize the initial outlay of funds. The executives also anticipated a steady growth of sales of other products in the immediate future and some broadening of manufacturing activities, which would exert heavy pressures on working capital.

The members of the sales department, in computing their measure of the desirability of the purchase, included as an expense a figure of $600 per year for normal maintenance of the cars, estimated on the basis of the company's average experience with its existing fleet. Nothing was allowed for major rebuilding costs, which were incurred irregularly and unpredictably, especially with respect to the individual car. Mr. Haig learned that in the company's recent experience as much as $3,700 had been spent on an individual car in a single year. Total maintenance and rebuilding charges for the last 3 years had been as follows:

1963	$133,172
1964	321,574
1965	87,092
Total	$541,838

Costs in 1964 were inflated by an accelerated maintenance undertaking involving the entire fleet. No overhead was included in the totals. The 149 cars in the fleet in 1965 were about 10 to 12 years of age on the average.

Although a useful life of 20 years had been assumed, the sales department, in its calculations showing the desirability of the cars, used straight-line depreciation over 15 years, the period permitted by the U.S. Treasury *Guide Lines*. For tax purposes, however, the Ballantine Corporation used the double declining balance method of depreciation, because it was the only one of the permissible methods that could be applied to the total cost of the asset in the first years. The estimation of salvage value could be deferred until the annual charges were shifted to a straight-line basis. The experience of several companies showed that an estimate of 20% salvage value was appropriate for either 15- or 20-year life.

The schedule of annual depreciation charges for a $17,400 car, and the related tax shields resulting from this policy, appear in Exhibit 1. This schedule would be applied, no matter how the cars should be financed, unless they should be leased.

The company planned to use the 7% investment credit against its tax liability in the first year of ownership, as provided in the Revenue Act of 1964. This credit is also shown in Exhibit 1.

Direct Purchase from Manufacturer—Alternative I

After he had collected the alternatives to be described below, Mr. Haig's first step was to analyze the problem under the assumption that the cars would be purchased outright from the manufacturer through utilization of funds from working capital. He talked with several manufacturers of rail equipment and learned that a price of about $17,400 a car could be expected. Clearly, the pattern of cash flows created by this choice would be the outflow of a single sum, $17,400, at the beginning of the first year of ownership.

Use of General Credit—Alternative II

Mr. Haig next considered the use of the Ballantine Corporation's general credit position, which he knew was strong enough to permit the borrowing of the needed funds. From this point of view, it was in his opinion of no importance what maturity might be negotiated in a particular loan, since any repayments could be replaced by a new loan, and so on perpetually. The interest cost of such debt, Mr. Haig estimated, on the average, would not exceed 5% before taxes, although rates currently were higher. Cash outflows for 20 years on this assumption would be $870 per year before, and $452 per year after, taxes at 48%.

Ten-Year Mortgage Plan—Alternative III

Mr. Haig then considered the possibility of acquiring title to the cars through a mortgage arrangement. The Ballantine Corporation was limited in regard to debt financing by a term loan agreement with the Arcadia Life Insurance Company. Under the agreement the company could not undertake any further mortgage financing in cases where it proposed to pay less than 40% of the value of the asset at the time of purchase. Hence, an initial outlay of a minimum of $6,960 a car would be necessary. Mr. Haig learned that a mortgage loan for 60% of the cost of the new cars could be obtained at an interest rate of 6%. The principal would be repaid in 10 equal annual instalments, and the interest would be paid on the actual loan balances. Utilizing these assumptions, Mr. Haig made the cash flow table in Exhibit 2.

Conditional Sale—Alternative IV

The manufacturer of the cars was prepared to deliver the cars to the Ballantine Corporation without down payment, under a 10-year conditional sale agreement which required annual payments of $2,477. (Using compound interest tables, Mr. Haig discovered that an interest rate of 7% was implicit in this arrangement.) Exhibit 3 was prepared to show the cash flow consequences of this arrangement.[1] The investment credit would remain to benefit the Ballantine Corporation.

---

[1] It was assumed that, in the final form of the conditional sale agreement, the interest charge would be made explicit enough to qualify as an income deduction for tax purposes.

During the period of the conditional sale, the manufacturer would assume the responsibility for normal repairs, and would overhaul the cars during the tenth year. To show the difference in the treatment of maintenance in this scheme, an appropriate after-tax amount was entered by Mr. Haig as income to represent the cost that was assumed by the manufacturer. He did not include a savings for the overhaul in the 10th year, because this figure was uncertain. In the event it appeared that, if a savings for the overhaul were included, the conditional sales contract might be the most attractive financing, Mr. Haig would estimate possible levels of this expenditure.

The cash flows worked out by Mr. Haig for the various alternatives are shown in cumulative form in Exhibit 4.

Exhibit 1

BALLANTINE CORPORATION (A)

INVESTMENT CREDIT AND DEPRECIATION SCHEDULE
PER CAR COSTING $17,400, WITH SALVAGE VALUE OF 20%

Year	Credit Expense, or Terminal Value	After-Tax Cash Flow*
1 ⎰	$ 1,220	$ 1,220
1 ⎱	2,320	1,114
2	2,011	965
3	1,743	837
4	1,510	725
5	1,309	628
6	1,134	544
7	983	472
8	364	175
9	↑	↑
10		
11		
12		
13		
14	↓	↓
15	364	175
Termination†	20,000	20,000

* Assuming, in the case of depreciation expense, that the company has income enough to absorb this expense.
† Same value for any year between 15 and 20.

Exhibit 2

BALLANTINE CORPORATION (A)

COMPUTATION OF ANNUAL FUNDS FLOWS
RESULTING FROM CAR ACQUISITION

(Per Car)

Alternative III: 10-Year Mortgage Plan

Year	Principal	Interest	Total	Tax Shield* from Interest (48%)	Total After Tax
0	($6,960)←Down payment		($6,960)		($6,960)
1	(1,044)	($626)	(1,670)	$ 300	(1,370)
2		(564)	(1,608)	270	(1,338)
3		(501)	(1,545)	240	(1,305)
4		(438)	(1,482)	210	(1,272)
5		(376)	(1,420)	180	(1,240)
6		(313)	(1,357)	150	(1,207)
7		(251)	(1,295)	120	(1,175)
8		(188)	(1,232)	90	(1,142)
9		(125)	(1,169)	60	(1,109)
10	(1,044)	(63)	(1,107)	30	(1,077)
11	(0)	(0)	(0)	0	(0)
12					
13					
14					
15					
16					
17					
18					
19					
20	(0)	(0)	(0)	0	(0)
	$17,400	$3,445	$20,845	$1,650	$19,195

* Tax rate 48%.

Exhibit 3

BALLANTINE CORPORATION (A)

COMPUTATION OF ANNUAL FUNDS FLOWS
RESULTING FROM CAR ACQUISITION

(Per Car)

Alternative IV: Conditional Sale by Manufacturer

Year	Annual Payment	Payment		Tax Shield of Interest*	After-Tax Repairs Borne by Manufacturer*	Total After Tax
		Principal	Interest			
1	($2,477)	($1,259)	($1,218)	$ 585	$ 312	$ 1,580
2		(1,347)	(1,130)	542		1,623
3		(1,442)	(1,035)	497		1,668
4		(1,543)	(934)	448		1,717
5		(1,651)	(826)	396		1,769
6		(1,766)	(711)	341		1,824
7		(1,890)	(587)	282		1,883
8		(2,022)	(455)	218		1,947
9		(2,163)	(314)	151		2,014
10	(2,477)	(2,315)	(162)	78	312	2,087
11	0	0	0	0	0	0
12						
13						
14						
15						
16						
17						
18						
19						
20	0	0	0	0	0	0
	$24,770	$17,398	$7,372	$3,538	$3,120	$18,112

* Tax rate 48%.

Exhibit 4

BALLANTINE CORPORATION (A)

COMPARISON OF CUMULATIVE NET OUTFLOWS (AFTER TAX) OF ALTERNATIVE
METHODS OF FINANCING

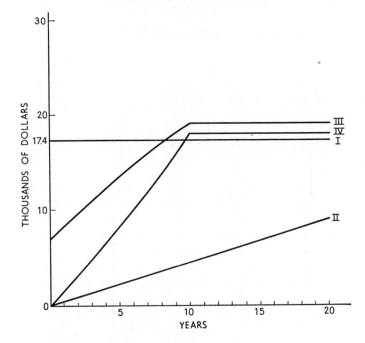

Case 32

Monitor Textile Company *

IN JANUARY, 1965, the Monitor Textile Company was considering replacement of one of its industrial forklift trucks. The desired machine was to be gasoline powered, and it had been determined that its cost, together with necessary parts would be $3,600. When considering buying the truck, the plant superintendent had been informed that the company was currently paying income tax at the rate of 48%, and that it would use the sum-of-the-years'-digits method of depreciation for a 5-year life to an estimated scrap value of 10% of original cost. The service life was estimated to be 6 years, with the same scrap value.

The Monitor Company enjoyed a strong working capital position, and funds were available for the purchase. On the other hand, the Stevens Company also offered to lease a truck to Monitor under two different leasing plans. Regardless of the plan chosen, Stevens would maintain the equipment and guarantee to keep it in serviceable condition at all times. This arrangement would relieve Monitor of a $15 per month charge for a blanket service contract, $24 per year taxes and insurance, and an estimated $200 overhaul at the end of the third year of operation.

In the event of a major breakdown, Stevens would provide a replacement truck, at its expense, within 4 hours. The cost of the lease plans, summarized below, varied depending on the minimum terms of the contract signed by the lessee.

Plan	Term of Contract	
1	3 years minimum, 30-day cancellation thereafter	145/month
2	5 years minimum, 30-day cancellation thereafter	132/month

It was company policy that funds committed to machine replacements should earn at least 10% after taxes. On the other hand, the company's debenture bonds were selling in the bond market to yield 5%.

---

* Abridged.

Case 33

Ballantine Corporation (B)

IN ADDITION to the alternatives described in the case Ballantine Corporation (A), Mr. Haig discovered the following:

A Financial Lease—Alternative V

A company which was in the business of arranging leases offered the following arrangement for a financial lease, that is a net lease in which the lessor would use the investment credit and the lessee would carry all the costs to maintain, etc., the cars. For the first 15 years, the payment would be constant at $1,460 per year. (A 3% rate was applied to the original cost.) At the end of the 15th year, the Ballantine Company could cease to use the cars, buy them at 20% of original cost, or rent them on a year-to-year basis at 5% of original cost per year.

Mr. Haig's calculations of cash flows under this arrangement are shown in Exhibit 1.

If the Ballantine Corporation should wish to retain the benefit of the investment credit the financial lease would remain as described, except that a 9% rate would be applied to the original cost in order to determine the annual rate for the first 15 years. Mr. Haig put this alternative aside without any alternative.

A Maintenance Lease—Alternative VI

A railroad car leasing company offered to rent the cars to the Ballantine Company indefinitely at $2,160 per year, on a minimum lease of 15 years. The lessor would assume all maintenance costs, including major rebuilding. The cash flows under this arrangement appear in Exhibit 2. As before, Mr. Haig omitted an estimate for major overhauls.

Mileage Allowances

Mr. Haig believed that the methods used by the railroads to bill customers might be crucial with respect to the estimation of costs under either lease alternative. The method of railroad building had developed from the fact that railroads were often using the rolling stock of other railroads in the daily course of their business. Therefore, they followed the practice of charging a shipper irrespective of who owned the railroad equipment and then "renting" the rolling stock used from the owner. For example, a railroad would first charge Ballantine Corporation for use of the company-owned equipment over its lines in the same manner as though railroad-owned cars had been used. Then it would pay rental at a specified rate per mile. The rate per mile depended upon the depreciated reproduction value of the car employed.

Cars that had a depreciated reproduction value in excess of $16,000 (which applied to the cars in question) were paid 18 cents per loaded mile. Under these rules, there was no payment for empty miles.

Should the Ballantine Corporation purchase the cars, the mileage allowances would accrue directly to the company and would serve to reduce operating costs. Under the leasing alternatives, the leasing corporation would be reimbursed. The lessor would apply these reimbursements to reduce the rentals paid by the Ballantine Corporation, but only to the extent of the rental charge.

Mr. Haig was not certain how to handle this problem; average mileages based on past experience obviously were not directly applicable. In his calculations he assumed that the effects would be negligible, although admittedly this treatment was open to question. During 1965, Ballantine sent its fleet of 149 cars on a total of 1,309 round trips for a total of about 3,239,000 miles. Per car, the average loaded trip length was about 1,080 miles.

The cash flows worked out by Mr. Haig for the two new alternatives are shown in cumulative form in Exhibit 3, together with the alternatives he had already analyzed. The residual values, of $20,000, are not charted.

Exhibit 1

BALLANTINE CORPORATION (B)

COMPUTATION OF ANNUAL FUNDS FLOWS
RESULTING FROM CAR ACQUISITION

(Per Car)

Alternative V: Financial Lease

Year	A: Gross Payments	B = A(0.52) After-Tax Expense of Rental	C: Lost Tax Shield of Investment Credit and Depreciation*	D = B + C Total
1	($1,460)	($759)	($2,334)	($3,093)
2	↑	↑	(965)	(1,724)
3			(837)	(1,596)
4			(725)	(1,484)
5			(628)	(1,387)
6			(544)	(1,303)
7			(472)	(1,231)
8			(175)	(934)
9			↑	↑
10				
11				
12				
13				
14			↓	↓
15	(1,460)	(759)	(175)	(934)
16	(870)	(452)	0	(452)
17	↑	↑	↑	↑
18			↓	
19	↓	↓	0	(452)
20	($870)	($452)	($20,000)	($20,452)

* From Exhibit 1, column 2, Ballantine Corporation (A).

Exhibit 2

BALLANTINE CORPORATION (B)

COMPUTATION OF ANNUAL FUNDS FLOWS
RESULTING FROM CAR ACQUISITION

(Per Car)

Alternative VI: Maintenance Lease

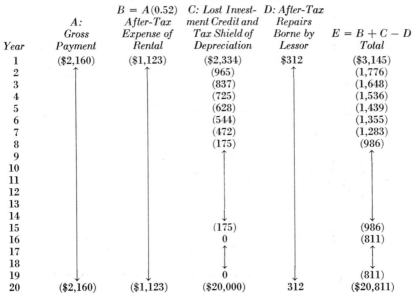

Year	A: Gross Payment	B = A(0.52) After-Tax Expense of Rental	C: Lost Invest- ment Credit and Tax Shield of Depreciation	D: After-Tax Repairs Borne by Lessor	E = B + C − D Total
1	($2,160)	($1,123)	($2,334)	$312	($3,145)
2			(965)		(1,776)
3			(837)		(1,648)
4			(725)		(1,536)
5			(628)		(1,439)
6			(544)		(1,355)
7			(472)		(1,283)
8			(175)		(986)
9					
10					
11					
12					
13					
14					
15			(175)		(986)
16			0		(811)
17					
18					
19			0		(811)
20	($2,160)	($1,123)	($20,000)	312	($20,811)

Exhibit 3

BALLANTINE CORPORATION (B)

COMPARISON OF CUMULATIVE NET OUTFLOWS (AFTER TAX) OF
ALTERNATIVE METHODS OF FINANCING

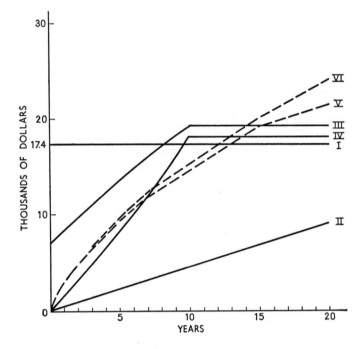

Case 34

The Prudential Insurance Company of America

Introduction

IN JANUARY, 1962, Mr. David Lloyd, an investment analyst in the Minneapolis office of The Prudential Insurance Company of America, was attempting to draw up a set of loan terms for a prospective new borrowing customer, Alliance Dairy Company. Alliance had asked for a loan of $340,000 on a long-term basis to help finance the construction of new plant facilities.

Alliance Dairy Company

Alliance Dairy Company was incorporated in Illinois in 1950, as Alliance Cooperative Dairy Company, to process and distribute dairy products at wholesale to independent member grocers. Initially, milk and butter were sold to 59 customers in Urbana, Illinois. The dairy's sales volume had grown steadily, aided by the broadening of its product line to include ice cream, cottage cheese, and a variety of other dairy products and by the addition of new member-customers. Alliance had been first in its area to use bulk tank milk pickup from its dairy farm supplies and to supply milk to its customers in half-gallon containers.

By 1962 Alliance distributed its products over an area within a 50-mile radius of Urbana with a population of 440,000. Its 165 independent grocer customers were at the same time stockholders, since each was required to purchases shares of Alliance's common stock. This stock served as collateral for payables due Alliance. Milk was purchased directly from about 80 dairy farmers, collected by Alliance tank trucks, and processed at the Alliance plant.

Alliance was the second largest of the 35 dairy processing firms

853

operating in the Urbana area, with 11% of the milk products business. Foremost Dairies, which had recently moved a milk-processing facility from Urbana to Stoneham—60 miles away—was Alliance's largest competitor, with 18% of the area business. Two other dairies each had about 10% of the market.

Alliance's net income was subject to the usual corporate income taxes, but under current tax regulations, rebates distributed to stockholders on the basis of their patronage were deductible as a business expense. To minimize its tax liability, therefore, the dairy made a practice of rebating all net proceeds from operations which were not needed to operate the business. Working capital needs were small, since accounts receivable were settled weekly and payments to dairy farmers for raw milk were made on a twice-monthly basis. (See Exhibits 1 and 2 for comparative financial data.)

Although Alliance enjoyed a reputation as an aggressively and skillfully operated business, its management in recent years had been increasingly dissatisfied with its antiquated milk-processing plant, which was both inefficient and limited in capacity. In November, 1960, therefore, the owner-patrons of Alliance had voted to build and equip a new bulk milk-processing and storage plant of sufficient capacity to permit continued expansion of operations. The old plant building was expected to have little value in a resale, but some of the equipment being used there could be transferred to the new facility. Because Alliance did not have sufficient funds available to finance the undertaking, the membership agreed to have an overcharge levied on them for milk and ice cream purchased from the dairy, beginning in December, 1960. In this way it was expected that $200,000 could be raised during the next year to help finance part of the $950,000 undertaking. The overcharge was to be returned to the owner-patrons in the form of preferred stock.

Soon after the membership had voted in favor of the surcharge, Alliance's commercial bank, the Peoples National Bank of Urbana, agreed to provide construction credit up to $150,000 to permit the building operation to be started immediately. In addition, it had agreed to supply $160,000 of the permanent financing needed and to assist Alliance in locating the $380,000 additional long-term funds required to complete the financing of the project, which would be finished by September, 1962. Alliance's management hoped to obtain an 8- to 10-year loan on terms which would not unduly burden them with constricting covenants and which recognized the somewhat distinctive nature of its operations and financing.

The Prudential Insurance Company of America

The Commercial and Industrial Loan Department of Prudential had been established in 1956 to extend financing to small companies whose capital needs had heretofore been considered too modest to warrant the time and attention of institutional lenders. By the end of 1961 the department had loans outstanding of $428 million and had been allocated $130 million in new funds to invest in 1962. This allocation provided strong incentive to accommodate as many loan requests as it could, within reason. In as many applications as possible the department sought to answer the question, "HOW can the loan be made?" rather than "CAN it be made?" The department had been organized into eight regional offices, each staffed with from two to six representatives. These offices initiated all departmental loan proposals and competed aggressively with other lending institutions for the business in their areas. Once a regional office had satisfied itself as to the soundness of a loan opportunity, it forwarded the pertinent financial data, along with tentative loan terms, to Prudential's home office in Newark, New Jersey, where it was reviewed by the loan officers there. The corporate office could deny further consideration of a loan proposal sent in by one of the regional offices but could not on its own authority grant a loan. If it judged that the proposal merited it, the pertinent data and recommended loan terms were summarized for presentation to Prudential's Finance Committee, which made the final decision on all loan proposals.

When Mr. Lloyd had first been asked by the Peoples National Bank to consider the Alliance loan request, several questions had arisen in his mind. Noting that the owner-patrons had voted to levy on themselves a surcharge on each half gallon of milk purchased from Alliance, Mr. Lloyd had queried what would prevent some or all of these owner-patrons from switching to competitive suppliers. Several inquiries about this convinced Mr. Lloyd that customer loyalty to Alliance had been strong. An executive of a competing dairy expressed the opinion that because of the dual role as owner and customer, it was practically impossible for other dairy processors to compete with Alliance for its customers' business. When Mr. Lloyd talked to the loan officer at the Peoples National Bank, he was told that the bank, in a move to demonstrate to Prudential its confidence in Alliance, was prepared to increase its participation in the long-term financing from $160,000 to $200,000, its legal lending limit. Thus, the size of the loan being requested from Prudential was reduced by $40,000 to $340,000. The bank had also agreed to accept security and repayment guarantees on a pro rata basis with the insurance company.

Mr. Lloyd has also raised questions about the reliability of Alliance's source of raw milk. Alliance's management conceded that there had been some dissatisfaction among the local dairy farmers over the price received for milk they produced for Alliance and other dairy processors. Management did not believe, however, that there was a serious possibility of a disruption in the supply of milk.

Having determined that the loan opportunity was worthy of further consideration and that if satisfactory terms could be worked out, a 6%

interest rate would be appropriate, Mr. Lloyd turned to the task of composing a set of covenants which would protect Prudential adequately yet not unduly restrict Alliance. He knew that several other institutional lenders had expressed preliminary interest in the dairy's capital needs and that if the proposed terms were unsatisfactory to Alliance, it might attempt to obtain financing from one of Prudential's competitors. To aid him, Mr. Lloyd had Prudential's manual of guidelines for framing loan covenants, excerpts from which are presented in Exhibit 3.

Exhibit 1

THE PRUDENTIAL INSURANCE COMPANY OF AMERICA

ALLIANCE DAIRY COMPANY

COMPARATIVE OPERATING DATA—YEARS ENDING NOVEMBER 30

(Dollar Figures in Thousands)

	1952	1953	1954	1955	1956	1957	1958	1959	1960	1961
Gross sales	$646	$744	$823	$991	$1,209	$1,331	$1,499	$1,873	$2,352	$2,640
Less: Cost of sales	570	650	717	873	1,059	1,135	1,254	1,567	1,914	2,043
Gross margin	76	94	106	118	150	196	245	306	438	597
Less: Selling, general and administrative expense (excluding depreciation)	38	56	73	83	97	126	158	189	259	309
Operating profit before depreciation	38	38	33	35	53	70	87	117	179	288
Less: Depreciation and amortization	5	7	8	12	17	19	21	27	34	36
Interest expense	3	1	0	1	5	4	3	2	3	4
Retained overcharges paid in cash or in stock	0	9	9	5	10	28	39	74	127	221
Plus: Other income	2	0	0	0	2	0	2	7	9	3
Taxable income	32	21	16	17	23	19	26	21	24	30
Less: Income tax paid	5	5	4	5	7	6	8	6	7	11
Net income after tax	27	16	12	12	16	13	18	15	17	19
Less: Preferred dividends	1	0	1	0	1	0	1	1	4	16
Common dividends	0	0	0	0	1	1	0	0	0	0
Net income after dividends	26	16	11	12	14	12	17	14	13	3
Previous earned surplus	(12)	14	30	41	53	67	79	96	110	123
Earned surplus at end of year	14	30	41	53	67	79	86	110	123	126

Exhibit 2

THE PRUDENTIAL INSURANCE COMPANY OF AMERICA

ALLIANCE DAIRY COMPANY

COMPARATIVE BALANCE SHEETS—AS OF NOVEMBER 30

(Dollar Figures in Thousands)

ASSETS	1952	1953	1954	1955	1956	1957	1958	1959	1960	1961
Cash	$ 8	$ 7	$ 20	$ 17	$ 27	$ 42	$ 59	$ 47	$183	$ 61
Accounts receivable	23	17	30	30	36	19	34	52	87	96
Inventory (lower of cost or market)	24	28	34	32	40	47	55	83	73	84
Prepaid expenses	2	1	2	2	2	3	3	3	7	9
Total current assets	$ 57	$ 53	$ 86	$ 81	$105	$111	$152	$185	$350	$ 250
Net plant	62	59	61	152	169	172	173	192	237	224
Construction in process	0	0	0	0	0	0	0	0	0	576
Bulk milk tanks	0	0	0	0	0	3	23	75	70	63
Miscellaneous assets	0	4	4	11	13	13	14	12	18	0
Total assets	$119	$116	$151	$244	$287	$299	$362	$464	$675	$1,113

LIABILITIES	1952	1953	1954	1955	1956	1957	1958	1959	1960	1961
Notes payable	40	14	0	20	25	0	0	0	0	0
Accounts payable and accrued	36	33	61	70	77	77	91	139	94	159
Reserve for income tax	5	5	4	5	7	6	8	6	7	11
Debt due within one year	0	0	0	0	0	0	0	28	32	28
Total current liabilities	$ 81	$ 52	$ 65	$ 95	$109	$ 83	$ 99	$173	$133	$ 198
Deferred income	0	0	0	2	2	1	0	0	3	2
Funded debt	0	0	0	44	50	50	46	22	45	179
Deposits for purchase of stock	0	3	6	11	15	14	52	56	62	97
Preferred stock	10	10	10	10	10	10	10	10	181	373
Common stock	14	21	29	29	34	62	59	93	128	138
Surplus	14	30	41	53	67	79	96	110	123	126
Total liabilities and equity	$119	$116	$151	$244	$287	$299	$352	$464	$675	$1,113

Exhibit 3

THE PRUDENTIAL INSURANCE COMPANY OF AMERICA

EXCERPTS FROM MANUAL ON FRAMING LOAN COVENANTS

1. Maturity—Generally ten years to fifteen years. The long-term predictable nature of life insurance policy claims has demanded that we take a long-term point of view toward investments.
2. Interest Rate—The interest rate should be related to the current money market. It should be borne in mind that direct placements usually command a higher rate than public offerings because of the elimination of substantial costs associated with public financing, and that our rates reflect the inherently greater risk associated with the smaller industrial concern, too small for public financing.
3. Price—At 100, except in very unusual circumstances.
4. Standby Fee—One-half of one per cent to one per cent per year.
5. Security—A mortgage or pledge of collateral gives The Prudential a preferred position with respect to the company's assets covered by the lien or pledge and may be desirable even though value alone would not justify the loan. In some instances, very attractive real estate may justify the investment where credit is borderline.
6. Concurrent Financing and Participations—Normally Prudential will purchase the entire issue; however, we will be happy to cooperate with the other lending institutions either on a *"pari passu"* basis, or in the later maturities where commercial banks are involved, providing we are not placed in a subordinate position at any time during the life of the loan.
7. Principal Payments—Generally, principal payments should be made in even thousands of dollars, in a constant amount, and payable on a semiannual or annual basis. Balloons or delays in the start of the principal payments may be applied in meeting special problems and in those instances where justified.
8. Optional Prepayments—Optional prepayments should be held to a minimum. However, the right to repay, at any time, at 100, in whole but not in part, if Prudential refuses consent to additional funded debt, shall be considered a standard provision. Such additional debt need not be offered to The Prudential, but the borrower must have a bona fide offer from another source. This provision does not apply if the borrower seeks merely to replace the Prudential loan.

   Where there is a participating lender, it is important that funds are not permitted to be paid out to the detriment of our position by reason of more liberal prepayment options than are granted by our terms.
9. Financial Statements and Audits—The loan terms will also include standard provisions for submission of annual audits, four quarterly interim financial statements and "Certificates of No Default."

Negative Covenants:

10. Working Capital Tests.
    a) Default level—The default level is based on the pro forma working capital and gives The Prudential protection against a continuing deterioration in the balance sheet. A high default level set close to

Exhibit 3 (Continued)

pro forma level is usually desirable for the following reason: The fact that a company may be borrowing the money for working capital shows that it needs working capital at the pro forma level; if the company grows as expected, it will need *more* rather than *less* working capital; and except for operating losses and debt retirements, reductions in working capital are controllable and limited to capital expenditure and restrictive payments.

   b) Dividend Test—A working capital minimum as a dividend test is generally used in those rare situations when a realistic default level cannot be obtained.

11. Dividends and Other Restrictive Payments—The primary purpose of this covenant is to protect Prudential against excess payout of earnings, to insure maintenance of net worth, and to provide the wherewithal for future company growth. Limitation on restrictive payments depends on the types of credits involved. A mathematical evaluation of the disposition of the earnings should be made, taking into account requirements for (*a*) debt repayment, (*b*) restricted payments, and (*c*) retention for reasonable growth.

    The covenant should provide that restrictive payments be limited to a percentage of the net earnings available for distribution to stockholders. Where the company is small or the funded debt heavy, the percentage should, of course, be smaller than that permitted for the stronger companies. On larger and stronger credits, and companies which are publicly held, it is sometimes necessary to permit a dollar cushion or to defer application of the dividend test for one year in order to permit the borrower to build up a reasonable amount of retained earnings available for dividends.

    "Stockholders compensation" may be eliminated entirely from the restricted payment clause where the company is essentially publicly held. Where the company is not publicly held and such control is deemed necessary, a fixed dollar limit on compensation should ordinarily be incorporated in a separate covenant, but may alternatively be included in restricted payments.

    Normally, preferred dividends, if not too large, are permitted regardless of the operation of the dividend formula, but such payments should be included in computations of surplus available for common dividends.

12. Funded Debt—Additional funded debt is prohibited without consent of The Prudential. This is a basic requirement except for finance companies and other highly specialized situations. The Prudential prefers use of this outright prohibition to the formula approach used by other lenders, due to the difficulty in developing a formula which would give The Prudential adequate protection in the average industrial case and still leave the borrower with any significant freedom. Debt fully subordinated as to principal and interest, with principal and interest payable only under the dividend formula, may be issued.

13. Current Debt—It is important that no creditor be placed in a preferred position over The Prudential. Normally, if current debt is secured, it is

Exhibit 3 (Continued)

secured by a pledge of the company's current assets; other general creditors, including The Prudential, would therefore have no recourse to the company's most liquid assets.

    a) Maximum Limitation—The maximum amount of unsecured and unendorsed current borrowings permitted should generally reflect the company's present and reasonably expectable seasonal requirements.

    b) The borrower is generally required to be completely free of bank loans for 90 consecutive days in either the fiscal or calendar year.

14. Discounting or Sale of Receivables with Recourse—The sale of receivables with recourse or discounting is prohibited except in unusual circumstances since it is another form of current borrowing in which the purchaser of the receivables has the right of selection to the highest quality assets against general creditors including The Prudential. Moreover, this is usually an expensive way of borrowing. An exception may be made in the case of installment receivables with appropriate safeguards.

15. Loans, Advances and Investments—Except for U.S. Governments, these are usually limited to a moderate dollar amount depending on individual circumstances. This provision prevents investments in unrelated ventures by acquisition-minded management, without the consent of The Prudential. Prime commercial paper maturing within one year from date of acquisition is excluded from this restriction.

16. Mergers, Consolidations or Sale of a Substantial Part of Assets—All of these actions are to be prohibited except where subsidiaries are absorbed by the parent or each other. These provisions protect The Prudential against loss of corporate identity and disposition of important earning assets. It may be necessary, however, to give more leeway to larger, more established concerns with adequate management depth.

17. Subsidiaries—Consolidated subsidiaries are to be only United States or Canadian companies wholly, or very nearly wholly owned. If a minority equity is substantial, there is a possibility of difficulty in any transfer of assets to the parent to meet its financial requirements. Any borrowings by a subsidiary other than from the parent company are prohibited since a creditor of a subsidiary would have a prior claim on the subsidiary's assets over a creditor of the parent.

18. Lease Rentals—A maximum dollar limit is to be placed on lease rentals involving real estate and major production equipment where such facilities are essential for the successful operation of the business. Short-term leases up to three-year duration ordinarily should be excluded from the lease rental limitation. The limitation is usually an amount reasonably in excess of present rentals. Rentals are another fixed operating charge of a company and should be kept within reason. The Prudential expects, however, to have a voice in any substantial expansion program involving large increases in rental obligations. Retail chain operations are a special situation, to be considered on an individual case basis.

19. Sale and Leaseback Transactions—Sale and leaseback of presently owned property or those to be financed with the proceeds of our loan are to be prohibited. These transactions are simply another form of a fixed obligation which does not appear on the company's financial statement. No

Exhibit 3 (continued)

prohibition is normally required on future acquired properties. Our protection in this instance will be a dollar limitation on rents. In purchase agreements which tightly restrict lease obligations, the covenant may be eliminated.

Other Covenants:

20. Closely Held Businesses—Small, closely held businesses present problems due to their size and ownership which must be anticipated by the investor. For this reason, it is desirable to include such covenants as:

    a) Hazard Insurance—As small companies particularly could be underinsured, it is desirable to require that adequate hazard insurance be carried and, in particular, use and occupancy, along with customary extended fire insurance. Otherwise, a severe loss could have disastrous financial consequences.

    b) Management Clauses—In cases where a company is particularly thin in management, dominated by one individual or dependent on the continuation of an important franchise or customer, The Prudential should have the right to mature the debt if that officer ceases being active in management. Likewise, if the company loses a key contract which we considered vital to the company's earning power at the time the loan was approved.

    c) Life Insurance on Officers—Life insurance on officers is important where one or a few men appear vital to the success of a business. Such insurance may also help in those cases where there are special problems arising out of death of a controlling or substantial stockholder in companies which are closely held. Note, however, we do not require that the insurance be taken with The Prudential.

    d) Control of transactions with stockholders and affiliated concerns.

21. Special Provisions Involving Bank Participations:

    a) It is desirable, particularly on borderline cases in which a bank is closely identified with the company, for The Prudential to share in the bank's right of offset applicable to the bank's long-term loan on a pro rata basis. This right of offset gives the bank the right to apply the company's deposits in that bank to a liquidation of the company's indebtedness to the bank in the event of default.

    b) Optional prepayments should be made pro rata to the bank and to The Prudential.

Case 35

Sun Stores, Inc.*

In November, 1957, Mr. David Stevens, an associate with the investment banking firm of Hanson and Company, was reviewing his analysis of alternative securities which Sun Stores, Inc., might sell in order to obtain $3,500,000 as a second step in financing its 3-year expansion program. Mr. Stevens was expected to recommend a specific security issue to the management of Sun Stores, for their choice.

Sun Stores, Inc., operated 146 retail stores in Iowa, Missouri, Nebraska, Kansas, Wyoming, and Colorado, with about 15% of these stores concentrated in and around Kansas City, Missouri. In addition to these "corporate" stores, the company sold at wholesale to 419 independently owned, franchised "agency" stores. Total sales of the company exceeded $150 million in fiscal 1957, representing a gain of 25% over the previous year's sales volume. The company had experienced a steady growth during the past 5 years, as earnings more than doubled, and the stockholders' equity in the company increased by nearly 60%.

Anticipating further expansion, Sun Stores had projected its external funds needs over the 3-year period starting in March, 1957, at $6,900,000, and Hanson and Company estimated that the cost of raising these funds would require an additional $400,000, making the total new funds requirement $7,300,000. After deducting the $3,000,000' of recently sold debentures, the company planned to obtain $3,500,000 by February 28, 1959,[1] and the remaining $800,000 in fiscal 1960. The following table summarizes this financing program:

---

* Abridged.←

[1] Unless otherwise noted, all references to years are in terms of Sun Stores' fiscal periods ending about February 29. Thus "1958" refers to the fiscal year ending March 1, 1958.

External requirements of expansion program........$6,900,000
Cost of raising funds............................   400,000
Total funds requirements.........................$7,300,000
To be met as follows:
Fiscal 1958................................. 3,000,000
Fiscal 1959................................. 3,500,000
Fiscal 1960.................................   800,000
                                             $7,300,000

This program, and the methods to be used in obtaining the funds, had been developed by Sun Stores and Hanson and Company after careful analysis of the company's financial needs. In March, 1957, the decision was made to obtain the 1958 requirements through a term loan. Hanson and Company prepared the selling memorandum and assisted in the negotiations that culminated in the placing of $3,000,000 of unsecured notes with seven institutional investors in October, 1957. The second stage financing to raise the $3,500,000 needed in fiscal 1959 was to utilize an equity-type security, and the final $800,000 would be raised with a term bank loan. With the initial financing successfully completed, Sun's management turned its attention to the second phase and requested Hanson and Company to appraise three equity-type securities for obtaining the $3,500,000—convertible subordinated debentures, convertible preferred stock, and common stock.

To assist him in his analysis, Mr. Stevens first developed a tabulation of the annual costs to the company of each of these securities, using assumed interest and dividend rates of $5\frac{1}{2}\%$ for the convertible debentures and $5\frac{3}{4}\%$ for the convertible preferred stock (Exhibit 1). Next, after assuming selling or conversion prices for each of the issues, he projected the number of additional common shares that would ultimately be required (Exhibit 2). With these tabulations, he then summed up the principal advantages and disadvantages he saw in each of the three types of securities:

CONVERTIBLE SUBORDINATED DEBENTURES

Advantages:

1. Convertible debentures, although a relatively new security, were currently a "fashionable" instrument for financing rapidly growing companies and had recently received favorable comment in the financial press.
2. Subordinated convertible debentures are viewed by institutions as enlarging the base for private senior borrowing almost to the same extent capital stock financing does.
3. Both dilution of per share earnings and added dividend costs are minimized (Exhibit 1). Conversion would probably not take place prior to the expected dramatic earnings increase during fiscal 1960. And even

then, conversion may be gradual in consequence of acts or policy decisions initiated by management. Furthermore, once the debentures are selling substantially above conversion parity, the company would be in a position to force conversion by a call for redemption.

4. Prior to conversion, net interest cost (after 54% tax saving) would be about half of the dividend cost under the convertible preferred and common stock plans.

5. The announcement of convertible debenture financing for the expansion program should not cause any significant decline in the market price of the common stock, because such debentures would be convertible at a premium above the existing market price of the common stock. Also, it is realized that conversion usually takes place when earnings per share and the stock price have risen substantially above existing levels. As a consequence, the present stockholders' current position would not be impaired.

6. The number of additional shares involved would be less than under the common stock plan (Exhibit 1).

7. There is a reasonable chance that the debentures will be partially converted during fiscal 1960.

Disadvantages:

1. Until the debentures are converted, the company will tend to be limited to the issuance of senior debt to obtain additional financing at a reasonable price.

CONVERTIBLE PREFERRED STOCK

Advantages:

1. Similar to the subordinated debenture, the conversion price assigned to the preferred stock would represent a premium over the prevailing market price at the time of the offering. Thus, if the preferred stock were converted, the company could view the transaction as a means of selling common stock above the prevailing market price, whereas direct sale of common stock would involve a price below the present market (Exhibit 2).

2. Preferred stock would be an addition to equity, whereas convertible subordinated debentures are viewed by Moody's and Standard and Poor's as part of overall debt in rating public issues of senior debt.

Disadvantages:

1. It is more expensive than the debenture issue, as previously noted.

2. Although dividend payments can be deferred in times of financial stress, they represent an obligation of the company which must be paid in full before any resumption of dividends to the common stock.

3. As is true with a convertible debenture, a convertible preferred stock tends to limit the company's choice of subsequent financing to senior obligations until the preferred is converted.

Common Stock

Advantages:

1. Sun stock is currently selling at about 1.5 times its book value. If common stock were offered, the new investor would be putting funds into the company directly and immediately at a premium over the funds invested previously by stockholders.
2. It is the safest medium. In future financing, the management would be freer to choose a medium other than senior debt.
3. Common stock financing would immediately broaden the market for Sun stock by the very fact of the issuance of 125,000 additional shares. This would be the first underwritten distribution of the common stock through a national syndicate.

Disadvantages:

1. An issue of common stock would reduce 1958 earnings per share immediately (Exhibits 1 and 2), and would drive down the market price of the outstanding common stock to, say, 27 or 28.
2. Earnings per share during subsequent fiscal years would be about 12% lower than they would be if a comparable issue of convertible debentures or preferred were outstanding.

The $3\frac{7}{8}\%$ notes of 1966, which were sold in 1951, and the recently sold $5\frac{1}{2}\%$ notes of 1972 had been placed privately with institutional investors, and Sun's management had been pleased with the success of these issues. Regarding the present financing, Mr. Stevens estimated that the cost of a private placement would be about $61,000 or 1.75% of the principal amount of the issue, whereas a public offering would cost about $103,000. However, the interest rate on a private placement of notes would probably be about $\frac{1}{4}\%$ higher than on a similar public offering, and a privately placed preferred would also require a similarly higher dividend rate.

Mr. Stevens believed that a private placement was especially suited for the smaller, lesser-known companies, and for this reason it might be the best method for Sun to use in obtaining its funds. On the other hand, both the earnings and the equity of the company had doubled since 1954, and this performance suggested that a public issue of the company's securities might be well received in the financial markets.

The success of any offering would be influenced to some extent by the current trends in the stock market. In recent weeks the market seemed to be showing signs of recovering from the decline that began in late July. On July 12, the Dow-Jones Industrial Average had reached 520.77, which was just a fraction less than its all-time peak, and then started to fall sharply. In the face of this general market decline, market prices of many food store shares had shown a moderate increase (Exhibit 3). Recent comments by various market observers suggested even more than normal uncertainty regarding the future action of the market. The currently unsettled market conditions raised questions as to how a public offering of any type of Sun Stores security would be received by the financial community.

Also inherent in the problem of choosing and selling the security, Mr. Stevens believed, was the question of whether Sun Stores' common stock should be listed on a national security exchange. The company's stock was presently traded over the counter, and its relatively small trading volume had been a continuing obstacle in broadening the ownership, and consequently the knowledge, of Sun Stores. Mr. Stevens decided, however, that action on this question could be deferred for the present. Although listing might conceivably encourage a broader distribution of Sun's common stock, and thus bring the Sun name to a larger number of potential investors, Mr. Stevens believed that this could be accomplished equally well by the active support of some of the leading over-the-counter wire houses. These firms, which maintained positions in unlisted securities, were able to create active markets by virtue of their close communications with brokers and dealers throughout the country.

Exhibit 1

SUN STORES, INC.

ANNUAL COST OF $3.5 MILLION NEW CAPITAL AND
PROJECTED EARNINGS PER SHARE, 1958–60

	Excluding Impact of New Financing	Convertible Subordinated Debentures		Convertible Preferred Stock		Common Stock
		Before Conversion	After Conversion	Before Conversion	After Conversion	
Face interest rate		5½%		5¾%		
Face interest or dividend cost (thousands)		$193	$147*	$201	$147*	$175*
Less: Tax saving on interest (54%) (thousands)		104	...	...	...	...
Net cost after taxes (thousands)		$ 89	$147	$201	$147	$175
Net rate of cost		2.53%	4.20%	5.75%	4.20%	5.00%
Net cost per present common share†		15¢	46¢	33¢	46¢	53¢
Cash outlay by company						
Net interest or dividend cost (as above) (thousands)		$ 89	$147	$201	$147	$175
Plus sinking fund (thousands)		175‡	...	70§	...	...
		$264	$147	$271	$147	$175
Company estimates of future earnings per common share						
Fiscal 1958	$3.11**	$2.96	$2.65	$2.78	$2.65	$2.58
Fiscal 1959	3.53**	3.38	3.01	3.20	3.01	2.93
Fiscal 1960	4.84**	4.69	4.14	4.51	4.14	4.02

* Based on present dividend rate of $1.40 per share and conversion or offering prices as estimated in Exhibit 2. In subsequent columns, the numbers are after the deduction of the annual interest or the preferred dividend appropriate to the choice indicated.

† Based on 609,000 shares outstanding and $3.11 earned per share if no financing takes place.

‡ No sinking fund for first 10 years.

§ No sinking fund for first 5 years.

** Numbers in this column exclude the changes due to new financing.

Exhibit 2

SUN STORES, INC.

Pʀᴏ Fᴏʀᴍᴀ Aᴅᴅɪᴛɪᴏɴ ᴛᴏ
Nᴜᴍʙᴇʀ ᴏꜰ Sʜᴀʀᴇs Oᴜᴛsᴛᴀɴᴅɪɴɢ

	Convertible Debentures or Preferred	*Common Stock*
Amount of issue.......................	$3,500,000	$3,500,000
Conversion or offering price.............	33⅓*	28†
Number of shares to be issued............	105,000	125,000
Number of shares now outstanding........	609,000	609,000
Number of shares, pro forma.............	714,000	734,000
Additional shares as percent of total......	14.7%	17.0%

* Assuming 11% premium over current market price of 30.
† Assuming spot offering at market price of 28—a discount of 6% from the current market price of 30.

Exhibit 3

SUN STORES, INC.

Iɴᴅᴇxᴇs ᴏꜰ Dᴏᴡ-Jᴏɴᴇs Iɴᴅᴜsᴛʀɪᴀʟ Aᴠᴇʀᴀɢᴇs ᴀɴᴅ 10 Lᴇᴀᴅɪɴɢ
Fᴏᴏᴅ Cʜᴀɪɴ Sᴛᴏᴄᴋ Pʀɪᴄᴇs, Jᴀɴᴜᴀʀʏ–Nᴏᴠᴇᴍʙᴇʀ, 1957

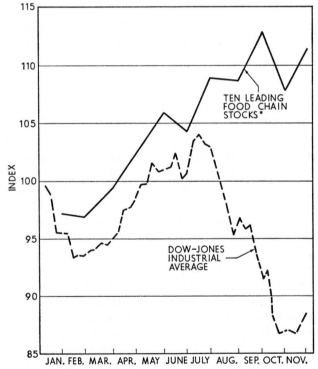

* 1. American Stores
2. First National Stores
3. Food Fair Stores
4. Grand Union
5. Great A & P Tea Co.
6. Jewel Tea
7. Kroger
8. National Tea
9. Safeway
10. Colonial Stores

Case 36

Standard Light and Electric Company

In February, 1953, the Standard Light and Electric Company was the owner of all of the outstanding securities of Municipal Utilities, Inc. Both organizations were subject to the jurisdiction of the Securities and Exchange Commission, which had ordered[1] that Standard Light and Electric Company divest itself of its interest in the wholly owned subsidiary. It had been decided to carry out the divestment by selling to the public newly issued securities of Municipal Utilities. The cash proceeds of the sale would be used by the parent company for general corporate purposes.

As the first step in carrying out this plan, Municipal Utilities would create whatever securities were decided upon as best for it to issue, and it would exchange these for its outstanding securities now held by Standard Light and Electric Company. Public sale would then be arranged by the latter company. Thus, the opportunity existed to recapitalize this going concern in the most satisfactory way, and Mr. Fliegler, the chairman of the Finance Committee of the board of directors of both companies, was working on the plan.

Municipal Utilities, Inc., had enjoyed profitable operations since its inception in 1923, allowing an unbroken record of dividends and interest payments. In addition, it served a fast-growing community and had a reputation for progressive management policies; for these reasons, Mr. Fliegler felt quite sure that its securities, when offered to the public, would be rated "high grade" by the market, providing that the proportion of debt to equity in the revised capitalization was reasonable.

Municipal Utilities, Inc., had been organized to serve the needs of an expanding eastern city with a population, according to the 1950 census, of 885,000. For the past few years, the company's earnings had stabilized

---

[1] Under the "death sentence" provisions of the Public Utility Holding Company Act of 1935.

at approximately 13% (before income taxes) on its capitalization, and the management had used this rate of return as a basis for plans up to 5 years in the future. The company's financial condition and earnings record are summarized in Exhibits 1 and 2.

The Bureau of the Census had predicted, in 1950, a population growth to a 1960 level of 1,425,000 in the area served by Municipal Utilities, Inc. The directors, with this growth in mind, had recently approved an expansion program (shown in Exhibit 3), totaling $82,600,000 for 1953–55, covering increased capacity in electric generating, transmitting, and distributing facilities. Though a part of the funds required for this program would be generated internally through retained earnings and depreciation allowances, it was estimated that a substantial portion of the new money would have to be obtained through new financing during the period.

In the latter part of 1952, all litigation in connection with the separation had been resolved. Mr. Fliegler had noted that the securities market had become actively interested in utility issues, and he believed that the time was appropriate to undertake the refinancing program. He believed that the first step in the transfer of ownership to the public should be the sale of common stock; negotiations with underwriters had begun, and it had been decided that the official offering could be made in the early part of May.

In considering the proportions of the various securities which would comprise the new capital structure of Municipal Utilities, Inc., Mr. Fliegler had to contend with two conflicting interests. On one hand, sale of the securities should produce a maximum return to the present owner, Standard Light and Electric; therefore, maximum net sale prices for the "package of new securities" were desired. On the other hand, the new capitalization must take into account the long-run interests of the future owners of Municipal Utilities; the capital structure must be so arranged as not to restrict operations or subsequent financing. Translating the latter objective into financial policy, Mr. Fliegler thought that flexibility would be assured if the company's needs for external funds (as distinguished from reinvested earnings) could be met by floating securities that would be considered "high grade" on the basis of current levels of earnings actually established plus 5% (before taxes) on new assets.[2]

The Securities and Exchange Commission held overall supervisory powers regarding new capitalizations resulting from a "death sentence" proceeding. Decisions relating to individual programs were made largely on an *ad hoc* basis, though it had been generally held that bonds and preferred stocks, treated as a group, should constitute no more than 70%

---

[2] Earnings on new assets were estimated at less than one half the earnings on existing assets for 3 years from installation, since these new assets typically did not produce their ultimate rate of return at once.

to 75% of the total capitalization. In the case of Municipal Utilities, Inc., the Commission had indicated that it would not approve a proportion of over 70%.

Mr. Fliegler knew that there had been a great deal of activity in utility financing since the end of World War II and that at present the market for all utility securities was active and rising. He felt that he could predict with some accuracy the terms which the company could obtain, and he had reached the following conclusions about securities.

Public utilities were characteristically financed with a substantial proportion of fixed debt, since their earnings were relatively stable and little risk to investors was involved. Further, the sale of debt securities represented the lowest-cost form of financing and was attractive to utilities for this reason. Mr. Fliegler thought that under present market conditions, it would be possible to sell a large first-mortgage bond issue to the public. The utilities industry had not suffered a truly "poor year" since 1938, when the earnings of Municipal Utilities, Inc., had dropped 23% under the level of the previous year.

Mr. Fliegler thought that savings banks and insurance companies would be large purchasers of Municipal Utilities' bonds. While state banking and insurance company statutes placed numerous restrictions on the eligibility of securities for investment by banks and insurance companies, Mr. Fliegler thought that a Moody's "Aaa" rating would qualify these bonds as legal investments for these institutions in most states.[3]

In the analysis of corporate bonds for rating purposes, Moody's took into consideration a wide variety of factors, including the nature of the business, the importance of its products in the economy, the history of the company, past record, significant statistical ratios, indenture provisions, and intangible factors. In connection with statistics, however, they did not attempt to reduce such ratios to any simple form of measurement that would quickly identify an issue with a specific rating group. "Aaa" was assigned only to those issues where protection was strong, where future changes were likely to be small, and where the element of long-term risk was at a minimum.

Mr. Fliegler thought that the conservative financial practice which he felt the company should follow would require that any bonds should have their interest payment requirements earned 6 to 7 times in average earnings years, and 3 to 4 times in poor years. The bonds should have a senior lien on a value of the company's fixed assets well in excess of the amount of the issue and should represent no more than 50% of the company's capitalization. If a sinking fund requirement existed, such requirement should be covered 3 times after taxes and before preferred dividend requirements in good years, 2 times in poor years.

---

[3] Bond ratings are published in *Moody's Investors Service*, and are widely recognized as expert judgment regarding the quality of a given bond issue.

The cost to the company of issuing Aaa bonds would be about 3⅝% ✗ on an annual basis after usual fees and expenses of issue. Any interest payment would be considered as an expense for tax purposes. Mr. Fliegler thought that purchasers would require a sinking fund arrangement; for planning purposes, he projected an annual sinking fund requirement equal to 2½% of the face value of the issue. With a 30-year bond maturity, this sinking fund would leave a balance of 25% of the value of the issue at maturity. This balance could be refunded by the sale of an appropriate security issue at that time.

A number of utility preferred issues had been placed in recent months, and Mr. Fliegler thought that some preferred stock could be included in the revised capitalization. For the purposes of planning, he used the figure of 4.5% dividend cost after expenses of issue. Under current market conditions, he thought that an annual retirement fund of about 2% of the original issue would be necessary. The principal buyers of such an issue would be trusts and insurance companies.

Mr. Fliegler knew that bonds and preferred stock, treated as a group, could not exceed 70% of total capitalization. He felt, furthermore, that sound financial practice required that bond interest and preferred dividends together should not exceed 65% of net earnings after taxes in an average year, and that preferred dividends should be assured if a 15% drop in gross income (as the term is used in Exhibit 2) below the trend were experienced.

Under current tax regulations, public utilities could deduct a portion of preferred dividends paid as if they were interest expense. The company's tax counsel had told Mr. Fliegler that such credits could be expected in a future issue to the extent of 65% of dividends. The remaining portion of the preferred dividends, and all other taxable earnings, were currently subject to an income tax rate of 50%.

Market demand for utility common stocks was, and had for some time been, encouraging, particularly after a number of important state utility regulatory commissions had started what appeared to be a nationwide trend in allowing rate increases, thus foreshadowing more generous common stock earnings. Mr. Fliegler knew, from experience, that it was easier for utilities to plan on future expansion financed by the sale of common stock than it was for industrial firms, provided that the outstanding stock of the utilities showed an attractive dividend record.

As previously mentioned, the first step in the recapitalization of Municipal Utilities, Inc., was to be the sale of common stock. Negotiations with underwriters had begun; the tentative price to the public would be $29.75, with proceeds to the company of $29.20 per share. It was planned to assign no par value to the stock; this was common practice in the company's state of incorporation. An annual cash dividend rate of $2 which would yield 6.7% at a price of $29.75 was planned. Mr. Fliegler thought that the company could pay out as much as 75% of earnings after sinking funds and still have the dividend considered reasonably safe. The underwriters had indicated that a very large issue could be sold to the public without prejudicing further issues during the following 3-year period. Such a stock would be bought by many individuals seeking income, as well as by trusts and certain insurance companies.

With this information at hand, Mr. Fliegler began the determination of the capitalization which Municipal Utilities, Inc., should create and which Standard Light and Electric Company should sell.

Exhibit 1

THE STANDARD LIGHT & ELECTRIC COMPANY

CONDENSED BALANCE SHEET ON 12/31/52
OF MUNICIPAL UTILITIES, INC.

ASSETS

Current assets..................	$ 19,308,656	
Fixed assets (net)...............	208,893,866	
Total assets..............		$228,202,522

LIABILITIES

Current liabilities...............	$ 34,919,820	
Capitalization..................	193,282,702	
Total liabilities...........		$228,202,522

Exhibit 2

THE STANDARD LIGHT & ELECTRIC COMPANY

CONDENSED INCOME STATEMENTS 1947–53
OF MUNICIPAL UTILITIES, INC.

(Dollar Figures in Millions)

	1947	1948	1949	1950	1951	1952	1953*
Gross sales................	36.6	40.1	51.1	57.9	60.0	64.2	68.6
Operating expenses.........	20.1	23.9	31.3	35.1	37.3	39.2	41.4
Operating income..........	16.5	16.2	19.8	22.8	22.7	25.0	27.2
Other income..............	.4	.2	.3	.3	.5	.6	1.0
Income before interest and							
tax (gross income).......	16.9	16.4	20.1	23.1	23.2	25.6	28.2
Interest expense...........	1.8	1.9	2.2	2.6	2.8	2.8	3.0
Gross profit...............	15.1	14.5	17.9	20.5	20.4	22.8	25.2
Income taxes..............	6.9	7.7	9.1	10.2	13.3	13.8	14.0
Net profit.................	8.2	6.8	8.8	10.3	7.1	9.0	11.2

* Estimated without allowance for expansion program.

Exhibit 3

THE STANDARD LIGHT & ELECTRIC COMPANY

EXPANSION PROGRAM SUMMARY 1953–55
MUNICIPAL UTILITIES, INC.

(Dollar Figures in Millions)

	1953	*1954*	*1955*	*Totals*
Requirements				
Production Facilities.............	$18.00	$ 4.20	$ .20	$22.40
Transmission Facilities...........	.40	6.28	8.00	14.68
Distribution Facilities...........	1.00	.79	2.80	4.59
Smoke Control Program.........	1.75	1.75	1.75	5.25
System Rehabilitation...........	5.20	8.75	10.40	24.35
Miscellaneous Expense...........	2.00	3.03	6.30	11.33
Totals....................	$28.35	$24.80	$29.45	$82.60
Sources				
Depreciation...................	$ 8.00	$ 8.25	$ 9.00	$25.25
Other........................	20.35	16.55	20.45	57.35
Totals....................	$28.35	$24.80	$29.45	$82.60

Case 37

Boxer Corporation

IN APRIL, 1966, the management of the Boxer Corporation, a manufacturer of kraft paper, corrugated board, and boxes, all of which were widely used for commercial purposes, was considering whether under the circumstances it should continue to appropriate funds for the purchase and subsequent retirement of the preferred stocks of the company. If such a policy were continued, the management would be required to decide whether it should continue purchasing shares in small lots from time to time or whether it should call both issues of the outstanding preferred stocks at the redemption prices. In either case the company would need to obtain funds to provide for the acquisition of the shares.

As will appear below, the treasurer of the company had explored possibilities of financing and had developed an offer of a refunding issue of 20-year debenture bonds to raise a maximum of $6 million.

Balance sheets for the years 1963–65 and the current position at March 31, 1966, will be found in Exhibit 1. Exhibit 2 contains a summary of income figures and dividend payments from 1956 through 1965, and Exhibit 3 gives more detailed earnings statements for the years 1963–65. A change in the efficiency of operation will be noted. In 1963 the company had made a careful study of its production costs and sales margins and subsequently had made substantial changes in policy, the results of which were reflected in the increased rate of earnings in 1964. It was believed that this increase in efficiency could be maintained in future years. On such a basis, the management felt that at an annual sales volume of $15 million, net profits would be adequate to provide not only for preferred dividends but also for dividends of at least $0.30 a share on the common stock. Plans in regard to the financial needs of the next few years had been made in 1963 on the assumption that an annual sales volume of $15 million was a practical goal, at least in the immediate future. There would be no need to force sales, by cutting margins, to reach higher totals.

The company maintained principal banking relationships with two large city banks and had been told regularly by them that its credit was so strong that the seasonal loans requested were well within the limit that the company would be able to borrow. The company also had been able to obtain occasional temporary loans to permit the purchase of blocks of its own stock. These loans had to be repaid, when due, out of earnings.

The high volume of business activity in the 1960's led to an increased volume of orders for the standard products of the company. Some novelty lines with low margins were cut out, but demands for special types of containers developed so rapidly that sales for 1965 were approximately $18,600,000. During the first 3 months of 1966 the sales of the Boxer Corporation were $5,456,000, an increase of $1,272,000 over the same period in 1965. Unfilled orders at April 1 totaled $4,104,000. It was estimated that the year's sales would exceed $20,500,000. The rate of net profits on sales, which was 9.9% before taxes and 4.7% after taxes in 1965, was maintained in the first quarter of 1966, and management expected to earn about the same rate for the rest of the year. The director of marketing believed that sales in 1967 and 1968 would probably total about $20 million and $21 million, respectively.

Pending a determination of policy, the treasurer did not include in his budget any provisions for the continued purchase of shares of the company, as had been a recent policy.

The treasurer talked with investment bankers about refunding the two types of preferred stock outstanding with an issue of 20-year debenture bonds. It was understood that a $6 million issue of bonds with a 5¾% coupon could be sold to net the company the par price. The bonds would have a sinking fund requiring annual retirement of $200,000 principal, beginning in 1971. Although further details had not been worked out, the bankers had stated that three provisions would have to be included in the indenture: (1) that all debt, current and fixed, should not exceed 200% of the current assets; (2) that the company could not mortgage any property while any of the bonds were outstanding; (3) that the bonds would be callable in whole or in part at 105% of the public issue price, except that the call would not be permitted for the purpose of refunding at a rate lower than 5¾%.

The 8% first preferred stock and the common stock of the company were listed on an organized exchange and were widely held, although infrequently traded. The 7% preferred stock was unlisted and had been almost completely inactive since 1963.

Through occasional public tender offers, the company had begun to acquire shares of various classes of its stock in the open market as part of a plan to simplify its capital structure and reduce its outstanding capitalization by the retirement of the stock so purchased. Exhibit 4 tabulates the number of shares of the various classes of stock retired and the average prices paid in the years 1964 and 1965. No purchases of any class of stock had been made to date in 1966.

By April, 1, 1966, it was clear that few, if any, more shares of the 7% preferred stock could be obtained without call. Small blocks of shares of the 8% first preferred stock continued to come on the market from time to time, principally from trust accounts and estates liquidating some of their investments. The only quotation so far recorded in 1966 was in the week of March 19, at $123 a share. The number of shares traded in this week was 10.

The provisions of the capital stock issues are summarized in Exhibit 5.

Because of the heavy burden of the preferred dividends, the company had not made any payments to the common stockholders since 1954. The management was anxious to clear the way for dividends on the common stock in the immediate future. Further purchases of common shares did not seem advisable in view of the need to conserve cash.

Exhibit 1

BOXER CORPORATION

BALANCE SHEETS AS OF DECEMBER 31, 1963–65, AND CURRENT POSITION,
MARCH 31, 1966

(In Thousands)

	1963	1964	1965	March 31, 1966
ASSETS				
Current Assets:				
Cash and deposits...................	$ 1,013	$ 1,893	$ 801	$ 723
U.S. government securities............	60	150	150	50
Accounts receivable.................	2,466	2,264	2,907	1,953
Inventories*.......................	2,647	2,735	3,532	4,136
Total current assets.............	$ 6,186	$ 7,042	$ 7,390	$6,862
Investment in subsidiaries, etc.†.........	855	855	350	
Land†..............................	226	198	438	
Buildings, machinery, equipment†......	$10,624	$10,683	$11,031	
Less: Allowance for depreciation.......	6,920	7,240	7,677	
	$ 3,704	$ 3,443	$ 3,354	
Deferred charges and supplies..........	283	237	374	
Total assets....................	$11,254	$11,775	$11,906	
LIABILITIES AND CAPITAL				
Current Liabilities:				
Accounts payable...................	$ 510	$ 555	981	$ 838
Accruals...........................	253	303	707	756
Estimated income tax liability.........	666	961	1,031	816
Total current liabilities...........	$ 1,429	$ 1,819	$ 2,719	$2,410
8% first preferred stock, $100 par........	$ 4,584	$ 4,584	$ 4,584	
Less: Par value in treasury...........		83	736	‡
	$ 4,584	$ 4,501	$ 3,848	
7% preferred stock, $100 par..........	$ 183	$ 183	$ 183	
Less: Par value in treasury...........		98	171	‡
	$ 183	$ 85	$ 12	
Common stock, $5.00 par..............	$ 2,120	$ 2,120	$ 2,120	
Less: Par value in treasury...........		52	58	‡
	$ 2,120	$ 2,068	$ 2,062	
Difference between par value and cost of treasury stock.....................		(149)	(298)	
Earned surplus......................	2,938	3,451	3,563	
Total liabilities and capital.....	$11,254	$11,775	$11,906	

* Lower of cost or market.
† Cost.
‡ No shares were purchased or retired after December 31, 1965.

Exhibit 2

BOXER CORPORATION

SUMMARY INCOME STATEMENTS FOR YEARS ENDED DECEMBER 31, 1956–65

(Dollar Figures in Thousands)

Year	Sales	Net Income before Taxes	Tax Rate	Net Income after Taxes
1956	$ 9,516	$ (899)[d]	. .	$(561)[d*]
1957	9,356	111	38%	69
1958	11,897	839	38	520
1959	12,471	924	38	573
1960	14,073	1,398	47	741
1961	15,085	1,400	62	532
1962	13,377	171	52	82
1963	14,991	850	52	408
1964	15,049	1,774	50	887
1965	18,577	1,831	48	952

* After-tax loss carry-back.
[d] Deficit.

Exhibit 3

BOXER CORPORATION

INCOME STATEMENTS FOR YEARS ENDED DECEMBER 31, 1963–65, AND
DIVIDENDS PAID IN FIRST QUARTER OF 1966

(In Thousands)

	1963	1964	1965	1st Quarter 1966
Sales	$14,991	$15,049	$18,577	$5,456
Cost of goods sold*	9,448	9,039	11,976	
	$ 5,543	$ 6,010	$ 6,601	Figures not yet available
Selling and administrative expense*	4,600	4,203	4,798	
	$ 943	$ 1,807	$ 1,803	
Other income	(14)	(8)	(57)	
Other expense	107	41	29	
Net income before income tax	$ 850	$ 1,774	$ 1,831	
Estimated federal income tax	$ 442(52%)	887(50%)	879(48%)	
Net income available for dividends	$ 408	$ 887	$ 952	
Dividends paid:†				
8% first preferred stock	$ 367	$ 365	$ 332	$ 77
7% preferred stock	55	9	3	0.2
Total dividends paid	$ 379	$ 374	$ 335	$ 77.2
Income transferred to surplus	29	513	617	

* Depreciation expenses included as follows:
    1963 . . . . $408,000
    1964 435,000
    1965 552,000
† 8% first preferred stock, average number of shares outstanding:
    1956–63 . . . . 45,840 shares
    1964 45,425
    1965 41,745

Exhibit 4

BOXER CORPORATION

ACQUISITIONS BY THE COMPANY OF ITS OWN STOCK, 1964 AND 1965

Class of Stock	Number of Shares Acquired	Total Par Values Acquired	Average Cost per Share	Total Cost
1964:				
1. 8% first preferred.....	830	$ 83,000	$ 96.91	$ 80,435
2. 7% preferred.........	980	98,000	80.15	78,900
Total preferred......		$181,000		$159,335
3. Common.............10,400		52,000	21.40	222,560
				$381,895
1965:				
1. 8% first preferred.....	6,530	$653,000	118.75	$775,438
2. 7% preferred.........	730	73,000	111.93	81,709
Total preferred......		$726,000		$857,147
3. Common.............	1,240	6,200	19.40	24,056
				$881,203

Exhibit 5

BOXER CORPORATION

CERTAIN PROVISIONS OF OUTSTANDING CAPITAL STOCK, APRIL 1, 1956

	8% First Preferred Stock, Par $100	7% Preferred Stock, Par $100	Common Stock Par $5
Actually outstanding	38,480 shares	120 shares	365,800 shares
Redemption provisions	Callable on 90 days' notice at $150 and accumulated dividends. Not redeemable in part, (38,480 × $150 = $5,772,-000).	Callable on 90 days' notice at $115 and accumulated dividends. Not redeemable in part, (120 × $115 = $13,800).	None
Voting power	Obtains 10 votes per share whenever dividends are $12 or more in arrears and also the right to elect two thirds of the board of directors. Otherwise, does not vote.	None	One vote per share
Dividend priority	8%, senior to all other classes, fully cumulative (8% of $3,848,-000 = $307,840).	Junior to first preferred, senior to all others. 7% fully cumulative (7% of $12,000 = $840).	Dividends may not be paid unless remaining surplus would amount to at least 1 year's dividend requirement on both preferred stocks.
Dividend record	No arrearages	No arrearages	No dividend since 1954.

Repurchase of your securities may be a refinancing effort

Case 38

Extone Chemicals, Inc.*

THE DECISION, taken June 24, 1963, by the board of directors of Extone Chemicals, Inc., to instruct the treasurer to buy up to 60,000 shares of its common stock marked an important change in the policy of the company. Although shares had previously been purchased in annual amounts ranging from 14,000 to 25,000 shares, these purchases had been roughly equal in magnitude to the number of shares required to be issued to meet obligations under the restricted stock option plans approved by the stockholders from time to time. There had been no intention to acquire treasury stock for any other reason, and the board had previously rejected all suggestions for additional purchases. There was a strong undercurrent of feeling on the board that such purchasing "smelled of manipulation by insiders" for their benefit. Holders of stock options, for instance, might be such beneficiaries.

The new policy was announced to the stockholders in the annual report covering the fiscal year ended June 30, 1963, which was mailed so as to reach the holders on August 26, 1963, in the following words:

Stock Purchase

During July, the company acquired 10,780 shares of its common stock which are being held in the Treasury. These purchases are part of a program to reacquire shares previously issued in connection with an acquisition. The Board of Directors, because of this and other considerations, has authorized the purchase of up to 60,000 shares of the company's common stock in the open market, but there is no assurance that this number of shares will in fact be purchased. The Board of Directors, however, may in the future approve the purchase of shares in addition to those for which purchase has been authorized.

It was the opinion of counsel for the company that this decision did not require stockholder approval; so no formal motion on the subject was

---

* Abridged.

put before the annual stockholders' meeting that took place September 17.

Although there had been considerable discussion of the desirability of the new policy, and opinions among directors and officers were not unanimous, there is no need to record the differences here, because all the arguments were revived in the spring of 1964, when the recommendation to continue with further stock purchases was under discussion.

Recent Events in Company History

With the exception of a small rise in 1961, the earnings available for the common stock of Extone Chemicals, Inc., had declined steadily from the all-time high of \$4.70 a share[1] in the fiscal year 1958–59 to \$2.61 in the fiscal year 1961–62. A sharp recovery, to \$3.97 a share in the fiscal year 1962–63, gave rise to the expectation that the company had removed the drains on its profitability that, in the opinion of the management, had been due to the operations of certain unprofitable divisions, whose liquidation was well under way by the spring of 1963.

In the early 1950's Extone Chemicals, which already manufactured a broad line of specialized chemicals, had extended its interests into certain mechanical and electronics fields. The new lines were by-products of research work in the Extone laboratories. They soon proved to be outside the management's main competence, however, and were not profitable. In recent years, therefore, on the advice of the president and other officers, the board of directors had decided that the company should concentrate on specialized areas of chemistry, where Extone Chemicals had proven strength. Accordingly, while new and profitable products were being introduced into these divisions of the business through company research, there were liquidations, both piecemeal and by the sale of operating units, of other activities.

The Middlesex division, acquired through the issuance of 60,000 shares of Extone common stock in the fiscal year 1959–60, was sold as a unit for cash in the fiscal year 1962–63.

The annual report of the fiscal year 1962–63 stated:

. . . orderly liquidation [of the electronics division] . . . is now in progress. . . . As a result of the liquidation, substantial cash will be available for reinvestment in other areas in our business which promise greater return on our capital.

Other liquidations took place and were planned so that by the end of the fiscal year 1963–64 Extone Chemicals was expected to have sold all its units in the mechanical and electronics divisions and to have entirely completed the program of disinvestment that had been decided upon.

Dividends, established at the rate of \$2.50 a share in the fiscal year

---

[1] All per share figures used in this case have been adjusted for all stock splits occurring in the period.

1959–60, were maintained at this rate according to a policy several times stated to the stockholders in annual reports:

Extone Chemicals, Inc., has followed a policy of paying consistent, regular dividends on its common stock. After a regular rate has been established, it has never been reduced. At the same time, the company has endeavored to diversify and expand mainly through the use of retained earnings. The amount of this reinvestment has varied from year to year, but has averaged 37% of earnings for the last 10 years.

Viewing the response of the market price of the stock to declining earnings, and considering the company's future needs, the financial officers of the company had decided to continue the announced dividend policy, to plan on an average dividend payout of 50%, and to emphasize the creation of earnings per share as the primary objective of financial policy in the stockholders' interest. Investment bankers advising the company endorsed these decisions but emphasized that a steady increase of dividend in proportion to growth seemed to be given high value by investors in the stocks of the chemical industry. Pertinent data on the common stock for the last 5 fiscal years, together with estimates for the year ending June 30, 1964, are given in Exhibit 1.

Despite the dividends paid and the considerable sums spent on capital investment, and as a result of the retention of earnings and the program of disinvestment, Extone Chemicals became possessed of a high level of liquid resources during the fiscal years under discussion in this case. The condition is indicated by the figures in the following table, which include also the comptroller's estimate for the end of the next fiscal year (figures in thousands, taken from consolidated balance sheets):

	1959	1960	1961	1962	1963	1964*
Net working capital....	$ 84,131	$ 71,691	$ 70,313	$ 76,575	$ 85,478	$ 83,900
Cash.................	17,436	14,603	12,039	12,833	14,358	12,000
Short-term investments	11,557	...	...	...	35,053	42,200
Sales volume..........	524,158	516,305	552,492	524,545	502,988	518,400

    * Estimated.

Stock Acquisition Policy, 1963

During the fiscal year 1962–63 the treasurer of the company, under instructions from the financial vice president, undertook a program of investing surplus funds, which produced an average return of 4% before income taxes. Impressed by the relatively low level of this return, and recognizing that the company's policy of expanding in its chosen fields of concentration would not require funds shortly, the financial officers succeeded, over some opposition, in persuading first the president, then the Finance Committee of the board, and finally a majority of the board of directors to approve, as a first step to be followed by more thorough study, the reacquisition of 60,000 shares, an amount equal to the shares that had been issued in the Middlesex acquisition. Consequently, the announcement was made to stockholders in 1963, and the purchasing was subsequently carried out by the treasurer (who dealt with several brokerage firms personally) under the following conditions, which had been voted by the board of directors after review by counsel:

1. No purchase price should exceed $ 83 a share.
2. Purchases on the New York Stock Exchange should not be in excess of one third of the daily volume, or 30% of the monthly volume, of sales, and should be at a price within the range of trading on the Exchange. [A study of volume records for the previous 2 fiscal years showed a daily average of 1,800 to 2,300 shares traded. The investment banking firm with which the financial officers had consulted on the details of the proposed operation had recommended the 30% limit as one which had served well in a number of situations where buyers wished to accumulate stock in a way that would not attract the attention of specialists or other traders.]
3. Purchases of secondary offerings of blocks of stock should be exempt from the volume limitation.

Purchasing began at the beginning of July, 1963, and continued almost daily until the middle of February, 1964. Seldom (except for taking advantage of a few secondary offerings) did a daily purchase reach 450 shares. The total cost of the 60,000 shares was $4,624,800 at the average price of $77.08 a share. The treasurer was satisfied that his purchases could have had no noticeable effect on the general movements of the market price of Extone stock. Market prices by months for the period January 1962–April 1964 appear in Exhibit 2, compared with the Standard and Poor's stock price indexes for 11 chemical companies (excluding Du Pont). These data are charted in Exhibit 3.

There was an easy flow of ideas in the Extone Chemicals organization, and those which had to do with financial policy questions came to Mr. Prouse or Mr. Blaine. These officers were acquainted not only with the formally adopted policies of the board of directors but also with underlying attitudes, since Mr. Prouse was secretary of the board's Finance Committee, and Mr. Blaine attended meetings to present the most recent financial results. Using such background, they could make choices about which ideas were worth pursuing, and which had no chance of survival.

For example, when the purchase of 60,000 shares neared completion in February, 1964, Mr. Blaine once more pointed out to Mr. Prouse that the liquid position of Extone Chemicals continued to be very generous, and that short-term forecasts were for a further increase in cash items on hand. With Mr. Prouse's approval, he instructed Mr. Gibson to prepare a report discussing the amounts involved and the alternatives to be considered. Mr. Gibson was specifically instructed to consider the desirability of calling the company's preferred stock for redemption, as this alternative had been suggested by certain directors when the matter had been under discussion in the spring of 1963, and it was to be expected that the proposal would be raised once more.

The 5% cumulative preferred stock, with a par value of $21,261,400, had been issued in 1928. Dividends on this stock had never been in arrears. It had been deemed advisable in 1928 to set a high call price, $115 a share, to aid in making the offer attractive. Thus, with $115 a share required to eliminate a dividend of $5 a share, this alternative investment of $24,450,610 could be said to offer a return of 4.35%, after income taxes. Another measure of the consequence of retiring the preferred stock was to say that it would increase the earnings on the common stock outstanding in February 1964 (approximately 3,285,500 shares) by $0.17 a share, a number obtained by deducting from the amount of the preferred dividend ($1,063,070) 2% of $24,450,000, or $489,000, to represent the after-tax income from surplus fund investments.

The development of comparable figures for the alternative of expending $24,450,000 on the purchase and retirement of common shares proved more difficult for Mr. Gibson because of the anticipated growth of the company.

After study of the record of market prices for the stock in recent months, and giving consideration to the continued gain in earnings (7% higher in the last 6 months of 1963 than in the same period of 1962), and consultation with Mr. Blaine, Mr. Gibson decided that an average purchase price of $89½ a share could be assumed, if the buying was undertaken promptly. Higher prices were expected for later years. Under this assumption, 273,184 shares would be purchased, relieving the company of $682,296 in dividends at the current rate.

In the fiscal year 1962–63, earnings available for common shares were $13,252,677. Deducting 2% of $24,450,000, or $489,000, to represent the after-tax income from the investment of surplus funds, and rounding, Mr. Gibson obtained $12,764,000. He then prepared the following comparison:

$$\frac{1962\text{–}63 \text{ Earnings}}{\text{February, 1964 Number of Shares}} = \frac{\$13,252,677}{3,285,500} = \$4.03 \text{ per share}.$$

$$\frac{1962\text{–}63 \text{ Earnings, Adjusted}}{\text{Reduced Number of Shares}} = \frac{\$12,764,000}{3,012,316} = \$4.24 \text{ per share}.$$

As the earnings of Extone Chemicals were expected to grow, Mr. Gibson performed a similar calculation for increases in operating earnings of 15%, 30%, and 45%.[2]

---

[2] AUTHOR'S NOTE: Actually, forecasts made by the comptroller's department were available that permitted Mr. Gibson to put dates on the occurrence of these amounts of growth. They have been omitted here, in order not to reveal the planning factors of the company.

Operating earnings	F/Y 62–63	+15%	+30%	+45%
E.P.S. 3,285,500 shares....	$4.03	$4.62	$5.20	$5.78
E.P.S. 3,012,316 shares....	4.24	4.87	5.51	6.14
Gain from repurchase of 273,184 shares..........	$0.21	$0.25	$0.31	$0.36

Knowing Mr. Prouse's interest in the computation of "return on investment" figures, Mr. Gibson then proceeded as follows. He computed the amount of earnings, after taxes, necessary to make $4.24 earned per share on 3,285,500 shares. The product of these numbers was $13,930,-520, a quantity $1,166,520 greater than the $12,764,000 actually earned. He related this number, $1,166,520, to $24,450,000 to obtain the rate of 4.8% after taxes. From a similar computation, he found an indicated rate of return of 6.8%, after operating earnings had increased by 45%.

Upon reviewing the study made by Mr. Gibson, Mr. Blaine concluded that the purchase of common stock would be preferable to the retirement of the preferred issue. The figures showed a small immediate advantage both in earnings per share and in rate of return for the policy, and the advantage would become greater as the earnings of Extone Chemicals grew larger. Mr. Blaine also was well aware of the steady growth in stock repurchases by corporations generally.

Mr. Blaine felt that as much as $34 million could be used (379,888 shares at $89½), after considering forecasts of future funds flows as well as the existing amount of temporary investments, even after allowing $12 million for cash to support operations. He noted that, even at the rate of 450 shares purchased per day, it would take a long time to accomplish the desired result, and he therefore gave favorable consideration to acquiring the shares through an invitation to the shareholders to tender them to the company.

The investment bankers advising the company had reported that few companies had chosen to ask for tenders as a means of acquiring shares, but that the practice was by no means unknown. Their advice, however, was against the practice because: (1) A tender offer was unusual, and therefore would attract comment and, perhaps, unfavorable gossip, especially in view of recent publicity given to the sale of several parts of the business. (2) It required setting a price, which was not an easy operation, though possible. The price would certainly have to be higher than market, to attract the volume of shares desired. But at the price offered, the desired quantity might not be obtained. Offerings of too few or too many shares might produce unfavorable comment. (3) Although the company and its advisers would offer a price that was an appraisal of the current market situation, there was no way to avoid having some shareholders interpret it as an official statement of the "value" of their stock—with misunderstandings and complaints to follow, whichever way the market value might move. (Usually, tender offers were followed by increases, because the normal supply to the market was absorbed.)

Nevertheless, Mr. Blaine was favorably disposed toward the use of tenders. His reasons included: (1) The transaction could be completed quickly, as contrasted with the long time needed by purchasing small quantities in the open market. If it affected price, its effect would soon be over. (2) It would create immediately the full effect on earnings per share. (3) It gave the maximum assurance of full disclosure to share-holders, since each listed owner would receive a description of the offer directly from the company and could hardly avoid considering the matter.

Mr. Blaine knew that some companies made use of tender offers. For example, in March he noted in *The Wall Street Journal* an invitation from Thompson Ramo Wooldridge, Inc., to its stockholders to tender shares. The announcement of the invitation is reproduced in Exhibit 4. The invitation had had the desired results.

When Mr. Blaine discussed the matter with Mr. Prouse, however, he learned that the board of directors would surely be unfavorable to the idea of using tenders. In addition to the reasons given by the investment bankers, Mr. Prouse emphasized that: (1) A sudden distribution of a very large quantity of funds scarcely fitted the image of the dynamic company that Extone Chemicals was, in fact. (2) A number of investing institutions held large blocks of Extone stock, and the tender scheme would offer them too easy an opportunity to take capital gains on their entire holding. (3) Also, once the invitation was issued, there was no flexibility, as to either price or quantity of shares. Extone Chemicals was actively following a policy leading to acquisitions, and therefore might wish to revise its stock repurchase policy in one way or another. (4) A single tender offer might be considered, but the method did not offer a basis for any continuing policy. (The rumor of a tender offer usually caused price increases, and so no inference of a policy of repeated tenders could be permitted.)

At the same time as the studies on repurchase of stock were under way, Extone Chemicals arranged to purchase a company that would make an important addition to its line of chemical specialties. The purchase was to be accomplished by issuing to the sellers 264,000 shares of Extone common stock. This transaction emphasized in Mr. Prouse's and Mr. Blaine's minds the importance of having on hand a substantial number of treasury shares to permit acquisitions without any immediate dilution. They also felt that it would be desirable to put the pending acquisition "on a cash basis" at current levels in the stock market. In this case, as in several that were under consideration, the terms of exchange depended on the market values of the shares of the two companies. With Extone stock selling at low price-earnings multiples, it was hard to find desirable acquisitions that did not seem high priced, in terms of dilution.

With such information at hand, Mr. Blaine prepared a formal recommendation to Mr. Prouse that the board of directors be asked to approve further acquisitions in the manner previously used. In his memorandum, Mr. Blaine said:

I would certainly recommend that we continue the rules relating to the volume of daily purchasing and the range within which purchases should be made.

I would not like to see a definite maximum set and I definitely do not recommend that any further notification of our intention to purchase should be given to stockholders. Such an announcement would give all and sundry definite knowledge of our intention to purchase and might also in some way be construed as support of the market.

The purchase program could be said to be a mechanism by which we could reacquire equity capital formerly directed to the mechanical and electronics phases of our business, allowing it to be redirected to chemicals without seriously penalizing our stockholders.

As he prepared to draft his own recommendation to be presented to higher officers, Mr. Prouse recalled certain negative views that had been argued in the previous year. Most, if not all of them, could be expected once more, and he wanted to consider how they could be compromised or overcome in order to obtain the repurchase policy, which he favored strongly. These negative views were:

1. It was desirable to retire the preferred stock, which was an obsolete and expensive kind of financing. If necessary, it should be retired by refunding into some sort of debt.

2. Although both the long-term debt and the preferred stock contracts contained the same maximum for long-term debt of $50 million (and Extone Chemicals was currently obligated for about $43,875,000), the preferred stock was held by many owners. It would be hard, therefore, to get the restriction in the preferred contract changed. The debt contract containing this restriction, on the other hand, was held by one insurance company, which was expected to be reasonable about changes. (The company's debt ratio was not "out of line" in the industry.)

3. The price of the common stock was above book value, and it was unfair to the remaining shareholders to reduce their book values by the proposed repurchases.

4. The board ought not to approve repurchases unless a new statement of intent, similar to the 1963 statement specifying the number of shares to be acquired, was made before any purchases began. Directors with this opinion believed that any purchases, no matter how carefully made, would inevitably affect market prices if they were continued over many days, as would be the case for the current proposal. Therefore, they wanted as explicit a statement as possible, and they wanted it renewed each time the board of directors authorized a new number of shares to be purchased. One of these directors went so far as to propose that the nature of the restrictions on the treasurer's buying should also be made public.

An opinion of company counsel was obtained, that the 1963 announcement met all legal requirements for publicity, so long as similar quantities and methods of purchase were involved. If, however, more than 5% of the shares were to be retired, an announcement in advance of any buying would remove any question of inadequate disclosure under SEC rulings.

The studies and discussions described above, which had begun in February, 1964, lasted until early May. At this date, the end of the fiscal year was approaching. Earnings per share for the year 1963–64 were estimated at $4.39 on the 3,513,416 shares outstanding. The directors would next meet early in June, and the text of the annual report would be open to changes until early in July.

Exhibit 1
EXTONE CHEMICALS, INC.
DATA ON COMMON STOCK, FOR YEARS ENDED JUNE 30, 1959-64

	6/30 1959	6/30 1960	6/30 1961	6/30 1962	6/30 1963	6/30 1964*
Net earnings for common stock.	$15,082,172	$9,991,474	$11,256,374	$8,686,417	$13,252,677	$15,435,000
Number of common shares, end of year†	3,208,816	3,289,477	3,314,563	3,328,995	3,341,206	3,513,416
Earned per share†	$4.70	$3.04	$3.40	$2.61	$3.97	$4.39
Dividends per share†	$2.20	$2.425	$2.50	$2.50	$2.50	$2.50
Percentage of common stock earnings paid out	46.8%	79.8%	73.5%	95.8%	63.0%	56.9%

CALENDAR YEARS

	1959	1960	1961	1962	1963	Jan.–Apr. 1964
Market prices						
High	$83⅝	$69¾	$80¾	$70⅝	$89	$88¼
Low	$61¼	$49¾	$64⅝	$44¾	$65⅜	$75
Standard & Poor's weekly stock price indexes for 11 chemical companies, excluding Du Pont (1941–43 = 10). Average of weekly indexes	45.76	42.77	44.68	35.44	39.94	45.92

* Estimated.
† Adjusted for all stock splits.

Exhibit 2

EXTONE CHEMICALS, INC.

MONTHLY HIGH AND LOW MARKET PRICES OF COMMON STOCK, 1962–APRIL, 1964

	1962		*1963*		*1964*		*Standard & Poor's Stock Price Index for Chemical Companies* (1941–43 = 10)*		
	Low	*High*	*Low*	*High*	*Low*	*High*	*1962*	*1963*	*1964*
January	60⅝	70⅝	65⅜	70⅞	79⅝	84⅛	41.41	37.95	45.16
February	60⅞	63½	66⅝	71⅜	76½	81¾	41.59	38.28	45.17
March	60⅜	66⅝	69¾	73¾	79⅛	88¼	40.19	38.05	46.09
April	58⅜	62½	73⅛	79⅛	75	86¼	37.91	39.94	47.24
May	44¾	61¼	71⅜	77⅝			34.86	40.54	
June	50	57¾	71⅞	77⅞			30.61	39.80	
July	46⅛	53⅛	67½	75			30.45	38.83	
August	49	57	71⅞	81¼			31.33	39.73	
September	53⅛	59⅜	76½	85⅛			32.05	40.81	
October	52⅛	57	82	89			32.07	40.49	
November	55¼	64⅜	75	83⅛			36.05	41.21	
December	63¼	67⅛	80¾	84⅞			36.76	43.63	

* Composite of 11 stocks, excluding Du Pont. Monthly averages of weekly indexes.

Exhibit 3

EXTONE CHEMICALS, INC.

SHARE VALUE INDICES

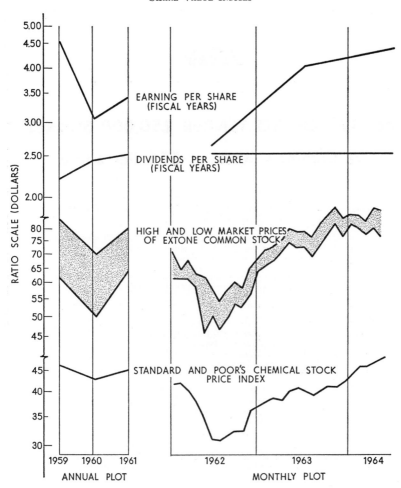

Exhibit 4

EXTONE CHEMICALS, INC.

A TYPICAL INVITATION TO TENDER SHARES

THOMPSON RAMO WOOLDRIDGE INC.

INVITATION TO TENDER 250,000 SHARES

of Common Stock at $56 Per Share

By letter dated March 2, 1964, the company has invited its shareholders to tender 250,000 shares of its Common Stock, at a price of $56 per share. The company will pay any Federal and State Transfer Taxes involved in its purchase of shares.

The invitation to tender will expire at 3:30 pm., EST, on March 17, 1964 unless extended for a period of not more than ten days. The company reserves the right to purchase more or less than 250,000 shares, but in no event less than 100,000 shares.

All tenders are invited in accordance with the terms and conditions specified in the formal invitation to tender and accompanying tender form mailed to shareholders of record.

To accept this invitation, shareholders should send the prescribed letter of transmittal accompanied by their stock certificates to:

The National City Bank of Cleveland
Corporate Trust Department
623 Euclid Avenue
Cleveland, Ohio 44101

or

Morgan Guaranty Trust Company of New York
Corporate Trust Division
23 Wall Street
New York, New York 10015

Additional copies of the invitation to tender and tender form may be obtained from either of such banks, or by writing to or telephoning the undersigned at 23555 Euclid Avenue, Cleveland, Ohio 44117 — Phone: Area Code 216, 383-2257.

THOMPSON RAMO WOOLDRIDGE INC.

P. W. Schuette, Secretary

SOURCE: *The Wall Street Journal*, March 4, 1964, p. 16.

Case 39

John F. Childs

In September, 1956, the director of the Division of Corporate Regulation, Securities and Exchange Commission, sent out a letter and questionnaire asking for views on the capital structure of public utilities. The SEC wished to sample informed opinion of regulatory officials, investors, underwriters, utility officers, educators in finance, and others on the question of appropriate capitalization ratios for those public utilities coming under SEC jurisdiction. The survey was in anticipation of a policy statement to be made by the SEC on this question.

Exhibit 1 presents the questionnaire. Exhibit 2 gives the answer made by Mr. John F. Childs, a vice president of the Irving Trust Company.

Exhibit 1

SECURITIES AND EXCHANGE COMMISSION

Study of Capitalization Ratios (1956), File No. S7–148

The Division of Corporate Regulation of the Securities and Exchange Commission is studying the advisability of recommending that the Commission issue for comment by interested persons a proposed Statement of Policy relative to appropriate capitalization ratios for registered holding companies and their subsidiary operating companies subject to the Public Utility Holding Company Act of 1935. Any Statement of Policy ultimately adopted would be applicable to declarations regarding security issuances filed by registered holding companies or their subsidiaries under Section 7 or to applications for exemption filed under Section 6 (b).

Section 7 provides, in subsection (d) (1), that the Commission shall permit a declaration regarding the issue or sale of a security to become effective unless the Commission finds that "the security is not reasonably adapted to the security structure of the declarant and other companies in the same holding-company system." Section 6 (b) provides that in granting an application under Section 6 (b) for exemption of a security issuance from the requirements of Section 7, the Commission may impose such terms

895

Exhibit 1 (Continued)

and conditions as it deems appropriate in the public interest or for the protection of investors or consumers.

In its Tenth Annual Report to Congress for the fiscal year ended June 30, 1944, the Commission stated, at page 99:

"A balanced capital structure provides a considerable measure of insurance against bankruptcy, enables the utility to raise new money most economically, and avoids the possibility of deterioration in service to consumers if there is a decline in earnings."

Similarly, in a report for the SEC Subcommittee of the House Committee on Interstate and Foreign Commerce on the Public Utility Holding Company Act of 1935, dated October 15, 1951, the Commission stated, at page 27:

"An adequate equity cushion to absorb the vagaries of business conditions is an important attribute of a good security."

The Commission has heretofore expressed and applied its views on minimum standards of capitalization ratios on a case-by-case basis. Thus, for example, in *General Public Utilities Corporation et al.*, 30 S.E.C. 587 (1949), the Commission stated, at page 601, that although it had generally required the insertion in charters upon the issuance of preferred stock a provision limiting the payment of common stock dividends when the ratio of common stock equity to total capitalization and surplus is less than 25%, it had never regarded a 25% common stock equity ratio as being anything other than a floor below which existing common stock equity ratios should not drop or to which existing lower ratios should, *as a minimum*, increase. The Commission added that it had continuously striven to have common stock equity ratios maintained at, or increased to levels substantially above, 25% of capitalization and surplus. Subsequently, in *Eastern Utilities Associates* (Holding Company Act Release No. 11625 [1952]), the Commission stated, at page 55, that, generally speaking, long-term debt should not exceed 60% of capitalization and surplus and common stock equity (including surplus) should not be less than 30% thereof.

In a memorandum submitted May 24, 1956 to a Subcommittee of the Committee on Interstate and Foreign Commerce of the United States Senate (84th Congress, 2nd Session), on S. 2643, the Commission again emphasized the need for balanced capital structures for public utility companies and public utility holding company systems and discussed the substantial improvement in capitalization ratios which has taken place in the public utility industry since the enactment in 1935 of the Public Utility Holding Company Act. (See Senate Subcommittee Hearings on S. 2643 [84th Congress, 2nd Session] at pages 397–406.) The Commission also discussed situations in which two or more electric utility companies organize, and own all the common stock of, a subsidiary generating company which sells all or substantially all of its electrical generation to the parent companies, and in connection therewith the Commission explained the analytical technique of proportional consolidation pursuant to which there are added to the corporate figures of the parent company the senior capitalization, earnings, and fixed charges of the subsidiary, but only to the extent of the

Exhibit 1 (Continued)

percentage representing the parent company's ownership of the common stock. (*Id.,* at pages 406–408.)

The Division considers that an administrative determination by the Commission through a Statement of Policy on capitalization ratios may be a desirable means of apprising issuers subject to the Act and investors and consumers of the standards which the Commission would generally apply in determining (1) whether to impose terms and conditions in granting applications under Section 6 (b) or (2) whether to make adverse findings in respect of declarations pursuant to Section 7 (d). Accordingly, in order that the Division may be adequately advised prior to making any recommendations to the Commission on this matter, it would be greatly appreciated if you would submit in writing, on or before November 1, 1956, your views and comments on the following items:

1. What should be the appropriate maximum proportion of total capitalization and surplus (excluding notes payable due within one year) represented by long-term debt and the minimum proportion represented by common stock and surplus, both where there is and where there is not preferred stock outstanding? Consider this question separately for a company which is (a) principally an electric utility company other than a company described in (b) hereof; (b) a company which is essentially an electric generating company supplying the power requirements of one or more electric utility companies which own all or substantially all of the common stock of such generating company; (c) principally a gas distribution utility company; and (d) principally a natural gas pipe line company.

2. What should be the appropriate maximum ratio of long-term debt to net utility plant (after deduction of reserves) for the types of companies referred to in item (1)?

3. In determining the ratio limitations in items (1) and (2) above, what adjustment, if any, should be made with respect to any amounts on the books of the company in excess of original cost of used or useful utility plant?

4. What should be the appropriate maximum proportion of total consolidated capitalization and surplus (excluding notes payable due within one year) of a holding company and its subsidiaries represented by consolidated long-term debt and the minimum proportion represented by consolidated common stock and surplus, both where there is and where there is not preferred stock outstanding? Consider this question separately where (a) the holding company controls a system which is principally an electric utility system; (b) the holding company controls a system which is principally a gas distribution utility system; and (c) the holding company controls a system comprised of both gas distribution utility companies and natural gas pipe line companies.

5. In applying the ratio limitations in item (4) above to a holding company and its subsidiaries on a consolidated basis, what adjustment, if any, should be made for any excess of carrying amounts (cost) of investments in the common stocks of subsidiaries over the underlying book values thereof at dates of acquisition?

6. Where two or more electric utility companies own all or substantially

Exhibit 1 (Continued)

all of the common stock of an electric generating company which sells all or substantially all of its generation to such parent companies, what consideration should be given, in determining appropriate capitalization ratios for such parent companies, to including as part of the capital structure of each parent company all or a proportionate share of the senior capitalization of the generating company? Distinguish between (a) a case in which one of the parent companies owns a majority of the common stock of the generating company and the balance of the stock is owned by one or more parent companies, and (b) a case in which no single parent company owns a majority of the common stock.

7. Would your answer to item (6) above be different if the electricity generated by the subsidiary generating company were contracted to be sold substantially to a single nonaffiliated purchaser, such as a Governmental agency, with the parent companies (either directly or through subsidiary electric utility companies) supplying any needed backup power and purchasing any surplus power not required by the single purchaser? Please state your reasons. (Assume herein that one or more of the parent companies may be solely a holding company rather than an operating electric utility company.)

8. What should be the appropriate maximum proportion of notes payable due within one year to total capitalization and surplus exclusive of such notes payable?

9. What do you consider to be the ideal or optimum capitalization ratios for the types of companies or systems referred to in items (1) and (4) both where there is and where there is not preferred stock outstanding?

10. At what point do you consider the ratio of common stock and surplus to total capitalization and surplus (excluding notes payable due within one year) for the types of companies or systems referred to in items (1) and (4) to be, both where there is and where there is not preferred stock outstanding:

   a) Minimum acceptable.
   b) Good.
   c) Very good.
   d) Unduly high.

11. State any factors or consideration which the Commission should take into account in connection with promulgating a Statement of Policy regarding capitalization ratio standards.

Your reply will be considered available for public inspection unless you request that it not be disclosed. In replying please refer to file number S7–148.

Exhibit 2
LETTER TO THE SECURITIES AND EXCHANGE COMMISSION
IRVING TRUST COMPANY
ONE WALL STREET
NEW YORK 15, N.Y.

JOHN F. CHILDS   October 31, 1956
VICE PRESIDENT

Securities and Exchange Commission
Division of Corporate Regulation
Washington 25, D.C.

Re: Study of Capitalization Ratios
File No. S7–148

DEAR SIR:

First, I would like to make some preliminary general remarks about the survey:

1. Managements should be allowed to determine their own policies within wide limits. The survey should not be used to set specific rigid standards so as to interfere with managements' prerogative.

2. Each company should be allowed wide flexibility, and decisions regarding each company's capital structure should be based upon adequate testimony at the particular time which takes into account the individual differences. Once averages have been established, there may be an unwarranted tendency to place too much reliance on such averages.

3. Unless a person has had long experience in finance and matters of "fair return," his answers will be worthless. The survey does not require any statement of qualifications for answering the questionnaire. Apparently the survey has been distributed rather widely since some instances have come to my attention in which recipients of the questionnaire have not felt qualified or had the time to give their own answers. They have sought advice as to what to include.

4. Unless there is included the reasoning behind the answers, there will be no indication as to whether the answers are based on sound judgment. The obvious answer is to use a lot of debt because of the tax savings of interest and because debt may be five times cheaper than equity. The fallacy of this answer is only apparent if a long and careful explanation is given.

5. The survey could be affected by where we are in the business cycle when the survey is made unless stress is laid on the fact that the ratios should be established under average circumstances. For example, a survey in boom times, when some investors want leverage, will produce one result. A survey made under adverse market conditions could produce another.

6. The answers must be based on a long-term view, since bonds are issued for 20 and 30 years and preferred and common stocks are outstanding indefinitely. No one can tell what will happen to the industry except in the near future. Answers based on the exigencies of the near future will be absolutely useless. Many who answer the survey will be inter-

Exhibit 2 (Continued)

ested only in the short run benefits. There is nothing in the survey suggesting the importance of the long run point of view.

Thus, while I have the above reservations with regard to the survey, I will try to answer the questions in order to at least give some indication of my thinking. Actually my views are public knowledge since I have testified before government authorities on the subject.

On the matter of capital structure ratios, I expressed myself as given below in recent testimony. I include it merely to confirm that I have previously furnished this information under oath.

"A. This is an exhibit . . . made some time ago to illustrate the relationship of debt ratio and ratings for electric and telephone bonds. It shows quite clearly that for telephone bonds to have the same rating, the debt ratio must be lower than for electric. For example, the debt ratio shown for double A bonds is about 50% as compared to 35% for the telephone. Another way to say it is that a telephone bond must have a lower debt than a triple A electric even to qualify as a double A. . . ."

"Q. . . . . Mr. Childs, do you have any thoughts on appropriate debt ratio?"

"A. Yes, and I would like to review the points on the subject as covered in my discussion at the Financial Seminars, conducted by me for the Irving Trust Company for utility people. . . . No rigid rules can be laid down regarding these ratios because all the facts surrounding a particular company at a particular time must be weighed. Special circumstances may justify unusual treatment. However, there are certain basic principles that are generally applicable to all utilities over the long run because of their special nature. Utility companies require unusually large amounts of long-term capital. They must be prepared to provide service under all conditions. If the utility in a particular area doesn't adequately supply service there is no other utility to step in and meet the consumers' needs, the only alternative is government service which is socialism. The financial policy should not be established on the basis of boom times. The utility must be in a position to finance new construction and to meet the payment of large bond maturities without damage to its financial strength under every conceivable circumstance, including: adverse conditions in the securities market; adverse conditions for the particular company; adverse conditions in the utility industry; adverse general conditions.

Since utilities must supply service for an indefinite period, and this is important, and is inevitable, that sometimes these conditions will be encountered by most companies. The only way in which a company can be prepared to meet these conditions and still be in a position to serve the consumer adequately, is to follow a sound financial policy.

Some of the basic factors which must be kept in mind in determining debt ratio are as follows:

1. Financial policy should be based on long-range point of view rather than the exigencies of the moment. Character in financing and investors' faith in a company are only built up over a long period of time after a company has demonstrated its ability to withstand adversity. Capital structures ratios can be allowed to get out of line temporarily. It is the average capital structure ratios and the long-range goal of the management which investors study closely.

Exhibit 2 (Continued)

2. After a certain point, as debt is added, the cost of the debt increases, but more important, the added risk results in increased cost of common stock capital and the increase in cost of common stock is not deductible for tax purposes. Remember that basically the economic risk of an enterprise determines the cost of capital and not the way the capitalization is divided between the various groups of security holders. As a practical matter for a company with relatively little risk, debt can be added up to a certain point without adding to the overall risk of the company, but should not be added further than that point. The proof of this economic principle must be done over a long period of time under average conditions in the securities market. Obviously a distortion will result if resort is made to security prices in a bull market. . . .

3. As indicated above, the test of how much debt is appropriate should be made during a period of adverse circumstances rather than a period of favorable conditions. The time when that really becomes burdensome is when trouble is encountered; also, as indicated above, debt carries with it the problem of payment at maturity under conditions which cannot be predicted.

4. Equity markets disappear quite rapidly. A company should be in a position to raise outside capital practically at any time. High-grade debt issues can generally be sold even under adverse conditions. Therefore, it is advantageous to keep a low debt ratio with a high credit standing so that if an emergency arises and capital is needed, debt financing can be resorted to without impairing a company's credit standing. This is what is known as maintaining a borrowing reserve.

5. A conservative financial structure provides insurance against unforeseen difficulties.

6. Debt is a relatively cheap form of capital even with high money rates and interest is deductible for tax purposes. This might appear to allow cheaper rates but in the long run, as I have previously explained, high debt might well result in higher rates for the consumers.

   Of course, particular allowance must be made for the differences between the companies engaged in various types of utility business. They may be ranked in the following order as to their ability to carry debt, other things being equal; water, electric, gas distribution, telephone and traction."

"Q. Mr. Childs, what do you think is an appropriate debt ratio of a telephone company?"

"A. As I have indicated above, I believe that the utility company should maintain a high credit rating which means certainly no lower than a double A. For a telephone company this requires debt somewhat less than 35%."

The above might be restated in another way. There is a simple unstudied argument in favor of high debt—the cost of debt money is cheap as compared to equity capital and interest is deductible for tax purposes. For example, long-term bonds might be sold at an interest rate of 4%, which means a net cost of only 2% after allowing for an assumed federal income tax rate of 50%. Common stock money may cost 10%. Thus capital raised through common stock is five times more costly than the net cost of bond money. For this reason, it is contended that a company should issue a lot of debt.

Exhibit 2 (Continued)

This argument is a naïve approach for the following reasons:
1. It combines a number of elements of cost which are totally different and must be considered separately.
2. It uses incorrect cost figures. Correct cost figures show that the tax factor, as far as the consumers are concerned, is so small as to suggest in no way the use of high debt.
3. It leaves out fundamental financial policy considerations suggested above, which are all important.
4. It is an argument which appears correct in boom times, but proves unsound over the long run.

In determining capital structure ratios, I believe that the long range average is the most important consideration and that depending on market conditions, business conditions, etc., a company should only vary from the long term goal provided it has plans to get back to that long term goal. The best example of such a policy exists in the Bell System. It has as a goal ⅓ debt on a consolidated basis and the balance in common equity. After World War II, it had to run its debt up to slightly over 50% of total capitalization because its earnings were inadequate and it could not sell common stock directly. Since then it has reestablished the ⅓ debt ratio and again has necessary "borrowing reserve."

My answers to the questions in the survey follow:

1a. (see 10 below)
1b. *An electric generating company supplying power to owning companies.* Such a company can have high debt depending on its contracts for power. However, the debt ratio of such a company is meaningless in itself. The debt of the generating company should be apportioned to the owning companies on the basis of their contracts with the generating companies which provide for service of the debt. Then the overall debt ratios should be considered on the basis for the figures suggested below.
1c. (see 10 below)
1d. (see 10 below)
2. I prefer capital structure ratios rather than debt to property.
3. *Adjustments for amounts above original cost*
   If the amounts are pure write-ups they should be deducted from equity. If the amounts represent actual expenditures and are being written off like account no. 100.5 they should not be deducted. However, a judgment must be applied when comparing a company with no such write-up and a company with such a write-up.

Adjustments to original cost for analytical purposes should not be interpreted as justifying use of original cost for rate base purposes.

4. A well integrated holding company should generally have the same ratios as an operating company.
5. Excess of carrying amounts of investments in the common stocks of subsidiaries over underlying book values thereof at dates of acquisition, should generally be deducted from equity, but it depends on the basic reasons which gave rise to the excess, and whether they are being written off.
6a. and b. In both instances, debt etc., of an electric generating company

Exhibit 2 *(Continued)*

should be allocated to the owning companies to the extent that they are obligated to buy power or to take care of the debt, either directly or indirectly.

7. My answer to 6a and b would be different if the government authority were solely responsible for the debt of the generating company. But if ultimately the owning companies are responsible for the debt then it should be allocated to the owning companies with "judgment" allowance being made for the fact that the government has an original responsibility.

8. Generally the maximum portion of notes payable within one year should be about 10% to 15% to take care of construction requirements, but special circumstances might justify a higher figure, say 20%. Therefore, companies should not be straightjacketed with one of the lower figures.

9. (see 10 below)

10. *Large, well-situated electric operating company*
    Long Range Goal

	Debt Rating	Debt	Preferred	Common
a) Minimum acceptable..		(see below)		
b) Good (Optimum).....	Aa	50%	15%	35%
c) Very good..........	Aaa	45	15	40
d) Unduly high........ (less than)	40	15 (above)	45

Debt can be allowed to vary from a minimum of 40% and a maximum (if absolutely necessary under special circumstances) of 60%, but plans should be established to get back to the goals of (b) or (c) above with a preference for the latter.

I definitely favor the use of preferred stock for an electric operating company. If preferred is not used, then the debt ratios under (b) and (c) above might be allowed to go a little higher.

For an electric generating plant see comments under 1b above.

A gas distribution company should generally have somewhat lower debt ratios than an electric company because of the nature of the business.

A gas pipeline may justify higher debt because of contracts on both ends of the pipeline for gas supply and sales for the duration of the bonds, and because pipeline bonds generally contain 100% sinking funds. However, the circumstances surrounding each pipeline company are quite different and therefore it is difficult to generalize for such companies.

11. I do not believe that the commission should promulgate a statement of policy as indicated above in my preliminary remarks. The most that the Commission might do is to suggest minimum allowances for common equity and maximum for debt applicable to a large, well situated electric operating company. Then some general statement might be made as to whether other types of companies might have lower or higher ratios. However, I feel that it would be preferable to avoid even a policy statement in terms of minimums and maximums. Each

Exhibit 2 (Continued)

piece of financing should be decided at the particular time after adequate testimony has been presented to warrant a decision.

I would like to conclude with two more general comments.

I think it is most important that the survey in no way be concerned with the matter of cost of capital. As I understand it, the basic purpose for which the SEC was established was to assure full disclosure in security offerings, and under the holding company act to assure that issues are "reasonably adapted to the security structure."

I do not believe that the SEC is required to consider capital structure from the point of view of overall cost of capital nor need do so. The Federal Power Commission and state regulatory authorities have adequate jurisdiction over matters of rates of return to protect the consumers. Furthermore, cost of capital is a very complicated subject, and I do not think the survey was so designed as to include this as a consideration. Therefore, I think it would be most unfortunate if this question should become interjected.

The utility industry as a whole, has done an excellent job in strengthening capital structure. For example, Illinois Power Company and Indianapolis Power and Light Company have recently improved their bond rating from A to Aa by reduction of debt. There are other companies such as Interstate Power Company and Pennsylvania Power and Light Company which have substantially improved their capital structure. Conservative financial policy seems so essential for the good of the utility investors and consumers that it would be too bad to encourage in any way laxity in capital structure or a swing toward more leverage. Unsound finance was one of the principal reasons for the Holding Company Act.

Very sincerely yours,
(*Signed*) JOHN F. CHILDS
Vice President

SOURCE: U.S., S.E.C., File No. S7-148, "Study of Capitalization Ratios—Public Letters of Comment . . . ," Vol. 1, pp. 270–80.

Case 40

Upstate Canning Company, Inc.

DURING THE PERIOD following his graduation from a business school in 1950, Mr. Nelson Shields had attempted to prepare himself for the opportunity of becoming the manager and sole or part owner of a company with real growth possibilities. Because he lacked financial resources, he had sought employment which offered substantial immediate income as well as managerial experience which would be useful in later years. This search led him successively through positions in three distinctly different businesses, in each of which experience was largely concentrated in the sales and sales management areas. By 1956 he had accumulated personal savings of $15,000, which, added to some family money placed at his disposal, gave him an investment fund of $35,000.

At this point, Mr. Shields had begun an active search for opportunities to purchase an existing business. In the course of the year he looked into about 25 possibilities which came to his attention. Some of these were quickly rejected; others involved the expenditure of considerable time and some money before a negative decision was reached. While looking for business possibilities, Shields also sought to develop contacts with business and professional men who might be induced to invest equity capital in an attractive opportunity, should one be found requiring more capital than he possessed. By the end of 1956 Mr. Shields was still investigating business leads, but with no real prospect in sight. Meanwhile, the pressure to settle on a business was increasing. Shields had given up employment in October in order to devote full time to his search, and he realized that he could not afford many months of unemployment without eating into the sum set aside for investment.

In February of 1957 a business broker called Shields to advise him that a small cannery had just come up for sale. The property consisted of two plants, equipped for the canning of fruits and vegetables, which were located close to the source of supply in rural towns in New York State. The business, known as the Upstate Canning Company, Inc., was owned and managed by Mr. A. C. Fordham. Mr. Fordham's health was uncertain and, at 55, he had decided to sell out because he had no relatives to take his place in the business. The broker urged Shields to investigate this opportunity because it looked as though it might fit his circumstances.

Mr. Shields immediately set out to learn what he could about the fruit and vegetable canning industry in general and this business in particular. The broker arranged a meeting with Mr. Fordham; and from this and subsequent meetings and telephone conversations, Mr. Shields assembled a picture of the business.

In general, Mr. Fordham was very cooperative in providing the information requested from him. He was reluctant, however, to disclose the financial details of operations for the 3 years prior to 1956. During 1952 Fordham had brought in a general manager on a 3-year employment contract as a means of easing himself out of the day-to-day responsibilities of the business. The new man had not worked out well, and sales and profits had suffered as a result. Upon the termination of this contract, Fordham had again assumed full management responsibilities, and results in 1956 improved substantially over those of 1953, 1954, and 1955. Fordham argued that these years were not representative of the earnings potential of the business and that 1956 should be taken as the most accurate measure of its possibilities. From what Shields had been able to find out about the business from other sources, he was inclined to accept Fordham's explanation and to base his estimates on the figures for 1956.

The physical plant of the business appeared to be in very good condition. The two buildings had been kept in excellent repair, and the canning equipment was modern. The combined plant and equipment had recently been appraised for insurance purposes, and their value had been placed at $200,000. Shields was assured that no major repairs would be necessary over the next few years.

Mr. Fordham had been accustomed to operating the plants only during the limited harvest season for the fruits and vegetables which he canned. The season lasted for 4 months, from July through October, with August and September normally accounting for two thirds of the company's total production. At times, Fordham had considered stretching out the production period with other canning operations, but he had never taken any action on the idea. During the 1956 season Upstate had produced canned fruits and vegetables with a total value of $850,000 (valued at Upstate's selling price). This production represented only about 50% of combined productive capacity of the plants during the production season. Excess capacity was attributed to the substantial expansion of facilities which had been undertaken to meet wartime demands.

The vegetables and fruits canned by Upstate were bought on a contract basis from farmers in the surrounding area; farmers were paid cash on delivery on the basis of prevailing market prices at the time of delivery. The quantities canned by Upstate varied to some extent with the crop conditions from year to year; normally, output could be increased considerably, however, by noncontract purchases, if good marketing opportunities existed. The production process was almost entirely mechanical, and the towns and surrounding areas offered an ample supply of seasonal labor sufficiently skilled to perform the various operations in the plant. Labor was paid on a weekly basis.

The products of the Upstate Canning Company were marketed primarily under the Upstate brand through jobbers. It was the normal practice to sell the entire season's pack before the next canning season began, so that little inventory would be carried over from one year to the next. Sales tended to be concentrated during and immediately following the production period. Fordham indicated that about 50% of the pack would normally be sold by the end of the canning season (October) and 70% by the end of December. The balance of sales was customarily spread rather evenly over the remaining months through June.

Mr. Shields was particularly attracted by the marketing opportunities of the business. It was his impression that Fordham had not been aggressive in sales promotion—that much better use could be made of the company's productive capacity. Shields believed that he could greatly increase the scale of operations by undertaking an active but relatively inexpensive sales program. He had in mind direct sales to supermarket chains of both Upstate and private brands, to be obtained largely through his own efforts with no significant increase in present selling costs.

Relying on these expectations, Shields prepared a 5-year sales program (see Exhibit 1) which he planned to use as the basis of his estimates of profits and working capital requirements. He was informed by Fordham that collections on accounts receivable caused little trouble in this business; bad-debt losses were rare, and accounts were normally collected within 30 days. Shields expected that the planned expansion would not affect this collection period and might even improve it, because he would be increasing direct sales to large accounts.

In examining the cost aspects of the business, Shields soon became aware of the high proportion of variable costs. The principal items were the fruits and vegetables and other ingredients, cans, and direct labor. As previously indicated, fruits and vegetables were bought on a cash basis, labor was paid weekly at fixed hourly rates, and cans and "other ingredients" were purchased on normal terms of 2/10, net 30 days. The details of revenues and costs for 1956 are shown in Exhibits 2 and 3.

As negotiations proceeded, it became evident that Fordham was anxious to sell the business as soon as possible. The new crop season was coming on; and Fordham felt that if he were to operate the business for another year, it would soon be necessary to sign contracts with farmers for the year's production. After 3 weeks, during which Shields was gathering and studying information and talking to bankers, can company officials, government agencies, and others, Fordham came forward with a specific proposal for the sale of the business (see Exhibit 4).

The plan anticipated that Shields would organize a new company and purchase certain Upstate assets, namely, its plant and equipment, a small amount of finished goods inventory, and the right to use the Upstate brand names. Current assets (other than the inventory mentioned above) and liabilities of the old company would not pass to the new company. It was apparent from the plan that Fordham had guessed that Shields had very limited resources and, accordingly, had provided for an instalment purchase of Upstate assets through the gradual redemption of $300,000 of income bonds to be issued to Fordham. By this time, Shields had become convinced that this business was sufficiently promising to justify a full and detailed study of Fordham's proposal.

Before accepting Fordham's proposal or making a counterproposal, it was necessary for Shields to determine how the new company was to be financed. His best lead for additional equity capital was a professional man who had indicated that he was prepared to invest as much as $100,000 if the right opportunity came along. This man was 50 years of age, and his investment goal appeared to be that of capital appreciation over the years rather than immediate income.

Shields was determined that the plan for the new company would include a means by which he could become the owner of 51% of the voting stock as soon as possible. More specifically, he hoped to obtain control within 5 years, and hence was intent on arranging a compensation plan for himself as manager which would enable him to accomplish this objective. Shields's plan, as tentatively formulated, provided for a basic salary of $15,000 plus 5% of profits before taxes; these figures took account of his estimate that roughly 60% of his annual income would be absorbed by living expenses and tax payments. His plan also included an option to buy enough additional shares—either new shares to be issued by the company or outstanding shares held by his associate(s)—to raise Shields's holdings to 51% of all outstanding voting stock. It was clear, however, that the exact details of the final plan would have to be worked out with the other shareholder or shareholders before arrangements could be completed with Fordham.

As part of his program to assure an adequate supply of capital, Mr. Shields obtained an introduction, through a mutual friend, to one of the officers of a medium-sized bank in a nearby city. This officer indicated that it was the bank's normal policy to avoid substantial loans to new enterprises, but that exceptions were occasionally made where there was adequate security. Canning operations were important to the surrounding area, and he suggested that the bank might consider a secured loan to the new company if it looked promising on closer examination. From further conversation, Shields concluded that the best possibility would be a loan of up to 75% of the cost of finished goods inventory under a field warehousing arrangement. The cost of this kind of financing, including field warehousing expenses, which would not otherwise have been incurred, would be about 6% per annum. In addition to the bank loan, Shields also believed that it might be possible to stretch the payment period on cans to 60 days without creating serious credit problems.

In considering his preliminary calculations, Shields planned to make a detailed study of the year 1957–58 and to use this as a basis for approximating the necessary figures for the fiscal years 1958–59 through 1961–62. He had in mind a fiscal year beginning July 1.

Shields was aware that the next move was up to him. As he saw it, there were three obvious courses of action: (1) accept Fordham's proposal as presented; (2) reject the proposal and look for another business; (3) propose a compromise plan which would have a reasonable prospect of meeting the objectives of all interested parties.

Exhibit 1

UPSTATE CANNING COMPANY, INC.

PLANNED SALES VOLUME, 1957–62

1957–58	$ 850,000
1958–59	1,050,000
1959–60	1,250,000
1960–61	1,450,000
1961–62	1,650,000

Exhibit 2

UPSTATE CANNING COMPANY, INC.

INCOME STATEMENT FOR YEAR ENDED DEC. 31, 1956

(Dollar Figures in Thousands)

		Amount	Percent of Sales
Sales (net after returns and allowances)		$850	100%
Less: Cost of goods sold			
Beginning inventory, Jan. 1, 1956	$257		
Add: Cost of goods manufactured	630		
	$887		
Less: Ending inventory, December 31, 1956	254	633	74
Gross profit on sales		$217	
Less: Selling and administrative expense			
Selling and delivery	$ 64		8
Administrative and general (including salary to Fordham of $20,000)	56	120	7
Profit before taxes		$ 97	
Less: Federal income tax*		45	5
Net profit after taxes		$ 52	6

* Federal income tax is computed on the basis of 30% of the first $25,000 of taxable income plus 52% of income in excess of $25,000. For companies of this size the tax is payable in the succeeding fiscal year as follows: 50% on the 15th day of the 3d month following the end of the tax year and 50% on the 15th day of the 6th month following.

Exhibit 3

UPSTATE CANNING COMPANY, INC.

STATEMENT OF COST OF GOODS MANUFACTURED FOR
YEAR ENDED DEC. 31, 1956

(Dollar Figures in Thousands)

	Amount		*Percent of Total Cost of Goods Manufactured*
Direct costs			
Vegetables and fruit................................	$232		
Labor..	138		
Cans...	112		
Other ingredients.................................	36	$518	82%
Variable overhead			
Fuel oil..	$ 17		
Electricity and water..............................	7		
Factory supplies..................................	5		
Payroll taxes.....................................	7		
Truck and auto expenses...........................	2		
Gas and oil.......................................	5	43	7
Fixed overhead			
Repairs and maintenance..........................	$ 18		
Insurance..	12		
Property taxes....................................	10		
Depreciation—plant and equipment..................	24		
Machinery rental.................................	5	$ 69	11
Total cost of goods manufactured......................		$630	100%

Exhibit 4

UPSTATE CANNING COMPANY, INC.

INITIAL PROPOSAL BY MR. FORDHAM FOR THE PURCHASE OF CERTAIN ASSETS OF
THE UPSTATE CANNING COMPANY, INC., BY MR. SHIELDS AND ASSOCIATE(S)

1. New corporation to be formed with capitalization of $400,000 and with a capital structure as follows:

    a) $100,000 of common stock, $1 par, one vote per share, to be issued to Shields and associate(s) for $100,000 cash. Cash to be retained in new corporation.

    b) $300,000 of income bonds due on June 1, 1967; 3% interest per annum, payable semiannually (June 1 and December 1) if and when earned, cumulative, to be issued to Fordham in exchange for all plant and equipment of Upstate Canning Company, $50,000 of salable finished goods inventory, and the right to use the brand names of the Upstate Canning Company. (Prior to the exchange, the Upstate Canning Company will be liquidated and the assets distributed to Fordham as sole owner.)

2. Repayment provisions of income bonds:

    a) Company to repurchase $50,000 of income bonds on or before June 1, 1958.

    b) In succeeding years, company to repurchase income bonds equivalent in par value to 50% of the net profit after taxes, provided that the amount in any year will be no less than $15,000. The $15,000 will be due on June 1, and any balance within 30 days after the close of the fiscal year.

    c) Company to have the option of purchasing any amount of income bonds in excess of the minimum requirements according to a schedule of discounted prices as follows: in the first year at 80% of par, in the second year at 82½% of par, in the third year at 85% of par, and so on.

3. No fixed assets to be sold or encumbered in any way without the consent of the income bondholders.

4. Control of the company to be divided equally between the income bondholders and the common shareholders until the income bonds have been completely retired. Each group will elect two directors to a four-man board.

5. Fordham to act as chairman of the board and receive compensation for whatever time he spends on operating matters, beyond board meetings, on a basis to be determined in further negotiations.

6. Shields to act as president and general manager.

7. New company to be incorporated and assets of Upstate to be acquired on or about June 1, 1957. In the meantime, it is to be understood that Fordham and Shields will work together in negotiating contracts with farmers and arranging for an orderly transfer of ownership.

Case 41

Midland Spark Plug Company

"Lou, this is a real good outfit. All and all I think you'd do well to join us and take a part of it. It seems to me a unique opportunity to make a highly leveraged investment in a company that's had a long record of good earnings. Unlike the new concerns both you and I have been investing in, Midland has the cash flow to service a large debt. Besides, it's darn hard to kill an old company like this while one of our new 'glamour' companies can make a bad decision and go broke overnight!

"In addition to the stability of its present business, Dr. Zimmer thinks Midland has good prospects in some new products he's looked into. His report on the company shows that with even very conservative assumptions, Midland should earn a quarter of a million next year and that's on only $100,000 of equity. I'll put a copy of the report in the mail for you today.

"I'm sorry, though, to have to press you for a decision on such short notice, but since the Superior National Bank backed out last week, we've been under a lot of pressure to find someone to fill their shoes. Mr. Bruce Tanner who now owns most of the Midland stock seems to be a pretty unpredictable guy, so we don't want to tread on his toes by asking for another delay."

On April 5, 1961, Mr. Louis Cushman recalled this conversation he had 2 weeks earlier with Mr. Graham McMillan, president of Mid-Continent Capital Corporation of Chicago. Mr. Cushman was chairman and president of Great Lakes Capital Corporation of Milwaukee which, like Mid-Continent, was a large, publicly held small business investment company. Since Mr. Parton, vice president of Great Lakes had returned the day before from a visit to the Midland Spark Plug Company in Midland, Michigan, Mr. Cushman thought he had all the material that would be available to him for making a recommendation to Great Lakes' board of directors. Mr. Cushman had already received the Zimmer report which

Mr. McMillan had promised to send him, and with it an appraisal of Midland's assets by Harris Brothers, Inc., a well-regarded and reliable rebuilder and purveyor of used machinery (see Exhibits 1 and 2).

Recent Events

Mr. McMillan had called Mr. Cushman to offer Great Lakes a chance to loan $300,000 at 8% to the Midland Spark Plug Company and to buy 30 of its 100 shares of common stock for $30,000. Midland was a new company formed by Dr. Zimmer and two other investors to buy the assets of another company of the same name. Mr. Tanner, the present owner, had managed the old Midland Spark Plug Company since 1929, when its creditors had installed him as president after it had been declared bankrupt. In 1961 Midland produced a proprietary line of replacement spark plugs, specialty igniters, and related electrode connectors and in addition did a large volume of contract precision machining.

Late in 1960 Dr. Zimmer had learned that Mr. Tanner, then in his late 60's and in poor health, wanted to sell Midland. After doing the research summarized in the report shown in Exhibit 1, Dr. Zimmer had formed a syndicate to purchase Midland's assets. The $650,000 purchase price net of redundant working capital (see pro forma balance sheet in Exhibit 3) was to have been financed as follows:

Superior National Bank—20-year mortgage secured by land and building	$250,000
Mid-Continent Capital Corporation—6-year equipment note @ 8%, amortization beginning in the 27th month.	
Warrants to purchase one third of the common stock	300,000
Zimmer group—common stock	100,000
	$650,000

After Superior National had declined to participate, Great Lakes was invited, and the proposed capitalization was altered to accommodate them:

Great Lakes—8% first-mortgage note* with limited subordination to be amortized by 1968	$300,000
Common stock	30,000
Mid-Continent—8% first mortgage note* with limited subordination to be amortized by 1968	300,000
Common stock	30,000
Zimmer group:—common stock	40,000
	$700,000

* Notes would be secured by land, building, and equipment.

Background of Great Lakes Capital Corporation

Great Lakes had been formed in 1959, when Mr. Cushman, Mr. Parton, and several other investors obtained a charter from the Small Business Administration to take advantage of opportunities offered by the Small Business Investment Act of 1958. In September, 1960, Great Lakes had publicly sold 500,000 shares of common stock, netting it $5 million.

By March, 1961, Great Lakes had invested $1.7 million in four small businesses. The balance of its funds was in liquid assets (see Exhibits 4 and 5 for financial statements of Great Lakes). In Great Lakes' 1961 annual report, Mr. Cushman had told shareholders:

When public participation in the financing of the expansion of Great Lakes Capital Corporation was successfully achieved last September, the first of two objectives we established as early as 1959 was realized. The second was to invest our present capital of approximately $5,550,000 in companies having unusual growth potential, so that the leverage available to the company may be employed as soon as possible.

Reflecting on what he had told the public, Mr. Cushman emphasized the desirability of putting Great Lakes' funds to work. "The public didn't give us their money to invest in Treasury bills. They're looking for capital gains. That's why we've got to invest in good small businesses as soon as possible. Besides, once we've invested our original capital we can get some more money from the SBA at pretty good terms.[1] As I see it, we're responsible both for getting this money to work and also for making the investments good ones. If the opportunities aren't there, we can't let the money burn a hole in our pockets!"

To make possible capital gains, Great Lakes had purchased 30% of the common stock of one of the four companies in which it had invested and had received warrants to purchase from 6%–30% of the common shares of the other three.

Mr. Cushman summed up Great Lakes' brief history, "We didn't have much experience in venture capital when we really got going last year so we've had to feel our way along, trying to work out the best way to make money. So far we've invested in combinations of common stock and debt or debt with detachable warrants. We're still experimenting though, still looking for ways to get more for each dollar we put in.

"As far as a target rate of return—we haven't really picked one yet. Anything would be better than the 3%–4% we get on governments, but then we won't always have this cash. It's pretty hard to pick a goal. When we get some equity in a promising company, our hopes are unlimited. In most cases capital gains seem to be pretty far in the future, though, so we have to depend on interest income for the time being. That should be

---

[1] The Small Business Investment Company Act of 1958 permitted SBIC's to borrow from the SBA an amount equal to the SBIC's capital up to a maximum of $400,000 in the form of 5% subordinated debentures. In addition, SBIC's could obtain a 5% secured loan from the SBA equal to one half of total capital (including subordinated debentures) to a maximum of $4 million.

8%–10%. I guess you could say we demand 8%–10% and then hope our capital gains will be greater than our capital losses."

Present Decision

After reviewing Dr. Zimmer's report once more, Mr. Cushman called Mr. Parton into his office for a report on his trip to Midland.

"Tanner's not selling out because there's anything wrong with the company," Mr. Parton began. "He's just tired of running it. He said he had tried to figure how he could have his sons-in-law take over, but in the end, I think he figured his grandchildren would be better off with cash than with Midland stock.

"What bothers me about the company, though, is their product line. The three big O. E. M. makers of spark plugs are tough competitors. Furthermore, competition is cutthroat in contract precision machining and that's an even bigger part of their business than spark plugs. In that business if demand for your customers' products falls off, there's nothing you can do about it. You can't even look for much new business because it's hard to compete more than one or two hundred miles from home. Then, too, price competition is sharp where the machining business is bid for. Unless Midland can do something no one else can, margins are pretty slim.

"In my way of thinking, any real future for Midland lies in developing new proprietary products which would capitalize on their skills. Their machines are modern and well kept up. What's more, they have some production and engineering people who seem pretty able. However, Bruce Tanner has dominated that company for 30 years. If it's to be turned around, I think someone from outside the company will have to come in and provide some sort of leadership."

Weighing this information on the Midland Spark Plug Company, Mr. Cushman was still unclear what he should conclude. He did know that Mr. McMillan was anxious to hear from him so that the deal could be closed. He worried that if Great Lakes put their decision off any longer, the offer inviting them to participate might be withdrawn. Mr. Cushman was also not sure at that point what Great Lakes' bargaining position was with the other investors.

Exhibit 1
MIDLAND SPARK PLUG COMPANY
REPORT ON MIDLAND SPARK PLUG COMPANY PREPARED FOR INVESTORS BY DR. OTTO ZIMMER

A group headed by Otto F. Zimmer intends to purchase and operate the Midland Spark Plug Company. In that connection the group has requested a $300,000 loan from the Mid-Continent Capital Corporation. This memorandum is intended to furnish a brief description of the company, its financial background, earnings prospects, and related information.

Exhibit 1 (Continued)

Business of Midland Spark Plug Co.

The Midland Spark Plug Co. has been owned by the Tanner family in Midland since 1930. Its business falls in three major categories, each accounting for the following approximate percentage of total sales:

	Percent
Replacement spark plugs	40
Precision screw machine products	35
Custom manufactured screw machine parts	25

The largest individual customer is IBM, for whom custom precision screw machine parts are made.

Mr. Bruce Tanner, the active head of the company, is in his late 60's and in poor health and is therefore eager to sell the business at this time.

Acquiring Group

Dr. Otto F. Zimmer, age 47, who heads the acquiring group, is a chemical engineer, graduate of Lehigh University and Oxford University (which he attended as a Rhodes scholar), formerly an assistant vice president of Westinghouse, originally in charge of purchases and traffic and then assigned to supervise their Mexican operations. More recently he was a group vice president of Olin Mathieson Corporation in charge of chemicals, metals, and fissionable materials. Dr. Zimmer at this time is president of Zimmer, Inc., engaged in industrial management and consultation, and is a director of Consolidated Diesel Electric Corporation, F. H. McGraw Co., and Wagner Baking Corp.

Associated with Dr. Zimmer in the acquisition will be Mr. Dudley Smith, vice president of Revere Equipment Corporation and formerly vice president of Morey Machinery Corporation; Mr. Fred Manners, a senior partner in the certified public accounting firm of Manners & Manners; and Mr. Jesse Cooper, a vice president of Zimmer, Inc.

Active management of the corporation will be under the direction of a former associate of Dr. Zimmer at Olin Mathieson and at Westinghouse who has had broad-gauge experience at top-management levels in metal fabrication and other industrial activities and who, in recent years, has been active chiefly in sales promotion. This gentleman will move to Midland, Michigan, and devote his full time to the affairs of the company. Dr. Zimmer will devote such time as is necessary to effect the rehabilitation and expansion of the company, as will the other principals, along the lines outlined subsequently in this memorandum.

Past Earnings and Potential

As indicated in the following tabulation, the company showed substantial earnings in 1952 and 1953, but since then its reported earnings have been relatively drab. However, the present management and family owners have enjoyed substantial salaries and other benefits. The present head will remain for 2 years at a substantial reduction in salary, and nonproductive family salaries will be terminated. As a result of the foregoing,

Exhibit 1 (Continued)

executive compensation and expenses will be reduced $40,000 to $50,000 from present amounts after providing for compensation to the new president to be installed by the Zimmer group. The present chiefs of the three operating divisions (all competent men between 35 and 45 years of age) will remain.

Year	Gross Sales	Gross Profit		Selling and Administrative	Net Income after Other Income and Other Expenses (before Federal Income Taxes)
		Amount	%		
1952	$2,044,475	$468,309	23.0	$297,257	$167,217
1953	2,305,214	506,999	22.0	316,946	181,217
1954	1,607,565	246,524	15.3	239,923	2,136
1955	1,750,585	246,529	14.1	236,356	1,980
1956	1,767,904	263,932	14.8	229,691	20,345
1957	1,749,954	295,233	16.9	259,652	23,175
1958	1,574,012	263,996	16.7	237,001	23,469
1959	1,801,963	342,658	19.0	265,001	75,308
10 mos. to 10/31/60	1,197,153	309,763	26.9*	194,636	110,883

* Interim figures subject to year end audit (actual gross may be several points less).

The Zimmer group is confident that it can achieve immediate and substantial increases in sales volume of items presently produced. Such increases would be achieved principally by acquiring major new customers, especially for precision screw machine products (notably Westinghouse). Based on expected increases in sales of present items coupled with minimum anticipated economies in executive management costs, the following results are projected for 1961 through 1963. (There may be additional reduction of costs not taken into account; the union has agreed to a discontinuance of the profit-sharing arrangement, and economies in plant operation are expected from tighter supervision.)

Projected:

Year	Gross Sales	Gross Profit		Selling and Administrative	Net Income after Other Income and Other Expenses (before Federal Income Taxes)
		Amount	%		
1961	$2,000,000	$400,000	20	$225,000	$175,000
1962	2,250,000	450,000	20	250,000	200,000
1963	2,750,000	550,000	20	300,000	250,000

Over and above the preceding projections, the new owners plan expansion along these lines:

1. Original equipment market (OEM) sales of spark plugs to be instituted to automotive and marine engine builders.
2. New product lines in marine and instrument fields to be introduced. Presently under contemplation are a variable pitch propeller and a viscosimeter, a device

Exhibit 1 (Continued)

used for detecting the maintenance needs of diesel motors. The company's diversified plant facilities can be utilized to produce many other new items if they are economically attractive. Sales of a fire detection device presently produced by the company will be promoted more aggressively.

Balance Sheet Items

	At Book Values	At Estimated Minimum Liquidation Values	Comments Re: Liquidation Values
Current assets			
Cash....................	$170,939	$ 170,939	
Cash surrender value of life insurance............	199,400	199,400	
Accounts and notes receivable...............	119,921	119,921	To be guaranteed by seller
Inventories..............	204,188	264,188	
Investments.............	19,380	37,000	
Airline deposit...........	425	425	
	$714,253	$ 791,873	
Fixed assets			
Land..................	$ 5,000	$ 65,000	13 acres valued @ $5,000 each
Buildings......$150,439 Less: Accumulated depreciation.. 90,632	59,807	100,000	50,000 sq. ft.: appraisals—replacement value—$439,000 insurable value— 357,000
Machinery and equipment...$718,519 Less: Accumulated depreciation....... 598,855	119,664	300,000	= Minimum forced sale liquidation value: appraisals—replacement value—$1,921,000 insurable value— 1,484,000
Furniture and fixtures, autos, etc.—depreciated..........	7,453	5,000	
	$191,924	$ 470,000	
Prepaid items............	$ 12,125	$ 12,125	
Total assets..........	$918,302	$1,273,998	
Current liabilities......	124,445	124,445	
Net worth...........	$793,857	$1,149,553	Subject to tax on excesses above book value

Acquisition Price and Terms

The purchase price is $950,000. It is presently contemplated that the purchase would take the form of the acquisition of 100% of the assets. The seller will warrant net book assets of at least the October 31, 1960, values with a reduction in price should net book assets be less at closing date, but no upward revision if they have increased. Inasmuch as cash, cash surrender value of life insurance, and investments total over $400,000, the price for the working assets and business is actually $550,000. The Zimmer

Exhibit 1 (Continued)

group recognizes that this may not be a "bargain price," based on earnings in recent years, but feels that it is a very attractive price in the light of the excess of realizable value of assets over purchase price and the excellent earnings potential under new management. The sales and earnings forecast for the next 3 years are regarded as very conservative and are based only on present product lines. The company enjoys an excellent reputation for product quality, which has been maintained by the present management. Sales promotion and new product development, however, have been given no more than minimal attention. The Zimmer group is confident that it can profitably utilize the substantial excess plant capacity to increase sales of present items and to produce related new items. Moreover, it feels that with this physical plant and a vigorous sales organization, an aggressive top management can use Midland as a springboard for the acquisition of other companies.

As indicated above, the purchase price, net of corporate cash and equivalent, is $550,000. The Superior National Bank will assume a mortgage for $250,000.* Thus the acquisition would require $300,000 net, and it is estimated an additional $100,000 would be needed for working capital, closing costs, etc. Of the total of $400,000 needed, the Zimmer group intends to invest $100,000 in capital stock and seeks to borrow $300,000 from Mid-Continent Capital Corporation on 8%, 5-year notes, with amortization beginning quarterly in the second year. Mid-Continent would also receive warrants to purchase one third of the total capital stock.

FR:BL
February 27, 1961

---

* Superior National has since declined to take mortgage.

Exhibit 2

MIDLAND SPARK PLUG COMPANY

APPRAISAL OF MIDLAND'S ASSETS

HARRIS BROTHERS, INC.
624 SUMMER STREET
HARTFORD, CONNECTICUT

March 13, 1961

MID-CONTINENT CAPITAL CORPORATION
3 WEST 4th STREET
CHICAGO 22, ILLINOIS

GENTLEMEN:

We submit the following report as a result of our visit to the Midland Spark Plug Company in Midland, Michigan.

The operation itself is an excellent one. We found all the equipment to be in excellent condition, which is an indication that the maintenance practiced is thorough and good. The automatic screw machines are all late and excellent. As a matter of fact, we believe that there is very little

Exhibit 2 (Continued)

room for improvement in this department. The present machines have in almost every case the speed and capacity of new machines.

The toolroom we consider to be very adequate and very well equipped for the work that is being done in this plant. The tool crib, including the area that is used for tool classification and tool cam storage, is a very fine operation, and we consider it to be above the standards generally found in a job shop operation. The material handling and steel storage department is also very well laid out, and there is good material handling equipment in use in order to do the job that is being done. The inspection equipment we consider also to be of very high caliber.

We have no figures as far as the spark plug production is concerned but do feel that if production were increased materially, it might warrant considering a better or more efficient internal material handling or some type of "automation."

As far as prices are concerned, in figuring the equipment that was used solely in the spark plug division, we considered this at scrap prices or very little above. We feel that under a slow, orderly liquidation the equipment at today's prices would bring approximately $350,000. For an auction-type liquidation, where everything went and no equipment was protected, we feel that this equipment would bring approximately $300,000. All the equipment in the plant was considered, including office equipment, compressors, etc. However, we did not figure into our computation any fluorescent lights, bus duct, or any equipment that we felt might be included with the real estate.

You will note that there is a difference between the two figures given, and this is due mainly to the fact that there are many duplications in the equipment, and in order to realize the highest amount of money from any kind of liquidation, it would be best to try to dispose of the equipment in an orderly fashion. However, we feel that it could be disposed of under an auction type of liquidation but would not bring the same price.

Should you have any question on our inspection or comments or should you desire any further information, please do not hesitate to contact us. We certainly appreciate the opportunity of being of service to you, and trust that if any other situation should develop, we will be called upon again.

Very truly yours,
HARRIS BROTHERS, INC.

JOSEPH B. HARRIS
President

JBH/lb

Exhibit 3

MIDLAND SPARK PLUG COMPANY

PRO FORMA BALANCE SHEET OF FINANCING AS ORIGINALLY CONCEIVED

(Using April, 1961, Figures)

(Dollar Figures in Thousands)

Current assets			Current liabilities		
Cash*	$	93	Accounts & notes payable	$	35
Accounts & notes receivable		134	Accrued payroll		10
Inventories		194	Accrued taxes & insurance		14
Investments and deposits		1	Total current liabilities	$	59
Total current assets	$	422			
			Long-term debt*		
Fixed assets			20-year mortgage†	$	250
			6-year equipment note‡		300
Land and building, net	$	400	Total long-term debt	$	550
Machinery and equipment, net		300			
Other fixed		6	Net worth		
Total fixed assets	$	706	Capital stock	$	100
Prepaid items		10	Revaluation surplus§		429
Total assets	$1,138		Total net worth	$	529
			Total liabilities and net worth	$1,138	

* With participation by Great Lakes the cash account would be increased by $50,000 and long-term debt would consist of $600,000 of 8% first-mortgage notes with limited subordination.

† Secured by land and building.

‡ Amortization starts in the 27th month.

§ Revaluation of land, building, and equipment is based on appraisals giving effect to insurable value on the building, a minimum sales price on land, and liquidation value of equipment.

Exhibit 4

MIDLAND SPARK PLUG COMPANY

BALANCE SHEETS OF GREAT LAKES CAPITAL CORPORATION
(Dollar Figures in Thousands)

March 31	1960	1961
ASSETS		
Current assets		
Cash	$152	$3,815
Accrued interest and other receivables	...	25
Total current assets	$152	$3,841
Investments in small business concerns, at cost	...	1,730
Less: Allowance for losses on investments	...	2
	...	$1,728
Furniture and equipment net of depreciation	...	4
Other assets	1	3
Total assets	$153	$5,576
LIABILITIES		
Accounts payable	$...	$ 2
Accrued liabilities	...	21
Total liabilities	...	$ 23
EQUITY		
Common stock, $1 par	$ 15	$ 560
Paid-in surplus	136	4,991
Earned surplus	2	2
Total equity	$153	$5,553
Total liabilities and equity	$153	$5,576

Exhibit 5

MIDLAND SPARK PLUG COMPANY

INCOME STATEMENTS OF GREAT LAKES CAPITAL CORPORATION
(Dollar Figures in Thousands)

Years Ended March 31	1960	1961
Interest income	$ 3	$ 81
Expenses		
Officers' salaries	$...	$ 17
Other expenses	1	62
Total expenses	$ 1	$ 79
Operating income	$ 2	$ 2
Provision for losses on investments	...	2
Net income	$ 2	$...

Case 42

Lestoil Products, Inc.

In early June, 1960, Mr. John Bolten, Sr., and Mr. Daniel E. Hogan, Jr., members of the executive committee of Lestoil Products, Inc., were studying the details of a proposed offering of the company's capital stock, which was to be traded over the counter. In light of the company's past record, its potential future earnings, and the terms of the issue, they were confident that the proposed stock would be sold with little difficulty. In this final analysis of the offering, they concentrated particularly on the price of the stock to the public. They believed that the offering price would certainly be attractive. They thought, however, that the offering was perhaps underpriced and questioned whether the company should offer fewer units at a higher price to raise the necessary funds.

Company Background

Lestoil Products, Inc., was organized in the spring of 1960 for the purpose of purchasing Adell Chemical Company, Inc.; its wholly owned advertising affiliate, Jackson Associates, Inc.; and its wholly owned real estate subsidiary, J.L.B. Realty Trust. Adell Chemical Company had been organized in 1933 by Mr. Jacob L. Barowsky to manufacture and sell a synthetic liquid detergent. Until 1954, sales had been made primarily to commercial laundries and the paper and textile industries. In that year the Adell Company brought its detergent to the attention of the household trade through spot television advertising. The company later added several other items, including a concentrated, premeasured dry bleach sealed in individual, water-soluble packets. The two principal products, the detergent and the bleach, were widely advertised and known under the trade names of "Lestoil" and "Lestare." The company's offices and manufacturing facilities were located in Holyoke, Massachusetts. Financial data for Lestoil Products' predecessor are presented in Exhibits 1 and 2.

Acquisition of Adell Chemical Company, Inc.

In early 1960 Mr. Barowsky, the president and founder of Adell Chemical Company, decided to find a buyer for the company. He turned down several offers. One company, for instance, offered $8 million in its own stock and $4 million in cash, but Mr. Barowsky wanted a cash sale. Another company offered $7 million in cash, but Mr. Barowsky thought that this amount was not enough. Mr. Samuel S. Dennis III, a member of the law firm of Hale and Dorr of Boston, Massachusetts, who had been counsel to the Adell Company, had been attempting to aid Mr. Barowsky in finding a buyer.

Mr. Dennis was also associated with a family group in Andover, Massachusetts, headed by Mr. Bolten, Sr., and Mr. Hogan, respectively chairman of the board and president of the Standard International Corporation. This corporation was a closely held investment company with substantial interests in a number of corporations. During the time that Mr. Dennis was trying to locate a buyer for Adell Chemical Company, he, Mr. Bolten, and Mr. Hogan concluded that perhaps a group associated with Standard International would find it worthwhile to buy the company. Recognizing a possible conflict of interest, Mr. Dennis immediately notified Mr. Barowsky that he should obtain new legal counsel to represent him in this transaction.

As the result of further negotiations a contract, dated March 25, 1960, was entered into between Adell Chemical Company and its stockholders as sellers and Standard International Corporation and Mr. Hogan, acting for himself and as agent for Mr. John Bolten, Sr., Mr. John Bolten, Jr., and Mr. Dennis, as purchasers. Lestoil Products, Inc., was formed subsequently by the purchasing group to become the acquiring corporation.

Lestoil Products agreed to pay the sellers a cash price of $8 million and also agreed to assume a conditional liability to pay an additional sum in the maximum amount of $4 million. Payments on the conditional obligation were required to be made annually but only to the extent of one half of annual net profits in excess of $1,500,000 after income taxes. The obligation would expire on October 31, 1969, whether or not the maximum amount had been paid in full.

The purchase and sale agreement called for a deposit of $150,000 as option money and gave the purchasing group 90 days to complete the transaction. This sum was to be forfeited as damages in the event that the transaction was not completed within this period. The Standard International Corporation advanced the option money. In addition, employment contracts were made with three of the former officers for 5 years, beginning on June 1, 1960, and the following salary schedule had been established.

	First Year	Annually, Last 4 Years
Jacob L. Barowsky	$100,000	$ 50,000
Isaac L. Eskenasy	30,000	30,000
Aaron L. Kingsberg	20,000	20,000
	$150,000	$100,000

These officers had received compensation at a higher rate in recent years.

Mr. Hogan had always kept a business diary. The entries in the spring of 1960 included a chronological account of the important dates and events in connection with the acquisition of Adell Chemical Company. A summary of these entries from February 1 to March 25 is given below:

1960

Monday, February 1—In Palm Beach with Sam Dennis. He called the president of a chemical company in New York and told him about the availability of Adell Chemical and suggested that his company consider the possibility of adding it as one of their divisions.

Friday, March 4—While in New York on another matter with Mr. Dennis, we decided to visit the president of the chemical company personally and tell him the latest news about Adell Chemical and give him the reasons why his company should buy it, etc. En route to Boston the next day, the thought occurred to us that maybe we could put together a group or a transaction that would be attractive to all concerned, and where Standard International and its stockholders could end up with a fairly good-sized piece of the Adell equity.

Tuesday, March 8—Visit to Boston and preliminary discussions with Mr. William L. Brown, vice president of the First National Bank of Boston, regarding interim financing.

Wednesday, March 9—Visit to Holyoke and preliminary discussion with Mr. and Mrs. Barowsky.

Thursday, March 10—Conferences in Boston regarding the amount and terms of the loan which the bank was willing to give us to finance the purchase.

[At this early stage of negotiations the bank indicated a willingness to provide $7–$8 million in "turnaround money" at an interest rate of 5½%. The stocks of Lestoil Products and of Standard International were to be pledged as security.]

Friday, March 11—Conferences in Boston with law firm of Hale and Dorr to go over the preliminary drafts of the proposed employment contract for the owners of Adell Chemical.

Saturday, March 12—Skiing at Mittersill and met Mr. [X] of a law firm in New York with contacts which might be helpful in a public underwriting.

Monday, March 14—Conferences at Holyoke with Mr. and Mrs. Barowsky.

Tuesday, March 15—Conference at the First National Bank of Boston with the senior loan officer.

Wednesday, March 16—Conference at Andover with Gale Deam and

Charles McCarthy, who would be the vice presidents for manufacturing and sales in the new Lestoil organization. Aaron Kingsberg of Adell phoned to emphasize the fact that we would have to show them definitely where the $8 million is coming from fairly soon.

Thursday, March 17—With McCarthy, Deam, and Sol Sackell, who will be in charge of advertising activities, to Holyoke for more negotiations regarding the purchase and sale contract.

Friday, March 18—In Andover and Boston, going over the various projections involved in paying off the interim bank loan.

Sunday, March 20—Conversations with S. Dennis about various financing alternatives.

Monday, March 21—In New Hampshire, conversations with Mr. [M] regarding the possibility of his firm's joining in an underwriting group re: Lestoil Products, Inc.

Tuesday, March 22—In Jackson, New Hampshire, more conversations with Mr. [M].

Wednesday, March 23—In New York City, initial conferences with institutional lenders regarding the possibility of their putting up $3–$4 million of subordinated funds.

Thursday, March 24—In Andover, conversations with Mr. Bolten, Sr. and Mr. Bolten, Jr., regarding progress of the Lestoil situation.

Friday, March 25—Signing of purchase and sale agreement of Adell Chemical.

Financing the Acquisition

The formal closing of the purchase and sale transaction took place on May 31, 1960, when Lestoil Products paid $8 million in cash to the sellers. It had raised the necessary funds to finance the acquisition of Adell Chemical Company in the following manner:

Sale of Lestoil common stock at 60 cents a share:

Purchasers	Shares	Amount
Standard International Corporation	249,406	
John Bolten, Sr.	396,599	
John Bolten, Jr.	396,598	
Daniel E. Hogan, Jr.	396,599	
Samuel S. Dennis, III	396,598	
Total	1,835,800	$1,101,480
Loan to Lestoil Products from the First National Bank of Boston on a demand promissory note		6,900,000
		$8,001,480

The bank loan was a temporary one, which had been granted to serve only as "turnaround money" while Lestoil Products raised permanent capital to finance the acquisition. The purchasers had spent the past 2 months working out the details of the permanent financing.

As one part of the financing, on May 27, 1960, the company received letters of commitment from representatives of institutional investors (several pension funds) stating their intention to purchase $3,200,000 principal amount of the company's 6¼% notes due in 1970, together with detachable and transferable 10-year warrants, protected against dilution, for the purchase of a total of 339,200 shares of common stock at $7.50 a share.[1] The agreement provided that the obligation of the institutional lenders was conditional on the sale by Lestoil Products to the public of certain of its equity securities as outlined in management's proposal for a public offering to raise approximately $4 million. Any excess over the $6,900,000 needed to repay the bank loan was to be used for general corporate purposes.

Important provisions of the loan agreement relating to the 6¼% notes to be purchased by the institutional lenders were as follows: Annual instalments on principal were payable in the amount of $300,000. The notes were redeemable for the first 2 years at a premium of 10%; the premium would be 4% for the third year, and then would diminish annually at the rate of 1% a year until 1966, after which date the notes would be redeemable at par. The company could not create liens or mortgages other than for the purpose of financing a maximum of 70% of plant and equipment purchases. It was required to maintain a minimum net working capital balance of $1,200,000 during the period July 1, 1961–June 30, 1962, and $1,500,000 after June 30, 1962. It was prohibited from making distributions on account of the common stock until such time and also thereafter if, as a result, consolidated net working capital would be less than $2,500,000. The notes were subordinated to bank loans up to a maximum of $3 million, which under certain circumstances could be increased to a maximum of $5 million.

The Public Offering of Equity Securities

The major part of the funds needed were to be raised by a public offering of equity securities. Mr. Hogan and a representative of one of the two underwriting firms involved had conceived a plan that they believed would aid in assuring the success of the offering. The securities designed for the public sale were to be split into class A shares and common shares and sold in units consisting of one common share and one class A share. Certificates representing units were to be issued to purchasers. On January 2, 1961, the shares of class A and common stock composing a unit would become separately transferable, and certificates representing units would become exchangeable for separate certificates for shares of class A and common stock.

A complex of factors actually determined the size and price of the offering. The offerors naturally wanted the offering to be successful and hoped, therefore, that no questions would be raised regarding its attractiveness. At the same time, they wanted to hold dilution of their

---

[1] When the financing was completed, 339,200 shares would be approximately 14% of the common stock before conversion of the class A shares, and approximately 11% after conversion.

equity within reasonable limits. They knew that Mr. Barowsky had talked earlier with several investment banking houses regarding the possibility of selling the stock of Adell Chemical Company publicly. These discussions had indicated some interest on the part of investment bankers in underwriting such an issue at a price-earnings ratio of 15/1. Thus, from the start, the Standard International group had based its thinking on a price-earnings ratio in this range.

In preliminary talks with representatives of underwriting firms, an offering of only one class of common stock had been proposed. After a review of the situation the underwriters replied that, in their opinion, the company's earnings were not sufficiently stable to jusitfy a 15/1 price-earnings ratio on a straight common issue. The package of two classes of stock was then conceived and decided upon, one class bearing a fixed and cumulative preferred dividend obligation, to add the appeal of an assured return to the offering for the investing public. As an additional capital gains incentive, the class A stock would be made convertible into common stock at any time prior to redemption and within a limited time after any call for redemption.

On the basis of earnings after taxes in the year ended October 31, 1959, adjusted to allow for $6\frac{1}{4}\%$ interest payments on the notes to be purchased by institutional lenders, it was estimated that earnings after interest and taxes in future years were likely to be at least $1 million. The offerors and underwriters agreed that a fixed dividend commitment on class A stock should be covered a minimum of four times if it and the common stock were to be looked on with favor by investors. A computation revealed that it would be possible to maintain this coverage and still offer as much as a 6% return on the total funds to be raised through the offering ($4 million).

With this information at hand, specific details of the offering were "backed into." The conversion ratio of the class A stock was set at two shares of common stock for each share of class A, and a price of $14.40 and 60 cents, respectively ($15 a unit), was placed on the class A and common shares on a total offering of 275,000 units—primarily on the following basis: It was determined that a fair offering price for the common shares would be the same as the Standard International group had paid for their shares, namely, 60 cents. The price and conversion ratio of the class A stock were then determined at the amount per share that would give a price-earnings ratio of approximately 15/1 on the whole package, allowing for probable future dilution from the warrants issued to institutional investors. This automatically gave an acceptable result in terms of equity dilution on the basis of a $4 million offering. The preferred dividend was then determined at 90 cents, to give a 6% plus return on the class A shares. Other factors involved in setting the conversion privilege at two shares of common for each share of class A were (1) to give additional desirability to the offering and (2) to be substantially consistent with the $7.50 warrant price to institutional investors.

	Shares of Common Stock	Percentage
Owned by promoting group	1,835,800	61.2
Reserved for exercise of warrants	339,200	11.3
Sold to public (275,000 units):		
Common stock	275,000	9.2
Reserved for conversion of class A shares	550,000	18.3
Total	3,000,000	100.0

Earnings for year ended October 31, 1959 (adjusted)	$1,000,000
Total shares of common stock to be outstanding	3,000,000
Earnings per share	$ 0.333
Offering price per unit	$ 15.00
Effective cost to public per share of common stock	$ 5.00
Effective price-earnings ratio (after dilution)	15/1

Both the Standard International group and the underwriters were confident that this combination would make an attractive package for sale to the public.[2]

The "red-herring" prospectus[3] for the public offering was completed early in June, 1960. Other provisions of the two classes of stock were described as follows: A provision was included for adjustment of the conversion ratio to prevent dilution of the rights of class A shareholders. The class A stock had a liquidation and redemption value of $15 a share. No dividends could be paid on the common stock while any shares of class A stock were outstanding, and the prospectus stated that no dividends on the common stock should be expected in the near future. Management intended to retain all earnings until a substantial amount of working capital had been accumulated. The common shares and the class A shares were entitled to one vote each and would vote together as a single class except where the separate consent of class A shares was required.

Conferences with underwriters indicated an underwriting commission

---

[2] Exhibit 3 presents selected data on certain other companies, and Exhibit 4 gives data from *Moody's Industrial Stock Averages.*

[3] Eric L. Kohler, *A Dictionary for Accountants* (2d ed.; Englewood Cliffs, N.J.: Prentice-Hall, Inc., 1957), p. 410, defines *red-herring prospectus* as follows: "An announcement and description of an anticipated issue of securities, given restricted circulation during the 'waiting' period of 20 days or other specified period between the filing of a registration statement with the U.S. Securities and Exchange Commission and the effective date of the statement. It generally takes the form of the final prospectus except that the offering price, commissions to dealers, and other data dependent on price are omitted; also emblazoned across each page is an inscription printed in red, stating that the document is not an offer to sell or the solicitation of an offer to buy and that neither kind of offer may be made until the registration statement has become effective."

of 8%. Net proceeds to the company would therefore amount to $3,795,000. The effects of the proposed financing on the company's balance sheet and earnings statements are shown in the pro forma financial statements presented as Exhibits 5 and 6.

Mr. Hogan's business diary noted the development of the plans for the permanent financing:

Saturday, March 26—Conference in New York City with underwriters' representatives re: first studies as to the various methods that could be used in the Lestoil underwriting. We first came up with the possibility of the class A and common stocks package at this conference.

Sunday, March 27—More conferences, New York City—conversations with Sam Dennis regarding the present proposal for the packaged security.

Monday, March 28—Additional conferences in New York City with representatives of the two underwriting firms.

Tuesday, March 29—We are now in effect running Lestoil. Held conferences with McCarthy, Deam, and others regarding immediate steps that should be taken to strengthen the business.

Wednesday, March 30—Conferences with the Barowskys at Holyoke on what is needed in Lestoil.

Friday, April 1—Finalized the arrangements with underwriters.

Monday, April 4—Conferences in New York with institutional lenders to discuss the intermediate financing plans and subordinated notes.

Tuesday, April 5—At Holyoke planning Lestoil strategy.

Wednesday, April 6—Left Holyoke with Mr. Barowsky, to packaging show in Atlantic City.

Thursday, April 7—Conference in New York City with a chemical company regarding possibility of bringing out a liquid starch made from their synthetic resins.

Tuesday, April 12—Picked up representatives of the pension funds in Morristown, New Jersey, and flew them to Lestoil at Holyoke for the day. [One of the corporations controlled by Standard International owned an airplane as its only asset. Mr. Hogan held a pilot's license and often flew the plane on such trips.]

Thursday, April 14—Conferences in Boston regarding the closing of the Lestoil deal and the details of the underwriting.

Friday, April 15—In Andover and Boston, discussing details of financing with Messrs. Bolten, Senior and Junior. Then a luncheon conference with firm of Hale and Dorr to begin giving them the background work for the registration statement.

Monday, April 18—On the phone most of the day with representatives of pension funds trying to work out the details of their financing versus the underwriting. Pension funds thought the underwriters' deal was too rich, and the underwriters felt that the pension funds were asking for too much. [The institutional lenders thought that the underwriters were making the package more attractive than necessary to raise $4 million. The underwriters thought that the institutional lenders were getting too many warrants for purchase of stock at $7.50 a share.]

Tuesday, April 19—Writing up the brochure for consideration by the pension funds committees to help push the financing of the subordinated notes.

Thursday, April 21—Conferences in Boston with the underwriter. Then meeting with president of [XYZ Company]. He was interested in buying Lestoil. We had many feelers from various companies wanting to know if we would like to turn over our deal to them. [Mr. Hogan did not investigate any of these offers in any depth.]

Friday, April 22—Conferences with underwriter in Boston.

Saturday and Sunday, April 23 and 24—Revising the brochure for the underwriters and the pension fund.

April 25–May 31—A lot of activity on the promotions at Lestoil, details of the underwriting, preparing the details for the SEC, etc.

Tuesday, May 31—We had the closing at The First National Bank of Boston.

Future Prospects

Lestoil Products maintained a research department to study production methods, quality controls, and development of new products by applying to practical uses current discoveries and developments in chemical science. The management intended to place the emphasis almost entirely on development and improvement of discoveries made by others in the field, rather than emphasizing basic research. The policy of the company would be to add new items for family and household use to its product line if and when suitable products were developed and proved. Management's objective was to develop and market companion products to Lestoil and Lestare, and thus offer a "family" of Lestoil products to the consumer.

In 1959 some of the major soap and detergent companies had introduced new brands of heavy-duty liquid detergents, accompanied by extensive television advertising and other unusually intensive methods of sales promotion. Partly as a result of this competition, sales of Lestoil had declined since September, 1959. Industry sales were also seasonally lower during the winter months. The new owners believed, however, that no permanent or continuing adverse trends in sales volume were necessarily indicated. In fact, they thought that a seasonal increase in industry sales, improvements in sales management, rapidly increasing sales of Lestare, and plans to advertise and market company products in the western and southwestern parts of the United States in the immediate future would push sales volumes to new highs. They felt that company profits before taxes during the calendar year 1960 could reasonably be expected to reach a level of $3 million, and that the before-tax profits for 1961 were likely to show an increase over the 1960 level. In their opinion, existing plant facilities would be adequate for some time. The company's net cash inflow during the next few years would therefore be substantial.

At this time the Standard International group foresaw no need for additional common stock issues in the future. In fact, they had stated that company policy would be to avoid any such dilution if at all possible. Acquisitions by or additions to Lestoil Products would be made with cash and new debt, with sale of equity only as a last resort.

Exhibit 1

LESTOIL PRODUCTS, INC.

CONSOLIDATED STATEMENT OF FINANCIAL CONDITION OF
ADELL CHEMICAL COMPANY, INC., AND SUBSIDIARIES
ON MARCH 31, 1960

(Dollar Figures in Thousands)

ASSETS

Current assets:

Cash and U.S. Treasury bills	$1,614	
Accounts receivable	1,605	
Inventories (at lower of cost or market)	1,304	
Other	65	
Total current assets		$4,588
Fixed assets (net)		3,415
Other assets		184
Total assets		$8,187

LIABILITIES AND CAPITAL

Current liabilities:

Notes payable (banks)	$1,140	
Other	2,465	
Total current liabilities		$3,605
Noncurrent liabilities*		1
Capital stock and retained earnings		4,581
Total liabilities and capital		$8,187

* Commitments for noncancelable media advertising for a three-month period amounted to approximately $1,500,000.

Exhibit 2

LESTOIL PRODUCTS, INC.

CONSOLIDATED STATEMENTS OF INCOME AND EXPENSE OF ADELL CHEMICAL COMPANY, INC., AND SUBSIDIARIES, 1955–60

(Dollar Figures in Thousands)

	Year Ended October 31					Five Months Ended March 31	
	1955	1956	1957	1958	1959	1959	1960
Net sales	$474	$1,641	$7,220	$19,945	$22,467	$9,158	$8,719
Cost of sales*	218	625	2,553	7,319	8,731	3,399	3,959
Gross profit	$256	$1,016	$4,667	$12,626	$13,736	$5,759	$4,760
Advertising expense	$125	$ 497	$2,033	$ 6,008	$ 9,562	$3,648	$3,027
Selling, general, and administrative expenses	100	191	650	1,666	1,974	859	825
	$225	$ 688	$2,683	$ 7,674	$11,536	$4,507	$3,852
Net operating income	$ 31	$ 328	$1,984	$ 4,952	$ 2,200	$1,252	$ 908
Other income (expense):							
Interest income	$.....	$.....	$ 6	$ 9	$ 7	$ 6	$ 5
Miscellaneous	(2)	5	14	80	113	41	26
Interest expense		(1)	(3)	(14)	(26)	(7)	(24)
	$ (2)	$ 4	$ 17	$ 75	$ 94	$ 40	$ 7
Net income before taxes	$ 29	$ 332	$2,001	$ 5,027	$ 2,294	$1,292	$ 915
Provision for federal and state income taxes	10	178	1,091	2,763	1,226	695	499
Net Income	$ 19	$ 154	$ 910	$ 2,264	$ 1,068	$ 597	$ 416

* Depreciation charges included:

Year ended October 31:
- 1955 ... n.a.
- 1956 ... n.a.
- 1957 ... $ 49
- 1958 ... 192
- 1959 ... 318

Five months ended March 31:
- 1959 ... n.a.
- 1960 ... $168

Exhibit 3

LESTOIL PRODUCTS, INC.

SELECTED DATA ON CERTAIN COMPANIES IN THE SAME AND RELATED FIELDS OF BUSINESS

	Where Traded	Price-Earnings Ratios (1)*	Price-Earnings Ratios (2)†	Cash Dividend Yield on Common Stock, 1959‡	Sales Year Ended	Sales Amount (Millions)	Date	Capitalization Long-Term Debt	Capitalization Preferred Stock	Capitalization Common Stock and Surplus
Lestoil Products Inc. (pro forma)	O.C.	15§		6.0%#	10/31/59	$22.5	3/31/60	39.5%	45.0%	15.5%
Purex Corporation, Ltd.	O.C.	20	18	2.4%	6/30/59	$71.4	6/30/59	39.1%	.....	60.9%
Manufactures and sells bleaches, disinfectants, synthetic detergents, ammonia, and other soaps, cleaners, and toiletries. Products are sold under a variety of trade names. Company was established in year 1927.										
Procter & Gamble Company	NYSE	20	24	2.7%	6/30/59	$1,368.5	6/30/59	14.7%	0.3%	85.0%
Constitutes the largest factor in the domestic soap industry. Manufactures and sells soap, toothpaste, synthetic detergents, household cleansers, glycerine, cooking fats, peanut butter, cake mixes, and a variety of other products. Its products are marketed under numerous trade names. Company was established in year 1905.										
Stepan Chemical Company	O.C.	21	18	0.0%	12/31/59	$19.4	12/31/59	36.2%	.....	63.8%
Manufactures organic chemicals which are sold primarily to processors and industrial users. Products include liquid detergents, chemicals for cosmetics, emulsifiers, insecticides, flavoring compounds, liquid fertilizers, and others. Company was established in year 1932.										
Wyandotte Chemical Corporation	O.C.	20	28	1.9%	12/31/59	$93.9	12/31/59	10.1%	14.8%	75.1%
Produces cleansing products, sanitizing products, soda ash, caustic soda, chlorine, glycols, coke, cement, and other products. Sales are made primarily to industrial users. The existing company was incorporated in year 1942.										
Witco Chemical Company, Inc.	O.C.	17	11	2.5%	12/31/59	$51.2	12/31/59	.....	.....	100.0%
Produces chemicals, synthetic detergents, metallic stearates, emulsifiers, plasticizers, asphalts, and other products. Sales are made largely to industrial users. Company was formed in year 1920.										

* Bid prices (or closing prices) on December 31, 1959, divided by earnings for year ended December 31, 1959.
† Bid prices (or closing prices) on May 31, 1960, divided by earnings for quarter ended March 31, 1960, on an annual basis.
‡ Annual cash dividend rate, divided by average of high and low market prices for the year.
§ Effective price/earnings ratio (after dilution) based on effective offering price per share of common stock ($5.00) divided by earnings for year ended October 31, 1959.
# Yield on offering price of unit.
SOURCE OF BASIC DATA: Moody's Industrials.

Exhibit 4

LESTOIL PRODUCTS, INC.

SELECTED DATA FROM "MOODY'S INDUSTRIAL STOCK AVERAGES"
MOODY'S INDUSTRIAL STOCK AVERAGES—
PRICE-EARNINGS RATIOS*

1955	12
1956	14
1957	14
1958	18
1959	19

* Moody's annual composite weighted average prices, divided by composite weighted average earnings for corresponding years (125 common stocks).

MOODY'S PREFERRED STOCK YIELD AVERAGES

	10 Medium-Grade Industrials	*10 Speculative-Grade Industrials*
1959	4.99%	5.58%
1960:		
January	5.23	5.78
February	5.22	5.72
March	5.21	5.79
April	5.25	5.80

Exhibit 5

LESTOIL PRODUCTS, INC.

PRO FORMA BALANCE SHEET GIVING EFFECT TO THE PROPOSED FINANCING
AS IF THE ACQUISITION TRANSACTION HAD BEEN COMPLETED
ON MARCH 31, 1960

(Dollar Figures in Thousands)

ASSETS

Current assets:

Cash and U.S. Treasury bills	$1,889	
Accounts receivable	1,605	
Inventories (at lower of cost or market)*	1,374	
Other*	58	
Total current assets		$ 4,926
Fixed assets (net)*		4,077
Other assets†		2,760
Total assets		$11,763

LIABILITIES AND CAPITAL

Current liabilities:

Notes payable (bank)	$1,140	
Other‡	2,525	
Total current liabilities		$ 3,665
Noncurrent liabilities:		
6¼% notes		3,200
Other§		1
Capital stock:		
Class A (convertible, no par value; 275,000 shares)	$3,644	
Common stock (50¢ par value; 2,110,800 shares)	1,055	
		4,699
Capital paid in in excess of par value of common stock		198
Total liabilities and capital		$11,763

* Reflects adjustments made on the basis of values as determined by the new management and supported by independent appraisal.

† Reflects excess of cost of total assets over the amount allocated to tangible assets. Payments on the $4 million conditional liability were to be allocated to intangible assets also.

‡ Reflects adjustment for estimated organization and financing charges in connection with acquisition transaction.

§ Commitments for noncancelable media advertising for a three-month period amounted to approximately $1,500,000.

Exhibit 6

LESTOIL PRODUCTS, INC.

PRO FORMA EARNINGS AS IF THE ACQUISITION TRANSACTION HAD BEEN EFFECTIVE
DURING THE PERIODS COVERED

(Dollar Figures in Thousands)

	Years Ended October 31		Five Months Ended March 31,
	1958	1959	1960
Net income after taxes (as reported)	$2,264	$1,068	$ 416
Pro forma adjustments:			
Interest on 6¼% notes	$ (200)	$ (200)	$ (83)
Amortization of estimated organization and financing expenses	(12)	(12)	(5)
Changes in depreciation charges resulting from revaluation of assets and change in method*	24	54	58
Estimated reduction in income taxes resulting from additional expenses	104	87	16
	$ (84)	$ (71)	$ (14)
Pro forma net income after taxes	$2,180	$ 997	$ 402
Dividends on 275,000 Class A shares	$ 248	$ 248	$ 103
Pro forma net income on common stock	$1,932	$ 749	$ 299
Pro forma net income per share—based on 2,110,800 common shares	$ 0.92	$ 0.35	$0.14

* Lestoil Products, Inc., would not be permitted to use accelerated methods used by the predecessor company.

Case 43

Head Ski Company, Inc.

In LATE February, 1960, Mr. Thomas Long, a partner in the Baltimore investment banking firm of Robert Garrett & Sons,[1] was nearing a decision on the price at which Robert Garrett would offer to underwrite and sell publicly a certain number of shares of the common stock of the Head Ski Company (HEAD). Since December, 1959, Mr. Long had been negotiating with Mr. Howard Head, president and chief stockholder of HEAD, in an attempt to arrive at the most suitable plan for the first public offering of that company's stock. The proposed offering would total approximately $280,000. Since the size of the offering was less than $300,000, HEAD would be exempt from a complete and costly Securities and Exchange Commission registration requirement. The company desired to raise approximately $162,000 in net proceeds (after underwriting commissions) to supplement existing working capital. In addition, certain selling stockholders wished to raise $90,000 in net proceeds through a secondary offering; thus, the proposed new issue would include both a corporate and a secondary offering of HEAD's common stock. It was Mr. Long's responsibility to determine the number of new shares to be issued by the company, the number of shares to be sold by the selling stockholders, and the price at which Robert Garrett & Sons would be willing to underwrite and offer to the public the Head Company stock.

The Company

The Head Ski Company was founded in Baltimore, Maryland, in 1947 by Mr. Howard Head, then 32 years old, and was operated as an individual proprietorship until 1953. Between 1947 and 1950 Mr. Head concentrated on the development of a ski radically different from the traditional hickory skis in wide use at that time. By 1950 the Head ski had been developed—a composite design of aluminum alloy, plastic,

---

[1] In this case, names of officers of Robert Garrett & Sons have been disguised.

steel, and wood. Head skis were placed on the market during the 1950 winter skiing season. Their acceptance was immediate; sales rose from 300 pairs in the 1950–51 skiing season to 8,000 pairs in 1954–55 and 33,000 in 1958–59. During this period the demand for Head skis consistently outstripped the company's production capabilities. By 1959 Head skis had developed a wide reputation in the United States, Canada, and abroad as strong, lightweight, and easily maneuverable skis, suitable for experts as well as beginners. Mr. Head estimated that sales during the 1959–60 season would approximate 40,000 pairs of skis.

HEAD currently manufactured and sold two models—the "Standard," retailed at $89.50, and the "Vector," which sold for $107.50. The Vector model was introduced in 1959 for use by more experienced skiers. With the increased interest in racing arising out of the 1960 Winter Olympics, HEAD accelerated its work on the development of an international racing ski. Three Olympic skiers visited the company after the winter games to assist on this project and won several international races on Head skis late in the 1960 skiing season. Mr. Head thought that a product line which included a racing ski as well as the Standard and Vector models would enable Head to serve most classes of skiers.

Currently, the company employed 140 people in a new 27,000-square-foot plant constructed in 1959 near Baltimore; the new facilities would accommodate an annual production level of up to 160,000 pairs of skis. Although Mr. Head had designed the original Head ski, the company currently employed six engineers and technicians who assisted Mr. Head in the research and development of new products and in refinement of existing products. Sixty-five percent of present sales were made in the United States and Canada through 500 franchised dealers selected for their wide experience in the sale of skis and ski equipment. One distributor in Switzerland accounted for 30% of HEAD's total sales; this dealer had established subdistributorships for sales throughout Western Europe. The remaining 5% of the company's sales were to other countries outside of Europe and North America. HEAD rigidly enforced the retail prices on its Standard and Vector model skis in order to eliminate the possible unfavorable aspects of price cutting on its product line.

The competition for Head skis came from the manufacturers of traditional hickory skis and the makers of other metal-plastic composite skis. Traditional hickory skis had for many years enjoyed popularity in the inexpensive ski field and as special-purpose racing skis. The volume of sales achieved by HEAD, however, indicated that the Head design was continuing to overtake major parts of the hickory ski market. The success of the Head design had also promoted the establishment of a number of manufacturers of metal-plastic composite skis both in the United States and abroad. Mr. Head had patented certain aspects of the Head ski, but his patent protection could not prevent the development of slightly different competitive designs. This competition, however, had not prevented

HEAD from selling all the skis it could produce prior to the move to its new plant in 1959. Mr. Head estimated that the second largest metal ski manufacturer produced approximately 20% of HEAD's volume, and that the volume of all such manufacturers was approximately 50% of that of HEAD.

Financial History

The company was incorporated in 1953; at that time Mr. Head was issued 900 shares of cumulative preferred stock and 825 shares of common stock in exchange for assets valued at $90,825. Later in 1953 the requirements for additional working capital to finance expanding production levels resulted in the addition of $60,075 in equity funds through the private sale of 600 shares of cumulative preferred stock and 675 shares of common. In 1955, $7,500 was raised through the private sale of 50 shares of cumulative preferred stock and a like amount of common stock. These capital additions represented the extent of equity financing in HEAD's growth from 1947 to early 1960. As of April 25, 1959, HEAD's capital stock consisted of 1,550 shares of cumulative preferred and 1,550 shares of common stock. Changes in the company's capital accounts between April, 1959, and January, 1960, reflected the retirement of the preferred with accumulated dividends and the no par value common stock in exchange for new shares of $1.50 par value common stock (Exhibit 1). Currently, Mr. Head owned 57.6% of HEAD's outstanding common stock.

Other than by the additions to equity capital between 1953 and 1955, HEAD's growth had been financed entirely out of retained earnings and short-term bank borrowings. By the nature of its business, HEAD's sales and heavy shipments out of inventory began in August and September, reached peak levels in October and November, and declined gradually to the end of its shipping season in early March. In the past a substantial portion of the company's seasonal cash requirements had been provided through an unsecured line of credit from a Baltimore bank. Borrowing normally began in August, peaked in December, and declined thereafter to complete pay-out by the end of March. Because of its rapid growth in sales, HEAD's credit line had increased each year since 1953 and reached a high of $450,000 in December, 1959; at that time the company's accounts receivable totaled $690,000 and inventories $263,000.

With sales showing no tendency to level off, Mr. Head anticipated that the company's need for bank credit would continue to increase. Earnings retention during the next few years appeared insufficient to meet expected increases in working capital requirements, and he estimated that the company would require credit accommodations of between $700,000 and $750,000 within the next 2 or 3 years. In early December, 1959, when HEAD's borrowing had reached $450,000, its bank had stated that that level represented the reasonable maximum credit the bank would be willing to extend on the basis of the company's net worth. HEAD's net worth was then slightly over $500,000, and the bank had been following a policy of placing an upper limit on the company's credit of slightly less than its net worth. At that time HEAD's banker suggested that additional equity capital would not only strengthen the company's working capital position but also provide a larger equity base, and one upon which the bank would be willing to increase its maximum credit line to the company.

The Proposed Common Stock Offering

It was on the basis of the preceding considerations that Mr. Head approached Mr. Long of Robert Garrett & Sons early in December, 1959. The two men quickly agreed that the sale of common stock would provide the most practical method of raising additional capital. The alternative of raising debt capital was clearly undesirable in view of HEAD's seasonal borrowing requirements and was considered inappropriate in view of the need for larger amounts of permanent capital. Mr. Head was also averse to selling preferred stock, since the company had just recently retired the 1,550 shares of preferred that had been outstanding since 1956. Mr. Head was receptive to Mr. Long's suggestion that a public offering of HEAD's stock would satisfy the objectives of raising new capital and would also facilitate, for the first time, a trading market in the company's stock. The two previous stock sales, in 1953 and 1955, had been private sales to a limited number of investors who had not traded actively in the stock. Between December, 1959, and February, 1960, negotiations between Mr. Head and Mr. Long were continued on the assumption that HEAD's new capital would be raised through a public stock offering underwritten by Robert Garrett & Sons.

A preliminary consideration in establishing the size of the proposed offering was the amount of capital that HEAD would need in order to raise its borrowing capacity from $450,000 to the $700,000–$750,000 range. The company's net worth of $534,000 on January 2, 1960 (Exhibits 2 and 5) reflected an addition to retained earnings from net profits since April 25, 1959, of $62,500. Mr. Head estimated that total net earnings for the year ended April 30, 1960, would approximate $75,000. This would be lower than the $95,000 earned in 1959, despite an increase in sales, because HEAD had experienced nonrecurring expenses associated with the move to its new plant and with the development of the Vector model ski. Since HEAD paid no dividends on its outstanding common stock, estimated earnings of $75,000 for fiscal 1960 would produce a net worth on April 30, 1960, of approximately $546,000 (exclusive of the proposed offering). In discussing these projections with the company's commercial bank, Mr. Head was informed that the addition of between $160,000 and $170,000 in equity funds would enable the bank to increase HEAD's line of credit to a maximum of $700,000.

Mr. Head and Mr. Long next discussed the possibility of including a secondary offering by the existing stockholders in the proposed new issue. This appeared to be an attractive opportunity in light of the relatively small amount of capital required by the company for corporate use. A secondary offering would increase the size of the issue and make more shares available for sale; it was hoped that such a plan would stimulate increased trading activity in the stock among a wider group of investors.

An important consideration relative to a combined corporate and secondary offering involved the expense to HEAD of registering a new issue with the SEC. Mr. Head desired to keep this expense as small as possible. Under the terms of the Securities Act of 1933, a public security offering was exempt from full registration requirements if the aggregate amount of the issue offered to the public did not exceed $300,000. Mr. Long estimated that such an exemption in the case of HEAD's proposed offering would save the company between $5,000 and $10,000. According to HEAD's legal advisers, an additional consideration under such a partially exempt registration was that a secondary offering would be limited to $100,000.

On the basis of the preceding factors, Mr. Head and Mr. Long decided to limit the combined corporate and secondary offering to less than $300,000. Tentative agreement was also reached on a 10% underwriting commission to Robert Garrett & Sons as compensation for accepting the responsibility of buying and then reselling HEAD's stock to security dealers and to the public. With these stipulations as guidelines, the two men were able to define within fairly narrow limits those portions of the proceeds from the proposed issue to be allocated to the company, to the selling shareholders, and to underwriting commissions. The size of the issue would be approximately $280,000; $162,000 would represent net proceeds to the company, $90,000 would go to the selling shareholders, and $28,000 would represent the 10% underwriting commission.

By late February, 1960, the remaining issue of major importance concerned Mr. Long's recommendation to Mr. Head as to the price at which Robert Garrett & Sons would offer to sell HEAD's stock to the public. The determination of the offering price would enable Mr. Long to calculate the number of new shares to be offered by the company and the shares to be sold by the selling shareholders in arriving at the total offering price of $280,000. Mr. Head had contacted the company's major stockholders, and each had agreed to sell the same percentage of his stock ownership as the percentages sold by the other members in arriving at the gross figure of $100,000 under the secondary offering. Conceivably, Mr. Head's ownership in the company could fall below 50% after the proposed new issue, depending upon the offering price of the stock. The offering price would, in turn, determine the number of shares to be sold by Mr. Head as part of the secondary offering and the dilution in his stock ownership resulting from the new corporate issue. Mr. Head did not consider such a possibility a major drawback to the proposed offering; he indicated that he would continue to receive the backing of the present stockholders and that the combined holdings of this group would represent well over 50% of the stock outstanding subsequent to the issue. (Exhibit 3 describes HEAD's common stock and the rights associated therein.)

An important factor relative to Mr. Long's pricing recommendation to Mr. Head concerned HEAD's past earnings record (Exhibits 4 and 5). Potential investors would, as one method of evaluation, concern themselves with the offering price of HEAD's stock in relation to the company's past earnings per share. In order accurately to reflect HEAD's earnings relative to the proposed offering, Mr. Long realized that the company's past per share earnings would have to be adjusted downward on the basis of the larger number of common stock shares that would be outstanding subsequent to the offering. An additional consideration concerned the company's dividend policy; Mr. Head desired to continue the policy of reinvesting all earnings in order to strengthen the company's working capital position in anticipation of increased sales and production levels. Mr. Long did not feel that such a policy would have an adverse effect upon the marketability of HEAD's stock, however, since the reinvestment of all earnings had become an accepted policy of many companies which were expanding rapidly and whose stock was actively traded.

To aid him in his pricing decision, Mr. Long had compiled comparative financial and descriptive data on selected companies in the recreational and amusement fields (Exhibits 6, 7, and 8). None of these companies concentrated solely on the manufacture and sale of skis since, to Mr. Long's knowledge, all such companies were either privately owned or were subsidiaries of larger, publicly owned corporations. Mr. Long had also compiled published statements regarding the future prospects for the amusement industry (Exhibit 9).

A corollary consideration in Mr. Long's pricing recommendation concerned the present conditions in the capital stock markets. The number of relatively small companies issuing stock publicly for the first time had shown a marked increase since the fall of 1959. According to many underwriting firms and security dealers, this had produced an oversupply of stocks in the new issues market, promoting lower prices for the stocks of many companies in relation to their past earnings records. On the other hand, Mr. Head anticipated that HEAD's new issue would generate considerably more investor appeal than the moderate interest expressed in some current new issues. He thought that many owners of Head skis would be potential buyers of HEAD's stock; this, coupled with the relatively small supply of stock anticipated in the proposed offering, would, he hoped, stimulate an active buying interest in the issue.

If Robert Garrett & Sons was accepted as HEAD's underwriter, it was

Mr. Long's intention to distribute the stock to security dealers for resale to the public in those areas of the country where interest in skiing was most pronounced; specifically, he would allocate approximately half of the stock to dealers in California and Colorado and the remainder to dealers along the east coast. The offering would be scheduled for early April, 1960, and would be traded in the over-the-counter market. Under the terms of the proposed underwriting agreement, the selling stock-holders would be restricted from selling additional stock for a period of one year from the date of the issue. During that period, then, the trading activity in HEAD's stock would be confined to the number of shares offered through the underwriting.

Mr. Long's most important objective in his recommendation to Mr. Head was the determination of that price for HEAD's stock that would result in the highest proceeds and lowest dilution in earnings per share to the company and the selling shareholders, consistent with a price that would stimulate active and continued investor appeal. He would consider the issue successful if the stock rose to a premium of one or two points above the offering price in the trading market after the offering. If HEAD continued to grow at its present rate, the company might wish to return to the equity markets in the future; a successful offering at this time would certainly make it easier for HEAD to consider future public offerings of common stock.

Exhibit 1

HEAD SKI COMPANY, INC.

Net Worth and Capital Stock Outstanding

April 30, 1955–January 2, 1960

	4/30/55	4/30/56	4/30/57	4/26/58	4/25/59	6/10/59	1/2/60
Net worth:							
Common stock	$ 1,500	$ 4,000	$ 4,000	$ 4,000	$ 4,000	$158,400	$167,400
Preferred stock—5% cumulative	149,400	154,400	154,400	154,400	154,400	…	…
Surplus	63,051	154,075	135,077	207,841	302,731	n.a.	366,340
Total	$213,951	$312,475	$293,477	$366,241	$461,131	n.a.	$533,740
Preferred stock dividends earned but not declared	$ 15,375	$ 23,062	$ 30,812	$ 38,562	$ 46,312	…	…
Capital stock outstanding (number of shares):							
No par value common	1,500	1,550	1,550	1,550	1,550	…	…
No par value new common	…	…	…	…	…	74,400*	…
$1.50 par value common	…	…	…	…	…	…	111,600†
No par value preferred	1,500	1,550	1,550	1,550	1,550	…	…

* 74,400 no par shares new common stock outstanding following issuance of (1) 13 shares for each share of preferred stock and accumulated dividend arrearages thereon and (2) 35 shares for each share of old common stock.

† 111,600 shares of $1.50 par value common stock outstanding following issuance of 1½ shares of $1.50 par value common for each one share of nopar value common.

Exhibit 2

HEAD SKI COMPANY, INC.

BALANCE SHEET* AS AT JANUARY 2, 1960

(Unaudited)

ASSETS

Current assets:

Cash in bank and on hand	$ 64,107	
Trade acceptances	17,054	
Accounts receivable (net)	543,315	
Inventories (see Note A)†	316,251	
Prepaid expenses and other	$ 33,341	
Total current assets		$ 974,068

Fixed assets:

Machinery and equipment	$211,477		
Less: Depreciation to date	100,847	$110,630	
Other	$ 40,472		
Less: Depreciation and amortization to date	16,195	24,277	
Building	$261,476		
Less: Depreciation to date	10,644	250,832	
Total fixed assets			385,739

Other assets:

Cash surrender value—life insurance (see Note B)†	$ 36,918		
Miscellaneous	26,306	63,223	
Total assets			$1,423,031

LIABILITIES AND NET WORTH

Current liabilities:

Vouchers payable	$206,839	
Notes payable	300,000	
Mortgage payable—current portion (see Note C)†	8,820	
Customers' advance payments	14,153	
Estimated federal and state income taxes payable	63,388	
Other	94,911	
Total current liabilities		$ 688,111

Long-term debt:

Mortgage payable—noncurrent portion (see Note C)†		201,180
Total liabilities		$ 889,291

Commitments and contingent liabilities (see Note D)†

Net worth:

Common stock, $1.50 par value, authorized, 200,000 shares; issued and outstanding, 111,600 shares	$167,400	
Retained earnings	366,340	
Total net worth		533,740
Total liabilities and net worth		$1,423,031

* Figures are rounded and therefore may not add to totals.

† The notes to financial statements (see Exhibit 5) are an integral part hereof.

Exhibit 3

HEAD SKI COMPANY, INC.

DESCRIPTION OF COMMON STOCK, AS OF FEBRUARY, 1960

Prior to June 10, 1959, the authorized capital stock of the company consisted of 1,550 shares without par value of preferred stock and 1,550 shares without par value of common stock, all of which shares were issued and outstanding. By amendments of the charter and stock splits since that date, these shares have all been reclassified into the now outstanding 111,600 shares of the par value of $1.50 per share of common stock of the company; and the authorized capital stock has been increased to the present 200,000 shares of common stock, all of one class.

All shareholders will participate equally, share for share, in any dividends which may be paid or on liquidation. On all matters of voting, each shareholder is entitled to one vote for each share of stock standing in his name. Cumulative voting for directors is not provided for by the charter or by the bylaws, and the shares have noncumulative voting rights; that is, the holders of more than 50% of the shares voting for the election of directors can elect 100% of the directors if they choose to do so; and in such event, the holders of the remaining less than 50% of the shares voting for the election of directors will not be able to elect any person or persons to the board of directors. The holders of the common stock have under the charter of the company no pre-emptive rights.

Exhibit 4

HEAD SKI COMPANY, INC.

STATEMENTS OF INCOME FOR THE PERIODS INDICATED BELOW

(Unaudited)

	Fiscal Year Ended April 30, 1957	52 Weeks Ended April 26, 1958	52 Weeks Ended April 25, 1959	36 Weeks Ended January 2, 1960
Sales	$1,076,652	$1,315,063	$1,613,872	$1,514,181
Less: Cost of sales	800,190	919,762	1,122,578	1,085,095
Gross profit	$ 276,462	$ 395,301	$ 491,294	$ 429,086
Less: Expenses:				
Selling expenses	$ 76,848	$ 101,187	$ 109,305	$ 97,800
Administrative expenses	77,809	92,751	107,405	91,614
Corporate expenses	26,951	39,987	77,459	113,870
Total expenses	$ 181,608	$ 233,926	$ 294,168	$ 303,284
Net profit before income taxes	$ 94,854	$ 161,375	$ 197,126	$ 125,802
Federal and state income taxes	49,988	88,611	102,236	63,388
Net profit after income taxes (see Note E)*	$ 44,866	$ 72,764	$ 94,890	$ 62,414
Earnings per share (based upon 111,-600 shares outstanding on January 2, 1960, giving retroactive effect to recapitalization)	$0.40	$0.65	$0.85	$0.56

* The notes to financial statements (see Exhibit 5) are an integral part hereof.

Exhibit 5

HEAD SKI COMPANY, INC.

NOTES TO FINANCIAL STATEMENTS

Note A—Inventories

Inventories are valued at lower of cost or market and are detailed below:

Finished goods	$ 75,985
Goods in process	98,259
Raw materials	125,127
Manufacturing supplies	16,880
Total	$316,251

Note B—Cash Surrender Value of Life Insurance

The company is the owner and beneficiary of life insurance contracts in the face amount of $500,000 on the life of its president, Howard Head. The cash surrender value of these policies was $36,918 on January 2, 1960.

Insurance owned by the corporation on the life of its president, with maturity value of $50,000 and cash surrender value of $3,463 at January 2, 1960, has been pledged as additional security for the mortgage loan payable to Loyola Federal Savings and Loan Association.

Insurance owned by the corporation on the life of its president, with maturity values of $400,000 and aggregate cash surrender value of $28,581 at January 2, 1960, is held by a trustee pursuant to the terms of a stock redemption contract between the company and its president. The company is permitted by this contract to exercise various rights with respect to such policies, including the right to borrow and the right to change beneficiaries. The company is obligated to purchase only as much of the president's stock as the insurance proceeds can buy. Shares which are subject to the agreement are in the custody of the trustee. The president has limited rights to withdraw some of his shares from the trustee, thereby removing these shares from the effects of the contract.

Note C—Mortgage Payable

The company plant at Timonium, Maryland, and a life insurance contract owned by the company are pledged to secure a 6% mortgage loan payable in monthly instalments to Loyola Federal Savings and Loan Association. The last monthly payment will be due on December 1, 1974.

Note D—Long-Term Leases, Commitments, Contingent Liabilities

The company, prior to moving into its present facilities, occupied premises at 1507 Roland Heights Avenue in Baltimore under a lease which will expire on March 31, 1964. The rental under such lease is $7,520 per annum. The company has subleased said premises for the remaining term of the lease at an annual rental of $7,800.

Land upon which the company has constructed its plant is leased for twenty years beginning on September 1, 1959, at an annual rental of $7,200, subject to reduction until certain utilities and grading have been supplied by the lessor, and subject to an increase of $1,152 per acre in the annual rental to the extent that a portion of the leased tract, consisting of 1.562 acres and reserved for storm drainage, is made available for company use. The lease gives the company options to renew for three successive 20-year terms followed by a final term of 19 years. In addition, the company has the option to purchase the land at any time during the last 15 years of the initial 20-year term of the lease at a price of $25,000 per acre of land not reserved for Baltimore County storm drainage less the sum of $12,500. If the present reservation for storm drainage purposes is not changed, upon exercise of the purchase option the company would acquire 6.25 acres, not subject to storm drainage use, for a price of $143,750.

Skis sold by the company bear a guaranty for one year from the retailer's sales date. The financial statements make no provision for the contingent liabilities created by such guaranties, since the extent of such liability is indeterminate and, in the opinion of the company's officials, based upon past experience, is not considered material.

Note E—Statements of Income and Retained Earnings

Examination indicates a correction is needed to the company's opening inventory for the 36-week fiscal period ended January 2, 1960, and here reported. Inventories as of April 25, 1959, were undervalued by $38,850. As a consequence, net profit after income taxes for the fiscal period April 26, 1959, to January 2, 1960, includes $11,888 which was earned prior to April 26, 1959, and which is computed as follows:

Increase in current-period income because of inventory undervaluation	$38,850
Less: Increase in current-period profit sharing and incentive bonus expenses as result of above increase	12,781
Increase in net profits before income taxes	$26,069
Less: Income taxes on above income	14,182
Increase in net profits after taxes	$11,888

During the fiscal period April 26, 1959, to January 2, 1960, depreciation charges amounted to $47,117, and the following extraordinary expenses were incurred and charged off:

Expenses of moving plant from Baltimore to Timonium (included in corporate expenses)	$20,896
Contribution to Winter Olympic Ski Team (included in administrative expenses)	2,500
Total	$23,396

Testing and research expenses are included in corporate expenses. For the 52 weeks ended April 25, 1959, these expenses amounted to $28,417. Because of increased experimentation, research, and product development, testing and research expenses aggregated $36,147 for the 36 weeks ended January 2, 1960.

Because of increased borrowings, including interest paid on construction loans, interest expense for the 36 weeks ended January 2, 1960, was $19,471, as compared with $11,068 for the 52 weeks ended April 25, 1959. Interest expense is included in corporate expenses.

Exhibit 6

HEAD SKI COMPANY, INC.

COMPARATIVE STOCK PRICING AND FINANCIAL DATA ON SELECTED COMPANIES

February 26, 1960

	Head Ski Company, Inc.	MCA, Inc.	Shakespeare Company	Highbie Mfg. Company	A. G. Spalding & Bros., Inc.	Milton Bradley Co.	Murray Ohio Mfg. Co.	U.S. Playing Card Co.	Brunswick-Balke-Collender Co.	Outboard Marine Corp.
Fiscal year end	4/25	12/31	7/31	7/31	7/31	12/31	12/31	12/31	12/31	9/30
Latest complete year	4/25/59	12/31/59	7/31/59	7/31/59	7/31/59	12/31/59	12/31/59	12/31/59	12/31/59	9/30/59
Sales (000)	$ 1,614	$ 56,929	$ 14,954	$ 7,748	$ 14,954	$ 12,336	$ 33,178	$ 21,547	$ 275,100	$ 171,569
Net income (000)	95	5,186	1,378	593	1,378	746	1,243	2,204	26,859	13,785
Net income/sales	5.9%	9.1%	9.2%	7.7%	9.2%	6.1%	3.8%	10.2%	9.7%	8.0%
Net income/net worth	20.5%	17.8%	10.6%	11.2%	8.2%	18.6%	10.0%	15.6%	26.6%	16.8%
Earnings per share:										
1959	$0.85	$1.28	$2.85	$1.64	$1.35	$6.87	$4.23	$1.43	$3.42	$1.76
1958	0.65	1.18	2.73	0.74	1.21	3.02	2.74	1.40	2.13	1.16
1957	0.40	0.12	2.59	0.98	0.79	2.38	2.12	1.22	1.38	1.67
1956	0.82	0.74	2.00	0.96	1.32	2.60	2.28	1.18	0.77	1.69
1955	0.22	0.61	2.38	1.10	1.05	2.06	3.42	1.10	0.32	1.23
1959 versus 5-year average	143%	130%	114%	151%	118%	202%	142%	113%	213%	117%
Market price[p]		25	28½[b]	15¾	23⅝	57[b]	31½	32⅜	58⅝	34¼
Price/earnings:										
1959		19.5	10.0	9.6	17.5	8.3	7.5	22.6	17.2	19.5
5-year average, 1955–59		25.4	11.4	14.4	20.6	16.8	10.6	25.6	36.5	22.6
Current cash dividend rate	$ 0.00	$ 0.00	$ 1.80	$ 0.60	$ 0.00	$ 0.95	$ 2.00	$ 1.25	$ 0.53	$ 0.80
Current cash yield	0.00%	0.00%	6.3%	3.8%	0.00%	1.7%	6.3%	3.9%	0.9%	2.3%
Market price net tangible assets per share (Common)[n]		366%	128%[e]	168%[e]	118%[e]	167%	074%	353%	460%	330%
Common shares:										
Total outstanding	111,600	3,996,000	483,000	363,000	855,000	106,000	294,000	1,540,000	7,823,000	7,854,000
Recent offering		400,000								
Date of offering		10/8/59								
Offering price		$17.50								
Traded	NYSE	O.C.	O.C.	ASE	NYSE	O.C.	ASE	NYSE	NYSE	NYSE

Symbols:
p = Closing quotations February 26, 1960.
b = Bid prices.
n = Based on capitalization 12/31/59.
e = Estimated.

Exhibit 7

HEAD SKI COMPANY, INC.

COMPARATIVE FINANCIAL DATA ON SELECTED COMPANIES

(Dollar Figures in Thousands)

Balance Sheet Analysis	Head Ski Company, Inc. 1/2/60	MCA, Inc. 12/31/59	Shakespeare Co. 7/31/59	Outboard Marine Corp. 9/30/59
ASSETS				
Cash	$ 64	$ 2,753	$ 2,579	$ 15,518
Marketable securities	......	2,407	2,384	5,424
Accounts receivable (net)	539	4,592	1,642	14,049
Inventories	316	18,786	3,280	37,468
Other current assets	55	354	128	......
Total current assets	$ 974	$28,892	$10,013	$ 72,459
Land, buildings, etc.	$ 514	$17,537	$ 5,160	$ 62,804
Depreciation	128	3,122	2,278	22,394
Net property	$ 386	$14,415	$ 2,882	$ 40,410
Unamortized assets	......	25,093	......	......
Other assets	63	2,123	106	6,432
Total assets	$1,423	$70,523	$13,001	$119,301
LIABILITIES AND CAPITAL				
Notes payable	$ 300	$ 3,000	$	$ 3,500
Accounts payable	207	6,915	428	6,672
Federal income taxes	63	4,020	1,203	998
Accruals and other	118	4,241	669	5,899
Total current liabilities	$ 688	$18,176	$ 2,300	$ 17,069
Contracts or notes payable, other long-term debt	$ 201	$23,232	$	$ 20,779
Preferred stock	......	1,799	......	......
Common stock	167	7,476	2,417	2,356
Retained earnings and surplus	367	19,840	8,284	79,097
Total liabilities and capital	$1,423	$70,523	$13,001	$119,301

Exhibit 7 (Continued)

Head Ski Company, Inc.

Year	Sales	Increase over Previous Year	Net Earnings	Increase over Previous Year
1959	$1,614	23%	$ 95	30%
1958	1,315	22%	73	62%
1957	1,077	28%	45	(51%)
1956	839	294%	91	264%
1955	213	.....	25	.....

MCA, Inc.

Year	Sales	Increase over Previous Year	Net Earnings	Increase over Previous Year
1959	$56,929	20%	$ 5,106	20%
1958	47,473	22%	4,328	5%
1957	38,878	24%	4,121	49%
1956	31,392	31%	2,758	21%
1955	23,895	.....	2,286	.....

Shakespeare Co.

Year	Sales	Increase over Previous Year	Net Earnings	Increase over Previous Year
1959	$14,954	7%	$ 1,378	4%
1958	13,962	(1%)	1,320	5%
1957	14,099	13%	1,253	29%
1956	12,456	3%	969	(16%)
1955	12,112	.....	1,154	.....

Outboard Marine Corp.

Year	Sales	Increase over Previous Year	Net Earnings	Increase over Previous Year
1959	$171,569	8%	$ 13,785	52%
1958	158,713	6%	9,095	(30%)
1957	150,476	23%	13,071	8%
1956	122,045	42%	12,098	54%
1955	85,856	.....	7,864	.....

Exhibit 8

HEAD SKI COMPANY, INC.

DESCRIPTIONS OF COMPANIES LISTED IN EXHIBITS 6 AND 7

Music Corporation of America, Inc. (MCA), produced television film series and distributed these films throughout the United States and to foreign countries. The company also acted as agents for artists in the entertainment business. On October 8, 1959, MCA's common stock became publicly owned through an issue of 400,000 shares at $17.50 a share.

The *Shakespeare Company* manufactured and sold steel tubing and fishing reels. Over 50% of the company's operations were devoted to the manufacture of small-diameter welded steel tubing, of which 80% was sold to the automobile industry. Fishing reels represented between 35% and 40% of the company's business.

A. G. Spalding & Bros., Inc., was a well-known manufacturer of a varied line of sporting goods.

Milton Bradley Company manufactured school materials, display booths, and a varied line of additional amusements, toys, and novelties.

The *Murray Ohio Manufacturing Company* manufactured a complete line of juvenile automobiles, bicycles, wagons, scooters, etc. In 1957, over 45% of the company's sales were to Sears Roebuck & Co.

U.S. Playing Card Company manufactured and sold all types of playing cards.

Brunswick-Balke-Collender Company was the largest manufacturer of bowling equipment in the United States. The company also manufactured and sold school furniture, sports equipment, nonpharmaceutical laboratory supplies, and various defense products.

Outboard Marine Corporation was the largest domestic producer of outboard motors. The company also manufactured power lawn mowers, chain saws, and similar types of equipment.

Exhibit 9

HEAD SKI COMPANY, INC.

SELECTED COMMENTS ON THE AMUSEMENT INDUSTRY*

All indications point to the greatest boom in the history of the amusement industry over the next decade and longer. . . .

Factors are:

. . . . current projections for a 41% rise in the number of persons between 15 and 29 years old in the 1960–70 period. . . .

. . . . the substantial increase in consumer income anticipated in coming years. . . .

. . . . the growing amount of leisure time enjoyed by the average working man.

Current indications suggest the largest relative gains in sales and earnings will be experienced by those segments of the entertainment industry in which individuals are involved as participants rather than as spectators. . . .

. . . . Total spending on sporting goods in 1959 is expected to rise roughly 8% to a new peak of $1.97 billion. . . .

---

* Standard and Poor's Corporation. *Industry Surveys: Amusements*, May 21, 1959.

Case 44

Wizard Corporation

ON DECEMBER 27, 1961, David Prescott, president of Cutter & Dunlop, Inc., of Lynn, Massachusetts, was negotiating to acquire the assets and business of the Wizard Corporation of Framingham, Massachusetts. James Gruber, president and sole owner of the Wizard Corporation, had found Mr. Prescott's first three offers unacceptable, and negotiations had reached the point where Mr. Prescott was certain that his next bid must be final. He was also aware that any commitment resulting from the negotiations would have to be approved by both the board of directors of Cutter & Dunlop and two thirds of its stockholders.

History of Cutter & Dunlop

Cutter & Dunlop was incorporated on March 27, 1951, to succeed a partnership formed in 1946 by James Cutter and Foster Dunlop. The company designed, developed, and manufactured measuring instruments and miniature assembly lighting and control equipment. Virtually all of Cutter & Dunlop's products were proprietary items developed internally. Profits were volatile, and sizable losses were recorded in 1955 and 1957. In early 1958 David Prescott, production manager of Inca Camera Corporation, purchased Mr. Cutter's interest and became executive vice president of Cutter & Dunlop. He was elected president the following year. For the year ended December 31, 1960, Mr. Prescott received a salary of $15,000, and Mr. Dunlop received $10,000. Otherwise, no employee of the company received remuneration in excess of four figures.

Under Mr. Prescott's leadership Cutter & Dunlop completely revised operating policies and procedures. In addition to a cost-cutting program, the president started a research and development program aimed at servicing the needs of the electronics and miniaturization industries. By the end of 1960, despite heavy research expenditures, the company had achieved record-breaking sales and profits. Exhibits 1 and 2 present balance sheets and profit and loss statements for the years 1958–60.

Much of this success was attributable to customer acceptance of the company's new line of optical comparators and projectors. These products were measuring devices which, with the use of light and optics, permitted gauging to very close tolerances. They were also used as quality control instruments, as devices for assembling intricate and minute parts, and as a means of monitoring parts in process. An optical comparator might be described as a microscope in which a magnified image of a part is reflected on a screen marked with a precise measuring scale to test the conformity of the manufactured product to established standards.

As an adjunct to precision measuring and control equipment, Cutter & Dunlop had also developed optically ground and polished lenses coupled with high-intensity fluorescent lamps to provide a wide, uniformly illuminated magnified area for examination of precision parts. Like the optical comparators and projectors, these products were designed for industries requiring a concentrated source of localized lighting.

The company's largest customers, for all products, were major optical manufacturers and missile and electronics firms. Cutter & Dunlop's sales for the year ended December 31, 1960, were divided among its products as follows:

Comparators and projectors............	35.8%
Lighting aids........................	63.9
Special designing and consulting..........	0.3
	100.0%

Management believed that most of the company's future growth would come from expansion of its interest in optical instrumentation rather than from lighting aids.

In Mr. Prescott's opinion, the continued success of Cutter & Dunlop depended upon the company's ability to strengthen its marketing facilities in order to capitalize fully on several new products: a large-screen machine tool projector, an audiovisual projector, and a projection microscope. The markets for these products were considered by management to be almost insatiable.

The company had no collective bargaining agreements with any union and had never had a strike. Production facilities, leased for $3,600 a year, consisted of 12,000 square feet of space on the first, third, and part of the fourth floors of a factory building located in Lynn, Massachusetts. Housed in these quarters Cutter & Dunlop had a well-equipped general machine shop capable of producing most of its products. The remainder were subcontracted to several local job shops.

In June, 1961, Cutter & Dunlop successfully sold 100,000 shares of common stock to the public at $3 a share through Crane Bros., an investment banking firm of New York. The issue was quickly oversubscribed, and trading opened at $6 a share. After underwriting commissions and expenses, the company netted $242,000. As additional compensation, Cutter & Dunlop granted the underwriter a 5-year option to purchase 20,000 shares of the company's common stock at $3 a share, exercisable 13 months after the date of the public offering.

A monthly history of the market price of Cutter & Dunlop stock appears below:

BID AND ASKED PRICES OF CUTTER & DUNLOP SHARES
BY MONTH FOR THE PERIOD JUNE TO DECEMBER 15, 1961

Month	Bid	Asked
June	6	7
July	8½	9
August	7	7½
September	6½	7
October	5½	6
November	6	6½
December 15	6	6½

Following the public offering, Cutter & Dunlop's shareholder distribution appeared as follows:

	Number of Shares	Percentage of Total
David Prescott	43,700	16.7%
Nancy Prescott	85,100	32.6
Foster Dunlop	27,600	10.6
Employees of company	4,600	1.8
Public investors	100,000	38.3
Total shares issued and outstanding	261,000	100.0%
Total shares authorized	300,000	

In addition to Mr. Prescott, the board of directors of Cutter & Dunlop included Peter Mann, a senior partner of the law firm of Wellington, Creme, and Mann, counsel for the company; Clarence Bedash, treasurer of the company; and Basil Haliday, a friend of Mr. Prescott's and sales manager of Filter Corporation of America. Mr. Mann and Mr. Bedash each held 200 shares of Cutter & Dunlop stock. Mr. Haliday was not a stockholder.

Proposal of Merger

In early November, Roger Crane, a partner of Crane Bros., telephoned to Frederick Ingalls, a prominent tax consultant in the Boston area. Over the past several years Mr. Ingalls had built a reputation for his ability in finding and negotiating mergers and acquisitions for several small "scientific" companies. Mr. Crane explained that he was very anxious to have Cutter & Dunlop acquire a small but profitable optical company or a manufacturer of miniature electronic components. Mr. Prescott had mentioned, on his previous visit to Crane Bros. in New York, that his company would be interested in acquiring a firm in one of these two industries. The banker continued by saying that heavy start-up production costs and promotional expenses related to new products, plus a poor year for the economy in general, had prevented Cutter & Dunlop from realizing its profit forecasts. Even though 1961 would probably be a record sales year, the currently high market price of the shares indicated that investors were expecting a more favorable profit report for the current period than would actually appear. A merger at this time would be considered a constructive step in offsetting the interruption of the company's growth trend. A flood of new orders suggested that the company would meet its 1962 sales and profit goals and might even exceed forecasts.

Mr. Ingalls replied, "At the moment I have nothing in mind, but I will talk to David Prescott personally if an attractive situation comes up." The following week Mr. Ingalls telephoned Mr. Prescott and briefly described the Wizard Corporation, the owner of which wanted to merge with an aggressive, publicly held company. When Mr. Prescott expressed an interest in the situation, Mr. Ingalls offered to arrange a meeting between the management of both organizations. If progress was made, he would assist in the negotiations and act as an intermediary between the two parties. In return, he expected a customary finder's fee of 5%, in cash or stock, whichever was the vehicle used by the participants to consummate the merger. In the event that the proposed merger fell through, Mr. Ingalls did not expect any compensation for the time or effort expended in bringing the parties together. Mr. Prescott agreed to these terms.

History of the Wizard Corporation

The Wizard Corporation was founded as a sole proprietorship by James Gruber in 1955 and was incorporated in 1959. The company designed and manufactured precision components of a miniature nature for the electronics, missile, electrical appliance, and related industries. Before forming his own business, Mr. Gruber had been production manager of the Munster Watch Co. He had been associated with this organization for over 20 years, working up from skilled machinist to production manager with a yearly salary of $18,000. Nevertheless, the desire to be his own boss led Mr. Gruber to establish a company engaged in the fabrication of small metal products. The initial capital he ventured was $40,000, a substantial part of his life savings.

The Wizard Corporation quickly made substantial progress in penetrating the precision parts market, which was growing rapidly in eastern Massachusetts. Sales in 1959 and 1960 were $127,000 and $362,000, respectively. Profits were difficult to judge because the business filed its corporate tax returns on a cash rather than an accrual basis.

The Wizard Corporation employed 40 full-time people, of whom 32 were skilled machinists and 8 were supervisory and clerical help. Over the past year and a half the company had been running two 10-hour shifts. Mr. Gruber expected to continue this high rate of production well through 1962.

Mr. Gruber commented, "I believe our growth rate over the next 5 years will level off to 10% a year. Profit margins will remain at their current levels. For 1962 we have conservatively estimated sales at $450,000. Since I bring in 95% of the business, selling expenses are kept at a minimum. We have sales representatives on a commission basis, but they are ineffective. The secret of our success is that we hold overhead down. Wizard's market is very competitive but, because of our skill in manufacturing, we can do jobs others turn down. I have the best machinists in the country and pay top wages."

The Wizard Corporation was nonunion and had never had a strike. The company rented 15,000 square feet of a factory building on a long-term lease for $800 a month. There was adequate space for expansion.

Merger Negotiations

A history follows of the events leading up to the final merger talks between the two companies:

November 17—Mr. Prescott, Mr. Roger Crane, and Mr. Ingalls visited the Wizard Corporation. Mr. Gruber escorted the group around the plant and showed them some finished products. He told them that the company was currently highly profitable, still expanding, and in a strong competitive position as a result of its unique production ability.

November 21—Mr. Gruber visited Cutter & Dunlop. Mr. Prescott carefully showed him the plant and demonstrated several of the company's optical instruments. He also detailed his plans for expansion over the next 5 years.

December 3—Mr. Ingalls met with Mr. Prescott. The finder indicated that Mr. Gruber had checked references on Cutter & Dunlop and was pleased with the results. Mr. Prescott had also investigated the Wizard Corporation and found that Mr. Gruber had the reputation of being a tough competitor, a top salesman, and well liked by the trade. Mr. Prescott said, "Arrange another meeting for the day after tomorrow and we will talk numbers."

December 5—Mr. Prescott and Mr. Morganstern, Cutter & Dunlop's accountant, handed Mr. Gruber the financial statements and estimates appearing in Exhibits 1, 2, and 3. Mr. Morganstern said that the Wizard Corporation's statements, being prepared on a cash and not an accrual basis, were unacceptable for valuation purposes in their existing form. Although Mr. Prescott desired financial statements for the Wizard Corporation since its incorporation, the cost of reauditing the books was considered by Mr. Gruber prohibitive. After a 2-hour bargaining session, Mr. Gruber agreed to let Mr. Morganstern examine the company's statements for the last year and draw up a 1961 balance sheet and profit and loss statement. The cost of these financial statements to the Wizard Corporation was estimated at $2,500. Mr. Prescott expected that he could accurately value the Wizard Corporation from the financial data prepared by the accountant.

Mr. Prescott also said, "If we can agree on valuation, I should be interested in acquiring all the stock of the Wizard Corporation. We should then operate the company as a division of Cutter & Dunlop. The staff and management would be completely retained." Mr. Gruber nodded in approval and added, "What I really want is to be left alone to run my own show."

December 17—Mr. Morganstern delivered the financial and operating statements appearing in Exhibits 4, 5, and 6. The accountant pointed out that on Mr. Gruber's sales estimate for 1962 of $450,000, net profits on an accrual basis should reach $50,000. Mr. Gruber later confirmed this figure. After carefully examining the statements, Mr. Prescott mapped out in detail the advantages of the merger.

1. The Wizard Corporation had the production "know-how" and capacity, without reducing external sales, to manufacture the precision parts that Cutter & Dunlop was now purchasing from outside sources for use in its optical comparators. Mr. Prescott estimated that he could give the Wizard Corporation $100,000 worth of business in 1962.
2. The Wizard Corporation had access to an empty building that provided more than adequate physical room for expansion of both companies. Cutter & Dunlop could avoid moving its complete plant and facilities to larger quarters, since this additional space adjoining the Wizard plant could be rented for the manufacture of several of Cutter & Dunlop's products.
3. The Wizard Corporation had certain machinery and equipment costing about $50,000, which Cutter & Dunlop needed in order to manufacture precision parts for its new line of audiovisual projectors.
4. Since both companies called upon many of the same customers, some sales economy might result.
5. And, lastly, several of the Wizard Corporation's customers were potential customers of Cutter & Dunlop. Mr. Prescott believed that his sales force might be in a stronger selling position if the company was already a supplier. Sharing knowledge of potential customers could prove valuable in increasing sales of both companies.

In Mr. Prescott's opinion, the only disadvantage of the proposed merger was the possibility that the two managements might not function together harmoniously. He thought, "Of course, only time will tell. We are basically a scientific organization, working hand in hand with young men of proved managerial capacity. Our staff is proud of its educational and engineering accomplishments. Jim Gruber's operation, when you trim the fat off, is a highly efficient job shop with no really sophisticated engineering talents. Some friction could develop even if Wizard remains autonomous. In the last analysis, however, Jim Gruber's influence will be in direct proportion to the terms of the deal."

Mr. Prescott next telephoned Mr. Ingalls to inquire whether he knew how much money and what kind of arrangement Mr. Gruber desired. The finder replied that the Wizard Corporation could be acquired for 125,000 shares of Cutter & Dunlop stock. Since the market that morning quoted the shares at 6 bid, 6½ asked, Mr. Prescott deduced that Mr. Gruber valued his company at about $750,000.

December 18—Mr. Prescott decided to start the negotiations by offering exactly half of the number of shares the finder indicated would be acceptable to Mr. Gruber. He therefore formally offered 62,500 shares of Cutter & Dunlop stock for all the stock of the Wizard Corporation.

December 19—Mr. Gruber turned the offer down. To protect his interests he asked for 128,000 shares, the same number as those held by the Prescott family.

December 20—Mr. Prescott talked with Roger Crane, who strongly urged that Cutter & Dunlop acquire the Wizard Corporation. He further suggested that Mr. Prescott offer a cash deal, since stock might dilute earnings per share.

December 22—Mr. Prescott offered Mr. Gruber $250,000 in cash, believing that if it was accepted, the cash from the combined companies plus a bank loan would be adequate to meet the purchase price. Mr. Gruber refused to consider a straight cash transaction because of the capital gains tax, which would have to be paid immediately.

Mr. Prescott again conferred with Roger Crane, who suggested that both for the sake of control and to avoid dilution Cutter & Dunlop offer Mr. Gruber cash and stock over a period of years. This type of payment would lessen taxes.

December 23—Mr. Prescott offered Mr. Gruber a combination of stock and cash: each year over the next 5 years Mr. Gruber would receive 4,000 shares of Cutter & Dunlop stock and $60,000 cash.

December 24—Mr. Gruber refused the last offer and indicated that unless Mr. Prescott took a more realistic view of the value of his company, negotiations would end at once. During this talk with Mr. Gruber, Mr. Prescott realized that one area of substantial difference between them was the determination of real earnings. Mr. Prescott, thinking in terms of the profit and loss statements, had decided upon $40,000 net earnings as the point of valuation. Mr. Gruber, on the other hand, believed that $100,000 was a truer figure, contending that depreciation and his own salary of $39,600 should also be included in arriving at the profitability of the company. When Mr. Prescott inquired whether Mr. Gruber expected to draw this salary in the event of a merger, he said, "I will sign a 5-year employment contract at a fixed salary of $29,000. Also, even though our fixed equipment is in excellent condition, it has been largely written down. A careful examination of the machinery should indicate that it could not be replaced for less than $100,000."

December 26—Mr. Prescott and Mr. Ingalls met in conference. When asked about the bargaining strengths of the two parties, the finder remarked, "The Wizard Corporation has been offered merger opportunities by two medium-size electronics companies. Although Mr. Gruber has tentatively turned both offers down, they indicate that he is placing an attractive package on the market. Last month he talked with a local underwriter, Wieler & Co., which valued the company at $1,500,000. Harold

Wieler wished to sell one third of the company to the public for $500,000 on a best-efforts basis to net the Wizard Corporation $400,000. Mr. Gruber felt that the commissions were exorbitant and also questioned the ability of the investment banker to sell the issue. He said further that if he were to merge or to 'go public,' he wanted to do so immediately. Considering the backlog of registration statements filed with the Securities and Exchange Commission, it is likely that a public offering by the Wizard Corporation may be held up by red tape for a period of 6 months."

Mr. Ingalls appeared unwilling to reveal any additional information about the alternative offers to the Wizard Corporation, and Mr. Prescott was unable to learn any more through other means.

"Looking at your side of the coin," Mr. Ingalls continued, "Cutter & Dunlop's strength is that you are a growth company in a glamorous industry. I have never heard of another company of your size that can boast of such management and scientific abilities as Cutter & Dunlop employs. Jim knows this and fully realizes that Cutter & Dunlop may some day blossom into a large, successful company. In other words, Jim is willing to gamble his strong balance sheet position of today for a piece of the future.

"Also, an exchange of stock with Cutter & Dunlop would simplify estate valuation for the Gruber family in the event of death. Jim is a married man in his middle 50's, with two teen-aged sons. He believes that his estate would be in a stronger and more liquid position if it held stock in a publicly traded company."

Later that afternoon Mr. Prescott telephoned Roger Crane to discuss the situation. The banker pointed out that common stocks of publicly traded companies similar to the Wizard Corporation were then selling at approximately 15 times earnings. He also said, "By merging with Wizard you will be increasing the size of Cutter & Dunlop's capitalization as well as its assets and earning power. The larger Cutter & Dunlop becomes, by either internal or external means, the more solid the company will appear to investors. I should then expect the market price of the shares to be less volatile than in the past."

On several occasions Mr. Prescott had examined his company's transfer records and had been disturbed by the heavy trading volume in Cutter & Dunlop securities. Crane Bros. estimated that a total of 200,000 shares, or twice the number of shares sold to the public, had changed hands in the 6-month period following the public offering. To counteract this speculative fervor, Mr. Prescott had recently employed a public relations firm, C. D. LaVine & Co., to establish a stockholder relations program. Mr. LaVine suggested, however, that Cutter & Dunlop wait until 1962 before taking an active interest in this area so that company publicity would be concurrent with an improved profit picture.

Mr. Crane thought that the market place would probably place the same price-earnings multiple on the combined companies as it did on Cutter & Dunlop alone. This, in the banker's opinion, would create a strong upward pressure on the shares and would put the company in a stronger position to negotiate other acquisitions. Mr. Crane was anxious for Mr. Prescott to complete the merger immediately so that the Wizard Corporation's earnings could be consolidated with Cutter & Dunlop's for the year ending December 31, 1961. In this way, the profit and loss statement for the combined companies would appear in the annual report and in the newspapers.

Exhibit 1

WIZARD CORPORATION

BALANCE SHEETS OF CUTTER & DUNLOP, INC.,
AS OF DECEMBER 31, 1953–1960, AND NOVEMBER 30, 1961

ASSETS	12/31 1958	12/31 1959	12/31 1960	11/30 1961
Current assets				
Cash	$ 6,192	$ 2,191	$ 9,724	$129,795
Accounts receivable	40,102	59,394	55,375	63,834
Inventory	55,453	93,838	110,891	141,170
Prepaid expenses and deposits	4,092	1,980	1,932	24,058
Advances—officers and employees	456	983	89	176
Due from officers	...	...	8,938	16,015
Total current assets	$106,295	$158,386	$186,949	$375,048
Machinery and equipment (net)	19,979	19,894	24,556	47,563
Total assets	$126,274	$178,280	$211,505	$422,611

LIABILITIES AND CAPITAL				
Current liabilities				
Notes payable	$ 25,000	$ 15,507	$ 25,000	$ ...
Accounts payable	11,239	57,916	24,009	21,244
Advance on contracts	400	3,201		...
Accrued salaries, wages, and commissions	8,031	9,715	9,581	7,231
Withheld and accrued taxes	3,175	5,258	9,894	8,642
Reserve for federal taxes	...	...	12,000	4,406
Deposits on projectors	1,100	1,100	1,100	1,100
Loans payable—officers	746	312	...	...
Due to officers	...	...	2,245	117
Total current liabilities	$ 49,691	$ 93,009	$ 83,829	$ 42,740
Capital				
Common stock, no par value*	60,200	60,200	60,200	301,947
Surplus	16,383	25,071	67,476	77,924
Total liabilities and capital	$126,274	$178,280	$211,505	$422,611
Book value per share—based on 261,000 shares	$0.29	$0.33	$0.49	$1.46

* 1,400 shares outstanding, 1958–60. In March, 1961, authorized common stock was increased to 300,000 shares, and the 1,400 outstanding shares were exchanged for 161,000 shares. In June, 1961, 100,000 common shares were sold to the public; upon completion of the offering there were 261,000 shares issued and outstanding. In addition, Crane Bros. was granted five-year warrants to purchase 20,000 shares of authorized but heretofore unissued common stock.

Exhibit 2

WIZARD CORPORATION

PROFIT AND LOSS STATEMENTS OF CUTTER & DUNLOP, INC.,
FOR YEARS ENDED DECEMBER 31, 1958–60

	1958	1959	1960
Net sales	$287,985	$372,785	$629,759
Cost of goods manufactured and sold	194,393	272,760	425,765
Gross profit	$ 93,592	$100,025	$203,994
Selling and administrative expenses	93,672	90,619	144,065
Operating profit (loss)	$ (80)	$ 9,406	$ 59,929
Total other income (charges)	(783)	482	(524)
Net income (loss) before taxes	$ (863)	$ 9,888	$ 59,405
Income taxes	500	1,200	17,000
Net income (loss) after taxes	$ (1,363)	$ 8,688	$ 42,405
Earnings per share—based on 261,000 shares	—	$0.03	$0.16

Exhibit 3

WIZARD CORPORATION

ESTIMATED PROFIT AND LOSS STATEMENTS OF CUTTER & DUNLOP, INC.,
FOR YEARS ENDED DECEMBER 31, 1961–63

	1961*	1962*	1963*
Net sales	$795,000	$1,740,000	$2,845,000
Cost of goods manufactured and sold	505,000	1,068,000	1,720,000
Gross profit	$290,000	$ 672,000	$1,125,000
Selling and administrative expenses	190,000	450,000	670,000
Net income before taxes	$100,000	$ 222,000	$ 455,000
Provision for state and federal taxes	35,000	122,000	252,000
Net income	$ 65,000	$ 100,000	$ 203,000
Depreciation	$ 5,400	$ 6,100	$ 5,600
Earnings per share—based on 261,000 shares	$0.25	$0.38	$0.78

* Estimates prepared in April, 1961.

Exhibit 4

WIZARD CORPORATION

ESTIMATED BALANCE SHEET AS OF DECEMBER 31, 1961, BASED ON ACTUAL BALANCE SHEET AS OF DECEMBER 15, 1961

ASSETS

Current assets		
Cash		$ 75,405
Accounts receivable		93,053
Due from employees		1,022
Due from officer		170
Prepaid expenses		6,094
Total current assets		$175,744
Fixed assets		
Cost		$106,675
Less accumulated depreciation		55,142
Net fixed assets		$ 51,533
Total assets		$227,277

LIABILITIES AND CAPITAL

Current liabilities		
Accounts payable		$ 444
Notes payable (Note 1)		12,784
Accrued payroll		2,600
Accrued and withheld taxes		14,977
Federal income taxes (Note 2)		46,436
Total current liabilities		$ 77,241
Deferred notes payable (Note 1)		5,894
Capital:		
Common stock (no par value)—115 shares outstanding		15,300
Surplus		128,842
Total liabilities and capital		$227,277

NOTE 1—Machinery and equipment in the amount of $87,115 was pledged to secure notes payable in the amount of $18,678 on conditional sales contracts.

NOTE 2—The Wizard Corporation had filed its corporate state and federal returns on a cash basis since its inception on February 5, 1959. At this report date, there had been no examination by either the state or the federal taxing authorities. If at some future time, within the statutory period, the taxing authorities, upon examination, did not concur with the basis used by the corporation in filing its returns, there might be possible additional state and federal assessments of approximately $55,000.

Exhibit 5

WIZARD CORPORATION

ESTIMATED PROFIT AND LOSS STATEMENT FOR THE YEAR ENDING DECEMBER 31, 1961,
BASED ON ACTUAL RESULTS UP TO DECEMBER 15, 1961

			Percentage of Sales
Net sales		$423,160	100%
Cost of goods manufactured and sold:			
Raw materials	$20,652		4.9
Direct labor	84,790		20.0
Subcontract	68,740		16.2
Shop burden	97,033		23.0
Total cost of goods manufactured and sold		$271,215	64.1
Gross profit on sales		$151,945	35.9
General, selling, and administrative expenses		77,959	18.4
Total income		$ 73,986	17.5
Other charges (net)		(1,003)	(0.2)
Net income before federal taxes		$ 72,983	17.3
Provision for federal taxes		32,452	7.7
Net income after taxes		$ 40,531	9.6%
Depreciation		$ 19,520	4.6%

Exhibit 6

WIZARD CORPORATION

ESTIMATED SCHEDULE OF SHOP BURDEN, GENERAL, SELLING, AND ADMINISTRATIVE
EXPENSES FOR THE YEAR ENDED DECEMBER 31, 1961, BASED ON ACTUAL RESULTS
FOR THE PERIOD ENDED DECEMBER 15, 1961

		Percentage of Sales
Shop burden		
Supervisory salaries	$25,400	6.0%
Depreciation—machinery and equipment	18,753	4.4
Mill supplies	12,075	2.8
Product inspection	9,139	2.2
Rent	7,641	1.8
Tooling	7,554	1.8
Insurance	4,973	1.2
Payroll taxes	4,585	1.1
Maintenance and repairs	2,934	0.7
Production clerk	1,986	0.5
Light, heat, and power	1,547	0.4
Amortization—lease improvements	446	0.1
Total shop burden	$97,033	23.0%
General, selling, and administrative expenses		
Officers' salaries	$39,600	9.4%
Professional fees	10,525	2.5
Promotion, travel, and entertainment	7,777	1.8
Taxes	6,701	1.6
Office salaries	3,795	0.9
General and office expenses	2,500	0.6
Commissions	2,352	0.6
Motor vehicle expenses	1,575	0.4
Telephone	1,234	0.3
Postage and express	1,133	0.2
Depreciation—motor vehicle	607	0.1
Depreciation—office equipment	160	—
Total general, selling, and administrative expenses	$77,959	18.4%
Other income (charges)		
Interest expense	$ (3,020)	(0.7)%
Sales discounts	(2,690)	(0.6)
Interest income	2,362	0.6
Sale of scrap	1,446	0.3
Rental income	550	0.1
Miscellaneous	349	0.1
Total other charges	$ (1,003)	(0.2)%

Case 45

Fairview Motors, Inc.

In February, 1955, Mr. Elwood, president and treasurer of Fairview Motors, Inc., was giving serious consideration to liquidation of his automobile dealership which he had operated since December, 1934. The pro forma income statement for 1955 anticipated a net loss from operations; and in view of the poor performance of the preceding 3 years (see Exhibit 1), he had become quite pessimistic about the future prospects for this line of business.

Mr. Elwood had first entered the automobile business in 1921 as a new-car salesman. Between 1921 and 1934 he worked in a variety of jobs in the industry, primarily as an employee of automobile manufacturers. This experience included assembly-line work, parts sales and service promotion, and positions as regional service manager and warehouse manager. In 1933 his employment with the second of two manufacturers for which he had worked was terminated, and in 1934 he became established as a dealer in the town of Fairview, Ohio, under the name of Fairview Motors, Inc. The dealership was acquired with $2,700 of personal funds, assistance from relatives and friends, and an unsecured bank loan. The dealer franchise was for the sale of a medium-priced car produced by one of the "Big Three" manufacturers.

In its early years Fairview Motors, Inc., barely managed to survive the difficult and uncertain economic circumstances following the severe depression of the early thirties. In 1937 the company sold 127 new cars at a total profit of $126. The recession of 1938 cut sales of new cars back to 40. In 1941 Mr. Elwood joined the Army, leaving the business in the hands of employees. On his release in 1944 he returned to the company and immediately began the job of rebuilding it. The profit record of the company since incorporation in 1938 (shown in Exhibit 2) indicates the extent to which profits recovered through 1950. The results of this recovery period are reflected in company balance sheets, which are shown in Exhibit 3 for the years 1951 to 1954, inclusive. Throughout the life of the business, Mr. Elwood had remained sole owner. In recent years he was assisted in its management by his son.

Because of what he considered to be highly unsatisfactory prospects for 1955, Mr. Elwood decided to discuss the matter with the automobile manufacturer's regional financial representative, Mr. Fairfax. After reviewing Mr. Elwood's financial statements and forecast, Mr. Fairfax suggested that there were three aspects of his business which Mr. Elwood should examine closely before coming to any final conclusions. These were: (1) pricing and bargaining with the customer, (2) cost control, and (3) the maximum investment necessary to operate the business. Mr. Fairfax stated that the manufacturer expected a well-managed dealership to return at least 15% on the owner's investment (after taxes and bonuses).

On the subject of pricing, Mr. Fairfax suggested that Mr. Elwood consider the practice of "packing." This was a practice in general use in the automobile business at the time whereby the list price of a new car quoted the customer was increased by what was known as a "pack" of, say, $200 to give the dealer more of a margin within which to bargain. With the shrewd bargainer, the dealer could make what appeared to be substantial concessions either in trade-in price or in the form of a cash discount in order to close the sale. The customer who failed to bargain effectively would pay the inflated price, thus increasing the overall margin of profit on new-car sales. Mr. Elwood had very strong views on the use of the pack, feeling that it favored some customers at the expense of others on an unfair basis, and he had steadfastly refused to resort to it up to this point. These views were known to Mr. Fairfax from previous discussions with Mr. Elwood.

Mr. Fairfax also suggested that in some respects, Mr. Elwood's costs of operating the dealership were unnecessarily high. In particular, he took exception to the item: salaries—officers. It was his contention that the annual salary of the owner and manager of a dealership of this size (an average of 150 new cars sold per year) should not exceed $9,000. In addition, he objected to expenditures on leasehold improvements. Automobile manufacturers encouraged dealers to rent rather than own their own buildings and, in line with this, discouraged leasehold improvements as being just another way of investing in real estate. Countering this, Mr. Elwood insisted that he had not made any such expenditures that were not absolutely necessary to a well-run automobile business. Other items, such as travel and entertainment, were also questioned by Mr. Fairfax. On balance, he contended that Mr. Elwood could help his profit performance substantially by a more careful control of costs.

Subsequently, Mr. Elwood undertook to analyze his costs for 1954 to see how the profit would have appeared according to the line of reasoning taken by Fairfax. In doing so, he reduced certain costs by the following amounts:

Salaries and wages:
Officers' salaries.....................$11,200
Officers' bonuses.................... 5,800
Training school.....................   400
Other semifixed expenses:
Company car.......................   400
Advertising........................ 1,200
Travel and entertainment............. 1,100
Memberships......................   300
Fixed expenses:
Maintenance—buildings............... 1,200
Maintenance—equipment............. 1,300
Total reduction.................$22,900

The third aspect of the business questioned by Mr. Fairfax was the owner's investment. It was a basic policy of the manufacturer to discourage the dealer from investing any more than absolutely necessary. Fairfax drew up a balance sheet which, in his view, reflected the investment required to carry on a 200-car dealership (see Exhibit 4). In view of the fact that Mr. Elwood's agency was at a current level of 150 new cars a year, this balance sheet clearly suggested that his investment was excessive. The suggested balance sheet did not provide for any investment in new-car inventory, on the assumption that all new cars would be financed in full through a bank or other lending agent. The investment in used-car inventory was taken at a maximum 30 days' inventory of 25 cars. Mr. Fairfax pointed out that if this excess investment were withdrawn, the rate of return on the remaining investment would be proportionately improved.

Mr. Elwood came away from the interview with Mr. Fairfax feeling that the latter was not recognizing the "facts of life" of the automobile agency business. He felt that Fairfax had in mind a stripped-down, "shoestring" kind of dealership, whereas his objective had been to develop a well-equipped, well-run dealership which would justify a permanent and respected place in the business community. In particular, he rejected the idea that $9,000 was an adequate salary for the manager of an $800,000-a-year business. He also questioned 15% as an adequate rate of return, particularly in view of the minimum investment suggested by Fairfax. Experience had taught him that there were considerable risks inherent in the business of selling automobiles.

In order to gain additional perspective on his problem, Mr. Elwood proceeded to gather information on other dealerships. In doing so, he interviewed other dealers and also sought the help of the National Automobile Dealers Association (NADA). In particular, he wanted to know whether he was justified in his beliefs that he was above average in overall efficiency of operations and that his investment was not excessive.

His primary source of information in this regard was NADA. From this organization, he obtained national averages on costs as a percentage of sales for dealers in his make of car and in his size group. These figures were for 1954, and he proceeded to make similar calculations from the 1954 income statement of Fairview Motors, Inc. (see Exhibit 5). These comparisons were interpreted by Mr. Elwood as further evidence that he was above average in terms of operating efficiency. In previous years he had shown up very favorably in dealer comparisons drawn up by the manufacturer and on more than one occasion had been "exhibited" as a sample of what could be done in the business.

In reviewing the industry cost figures supplied by NADA, Mr. Elwood noted a downward trend in profit margins beginning in 1950:

	Gross Profit	Operating Profit As a Percent of Sales	Total Expenses
1950	18.6%	6.3%	12.3%
1951	18.2	4.9	13.3
1952	17.2	3.6	13.6
1953	15.2	2.2	13.0
1954	14.8	0.6	14.2

Information on the average investment by automobile dealers was more difficult to find. NADA had only commenced collecting such information in 1954. The figures available for 1954 were on an industry-wide basis and showed an average per dealer net worth of $108,933 (average sales: 101 new cars). On this basis the ratio of operating profit to net worth was 5.83% (before federal income taxes).

Mr. Elwood was also giving some thought to the probable outcome of a decision to liquidate. He was certain that if he did so, he could work for another dealer as manager at a minimum salary of $15,000. On the other hand, he was quite uncertain as to what he could get for the business, in view of the special circumstances of the agency relationship. To clarify his thinking on this point, Mr. Elwood and his service superintendent took an inventory of all machinery, equipment, office furniture, and fixtures. They priced each item at replacement cost, taking into consideration the percentage of useful life remaining in each piece of equipment. This gave a figure that Mr. Elwood thought was a fair selling price for these assets. He also inventoried his spare parts, accessories, and supplies, which at cost would be valued at about $10,000. The manufacturer would buy back practically all of this at cost price if Mr. Elwood closed out the business without someone taking over as a dealer.

The total value of the physical assets of the business to be offered for sale was estimated as follows:

Machinery, equipment, office furniture, and fixtures	$47,000
Spare parts, accessories, and supplies	10,000
Company cars	4,000
	$61,000

If the business was to be sold as a going concern, Mr. Elwood felt he was justified in asking a price in excess of $61,000 in order to reimburse him for the expense of the development of the business which he had incurred over a 20-year period. He was willing to spread the payment for the assets over a 5-year period. He thought there would be several people interested in buying in on this basis. On the other hand, he was uncertain as to whether the manufacturer would be willing to franchise a new dealer on these terms. Previous experience of other dealers indicated that the manufacturer took an active interest in the price at which the dealership was to be sold and that it appeared to consider depreciated book value as the proper basis, with no allowance for goodwill.

Exhibit 1

FAIRVIEW MOTORS, INC.

INCOME STATEMENTS FOR YEARS ENDING DECEMBER 31, 1951–55

	Actual				*Pro Forma*
	1951	*1952*	*1953*	*1954*	*1955*
Net sales	$486,800	$579,100	$698,400	$803,800	$753,600
Less: Cost of sales	381,600	474,800	563,400	665,300	624,700
Gross profit on sales	$105,200	$104,300	$135,000	$138,500	$128,900
Less:					
Variable expenses[1]	$ 11,700	$ 16,600	$ 21,400	$ 28,300	$ 31,900
Semifixed salaries and wages[2]	54,900	54,100	67,600	68,900	60,500
Other semifixed expenses[3]	12,200	15,400	20,100	20,500	15,700
Fixed expenses[4]	16,000	17,000	24,000	26,500	22,200
Total expenses	$ 94,800	$103,100	$133,100	$144,200	$130,300
Net profit (loss) from operations	$ 10,400	$ 1,200	$ 1,900	$ (5,700)	$ (1,400)
Add other income[5]	4,500	4,400	9,700	10,400	9,000
	$ 14,900	$ 5,600	$ 11,600	$ 4,700	$ 7,600
Less: Other expenses	400	500	1,400	1,000	...
Net profit before taxes	$ 14,500	$ 5,100	$ 10,200	$ 3,700	$ 7,600
Federal taxes	4,200	1,500	3,000	1,000	
Net profit after taxes	$ 10,300	$ 3,600	$ 7,200	$ 2,700	

[1] Includes salesmen's salaries and commissions ... $ 6,000 $ 8,000 $ 10,000 $ 13,000 $ 12,500

[2] Includes officers' salaries ... 28,000   28,700   28,700   23,200   25,200

and bonus ...   5,800

NOTE: Of the sum paid as officers' salaries and bonus, a part was paid to individual members of the Elwood family who served in management in some capacity. In recent years the amount paid to these individuals other than Mr. Elwood was approximately $10,000.

[3] Major item—advertising ... 4,300   4,800   5,400   6,600   4,800

[4] Includes rent, amortization of improvements, depreciation, etc.

[5] Includes revenue received in connection with the financing of customer installment contracts ... 500   400   4,900   5,900

Exhibit 2

FAIRVIEW MOTORS, INC.

Net Profit after Taxes, 1938–50

For Year	Net Profit (Loss) after Taxes	Salaries and Bonuses Paid to Owner and Officers
1938	$ (1,400)	$ 2,700
1939	(4,000)	3,200
1940	500	5,600
1941	500	9,600
1942*	...	...
1943*	...	...
1944*	...	...
1945	1,200	7,500
1946	10,800	12,600
1947	13,600	21,000
1948	8,100	32,100
1949	14,500	25,700
1950	16,700	25,700

* Not given—period when Mr. Elwood was absent from the business.

Exhibit 3

FAIRVIEW MOTORS, INC.

BALANCE SHEETS, 1951–54

ASSETS	1951	1952	1953	1954
Current				
Cash............................	$ 6,800	$16,200	$ 21,800	$ 16,800
Contracts in transit.................	1,500	1,400	2,300	2,700
Customers' accounts less reserve......	9,400	10,700	13,200	11,500
Inventories: New cars...............	2,100	2,100	10,500	13,300
Used cars...............	14,400	14,400	7,500	7,100
Other..................	12,400	13,500	12,600	19,500
Securities at cost...................	14,100	10,100	10,100	8,300
Miscellaneous.....................	900	1,900	2,300	2,800
Total current assets............	$61,600	$70,300	$ 80,300	$ 82,000
Fixed (net of depreciation)				
Machinery and equipment...........	$ 6,800	$ 6,500	$ 7,000	$ 6,300
Furniture and fixtures..............	2,300	2,600	3,600	3,900
Service cars......................	100	1,900	1,400	4,300
Leaseholds and improvements........	5,400	4,700	18,800	16,200
Total fixed assets..............	$14,600	$15,700	$ 30,800	$ 30,700
Other				
Repossession reserve................	$ 2,300	$ 3,500	$ 4,800	$ 5,500
Miscellaneous.....................	700			
Total other assets..............	$ 3,000	$ 3,500	$ 4,800	$ 5,500
Total assets.................	$79,200	$89,500	$115,900	$118,200

LIABILITIES AND NET WORTH	1951	1952	1953	1954
Current liabilities				
Accounts payable..................	$ 800	$ 1,800	$ 7,600	$ 7,700
Accounts receivable—credit balance...	1,800	2,100	8,200	200
Service contract deposits............	400	500	600	1,700
Accrued payroll and bonuses........	1,100	800	7,600	600
Accrued taxes other than federal.....	4,500	3,900	4,100	2,500
Accrued federal income tax..........	4,700	1,500	3,000	...
New cars financed..................	...	...	...	13,200
Due officers......................	...	3,700	3,500	...
Total current liabilities..........	$13,300	$14,300	$ 34,600	$ 25,900
Current asset reserves................	$ 300	$ 800	$ 200	$ 9,400
Net worth				
Capital stock—common.............	$19,200	$26,600	$ 26,600	$ 26,600
Earned surplus....................	46,400	47,800	54,500	56,300
Total net worth...............	$65,600	$74,400	$ 81,100	$ 82,900
Total liabilities and net worth..	$79,200	$89,500	$115,900	$118,200

Exhibit 4

FAIRVIEW MOTORS, INC.

PROPOSED BALANCE SHEET, 200 CAR DEALERSHIP

ASSETS

Current assets
Cash..$ 15,000
Accounts receivable.............................. 12,000
Inventories: New cars...............................   ....
            Used cars........................... 25,000
            Other............................... 23,000
Securities..   ....
Due from finance companies........................ 10,000
Other... 5,500
     Total current assets........................$ 90,500
Fixed assets....................................... 25,000
                                                 $115,500

LIABILITIES AND NET WORTH

Current liabilities...................................$ 15,500
Net worth.. 100,000
                                                 $115,500

Exhibit 5

FAIRVIEW MOTORS, INC.

COSTS AND REVENUES AS PERCENT OF TOTAL SALES, 1954

	Fairview Motors, Inc.	The Industry Average	
		150–399 New Cars	1–149 New Cars
	% of Sales	% of Sales	% of Sales
Salaries, commissions and other compensation to salesmen.........................	1.60	2.53	1.83
Salaries and wages			
Owners or officers.......................	2.90	1.49	1.68
Supervision.............................	1.25	1.45	1.10
Other...................................	3.26	2.46	2.30
Total salaries and wages..............	7.41	5.40	5.68
Rent plus expenses in lieu of rent..........	1.15	1.25	1.21
Advertising, local........................	.82	1.11	.84
Total expenses.........................	16.90	15.16	14.39
(Variable expense).....................	3.54	4.05	3.30
Total gross profit.......................	17.30	16.09	14.77
Operating profit.........................	.39	.93	.38
Operating profit before owners' and officers' salaries...............................	3.29	2.42	2.06
Percent return on invested capital*.........		5.1	2.1
Percentage of dealers who reported an operating loss...........................		26.2	34.6

* Before income taxes.
SOURCE: National Automobile Dealers Association, based on nationwide information from dealers in the same make of car and in comparable size groups.

Case 46

Bauman's, Inc.

In late May, 1952, Mr. Frank Preston, credit manager of the James W. Saxton Company, Rocky Mount, North Carolina, manufacturers of fine home furniture, had completed one year's activity as a representative for an informal creditors' committee. The committee had been formed for the purpose of reestablishing a sound financial position for Bauman's, Inc., leading retailers of quality home furnishings in St. Louis, Missouri. After the creditors' committee had disbanded and all old obligations of Bauman's had been discharged, Mr. Preston received an order in June, 1952, amounting to $4,300 and pondered what terms of sale to grant on the order. Typically, terms of sale were 1% 10, net 30.

Bauman's had handled its financial affairs in a satisfactory manner for a number of years, but in early April, 1951, Mr. Preston became concerned about the account when he reviewed the trial balance of his company's accounts receivable for March, 1951, and noted that the Bauman's account stood as follows:

Total	Mar.	Feb.	Jan.	Dec., 1950
$11,268.82	$1,028.01	$3,524.37	$913.30	$5,803.14

Mr. Preston checked with the credit managers of several other large suppliers to Bauman's and learned that their accounts were similarly delinquent. One organization reported a bill of over $4,000 extending back to November of 1950. Although no financial statements had been issued to trade creditors for a number of years, this had not disturbed the several credit managers because of the long-standing relationship and the manner in which Bauman's had handled its accounts. As a result of the telephone conversations, Mr. Preston and Mr. Carl Runstedt, another credit manager, decided to visit the company. When the two men met Mr. Harold Bauman, the president, he told them that the company had done some overbuying and was simply experiencing an unusually slow season. He said the company would be "squared away shortly." The two credit managers wanted more specific information on the company's position and accordingly checked with the company accountant, who showed them audited statements as of January 31, 1951 (see Exhibits 1 and 2).

A cursory review of the financial statement by the two credit managers indicated that Bauman's had more problems than its president was willing to acknowledge. They asked to look at the accounts payable ledger and noted the following figures which were current at the time of their visit (about the middle of April):

Total Payables Outstanding	Mar.	Feb.	Jan.	Dec., 1950	Nov.	Prior Months
$178,752	$46,544	$58,477	$32,100	$25,927	$15,339	$365

Although some of Bauman's purchases were made on varying terms, the bulk of the purchases called for payment within 30 days, thus most accounts prior to February were past due.

The two credit managers knew that one-half interest in Bauman's, Inc., had been sold by two of the four owners, but they were not aware of the terms of the purchase agreement. The item in the balance sheet, "Mortgage notes payable—purchase obligation, $296,700," therefore caused them to raise questions regarding the manner in which title was transferred. By questioning Mr. Bauman, the two men learned that the total purchase price for the one-half interest in the firm amounted to $310,500. The sellers received a second mortgage on four parcels of real estate. The mortgage carried 5% interest, and the principal was payable at the rate of $1,725 per month starting in June of 1950.

The two credit managers also learned that the company had borrowed from its bank of account, the River Trust Company in St. Louis, $144,900 obtained on an open line of credit secured by accounts receivable. The corporation also owed $141,738 on the original purchase of some real estate, which was secured by a first mortgage and was payable at the rate of $16,675 annually.

This information, together with the financial statements for the year ended January 31, 1951, forced the two credit managers to conclude that drastic steps were necessary. After an extended discussion with Harold Bauman, the president, and his nephew, Jeffrey, the vice president, Mr. Preston and Mr. Runstedt convinced the Baumans of the seriousness of their company's position. The Baumans then agreed to a program of action which called for the following:

1. Holding a tremendous store-wide sale to reduce inventory as quickly as possible to free cash.
2. Paying cash for necessary purchases but buying only for "fill-ins."
3. Renegotiating the loan with the bank to free some accounts receivable.
4. Attempting to sell or pledge the freed accounts receivable to a finance company, using these funds to reduce the bank loan, thereby gradually

eliminating the bank loan and transferring the financing on accounts receivable to a finance company which would give more liberal credit.

5. Selling two pieces of store real estate not essential to the business.
6. Selling some personal property of Harold Bauman worth approximately $34,500 and applying this to the business to reduce the item entitled "Due from officers."
7. Paying off all creditors owed $100 or less.
8. Effecting an informal agreement with all other creditors to handle the outstanding accounts on a deferred basis.

When a list of creditors was completed, as of the end of April, the accounts payable were as follows:

Total	April	Mar.	Feb.	Jan.	Dec., 1950	Nov.
$211,883	$79,156	$37,126	$48,361	$24,470	$15,106	$7,664

The total accounts numbered 345, of which only 37 were over $1,000 each.

At the end of the first week in May, the board of directors of Bauman's passed a resolution naming Mr. Preston and Mr. Runstedt from among the large creditors of the corporation to act as trustees for all monies of the company to prevent independent action by any creditor to secure a preferred status. These trustees, appointed for one year or until final settlement, had been previously designated by the informal creditors' committee as their representatives.

One of the first acts of the trustees was to pay all creditors whose accounts amounted to $100 or less. This reduced the 345 accounts to 204. The trustees appointed the company accountant as their agent to sign checks and maintain records. Furthermore, one of the merchandise managers was appointed general manager of the store by joint agreement between trustees and the Baumans. All purchases and expenses were to be passed upon by both the new general manager and the president, Mr. Harold Bauman.

A finance company was contacted and arrangements made to handle all current accounts receivable on a 70% basis, thereby gaining about $46,000, which was applied against the bank loan and creditors' past-due accounts. The finance company also agreed to buy the time-payment accounts on a nonrecourse basis.

The new general manager and the accountant were instructed to supply the two trustees with brief summary financial reports on a weekly basis. They also agreed not to purchase any merchandise for 30 days, thereafter to purchase only for "fill-ins" and to discount all new purchases. The trustees estimated gross sales for the year at $850,000 and concluded that Bauman's could turn its inventory about four times per year.

On May 15 the president of Bauman's sent out the following letter:

May 15, 1951

GENTLEMEN:

Because of an extremely slow season and purchases made in good faith, but beyond present requirements, we find that instead of being able to pay our obligations on our usual discount or prompt basis, we now have an accumulation of past-due accounts payable. Naturally we regret this very much.

In view of this situation, we felt it proper to confer with some of our largest creditors. As a result of their advice, and with their approval we would like to request your cooperation in granting us additional time to correct our condition. We have requested Mr. Frank Preston of the J. W. Saxton Company and Mr. Carl Runstedt of K. K. Kramer, Inc., to work with us in this connection. These two gentlemen have agreed to oversee the disbursement of funds to all creditors on a proportional basis with preference to none.

Our proposal for settlement of our present indebtedness to you is as follows: on or before July 1, 25% of the balance outstanding, and for the remainder, 12 notes carrying 6% interest to be retired within one year, with the understanding that we may retire these notes before maturity.

All purchases made from and after May 15 will be on a discount basis, so that you will not be adding to the amount of your account. Purchases will be limited to "fill-ins" and items absolutely necessary to complete constructive sales.

We are confident that we can carry out the program above outlined. We are listing some real estate, which is not essential to the operation of the business and we are hopeful that we may effect a sale within 60 days. We have reduced our expenses to the minimum, and we will maintain such reductions consistent, of course, with a good selling program. A careful budget has been prepared which we will follow.

We have a good organization. Everyone from top to bottom is dedicated to the task of getting us into a current position, and you may be assured of our genuine and wholehearted efforts.

We need and desire greatly to have your cooperation so that we may continue to provide you with a profitable outlet for your merchandise. If there is any difference between the amount of your account given below and that shown on your records, kindly communicate with us.

Very truly yours,

HAROLD BAUMAN

President

In response to the May 15 letter, about 90% of the creditors agreed to accept a deferred claim; the remainder demanded immediate payment. Some of the accounts not desiring to "go along" represented small amounts up to $200; these were paid off.

In addition to the refinancing of a portion of the accounts receivable, the nonessential real estate was sold. Although the proceeds were primarily used to pay the mortgages on the property, the elimination of the fixed obligation eased the working capital position of the company.

By June 15 there was enough money to permit the payment in full of accounts up to $600, and the payment of notes one and two to the deferred creditors.

There were a few creditors who for some time declined to go along with the arrangement. These kept writing and contacting by phone or telegram the trustees of the creditors' committee to effect payment of their accounts. Typical of these creditors was the Sunflower Appliance Company, Kansas City, Missouri. Their letter to Mr. Preston read as follows:

June 6, 1951

DEAR SIR:

On May 15, Bauman's, Inc., wrote us to ask that we accept a series of notes in payment of their account with us. We beg to inform you that we do not wish to accept the plan.

Our reason for nonacceptance of this plan is based primarily on the fact that we are appliance distributors, and Bauman's have indicated to us that they are not planning to push their appliance business and particularly the products that we sell. We, therefore, feel that since this account doesn't offer future possibilities for us, we would be assuming an unjustified burden to go along on this program. We believe that suppliers like yourselves have a definite interest in this company, for, if you help them with their temporary problems, they will continue in the future to be substantial outlets for your merchandise. If that were true in our case, we would look more favorably upon their plan.

Electrical appliance selling is usually based on much shorter terms than is furniture and other items that furniture stores sell. It is very important that accounts be paid promptly for appliances. The merchandise for which Bauman's owes us represents purchases of January, February, and March of this year, and we feel that we have already waited quite some time for our money.

We frankly admit that in some instances in the past we have tried to work out methods for dealers to liquidate their obligations over a period of time, and many dealers with whom we have gone through such plans are today substantial customers. However, Bauman's discouraged us from entering into any such arrangement when they told us that they are not particularly interested in our products for the future. Accordingly, we return herewith the notes sent us.

Very truly yours,

JOHN M. LESTER
Vice President

Mr. Preston responded:

June 12, 1951

DEAR MR. LESTER:

I have just returned from a trip to Bauman's and went over the situation there as to the volume of business they have been doing with you, and found that they have done nearly $3,000 in the last 60 days. I, therefore, decided that as long as you are still a supplier and have already cashed their check for 25% of the settlement, I would forward to you the notes covering the unpaid portion of their obligation.

I am very pleased to say at this time that you may present notes one and two at once for payment. We hope they will be able to pay off the balance of these notes as rapidly in the future as they have up to the present.

Yours truly,

FRANK PRESTON

With the new general manager keeping a tight rein on the company's operations and frequent visits by the two trustees, the company made sufficient progress during the year to pay the numbered notes on the following dates: On August 28, notes three and four; on September 28, note five; November 15 and December 15, notes six and seven, respectively.

Mr. Runstedt, who lived in the St. Louis area, wrote to Mr. Preston on November 20 as follows:

November 20, 1951

DEAR FRANK:

Things seem to be progressing. Sales are holding up and there is a good cash balance in the bank. If this situation continues to the end of the month, I would suggest that we attempt to pay off one or two more notes. Frankly, I would like to see all of these notes liquidated by the first of the year if it can be done. I fully realize that we cannot in any way jeopardize current purchases, but if sales continue at a good rate, I would not be the least averse to taking this cash out of the bank, so that it cannot be spent for any other purposes.

From recent conversations with Joe Jackson [the recently appointed general manager] I fear he is becoming a bit uneasy and disturbed. This is especially true in respect to his relationship with Harold, who appears to feel that the company has about corrected the condition in which they found themselves. Harold is increasingly taking over again as of old. Joe cited several examples which seem to bear out his thinking.

I have persuaded him not to become involved in too serious a conflict with Harold for the next few weeks, and until I have had the opportunity to bring this condition to your attention. Perhaps, under the circumstances, you might like to come to St. Louis.

Cordially,

CARL

At the meeting held in St. Louis in early December, the trustees learned that the item on the balance sheet, "Notes payable—employees, $12,650," represented some back salary due the general manager, Joe Jackson. Since the top executives of the firm had been receiving full salary, although on a reduced basis, the trustees demanded payment for the general manager. This was accomplished in early January, 1952. In addition, the salaries of the Baumans were increased to their former basis retroactive to June, 1951. The increases, however, were not paid in cash; the differences between the old and new salaries were credited to their obligations to the company. This reduced the tax liability of the corporation and forced the reinvestment of funds which had earlier been withdrawn from the business.

Mr. Preston also learned that upon two occasions in November, Mr. Bauman had initiated purchases involving moderate amounts without the approval of Mr. Jackson. Mr. Preston explained that he expected the purchase orders to be routed through Mr. Jackson for his initials or signature to avoid any misunderstanding.

On February 21, 1952, note number nine was called for payment. On March 8 and March 28, notes numbered ten and eleven were paid, respectively.

Mr. Preston was surprised on March 30, 1952, to receive from the legal firm representing Bauman's, Inc., formal notice that the arrangement which the board of directors of Bauman's made with the creditors' committee was ended and that the powers of trustees were revoked. Mr. Preston wrote immediately to Mr. Bauman and the latter's lawyers indicating that he and Mr. Runstedt could not accept the action by the corporation until all funds were paid or the agreed-upon one-year period had elapsed. He cited the board of directors' resolution which supported his stand. Finally on May 5, 1952, note number twelve was called for payment. At this time the resolution was formally revoked and the trustees dismissed.

On May 20, Mr. Jackson resigned, telling his friends the move was prompted by his inability to get along with the president and his nephew. He declared his intention of going into business for himself in a nearby community.

In late May Mr. Preston talked with the sales manager of his company regarding the desirability of retaining Bauman's as a sales outlet for the Saxton line of home furnishings in the St. Louis area. The sales manager stressed strongly the desirability of having the Saxton line in the Bauman locations, noting that it had been for a number of years a highly successful merchandising organization and had purchased and sold more than $60,000 of Saxton furniture in the year ended January, 1950. No other organization in the St. Louis area, according to the sales manager, was able to get the volume and to handle its affairs with the sales department in such a satisfactory manner.

During the period of the "workout," Bauman's, Inc., had purchased from the Saxton Company $23,216 of furniture on a discount basis. Saxton's net profits on sales varied with the items sold from 2% to 7%, averaging 5%. Saxton's costs were composed of 80% variable and semivariable and 20% fixed.

Monthly financial statements had not been made available to the trustees after January, 1952, when the annual report was rendered. To learn specifically of the current financial position of Bauman's, Mr. Preston wrote to Mr. Harold Bauman asking for a statement. He was surprised to have his request denied. Mr. Preston then contacted one of his banking friends who was able to get a brief unaudited financial statement as of May 31, 1952 (see Exhibit 1).

Thus in early June, 1952, with the limited financial information available, Mr. Preston faced the question of what terms to place on the $4,300 order from Bauman's and the manner in which to handle other future orders.

Exhibit 1
BAUMAN'S, INC.
BALANCE SHEETS

ASSETS	Audited as of Jan. 31, 1951	Audited as of Jan. 31, 1952	Unaudited as of May 31, 1952
Cash	$ 8,311	$ 44,659	$ 20,125
Accounts receivable, net (assigned)	268,415	163,542	126,500
Inventory	304,100	191,639	189,750
Total current assets	$580,826	$399,840	$336,375
Land	$ 58,603	$ 49,993	$ 51,750
Buildings, fixtures and equipment	263,027	244,826	....
Less: Depreciation reserve	65,915	76,479	....
Net buildings, fixtures, and equipment	$197,112	$168,347	$164,450
Investments	10,631	5,175	5,175
Due from officers	47,471	37,309	27,245
Deferred charges	3,128	3.930	4,600
Total assets	$897,771	$664,594	$589,595

LIABILITIES			
Accounts payable	$154,496	$ 19,950	$ 28,750
Notes payable—trade creditors	....	43,906	....
Notes payable—employees	12,650	....	....
Salaries, wages, commissions accrued	3,270	1,914	1,725
Estimated federal income tax	......	1,749	2,300
Current maturities on long-term debts	37,375	37,375	35,650
Miscellaneous accruals	7,582	4,200	4,025
Total current liabilities	$215,373	$109,094	$ 72,450

Exhibit 2

BAUMAN'S, INC.
PROFIT AND LOSS STATEMENTS

	Year Ended Jan. 31, 1951	Year Ended Jan. 31, 1952
Gross sales.............................	$1,501,506	$986,078
Less: Returns and allowances............	121,654	183,194
Net sales..............................	$1,379,852	$802,884
Cost of goods sold......................	858,566	485,571
Gross profit...........................	$ 521,286	$317,313
Less: Operating expenses...............	498,513	279,923
Operating profit........................	$ 22,773	$ 37,390
Other income..........................	14,519	10,761
Net after other income..................	$ 37,292	$ 48,151
Interest and other deductions............	43,011	31,872
Net profit (loss).......................	$ (5,719)	$ 16,279

TABLE A
PRESENT VALUE OF $1

Periods until Payment	1%	2%	2½%	3%	4%	5%	6%	8%	10%	12%	14%	15%	16%	18%	20%	22%	24%	25%	26%	30%	40%	50%
1	0.990	0.980	0.976	0.971	0.962	0.952	0.943	0.926	0.909	0.893	0.877	0.870	0.862	0.847	0.833	0.820	0.806	0.800	0.794	0.769	0.714	0.667
2	0.980	0.961	0.952	0.943	0.925	0.907	0.890	0.857	0.826	0.797	0.769	0.756	0.743	0.718	0.694	0.672	0.650	0.640	0.630	0.592	0.510	0.444
3	0.971	0.942	0.929	0.915	0.889	0.864	0.840	0.794	0.751	0.712	0.675	0.658	0.641	0.609	0.579	0.551	0.524	0.512	0.500	0.455	0.364	0.296
4	0.961	0.924	0.906	0.888	0.855	0.823	0.792	0.735	0.683	0.636	0.592	0.572	0.552	0.516	0.482	0.451	0.423	0.410	0.397	0.350	0.260	0.198
5	0.951	0.906	0.884	0.863	0.822	0.784	0.747	0.681	0.621	0.567	0.519	0.497	0.476	0.437	0.402	0.370	0.341	0.328	0.315	0.269	0.186	0.132
6	0.942	0.888	0.862	0.837	0.790	0.746	0.705	0.630	0.564	0.507	0.456	0.432	0.410	0.370	0.335	0.303	0.275	0.262	0.250	0.207	0.133	0.088
7	0.933	0.871	0.841	0.813	0.760	0.711	0.665	0.583	0.513	0.452	0.400	0.376	0.354	0.314	0.279	0.249	0.222	0.210	0.198	0.159	0.095	0.059
8	0.923	0.853	0.821	0.789	0.731	0.677	0.627	0.540	0.457	0.404	0.351	0.327	0.305	0.266	0.233	0.204	0.179	0.168	0.157	0.123	0.068	0.039
9	0.914	0.837	0.801	0.766	0.703	0.645	0.592	0.500	0.424	0.361	0.308	0.284	0.263	0.225	0.194	0.167	0.144	0.134	0.125	0.094	0.048	0.026
10	0.905	0.820	0.781	0.744	0.676	0.614	0.558	0.463	0.386	0.322	0.270	0.247	0.227	0.191	0.162	0.137	0.116	0.107	0.099	0.073	0.035	0.017
11	0.896	0.804	0.762	0.722	0.650	0.585	0.527	0.429	0.350	0.287	0.237	0.215	0.195	0.162	0.135	0.112	0.094	0.086	0.079	0.056	0.025	0.012
12	0.887	0.788	0.744	0.701	0.625	0.557	0.497	0.397	0.319	0.257	0.208	0.187	0.168	0.137	0.112	0.092	0.076	0.069	0.062	0.043	0.018	0.008
13	0.879	0.773	0.725	0.681	0.601	0.530	0.469	0.368	0.290	0.229	0.182	0.163	0.145	0.116	0.093	0.075	0.061	0.055	0.050	0.033	0.013	0.005
14	0.870	0.758	0.708	0.661	0.577	0.505	0.442	0.340	0.263	0.205	0.160	0.141	0.125	0.099	0.078	0.062	0.049	0.044	0.039	0.025	0.009	0.003
15	0.861	0.743	0.690	0.642	0.555	0.481	0.417	0.315	0.239	0.183	0.140	0.123	0.108	0.084	0.065	0.051	0.040	0.035	0.031	0.020	0.006	0.002
16	0.853	0.728	0.674	0.623	0.534	0.458	0.394	0.292	0.218	0.163	0.123	0.107	0.093	0.071	0.054	0.042	0.032	0.028	0.025	0.015	0.005	0.002
17	0.844	0.714	0.657	0.605	0.513	0.436	0.371	0.270	0.198	0.146	0.108	0.093	0.080	0.060	0.045	0.034	0.026	0.023	0.020	0.012	0.003	0.001
18	0.836	0.700	0.641	0.587	0.494	0.416	0.350	0.250	0.180	0.130	0.095	0.081	0.069	0.051	0.038	0.028	0.021	0.018	0.016	0.009	0.002	0.001
19	0.828	0.686	0.626	0.570	0.475	0.396	0.331	0.232	0.164	0.116	0.083	0.070	0.060	0.043	0.031	0.023	0.017	0.014	0.012	0.007	0.002	
20	0.820	0.673	0.610	0.554	0.456	0.377	0.312	0.215	0.149	0.104	0.073	0.061	0.051	0.037	0.026	0.019	0.014	0.012	0.010	0.005	0.001	
21	0.811	0.660	0.595	0.538	0.439	0.359	0.294	0.199	0.135	0.093	0.064	0.053	0.044	0.031	0.022	0.015	0.011	0.009	0.008	0.004	0.001	
22	0.803	0.647	0.581	0.522	0.422	0.342	0.278	0.184	0.123	0.083	0.056	0.045	0.038	0.026	0.018	0.013	0.009	0.007	0.005	0.003	0.001	
23	0.795	0.634	0.567	0.507	0.406	0.326	0.262	0.170	0.112	0.074	0.049	0.040	0.033	0.022	0.015	0.010	0.007	0.006	0.005	0.002		
24	0.788	0.622	0.553	0.492	0.390	0.310	0.247	0.158	0.102	0.066	0.043	0.035	0.028	0.019	0.013	0.008	0.006	0.005	0.004	0.002		
25	0.780	0.610	0.539	0.478	0.375	0.295	0.233	0.146	0.092	0.059	0.038	0.030	0.024	0.016	0.010	0.007	0.005	0.004	0.003	0.001		
26	0.772	0.598	0.526	0.464	0.361	0.281	0.220	0.135	0.084	0.053	0.033	0.026	0.021	0.014	0.009	0.006	0.004	0.003	0.002	0.001		
27	0.764	0.586	0.513	0.450	0.347	0.268	0.207	0.125	0.076	0.047	0.029	0.023	0.018	0.011	0.007	0.005	0.003	0.002	0.002	0.001		
28	0.757	0.574	0.501	0.437	0.333	0.255	0.196	0.116	0.069	0.042	0.026	0.020	0.016	0.010	0.006	0.004	0.002	0.002	0.002	0.001		
29	0.749	0.563	0.489	0.424	0.321	0.243	0.185	0.107	0.063	0.037	0.022	0.017	0.014	0.008	0.005	0.003	0.002	0.002	0.001			
30	0.742	0.552	0.477	0.412	0.308	0.231	0.174	0.099	0.057	0.033	0.020	0.015	0.012	0.007	0.004	0.003	0.002	0.001	0.001			
40	0.672	0.453	0.372	0.307	0.208	0.142	0.097	0.046	0.022	0.011	0.005	0.004	0.003	0.001	0.001							
50	0.608	0.372	0.291	0.228	0.141	0.087	0.054	0.021	0.009	0.003	0.001	0.001	0.001									

SOURCE: Jerome Bracken and Charles J. Christenson, *Tables for Use in Analyzing Business Decisions* (Homewood, Ill.: Richard D. Irwin, Inc., 1965), except for the data on 2½%, the source for which is *Mathematical Tables from Handbook of Chemistry and Physics* (6th ed.; Cleveland: Chemical Rubber Publishing Co. 1938).

AUTHORS' NOTE: These values are obtained by compounding at the end of each period. Other tables use different schemes of compounding, without changing the magnitudes greatly.

TABLE B

PRESENT VALUE OF $1 RECEIVED ANNUALLY

Periods to Be Paid	1%	2%	2½%	3%	4%	5%	6%	8%	10%	12%	14%	15%	16%	18%	20%	22%	24%	25%	26%	30%	40%	50%
1	0.990	0.980	0.976	0.971	0.962	0.952	0.943	0.926	0.909	0.893	0.877	0.870	0.862	0.847	0.833	0.820	0.806	0.800	0.794	0.769	0.714	0.667
2	1.970	1.942	1.927	1.914	1.886	1.859	1.833	1.783	1.736	1.690	1.647	1.626	1.605	1.566	1.528	1.492	1.457	1.440	1.424	1.361	1.224	1.111
3	2.941	2.884	2.856	2.829	2.775	2.723	2.673	2.577	2.487	2.402	2.322	2.283	2.246	2.174	2.106	2.042	1.981	1.952	1.923	1.816	1.589	1.407
4	3.902	3.808	3.762	3.717	3.630	3.546	3.465	3.312	3.170	3.037	2.914	2.855	2.798	2.690	2.589	2.494	2.404	2.362	2.320	2.166	1.849	1.605
5	4.853	4.713	4.646	4.580	4.452	4.330	4.212	3.993	3.791	3.605	3.433	3.352	3.274	3.127	2.991	2.864	2.745	2.689	2.635	2.436	2.035	1.737
6	5.795	5.601	5.508	5.417	5.242	5.076	4.917	4.623	4.355	4.111	3.889	3.784	3.685	3.498	3.326	3.167	3.020	2.951	2.885	2.643	2.168	1.824
7	6.728	6.472	6.349	6.230	6.002	5.786	5.582	5.206	4.868	4.564	4.288	4.160	4.039	3.812	3.605	3.416	3.242	3.161	3.083	2.802	2.263	1.883
8	7.652	7.325	7.170	7.020	6.733	6.463	6.210	5.747	5.335	4.968	4.639	4.487	4.344	4.078	3.837	3.619	3.421	3.329	3.241	2.925	2.331	1.922
9	8.566	8.162	7.971	7.786	7.435	7.108	6.802	6.247	5.759	5.328	4.945	4.772	4.607	4.303	4.031	3.786	3.566	3.463	3.366	3.019	2.379	1.948
10	9.471	8.983	8.752	8.530	8.111	7.722	7.360	6.710	6.145	5.650	5.216	5.019	4.833	4.494	4.192	3.923	3.682	3.571	3.465	3.092	2.414	1.965
11	10.368	9.787	9.514	9.253	8.760	8.306	7.887	7.139	6.495	5.938	5.453	5.234	5.029	4.656	4.327	4.035	3.776	3.656	3.544	3.147	2.438	1.977
12	11.255	10.575	10.258	9.954	9.385	8.863	8.384	7.536	6.814	6.194	5.660	5.421	5.197	4.793	4.439	4.127	3.851	3.725	3.606	3.190	2.456	1.985
13	12.134	11.348	10.983	10.635	9.986	9.394	8.853	7.904	7.103	6.424	5.842	5.583	5.342	4.910	4.533	4.203	3.912	3.780	3.656	3.223	2.468	1.990
14	13.004	12.106	11.691	11.296	10.563	9.899	9.295	8.244	7.367	6.628	6.002	5.724	5.468	5.008	4.611	4.265	3.962	3.824	3.695	3.249	2.478	1.993
15	13.865	12.849	12.381	11.938	11.118	10.380	9.712	8.559	7.606	6.811	6.142	5.847	5.576	5.092	4.676	4.315	4.001	3.859	3.726	3.268	2.484	1.995
16	14.718	13.578	13.055	12.561	11.652	10.838	10.106	8.851	7.824	6.974	6.265	5.954	5.668	5.162	4.730	4.357	4.033	3.887	3.751	3.283	2.488	1.997
17	15.562	14.292	13.712	13.166	12.166	11.274	10.477	9.122	8.022	7.120	6.373	6.047	5.749	5.222	4.775	4.391	4.059	3.910	3.771	3.295	2.492	1.998
18	16.398	14.992	14.353	13.754	12.659	11.690	10.828	9.372	8.201	7.250	6.467	6.128	5.818	5.273	4.812	4.419	4.080	3.928	3.786	3.304	2.494	1.999
19	17.226	15.678	14.979	14.324	13.134	12.085	11.158	9.604	8.365	7.366	6.550	6.198	5.878	5.316	4.844	4.442	4.097	3.942	3.799	3.311	2.496	1.999
20	18.046	16.351	15.589	14.877	13.590	12.462	11.470	9.818	8.514	7.469	6.623	6.259	5.929	5.353	4.870	4.460	4.110	3.954	3.808	3.316	2.497	1.999
21	18.857	17.011	16.185	15.415	14.029	12.821	11.764	10.017	8.649	7.562	6.687	6.312	5.973	5.384	4.891	4.476	4.121	3.963	3.816	3.320	2.498	2.000
22	19.660	17.658	16.765	15.937	14.451	13.163	12.042	10.201	8.772	7.645	6.743	6.359	6.011	5.410	4.909	4.488	4.130	3.970	3.822	3.323	2.498	2.000
23	20.456	18.292	17.332	16.444	14.857	13.489	12.303	10.371	8.883	7.718	6.792	6.399	6.044	5.432	4.924	4.499	4.137	3.976	3.827	3.325	2.499	2.000
24	21.243	18.914	17.885	16.936	15.247	13.799	12.550	10.529	8.985	7.784	6.835	6.434	6.073	5.451	4.937	4.507	4.143	3.981	3.831	3.327	2.499	2.000
25	22.023	19.523	18.424	17.413	15.622	14.094	12.783	10.675	9.077	7.843	6.873	6.464	6.097	5.467	4.948	4.514	4.147	3.985	3.834	3.329	2.499	2.000
26	22.795	20.121	18.951	17.877	15.983	14.375	13.003	10.810	9.161	7.896	6.906	6.491	6.118	5.480	4.956	4.520	4.151	3.988	3.837	3.330	2.500	2.000
27	23.560	20.707	19.464	18.327	16.330	14.643	13.211	10.935	9.237	7.943	6.935	6.514	6.136	5.492	4.964	4.524	4.154	3.990	3.839	3.331	2.500	2.000
28	24.316	21.281	19.965	18.764	16.663	14.898	13.406	11.051	9.307	7.984	6.961	6.534	6.152	5.502	4.970	4.528	4.157	3.992	3.840	3.331	2.500	2.000
29	25.066	21.844	20.454	19.188	16.984	15.141	13.591	11.158	9.370	8.022	6.983	6.551	6.166	5.510	4.975	4.531	4.159	3.994	3.841	3.332	2.500	2.000
30	25.808	22.396	20.930	19.600	17.292	15.372	13.765	11.258	9.427	8.055	7.003	6.566	6.177	5.517	4.979	4.534	4.160	3.995	3.842	3.332	2.500	2.000
40	32.835	27.355	25.103	23.115	19.793	17.159	15.046	11.925	9.779	8.244	7.105	6.642	6.234	5.548	4.997	4.544	4.166	3.999	3.846	3.333	2.500	2.000
50	39.196	31.424	28.362	25.730	21.482	18.256	15.762	12.233	9.915	8.304	7.133	6.660	6.246	5.554	4.999	4.545	4.167	4.000	3.846	3.333	2.500	2.000

SOURCE: Jerome Bracken and Charles J. Christenson, *Tables for Use in Analyzing Business Decisions* (Homewood, Ill.: Richard D. Irwin, Inc., 1965), except for the data on 2½%, the source for which is *Mathematical Tables from Handbook of Chemistry and Physics* (6th ed.; Cleveland: Chemical Rubber Publishing Co., 1938).

AUTHORS' NOTE: These values are obtained by compounding at the end of each period. Other tables use different schemes of compounding, without changing the magnitudes greatly,

Tax Table

FEDERAL TAX RATES ON CORPORATE INCOME, AND PAYMENT DATES

(To be used in connection with cases in this book. This is not a complete statement of applicable rates, and it should not be used as a reference for general purposes.)

Income Years	Rate	Income Years	Rate	Income Years	Rate
1940*	24.0%	1949	38.0%	1958	52.0%
1941*	31.0	1950*	47.0	1959	52.0
1942*	40.0	1951*	52.0	1960	52.0
1943*	40.0	1952*	52.0	1961	52.0
1944*	40.0	1953*	52.0	1962	52.0
1945*	40.0	1954	52.0	1963	52.0
1946	38.0	1955	52.0	1964	50.0
1947	38.0	1956	52.0	1965	48.0
1948	38.0	1957	52.0	and later years	

* Excess profits tax also applied for at least part of year.

The 52 per cent rate broke down into a normal tax of 30 per cent of taxable income and a surtax of 22 per cent of taxable income in excess of $25,000. The 50 per cent rate broke into a normal tax of 22 per cent and a surtax of 28 per cent; and the 48 per cent rate into a normal tax of 22 per cent and a surtax of 26 per cent.

Recent revenue acts have moved corporate income tax payments close to current payment. Beginning in 1950, payments were gradually accelerated until in 1954 they were brought entirely within the first half of the year following the tax liability. The Revenue Acts of 1954 and 1964 and the Tax Adjustment Act of 1966, which became law on March 15, 1966, set up even more accelerated schedules. All tax liabilities up to $100,000 are payable in equal amounts on March 15 and June 15 of the year following the tax liability. Tax liabilities over $100,000, for companies on a calendar year, are payable according to the following schedule:

	Percentage Paid in Income Year*				Percentage Paid in Following Year†			
Year	Apr. 15	June 15	Sept. 15	Dec. 15	Mar. 15	June 15	Sept. 15	Dec. 15
1949......	—	—	—	—	25%	25%	25%	25%
1950......	—	—	—	—	30	30	20	20
1951......	—	—	—	—	35	35	15	15
1952......	—	—	—	—	40	40	10	10
1953......	—	—	—	—	45	45	5	5
1954......	—	—	—	—	50	50	—	—
1955......	—	—	5%	5%	45	45	—	—
1956......	—	—	10	10	40	40	—	—
1957......	—	—	15	15	35	35	—	—
1958......	—	—	20	20	30	30	—	—
1959......	—	—	25	25	25	25	—	—
1960......	—	—	25	25	25	25	—	—
1961......	—	—	25	25	25	25	—	—
1962......	—	—	25	25	25	25	—	—
1963......	—	—	25	25	25	25	—	—
1964......	1%	1%	25	25	24	24	—	—
1965......	4	4	25	25	21	21	—	—
1966.........12		12	25	25	13	13	—	—
1967.........25		25	25	25	—	—	—	—
and subsequent years‡								

* These are percentages of the estimated tax liability on income of the current year.
† These are percentages of the tax liability on income of the previous year.
‡ Until passage of the Tax Adjustment Act of 1966, the payment schedule for 1966–70 was as follows:

	Percentage Paid in Income Year				Percentage Paid in Following Year			
Year	Apr. 15	June 15	Sept. 15	Dec. 15	Mar. 15	June 15	Sept. 15	Dec. 15
1966.........	9%	9%	25%	25%	16%	16%	—	—
1967.........14		14	25	25	11	11	—	—
1968.........19		19	25	25	6	6	—	—
1969.........22		22	25	25	3	3	—	—
1970.......	25	25	25	25	—	—	—	—

Sources: Derived from *Prentice-Hall Federal Taxes* (Englewood Cliffs, N.J.: Prentice-Hall, Inc., 1965); *Prentice-Hall Federal Taxes*, Vol. XLVII, No. 7 Extra Issue, February 18, 1966; and *Wall Street Journal*, March 16, 1966.

Some References for Additional Reading*

NOTE: In general, this bibliography gives each reference only once, the first time it is relevant. The reader will easily see, however, that some of the references are also applicable to later sections of the book.

PART I. INTRODUCTION

1. General Textbooks of Corporate and Business Finance

ARCHER, STEPHEN H. and CHARLES D'AMBROSIO. *Business Finance: Theory and Management.* New York: Macmillan Co., 1966.

BERANEK, WILLIAM. *Analysis for Financial Decisions.* Homewood, Ill.: Richard D. Irwin, Inc., 1963.

BOGEN, JULES I. and SAMUEL S. SHIPMAN (eds.). *Financial Handbook.* 4th ed. New York: Ronald Press Co., 1964.

BRADLEY, JOSEPH F. *Administrative Financial Management.* New York: Holt, Rinehart & Winston, Inc., 1964.

BRANDT, LOUIS K. *Business Finance: A Management Approach.* Englewood Cliffs, N.J.: Prentice-Hall, Inc., 1965.

COHEN, JEROME B. and SIDNEY M. ROBBINS. *The Financial Manager.* New York: Harper & Row, Publishers, 1966.

DAUTEN, CARL A. and MERLE T. WELSHANS. *Principles of Finance: Introduction to Capital Markets.* 2nd ed. Cincinnati: South-Western Publishing Co., 1964.

DONALDSON, ELVIN F. and JOHN K. PFAHL. *Corporate Finance: Policy and Management.* 2nd ed. New York: Ronald Press Co., 1963.

GUTHMANN, HARRY G. and HERBERT E. DOUGALL. *Corporate Financial Policy.* 4th ed. Englewood Cliffs, N.J.: Prentice-Hall, Inc., 1962.

JOHNSON, ROBERT W. *Financial Management.* 3rd ed. Rockleigh, N.J.: Allyn & Bacon, Inc., College Division, 1966.

LINDSAY, ROBERT and ARNOLD W. SAMETZ. *Financial Management: An Analytical Approach.* Homewood, Ill.: Richard D. Irwin, Inc., 1963.

WESTON, J. FRED and EUGENE S. BRIGHAM. *Managerial Finance.* 2nd ed. New York: Holt, Rinehart & Winston, Inc., 1966.

2. Additional References

AMERICAN MANAGEMENT ASSOCIATION. *New Responsibilities in Corporate Finance.* AMA Management Report No. 71. New York, 1962.

---

* For a more detailed topical bibliography, see *Corporate and Business Finance: A Classified Bibliography,* compiled by Gordon Donaldson and Carolyn Stubbs. (Boston: Baker Library, Graduate School of Business Administration, Harvard University, 1964.)

ARANOW, EDWARD R. and HERBERT A. EINHORN. *Proxy Contests for Corporate Control: A Treatise on the Legal and Practical Problems of Management and Insurgents in a Corporate Proxy Contest.* New York: Columbia University Press, 1957.

BAUM, DANIEL JAY and NED B. STILES. *The Silent Partners: Institutional Investors and Corporate Control.* Syracuse, N.Y.: Syracuse University Press, 1965.

CURTIS, EDWARD T. *Company Organization of the Finance Function.* AMA Research Study No. 55. New York: American Management Association, 1962.

"Developments in Financial Organization, 1915–1965," a Supplement to *Financial Executive,* Vol. XXXIII (September, 1965).

EELLS, RICHARD. *The Meaning of Modern Business: An Introduction to the Philosophy of Large Corporate Enterprise.* New York: Columbia University Press, 1960.

FINLEY, JAMES A. and MALCOLM C. NEUHOFF. *The Duties of Financial Executives.* Studies in Business Policy No. 56. New York: National Industrial Conference Board, Inc., 1952.

GILBERT, LEWIS D. and JOHN J. GILBERT. *Twenty-Sixth Annual Report of Stockholder Activities at Corporation Meetings during 1965.* New York, 1965.

HUNT, PEARSON. "A Program for Stockholder Relations," *Harvard Business Review,* Vol. XXX (September–October, 1952), pp. 99–110.

KINLEY, JOHN R. *Corporate Directorship Practices.* Studies in Business Policy No. 103. New York: National Industrial Conference Board, Inc., 1962.

LIVINGSTON, JOSEPH A. *The American Stockholder.* Philadelphia: J. B. Lippincott Co., 1958.

MASON, EDWARD S. (ed.) *The Corporation in Modern Society.* Cambridge, Mass.: Harvard University Press, 1959.

MCCORMICK, W. F. "The Corporate Treasurer's Role," *Financial Executive,* Vol. XXXI (January, 1963), pp. 27–32.

"The New Power of the Financial Executives," *Fortune,* Vol. LXV (January, 1962), pp. 81–85.

PLUMMER, GEORGE F. and GEORGE MOLLER. "Financial Executive; His Role in the Corporate Organization and in Over-All Company Planning," *Controller,* Vol. XXX (January, 1962), pp. 16–18.

WHETTEN, LELAND C. *The Rise of Professional Proxy Solicitors: Georgeson & Company of Wall Street et al.* Studies in Business and Economics, Bulletin No. 12. Atlanta, Ga.: Bureau of Business and Economic Research, Georgia State College of Business Administration, 1961.

WILLIAMS, CHARLES M. *Cumulative Voting for Directors.* Boston: Division of Research, Harvard Business School, 1951.

PART II. THE MANAGEMENT OF ASSETS AND THE NEED FOR FUNDS

ANDERSON, CLAY J. "Managing the Corporate 'Money' Position," *Business Review* of the Federal Reserve Bank of Philadelphia, March, 1961, pp. 3–10.

BAUMES, CARL G. *Inventory Management in Industry.* Studies in Business Policy No. 88. New York: National Industrial Conference Board, Inc., 1958.

BECKMAN, THEODORE N. *Credits and Collections: Management and Theory.* 7th ed. New York: McGraw-Hill Book Co., 1962.

BIERMAN, HAROLD, JR., and ALAN K. MCADAMS. *Management Decisions for Cash and Marketable Securities.* Cornell Studies in Policy and Administration. Ithaca, N.Y.: Graduate School of Business and Public Administration, Cornell University, 1962.

BROWN, ROBERT G. *Statistical Forecasting for Inventory Control.* New York: McGraw-Hill Book Co., 1959.

CREDIT RESEARCH FOUNDATION (ed.). *Credit Management Handbook.* (A publication of the National Association of Credit Management.) Rev. ed. Homewood, Ill.: Richard D. Irwin, Inc., 1965.

ETTINGER, RICHARD P. and DAVID E. GOLIEB. *Credits and Collections.* 5th ed. Englewood Cliffs, N.J.: Prentice-Hall, Inc., 1962.

FEDERAL RESERVE BANK OF CLEVELAND. *Money Market Instruments.* 2nd ed. Cleveland, 1965.

FOULKE, ROY A. *Current Trends in Terms of Sale.* New York: Dun & Bradstreet Publications, Inc., 1959.

———. *Inventories and Business Health.* New York: Dun & Bradstreet Publications, Inc., 1960.

HADLEY, GEORGE and THOMSON M. WHITIN. *Analysis of Inventory Systems.* Englewood Cliffs, N.J.: Prentice-Hall, Inc., 1963.

HOFFMAN, RAYMOND A. *Inventories: A Guide to Their Control, Costing, and Effect Upon Income and Taxes.* New York: Ronald Press Co., 1962.

HORN, FREDERICK E. "Managing Cash," *Journal of Accountancy,* Vol. CXVII (April, 1964), pp. 56–62.

JOHNSON, ROBERT W. "More Scope for Credit Managers," *Harvard Business Review,* Vol. XXXIX (November–December, 1961), pp. 109–20.

LANGER, LEONARD C. R. and LAWRENCE E. THOMPSON. *A Study on Measurement of Credit Department Effectiveness.* New York: Credit Research Foundation, Inc., 1954.

LAW, WARREN A. and M. COLYER CRUM. "New Trend in Finance: The Negotiable C.D.," *Harvard Business Review,* Vol. XLI (January–February, 1963), pp. 115–26.

LEONE, EDMUND. "Techniques for Improving Cash Turnover," *Financial Executive,* Vol. XXXII (January, 1964), pp. 38–42.

MAGEE, JOHN F. *Production Planning and Inventory Control.* New York: McGraw-Hill Book Co., 1958.

MORGAN GUARANTY TRUST COMPANY. *Money-Market Investments: The Risk and the Return.* New York, 1964.

PFLOMM, NORMAN E. *Managing Capital Expenditures.* Studies in Business Policy No. 107. New York: National Industrial Conference Board, Inc., 1963.

———. *Managing Company Cash.* Studies in Business Policy No. 99. New York: National Industrial Conference Board, Inc., 1961.

PRICHARD, JAMES W. and ROBERT H. EAGLE. *Modern Inventory Management.* New York: John Wiley & Sons, Inc., 1965.

ROBBINS, SIDNEY M. "Getting More Mileage out of Cash," *N.A.A. Bulletin,* Vol. XLII, No. 1, Sec. 1 (September, 1960), pp. 65–74.

STANBACK, THOMAS M., JR., *Postwar Cycles in Manufacturers' Inventories.* Studies in Business Cycles No. 11. New York: National Bureau of Economic Research, Inc., 1962.

STARR, MARTIN K. and DAVID W. MILLER. *Inventory Control: Theory and Practice.* Englewood Cliffs, N.J.: Prentice-Hall, Inc., 1962.

PART III. ANALYSIS OF PAST FINANCING AND FUTURE FUNDS NEEDS

CREDIT RESEARCH FOUNDATION. *Cash Flow Projection—A Tool of Credit Management.* New York, 1961.

EDWARDS, GROVER E. "Structure and Services of the Cash Budget," *N.A.A. Bulletin,* Vol. XXXIX, No. 3, Sec. 1 (November, 1957), pp. 67–73.

FOULKE, ROY A. *Practical Financial Statement Analysis.* 5th ed. New York: McGraw-Hill Book Co., 1962.

HELFERT, ERICH A. (ed.). *Techniques of Financial Analysis.* Homewood, Ill.: Richard D. Irwin, Inc., 1963.

JAEDICKE, ROBERT K. and ROBERT T. SPROUSE. *Accounting Flows: Income, Funds, and Cash.* Englewood Cliffs, N.J.: Prentice-Hall, Inc., 1965.

KENNEDY, RALPH D. and STEWART Y. MCMULLEN. *Financial Statements: Form, Analysis, and Interpretation.* 4th ed. Homewood, Ill.: Richard D. Irwin, Inc., 1962.

MASON, PERRY E. *"Cash Flow" Analysis and the Funds Statement.* Accounting Research Study No. 2. New York: American Institute of Certified Public Accountants, 1961.

MCFARLAND, WALTER B. "Review of Funds-Flow Analysis," *Harvard Business Review,* Vol. XLI (September–October, 1963), pp. 162–73.

MYER, JOHN N. *Financial Statement Analysis: Principles and Technique.* 3rd ed. Englewood Cliffs, N.J.: Prentice-Hall, Inc., 1961.

NATIONAL ASSOCIATION OF ACCOUNTANTS. *Cash Flow Analysis for Managerial Control.* N.A.A. Research Report No. 38. New York, 1961.

WESTON, J. FRED. "Forecasting Financial Requirements," *Accounting Review,* Vol. XXXIII (July, 1958), pp. 427–40.

PART IV. SHORT-TERM SOURCES OF FUNDS

AMERICAN BANKERS ASSOCIATION. *The Commercial Banking Industry.* (Prepared for the Commission on Money and Credit.) Englewood Cliffs, N.J.: Prentice-Hall, Inc., 1962.

BAXTER, NEVINS D. *The Commercial Paper Market.* Research Memorandum No. 69. Princeton, N.J.: Princeton University, Econometric Research Program, 1964.

BECKHART, BENJAMIN H. (ed.). *Business Loans of American Commercial Banks.* New York: Ronald Press Co., 1959.

DIENER, ROYCE. *How to Finance a Growing Business.* New York: Frederick Fell, Inc., 1965.

DOUGLAS-GUARDIAN WAREHOUSE CORPORATION. *How to Finance Business by Field Warehousing Inventory; Facts and Information for Borrowers, Banks, and Lending Agencies.* New Orleans, La., 1962.

FALCON, WILLIAM D. (ed.). *Financing International Operations: A Guide to Sources and Methods.* AMA Management Report, No. 82. New York: American Management Association, 1965.

"Financing Inventory through Field Warehousing," *Yale Law Journal,* Vol. LXIX (March, 1960), pp. 663–708.

HAYES, DOUGLAS A. *Bank Lending Policies: Issues and Practices.* Ann Arbor, Mich.: Bureau of Business Research, School of Business Administration, University of Michigan, 1964.

HODGMAN, DONALD R. *Commercial Bank Loan and Investment Policy.* Champaign, Ill.: Bureau of Economic and Business Research, University of Illinois, 1963.

LUCKETT, DUDLEY G. (ed.). *Studies in the Factor Markets for Small Business Firms: Internal and External Aspects of the Capital, Labor and Management Markets.* Small Business Management Research Reports. Ames, Ia.: Iowa State University, 1964.

MACHINERY AND ALLIED PRODUCTS INSTITUTE. *Financing U.S. Exports and Overseas Investment: A MAPI Study and Guide.* Washington, D.C.: Machinery and Allied Products Institute and Council for Technological Development, 1964.

MOORE, CARROLL G. "Factoring—A Unique and Important Form of Financing and Service," *Business Lawyer,* Vol. XIV (April, 1959), pp. 703–27.

PHELPS, CLYDE WILLIAM. *Accounts Receivable Financing as a Method of Securing Business Loans.* Studies in Commercial Financing No. 2. 2nd ed. Baltimore, Md.: Educational Division, Commercial Credit Co., 1961.

PROCHNOW, HERBERT V. and ROY A. FOULKE. *Practical Bank Credit.* 2nd rev. ed. New York: Harper & Row, Publishers, 1963.

SEIDMAN, WALTER S. *Accounts Receivable and Inventory Financing.* Ann Arbor, Mich.: Masterco Press, Inc., 1957.

SELDEN, RICHARD T. *Trends and Cycles in the Commercial Paper Market.* Occasional Paper No. 85. New York: National Bureau of Economic Research, Inc., 1963.

WILLIAMS, CHARLES M. and HOWARD A. WILLIAMS. "Incentive Financing—A New Opportunity," *Harvard Business Review,* Vol. XXXVIII (March–April, 1960), pp. 123–34.

PART V. THE SOURCES OF LONG-TERM CORPORATE CAPITAL

1. *Dividend Policy*

BRITTAIN, JOHN A. "The Tax Structure and Corporate Dividend Policy," *American Economic Review,* Vol. LIV (May, 1964), pp. 272–87.

GORDON, MYRON J. *The Investment, Financing, and Valuation of the Corporation,* chap. v. Homewood, Ill.: Richard D Irwin, Inc., 1962.

LINTNER, JOHN. "Distribution of Incomes of Corporations among Dividends, Retained Earnings, and Taxes," *American Economic Review, Papers and Proceedings,* Vol. XLVI (May, 1956), pp. 97–113.

———. "Optimal Dividends and Corporate Growth under Uncertainty," *Quarterly Journal of Economics,* Vol. LXXVIII (February, 1964), pp. 49–95.

WALTER, JAMES E. "Dividend Policy: Its Influence on the Value of the Enterprise," *Journal of Finance,* Vol. XVIII (May, 1963), pp. 280–91.

2. *Capital Markets*

AMERICAN MUTUAL INSURANCE ALLIANCE, and OTHERS. *Property and Casualty Insurance Companies: Their Role as Financial Intermediaries.* (Prepared for the Commission on Money and Credit.) Englewood Cliffs, N.J.: Prentice-Hall, Inc., 1962.

ANDREWS, VICTOR L. "Pension Funds in the Securities Markets," *Harvard Business Review,* Vol. XXXVII (November–December, 1959), pp. 90–102.

BRIMMER, ANDREW F. *Life Insurance Companies in the Capital Market.* East Lansing, Mich.: Bureau of Business and Economic Research, Michigan State University, 1962.

CHRISTENSON, CHARLES. *Strategic Aspects of Competitive Bidding for Corporate Securities.* Studies in Managerial Economics. Boston: Division of Research, Harvard Business School, 1965.

COHAN, AVERY B. *Cost of Flotation of Long-Term Corporate Debt since 1935.* Research Paper No. 6. Chapel Hill, N.C.: School of Business Administration, University of North Carolina, 1961.

————. *Private Placements and Public Offerings: Market Shares since 1935.* Technical Paper No. 1. Chapel Hill, N.C.: School of Business Administration, University of North Carolina, 1961.

————. "Yields on New Underwritten Corporate Bonds, 1935–58," *Journal of Finance*, Vol. XVII (December, 1962), pp. 585–605.

COREY, E. RAYMOND. *Direct Placement of Corporate Securities.* Boston: Division of Research, Harvard Business School, 1951.

DOUGALL, HERBERT E. *Capital Markets and Institutions.* Englewood Cliffs, N.J.: Prentice-Hall, Inc., 1965.

FLOYD, JOE S., JR., and LUTHER H. HODGES, JR. *Financing Industrial Growth: Private and Public Sources of Long-Term Capital for Industry.* Research Paper No. 10. Chapel Hill, N.C.: School of Business Administration, University of North Carolina, 1962.

FRIEND, IRWIN. *Investment Banking and the New Issues Market: Summary Volume.* Philadelphia: Wharton School of Finance and Commerce, University of Pennsylvania, 1965.

————, and OTHERS. *Private Capital Markets.* (Prepared for the Commission on Money and Credit.) Englewood Cliffs, N.J.: Prentice-Hall, Inc., 1964.

GAGNON, JOAN M. *Bond Financing by Corporations through the Medium of Direct Placement.* Wisconsin Selected Papers, Vol. 1, No. 2. Madison: University of Wisconsin, 1963.

GOLDSMITH, RAYMOND W. *Financial Intermediaries in the American Economy since 1900.* National Bureau of Economic Research Studies in Capital Formation and Financing No. 3. Princeton, N.J.: Princeton University Press, 1958.

————. *The Flow of Capital Funds in the Postwar Economy.* Studies in Capital Formation and Financing No. 12. New York: National Bureau of Economic Research, 1965.

HANSON, WILLIAM C. *Capital Sources and Major Investing Institutions.* New York: Simmons-Boardman Publishing Corp., 1963.

HORVITZ, PAUL M., and OTHERS. *Private Financial Instiutions.* (Prepared for the Commission on Money and Credit.) Englewood Cliffs, N.J.: Prentice-Hall, Inc., 1963.

ISRAELS, CARLOS L. and GEORGE M. DUFF, JR. (eds.). *When Corporations Go Public.* New York: Practising Law Institute, 1962.

JOHNSON, STEWART, and OTHERS. *Federal Credit Programs.* (Prepared for the Commission on Money and Credit.) Englewood Cliffs, N.J.: Prentice-Hall, Inc., 1963.

KATONA, GEORGE. *Private Pensions and Individual Saving.* Monograph No. 40. East Lansing, Mich.: Survey Research Center, Institute for Social Research, University of Michigan, 1965.

LIFE INSURANCE ASSOCIATION OF AMERICA. *Life Insurance Companies as Financial Institutions.* (Prepared for the Commission on Money and Credit.) Englewood Cliffs, N.J.: Prentice-Hall, Inc., 1962.

LUDTKE, JAMES B. *The American Financial System: Markets and Institutions.* Rockleigh, N.J.: Allyn & Bacon, Inc., College Division, 1961.

NEW YORK UNIVERSITY, C. J. DEVINE INSTITUTE OF FINANCE. *New Forces in the Money and Capital Markets.* Bulletin No. 23. New York, 1963.

ROBINSON, GERALD J. *Going Public: Successful Securities Underwriting.* New York: Clark Boardman Co., Ltd., 1961.

ROBINSON, ROLAND I. *Money and Capital Markets.* New York: McGraw-Hill Book Co., 1964.

U.S. SECURITIES AND EXCHANGE COMMISSION. *Report of the Special Study of Securities Markets,* Part 2. (88th Cong., 1st sess., House Doc. 95.) Washington, D.C.: U.S. Government Printing Office, 1963.

WATERMAN, MERWIN H. *Investment Banking Functions: Their Evolution and Adaptation to Business Finance.* Michigan Studies in Business, Vol. 14, No. 1. Ann Arbor, Mich.: Bureau of Business Research, School of Business Administration, University of Michigan, 1958.

WHEAT, FRANCIS M. and G. A. BLACKSTONE. "Guideposts for a First Public Offering," *Business Lawyer,* Vol. XV (April, 1960), pp. 539–64.

PART VI. THE LONG-TERM CAPITAL STRUCTURE

BERANEK, WILLIAM. *Analysis for Financial Decisions,* chaps. viii and ix. Homewood, Ill.: Richard D. Irwin, Inc., 1963.

CHILDS, JOHN F. *Long-Term Financing.* Englewood Cliffs, N.J.: Prentice-Hall, Inc., 1961.

DONALDSON, GORDON. *Corporate Debt Capacity: A Study of Corporate Debt Policy and the Determination of Corporate Debt Capacity.* Boston: Division of Research, Harvard Business School, 1961.

———. "In Defense of Preferred Stock," *Harvard Business Review,* Vol. XL (July–August, 1962), pp. 123–36.

JOHNSON, ROBERT W. "Subordinated Debentures: Debt That Serves as Equity," *Journal of Finance,* Vol. X (March, 1955), pp. 1–16.

LINTNER, JOHN. "The Cost of Capital and Optimal Financing of Corporate Growth," *Journal of Finance,* Vol. XVIII (May, 1963), pp. 292–310.

MODIGLIANI, FRANCO and MERTON H. MILLER. "The Cost of Capital, Corporation Finance, and the Theory of Investment," *American Economic Review,* Vol. XLVIII (June, 1958), pp. 261–97.

ROBICHEK, ALEXANDER A. and STEWART C. MYERS. *Optimal Financing Decisions.* Englewood Cliffs, N.J.: Prentice-Hall, Inc., 1965.

SAMETZ, ARNOLD W. "Trends in the Volume and Composition of Equity Finance," *Journal of Finance,* Vol. XIX (September, 1964), pp. 450–69.

SOLOMON, EZRA. "Leverage and the Cost of Capital," *Journal of Finance,* Vol. XVIII (May, 1963), pp. 273–79.

STEVENSON, HAROLD W. *Common Stock Financing.* Michigan Business Reports No. 29. Ann Arbor, Mich.: Bureau of Business Research, School of Business Administration, University of Michigan, 1957.

PART VII. CAPITAL BUDGETING

BARGES, ALEXANDER. *The Effect of Capital Structure on the Cost of Capital: A Test and Evaluation of the Modigliani and Miller Propositions.* Ford Foundation Doctoral Dissertation Series. 1962 Award Winner. Englewood Cliffs, N.J.: Prentice-Hall, Inc., 1963.

BIERMAN, HAROLD, JR., and SEYMOUR SMIDT. *The Capital Budgeting Decision: Economic Analysis and Financing of Investment Projects.* 2nd ed. New York: Macmillan Co., 1966.

EISNER, ROBERT. *Determinants of Capital Expenditures: An Interview Study.* Studies in Business Expectations and Planning No. 2. Urbana, Ill.: Bureau of Economic and Business Research, University of Illinois, 1956.

FARRAR, DONALD E. *The Investment Decision under Uncertainty.* Ford Foundation Doctoral Dissertation Series. 1961 Award Winner. Englewood Cliffs, N.J.: Prentice-Hall, Inc., 1962.

GRANT, EUGENE L. and W. GRANT IRESON. *Principles of Engineering Economy.* 4th ed. New York: Ronald Press Co., 1960.

HILLIER, FREDERICK S. "The Derivation of Probabilistic Information for the Evaluation of Risky Investments," *Management Science*, Vol. IX (April, 1963), pp. 443–57.

ISTVAN, DONALD F. *Capital-Expenditures Decisions: How They Are Made in Large Corporations.* Indiana University Business Report No. 33. Bloomington, Ind.: Bureau of Business Research, Indiana University, 1961.

LESSER, ARTHUR, JR. (ed.). *Decision-Making Criteria for Capital Expenditures.* Fourth Summer Symposium Papers. Hoboken, N.J.: *The Engineering Economist*, Stevens Institute of Technology, 1965.

MASSÉ, PIERRE. *Optimal Investment Decisions: Rules for Action and Criteria for Choice.* Trans. Scripta Technica, Inc. Englewood Cliffs, N.J.: Prentice-Hall, Inc., 1962.

PORTERFIELD, JAMES T. S. *Investment Decisions and Capital Costs.* Prentice-Hall Foundation of Finance Series. Englewood Cliffs, N.J.: Prentice-Hall, Inc., 1965.

SOLOMON, EZRA (ed.). *The Management of Corporate Capital.* Glencoe, Ill.: The Free Press of Glencoe, 1959.

SOLOMON, EZRA. *The Theory of Financial Management.* New York: Columbia University Press, 1963.

WEINGARTNER, H. MARTIN. *Mathematical Programming and the Analysis of Capital Budgeting Problems.* Ford Foundation Doctoral Dissertation Series. 1962 Award Winner. Englewood Cliffs, N.J.: Prentice-Hall, Inc., 1963.

PART VIII. THE BARGAIN FOR FUNDS

BARKER, C. AUSTIN. "Effective Stock Splits," *Harvard Business Review*, Vol. XXXIV (January–February, 1956), pp. 101–06.

———. "Evaluation of Stock Dividends," *Harvard Business Review*, Vol. XXXVI (July–August, 1958), pp. 99–114.

BELLEMORE, DOUGLAS H. and LILLIAN H. BLUCHER. "A Study of Stock Splits in the Post War Years," *Financial Analysts Journal*, Vol. XV (November, 1959), pp. 19–26.

BERANEK, WILLIAM. *Common Stock Financing, Book Values and Stock Rights: The Theory and the Evidence.* Wisconsin Commerce Reports, Vol. 6, No. 3. Madison, Wisc.: Bureau of Business Research and Service, University of Wisconsin, 1961.

GREENFIELD, HARVEY and FRANK K. GRIESINGER. *Sale-Leasebacks and Leasing in Real Estate and Equipment Transactions.* New York: McGraw-Hill Book Co., 1958.

Loss, Louis. *Securities Regulation.* 2nd rev. ed. Boston: Little, Brown & Co., 1961.

Myers, John H. *Reporting of Leases in Financial Statements.* Accounting Research Study No. 4. New York: American Institute of Certified Public Accountants, 1962.

Pilcher, C. James. *Raising Capital with Convertible Securities.* Michigan Business Studies, Vol. 12, No. 2. Ann Arbor, Mich.: Bureau of Business Research, School of Business Administration, University of Michigan, 1955.

Robbins, Sidney M. "A Bigger Role for Income Bonds," *Harvard Business Review,* Vol. XXXIII (November–December, 1955), pp. 100–114.

Schlei, Norbert A. *State Regulation of Corporate Financial Policies: The California Experience.* Boston: Harvard Graduate School of Business Administration, 1962.

Sussman, M. Richard. *The Stock Dividend.* Michigan Business Studies, Vol. 15, No. 5. Ann Arbor, Mich.: Bureau of Business Research, School of Business Administration, University of Michigan, 1962.

Vancil, Richard F. *Leasing of Industrial Equipment* (with tables for the analysis of financial alternatives and capital expenditures by Jerome Bracken and Charles J. Christenson). New York: McGraw-Hill Book Co., 1963.

Weston, J. Fred. "The Timing of Financial Policy," *Controller,* Vol. XXIX (December, 1961), pp. 596–600.

Winn, Willis J. and Arleigh Hess, Jr. "The Value of the Call Privilege," *Journal of Finance,* Vol. XIV (May, 1959), pp. 182–95.

Part IX. Financing Growth and Development

1. *Financing the New, Small-Scale Enterprise*

Flink, Salomon J. *Equity Financing for Small Business.* New York: Simmons-Boardman Publishing Corp., 1962.

Hayes, Samuel L. and Donald H. Woods. "Are SBICs Doing Their Job?" *Harvard Business Review,* Vol. XLI (March–April, 1963), pp. 6–19.

Hungate, Robert P. *Interbusiness Financing: Economic Implications for Small Business.* Small Business Research Series, No. 3. Washington, D.C.: U.S. Small Business Administration, 1962.

McKinley, Gordon W. "Life Insurance Company Lending to Small Business," *Journal of Finance,* Vol. XVI (May, 1961), pp. 291–303.

Miller, Glenn R. "Long-Term Small Business Financing from the Underwriter's Point of View," *Journal of Finance,* Vol. XVI (May, 1961), pp. 280–90.

U.S. Board of Governors of the Federal Reserve System. *Financing Small Business.* (Report of the Committee on Banking and Currency and the Select Committees on Small Business, 85th Cong., 2nd sess., 1958), Parts 1 and 2. Washington, D.C.: U.S. Government Printing Office, 1958.

2. *Business Mergers*

Bosland, Chelcie C. *Valuation Theories and Decisions of the Securities and Exchange Commission.* New York: Simmons-Boardman Publishing Corp., 1964.

Butters, J. Keith, John Lintner, and William L. Cary. *Effects of Taxation: Corporate Mergers.* Boston: Division of Research, Harvard Business School, 1951.

Drayton, Clarence I., Jr., and Others. *Mergers and Acquisitions: Planning and Action.* New York: Financial Executives Research Foundation, Inc., 1963.

MACE, MYLES L. and GEORGE G. MONTGOMERY, JR. *Management Problems of Corporate Acquisitions.* Boston: Division of Research, Harvard Business School, 1962.

McCARTHY, GEORGE D. *Acquisitions and Mergers.* New York: Ronald Press Co., 1963.

PART X. BUSINESS FAILURE

CREDIT RESEARCH FOUNDATION (ed.). *Credit Management Handbook.* (A publication of the National Association of Credit Management.) Rev. ed. Homewood, Ill.: Richard D. Irwin, Inc., 1965.

MASSON, ROBERT L. *New Shares for Old: The Boston and Maine Stock Modification.* Boston: Division of Research, Harvard Business School, 1958.

SCHINDLER, JAMES S. *Quasi-Reorganization.* Michigan Business Studies, Vol. 13, No. 5. Ann Arbor, Mich.: Bureau of Business Research, School of Business Administration, University of Michigan, 1958.

Indexes

Index

Index of Cases

*This book has been set on the Linotype in 11
and 10 point Bodoni Book, leaded 1 point.
Part and chapter numbers and titles are in
assorted Bodoni display faces. The size of the
type page is 27 by 47½ picas.*